HISTORY

OF

THOMASTON, ROCKLAND,

AND

SOUTH THOMASTON,

MAINE,

FROM THEIR FIRST EXPLORATION, A. D. 1605; WITH FAMILY GENEALOGIES.

By CYRUS EATON:
Cor. Member of the Mass. Hist. Society, also of the Wisconsin Hist. Society, and Member Elect of the Maine Hist. Society.

"Gather up the fragments, that nothing be lost." —*John* 6, 12.

IN TWO VOLUMES.

VOL. II.

HALLOWELL:
MASTERS, SMITH & CO., PRINTERS.
1865.

CONTENTS.

HISTORY

OF

THOMASTON, ROCKLAND AND SO. THOMASTON.

CHAPTER I.

EAST THOMASTON AND ROCKLAND CITY.

East Thomaston, after being separated from the parent town, July 28, 1848, proceeded to the election of the usual town officers and transacting other business incumbent upon her as an incorporated town. The first meeting was held on the 23d of August, in the vestry of the Congregational meeting-house; and a vote was passed "to accept the Act" of incorporation passed by the Legislature.

In 1848, a scheme was broached for making a new *collection* district, and locating the *custom house* in this place. This having met with some opposition, a compromise was effected by establishing a *deputy's* office here, under the old Waldoboro' district. Of this, Dr. John Merrill was appointed the first deputy collector, his first entry having been made in March, 1849. He was succeeded in May by Elkanah Spear, Jr., who was followed by Walter E. Tolman, in July, 1853, Thos. K. Osgood, in May, 1857, and Geo. W. Kimball, Jr., in June, 1861,—at which time Davis Tilson of this place was appointed collector of Waldoboro' district. The office is now kept in the Custom House block, so called, on Main street.

On the establishment of the Maine *Telegraph* Company, Hon. Knott Crockett with his usual promptness made himself responsible for the portion of stock assigned to this place, was appointed one of its directors, and, in consequence, an office was opened here. The first message received was from Belfast, at nine on the morning of Nov. 29th. A. D. Nichols was appointed the first operator; who was succeeded in 1853 by Sears Ulmer, J. C. Upham, and perhaps some others who staid but a short time, till the present operator, E. W. Austin, took charge of the office. It pays a salary of $500, and its income is about $1800, yearly. The office was removed in Jan. 1857, from the Lime Rock Bank building to the second story of Berry's new block.

A number of citizens of this place obtained, Aug. 10th, an act of incorporation for the *East Thomaston Bank*, with a capital of $50,000; — but the projected institution never went into operation. B. W. Lothrop & Co. this year erected the *Spofford block*, so called, on land leased for the purpose by the heirs of C. Spofford, at the corner of Main and School streets, containing four stores.

1849. A *Town Court* for East Thomaston was established by an Act of Aug. 13th, which required one justice of the peace and quorum to be chosen once in three years by the town, who, as Judge of said court, was to have concurrent jurisdiction in the county of Lincoln, and exclusive jurisdiction in the town, over all matters triable by justices of the peace, and over all actions wherein the debt or damage did not exceed $100, provided the defendant resided in the town; also to take cognizance of all larcenies not exceeding $50. A court room was to be provided and expenses defrayed by the town. The act was repealed July 29, 1850, and a *Municipal Court* for the town of Rockland established in its stead, not materially differing from it, except that the Judge was to be appointed by the Governor and Council and hold his office for seven instead of three years. John C. Cochran was the judge, elected Sept. 17, 1849, for the town court, and the same gentleman first judge of the municipal court, appointed for seven years, August, 1850. In the mean time the place having received a city charter, the first judge under it, Feb. 1, 1855, was Wm. G. Sargent; succeeded by election of the people, 1856, by Wakefield G. Frye, who, receiving an advantageous offer out west, relinquished the office April 4th, to John A. Meserve; S. C. Fessenden was appointed, April 17, 1857, by the Governor and Council, succeeded March, 1858, by Nathaniel Meservey. In March, 1861, the Municipal Court was abolished by act of legislature, and a *Police Court* with enlarged jurisdiction substituted, of which M. W. Farwell, the present incumbent, was appointed judge for one year, and at the end of that time was elected by the people to the same office for four years. This court has a good reputation, and is said to have been lately complimented by Judge Cutting as the best in the State except the Supreme Court.

At a meeting called June 4th, the town instructed the licensing board to grant no further licenses; to notify all those selling liquors contrary to law, to cease from the traffic; to prosecute all who, after such notice, continue in the same; to watch all places where such sale is suspected on the Lord's day; and to regard the written allegations of five citizens as sufficient ground for commencing action against suspected venders. These energetic measures, of course, awakened resentment in those interested, insomuch that, in revenge, an unsuccessful attempt was made, November 9th, to blow up the store of F. Cobb, with the families of C. G. Moffitt and A. S. Richmond residing over it; but this only led to more strenuous efforts to detect the perpetrator and suppress the traffic. On September 17th, a judicious and salutary system of by-laws for preventing improper obstructions, disorderly conduct, and disturbances, in the streets, cruelty to animals, indecent exposure in bathing, interruption of meetings, and other offences, was adopted; and 21 police officers were chosen to carry the same into effect.

The *Partridge and Harden Wharf and Lime-kiln Company* was incorporated July 17th, with power to hold real and personal estate not exceeding $15,000. The discovery of gold in California caused, in this and the preceding year, the loss by emigration of some twenty or more of the enterprising young men of the place; and the loss has been more or less continued in later years. But the town still manifested a healthy growth, and about 125 dwellings were erected.

Education continued to advance in the place. In November a new and commodious school-house was finished in Grace street; and Thomas K. Osgood came from New Hampshire, and commenced his labors here as a teacher, which he has since conducted with eminent success when not diverted from them by more profitable or less fatiguing pursuits. A series of lectures, by Rev. E. G. Brooks, was delivered in this place, on Common Schools and in favor of the *Grade* or Prussian *system*. These were followed in the winter by meetings of the citizens, at which the subject underwent a thorough discussion, which finally led to a partial adoption of that improved system.

An attractive temperance celebration of the 4th of July, here, drew large crowds from this and the neighboring towns. A long procession, marshalled by H. G. Berry, with banners and significant mottoes; a fine oration at Rankin's Orchard, by Rev. Mr. Brooks of Bath; and a dinner by E. W. Pendleton, in a spacious pavilion, were its principal features; and one occurrence only, marred its pleasure. This was the premature discharge of a cannon by which the right arm of Robert Thomas was so badly mangled as to require amputation. A small one-story house, at the North End, owned by Capt. N. Marshall, was consumed by fire on the night of May 30th; insurance, $600. A shocking injury occurred to Reuben Hanson, September 6th, in a lime quarry, by which both of his eyes and one hand were destroyed. Another more fatal accident occurred September 1st, by which Capt. John Booker was drowned from a vessel in the harbor, being drawn overboard by the entanglement of his foot when dropping the anchor. On the 30th November, also, a fatal accident occurred in the fall of an old wooden building on Sea street; crushed by the weight of corn and flour stored above. It was occupied below as a boat-builder's shop by E. M. Merrill, who was instantly killed.

The year began with fine sleighing and severe weather; the harbor, Feb. 22d, being frozen over further than the eye could see. The week ending August 17th was most oppressive; the thermometer indicating 95° and 103° of heat, with an atmosphere of lime dust by day and fog by night.

1850. At an adjournment of the annual meeting, May 15th, a vote was passed to change the name of the town from East Thomaston to ROCKLAND, and instructing the Selectmen to petition the Legislature accordingly. This was done, and the petition complied with by an Act passed July 17, 1850; since which the town, now city, has rejoiced in its chosen name, which, when it is considered that its quarries of lime-rock are the foundation on which the prosperity of the place rests, all must acknowledge to be an appropriate one. Its lime, heretofore known as that of Thomaston, now took the name of *Rockland lime* in the market; and the place has since by common consent been considered the principal manufactory and depot of lime for the United States. During this year of 1850, there was inspected and sent off the enormous amount of 800,000 casks; which, at 60 cents, the average price on the wharves, amounted to $480,000. The casks used, at their average price for that year, 18 cents, amounted to $144,000; the stone, at 9 cents in the quarry, to $72,000; transporting the same to the kilns, at 6 cents, to $48,000. There were then in use 125 kilns, which, at each burning, on an average, turned out 420 casks, consumed 30 cords of wood, at the average price of $2,50 per cord, and employed two men four days and five nights. The transportation of this lime to market, and the back freights usually obtained, employed 120 coasters, and as many more in bringing the wood from the eastern coast and islands; over 200 sail of vessels being owned here. Business in general, this year, was good,—three ships going up; a steam mill put in operation by Ambrose Colby, since of Portland, for grinding, sawing, planing and other purposes; the clothing store of O. H. Perry, enlarged, and other mercantile establishments thriving; and many new buildings appearing, among them one of three stories, at the meadows, by Ephraim Ulmer.

Among the pleasant things of the season, was a May-day festival held by the ladies in Eagle Hall. On the 29th Aug., also, a grand pic-nic, free, to which all the town was invited and all the world made welcome, was held in the oak grove on the eastern shore of Tolman's Pond, which, on this occasion, was rebaptized by the euphonious name of *Chikawauka Lake*, or, by interpretation, (somewhat apocryphal,) "the lake of smiling waters." About 2000 citizens were present, Larkin Snow presided, speeches were made by Messrs. Kalloch, Osgood, Farwell, Richmond and Holmes, the new name was reported by a committee of which R. T. Slocomb was chairman, and all departed well pleased with the good cheer, joyous greetings, and magnificent scenery.

The summer of 1850 was variable, with many long rains and high freshets. During a terrible storm of wind and snow, Dec. 23d, the schooner Niagara, lying in the harbor, and lime-loaded, dragged her anchors, struck a ledge, and, taking fire, was a total loss,—the captain and crew having been taken off, many of them insensible from cold and 12 hours' exposure. Schooner Violet drove ashore and was left high and dry on the beach, uninjured, as was also a brig with masts cut away, at Clam Cove. This storm called out an article in the GAZETTE advocating the erection of a *Breakwater* to protect the harbor from storms; which was followed, in 1852, by a petition to Congress, of Knott Crockett and 807 other citizens of this place, for the construction of such a work; but there was no report in its favor, and nothing has yet been obtained. In 1855, a bill making appropriation for this purpose, among others, was introduced into the U. S. Senate by Hon. W. P. Fessenden, and passed there, but failed in the House. The first step towards this desirable improvement of the harbor had been taken by Government as early as 1835; when a survey was made by Ward B. Burnett, 2d Lieut. in U. S. army, on topographical duty. This officer reported in favor of the project, having found an eligible site for constructing a breakwater 825 yards long in the central part of the harbor, on a shoal consisting of rocks, more or less covered with smaller rocks and stones, and estimating the cost at $1,000,000; but, in consequence of the rival claims of Owl's Head harbor for a similar work, no appropriation was at that time made for either. It remains to be settled whether this object is to be accomplished by the General Government, the people of this city, the joint action of both, or given up altogether.*

On the morning of Nov. 7th, a fire broke out at the rear of the Rockland House in the boat-builder's shop of the Messrs. Dyer. This building and its contents were completely destroyed to the value of about $3000, the heaviest loss falling on Chas. S. Cables, who occupied the upper part as a carriage shop. Although hotel stables and piles of seasoned lumber were in close proximity, yet by the active exertions of the two fire companies nothing further was even scorched. This fortunate escape, due in a great measure to the tide being in at the time, had the effect to awaken the citizens to a sense of their danger and the necessity of a better supply of water at all times. At a meeting for the purpose, Nov. 28th, $400 in addition to $200 at the annual meeting, were raised by the town for repairing engines, purchasing hooks and ladders, and constructing reservoirs, to be expended under direction of Jona. White, C. Holmes, and John S. Coburn, committee. A voluntary night-watch was also organized Dec. 1st; Dr. G. Ludwig, S. H. Fuller, and F. Harden, were chosen officers; hooks were provided; and members classified to serve by rotation.

The *Rockland Water Company* was created by an Act passed August 20, 1850, with power to construct an aqueduct from Chikawauka Lake into and through the village of Rockland, to regulate the use, distribution, and prices of said water, and to hold real and personal estate not exceeding $75,000; on condition, however, that at the end of ten years, on the refunding all the expenditures and ten per cent. in addition, the town, at its option, was to have the right to take and control all the property and privileges of said corporation. A preliminary survey by R. T. Slocomb, and estimate of cost was made; and the subscriptions to the stock, by exertions of Jere. Berry, and others, soon amounted to within $4000 of the sum required. This balance was taken by the New York firm of Ball & Co., in part payment for a supply of their newly invented Indestructible Water-pipe, of which it was

* Burnett's Report to Lt. Col. Long, Topog. Engineer, dated Concord, N. H., Nov. 20, 1835.

computed that 30,898 feet would be required, from one to nine inches bore. The company was, in February, 1851, duly organized by choice of I. K. Kimball, president, C. Holmes, treasurer, and C. L. Lowell, clerk. Mr. Ball contracted to excavate the trenches,—six miles, for $4000, and, all over that distance, for $1 a rod. This was completed, and the Chikawauka water reached the city, through its subterranean channel, by the middle of November. The $30,000 stock being thus expended, a further subscription of $10,000 was obtained; and, in October, 1852, the directors reported that 14 miles of pipe had been laid, 225 rods of which, on account of deep cutting and rock, had been subjected to an extra expenditure of $5000, that the whole cost amounted to $46,000, that the number of takers was 400, and rapidly increasing, at $6 per family, and that, from the first nine month's profits, a dividend of four per cent. had been declared. McLain's mill at the outlet of the lake was purchased, and in 1855 rebuilt, at a cost of $10,185; and the whole expenditure of the company up to 1855, at which time Wm. A. Farnsworth was president and M. Sumner secretary and treasurer, amounted to $67,411; capital stock, increased by that year's dividend, $55,000, leaving a debt of $11,821. Continuing to apply its income to the reduction of the company's debt, and paying off the dividends by new certificates of stock, the latter was increased to over $70,000. The stockholders becoming impatient of slow returns, in the spring of 1857 the rates were raised to $10 per family. This gave great dissatisfaction, which continued till the rates were reduced in the following August.

Soon after the separation of the town, the subject of a *Poor-house* and *farm* was agitated; and, at the April meeting of this year, it was voted to offer Lewis McLain the sum of $2500 for his (the Mosman) farm, with the reversion of the widow's dower. This offer was at that time rejected; but the farm was finally purchased in the fall; and the house upon it furnished ample accommodation as an almshouse till 1860; when, from the increased number of paupers, consequent on the increase of intemperance, it was found to be too small, and a large addition was built.

At a meeting, March 25th, the town voted $500, (increased, May 15th, by $100 more,) for the purchase of a *cemetery;* and the selectmen were instructed to lay out such portion of the same as they thought proper, and dispose of the lots at auction,—fencing and ornamenting the grounds with the money given for the right of choice. The ground purchased was five acres, at Jameson's Point, within the limits of Camden, in a beautiful situation, commanding, in some portions, a view of Rockland and the intervening water; and which is capable, by the addition of trees and shrubbery in connection with the adjacent forest, of being made a lovely and congenial place for depositing the ashes and communing with the spirits of the sacred dead. An ordinance respecting the sale and conveyance, fencing and ornamenting of this cemetery, was passed by the City Council in 1859.

The former pastor of the 1st Baptist church of this place, Rev. Amariah Kalloch, died June 16th, of this year, near Sacramento City, California, just as his numerous friends here were expecting his return. He was an able and successful minister, of great mental power, and of a winning and prepossessing appearance. His loss was deeply lamented not only by the church that had grown up with him here, but by the citizens and community at large, and particularly his own denomination, in whose Associations he had frequently presided and always been an efficient member. The death of President Taylor was duly noticed in this place, and an oration or eulogy delivered by T. K. Osgood, at the 1st Baptist church on the evening of August 18th.

1851 opened with frequent storms, obstructed mails, and greater depth of snow than had been known for eight or ten years.

At the close of July and first of August, the bay and harbor here were literally alive with mackerel, affording the citizens sport even to weariness in taking them. On the 27th of August the house occupied by Mrs. Rhoades was struck by lightning, which demolished the chimney, tore off the plastering, set fire to a bed, rudely knocked down a lady, and finally, after assaulting a stove and silencing a tea-kettle, made a hasty exit through the cellar. At the same time there was a flash and explosion like that of a pistol, in the Telegraph office near by. Then followed a season of severe heat, dust, and drought, which was not broken by rain till Sept. 23d; but which was borne patiently on account of the facilities it afforded for laying the pipes of the aqueduct. On Sunday, Sept. 14th, the dwelling of John Keen in the northwestern part of the town, took fire whilst the family were all absent, and, with the furniture, papers, accounts, and notes, was wholly consumed. The schooner Fortune of this port having on board Thomas M. Stearns, master, and Wm. H. Stearns, mate, of this town, and two others, left New York for this place with a cargo of corn and flour; was last seen off Chatham, Nov. 25th; and was supposed to have been lost in the snow storm of that evening.

The strong and general interest in the temperance cause, characteristic of Rockland, was more strongly manifested this year by a number of crowded mass meetings under direction of the different temperance organizations. Nor was the movement confined to this place, but a general interest seemed to be awakened through the State, more especially by means of the Sons of Temperance. At the State celebration of this order held here July 11th, a procession, marshalled by Messrs. F. Cobb, C. Holmes, and E. W. Pendleton, and consisting of *Lime Rock*, *Farmer's and Mechanics*, *Oak*, and *Hyperion* Divisions, *Cadets of Temperance*, *Temple of Honor*, and *Watchman's Club*, (all, except the first, being new organizations formed within the two preceding years) with the fire companies, brass band, committee of arrangements, clergy, and the Grand Division, marched to Rankin's Grove; where a concourse of 5000 people listened to eloquent addresses from Arnold S. Richmond, president of the day, Revs. Fessenden and Kalloch of this place, and many gentlemen from other parts of the State. The mass meetings continued every fortnight through the winters of 1851 and 1852; and, with strict watchfulness and prompt prosecutions under the new Maine Law, effected almost a complete annihilation of the baneful traffic. Every influential business man, it was stated, was in favor of temperance; and, instead of the great number of paupers formerly maintained, there was now but a solitary one, remaining in the poor-house.

A young men's *Literary club* was formed in the autumn of 1851; $200 were raised by sale of tickets, and a course of lectures provided; which were by Rev. Messrs. Wm. Ware of Cambridge, on "Kossuth," November 25th; William A. Drew, on the "world's fair," December 5th; Chas. F. Allen of Bath, on "Cromwell," December 11th; Prof. Packard of Bowdoin College, on "nationality," January 7, 1852; J. W. Chickering of Portland, on "Switzerland," January 23d; Sylvester Judd of Augusta, on "the beautiful," February 2d; George Shepard of Bangor, on "reading," March 6th, and April 20th; and Theodore Parker of Boston, on "false and true idea of a gentleman," March 9th.

This year was distinguished for business prosperity and the rapid growth of the place. The spacious *Kimball block*, of brick, three stories in height, on the eastern side of Main street, having been in progress since 1848, was now opened, furnishing six new stores on the first floor, and on the second floor accommodations for the Bank, Insurance, lawyers' and other offices. A large number of buildings of different descriptions were going up. The Lindsey field, of 14 acres, a short distance north of Lime Rock and Main streets, was purchased by A. H. Kimball and Isaac C. Abbott, laid out in some 75 building lots, and four or five of them improved as such not long after by the owners. The Crockett *pasture* (as it was six years earlier) was now also in demand for building purposes; and to facilitate renting, the first *house-brokerage* office was opened by M. S. Whiting, at his law office in the Spofford block. Two large ships, one of them of 1700 tons—the largest ever before built in Maine—and other vessels, building; the manufacture of 741,000 casks of lime and the construction of the water works, rendered business unusually lively. Of the merchants in the place, (nearly 100,) not a single failure occurred during the year. The *Rockland Bank* was incorporated, May 31st, with a capital of $50,000, and the right of increasing it to $100,000 on or before April 1, 1853. The stock was taken up almost wholly by citizens of the place; and the bank went into operation the following October. The present capital is $150,000, the number of stockholders 168, and its annual dividend 6 per cent. Alfred H. Kimball has been president and Wm. H. Titcomb cashier, from the beginning. The office is kept in the Kimball block, Main street; discount day, Tuesday.

Nor was this prosperity confined to business alone; a marked improvement was manifest in the cause of education, public morals, mental culture, and social intercourse. The East Thomaston, now *Rockland Athenæum*, an association for forming a library, after a preliminary meeting of seven individuals, had met Feb. 7, 1850, and chosen for president Jas. O. L. Foster, then in the practice of law here; A. C. Spalding, vice president, W. H. Titcomb, secretary, C. Holmes, treasurer, and a board of seven directors. It commenced with a capital stock of $1000, and 100 share-holders, who were to pay an annual tax of two dollars each, and other subscribers to share its privileges by paying $3 a year or $1 a quarter. A suitable room was provided in the Kimball block and fitted up at a cost of $157, carpeted by the ladies, hung with engravings, and furnished with nearly 1000 standard volumes, and the periodicals of the day,—of which the British Quarterlies and Hunt's Merchant's Magazine were gratuitously bestowed by Col. C. A. Macomber. This library was removed, in Jan., 1857, to Berry's new block, where it still retains some 1800 volumes of standard works, and is one of the most valuable institutions of the city.

By council duly called, the *Second Baptist Church* in Rockland was formed, Nov. 26th of this year, consisting of 12 male and 8 female members of the 1st church, cordially dismissed for the purpose, together with three from churches in other towns, — mostly residents at the North End. At the first church meeting, Dec. 13th, John Porter and J. Riley Bowler were chosen deacons; succeeded, Feb. 12, 1859, by Waterman Fales and Joseph R. Walker. Rev. Winthrop O. Thomas, dismissed from Lincolnville church, was pastor in 1852 at $300, the two following years at $400, and 1855 at $500, — continuing his very acceptable services till Dec. 26, 1858, and then removing for a time to Leavenworth, Kansas. On the 29th Dec. 1852, their church edifice, standing in a commanding situation at the North End, was dedicated; having been built on contract for $8000 by Col. H. G. Berry, and furnished with a town clock by subscription of the citizens at large, a communion service by Mrs. Geo. Thomas, a sofa by H. G. Berry, two stuffed chairs by Messrs. Sawyer & Colson, a table by H. Burpee, a chandelier and pulpit lamps by Secomb & Taylor of Boston, a bible by Dr. J. M. Blaisdell and W. G. Sargent, Esq., and a copy of the Psalmist by T. K. Osgood. The pews sold for a sum sufficient to cover the cost of the house. In March, 1859, Rev. Joseph Kalloch became the pastor, and still continues his services. The church has suffered somewhat from the death or removal of members; but the whole number in 1863 was 109, and its number of S. S. scholars 110, with a library of 400 volumes.*

An Antiquarian Singing Choir under the lead of Mr. Harrington, gave repeated and very successful concerts in the winter of 1851–2, the proceeds of which were distributed among the poor and needy families.

1852. For a week or more prior to April 22d, there was a constant succession of east and north-east gales and storms; one of which lasted from Sunday till Wednesday, so violent that few could stand against it, and the steamers Governor, Boston, and Eastern State, were obliged to seek shelter till it was over. A drought succeeded; during which, June 6th, a fire broke out at Brown's Corner, in a barn, from which it rapidly spread to the store and dwelling of Wm. Lovejoy, and thence to the dwelling of Edward Lovejoy; which were consumed, but the goods and furniture saved. Loss about $3000. The greatest exertions of the citizens were necessary to save the neighboring buildings. During a protracted shower, June 22, the schooner Rio Grande, Capt. Hix, at anchor in this

* Church records; Minutes of the Association.

harbor, was struck by lightning, her masts shattered, and house split its whole length. On the morning of December 28th, a fire broke out in the dwelling of D. C. Dinsmore, at the North End, which, with its contents and the furniture of a Mr. Lord, stored there, was consumed. The loss to this industrious mechanic, $1500, not being insured, the citizens with their characteristic liberality immediately raised a handsome sum for his relief and something towards that of Mr. Lord.

Among the other signs of progress, was the building of a number of new stores on the west side of Main, below Spring street, three in one block, by Mitchell & Young, with a large hall above called *Beethoven;* another block by Wm. Wilson; and still another, by G. W. Palmer. New streets were laid out in various directions; and it was said that some 300 dwellings, stores, and other buildings, besides two churches elsewhere mentioned, were going up. Among others, George Lindsey repaired and enlarged his dwelling, which has since been converted into a tavern known as *the Lindsey House*, and which he had erected in 1835, — himself burning the lime, making the brick, and hauling the materials. A *marine railway*, wharves, kilns, and ship-yards, were built at the southern end of the harbor; and no less than 1,000,000 casks of lime were burnt during the year.

The *Rockland Lime Rock Company* was incorporated March 23d, with a capital not exceeding $10,000, for draining or otherwise removing the water from the range of quarries near Alden Ulmer's and improving the same. A plank road having been in agitation and advocated by many, was, as early as April 15, 1850, voted by the town to be built for twenty rods on Lime Rock street, by way of experiment; and now, April 13, 1852, the *Rockland Plank Road Company*, with a capital of $25,000, was incorporated for the purpose of constructing a plank road from the Austin quarries near the Thomaston line, to the lime kilns near the shore, with a branch to the quarries at Brown's Corner. But, in the mean time, the result of the town's experiment began to appear. It was found that the three-inch planks used, were, in less than two years, cut through by the heavily loaded wheels employed in the transportation of limestone; and the plan was abandoned. In 1853 an additional Act authorized the company to substitute a macadamized for a plank road, on any portion of the same; and, in 1864, on petition of F. Cobb and others, a railroad was granted by the legislature from the quarries to the wharves.

Mr. Colby's steam engine, of 25 horse power, was purchased this year by the *Rockland Steam Manufacturing Company*, consisting of I. K. and A. H. Kimball, Jos. C. Libbey, and H. G. Berry, which was incorporated April 2d, with power to hold property not exceeding $30,000, and to manufacture wood, iron, &c. It did a good business, especially in the manufacture of doors, sashes and blinds, till destroyed by fire in 1855.

The *Rockland Fire and Marine Insurance Company* was incorporated Feb. 7th, with a capital of $50,000; and in March following duly organized by the choice of N. A. Farwell, John Gregory, Jona. White, A. H. Kimball, F. Cobb, C. W. Shaw, and C. McLoon, directors; Mr. Farwell was appointed its first and, as yet, only president; and E. Spear, Jr., secretary, succeeded, Jan. 1854, by Maynard Sumner, the present incumbent. It has been very prosperous in its operations.

In Dec. 1852, the Advertiser, a small weekly sheet which had been published nearly a year at Camden, was removed to this place and here issued under the new name of COMMERCIAL ADVERTISER. It was published by F. C. Messenger, and continued till 1854. Aug. 31st of the same year, appeared the PINE TREE STATE, a political campaign paper, published six weeks here and at Camden, under patronage of Hon. E. K. Smart, of the latter place. The year was somewhat memorable for political excitement, no less than three congressional conventions being held in this place; one, the democratic, proving very stormy and at length splitting into two, and nominating Hon. Iddo K. Kimball of Rockland and Hon. M. H. Smith of Warren as their respective candidates. Jas. O. L. Foster, Esq., was nominated for the same office by the free soil convention; but, in consequence of these divisions, Hon. E. W. Farley, the whig candidate, was elected.

The Rockland Lyceum was organized in the fall of 1852, and, under its auspices, lectures delivered, by Messrs. Joseph Harvey of Amherst; E. G. Brooks of Lynn; Geo. Shepherd of Bangor; Wm. Smyth of Brunswick; C. F. Allen of Bath; E. B. Webb and Asa Dalton of Augusta; G. F. Talbot of E. Machias; J. W. Hanson, Gardiner; J. P. Skeele; Henry Giles of Bucksport; U. Balkam of Wiscasset; E. Whittlesey of Bath; W. A. Drew of Augusta; and closing with H. Giles again, April 8, 1853.

The *Youth's Educational Union* was organized this year, by Z. Pope Vose and seven other young people of the place, for purposes of self-improvement. It continued for some four or five years, and contained considerable native talent; publishing in 1854 a small volume of 218 pages of original compositions, under the title of *The Stray Sunbeam*, edited by Mr. Vose, Cynthia I. McIntosh, H. F. Perry, and S. Francis White; which, though now regarded by some of its widely scattered members as a youthful indiscretion, is a pleasant memento of happy hours, and exhibits marks of fine feeling, taste, and the germs of genius, since more amply developed and appreciated. About the same time, *The Dial*, of 29 pages, was published; being a creditable number of a semi-monthly paper got up by Mr. Osgood's pupils, at Grace street school.

The *Methodist Episcopal Society* of Rockland, whose house of worship here was erected in 1829 or '30, and whose history has been already brought down to 1838, in chapter XVI, had continued to thrive under the preaching of Revs. A. Caldwell, 1839-40; John Atwell, 1841; Thomas Greenhalgh, 1842; C. C. Cone, 1843; J. C. Perry, 1844-5; Charles Baker, 1846; L. P. French, 1847-8; J. Atwell, 1849-50; and Geo. Pratt, 1851-2. Having now, from a handful of humble believers, become a numerous and able body, they put up the present year an addition to their chapel, of 12 or more feet, making a commodious and neat church, with sittings for 500 persons, which, in 1862, was valued at $5000. Mr. Pratt has been succeeded by Revs. H. C. Tilton, 1853-4; A. Church, 1855-6; C. F. Tupper, 1857-8; Wm. H. Crawford, 1859; C. B. Dunn, 1860; Barnet M. Mitchell, 1862; and E. W. Hutchinson, 1863. In 1862, the number of church members was 107; probationers, 24; Sabbath School scholars, 75; volumes in library, 200; preacher's receipts, $346; value of parsonage, $1200.*

1853. The year opened sadly in this place; — a fire breaking out at eleven o'clock on New Year's eve, in the attic of the northern half of the Kimball block. When first discovered, such damage was done to the roof and upper story, that strong fears were entertained for the whole block and the wooden buildings across the narrow street; but, by exertions of the fire companies and citizens at large, among whom Messrs. Chas. S. Crockett, J. Cables, Israel Perry, J. S. Coburn, and I. Gregory were particularly noticed, aided by full hydrants and a storm of sleet which covered every wall with ice, the fire was arrested and finally got under. The loss was estimated at $7000 to I. Kimball on the building; $1500 to

---

* Church Records, Mr. S. Albee, Conference Minutes.

Kimball & Tate, hardware merchants, both uninsured; $4500 to B. W. Sawyer & Co., furs, &c.; $10,000 or $12,000 to E. Barrett, dry goods, on the first floor, insured; while on the second floor the Municipal Court room, the law office of C. L. Lowell, Esq., dentist's office of Dr. J. E. Hunt, with their contents, were all destroyed; as well as the hall and rooms occupied by Relief Lodge of I. O. of O. F., Lime Rock Div. S. of T., and a chapter of the Temple of Honor, on the third floor. Much damage also was sustained by others in the removal of goods, and the pilfering, which was carried on to so great an extent that strong suspicions of incendiarism were awakened.

Roused to a sense of danger by this occurrence, the town, at a meeting called Jan. 29th, voted that the selectmen and auditors of accounts purchase two fire engines and necessary apparatus; provide and locate suitable engine houses; and hire the amount of money necessary, to be paid in four annual instalments. This action, though prompt, was altogether too tardy for the events which followed. A second fire succeeded on the morning of Feb. 28th, in the clothing store of S. E. Benson, Jr., which was totally consumed, with most of his stock in trade, estimated at $3000, insured $2000. The adjoining establishment of M. E. Thurlo and the office of W. G. Sargent over it, were torn down to prevent extension of the flames; whilst a barber's shop and two shoemaker's shops were wholly destroyed, without any insurance. Just one month later, March 28th, still another fire occurred in and totally consumed a wooden building on Main street, belonging to S. Rankin, the lower part being occupied as a provision store by the owner, and as a variety store by Ephraim Gay, who lost a new stock of goods worth $5000, wholly uninsured; and the upper story occupied as dwellings by Wm. O. Fuller and M. C. Andrews, who lost all their clothing and furniture, Andrews only being insured for $250. But the greatest fire of the season and most destructive one ever before experienced here or perhaps in any part of the State, took place at three o'clock in the morning of May 22d. It broke out in the rear of S. Pillsbury's store on Main street, consuming all the buildings on the west side of that street from the store of Larkin Snow on the corner of Spring street to Holmes's block on Lime Rock street inclusive,—the Commercial and Rockland hotels, Holmes's, Thorndike's, Spofford's, and Shipbuilder's Bank, blocks; and all immediately opposite on the east side;—including Berry's stables, and those of Dennis, Thorndike, and Young; 23 stores; and a large number of dwellings and other buildings. The total loss was estimated at from $150,000 to $200,000, and the insurance on the same at about $60,000. The causes which led to so extensive a destruction of property, were, the strong wind blowing at the time; the lack of water in the hydrants, from its having been shut off a few days before, and the tide being out; together with a want of engines; — the only one in town not being in good working condition, and the two new ones ordered not having yet arrived, though both those from Thomaston with many of its citizens came and rendered effective aid. Notwithstanding the hurry and confusion of the crowds engaged in arresting the flames and removing goods, no serious accident to life or limb happened, except that J. Spofford, Esq., broke his shoulder blade and arm in falling through the scuttle of a store, John Bennett had his face and hands badly burnt in rescuing some hose, and Mrs. T. Frye was slightly injured in escaping from her burning house.

The two new engines being at length received and named, the one *Dirigo, No.* 3, and the other *Defiance, No.* 4, measures were immediately taken to form a company for the management of each of them. Two effective companies were accordingly organized, the former under Wm. G. Berry and Elijah Walker, first and second foremen, with G. L. Smith and C. S. Crockett, foremen of the hose; and the latter, under officers not ascertained. These did good service without any compensation, till the city council made, in April, 1855, an appropriation of $150 for each company. This sum not proving satisfactory, the Dirigo company refused further service and voted to disband. It, or a new one, was immediately re-organized, however; and both companies have continued their organization to the present time, contributing much to the security of life and property, as well as to the general credit and respectability of the city.

The business of Rockland was never more prosperous than in 1853; though its usual substratum, that of lime, fell off this year, on account of the scarcity of eastern wood, to 613,323 casks. Yet 40 or more new kilns for its manufacture were built, at an average cost of $800 or $900. Ship-building was also actively prosecuted; one of its distinguished exploits being the clipper ship Red Jacket, of 2500 tons, which, a few months after, performed the passage from New York to Liverpool in thirteen days, one hour and twenty-five minutes; the quickest, it was then said, on record. Many stores and other buildings, also, were going up in various parts of the village. Among these last, were a brick block by Capt. John Spear, on Main street, with three spacious stores below and dwellings above; and, in the northern part of the village, a like block, by Jos. Hewett, and another, of four stores, by Constant Rankin. At Ingraham's Point, great improvements were made, especially by the *Atlantic Ship Wharf and Lime Manufacturing Company*, which was incorporated March 19th, with a capital of $50,000, and power to construct a wharf not exceeding 800 feet into tide waters. It was organized April 30th, by the choice of H. Ingraham, president, and F. Cobb, treasurer, and the same with Sidney B. Morse of Boston, and H. C. Lowell and Thomas Colson, directors. After the burning of the public houses mentioned, the large wooden dwelling, recently owned by Charles Holmes, on Lime Rock street, was fitted up for a hotel, and opened June 13th, by J. C. Merrill, last from Gardiner. Adjoining the Kimball block, which was also enlarged, a block was built by Berry & Abbott, of brick, with a cast iron front to the second story, containing three stores, with offices above; a large wooden store by W. A. Farnsworth, on the site formerly occupied by him on Main street, at the head of Sea street; and a block of three very large and fine stores by Jeremiah Berry, on the site of the late Commercial House. Messrs. Dyer & Co. of Portland, established themselves, in the spring, as brass founders and machinists, at the North End. The steamboat *Rockland*, of 195 tons, was this year built at Hoboken, N. Y., and, August 21st, entered upon her route between Rockland and Machias, under the command of Capt. E. S. Blaisdell of this place; and has proved a popular little steamer for various excursions with our citizens. For this, or some kindred enterprise, the *Maine Steam Navigation Company*, comprising many leading men of this place and Camden, was incorporated Jan. 31st. The "Rockland" was, for some reason, sold in 1858,—and bid off by F. Cobb and others of this place, for $7800. The *Rockland Gas Light Company* was incorporated March 5, 1853, and, under the care of R. Young, superintendent, commenced making gas at 9, A. M., Jan. 13, 1855,—lamp-posts being erected in different places, and the city first lighted up by its means in June, 1855. An Act for the protection of the shores, docks and harbor of Rockland from injury, by the deposit of core and other waste matter from the lime kilns, was passed March 10th, and a fine of ten dollars imposed for every offence of the kind.

The *Ship-builders' Bank* in Rockland was incorporated March 7th, with a capital of $100,000; and such was its prestige that its stock was rapidly taken up, and its business commenced in June, auspiciously, under direction of Henry C. Lowell, president, and Wm. L. Pitts, cashier. Some obscurity has ever rested upon the affairs of this Bank; but it would seem that the confidence reposed in these officers was such that the directors neglected the ordinary precautions against their mismanagement. The bonds given by the cashier were not renewed at the expiration of his first year, and he, with or without the knowledge of the president, rushed into hazardous speculations with the funds of the Bank, to supply the loss of which a vast and unknown amount of its bills were put in circulation without the knowledge of the directors, or any record by which the amount could be ascertained. These circulated for a time without suspicion; but, as they began to return faster than the Bank was able to redeem them, embarrassments arose. New officers (viz., A. K. Kimball, president, and A. W. Kennedy of Warren, cashier,) were appointed, and attempts were made to examine into the cause of defalcation. These attempts resulted in nothing certain, except that the funds of the Bank had disappeared, a large amount of its paper had been clandestinely put in circulation, no bondsmen were found liable, its credit was gone, and the former cashier had absconded to avoid arrest. Its affairs were put into the hands of receivers, Jan. 10, 1855; and Mr. Lowell, unable to face the defrauded stockholders and an indignant public, whose confidence and esteem he had till then fully enjoyed, sought a retreat for his family and his mortification in the far West.

On the 13th of January, the house of the *Free-Will Baptist Society* of Rockland, completed and finished, was dedicated to the worship of God by the usual services, including a sermon by Rev. P. Weaver, address to the church and society by Rev. J. Mariner, and dedicatory hymn written for the occasion by Mrs. Ramsey. The edifice is situated on Camden street, in the north-eastern part of the city, and has accommodations for 200 persons, being valued, by the census of 1860, at $2000. An elegant bible was presented to the society by Dr. Thos. Frye, a choice table by Franklin N. Brown, and $257 contributed for the purchase of a bell. The church was organized as early as June 27, 1851, and consisted of seven members only, of whom J. H. Young was chosen standing clerk, and Hollis Kirkpatrick, deacon. Its members, in 1862, amounted to 120, — Jacob Thomas and Stephen Prescott being then deacons, and Abel Walker standing clerk. The pastors of this society have been, Rev. Wm. H.

Littlefield, from June, 1852, to April, 1859; Rev. Jason Mariner, from June, 1860, to June, 1862; and, in Nov., 1862, Rev. Ebenezer Knowlton, succeeded, in 1864, by Rev. Albert P. Tracy.*

The corner stone of an *Episcopal Church*, also, named *St. Peters*, on Park street, was laid, July 11th of this year, with appropriate ceremonies by Rt. Rev. Bishop Geo. Burgess. Notwithstanding the discouragement consequent on the great fire in May preceding, in which were totally destroyed the temporary place of worship and church furniture of the small band which, on the 18th of January, had been organized into the parish of St. Peters and obtained the services of a rector, the building was, under the advice and generous gift of Bishop Burgess, now commenced and by the end of February, 1854, brought to a successful close. This edifice, in Gothic style, 65 feet long by 35 feet wide, with four buttresses on each side and at the gable an octagonal tower surmounted by a cross, with a stained glass window, ornaments, and devices, is capable of seating 300 persons; and cost between $3000 and $4000. Much of the expense was defrayed by contributions from churches of the order in Boston, New York, and Philadelphia. A tower and spire were added in May, 1858. The first and only rector, thus far, of this church, was Rev. George Slattery, who came from Saco, preached his first discourse here July 11, 1852, and continued the duties of his office till his resignation was, April 10, 1860, accepted with much regret by his parish. The wardens, senior and junior, of this church have been in different years, N. G. Bourne, W. L. Pitts, C. N. Germaine, Richard Walker, Lewis Hall, Chas. A. Reed, Jos. Benson, O. G. Hall, and S. H. Holbrook.

There were interesting temperance lectures this season by Rev. S. C. Fessenden, John Hawkins, the reformed drunkard, and others; and, under the operation of *the Maine law* and its faithful execution, during two months from July 1st, by I. G. Day, constable and keeper of the lock-up, (for the erection of which $200 had been voted the previous year,) it appeared that there was 60 per cent. less of drunkenness in the place than in the months preceding. The Lime Rock and Hyperion divisions of S. of T. held a pleasant celebration, Dec. 24th, with a procession, appropriate addresses, and refreshments at Beethoven Hall; and a series of bi-monthly mass meetings commenced Jan. 18, 1854.

The *Benevolent Union Association*, for the relief of the

---

* Rockland Gazette, communication of Abel Walker, Esq.

destitute, was formed at the close of Nov. 1853, with Messrs. N. A. Farwell, G. J. Burns, T. K. Osgood, and J. Wakefield, as officers.

On the evening of January 3, 1853, two young men, gunning on Jameson's Point, discovered the dead bodies of a man and woman, their broken boat and its contents, in the surf on and near the shore. They proved to be those of John Smith and his wife, long the only occupants of Laisdell's Island, who had visited Camden for a few New Year purchases, on the 31st, starting for home and their lonely children just before dark; had met a head wind and some sea, and, running for Rockland harbor, had kept in too near the Point, struck a rock, and, bewildered by the darkness and chilled by the cold, failed to reach the shore. On the the 16th July, during a heavy shower, one barn and four dwellings were struck by lightning; and, on the evening of September 6th, the place was again visited by a smart thunder shower, during which, a horse belonging to J. Wakefield was supposed to have been killed by the lightning, though the building, a few feet from which he stood, was not struck. As Oliver Gay of this place, and Chas. Winslow, formerly of Waldoboro', were engaged in blasting rock at the marine railway, on Ingraham's Point, September 19th, having put in a charge and ignited the fuse, they withdrew a sufficient time, as they supposed, but unfortunately returned at the moment of its explosion. Gay was much injured, and Winslow's skull so badly shattered that he died the next day. On the 7th October, Joseph D. Thurston, employed at the machine shop of Thurston & Ingraham, at the North End, whilst under derangement in a typhoid fever, during the temporary absence of his brother, left his room in the night time; and, notwithstanding an immediate search, no trace of him was discovered till Sunday, when he was found dead, having made his way 120 feet up into a subterranean passage, which crossed the street in the immediate vicinity of the work-shop. A storm of snow with a violent north-east wind occurred December 29th, blocking up the roads and stopping the mails west of Bath for six days, so that 14 mail-bags arrived at this place simultaneously. Much shipping suffered along the coast; and, in this harbor, among other slight damages, the schooners Edwin of Sullivan, and Richmond of this port, went ashore and were wrecked or burnt. The schooner Henry Franklin of this place, loaded with moulding sand, was lost on Race Point with all on board except the Captain, Samuel Thomas, who succeeded with great difficulty in reaching the shore through the surf. Those who perished were Nathan A. Saunders, mate, and his father, both of Rockland, and Charles Merrill of Augusta.

1854. An Act to incorporate the town of Rockland into a city, was passed by the Legislature at its session of 1854, subject to a vote of the inhabitants, accepting or rejecting the same. This was decided at a town meeting duly called on the 3d of June, by the following vote; for accepting, 238; against, 110; and the event was greeted in the evening by martial music of the brass band, through the streets, ringing of bells, firing of cannon, sending up of rockets and Roman candles, a huge bonfire of tar-barrels, and other demonstrations of joy. In the course of two or three weeks the selectmen proceeded to divide the city, by specific boundaries, into seven wards, preparatory to an election of city officers, which was made July 8th, 1854; handsome rooms were provided for the city council, in the Berry block; and the city of Rockland, with the Hon. Knott Crockett as its mayor, commenced its career, as the 8th city chartered in the State and the 5th in population.

At the annual meeting in March, 1854, the town had voted that the selectmen cause a survey to be made of the town lines and all the different roads and streets, designate the latter by names and guide-boards, and produce a plan of the same; but, by a subsequent vote, this work was postponed till after the adoption of the city charter. Applications for building side-walks in many of these streets had been frequently made since the separation of the place from Thomaston, and usually referred to the selectmen; but, in 1853, $1000 had been appropriated for their construction.

The *North Bank* of this city was incorporated March 20th of this year, with a capital of $50,000; and, in October, chose its directors and went into operation, with John Bird, president, and Stephen N. Hatch, cashier, both of whom still continue. This bank is located in the Crockett block, discounts on Monday, and pays at present an annual dividend of six per cent. to its 132 stockholders.* Of *Patent* or *Improved Lime Kilns*, a newly invented one, by Messrs. A. D. Nichols and Davis Tilson, was tried this year and promised to be valuable and important; another was introduced the following year by Hon. Chas. Crockett, which was thought to save fifty per cent. in the amount of fuel; and still another in 1857, patented by Mr. Abner Weeks, saving the time and expense of cooling and re-heating the kiln. But,

---

* Report of Bank Commissioners, 1863.

of the improved kilns, that now most generally used in the place is the *Snow kiln*, introduced from Glen Falls, N. Y., by Chas. W. Snow, Esq., about 1857; upon which, we believe, no patent fee is paid by builders here. A new brick block was this year erected by Larkin Snow, on the corner of Main and Spring streets, containing a store in the first story, offices in the second, and the armory of the City Guards in the third; also, at the North End, the spacious *Crockett block*, by Charles Crockett, containing, among its apartments, "*the Granite Hall*"; also, the *Thorndike block* of stores on the corner of Main and Sea streets. The *Rockland Hotel Company*, with a capital of $40,000, having been incorporated, March 30, 1852, organized the present year by choosing a body of directors; but we are not aware that anything further was done.

The *Rockland City Guards*, a light infantry company, after instruction by Davis Tilson, graduate of West Point, and receiving from the State the requisite number of muskets, organized by choice of Col. H. G. Berry, captain, G. J. Burns, Jona. Spear, and A. S. Dyer, lieutenants, Wm. H. Titcomb, orderly sergeant, and O. J. Conant, ensign; and, attired in its handsome uniform of blue and gold, was soon attracting general admiration. It was presented with a beautiful flag, May 8, 1855, by his Honor the Mayor, as was Capt. Berry, in Aug., 1855, with a silver pitcher and gold chain and plate attached, by members of the company.

A week of extreme cold occurred between January 19th and 27th, the mercury in this city falling at sunrise, for the most part, below 10° minus. On the 30th and 31st of March, fifteen inches of snow fell, and, followed by cold weather, made excellent sleighing. Dirigo Engine Company caused a fine flag-staff to be erected, May 1st; but the joy of the occasion and the day was interrupted by the fall of the shears used, which struck and seriously injured Frederic Sweetland. The company's contemplated ball was, in consequence, postponed, and a substantial token of sympathy in a handsome subscription tendered the sufferer Knott C., a little son of Isaac Simmons, was accidently drowned, July 29th, in Chickawauka Lake. On the 30th September, the schooner Ontario, Capt. H. G. Penniman, on her passage out from Boston to this port, went on to the ledge called the Devil's Back; where, after lying with bow and stern afloat three hours, she broke in two, precipitating the crew into the sea; all four of whom, including the mate, David Beals of this city, perished; the captain alone retaining his hold on the wreck till morning, when he was taken off by a passing fisherman.

Among the lectures at Beethoven Hall, may be mentioned an attractive poem on "the past and present," by W. C. Williamson of Belfast, February 14th, repeated the 28th; and, on the week ending February 22, a series of lectures on "sympathy or no sympathy," on "civil liberty," and on "true greatness of soul," by Charles Lowell, Esq., a native of South Thomaston. A crowded audience also assembled, August 5th, to hear a lecture on temperance, from Hon. Neal Dow, the celebrated author of the Maine Law, which was followed by lectures against the same, August 12th, by S. Carey of Houlton, and L. D. Wilkinson of Saco.

1855. The storm of Jan. 19th, with a strong north-east gale and very high tides, swept disastrously over the whole shore border of the city, destroying property to the amount of $20,000, distributed among the owners of wharves, lime-sheds, kilns, wood, lime, and coal, as well as the Marine Railway company, whose entire works were swept away. The tide at Matinicus was three feet higher than ever known before; and buildings that had stood 40 years were carried away by its fury. The first week in February was cold, the mercury falling to 16° minus, at one time, and the bay, on the 7th and 8th, freezing over as far out as Owl's Head; but the whole winter was nearly destitute of sleighing. On March 14th, much damage was done by a storm to the shipping; two schooners were sunk or went to pieces at the wharves, — one, the Minerva, lime-loaded, went ashore at Ingraham's Point, as did also a sloop. Capt. John Hart of this place was so badly injured on board his vessel, that, after lingering about a fortnight and undergoing amputation, mortification set in and caused his death, March 25th, — leaving a wife and two young children. In a violent gale, April 2d, also, the brig Duncan, Capt. Isaac A. Porter, master, and Henry S. Verrill, mate, both of this place, from Philadelphia for Bath with coal, went down with every soul on board, in sight of the schooner Elvira, which lay by her four hours unable to render any aid, from the violence of the waves. The early spring was dry, but hay and most crops were good. In July the harbor swarmed with mackerel.

The *North Fire and Marine Insurance Company* in Rockland was incorporated March 12th; but its principal mover, John Bird, having become interested in the Lime Rock Insurance Company, it never went into operation. Among the losses by fire this year was that of the steam-mill on Main street, before mentioned, on the evening of Oct. 25th, the owners losing about $12,000, while O. P. & J. Merriam, manufacturers of doors, sash and blinds, and in part occupants, lost $400,—none of the parties being insured. The fire originated near the boiler. As an additional means of safety against such occurrences, the mayor and aldermen made an arrangement with the Water Company by which twenty hydrants attached to the Company's pipes were put down in convenient places through the most compact portions of the city. A *Watch* was also appointed, for the nightly protection of the city; which has, more or less, been continued, through the winter at least, in succeeding years.

A Temperance Jubilee was held in Crockett's block March 16th, when well spread tables did honor to the ladies who prepared the feast for a gratified and crowded assemblage, who listened to eloquent speeches from several gentlemen called out by the promptness and wit of the president, Freeman Harden, who, among other sentiments gave the following: "our worthy mayor; a hard *knot* for the rummies." A grand festival, procession, and collation at Granite Hall, was held, July 17th, on the meeting of the Grand Division of the S. of T. with the Lime Rock and Hyperion Divisions of this city. By the energetic labors of David M. James, city marshal, violators of the law were prosecuted and liquor selling kept to a good degree in check, till "after the September election, when the flood-gates of intemperance were opened anew, more especially by the refusal of the Grand Jury to do their duty in sending for witnesses in cases of persons who had been tried in the Municipal Court; and, on clear and conclusive evidence, bound over for appearance at the October term of the Supreme Court."*

On the 15th Jan. 1855, the City Council authorized the treasurer to procure by loan $10,000 to pay outstanding orders and town liabilities. This indebtedness of the city has, of course, increased since,—especially within the last few years, in consequence of soldiers' bounties, and other expenditures incident to a state of war; and a permanent loan of $30,000 has of late been effected at 5 per cent.,—all of which is taken by residents of the place. The entire indebtedness of the city, was in 1863, about $60,000.†

In a tax of seven mills on a dollar this year (1855) assessed, 105 individuals paid over $50, forty-five paid over

---

*Report of City Marshal, for 1855.
† Mayor Wiggin's address of March, 1863

$100, and three over $500; whilst the number of those paying $20 and upwards was very large.

Ship-building, which was very flourishing this year, by the high wages it offered, drew off many workmen from other pursuits and somewhat lessened the lime product, which was still further decreased by the high prices of provisions, dulness of trade, and the want of building in New York. New buildings, however, still went up in this city. The *Thorndike hotel*, built the past year of brick, covered with mastic cement, three stories in front and four in the rear, extending 80 feet on Main and 60 on Sea streets, with ample accommodations for a first class hotel, and several stores on the first floor, was opened, May 8th, by Capt. Wm. H. Thorndike, proprietor. The hotel kept by J. C. Merrill before mentioned, which had taken the name of its predecessor, the *Commercial House*, was also this year enlarged by an additional wing of eight suits of rooms, and put in first rate condition. Both houses, were, it is believed, well patronized by the large number of steamboat travellers and the public generally. The new, beautiful, and well-appointed schooner *Greyhound*, in August commenced running as a regular packet between this place and Vinalhaven. The *North Marine Railway* was this year constructed, being commenced in June and completed by December, at a cost of $11,000, and fitted to receive ships of 1400 tons. The company was incorporated the following winter, with a capital of $75,000. The first *Savings Bank*, incorporated February 28, 1855, consisted of Chas. W. Snow and 27 others, principal citizens of the place, who met April 13th; and, after voting in eight new members, accepted the charter and chose a committee on by-laws. The beneficent institution, however, seems never to have gone into operation; and a second one, incorporated in 1861, in which Mr. Titcomb was principal mover, shared a like fate in consequence of the supervening troubles growing out of the rebellion.

A new volunteer militia company was this year organized by the name of the *Mechanic's Rifle company*, whose uniform was gold-laced black velvet caps and grey clothes trimmed with black. Its first officers were E. C. Spalding, captain, succeeded before the close of the year by Joseph Farwell; with Samuel J. Erskine and Gilbert Perry, lieutenants.

In November, a new weekly paper, the UNITED STATES DEMOCRAT, with 150 subscribers, was commenced in this city by A. & E. Sprague, printers and publishers. It was of good appearance, ably conducted, and warmly devoted to the support of the Democratic party. After a time, March, 1858, its subscription list, having increased to about 1000, was further swollen by the transfer to it of about 800 more from the MAINE FREE PRESS, a paper which had been established at Belfast in support of Pierce's administration. After this, it took the name of the DEMOCRAT AND FREE PRESS; is now devoted to the cause of the Union and Freedom; and has a circulation of about 1400.

The Youth's Educational Union, in default of other effort, this year engaged public lecturers, and devoted the proceeds to the benefit of its library. These were Capt. Stehendsohn, a Hungarian exile; Rev. I. S. Kalloch, Feb. 13th, and again Jan. 10th; J. G. Saxe, on "the money-king," Aug. 9th; Rev. Jas. Belcher of Oldtown, on "the bible in our common schools," April 13th; Mrs. E. Oakes Smith, on "woman and the times," a poem, Nov. 27th, and "the dignity of labor," Nov. 28th; and Rev. J. O. Skinner, on "the unity of the human race," Dec. 27th.

1856. There was a severe storm Jan. 13th, in which the roads were so blocked up that the western mails did not reach here till the 16th. A similar interruption occurred from Feb. 17th to the 20th. On the extremely cold night of Jan. 28th, a fire destroyed the wooden blocks of G. W. Palmer and Wm. Wilson, on Main street, each valued at $2000 and insured for $1500. The principal sufferers were, E. R. Spear, bookseller, F. G. Cook, druggist, Thos. Wiggin, shoe dealer, C. N. Germaine, physician, E. A. Mansfield, H. P. Wood & Son, hardware, C. G. Moffit, clothing, and N. A. & S. H. Burpee, furniture dealers. January was remarkable for being entirely destitute of its usual thaw. The whole winter is memorable for its immense depth of snow, enormous drifts, and uneven roads, over which passing sleighs rose and plunged like ships in a stormy sea. The fine sunny weather of March and April, upon the great body of snow, produced, especially in this city, bad travelling and some stage accidents. April 4th, the two story house of John Porter (2d), at the extreme South End, took fire, from some unknown cause, at two in the morning, and, the state of the streets preventing the engines getting to it, was totally consumed. Loss $1800, insured $1500. A sound resembling the explosion of a powder mill, was, at 9 A. M., of April 11th, distinctly heard in this city, and more especially at Belfast, where it shook the houses, and was supposed to be caused by a meteor falling south of that place. There was some hot weather June 22d, when the mercury stood at 99° here; and again in July, followed by dense fogs and bad hay weather. Mackerel were abundant in the harbor and caught from the wharves. A small two-story building owned by Pendleton & Howes, occupied as a variety store by Joseph Farnham, on North Main street, was burned at two o'clock in the morning of December 2d; valued, building $575, insured, $375, and stock at $500, not insured. The 18th December was severely cold; the mercury being 14° minus at sunrise, in this city. During the violent gale which accompanied this severe cold, the schooner Belcher struck on Race Point, and, but for the almost superhuman exertions of the mate, A. T. Spear of this city, who cut off his frozen overcoat with a hatchet, and succeeded in reaching the shore with a line, all on board had perished. About the same time, the schooner *Excelsior* of this city was lost on her passage from Aux Cayes to New York, together with her captain, Alfred Babbidge, Jr., his wife, his brother, his sister, and his child.

The business of the place was this year rather inactive, both in commerce and manufactures, especially ship-building. Many private residences, some of them elegant, were erected, and two or three brick blocks; one by the Berrys, on the corner of Main and Lime Rock streets; and one by Wilson and White, north of the Thorndike hotel on Main street, containing *Phœnix Hall.* A new steam mill was also constructed on the corner of Main and Willow streets, at a cost of $5000, and owned by K. Crockett, F. Harrington, G. A. Stevens and I. Gregory. The wooden block of Palmer and Wilson was rebuilt, and a new one, also, by Richard Walker, opposite the Spear block, at the raising of which the owner was severely injured by a fall of part of the frame. The Palmer & Wilson block has been since, in June, 1862, again burnt, and again immediately rebuilt in a handsome manner, three stories high, containing four stores, and owned by Wood & Sons, C. G. Moffit and Dr. Frye.

A petition in favor of setting off the 7th ward, which contains all the rural portion and about two-thirds of the whole territory of the city, into a new town, and remonstrances against the same, were got up and presented to the Legislature in Feb., 1856, but resulted in the petitioners having leave to withdraw. The outrage upon free speech in the person of Senator Sumner, called out in this city, May 31st, a large meeting of citizens in Beethoven Hall, without respect to sect or party, who unanimously passed strong resolutions of condemnation. This, with the recent events in Kansas,*

* Among the first to respond to the call to save this territory to freedom

fanned the flames of opposition to the party in power, and, the new Republican party being formed, gave unusual spirit to the elections here as elsewhere. Beautiful flags, bearing the names of the opposing candidates, were suspended across Main street, from the Kimball block, and many mass meetings were held. This spirit, however, did not prevent a harmonious celebration of the Fourth of July. A long procession of S. S. scholars, truckmen, military companies, fire companies of this city and Thomaston; the beautiful ship Independence, manned and officered, drawn by four horses; the car of beauty containing 31 young ladies, representing the several States; &c., marshalled by J. T. Berry, moved to the Lindsey grove, where prayer was offered by Mr. Fessenden, and "America" by the children, the declaration by T. S. Osgood, ode on freedom by the Antiquarian choir, and an oration by I. S. Kalloch, then of Boston, with music by the brass band, were listened to; the whole closing with dinner provided by C. A. Harrington in a pavilion near, the ringing of bells, a salute of 31 guns, and fine display of fireworks. From 8000 to 10,000 people were estimated to be present on the grounds. On the 16th and 17th September, the 1st regiment of the 2d brigade and 4th division of the volunteer militia of the State, was mustered for camp duty in this city, under Col. Burns; consisting of nine well drilled companies, with three brass bands, including that attending the Portland Rifle guards, who were invited guests; and, after drill the first day, was, on the 17th, reviewed by Maj. Gen. Cochran, and Adj. Gen. Atwood, — viewed by thousands of spectators.

A *Teachers' Association* or lyceum, comprising a large portion of the male and female instructers of the place, was organized in December for weekly discussions, essays, &c., on subjects connected with their vocation. Under its auspices, lectures were delivered Jan. 31, 1857, by Rev. N. Butler, on "the anglo-saxon race;" Feb. 20th, by Rev. J. O. Skinner, on "common schools;" and, March 13th, by Rev. F. Wallace, on "John Knox."

1857. In the severe gales prevailing in January, much shipping was destroyed; among others, the schooners *John*

---

was Dr. John W. Robinson of this city, who received a medical degree at Bowdoin in 1849, and came from Richmond here, where he practised medicine and was surgeon of the State Prison. In Kansas his services were highly appreciated, and he was chosen its first Secretary of State. On the breaking out of the rebellion, he left his new and happy home, became surgeon of the 2d Kansas Cavalry, and, after more than a year's faithful service, died Dec. 10, 1863.

B. and *Sam'l Rankin* of this city; and among the sad losses of life, was that of James P. Haskell, lost overboard, together with the mate, from the barque *Tidal Wave*, Jan. 19th. On the 5th Jan. fire was discovered in the Crockett block, but soon extinguished; the chief damage being to the millinery goods of Miss F. Kirkpatrick & Co.,—$314, with no insurance. The barn and shed connected with the house of Dr. J. E. Hunt, corner of Union and Grace streets, were totally consumed and the house considerably damaged by fire, on the night of March 12th, together with a fine horse owned by F. Case. On the 24th of March, John L. Craig, a lad of 15 years, and the only son of his parents, was accidentally shot by a gun which another boy was loading, and the iron ramrod driven through his right eye and passing out some four inches beyond the back part of the head. He died five days afterwards. On June 13th, by a premature explosion of powder in Munroe's quarry, south of the head of Pleasant street, John Murray, a native of Ireland, was so badly injured as to lose one hand. This was followed, July 25th, by a more fatal occurrence in Ulmer's quarry. Reuben T. Jacobs, 27 years of age, had ignited the fuse of a charge, and, after waiting long and supposing it gone out, returned to relight it, when it exploded and so shattered one of his legs as to render amputation necessary, from the effects of which he died the next morning. Sept. 12th, a wooden block of four tenements, belonging to Rufus Carll, on Warren street, was nearly destroyed by fire. Insurance $2300. In the store of Bills & True, North Main street, their shoe stock was damaged by fire, Nov. 29th, about $400.

A daring attempt to break open and rob the Lime Rock Bank, at the corner of Main and Summer streets, was made on the night of May 19th, the miscreants entering through a back window and trying, by means of an iron bar, a sledge, and gunpowder, to wrench the locks from the iron door of the specie vault. But, after succeeding with the two lower locks, the upper one resisted their efforts; and, from some alarm or the approach of daylight, they decamped, leaving their tools, and the old bags which they had hung at the windows. Much disorderly conduct, and several cases of assault, and even stabbing, perpetrated in the summer and autumn of this year, gave sufficient evidence of an inefficient police system and the non-execution of the liquor law, complained of at this time.

The 4th of July was celebrated not by a formal oration and dinner, but by the usual procession, with prayer by Rev.

Wm. H. Littlefield, speeches from Revs. N. Butler, and J. O. Skinner, the declaration by Rev. S. C. Fessenden, interspersed with music from the Thomaston Cornet, Rockland, and Camden bands, in front of the Congregational Church; and, in the afternoon, by the less elevating exercises of a trotting match and a foot-race on Jameson's Point; the latter performed by a Penobscot Indian, 5 miles in 29 minutes 24 seconds. A pleasing union pic-nic celebration of the Congregational, 1st Baptist, and Universalist sabbath schools, was held in Lindsey Grove, September 10th. The *Young Men's Forensic Union*, for debating and literary improvement, organized the preceding December 18th, also provided a course of free lectures; viz.: March 26, 1857, on "the true education" by T. K. Osgood; April 16th, on "success in life" by Rev. A. Church; and, besides private lectures by their own members, aided by the sale of tickets, procured, November 10th, the reading of the poem "Yankee land," by J. G. Saxe; lecture on "the physiology of nations" by Elihu Burrett, November 17th; "bibliography," by I. Sawyer, December 17th; "cemeteries and epitaphs" by I. S. Kalloch, January 6, 1858; "compensated emancipation," by E. Burritt, March 12th; and closing the season, March 18th and 19th, with an unusually gratifying exhibition of home talents in music, declamation, original poetry, and the dramatic art.

A loss befel the city, this autumn, in the death of Hon. Knott Crockett; who, from an orphan boy, gradually rose by his industry, honesty, gentle demeanor, liberality, and good judgment, to the first rank among his fellow citizens. Though only sixty-five years of age, he remembered the city when it consisted only of woodlands and fields of grass and grain. Here, at the age of 15, he began his humble labors by teaching, farming, and burning lime in the little old-fashioned kiln of less than 100 casks, hauling his rock and wood himself with a single horse, maintaining the family of his deceased father, and freeing the estate from its encumbrances. In 1817, at the age of 25, having acquired a little capital, he commenced trade in a store at the corner of Main and Lime Rock streets, where the Berry block now stands; in 1838 took into partnership Wm. Thomas, afterwards a prominent and influential citizen; and, after a course of uniform success, withdrew from mercantile business in 1841. He was, as before stated, the first president of the first bank established in the city, the first Mayor of the city, and among the first in almost every plan to promote its prosperity. In 1856, he was chosen one of the Presidential electors, voting for J. C. Fremont. After disposing of his ample property in legacies to relatives and friends, he devised to Lime Rock Bank, over whose doings he had presided for 21 years, the sum of $5000 — partly in acknowledgment of the confidence reposed in him, and partly to cover any possible loss the institution might sustain from his natural leniency and accommodating disposition towards its debtors.

1858. The winter was unusually mild, with bare ground; and robins were heard, Jan. 28th, singing in the gardens of the city. But after the 11th February, snow, sleighing, and cold weather prevailed. On Feb. 20th, the dwelling on Pleasant street, owned and occupied by Wm. Haskell, was wholly consumed by fire from a cause not ascertained; loss about $2500. On the afternoon of June 5th, the building known as the old steam mill, situated between the South Point kilns and the Atlantic wharf, was destroyed by fire. It was owned by Sam'l Pillsbury, had been erected by Capt. Lemuel Andrews, 12 or 15 years before, and had never been a good investment. The house of Capt. Robt. Wheeler was much injured by fire on the afternoon of June 30th, and on the night of July 3d the bake-house of Ephraim Perkins was entirely consumed.

On the 30th of June, 1858, the schooner Laura Frances, Capt. H. W. Bullock of this city, while on her passage from Salem, was struck by a sudden squall off Cape Elizabeth, thrown upon her beam ends and soon after, by a lurch of the sea, bottom up. The boat, which had broken from the davits and was floating loose full of water, was reached by the captain and two of his men, Edward Cobb, Jr. and Albion K. P. Duncan, where they remained till the two last successively expired in the arms of the captain. The only other person on board, a Scotchman, whose name we have not learned, was drowned; and the captain was taken off at half past eight the next morning by a passing vessel. Nov. 17th, a two-story building at the Brook, occupied as a joiner's shop and store for sash and blinds, by Messrs. Hemenway and Jones, was totally consumed; loss $1700; insured $1000. A number of new hydrants were this year put down by the city authorities. In removing the staging of the barque Orraville, Nov. 2d, R. Trowbridge, master builder, narrowly escaped death; being precipitated from it more than 26 feet.

A commodious block, at the corner of Main and Sea streets, was this year erected by Henry and Bernard Ulmer, the whole upper portion consisting of a fine hall, called the *Ul-*

mer Hall; also a block of stores, built on Lime Rock street, by O. H. Perry.

A series of temperance meetings in the autumn of this year, was commenced with a view of preparing the public mind for the prompt and vigorous execution of the liquor law, now permanently established by a vote of the people of the State. These were largely attended and addressed by most of the leading men of the city; continuing with much spirit through the winter, and into 1859, when the Lime Rock Div. Sons of Temperance, which had suspended its meetings in 1856, was again revived, and has since continued its efforts in the good cause with renovated vigor.

The death of Oliver Fales, a quiet, honest and honored citizen, long regarded as one of the fathers of the business and society of the place, respected by all, beloved by many, through a long life of eighty years, took place on the 10th of December. " To do good, to *be* and not to *seem*, was the religion of his heart as of his daily life."*

A Roman *Catholic Church* which had been in process of building since autumn, was this year completed on Park street; being a handsome edifice, with tower and spire, and costing about $5000. It was named *St. David's* church, and dedicated Aug. 1st, by Rev. Andrew Barron, who was, the preceding summer, appointed to the office of priest, the first in the vicinity, and who was at this time doing a good work among the people of his charge. These still remain under his care. Not far from the same time also, a new diocese was formed and the Bishop of Portland appointed,—his jurisdiction extending to those of the Catholic faith in this vicinity, who were formerly under that of the Bishop of Boston.

The city having at the preceding session of the Legislature been made a *half shire town* of Lincoln county, Phœnix Hall was prepared by the city government as a Court room; and was first occupied by the Supreme Judicial Court, which opened its session, Jan. 25, 1859.

The excellent Rockland Band had, this year, a stand erected in a vacant lot opposite the head of Sea street, and held a series of out-door concerts, weekly, on fine evenings through the summer. National Independence was celebrated July 5th in this city; the principal features being the fantastics from Ward 7; oration by Rev. I. S. Kalloch; reading of the Declaration by L. G. Howes, Esq., now established here

---

* Obituary notice in Rockland Gazette.

as a lawyer; a procession of military, firemen, civic authorities, &c., to Lindsey grove; after which the two Fire companies with their invited guests dined, the one at the Commercial House, and the other in a tent near the Rockland Exchange at the North End. A silver trumpet was presented earlier in the day to the Dirigo Engine Company, in behalf of citizens, by T. K. Osgood; who was fittingly responded to by foreman E. Walker.

1859. In January, the MAINE SPECTATOR, a weekly literary paper for youth and the home circle, was commenced, and conducted in such a manner, through the taste and talent of its accomplished editor, Z. Pope Vose, that it gave promise of much usefulness to the community; but it was discontinued at the end of six months.

The *Young Ladies' Aid Society*, for the benefit of the destitute, held an entertaining levee of tableaux and other entertainments, Feb. 21st, the receipts of which amounted to seventy-five dollars.

The first annual public meeting of the *Rockland Bible Society*, which was formed by a union of all the protestant churches of the city, was held Feb. 27th, and, having purchased bibles and testaments to the amount of $200, measures were taken to supply, by sale or gift, every family destitute of a bible. On the breaking out of the rebellion and the mustering of a regiment of volunteers in this place, this society presented, by the hands of Rev. Jos. Kalloch, a neat copy of the Testament and Psalms to each of the soldiers.

Among the various temperance associations of the city, the *Rockland Band of Hope* was organized, which, at its third meeting, June 11th, numbered 580 youths of both sexes. These, on the 4th of July, held a grand pic-nic celebration, when, after the usual ushering in of the morning and the public presentation of a silver trumpet to the Defiance Engine company by Rev. Jos. Kalloch, the children, numbering about 700, after appropriate exercises in the Methodist church, marched in four divisions, with banners and appropriate mottoes, escorted by the Juvenile Fire King Engine Company, through the principal streets to Lindsey grove, where tables 450 feet in length, enclosing a circular area, were bountifully spread and enjoyed by the happy company. The ladies of the Episcopal church, also, on the same day held a successful strawberry festival in the same grove.

A new brick block, with an iron front to the first story and a French roof, was this year erected by Samuel Pillsbury, at the corner of Main and School streets; containing three large stores below, offices on the second story, a large hall on the third, and several rooms on the fourth. But from the commercial embarrassments of the country and the falling off of business here, the value of real and personal estate owned in the city had suffered a decline since 1857; when, by the assessors' cash valuation, it exceeded $3,000,000. The lime this year manufactured, amounted to about 815,000 casks.

By fires, May 26th and June 1st, the houses of David Kidd and William Flagg were nearly destroyed; both on North Main street; and, August 17th, the house owned and occupied by John Knights and widow Seavey, was nearly consumed, and the barn, with its contents, wholly so, — the flames also communicating to and damaging the house of J. S. Kenniston. On the 21st of July, James Toner and James Latta, employed in Thurston's iron foundry, at the North End, lost their lives by the upsetting of a sloop-rigged sail-boat, laden with 500 lbs. pig iron and two or three bags of sand, which, being struck with a squall, two miles from Camden harbor, immediately filled and went down. Sunday morning, December 18th, the vestry of the Congregational church was damaged by fire to the amount of $500; followed, two days later, by a more destructive and fatal occurrence. A fire, on the evening of the 20th, broke out in the Commercial House, on the second floor, which, after an ineffectual attempt to subdue, without alarming the inmates, spread so rapidly between ceiling and floors through the building, that though the engines speedily arrived and were well served, they failed to extinguish the flames till the main building was wholly destroyed, with most of its furniure and the wearing apparel and other effects of its boarders. By the great exertions of both the engine companies, together with the damp snow and rain that was falling at the time and covered the adjoining wooden buildings, the flames were arrested without spreading further; — the Beals Hall even, though connected with the hotel, being saved. This hotel was owned by Horace Beals of New York, and kept by S. G. Dennis, both of whom were losers; $5000 only being insured on the house, and $3800 on its contents. But the most mournful part of this catastrophe was the accident which befel three brave and active young men of this place, members of Dirigo Engine Company. James F. Sears, Edward Love, and James B. Ulmer, had erected a ladder against the building and carried up their hose to the eaves to pour a stream of water on the burning roof. While the first held the pipe at the eaves and the others were below him on the ladder almost in the midst of the flames, the heavy chimney was observed to totter, a shriek of alarm rose from the crowd, the victims looked up, and in a moment the whole upper mass breaking off just below the roof, fell upon them, broke the ladder, and precipitated all to the ground. They were immediately extricated from the ruins in a crushed and mangled condition; Sears, in a state of unconsciousness, died in the course of an hour; and Love was so badly injured that his life was for a time despaired of, though he finally recovered, and was able to be out in March, when $250 were voted him by the city council. Ulmer, whose external injuries were greater than those of either, recovered sooner, went to sea, and, strange to say, met his death by a fall from aloft a year later. Much sympathy was felt for the sufferers, and the death of young Sears greatly lamented, particularly by the Fire companies, who, on the following Sabbath, Jan. 1, 1860, crowded the 1st Baptist church to listen to the funeral discourse pronounced by Rev. Jos. Kalloch, from the text, "for I reckon that the sufferings of this present time are not worthy to be compared with the glory that shall be revealed in us."

Among other valued matters destroyed in this fire, was a highly prized relic of the Knox mansion, in the form of a large American eagle beautifully carved in wood, originally surmounting the General's arched gateway at the approach to the mansion through the lane, now Knox street, and which, after the transfer of the property and the changes incident to its passing into the hands of strangers, was brought to this city and placed above a dormer window on the roof of the Commercial House. So perish alike the gains of industry and the adornments of renown!

On the 1st August there was a slight shock of an earthquake felt in this city about 9 o'clock, P. M. On the evening of August 14th a lunar rainbow was observed by many in the place; and, on the 1st and 2d of September, the most brilliant exhibitions ever witnessed here of the aurora borealis, with varied colors and ever changing coruscations.

The project, in 1858, of forming a new county with Camden for its shire town, not having succeeded, a movement was this year made for the same purpose, but with this city for the seat of justice. This was deemed of so much importance to the public at large, and to this city in particular, that, in compliance with a unanimous recommendation of a citizens' meeting, called for the purpose, Dec. 12th, the city council appropriated $500 to further it. The measure was prosecuted with zeal; was adopted by the Legislature; and the new

County of Knox commenced its judicial corporate existence; its several officers being appointed by the Governor, March 21, 1860, and its first court held here on the 8th of May. Thus this place, with the rest of old Thomaston, after peaceably abiding in the county of Lincoln just 100 years, found itself embarked on a new bottom and sailing under the new and justly honored name of Knox.

1860. On the 10th February, a small house on Gay street, owned by T. Lane and occupied by Henry Corson, was destroyed by fire. A woman named Mary Curtis, employed as a cook in the Thorndike Hotel, was found on Monday morning, February 20th, in the rear of Eli Sprague's blacksmith shop, at the foot of Winter street, frozen to death while in a state of intoxication. On the morning of June 1st, a double one-and-a-half story house on Masonic street, owned and occupied by S. M'Cann and a Mrs. Crawford, was consumed by fire, supposed to be set by an incendiary. Another fire on the same street and from the same cause, took place two days after, at nearly the same hour, 2 A. M. by which a two story house, with new porch and stable, belonging to Walter J. Wood, was totally consumed, with the furniture, besides joiner's tools worth nearly $500. Insurance on buildings, $1200. These, and other less successful attempts at arson, induced the mayor to offer $100 for the detection of any perpetrator of that crime in the city. On Sunday, September 9th, a fire broke out in the range of large sheds connected with the five patent kilns known as the Haskell privilege, destroying sheds, lime, wood, and casks, and injuring kilns to the amount of $10,000 or $12,000. The principal losers were Messrs. F. Cobb, Wm. McLoon, Wm. O. Fuller, and the firm of Spalding & Haskell, all uninsured. A similar fire took place at the North End, Jan. 26, 1862, in the lime sheds of Messrs. Bird, Fales, Crockett, and Dean, occasioned by contact of water with lime in a storm, by which $3000 worth of property was lost. Other losses by fire have taken place in the last two years, especially in 1862, when incendiarism prevailed to some extent; and Rockland, on the whole, has usually been largely a sufferer from fire. From her Chief Engineer's reports, which are before me with exception of those of 1859 and 1860, it appears that the losses from this cause, for the year ending March, 1856, were $24,463, insurance, $8,778; ditto, 1857, $3,389, insurance, $2,219; 1858, $5,700, insurance not given; 1861, $12,075, insurance, $1,865; 1862, $5,230, insurance, $1,040; and 1863, $17,940, insurance $8,500.

On Sept. 8th, as Amos Thompson and his wife, the wife of Dr. Zenas Colby, the wife of Chas. Hopkins, and Miss Mary Jameson, all of this city, were returning by water from a camp-meeting in Northport, the boat, when off Camden harbor, was capsized; and three of the party, Mrs Colby, Mrs. Hopkins, and Miss Jameson, were drowned. Mrs. Thompson was much bruised and exhausted, but was rescued with her husband, and the body of Mrs. Colby recovered, by the crew of a schooner under way in the harbor. The bodies of Mrs. Hopkins and Miss Jameson were recovered, the former Oct. 1st, and the latter about a week after, washed ashore on one of the Muscle Ridge Islands.

In February a new periodical was started by Z. Pope Vose, editor and proprietor, denominated the YOUTH'S TEMPERANCE VISITOR, a monthly quarto, devoted to the temperance culture of the young, everywhere. It was published in this city at the office of the Gazette, of which also Mr. Vose was now the editor, and proved a valuable auxiliary to the cause it advocated. In consequence of the disturbed state of the times, it was discontinued in July, 1861, but is again revived and flourishing. A new temperance association was organized on the 3d Dec., 1860, under the name of the *Rockland Temperance League*, which embracing, as it did, a large proportion of the active, leading, and respectable citizens, bade fair to free the city from the intemperance which had again insinuated itself into the community by means of the ale and beer traffic. But from the supervening war and its excitements, these efforts were probably relaxed; and it seemed to be a generally acknowledged fact that intemperance had again come in like a flood upon our people, insomuch that the City Marshal of Rockland was obliged to say in his report of March 1, 1863, that "there has never been a time when rum held such complete sway as at present." This state of things, however, has been greatly modified in 1864 by a rigid and faithful execution of the law on the part of the grand jury and prosecuting officer of the county.

Notwithstanding the increased attention paid to education for some years past, the city has not yet succeeded in bringing its schools under any entire, complete, and permanent system, adequate to the wants and ability of the population. In the thickly settled portion of the city the grade system, working its way through many difficulties, has at length been satisfactorily adopted; and one high school, six grammar schools, two intermediate, and nine primary schools have been provided. In the suburban portion of the city, consisting of six school districts, the old system has been continued. The war has drawn heavily upon the corps of High School teachers employed here since 1859; — of whom, Ellis Spear is now Lieut. Colonel, Nath'l A. Robbins, lieutenant, T. K. Osgood, paymaster, E. T. Chapman, paymaster in the navy, and A. J. Pickard, lieutenant of cavalry; all of whom have found more lucrative employment, some of them wounds, one a prison, and one a grave, in the public service. In the troubles that have succeeded 1860, but little change has taken place in the condition of the schools, though the city rose in the scale of liberality towards them, from the 89th town or city in the State in 1860, to the 23d in 1861.

Some increase of business was this year manifested; especially in the manufacture of lime, which amounted to 899,460 casks. There were, at this time, 35 patent kilns in operation; and about one-fourth of the above amount was manufactured in those of F. Cobb & Co. But, as the census of 1860 gives a very meagre and manifestly imperfect return of this manufacture, we substitute an account of it in the year 1863, when partially recovering from the great depression occasioned by the rebellion and the loss of the Southern market. In that year the principal manufacturers were F. Cobb, who burnt 46,777 casks; Cobb, Wight & Case, 25,238; Cobb & Colson, 900; Jona. White, 27,197; J. Bird & Co., 25,062; C. W. Snow, 24,779; W. A. Farnsworth, 24,181; John J. Perry, 23,486; J. H. Wheeler & Co., 22,588; A. J. Bird, 19,792; Albert F. Ames, 21,260; D. C. Haskell & Co., 19,115; William Wilson & Co., 29,386; C. R. Whitney, 19,095; Calvin Hall, 18,226; Joseph Spear, 16,001; G. L. Snow, 13,807; S. Gould, 11,038; Cornelius Henrahan, 23,518; Thos. Lothrop, 10,877; Sumner Whitney, 18,007; J. W. Hunt, 11,159; R. P. Thomas, 8,909; Thos. Walsh & Co., 7,531; John Hall, 6,015; B. Clark, 9,352; Bowler & Abbott, 6,768; J. S. Wheeler, 9,084; Jona. Spear & Co., 3,388; R. Sherer, 2000; Henry Howard, 7,263; and O. Sherer, 347; making a total of 527,193 casks.

The 8th annual Cattle-show and Fair of the Lincoln Co. Agricultural and Horticultural Society was held here on the 2d, 3d, 4th and 5th days of October. The live stock was exhibited on the grounds prepared for the purpose on Lime Rock street, and the other articles in the hall and adjoining rooms of the Pillsbury block. Few animals were brought on, till the second day; when a ploughing-match and procession took place, the streets were crowded with people, the receipts of the society were large, and the Fair altogether successful.

The two last days, however, proved rainy, and in consequence, the address by T. K. Osgood, and the equestrian exercises were deferred. The ox-teams of this city have usually been the most distinguished of any in these Fairs. In agriculture, the census enumerates in Rockland, 47 farms, cash value $200,000; value of farming implements, &c., $4,730; live stock, $17,757; animals slaughtered, $3,323; products of market garden, $1,733; orchard, $295; hay, 1,034 tons; butter, 19,075 lbs.; cheese, 1,700 lbs.; wool, 220 lbs.; and wine, 40 gallons; besides what will appear in the valuation, Table II. It appears by the returns furnished the Maine Board of Agriculture, 1863, that Rockland exceeds every town of the county, in the number of its *horses*, viz.: 393, and in *beets* raised, viz.: 1582 bushels.

The year 1860 is chiefly memorable for the animated and exciting efforts of the different political parties, the imposing mass meetings, the picturesque array and torch-light processions of the *Wide Awakes*, and the eloquent harangues and addresses, ending in the triumphant election of Mr. Lincoln and the Republican candidates; in all which the people and parties of this city more or less largely participated.

At ten o'clock on the evening of July 20th, the splendid meteor, seen all over the country as far south as Philadelphia, was observed in this city. It appeared here about a fourth of the size of a full moon in the N. W. quarter of the Heavens, passed horizontally round toward the E. at the height of about 20^0 or 25^0 with a uniform motion apparently slower than that of a rocket, and when in the S. W. divided into two equal portions, which passed on in the same direction near each other, and, emitting sparks the whole distance, disappeared in the S. E.* This, and a small comet in June, followed by another, more splendid, which appeared about the 4th of July in the succeeding year, while they added to the fears of the timid and superstitious, who regarded them only as omens of approaching trouble, were viewed with delight by the admiring students of nature, and imparted to the Christian fresh confidence that the same unerring hand which guides these apparently lawless wanderers of the sky on their destined errands, will, and does, equally guide cities, States, and empires to the accomplishment of His wise and beneficent purposes.

* Rockland papers of the day.

CHAPTER II.

MILITARY EVENTS AND ROCKLAND VOLUNTEERS.

THE original intention of the compiler was to terminate this history with the year 1860; but the events, civil, military, and naval, since transpiring, have been of so interesting and thrilling a character and so largely participated in by the citizens of Rockland, that some account of those who so promptly volunteered their services and so heroically shed their blood in defence of law, liberty, and the Union, seems absolutely indispensable.

The first note of preparation for the approaching conflict was sounded here on the 8th of Jan. 1861, when, by order of the Governor, a salute of 33 guns was given by Maj. Gen. Titcomb, in honor both of the battle of New Orleans and the occupation of Fort Sumter by the faithful Major Anderson; and when, April 17th, news arrived of the attack and capture of that fortress and the nation's flag desecrated by the infatuated rebels of Charleston, S. C., one burst of indignation arose from the whole population of the city. The national flag was soon floating from the rooms of the city government, was saluted by the "Star Spangled Banner" and other patriotic airs by the Rockland Band, and cheered by a crowd of assembled citizens. Deputy Collector Osgood displayed the stars and stripes from the Custom House, and, with a few solitary exceptions, one sentiment of fidelity to the Union pervaded the city. On the evening of the same day a citizens' meeting irrespective of party and of which the editors of both the Gazette and Democrat acted as secretaries, was held at Atlantic Hall, when eloquent speeches were made, and a series of patriotic and government-sustaining resolutions adopted. A few days later, no less than 20 large and beautiful flags were raised in different parts of the city; numerous gatherings were held, and national salutes fired. On Tuesday, the 23d, another large citizens' meeting was held at the Court Room, at which the City Council was instructed to appropriate $10,000 for the support of the families of such as shall volunteer to serve in defence of the Government and Union; strong resolutions were passed; Stephen H. Chapman came forward as the first volunteer soldier, as such receiving the $20 premium offered by Capt. C. F. Hodgdon; and foreman Elijah Walker tendered 25 of his Dirigo Engine Company, as now ready to enlist against treason as they had done against fire. Soon after, Mrs. R. S. Mayhew, a valued teacher in the graded district, together with Miss Orissa A. Packard and Miss Jennie Grafton, tendered their services to the State to attend the Maine volunteers as nurses; and in less than a week three companies of volunteers, numbering many of the best young men as well as older and respected citizens, were filled and organized;— under Captains E. Walker, O. J. Conant, and L. D. Carver. These, on Sunday, April 28th, attended divine services conducted by Rev. J. Mariner, in the open air at the foot of Lime Rock street. By the end of the first week in May, a fourth company was raised by Col. Geo. J. Burns, of which he was elected captain; and by May 16th, all these, followed by the other companies composing the 4th Maine Regiment, went into camp on Tilson's Hill. This was denominated Camp Knox, a name which they carried with them to the banks of the Potomac. The tents for this and the other Maine regiments were furnished on contract by Gen. Wm. S. Cochran, who employed in this city between 100 and 200 persons, and, as the reputation of his tents extended and further contracts were obtained, increased the number to nearly 500, mostly women and girls, continuing the business far into the winter, and using, a portion of the time, 8000 yards of duck, and turning out 100 tents per day.

The $10,000 recommended, were appropriated by the city council to relieve the families of such volunteers as should give for the same purpose one half their bounty and $6 per month of their wages. To aid the city in this and other expenditures, Defiance Engine Company, as well as Dirigo Engine Company, now decimated by enlistments, relinquished all compensation for their services during the year; Cornelius Henrahan and a number of other citizens offered to labor gratuitously with their teams in repairing Pleasant, Park and Lime Rock streets; while the ladies assembled daily for six weeks, in numbers varying at times from 25 to 150, at Pillsbury hall, making up about 800 shirts, 400 havelocks, and nearly 2000 towels, for the regiment; 52 bed-sacks and pillow ticks with 75 yards of new cloth and large quantities of old into bandages for the hospital; together with a hold-all, and two handkerchiefs for each soldier of the Rockland companies, exclusively. These articles were, June 14th, publicly presented at Camp Knox, by J. Farwell, in behalf of the fair donors, a large number of whom were present; and his appropriate remarks were happily responded to by Capt. Carver of company D. On the 15th, the regiment in dress parade was mustered in, reviewed, and addressed by Gov. Washburn, who pronounced it the best looking body of men Maine had yet sent to the service. On Sunday, the 16th, religious services, which had heretofore been conducted by most of the city clergy in rotation, were performed by Rev. Mr. Mitchell, of the Methodist church, after which, a presentation of swords, procured by subscription among the citizens, was made, with a stirring address by Mr. Osgood, to the commissioned officers of the four Rockland companies, responded to in an earnest and fitting manner by Capt. Walker of company B. And, on the 17th, the reveille sounded at four o'clock; at five the soldiers ate their last breakfast in the camp here; received a day's rations; struck and packed their tents; and at nine, with a large white banner bearing the inscription "FROM THE HOME OF KNOX," took up their line of march down Middle street, and through Main street to Atlantic wharf, where the steamer Daniel Webster was waiting to receive them. At Main street they were joined by the Rockland band in full uniform, who volunteered to accompany them on to Washington; and, opposite the Kimball block, a halt was made, and a second banner bearing the motto and arms of the State, was presented the Colonel by Maj. Gen. Titcomb. The camp grounds, the streets, windows and avenues along the whole line of march, and especially the wharf, buildings, and shipping near the place of embarcation, were densely thronged with weeping friends, relatives, and interested spectators. Under a salute from the ship Alice Thorndike, the troops were all embarked, when an address was made by Maj. Gen. Titcomb to the assembled crowds, who gave "three times three hearty cheers to the Fourth Regiment, which were returned by the soldiers,—and the boat moved away, the band playing, handkerchiefs waving, hearts throbbing, and tears falling, as she bore our brave volunteers away to the soldier's work."

The field officers of this regiment, which has ever been distinguished for its cleanliness and health, correct discipline, and bravery, were, at the time of leaving, as follows: Hiram G. Berry of this city, colonel; Thomas F. Marshall of Belfast, lieutenant colonel; F. S. Nickerson of Searsport, major; J. B. Greenhalgh of this city, adjutant; Stephen H. Chapman, ditto, sergeant major; Wm. A. Banks, ditto, acting surgeon; Elisha Hopkins, soon supplanted by S. C. Hunkins of Windham, assistant surgeon; Isaac C. Abbott of this city, quartermaster; J. H. Crowell of Winterport, quartermaster sergeant; Julius A. Clark, commissary sergeant;

Charles S. McCobb, hospital steward; and B. A. Chase of Unity, chaplain. Besides the officers already mentioned, the following citizens of this place were enrolled as officers or privates: —

In the Regimental band, John F. Singhi, leader, discharged in 1862; John R. Burpee, discharged Sept. 5, 1862; Henry G. Tibbetts, afterwards wagoner of company B, then its principal musician; John Brennan, transferred as musician to company D, left the service, Sept. 15, 1862; Sullivan K. Whiting, discharged in 1862.

In *company A*, Benjamin F. Philbrick, wounded in May, 1864; Wm. Thompson, died Sept. 16, 1862; and William Crosby, captured at Gettysburg.

. In *company B*, Elijah Walker, captain, promoted to colonel; Orren P. Mitchell, lieutenant, promoted to captain, discharged July 31, 1862; Julius P. Litchfield, lieutenant, promoted to captain, captured at Gettysburg; Arthur Libby, sergeant, promoted to captain of company A, wounded slightly in May, 1864; Harrison U. Cowing, sergeant, killed at Malvern Hill; Wm. E. Crockett, sergeant, returned to the ranks, left the service August 20, 1861; Heman H. Burpee, promoted to sergeant, captured August 29, 1862, discharged for disability Dec. 19, 1862; Eben. Harding, corporal, promoted to lieutenant, dismissed from service May 4, 1863; John Butler, corporal, promoted to sergeant, discharged for disability Nov. 15, 1862; Madison Stevens, corporal, killed in battle Sept. 1, 1862; Havilah Pease, corporal, promoted to lieutenant; Otis G. Spear, corporal; Henry T. Mitchell, corporal, captured July 2, died at Richmond, Dec. 16, 1863; Henry O. Ripley, corporal, promoted to lieutenant, wounded May 10, 1864, and died June 7th, at Washington; Chas F. Sawyer, corporal, promoted to sergeant major, and, in 1863, to adjutant; Robert Anderson, Jr., transferred to invalid corps; Chas. Baker; Wm. A. Barker, promoted to lieutenant of company G, and captain of company H, wounded May, 1864; Edwin R. Blackington, discharged for disability; Morton A. Blackington, sent to general hospital, October 15, 1863; George A. Bramhall, discharged for disability, December 7, 1862; Edwin E. Brown, wounded September 1, and discharged for disability, December 30th, 1862; Robert Christy, wounded in left side, promoted to corporal, transferred to invalid corps; James W. Clark; Edmund S. Cowing, wounded August 29, 1862, transferred to invalid corps; Herbert J. Dow, wounded August 29, 1862, on duty Nov. 1863; George H. Dunbar, wounded September 1, 1862; Theodore H. Farnsworth, discharged for disability, March, 1862; Wm. J. Flanigan, died of disease, October 1, 1863; Bryan W. Fletcher, killed July 21, 1861; George Foreman, left sick at Cumberland Landing; John W. Haskell, discharged for disability, December 2, 1861; Artemus Heald, left the service, September 12, 1862; Rufus C. Ingraham, discharged for disability; John L. Kalloch; Edgar L. Mowry, promoted to sergeant; Wm. A. Philbrick, died of fever Dec. 16, 1861; Thaddeus S. Pillsbury, promoted to sergeant, wounded May, 1864; Harrison A. Pitcher, left the service July 27, 1861; Franklin W. Potter, discharged for disability, November 17, 1862; Royall Prescott, discharged for disability, July 1, 1862; Hanson B. Simmons, wounded July 2, 1863; Josiah C. Spear, wounded May, 1864; Thomas B. Spear, discharged for disability, October, 1862; Elery G. Stevens, wounded in battle September 1, 1862, transferred to invalid corps; George F. Stetson, wounded at Gettysburg, July 2, 1863; George F. Taylor, wounded July 2, 1863, and severely, May, 1864; Geo. H. Tighe; John W. Titus; Samuel S. Totman; Asahel Towne, killed by a cannon ball, July 21, 1861; Alonzo N. Ulmer, wounded July 2, 1863; Wyman W. Ulmer, promoted to corporal; George E. Wall, wounded September 1, 1862, promoted to sergeant, wounded May, 1864; Aruna Willis, wounded May, 1864; Charles F. Wood, wounded in battle, July 1, 1862, promoted to corporal, discharged for disability September 11, 1862; and Alden F. Wooster, reported missing, after the battles of May, 1864.

In *company C*, Oliver J. Conant, captain, resigned from ill health August, 1861; Charles B. Greenhalgh, lieutenant, promoted to captain, resigned April 28, 1862; George T. Crabtree, sergeant, promoted to lieutenant, wounded Sept. 1, 1862, promoted to captain, and resigned July 21, 1863; Charles H. Conant, sergeant, promoted to captain 1863; Franklin Achorn, promoted to sergeant, killed in battle August 29, 1862; Elisha S. Rogers, sergeant, promoted to lieutenant of company H; John H. Young, sergeant; Joseph R. Conant, corporal, promoted to lieutenant, wounded May 5th, and May 6, 1864 died at Fredericksburg; K. K. Rankin, corporal, promoted to lieutenant and quartermaster; Eugene Waters, corporal, wounded Sept. 1, discharged Oct. 4, 1862; George A. Staples, corporal, returned to ranks at his request; John Colburn, corporal, wounded at Gettysburg; Eben L. Higgins, corporal, wounded at Chantilly, discharged Feb. 8, 1863; Horatio G. Collins, corporal, returned to ranks at his request; Oliver N. Blackington, promoted to sergeant, wounded at

Fredericksburg and discharged for promotion in corps d'Afrique; John F. Walker, and Nathaniel C. Mathews, musicians, returned to ranks, the latter wounded May, 1864; George A. Barker, and Samuel P. Boynton, both discharged for disability 1862; James M. Bragg, killed at Fredericksburg, Dec. 13, 1862; Orlando F. Brown; Avery L. Candage, promoted to corporal, killed at Fredericksburg, Dec. 13, 1862; Dennis Canning, killed by a cannon ball July 21, 1861; Henry Carson, honorably discharged March 26, 1863; Wm. Chapman, left the service March 18, 1862; Horatio G. Collins, detached to other service; Alden Crockett, mostly on detached service; McCobb Cushing, discharged for disability Dec. 28, 1862; Allen A. Dickey, died Jan. 26, 1862, at Alexandria; Michael N. Feyler, discharged for disability Sept. 10, 1862; Nathaniel B. Gowen, captured July 21st, and died in Oct. 1861; John F. Grant, detached on gunboat service; Jarvis B. Grant, killed July 21, 1861; Sewall Hewett, captured July 21, 1861, supposed to be dead; Samuel C. F. Hills, enlisted at Harrison's Landing, discharged for disability Dec. 3, 1862; John A. Kalloch, promoted to corporal, killed at Fredericksburg; Thomas Kalloch, captured at Gettysburg; Daniel Kennedy, discharged for disability July 19, 1862; Charles A. Libby (2d), wounded at Manassas August 29, 1862; James Macovey, left service July 23, 1861; Francis G. Mellus, detached on gunboat service, discharged Sept. 25, 1862; Ambrose P. Melvin, discharged for disability Feb. 11, 1863; Charles H. Miller, promoted to sergeant; Levi Murphy, discharged for disability Nov. 8, 1862; Moses Nickerson, discharged Sept. 10, 1861; Lorenzo Packard (2d), wounded in battle Sept. 1st, and discharged Dec. 27, 1862; Charles C. Perry, sick at home in Nov. 1863; Adelbert S. Pitcher, discharged for disability Sept. 26, 1862, died at Rockland Dec. 30, 1863; Andrew Pottle, captured at Gettysburg; Benj. F. Pottle, died of fever at Harrison's Landing July 12, 1862; Andrew B. Pressey, detached on gunboat service and discharged; John Purcell, left service Nov. 9, 1861; Leonard C. Rankin, killed in action May 5, 1864; Rufus Robbins, on detached service; Walter Sutherland; George W. Thomas, killed in action May 5, 1864; John H. Thomas, wounded in battle Sept. 1, 1862, honorably discharged Jan. 1, 1863; Ezekiel M. Titus, discharged on account of wounds Jan. 1, 1863; James F. Tuttle; Abijah Veazie; Edwin Wade; Jos. Weed, discharged for disability Feb. 20, 1863; Thurlow Weed, wounded in battle Sept. 1, 1862, and left from the hospital at Washington; Joshua G. Whitney; Jacob Winslow, mostly on detached service; and, enlisted March 25, 1862, James P. Wentworth, wounded in battle Sept. 1, 1862.

In *company D*, Lorenzo D. Carver, captain, promoted to lieutenant colonel, discharged for disability Dec. 16, 1863; Thomas B. Glover, lieutenant, captured at Bull Run, promoted to captain, resigned; Charles L. Strickland, lieutenant, resigned; Edwin Libby, sergeant, promoted to adjutant, joined again as captain, killed in action May 5, 1864; Sam'l L. Meservey, corporal, promoted to sergeant, wounded May, 1864; Mark Perry, promoted to sergeant, detached; Hosea Coombs, corporal, captured, discharged Nov. 20, 1861, re-enlisted in a Pennsylvania regiment, and again captured; Allen P. Farrington, promoted to sergeant; William Norton and Thomas Wyatt, both promoted to corporals, detached to gunboat service, the latter killed in the *Mound City* at the attack on Fort Charles, on the Mississippi, June 16, 1862; Rufus F. Day, corporal, promoted to sergeant, died of fever Aug. 18, 1862; William Fountain, corporal, promoted to sergeant, wounded May, 1864; and Levi G. Perry, corporal, enlisted Oct. 28, 1862; Charles P. Burns, wagoner; Benj. Bartlett, discharged Aug. 23, 1862; Charles Bowden, killed in battle Sept 1, 1862; Barzillai E. Bragg, injured by exposure, discharged Dec. 28, 1861; Jacob C. Cunningham, transferred to and from 38th New York regiment; Charles A. Davis, wounded at Gettysburg and discharged Oct. 12, 1863; Henry O. Davis; William B. Foss, killed July 21, 1861; Ezekiel P. Hager, wounded and discharged; Edward Hall, promoted to corporal; Augustus Hanley, transferred to U. S. regular battery; Samuel Heath, died Oct. 1, 1862; John O. Johnson, transferred to 38th New York regiment; Alex. B. Kieff, transferred to invalid corps; Silas E. Labe, discharged Jan. 5, 1862; Daniel Martin, left the service May 12, 1862; John Miller, mostly on detached service; Parker Miller, discharged Dec. 7, 1862; John Morrissey; Charles Mudgett, left the service Aug. 25, 1862; John Murphy, straggled from ranks July 21, 1861; Patrick O'Brien, transferred from company H, missing in action June 30, 1862; Wm. H. O'Niel, detached to Heintzelman's headquarters, died Sept. 7, 1862; William Perkins; Horatio Richards, transferred to and from 38th New York regiment; Lafayette Richards, captured July 21, 1861, wounded May, 1864; James P. Robbins, discharged Dec. 7, 1862; Sylvanus N. Saddler, wounded near Richmond, and left the service Oct. 29, 1862; James C. Sholler, promoted to sergeant, returned to ranks, wounded and transferred to invalid corps; John Smith, Edwin Snow,

Joseph E. Stimson, all transferred to 38th New York; Jacob A. Sparhawk, captured and wounded July 21st, died at Richmond Aug. 15, 1861; Hiram Stevens, died Oct. 24, 1862; Simon P. Taylor, wounded May, 1864; Orren O. Thomas, transferred to U. S. regular battalion Jan. 19, 1863; Edward W. Thomas, discharged Aug. 9, 1861; Joseph Thompson; Samuel A. Wood, wounded at Bull Run, wounded at Fredericksburg Dec. 12th, and died the 13th, 1862; Jerome Watson, wounded May, 1864.

In *company E*, Ensign Coombs; W. M. Packard, captured at Bull Run, discharged.

In *company F*, Ephraim Langell, wounded and captured June 30, 1862, paroled, discharged for disability, October 24, 1862; James Rackliff, (2d,) discharged July, 1862.

In *company H*, Geo. J. Burns, captain, discharged October 4, 1861; Benaiah C. Brackley, lieutenant, discharged Oct. 21, 1861; William Shields, sergeant, transferred to company D, promoted to lieutenant, wounded at Fredericksburg, resigned September 7, 1863; John Copeland, sergeant, discharged for disability, March 16, 1862; Andrew A. Neubert, discharged for disability; Thomas A. Neubert, not mustered in; Edwin Keizer, corporal, transferred with the 22 who follow, to the 38th New York; Daniel B. Barter, discharged for disability; John Butler, and John Kiff, returned and wounded, May, 1864; Horace C. Clough, returned, promoted to corporal; James M. Eugley, Alonzo E. Martin, Orlando Martin, Wm. B. Morse; Patrick Crowley, returned, wounded in battle and died at Washington, May 29, 1864; John Bean, Daniel Bean, Isaac J. Fields, James McDavit, Jeremiah Sullivan, Thomas O'Brien, Isaac S. Saunders, Augustus Studley, Benj. C. Studley; Isaac Stahl, returned; John Cokely and John H. Ham, both wounded at Williamsburg and discharged; William H. Ames, transferred to company K, wounded at Spotsylvania, May 9, 1864, and died June 17th, at Philadelphia; Benj. Burr and John J. Seamore, dropped from the rolls; George M. Smith, transferred to company K, and invalid detachment; James Turner, died August 30, 1861; William Fountain, corporal; S. L. Young; Hiram Holmes, Samuel Jackson, and Amasa Jackson, who died in Baltimore, Nov. 29, 1862, all three transferred to company K; Jas. McLaughlin, Simon McCann, Daniel Martin, all three transferred to company D, the last left the service May 12, 1862; the second, discharged November 16, 1862; and the first promoted to lieutenant; Robert Walsh, left the service, July 25, 1861; and, joined since the company's re-organization, Jabez

Greenhalgh, lieutenant; Abram J. Furbish, wounded May, 1864; Thomas C. Saunders, wounded May 2, 1863; and Horatio A. Ulmer, detached on gunboat service.

This regiment, after arriving at Washington, spent the time in further improvement in drill and discipline at different places of encampment. At one of these, July 13th, the first rebel prisoners by Maine regiments, were taken by John Butler, Corporal Stevens, W. E. Crockett, and John McKeen of Capt. Walker's company; and their weapons were distributed by Col. Berry among the captors. In the disheartening battle of Bull Run, July 21st, this regiment (scarcely more than one short month from peaceful homes) took an active part, and was the last to leave the field — having in connection with the 2d Vermont, made a desperate charge up the hill, and, for half an hour after its lines were partially broken by retreating cavalry and the battle was lost, stood the fire of shot and shell till ordered to retreat; and then, with the rest of Howard's brigade, came in from Centreville to Alexandria, in good order, under command of its officers. Its loss was 23 killed, 24 wounded, and 42 missing. Among the killed, this city had to lament the loss of several valuable citizens. Sergt. Major Chapman, a man of literary and musical talents, whose letters published in the Gazette, giving an account of the journey to Washington and all the movements of the soldiers, were so much prized by their friends and the community, was the first of the regiment to lay down his life as he had been the first to enlist in the cause of his country. He was killed instantly by a rifle ball, soon after the regiment came under fire, — thus giving a noble answer to the question which appeared in his latest published letter, written just before the battle, "how *can* one better or more gloriously die, than for his country?" Asahel Towne, also, B. W. Fletcher, Wm. B. Foss, Dennis Canning, Jarvis B. Grant, and Sewall Hewett, all in various ways, contributed their lives to the great ransom paid for the Nation's integrity and freedom. Nathaniel B. Gowen, who had been an estimable member of the first Baptist church and an active teacher in its Sabbath school, and Jacob A. Sparhawk, were wounded and carried prisoners to Richmond, where they subsequently died. The various instances of individual bravery and daring, in this battle, as in the many that have followed, would fill volumes; but we have not space for them.

Subsequent to the retreat, the Fourth returned to the station it had previously occupied at Bush Hill, south of the Potomac, and several changes took place among its officers.

Lt. Col. Marshall being appointed colonel of the 7th Maine, his place was supplied by Major Nickerson, and that of the latter by Silas M. Fuller. Company H, having become reduced in consequence of a misunderstanding among the men in regard to the time of service enlisted for, was broken up, and the men, with some others in the regiment, transferred to the 38th New York, or distributed in other companies. It was, however, replaced in November by another, of new recruits under Capt. W. L. Pitcher of Bangor. Before the close of the year, Capt. Walker of company B, became major; and, to the regret of the regiment, Col. Berry, its active, popular, and meritorious commander, left in March, 1862, on being promoted to the office of brigadier general. Major Walker relinquishing his place to Capt. Pitcher, succeeded as colonel, and Capt. Carver of company D, as lieut. colonel.

The eagerness of this regiment for action was evinced in the fact that more than 100 of its men volunteered early in Feb., 1862, to join the gunboat fleet at Cairo; but only 30 from any one regiment were allowed to leave. On the 17th March it went to Old Point Comfort, thence to the plains beyond Hampton, and on the 4th April advanced towards Yorktown. In the operations of our army between Yorktown and Richmond, it was most frequently drawn upon for men to do special duties requiring marked heroism and despatch; and Gen. Heintzelman is reported to have said of it, "it could furnish a corps of brigadiers as good as any in the army."

In the battle of Williamsburg, May 5, 1862, from the position assigned to it on the left flank which was not attacked, it did not materially suffer; yet its flag was the first the next morning to float over the abandoned defences of Williamsburg. Still, as many of Co. H had been transferred to the New York 38th regiment, which behaved so nobly and was so terribly cut up amidst the storm of deadly hail which assailed them, some of our Rockland boys suffered. At Seven Pines the regiment was engaged. At the battle of Fair Oaks, May 31st, it suffered but little; as, in the afternoon of the first day, Gen. Birney failed to bring the brigade into action; and, on the second day, though, under another commander, doing good execution on the enemy, it was protected by the railroad embankment which formed a breast-work from behind which the men poured a constant shower of bullets upon the foe whilst remaining in comparative safety themselves. Col. Walker stood in an exposed situation on the railroad, directing the fire of his men, and, together with Lieut. Col. Carver and Maj. Pitcher, received honorable mention in Gen. Ward's official report. Two only of the Fourth were killed and seven wounded. On the 25th of June, the Fourth was engaged with the enemy in the afternoon and evening, holding a most difficult position in face of the rebel force through the night; on the 28th, it was detached from its brigade to build a bridge across Jordan's Ford in White Oak Swamp, where, the remainder of the brigade having joined them, they held back the enemy until the main force had crossed, when they joined the retreat as the extreme rear guard; and it bravely bore its part in the several succeeding battles which were fought before Richmond. At Charles City Cross Roads it was in action; and at Malvern Hill, July 1st, supported the artillery planted on the heights. Though often wonderfully and providentially preserved from exposure, it did not escape a share of the casualties; among which, at the latter place, Sergeant Cowing of this city, much respected and beloved, was killed instantly by a piece of shell. On the 4th of July the regiment reached the place of retreat, Harrison's Landing, completely exhausted. On the 15th of August it again left its encampment; and, in the various and severe engagements which, from August 27th to September 1st, attended McLellan's retreat from before Richmond, the Maine 4th bore itself in its usual faithful and energetic manner; — being thus spoken of in Gen. Kearney's report. "The staunch 4th Maine, under Walker and Carver, true men, of rare type, drove on through the stream of battle irresistibly." It suffered severely, though, — having at the second Bull Run seven killed, (among them Sergeant Achorn, Corporal Stevens and Charles Clark of this city,) thirty-three wounded and seven missing, and, at Chantilly, eight killed, fifty-four wounded and two missing. An exploit of two young men of this city, Orlando H. Brown and George H. Dunbar, may deserve mention. Being left behind with two other videttes, on the 30th, in the retreat toward Centreville, they succeeded in capturing a party of the enemy consisting of one assistant adjutant general, one lieut. of cavalry, one orderly and two negroes, with six horses and sets of horse equipments, all of which they brought into camp. After this, till December, the Fourth was actively employed at various important points along the Potomac, guarding the fords.

In the battle of Fredericksburg, commencing Dec. 13, 1862, it is doubted if any regiment participating displayed more indomitable courage, or suffered a severer loss than did the Fourth Maine. In Ward's brigade and Birney's division, they made the first charge upon the rebels; and it was they who drove them back through a dense piece of woods on the right of where the division entered the engagement, through an open field and back of the embankment which there formed a part of the railroad. But as soon as they reached the rear of this embankment, the rebels who had been driven, fell flat on their faces, while others rose fresh in their rear and poured in so murderous a fire that our Maine boys were compelled to retreat; though their left nobly continued to hold the foe in check, till, being joined by their right, and the rebels driven back by Gen. Berry, who came with his brigade to their relief, they retired, bringing off many of their wounded or dying comrades. Of the 211 men which went into the fight, but 124 returned in safety; and of the 23 field and line officers, but five escaped uninjured. Of those belonging to this city, Avery L. Candage and John A. Kelloch, corporals, James M. Bragg, Moses D. Bartlett, and Samuel A. Wood, privates, were killed, falling, like their gallant Major Pitcher, "with breasts to the foe, doing their whole duty."

At Chancellorsville, the Fourth "did good service to retrieve our position"; the desperate charge of Ward's brigade on the night of May 2d, 1863, costing its chief loss of 32 killed, wounded and missing, — only a few, comparatively, being wounded in the main battle on Sunday. None of those from this city were killed; but the whole regiment, as well as the people of Rockland and the community at large, were most deeply affected by the loss, in this battle, of its early commander, — the brave, exemplary, and eminently successful Major General Hiram G. Berry. After his promotion to the command of a brigade, he had, at the battle of Williamsburg, by a forced march through the rain and mud in double quick time, passing three other brigades on his way, arrived at a critical moment to the relief of the right wing of our army exhausted by a bloody conflict and about giving way, and, by a gallant and successful charge upon the fresh troops of Johnston, turned the scale of victory and won for himself and his brave command the highest honor. Thus having obtained the soubriquet of "the hero of Williamsburg," he again, at the battles of Fair Oaks, White Oak Swamp, Nelson's Farm, and Malvern Hill, managed his brigade with the same promptness, skill, and courage, rendering signal service at the right time and situation to prevent imminent disasters; so that on his return home, Aug. 6th, to recruit his health and recover from a slight wound and injuries occasioned by a fall from his wounded and plunging horse, Rockland was proud to give him, her favorite son, a public and very flattering reception. Mayor Wiggin's address of welcome on the occasion was appropriate, warm, and deeply affecting. On the 29th of January, his gallant services were rewarded by an appointment to the office of major general, in which capacity his services were equally appreciated. But the end of his career was approaching. On Sunday morning, the 3d of May, while posted to the right of Chancellorsvile, Gen. Howard, whose division had been put to flight, rode up and said, "Gen. Berry, I am ruined!" Berry replied, "Oh no, General; I have a division that never was driven an inch; I will put them immediately into the breach and regain what you have lost." 'Twas said, 'twas done. He put himself at the head of his brave men, and, with an irresistible charge, they drove back the rebels at the point of the bayonet and retook the ground which had been lost. In the temporary hush of battle that followed this successful onset, Gen. Berry directed Capt. Greenhalgh to ride to Hooker's headquarters, for orders as to whether he should hold his position or not. Then dismounting with the remainder of his staff, he walked a few rods to confer with Gen. Mott, the senior officer of his division, and, on his return, when but a short distance from where the members of his staff stood, was struck in the arm close to the shoulder by a rifle minnie ball, which passed downwards through his vitals, lodged in his hip, and killed him almost immediately. "I am dying," he murmured, "carry me to the rear;" and indicating by a feeble shake of the head to his inquiring aid that he had no particular wish to express, his spirit ascended to its reward. His body, after being greeted with an outburst of regret and sorrow from Gen. Hooker at the Chancellor house, was conveyed back to Falmouth. On the way, it was met by a squad of the Fourth regiment, who, learning that the body of their former commander was being carried by, desired to have it laid down, and each one of the brave fellows came forward, kissed the cold brow of the man they had loved and first followed into the battle field, and then silently and tearfully took their places in the ranks. The corpse, under the care of Capt. Greenhalgh, after being embalmed, and receiving the highest honors, civil, military, and masonic, at Washington and Portland, arrived in this city May 9th, in charge of the committee which had been sent on to Portland for that purpose. On the appearance of the steamer, minute guns were fired and the bells of the churches tolled, the flags of the shipping displayed at half mast, the stores and principal buildings in Main street draped in mourning. At the Atlantic wharf, with a brief address from its chairman, Joseph Farwell, Esq., the committee, which had been sent on to Portland, delivered over its precious charge to the committee in waiting as representatives of the city, in whose behalf a response was made by Hon. S. C. Fessenden; and the coffin in a hearse draped with national flags, attended by the guard of honor with reversed arms, and followed by the family of the deceased and a long train of citizens in carriages, was conveyed to the family residence. After lying in state there, in the full uniform of his rank, adorned with bouquets, and on his breast the Kearney badge, with the beautiful wreath of flowers offered by the President at Washington, until Thursday the 14th, the body, beneath a gloomy sky and the moaning of the ocean wind, was deposited with parental dust in the Achorn cemetery* at Blackington's Corner. The obsequies which preceded were performed in front of the house, from a platform on which were seated Gov. Coburn, Ex-Gov. Washburn, and other distinguished personages, and consisted of scripture readings by Rev. Mr. Hart, prayer and eulogy by Rev. N. Butler, benediction by Rev. Jos. Kalloch; succeeded by the procession, comprising the military and masonic bands, the Bangor and Rockland bands of music, military officers and guard of honor, and, following the funeral car, the General's three war horses, his family and relatives in carriages, his military staff, various official personages, guests and citizens, which moved down Lime Rock and up Main and North Main streets to the cemetery, where the usual masonic and military ceremonies were performed. The half-hour guns, the tolling bells, the closed places of business, and the assembled crowds, variously estimated at from 5000 to 8000, testified the general regret of the city and whole community, which was well expressed by his fellow citizen, Z. Pope Vose, Esq., in a requiem, the second and last stanzas only of which our space allows us to give.

"Toll! bells, in sadness, toll!
Your solemn anthem roll!
City that gave him, weep!
Claiming this mournful trust,
Take back his lifeless dust,
Safely to guard and keep.
When Sumter's cannon spoke,
And at that summons woke

* This is a private cemetery, laid out on the estate of the late Michael Achorn, first used on the death of his daughter, 1842.

Thousands to Freedom's call,
He went to win or fall,
Where treason's fire outbroke;
Toll! toll!"
Speak from each iron tongue
Grief that our hearts has wrung, —
Toll! bells, in sadness, toll!

Write! pen of History, write!
In words of burning light,
Deeds of this mighty day:
And to the brave and free,
Saviors of Liberty,
Millions shall praises pay.
Tell how the wrong assailed;
Tell how the Right prevailed;
And on thy deathless page,
Bright'ning from age to age,
Be its defenders hailed!
Write! write!
High on the roll of fame
Blazon our hero's name!
Write! pen of History, write!

The colors of the Fourth regiment, rent, marked with bullet holes, and stained with the smoke of battle, but never with disgrace, were received in this city on the same day, May 9th, with the remains of the gallant General who nobly led it forth and so faithfully watched over its welfare. Beneath these banners, the regiment had fought in no less than 15 encounters with the rebels, from that of Bull Run to Chancellorsville; till, worn and shattered like many of those who followed them, they were sent home as proud trophies of the bravery and endurance of our citizen soldiers. Since then, the Fourth has continued to show a bright and untarnished record. At Gettysburg it was in the thickest of the fight on the right and front, going in with 299 men and coming out with only 211 men, Capt. Libby taking command after the colonel and major were successively wounded. At Rappahannock Station it fought with its accustomed bravery in Ward's brigade; and in 1864 it shared and severely suffered in all the battles of Grant's army from the Rapidan to the James, till the 15th of June, — when its war-worn remnant was ordered out of the line, 217 of its unflinching re-enlisted veterans and later recruits were transferred to the 19th Maine, and the remainder, numbering 13 officers and 132 privates, returned to this city "without a stain upon their banner and with a history that will never die." Here a public reception, heartfelt and appropriate, was tendered them by the city fathers; a procession of the Rockland Band, State Guards, Fire Department, and City Council, under direction of Gen. Titcomb, escorted them to a bountiful collation at Atlantic Hall, — after a few hearty words of welcome from Hon. N. A. Farwell, salutes from the batteries, and rejoicings mingled with tears of the assembled crowds as they welcomed the brave boys back. The regiment was mustered out, here, July 19th, — having, out of its whole number, viz., 1525, lost 153 officers and privates killed in battle or died of wounds, and 114 who perished by disease.

These gallant soldiers of the 4th regiment, as well as their suffering companions in arms, have never been forgotten by the humane and generous ladies of Rockland. Their hands have been untiring, and their exertions almost uninterrupted. Besides their labors already noted, and the addition of three boxes containing 624 garments sent on to the Sanitary Commission, they, in July, 1862, transmitted four large boxes of hospital clothing, bedding, soap, sponges, spices, corn starch, farina, &c.; with two boxes of wines and jellies, to the State Relief Society. The city was at the same time canvassed in the several wards and $500 contributed to aid the Sanitary Commission. In answer to the appeal of the Surgeon-general for aid in mitigating the sufferings of the wounded in the battles which so mournfully closed the month of August, 1862, the ladies, misses, and children of this city set themselves promptly at work preparing lint and bandages, gathering every evening at various places, whilst the members of the Universalist Sewing Circle and the children of Miss Eaton's school devoted their Wednesday afternoon to the same purpose; so that on the evening of that day, Sept. 3d, two large dry-goods boxes were forwarded, and the work still went on. Mrs. C. N. Germaine of this city, associate manager of the Commission, herself alone, from the time the 4th regiment left Rockland till July, 1863, cut, rolled, and put up in packages for hospital use, 3824 yards of bandages. During the winter of 1862–3, the Rockland ladies, having formed a Soldier's Aid Society, supplied their peculiar charge, the soldiers of the 4th regiment, with 165 pairs of woolen stockings; and, by April 6th, had finished and forwarded in response to the appeal of the New England Women's Association for sick and wounded soldiers, 30 cotton shirts, 15 flannel ditto, eight cotton flannel ditto, 16 pairs cotton flannel drawers, 12 bed-sacks, two sheets, two towels, six pillows, eleven pairs socks, seven pairs slippers, eight quilts, besides lint, bandages, reading matter, &c. On the 11th July, another box, containing $100 worth of bedding, with stockings, dried apples, pickles, corn starch, sugar, tea, &c., purchased with money collected by Mrs. Germaine from the business men of the place, was added. A barrel also of supplies was sent on to Mrs. Mayhew by the same society in Sept., 1863, which, through her ministering hands, supplied to many of the wounded cavalry soldiers a most timely relief. Beyond this, our information does not extend; but it is presumed that the louder calls in 1864 from bloodier battle fields, have not been unheeded. In June the city was canvassed by a committee, and several hundred dollars collected in answer to the appeal of the Christian Commission.

The two companies of *Home Guards* under Capts. Wm. H. Luce and Wm. Farrow, Jr., formed in August, 1862, having declined with the apprehensions of danger from Southern privateers of that season, a company of *State Guards* (100 men) was formed in 1863, under F. Cobb, captain, O. J. Conant (since O. P. Mitchell) and E. E. Wortman, lieutenants. Rifles, &c., were supplied by the State. The same season, government also caused the harbor to be defended by two batteries, — one on Jameson's Point, and the other at Half-way Point, on the opposite side towards Owl's Head, the distance between them being three miles. These were completed in 1864, supplied with five 32 and 24 pound guns, each, and garrisoned with a lieutenant and 25 soldiers.

The commerce and navigation of this place has suffered far less than might have been anticipated. Early in 1861, the barkantine *Ocean Eagle*, of this port, Capt. William H. Luce, bound to New Orleans with a cargo of lime, was taken at the Balize by a rebel steamer, being the first vessel captured on the Mississippi. The captain, however, having been released on parole, returned home, and, in full confidence of regaining the vessel, valued at $12,000, the property of his widowed mother, watched the course of events, and on the occupation of New Orleans, April 25, 1862, by our forces, was there almost as soon, found his barque safe among the only three Northern vessels saved from the flames, which, with such articles of property taken from him and sold as could be looked up, being restored by Gen. Butler's order, he was soon on his way to New York, with a fine freight of sugar, at $13 a hogshead. The ship *Chas. A. Farwell*, at the time of her capture valued at $40,000, mostly owned in this city, and supposed to have been destroyed with the other shipping by order of the rebels, was also found safe, on the occupation of New Orleans, and Capt. Amsbury was immediately sent out for her recovery. She had been purchased and was then claimed by a British merchant, who, at first, treated Amsbury's demand, as well as a subsequent order from

Gov. Shepley, with supercilious contempt; but a file of soldiers with an order from Butler to deliver her up, together with everything belonging to her and to bring the merchant before the Governor for his conduct, had its immediate effect, and everything was restored except an anchor and cable which had been taken away for a rebel gunboat. On the 3d of June, 1861, the brig *Joseph*, of 170 tons and valued at $4000, owned by S. N. Hatch, John and Geo. F. Cables, R. Sherer, and Joseph Ingraham, and commanded by Capt. N. Myers, on her passage from Cardenas, with a cargo of sugar, was captured by the rebel privateer Savannah, sent into Georgetown, S. C., condemned by the confederate court at Charleston, June 21st, and her cargo ordered to be sold. And, among the many vessels that have fallen a prey to the piratical steamer Alabama, were the ship *Bethia Thayer*, owned by Hon. Wm. McLoon of this city, which was captured in the spring of 1863, when bound for Nantes, with a cargo of guano, and allowed to go on her way on giving a bond for $40,000; and the *Louisa Hatch*, Capt. Grant, loaded with coal, captured April 4th, taken to the convict island near Pernambuco, and burnt.

Not content with her contribution to the Fourth, Rockland was not slow to aid in the formation of other corps. Of the *First Regiment Cavalry*, this city furnished the following: Samuel C. Lovejoy, hospital steward. In Co. A, Edgar F. Comstock, discharged for disability Nov. 25, 1862. In Co. B, Joshua A. Fessenden, sergeant, promoted to lieutenant in U. S. army; Edmund C. Grafton, musician, died July 30, 1862, from injury on railroad; Jos. McAllister; John McLoud, wounded June 17, 1863; Wm. J. Philbrook, died on his way to hospital, March 1, 1863; Burnham C. Sleeper; and Ezekiel Winslow, detached to quartermaster's department. In Co. D, Clarence D. Ulmer, promoted to quartermaster March 9, 1863. In Co. E, Antoine Schouton, bugler, captured June 9, 1863, exchanged. In Co. F, Ephraim Hewett, left the service in Camp Penobscot, Feb. 14, 1862; and Frank Pacott. In Co. I, Levi Crowell, farrier; and Co. L, Charles B. Clarkson.

In the Maine volunteer company, D, of the 2d regiment U. S. *Sharpshooters*, have been the following citizens of Rockland: Jacob McClure, lieutenant, wounded at Gettysburg, promoted to captain, major, and lieut. colonel; Lorenzo Hall, sergeant, discharged for disability; Edwin P. Morse, corporal, discharged for disability March 27, 1863; Barzillai E. Bragg, transferred to invalid corps; Henry Brown, a valued adopted citizen from Bremen, Europe, died at Finley hospital, Washington, Dec., 1863; Edgar Crockett, promoted to sergeant; Alex. C. Crockett; Nelson Hall, promoted to corporal, discharged for disability Aug. 10, 1863; Rufus T. Hall, discharged for disability; John S. Hall and Thos. J. Henderson, both on detached service in invalid corps; Martin Hopkins, left the service Dec. 31, 1862; John M. Jameson; Edward Lindsey, captured at Manassas; Jas. M. Mathews, promoted to sergeant; Argyl D. Morse, promoted to corporal, captured and paroled; John E. Wade, promoted to sergeant; John M. Wilson, in quartermaster's department; James N. Pendleton, wounded July 4, 1863; and Wm. Eugene Conant, whose record may be briefly given as a specimen of the spirit that has animated so many. He had with difficulty, one year before, been prevented from enlisting—a stripling of 18 years—in the 4th regiment, with his three elder brothers. But on the prospect of a draft, in July, 1862, the brave youth wrung from his father a reluctant consent, and did active service in three battles previous to that of Antietam, September 17th, where, while gallantly facing the foe, he received a cruel wound in the thigh, and fell. After he fell, he was struck four times more, one ball passing through his wrist; and there he lay twenty-four hours, without covering, nourishment, or care, suffering what none can describe. Thence, he was taken a mile and a half to a hospital, where he had good care, and, in his last days, the loving attentions of his only sister. But all could not save him. No word of complaint passed his lips; no suffering could force him to say he regretted his enlistment. Heroic through all and to the last, perfectly sensible as the shades of death crept over him, his soul went up to a patriot's rest. His body was brought back to his home; and November 30th, funeral services were performed by Rev. Joseph Kalloch, at the second Baptist church, which was thronged by citizens eager to pay respect to, and take their last look at the young private who had died for his country.

In November, 1861, a battery of Light Artillery was formed by enlistments in this city and the neighboring towns, under the command and by the active exertions of Davis Tilson of this place, who had been educated at West Point, was lately Adjutant General of the State militia, and, at the time, Collector of Customs in this district. It was known as the *Second Battery*, in 1st regiment of Mounted Artillery, Maine Volunteers; and was mustered into the U. S. service, Nov. 30, 1861. Besides the commander, this city contributed to its formation the following volunteers: — Junior 2d lieut. William A. Perry, promoted to 1st lieutenant, since on Brig. Gen. Tilson's staff; 1st sergeant Wm. N. Ulmer, promoted to captain; 3d sergeant Benj. Kirkpatrick, dropped to ranks at his request; 7th corporal Lewis L. Smith, ditto, discharged for disability May 8, 1863; 12th corporal Samuel Wier, reduced to ranks, discharged for disability Jan. 27, 1863; artificers, Percy Montgomery; James E. Thorndike, discharged June 12, 1862; and Anson Hewett, returned to ranks; privates, Washington Achorn; Charles Allen, promoted to corporal; John Barrington; William N. Benner; Alvra E. Boynton, discharged for disability Jan. 17, 1862; George Bunker; Benjamin A. Chaples, transferred to invalid corps; Nathan F. Clark, discharged for disability Feb. 13, 1862; Jewett F. Cotton, died at Washington Feb. 6, 1863; Samuel Derby; Charles H. Derby, died Sept. 17, 1862; Alden L. Farrington, discharged for disability March 30, 1863; Jacob U. Farrington; Benj. B. Gardner; Anthony N. Greely, promoted to sergeant; Almond Greely; Alva F. Green; Samuel W. Hewett, discharged Oct. 12, 1862; Charles A. Jameson; John M. Kalloch; Allen Kelly, left the service Jan. 13, 1862; Frank A. Knight, discharged July 30, 1862; Joseph P. Knowles, wounded July 1, 1863; Robert N. Marsh; Lorenzo D. Martin, discharged for disability Jan. 27, 1863; Cyrus N. Mills, promoted to corporal; Simon Morang and Dennis Murphy, left the service, one April 9, 1862, the other June 30, 1863; Enoch S. Philbrook, discharged Oct. 5, 1862; Adolphus Richards, promoted to corporal, transferred to invalid corps; Henry Richardson and Daniel Robbins, discharged for disability May 5th, and June 20, 1862; Charles H. Spalding; Robert Spalding; Oliver B. Spear, discharged Sept. 11, 1862; Alden W. Thorndike, wounded at Manassas, discharged Dec. 24, 1862; George F. Thomas, promoted to corporal; Amos L. Thompson, discharged May 5, 1862; James L. Thompson; Franklin Tolman, promoted to corporal; Frank H. Ulmer; Frederic H. Ulmer, missing since battle of Gettysburg; Spencer G. Walsh; Jacob Welman, left the service Feb. 13, 1862; Odbrey Witham; Franklin P. Witham; and Jerome B. Wood. In May, 1862, Capt. Tilson was appointed major of the Maine Volunteer Artillery, and in August following was raised to the position of Chief of Artillery in McDowell's army corps; since which he has been appointed Brigadier General, and put in charge of the department of Ohio as Chief of Artillery. At its first engagement the Second Battery did gallant service at Cedar Mountain, Va., Aug. 9, 1862, opening near morning upon the flank of the rebel camp. Its first shot killed the Confederate Gen. Winder, at the same time killing or wounding his whole staff, thus throwing the right wing of the rebel army into confusion. At Fredericksburg also, though it suffered more, having two men killed and fourteen wounded, this battery's services were equally gallant; at Chancellorsville it held an important position on the extreme right of the army; and at Gettysburg it was engaged, July 1, 1863, fully two hours before any other batteries arrived; but, insufficiently supported by infantry, came out of a double charge upon it by the enemy with all its guns safe, though reduced in men and horses and with carriages badly smashed. Later in the day however, three of its guns were the first to be posted in the grave-yard on Cemetery Hill; and under its successive commanders Hall, Ulmer, and Thomas, and through all the battles of 1864 around Richmond and Petersburg, it has ever sustained a distinguished reputation for promptness, discipline, and courage.

On the President's call in July, 1862, for 300,000 men, this city, to avoid the necessity of drafting, voted to give to all who should voluntarily enlist to make up its quota of 80 men a bounty of $125 each; and, before August 9th, the whole number was obtained, including some of the best young men of the city. These went mostly to form *company I* of the 19th Maine regiment, and were mustered into service August 25th. They were Edward A. Snow, captain, discharged for disability Feb. 23, 1863; George D. Smith, lieutenant, promoted to captain, killed July 3, 1863; Henry H. Earle, sergeant, discharged for disability Dec. 9, 1862; James M. Higgens, sergeant, died Dec. 8, 1862; Edgar A. Burpee, corporal, promoted to captain, wounded at Gettysburg; William E. Barrows, corporal, promoted to sergeant, killed July 3, 1863; James W. Packard, musician, died Dec. 18, 1862; Hiram Whitten, wagoner; Gorham L. Black, wounded at Gettysburg; John H. Cables, sick in Washington; Joseph L. Clark, promoted to lieutenant; Luther Clark, and Adrian C. Dodge, both wounded at Gettysburg; George E. Holmes, promoted to sergeant, wounded and died June 15, 1864; Nahum R. Jackson, died Jan. 7, 1863, from cold taken in the exhaustion of retreat after the battle of Fredericksburg; Jas. H. Place, discharged for disability May, 1863; William N. Rackliff, in ambulance corps; Charles S. Richardson, discharged for disability, May 13, 1863; Solomon Taylor, sick at Washington Nov. 1863; and Hosea West, discharged for disability March 31, 1863. Rev. W. A. Smith of the Rockland Congregational Church was, in May 1863, appointed chaplain of the regiment. Others of this quota joined other regiments, and their names will be found on other pages. This company I was put to a severe trial at the battle of Gettysburg, Pa., July 2d and 3d, 1863, in which its brave commander Capt. G. D. Smith, long an esteemed teacher of music in this city, and Serg't Barrows, both endeared to many hearts, were killed.

Before this July quota was wholly raised, an additional draft was ordered of another 300,000, to serve for nine months only. In consequence of the spirited exertions of a number of influential citizens, the quota of this city in consideration of the large number already furnished to the army, was reduced to 58; and, although $200 bounty was voted by the City Council Sept. 1, 1862, these were not readily obtained by voluntary enlistments, so that a draft was resorted to Sept. 10th, but with a general understanding that no man should be allowed to go on compulsion. Volunteers were easily found, and the city's quota left for Augusta, Sept. 11th, forming with those of South Thomaston and Vinalhaven, Co. G, of the 28th Maine regiment. Those of this city were Augustine Thompson, captain, Edward A. Sprague, William Thurston, William H. Morse, and Augustus Luce, sergeants; Edgar A. Hanaky, and Edgar O. Ulmer, corporals ; Benjamin Studley, musician; James G. Simonton, wagoner; Danforth B. Blackington; John Clifford, Amos Eldridge, Nahum H. Hall, promoted to corporal; Charles Haskell, Joshua H. Kalloch, Alfred N. Kalloch, Adolphus A. Leavitt, Benjamin P. Mitchell, Charles H. Nickerson, Josiah H. Paine, George H. Place, Andrew D. Pottle, Ezekiel I. Perry, enlisted in U. S. navy; James Simmons, Charles Titus, Augustus H. Ulmer, and Leander Wall. In the extraordinary and almost unparalleled defence of Fort Butler at Donaldsonville, June 28, 1863, Capt. Thompson and his company won undying honors, but at the expense of hard fighting and many casualties. Besides Lieut. I. Murch, and C. V. Smith of Vinalhaven, Sergeant Morse, and Alfred N. Kalloch fell gloriously in the thickest of the fight; while, among many others, Joshua A. Kalloch of this city was wounded in the head so that he died a few days after, and R. A. Palmer, commissary sergeant of the regiment, received two bullets in the hand. After their term of service had expired, the soldiers of this regiment were received with many honors at Augusta, and returned to their homes in August, 1863.

The following from this city have enlisted in other Maine regiments,—as collated from the Adjutant General's report, giving their standing in Nov., 1863,—viz.: In the *Second*, Co. E, James Wright, musician; Co. K, Richard D. Pickard, discharged for disability Nov. 13, 1862; Albert H. Tarr, corporal, promoted to sergeant. In the *Third*, Wm. S. Heath, of the law firm of Heath & Miller, though incurring popular indignation here as an apologist for secession, on the fall of Sumter went to Waterville, raised a company of volunteers, was promoted for gallant conduct at Bull Run to lieut. colonel, and was one among the many who gave up their lives for their country, near Richmond, Va., in 1862; in Co. A, John Stevenson; Co. F, James Corcoran, Joseph Coad; Co. H, Henry H. Ferguson; Co. K, James P. Flagg, Levi F. Howard, and John W. Spruce. In the *Fifth*, Thomas Jewett, shot by sentence of general court martial, Aug. 14, 1863. In the *Sixth*, Fred. W. Libby, musician, mustered out in 1862; Ralph W. Young, captain of Co. G, killed at Fredericksburg May 3, 1863. In the *Seventh*, Franklin B. Thomas, Chas. O. Wentworth. In the *Eighth*, Edgar A. Perry, sergeant major, died at Tybee Island, May 22, 1862; in Co. B, Robert E. Wentworth; Co. H, George Wasgatt. In the *Ninth*, Dr. Joel Richardson, surgeon, resigned Dec. 19, 1862; Co. H, John W. Pomeroy, died Dec. 19, 1861, Alexander Hart. In the *Tenth*, Co. E, Joseph Benson, discharged for disability, Sam'l Wilson; Co. F, Benj. F. Hutchinson. In the *Eleventh*, Co. G, Theodore Bunker, supposed discharged. In the *Twefth*, Co. I, Simon Gordon, died at New Orleans, Sept. 25, 1863, after two years brave service. In the *Fifteenth*, Rev. J. I. Brown, a former resident here, appointed chaplain, and besides his regular duties, saved the life of a federal officer at New Orleans, it is said, by shooting a rebel who was attempting to stab him with his bowie knife; in Co. A, Charles S. Williams, left the service March 4, 1862; in Co. G, Ransom N. Pierce, lieut.; in Co. I, Charles Conner, Thomas Toburn, both sick in 1863 at New Orleans, and Charles Wood. In the *Sixteenth*, Co. H, John E. Haley, Robert Jenkins, discharged Dec. 27, 1862. In the *Nineteenth*, Co. D, Henry D. Byard, wounded at Gettysburg, Ezekiel Rackliff; in Co. E, Benjamin Burgess. In the *Twenty-First*, Co. F, Charles V. Grey. In the *Thirtieth*, Co. I, Charles Clements. In the *Sixth battery of Mounted Artillery*, Timothy Driscoll. In the *First regiment Heavy Artillery*, Co. F, James McLellan. In the *Twentieth* regiment, Alden Litchfield, quartermaster; in Co. D, Samuel H. Gregory; in Co. K, Robert Anderson, corporal, discharged Aug. 3, 1863, John H. Ames, Erastus C. Anderson, detached, Frederic H. Cross, sick in Washington, Asa Cunningham, discharged for disability Dec. 25, 1862, Jas. S. Durgin, Joel S. Hart, in convalescent camp, Charles Rhoades, detached to brigade headquarters, and Vinal E. Wall, promoted to corporal. The first colonel of this regiment was Adelbert Ames of this city, who, on the breaking out of the rebellion, had just graduated at West Point, entered the regular U. S. army, and, in command of the third gun of Griffin's battery, was wounded at Bull Run, by a minie rifle ball through his thigh, and though ordered to leave the field, remounted his horse and kept his piece going till unable to ride from loss of blood, when he got upon the box of a gun and gave orders to his gunners till his boot ran full of blood and he was completely exhausted. Capt. Griffin wrote of him, "I never saw more fortitude and courage displayed." Promotion soon followed, and in Oct., 1861, he was assigned the command of a battery of light artillery called Ames', or Battery A of U. S. Artillery. In the battles of the Chickahominy, and especially Malvern Hill, he performed signal service, had two horses shot under him as he rode from gun to gun, cheering on his men and handling his battery with great skill, which was on the field the entire day and expended 1300 rounds of ammunition.* Soon after taking command of the 20th regiment, he was promoted to a brigadier general; and, acting as major general, commanding the 1st division of the 11th army corps, greatly distinguished himself at Gettysburg, as on more recent occasions.

Among the volunteers of other States, Rockland has contributed the following; viz.: Samuel Smith, 17th Mass. regiment; D. M. Spear, N. Y. cavalry; Jos. Verrill, Mass. regiment; Fred. M. Sawyer, 5th N. Y. cavalry; Jas. Cotter, 32d Mass. regiment; Weston W. Dow, California regiment; Chas. H. Huntley, 8th N. H. regiment; John E. Young, 2d Mass. regiment; Geo. W. Haskell, Ohio regiment; James Miller, N. Y. battery; Wm. M. Snow, 3d Wisconsin regiment; James L. Smith, 17th Mass. regiment; Niles T. Crocker, 3d N. Y. artillery, company B; David E. Davis, 11th Mass. regiment, and Ira O. Rhoades of the Nebraska regimental band, who died of typhoid at Cincinnati, O., May 11, 1862.

In the U. S. army, regulars, this city has Adam G. Bridges, Charles Bunker, Sewall L. Day, Charles B. Fuller, Ephraim

---

* Col. Gerty's Report.

M. Hewett, Wm. Knowlton, Lorenzo Lothrop, Collamore McLane, Nathaniel C. Stubbs, and John Vandergill, of the 17th regiment; Wm. W. Place; Wm. Fessenden, paymaster; and Thos. K. Osgood, paymaster; besides Lieut. J. A. Fessenden, before mentioned, who was wounded in the midst of his brave service at the battle of Stone River, Chickamauga, when, after the death of the captain and capture of the 1st Lieutenant, the command devolved upon him.

To the U. S. naval service, Rockland has supplied the following: Daniel J. Adams, Alden C. Andrews, Henry Andrews, Edwin Banks; Richard Bartlett, Lucius Beattie, sailing master of *Sabine*; Wm. A. Beattie, J. Warren Bragg, Wm. D. Branard, Orris Brewer, Newell W. Brown, John G. Brown, master's mate; Arthur K. Brown; Heman H. Burpee, Edward A. Butler, master's mate; Geo. Cables, acting master; Geo. W. Caliph; Sewall Cates, E. T. Chapman, paymaster, perished in the *Commodore Jones;* James Cottar, Joseph C. Cotton, Niles T. Crocker, Jonathan W. Crocker, Charles S. Cutler, Sewall L. Day, Thomas W. Devons, Timothy Downey; John M. Eastman, Jos. Warren Edgcomb, Wm. F. Elliott, Royal G. Erskine, James Foeman, George Foreman, Frank M. Foster, Frederic Furbish, acting ensign, died at New Orleans. Wm. Galland, Francis Gildy, John F. Grant, Weston Gregory, master's mate, John H. Ham, Wm. Hanson, John F. Harden, Edward C. Healey, acting master in steamer Somerset, Wm. T. Higgens, Eben L. Higgens, John T. Irons, Daniel W. Jackson, Martin Jackson, Henry T. Keene, Frederic W. Libby, John McKean, Francis G. Mellus, Chas. H. Miller, Oliver B. Mills, James Mullen, Theirs N. Myers, Edward Norton, paymaster's clerk, Frederic Ordway, Albert L. Pendleton, Joseph H. Pierce, Joseph O. Pierce, Harrison A. Pitcher, Andrew B. Pressy, John W. Rich, Dodipher Richards, Edward Rogers, Joshua N. Rowe, master's mate, Adelbert Rowe, Wm. Sansom, Thomas Saunders, Chas. Vincent Shelden, Martin U. Singhi, Henry J. Sleeper, Henry A. Smith, Lewis L. Smith, Wesley Smith, Chas. W. Snow, (2d), acting ensign, died at New Orleans of fever; Alden T. Spear, in command of ship *Nightingale*, died of yellow fever at Santa Rosa Island, 1863, after a brilliant career, Otis G. Spear, Francis M. Staples, Albert H. Tarr, Nelson Tate, Harry Thompson, Jas. E. Thorndike, Edward E. True, Benj. F. Trundy, Orlando S. Trussell, Bolin F. Tucker, Albert F. Ulmer, Arthur Ulmer, Horatio A. Ulmer, Harvey S. Walsh, Patrick Walsh, Chas. B. Washburn, J. A. Wentworth, John Wilson, Ephraim Wiley, Henry

Woods, and Edward R. Wooster. [The list furnished the compiler, did not mention the offices and stations held by each, so those only are noted which happened to be picked up from other unofficial sources.] There were also enlisted into the navy under the call of July 18, 1864, Josiah Achorn, Jr., John H. Adams, Issac Adams, J. G. Babbidge, Charles C. Baker, Hudson Barker, Theodore S. Brown, Chas. E. Burpee, Austin Buckland, B. W. Candage, Seth E. Condon, Frank S. Coombs, Jos. C. Cotton, reinlisted, Alex. C. Crockett, Albert J. Crockett, Alfred Crockett, Henry O. Davis, Henry T. Dunning, Amos Eldridge, Iddo K. Elwell, John E. Ellems, Albert N. Fales, John H. Grafton, Iddo K. Graves, Samuel L. Hall, W. W. Hardy, Zenas H. Higgens, Jairus M. Healey, Bradford K. Holmes, Orris J. Jameson, Leonard Jameson, F. C. Knowlton, Eugene Mills, Amos Nash, ——— Packard, Albert N. Pendleton, Abner A. Perry, Jos. O. Pierce, Mauton M. Pillsbury, Greenleaf Porter, William A. Pressey, Galen Rhoades, John B. Rogers, Josiah Sherer, G. T. Simmons, A. K. Simonton, Geo. S. Slocum, William H. Snow, Frederic Snow, Timothy Smith, Geo. E. Williams, Ichabod Y. Wing, Amos P. Wood, and Edgar O. Ulmer.

On a call for a draft of 300,000 in July, 1863, this city's quota was 183, of whom two, viz., Albert E. Smith and John Coakley, entered service; 71 furnished substitutes, of whom one only, Michael Martin, was of this city; 74 were exempted for physical disability, &c.; one had been paroled by rebels; two were in service March 3, 1863; and 32 failed to report. On the President's later calls for volunteers, many of the young men of this city enlisted, of whom the following joined the *2d Regiment Cavalry;* viz., Charles A. Miller, major; in Co. D, Albion C. Colby; in Co. E, Adoniram J. Pickard, lieutenant; Edgar A. Hanaky, sergeant; Adolphus A. Leavitt, Cyrus Harding, and James P. Robbins, corporals; Benjamin Bartlett; Jonathan Crockett; John H. Dean; Ambrose Dill; Melzar T. Dyer, Albert L. Fields, Samuel W. Hewett, Nathan A. Hewett, Frank A. Knight, Francis G. Mellus, Sanford H. Pendleton, Josiah Peabody, David M. Robbins, John E. Sanders, Ashley St. Clair, Pearl Spear, Michael Tracy, William Wasgatt, Charles O. Wentworth, and Charles P. Wood; and, in Co. M, Thomas Barney, Stephen O. Young, and William S. Farwell, corporal, transferred to Capt. Chase's company of District Columbia cavalry and promoted to lieutenant.

The following were enrolled in the *Coast Guards:* Philip Achorn, Manasseh E. Andrews, John M. Bachelder, Oliver D.

Brown, Alphonzo Brown, Wm. J. Cotton, Byron J. Erskine, George Johnson, Benjamin Jones, Oscar R. Perry, Israel Rivers, Wm. A. Rackliff, Augustus Studley.

The following enlisted in the 30*th regiment;* viz., Charles Clemmons, company I; Joel P. Quimby, company D; and in company F, Charles E. Haskell, George F. Stewart, and Edward A. Sprague, the latter probably transferred to the 31st regiment, in which, as stated in the papers, he was the color bearer, greatly distinguished for his coolness and bravery in all the battles of the Potomac army from the Wilderness to Petersburg, in the assault on which, after the mine explosion, he was the first to plant the Union flag on its breastworks, for which he has since been promoted to 1st lieutenant of his company.

The remainder of those enlisted since Jan. 1, 1864, whose regiment and companies, not being found in the last Adjutant General's Report, we are unable to give, are as follows: Washington Achorn, Wm. H. Ames, Wm. Anderson, Thos. Anderson, John Adley, Jr., Benjamin L. Babbidge, Alvin Barnoul, Peter Blake, Warren Blake, George S. Bond, Enos C. Bridges, Wm. H. Britto, Benaiah P. Brackley, Wm. J. Brown, John E. Burrill, George Bunker, Michael Cassady, Cornelius Cauhalen, Abiel B. Clark, Orrin S. Clossen, Wm. J. Collamore, Frederic Colombe, Edgar Crockett, Norman L. Crockett, James B. Cushing, Samuel Derby, Thomas Devens, Leander Elwell, Samuel Fessenden, Alva F. Furbish, Joseph F. Gerry, Henry H. Gilpie, John Graves, Jr. Almond Greeley, Anthony N. Greeley, Alva F. Green, Alex Hall, Frank W. Ham, James Harriman, Robert Hill, Jacob B. Holmes, Wm. T. Higgins, Daniel L. Howe, Charles A. Jameson, Edward E. Jennison, Charles Jones, Peter Kaler, John M. Kalloch, Wm. H. Kenneston, John S. Kenneston, Joseph Knowles, Edgar C. Kirkpatrick, Benjamin Leach, Thomas W. Lee, Adolphus A. Leavitt, Charles H. Leighton, Robert N. Marsh, J. A. Marshall, James M. Mathews, Samuel L. Meservey, Edwin P. Merrill, Cyrus N. Mills, Charles H. Miller, Charles A. Moore, Eugene Moffitt, Myrick H. Nash, Daniel C. Norris, Frederic Ordway, Wm. A. Orne, Thomas Powers, Eli R. Perry, James Rackliff, Jere. P. Rackliff, Charles H. Raye, Charles C. King, Thomas Riley, James E. Rhoades, Daniel Robbins, Andrew H. St. Clair, Thomas C. Saunders, Robert Spalding, Jr., Charles H. Spalding, Otis G. Spear, Robert C. Stacy, Dennis A. Sullivan, George F. Thomas, Zebulon F. Thompson, Alden U. Thorndike, James E. Thorndike, Edward Titus, Charles B. Titus, Franklin Tolman, Michael

E. Towne, John W. Turner, F. H. Ulmer, Abiezer Veazie, James Walden, Abiathar K. Wiggin, John M. Wilson, Odbrey Witham, Daniel Whalen, Jerome B. Wood, and George W. Wood. Rockland being thus credited with so large a number of volunteers, was not subject to the draft of Oct. 5, 1864.

Besides this long list of her most precious treasures, torn from the peaceful pursuits of civil life, the city has contributed from her pecuniary resources, for soldiers' bounties, prior to Feb., 1864, $77,175; for the support of soldiers' families, $9,220,32; and her citizens, for one year ending Aug. 31, 1863, were called upon to pay internal duties, licenses, &c., to the amount of $7,296,82, of which $2,814,-96 were paid by 86 individuals as an income tax, — an amount said to be nearly double that paid by any other town or city in this the 5th district of Maine. The remainder was assessed on 13 wholesale dealers, one wholesale liquor dealer, 90 retail dealers, 24 retail liquor dealers, eight third class peddlers, four fourth class peddlers, three seventh class and two eighth class hotel keepers, five livery stable keepers, seven manufacturers, three photographers, seven lawyers, nine physicians and surgeons, and four apothecaries. The same taxes for 1864, amounting to $4434,67, together with the tonnage duties on vessels, had their amount been received in season to be here inserted, to say nothing about the derangement of business from fear of piratical cruisers, and other like causes, added to the preceding sums and individual contributions, would exhibit sufficient evidence that the people of this city have borne their full share of the burdens, privations, sorrows, and sufferings growing out of the present conflict — a willing sacrifice for liberty, union, and the institutions established by our forefathers.

TABLE I.

HIGHWAYS LAID OUT BY THE TOWN OF THOMASTON.

LAID OUT.			ACCEPTED.
1778,	From	Warren line to Camden line,	Mar. 29, 1779.
"	"	Old saw-mill to Wessaweskeag,	
1783,	"	Camden road W. of Madambettox meadows,	Mar. 20, 1784.
1786,	"	James Brown's to line between Thomaston and St. George,	May 6, 1788.
May 29, 1786,	"	Head of Owl's Head Bay to Jona. Crockett's,	" "
Dec. 1787,		The same laid out by D. Fales, and again by Gleason,	1806.
May 29, 1786,	"	Main road to N. Fales's or Beech Woods,	May, 1788.
"	"	Bridge, O. Head Bay, to Rendall's at O. Head Harbor,	" "
"	"	Bridge, O. Head Bay, to Heard's at Ash Point,	April 1, 1793.
"	"	Near Crockett's at Ash Point to Wessaweskeag,	May 6, 1788.
		Alteration in same,	April 1, 1793.
"	"	Bridge near Coombs's, S. to town line,	Mar. 9, 1789.
	"	Abiathar Smith's to Watson's ferry,	May 4, 1789.
1794,	"	Isaiah Tolman's to Camden line, W. of pond.	
	"	Eph. Snow's ship-yard, at Gig, to Jas. Brown's,	May 10, 1797.
	"	S. Tolman's, W. of Meadows, to D. Creighton's,	" "
	"	G. Ulmer's to Lindsey's to road at Lermond's Cove, (subject to gates,)	" "
	"	D. Fales to Josiah Ingraham's,	" "
	"	Jos. Perry's S. line, to Wessaweskeag bridge, below mills,	May 13, 1799.
	"	Camden road, or line, toward Curtis Tolman's,	April 7, 1800.
	"	Woodcock's land to Warren line at Oyster River bridge,	May 5, 1800.
Jan. 20, 1802,	"	Camden line at R. Jameson's, to Jas. Fales's on the road leading from J. Crockett's to Co. road,	April 5, 1802.
	"	John Fales's, by Healey's, Blackington's mill-dam, &c. to Camden line at John Keen's,	April 4, 1803.
	"	Mill river bridge to Oyster river bridge, 2d laying out,	" "
Sept. 9, 1802,	"	Lindsey's corner to Eph. Gay's,	" "

TABLE I. (*Continued.*)

LAID OUT.			ACCEPTED.
Sept. 9, 1802,	From	Owl's Head at F. Reed's, to N. Emery's, on road from Ash Point to Owl's Head Bay,	April 4, 1803.
May 2, 1803,	"	Wessaweskeag mills to St. Geo. line,	May 2, "
Aug. 3, 1803,	"	Camden line to Wheaton's bridge,	Aug. 8, "
Jan. 20, 1802,	"	Camden line to road from Shore to road by Crockett's,	March, "
Mar. 19, 1804,	"	Lermond's Cove to Geo. Ulmer's,	April 2, 1804.
Nov. 30, 1803,	"	Sam'l Tolman's, W. of Meadow, to James Howard's,	" "
Apr. 29, 1803,	"	Camden line N. W. of Tolman's Pond, to John Blackington's,	May 4, "
May 28, 1804,	"	Fogler's shop to Eph. Gay's, near Shore, provided John Crockett gives a town-landing,	May 30, "
Aug. 10, 1806,	"	N. Parish house to Owl's Head Bay road,	Aug. 23, 1806.
		Same, shifted from Fales's to Dr. Webb's land,	May 4, 1807.
		Same, or Butler road, re-accepted and described,	June 30, 1808.
	"	Mosman's mills, by Pond, to Camden. By order Court,	1804.
		Road at Owl's Head Harbor,	April, 1809.
	"	John Snowdeal's to St. George's line,	May 4, 1812.
	"	Between P. Ulmer and W. Tilson, to L. Smith's,	May 6, 1816.
	"	Cushing line to river opposite King's wharf,	May 10, 1819.
	"	Paine's store to the toll-bridge,	July 26, 1819.
Sept. 5, 1819,	"	J. Dean's gate to Butler road.	
	"	I. Snow's N. line to Brin. Butler's S. line,	Nov. 6, 1820.
Oct. 1, 1820,	"	Timothy Spalding's to Wessaweskeag road,	" "
Nov. 1, 1820,	"	S. Rankin's to W. of Jas. Fales's house, three rods wide,	April 2, 1821.
	"	N. Parish church to Schoolhouse near Mrs. Dodge's,	" "
	"	Lampson's by L. Smith's to Beech Woods,	" "
Oct. 24, 1824,		Alteration in ditto,	Nov. 1, 1824.
	"	J. Sprague's to King's wharf,	April 8, 1822.
	"	John Gleason's to King's wharf,	Sept. 9, 1822.
	"	King's wharf to Mrs. Knox's or Fort wharf,	" "
	"	D. Gay's to County road near Austin's (a bridle road,)	April 4, 1825.
	"	Town road near R. Lowell's to N. Sleeper's,	" "

TABLE I. (*Continued.*)

LAID OUT.			ACCEPTED.
April 2, 1825,	From	B. S. Dean's to road leading to wharf,	April 4, 1825.
Mar. 11, 1826,	"	Opposite Beech Woods road, S. and S. W. to Knox lane,	April 3, 1826.
April 3, 1826,		Beech Woods road altered,	" "
Sept. 2, 1826,	"	Knox lane to J. Morton's land, (now Elliott street,)	April 2, 1827.
Sept. 7, 1827,	"	O. Jordan's to D. Henderson's, (now the N. side of Mall,)	Sept. 1827.
"	"	60 rods W. of Cong. church to road leading to Fort wharf,	" "
June 14, 1827,	"	Between M. Ulmer and J. Blackington's to the Shore road,	" "
	"	Curtis Tolman's to Widow Eaton's, altered,	April 2, 1827.
Aug. 19, 1828,	"	The Northern Branch road to Warren line,	Sept. 1828.
Sept. 5, 1828,	"	The Town Landing to Morton's road,	" "
" "		West of Stimpson's store, southerly,	" "
" "		West of the Meeting house lot to road No. 73,	" "
" "	"	O. Robbins's store to the river at ship-yard,	" "
Oct. 31, 1828,	"	Main road to D. N. Piper's,	Nov. 3, 1828.
" "	"	Tilson's barn to Piper's Slaughter house,	" "
" "	"	The Bank and Fort wharf road to Foster's wharf,	" "
Mar. 28, 1831,	"	Road by David Gay's to the Shore road,	April 11, 1831.
Mar. 14, 1831,	"	Between M. Ulmer's and John Blackington's, to Shore road,	" "
Mar. 31, 1832,	"	J. Partridge's shop, by J. Berry's to Camden road,	April 2, 1832.
May 5, 1832,	"	W. Mosman's to Tolman's pond. By County Commissioners,	April 17, 1832.
April 24, 1832,	"	Mrs. E. Scott Young's to Bartlett Oliver's. By Co. Com.,	Sept. 4, 1832.
Sept. 7, 1832,	"	M. Mosman's house to E. G. Dodge's house,	April 22, 1833.
April 12, 1833,	"	O. Robbins's store to ship-yard Landing,	" "
	"	Wm. Mosman's to Tolman's p'd, alteration,	July 3, 1833.
Aug. 10, 1833,	"	County road to Beech Woods road,	Aug. 29, 1833.
Aug. 22, 1833,	"	Camden line in O. Holmes's pasture to Tolman's pond road,	" "
" "	"	Dr. Lovejoy's to B. Blackington's barn-yard,	" "

TABLE I. (*Continued.*)

LAID OUT.			ACCEPTED.
	From	Geo. Emery's house to the main road,	April 14, 1834.
April 9, 1834,	"	Town Landing to, or across B. Bussy's land,	" "
Sept. 3, 1834,	"	Near J. & C. Thorndike's house lot on to Ulmer's Point,	Sept. 20, 1834.
" "	"	Jas. Crockett's to Spofford kiln lot, on Ulmer's Point,	" "
	"	Alden Gay's to Mrs. Colley's; widened,	April 18, 1836.
	"	The lane at Owl's Head to Dodge's line,	" "
April 18, 1835,	"	Beech Woods to Warren line,	" "
" "	"	Kalloch & Perry's house to Jos. Hasty's land at Shore village,	" "
Mar. 22, 1836,	"	C. Spear's house lot, N. E. to land of J. Spofford,	" "
" "	"	Meth. church, E. Thomaston, to Shore road, intersecting the preceding,	" "
	"	A. Levensaler's N. W. corner, southerly to Fort wf. alteration,	" "
	"	Main road leading to Warren toward Upper Toll bridge,	" "
July, 1836,	"	Beech Woods to Warren line, alteration,	Aug. 6, 1836.
	"	E. Perry's house to road near K. Crockett's wharf,	April 17, 1837.
April 12, 1837,	"	I. Willis's house across to the road to Jacob Ulmer's mill,	" "
		Again accepted,	April 16, 1838.
" "	"	R. Robinson's on W. Meadow road to Gallop's blacksmith shop,	April 17, 1837.
" "	"	J. Turner's to the road that leads from Shore road to Meadow road,	" "
" "	"	Fort wf. to Elisha Fales's house, old road discontinued,	" "
		Leading by O. Holmes's house,	" "
	"	Richard Robinson's to Gallop's shop, discontinued,	May 15, 1837.
	"	Richard Robinson's to Gallop's shop, re-accepted,	April 16, 1838.
		Denominated the Snow road, probably Booker street,	" "
	"	Lewis Smith's across Crockett's land to road from E. Brown's to D. Gay's store,	" "
	"	Owl's Head road near Jno. Hall's land S. Easterly, with bridle roads, &c.,	" "

TABLE I. (*Continued.*)

LAID OUT.			ACCEPTED.
		To Sherer & Ingraham's saw-mill, discontinued and made a bridle road,	Aug. 16, 1838.
July 12, 1836,	From	Camden to D. Gay's in Thomaston. By Co. Com.,	
	"	Willis's at Meadow to Sherer & Ingraham's mill, re-opened,	April 15, 1839.
March, 1839,	"	Granite post, near Singhi's, to land of P. Ulmer,	" "
" "	"	Between Ingraham & Godding lots to sea shore,	" "
" "	"	L. Snow's store, to road leading by Methodist church,	" "
" "	"	N. Spear's corner, W. to a reserve for cross road,	" "
" "	"	N. W. corner of A. Drake's land, northerly 22 rods,	" "
" "	"	McIntosh's shed N. 46 rods to road,	" "
" "	"	E. corner of S. Partridge's land, N. W. 17 rods,	" "
June 8, 1839,	"	J. Pillsbury's store, to Universalist church and school house,	June 8, 1839.
" "	"	C. Spofford's house lot, to land of J. Spofford,	" "
	"	Near J. Ulmer's grist mill, to O'Brien's marble Mill,	April 12, 1841.
	"	Dodge's Mountain, to road near M. Mosman's,	June 8, 1839.
	"	Lime Rock Bank N. 50 rods to Lindsay's Brook,	April 6, 1840.
	"	Elibeus Fales's house to the town road,	April 12, 1841.
	"	Near Waterman Fales's, bridle road, discontinued,	" "
1840,	"	I. Kimball's store to Wm. Tilson's corner,	" "
	"	Dodge's Mountain to road near M. Mosman's, alteration,	" "
	"	Jameson's Point to county road near Chas. Jameson's,	June 1, "
	"	E. Perry's store to Meadow road, (now Pleasant st.,)	" "
		passing by Universalist church, conditionally,	April 11, 1842.
	"	D. Thomas's to S. Rankin's,	" "
	"	near J. Ulmer's grist-mill to O'Brien's Marble mill,	July 14, "
	"	near J. Ulmer's grist-mill, part discontinued, and in lieu thereof, road built by L. Andrews accepted,	" "

TABLE I. (*Continued.*)

LAID OUT.			ACCEPTED.
	From	Philip Ulmer's mill, alteration in, conditionally,	April 10, 1843.
		by Universalist church, accepted by County Commissioners,	Oct. 21, 1842.
	"	the highway to Geo. Emery's, discontinued,	April 15, 1844.
	"	E. S. Hovey's, westerly, to M. E. Thurlo's,	" "
	"	outlet of Tolman's pond to road near Calvin Tolman's,	" "
August 6, 1844,		at Shore village to Crockett's Pt., alteration and straitening,	" 14, 1845.
" "	"	George Spears' to Pleasant st., Shore village,	" "
April 7, 1845,	"	Achorn's wh'f privilege to Camden and Eph. Perry's road,	" "
" "	"	near E. S. Smith's to steam mill and road to Ingraham's Pt.,	" "
March 24, 1845,	"	M'Kellar's store to Geo. Thorndike's house,	" "
" "	"	the post office in South Thomaston, southerly, 30 rods, by County Commissioners,	August 25, "
May 2, 1846,	"	Eph. Dean's to South Parish church, Westkeag,	July 2, 1846.
Feb, 26, 1847,	"	R. Sherer's barn to Tolman's line, alteration,	March 8, 1847.
" "	"	Camden line, by the Jameson's, to new county road,	" "
March 1, 1847,	"	Col. H. Healey's to Main st., W. Thomaston,	" "
Feb. 26, "	"	Leprelet Smith's house to steamboat pier,	" "
" "	"	J. Crockett's house to Cole & Lovejoy's wharf and kiln privilege,	" "
March 1, 1848,	"	Mill river bridge to Morse & Ferrend's wharf, and to Knox st.,	" "
Dec. 4, "	"	E. S. Smith's, E., to land of D. Haskell, Spear and others,	" "
Feb. 29, "	"	the main road in Shore village, easterly, to E. Andrews,	" "
Feb. 16, "	"	C. McLoon's, northerly, to Israel Dean's,	" "
March 6, "	"	the David Gay road to Blackington's Corner,	" "
" "	"	Jas. Henderson's S. Westerly to land of Polly Hyler,	Mar. 18, 1850.
		On petition of Sanford Williams, &c, as per plan No. 1,	Mar. 22, 1852.
		On petition of J. O. Sprague, and others, as per plan No. 2,	" "

TABLE I. (*Continued.*)

LAID OUT.			ACCEPTED.
		On petition of Abel Hildreth, and others, as per plan No. 3,	" "
		On petition of Geo. W. Robinson, and others,	Mar. 21, 1853.
		All the roads in town as resurveyed by E. Rose,	Mar. 20, 1853.
	From	Main street by L. B. Gilchrist's, to school street,	Mar. 19, 1855.
	"	Land of Sam'l Watts, N. into road from Knox to Green st.,	" "
		Built by J. Barnard, called North street,	Mar. 24, 1856.
	"	Main street to Chapman & Flint's yard,	" "
	"	Knox street to Fish street,	" "
	"	Mill River to Rockland, voted to be built,	Aug. 26, 1857.
		On petition of John Morse and others, and discontinuing the old,	Mar. 22, 1858.
		On petition of Ranlett, Jordan & Co.,	" "

BY EAST THOMASTON OR ROCKLAND.

Sept. 1, 1848,	From	Main St. near I. Ames's, N. W. to D. F. Conant's; by County Commissioners,	Nov. 29, 1848.
Mar. 14, 1849,	"	Main St. near W. Blaisdell's to A. Achorn's on ship-yard road,	Mar. 26, 1849.
" "	"	Near W. Perry's to Gay's and Blackington's corner road,	" "
April 7, 1849,	"	East terminus of Starret ship-yard road to Ingraham's wharf road,	April 16, 1849.
March, 1849,	"	Shore road at Waterman's store to the Gay & Bl. Corner road,	" "
	"	West side Main St. near G. W. Pillsbury's, N. W., 35 rods,	" "
	"	Shore road, westerly by J. W. Sayward and A. Rankin,	" "
April 10, 1849,		Shore road on Main St. as resurveyed,	" "
Dec. 5, 1849,	"	Yellow school-house, Lime Rock St., N. E. to near Crocker's, by County Commissioners,	Nov. 15, 1849.
Mar. 15, 1850,	"	Pleasant Street near Hix's, to Holmes farm near G. Spear's,	April 1, 1850.
" "	"	Holmes farm near J. Wheeler's to A. Simonton, Jr.'s,	" "
Mar. 17, 1851,	"	South side Meth. church to reserved road of Ulmer heirs,	April 7, 1851.

TABLE I. (*Continued.*)

LAID OUT.			ACCEPTED.
March, 1852,	From	N. W. corner Jona. Spear's land to Marsh's Mt. road,	April 19, 1852.
April 8, 1852,	"	Cam. road near S. McLaughlin's S. E. to Jameson's Pt. road,	" "
" "	"	Joseph Furbish's N. E. to Eph. Perry's,	" "
March 25, 1853,	"	J. Furbish's, easterly, to J. Gregory's store,	" 25, 1853.
" "	"	near Nat. Nichols's house to C. Starrett's ship-yard,	" "
March 28, "	"	near S. Starrett's to South Cove on Ingraham's Pt.,	" "
March 29, "	"	Warren st., near J. Knight's, to Cedar st.,	" "
" "	"	Warren st., across Cedar st., to Blackington's corner road,	" "
March 30, "	"	Warren st., near G. Smith's, to Cedar st.,	" " " "
April 5, "	"	near L. Pendleton's to town way near C. Crockett's,	" "
April 8, "	"	Sherer & Ing. mill to Warren line,	" "
April 9, "		straightened from Simonton's Corner to Mrs. S. J. Pierce's,	" "
Aug. 25, "	"	W. end of st. by I. K. Kimball's to near G. D. Martin's,	Sept. 3, "
Aug. 26, "	"	Pleasant st., near B. Sweetzer's, southerly, to Holmes' farm,	" "
" "	"	the Deep Gully, Pleasant street, easterly to Union street,	" "
" "	"	E. S. Smith's, Main st., easterly to H. Ingraham road, straightened,	" "
Mar. 17, 1854,	"	a street leading N. from Lime Rock st. N. W.'ly to Lindsey Brook,	Mar. 27, 1854.
Mar. 18, 1854,	"	the Marine Railway road to the South Thomaston road,	" "
" "	"	the Simonton Corner and Ingraham Pt. road, to a street laid out by heirs of Sally Partridge,	" "
April 6, 1854,	"	W. end of Granite street N. W. to new town road,	April 15, 1854.
May 1, 1854,	"	Ocean street southerly to Ingraham Point road. Referred to city government,	
May 20, 1854,	"	Pleasant street to Park st. near Episcopal church, do.	
May 22, 1854,		Private way from barn, formerly J. Ulmer's, to quarry of the J. W. Blackington heirs, do.	

TABLE II.

VALUATION OF THOMASTON, ROCKLAND, AND SOUTH THOMASTON.

	BEFORE DIVISION.								AFTER DIVISION.					
Articles.	1780.	1784.	1790.	1800.	1810.	1820.	1830.	1840.	1850.			1860.		
									Thomaston	Rockland.	S. Thomast.	Thomaston	Rockland.	S. Thomast.
Polls,	80	80	203	311	457	417	616	1157	466	982	250	656	1697	314
Dwellinghouses,	35	58	85	155	215	242	423	684	300	716	167	444	1162	260
Barns,	35	45	40	115	185	228	292	408	176	273	135	276	766	190
Stores, Shops, &c.,			10	24	22				47	119	15	53	281	20
Saw and Grist Mills,	2	3	8	7	9							5	4	2
Acres Tillage Land.	150	70	230	291	418	415	482	548						
" English Mowing,	150	210		1107	1804	1769	2720	3622						
" Fresh Meadow,	150 (Fresh and Salt Meadow)	83	190	214	251	373		218						
" Salt Meadow,		129	166	176	74	70	104	147	5223 (all Acres)	6535 (all Acres)	9025 (all Acres)	4844 (all Acres)	5873 (all Acres)	9837 (all Acres)
" Pasturing,	200	99	808	1047	1948	1924	4299	4671						
" Wood & unimp'd,	20000	21696	21283	15685	12918	1653	1036	1450						
" Unimprovable,		2670	874	2390	605	1209	422	1188						
Tons of Hay,				1346	1978	1922	2618	3714				1077	1034	934
Bushels of Rye,				142	365							50	42	72
" Wheat,				105	1191	1692		998				39	56	156
" Oats,				88	266							79	495	247
" Indian Corn,				2348	2014	1701		965				320	830	420
" Barley,				208	504	692						883	960	495
" Peas and Beans,				164	68	116	40	86				191	201	830
" Potatoes,							25850	36219				2725	3986	960
Horses 3 yrs. & upwards,	36	19	31	114	193				122	261	61	185	379	102
Oxen 4 do. do.	88	58	189	311	304				140	269	104	53	118	72

Steers and Cows,	150	191	398	509	699				235	350	313	318	387	291
Sheep,	304								101	140	562	60	51	450
Swine 6 months old,	81	53	151	273	349				39	104	54	116	110	73
Stock in trade,		£80	£343	$4775	11694				17450	149312	1250	54225	115705	2200
Money,		£55	£147	$4335	1265				31750	74738	1250	68300	68196	13200
Bank Stock,						1000	9000	49360	12502	36230	6615	51500	99745	7331
Public Stock,			£12		2				1705	.5100	1340	34070	21200	575
Tons of Vessels,			312	332	1415								24140	
Value of do.						14668		181700	298756	336385	84299	828715	544643	59647
Pleasure Carriages,						15	49	85	24	97	35	39	77	3
Ounces of Plate,			32	200	14	150		146						
Piano Fortes, &c.,									22	16		44	74	6
Square feet of Wharf,				9927	6635		Wharves,		18	38	7			6
Total value of Real & Personal Estate,						$162504	1085823		740876	1166475	285073	2053573	2699611	289622

NOTE.—To Rockland, in 1860, should be added privileges, including wharves, kilns, quarries, &c., value, $336,365; value of carriages, $5,855; of house furniture and musical instruments, $16,920. The number of houses in Rockland, for 1850, is from valuation of 1851, the former being destroyed by fire; the crops raised in 1860, from the census.

TABLE III.

POPULATION OF THE TOWN OF THOMASTON FROM THE CENSUS RETURNS FOR THE YEARS

	1790.	1800.	1810.	1820.	1830.	1840.	1850.	1860.	Engaged in	1820.	1840.	1860.
White Males,	416	737	1101	1343	2218	3159	1419	1453	Agriculture,	152	540	69
White Females,	379	660	998	1308	1997	3061	1297	1626	Commerce,	63	106	68
Colored Persons,	4	5	1		6	7	7	6	Manufactures,	129	866	300
									Ocean Navigation,		456	201
Total,	799	1402	2100	2651	4221	6227	2723	3085	Learned professions,		44	22

In 1840, Thomaston had 13 military pensioners, 5 deaf mutes, 2 blind, 4 insane and idiotic.

In 1860, 24 gentlemen, 19 officials, prison guards, &c., 27 teachers, 224 day laborers and domestics, 1 blind, 2 deaf mutes, 6 insane and idiotic.

TOWN OF SOUTH THOMASTON, AFTER DIVISION.

	1850.	1860.	Engaged in	1860.
White Males,	721	822	Agriculture,	57
White Females,	699	793	Commerce,	14
			Manufactures, stone cutting, mechanism, &c.,	136
Total,	1420	1615	Ocean Navigation,	167

In 1860, South Thomaston had 3 officials, 2 in learned professions, 7 teachers, 1 artist, 26 in fishery, 67 day laborers and domestics, 2 blind, 2 deaf mutes, and 2 idiotic.

CITY OF ROCKLAND, AFTER DIVISION.

	1850.	1860.	Engaged in	1860.
White Males,	2621	3591	Agriculture,	166
White Females,	2420	3725	Commerce,	231
Colored Persons,	11	1	Manufactures and mechanical pursuits,	815
			Ocean Navigation,	553
Total,	5052	7317		

Besides which, Rockland had in 1860, 32 officials, 37 teachers, 39 in learned professions, 21 in fishery, 370 day laborers and domestics, 4 blind, 4 deaf mutes, 8 insane and idiotic, and 1 in Reform School.

TABLE IV

AMOUNT OF TAXES VOTED TO BE RAISED FROM 1777 TO 1862.

THOMASTON.

Years.	For Schools.	Highways.	Town Charges.	Years.	For Schools.	Highways.	Town Charges.
1777		£ 100	£ 100	1815	$1000	$2000	$1000
1778			50	1816	1000	2000	1000
1779			100*	1817	1000	2000	1000
1780			600	1818	1000	2000	1000
1781		90 silv.	60 silv.	1819	1000	2300	1500
1782			75 "	1820	1000	1500	1000
1783			10 "	1821	1100	1500	1200
1784				1822	1500	2150	2000
1785			40	1823	1100	3000	1100
1786		100	20	1824	1500	2000	1800
1787		150	30	1825	1100	2500	1500
1788	£20	100	50	1826	1500	2500	1500
1789	60	100	60	1827	1500	2500	1000
1790	60	100	30	1828	1500	3000	1200
1791	26	100	50	1829	1500	3000	1200
1792	26	150	40	1830	1500	3000	1000
1793	60	150	45	1831	1800	3500	1200
1794	60	150	45	1832	1800	3800	2000
1795		150	90	1833	2000	4300	1500
1796		$ 600	$ 200	1834	2000	3500	2000
1797		600	200	1835	2000	4000	3500
1798	$ 300	1400	350	1836	2000	4500	4500
1799	600	1600	350	1837	2500	5000	5000
1800	600	1600	300	1838	2500	5000	4000
1801	600	1600	300	1839	2500	5000	5000
1802	1000	1600	400	1840	2500	5000	6000
1803	1000	1600	500	1841	2500	5000	5000
1804	1000	1600	1000	1842	2500	5000	3500
1805	1000	1600	500	1843	3000	6000	2000
1806	1500	1600	1500	1844	3000	6000	2500
1807	1500	1400	800	1845	3000	6000	2000
1808	1000	1600	500	1846	3500	6000	2500
1809	1500	2000	600	1847	3500	8400	4800
1810	1000	1500	700	1848	3500		3000
1811	1000	1500	1500	1849	1200	2700	1200
1812	500	1500	2200	1850	1500		1700
1813	500	1800	1000	1851	1500	1600	1800
1814	500	2000	1000	1852	1500	1600	1800

* Including ministry, schools, &c.

TABLE IV. (*Continued.*)

Years.	For Schools.	Highways.	Town Charges.	Years.	For Schools.	Highways.	Town Charges.
			THOMASTON.				
1853	$1600	$1700	$2500	1858	$2000	$4000	$3000
1854	2000	1600	2000	1859	2500	2900	3200
1855	2000	1600	2000	1860	2500	3200	0540
1856	2000	4000	2500	1861	2500	2500	3700
1857	2200	3000	2500	1862	2200	1800	4350
			EAST THOMASTON.				
1849	$3000	$5000	$2700	1852	$3750	3000	3200
1850	4000	3000	2200	1853	4000	6000	2700
1851	3000	3000	4300	1854	5000	10000	6200
			ROCKLAND CITY.				
1855	$3486	$8387	$4896*	1859	$6000	$5000	$8700
1856	5267	7101	†8242	1860	4000	5500	8250
1857	5500	6000	7800	1861	5000	4000	7600
1858	5000	5000	8550	1862	4400	3500	9850
			SOUTH THOMASTON.				
1849	$700	$1000	$500	1856	$800	$1200	$750
1850	700	1000	500	1857	900	1200	900‡
1851	800	1000	600	1858	900	1400	1000
1852	700	1000	600	1859	900	1400	1000
1853	800	1000	550	1860	900	1600	1000
1854	900	1300	650	1861	1000	1400	1000
1855	1000	1200	700	1862	1000	1400	1400

* Including Watch, Fire, and Police expenditures.
† Including road damages and contingent fund.
‡ With the addition of $599,99 for outstanding liabilities in 1857, $500 in 1858, and $100 in 1859.

TABLE V.

PRINCIPAL TOWN OFFICERS.

Years	Town Clerk.	Treasurer.	Representative.
1777.	David Fales,	Mason Wheaton,	None sent.
1778.	James Stackpole,	John Mathews,	do.
1779.	David Fales,	Elisha Snow,	Mason Wheaton.
1780.	do.	do.	None sent.
1781.	do.	David Fales,	Oliver Robbins.
1782.	do.	do.	Mason Wheaton.
1783.	Israel Lovett,	Isaiah Tolman,	do.
1784.	John Dillaway,	James Stackpole,	John Dillaway.
1785.	Dea. Samuel Brown	Israel Lovett,	Samuel Brown.
1786.	do.	do.	do.
1787.	do.	David Fales,	do.
1788.	do.	Nathaniel Fales,	No choice.
1789.	do.	do.	Samuel Brown.
1790.	John Dillaway,	Samuel Brown,	do.
1791.	do.	do.	do.
1792.	do.	do.	do.
1793.	do.	do.	Josiah Reed.
1794.	do.	do.	None sent.
1795.	do.	David Fales,	Samuel Brown.
1796.	do.	do.	
1797.	do.	do.	Samuel Brown.
1798.	David Fales,	do.	Josiah Reed.
1799.	John Dillaway,	do.	do.
1800.	Josiah Reed,	Ephraim Snow,	Gen. Henry Knox.
1801.	do.	David Fales,	do.
1802.	do.	James Stackpole,	do.
1803.	do.	Joshua Adams,	do.
1804.	do.	do.	Joshua Adams.
1805.	Joseph Ingraham,	William Tilson,	Isaac Bernard.
1806.	do.	do.	I. Bernard, M. Wheaton.
1807.	do.	do.	M. Wheaton, E. G. Dodge.
1808.	do.	do.	M. Wheaton, J. Adams.
1809.	do.	Martin Marsh,	E. G. Dodge, I. Bernard.
1810.	do.	Josiah Ingraham,	do. do.
1811.	do.	do.	do. do.
1812.	do.	Joseph Ingraham,	E. G. Dodge, I. Bernard, Charles Spofford.
1813.	do.	do.	E. G. Dodge, Sam. Baker.
1814.	do.	Martin Marsh,	J. Gleason, E. Thatcher.
1815.	do.	do.	I. Bernard, John Spear.
1816.	Charles Spofford,	do.	do. do.
1817.	do.	Elkanah Spear,	Isaac Bernard.
1818.	do.	do.	John Spear.
1819.	do.	John Spear,	I. Bernard, John Ruggles.
1820.	Joseph Ingraham,	do.	Isaac Bernard.
1821.	do.	James D. Wheaton,	Martin Marsh.
1822.	Oliver Fales,	Joseph Sprague,	do.
1823.	do.	do.	John Ruggles.
1824.	do.	John Spear,	do.
1825.	do.	do.	do.
1826.	do.	do.	do.
1827.	do.	do.	do.
1828.	do.	John Spofford,	do.

TABLE V. (*Continued.*)

Years	Town Clerk.	Treasurer.	Representative.
1829.	Oliver Fales,	John Spofford,	John Ruggles,
1830.	do.	do.	do.
1831.	do.	Charles Holmes,	E. Spear, Jona. Cilley.
1832.	do.	do.	
1833.	do.	do.	E. Spear, Jona. Cilley.
1834.	do.	Hezekiah Prince,	Jona. Cilley, E. Spear.
1835.	do.	do.	J. Cilley, N. C. Fletcher.
1836.	do.	do.	A. Levensaler, do.
1837.	do.	do.	do. Jos. Hewett.
1838.	do.	do.	do. do.
1839.	do.	do.	L. Wilson, I. K. Kimball.
1840.	do.	do.	Jos. Gilchrist, do.
1841.	Walter E. Tolman,	Oliver Robbins,	do. H. Stevens.
1842.	do.	do.	Beder Fales, Isaac Ames.
1843.	do.	do.	Joseph Berry, do.
1844.	Nath'l Meservey,	do.	J. C. Adams, Jos. Berry.
1845.	do.	do.	A.Levensaler, O.B.Brown.
1846.	do.	do.	W. Thomas, J. W. Dodge.
1847.	do.	do.	J. C. Cochran, A. Coombs.
1848.	do.*	do.	do. Thos. O'Brien.
1849.	George A. Starr,	do.	Jer. Tolman, J. C. Adams.
1850.	do.	do.	do. Thos. O'Brien.
1851.	do.	O.Robbins, S.Waldo	
1852.	do.	Shubael Waldo,	Oliver Robinson.
1853.	do.	do.	George A. Starr.
1854.	do.	do.	Edward O'Brien.
1855.	do.	Alex. W. Brown,	Atwood Levensaler.
1856.	do.	do.	Samuel H. Allen.
1857.	do.	Shubael Waldo,	Robert Walsh.
1858.	do.	Edward E. O'Brien,	Samuel Watts.
1859.	do.	do.	Moses R. Ludwig.
1860.	Elisha Linnell,	do.	Albert P. Gould.
1861.	George A. Starr.	do.	do.
1862.	do.	Joshua A. Fuller,	Charles E. Ranlett.
1863.	Edw. R. Levensaler,	Edward E. O'Brien,	Thomas O'Brien.
1864.	do.	do.	Edmund Wilson.
	EAST THOMASTON.		
1848.	Nath'l Meservey,	Charles Holmes,	J. C. Cochran, T. O'Brien.
1849.	do.	do.	Jer. Tolman, J. C. Adams.
1850.	do.	do.	do. Thos. O'Brien.
1851.	do.	do.	
1852.	do.	do.	Hiram G. Berry.
1853.	do.	do.	Nathaniel A. Burpee.
1854.	do.	Maynard Sumner,	do.
	ROCKLAND CITY.		
1854.	Wakefield G. Frye,	Charles R. Mallard,	Nathaniel A. Burpee.
1855.	do.	do.	John Merrill.
1856.	do. E. R. Spear,	do.	Jeremiah Tolman.
1857.	Edward R. Spear,	Maynard Sumner,	Davis Tilson.
1858.	Alden Sprague,	Walter E. Tolman,	John T. Berry, resigned, Timothy Williams, el.

* After division of town, George A. Starr.

TABLE V. (*Continued.*)

Years	Town Clerk.	Treasurer.	Representative.
1859.	Oliver G. Hall,	Leander Weeks,	Timothy Williams.
1860.	do.	do.	Nathan A. Farwell.
1861.	do.	do.	A. Stanley, Francis Cobb.
1862.	do.	do.	Oliver J. Conant, do.
1863.	do.	do.	do. N. A. Farwell.
1864.	do.	do.	N. A. Farwell, Calvin Hall.
		SOUTH THOMASTON.	
1848.	Arch. McKellar, jr.	Ezekiel Hall,	J. C. Cochran, T. O'Brien.
1849.	do.	do.	Jre. Tolman, J. C. Adams.
1850.	do.	do.	do. Thos. O'Brien.
1851.	do.	Asa Coombs,	
1852.	do.	do.	Geo. Gilchrist of St. Geo.
1853.	do.	do.	Henry Spalding.
1854.	do.	Allen F. Martin,	Geo. Gilchrist of St. Geo.
1855.	do.	do.	Rich. R. Wall of St. Geo.
1856.	do.	do.	William Rowell.
1857.	Charles G. Snelling,	do.	Sam'l Trussell of St. Geo.
1858.	do.	James Newhall,	Samuel F. Coombs.
1859.	James Newhall,	do.	Matthew Kinney of St. Ge.
1860.	do.	do.	Richard R. Wall.
1861.	do.	John Dean,	Dav. Vinal of Vinalhaven.
1862.	do.	John H. Dean,	Jesse Sleeper.
1863.	do.	John Dean,	W. Thomas of No. Haven.
1864.		E. D. Hall,	

SELECTMEN.

1777. Col. Mason Wheaton, Lieut. John Mathews, David Fales.
1778. David Fales, Mason Wheaton, Samuel Brown.
1779. David Fales, Elisha Snow, Jonathan Crocket.
1780. Elisha Snow, David Fales, Jonathan Crocket.
1781. Samuel Brown, Jeremiah Tolman, Israel Lovett.
1782. David Fales, Israel Lovett, Jeremiah Tolman.
1783. John Simonton, Samuel Brown, Oliver Robbins, jr.
1784. John Dillaway, John Simonton, Jeremiah Tolman.
1785. Israel Lovett, Joseph Ingraham, Nathaniel Fales.
1786. Nathaniel Fales, Jeremiah Tolman, Ephraim Snow.
1787. do. do. John Simonton.
1788. John Dillaway, John Simonton, William Spear.
1789. do. do. do.
1790. Ambrose Snow, Israel Lovett, D. Fales, T. Hix, O. Robbins, jr.
1791. Samuel Brown, Mason Wheaton, Jeremiah Tolman.
1792. David Fales, Jeremiah Tolman, Mason Wheaton.
1793. Josiah Reed, William Rowell, John Crockett.
1794. do. do. do.
1795. Jeremiah Tolman, John Crockett, Joseph Ingraham.
1796. John Crockett, David Fales, Jr., William Spear.
1797. Ephraim Snow, do. Jonathan Spear, Jr.
1798. do. do. do.
1799. do. do. do.
1800. do. do. do.
1801. Josiah Reed, David Jenks, Jeremiah Tolman.

TABLE V. (*Continued.*)

1802. David Jenks, Jeremiah Tolman, Joshua Adams,
1803. do. Joshua Adams, Jere. Tolman, J. Reed, N. Emery.
1804. do. Josiah Reed, Jeremiah Tolman.
1805. Jeremiah Tolman, Perez Tilson, Richard Keating, Jr.
1806. Joshua Adams, David Jenks, Perez Tilson.
1807. Jeremiah Tolman, Jonathan Spear, Jr., John Blackington.
1808. do. J. Ingraham, I. Bernard, E. Snow, Jr., D. S. Fales.
1809. do. Isaac Bernard, Joseph Ingraham.
1810. do. Charles Spofford, Maj. Otis Robbins.
1811. do. do. Martin Marsh.
1812. Isaac Bernard, Martin Marsh, David Crockett.
1813. Martin Marsh, David Crockett, James D. Wheaton.
1814. do. do. do.
1815. David Crockett, John Spear, John Barnard.
1816. John Spear, David Crockett, Joseph Ingraham.
1817. David Crockett, Joseph Ingraham, Job Washburn.
1818. do. do. Halsey Healey.
1819. do. do. do.
1820. Job Washburn, William Heard, Elkanah Spear.
1821. William Heard, Job Washburn, Martin Marsh.
1822. do. do. do.
1823. John Spear, Wm. Stackpole, Enoch Lovejoy.
1824. Enoch Lovejoy, John Spofford, Wm. Stackpole.
1825. H. Prince, T. Tolman, J. Ingraham, A. Hall, I. Brown, (2d).
1826. do. do. do.
1827. do. do. Philip Ulmer.
1828. do. Wm. Heard, do.
1829. do. John Spear, do.
1830. do. do. do.
1831. do. Wm. Heard, James Partridge.
1832. Wm. Heard, John O'Brien, John Spofford.
1833. Elkanah Spear, Israel J. Perry, Atwood Levensaler.
1834. Thomas Tolman, do. do.
1835. do. do. do.
1836. Atwood Levensaler, Thomas Tolman, Asa Coombs.
1837. do. Joseph Hewitt, Harvey H. Spear.
1838. Timothy Fogg, Henry Ingraham, do.
1839. Harvey H. Spear, Timothy Fogg, Asa Coombs.
1840. Timothy Fogg, Isaac Ames, Harvey H. Spear.
1841. do. do. William McLoon.
1842. Isaac Ames, Wm. McLoon, Timothy Fogg.
1843. Thomas O'Brien, Oliver B. Brown, Wm. McLoon.
1844. Wm. McLoon, Thos. O'Brien, Oliver B. Brown.
1845. Thos. O'Brien, Ezekiel Perry, do.
1846. Chas. Harrington, Rowland Jacobs, Jr., Freeman Harden, Jr.
1847. do. do. do.
1848. Rowland Jacobs, Jr., Elkanah Spear, Jr. do.
" June. do. Joseph S. Burgess, Josiah W. Dodge.
1849. do. do. Merritt Austin.
1850. do. Thomas O'Brien, do.
1851. do. Merritt Austin, Thomas O'Brien.
1852. do. do. do.
1853. do. do. do.

TABLE V. (*Continued*)

1854. Thomas O'Brien, Chas. T. Starrett, Atwood Levensaler.
1855. Atwood Levensaler, do. John D. Barnard.
1856. do. Rowland Jacobs, Jr., Wm. Flint, Jr.
1857. Merritt Austin, Joseph Maxey, Rowland Jacobs, Jr.
1858. Rowland Jacobs, Oliver W. Jordan, James M. Beverage.
1859. do. do. do.
1860. do. do. do.
1861. do. do. do.
1862. Charles E. Ranlet, Wm. Stackpole, Chas. T. Starrett.
1863. Atwood Levensaler, James O. Cushing, James M. Beverage.
1864. do. do. do.

EAST THOMASTON.

1848. Joseph Hewett, Oliver B. Brown, Elkanah S. Smith.
1849. Elkanah S. Smith, do. Elkanah Spear, Jr.
1850. do. Chas. A. Macomber, George S. Wiggin.
1851. George S. Wiggin, Elkanah S. Smith, Timothy Williams.
1852. do. do. do.
1853. do. Alden Ulmer, A. J. Bird.
1854. do do. do.

SOUTH THOMASTON.

1848. Charles McLoon, George Thorndike, Joshua C. Adams.
1849. Joshua C. Adams, Peter Williams, Jr., George Thorndike.
1850. Peter Williams, Jr., James Sweetland, Jr., George Emery.
1851. George Thorndike, Charles McLoon, Peter Williams, Jr.
1852. do. do. do.
1853. do. William D. Graves, Isaac Tolman, (3d).
1854. do. do. do.
1855. do. do. do.
1856. William D. Graves, Ephraim Dean, Jr., Calvin C. Ingraham.
1857. Henry Spalding, do. Joseph M. Emery.
1858. Ephraim Dean, Jr., Joseph M. Emery, Mark Ames.
1859. do. do. do.
1860. do. James Sweetland, Ezekiel Doe.
1861. do. do. Calvin Ingraham.
1862. Jesse Sleeper, Jr., do. Jeremiah Sleeper.
1863. Ephraim Dean, Jr., J. A. Emery, Isaac Tolman.
1864. Joseph Emery, Elias P. Sleeper, George S. Williams.

ASSESSORS, FOR THOSE YEARS WHEN CHOSEN SEPARATE FROM THE SELECTMEN.

1778. David Fales, Israel Lovett, Samuel Brown.
1781. do. Jeremiah Tolman, do.
1782. do. Thomas McLellan, Elisha Snow.
1802. do. Thomas Vose, Josiah Reed.
1806. Martin Marsh, Jackson Durand, Jeremiah Tolman.
1807. Jeremiah Tolman, David Crockett, Jr., Benjamin Webb.
1808. J. Bentley, M. Marsh, J. Tolman, J. Adams, G. Coombs.
1809. Jeremiah Tolman, Isaac Bernard, Joseph Ingraham.
1810. Benjamin Webb, John Barnard, Capt. David Crockett.
1811. John Gleason, William Heard, John Spear.

TABLE V. (*Continued.*)

1813. William Heard, William M. Daws, David Crockett.
1814. do. do. Timothy Wellman.
1824 do. Knott Crockett, Hezekiah Prince.
1831. Isaac Brown, (2d,) George Emery, jr., N. Meservey, Asa Coombs, M. R. Ludwig
1832. Isaac Brown, (2d.) Iddo Kimball, Richard Robinson.
1836. Charles Harrington, Oliver Heard, William Singer.
1837. do. Samuel Fuller, William Heard.
1833. Samuel Fuller, Nathaniel Meservey, Asa Coombs.
1840. Atwood Levensaler, Iddo Kimball, Elkanah S. Smith.
1841. do. Jeremiah Tolman, do.
1842. Beder Fales, do. do.
1843. Joel Miller, Atwood Levensaler, do.
1844. do. do. do.
1845. do. do. do.
1846. Charles McLoon, Charles Crockett, Isaac Brown.
1848. Charles Harrington, Rowland Jacobs, Jr., Freeman Harden, Jr.
1853. Atwood Levensaler, Joseph Gilchrist, Oliver W. Jordan.

ROCKLAND CITY.

1855. Jeremiah Tolman, (3d), Isaac Gregory, Freeman Harden.
1856. do. do. do.
1857. Freeman Harden, Davis Tillson, E. W. Pendleton.
1858. Richard Walker, Azariah Stanley, Oliver B. Brown.
1859. Freeman Harden, Jeremiah Tolman, George D. Wooster.
1860. do. do. do.
1861. do. do. do.
1862. Jeremiah Tolman, Rufus C. Thomas, M. A. Achorn.
1863. Freeman Harden, Oliver J. Conant, W. J. Bond.

SOUTH THOMASTON.

1862. Charles P. Redman, Harrison P. Babb, John A. Emery.

TABLE VI.

MAYORS, ALDERMEN, AND MEMBERS OF THE COUNCIL, ROCKLAND.

MAYORS OF THE CITY OF ROCKLAND.

1854.	Knott Crockett,	1858.	Geo. S. Wiggin,	1862.	Geo. S. Wiggin.
1855.	do.	1859.	do.	1863.	do.
1856.	H. G. Berry,	1860.	do.	1864.	do.
1857.	Chas. Crockett,	1861.	do.		

TABLE VI. (*Continued.*)

ALDERMEN OF ROCKLAND.

Yrs.	Ward 1.	Ward 2.	Ward 3.	Ward 4.	Ward 5.	Ward 6.	Ward 7.
1854.	A. J. Bird,	Isaac Gregory,	G. S. Wiggin,	Thomas Colson,	T. W. Hix,	A. C. Spalding,	J. Tolman.
1855.	do.	do.	do.	do.	Ephraim Hall,	H. Ingraham,	do.
1856.	J. Achorn,	E. C. Healey,	A. H. Kimball,	W. E. Tolman.	S. Libbey,	E. S. Smith,	J. Bird.
1857.	Calvin Hall,	Isaac Gregory,	do.	B. Litchfield, jr.,	J. A. Ingraham,	do.	O. B. Brown.
1858.	P. T. Prescott,	do.	A. L. Lovejoy,	M. E. Thurlo,	do.	S. Starrett,	J. W. Ormsby.
1859.	Calvin Hall,	C. Crockett,	W. H. Titcomb,	C. G. Moffit,	Ephraim Hall,	S. H. Burpee,	T. Williams.
1860.	do.	do.	do.	do.	do.	do.	do.
1861.	P. Thurston,	do.	do.	do.	C. R. Whitney,	F. Harden,	Wm. Thompson.
1862	do.	A. T. Low,	C. R. Mallard,	W. J. Bond,	I. Snow,	J. Kalloch,	do.
1863.	do.	C. Crockett,	C. W. Snow,	do.	L. Weeks,	do.	C. C. Lovejoy.
1864.	C. L. Allen,	R. Crockett,	do.	J. P. Wise,	do.	Ira B. Ellems,	Alden Ulmer.

COMMON COUNCILMEN OF ROCKLAND.

Yrs.	Ward 1.	Ward 2.	Ward 3.	Ward 4.	Ward 5.	Ward 6.	Ward 7.
1854.	Calvin Hall,	Charles Crockett,	Samuel Rankin,	Elijah Walker,	Ephraim Hall,	F. W. Rhoades,	Jonathan Spear,
	Azariah Stanley,	C. L. Allen,	John Wakefield,	John Spofford,	David Robinson,	Dan'l C. Haskell,	O. B. Brown.
	Patr'k Simonton.	Isaac Ingraham.	John S. Case.	George J. Burns.	Jeremiah Berry.	Sam'l H. Burpee.	John Bird (2d).
1855.	Calvin Hall,	Charles Crockett,	John S. Case,	George J. Burns,	David Robinson,	Sam'l H. Burpee,	Oliver B. Brown,
	Azariah Stanley,	I. Ingraham (2d),	John Wakefield,	Elijah Walker,	Samuel Libbey,	Freeman Harden,	John Bird, jr.
	Geo. D. Wooster.	C. L. Allen.	Samuel Rankin.	F. Harrington.	Maynard Sumner.	D. H. Ingraham.	Jonathan Spear.
1856.	Geo. D. Wooster,	Geo. A. Stevens,	A. L. Lovejoy,	O. P. Mitchell,	O. B. Fales,	John C. Hilt,	O. B. Brown,
	Hiram Brewster,	Charles Crockett,	L. Campbell,	F. Harrington,	Larkin Snow,	Sanford Starrett,	Jona. Spear,

	Calvin Hall.	W. B. Robinson.	O. J. Conant.	G. J. Burns.	John Merrill.	Benj. Hardy.	Jas. Ormsbee.
1857.	J. T. Young,	W. B. Robinson,	L. Campbell,	C. G. Moffit,	C. R. Whitney,	J. C. Hilt,	J. W. Ormsbee,
	A. L. Tyler,	E. W. Pendleton,	O. J. Conant,	A. C. Wicker,	Leander Weeks,	S. Starrett,	S. B. Ulmer,
	Hiram Brewster.	Demerrick Spear.	A. L. Lovejoy.	G. J. Burns.	J. R. Richardson.	T. B. Glover.	A. J. Hewett.
1858.	J. T. Young,	Nathan Sleeper,	P. W. Walsh,	G. J. Burns,	C. R. Whitney,	T. B. Glover,	John Bird, jr.
	A. L. Tyler,	W. B. Robinson,	Ephraim Gay,	H. H. Burpee,	Leander Weeks,	Alfred Keene,	Chs. C. Lovejoy,
	Hiram Brewster.	B. B. Dean.	F. G. Cook.	O. H. Perry.	A. B. Cobb.	Wm. Butler, jr.	Jno. Brown (2d).
1859.	J. T. Young,	A. T. Low,	Allen Bowler,	Wm. J. Bond,	John Lindsey,	Freeman Harden,	H. Ferrand,
	A. L. Tyler,	R. C. Rankin,	Charles Clark,	F. B. Farwell,	Leander Weeks,	Charles Glover,	R. Crockett,
	C. L. Allen.	Nathan Sleeper.	Heman Burpee.	John Crockett.	J. R. Richardson.	H. E. Ingraham.	Z. C. Shuman.
1860.	C. L. Allen,	Wm. Wilson,	L. C. Pease,	Wm. J. Bond,	J. R. Richardson,	Freeman Harden,	R. Crockett,
	Walter Philbrick,	A. T. Low,	G. W. Kimball, jr.	John Crockett,	Alex. M. Snow,	H. E. Ingraham,	Wm. Russell,
	Geo. D. Wooster.	Benj. Knowlton.	E. R. Spear.	O. C. Ludwig.	M. L. Simmons.	Charles Glover.	Alden Ulmer.
1861.	C. L. Allen,	A. T. Low,	L. C. Pease,	John Crockett,	M. L. Simmons,	Thomas Colson,	James Ulmer,
	S. T. Cleaveland,	Leander Thomas,	G. W. Kimball, jr.	Wm. J. Bond,	Oliver P. Hix,	Denny F. Miller,	Wm. Spofford,
	W. O. Hewett.	Rufus C. Thomas.	E. R. Spear.	O. C. Ludwig.	Chas. H. Cables.	A. McKellar, jr.	O. P. Tolman.
1862.	C. L. Allen,	Rufus C. Thomas,	G. W. Kimball, jr.	John Crockett,	M. L. Simmons,	Thomas Colson,	Alden Ulmer,
	Walter Philbrick,	C. A. Keen, jr.	E. R. Spear,	J. P. Wise,	O. P. Hix,	Ira B. Ellems,	Jona. Spear,
	W. O. Hewett.	Joseph Furbish.	John S. Case.	Nat. Meservey.	Geo. W. Berry.	Jos. C. Ingraham.	O. P. Tolman.
1863.	C. L. Allen,	Joseph Furbish,	John S. Case,	John Crockett,	Geo. W. Berry,	Ira B. Ellems,	M. S. Adams,
	J. T. Young,	Geo. W. White,	Allen Bowler,	John P. Wise,	Oliver P. Hix,	Jos. C. Ingraham,	O. P. Tolman,
	Jackson Weeks.	Benj. Knowlton.	Albert F. Ames.	R. M. Pillsbury.	Edwin Sprague.	Wm. H. Glover.	O. D. Brown.
1864.	Jackson Weeks,	Isaac Gregory,	Albert F. Ames,	R. M. Pillsbury,	Seth E. Benson,	Wm. H. Glover,	E. P. Lovejoy,
	F. B. T. Young,	Aaron Howes,	G. W. Kimball, jr.	John Crockett,	C. N. Germaine,	I. A. Jones,	C. Hanrahan,
	S. N. Hatch.	Geo. A. Stevens.	Allen Bowler.	E. E. Wortman.	Lewis M. True.	Freeman Harden.	Sidney M. Bird.

TABLE VII.

LICENSES GRANTED BY COURT OF SESSIONS TO RESIDENTS OF THOMASTON, FROM ITS INCORPORATION TO 1800.

Nathaniel Fales,* 1778, and '79.
M. Wheaton,* 1779, retailer '93.
D. Fales,* 1784 to 9, '93, '94, '96, retailer, '90, '91.
James Fales, Jr., 1785.
James Fales, 1786 and '90.
David Jenks,* 1786 to '93, and '98.
I. Barrows, 1787, '92, and '93.
J. Stackpole, 1788, '90, '91, '92 '93.
David Fales, Jr., 1789, and '95.
Jos. Coombs,* 1793, retailer, '90, and '91.
J. Ingraham,* 1795, ret., '91 and '93.
James Wheaton, 1792.
John Blackington, 1792, and '94.
J. Spear, Jr.,* 1794, ret., '92, and 93.
I. Tolman,* 1793, '94, and '95.
J. Reed,* 1795, retailer, '93.
G. Ulmer,* 1796, retailer, '93.
Jonathan Crockett,* 1793.
Frederic Reed,* 1794.
John Ulmer,* 1795, '96, and '98.
Spencer Vose,* 1795, and '96.
Ebenezer Jones, 1795.
William Rowell, 1795.
Joseph Ingraham,* 1796.
Walter Hatch,* 1796, and 1797.
Samuel M. Martin, 1796 and '97.
Wm. Tilson,* 1799, retailer, '97.
Joshua Adams, 1797.
Ebenezer Dunton, 1799.
Perez Tilson, 1799.

LICENSES GRANTED BY THE SELECTMEN OF THOMASTON, FROM 1821 TO 1829.

Halsey Healey, 1821, '2, '4, '5, '6, '7, '8, and '9.
H. Prince, 1821, '2, '3, '5, and '6.
Iddo Kimball, from 1821 to '28.
Joshua Adams, " 1821 to '29.
William Cole, " 1821 to '29.
Eusebius Fales, 1821, '2, '3, '4, '8, and '9.
Gleason & Keith, from 1821, to '23.
John Blackington, do.
Joshua Jordan, 1821, '2, '3, '4, '5, '6, '7, and '9.
Knott Crockett, from 1821 to '29.
James Stackpole do. '26.
John Lovejoy, do. '29.
Elisha Snow, do. '22.
Wm. Killsa, do. do.
Geo. McLellan, do. '26.
Gideon Seavey, 1821.
Oliver Fales, from 1821 to '29.
Chas. Holmes, do. do.
Green & Merrill, 1821.
Eli Merrill, from 1821 to '22.
James Tolman, do. '23.
Ephraim Perry, do. '28.
Patrick Keegan, 1821 to '29.
Samuel Fuller, 1821.
Wm. Tilson,* from 1821 to '28.
Josiah Ingraham (3d), 1823.
Green & Foster, from 1823 to '25.
Jerusha Hastings, 1823.*
John G. Paine, from 1823, to '29.
Jas. Vanstone,* from 1823 to '25.
John Spear, from 1824 to '25.
Tolman & Barrows, 1824.
C. Harrington, from 1824, to '29.
Wm. McLellan, 1825.
Wm. R. Keith, from 1824 to '25.
John Copeland,* from 1825 to '2[illegible].
Anthony Hall, 1824.
B. Stimpson, from 1824 to '26.
J. Crockett, (2d), f'm 1824 to '27.
Nathaniel Wells, f'm 1825 to '27.
Coombs & Mann, 1825.
B. T. Levensaler, f'm 1825 to '29.
Ephraim Bartlett, 1825.
Isaac Bunker, from 1825 to '27.
Alex. Barrows & Co., 1825.
Perry & Amsbury, 1825.
Rice & Beirce, 1825.

* Innholders.

TABLE VII. (*Continued.*)

T. McLellan, from 1825 to '27.
Dean & Hall, 1825.
Wm. Stackpole, from 1825 to '27.
Amos Barns, 1825.
John Barnard, 1825.
Joshua C. Adams, 1826.
Geo. W. Fales, from 1826 to '28.
O. Robbins, (4th),f'm 1826 to '29.
W. T. Hewett, from 1826 to '27.
Josiah Achorn, from 1826 to '28.
Nelson Spear, from 1826 to '28.
H. S. Kenneston, f'm 1826 to '29.
Ezekiel & Lewis Hall, 1826.
Samuel Albee, from 1826 to '27.
A. Levensaler, f'm 1826 to '27.
Robert Foster, do. '29.
Ballard Green, do. do.
Phineas Tyler, do. do.
John Haskell,* do. 1827.
David Shaw, 1827.
Eli Perry, from 1827 to '28.
Hannah Haskell, from 1827 to '29.
Ephraim Hall, do. do.
Charles Pope, from 1827 to '28.
Oliver White, 1827.
Lucy Spofford,* 1827.
Benjamin Robinson, 1827.
Isaac Stearns, from 1827 to '29.
H. C. Lowell, from 1827 to '29.
David Gay, from 1827 to '28.
Archibald Robinson, 1827.
John P. Cole, 1827, '28, '29.
C. Sampson,* from 1827 to '28.
Joseph Fowler, 1828.
Charles Loring, from 1828, to '29.
Ezekiel Hall, 1828.
William Tate, 1828.
Israel J. Perry, from 1828 to '29.
Jeremiah Berry*, 1828.
Joseph Berry,* 1829.
Elkanah Spear, Jr., 1829.
Snow Paine, 1829.
Lewis Fales, 1829.
John B. Sears, 1829.
Kimball & Robbins, 1829.
Josiah W. Dodge, 1829.

TABLE VIII.

VOTES FOR GOVERNOR, &C. GIVEN IN THIS PLACE, FROM 1788 TO 1864.

Years.	Governor.	Votes.	Party.		Lieut. Governor.	Votes.
1788.	John Hancock,	23		el.	Benjamin Lincoln,	23
1789.	do.	26		el.	do.	12
					Samuel Adams,	11
1791.	do.	43		el.	do.	39
1792.	do.	30		el.	do.	30
1793.	do.	25		el.	do.	23
1794.	Samuel Adams,	41	R.	el.	James Warren,	38
1795.	do.	40	R.	el.	Moses Gill,	39
1796.	do.	36	R.	el.	do.	33
	Increase Sumner,	10	F.		Elisha Sumner,	1
1797.	do.	16	F.	el.	Increase Sumner,	10
	Moses Gill,	16	F.		Moses Gill,	19
1798.	Increase Sumner,	37	F.	el.	do.	30
1799.	do.	42	F.	el.	do.	42
1800.	Moses Gill,	24	F.		do.	41
	Caleb Strong,	21	F.	el.	Caleb Strong,	8
	Elbridge Gerry,	15	R.		Elbridge Gerry,	3
1801.	Caleb Strong,	21	F.	el.	William Heath,	42
	Elbridge Gerry,	45	R.		Edward H. Robbins,	19
1802.	Caleb Strong,	51	F.	el.	do.	47
	Elbridge Gerry,	12	R.		William Heath,	12

* Innholders.

1803.	Caleb Strong,	71	F.	el.	Edward H. Robbins,	71
	Elbridge Gerry,	1	R.		James Bowdoin,	1
1804.	Caleb Strong,	59	F.	el.	Edward H. Robbins,	62
	James Sullivan,	12	R.		William Heath,	10
1805.	Caleb Strong,	85	F.	el.	Edward H. Robbins,	85
	James Sullivan,	56	R.		William Heath,	56
1806.	Caleb Strong,	82	F.	el.	Edward H. Robbins,	71
	James Sullivan,	127	R.		William Heath,	142
1807.	Caleb Strong,	74	F.		Edward H. Robbins,	55
	James Sullivan,	135	R.	el.	Levi Lincoln,	141
1808.	Christopher Gore,	53	F.		David Cobb,	51
	James Sullivan,	133	R.	el.	Levi Lincoln,	125
1809.	Christopher Gore,	85	F.	el.	David Cobb,	87
	Levi Lincoln,	165	R.		Joseph B. Varnum,	159
1810.	Christopher Gore,	81	F.		David Cobb,	77
	Elbridge Gerry,	165	R.	el.	William Gray,	166
1811.	Christopher Gore,	48	F.		William Phillips,	47
	Elbridge Gerry,	127	R.	el.	William Gray,	128
1812.	Caleb Strong,	101	F.	el.	William Phillips,	90
	Elbridge Gerry,	180	R.		William King,	179
1813.	Caleb Strong,	103	F.	el.	William Phillips,	94
	Joseph B. Varnum,	155	R.		William King,	140
1814.	Caleb Strong,	102	F.	el.	William Phillips,	101
	Samuel Dexter,	169	R.		William Gray,	163
1815.	Caleb Strong,	82	F.	el.	William Phillips,	81
	Samuel Dexter,	144	R.		William Gray,	144
1816.	John Brooks,	64	F.	el.	William Phillips,	60
	Samuel Dexter,	143	R.		William Gray,	145
1817.	John Brooks,	70	F.	el.	William Phillips,	73
	Henry Dearborn,	119	R.		William King,	115
1818.	John Brooks,	35	F.	el.	William Phillips,	36
	B. W. Crowninshield,	79	R.		Thomas Kittredge,	78
1819.	John Brooks,	69	F.	el.	William Phillips,	63
	B.W.Crowninshield,	128	R.		Benjamin Austin,	121

Yrs.	Governors.			Yrs.	Governors.		
1820.	William King,	201	R. el.	1830.	Jona. G. Hunton,	185	N. R.
	Ezekiel Whitman,	2	F.	1831.	Samuel E. Smith,	359	D. el.
1821.	Albion K. Parris,	106	R. el.		Daniel Goodenow,	89	N. R.
	Ezekiel Whitman,	60	F.	1832.	Samuel E. Smith,	496	D. el.
	Joshua Wingate, jr,	36	R.		Daniel Goodenow,	210	N. R.
1822.	Albion K. Parris,	134	R. el.	1833.	Samuel E. Smith,	279	D.
	Ezekiel Whitman,	31	F.		Daniel Goodenow,	174	N. R.
	Joshua Wingate, jr.	4	R.		Robert P. Dunlap,	162	D. el.
1823.	Albion K. Parris,	236	R. el.	1834.	Robert P. Dunlap,	459	D. el.
	Scattering,	11		1834.	Peleg Sprague,	276	N. R.
1824.	Albion K. Parris,	160	R. el.	1835.	Robert P. Dunlap,	319	D. el.
	Scattering,	11			William King,	94	N. R.
1825.	Albion K. Parris,	198	R. el.	1836.	Robert P. Dunlap,	323	D. el.
1826.	Enoch Lincoln,	131	R. el.		Edward Kent,	118	W.
	Scattering,	2		1837.	Gorham Parks,	398	D.
1827.	Enoch Lincoln,	136	R. el.		Edward Kent,	325	W. el.
	William P. Preble,	1		1838.	John Fairfield,	617	D. el.
1828.	Enoch Lincoln,	189	R.el&d		Edward Kent,	410	W.
	Scattering,	2		1839.	John Fairfield,	605	D. el.
1829.	Samuel E Smith,	234	D.		Edward Kent,	330	W.
	Jona. G. Hunton,	103	N.R.el.	1840.	John Fairfield,	654	D.
1830.	Samuel E. Smith,	412	D. el.		Edward Kent,	452	W. el.

TABLE VIII. (*Continued.*)

Yrs.	Governors.				Yrs.	Governors.			
1841.	John Fairfield,	615	D.	el.	1845.	Hugh J. Anderson,	497	D.	el.
	Edward Kent,	361	W.			Freeman H. Morse,	282	W.	
	Jeremiah Curtis,	10	A.			Samuel Fessenden,	5	A.	
1842.	John Fairfield,	603	D.	el.	1846.	John W. Dana,	474	D.	el.
	Edward Robinson,	218	W.			David Bronson,	258	W.	
1843.	Hugh J. Anderson,	374	D.	el.		Sam'l Fessenden,	8	A.	
	Edward Robinson,	134	W.		1847.	John W. Dana,	401	D.	el.
1844.	Hugh J. Anderson,	850	D.	el.		David Bronson,	242	W.	
	Edward Robinson,	432	W.			Sam'l Fessenden,	8	A.	

IN THOMASTON, AFTER DIVISION.					ROCKLAND.	S. THOMASTON.
Years.	Governors.	Votes.	Party.		Votes.	Votes.
1848.	John W. Dana,	244	D.	el.	417	122
	Elijah L. Hamlin,	140	W.		229	60
	Samuel Fessenden,	4	A.		14*	4
1849.	John Hubbard,	132	D.	el.	268	128
	Elijah L. Hamlin,	95	W.		189	59
	George F. Talbot,	1	A.		2	
1850.	John Hubbard,	211	D.	el.	433	127
	William G. Crosby,	90	W.		284	60
	George F. Talbot,	1	A.		2	
1852.	John Hubbard,	154	T. D.		473	64
	Anson G. Chandler,	125	D.		135	47
	William G. Crosby,	133	W.	el.	414	102
1853.	Anson P. Morrill,	19	T. D.		106	13
	Albert Pillsbury,	300	D.		431	72
	William G. Crosby,	114	W.	el.	338	83
	Ezekiel Holmes,	10	A.		44	16
1854.	Anson P. Morrill,	61	T. D.		464	43
	Albion K. Parris,	167	D.		269	77
	Isaac Reed,	130	W.		210	100
	Shepherd Carey,	90				2
1855.	Anson P. Morrill,	211	T. D.		481	150
	Samuel Wells,	273	D.	el.	582	119
	Isaac Reed,	42	W.		144	24
1856.	Hannibal Hamlin,	346	R.	el.	863	185
	Samuel Wells,	126	D.		444	119
	George F. Patten,	20	W.		51	13
1857.	Lot M. Morrill,	284	R.	el.	509	131
	Manasseh H. Smith,	255	D.		494	88
1858.	Lot M. Morrill,	251	R.	el.	657	166
	Manasseh H. Smith,	320	D.		553	109
1859.	Lot M. Morrill,	218	R.	el.	554	136
	Manasseh H. Smith,	291	D.		460	94
1860.	Israel Washburn, jr.	242	R.	el.	759	164
	Ephraim K. Smart,	306	D.		583	127
	Phineas Barnes,	23	A.		20	
1861.	Israel Washburn, jr.	156	R.	el.	438	110
	Charles D. Jameson,	191	U. D.		336	63
	John W. Dana,	62	D.		27	10
1862.	Abner Coburn,	142	R.	el.	348	73
	Charles D. Jameson,	71	U. D.		182	42
	Bion Bradbury,	125	D.		81	36
1863.	Samuel Cony,	211	R.	el.	739	158
	Bion Bradbury,	297	D.		333	88
1864.	Samuel Cony,	189	R.	el.	728	124
	Joseph Howard,	289	D.		321	69

*And Joshua A. Lowell, 34 votes.

TABLE IX.

VESSELS BUILT AT THOMASTON, BEFORE ITS DIVISION.*

Yrs.	Class.	Names.	Tns	Builders.	Chief Owners.
1787.		(unknown,)			Elisha Snow, capt. also.
178-.		Experiment,			Joseph Coombs.
179-.		Little Sally,			do.
		Arthur,			do.
1795.	Slp.	Olive,			Ichabod Barrows.
	Sch.	Betsey & Jenny,	90		Snow. Coombs, I Snow, c.
		Friendship,			J Crockett, J. Mathews, c.
	Slp	(unknown,)			John Ulmer
1796.	Sch	Jane,	100		E Snow & Sons. J. Snow, c.
		Friendship,			do Jos. Mathews.
	Slp.	(unknown,)			John Ulmer.
1797.	Sch.	Sally,	95?		E Snow & Sons.
1798.	Slp.	Miriam,	80		Richard Keating, c. also.
		(unknown,)			James Weed.
	Sch	Columbus,			Robert Dunning, c.
		Rebecca,			S & J Brown, Lovett, S. Martin, c.
1799.	Slp.	Dolphin,			W Spear, M Dexter.
1803.		Richard,	80		Keating. R Keating, jr., c.
	Sch.	Hannah & Polly,	104		Snow & Sons, I. Snow, c.
		Montpelier.	110	H. Rogers,	Henry Knox.
		(unknown.)			Philip Hanson.
1804.		Wessaweskeag,	100		Jas Spalding, capt.
	Brig	Quantabacook,	140	H. Rogers,	Henry Knox.
	Ship	(unknown,)	200	J. Bryant,	P. Hanson &c.
1804?		Dolphin,			Josiah Ingraham, c. also.
1805.	Slp.	Quicklime,	93	H Rogers,	Henry Knox.
1805?	Sch	Increase,			James Stackpole &c.
	Ship	(unknown,)		built by Snow,	Spalding, &c for Boston men.
1806	Slp.	Hannah,	56	J Ulmer,	Ulmers, M. Ulmer, c.
1807.		Polly,	99		Wm. Spear.
		Fair Play,	70	W. McLoon,	J Adams, J Robinson, c.
		Asa,	80		Coombs, A. G. Coombs. c.
1808.	Sch.	Aurora,		J. Stackpole.	b. J. Keith. R. Jacobs, &c.
1808?		Good Intent,	74	den,	J. & W Spear, Brewster.
1809.	Ship	Holofernes,	500	McLoon, Hay-	E Phinney & Brother.
		Bristol Trader,			C & W. Pope, J. Spalding, c.
	Sch.	Oliver,	80	L. Hayden,	Oliver Fales &c.
		Industry,	115		R. Jordan. W. Keating, c.
1810.	Brig	Wm. Henry,	197	J. Barnard,	John Paine.
1811.		Elder Snow,	13·	R. Wade,	Joshua Adams. J. Gray. c.
		Catharine,	175	Achorn.	John Paine, J Spalding, c.
	Sch.	(unknown,)		at Westkeag,	Oliver Fales
1815.		Jane.	80	Spear,	Wm. Spear. M Spear, c.
		Mary Spear,	98	J H. Counce,	W & J. Spear, J.Spear, jr. c.

* The records at Waldoboro' in whole, and Washington in part, having been burnt, the first of this table is necessarily imperfect. b. in the 6th column stands for *builder*, as being also a chief owner, and c. for *captain* or master.

TABLE IX. (*Continued.*)

Yrs.	Class.	Names.	Tns	Builders.	Chief Owners.
1815	Sch.	Four Brothers,	60	at Weir Cove,	E. I & Is. Snow, Spalding, c.
1816.		Catharine,	105	J. H. Counce,	H Healey, Dodge Webb, c.
		Lavinia,	88	J. Stackpole,	b Blackington, Wheaton, Hawke, c.
1817.		Thomas,	72		G. Coombs, J. Spalding, c.
		Milo,	80	W. McLoon.	E. Snow, F. Haskell, c.
		Dodge Healey,	80	Counce of W.	Healey, Dodge, J. Hathorn, c.
		Three Brothers,	80	Counce of W.	
1818.	Slp.	Shelburn,	47		I. Lovett. c.
	Sch.	John Gilman,	66		I Kimball, J. Crockett, c.
		Halsey,	145	Counce of W.	Healey, R. Robinson, c.
1819.	Slp.	Seven Brothers,	73		Elisha Snow.
		Alfred,	75		Fales & Kimball, Wm. Spear, jr., c.
	Sch.	George,	100	Counce of W.	John Gleason, J. Tobey, c.
		Ann,	134	Counce of W.	Webb, c., Healey, Cole, E. Brown.
		Nancy,	138		Spofford, K. Crockett, E. Crockett, c.
	Brig	Adams,	139		J Adams, E Thorndike, c.
1820.		Sylvester Healey	143	Counce of W.	Healey, Edw. Robinson, c.
	Slp.	Mary Snow,	45		E. Snow. Getchell. c.
1821.		Lucy Healey,	86	R. C. Counce,	Healey, J. D. Wheaton, Hawk, c.
	Brig	Belvidere,	167		
		John,	144	Counce of W.	I Kimball. J. Spear, c.
		Shawmut,	151		Elisha Snow, jr
	Sch.	John,			Geo. Coombs. Marshall, c.
1822.	Brig	Scio,	165		Elisha Snow, jr.
		Iddo,	197	Counce of W.	I Kimball. J. Spear, c.
1823.		Montpelier,	199	Counce of W.	Webb, c , Sprague, Healey, &c.
	Sch.	Leo,	89		J. Lovejoy, Fales, Kimball, Perry, c.
		Francis,	83	A. Hall?	Snow, E. Crockett, Dean, Haskell. c.
1824.	Brig	Dodge Healey,	200	Counce of W.	Healey, &c. A. Hathorn, c.
		Mark,	158		F. Harden, Fales, Spear, J Crockett, c.
	Ship	Georges,	319	Counce of W.	Healey, Foster, R. Robinson, c.
	Sch.	Lafayette,	103		E. Perry, Ingraham, J. Lindsey, c.
		Charles,	65		Thorndikes, Snow, &c.
1825.	Brig	Knott,	174		Crocketts, Lovejoy, G. Wooster, c.
		Brandywine,	179		Perry, Burrows, Holmes, R Perry. c.
		Mary Cole,	174	R. C. Counce,	Healey, Sprague, W. Singer. c.
	Sch.	Mary Thomas,	75		Oliver Fales.
		Georges,	72		Ludwig. Tilsons, Rice, Hathorn, c.
		Lincoln,	127	R. C. Counce,	Healey, T. Colley, c.
		George,	65	G. Thorndike,	b. Snow, c., Crockett, Dean, &c.

TABLE IX. (*Continued.*)

Yrs.	Class. Names.	Tns	Builders.	Chief Owners.
1825.	Slp. Mary Ann,	75	J. Stackpole,	J. Stackpole, A. Boyd, c.
1826.	Brig Brutus,	186	E. O'Brien,	T. McLellan, jr., A. Robinson, c.
	Belvidere,	182	R. C. Counce,	b. Healey, &c., B. Vose, c.
	William,	170		Chas. Thorndike, &c.
	Eliza,	129		I. Perry, O. Fales, Job Perry, c.
	Mechanic,	218	Joshua Morton,	P. Williams, Cole, &c., L. Wilson, c.
	Sch. John & Nancy,	110		Asa Coombs.
	Michael,	81		K. Crockett, Achorns, &c.
	Denny McCobb,	100		E. Perry.
	Margaret,	72	L. Hayden,	Spofford, Robbins, L. Ulmer, c.
1827.	Ship Hewes,	298	Counce of W.	Kimball, Lovejoy, Tolman, J. Spear, Jr., c.
	Brig Pulaski,	235	R. C. Counce,	b. Webb, c. Singer & Robinson, &c.
	Jos. Sprague,	183		Sprague, Healy, Hawk, c.
	Sch. New York,	126	J. Morton,	Wm. Robinson, c. also.
	Thomas,	85	Geo. Thomas,	R. Jameson, &c.
	Atlantic,	100		O. Fales, &c.
	Wm. Harris,	133	J. Morton,	b. W. Robinson, c. &c.
	John,	102		T. McLellan, jr., J. Burton, c.
	Gen. Jackson,	108	W. McLoon, jr.	b. Sleeper, Dean, T. McLellan, c.
	Peggy Thomas,	108	G. Thomas,	b. Tolmans, Bird, Keen, Thorndike, c.
	Maria,	133	Wade,	b. Snows, Hall, I. Snow, c.
	Sl. Hannah&Clarissa	56		B. & L. Ulmer, M. Ulmer, c.
	Bt. John,	21		Joel Miller.
1828.	Ship Majestic,	297	J. Morton,	b. McLellan, c. Morse, Jordan, &c.
	Brig Moscow,	222	R. C. Counce,	b. Singer, c. Robinson, Webb.
	Sch. Martha,	125	L. Hayden,	b. Wade, Heard, Hayden, jr., c.
	Volant,	87	G. Thomas,	b. Crockett, Amsbury, Wooster, c.
	Bradford,	121		Iddo Kimball. [c.
1829.	Brig Pensacola,	232	R. C. Counce,	b. Gregory, Cole, R Spear,
	Sch. Miner,	73	L. Hayden,	b. McLoon, A. C. Spalding, c.
	Thomaston,		Kalloch,	Crockett, Pease, Sleeper.
	Enterprise,	74	Sweetland,	Sleeper, Coombs, I. Thorndike, c.
	Cashier,	102	J. Morton,	W. R. Keith, &c. H. Peabody, c.
	Slp. Two Friends,	35		James Crockett.
	Franklin,	61	J. Morton,	W. Watts, c. J. Miller.
1830.	Brig Sherer,	144		Ingraham, Sherer, Spalding, c.
	Sch. Alfred,	74		Kimball, Fales, C Dyer, c.
	Romp,	77	W. McLoon,	b. A. Hall, c. Gray, Kellogg.

TABLE IX. (*Continued.*)

Yrs.	Class. Names.	Tns	Builders.	Chief Owners.
1830.	Sch. Dime,	95	G. Thomas,	b. O. Amsbury, c.
	Slp. Mary Snow,	54		L., C. W. & A. Snow.
	Ann Sarah,	85		Sears, R. S. Blasdell, &c.
1831.	Sch. Hope,	22		K. Crockett.
	Industry,	48	R. C. Counce,	b. Singer, Robinson, Watts, c.
	Freeman,	106	G. Thomas,	Crockett, Harden, A. G. Spear, c.
	Gen. Wayne,	137	R. C. Counce,	b. Singer & Co., Austin, Vose, c.
	New Sally,	65	J. Morton,	S. & L Harris, T. A. Snow, c.
	Mary,	92	W. Hayden,	G. Gault, c. &c. of Boston.
	Bt. Juno,	13		David Hall.
1832.	Ship Brunette,	333	R. C. Counce,	b. Singer & Co., W. J. Fales, c.
	Brig Arria,	136	J. Morton,	Thorndike, Lovejoy, J. Thorndike, c.
	Mary Kimball,	159		Kimball, B. & J. Wooster, c.
	Sch. Emeline,	115		D. Robinson, C. Holmes.
	Wm. Henry,	105		Ulmer, c. W. McLoon.
	Richmond,	98		W. & L. Hayden, c.
1833.	Brig Com. Tucker,	185	R. C. Counce,	b. Singer & Co., Austin, O. Robinson, c.
	Paragon,	241	J. Morton,	Cole, Jacobs, Hatch, D. Healey, c.
	Zealand,	189	F. Seiders,	McLoons, J. Sleeper, c.
	Snow,	198	P. Lermond,	E. & I. Snow, Is. Snow. c.
	Sch. Fair Play,	116		Miller, Gilchrist, W. Gilchrist, c.
	Tremont,	120	G. Thomas,	Achorn, Dean, B. Ulmer, c.
	Orion,	49		A. G. Spear, c., E. Hall.
	Vincent,	148		O. Robinson, &c.
1834.	Minerva,	100		L. & O. Gray, c. Ez. Hall.
	Olive Branch,	21		J. W. Dodge.
	Ariadne,	51	E. & P. Tilson,	b. Rollins, Harrington, c.
	Curlew,	76		J. Crockett, c C. Holmes.
	Solidus,	83	J. Morton,	W. & J. P. Cole, Burton, c.
	Brig Majestic,	156		Crockett, Sherer, Perry, c.
	Julia & Helen,	193		J. Thorndike, J. Bartlett, c.
	Raymond,	205	F. Seiders,	Gilchrist, C. Levensaler, c.
1835.	Sch. Effort,	78	I. J. Perry,	b. Ingraham, Hill, R. Perry, c.
	Gen. Knox,	149	R. C. Counce,	Singer & Robinson, Cutler, Snow, c.
	Brig Zoroaster,	159	J. Morton,	b. Ludwig, Keegan, &c.
	Lincoln,	130		Kimball, White, Lovejoy.
	Ship Peruvian,	476	G. Thomas,	J. Spear. c. Kimball, Tolman.
1836.	Sch. Dav. R. Kalloch,	129	W. McLoon,	W. McLoon.
	Richard Taylor,	121		Rankins, White, J. Crockett, c.
	Molaeska,	152	J. Morton,	Keith, Miller. Boynton.
	Corvo,	128		Crocketts, Sherer, Ingraham.
	D. B. Keeler,	128	W. McLoon,	b. Keeler, H. H. Ulmer, c.

TABLE IX. (*Continued.*)

Yrs.	Class.	Names.	Tns	Builders.	Chief Owners.
1833.	Sch.	Candidus,	396	R. C. Counce,	b. Webb, c. Singer, Robinson.
1837.	Bt.	Maria Jane,	5		
	Sch.	Shakespear,	126		M. Achorn, O. Holmes, B. Ulmer, c.
	Brig	Voltaire,	144	G. Thorndike,	b. E. P. Sleeper, c. R. Jacobs.
1838.	Sch.	Hero,	100		J. Duncan.
		Challenge,	95		
		Geo. & James,	54		J. Dow, G. C. Dow, c.
		Potomac,	128	Ames,	Dean, C. Tolman, Penniman, c.
		John Spofford,	100		J., P., & D. Spofford, c.
	Brig	Lime Rock,	174	J. Morton,	R. Robinson, Keith, Allen, A. Butler, c.
	Ship	Tyrone,	538	G. Thomas,	Kimball, Spear, Tolmans, Gregory, c.
		Talleyrand,	549	R. C. Counce,	b. Webb, c. Jordan, Singer & Robinson.
1839.	Sch.	Glide,	38		E. Robinson.
		Nancy Hewett,	69		Sleeper, c. Crockett, Hewett, Gregory.
		Extio,	149	R. Walsh,	b. Read, Boynton, S. Robinson, c.
	Brig	Francis P. Beck,	249	R. C. Counce,	b. E. Stackpole, c. Webb, Jacobs, etc.
		Carleton,	24[illegible]	J. & C. C. Morton,	b. Carleton, Watermans.
		Growler,	247		K. Crockett, Bird, Ulmer, c.
	Brk.	Chas. William,*	298	J Sweetland, jr.	b. A. C. Spalding, Gregory, McLoon, &c.
	Ship	European,	593	W. Stetson,	b. Ludwig, Cole, T. McLellan, c.
1840.	Bt.	Hope,	14		J. Hewett,
		Marion,	16		J. Norton.
	Sch.	Mars Hill,	25		M. Burton, Webster, R. Hawes, c.
		Iowa,	149	Mortons,	b. Levensaler, G. L. Carney, c., Abbott.
		Edinburg,	195	E. Andrews,	Crocker, c., Kimball, &c.
		Oneco,	198	W. Stetson,	b Cole, Hatch Hodgman.
		Puritan,	229	J Sweetland, jr.	W. McLoon, H. H. Ulmer, c
		Loretto,	241	R. Walsh,	b J. Henderson, c., Singer, Elliott.
	Brk.	Suwarrow,	292	G. Thorndike,	Sleeper, c., Thorndikes, Bartlett, &c.
1841.	Sch.	Sabine,	164	J. M. Blackington,	Cole, Hatch, Robbins.
	Brig	Homer,†	199	R. Walsh,	b. E. Robinson, Elliott, Watts, c.
		Pantheon,	196	R. C. Counce,	b. A. M. Fales, c., Jacobs, Singer, &c.

* Being the 79th vessel that had been launched into the Wessaweskeag waters, as it was said.

† At this brig's launching a bottle of good *water*, for the first time on Georges River, it is said, was thrown with the usual ceremonies instead of a bottle of spirits.

TABLE IX. (*Continued.*)

Yrs.	Class.	Names.	Tns	Builders.	Chief Owners.
1841.	Brk.	Weskeag,	248	J.Sweetland, jr.	b. C. McLoon, A. C. & H. Spalding. c.
		Washington,	186	G. Thorndike,	b. Jacobs, Kimball, Cushing.
		Mandarin,	275	J. & C. C. Morton,	Keith, Merriam, J. Berry, &c.
		Baltic,	302	C. Starrett,	b. Kimball, J. Gregory, c.
		Teazer,	249	G. Thomas,	Crocketts, c., Sherer, Ingraham.
		Mallory,	300	N. A. Read,	b. Ludwig, Fuller, Brown, c.
1842.	Sch.	Alexander,	144	J. & C. C. Morton.	Linell. Boynton, & Co.
		Lightfoot,	149	E. Andrews,	b. B. & L. Ulmer, c., Bird, &c.
		Wilder,	122		W R Keith, S. M. Shibles. c.
	Brig	Susan Spofford,	199	C. & S. Starrett,	b. J. G. Lovejoy, Colson, W. Spofford, c.
		Atakapas,	149	W. Hayden,	b. McLoon, Rowell, L. Hayden, c.
		Saline,	199	R. Walsh,	b. Elliotts, Brown. Fales, c.
	Brk.	Epervier,	234	G. Thomas,	b I. Ingraham, J. C. Libby, Verrill, c.
1843.	Sch.	John Frederic,	102	J. Morton,	b. Lermond, Jacobs, Wheeler, c.
		John Kendall,	169	C. & S. Starrett.	White, Kimball, Ferrand.
		Swallow,	157	E. Andrews,	b. Bird. Caswell, Holb'k, c.
	Brig	Chinchilla,	139	W. Stetson ?	b. Jacobs, Williams, O. Robinson, c.
	Brk.	Louisiana,	249	J. Sweetland,	b. McLoon, Vose, W. S. Emery, c.
	Ship	Alvum,	364	G. Thomas,	b. Allen, Fisher, W. Smith, c.
		Charlemagne,	742	R. C. Counce,	b. Webb, Singer, R. Robinson, c.
1844.	Sch.	Willow,	100	N. A. Read,	Roney, c., Rice, Shibles, Catland.
		New York,	133		W. Thomas, Hewett, Beverage.
	Brig	Rowland,	230	R. Walsh,	Browns, Overlock, A. Watts, c.
		Maine,	222	Thorndike,	W. McLoon, C. W. Thorndike, c.
		Marsellois,	220	G. Thorndike,	b. Sleeper. c., Snows, Kelloch. Alden.
		Mary Jane,	148	J. & C. C. Morton.	Lermonds, E. G., c., Wyllies. Spear.
		Four Brothers,	199	do.	builders, W. Slater. c.
		Kimball,	182	C. Starrett,	b. Kimballs, Sawyer & Colson.
	Ship	Medora,	400	G. Thomas,	b. W. Thomas, K. Crockett, J. Crockett, c.
1845.	Sch.	Gulnare,	150	G. Thomas,	b. Luce. Ingraham, Berry, Spalding, c.
		Peru,	88		
		Lydia & Mary,	29		C. Holmes, J. Rackliff, c
		Avenger,	105		

TABLE IX. (*Continued.*)

Yrs.	Class. Names.	Tns	Builders.	Chief Owners.
1845.	Sch. Lucy White,	94		White, Kimball, O. Jameson, c., Rankin.
	Mary George,	148		
	Leprelet,	100		Litchfield,Smith,Sleep'r,c.
	Adelaide,	116	W. Stetson,	b. Cole, Williams, Sumner, H. Stackpole, c.
	Queen Pomare,	95	N. A. Read,	Singer, Jordan, Snow, E. L. Snow, c.
	Mary Langdon,	100	G. Thomas,	b. F. Cobb, Torry, Flint E. Cobb, c.
	Floreo,	120	G. Thomas ?	b. Libby & Fuller, Arey, S. Thomas, c.
	Frances Colley,	167		Rice, Nelson, Mathews, O. Robinson, c.
	Brig Annawon,	147	E. Andrews,	b. J. Bird, H. G. Bird, c., Ingraham, Brewster.
	Joseph,	178		Crockett, Ingraham, Sherer. Kalloch, c.
	Almira,	194	J. Morton,	T. O'Brien, Ludwig, Boynton, S. Curling, c.
	Alida,	234	R. Walsh,	b. Fales, c., Jacobs, Elliott, E. Robinson.
	Hamlet,	219	Walker, Maxy,	b. R. Robinson, jr., c., Jacobs.
	Martha Sanger,	188	Starretts,	Keen, Achorn, Burpee, etc.
	Ashland,	194		I. Snow, Thorndike, c., Dennis, Abbott.
	Kedron,	200	J. & C. C. Morton,	b. Carney, c., T. O'Brien, Boynton.
	Patrick Henry,	148	C. Starrett,	b. Cole, Lovejoy, Hewett, Packard, c.
	Brk. Algoma,	293	J. Sweetland,	b. H. Spalding, c., W. Vose, Martin, Graves.
	Alvarado,	299	G. Thomas,	b. K. Crockett, W. Thomas.
1846.	Sch. Eagle,	98	Harrington, &c.	J Farwell, E. Snow, J. W. Haskell, c.
	Linnell,	144	J. & C. C. Morton,	b. Welsby, c., Watts, Elliott, &c.
	Santiago,	99	S. Starrett,	Abbott, Spofford, Kimballs, Ingraham, c.
	Niagara,	122	Harrington, &c.	Cobb, Spaldings, C., c., Hunt.
	Isaac Achorn,	98	H. Merriam,	Fales, Mossman, Stevens, R. Crockett, c.
	Bengal,	97	G. Thomas,	Kimb'ls, Fer'nd, Crouch, c.
	Pawtucket,	100	C. Starrett,	Dean, Smith, Ormsby, c.
	Brig Reveille,	183	G. Thorndike,	b. Sawyer, F. Colson, Vose, Sleeper, c.
	Florence,	175	E. Andrews,	Fogg & Fales, Ulmer, W. Fales, c.
	Irving,	236	R. Walsh,	Curling, McLellan, W. & J. Robinson, c.
	Monterey,	200	J. Sweetland, jr.	b. C. McLoon, J. S. Kalloch, c.
	Susan Ingraham	176	G. Thomas,	b. Ingraham, S. N. Hatch, A. O Blackington, c.
	Benj. Litchfield,	190		Litchfields, Sawyer, Colson, Smith, c.

TABLE IX. (*Continued.*)

Yrs.	Class. Names.	Tns	Builders.	Chief Owners.
1846.	Brig Pulaski,	249	A. Walker,	b. Norris, c., Walsh, Vesper, &c.
	H. R. Hyler,	242	J. & C. C. Morton,	b. R. Anderson, c., Snow, &c.
	Brk. Georges,	267	J. Maxey,	Jacobs.Elliott, Robinsons, O. Robinson, c.
	Leopard,	263	N. A. Read,	Snow, Burgess & Co., P. Vesper, c.
	John Stroud,	268	Rhodes, Alden,	Snow & Dennis, Spalding, Brown, c.
	Mary Kendall,	274	C. & S. Starrett,	b. Dow, Bond, &c , Crocker, c.
	Miltiades,	447	W. Stetson,	b. Ranlet, c., Lermond, &c.
	Ship Thorndike,	399	G. Thorndike,	b. Stone of Boston, S. Child, c.
1847.	Slp. Peace,	69		
	Sch. Melbourne,	132	F. Rhoades ?	Libby & Co., S. Libby, T. Williams, etc.
	Thomas Hix,	126	G. Thomas,	Hix, Condon, Robbins; H. Hall, c.
	Bengal,	97		Colson & Sawyer, Ferrand, Crouch, c.
	Sea-Gull,	124		Crockett, W. Thomas, I. Gregory, Verril, c.
	Brig John Kendall,	180		Libby & Kimball, &c.
	Azores,	274		W. McLoon, O. Amsbury, c.
	Highlander,	206	J. & C. C. Morton,	b. Snow, Burgess, Anderson, c.
	Tartar,	199	S. Starrett,	Kimballs, Paul, c., Ulmer.
	Amulet,	199	C. Starrett,	Spoffords, J. P. c., Kimballs, &c.
	Swan,	231	G. Thomas,	b. Nesmiths, Walsh, J. Pierce, c.
	Elizabeth Watts	225		O'Brien, Watts, Burgess, &c.
	Matinic,	192		F. Kalloch, Thorndikes, W. H. c., Snow.
	Lucy Spear,	202	C. Starrett,	Spear, Ingraham, Kimball, Robbins, c.
	H. Kalloch,	217	Morton & Lermond,	b. Burgess, Snow, A. B. Kalloch, c.
	Brk. Marmion,	358	W. Stetson,	b. Flint & Chapman, &c., I. N. Jackson, c.
	Star,	298	G. Thorndike,	Thorndikes, Sweetland, I. Snow, c.
	Catharine,	316	W. Stetson,	Wattses, Elliotts, &c., J. Watts, c.
	Robert Walsh,	282	R. Walsh,	b. W. J. Singer, c., Fales, Henderson, &c.
	Ship Walter R. Jones	400	A. Walker,	b. Counce, Ludwig, &c., J. Colley, c.
	Nisida Stewart,	565	J. Maxey & Co.	b. Webb, Or. Fales, c., Jacobs, &c.

TABLE IX. (*Continued.*)

VESSELS BUILT IN THOMASTON, AFTER ITS DIVISION.

Yrs.	Class. Names.	Tns	Builders.	Chief Owners.
1848.	Sch. Sarah Lewis,	172	S. Williams,	Watts, Robinson, Miller, Washburn, c.
	Anita Damon,	137	R. C. Counce, [ton.	Linnell, Hodgkins, J. Bently. c.
	Brig Bryant,	177	J. & C. C. Mor-	Keith, &c , J. Bryant, c.
	Denmark,	219	[Co.	Rice, Catland, J. W. Jacobs, Roney, c.
	Rainbow,	248	Morton, Ler. & [ton,	Elliott, Chapman, Stackpole, c.
	Brk. California,	310	J. & C. C. Mor-	b. Slater.c., T. O'Brien.&c.
	Theoxena,	398	J. Small,	Jacobs.Elliott, Smith,Borland, c.
	Ship Pyramid,	741	N. A. Read,	Singer, Ludwig, Snow, R. Robinson, c.
	John Hancock,	746	W. Stetson,	Gilchrist, Levensaler, A. Snow, c.
	Str. Gold Hunter,	23	[Co	G. C. Dow, c., Sterling, Morse, &c.
1849.	Brk. S. H.Waterman,	480	Lermond, M. &	b. L B Gilchrist, c., Cushing, Waterman.
	Ithona,	315	R Jacobs & Co.	Boston men, J. Lukie, c.
	Ship Ionian,	749	W. Stetson,	Chapman & Flint, Jordan, Ranlet, c.
	S. Carack,	874	R. Walsh,	b. W. J. Fales, Robinson, Snow, c.
1850.	Brg Frederic Eugene	126	J. W. Small, [ton,	Jacobs, Maxey, Starrett, &c.
	Brk. Culloma,	360	J. & C. C. Mor-	Sold in N. Y.
	Ship Jas. Nesmith,	991		Stetson,Walker, Mills.&c.
	Vaucluse,	699	C. Lermond,	Gilchrist, Lermond & Co.
1851.	Sch. Marcelia,	142	A. Walker, [ton,	Jacobs, Starrett, Dunn, Ellems, c.
	C. bk. Racehound,	506	J. & C. C. Mor-	Sold in N. Y.
	Ship Rochambeau,	866	Mor. Ler. & Co.	b. Stackpole, Overlock, Hallowell, c.
	Wm. Stetson,	1146	W. Stetson,	b. Flint Mathews, Creighton, c.
1852.	Slp. Gen. Washington	43		M. J. Stearns, E. Baker,c.
	Brig Caroline,	221	Lermond & Co	Cushing, Oliver, Bryant, c.
	Brk. Linden,	440	A. Walker, [ton,	R. & W. Jacobs, Starrett, Flinton, c.
	Ship Hyperion,	838	J. & C. C. Mor-	Sold in Boston, named Golden Racer.
1853.	Slp. Nevis,	58	A. Walker,	b. Edwin Starrett.
	Ship Oracle,	1200	R. Walsh, [ton,	b. Chapman & Flint, Ranlet, c.
	Ocean Chief,	1229	J. & C. C. Mor-	Mortons, Curling, c.
	Germanicus,	1167	W. Stetson,	b. Chapman, Creighton, Fales, c.
	Juventa,	1187	W. Stetson,	Webb, Watts, A. Watts,c.
	Mulhouse,	1130	J. Small,	J. W. &. R. J'bs, Healey,c.
	L. Gilchrist,	1198	Ler. Mor. & Co.	b. Gilchrist, R. L. Gilchrist, c.
	Alice Counce,	1157	A. McCallum,	Singers, W. J., c., R. Robinson, Metcalf, &c.

TABLE IX. (*Continued.*)

Yrs.	Class.	Names.	Tns	Builders.	Chief Owners.
1854.	Brig	George Albert,	241	S. Williams,	not ascertained, I. Wyllie. c.
	Ship	Sebastian Cabot,	1336	Ler. Mor. & Co.	b. Fish, Washburn, J. Watts, c.
		Baden,	1200	J. Small,	J. W. & R. Jacobs, D. Healey, c.
		S. Curling,	1468	J. Hilt,	E. & T. O'Brien, Watts, Curling. c.
		R. Robinson,	1458	W. Stetson,	Stetson, Gerry & Co., R. Robinson, jr., c.
1855.	Brig	Austins,	292	Copeland and Small,	Stackpole. Morse, Ferrand, Ellems, c.
		C. F. O'Brien,	283		Burgess & O'Brien, Watts, &c.
		Almira,	194	Ler. Mor. & Co.	Ludwig, O'Brien, Watts, Curling, c.
	Brk.	Mary Bentley,	396	Waterman, &c.	Olivers, Cushing, Jacobs, &c.
		Nineveh,	439	A. Walker,	H. Stackpole, c., Morse, Prince, &c.
	Ship	J. F. Chapman,	1035	R. Walsh,	b Walsh, Chapmans, J. F., c., Levensaler.
		Leona,	1149	A. McCallum,	Robinson, Fales, Webb, J. Norris, c.
		R. Jacobs,	1122	Cope'd & Small,	Webb, Gilchrists, Elliott, Henderson, c
		Jas. R. Keeler,	1292	J. & C. C. Morton,	Sold in New York, H. M. Allen, c.
		Samuel Watts,	1249	W. Stetson,	S. Gerry & Co., Webb, Smith, Mills, c.
		Vesper,	1497	H. Benner,	O'Brien, Watts, Hilt, Vesper, c.
1856.	Brig	Lorana,	339		Shibles.&c , sold in Boston
	Brk.	Livorno,	456	Oliver & Co.	Montgomerys, Payson, Hewett, &c.
	Ship	Barnabas Webb,	1342	A. McCallum,	b. Webb. A. Watts, c., Hilt, Young.
		Jos. Gilchrist,	1444	Mor.& Lermond	Gilchrists, R. L., c., Hewes, &c.
		J. Morton,	1149	J. & C. C. Morton,	b. Hallowell, Mathews, Gilley, c.
		Wm. Singer,	1049	Cope'd & Small	Jacobses, Singer, C. Farley, c., &c
		Marquette,	1199	Cushing & Waterman,	Creighton, O. Robinson, Watts, c.
		Aldanah,	1048	Pattersons,	Walsh, Walker, Oliver, Bunker, c.
		Mary O'Brien,	1297	H Benner,	Vesper, c ,O'Brien, Watts, &c.
		James Colley,	1175	McDonald & H Lermond.	Chapman & Co., Tobey, J. Colley, c.
1857.	Ship	Bolina,	1199	Hilt&McCallum	Webb, Fales. Counce, &c.
		S. Emerson Smith,	1260	H. Benner,	Burgess & O'Brien, Campbells, Creighton, c.
		Holy-Rood,	1048	Small & Cope'd,	Ranlet, Jordan & Co., S. C. Jordan, c.
		Frank Flint,	1193	McDonald and Lermond.	Chapman & Co., E. A. Robinson, c.

TABLE IX. (*Continued.*)

Yrs.	Class. Names.	Tns	Builders.	Chief Owners.
1858.	Ship Joseph Fish,	1199	J. Hilt,	Watts, Gould, Webb, Mehan, &c.
	Mary E. Campbell,	1374	H. Benner,	O'Brien, S. B. Starrett, Morse, c.
1859.	Sch. Nautilus,	136	J. Small,	Ranlet, Tobey, Dunn, Small, c.
	Ship Eagle,	1448	H. Benner,	O'Briens, Bliss, Nicholson, &c.
	Montebello,	1050		Levensaler & Webb, Walsh, Henderson, c.
	Spiridion,	1149	Small & Cope'd,	Jacobs, W. Jordan, c., Whitcomb, &c.
1860.	Sch. Gen. Knox,	219		Stetson, Sherman, Gerry, Small, c.
	Ship St. Mark,	1448	McDon. & Ler.	Flint & Chapman, Colley, c.
	Col. Adams,	1314	J. Hilt,	b. Webb, Watts, Fish, Mills, c.
	E. Creighton,	1286	H. Benner,	E. O'Brien, Creighton, c.
1861.	Gunboat Kennebec,		J. Hilt,	U. S. A.
1862.	Brk. Sea Bird,	535	W. Morse,	W. Morse, also c.
	Ship Gen. McLellan,	1349	J. Hilt,	b. A. Watts, c., Hewes, Prince, Hill.
1863.	Brk. Sunbeam,	654	C. E. Ranlet,	C. E. Ranlet, c. also.
	Glen Avon, or Glen Alvon,	718	H. Lermond,	Burgess, O'Brien & Co., J. Watts, c.
	Ship Edward O'Brien	1552	H. Benner,	E. O'Brien, G. Gilchrist, c.
	Gen. Berry,	1197	J. Hilt,	S. Watts, Hilt, &c., J. Watts, c.
	Oracle,	1196	McDon. & Ler.	Chapman & Flint, A. Wood, c.
	Ne Plus Ultra,	1396	J. McDonald,	Gilchrist & Walsh, sold in N. Y. for about $100 000.
	E. Pluribus Unum,	1370	J. Small ?	R. & J. W. Jacobs, W. Jordan, c.
1864.	Sch. Seventy-Six,	234	Simmons,	Walsh, Simmons & Co. J. Teal, c.
	Carrie Melvin,	275		Stetson, Gerry, &c. Watts, c.
	Brk. Singapore,	751		L. B. Gilchrist, W. Hewes, c.
	Ship	1200	McDon. & Ler.	Chapman, Flint & Co.
		1500	J. Small ?	Samuel Watts.

VESSELS BUILT AT SOUTH THOMASTON.

Yrs.	Class. Names.	Tns	Builders.	Chief Owners.
1848.	Sch. Gen. Cass,	123	W. McLoon,	b. R. Hayden, J. Kelloch. c.
	Brk. Laura Snow,	293	G. Thorndike,	b. Sleepers, J. Crockett, c.
	Clœlia,	249	J. Sweetland,	b. McLoon, J. K. Bartlett, c.
1849.	Sch. Vendovi,	185	O. Sweetland,	b. Kimball, &c., J. G. Bray, c.
	Brig Sarah Cushing,	234		W. McLoon, R Keating, c.
	Brk. Emma Lincoln,	299	O. Sweetland,	Vose, Graves, &c , E. Bartlett, c.
	Mary Adelia,	325	J. Sweetland,	b. C. McLoon, H Spalding, c. etc.
	Geo. Leslie,	288	G. Thorndike,	b. Sleepers, &c., E. P. Sleeper, c.

TABLE IX. (*Continued.*)

Yrs.	Class. Names.	Tns	Builders.	Chief Owners.
1850.	Sch. Silas Wright,	142		W. McLoon, O. Cowl of N. Y., L. Johnson, c.
	Charles William	141	G. Thorndike,	b. Spear, Ingrahams, A. Pendleton, c.
	Brk. Golden Era,	443	G. Thorndike,	b. &c., W. H. Thorndike, c.
	Jo,	287	Elisha Brown,	sold in Boston, E. Brown, c.
	Mary Annah,	449	W. McLoon,	b. H. P. Williams, &c., R. Keating, c.
	Atlantic,	300	G. Stetson,	not ascertained, Brown, c.
1851.	Sch. Arcularius,	128		S. O. Pierce, c. I. & I. L. Snow, etc.
	Melita,	198	E. Brown,	E. Brown, c. sold Boston.
	Julien,	125	J. Sweetland,	McLoon, Martin, etc., I. Snow, c.
	Brk. Chas. Brewer,	319	W. McLoon,	b. H. P. Williams, C. Brewer, etc.
	Ship Empire,	1273	G. Thorndike,	G. Thorndike, E. A. Thorndike, c.
1852.	Sch. Harbinger,	98	E. Brown,	b. N. P. Webster, B. Lewis, Hooper, c.
	E. Brown,	40		Elisha Brown, J. T. Coombs, c.
	Orrin Cowl,	137	W. McLoon,	b. H. W. Miller, c., White of N. York.
	Samuel Rankin,	150		McLoon, Hayden, T. M. Brown, c.
	Usher,	144		E. Brown, c. also.
	Kingfisher,	125		Brown, W. Barrett, J. Sleeper, Hooper, c.
	Brk. Charm,	312	G. Thorndike,	W. Kelloch, L. Hall, A. Sleeper, c.
	Satellite,	450	W. McLoon,	b. etc., O. Amsbury, c.
	Ship Kate Sweetland,	527	J. Sweetland,	b. McLoon, J. Sleeper, etc. Keating, c.
1853.	Sch. Lane,	163	G. Thorndike,	b. R. W. Trundy of N. Y. J. P. Allen, c.
	Wm. Woodbury,	139		Wm. McLoon, J. Manning, c.
	Israel L. Snow,	95		Snows, Sargent, etc., Conery, c.
	Trident,	235	J. Sweetland,	b. C. McLoon, I. Snow, c.
	Chas. Richard,	213	R. Hayden,	b. S. R. Ulmer, c., Small, Graves, etc.
	Cerito,	257		E. Brown, c. also.
	W. H. Titcomb,	199		McLoon, H. Williams, etc. Johnson, c.
	John Hart,	180		Hart, Dyers, S. N. Smith, c.
1854.	Slp. Westkeag,	53	W. Newhall,	J. & W. Newhall, b. was c.
	Sch. Helen,	272	E. Brown,	E. Brown, c. also.
	Elvira,	174	J. Sweetland,	Allen, c. E. Dean, Jr. & Co.
	Brig Newsboy,	300		E. Brown, c. also.
	Brk. Fleet Eagle,	381	A. J. Sweetland,	Emery, B. Lewis & Co., Brown, c.
	Wm. A. Banks,	470	G. Thorndike,	b. Jackson, etc., E. Bartlett, c.
	Clementine,	411	H. Williams,	b. & Co., McLoon, Joseph Wade, c.

TABLE IX. (*Continued.*)

Yrs.	Class. Names.	Tns	Builders.	Chief Owners.
1854.	Brk. Growler.	484		T. K Pillsbury, c.
	Pathfinder,	421		Hayden, Graves, Small, etc., R. Kelloch, c.
	Ship Cincinnatus,	1144		S. Pillsbury, c.
	Alice Thorndike	848	J. Sweetland,	Thorndike, E. P. Sleeper, c., Johnson, etc.
1855.	Sch. Georgiana,	276		E. Brown, E. T. Emery, c.
	Brig Golden Lead,	299		Thorndike, H. Johnson, c.
	Brk. Architect,	399		Merriam, Beans, etc., Bailey, c.
	Ship Octavius,	868		E. Brown. also c., Emery, Hall & Co.
1856.	Sch. Cherokee,	96		W. Newhall, c. W. K. Bartlett.
	Wm. Woodbury,	139		W McLoon, J. Savage, c.
	Princess,	247		F. Cobb, I. L. Snow, c.
	Ship Lizzie Spalding,	792	J. Sweetland,	H. & J. Spalding, c., McLoon, Bartlett, etc.
	Bethia Thayer.	896	H. Williams,	H. Williams, etc.
1857.	Sch. Laura Frances,	142		Rockland owners, J. B. Higgens, c.
	Hunter,	37		O. B Pillsbury, J. K. Mathews, Brown, c.
1858.	Ship Juliet Trundy,	899		Rockland owners, T. R. Pillsbury, c.
1860.	Sch. Helen,	134		W. McLoon, J. W. Carrol, c.
	J. B. Litchfield,	230		Litchfields, etc., W. S. Crockett, c.
1861.	Brig Josephine,	259		Deans, McLoon, Babb, etc , Allen, c.
1864.	Brk. Fighting Joe,	574	E. Dean, jr.	E. Thorndike, & als., E. Bartlett, c.

VESSELS BUILT IN ROCKLAND AFTER THE DIVISION.

Yrs.	Class. Names.	Tns	Builders.	Chief Owners.
1848.	Sch. Lanson Dean,	103	C. Starrett,	Dean, McLain, etc., Packard, c.
	Mary Wise,	125	G. Thomas,	J. Crockett, Farwell, etc. Brewster, c.
	Sarah Hamilton,	123	E. Andrews,	b. Achorn, B. & J. Clough, c., Gregorys.
	H. C. Lowell,	136	F. W. Rhodes,	Libby, Kimball, Case, etc., Thomas, c.
	Ophir,	118	I. Ames,	b. Blackintons, White, Packard, c.
	Brig Geo. S. Abbott,	208	C. Starrett,	A. H. Kimball, I. Abbott, Stanley, c.
	Brk. Norumbega,	325		Libby & Kimball, A. Spear, c
	A. H. Kimball,	283	S. Starrett,	Kimball, Sawyer & Colson, Sleeper, c.
	Helen,	316		I., I. K & A. H. Kimball, Ulmer, c.
	George Thomas,	290	G. Thomas,	b. Gregory, Sawyer & Colson, Fisk, c.
	Telegraph,	224	H. Merriam,	O. B. Fales, Flint, etc., R. Crockett, c.

TABLE IX. (*Continued.*)

Yrs.	Class. Names.	Tns	Builders.	Chief Owners.
1848	Ship Henry Nesmith,	478	G. Thomas,	b. Kimballs, H. H. Ulmer. c.
1849.	Sch. Oliver H. Perry,	129	C. Starrett?	Kimball, Williams, H. H. Burpee, c.
	Gertrude Horton,	123	Mer.&Andrews,	Crockett, Pillsbury, Alden, Pendleton, c.
	Brig Edgar,	144	S. Starrett,	S Starrett, R. Smith, c.
	Brk. John Bird,	278	C. Starrett?	Birds, Jackson, etc., H. Bird. c.
	Golden Age,	311	I. Ames,	Ames & Farnsworth, Arey, c.
	Marmora,	388	Andrews & Mer.	Sawyer. Colson, Allen, Duncan. c.
	Ship Equator,	876	G. Thomas,	Boston Owners, I. Taylor, c
	John Spear,	629	F. W. Rhoades,	Kimball, J. C. Libby, Spears, c.
1850.	Sch. Rockland,	48		Jos. Hewett, S Welch, c.
	James R.	52		Farnsworth, J. Getchell, c.
	Celestial,	116	S. Starrett?	Spears, Ingrahams, Pendleton, c.
	Ship Mary Crocker,	549	C. Starrett,	J. Crocker, c. Starrett, etc.
	Crescent,	753	Mer. & Andrews	Merriam & Andrews, Forbes, c.
	Rockland,	1000	Geo. Thomas,	
1851.	Sch. R. B. Pitts,	82		Berry, Coburn, Wheeler, Verrill, c.
	Lion,	150	Jas. Crockett,	Jas. & K. Crockett, E. C. Healy, c.
	Superior,	98	Merriam & And.	Achorn, Burpees, Robinson, c.
	B. B. Whitlock,	150	Merriam & And.	b. Jos. Packard, c.
	Ann,	157		J. White, Sherers, etc. Daggett, c.
	Louisa Dyer,	145		Dyers, Coombs, Ludwig, Ames, c
	Onatavia,	137		Kimball, Rankin, Snow, Simonton, c.
	Wm. Gregory,	149		McLoon, F. Gray, etc., Bucklin, c
	Brk. Geo. W. Horton,	299	C. Starrett,	J. Bird, Atkins, etc., Packard, c.
	Harriet Spalding,	299	S. Starrett,	Cobb, Ingraham, etc, C. Spalding, c.
	Iddo Kimball,	474	C. Starrett,	b. Kimballs, S. L. Ingraham, c.
	Springbok,	370	G. Thomas,	Secomb & Taylor of Boston.
	Ship Chas. Holmes,	792	Andrews & Mer.	R. Crockett, c., Pillsbury, etc.
1852.	Sch. Rebecca,	115		A G. Luce, T. Thurston, c
	Wm S. Brown,	146	H. Merriam,	Crockett, Furbish, etc., Holbrook c.
	Lucy Ames,	150	S. Starrett,	Berrys. D. Ames, c.
	Jane Ingraham,	148	S. Starrett,	Ingrahams, J. Stevens, etc Wheeler. c.
	Isaac Cohen Hertz,	149	C. Starrett,	Kimballs, Burpees, Bullock, c.

TABLE IX. (*Continued.*)

Yrs.	Class. Names.	Tns	Builders.	Chief Owners.
1852.	Sch. Marcia Ferrand,	175	C. & N. Dyer,	Whitney, Luce, Burpees, etc., Spear, c.
	Josiah Achorn,	124	H. Merriam,	Burpees, Grover, Fales, Merrill, c.
	Chas. Roberts,	149	C. & N. Dyer,	b. L. Snow, Wise, D. E. Post, c.
	Brk. Jenny Pitts,	540	H. Merriam,	Snows, Farwell, Pitts, Thorndike, c.
	Ship Paragon,	900	H. Merriam,	b. & S. Duncan, c.
	Anglo Saxon,	869	F. W. Rhoades,	b. & R. Keating, c.
	Defiance,	1691	G. Thomas,	G. Thomas, H. Vinal, c.
	Rattler,	1121	G. Thomas,	b. & J. O. Amsbury, c.
1853.	Sch. Empire,	218	H. Merriam,	Rollins York, c.
	Mary Farnsworth,	150	C. & N. Dyer,	Fales, Farnsworth, Hunt, Everett, c.
	Sarah L. Hills,	171		Snows, Pillsbury, Case, McKennon, c.
	Mountain Eagle,	196		David Ames, A. C. Ames, c
	Emma Furbish,	185	E. Andrews,	Ames, Lime Rock Bank. etc., Kendall, c.
	Hardscrabble,	126	H. Gregory,	b. McLain, C. Jameson, H. Gregory, Jr., c. etc.
	John Bell,	148	J. Achorn,	Starrett, Berry, Cobb, etc., Ham, c.
	Lewis McLain,	176	G. Thomas,	K. Crockett, A. C. Fales, etc., Bucklin, c.
	C. L. Allen,	155	C. & N. Dyer,	Achorn, Atkins, Rhoades, c
	F. L. Jones,	167	J. Achorn,	Achorn, G. Gregory, c., Osgood, Bean.
	Kate Holbrook,	169	S. Starrett,	E. Perry, G. L. Smith, etc., Hall, c.
	Brk. H. S. Bradley,	400	H. Merriam,	H. Merriam, etc., B. W. Conant, c.
	Mary J. Kimball,	398	C. Starrett,	Brewster, Lord, Fisk, c.
	Angelia Brewer,	422	S. Starrett,	Kimball, J. H. Butler, etc., Ulmer, c.
	Wm. T. Sayward,	462	Isaac Ames,	Jas. W. Sayward, c. also.
	David Kimball,	449	D. C. Dinsmore	J. Ames, c. Hewett, Pillsbury.
	Ship Live Yankee,	1638	H. Merriam,	G. W. Brown, c. & als.
	Charles Buck,	1424	J. Hilt,	Lawrence, Hilt, & Co., Smalley, c.
	Gazetteer,	1119	F. W. Rhoades,	b. R Crockett, c.
	Mary. T. Starrett,	625	C. Starrett,	b. A. H Kimball, H. Ulmer, c.
1854.	C. A. Libbey,	238	H. Merriam.	b James Wallace, c.
	Albert Jameson,	89	E. Andrews,	John Jameson, c. also.
	Excelsior,	174	[ener,	Watermans, etc., Sleeper, c
	Ella,	213	Starrett & Hav-	Crockett, Marston, Davis, etc , Ulmer, c.
	Sch. L. W. Alexander,	145	I. Ames,	Sherers, J. Tollman, Alexander, c.
	Ella May,	61	Lawrence & Co	b. Brackett, etc., Titus, c.
	Brig Ann M. Weeks,	198	J. Crockett,	Holmes, Crockett, etc., Marston, c.
	Mary Cobb,	285		J. A Creighton, Flinton, c
	Tyrant,	211	E. Andrews,	Bean, Osgood, Gregory, c.

TABLE IX. (*Continued.*)

Yrs	Class Names.	Tns	Builders.	Chief Owners
1854.	Brig Sarah E. Dix,	262	St. & Havener,	b. J. F. Cables, c.
	Brk. Rambler,	367	H. Merriam,	C. L. Allen, Bean, Packard, c.
	Samson,	456	L. D. Carver,	D. Robinson, Harden, Woods, Daily, c.
	Ship Yankee Ranger,	708	R. Trowbridge,	A. H. Kimball, I. C. Abbott, etc.
	Cavalier,	1286	Hilt & Co.	Dyer, Achorn, Atkins, Glover, c.
	Chs. A. Farwell,	1298	S. Starrett,	Farwells, Cobb, etc., Crocker, c.
	Clarissa Bird,	1064	C. Starrett,	b. H. Bird, c., A. H. Kimball.
	Oliver Jordan,	1219	C. Starrett,	Kimball, Abbott, Jordan, c
	Louisa Hatch,	854	W. McLoon,	b. etc., O. Amsbury, c.
	Young Mechanic,	1376	F. W. Rhoades,	b. etc., H. Spalding, c.
	John Cottle,	1200	Hilt & Co,	
	J. Wakefield,	1286	H. Merriam,	Wakefield, Berry, etc.
	Euterpe,	2000	H. Merriam,	G. W. Brown, & als. of N. York.
1855.	Sch. N. C. Fletcher,	96		J. Hewett, H. Rhoades, c.
	Ella Frances,	22		S. L. Treat, Penniman, c.
	Baltic,	148		Healey, Cates, Holbrook, c
	Hiawatha,	131	Jas. Crockett,	b. Page, Alden, Simonton, c.
	Brk. L. D. Carver,	414	L. D. Carver,	W. S. Carver, c. also.
	Hanson Gregory,	349	C. Starrett,	Alden, Thomas, Sylvester, c
	Caroline Ellems,	399	S. Starrett,	O'Neal, Glover, Ellems, c.
	Ship Squando,	1089		Kimballs, W. Jordan, c.
1856.	Sch. Uncle Sam,	57		A. G. Luce, Farnham, c.
	Brig Ocean Eagle,	290		A. G. Luce, c. also.
	Brk. Harriet S. Fisk,	564		Ingraham, Butler, etc., Fisk, c.
	Ship Julia Lawrence,	877	Lawrence & Co.	Cobb, Libby, etc, Spear, c.
	Forest Eagle,	1156	C. Starrett,	b. A. H. Kimball, Ulmer, c
1857.	Brk. Cephas Starrett,	424	C. Starrett,	Kimball, Bird, Gregory, c.
	Ship B. S. Kimball,	1192	R. Trowbridge,	Kimballs, etc., Hosmer, c.
1858.	Sch. B. B. Bean,	217		Bird, Duncan, A. Merrill, c
	Emeline McLain,	200		McLain, Perry, Sleeper, Bucklin, c.
	Brk. Orraville,	599		Farwells, Mallard, etc., Crockett, c.
1859.	Sch. Joseph Hewett,	122		H. J. Hewett, Bucklin, c.
	Minnie Cobb,	85		N. A. Farwell, Cobb, Ham, c.
	Caroline,	449		McLoon, J. Packard, c.
	Ship Jennie Beals,	1094	S. Starrett.	F. Cobb, H. Beals.
1860.	Sch. Ada Ames,	199	S. Starrett,	A. F. Ames, D. Ames, c.
	Leonessa,	223		Rokes, Beans, etc. Hupper, c.
	Convoy,	161		J. & H. Bird, J. Merrill, c.
	Fanny Keating,	237		I. Snow, c., Farwell, Hall, etc.
	Aurora,			
1861.	Trader,	75	S. Albee, jr.	W. A. Farnsworth, E. Crockett, c.
1862.	Lizzie Guptill,	74	A. Daggett,	M. Sumner, & als., R. Guptill, c.

TABLE IX. (*Continued.*)

Yrs.	Class.	Names.	Tns	Builders.	Chief Owners.
1862.	Sch	A. J. Bird,	178	H. Merriam,	J. Bird, & als., J. H. French, c.
	Brk.	Bradford,	284	S. Starrett,	Kimball, etc., J. F. Cables, c.
		Antietam,	222	R. C. Thomas,	W. A. Farnsworth, c. also.
	Ship	Martha Cobb,	1193	S. Starrett,	F. Cobb, & als., T. R. Pillsbury, c.
1863.	Sch.	Indomitable,	88	N. Beverage,	W. T. Cochran, etc., S. I. Brewster, c.
		Adrian,	109	Jos. Emery,	C. C. Ingraham, etc., S. E. Everett, c.
		Ned Sumter,	104	Is. Snow,	Lucy W. Snow, etc., Israel Thorndike, c.
		Vicksburg,	101	J. Mehan,	b. & als., N. P. Haskell, c.
		Catawamteak,	158	Lewis Brewer,	Israel L. Snow, c., & als.
	Brig	Nellie Hewett,	220		Hudson J. Hewett, W. Bucklin, c.
	Brk.	New York,	366	S. Starrett,	Jas. A. Borland, etc., J. Hooper, c.
1864.	Sch.	Concord,	62	Jos. Emery,	F. Cobb, A. G. Spear, c.
		G. W. Kimball, jr.	94	R. C. Thomas,	Olive C. Kimball, etc., A. W. Crockett, c.
		Fortuna Thompson	242	R. C. Thomas,	Geo. Holmes, c., & als.
	Ship	Ortago,	850	Jos. Emery,	Francis Cobb.

TABLE X.

NUMBER OF DEATHS AS NOTED BY HON. B. FALES WITHIN THE PRESENT LIMITS OF THOMASTON FOR EACH YEAR FROM 1836 TO 1862.

Years.	No.	Years.	No.	Years.	No.	Years.	No.
1836	9	1843	25	1850	25	1857	36
1837	8	1844	23	1851	29	1858	43
1838	20	1845	27	1852	36	1859	17
1839	14	1846	30	1853	53	1860	11
1840	22	1847	24	1854	44	1861	44
1841	14	1848	30	1855	46	1862	46
1842	41	1849	36	1856	28		

TABLE XI.

SHOWING THE STATE OF THE SCHOOLS IN THOMASTON, ROCKLAND, AND SOUTH THOMASTON, 1863.

	No. of children between 4 & 21 yrs.	Whole No. registered in summer schools.	Average attendance in summer schools.	Whole No. registered in winter schools.	Average attendance in winter schools.	Average length of summer schools in weeks.	Average length of winter schools in weeks.	No. of districts.	No. parts of districts.	No. school houses.	Do. in good condition.	Do. built last year.	Cost school house built last year.	Expenses for repairs, fuel, &c.	No. male teachers, summer.
Thomaston,	1103	688	560	666	499	10.0	15.0	1	3*	11	9	1	$700	$400	2
Rockland,	2757	1656	1240	1764	1315	13.3	17.0	5	2*	14	9				3
South Thomaston,	651	367	275	476	367	9.0	10.0	12		11	8				

	No. male teachers in winter.	No. female teachers in summer.	No. female teachers in winter.	Wages to male teachers per mo. exclusive of board.	Wages to female teachers pr week, ditto.	Average cost teachers' board per week.	School money raised in 1863.	Amount more than law requires	Amount per scholar.	Amount drawn from State.	Amount paid for private tuition within the State.	Amount paid ditto out of State.	Amount p'd to prolong pub. schools	Amount paid for school supervision.	No. of districts in which scholars are graded.
Thomaston,	4	11	9	$32,00	$4,25		$2,800	$628	$2,54	$387,00				$50	1
Rockland,	8	22	15	$30,40	$3,18	$2,00	$5,000	$611	$1,23	$972,48	$200	$100		$120	2
South Thomaston,	10	12	3	$22,50	$2,33	$1,84	$1,000	$31	$1,54	$239,94	$450		$45	$30	

* These fractional districts are united to others without the municipality.

TABLE XII

METEOROLOGICAL; COMPILED FROM OBSERVATIONS OF CAPT. GEO. PRINCE, IN THE YEARS 1850–1, MADE AT HIS RESIDENCE, MILL RIVER, AND THE THOMASTON INSURANCE OFFICE.

	Mean Monthly Temperature.	Greatest Heat.	Days.	Greatest Cold.	Days.	Greatest fall of barometer.	Strongest wind.*	Remarks.
1850, March,	29° $\frac{12}{31}$	50°	31st	4°	4th	1st	1st, E. S. E. 6	Snow and rain, the 1st.
April,	37° $\frac{28}{30}$	64°	26th	20°	8th, 9th, 17th	13th, 14th	14th, N NW 6	Rain, three inches, and thunder, the 28th.
May,	48° $\frac{28}{31}$	70°	13th	31°	3d	6th	1st, S. W. 5	Sev. thunder storm, 6th; flashes uninterrupted.
June,†		92°	20th	40°	1st		10th, E. 6	
July,‡		86°	23d	58°	3d		6th, N. W. 6	
Aug.	63° $\frac{13}{31}$	84°	6th	45°	28th		16th, S. W. 5	Squall of hail and rain at 3 P. M. of 16th.
Sept.	56° $\frac{14}{30}$	79°	1st	34°	30th		13th, N. W. 5	Rain from 4 P. M. of 7th to 2 A. M. 9th; 16 in.
Oct.	40° $\frac{26}{31}$	65°	23d	22°	30th		13th, N. W. 5	Four inches rain, the 18th.
Nov.	31° $\frac{2}{30}$	55°	11th	20°	12th		17th, N. E. 5	First snow the 21st; three inches.
Dec.	19° $\frac{29}{31}$	42°	5th	4°—	31st	23d	23d, E. 6	Snow from 1 P. M. to 4 A. M. 23d; 10 in.
1851, Jan.	18° $\frac{29}{31}$	40°	30th	12°—	30th, 31st	28th	29th, S. 5	Snow, 28th, warm rain, 29th, ch'g to sev. cold.

Feb.	24°	$\frac{16}{28}$	44°	15th	10⁰ —	1st, 7th, 8th	21st	25th, N.	6	Snow, 21st, changing, 23d, to drizzling rain.
March,	31°	$\frac{10}{31}$	55°	31st	4⁰	14th	13th	18th, N. E.	6	Four inches snow night of the 13th and 14th.
April,	40°	$\frac{29}{30}$	62°	27th	26⁰	13th		16th, N. E.	6	Very cloudy month; sun ap'd 22d, after 8 days.
May,	50°	$\frac{25}{31}$	75°	27th	32⁰	7th		5th, N. E.	6	
June,	58°	$\frac{7}{30}$	80°	29th	36⁰	17th	6th	4th, E.	4	Severe thunder storm, 3 P. M. of 13th.
July,	65°	$\frac{27}{31}$	87°	17th	47⁰	15th		20th, S. W.	5	Thunder tempest, night of 19th.
Aug.	34°	$\frac{20}{31}$	84°	3d	50⁰	27th	25th	26th, N N E	5	Shower 2 P. M. of 25th.
Sept.	58°	$\frac{7}{30}$	88°	7th	31⁰	23d	22d, 23d	24th, N.	5	First frost, 15th; heavy frost, 22d.

* *Figures* placed after the *direction* of winds indicate their force: a perfect calm being represented by 0.
† Imperfect; 11 days partially or wholly unobserved.
‡ Imperfect; 16 days in the month unobserved.

TABLE XIII.

JUSTICES OF THE PEACE IN THE TOWN OF THOMASTON, WITH THE DATES OF THEIR APPOINTMENT, WHEN ASCERTAINED.

David Fales, about 1767, 1789, and quorum 1800, 1807, 1814.
Mason Wheaton, Oct. 6, 1781, 1788, 1795, 1802, 1809.
Samuel Brown, 1800, 1812.
Josiah Reed, 1800, and quorum 1806.
Joshua Adams, 1804, 1811, and quorum 1818, Feb. 13, 1821.
Henry Knox, 1804.
Joseph Ingraham, 1805, 1812, and quo. March 13, 1821, Feb. 7, 1828.
Hezekiah Prince, in St. George, Feb. 24, 1804, in Thomaston, 1816, and quorum Feb. 5, 1825, dedimus Sept. 23, 1836, through the State Jan. 24, 1833, Jan. 1, 1840.
Ebenezer Thatcher, in Warren, 1805, in Thomaston, ditto & dedimus 1812, July 7, 1820, and quorum Oct. 13, 1821, Feb. 7, 1828.
Otis Robbins, jr., 1808.
Isaac Barnard, 1809, ditto & ded. Sept. 1, 1820, & quo. Feb. 23, 1821.
Elias Phinney, 1810.
Elisha Snow, jr., 1810, '17, and quorum Feb. 5, 1822, Feb. 13, 1829, Dec. 8, 1836.
John Gleason, 1811, and quorum March 3, 1821, Feb. 7, 1827.
David S. Fales, 1810, '17, Nov. 20, 1824, Oct. 5, 1831.
Ezekiel G. Dodge, 1811.
Charles Spofford, 1812.
Joseph Sprague, 1818, and quorum March 30, 1822.
David Fales, jr., Nov. 24, 1820, Oct. 27, 1827, Sept. 25, 1834, and quorum Oct. 3, 1838, Dec. 14, 1840.
John Ruggles, ditto & ded. Sept. 1, 1820, June 21, 1827, through the State Jan. 26, 1832, Jan. 4, 1842, Feb. 7, 1849, ded. Jan. 21, 1857.
John Spear, June 29, 1820, ditto and quorum June 21, 1827.
George Coombs, ditto and quorum Feb. 23, 1821.
John H. Ingraham, to solemnize marriages, Mar. 3, 1821, July 1, 1829.
Elisha Snow, " " " " " "
Job Washburn, " " " Oct. 10, 1822, Feb. 24, 1830.
Samuel Fogg, " " " Jan. 1, 1823.
Grenville Mellen, Jan. 1, M. Marsh, Jan. 30, Wm. Heard, May 20, 1823.
David Crockett, March 3, 1824, April 2, 1831, ditto and quorum June 28, 1838, June 15, 1848.
Philip Ulmer, June 20, 1824.
Eusebius Fales, June 21, and Waterman T. Hewett, Nov. 29, 1825.
Oliver Fales, June 29, 1826, June 29, '33, and quorum June 24, '40, July 1, '47.
Henry J. Knox, Feb. 18, 1826, dedimus Feb. 5, '32.
Benjamin A. Gallop, Jan. 24, 1827, Jan. 21, '36, to solemnize marriages Dec. 25, '41.
Timothy Wellman, quorum Feb. 24, 1827, March 14, '34, dedimus Feb. 25, '36, June 26, '42.
Jonathan Cilley, quorum Dec. 29, 1828, dedimus Jan. 31, '31, Jan. 21, '36, and, March 31, through the State.
Elijah Davis, quorum Feb. 15, 1828.

Henry Ingraham, June 28, 1828, Feb. 2, '43, in Rockl'd June 11, '50.
Daniel Rose, quorum Feb. 7, and Thomas P. Vose, Feb. 9, 1828.
James Crockett, July 7, 1830; March 12, '34.
Halsey Healey, quorum March 19, 1830.
Richard Woodhull, to solemnize marriages Oct. 27, 1830, June 20, '34.
Elisha Harding, Nov. 1, and Simeon B. Lowell, Dec. 14, 1830.
Samuel G. Adams, Jan. 21, and William Cole, June 29, 1831.
Asa Coombs, Oct. 5, 1831, March 21, '39, and quorum May 2, '46, and in South Thomaston May 10, '53.
William J. Farley, quorum Jan. 7, 1831.
Henry C. Lowell, Jan. 31, 1831, June 30, '45.
Hezekiah Prince, jr., Jan. 31, 1831, dedimus Oct. 5, '32, Mar. 23, '37.
Manasseh H. Smith, Jan. 21, 1831, quorum Jan. 21, '37.
Rufus C. Counce, Jan. 27, and Abner Knowles, Oct. 5, 1832.
John T. Gleason, March 2, 1832, and quorum June 27, '39.
Atwood Levensaler, June 23, 1832, and quorum March 16, '40, Mar. 4, '47, April 11, '54.
Nathaniel Meservey, jr., March 9, 1832, quorum '33, June 25, '40, June 24, '47.
John Stackpole, Jan. 2, and William Perry, jr., June 23, 1832.
Hermon Stevens, Mar. 9, 1832, quo. and ded. Oct. 22, '34, Oct. 23, '41.
Ivory T. Hovey, quorum June 29, 1833.
John C. Cochran, March 12, 1834, do. & quo. Mar. 14, '38, Mar. 6, '45.
Charles Harrington, Jan. 21, 1834, April 6, '41.
Oliver Heard, March 18, and Lewis Fales, Sept. 25, 1834.
Charles Holmes, March 14, 1834, do. and quorum June 25, '41.
Edwin S. Hovey, quo & ded. Oct. 19, 1834, Oct. 23, '41, May 26, '49.
Moses R. Ludwig, Jan. 21, and quorum Feb. 14, 1834.
Joseph H. Jenne, quorum through the State Oct. 16, 1834.
James Morse, Jan. 29, Asa Perkins, Feb. 19, Phineas Tyler, Dec. 31, '34.
Samuel Albee, do. and quorum, Feb. 19, 1835, in Rockl. Dec. 21, '59.
Harmon Moses, to solemnize marriages Sept. 23, 1836.
Abner Rice, March 5, 1835, March 17, '42, July 24, '48, Nov. 10, '51.
William Singer, March 19, 1835, quo. through the State Jan. 20, '42.
Lucius H. Chandler, Feb. 18, 1835, quorum March 9, '43.
George Emery, jr., June 20, 1836, and quorum March 14, '44.
Samuel Fuller, Dec. 8, 1836, Oct. 17, '43.
Nelson Spear, March 24, 1836.
James C. Cochran, quorum Feb. 23, 1837, June 7, '39, June 17, '45.
Nathan C. Fletcher, quorum Jan. 26, 1837, through the State Jan. 26, '41, Oct. 17, '43.
Joel Miller, quorum June 27, 1837, May 28, '46.
Henry Paddelford, Feb. 9, and William Masters, Feb 16, 1837.
Edmund Wilson, Dec. 27, 1837, and quorum Nov. 7, '39, July 1, '47, June 26, '54.
George Abbott, March 3, 1838, and quorum March 27, '45.
John D. Barnard, April 27, 1838, and quo. Mar. 27, '45, Mar. 16, '52.
William Beattie, Feb. 7, 1838, dedimus June 27, '38, quo. Feb. 7, '39, Nov. 20, '46.
John Holmes, ditto and quorum April 25, 1838.
Eliphalet Martin, Feb. 15, 1838, July 16, '46.
James Spalding, March 3, 1838.
John S. Abbott, do. & quo. Jan. 25, Jona. G. Dickenson, June 27, '39.
Ezekiel Hall, Mar. 26, Alonzo Emery, Nov. 7, S. B. Dodge, May 2, '39.
Nathaniel Liscomb, Nov. 7, 1839, May 28, '46, Sept. 27, '53.
Jeremiah To'man, March 26, 1839.

George A. Starr, Sept. 24, 1840, dedimus Mar. 29, '54, and quorum Aug. 3, '47, June 26, '54.
William R. Keith, ditto and quorum Jan. 21, 1840, Nov. 2, '47.
Walter E. Tolman, quorum Dec. 30, 1840.
Edwin Rose, Mar. 27, 1841, & quo. Oct. 17, '43, Nov. 19, '48, Dec. 2, '56.
Ephraim Wilder Farley, quorum April 21, 1841.
James O. L. Foster, April 22, and Joshua O. Le Fevre, April 22, 1841.
Jos. Gilchrist, Feb. 24, L. Levensaler, May 25, B. Hardy, May 31, 1852.
Israel J. Perry, June 13, and John Henderson, Nov. 10, 1842.
William Lamson, to solemnize marriages June 30, 1841.
Henry C. Leonard, " " March 4, '42.
Enoch Hutchinson, " " June 24, "
Timothy Fogg, Feb. 2, 1843.
Joseph Farwell, do. and quorum March 23, 1843, ded. July 11, '45,
Beder Fales, do. & quo. Mar. 23, 1843, Jan. 25, '50, July 1, '57, ded. Sept. 26, '59.
Rowland Jacobs, March 23, 1843, at same time James Fogg, do. & quo.
William T. Sayward, June 21, 1843, and quorum May 2, '46.
Merrick Mossman, Jan. 25, 1844, and, at same time, John T. Berry, Daniel Rose, (2d,) David N. Piper, and Albert G. Lermond.
Edward C. Tilson, March 21, and quorum July 1, 1844.
Joshua C. Adams, Feb. 13, 1845, and in South Thomaston Feb. 7, '53.
Thomas McLellan, March 6, 1845.
Archibald McKellar, " " & in S. Th. Ap. 26, & ded. Mar. 8, '52.
Orchard C. Ludwig, quorum April 3, Freeman Harden, Oct. 4, 1845.
Joseph H. Brackett, quo. Jan. 27, Joseph H. Beckett, May 2, 1845.
Thomas W. Hix, quorum August 12, 1846.
David O'Brien, quo. Nov. 20, 1846, April 23, '51, Dec. 30, '57.
Elisha Fales, June 14, and Albert Merrill, June 24, 1847.
Christopher Prince, June 14, 1847, and quorum April 18, 1854.
John Bird, July 11, 1848, in Rockland June 12, '55.
George Thorndike, June 15, 1848, at same time Knott C. Perry and James Jones.
James H. Rivers, July 24, 1848, and at same time Joseph W. Jacobs.
Oliver J. Fernald, to solemnize marriages, Oct. 21, 1848.
George Prince, quorum Nov. 19, 1850.
Benjamin Carr, quorum and through the State, March 2, 1852.
Ambrose Lermond, quorum Feb. 1, 1853, Feb. 29, '60.
Thomas Rose, quorum Feb. 21, 1854.
John O. Robinson, quo. March 13, Rufus Fales, quo. March 25, 1856.
Ezekiel Ross, quo. April 17, and Benj. A. Lowell, quo. April 9, 1857.
James McLean, to solemnize marriages, Sept. 26, 1859.
Ezra Sanborn, " " July 1, 1858.
George W. French, quorum Sept. 30, 1858.
Oliver Robinson, quo. Feb. 2, and Samuel H. Allen, March 30, 1859.
James M. Beverage, do. and quorum July 18, 1859.
Lysander Hill, do. and quorum Feb. 1, 1860.

IN SOUTH THOMASTON AFTER ITS SEPARATION.

William McLoon, Oct. 16, 1848, and, at same time, Daniel Vaughan.
George Thorndike, quorum May 26, 1849, April 2, '57.
Silas M. Arey, " July 30, '49.
William Perry, " Nov. 18, '54.
Samuel F. Coombs, " Mar. 2, '55.

J. Riley Bowler, to solemnize marriages, Oct. 3, 1854.
Benj. A. Chase, " " July 18, 1859.
Shubael A. Hinkley, quo. March 23, Jona. Newhall, April 6, 1859.
George W. White, quorum Sept. 26, 1859.

IN ROCKLAND AFTER ITS SEPARATION.

John Wakefield, quorum May 8, 1849, at same time Wm. L. Pitts, and, May 26, Emery Sawyer.
Henry Ingraham, quorum June 11, 1852, Jan. 19, '59.
Wm. H. Titcomb, " May 8, 1849, June 24, '56, ded. Mar. 29, '53.
John A. Meserve, " Jan. 16, '50, Feb. 17, '58.
Hermon Stevens, " May 2, '50, July 1, '58.
Joseph Farwell, " July 30, '50, Feb. 17, '59, for Waldo Co., Feb. 17, '58.
Charles L. Lowell, " June 10, and Josiah I. Brown, Aug. 25, '51.
Moses W. Farwell, " Nov. 26, '51, Jan. 19, '59.
Manasseh P. Whiting, " Aug. 16, and Wm. G. Sargent, Mar. 9, '52.
Davis Tillson, " Mar. 9, '52, Mar. 30, '59.
Jeremiah Tolman, " April 13, '52, May 11, '59.
John C. Cochrane, " April 26, and H. C. Lowell, Oct. 20, Chas. G. Cram, Dec. 28, '52.
Nathan C. Woodard, " Feb, 8, '53, Dec. 21, '59.
Larkin Snow, Mar. 8, 1853, Wm. P. Frye, Feb. 8, '53, Dec. 21, '59.
Thomas W. Hix, quo. Sept. 27, 1853, same time, Wakefield G. Frye.
William Beattie, " Oct. 20, "
James O. Skinner, to solemnize marriages, Feb. 21, 1854.
Henry E. Ingraham, quorum April 11, 1854.
Oliver Fales, quorum June 26, 1854, same time, Nathaniel Meservey.
Archibald C. Spalding, quo. Sept. 29, 1854, same time, C. Glover.
Peter Thatcher, quorum Dec. 29, 1854.
L. M. Howes, quo. May 8, 1855, same time, John King, K. C. Perry.
Charles A. Sylvester, quo. Aug. 6, J. Goodwin Day, Oct. 3, 1855.
Ralph P. E. Thatcher, quo. Dec. 9, 1855, Charles Coffran, Mar. 19, '56.
Walter E. Tolman, quorum Nov. 29, 1856.
Lewis Richardson, quorum Jan. 1, 1857.
Samuel C. Fessenden, quorum Feb. 9, 1857.
Erasmus H. Cochran, Feb. 25, 1857.
Ephraim W. Pendleton, quo. Mar. 26, Gershom Burgess, Ap. 2, 1857.
Oliver G. Hall, quo. April 17, 1857, William Fessenden, Oct. 10, '59.
William McLoon, quorum and through the State, Jan. 31, 1857.
Findley Wallace, to solemnize marriages, Feb. 12, 1857.
Andrew Barron, " " Jan. 27, 1858.
Ziba Pope Vose, quo. Jan. 5, and Alonzo D. Nichols, Feb. 17, 1858.
Geo. W. Kimball, jr., quo. Feb. 17, and T. K. Osgood, Feb. 24, 1858.
Chas. R. Mallard, quo. Feb. 2, and S. G. B. Coombs, Mar. 16, 1859.
Archibald McKellar, jr., quo. April 6, & Albert S. Rice, Oct. 17, 1859.
Ephraim C. Barrett, quorum Dec. 21, 1859.
William S. Heath, quorum Sept. 26, 1859, dedimus Jan. 19, 1860.

TABLE XIV.

OTHER CIVIL OFFICERS WITH DATES OF THEIR APPOINTMENT, SO FAR AS ASCERTAINED.

IN THOMASTON.

Mason Wheaton, coroner, Aug. 30, 1770.
Benjamin Webb, deputy sheriff, 1797.
Ephraim Snow, notary public, 1800.
Samuel M. Martin, coroner, 1800.
Leonard Fales, deputy sheriff, 1802 and 1804.
David Fales, notary public, 1803, '4, '5, '6, '7, '13, and '14; special Justice, 1808, '9, '10, and '11.
David S. Fales, coroner, 1804 to '10, inclusive; notary public, 1815 to '18, inclusive.
Willard Fales, deputy sheriff, 1805, '6, '7, '8, '9, and '10.
Jackson Durand, notary public, 1807.
Otis Robbins, jr., coroner, 1809 to '19, inclusive.
William M. Dawes, surveyor and inspector of customs, 1810 to '20; notary public, 1810, and '13.
Halsey Healey, coroner, 1812 to '20; Oct. 7, 1825; March 13, 1838; lime inspector, Feb. 26, 1856.
Charles Pope, deputy sheriff, 1813, '14, '15, '16, and '17.
Philip Ulmer, deputy sheriff, 1813, '14, '15, '16, '17, '18, and '19.
Joshua Adams, commissioner of wrecks, 1816, '17, '18, '19, and '20.
Ebenezer Thatcher, Associate Justice for 2d Eastern dist. C. C. P. 1819.
Samuel Fuller, deputy sheriff, 1819; pilot of the Port, June 20, 1834.
Hezekiah Prince, deputy collector, 1817 to '40.
Hezekiah Prince, jr., surveyor and inspector of customs, 1821 to '43.
John Ruggles, notary public, June 16, 1820, June 21, 1827; Judge of C. C. P., March 4, 1831.
Eliphalet Conner, fish inspector, May 11, 1821.
Samuel Rankin, fish inspector, Oct. 22, 1821; Nov. 1, 1826.
John Paine, notary public, Jan. 6, 1824; Feb. 13, 1831.
Daniel Rose, warden of State Prison, Mar. 23, 1824; Mar. 8, 1828; land agent, June 28, 1828; June 26, 1831.
Charles Ulmer, coroner, Feb. 26, 1824; lime inspector, June 20, 1824.
James Ulmer, lime inspector, June 20, '24; at same time, Alden Ulmer.
John Spear, inspector of State Prison, April 30, 1824, Mar. 28, 1828; inspector of lime, Feb. 15, 1825, Mar. 13, 1829, June 27, 1833.
John O'Brien, coroner, Feb. 28, 1827; inspector of State Prison, Apr. 2, '30, Jan. 26, '35; warden of ditto, June 30, '36, Feb. 13, '41.
Orchard C. Ludwig, coroner, Feb. 25, 1828, and Mar. 8th, Jonas Mason, coroner.
John Stackpole, coroner, March 9, 1829.
Beder Fales, coroner, March 19, 1831; deputy sheriff, 1831; register of Probate, March 21, 1844; Judge of Probate since.
John Copeland, deputy sheriff, 1831.
Timothy Wellman, notary public, Dec. 8, 1831, Dec. 24, 1838.
Freeman Harden, deputy sheriff, 1831.
Joel Miller, warden of State Prison, June 27, 1832; Judge of Probate, E. division, March 21, 1844.
Henry J. Knox, notary public, Feb 5, 1832.

Abner Knowles, inspector of state prison, Jan. 21, 1834.
Elkanah Spear, deputy sheriff, 1834.
Michael Achorn, lime inspector, June 20, 1834, same time, Ralph Chapman, Knott Bartlett, John S. Coburn, Briggs Butler, Jas. Cudworth, David F. Conant, William Butler, Tilley Clements, George W. Coombs, John Brown, and Willard Blackington, to the same office.
Daniel Cowing, lime inspector, June 20, 1834, and March 27, 1845.
James Dane, lime inspector, March 25, 1834.
John Butler, lime inspector, Sept. 25, 1834, Aug. 9, '48.
Alexander Barrows, lime inspector, Oct. 21, 1834.
John Ellems, lime inspector, June 20, 1834, and, at same time, to same office, Elisha Fales, Nathaniel Fales, jr., Philip Fales, Noyes Fales, and George Fales, who was re-appointed Dec. 31, '34.
Jeremiah Gilman, lime inspector, Dec. 26, 1834.
Ezekiel Hall, lime inspector, June 20, 1834, and, at same time, Chas. McLoon, Elijah Hall, Luther Lincoln, Wm. Ingraham, Isaac Ingraham, Bernard Ingraham, and John Ham, to same office.
William McLoon, lime inspector, Sept. 25, 1834.
Oliver Bartlett, lime inspector, June 20, 1834, and, at same time, Jerome Watson, Samuel Packard, George I. Williams, Patrick Woodcock, James Vose, Alibeus Partridge, Perez Tillson, John Sterling, Robert R. Richards, Lozier Packard, and Eli Perry, to the same office.
Nathaniel Meservey, jr., notary public, Mar. 5, 1834, Dec. 31, '42.
Thomas O'Brien, coroner, Jan. 21, 1834, May 28, '46.
Robert R. Richards, coroner, March 5, 1834.
Samuel Rankin, jr., lime inspector, Sept. 25, 1834, May 2, '39.
Constant Rankin, lime inspector, Sept. 25, 1834, at same time, Ebenezer Walker, together with Elbridge G. Shepherd, and William Walsh, jr., to same office.
Wm. K. Stevens, lime inspector, Oct. 26, 1834, Mar. 7, '42, resigned.
David Beals, lime inspector, Mar. 14, 1835, & Feb. 19th, David Jenks.
Enoch Post, lime inspector, June 19, & Dennis Smith, Mar. 19, 1835.
Henry Ingraham, inspector of state prison, Dec. 29, 1836.
Hanson Tolman, fish inspector, Feb. 25, 1836.
William Thomas, notary public, Jan. 21, 1837, Nov. 20, '46.
John D. Barnard, notary public, April 27, 1838, March 27, '45, March 16, '52, public administrator, May 8, '49.
George Miller, notary public, Feb. 9, 1838, Feb. 7, '39.
John Holmes, inspector of state prison, Jan., 1838.
John Prince, notary public, June 20, 1838.
Charles Harrington, inspector of state prison, Jan., 1838.
George S. Wiggen, " " " " "
John G. Lovejoy, notary public, May 2, 1839.
George A. Starr, inspector of state prison, Jan., 1839, Feb. 23, '43, Jan. 26, '46.
John Merrill, inspector of state prison, Jan., 1839, and Feb. 3, '42.
Joseph Spear, lime inspector, March 11, 1841.
George Thorndike, notary public, Dec. 20, 1841.
Joseph Ulmer, lime inspector, Feb. 18, 1842
Joshua C. Adams, notary public, Dec. 31, 1842.
Iddo Kimball, inspector of state prison, March 16, 1841.
Wm. R. Keith, " " " " "
Elisha Snow, " " " " "

Job Washburn, chaplain of state prison, April 21, 1841, '42, '43, '44, '45, '46, '47.
John T. Gleason, notary public, March 23, 1843.
George Prince, notary public, Oct. 17, 1843, Nov. 19, 1850.
James C. Madigan, notary public, Oct 17, 1843.
Ephraim M. Perry, notary public, Nov. 28, 1844.
Benjamin Carr, warden of state prison, 1839, and Jan. 22, 1846.*
Atwood Levensaler, public administrator, June 17, 1846.
Daniel Small, inspector state prison, Jan. 16, 1850; school commissioner, June 21, 1852.
Richard Woodhull, trustee of Insane Hospital, May 11, '53, June 17,'56.
Edmund Wilson, county attorney, Dec. 6, 1845; ditto, elected by people, 1842.
Oliver J. Fernald, chaplain of state prison, Feb. 21, 1853.
Wm. Bennett, warden of state prison, 1850, Feb. 28, '54, & Jan. 31, '56.
Charles T. Starrett, inspector of state prison, Sept. 29, 1854.
Alexander Young, coroner, Jan. 22, 1846, Jan. 16, 1850; deputy sheriff, April, 1854.
Edwin S. Hovey, notary public, June 24, 1847; register of probate, May 8, 1849.
George Abbott, notary public, July 20, 1848.
James W. Rivers, notary public, July 24, 1849.
Charles G. Smith, notary public, March 16, 1850; inspector of state prison, Nov. 2, 1858.
George Moody, inspector of lime, April 1, 1853.
Samuel E. Smith, notary public, Jan. 3, 1854.
Christopher Prince, notary public, April 18, 1854.
Isaac Sawyer, to solemnize marriages, Sept. 29, 1854.
Levi G. Marsh, to solemnize marriages, Dec. 19, 1855.
David O'Brien, notary public, Jan. 31, 1856.
Edward Robinson, commissioner on affairs of warden of state prison, resigned and was succeeded Jan. 1856 by George Crawford.
John C. Levensaler, notary public, Nov. 29, 1856.
M. R. Ludwig, commissioner on affairs of warden of state prison, Jan. 1856; trustee of Insane Hospital, Oct. 1864.
Asa C. Fuller, notary public, April 9, 1857; collector of internal revenue, 1863.
Joseph Fish, notary public, Feb. 10, 1858.
James Gilchrist, (2d), coroner, April 6, 1859.
Nathaniel Moody, coroner, Sept. 30, 1858, May 8, 1860; deputy sheriff, 1857 and 1863.
Oliver Robinson, notary public, March 9, 1859.
George Moody, lime inspector, March 21, 1859.
Edward Hills, high sheriff of Knox county about 1861.
Nathaniel Liscomb, assistant marshal for taking the census, 1860.
S. S. Gerry, county commissioner, Knox county, March 21, 1860.
Bartlett Jackson, treasurer of Knox county, March 21, 1860.
B. Webb Counce, assistant assessor of internal revenue, Sept. 1862.

---

* By this, as well as by the appointments of John O'Brien, it will be seen that the list of Wardens on page 336, vol. 1st, furnished by the Clerk from the Prison records, is at fault in omitting the re-appointment of Mr. O'Brien in 1841 and that of Mr Carr in 1846. The *year* only of Mr. Carr's first appointment is given in this Table, and that of some other wardens, because, not being then residents of Thomaston, they were not included in the list obtained from the Secretary's office.

IN SOUTH THOMASTON.

Archibald G. Coombs, lime inspector, Aug. 11, 1848.
William McLoon, lime inspector, Nov. 19, 1849.
Archibald McKellar, jr., notary public, June 11, 1850; in Rockland, July 18, 1859.
George Thorndike, notary public, June 11, 1850; inspector of state prison, Feb. 7, 1853; clerk of courts, Knox county, 1863.
Joshua C. Adams, notary public, July 10, 1850.
George W. Coombs, lime inspector, Feb 3, 1852.
Isaac Tolman, fish inspector, Jan. 2, 1857.
George W. White, register of deeds, Knox county, March 21, 1860.

IN ROCKLAND.

Alden Ulmer, lime inspector, Oct. 16, 1848, Oct. 20, 1852, Feb. 19, 1857, Feb., 1861.
William L. Pitts, notary public, May 8, 1849.
Charles R. Mallard, notary public, May 8, 1849, June 24, 1856.
Charles A. Sylvester, coroner, Oct. 16, 1849, March 29, 1854.
Nathan A. Farwell, coroner, Feb. 12, 1849.
Hermon Stevens, inspector of state prison, Jan. 16, 1850; notary public, May 1, 1857.
Charles A. Macomber, coroner, Aug. 31, 1850.
John C. Cochran, justice of municipal court, Aug. 13, 1850.
Wm. H. Titcomb, notary public, Nov. 26, 1851, Feb. 16, '59.
Charles Holmes, inspector of state prison, Oct. 19, 1852.
George J. Burns, inspector of lime, Feb. 8, 1853.
Maynard Sumner, notary public, March 1, 1853.
Alonzo D. Nichols, notary public, March 8, 1853.
David M. Mitchell, coroner, July 7, 1853, deputy sheriff, April, '54.
Jona. Spear, jr., inspector of state prison, May 11, 1853, Mar. 10, '58.
Joseph Farwell, high-sheriff, March 21, 1854.
Elkanah Spear, jr., deputy sheriff, April, 1854.
J. G. Lovejoy, notary public, April 11, 1854.
Stephen N. Hatch, notary public, Nov. 18, 1854.
Peter Thacher, notary public, Dec. 29, 1854.
Wm. G. Sargent, judge of municipal court, Feb. 1, 1855.
Edward L. Lovejoy, notary public, March 2, 1855.
James O. L. Foster, " " " "
John King, " " June 12, "
Ralph P. E. Thacher, " " Dec. 9, "
Lewis Hall, lime inspector, Jan. 24, 1856.
Nathan C. Woodard, notary public, March 25, 1856, assistant marshal for taking census, 1860.
John A. Meserve, judge of the municipal court, April 4, 1856.
William Beattie, notary public, April 4, 1856.
Walter E. Tolman, " " Jan. 1, 1857.
George W. Berry, " " March 2, 1859.
Thos. W. Chadbourn, " " 21, 1860, sheriff, 1858.
L. W. Howes, notary public, Mar. 23, 1858, county attorney, Feb. '62.
Charles A. Libbey, coroner, Jan. 27, 1858, May 8, '60.
Nathaniel Meservey, notary public, Aug, 25, 1851, May 11, '59, judge of the municipal court, March, '58.
Charles A. Miller, notary public, Sept. 26, 1859, clerk of courts, Knox county, '63.

Samuel C. Fessenden, judge of municipal court, April 17, 1857, inspector of state prison, Jan. 6, '57.
Thomas W. Hix, inspector of state prison, Sept. 21, 1854, warden do. March 20, '55, Jan. 6, '57.
J. Goodwin Day, coroner, July 1, 1857.
Moses W. Farwell, judge of police court, March? 1861.
Francis L. Jones, inspector of the customs, May, 1861.
Jeremiah Tolman, assistant assessor of internal revenue, Sept., 1862.
John Arnold and Eph. Hall, assistant collectors of ditto., Sept., ditto.

TABLE XV.

MILITIA OFFICERS OF THE OLD ORGANIZATION, IN THOMASTON, ROCKLAND, AND SOUTH THOMASTON, WITH THE DATES OF COMMISSIONS AS FAR AS COULD BE ASCERTAINED FROM THE ADJUTANT GENERAL'S OFFICE, ARRANGED ALPHABETICALLY; WITH SOME OBTAINED FROM OTHER SOURCES.

Achorn, Isaac, cornet of Cavalry, Oct. 17, 1828.
Achorn, Michael A., capt. co. A, Rockland, July, 1862.*
Adams, Joshua, lieut., Mar. 6, 1799, capt. Ju. 4, 1801, maj. Sept. 5, '5.
Adams; Joseph, lieut. Light Infantry, Aug. 26, 1817, capt. Oct. 7, '20.
Adams, Darwin, chaplain, Aug. 24, 1830.
Adams, Mark S., cornet, Cavalry, Feb. 26, 1842.
Adams, William, capt. co. D, Rockland, July, 1862.
Allen, Samuel H., aid-de-camp, May 8, 1860.
Andrews, Thomas S., 3d lieut. co. B, Thomaston, July, 1862.
Austin, Aaron M., capt. co. A, Thomaston, July, 1862.
Ayer, Benjamin, 1st lieut. co. B, Thomaston, July, 1862.
Baker, Samuel, chaplain, Aug. 1, 1812.
Banks, William A., 2d lieut., Rockland, Light Infantry, Aug. 6, 1858.
Barrows, Alexander, capt. Riflemen, July 18, 1826.
Barrows, Otis, ensign co. A, Aug. 23, 1827.
Bartlett, Benjamin, capt. co. A, Aug. 21, 1841.
Bean, B. B., capt. co. B, Rockland, July, 1862.
Bean, C. N., 1st lieut. co. C, Rockland, July, 1862.
Bernard, Isaac, 2d lieut. Cavalry, 1801, capt., Oct. 12, '8, maj. Nov. 18 '20.
Berry, William E., lieut. E. Thomaston Artillery, March 12, 1842.
Berry, Jeremiah, ensign, June 18, 1814.
Berry, Hiram G., capt. Rockland Light Infantry, Aug. 1858, having previously risen to colonel.†
Berry, George W., 2d lieut. co. E, Rockland, July, 1862.
Berry, Joseph T., capt. co. F, Rockland, July, 1862.

---

* Elected, but, with others of the same date, probably not commissioned, in consequence of some change in the law.
† Of this and some other commissions, no date can be given in consequence of defects in the Adjutant's General's records.

Bickford, William K., 2d lieut. co. B, Thomaston, July, 1862.
Bird, John, jr., capt. co. G, Rockland, July, 1862.
Blackington, James W., quarter master, Aug. 24, 1813.
Blackington, Nathan, ensign, Oct. 4, 1808.
Blackington, Willard S., lieut. Cavalry. July 26, 1834.
Blackington, Erastus F., lieut. co. B, Light Infantry, Feb. 22, 1840.
Blood, Simeon, ensign, Aug. 21, 1841.
Boyles, Edward, lieut., May 12, 1838.
Brown, Isaac, (2d), ensign, Nov. 29, 1823.
Brown, Oliver, ensign, April 30, 1824.
Brown, John, lieut. Rifle Company, July 28, 1826.
Brown, William, lieut. co. A, July 17, 1830.
Brown, H. M., 1st lieut. co. D, Rockland, July, 1862.
Butler, Phinehas, ensign, July 17, 1797, lieut., June 30, 1799.
Caldwell, Richard D., lieut., June 29, 1839.
Carr, Moses S., lieut. Cavalry, July 26, 1834.
Carver, Lorenzo D., paymaster, Sept. 1856.
Case, John S., division inspector, May 8, 1860.
Chandler Lucius H., capt. Thomaston Guards, June 29, 1839.
Chapman, Ralph, ensign, August 19, 1812.
Cobb, Francis, lieut. E. Thomaston Artillery, March 22, 1841, capt. March 12, 1842.
Coffin Edmund, surgeon's mate, Sept. 23, 1830.
Cole, William, lieut. Light Infantry, Dec. 19, '21, capt. Jan. 25, '23.
Coombs, Joseph, 2d lieut. August 14, 1785.
Coombs, Archibald G., capt. April 22, 1811, major, June 30, 1814.
Coombs, George, lieut. Ap. 22, 1811, capt. Sept, 1, '14, col., June 10, '17.
Coombs, Asa, ensign, Sept. 13, 1819, lieut., July 15, '22.
Coombs, George W., ensign, Dec. 30, 1831.
Counce, Rufus H., 1st lieut. co. A, Thomaston, July, 1862.
Crawford, Oliver, capt. Rifle Company, Dec. 31, 1831.
Crawford, William E., 4th lieut. co. A, Thomaston, July, 1862.
Crockett, Asa, lieut., Sept. 1, 1814.
Crockett, James, ensign, Riflemen, May 13, 1837.
Crockett, Jonathan, capt. East Thomaston Artillery, April 22, 1841.
Crockett, Charles, lieut. do. do. March 12, '42.
Crockett, C. S., capt. co. C, Rockland, July, 1862.
Cushing, Isaiah, lieut. Artillery, April 22, 1806.
Cushing, James O., ensign, Thomaston Guards, Feb. 22, 1820.
Davis, C. M., 4th lieut. co. B, Rockland, July, 1862.
Dean, Jonas, ensign, Mar. 6, 1799, lieut. Jan. 4, '01, capt. Mar. 7, '05.
Dean, Benjamin S., lieut. Sept. 22, 1818, capt. July 15, '22, col. Feb. 26, 1830.
Dean, Alanson, ensign, Rifle Company, July 28, 1826.
Dodge, Josiah W., 1st lieut. Artillery, May 15, 1824, capt. May 18, '25.
Dow, James, capt., March 28, 1835.
Durand, Jackson, ensign, May 6, 1806.
Dwight Sullivan, lieut. July 24, 1813, capt. Light Infantry, July 30, '17, major, August 16, '21, lieut. col. Feb. 9, '24.
Elwell, James H.. 1st lieut. co. B, Rockland, July, 1862.
Erskine, A. I., 1st lieut. Rockland Riflemen, Sept. 18, 1855.
Fales, Nathaniel, captain of Coast Guards, 1777.
Fales, David, jr., captain, May 15, 1797.
Fales, David S., adjutant Artillery, June 1, 1810.
Fales, Eusebius, lieut. Light Infantry, July 30, 1817, capt. Dec. 19, '21, later, major or aid-de-camp.

Fales, George W., lieut. Sept. 12, 1827.
Fales, Oliver, jr., lieut. co. B, Artillery, Mar. 31, 1829, capt May 31, '29.
Fales, Samuel H., ensign, May 7, 1836, lieut., June 27, '39.
Fales Philip A., capt. first co. Light Infantry, Dec. 31, 1831.
Fales, Lewis T., ensign first co. Light Infantry, Sept. 28, 1833.
Fales, George D., ensign co. B, Light Infantry, Aug. 3, 1836, capt. Sept. 25, '40.
Fales, Willard, jr., lieut. co. B, Artillery, Aug. 12, 1836.
Farnham, J. G., 3d lieut. co. B, Rockland, July, 1862.
Flint, Henry, 3d lieut. co. F, do. do. do.
Fuller, Sylvester H., division inspector, March 31, 1840.
Gay, David, cornet, Cavalry, Feb. 4, 1801, lieut. Oct. 5, '04,
Gay, Alden, do. do. July 11, 1835.
Gay, Ephraim, 3d lieut. co. C, Rockland, July, 1862.
Gloyd, George W., captain, August 26, 1830.
Graves, John, ensign, April 9, 1836.
Green, Ballard, capt. Thomaston Guards, August 22, 1825.
Green, Leonard, 3d lieut. co. A, Rockland, July, 1862.
Gregory, William, capt. Cavalry, 1800.
Gregory, John, ensign, Cavalry, 1801, capt., April 11, '03.
Hall, Eli P., 4th lieut. co. F, Rockland, July, 1862.
Hall, T. G., 4th lieut. co. E, do. do. do.
Hanson, Philip, first lieut. Cavalry, Jan. 19, 1801.
Harden, Freeman, cornet, Cavalry, 1815, lieut. March 20, '24.
Harden, Freeman, jr., lieut. Rifle Company, July 30, 1830, captain, May 18, '39.
Haskell, John, lieut. Artillery, Feb. 22, 1809, captain, August 23, '13, major, '17, col., Nov. 16, '18.
Hatch, George D., ensign, June 29, 1839.
Havener, R. H., first lieut. co. A, Rockland, July, 1862.
Healey, Halsey, adjutant, Sept. 1, 1818, Artillery, capt. June 11, '21. major, Feb. 18, '25, Lt. col., April 24, '26.
Henrahan, Cornelius, 4th lieut. co. G, Rockland, July, 1862.
Hewett, Samuel, cornet, Cavalry, June 30, 1828, capt., Mar. 20, '24.
Hewett, A. E., 2d lieut. co. B, Rockland, July, 1862.
Hinkley, Edmund B.. capt. co. B, Thomaston, July, 1862.
Hodgman, Isaac, ensign, co. B, Light Infantry, Sept. 25, 1840.
Hunt, A. G., 4th lieut. co. C, Rockland, July, 1862.
Ingraham, John H., chaplain, Nov. 25, 1820, Feb. 26, '30.
Ingraham, Henry, lieut. Cavalry, Oct. 17, 1828.
Ingraham John N., 2d lieut. co. F, Rockland, July, 1862.
Ingraham, Job P., first lieut. co. A, South Thomaston, July, 1862.
Jameson, Robert, first lieut., August 4, 1785.
Jones, Nathaniel, second lieut. co. D, Rockland, July, 1862.
Keen, Rufus, capt., July 16, 1830.
Kelloch, James, ensign Rifle Company. June 29, 1839.
Kellogg, David, surgeon, Dec. 18, 1820.
Killsa, Wm., ensign Light Infantry, June 22, 1822, lieut. July 26, '23.
Killsa, Wm. C., ensign, August 26, 1830, lieut. Dec. 31, '31, capt. March 20, '33.
Kimball, Iddo K., capt. Rifle Company, August 31, 1833, first lieut. Rockland Light Infantry, August 6, '58.
Kimball, George W., jr., aid-de-camp, May 8, 1860.
Levensaler, Barden, ensign, June 26, 1823, lieut. Light Infantry, Aug. 28, '23, capt. Sept. 12, '27.

Litchfield, Alden, third lieut. Rockland Riflemen, May 5, 1856.
Lovejoy, Enoch, surgeon's mate, Aug. 1, 1812, surgeon, Sept. 22, '17.
Lovejoy, Edwin P., capt. Cavalry, July 27, 1855.
Lovejoy, Arthur, capt. co. A, June 29, 1839.
Lovejoy, Edward L., aid-de-camp, Sept. 1, 1843.
Lovejoy, C. C., 2d lieut. co. G, Rockland, July, 1862.
Lowell, Simeon B., lieut., July 11, 1830.
Ludwig, Moses R., surgeon, August 25, 1825.
McIntosh, Wm. H., cornet, Cavalry, June 20, 1840, lieut., Feb. 26, '42.
McKellar, Archibald, jr., lieut. col., August 15, 1839.
McLellan, George, quarter master, Dec. 6, 1824.
McLoon, William, ensign, Sept. 6, 1805.
McLoon, William, (2d), ensign, June 23, 1829.
McLoon, Enos C., second lieut. co. A, South Thomaston, July, 1862.
Madagan, James C., aid-de-camp, Sept. 4, 1843.
Mathews, John, lieut., 1775 or earlier.
Merrill, Eli, adjutant, Artillery, Sept. 21, 1821.
Miller, Leander, lieut. Thomaston Guards, Feb. 22, 1820.
Miller, Charles A., judge advocate, May 8, 1860, Governor's aid, '62.
Moody, Edwin, ensign, Light Infantry, June 3, 1828.
Mosman, William., ensign, May 5, 1823, lieut., April 20, '24, capt., August 10, '26.
Nanson, George G., third lieut. co. A, Thomaston, July, 1862.
Newcomb, Charles, ensign, June 11, 1836.
O'Brien, John, lieut. Thomaston Guards, August 22, 1825.
O'Brien, E. K., second lieut. co. A, Thomaston, July, 1862.
Osgood, T. K., capt. co. E, Rockland, July, 1862.
Perry, Joseph, ensign, July 4, 1799, lieut., Sept. 6, 1805.
Perry, David, ensign, July 15, 1822.
Perry, Samuel P., capt. Rockland Riflemen, August 1, 1857.
Perry, G. K., second lieut. Rockland Riflemen, Sept. 18, 1855.
Perry, A. W., third lieut. co. E, Rockland, July, 1862.
Pope, William, ensign, Light Infantry, Dec. 19, 1821.
Porterfield, Robert, adjutant, August 4, 1785.
Ramsey, John, ensign of first Light Infantry, Aug. 2, 1834.
Read, Alvin A., fourth lieut. co. B, Thomaston, July, 1862.
Richardson, J. R., first lieut. co. E, Rockland, do. do.
Rider, John B., lieut. Artillery, Aug 23, 1813, capt., Oct. 13, '17.
Robbins, Otis, capt., Aug. 4, 1785, major, '98, resigned, Oct. 26, 1803.
Robbins, Otis, jr., lieut. April 22, 1811, first lieut. U. S. Infantry, July 11, '14, capt. militia June 7, '17.
Robbins, Arunah, lieut. Cavalry, Aug. 30, '27, capt., Oct. 17, '28.
Robbins, Isaac C., quarter master, Cavalry, March 7, '27.
Robinson, John W., surgeon, Sept., '56.
Rollins, Alfred, ensign, Dec. 31, '31, lieut., March 20, '33.
Rose, Daniel, jr,, ensign Thomaston Guards, March 29, '33.
Ruggles, John, aid-de-camp, Jan. 25, '27.
Russell, George W., capt. co. A, August 21, '41.
Sargent, William G., adjutant, Sept. '56.
Sawyer, David A., ensign, June 27, '39, lieut., Aug. 21, '41.
Sayward, William T., lieut. East Thomaston Artillery, April 22, '41.
Sayward, Albert, first lieut. co. F, Rockland, July, '62.
Shaw, Benjamin, jr., quarter master, August 24, '30.
Sherer, Josiah T., second lieut. co. A, Rockland, July, '62.
Simonton, T. E.. second lieut. co. C, Rockland, do. do.

Smith, Leonard, second lieut. Coast Guards, '12.
Smith, Richard, ensign, Sept. 22, '18, lieut., Oct. 7, '20.
Smith, Leonard, jr., lieut., April 8, '37, capt., June 27, '39.
Snelling, Charles G., capt. co. A, South Thomaston, July, '62.
Snow, Ephraim, capt., Dec. 1, 1798.
Snow, Rufus, capt. co. E, South Thomaston, March 6, 1841.
Spalding, Joseph A., lieut. co. A., May 28, '36.
Spear, John, ensign, June 30, 1799, lieut., May 6, '06, capt., April 22, '11, major, April 30, '12, capt. Coast Guards, '12, capt. again in militia, August 26, '17.
Spear, Jonathan, (2d), cornet, Cavalry, Feb. 12, '08.
Spear, Jonathan, (3d), lieut. Rifle Company, May 18, '39.
Spear, Elkanah, quarter master, August 1, '12.
Spofford, Charles, adjutant, Feb. 23, '13.
Spofford, William, ensign, co. A, July 17, '30.
Sprague, Joseph, paymaster, July 30, '22.
Stabler, Dean, fourth lieut. Rockland Riflemen, May 5, '56.
Starr, George A., lieut. Light Infantry, May 11, '33, capt., Aug. 2, '34. col., August 15, '39.
Stevens, George W. ensign, Oct. 7, '20, lieut., May 6, '22, capt., April 20, '24.
Stevens, William K., ensign Light Infantry, August 28, '23.
Stevens, Hermon, division advocate, July 11, '43.
Stover, Andrew W., fourth lieut. co. A, South Thomaston, July, '62.
Thatcher, Ebenezer, capt. Artillery, '06, maj., July 17, '09, lieut. col. commandant, August 16, '14, colonel, brevet, June 20, '16.
Thomas, Joel, fourth lieut. co. A, Rockland, July, '62.
Tillson, William F., lieut., August 10, '26.
Tillson, Edward C., lieut., August 26, '30, capt., March 30, '38.
Tillson, Charles S., lieut. co. B, Light Infantry, August 2, '34, capt., Oct. 8, '36.
Tillson, Perez, jr., ensign, March 30, '33, capt., May 7, '36.
Tillson, Davis, adjutant, Jan. 8, '59, adjutant general, '60.
Titcomb, William H., major general, March 23, '60.
Tolman, David, lieut. Cavalry, May 2, '15.
Tolman, Thomas, ensign Coast Guards, '12.
Tolman, Calvin, cornet, Cavalry, May 10, '17, lieut. June 30, '21.
Tolman, Elliott, quarter master, Cavalry, June 9, '21.
Tolman, David, cornet, Cavalry, July 24, '13.
Tolman, Calvin, jr , ensign, July 30, '30.
Tolman, Orrin P., fourth lieut. Rockland Light Infantry, Aug. 6, '58.
Tolman, Walter, do. do. co. D, Rockland, July, '62.
Tolman, O P., first lieut. co. G, do. do. do.
Ulmer, Philip, lieut. Cavalry, July 24, '13, capt., May 10, '15, major, Sept. 6, '23.
Ulmer, James, capt. Cavalry, Nov. 14, '32.
Ulmer, Enos C., lieut. Cavalry, June 20, '40.
Ulmer, William S., capt. co. A, April 26, '34, major, August 15, '39, brig. gen., July 13, 1843.
Ulmer, Charles, adjutant, Cavalry, April 2, '27.
Ulmer, Jacob, jr., lieut. Cavalry, June 21, '23, capt., August 30, '27.
Vose, Thomas P., ensign, Light Infantry, Nov. 27, '20.
Vose, Jas., ensign, Thomaston Guards, Aug. 22, '25, lieut., Mar. 29, '33.
Watson, David, jr., cornet, Cavalry, March 20, '24.
Wheaton, Mason, major, 1770, col., about '76.

Wight, John M., lieut., July 17, 1797.
Wilkinson, Samuel S., paymaster, Artillery, Sept. 11, '15.
Williams, Timothy, ensign, co. B, Light Infantry, Aug. 29, '35, lieut., Aug. 8, '36, promoted, Feb. 29, '40, to lieut. col. or col.
Williams, Fred. O., third lieut. co. A, South Thomaston, July, '62.
Wilson, William, quarter master, Sept. '56.
Witham, F. P., third lieut. co. G, Rockland, '62.
Wortman, E. E., third lieut. co. D, Rockland, July, '62.

Several of the above have since been further advanced in the volunteer service of the United States.

TABLE XVI.

VOTES GIVEN FOR PRESIDENTIAL ELECTORS AFTER THE SEPARATION OF MAINE, SO FAR AS APPEARS BY THE RECORDS OF

THOMASTON.

Year	Candidate	Votes
1828.	Andrew Jackson, el.	144
	John Q. Adams,	99
1832.	Andrew Jackson, el.	495
	Henry Clay,	171
1836.	M. Van Buren, el.	320
	Henry Clay,	93
1840.	Martin Van Buren,	627
	W. H. Harrison, el.	436
1844.	James K. Polk, el.	808
	Henry Clay,	286
1848.	Lewis Cass,	248
1848.	Zachary Taylor, el.	153
	Martin Van Buren,	2
1852.	Winfield Scott,	131
	Franklin Pierce, el.	259
1856.	John C. Fremont,	293
	Jas. Buchanan, el.	287
	Millard Fillmore,	19
1860.	Abraham Lincoln, el.	200
	Stephen A. Douglas,	163
	J. C. Breckinridge,	34
	John Bell,	17

ROCKLAND.

Year	Candidate	Votes
1848.	Lewis Cass,	470
	Zachary Taylor,	275
	Martin Van Buren,	8
1852.	Winfield Scott,	374
	Franklin Pierce,	603
	John P. Hale,	44
1856.	John C. Fremont,	788
1856.	James Buchanan,	382
	Millard Fillmore,	45
1860.	Abraham Lincoln,	619
	Stephen A. Douglas,	302
	J. C. Breckinridge,	53
	John Bell,	12

SOUTH THOMASTON.

Year	Candidate	Votes
1848.	Lewis Cass,	119
	Zachary Taylor,	61
	Martin Van Buren,	4
1852.	Winfield Scott,	81
	Franklin Pierce,	112
	John P. Hale,	8
1856.	John C. Frement,	170
	James Buchanan,	131
1860.	Abraham Lincoln,	136
	Stephen A. Douglas,	80
	J. C. Breckinridge,	10
	John Bell,	1

GENEALOGICAL TABLE

OF THE INHABITANTS OF THOMASTON, ROCKLAND, AND SOUTH THOMASTON, DOWN TO 1860, ALPHABETICALLY ARRANGED AND COMPILED FROM TOWN RECORDS, MONUMENTAL INSCRIPTIONS, NEWSPAPER NOTICES, AND OTHER SOURCES.

FROM the great deficiency of records of births and deaths in the three municipalities, and the want of personal acquaintance with families, many errors and omissions will doubtless be detected. Those births, given without specifying the day and month are merely approximations from census returns,&c. — EXPLANATIONS : — b. *born ;* ch. *child* or *children ;* m. *married ;* p. *published ;* d. *died ;* a. *aged* ; r. *resides, resided, resident of ;* rem. *removed to ;* ret. *returned to ;* c. *came ;* grad. *graduated at ;* ab. *about ;* dau. *daughter ;* U. *Union ;* Wal. *Waldoborough ;* W. *Warren ;* Cam. *Camden ;* Th. *Thomaston ;* S. Th. *South Thomaston ;* R. or Rock. *Rockland ;* C. *Cushing ;* St. G. *St. George ;* Linc. *Lincolnville ;* Dam. *Damariscotta ;* and their initial capitals for the months, except January, April, May and July. Doubt is denoted by an interrogation point.

ABBOT, Benjamin, m. Phebe, dau. of Hon. Jacob Abbot, of Wilton, N. H., & rem. 1803 to Temple, Me. Of their sons, there c. to Th., 1, John S., Esq., b. Jan. 6, 1807, grad. Bowd. Coll. 1827, att'ny at law in U. '31, Th. '33 ; m. Elizabeth T. Allen, p. S. 12, '35, rem. Norridgewock, '41. 2, George, Esq., b. Feb. 22, 1813 ; m. Melinda, or Melina Alden of U., May 25, '37 ; practised law & r. Main st., Th., where he d. A. 18, '50. 3, Ezra, admitted to the bar when in Th., 1842 ; practised law in Richmond, Me.

George, Esqr's, ch. 1, Lucy Ellen, b. J. 3, 1839 ; r. Th. 2 Capt. George Roscoe, b. Jan. 26, '42 ; a clerk in 1860 ; vol. in U. S. A. since.

ABBOTT ; of this Belfast family, two brothers c. to this place. 1, Capt. Isaac C., b. ab. 1817 ; m Harriet W. Pressey of Deer Isle, Jan. 7, '41 ; r. R., a joiner ; Quarter Master of Maine 4th Reg., promoted, '63. to Brigade Quarter Master. 2, William F., b. ab. 1822 ; m. Mary A. Sanborn of Knox, 2d, Frances A. Pendleton of Northport ; r. R., where he d. Oct. 23, '64.

Capt. Isaac C.'s ch. 1, Mary K., b. Jan. 24, 1843, d. Feb. 6, '46. 2. George L., b. ab. '46. The mother d. O. 2, '63, a 39.

William F.'s ch. 1, Mary E., b. ab. '49. 2, George W., b. ab. '52.

ABBOTT, Joseph, b. ab. 1830 ; c. from Albion ; r. R. ; a merchant, firm of Bowler & Abbott ; m. Emily Spear of W., J. 8, '57. Their ch. William Osgood, b. ab. '58.

ABBOTT, George, b. ab. 1833 ; m. Emeline Thompson, N. 27, '52 ; r. R. ; a lime burner. Their ch. 1, Ada A., b. ab. '57. 2, Harriet A., b. ab. '59.

ACHORN, (or Eichhorn, as originally spelled,) Jacob, (whose father, Jacob, and mother, Jane, c. from Germany to Broad Bay, now Wal., in 1753,) was b. M. 14, 1761 ; m. Margaret Ulmer ; c. from Wal. with wife and 5 chil. to what is now R., in 1796 ; & d. S. 19, 1836. Their ch. 1, Polly, b. J. 3, 1785 ; m. Josiah Tolman ; r. R. 2, Margaret, b. O. 6, '87 ; d. S. 25, 1800. 3, John, b. M. 14, '91 ; m. Betsey Porter of Cam., O. 21, 1813; r. & d. Cam. 4, Philip, b. S. 29, '93; m. Bethia French, M. 9, '15; r. R., & d. A. 11, '47. 5, Michael, b. in Wal., (as were the four preceding,) M. 16, '96; m. Celinda Gregory of Cam., May 29, '22; r. R. & d. M. 20, '49. 6, Jacob, (2d), b. here May 20, '98; m. Mary Brown of Cam.; p. May 15, '19; r. Cam. 7, Isaac, b. N. 30, 1800; m. Olive Currier, May 21, '22; r. & d. R. 8, Lucretia, b. May 23, '03; m. Benjamin Porter, M. 24, '25, 2d, Rev. Joseph L. Cilley, Ap. 12, '58; r. Cam. 9, Capt Josiah, b. May 6, '06; m. Orissa W. Tolman, Ap. 12, '32, 2d, Mrs. Elmira, (Tolman) Hillman; r. R. 10, Catharine, b. J. 18, '09; m. Oliver Holmes; r. R.

Of John's ch., Albion G. was at one time in R.; m. Lucy G. Partridge, F. 3, '46; rem. Cal.

Philip's ch. 1, Almira, b. S. 21, '15; m. Chas. W. Smith; and d. D. 4, '35. 2, Margaret, b. N. 19, '18; m. Jas. Turner, N. 2, '43; r. R. 3, Philip, (2d), b. D. 1, '22; m. Mary A. Richards, N. 27, '52; r. R., &c. 4, Cyrena, b. Ju. 15, '26; m. Wm. Wallace Gorden; r. R. 5, Mary F., b. S. 10, '33; m. Henry Brown; r. R. The mother d. M. 10, '44, a. 49.

Michael's ch. 1, Lucinda, b. Jan. 16, '23; m. Capt. Samuel Duncan; r. N. Y. 2, Frances B., b. F. 14, '25; m. Isaac Orbeton; r. R. 3, Mary G., b. F. 13, '27; d. by suicide, S. 2, '42. 4. Melinda, b. Jan. 13, '29; m. Wm. Thorndike; r. R. and d. Ap. 27, '48. 5, Catharine H., b. May 8, '31; m. Dr. A. D. Nichols; r. R. 6, Clara B., b. May 9, '33; m. John Collins, a music teacher, O. 11, '51; rem. N. Y. 7, Margaret E., b. S. 6, '35; m. Gen. Davis Tillson; r. R. 8, Almira A., b. May 24, '37; m. Geo. W. Kimball, (2d); r. R. 9, John E., b. Ju. 7, '39; r. R.; m. Adelaide E. Crockett, N. 24, '61; a mariner. 10, Lucretia P., b. N. 12, '41. 11, Michael J., b. ab. '45.

Isaac's ch. 1, Lucy, b. J. 21, 1822; m. Capt. Robert Crockett; r. R. 2. Lucretia, b. A. 13, '24; m. Mark S. Adams; r. R., & d. A. 20, '64. 3, Lavinia, b. A. 20, '26; d. N. 19, '30. 4, Franklin, b. S. 9, '29; m. Abby Grant, Oct. 23, '48; r. R.; a mariner, soldier in the 4th Me. reg., killed in Va., A. 29, '62. 5, Sophronia, b. O. 16, '31; m. Elliot T. Harrington, 2d, Chas. L. Allen; r. R. 6, Olive, b. A. 19, '33; m. Capt. George Gregory; r. R. 7, Isaac, (2d), b. & d. Ap. 1, '37. 8. Margie A., b. D. 18, '41. 9. Girard, b. ab. '44.

Capt. Josiah's ch. by 1st wife. 1, Caroline E., b. A. 28, '32; m. Capt. Elijah Crockett,; r. R., & d. O. 13, '61. 2, Michael A. b. J. 16, '34; m. Mary L. Ulmer, S. 18, '56; r. R., a merchant. 3, Josiah G., b. Apr. 14, & d. S. 28, '36. 4, Capt. William W., b. F. 25, '38; m. Jennie C. Crockett, D. 7, '61; r. R., appt. master's mate U. S. N. Feb. '62. 5, Melinda F., b. D. 28, '39; m. —— Brown of Wal.; r. Boston. 6, Margie D., b. D. 24, '41; m. Lieut. Kendall K. Rankin; r. R. 7, Josiah, (2d), b. ab. '44. 8, Isaac Alfred, b. ab. '50.

Philip, (2d,)'s ch. 1, Charles E., b. ab. 1854. 2, Mary F., b. ab. '56. 3, Thomas J., b. ab. '58. 4, Sarah Bethia.

Michael A.'s ch. 1, Nellie E., b. ab. 1858. 2, Charles A., b. Ap. 11, '60; d. May 2, '61.

ADAMS, Dea., or Esq., Joshua, b. ab. 1769; m. Miss Gray; c. from Cape Cod or Scituate, to Linc., thence to S. Th., Owl's Head; long a blacksmith, ship builder and merchant; d. O. 12, 1829. Their ch. 1, Nancy, b. F. 10, 1792; m. Joshua Fuller; r. Th., & d. Ap. 28, 1858. 2, Saba, b. J. 15, '95, probably d. young. 3, Mary, b. O. 15, '98; m. Samuel P. Ingraham, a merchant of Hallowell, Jan. 15, '25. 4, Lydia, b. Ap. 13, '01; m. Capt. Thos. McLellan; r. Th., & d. Jan.

29, '30. 5, Capt. Samuel Gray, b. S. 28, '03; m. Adeline Cushing of Cam., June 28, '27; rem. Cam., where he has been a representative, a successful business man, &c.; has 10 ch. 6, Capt. Joshua C., b. May 9, '06; m. Nancy Whitney of Castine, Jan. 19, '26, 2d, Mary Oakes, of U., M. 6, '55; r. Owl's Head, &c., and d. Jan. 26, '58.

Joshua C.'s ch. 1, Henry W., b. May 6, 1826. 2, Lucy Ann, b. A, 22, '27; m. Capt. Moses Gay, O. 18, '49; r. Castine. 3, Lydia McLellan, b. May 12, '30; m. Henry Pillsbury; r. S. Th. 4, Charles W., b. F. 19, '36; m. & r. N. Y. 5, Susan Frances, b. M. 23, '37; m. Henry E. Tolman; r. S. Th. 6, Phebe P., b. D 6, '39; m. Capt. Oliver B. Pillsbury; r. S. Th. 7, Clara, b. O. 9, '40. 8, Samuel, b. N. 19, '41. 9, John W., b. M. 1, '43. 10, Julia Helen, b. ab. '45. The mother d. D. 15, '51, a. 43.

ADAMS, Capt. Joseph, b. ab. 1782, of Irish or Scotch Irish descent; c. from N. H. in 1803 or '4; m. Nancy Hyler of C.; r. R., & d. J. 22, '37. Their ch. 1, Thomas, b. A. 9, 1807; m. Sabra Walton, Ap. 5, '34, 2d, Mary Jackson, Ap. 18, '52; r. R., a quarry man. 2, Hannah, b. O. 6, '09; m. Bernard Ulmer; r. R. 3, Luranah, b. A. 7, '12; m. James Boston, Jan. 17, '30; r. Biddeford. 4, Mark S., b. M. 31, '15; m. Lucretia Achorn, A. 30, '40; r. R., a lime manufacturer. 5, Sophia, b. D. 5, '18; m. Samuel L. Ingraham, Ju. 1, '39; r. R. 6, John H. b. ab. '24; m. Mary Hooper of St. G. F. 1, '52; r. R., a quarry man.

Thomas' ch. 1, Jacob H., b. A. 28, 1836; r. R., a mariner. 2, Lorana B., b. May 28, 1838. 3, Arletta A., b. Jan. 21, '40. 4, Delphina A., b. Ju. 18, '42; m. Geo. E. Hewett: r. R. 5, Elizabeth, b. ab. '46. 6, Bartlett, b. ab. '53.

Mark S.'s ch. 1, Issac A. b. F. 19, 1842; r. R., a mariner. 2, Samuel I., b. ab. '44, a mariner. 3, Lucy Helen, b. ab. '46.

John H.'s ch. 1, Simeon H., b. ab. 1854. The mother died Jan. 8, '60, aged 28.

ADAMS, William, b. O. 30, 1800; c. from Edgecomb? m. Sarah A. Fuller, 2d, Mary Emerson, N. 23, '31: r. Th. Beech Woods, a joiner. His ch. by 1st wife. 1, Eliza J., b. Ap. 11, '26; m. Anthony Perkins, Jan. 20, '48; r. San Francisco. 2, Olive F., b. O. 23, '17; m. Samuel H. Waterman; r. Th., & d. F. 26, '57. 3, William J., b. A. 11, '29; m. Cassandra (Hills) McIntyre, Jan. 15, '57; rem. San. Francisco. The mother d. May 16, '30, a. 24. By 2d wife. 4, Sarah E., b. N. 11, '32; Sarah C. Adams, m. Alexander Spear, (2d); r. Th. 5, Mary R., b. M. 5, & d. S. 26, '34. 6, John E., b. M. 10, '35. 7, Mary, b. Jan. 26, '37. 8, Rebecca E., b. May 5, '39; r. Th. 9, Laura. b. O. 13, '41; m. Nathan W. Fuller, D. 30, '63; r. Th. 10, Emma E., b. Ju. 15, '44. 11, Daniel, b. ab. '46. 12, Lewis B., b. Jan. 3, '48; d. S. 1, '58.

ADAMS, Capt. Daniel H., b. ab. 1834; c. from Unity; m. Mary E. Young, A. 27, '56; r. Th., a carpenter; soldier of the 4th Me. reg., rose rapidly, but d. Ap. 30, '63.

ADAMS, William, b. ab. 1822, in Union; m. Elizabeth H. Lermond of W.; r. R., a carriage manufacturer. Their ch. Cora M., b. ab. '55.

ADAMS, Capt. James, b. M. 2, 1819; c. from Lincoln; m. Mary Ann Dunton, N. 17, '44, 2d, Sarah (Gilman) Andrews, Jan. 4, '61; r. R. His ch. by 1st wife. 1, John Q. A., b. D. 22, 1845; r. R. 2, Israel B., b. Ap. 7, '47; d. Ju. 10, '48. 3 & 4, twins, b. Jan. 25, '49,

Adelia Ellen, d. Ap. 30, '59, Arinda Alice, r. R. 5, James Orson, b. May 11, '51, d. S. 5, '52. The mother b. S. 23, '24; d. Jan. 6, '60.

ALBEE, Rev. Samuel, b. S. 10, 1794, in Wiscasset; c. to Th. May 14, 1820; m. 1st, ——— ———, 2d, Jane R. Fales, A. 27, '22; r. Th., W., Monhegan, Starks, and now R.; a joiner, merchant, local preacher of the Meth. E. Church, &c. Mrs. Albee grad. N. E. Female Med. Coll., Boston, and is now in successful practice in R. His ch. by 1st wife. 1, Sophia; m. John Thompson; r. Salmon Falls, N. H. 2, William Harrison, b. 1815; d. O. 13, '31. By 2d wife. 3, Samuel, (2d), b. A. 1, '23; m Emily McKellar, Ap. 7, '47; r. R., a carpenter, &c. 4, Nancy Jane, b. S. 9, '25; m. Capt. Luke Andrews; r. R. 5, Alice V., b. Jan. 29, '28; m. Capt. Thomas F. Thurston; r. Wiscasset. 6, Capt. Parker Bishop, b. N. 16, '29; m. Rhoda G. Andrews of Boothbay, Jan. '52; r. Monhegan. 7, Nathaniel F., b. O. 12, '33; r. R., a joiner, &c. 8, Seth V., b. J. 22, '38; r. R., a photographist. 9, Martha Paulina, b. Ap. 6, '41; m. Ephraim A. Jordan of Belmont, May 19, '58, & d. Jan. 3, '59.

Samuel, (2d's), ch. 1, Mary Eliza, b. in Th., S. 23, 1848; d. A. 28, '49. 2. Everett S., b. Ju. 5, '53.

Capt. Parker B's ch. 1, Frank S., b. in R., F. 12, 1853. 2, Herbert W., b. R., M. 22, '55; d. Ju. 1, '60. 3, Jane A., b. O. 1, '57. 4, Samuel A., b. ab. '59. 5, Orilla A., b. ab. '60.

ALDEN, Ebenezer, b. at Middleborough, Mass., S 20, 1774, settled in Union, 1795; m. Patience Gilmore of Franklin, Mass., M. 4, 1799, & d. July 10, '62. Their ch. 1, Hon. Horatio, b. F. 4, 1800; m., 1st, Polly G. Bachelor, 2d, Sally Bachelor, p. D. 14, 1835, sisters, of Readfield; r. Th. or R.; rem. Cam.; first Judge of Probate for Knox Co. 2, Louisa, b. Jan. 30, '02; m. Phineas Tyler, '23; r. Th. & d. S. 29, '27. 3, Silas, b. J. 23, '04; m. Sarah Lindley; r. Bangor. 4, Selina, b. D. 26, '06; d. N. 15, '07. 5, Lyman, b. D. 1, '08; m. Sarah E. Williams of Orono; r. S. Union. 6, Melina, b. J. 16, '11; m. George Abbott, Esq.; r. Th. 7, Augustus, b. Ju. 3, '14; m. Margaret W. Williams; r. U. 8, Ebenezer, (2d), b. D. 14, '16; m. Caroline Snow, J. 29, '45; r. R.; a joiner. 9, James G., b. M. 1, '19; m. Alvitia C. Miller of Bangor; r. Janesville, Wis. 10, Dr. Edward, b. D. 13 or 21, '21. 11, Henry, b. A. 5, '24; d. A. 16, '47. 12, George A., b. July 29, '28; died May 9, '29.

Horatio's ch. by 1st wife. 1, John M., m. Sabra R. Ulmer, A. 17, 45; r. R., rem. and d. Cal. 2, Arrevesta C., b. Ju. 4, 1829; 3, Nathaniel A. b. S. 2, '30; 4, Horatio E., b. D. 11, '34; all probably rem. The mother d. F. 7, '35. By 2d wife. 5, Benjamin H., b. F. 24, '38; 6, William G., b. July 17, '40; all probably rem. to Cam. 7, Henry L., born Nov. 20, 41; died June 16, '42.

Ebenezer, (2d's), ch. 1, Francis Marion, b. May 23, '48, d. Aug. 26, '51. 2, Alex. S., b. June, 1850, d. Aug. 4, '51. 3, Willie P., b. July '52, d. S. 28, '53. 4, Adaline, b. ab. '54. 5, Fannie, b. ab. '57.

John M.'s ch. 1, Emma, b. ab. '46. 2, Frank D., b. ab. '48.

ALDREAD, James, with Ellaes his wife, r. in old Th. and had ch. recorded here. 1, James A., b. Sept. 18, 1840, d. April 16, '41. 2, Mary A. E., born July 29, '42.

ALLEN, Charles Leeds, b. 1824; c. from Matinicus Isl. where he m. 1st, Martha W. Beverage, Dec. 29, '45; 2d, Sophronia (Achorn) Harrington, Oct. 8, '55, r. R. a sailmaker. His ch. by 1st wife. 1, Clara Frances, b. ab. '47. 2, Martha Delia, b. Sept. 1849,

ALLEN; of this family, two brothers came from Buckfield to this place about 1819; viz.: 1, Joshua G., b. ab. 1791; m. Mary Gloyd, July 14, '22; r. Meadows, Th. a farmer. 2, Samuel, m. Mrs. Elizabeth Kelleran of C., Sept. 29, '25; r. Th. at Meadows, rem. Mill R. Of their brothers, 3, Jacob, r. in Buckfield, whose son, Samuel Fessenden, b. ab. 1818, c. hither; m. Larissa J. Kelleran; r. R., a lime manufacturer, rem. Th. 3, Stephen, r. Poland, whose son, Joseph F. c. to R., m. Marietta Tolman, S. 14, '45; rem. Cal. and d. at Sacramento, N 3, 1850.

Joshua G.'s ch. 1, Joshua, b. June 6, 1823; m. Mary A. Vinal of Cam. p. Oct. 12, '47; r. Th. a farmer. 2, Mary, b. Ap. 25, '25; m. Jos. Battles; r. R. 3, Edward, b. D. 4, '27; d. D. 14, 34, drowned by falling through ice in a pond; 4, Marcia, b. M. 20, '29; m. Charles Morse; r. Th. 5, Augusta W., b. O. 13, '30, d N. 9, '48. 6, Orrin, b. O. 6, '32; m. Lydia Moore, O. 19, '58; r. Th. 7, Edwin, b. Ap. 14, '34; rem. Cal. 8, George H., b. Ap. 13, '37; m. Lydia J. Prescott, J. 19, '55; r. homestead. 9, Jane, b. F. 9, '39; m. James Ballcom, O. 25, '56; and d. Jan. 4, '58. 10, Henry D., b, J. 9, '41. 11, Richard W., b. ab. 1845.

Samuel's ch. 1, Col. Samuel H., b. O. 17, '26; m. Adelia Ingraham, Jan. 8, '59; r. Th., deputy collector, 1861; officer in 1st Maine cavalry, resigned Jan. 5, '63, since visited Cal. 2, Ellen K., b. S, 15, '28; m. Capt. Bart. R. Robinson; r. Th. 3, Lucy V., b. Jan. 12, '31, d. Ju. 18, '54. 4, Sarah, r. Th.

S. Fessenden's ch. 1, Clarissa S., b. May 23, 1842. 2, Frank F., b. ab. '44. 3, Larissa K., b. ab. '52. 4, Artemas W., b. ab. '54.

Joshua (2d)'s ch. 1, C. Henry, d. Jan. 11, 1852. 2. Frederic, d .D 28, ' 51. 3, Samuel V., b. ab. 1849. 4, Mary E., b. ab. 1851.

Col. Samuel H.'s ch. Lucy A.; b. ab. 1859.

ALLEN, Andrew R., c. from St. George; m. Hannah T. Clark, J. 17, '35; & had recorded here, ch. 1, David C., b. Jan. 31, 1836. 2, Lorinda, b. May 13, '37. 3, Joshua C., b. Jan. 8, 39, d. D. 14, '41. 4, James E., b. Jan. 14, '40, d. N. 28, '41. 5, Andrew W., b. F. 21, '41; m. Amelia C. Brown of N. Islesboro', p. M. 4, '64; r. S. Th.

ALLEN, Sumner, c. from Belfast? m. Sarah W. ——; r. R. Their ch. 1, Russell, b. N. 7, 1840 2, Benjamin K., b. M. 23, 42; r. R., lost overboard from sch. *Silas Wright*, Oct. 1864. 3, Eliza, b. ab. 1849. 4, Ephraim W., b. ab. 1853.

ALLEN, Capt. John P., b. ab. 1816, son of John of St. G., grandson of Gideon, and great grandson of John of Allen's Isl., who was somewhat celebrated in the Revolution; m. Elvira Norton; r. S. Th. Their ch. 1, Horace C., b. ab. 1843. 2, Josephine B., b. ab. '45; m. Chas M. Wiggin; r. S. Th. 3, Abel A., b. ab. '48. 4, Deborah M. b. ab. '50. 5, Joseph H., b. ab. '52. 6, John L., b. ab. '55.

ALEXANDER, Capt. Ezekiel K., b. ab. 1820, in North Haven; m. 1st, Lucy W. Sampson of North Haven, (who d. D. 11, '56, a. 35,) 2d, Anna D. Field, D. 24, '62; r. R.; a master mariner.

AMES, Mark; m. 1st, Priscilla Howland; rem. from Marshfield, Mass., to North Haven, took up a large tract of land; m. 2d, Rebecca Crosbery, and d. North Haven. His ch. by 1st wife. 1, Mark, (2d), m. Mercy Perry; r. & d. Appleton. 2, Rev. Benjamin, b. Ap. 1774? m. 1st, Margaret Dyer, 2d, Olive Waterman; stud. theology in 1806, with Rev. Mr. Merrill, ord. Bap. Min. at North Haven, '09, was minis'r at St G., from '11 till his death, A 23, '45. 3. Experience, m. Nath. Lindsey; r. R., & d. Jan. 7, '42. 4, Anna, m. Wm. Dyer; r. & d. North Haven. 5, John, m. Hannah Perry; r. & d. N. Haven. 6, Isaac, m. Abigail Clark; r. & d. Machias. 7, Abraham, m. ——— Clark, 3d, Olive Drinkwater; r. & d. Machias. 8, Hezekiah, m. Betsey Fowler, 2d, Sally Scofield; r. & d. N. Haven.

Mark (2d)'s ch. 1, Doyle, m. Lydia Waterman; r. Appleton. 2, Priscilla, b. Ap. 1, 1801; m. Capt. David Grant, 2d, Stephen Prescott; r. R. 3, Jabez, m. Abby Hall; r. & d. N. Haven. 4, Abner, b. ab. 1799; m. 1st, Mary Ann ———, 2d, Mrs. Charlotte Sanders, Ap. 7, '58; r. R., a mariner. 5, Abby, m. Geo. Hall; r. & d. N. Haven.

Rev. Benjamin's ch. 1, Abby, m. Jos. Robinson; r. St. G., & S. Th. 2, Lydia, m. Elisha Ames; r. S. Th.. 3, Isaac, b. ab. 1805; m. Ann F. Sherer, Mar. 2, '34; r. R., a ship-builder. By 2d wife. 4, Margaret, b. S. 16, '12; m. Shepherd R. Small; r. S. Th., & d. N. 20, '51. 5, Sarah W., b. A. 11, '13; d. Jan. 16, '33. 6, Joseph W., b. 1815; m. Bethia Martin; r. S. Th., a joiner. 7, Benjamin, (3d), d. at N. O., 1833. 8, Olive, b. S. 25, '19; m. Shepherd R. Small; r. S. Th. 9, Rebecca, d. Jan. 19, '33. 10, Mark (3d), b. Ap. 11, '22; m. Emily Wadlin, S. 16, '61; r. S. Th., a joiner, &c.

John's ch. 1, Dura, d. young. 2, Capt. Jesse, b. ab. 1810; m. Martha Tolman, O. 27, '33; r. R., rem. Minnesota. 3, Charlotte, m. Hiram Brewster; r. R., & d. F. 27, '34. 4, Olive, m. Samuel Rankin, (2d); r. & d. R. 5, Capt. Jackson, b. D. 30, '15; m. Sally Thomas; r. R., & d. at Port au Prince, N. 22, '55. 6, Lucy, m. Nath'l Crockett, (4th); r. R. 7, Hezekiah, m. ——— Thomas; r. N. Haven; has 2 daus. & 1 son. 8, Otis, d. young. 9, David, m. Sally Dyer; r. N. Haven; & has 1 dau. & 2 sons. 10, Nancy P., m. Capt. Oliver J. Conant; r. R.

Hezekiah's ch. by 2d wife. 1, Capt. Mark, (4th), m. Nancy Mathews; r. Linc. & has a son George. 2. Rebecca, m. ——— Mathews; r. N. Haven. 3, Amanda; r. N. Haven, 4, Abby, m. Jos. Fish; r. R., & rem. 5, Nathan, m. Clara Ames; r. N. Haven. 7, Priscilla. 8, Lizzie. 9, Abraham. 10, John. 11, Benjamin; all r. North Haven.

Fourth Generation.

Of Doyle's ch. 1, Capt. Jabez Frank, b. ab. 1826; m. Huldah A. Spalding, Feb. 1850; r. Rock.

Abner's ch. by 1st wife. 1, Charles P., b. F. 3, 1838; r. R.; a mariner. 2, Roziltha, b. S. 10, '40. 3, William H., b. ab. '44; soldier of 4th Me.; wounded at Spottsylvania, May 8th, d. at Philadelphia, J. 18, '64. The mother d. A. 2, '56, a. 47.

Isaac's ch. 1, Margaret, b. N. 23, 1835; m. Capt. Charles H. Marston; r. R. 2, Reuben S., b. Ju. 7, '40; m. Almira M. Candage, Ju. 7, '61; r. R.; a mariner. 3, Georgiana, b. ab. '44. 4, Eva Ann, b. ab. 1854.

Joseph W.'s ch. 1. Olinda S., b. M. 23, 1846; d. S. 1847. 2, Benjamin S., b. J. 16, 1849. 3, Margaret S., b. May 4, 1853; d. A. 15, 1854. 4, Olive W., b. Dec. 4, 1855.

Mark, (3d)'s ch. May Emily, b. S. 18, 1862.

Capt. Jesse's ch. 1, John Thomas, b. F. 15, 1834; m. & r. Minnesota. 2. Gen. Adelbert, b. O. 31, 1835; grad. at West Point Acad., 1861, being number 5 in his class; commander of Ames's Battery, Col. of the 20th Me. reg., and since Brig. Gen. of volunteers.

Capt. Jackson's ch. 1, Samuel, r. R. & North Haven. 2, Oliver

C., b. S. 7, 1842, killed by a fall from a horse. 3, Clara; m. Nathan Ames. 4, a daughter. 5, Jesse, (2d). 6, Jackson, (2d), all r. North Haven.

Fifth Generation.

Capt. Jabez Frank's ch. 1, Asa F, b. ab. 1851. 2, Frederic E., b. ab. '53. 3, Ambrose N., b. ab. '55. The mother d. Jan. 17, '61, a. 34.

AMES; of this Brooksville family, three brothers c. to this place. 1. Capt. David, b. ab. 1821; m. 1st, Lucy Frye, A. 7, 1842, 2d, Augusta Hall, S. 19, 1863; r. R. 2, Capt. Albert F., b. ab. 1824; m. Margaret W. Verrill, O. 27, 1856; r. R. 3, Samuel V.; m. Sylvia N. ——— ; r. R., a mariner, & d. by intentional drowning, as supposed, near Steamboat wharf, May 16, 1852.

Capt. David's ch. by 1st wife. 1, Ada A., b. ab. 1843. 2. Lucy J., b. May, 1844, d. April 7, 1853.

Capt. Albert F.'s ch. 1, Charles, b. ab. 1857. 2, Brindah A., b. February, and died July, 1859.

Samuel V.'s ch. 1, Amos M., b. 1835, d. N. 28, 1848. 2, Capt. Alonzo, b. ab. 1837; r. R. 3, Frances H., b. O. 24, 1839; r. R., a miliner. 4, Henrietta E. b. A. 20, '41; r. R. 5, Nancy C., b. ab. '44.

AMES; of the ch. of Asa of Skowhegan, there c. hither, 1, Rachel, b. 1831; m. Jonas Wood; r. R. & d. J. 6, 1864. 2, David, (2d), b. ab. 1835; m. Elizabeth H. Bartlett; r. R., a quarry man. 3, Sarah, b ab. 1837; m. William Spalding; r. R. 4, George, r. Rock.

David, (2d's), ch. 1, Ada M., b. ab. 1855. 2, George W., b. 1860.

AMSBURY, Capt. Oliver, b. in Pawtucket, R. I., Dec. 16, 1785, son of Jeremiah of Pawtucket; rem. with his father & family to North Haven ab. 1800; m. there, Margaret Wooster, (who was b. Jan. 23, 1788,) c. to Th. as a machinist, was employed in making the machinery & superintending it some years after the cotton factory went into operation; ret. to North Haven, 1815; c. to R. 1828, where he r., a master mariner, & d. D. 24, 1832. Their ch. 1, Sally, b. N. 30, 1809; m. Nathaniel Crockett; r. Ohio. 2, Lydia W., b. Jan. 18, 1811; m. Hon. Geo. S. Wiggin; r. R. 3, Margaret S., b. N. 18, 1813; m. Benjamin Crockett; rem. & d. at Napoleon, O., S. 3, 1846. 4, Capt. Oliver, (2d), b. S. 24, 1815; m. Rozella C. Beattie, D. 25, 1842; r. R. 5, Mary Ann, b. N. 17, 1817; m. Capt. Jeremiah Sleeper; r. S. Th. 6, Cynthia, b. A. 15, 1820; d. J. 7, 1821. 7, Capt. Joseph Otis, b. May 14, 1822; m. Mary Ann Thomas of North Haven; r. Quincy, Mass. 8, Hannah, b. S. 26, 1825; d. Jan. 10, 1826. 9, Emily, b. July 1, 1827; d. Dec. 24, 1829.

Capt. Oliver, (2d)'s ch. 1, Almeda, b. ab. 1844. 2, Emily, b. ab. 1847. 3, Lucius H., b. ab. 1850. 4, Celeste B., b. ab. 1853. 5, George W., b. ab. 1855. 6, Oliver W., b. ab. 1857.

ANDERSON, Robert, b. in Lewiston, ab. 1812; m. Harriet T. Wallace of Bangor; r. R., a baker, deputy sheriff in 1857, &c. Their ch. 1, Leander D, b. ab. 1834; m. Rose M. Clark, Jan. 1, 1862; r. R., a baker, rem. Lynn. 2, Margaret D., m. John E. Wallace; r. Beverly, Mass. 3, Augusta H., m. Joseph H. Gould; r. Rock. 4, Mary M., b. ab. 1842; m. Mortier De Fontaine, Aug. 2, 1864; r. R. 5, Robert, (2d), b. ab. 1843; a soldier of 4th Maine reg. 6, Erastus C., b. ab. 1846. 7, Charles A., b. ab. 1850. 8, John W., b. ab. 1853.

ANDERSON, Richard, b. in Buckfield, m. & r. Peru, Oxford Co. Of his sons. 1, Daniel T., b. in Peru, Jan. 18, 1823; m. Sarah E.

Patten, p. May 22, 1851; r. R., a shoemaker; & d. M. 31, 1861. 2, James G., b. ab. 1830, in Peru; m. Lucinda Brazier of Montville, p. M. 4, 1854; r. R., a shoemaker.

Daniel T.'s ch. 1, Georgiana. 2, Enoch, b. ab. 1853. 3, Lucy, b. ab. 1855.

James G.'s ch. 1, William, b. ab. 1856. 2, Belinda, b. ab. 1858.

ANDERSON, Capt. Rasmus, b. ab. 1822, c. from Arendad, Norway, Eu., to this place as a seaman; m. Helen A. (Hyler) Leeds, S. 4, 1845; r. Th. & d. N. 28, 1852, lost overboard. Their ch. 1, Dodge Hyler, b. D. 8, 1847; d. by drowning, A. 14, 1852. 2, Rasmus, b. ab. 1849. 3, Alida G., b. Ap. 1, 1851; d A. 22, 1852.

ANDERSON, James, b. in Pennsylvania, c. with his wife from the British Provinces, r. R., a steamboat engineer, rem. Portland. Their ch. 1, James M., b. ab. '51. 2, William H. 3, George H. 4, Aurelia.

ANDERSON, John H. D., b. ab. 1836; c. from British Provinces; m. Statira P. Pillsbury, A. 19, 1854; r. R., a mariner, rem. Portsmouth, N. H. Their ch. 1, Fannie E. 2, Grace E.

ANDREWS; for this family in full, see Annals of Warren. Of the sons of Capt. Lemuel there c. hither. 1, Ellis, b. M. 31, 1808; m. Sarah H. Gilman of Searsmont, p. O. 10, 1836; r. Rock., a ship-builder; & d. N. 13, 1857, very suddenly of heart disease. Of the sons of James. 1, Alden, b. ab. 1815; m. Sarah Hartford; r. Th., a joiner; & d. J. 2, 1855. Of the sons of George, who himself now also r. in Th. 1, Miles Cobb, b. Ju. 29, 1819; m. Elizabeth Wakefield, May 20, 1846; r. R., a bookseller, postmaster, &c. 2, Orris S., twin to preceding; m. Lucy H. Glover of Camden, p. Ap. 29, 1854; built a house & r. on Masonic street, R., a bookseller & stationer. 3, William, b. Jan. 29, 1828; m. Harriet B. Carleton, p. S. 2, 1852; r. Th., a painter. Of the sons of John, (2d). 1, Joseph, b. ab. 1829; m. Selina Butler; r. Th., a joiner. 2, Thomas S., b. ab. 1831; m. Mary T. Levensaler, N. 30, 1863; r. Th., a joiner.

Ellis's ch. 1. Adelia J., b. J. 22, 1838; d. O. 17, 1842. 2, Henry H., b. S. 4, 1840; r. R., a mariner, U. S. N. 3, Frances E., b. D. 10, 1841; d. S. 14, 1842. 4, Lucy M., b. D. 14, '49; d. May 29, '58.

Alden's ch. 1, Ann Sarah, b. ab. 1842; r. R. 2, Leonidas, b. O. 1843; r. R., a mariner. 3, Alden, b. S. 19, 1845, is in U. S. Navy. 4, Edwin. 5. Alexander.

Miles C.'s ch. Julia Maria, b. ab. 1850.

Orris S.'s ch. 1, Adelaide, b. Jan. 1858. 2, Lucy F., b. Ap. 1860. 3, Jennie May, b. J. 1, 1862.

William's ch. 1, Charles J., b. Nov. 19, 1853. 2, Gorham C., b. Sept. 2, 1855. 3, Willie, b. Nov. 17, 1860.

ANDREWS, Winthrop, b. in Essex, Mass., Dec. 9, 1778; m. Rhoda Grover; settled in Boothbay; and d. there Jan. 1863. Their ch. 1, Capt. Luke, b. O. 2, 1818; m. Nancy J. Albee, S. 21, 1845; r. Rock. 2, Capt. William N., b. A. 18, 1827; m. Pamelia J. Gregory, M. 28, 1850; r. R., 3, Rhoda G., b. in Boothbay as well as the preceding; m. Capt. Parker B. Albee; r. Monhegan.

Capt. Wm. N.'s ch. 1, Inez Zorilda, b. May 22, 1851. 2, Edward M. b. Ap. 3, 1858.

ANDREWS, Marshall, b. ab. 1807, probably of a St. Geo. family, m. Zilpha ——; r. S. Th., a farmer. Their ch. Marshall A., b. ab. 1846.

AREY; of this Vinalhaven family, four brothers, sons of James,

c. to S. Th. 1, James, (2d) b. Ju. 29, 1793; m. Nancy Merrill, (who was b. J. 28, 1796) r. S. Th., a mariner. 2, Capt. John, b in Vin. Ap. 11, 1797; m. Sarah Creed (who was b. at Vin N. 11, 1805) c. to S. Th. about 1834; r. S. Th., Owl's H. 3, Capt. Lewis, b ab. 1813; m. Mary Calderwood; r. S. Th. 4, Alden B. b. ab. 1817; m. Hannah Emery, Ju. 1, 1841, and d. at Edgartown of yellow fever, N. 1, 1841.

James, (2d)'s ch. 1, Capt. James, (3d) b. D. 13, 1814; m. Nancy Wilson of St. G. p M. 13, 1838; r. S. Th. 2, Sophia, m. Jonas Mills, p. Ap. 12, 1838; r. Fox Is. 3, Martha, m. Asa C. Dyer; r. S. Th. 4, Rodney, b. ab. 1827; m. Margaret A. Farr, O. 8. 1848; r. S. Th., a mariner. 5, Nelson, b. D. 14, 1829; m. 1st, Almira Johnson, N. 14, 1849, 2d, Eliza A. York, D. 22, 1855; r. S. Th., a mariner. 6, Mary A., b. Jan. 13, 1833; m. Samuel P. Brown; r. So. Th. 6, Jonas M., b. July 26, 1836. 8, Jane C. b. Ap. 23, 1838; m. William H. Brown of R., p. O. 21, 1854; r. Fox Is.

Capt. John's ch. 1, Margaret L., b. F. 25, 1823; m. Calvin Birding; r. S. Th. 2, Capt. Wm. S., b. S. 22, 1825; m. Hannah Brown, p. N. 2, 1850; r. S. Th., Owl's Head, and d. in 1864. 3, Mary C., b. Ju. 11, 1827; m. Capt. Richard S. Blaisdell; r. R. 4, Jane C., b. S. 20, 1829; m. ——— Hunt; r. Ill. 5, Lucy A. b. F. 20, 1832, at Vinalhaven, as all the preceding; m. Gilbert F. Higgens, D. 12, 1852; r. R. 6, Eliza S., b. May 11, 1835; m. Henry Dunning; r. S. Th. 7, Bradford A., b. May 17, 1837. 8, H. Howard, b. Mar. 15, 1840; a mariner. 9, J. Vinal, b. M. 23, 1843; a mariner. 10, Faustina, b. ab. 1846.

Capt. Lewis's ch. 1, Melissa, b. May 26, 1830; m. John Emery; r. Owl's Head. 2, Capt. Seth C., b. J. 16, 1838; m. Lucy M. Pillsbury; r. Owl's Head, So. Th. 3, Sarah C., b. ab. 1843. 4, Amelia Marion, b. 1848. 5, Lewis A., b. ab. 1850.

Capt. James, (3d,)'s ch. 1, William D., b. Ap. 26, 1839; d. F. 26, 1847. 2, Catharine E., b. A. 20, 1840. 3, Martha M., b. ab. 1844; m. Clarence Ingraham; r. S. Th. 4, Lucy Adeline, b. Ap. 6, 1846; d. F. 26, 1847. 5, Adelaide, b. 1849; d. Ap. 17, 1859. 6, Jane, b. ab. 1849. 7, George P., b. ab. 1851. 8, David, b. ab. 1853.

Nelson's ch. by 2d wife. Laura A., b. ab. 1859.

Rodney's ch. Juliet, b. ab. 1857.

Capt. William S.'s ch. 1, Ada I., b. ab. 1853. 2, Adela S., b. 1855. 3, Lucy E., b. 1857. 4, Oscar B., b. 1859.

AREY, Ebenezer, of a different family; m. Cathleen B. Dyer, Ap. 16, 1848; r. So. Th., a mariner. Their ch. 1, Melvin W., b. ab. 1849. 2, Angie E., b. ab. 1851. 3, Leander B., b. ab. 1853.

AREY, Silas M. Esq., a son, it is believed, of Ebenezer; m. & r. Rock. Of his ch. 1, Robert A. B.; m. Cynthia I. McIntosh, July 2, 1854; r. Rock.

ARMITAGE, William, b. ab. 1825, in Leeds, Eng.; m. Diana ——, in N. Scotia; r. R., a mariner. Their ch. 1, William N., b. ab. 1853. 2, Sarah, b. ab. 1855. 3, Elizabeth, b. ab. 1857. 4, John, b. ab. 1859.

ARNOLD, John, son of Rev. Ambrose Arnold, a Baptist minister of Mercer; m. & r. in Mercer. His ch. 1, Ambrose, b. 1814, in Mercer: m. Mary E., dau. of Samuel G. Howard of Searsmont, July 1, 1840; r. R., a mason. 2, Abbie, b. 1819; m. Mr. Chamberlain; r. R., a widow. 3, John, jr., b. ab. 1822; m. Lydia Ann Hawes of W.; . R., a street agent.

Ambrose's ch. 1, Ellen L., b. 1841. 2, Mary J., b. 1843; m. Dr.

P. T. Prescott; r. R. 3, Samuel H., b. 1845. 4, Elliott, b. 1846. 5, Charles A., b. 1848. 6, Edgar A., b. 1849, d. M. 20, 1850. 7, Frank L., b. 1850. 8, Lucy Edna, b. 1852, d. S. 26, 1853. 9, Lucy Addie, b. 1854. 10, Alvin L., b. 1856.

John, jr.'s, ch. 1, James B., b. 1845. 2, Aldana A., b., 1847. 3, Fannie E., b. 1852. 4, Annie Bell, b. 1861.

ASH, Nathaniel, b. ab. 1816, in Sullivan; m. Julia Philbrook, J. 22, 1840; r. S. Th., a mariner.

ATHERN, William A., b. in Hope; m. Nancy W. Fuller; r. R.

ATHERTON, Gilbert L. b. ab. 1834, in Mt. Desert; m. Abbie S. Lufkin of Deer Isle; r. R., a blacksmith. Their ch. 1, Alvah A., b. ab. 1855. 2. Caroline A., b. ab. 1857. 3, Mabel, b. ab. 1859. 4, Charles G., b. F. 10, 1861, d. A. 27, 1862.

ATKINS, Capt. Robert, b. ab. 1805, in Ireland; m. Adaline A. Andrews, O. 19, 1859; r. R.

ATKINS, (changed from Joachin, a Portuguese name,) William J., b. ab. 1823, in W.; m. Olivia F. Blackington; r. R., a blacksmith. Their ch. 1, Minnie G., b. 1856. 2, Jenny L., b. Ap. 15, & d. A. 30, '59.

AUSTIN, Aaron, b. ab. 1779; c. from Wendell, Mass.; m. Olive White, p. A. 18, 1808; settled at the Meadows, & d. S 26, 1837. His widow d. O. 19, 1843, a. 64. Their ch. 1, Adaline, b. S. 1809, d. young. 2, Alden, b. S. 1810; m. Roxana Stevens, N. 1839; r. Th., a farmer. 3, Cordelia, b. M. 5, 1812; m. Franklin Ferrand; r. Th. 4, Meritt, b. S. 22, 1814; m. Eleanor Bartlett, F. 6, 1838; r. Th., a farmer. 5, Louisa, b. J. 6, 1816; m. William Stackpole, (2d); r. Th. 6, Warren, b. Ap., 1817, d. young. 7, Jane, b. S. 18, 1818; m. Daniel Morse, (3d); r. Th.

Alden's ch. 1, Sergeant Warren W., b. O. 25, 1839, a soldier of the 4th Maine, d. May 7th, from wounds received May 5th, 1864. 2, Mary Helen, b. N. 27, 1841. 3, Jane M., b. ab. 1844. 4, Emily Louisa, b. ab. 1847.

Meritt's ch. 1, Margaret E., b. M. 6, 1839. 2, Aaron, b. Ap. 26, 1840; r. Th. 3, Jacob B., b. M. 22, 1842. 4, John M., b. July 17, 1846. 5, Maynard S., b. Jan. 2, 1853.

AUSTIN, Erastus W. B., b. ab. 1836, son of William B. & Eliza Ann (Patten) Austin of Newcastle and Narraguagus; m. Sarah C. Reed of Belfast, May 1, 1861; r. R., a telegraph operator, &c.

AVERILL, Elijah M., b. ab. 1803; c. from Orono; m. Jane Brown, Jan. 29, 1834, 2d, Lucy (Simonton) Partridge, 3d, Nancy S. Helmerhausen, Ap. 23, 1855; r. R., a joiner. His ch. by 1st wife. 1, Capt. Cyrus B., b. ab. 1834; m. Hannah S. Anderson, A. 18, 1854; r. R. By 2d wife. 2, Frank B., b. ab. 1844, a mariner. By 3d wife. 3, Eunice Sawyer, d. Ap. 28, 1858.

AYER, Benjamin, b. ab. 1825; c. from Boston; m. Lavinia S. Cole, A. 22, 1853; r. Th., a merchant tailor.

AYERS, George F., b. at North Haven, ab. 1828, son of Samuel & Sarah Ayers of Camden; m. Harriet L. Hosmer; r. R., a lumber dealer. Their ch. 1, Lucy F., b. ab. 1850. 2, Charles F., b. ab. 1859. 3, Georgiana L., b. ab. 1859.

BABB, Harrison P., b. ab. 1825, in Boothbay; m. Harriet Newhall; r. S. Th.; a merchant. Alexander B., a cousin, b. in Boothbay, ab. 1833, c. here in 1848; m. Jane H. Smalley of Belfast, Ap. 2, 1853; r. R.; a mariner.

Harrison P.'s ch. 1, Adelbert, b. ab. 1856. 2, Minnie, b. ab. 1858.

Alexander B.'s ch. 1, Eva A., b. ab. 1856. 2, Freddy H., b. O., 1858, d. A. 20, 1859.

BABBIDGE; of this family two brothers c. from Deer Isle, viz.: 1, Levi, b. ab. 1815; m. Mary Joice of Deer Isle, S. 29, 1843; r. R., a whip sawyer, fireman, &c., d. very suddenly, M. 15, 1860. 2, Capt. Charles, b. ab. 1819; m. Clarissa Spencer of Bradley, Me.; r. R. A cousin of these, Capt. Alfred, c. from Swan's Isle; m. 1st, Hannah Hamilton, 2d, Mrs. Susan A. Perry, D. 29, 1843; r. R., & d. at sea in sch. *Chesapeake*, J. 12, 1853.

Levi's ch. 1, Gardner L., b. ab. 1845. 2, Frederic, b. ab. 1850. 3, Albert, b. ab. 1852. 4, Mary L., b. F. 28, 1860, d. Ap. 7, 1861.

Capt. Charles' ch. 1, Benjamin F., b. ab. 1846. 2, Clementine, b. 1848, d. May 19, 1851. 3, Clementine A., b. July, 1852, d. Feb. 14, 1853. 4, Alonzo, b. April 12, & d. July 18, 1854. 5, Charles A., b. ab. 1857. 6, Clara A., b. ab. 1859.

Capt. Alfred's ch. 1, Capt. Alfred, (2d), m. Sarah B. Staples, July 6, 1852; r. Rock., lost at sea in 1856. 2, Augustus, lost at sea with his brother. 3, A sister, lost at same time. 4, Hannah M., b. in Rock., Aug. 11, 1839. 5, John W, b. Oct. 31, 1841. The mother d. May 10, 1842.

Capt. Alfred, (2d)'s, ch. 1, Lydia M., b. Jan. 22, 1853, d. March 5, 1854. 2, An infant, lost with its parents, 1856.

BACHELDER, Hezekiah, c. before 1777 to S. Th.; m. Mrs. ——— Ross; followed fishing, &c.; rem. & d. Lincolnville. Their ch. 1, Sally; m. Jacob Counce; r. & d. Cushing. 2, Jane. 3, Daniel; rem. Belfast. 4, Ezekiel. 5, Dodge. 6, Miriam; m. William Mathews. 7, Joanna. 8, Fanny, & perhaps, others, mostly rem. Belfast or Linc.

BAILEY, John, b. ab. 1826; c. from Washington; m. Mary J. Snow, July 29, 1850, 2d, Sophia E. Marshall of Hallowell; r. Th., a teacher, shipbuilder, &c; rem. Georgia, & engaged in lumbering with his brother Frank, (who also c. to Th.,) and others. His ch. by 1st wife. 1, Sarah. By 2d wife. 2, Mary Josephine.

BAILEY, William, b. ab. 1809; m. Angeline Wall of St. G.; r. R., some time, & d. July 25, 1859. The family subsequently rem. St. G., & his widow d. March 1, 1863, a. ab. 40. Their ch. 1, Rovena. 2, Georgianna. 3, William. 4, Sidney. 5, Lemuel.

BAILEY, Lemuel, b. on Muscle Ridge Isl., April 13, 1819, son of Mrs. Sarah N. Patten, now of Rockland; r. Rock. went to California, where his widow remains; ret. and d. in Rockland, Dec. 18, 1859.

BAKER, Rev. Samuel, (son of Joseph, who originally came from Martha's Vineyard,) was b in Readfield, April 17, 1785; m. Dec. 1, 1808, Hannah Parker, (who was b. at Bluehill, April 8, 1785); c. to r. S. Th. 1808, was colleague five or six years with Rev. E. Snow, settled one year over Baptist church in Scituate, Mass., some years in Universalist connection, r. ten years in Dexter, but ret. & d. in Rock., May 10, 1859, having been some of his last years a free itinerant laborer & missionary at large. Their ch. recorded here. 1, Mary Wood, b. July 25, 1810; m. & r., it is believed, in Penobscot county. 2, Joseph S, b. July 25, 1812; m. and r. Mass. 3, Hannah P., b. July 24, 1814.

BAKER, Dr. Peyton R., b. ab. 1825, in Haverhill, N. H., son of Hosea & Fanny (Huntington) Baker, of puritan descent; grad. Dartmouth Coll. 1848, M. D. in N. Y. Coll. of physicians and surgeons; m. Catharine McCallum of W., Sept. 26, 1858; r. & prac. med. Th. Oliver, a brother, also came to Th., 1862, a jeweler, &c. Dr. Peyton R.'s ch. 1, Oliver, b. 1859.

BAKER, John, b. ab. 1822; m. Jane ——; r. R., a laborer.

BALLCOM, or Balkum, William, b. ab. 1838, in China or vicinity; c. here; m. Maria Moore, March 10, 1850; purchased the S. Creighton place at Meadows; r. Th., a farmer. Their ch. 1, Melissa, b. ab. 1853. 2, Josephine, b. ab. 1856. Balkum, James, (name changed from Coombs); m. Jane Allen, Oct. 25, 1856; r. Th., member of 4th Maine regiment.

BANKS, Dr. William A., b. in East Livermore, ab. 1821; M. D. at Jefferson Med. Coll. Philadelphia; prac. med. in W. & other places, & in R. since 1852; m. Mary A. Tillson, Nov. 6, 1854; r. R. Their ch. 1, Lucy C., b. Nov. 30, 1857. 2, William T., b. June 21, 1859.

BARKER, George R., b. in Fredericton, N. B., son of John, (who also c. hither from Fredericton; r. R. & d. Apr. 29, 1850, aged 77); m. Amelia H. Elwell of Northport; r. R. Their ch. 1, George H., b. Jan. 8, 1837; m. Clementine P. Richards, Sept. 7, 1856; r. Cam. 2, Henry L., b. May 30, & d. Sept. 6, 1838. 3, James A., b. Feb. 4, 1840; d. Nov. 4, 1841 4, Julia E., b. July 21, 1841. 5, Cynthia J. S, born Aug. 5, 1844; died June 22, 1846.

BARKER, Lieut. William A., b. ab. 1835, son of Dr. Barker of Bangor; m. Helen S. Porter, Feb. 14, 1863; r. R., a bookbinder, sergeant major of 4th Maine regiment, and May, 1862, lieut. Co. G.

BARKER, William, b. ab. 1832; m. Maria ——; r. R., a lime burner. Their ch. William, (2d), b. ab. 1856.

BARLOW, Francis R., b. ab. 1819, in Palermo; m. Lavinia W. Swift, Dec. 1844; r R., a teamster. Their ch. 1, Helen, b. about 1847. 2, Frederic W., b. about 1849. 3, Imogene, b. ab. 1853. 4, Frank W., born about 1855.

BARLOW, George, b. about 1823 in Ireland; m. Ellen ——; r. R., a laborer. Their ch. Joanna, born about 1860.

BARNARD, Dea. John, b. Mar. 12, 1773; m. Priscilla Doane; c. from Newburyport to W., where he worked as a shipwright in 1795, rem. to Th., where he was a member more than a half century of the 1st & 2d Th. Bap. churches, & d. Ap. 28, 1853. Their ch. 1, Anna, b. July 20, 1797; d. Jan. 31, 1800. 2, Samuel, b. Aug. 24, 1799; d. Nov. 29, 1819. 3, John D., b. Aug. 24, 1801; m. Lucinda Buxton of W., Sept. 18, 1834; r. Th., cashier of Th. Bank, &c.; and d. Sept. 12, 1858. 4, Mary Ann, b. Aug. 13, 1803; m. Lewis S. Kirkpatrick, Sept. 3, 1826; r. W. 5, Almira, b. March 3, 1806; m. John Porter of Belfast; r. Rock. 6, Susan E., b. 1808; d. Dec. 29, 1847; a life-long sufferer from epilepsy. 7, David D., b. Oct. 1809; d. April 21, 1812. 8, Hannah D, b. April 9, 1813; m. Elias H. Brown, May 29, 1836. 9, Charles, b. Mar. 24, 1815; m. & r. Bucksport. The mother died in Rockland, Aug. 23, 1858; aged 82 years, 1 month & 28 days. John D.'s ch. 1, Lucy D., b. Dec. 21, 1835; r. Th. 2, Mary A., b. 1837; m. Fred. A. Robinson; rem. to Vineland, N. J.

BARNES, Asa, b. 1795, at East Machias; m. Catharine Snowdeal of Wal.; r. Rock., a lime burner. Their ch. 1, Sarah A, b 1838.

2, Mary J., b. ab. 1841. 3, Elwilda C., b. ab. 1843. 4, William, b. ab. 1847. 5, Emma F., b. 1852.

BARRETT, Daniel, a descendant of Humphrey Barrett, (who came from England, 1640,) was born in Concord, Mass., 1760; m. Peggy Grose, 1794; r. & built turnpike in Cam. & d. Dec. 1, 1850. Of his 12 ch. 1, Daniel, (2d), m. Bethia Jordan; r. Cam. & a time in Northport. Of Daniel, (2d)'s ch. there c. to this place. 1, Daniel T., b. ab. 1825; m. Louisa Rhoades of Northport, 2d, Caroline M. Heald, Apr. 19, 1863, 3d, Mrs. Lucy A. Cushman, July 28, 1864; r. Rock., a mason, &c. 2, Robert J.; m. Sarah B. Gay, Dec. 19, 1858; r. Th. 3, Edward H.; r. Rock. 4, Nelson M.; r. Rock. Ephraim Barrett, a 4th cousin to those last named, was born Sept. 27, 1810, in North Haven; m. Charlotte A. P. Holt of Bluehill, Oct. 16, 1842; r. Rock., a dry goods dealer, & is a son of James Barrett, & his wife, Jenny, dau. of Maj. George White of North Haven, who served in the Revolution six and a half years under Washington, and was a commissary in the war of 1812.

Daniel T.'s ch. by 1st wife. 1, Idella, b. ab. 1856. 2, Walter T., b. ab. 1858. 3, Dura K., b. 1860. The mother died Oct. 29, 1862. The step mother died Jan. 10, 1864, aged 37.

Robert J.'s ch. Sarah E.

Ephraim's ch. 1, Frederic M., b. Sept. 1, & d. Sept. 28, 1843. 2, Frances A., b. Oct. 1845, d. Aug. 14, 1858. 3, Charles E., b. Feb. 1848, d. Aug. 31, 1852. 4, Louisa A., b. June 1, 1852, d. Jan. 12, 1854. 4, Emily A, b. ab. 1856. The mother d. Feb. 1857, aged 36.

BARRETT, John, son of Mrs. Ephraim Knowlton by a former husband; m. Sally Spalding, Dec. 2, 1824; r. Rock., and was lost at sea, March 26, 1830. Their ch. John (2d), born Feb. 27, 1827; m. Julia Lampson, March 8, 1848; r. Rock., a quarryman.

John, (2d)'s, ch. 1, John A., b. May 28, & d. Aug. 18, 1850. 2, Gilman U., b. Apr. 9, & d. Sept. 8, 1852. 3, Frederic A. b. June 26, & d. Aug. 13, 1855. 4, James T., b. June 28, & d. Sept. 28, 1859. 5, Arletta, b. May 7, 1862.

BARROWS; of this family, from Attleboro', Mass., we have account of six brothers. 1, Caleb, c. early to E. Th. & settled the farm now occupied by Otis Barrows, ret. & d. in Mass., his acct. with Jas. Fales being settled by his brother, in July, 1776. 2, Ichabod, b. Oct. 13, 1752 or 1756, in Cumberland; rem. Attleboro', c. to what is now Rock., about 1770; succeeded to Caleb's farm; m. Mary Young of Th., Jan. 3, 1804; & d. 1823. 3, Comfort, b. in Attleboro', Oct. 5, 1759; c. to r. W. of the Meadows in Rock., Oct. 3, 1778; m. Sabra Robbins, Oct. 2, 1788; & d. May 12, 1791. 4, Benajah, born June 1762; was in Th. 1790 with his family; rem. Cam. & d. Jan. 3, 1844, aged 81 years, 7 months. 5, Peter, settled in Camden. 6, Ezra, r. Mass., but became owner of the farm settled by one of his brothers, & transferred it to his son Otis. 7 & 8, Eunice & Chloe, sisters? also came hither & m. John Ulmer.

Ichabod's ch. 1, Comfort, (2d), b. 1805; r. Cam. 2, Margaret, b. 1807; d. in Th. about 1825. 3, Mary Ann, born 1809; r. Cam. 4, Ezra, (2d), b. 1811; m. C. D. Withington, 1842; r. Cam. 5, Jackson, b. 1815; m. Nancy Skinner of W.; r. Cam. 6, Philip, b. 1818; m. Elizabeth Young of Baltimore, Md., where he resides.

Comfort's ch. 1, Sabra, b. May 22, 1790; m. Reuben Sherer, Jan. 14, 1808; r. Rock., & d. Feb. 11, 1850. 2, Comfort, a dau. b. Aug. 21, 1791; d. Sept. 15, 1794.

Of Peter's ch. Capt. Alexander, b. 1797; m. Charlotte Killsa, p. Mar. 13, 1823; r. Rock., a cooper; rem. & d. Leominster, Mass., Sept. 23, 1864.

Of Ezra's ch. Otis, b. ab. 1803; m. Barbara Crockett; r. Rock., a farmer.

Third Generation.

Capt. Alexander's ch. 1, Angelia H., b. Oct. 30, 1823; 2, Amanda M., b. J. 30, 1826; 3, Clementine A., b. Feb. 21, 1828; all rem. Mass. 4, Susan E., b. Oct. 5, 1829; d. in Franklin, Mass., March 31, 1852. 5, Charlotte M., b. June 1, 1833; rem. Mass. 6, Albert A., b. Sept. 28, 1835; d. Aug. 2, 1856. 7, Alfred A., b. May 22, 1838; d. Aug. 7, 1843. 8, Harvey H., b. Nov. 28, 1841; d. Feb. 3, 1842. 9, Dora, born about 1844; rem. Mass.

Otis's ch. 1, Melinda, b. Aug. 13, 1824; d. Aug. 13, 1838. 2, Harriet, b. April 16, 1826; d. March 9, 1830. 3, Caroline R., b. Dec. 29, 1827; m. Lowton O. Corey of Bureau Co., Illinois, Dec. 25, 1860. 4, Serg't William Ezra, b. Oct. 5, 1829; m. Amanda M. Thompson of Montville, June 30, 1860; r. Rock., an officer in 19th Me. reg.; killed at Gettysburg, July 3, 1863. 5, George; m. Susan Fifield in Illinois. 6, Augusta; r. Rock. 7, Miranda; m. Joseph Whitcomb of Waldo, Nov. 9, 1860. 8, Frances; m. James C. Dexter of R. I. 9, Orissa A.; m. Dominicus Hovey of Dubuque Co., Iowa, Dec. 25, 1860. 10, Otis, jr.; died young. 11, Clara, born about 1845.

BARTER, Jacob, with Lucy his wife, was in old Th., and had one child recorded here, viz.: Isaiah, b. May 19, 1842. There were also in Rock. in 1860 two brothers, Pelatiah, and George J., with their families, who have returned to St. George, their place of origin.

BARTLETT, Samuel, b. 1754; c. from New Meadows? to Th. before its incorporation; m. 1st. ——— Hix, 2d, Eleanor (Martin) Kimball of Bristol, p. Jan. 7. 1788; settled at Head of the Bay, & d. Feb. 9, 1819. His ch. by 1st wife. 1, Priscilla; m. Brice Jameson; p. June 17, 1791; r. & d. W. 2, Capt. Joshua, b. July 6, 1780; m. Miriam Keating; p. May 19, 1804; r. S. Th., & d. Ap. 4, 1855. 3, William; m. Ruth Waterman; rem. and d. Ohio. 4, Samuel, (2d), m. Betsey Keating; p. June 24, 1799; r. & d. Ohio. 5, Lois; m. Rosamus K. Lowell; r. & d. Farmington. By 2d wife. 6, Jane; m. David Everett; r. S. Th. and d. March 19, 1855. 7, Thomas; m. 1st, Orinda Fletcher of Linc., June 5, 1816, 2d, ——— Parkman; r. & d. Hope. 8, Knott, b. Nov. 12, 1793; m. Hannah Ulmer, Feb. 15, 1816; r. Th. Meadows, & d. Nov. 21, 1842. 9, Richard, b. 1795; m. Margaret Crie of Matinicus, Oct. 27, 1820; r. at Head of the Bay, and d. Sept. 18, 1831. 10, Eleanor, b. June 17, 1799; m. Josiah Spalding; r. S. Th. & Cal. 11, Ephraim S.; m. Matilda Spalding, Dec. 14, 1820; r. S. Th., rem. Ohio. 12, Capt. George, b. 1805; m. Nancy D. Hall, July 6, 1847; r. S. Th. & d. Dec. 27, 1851. 13, Hannah, m. Ira M. Gilman from Mercer, N. H., May 10, 1827; r. St. G. 14, David, m. Nancy Lovett of Linc.; r. Cam., rem. Minnesota. The mother died Feb. 12, 1833, aged 73.

Capt. Joshua's ch. 1, Miriam, m. John? Wadlin; r. Northport. 2, Oliver, lost at sea or in Long Island Sound. 3, Susan, m. John Allen; r. & d. Hope. 4, Olive, m. Daniel Wadlin; r. Northport. 5, Capt. Joshua, (2d), b. 1814; m. Martha M. Hix, p. July 14, 1840; r. S. Th. & d. April 5, 1849. 6, Capt. Jonas K., b. Oct. 5, 1816; m.

L. Maria Chapman, Aug. 31, 1843 ; r. S. Th. 7, Capt. Ephraim, (2d), b. Oct. 30, 1819; m. Ruth Dean, Aug., 1846; r. S. Th. 8, Capt. Samuel, (3d), b. June 10, 1823 ; m. Antoinette Chapman, July, 1846. 9, Capt. William K., b. Sept. 5, 1824; r. Kansas. 10, Hannah J., b. Feb. 22, 1826; m. Amos Norton; r. S. Th. 11, Knott, (2d), b. June 7, 1830 ; d. at sea, Aug. 12, 1853.

Of Capt. Samuel, (2d)'s, ch. 1, Thomas Scott; 2, Elizabeth T.; 3, Edwin Wood; all were bap. April 6, 1826.

Knott's ch. 1, Margaret, b. Aug. 1, 1816; m. John Morse (2d); r. Th. & d. Aug. 18, 1854. 2, Jacob, b. June 24, 1818; d. Nov. 10, 1839. 3, Eleanor, b. Oct. 1, 1820; m. Merritt Austin; r. Th. 4, David M., b. Jan. 8, 1823; d. June 4, 1825. 5, David, b. May 25, & d. Aug. 24, 1825. 6, Knott M., b. Nov. 23, 1827 ; m. Caroline Ulmer, Dec. 5, 1847; r. Th., & d. Dec. 23, 1849. 7, Hannah U., b. Ap. 20, 1830, d. Apr. 5, 1834. 8, Richard, b. May 24, 1833 ; m. Frank E. McKenney of S. Th., Jan. 11, 1862; r. Rock., is in U. S. Navy. 9, Hannah E., b. Dec. 1, 1834; d. Sept. 24, 1835. 10, Oliver, b. March 13, 1836 ; m. Frances Burton ; r. Terre Haut, Ind.

Richard's ch. 1, Rufus Y., b. July, 1823; d. Sept. 8, 1826. 2, Eveline Margaret, b. Feb. 9, 1828.

Ephraim S.'s ch. 1, Mary Ellen, born Oct. 17, 1821; m. William Rowell; r. Ohio. 2, Francis H., b. Aug. 4, 1823 ; m. Elmira Snowdeal, July 31, 1848 ; r. Ohio. 3, Larkin S., b. Jan. 24, 1829 ; d. Sept. 17, 1841. 4, Matilda L., b. June 17, 1833; r. Ohio.

Fourth Generation.

Capt. Joshua, (2d)'s ch. 1, Emma L., b. ab. 1842. 2, Joshua, (3d) b. ab. 1847.

Capt. Jonas K.'s ch. 1, Lucinda A., b. Feb. 18, 1848 ; d. Nov. 25, 1863. 2, Linda W., b. ab. 1850. 3, Nelson, b. ab. 1853. 4, Margaret S., b. ab. 1855. 5, Warner, b. ab. 1859. 6, Charles.

Capt. Ephraim, (2d)'s, ch. 1, Elnora, b. ab. 1846. 2, Melvin, born ab. 1848. 3, Merrill, b. ab 1857.

Francis H.'s ch. 1, Larkin, b. April 10, 1849. 2, Eva, b. Jan. 1, 1852. 3 & 4, twins, b. Mar 29, 1856; Archibald & Alice. 5, Luella S., b. Aug. 26, 1859. 6, Frank, b. Nov. 18, 1861.

BARTLETT, Benjamin, b. ab. 1802 in Shapleigh; m. Mary Hammond, Sept. 16, 1827; r. Rock., in quarry business, &c. Their ch. 1, Mary, b. Dec. 7, 1827; d. July 28, 1829. 2, William, b. May 25, 1830; d. April 23, 1832. 3, Edward, b. Oct. 3, 1833; m. Mary J. Lawson; r. Rock., a quarryman. 4, Elizabeth H, b. Feb. 9, 1836; m. David Ames, (2d); r. Rock. 5, James, b. May 12, 1838; d. Feb. 2, 1839. 6, Oliver, b. Feb. 20, 1840; d. Mar. 7, 1842. 7, Benjamin, (2d), b. ab. '43; m. Eliza F. Ulmer, Nov. 28, '62; r. Rock., in army.

BARTLETT, Horatio N., b. 1820 in Worcester, Mass.; m. Margaret C. Morse, 1847, 2d, Mrs. Susan D. Levensaler, July 6, 1855; r. Th., a joiner; rem. Illinois. His ch. by 1st wife. 1, Edwin Burton, b. Sept. 3, 1848. 2, Lizzie Jane, b. Dec. 21, 1850. 3, Albert H., b. Sept. 12, 1852; d. Oct. 15, 1854. The mother died in Th., March 6, 1854. By 2d wife. 4, Rebecca C., b. 1859.

BARTLETT, Seth, Esq., b. in Plymouth, Mass., 1789; came with his family from Wiscasset here, practised law a short time in Th., and died May 9, 1827.

BARTLETT, Moses D., b. ab. 1822 in Hope; m. Nancy I. ——— ; r. Rock., was a soldier of 4th Me. reg., killed at Fredericksburg, Dec.

13, 1862. Their ch. 1, Bethiah, b. ab. 1846. 2, Whiting, b. 1849. 3, Emily, b. 1851. 4, Mary, b. 1853. 5, Sophronia, b. 1858.

BARTLETT, John, came from Shapleigh? m. Susanna R. Burton, Oct. 22, 1843; r. Rock. Their ch. 1, Mary F., b. Feb. 28, 1846. 2, John A., b. Sept. 3, 1847. 3, George E., b. May, 1849.

BARTON, Matthew P., b. ab. 1795; m. Hannah (Elliott) Jordan, r. S. Th., or Rock., a farmer.

BATTLES, Joseph, b. ab. 1826; c. from St. George; m. Mary Allen, p. Nov. 29, 1849; r. Rock., a lime burner. Their ch. 1, Adelaide A., b. ab. 1852. 2, Ella, b. ab. 1854.

BATTLES, William, b. ab. 1796, perhaps from the same town; r. with Mary his wife, in S. Th. Their ch. John R., b. ab. 1820.

BAXTER, Rev. Francis W., b. in Boston; was pastor of Universalist Society in Th.; m. Lucretia —— of Frankfort and had recorded here, ch. 1, Ann E., b. June 17, 1839. 2, Joseph G., b. June 8, 1841; but the mother d. & he m. again in New Portland and rem. subsequently to Illinois or other Western State.

BAYNES, Dr. R., b. in England; a surgeon dentist & homœopathic practitioner in Th. since 1850.

BEALS, David, b. ab. 1782; c. from Dedham? Mass.; m. Nancy Robinson, Nov. 9, 1823; r. Rock., a farmer, & d. Nov. 10, 1860. His widow r. in Boston. Their ch. 1, Susanna, b. May 27, 1825; m. Capt. John Hart of St. G. & has 3 ch., Helen, Agnes, and John. 2, Mary, b. March 7, 1827; r. Rock. 3, Lydia, b. April 30, 1829; m. George R. Post; r. S. Th. 4, David (2d), b. April 8, 1832; lost at sea, Sept. 30, 1851. 5, Joseph, b. Sept. 26, 1833; d. Aug. 3, 1834.

BEAN; of this family, three brothers c. from Belfast to this place. 1, Charles N., b. in B. ab. 1825; m. Carrie Kenister of Liberty; r. Rock., a blacksmith. 2, Benjamin B., b. in Belfast about 1827; m. Eunice White of B.; r. Rock., a blacksmith. 3, James O., m. Sarah Dickey of Belmont; soldier in the army.

Charles N.'s ch. John C., b. ab. 1851.

Benjamin B.'s ch. 1, Ada W., b. ab. 1852. 2, Fanny A. 3, Elizabeth. 4, Helen.

BEAN, Jonathan, of a different family, b. ab. 1821; m. Sarah A. ——; r. Rock., a blacksmith. Their ch. 1, Esther E., b. about 1850. 2, Elwildie, b. ab. 1853. 3, Eliza C., b. ab. 1857.

BEAN, Daniel F., b. in New York ab. 1827; m. Mary A. ——; r. Rock., a mariner. Their ch. Eugene, b. ab. 1859.

BEATTIE, William, Esq., b. Dec. 25, 1799, in Northport; (son of Robert of that place & grandson of John, a lawyer, who was born & educated in Glasgow, Scotland); m. Jane Doyle of Northport, Nov. 27, 1821; came to Rockland in 1837, studied law with H. C. Lowell, Esq.; admitted to the bar in 1839; r. & practises law in Rock. Their ch. 1, Angeline S., b. Aug. 27, 1822; m. John H. McClennan, Aug. 29, 1842; r. Boston. 2, Rozella C., b. Jan. 22, 1824; m. Capt. Oliver Amsbury; r. Rock. 3, Aurelia L., b. Nov. 30, 1825; m. Samuel C. Cobb of Boston, Nov. 21, 1848. 4, Justina A., b. Nov. 3, 1827; m. Rosamus C. Lowell; r. Rock. 5, Capt. Lucius H., b. Jan. 25, 1830; sailing master U. S. ship Sabine, &c. 6, Almatia L., b. June 9, & d. June 26, 1832. 7, Jennie C., b. Sept. 3, 1833; m. Gustavus A. Hilton of Boston, Nov. 2, 1853. 8, William A., b. Feb. 7, 1836; d. Oct.

31, 1837. 9, Frederic E., b. June 25, 1839. 10, William A., b. Jan. 5, 1842; enlisted in U. S. Navy. 11 & 12, twins, b. Oct. 9, 1844, Charles H. & Emma F.

BELL, John, b. ab. 1816; c. with his wife Ann & 3 ch. from Nova Scotia; r. Th., a blockmaker. Their ch. 1, Martha, b. ab. 1843. 2, John (2d), b. ab. 1845. 3, Amelia, b. ab. 1847. 4, Catharine, b. ab. 1850. 5, Elizabeth G., b. ab. 1854. 6, Albert, b. ab. 1857.

BENNER, Henry jr., son of Henry of Waldoboro'; German in descent; m. Mary Brown, Nov. 2?, 182?; r. & d. Rock. Their ch. 1, Reuben, b. March 14, 1824; m. Eliza F. Upham of U., r Rock., a mariner. 2, Hannah, b. Feb. 4, 1826; m. Capt. Andrew F. Dailey; r. Rock. 3, Leonard S., b. Oct. 28, 1827; m. Helen A. Lovejoy, June 15, 1852; r. Rock., a joiner. 4, Sarah, b. March 28, 1833; m. David Winslow; r. Rock.

Reuben's ch. Leroy M., b. ab. 1859.

Leonard S.'s ch. 1, Clara, b. ab. 1854. 2, William. 3, Mary. 4, Amasa.

BENNER, Simon, b. Waldoboro', m. Alice Walsh, p. Oct. 4, 1839; r. Rock. and d. Aug. 2, 1846. Their ch. 1, Charles H., born Dec. 10, 1839; r. Rock., a teamster; 2, William N., b. June 3, 1841; r. Rock., a soldier of 2d Me. Battery. 3. Henry T., b. ab. 1846.

BENNER, Jackson, son of Simon (2d), and grandson of John Martin Benner, of Waldoboro; m. Susan L. Robinson; r. Th., a carpenter.

BENNER, Gorham, b. ab. 1818 in Wal., m. & r. Rockland, a shop keeper. His ch. 1, Mary, b. ab. 1842. 2, Amelia, b. ab. 1844. 3, Louisa, b ab. 1851. Louisa, the mother, d. Oct. 1859, a. 38.

BENNER, Hermon, b. ab. 1824, son of Charles of Wal., m. Louisa K. ———; r. Th., a carpenter. Their ch. Idelle, b. ab. 1853.

BENNETT, James? m. Betsey Comstock, r. &. d. in Ashby, Mass. Of their 7 ch., the 3d, viz., Asa, came to Th., taxed 1791; was a cooper by trade; m. Mary, dau. of Resolved Healey of Providence, R. I., p. Nov. 24, 1796; r. & d. Th.

Asa's ch. 1, Capt. Almond, m. Betsey Smith, Nov. 10, 1820; r. Th. & d. Dec. 23, 1852. 2, Mark Dexter, b. ab. 1800; m. Julia Robinson Nov. 30, 1826; r. Th. 3, Marcus, m. Joanna Smith, Jan. 13, 1824; r. W. 4, Ann F., b. ab. 1807; m. William K. Stevens; r. Th. 5, Resolved, died young. 6, Margaret H, m. Alexander Spear; r. Th. 7, Mahala, m. James Mero; r. Th. 8, M. Antoinette, m. James Graffham; r. Th. 9, Catherine W., m. Capt. William Fales (2d); r. Thomaston.

Capt. Almond's ch. 1, Rufus S., b. Aug. 30, 1821, merchant at Mill River, 1855. 2, Almond F., b. Jan. 29, 1825, d. June 21, 1847. 3, Mary E., b. June 11, 1827; d. Oct. 1, 1828. 4, Julia A., b. July 18, 1829, d. Nov. 13, 1831. 5, Thomas S., b. Nov. 10, 1834, d. Feb. 8, 1836. 6, Mary Elizabeth, d. Feb. 7, 1853. 7, Lilias, m. William Needham of Cambridgeport.

Marcus's ch. 1, Asa, b. May 15, 1826, drowned at sea, or N. Y., Feb. 1845, from br. *Caucasian*. 2, Angelina, b. Oct. 22, 1830; m. 1st, Moses M. Smith, July 30, 1848, 2d, John Clark, of W. March 1, 1852.

BENNETT, Alexander R., b. ab. 1810, in Bristol; m. Mrs. Caroline Babb; r. Rock., a mariner. Their ch. 1, Analette, b. ab. 1845. 2, Arabelle, b. Feb. 10, 1846, d. Nov. 25, 1861.

BENNETT, Col. William, b. ab. 1807; c. from Elsworth, as Warden of State Prison, and held that office several years; m. 1st, ———, 2d, Susan L. Haskell of Th., Nov. 26, 1848, 3d, Ann E. Henderson, Aug. 2, 1854; r. Th. Of his ch. by 1st wife. 1, William, (2d), b. ab. 1832, d. Oct. 17, 1859. 2, Lucy L., b. ab. 1843. By 2d wife. 3, Woodbridge Odlin, b. Sept. 1849, d. July 23, 1850. 4, Anna H., b. ab. 1851.

BENSON, Seth E., b. Jan. 4, 1828, in Boston; m. Lizzie H. Hall, Dec. 21, 1852; r. Rockland, a dentist for a time, now a druggist.

BENSON, William S., b. 1804, c. from Bangor; m. Almira Tenhey, Nov. 18, 1854; r. Rock., a fisherman, ret. Bangor.

BENSON, Joseph, b. ab. 1822, c. from Bangor; m. Ann M———; r. Rock., a baker, some two years, and rem. Portland. Their ch. Abby M., b. ab. 1845.

BENTLEY, John, c. from Boston, burned lime for Knox, taught school, &c.; married Betsey Blye, June 9, 1792; r. Th. at Meadows, entered army and d. Sept. 11, 1812, being killed by a cannon ball at Burlington. Their ch. 1, Joshua, b. July 1, 1794; d. unm. Oct. 7, 1847. 2, Mary P., b. May 4, 1796; m. Jairus Munroe; r. Th. 3, Elizabeth F. b. Feb. 6, 1798; m. Capt. Burton Vose; r. Th. 4, Capt. John (2d), b Oct. 24, 1802; m. 1st, Elsie Lindsey, Aug. 9, 1827; 2d, Mary Lane of Cam., Aug. 11, 1850, r. Th. 5, Thos. J., b. June 17, 1805; m. Fanny L. Willis, Jan. 3, 1830; was lost at sea same year, mate of sch. *Bradford*. 6 & 7, twins, b. Oct. 26, 1808; Harriet, r. Th.; Wm. M. died at sea, March 16, 1825, in consequence of walking overboard in his sleep, when coming from Boston.

Capt. John (2d)'s ch. 1, John Thomas, b. July, 1829, d. Jan. 1833; 2, Mary E., b. April 25, 1832; m. Joseph L. O'Brien; and d. May 1, 1857. 3, Lucy Jane, b. Oct. 26, 1834; m. Elisha A. Gould of Rock. Jan. 20, 1856. 4, Rowena, b. Jan. 19, 183[illegible], d. Oct. 17, 1838. 5, Nancy R., b. April 25, 1837; m. Edward B. Dunham of Nantucket, Dec. 23, 1856. 6, John T., b July, 4, 1839, d. Jan. 29, 1842.

BERNARD, Dr Isaac, c to this place and studied medicine with Dr. Dodge; prac. in Union and Camden, settled finally at what is now Rock.; m. 1st, Catherine Tolman, ab. 1787, 2d, Mary (Hastings) Hanson, Nov. 23, 1806; and died Sept. 3, 1823. His ch. by his 1st wife, 1, Sophia, b. Oct. 9, 1788; m. Capt. James Sears; r. Rock., & d. Dec. 1845. 2, Harriet, b. March 3, 1793; m. 1st, Capt. Jacob Ulmer, 2d, Whitten Hillman; r. Rock. 3, Julia, b June 12, 1798; m. George Wooster; r. So. Th. 4, Isaac (2d), b. Jan. 18, 1802. The mother d. Jan. 1805. By 2d wife. 5, Charles, b. Jan. 1, and d. Jan. 4, 1808.

BERRY, Thomas, b. ab. 1745, probably at Falmouth, now Portland; m. at Brunswick, Abigail Coombs, August 15, 1773; was an officer in the Revolution, a pensioner; r. Portland, but died in Rock., Jan. 27, 1828. Their ch. 1, Samuel, b. May 4, 1774; m. Polly Gould; & d. in Georgetown, Me. 2, Lydia, b. Aug. 14, 1776. 3, Joshua, b. March 4, 1779; m. Fannie Coombs; r. & d. in Portland. 4, Thomas (2d), b. May 26, 1781; m. Miss Burgess; r. & d. in Brunswick. 5, George, b. Aug. 14, 1783; m. r. & d. in Topsham. 6, Abigail, b. April 26, 1785; m. Josiah Haskell; r. Rock., & d. Nov. 1, 1853. 7, Jeremiah, b. Sept. 8, 1787; c. to Th. now Rock., in 1812; m. Frances A. Gregory, April 27, 1815; r. R., a mason, inn keeper,

& active business man; d. March 11, 1857. 8, Joseph, b. Sept. 20, 1789; c. here in 1812; m. 1st, Abigail Coombs, March 12, 1815, 2d, Jane Ann Creamer, Dec. 1845; r. Th., a mason, &c.; & d. March 29, 1855. 9, Betsey, b. 1791. 10, Benjamin, b. May 11, 1795; m. in Brunswick, Dolly Murray, Dec. 21, 1820; came to Rockland, where he died June 27, 1856.

Jeremiah's ch. 1, Jeremiah (2d), b. Jan. 23, 1816; d. March 25, 1832. 2, John T., b. Feb. 12, 1818; m. Catharine C. Crockett, April 25, 1841; r. Rock., stage proprietor, mail contractor on Bath & Rockland route, &c. 3, William G., b. July 8, 1820; m. Mary M. Jones, Dec. 25, '45; r. Rock., an active business man in company with his elder brother, but d. March 15, '58. 4, Maj. Gen. Hiram G., b. Aug. 27, '24; m. Almira M. Brown, March 23, '45; r. Rock., president of Lime Rock Bank, officer in war for the Union, & d. May 3, '63; killed at the battle of Chancellorsville, Va. 5, George W., b. July 2, '28; m. Julia E., dau. of the late Robert P. Pote of Belfast, Aug. 27, '54; r. Rock., express agent, &c. 6, Frances E., b. Aug. 14, '31; m. Oct. 15, '51, Edward H. Fosdick, merchant of New Orleans, but now r. in Brooklyn, N. Y., and has 2 ch., viz.: Cornelia F., b. in Rock., June 2, '54, and William Berry, b. in Brooklyn, Dec. 10, '58.

Joseph's ch. (Adopted) Georgiana, b. June 1, '34; m. Charles L. Lowell; r. Faribault, Minnesota.

Benjamin's ch. 1, Abbie C., b. Oct. 1, 1821; m. Capt. William S. Hatch; r. Rock. 2, Benjamin (2d), b. Dec. 6, '23; d. in Brunswick, Nov. 1825. 3, Olive Jane, b. Feb. 6, '26; m. Capt. Jos. Ham; r. Rock. 4, Capt. Joseph T., b. in Brunswick, March 29, '28; m. 1st, Hester A. Perry, June 11, '51, 2d, Hattie E., dau. of Oliver Andrews of Rockport, Oct. 22, '60; r. Rock. 5, Henry U., b. in East Th., March 18, '40; r. Rockland.

Fourth Generation.

John T.'s ch. 1, Frederic H., b. ab. 1845. 2, Clara C., b. ab. '47. 3, Charles H., b. ab. '49.

William G.'s ch. 1, Lizzie, b. ab. 1847. 2, Ada, b. Dec. 1849, d. Oct. 19, '51. 3, Albert, b. ab. 1851. 4, Emma, b. Jan. 31, '53, d. Feb. 10, '55. 5, Annie M., b. ab. 1856.

Maj. Gen. Hiram G.'s ch. Lucy F., b. ab. 1847.

George W.'s ch. Edward F., b. ab. 1858.

Capt. Joseph T.'s ch. 1, Edward S., b. ab. 1855. 2, Arthur H., b. ab. '57. By 2d wife. 3, Everett H., b. Nov. 22, '63, d. Aug. 11, '64

BEVERAGE, Capt. Matthew, of Hope, b. in Topsham, or c. from there to Fox Islands; m. 1st, Abigail Dyer of Fox Islands, 2d, Clarissa Cobb of W. r. & d. Hope. His ch. by 1st wife. 1, Harrison, lost at sea. 2, Achsa, m. Chas. Heald of Belmont. 3, Louisa, d. young. 4, Mary Miles, m. Anselm Tucker; r. Portland. 5, Jas Madison, b. ab. 1813; m. Mary J. Taylor of Hope; r. Th, where he has been much in town office. By 2d wife. 6, Ezekiel G. D., m. Martha Gilmore; r. East Union. 7, Sarah Abby, d. young. 8, Thomas Jefferson, b. ab. 1820; m. Deborah M. Taylor of Hope, Nov. 17, 1842; r. Th. a joiner. 9, George W., b. ab. 1824; m. Martha Frances Piper, Jan. 11, 1846; r. Th., a shoemaker, 10, Martha W., m. Charles L. Allen; r. Rock. and died Nov. 7, 1849.

James M.'s ch. 1, Thomas T., b. ab. 1838, taught high school, and was nearly ready to grad. at Bowdoin Coll., but d. May 12, 1864. 2, John F., b. ab. 1840.

Thomas J.'s ch. 1, John Thomas, b. ab. 1847. 2, Charles Henry, b. 1849, d. Oct. 10, 1853. 3, Martha Frances, b. ab. 1852. 4, Franklin, b. ab. 1854. 5, Mary J., b. ab. 1857.

George W.'s ch. 1, Edwin, b. ab. 1849. 2, Flora, b. 1851. 3, Charles, b. June 22, and died Dec. 12, 1853. 4, Ida, b. ab. 1855.

BEVERAGE, Nathaniel, b. 1804, a nephew of Capt. Matthew; m. Sarah Alexander, a niece of ditto; c. from Fox Islands; r. Rock., at North End, a carpenter. Their ch. 1, Henry T., b. Nov. 29, 1841. 2, Mercy, b. ab. 1843. 3, Frederic, b. ab. 1847.

BICKMORE, William, b. 1805, c. from Appleton; m. Almira A———; r. Rock., a lime burner. Their ch. 1, Charles, b. ab. 1843. 2, Henry, b. 1848. 3, Abby, b. 1849. 4, William O., b. 1856.

BICKMORE, Oliver, b. ab. 1830; perhaps a son of preceding; m. Maria ———; r. Rock., a mariner. Their ch. Eva M., b. 1859.

BIRD, John, b. ab. 1798; came from Framingham or Needham in 1805, settled in Cam.; m. Clarissa Gregory, Dec. 20, 1821; rem. to Blackington's Corner, 1831; r. Rock., a merchant, lime manufacturer, pres. North Bank, &c. Their ch. 1, A. Jackson, b. ab. 1822; m. Hannah H. Miller of Linc., r. Rock., a grocer. 2, Capt. Hanson, m. Malvina Ulmer, Aug. 17, 1845; r. Rock. 3, Almond, m. Sarah S. Keen, Sept. 18, 1853; r. Cam. 4, John (2d); m. Abby A. Smith of Worcester, Mass., r. Rock., a variety merchant. 5, Harriet, m. Capt. Merrick M. Packard; r. Rock. 6, Clarissa, m. Jackson Weeks; r. Rock. 7, Lorinda, r. Rock. 8, Laura, m. Robert Messer; r. Cam. 9, Mary A. 10, J. Sidney M., b. 1840; m Anna E. Heard, Sept. 25, 1859; r. Rock.; in mercantile business.

Adoniram J's ch. 1, Emma C., b. ab. 1851. 2, Mary M., b. ab. 1853. 3, Augustus D. b. ab. 1855. 4, Ada C., b. ab. 1857. 5, Hanson G., b. Jan. 6, 1859. 6, Anna J., b. April 17, & d. Sept. 6, 1860. 7, Hattie M., b. Oct. 3, 1861.

John (2d)'s ch. 1, Adaline M., b. ab. 1858. 2, William H., b. ab. 1859.

BIRDING, or Burding; of this family 3 brothers came from Fox Islands, and settled in S. Th. 1, Calvin, b. ab. 1824; m. Margaret L. Arey; r. S. Th., a mariner. 2, George W., b. ab. 1828; m. Susan Frye, Sept. 26, 1850; r. S. Th., a joiner, and soldier of 20th Me. reg. 3, Hiram E., b. ab. 1836; m. Mary E. Constant of Fayal, p. Jan. 24, 1859; r. S. Th., a carpenter.

Calvin's ch. 1, George, b. ab. 1848. 2, Adelaide, b. ab. 1854. 3, a son, b. in 1860.

Hiram E.'s ch. 1, Euphemia A., b. ab. 1853. 3, Eveline B., b. ab. 1855. 3, Joseph A., b. ab. 1857.

BISKEY, William, a Frenchman by birth, and house joiner by trade, c. to St. George and m. Catharine Long. Their ch. 1, Capt. William, m. Hepzibah Nutting of C., July 8, 1821; r. Th., and d. at Norfolk Aug. 24, 1826, in the brig *Tobacco Plant*. 2, Michael, m. Hannah Bartlett of Th., p. July 23, 1822; r. St. Geo. 3, John.

Capt. William's ch. 1, Mary Catharine, b. April 21, 1822, d. May 13, 1843. 2, Sarah L., b. June 4, 1826, m. Capt. Judson R. Washburn; r. Th. 3, William B., b. May 1833, d. Aug. 13, 1838.

BLACK, (translated from SCHWARTZ, the original German name;) of this family three brothers c. here from Wal. 1, Samuel,

b. 1805; m. Elizabeth Kaler; r. S. Th., a farmer, & d. April 3, 1862. 2, Asa, b. ab. 1813; m. Agnes Benner; r. Rock., a truckman. 3, Stephen, b. ab. 1815; m. Sarah ——— ; r. Rock. Jacob, a brother, m. and r. Wal., whose son, Thomas, b. ab. 1828, m. Sarah J. Blackington; r. Rock., a joiner.

Samuel's ch. 1, Lebalister, b. ab. 1842. 2, Louisa, b. ab. 1844. 3, Martha E, b. ab. 1847. 4, Samuel G., b. ab, 1852.

Asa's ch. 1, Rhoda A., m. James W. Clark; r. Rock. 2. Mary J., b. ab. 1840; m. Joseph L. Clark; r. Rock. 3, Helen A., b. ab. 1842. 4. Gorham L., b. 1845. 5, Clara E., b. ab. 1853.

Stephen's ch. 1, Stephen, (2d), b. ab. 1841. 2, Caroline, b, 1843. 3, John H., b. 1846. 4, Mehitable, b. 1851. 5, Jane E., b. 1853.

Thomas's ch. Emma F., b. ab. 1857.

BLACKBURN, John, b. 1823, in Canada East; as was Elizabeth his wife; r. Rock., a lime burner. Their ch. 1, John, b. ab. 1845. 2, Delaith, b. '47. 3, George, b. '49. 4, Louisa, b. '52. 5, Frank, b. '53. 6, Georgiana, b. '55.

BLACKBURN, Thomas, b. 1829, in New York; as was Jane his wife in Canada West; r. Rock., a lime burner. Their ch. 1, Frank; b. ab. 1854. 2, Emma J., b ab. 1858.

BLACKINGTON; of this family, said to be of Italian descent, Benjamin, b. Jan. 28, 1750; m. Eunice Woodcock; came from Attleboro'; was here with his family in 1777; took up 3 adjoining lots W. of the Meadows on which he & his sons settled; died Sept. 6, 1812. His ch. 1, Benjamin (2d), b. Aug. 1775; m. Catharine Sterling of Meduncook, p. Oct 22, 1796; r. Rock., and died March 31, 1850. 2, Nathan, m. Hannah Stevens, p. March 30, 1798; r. West of Meadows; and died Feb. 28, 1839. 3, Rebecca, b. June, 1781; m. Daniel Palmer; r. Th., & d. Jan 9, 1853. 4? Eunice, m. Jonathan Ames; rem. Burnham. 5, James W., m. Hannah Keen; r. Rock., was deputy sheriff, &c.; died May 4, 1850. 6, Jemima, m. Welcome Healey; r. and died in Thomaston.

Benjamin (2d)'s ch. 1, Willard, b. Dec. 5, 1797; d. Aug. 10, 1800. 2, Sterling E., b. April 9, 1800; m. Elizabeth Pottle, Aug. 19, 1821; r. Th., & d. Sept. 18, '39. 3, Gilbert M., b. Aug. 13, '02; m. Lucy Robbins of Union, p. May 5, '24. 4, Russell G., b. Sept. 6, '04; d. young. 5, Danforth B., b. July 28, '06; m. Louisa Webster; r. U. 6, Bryant, b. Oct. 17, '08; m. Susan Chaples, p. July 31, '38; r. Th. 7, James W., (2d), b. July 17, '11; d. Nov. 8, '36. 8, Rufus K., b. Oct. 7, '13; m. Harriet S. Robbins, Jan. 14, '38; rem. to Cam. 9, Jane H., b. Jan. 18, '19; m. Col. Timothy Williams; r. Rockland. The mother died Oct. 5, '39, aged 66.

Nathan's ch. 1, Harriet, born April 19, 1799; m. Capt. John B. Hawk; r. Th. 2, Adaline, b. June 9, 1801; m. George Collins; r. Rock., & d. March 4, '63. 3, Ann, b. June 1, '08; m. Jos. Palmer; r. Th. 4, Sophia, b. April 7, '10; m. Benjamin B. Palmer; r. Th. 5, Rebecca, b. June 1, 1812; r. Rock. 6, Nathan (2d), born Dec. 14, '13; m. & d. in Boston. 7, Erastus F., b. April 23, '15; r. Th. 8, Alden, b. July 2, '16; m. Nancy Kalloch, Jan. 29, '37, & d. in Rock. 9, Capt. Edward F., b. Jan. 9, '18; m. Emily H. Ulmer, Aug. 27, '48; r. Rock., a farmer. 10, George, b. March 7, '20; r. Rock., a farmer. 11, Willard (2d), b. Nov. 15, '22; m. Eliza Plaiston, Jan. 1, '55; r. Rockland.

James W.'s ch. 1, Willard S., (natural or adopted), b. ab. 1805;

m. Julia G. Thomas, Dec. 25, '31; r. Rock., a farmer. 2, Susan, b. Feb. 18, '19; m. Isaac Ingraham (2d); r. Rock., & d. Feb. 7, '58. 3, Irvin K., b. Oct. 10, '20; d. Feb. 7, '45. 4, Olivia, m. William J. Atkins; r. Rock. 5, Alvan, b. July 21, '22; went south in 1850 or '52. 6, Jasper W., b. Dec. 28, '23. 7, Francis Otis, b. Feb. 12, '29; killed in 1859, by a fall into a shaft in California. 8, Emily A., born Nov. 7, 1831.

Fourth Generation.

Sterling E.'s ch. 1, Clementine, b Feb. 2, 1822; d. April 6, '26. 2, Orrin L., b. Feb. 3, '23; m. Rebecca Black of Wal., p. May 10, '53; r. Rock., a teamster. 3, Thomas T., b. Sept. 10, '24; m. Catharine Richards, Jan. 27, '52; r. Linc. 4, Emeline H., b. March 30, '26; m. Jefferson Kalloch; r. Rock., & d. Mar. 3, '49. 5, Benjamin W., b. July 5, '27; m. Dora Houston of Linc., Jan. 2, '54; r. Rock., a joiner. 6, Frances E., b. Feb. 25, '29; m. Elbridge G. Kalloch of Rock. 7, Sarah J., b. 1834; m. Thomas Black; d. Rock., July 30, '57. 8, Morton, A., b. 1835; m. Mary H. Black; r. Rock., soldier of 4th Me., &c. 9, Eliza A., b. April 6, '37; m. Edward Perkins of W. 10, Edward R, m. Abby Bailey of Wiscasset; r. Cam. and Rock., a blacksmith. The mother died March 14, '54, aged 55 years, 17 days.

Bryant's ch. 1, Mary M., b. Oct. 4, 1839; r. Rock. 2, Catharine S., b. Oct. 11, '42. 3, Helen L., b. June 30, '44. 4, Emma A., b. Oct. 16, '46. 5, Harvey A., b. May 10, '50. 6, Chester, b. Sep. 30, '58.

Rufus K.'s ch. 1, Sarah G., b. April 6, 1838. 2, Alda Eliza, b. Oct. 20, '40. 3, Alphene.

Alden's ch. 1, Adelaide T., b. Oct. 30, 1837; m. Theodore M. Davis, Sept. 23, 1859, r. Rock. 2, Sarah E., b. Nov. 24, 1839. 3, Frederic, b. Sept. 17, 1842. 4, Mary, b. ab. 1846. 5, Harriet, b. ab. 1849. 6, Ada, b. ab. 1851. 7 & 8, twins, b. ab. 1856; Cora E, and Frances E.

Edward F.'s ch. 1, Anson U., b ab. 1849. 2, Esther B., b. about '51. 3, William, b. ab. '53. 4, Frederic, b. ab. '55. 5, Almond H., b. '57. 6, John F., b. ab. '59.

Willard (2d)'s ch. 1, Calfrena, b. ab. 1857. 2, Nathan S., b. ab. '58. 3, George H., b. '60.

Willard S.'s ch. 1, Oscar E., b. Jan. 6, 1833; a silver ware pedler, &c. 2, Lucy K, b. Oct. 16, '34; m. John H. Additon, 1859, r. Dexter. 3, Mary T., b. Feb. 11, '38; m. Hanson A. Mills of Fox Is. Oct. 22, '59. 4, Oliver N., b. March 14, '40; a freight agent. 5, Lydia J., b. May 16, '42; m. John F. Fogler, Jan. 1, '60, r. Rock. 6, Olive, b. ab. '47. 7, Jerusha, b. ab. '49. 8, C. Jennette, b. ab. '52. 9, Anna Bell, b. ab. '55.

Fifth Generation.

Thomas T.'s ch. Cora B., b. April, 1854, d. May 6, '55.

Benjamin W.'s ch. 1, Alvah, b. ab. 1856. 2, Jennie, b. ab. '59.

Morton A.'s ch. 1, Hiram, b. ab. 1855. 2, Clarence E., b. May, '58, d. Aug. 12, '60. 3, Edgar L., b. Sept. '60, d. Nov. 17, '63.

BLACKINGTON, ———, a distant connection of the preceding family, m. Chloe ———, of Attleboro, Mass., where he r. & d. His widow m. 2d, Oliver Robbins of Th., and probably was followed here by her first children, viz,: 1, Sarah, m. Alexander Jameson of Camden, rem. Charleston. 2, John, born ab. 1756; came, it is thought, from Weymouth; m. Eleanor Spear, p. June 16, 1795; r. Th. Mill

13*

River; a merchant, &c., and d. Nov. 16, 1843, a. 87. 3, Barbara, m. Nathaniel Copeland, p. March 29, 1786; r. W., and d. Oct. 4, 1822. 4, Nancy, m. Marlboro Packard, r. and d. U. 5, Rebecca, m. John Crockett, r. & d. Rock. 6, Capt. James, b. 1766; m. Betsey Watson, p. Feb. 19, 1799; a soldier & officer in the revolution; r. Th., & d. Oct. 25, 1835.

John's ch. 1, Margaret, b. J. 14, 1797; m. 1st, Otis Harding, 2d, ——— Dyer, of Weymouth, Mass. 2, Capt. John (2d,) b. Feb. 13, 1799; m. Maria D. Howard, Jan. 3, 1830; r. Th., Mill River. 3, William, b. May, 1801, d. Oct. 1805. 4, Capt. Edward, b. May 27, 1805; m. Eunice Creighton, March 6, 1834; r. Th. & d. N. O. 5, George, b. July 14, '07; m. Sarah Calef, July 16, '29, & d. Dec. 15, '30, leaving 1 child who d. May 2, 1831, a. 9 mos. 6, Oliver, b. Jan. 18, 1810, d. at sea, April 24, '37.

Capt. James's ch. 1, John (3d) b. 1803, d. 1804. 2, Thos. Jefferson, b. 1805, d. at Charleston, S. C., July 29, '31. 3, Capt. James Madison, b. '07; m. 1st, Elizabeth B. Liscomb, Dec. 24, '36, 2d, Abby Haskell of W., May, 1860, 3d, Nancy Fales, Aug. 14, '64, r. Th., Mill River. 4, Barbara, b. 1809; m. Nathaniel Liscomb; r. Th. & d. March 4, '38. 5, Rebecca, b. 1811; m. Capt. James S. Colley; r. Th. & d. Feb. 3, '61. 6, Angelina, b. 1813; m. Alexander Young; r. Th. & d. Nov. 21, '51. 7, Benjamin Franklin, b. 1815, & d. April 13 '23. 8, Abby S., b. Feb. 1819, d. Aug. 29, '33.

Capt. John (2d)'s ch. 1, Margaret E., b. July 30, 1830, d. April 5, '55. 2, Caroline E., b. Dec. 11, 31; r. Th. 3, Abby M., b. Oct. 23, '34; r. Th. 4, Wm. John, b. Feb. 25, '36; r. Th., a mariner. 5, Horace H., b. May 14, '37, d. April 5, '60, lost overboard at sea. 6, Alfred P., b. Aug. 15, '39; r. Th., a returned soldier of 4th Me. reg. 7, Richard R., b. Aug. 16, '41, d. Feb. 25, '42. 8, Frank, b. ab. '43; r. Th., a mariner.

Capt. Edward's ch. 1, Helen, b. May 17, 1837. 2, George E., b. Jan. 5, '42.

Capt. J. Madison's ch. by 2d wife. James Madison (2d), b. June 9, and died Sept. 1861. The mother died Jan. 22, 1862.

BLACKINGTON, Francis M., b. ab. 1827; m. Margaret C. Kaler, Oct. 18, '49; r. Rock., a shoe manufacturer. Their ch. Ada F., b. about 1851.

BLAKE, William, b. ab. 1824, (native place not ascertained by the compiler); m. Deborah ———; r. S. Th., a farmer. Their ch. 1, William F., b. ab. '51. 2, Benjamin, b. ab. '54. 3 & 4, twins, b. ab. '58; Alphonso & Alonzo. 5, Marcia, born about '59.

BLANCHARD, Loring, m. Sarah F. Jackson, Oct. 25, '61, when he resided in Rockland.

BLANDEN, Jonas, b. ab. 1815 of a Southboro', Mass. family; m. Jane Ogier of Cam; r. Th., a carpenter. Their ch. 1, William L., b. ab. 1840. 2, E. Arvesta, b. ab. '42. 3, Cornelia K., b. '43, died Jan. 3, 1858.

BLAISDELL, or Blasdell, Richard S., b. in 1761; m. & r. Hampden, but died in Rock., Nov. 1, 1846. Of his sons there came hither; 1, William, b. 1794, c. here from Orland; m. Lucretia Spear, May 13, 1823; r. Rock., & d. Oct. 21, '58. 2, Capt. Richard S., m. Mary C. Arey, Sept. 14, '46; r. Rock., rem. for a time to California, but returned and resides in Rockland.

William's ch. 1, Mary F., b. Oct. 29, 1827; m. William Walsh (3d); r. Rock. 2, Dr. John M., b. April 28, '29; m. Roxana E. Weston of Salem, Mass., p. Dec. 14, '52; r. Rock., & d. at Havana of yellow fever, Nov. 23, '57, his wife having died by suicide, June 25, 53. 3, Caroline, b. April 29, '32; d. Feb. 26, '34. 4, Ann Eliza, b. March 3, '35. 5, William (2d), b. Dec. 29, '36; r. Rock., a mariner. 6, Susan, born Aug. 27, '42; r. Rockland.

Capt. Richard's ch. we have no record of, except these, deceased. 1, Edwin F., died at Whitneyville, April 9, 1852. 2, Lucy Helen, b. Sept. 1848, died at ditto, April 19, '50. 3, Mary Sophia, died August 22, '54. 4, John B., born Jan. 1853, died August 7, '54.

BLAISDELL, Sanborn, came from Hampden; m. Mary Miller of Th., April 15, 1821; r. here a time, but rem. to Camden. Their ch. 1, Sarah, born June 15, '23; m. Josiah Burleigh of Salem, Mass., Oct. 23, '45. 2, Sanborn (2d), born July 6, '27. 3, Alonzo S., born Sept. 21, '30. 4, David H., born Nov. 7, '33; all probably rem. 5, Rebecca, born March 23, '22, died Sept. 5, '26. 6, Harriet, born April 5, '25, died Sept. 4, '26. The mother died April 8, 1851, aged 55.

BLODGETT, George W, born about 1815 in Freedom; m. Mary H. Gregory; r. Rockland, a photographist.

BLOOD, Simeon, b. Sept. 1782, c. from Deering, N. H.; m. Lucinda Fales, Dec. 22, 1808; settled on the Meadows road, Th., was an excellent mechanic, and occasional mariner, in which capacity he went to sea and was taken captive in the war of 1812 and carried to England, where dining at an inn one day after his release, the landlord brought in his daughter who was anxious to see an *American* and expressed great surprise at not finding him *black*; returned in safety, r. Th. & d. March 1, 1857. Of his brothers, 1, Abel, m. Betsey Howard of St. George, p. Feb. 28, 1809, rem. & d. Hope. 2, Joel, m. Thirza Whitcomb of Hope, July 25, 1816; r. Th., soon removed to Hope. 3. Lemuel, c. to Th. but, after a year or two, ret. to N. H.

Simeon's ch. 1, Ezekiel D., born Dec. 7, 1814; m. Elmira Waugh of Readfield, Jan., 1, 1841; r. Th., a joiner, & d. in 1864. 2, Simeon (2d), born Oct. 29, 1817; m. Eunice Palmer, Aug. 4, 1839; r. Rock., of great mechanical genius, and made, in 1850, an entire gold watch, the first, probably, made in the State. 3, David K., born July 7, 1820; went to sea as mate, died in Havana, Cuba, 1847. 4, William H., b. April 29, '24; m. Cordelia A. Gallop, Sept. 27, '46; r. Th., a jeweller, &c. 5, Jane A., born Oct. 14, '26; m. Capt. Alexander C. Post; r. Th. 6, Arthur M., born Dec 8, '29; m. Mary L. Slatery, Feb. 16, '52; r. Sacramento city, California. 7, Nancy T, born April 28, '33; r. Th. 8, Lucinda, born Nov. 13, '36; m. Sears S. Ulmer; removed and resides near Presque Isle.

Ezekiel D.'s ch. 1, Charles Sullivan, born 1847. 2, Francis D., b. '49. 3, (adopted,) Melissa Howard. 4, Ira, born April 7, '54, died April 22, '56. The mother died May 5, '61.

Simeon, (2d's), ch. 1, Zulietta A., born April 11, 1841, died Sept. 24, '42. 2, Sarah R., born Sept. 25, '42. 3, Frank M., born '45. 4, An infant, died. 5, Simeon, (3d), born about '52. 6, Grace E. born June '55, died Sept. 9, '56. 7, Nellie I., born about '59.

William H.'s ch. 1, Helen A., born Oct. 25, 1847. 2, William H., (2d), born Feb. 18, '52, died Nov. 14, '56. 3, George A., b. Dec. 1, '56.

BLYE, Ebenezer, m. Mollie Bishop; c. early with his family from Attleborough, Mass., r. Th., on Meadows road, and died 1811. Their ch. 1, Nancy, born 1766; m. Nehemiah Stevens, & died at her son's in W., Oct. 1854. 2, A son, who went into the army of the Revolution and never returned. 3, Another son, who was drowned in the river, at the age of 7 years, before the landing of the family at Th. 4, Betsey, m. John Bentley; r. Th., & d. Nov. 8, 1854. 5, Mary, b. ab. 1781; m. Samuel Hammond; r. Rock. & died August 16, '56. 6, Cynthia, died in W. at Samuel Kelloch's.

BOGGS, Dr. Life W., born March 27, 1798, in Hope, son of William (2d) and Sarah (Jameson) Boggs; m. 1st, Susan S. Huse, 2d, Phebe A. ——— ; r. St. George, Warren, & Camden, came to Rockland where he successfully practised Botanic medicine till his death, May 11, 1861. His ch. by 1st wife. 1, James Harvey, m. Lilias Philbrook, 1850; settled on the Peabody farm, Th., 1862, a soldier, 21st Me. reg. 2, Sarah M., b. 1825, d. Oct. 12, '49. 3, William, b. ab. 1827; m. Margaret Davis of Camden, Feb. 22, '64; r. Rockland, a carpenter. 4, George, born about '29; m. Catharine Waldo; r. South Th., a carpenter. 5, Josiah M. 6, Wilson, born March 22, '39; m. Margaret A. Sherer, Oct. 31, '61; r. Rock. 7, Hannah E., born July 30, '41, died Dec. 20, '45. 8, Lewis K., born Dec. 15, '43; r. Rockland, a mariner.

George's ch. 1, Frederic G., born ab. 1855. 2, Emma, b. ab. '59.

BOHNDEL, Christian Henry, born in Denmark, Europe, 1816; m. Dorothea Martin of Otwilder, Germany; r. Th., a rigger. Their ch. 1, Josephine, born Dec. 9, '33, died Sept. 15, '40. 2, Mary E., born August 3, '41; m. Oliver Robinson (3d); r. Th. 3, Christian H., b. March 2, '43. 4, Hortense, born about '45. 5, Josephine, born about '47. 6, George M. born about '49. 7, Dorothea M., born June 16, and died Sept. 21, '52. 8, Roselia, born Jan. 17, and died August 16, '54. 9, Wilhelmina S., born about '55.

BOND, William J., born about 1822 in Jefferson; m. Rachel M. Weeks; r. Rockland, a provision dealer. Their ch. 1, Freddie R., born about 1850 2, Grace D., born about '52.

BOOKER, Capt. John B, born about 1789; m. 1st, Betsey Hutchings, (who died January 14, 1832, aged 40), 2d, Mary E. Thompson, March 9, '33; r. Th., rem. Rockland, where he died by drowning, Sept. 1, '49. Joseph, perhaps a brother, born about 1794; m. Nancy ———; came from Boothbay; r. Th., rem. Rockland and died May 9, 1862. From one of these two, Booker street in Th. was named.

Joseph's ch. 1, Capt. Baker H., born about 1822; m. 1st, Julia A. Boynton, (who died May 22, '53), 2d, Mrs. Sophia R. Sproul, June 5, '56; r. Rockland. 2, Barnard. 3, Joseph (2d), born about '34; m. Priscilla Bridges, Oct 3, '61; r. Rockland, a mariner. 4, Melissa A., born about '43. 5, Gardner L., born about '46.

BOWDEN, Silas, born in China, Maine; m. Vesta L. Heath; r. Rock. Charles, born about 1837; r. Rockland with Matilda his wife; was a soldier in Co. D, 4th Maine regiment, and was killed at the battle of Chantilly, Sept. 1, '62.

BOWERS, George W., came from Providence, R. I., to what is now South Thomaston; m. Nancy, daughter of Col. David Nutt of Camden, p. April 29, 1792; and died 1848. Their ch. 1, Jane, born Feb. 27, 1793; m. John Murch of Castine; r. Hampden & Brooklyn, N. Y. 2, Betsey, born Oct. 4, 1796; m. David Green; r. Norridgewock. 3, Mary, born Oct. 17, 1799, died Oct. 25, 1822. 4, Susan, born March 27, 1803; m. Capt. John G. Paine; r. Th. 5, Sylvester, born Feb. 26, 1806; m. Mercy Murray, Feb. 12, 1830, 2d, Elizabeth Davy, March 4, 1848; r. Beech Woods; and died Feb. 15, 1858. 6, George, born August 5, 1808, died June 18, 1813. 7, Isaac B., born June 18, '10; m. Lydia H. Post, Oct. 31, '47; r. S. Th., a mariner. 8, Sarah B., born May 1, '14, died Dec. 18, '38. 9, Content A., born March 28, '18; r. South Thomaston.

Sylvester's ch. 1, Mary, born Sept. 20, 1831. 2, Content, born Jan. 18, '36. 3, George, (3d), born ab. '43. By 2d wife. 4, Cassandra, born about '51. 5, Sylvester, born about '54.

Isaac B.'s ch. 1, Elbridge, died young. 2, William H., b. ab. '52.

BOWLER; of this family, two brothers c. from Palermo, Me., to this place, viz. 1, Allen, born about 1819 in Palermo; m. Lydia B. Abbott of Albion; r. Rockland, a merchant in firm of Bowler & Abbott. 2, Rev. James Riley, born about 1825; m. Adaline F. Turner of Palermo; was settled in South Thomaston as pastor of the 2d Baptist church; r. since in Rockland.

Allen's ch. 1, Clara E., born ab. 1849. 2, Eugene R., b. ab. '53.

Rev. James Riley's ch. 1, Albert O. born about 1854; deaf mute.

BOWMAN, John, born about 1823 in Ireland; m. Kate Carr; r. Th. Their ch. 1, John (2d), born about 1855. 2, Sarah, born about '57. 3, Mary, born about '60.

BOYD, Adam, (son of Adam of St. George who died there April 17, 1850, aged 84); m. Rachel Kelloch; r. Rockland. Their ch. 1, William, m. Lavinia Hewett; r. California. 2, George W., born ab. 1826; m. Nancy S. Farnham; r. Rock., a mariner. 3, Mary Ann, d. in Rockland, Feb. 31, '43. 4, Eliza J., m. William Gay; r. Rock. 5, Phinley, born July, 1830; m. M. Augusta Knowlton; r. Rockland, and died May 12, '56. 6, Rachel, m. Samuel F. Coombs; r. Oregon. 7, Louisa, m. Charles Hall; r. S. Th. 8, Susan, m. Capt. Jefferson Drinkwater; r. Rock. 9, Frances, born April 3, '39; r. Rockland

George W.'s ch. 1, John Edmund, born about 1854. 2, Mary Josephine, born about 1859.

BOYLES, Edward, born about 1811; came to Th. and r. many years, carried on baker's business, Georges hotel, &c.; m. 1st, Caroline McClintock of Wal., p. April 3, '30, 2d, Asenath M. Willis; rem. to Wal. and the Kennebec, but ret. and r. Rock. His ch. by 1st wife. 1, Charles. 2, Salome B., born April 21, '33. 3, Caroline M., born April 15, '35; m. Joseph Nichols of Th., May 7, '56. 4, Mary Ann, born March 6, '37; m James M. Elliott of Phipsburg, 1860. 5, Edward (2d), born Nov. 25, '39, drowned May 11, '50. 6, Hermon F., born Nov. 10, and died Nov. 18, '43. The mother died Dec. 9, 1851. By 2d wife. 7, Clara, born about 1858.

BOYNTON, Hon. Nehemiah, born in Rockport, Mass., 1804; came in 1825 to St George, engaged largely in the fish business under firm of N. Boynton & Co., nine years; m. Mary Jane Miller, May 1828; was town treasurer, post master, and representative; removed to Th. where he was in active business eleven years, at the stand since occupied by Hon. E. O'Brien, was president of the Lincoln Bible So., and treasurer of the Theological Seminary; removed in '45 to Chelsea, Mass., where he has since resided, and done business in Boston, (N. Boynton & Co., Commission Merchants and Manufacturers of Cotton Duck, 134, Commercial St.,) has been selectman of Chelsea, chairman of board of aldermen, president of Winnesimmet Benevolent So., a trustee of Newton Theological Seminary, state senator two years, one of the State valuation committee, treasurer of Am. Bapt. Missionary Union 7 years, and, in '62, one of Gov. Andrew's council for Dist. No. 1, embracing Suffolk Co. Their ch. 1, Elizabeth R., b. Jan. 4, 1830; m. in '50 A. F. Hervey, who is connected with Mr. B. in business; and has one son, Frank W., b. in 1854.

BOYNTON, Cyrus V. R., b. ab. 1820, in Brooks; m. 1st Delia E. W. Cochran, 2d, Mary Jones; resides Rockland, a cabinet maker. Of his children by first wife. 1, Louisa, was b. about 1842. 2, Alfred, b. about '44. By 2d wife. 3, Fanny K., b. April 12, '60, d. April 12, 1864.

BOYNTON, Hiram H., b. ab. 1827; m. 1st, Lucia M. Young, June 17, 1854, 2d, Albina F. Young; r. Th., a carpenter, &c.

BOYNTON, Samuel P., b. about 1817; m. Emeline P. Ames; resides Rockland, a lime burner, and now in the army. Their children, 1, Laura Ann, b. about 1840. 2, Georgia G., b. about 1844, m. Frank M. Boynton, of Rockland, Dec. 1 '62. 3, Emily F., b. about '46. 4, Lucy A., b. about '48. 5, Lizzie, b. about '50. 6, Addie, b. about '51. 7, Samuel K. b. '52. 6, Augusta J., b. '54. 9, David, b. '56.

BRACKETT, Joshua b. ab. 1805, came from Acton; m. Jane P. Kelleran, July 13, 1837; r. Thomaston, a mariner. Their ch. Eliza, b. about 1846.

BRACKETT, James, came from Warren, was a merchant some years in Rockland, but removed 1864 to Portland.

BRACKLEY, Lieut. Benaiah C., b. in Strong, came to Rockland, m. Fannie Ulmer, was officer for a time in 4th Me. regiment, since re-enlisted; r. Rockland. Rufus K. Brackley, m. Fidelia Kelley, Jan. 11, '51; r. Rockland, and of whose ch. Silas was b. Jan. and died June 14, '53.

BRADBURY, Wymond, came from Portland about 1804, m. Ruth Mathews, Sept. 11, 1810; settled at S. Thomaston in the house now occupied by John Robbins and formerly L. Wade's; was a shoemaker by trade; d. July 6, '37. Their ch. 1, Capt. Samuel Andrews, b. Sept. 28, 1811; m. Lucy R. Butler, April 5, '41; r. S Thomaston, & d. Nov. 16, '45. 2, Archibald M., b. April 19, '14; r. S. Thomaston, a mariner. 3, Rebecca, b, Aug. 16, '16; m. Abiezer Coombs, October 6, '44, 2d, David Owens; r. S. Thomaston. 4, Capt. Charles, b. May 25, '19; m. Nancy M. Butler, Oct. 4, '46; r. S. Thomaston. 5, Almira S., b. May 28, '22, d. Oct. 12, '25. 6, Henry K., b. May 20, '25; m. Nancy C. Suchforth, p. May 22, '52; r. S. Thomaston, a mason. 7, George, b. March 7, '28; m. Irene Kelloch, p. Jan. 28, '54; r. S. Thomaston, a mariner. 8, Caroline F., b. Dec. 13, '33, d. Feb. 1860. 9, Sarah W., b. Oct. 1, '37, d. young.

Samuel A.'s ch. Charles Herbert, b. April 5, 1843, d. June 25, '44.

Capt. Charles' ch. 1, Charles B., b. about 1849. 2, Ardelle M., b. about '52. 3, Almyn, b. about 1857.

Henry K.'s ch. Percy, d. young.

George's ch. 1, Augusta, b. about 1856. 2, Ida, b. about '58.

BRADFORD, Isaiah, a descendant of Gov. William Bradford, of the honored Plymouth Pilgrims, m. 1st, Hannah Rawley, 2d, Mrs. Asenath (Morton) Miller; r. Cushing, and d. Oct. or November, 1851.

His ch. by 1st wife. 1, Nancy, m. William Campbell; r. Th. 2, Paul, born Nov. 1801; m. Mary E. Jacobs, October, 15, '29; r. Gleason street, Th., a carpenter. 3, James, m. Hannah Seavey; rem. Wisconsin, & married twice. 4, Isaac, died young. By 2d wife. 5, Martha, married Joseph Davis; r. Cushing. 6, Lydia, married John Burton; r. C. 7, William, married Jane Lewis; r. C. 8, Oliver, died young. 9, Harriet, died young.

Paul's ch. 1, Adeliza, born Sept. 19, 1831; married Silas Hanly; r. Th. 2, Mary M., born July 27, '34; married Joseph Eastman,; r. Rockland. 3, Helena, born Dec. 10, '36; r. Th. and kept millinary establishment for some time on Main street, in company with Miss A. Keating.

BRADFORD, Dea. Charles, m. Mrs. Elizabeth P. (Brown) Clark, Oct. 28, 1802; succeeded to Clark's house & pottery business, but in 1813 rem. to Ohio with his family. Their ch. 1, Lucy H. 2, Harvey Stetson, bap. July 13, 1810. 3, Charles Otis. 4, Nancy L., bap. July 26, '12. 5, Sophia Maria, bap. June 20, '13.

BRADY, Henry, b. ab. 1827 in Ireland; came over about 1853; m. Catharine Feeley, August 26, '52; r. Th. Matthew, a brother, also came to Th., was accidentally killed in Virginia in 1853 or '4, leaving a widow and three children.

BRAMHALL, Cornelius, m. Jane Pierce, Oct. 18, 1804; came, it is believed, from Vinalhaven; r. Rockland, and he or a son of the same name, m. 2d, Priscilla McCoy, June 28, '62. Capt. Robert, probably a brother, m. Nancy I. Graffam, Dec. 23, '31; r. Rockland, a mariner, and died Jan. 25, '53.

Capt. Robert's ch. 1, Thomas S., born Sept. 25, 1832, and was drowned June 6, '45. 2, George A., born May 6, '35; m. Lillias Herrick, Jan. 16, '64; r. Rockland, a mariner. 3, Mary H., born July 21, '38; m. William Simmons of Rockland, Dec. 24, '55. 4, Freeman Robert, born Sept. 27, '41; r. Rockland, a mariner. 5, Frances D., born about '44. 6, Margaret M., born about '47.

BRANN, Daniel, born in Whitefield, Maine; m. Elizabeth S. Tibbetts. Their ch. 1, Robert C., born about 1828; m. H. Frances Ingraham, Dec. 31, '50; r. S. Th., a sailmaker. 2, Frances, m. I. M. Packard. 3, Jane, m. John C. Irish, both now deceased. 4, Alpheus C., born about '35; m. Susan E. Smith, Dec. 25, '60; r. Rockland, a sailmaker. 5, Alonzo R., m. Lauretta Mitchell. 6, Ann E., m. Columbus Dyer; r. Cape Elizabeth. 7, Addie V., m. and r California. 8, Alexander T. is in the army, lately wounded. 9, Hester, deceased. 10, William A., now in the army. 11, James W., deceased.

Abraham, a cousin of these, born about 1830; m. Hannah K. Pillsbury, May 26, '55; r. South Thomaston, a carpenter.

Robert C.'s ch. 1, Edward H., born March, and died Nov. 26, '52. 2, Frank R., born about '54.

BRAY, Joseph S., born about 1827, and with Sarah his wife, r. in 1860 in Rockland, a mason. Their ch. 1, Charles, born about '51. 2, Franklin, born about '54. 3, Georgiana, born Dec. 28, '55, died March 5, '61. 4, Edwin, born about '58.

BRECK, Edward, son of Jonathan of Union, r. with Roxana his wife, many years in Thomaston, a tanner, teacher, &c, removed and died, it is believed, in China, Me. Of their ch. there appear on the Thomaston records, 1, Edward, (2d), born Jan. 13, 1819. 2, Rebecca

Russell, born Oct. 25, '20, who, or another daughter m. William H. Healey of China. 3, Lucy C., born '22, died Feb. 20, '24. 4, Joseph, born April, died May, '27. 5, a daughter was bap. August 7, '31.

BRETT, William, born about 1822; married Melissa M. ——— ; r. Rockland, a carpenter. Their ch. 1, Margary E., born about 1852. 2, John M., born about '54. 3, Deborah C., born about '57.

BREWER, Josiah, m. and r. in Freeport, Me. Of his sons. 1, Josiah, (2d), born in Freeport, m. Abby Brackett; r. Rockland. 2, Lewis, b. in F. about 1830; m. Benedicta Hutchinson from England; r. Rock., a ship carpenter.

Josiah (2d)'s ch. 1, Robert, born Sept 4, 1841, died March 25, '61. 2, Orris? in U. S. Navy. 3, Louisa G., born Sept. 1846, died Feb. 16, '62. The mother died Oct. 31, '58, in Rockland.

Lewis's ch. 1, Clara E., born about 1850. 2, Charles, born July, '51, died June '54. 3, William, born about '54. 4, Octavia.

BREWSTER, Zadoc, was the eldest son of Joseph, who was the 4th son of Nathaniel, who was the 1st son of William of Duxbury, who was the only son of Freelove, who was the younger of the two sons of William, the world renowned Elder & Governor of the Pilgrim colony at Plymouth, who was a native of Scrooby, Nottinghamshire, England, & whose empty chair, of Mayflower notoriety, now stands in Pilgrim Hall. He, Zadoc, was born March 15, 1742; married, 1st, Lois Brewster, 2d, Lucy Knight; r. Duxbury, Mass., but c. ab. 1786 to Old Thomaston, now Rockland, and died May 21, 1811.

Zadoc's ch. by 1st wife. 1, Darius, born June 23, 1764; married, 1st, Esther Soule, May 8, 1791, 2d, Sarah Fales, Feb. 6, 1823; was a soldier of the Revolution, came hither in 1797, from Duxbury, and settled back of Madambettox Mt.; r. Rock., & d. Feb. 19, 1846, a. 81. 2, Eunice, born May 11, 1766; married James Jones of Camden, and died June 18, 1819. 3, Sarah, born May 15, 1768; married, it is believed, & died Oct. 8, '01. 4, Cyrus, born Dec. 7, 1772; married and resided Camden? died May 18, '54 5, Ira, born April 20, 1775; married Patience Crocker, of New Castle, published Oct. 23, 1796; r. Rockland, North End, some years, and built three vessels; removed to Camden, and died Sept. 15, 1830. 6 and 7, twins, born Nov. 5, 1777, Joseph died Nov. 12, 1846, Benjamin, married Elizabeth Tolman, January 1, 1808; resided Camden and died January 19, 1849. The mother died November 14, 1777. By 2d wife, 8, Daniel, born November 17, 1780; married Bethiah Packard; r. Hope, and died January 18, 1844. 9, Lois, born April 17, 1782; married Rev. Reuben Keen; r. Freedom, and died May 1, 1864. 10, Ruth, born October 1, 1784. 11, Samuel, born April 22, 1786, died April 2, 1804. 12, Capt. William, born May 27, 1789; married 1st, Martha Jameson, Dec. 22, 1814; 2d, Nancy Nutt; r. Camden, Jameson's Point, and died by suicidal hanging, February 23, 1852. 14, Lucy, born Nov. 30, 1791, died August 23, 1792. 15, Lucy, born May 1, 1795.

Darius's children by 1st wife. 1, Martin, born February 7, 1792, died young. 2, Asa, born Dec., 19, 1793, died Feb. 27, 1814. 3, Benjamin (2d), born February 13, 1796; married Hannah G. Keiff, July 8, 1821; resides Rockland, on the homestead, a farmer. The mother died January 13, 1821, aged 66.

Of Ira's children. 1, Elijah, born February, 1798, died September 26, 1800. 2, Ira (2d), married Mary Thorndike; r. Camden. 3, Hiram, married 1st, Charlotte Ames, 2d, Sarah A,(Cooper) Sleeper, February 16, 1836, resides Rockland, a caulker, &c. 4, Lorenzo, resides Camden.

Of Daniel's ch. 1, Samuel, b. ab. 1830; m. Sarah Keen; r. Rock., a mariner.

Of Capt. William's ch. 1, Isaac, b. Feb. 3, 1819; m. Jane Smith; r. Rock., & d. by drowning, Jan. 6, '63, in Rockland harbor. 2, Capt. Zadoc F., b. ab. 1829; m. Sarah Brown; r. Rock., a master mariner, of late in U. S. Navy.

Fourth Generation, or Eighth from Gov. William.

Benjamin, (2d)'s ch. 1, Asa, b. Jan. 25, 1822, d. May 8, '32. 2, Sarah, b. Dec. 28, '23; m. 1st, Hazen B. Nelson, Jan. 1, '46, 2d, Willis Fish; r. Easton, Mass. 3, Washington I., b. Jan. 23, '26; m. Rebecca G. Oxton, March 4, '49; r. Rock., a farmer. 4, Elitha G., b. Jan. 24, '28; m. Edwin J. Delano, May 23, '52; r. Hammonton, N. J. 5, Esther, b. March 30, '30, d. Nov. 13, '32. 6, Benjamin F., b. Mar. 4, '32; m. Emily Fish; r. Natick, Mass., Dedham, &c., an agent for patents, &c. 7, Hannah E., b. Jan. 9, '36. 8, Darius Z., b. Dec. 2, '37; r. a time at Hammonton, N. J., but returned.

Ira's ch. 1, Lorina, m. Huse Tolman; r. Cam. 2, Edward, rem. Cal. 3, Harriet W., m. George W. Story; r. Rock. 4, Mary Frank, m. Charles B. Watts of W.; r. San Francisco, Cal. 5, Charles, b. ab. 1854; r. Cam.

Hiram's ch. by 1st wife. 1, Malvina, b. March 4, 1832; m. Woodbury A. Dyer; p. Aug. 26, '53; r. Portland. 2, Capt. John J., b. Dec. 21, '33; m. Emeline P. Mariner of C. Elizabeth, '60; supposed to have been drowned in the Mediterranean Sea. The mother died Feb. 27, '34.

Samuel's ch. Leonard, b. ab. 1857.

Isaac, (2d,)'s ch. 1, Emma F., b. ab. 1844. 2, Abbie F., b. ab. '49.

Capt. Zadoc F.'s ch. 1, Sarah M., b. ab. 1855. 2, Philena M., b. ab. '58. 3, Zadoc F., b. April 3, '60, d. April 30, '63.

Washington I.'s ch. 1, Willis Franklin, b. Dec. 7, 1849. 2, Milton C., b. Dec. 22, '51. 3, Edwin D., b. Sept. 22, '53. 4, Hannah R., b. Aug. 30, '55. 5, Mary Eva, b. June 25, '59.

BRICKLEY, John, b. ab. 1815; c. with Catharine his wife from Ireland; r. Rock., a lime burner. Their ch. 1 & 2, twins, b. in Mass., 1848, Thomas & Ellen. 3, John, b. ab. '52. 4, Mary, b. ab. '54.

BRIDGES, Dea. John, b. at York, Nov. 16, 1751, O. S., c. early to Old Th.; m. Sarah Eastman, Jan. 6, 1774, by D. Fales, Esq.; r. & d. S. Th. His wife was born in Sandown, N. H., Oct. 6, 1751, O. S. Their ch. *1, Betsey, b. Feb. 19, 1775; m. Reuben Higgins of Duck Trap, p. Sept. 15, 1795. 2, Isaac, b. April 7, 1777; m. Linnity Stoddard; and rem. to British Provinces. 3, Sally, b. May 20, 1779; m. 1st, Henry K. Dunbar of W., 2d, Ebenezer Vose; r. Montville. 4, Susan, b. April 7, 1781; m. ——— Colson; and rem. Mass. 5, Hannah, b. May 1, 1783; m. and went to Mass. 6, John, (2d), b. Jan. 6, 1785; m. Priscilla Erskine, p. May 2, 1807; r. & d. S. Th. 7, Joseph, b. June 15, 1787; m. Susanna Norton, April 23, 1809; rem. and d. in Ohio. 8, Ruth, b. Aug. 15, 1789; m. Nathaniel Capen, in Mass. 9, Rebecca, b. April 7, 1791; m. Jesse Sleeper; r. S. Th., and d. Nov. 4, 1852. 10, Kingsbury, b. May 20, 1794; m. Sally Bryant, p. July 5, 1817; r. S. Th. & Ohio, now deceased. 11, Mary, b. June 20, 1796; m. Capt. William Singer, Sept. 27, 1818; r. Th.

Kingsbury's ch. 1, Ruth, m. Thomas Goldsmith; r. Mass. 2, Levi, m. Abby Hardy of Lawrence, Mass., and rem. 3, Nathaniel, m. thrice; r. Cairo, Ill. 4, Lucinda S., m. Sam'l S. Thayer; r. S. Th.

BRIDGES, Jesse, b. ab. 1807 in Sedgwick; m. Mercy Gray of Sedgwick; r. Rock., a mariner, &c. Their ch. 1, Dudley, b. in Penobscot; m. Cynthia Gray; rem. to Penobscot. 2, Priscilla S., b. in P.; m. Joseph Booker; r. & d. Rock. 3, Mercy, b. in P.; m. Warren Robinson; r. Rock. 4, Lewis G., born March, 1838; m. Lizzie Martin of Liverpool; r. Rock., and d. April 24, '62. 5, Adam, b. ab. '41, in P., rem. and d. in California. 6, Alzada D., m. Dec. 23, '63, Melzar T. Dyer of Vinalhaven, and of the 2d Me. Cavalry. 7, Enos C., b. ab. '48 in Penobscot, member of 6th Me. Battery. 8, L. Jennie, b. ab. '51 in Rock. 9, Addie B., b. ab. '54 in Rockland.

Lewis G.'s ch. Fannie A., b. ab. 1859.

BRIMIGION, Samuel J., m. and r. in China, Me. Of his sons by his first wife. 1, Stephen, b. ab. 1810 in Bowdoin; m. Hannah H. Hanson; r. Rock. Of his sons by 2d wife. 2, Thomas, m. H. Elizabeth Hammond, May 1, '48; r. Rockland.

Stephen's ch. 1, Caleb H., b. ab. 1830; m. Eunice F. Braley, July 31, '52; r. Rock. 2, Loudon, m. Anna Sullivan; r. Phillips. 3, Samuel, b. ab. '34; r. Rock., a teamster. 4, Sarah J. 5, Angeline, b. ab. '42. 6, Malvina. 7, William, b. ab. '47. 8, Almond W., b. ab. '50. 9, Alden U., b. ab. '52.

Thomas's ch. 1, Charles, b. ab. 1849. 2, Gardner, b. ab. '51. 3, Viola, b. ab. '54.

Caleb H.'s ch. 1, George, b. ab. 1856. 2, Cora, b. ab. '59.

BRITTO, William H., b. ab. 1835; r. Rock., with Eliza A., his wife; was a mariner in 1860, since enlisted in the army.

BROWN, Dea. Samuel, Esq., b. at Newbury, Jan. 12, 1749; c. to Georgetown; m. Reliance Weed, (who was b. at Brunswick, Oct. 7, 1754, & d. Dec. 5, 1776), c. to Th.; m. 2d, Prudence Thompson, pub. May 22, 1777; rem. Cam. before 1808, and afterward to Ohio, where he d. Dec. 18, 1831. James, a brother, b. at Georgetown, July 11, 1755; c. from New Meadows to what is now S. Th.; m. 1st, Ruth Weed, p. Nov. 14, 1778, 2d, Nancy Braison or Brison of W., July 30, 1789; r. S. Th., was wounded by the falling of a tree, and expired about two hours afterwards, July 6, 1803.

Dea. Samuel's ch. by 1st wife. 1, Jonathan, b. June 24, 1774; m. Sally Jones of U. in 1794; r. and d. in Bowdoinham. 2, James, (2d,) b. in Georgetown, March 19, 1776, d. in Th., July 19, 1777. By 2d wife. 3, Reliance, b. April 12, 1778; p. to John J. Lovett, March, 1798, and died July 7, 1798. 4, James, (3d,) b. May 24, 1780; m. Betsey Hall of Nobleboro', p. April 26, 1810. 5, Mary, b. April 13, 1782; m. Gideon Seavey; r. Th., and d. Dec. 1, 1840. 6, Elizabeth, b. May 19, 1784; m. Dea. J. Partridge; r. Rock., and died Dec. 9, 1837. 7, Prudence, b. May 4, 1786; m. Elibeus Partridge; r. Ohio, &c., and d. in Rock.? 8, Abigail, b. April 26, 1790; 9, Samuel, b. Aug. 20, 1792; 10, Joanna, b. Oct. 25, 1794; 11, Ephraim, b. Sept. 25, 1797; all probably removed with their parents.

James's ch. by 1st wife. 1, Lydia, b. Oct. 5, 1779, d. Feb. 22, 1800. 2, Lucretia, b. Jan. 24, 1782; m. James Thompson; r. and died in Union. 3, John, b. April 27, 1784, d. young. 4, William, b. Feb. 24, 1786; m. Sarah Hawes, Dec. 24, 1809; r. U., and d. Th., Aug. 16, 1822. 5, Nancy, b. May 27, and d. Oct 25, 1788. By 2d wife.

6, Isaac, b. May 24, 1790; m. 1st, Mercy Otis of St. Geo., Nov. 23, 1810, 2d, Margaret Stahl of W., Feb. 13, '48; r. S. Th., and d. Mar. 1, '54. 7, Ruth, b. March 9, 1792; m. John Stackpole; r. Th. 8, Nancy, b. April 14, 1794; m. Oliver Robbins, (3d); r. Th., and died Jan. 15, '48. 9, Bethiah, b. June 16, 1796; m. Joseph Tolman; r. Cam., and d. March 14, '32. 10, Hannah, b. March 26, and d. Oct. 1, 1798. 11, Amos, b. Nov. 30, and d. Dec. 20, 1800.

Isaac's ch. by 1st wife. 1, Jane, b. Nov. 6, 1811; m. Elijah M. Averill; r. Rock., and d. Dec. 7, '41. 2, Nancy, b. May 16, '15; m. ——— Clarey of Boston, rem. and d. in Wisconsin, Feb., 1844. 3, George, b. July 6, '17; went abroad. 4, Lucretia, b. Sept. 23, '20, d. March 18, '23. 5, Eben John, b. July 19, '23, d. Jan. 5, '33. 6, Frances A., b. June 5, '30; m. Samuel Johnson; r. Lynn, Mass. 7, James, (4th), b. June 2, '32; rem. California. The mother died Oct. 20, '49; aged 57.

BROWN; of this family two brothers c. from Ipswich, Mass. 1, Isaac, rem. to New Ipswich, when 12 years old, to Th., when 21; m. Mrs. Mary (Ulmer) Croner of Wal., p. Sept. 25, 1793; r. Brown's Corner, Rock., & d. July, 1835. 2, William, m. Sarah Ulmer; rem. and died in Camden.

Isaac's ch. 1, William, (2d), b. July 9, 1794; m. Margaret Hoch of Wal.; p. Nov. 16, 1816; r. Rock., & d. Nov. 22, '38, on the morning of which day he was found dead in the road. 2, Sally, b. Feb. 1796; d. in 1814 or 15. 3, John, b. March 6, 1798; m. Sophia Marshall; p. March 17, 1819, 2d, Sabra Sherer, Dec. 13, '49, 3d, Nancy D. (Hall) Bartlett, June 8, '53; r. Rock. 4, Oliver B., b. April 25, 1800; m. Rosanna F. Fogerty, Sept. 19, '22; r. Rock., a farmer, merchant, &c. 5, Eliza, b. Oct. 13, ['02?] d. unm. 6, Mary, b. Jan. 1, ['04?] m. Henry Benner. 7, Susan, b. Oct., (record defective,) probably d. young. 8, Lucy, b. Oct. (ditto.) d. young.

William, (2d)'s ch. 1, Isaac, (2d), b. Feb. 17, 1818; lost at sea. 2, Henry, b. Sept. 20, '19; m. 1st, Mary H. Crockett, Dec. 6, '46, 2d, Mary F. Achorn, March 14, '52; r. Rock., a quarryman. 3, William, (3d), b. April 8, '22, d. July 8, '40. 4, Susan Elizabeth, b. April 26, '24; m. Col. Elijah Walker; r. Rock. 5, Irason C., b. Aug. 1, '27; r. California. 6, Mary E., b. Nov. 1, '30, d. July 17, '31. 7, Eliezer, b. March 9, '35, d. July 1, '39.

John's ch. by 1st wife. 1, John, (2d), b. Nov. 27, 1820, d. Sept. 23, '25. 2, Almira M., b. Aug. 25, '24; m. Gen. Hiram G. Berry; r. Rock. 3, Lucy A., b. Sept. 18, '28; r. Rock. 4, James G., b. Aug. 18, '31, d. Sept. 30, '38.

Oliver B.'s ch. 1, Eliza, b. Jan. 8, 1823; m. William Whitney; r. Th., & d. May 12, '58. 2, Alden U., b. Feb. 10, '27; m. Harriet A. Ulmer; p. Sept. 15, '52; r. Rock., a mariner. 3, John, (3d), b. Oct. 27, '29; m. Margaret Robbins, Jan. 21, '52; r. Rock., a quarryman; rem. California. 4, Oliver D., b. April 6, '38, a farmer. 5, Sarah, or Lucy, b. Oct. 28, '31, d. young.

Fourth Generation.

Henry's ch. 1, Isaac A., b. Nov., 1847, d. Oct. 10, '49. 2, Laura E., b. ab. '53. 3, Lizzie F., b. ab. '55. 4, William H., b. ab. '57. 5, Cora A., b. ab. '59.

Alden U's ch. 1, Alda E., b. ab. 1853. 2, Mary M., b. ab. '57.

John, (3d)'s ch. 1, Lucy F., b. ab. 1853. 2, Charles, b. ab. '57.

BROWN, Jeremiah, b. ab. 1820, (adopted by Isaac row, ,);

m. Deborah Havener; p. Sept. 13, '45; r. Rock., a quarryman. Their ch. 1, Mary E., b. ab. '47. 2, Myra B., b. ab. '53.

BROWN, ———, m. Miss Fales; r. & d. in Ashby, Mass. Their ch. 1, Simon, m. Betsey Robbins, p. Feb. 13, 1795; rem. Brownsville, ab. 1816. 2, Boaz, b. 1766: m. Freelove Morse, Nov. 27, 1805; r. Th., Meadows; & d. Oct. 27, '27. 3, Joab, m. Elizabeth Ingraham, May 16, 1795; was blown up in a well & lost a leg; rem. Camden & Unity. 4, Luther, m. Hannah Bosworth of W.; rem. Ohio. 5, Betsey, m. ——— Messer.

Of Simon's ch 1, Capt. George W., b. in Rock., ab. 1812; ret. from Brownsville when ab. 15 yrs. old; m. Amanda M. Crockett; r. Rockland.

Boaz's ch. 1, Candace, b. May 14, 1807; m. 1st, Henry Creighton, 2d, William Giles; r. Worcester, Mass. 2, Henry, b. May 20, 1810; m. Hannah Morse, Apr. 21, '33; r. Th., & d. June 26, '59. 3, Sarah, b. Jan. 13, '12; m. Nathaniel Whitney; r. & d. Worcester. 4, William, b. April 29, '16; m. Ann Prescott, April 22, '44; r. Th. 5, Levi, b. Oct. 16, '20, d. Jan. 25, '22. 6, Mary A., b. April 22, '23; m. George H. Rugg; r. Westboro', Mass.

Joab's ch. 1, Lucy, b. in Rock., Feb. 5, 1796. 2, Joseph, b. in Rock., July 2, 1799. 3, Joab, (2d). 4, Rev. Josiah I., m. Esther E. Crie, June 20, 1845; r. Rock., a Methodist minister, chaplain of 15th Maine Reg., discharged on account of ill health; now a farmer at E. Pittston. 5, Isaac I., m. Nancy Carleton.

Fourth Generation.

Capt. George W.'s ch. 1, Dora, b. ab. 1838. 2? Carrie F., b. Dec. 31, '53, d. Feb. 17, '62.

Henry's ch 1, James M., b. ab. 1835; r. Th., a mariner, soldier of 4th Maine Reg., &c. 2, William, lost at sea with Capt. Washburn Fales, 1860. 3, Emma D., b. ab. 1839; m. Tileston H. Smith; r. Th. 4, Rowena, b. ab. '43. 5, George, b. ab. '46. 6, Elwin F., b. ab. '50. 7, Marietta, b. ab. '53.

William's ch. 1, Henry, (2d), b. ab. 1844. 2, Charles, b. ab. '47. 3, Melvin, b. ab. '49. 4, Eveline, b. ab. '51. The mother d. Sept. 22, '57.

BROWN, Edward, b. Sept. 11, 1771; came from Newburyport to Th., April 13, 1795, went to Warren, July 8, 1795, to work for Col. J. W. Head; ret. Th.; m. Elizabeth Watson, Feb. 20, 1800; settled at Watson's Point; m. 2d, Delia Gay of F., March 7, 1811, (who was b. April 13, 1784); was a caulker by trade, & d. Feb. 3, 1844. His ch. by 1st wife. 1, Anne Greenough, b. March 10, 1801; r. Th., and d. Feb. 4, 1861. 2, Margaret Lermond, b. Nov. 25, & d. Nov. 30, 1802. 3, Edward, (2d), b. Jan 1, & d. May 9, 1804. 4, Alexander W., b. Aug. 5, 1805; m. Sarah J. Fogerty, Dec. 21, '43; r. Th., a merchant. 5, Edward, (3d), b. Nov. 27, 1807; r. Th., on the homestead. By 2d wife. 6, Elizabeth W., b. Dec. 30, 1819; m. Capt. William Alfred Watts; r. Thomaston.

Alexander W.'s ch. 1, Delia Gay, b. Jan. 18, 1845, d. Feb. 14, '58. 2, Sarah J., b. Nov. 4, '46. 3, Anne G., b. May 26, '49, d. Sept. 13, '63. 4, Edward, (4th), b. Sept. 5. '51. 5, Elizabeth W., b. July 22, '55. 6, Alexander W., b. Nov. 30, '57, d. May 26, '60. 7, William W., b. Jan. 28, '60.

BROWN; of the sons of John of Wal., who was by trade a saddler, there c. to Th. 1, Capt. David D., b. ab. 1813; m. Lucina Paine, July 26, '51, & d. April 25, '58. 2, Capt. John M., b. ab. '18;

m. 1st, Eliza M. Hyler, June 17, '41, 2d, Priscilla Hyler, Oct. 3, '59; r. Th. 3, Henry, c. to Th., rem. to California, and d. June 26, '59.

Capt. John M.'s ch. by 1st wife. 1, Martha W., b. March 25, & d. April 6, 1842. 2, Simon L., b. Jan. & d. Sept. 28, '44. 2, Mary, b. ab. '47. 3, Catharine, b. ab. '49. 4, Helen, b. ab. '52. By 2d wife. 5, William Ballard, b. May 1, '64.

BROWN, Charles S., b. ab. 1803, son of Dr. Benjamin Brown of Waldoboro'; m. Susan N. Robinson of C., was deputy sheriff, &c., c. to Rock., keeps livery stable, & has six sons in the army & navy. His nephew, Hector M., grandson of Dr. Benjamin, and son of Hector M. of Wal., m. Clara A. Grant of St. Stephens; r. Rock., & in '60 kept fish market.

Charles S.'s ch. 1, James, m. and r. in C., a farmer & soldier. 2, Newell W., m. in Frankfort; r. Rock., now in U. S. navy. 3, Frank W., b. ab. 1832; m. Clara A. Cole of Wal.; r. Rock., a mariner, now in navy. 4, Theodore S., b. ab. '35; m. Laura V. F. Overlock of Wal. Nov. 11, '62; r. Rock., in U. S. navy. 5 & 6, twins, b. ab. '40; John G. in U. S. navy, Edwin in the army. 7, ?

Hector M.'s ch. 1, Mary E., b. ab. 1853. 2, Hector M., (2d), b. ab. 1856.

BROWN, Timothy F., b. ab. 1808 in Lincolnville; m. Ellen ——; r. Rock., a quarryman. Their ch. 1, Thomas Jefferson, b. ab. 1834; m. Hannah M. Rackliff, Nov. 6, '58; r. Rock., a cooper, &c. 2, Harriet, b. ab. 1839. 3, Angelia F., b. ab. '41. 4, Alphonso, b. ab. '46. 5, Orville, b. ab. '48. 6, Lucy, b. ab. '50. 7, Frederic, b. ab. '53.

Thomas Jefferson's ch. Frank W., b. ab. 1859.

BROWN, Franklin N., b. ab. 1820 in Montville; r. Rock. in 1860, a R. R. bridge builder; rem. New York with Laura his wife, and ch. 1, Filena S., b. ab. 1848. 2, Alfred S., b. ab. '52. 3, Charles A., b. ab. '55. 4, Agnes N., b. Nov. '58, d. Sept. 8, '60.

BROWN, Josiah B., b. ab. 1808, son of John of Portsmouth, N. H.; m. Ann B. ——; r. Rockland, a stone mason. Their ch. 1, Alzada F., b. ab. 1844. 2, William A., b. ab. '46, a deaf mute. 3, Charles V., b. '53.

BROWN, William S., came from New York; r. some years in Rock., ab. 1842; rem. to New York, where, in 1856, he was of the firm of Wm. S. Brown & Son. His ch. recorded here, were. 1, Geo. Ogden, b. Aug. 5, 1834, d. in New York, Aug. 20, '56. 2, Hannah M., b. Aug. 22, '38. 3, Charles M., b. Nov. 13, '40. 4, Hezekiah, b. —— 31, '42.

BROWN, Moses, b. ab. 1830, of a different family; m. Mary E. Maxwell, Nov. 11, '53; r. Rock., a mariner. Their ch. 1, Sarah M., b. ab. 1854. 2, Charles Keen, b. Oct. 1856, d. Oct. 5, 1857. 3, Moses, (2d), b. ab. 1859.

BROWN, Samuel P., b. ab. 1832; m. Mary A. Arey, p. Nov. 11, '52; r. S. Th., a mariner. Their ch. Jonas A., b. ab. 1853.

BROWN, Samuel, b. ab. 1810; m. Chloe ——; r. Rockland, a mariner. Their ch. Angeline, b. ab. 1839.

BROWN, William, b. ab. 1806, in Fox Islands; m. Mrs. Clementine Perry; r. Rockland, a shop keeper.

BROWN, William, (2d), b. ab. 1833, in the British Provinces, as was Mary J., his wife, in Scotland in 1837; r. Rockland, a mariner.

BROWN, Willard B., b. ab. 1832; m. Sarah Tinney; r. Rockland, a stevedore.

BROWN, James G., b. ab. 1825; m. Harriet ——; r. Rockland, a blacksmith. Their ch. 1, Charles W., b. ab. 1851. 2, Harriet E., b. ab. 1853. 3, George F., b. ab. 1857.

BROWN, David, b. ab. 1830 in Damariscotta; m. Hannah Spear; r. Rockland, a wheelwright, in 1860.

BRYANT, Charles, came from England; m. Jerusha Barstow; r. Newcastle, & d. in Th. Their ch. 1, Charles, (2d), m. Betsey Loudon of Belfast, April 1, 1798; entered the army of 1812, & never ret. 2, Joseph, came to Th., m. Sally Vose, p. Dec. 21, 1799; a joiner, built at Mill River the house since occupied by H. & C. Prince, Esqrs.; r. and d. Th. 3, Sarah, m. 1st, John Rigby of England, 2d, Benjamin Hussey; r. & d. Palermo. 4, Asenath, m. Eliphalet Conner of Th., rem. and d. in Belfast. 5, Betsey, m. David Conner; rem. and d. in Montville. 6, Seth, came to Th., m. Mary Ulmer, May 13, 1804; rem. W., and d. in Montville. 7, Mary, m. Friend Keith of Th.; r. Lynn, Mass.

Joseph's ch. 1, Catharine Lamb, b. Aug. 18, 1801; m. Levi Willey, a clothier, rem. Searsmont, and d. in 1862 or '3. 2, Clementina, b. Oct. 15, 1804; m. John F. Cole; r. California.

BRYANT, Capt. John, came from Saco, with his brother Joseph, about 1792 or '3; m. 1st, Ruth Spalding, March 19, 1795; 2d, Mrs. Eliza Foster of St. George, 1828; r. S. Th., at Spalding's Point, or Ballahack. William, a cousin, also came here; m. 1st, Sarah Hayden, 2d, Polly Carr, Nov. 2, 1797; r. S. Th.

Capt. John's ch. 1, Sarah, b. Jan. 17, 1806; m. Kingsbury Bridges, & rem. 2, Joseph, b. Aug. 18, 1809; m. Susan Lincoln; r. Machiasport. 3, Nancy, b. Oct. 15, 1811; m. John Robinson, (2d); r. S. Th. 4, Hannah, b. July 8, 1813; m. David Clark; r. and died S. Th. 5, Jane, b. Oct. 20, 1816, died Jan. 1855.

BRYANT, Jesse, son of Aaron Bryant of St. George; m. Caroline Wheeler, p. Oct. 7, 1838; r. S. Th. Their ch. 1, Henry H., b. Aug. 29, 1840. 2, Francis, b. Jan. 25, '43, d. Jan. 23, '49. 3, Caroline A., b. May, '48, d. Sept. 1. '49. 4, Mary E., b. Jan. and d. Aug. 13, '54.

BRYANT, Samuel, b. ab. 1824, in Montville; m. Elizabeth H. Prescott of S. Th.; r. Rockland, a ship chandler. Their ch. Laura A., b. ab. 1849.

BRYANT, Isaac S., was also in Rock., and m. Laura A. Wagner, Sept. 7, 1863.

BRYSON, Peter, b. ab. 1826, in Scotland; m. Susan C. Bean, March 21, 1854; r. Rockland, a rigger.

BUCKLIN; of the descendants of two brothers, who came from Rehoboth about 1764, and settled, Baruch in Camden and Nathan in Warren, there c. here, 1, Caleb, b. in W., m. —— Davis, who d. Oct. 24, 1848, 2d, Elvira Cooper, Sept. 9, '49, 3d, Mary E. Hall, July 27, '56, 4th, Eliza Babb; r. Th. & Rock., a sailmaker. 2, Edward B., son of Capt. Joseph C. of W., b. ab. '18; m. Abby Thomas of C., '39; r. Th., a blacksmith. 3, Moses R., a brother, b. ab. '27; m. Martha (Vinal) Gilchrist; r. Th., a carpenter. 4, Capt. Edward, b. in Cam., Nov. 25, '24; m. Emeline S. McLain, Nov. 8, '54; r. Rock. 5, Capt. Wilson, a brother, b. in Cam. '26; m. Victorine M. Keen; r. Rock.

6, Capt. Horace, a brother, b. in Camden, '28; m. Mary J. Healy; r. Rock., & d. Jan. 3, '64.

Caleb's ch. 1, Emily. By 2d wife. 2, Adelaide. By 3d wife. 3, George S. 4, Adelbert.

Edward B.'s ch. 1, Austin H., b. ab. 1842; r. Th., a mariner, entered U. S. navy. 2, Edwin C., b. ab, '50. 3, Henry H., b. ab. '56.

Moses R.'s ch. 1, Otis Gilchrist, b. ab. 1854.

Capt. Edward's ch. 1, Hattie M., b. Dec. 17, 1855. 2, Maggie L., b. March 1, '58. 3, Fannie H., b. March 27, '60. 4 & 5, twins, b. May 29, '63, Emeline, d. August 22, Edwinna, d. Sept. 1, '63.

BULLOCK, Capt. Isaac, b. Sept. 3, 1796; c. from Northport; m. Jane Simonton, August 15, 1822; r. Rock., & d. June 18, '38, lost at sea. Of their ch. 1, Barbara Jane, b. '23, d. Sept. 16, '25. 2, Capt. Francis S., b. ab. '25; m. Susan J. Rich, Jan. 2, '47, r. Rock. 3? Capt. Henry W., r. Rock., a master mariner. 4, Lucy Ann, b. June 1830, d. July, 1840.

Capt. Francis S.'s ch. 1, Susan J., b. May, 1851, d. Oct. '52. 2, Elizabeth, b. ab. '54. 3 & 4, twins, b. ab. '56, Francis W., d. August 10, '58, and Carrie; r. Rock. 5, Morton Y., b. ab. '59.

BUMPS, William K., b. ab. 1824, in Unity; m. Eliza A. Evans; r. Th., in Green st., a ship carpenter. Their ch. 1, Emma R., b. ab. '56.

BUNKER, Isaac, b. April 22, 1787; m. Mary King, (b. Jan. 16, 1788); c. from Edgartown, Mass., a joiner, bought the farm of Dea. Weed; r. S. Th., & d. Feb. 10, 1861. Their ch. 1, William J., b. Dec. 29, 1812; m. Jane M. Reed; r. Th., a blacksmith. 2, Rufus K., b. March 29, '15; d. unm., April 29, '44. 3, Eliza Ann, b. Oct. 17, '17; m. Capt. B. C. Gates; r Th. 4, John T., b. Aug. 22, '20; m. Sarah E. Colley, March 16, '48; r. Th., a seaman. 5, Susan S., b. April 7, '23; m. Capt. George A. Mitchell; r. Th., & d. Dec. 24, '53. 6, Nancy K., b. March 27, '26, d. Sept. 15, '51. 7, Mary K., b. Oct. 22, '29; m. Capt. George A. Mitchell; r. Th., and d. May 21, 1863.

William J.'s ch. 1, Melissa, b. Dec. 29, 1835; m. S. E. Kelloch, April 1862; r. Th. 2, Aroline L., b. Oct. 9, '37. 3, Oceana, b. ab. '40. 4, William, b. ab. '43. 5, Rufus, b. ab. '45. 6, Isaac, (2d), b. ab. '47. 7, Orient, b. ab. '50. 8, Ava, b. ab. '52. 9, Cora, b. ab. '55. 10, John, b. ab. '57.

John T.'s ch. 1, Aldana, b. ab. 1850. 2, John Thomas, b. May 28, 1853, d. March 15, 1854.

BUNKER, Silas, b. ab. 1814, in Gouldsboro'; m. Susan Wall of St. Geo., r. Rock., a limeburner. Capt. Charles, probably a brother, b. Feb. 1816; m. Lydia C. ——— -, r. Rock. and d. Sept. 1, 1858.

Silas's ch. 1? Charles, b ab. 1836; r. Rock., a limeburner. 2, ? Robert, b. ab. '38; d. April 21, '62. 3, Theodore, b. Jan. 26, '43; r. Rock., a limeburner. 4, George, b. ab. '46; m. Harriet L. Spalding, Jan. 10, '64; r. Rock., enlisted in the army '64. 5, Eliza, b. ab. '48. 6, Julia, b. ab. '50. 7, Thomas, b. ab. '53. 8, Warren, b. ab. '55. 9, Silas, (2d), b. ab. '57. 10, Leonard, b. March 8, died Dec. 20, 1860.

Capt. Charles's ch. 1, Abby N., b. ab. 1846. 2, Frederic, b. Jan., 1851, d. Feb. 19, '54. 3, Jennie E., b. ab. '55.

BUNKER, John, b. ab. 1828, r. with Laura, his wife, at Rock., in 1860, a joiner.

BURBANK, Fordyce C., b. ab. 1821, in Bethel, Me.; m. Drusilla P. Ingalls of Shelburne, N. H.; r. Rockland, in mercantile business. Their ch. 1, Nancy I., b. ab. 1849. 2, Charles F., b. ab. '57.

BURGESS; of this Warren family, 1, Capt. Joseph Swift, b. Oct. 6, 1813, son of Capt. Stephen C., and Elizabeth (Starrett) Burgess, of W.; m. Eliza Gilchrist, p. Aug. 27, 1836; master mariner, and merchant in Th., and commission merchant since in N. Y. 2, William Carey, b. Oct 17, '15; m. Ann O. Wakefield, June 3, '44; r. Th., a merchant, firm of Burgess, O'Brien & Co.

Capt. Joseph S.'s ch. 1, Thomas, b. April, 1837, d. Aug. 20, '40. 2, Levi G., b. March 4, '42.

William C.'s ch. 1, Ann P., b. May 27, and d. Dec. 14, 1849. 2, Maria O., b. ab. 1851. 3, Ann H., b. ab. '55. 4, Nellie B., b. ab. '57. 5, Edward O., b. ab. '60.

BURGESS, Gershom F., b. ab. 1831 in Fairfield, Me., m. 1st, Mrs. Hannah S. White, Oct. 1, 1857, 2d, Christiana F. Young, Aug. 22, '63; r. Rock. and Rockport; a teacher.

BURKE, Patrick, b. ab. 1827, in Ireland; m. in New Brunswick, Matilda Robbins, p. Jan. 9, '54, and, with his mother, r. Rock. . Their ch. 1, Thomas, b. ab. 1858. 2, Joseph, b. ab. '59.

BURKETT, Henry, of Waldoboro'; m. Eleanor Crawford of W., Jan. 29, 1809. Their ch. 1, James, b. ab. 1812; m. Louisa Feyler of Cam., r. Rock., removed St. Johns. 2, Henry A.; m. Abby W. Hemenway of Wal., Oct. 20, '46; r. Rock., a restaurateur, soldier, &c. 3, Lawrence C., m. Alma S. Ulmer, Sept. 6, '53; r. Rock., a grocer. Dexter, b. ab. '24, son of Jacob, of Wal.; m. Emeline Watts; r. Th., at Beech Woods, a cooper, &c.

James's ch. 1, Augusta A., b. ab. 1837. 2, Ellen L., b. ab. '39. 3, George H. P., b. ab. '47. 4, Edna F., b. ab. '52.

Henry A.'s ch. 1, Arabella, b. ab. 1847. 2, Augustus H., b. ab. '49. 3, Sarah E., b. ab. '51. 4, Frank P., b. ab. '53.

Lawrence C.'s ch. 1, Frederic H., b. ab. 1854. 2, Jessie H. born about '57.

Dexter's ch. Euphemia, b. ab. 1852.

BURNHAM, Capt. James, b. in Yarmouth, England, 1794; c. to Th. 1805; enlisted about 1811 on board the U. S. frigate *Constitution*, & served through the war; m. Harriet M. Shibles, Nov. 4, '21; r. Th., & d. Sept. 7, '26. Their ch. 1 & 2, twins, b. June 23, '22, Almira, m. John Peterson, r. Th., & Maria, m. Thomas H. Nichols, Sept. 28, '51, r. Boston, & d. July 2, '52, with both of her twin babes. 3, James, (2d), b. April 11, '25; m. Sarah Maxey, Sept. 15, '53; r. Th., a trader, &c., has ch. 1, Maria, b. ab. '55. 2, Frederic, b. ab. 1858.

BURNHAM, Jonathan, b. March 25, 1817; m. Helen M. Rowe, Sept. 17, 1848, r. Rock., and d. June 4, '56. Their ch. 1, Susan M., b. Sept. 22, '49, d. Feb. 5, '50. 2, William R., b. July '53, d. Jan. 2, '54. 3, Charles A., b. ab. 1852. 4, Robert H., b. ab. '55.

BURNS; of this family four brothers, sons of Samuel, of Anson, came to this place; viz.: 1, John W., b. ab. 1805, in Norridgewock; m. 1st, Lois Jones, 2d, Jane Post, p. Nov. 27, 1834, 3d Eunice S. Post, Dec. 8, '47; r. Rock., a truckman, &c. 2, Joseph, b. in Anson; m. Deborah Ranlet of Freeman; r. in Rockland where his wife d. Feb. 18, '52. 3, Ephraim Hildreth, b. ab. 1810; m. 1st, Hannah Luce, of

New Vineyard, 2d, Catharine Broadman of Wal., r. Rock., and d. Feb. 10, '56. 4, George W., r. Rock., city crier.

John W.'s ch. 1, James, b. April 7, 1829, d. March 17, '45. 2, William H., b. April 18, '30 ; m. Lucy D. Trussell of Belfast, p. April 30, '53 ; r. Rock. and d. Feb. 13, '57. 3 and 4, twins, b. April 29, '33, Orris, d. Feb. 8, '53, Orrin, d. July 17, '38. By 2d wife, 5, Lucinda S. b. June 2, '35 ; m. Silas D. Labe ; r. Rock. 6, Nancy J., b. May 3, '37 ; m. Capt. Gardiner Robinson, Jan. 7, '60 ; r. Rock. 7, Melinda A., b. May 17, '39, d. Mar. 24, '42. 8, Mary A., b. Nov. 1, '41 ; m. H. G. Tibbets ; r. Rock. 9, Adelaide, b. ab. '43 ; r. Rock. By 3d wife. 10, Hiram G., b. ab. 1849.

E Hildreth's ch. 1, Thomas A., b. Oct. 1837, killed in Boston, by being thrown from his wagon, July 23, '64. 2, Sarah A., b. Ap. 2, '40.

BURNS ; of this Waldoboro' family, two brothers came to this place. 1, Col. George J., b. ab. 1821 ; m. Frances (Ulmer) Penniman, p. Nov. 9, '45, r. Rock., a lime manufacturer, officer in the 4th Maine reg., &c. 2, John J., b. ab. 1825 ; m. Hannah F. ——— ; r. Rock., and d. April 4, '56.

Capt. George J.'s ch. 1, Sarah E., b. ab. 1847. 2, Frances A., b. Sept. 1848, d. Aug 14, '51.

John J.'s ch. 1, George G., b. ab. 1830, r. Rock. 2, Thomas A., 3, Drusilla D. 4, Emily L., b. ab. '56.

BURNS, Alfred K., b. ab. 1827, probably of the same family, m. Frances B. Gregory, Feb. 5, '56 ; r. and d. Rock., a joiner Their ch. 1, Frederic B., b. ab. 1858. 2, Alfred K., (2d), b. ab. '60.

BURNS, James, b. ab. 1828, in Ireland, r. with Ann, his wife, in Rock. Their ch. 1, Hannah, b. ab. 1855. 2, Catharine, b. ab. '57. 3, Mary Ann, b. ab., '58. 4, Patrick, b. ab. '59.

BURPEE, Heman, b ab. 1794, in Sterling, Mass. ; m. Statira Redding in Grafton, Mass. ; c. to Th, 1829, to Rock. '35 ; r. Rock., a painter. Their ch. 1. Hon. Nathaniel A., b. ab. '16 ; m. Mary J. Partridge ; r. Rock., a cabinet manufacturer, State Senator, '57–8, &c. 2, Samuel H., b. ab. '18 ; m. Abby W. Marshall, Dec. 2, '43 ; r. Rock., a cabinet maker. 3, Heman H., m. Mary C. Spear, Nov. 15, '46 ; r. Rock., a painter, now in U. S. navy. 4, John R., m. Abby M. Butler, Jan. 1, '64, ; r. Rock., a painter.

Hon. Nathaniel A.'s ch. 1, Capt. Edgar A., b. Dec. 19, 1839, officer in 19th Me. reg. 2, Emma E., b. Dec. 9, '41. 3, William P., b. ab. '46. 4, Mary C., b. ab. '50. 5, Frank L., b. '52.

Samuel H.'s ch. 1, Charles E., b. ab. 1845 ; r. Rock., entered U. S. navy. 2, Samuel A., b. ab. '49. 3. Richard H., b. ab. '51. 4, Alfred J., b. ab. '55. 5, Edwin W., b. Nov. 7, '58, d. Oct. 7, '61. 6, Annie, b. ab. '60.

Heman H.'s ch. 1, Frederic F., b. ab. 1849. 2, James S. W., b. ab. 1852.

BURRILL, John A., b. ab. 1835 ; m. Angeline Jameson, Mar. 13, '56 ; r. Rock., a blacksmith. Their ch. 1 & 2, twins, b. ab. 1859, Orris & Edith.

BURROWS, Jerome, b. ab. 1835; m. Sabra ——— ; r. S. Th., a peddler, &c. Their ch. 1, Emma, b. ab. 1855. 2, Ada F., b. ab. 1857. 3, a son, b. 1860.

BURTON, William, born 1754, (brother of Col. Benjamin, son of Capt. Benjamin of Cushing, and grandson of Benjamin who d. on his passage from Ireland to St. George's); m. 1st, Jane Robinson, 2d, Chloe Bradford; r. C. and d. March, 1842. His ch. by 1st wife. 1, Jane, d. young. 2, Nancy, m. Capt. Andrew Robinson; r. and d. St. George. 3, William, (2d), m. 1st, Elizabeth Parsons of C., 2d, Lucy Spear of W.; r. C. and d. Jan. 2, 1821. 4, Jane B., m. John Montgomery of Townsend; r. C. and now Th. 5, Isaac, m. Nancy Parsons; r. C. & d. Boston. 6, Matthew, b. May 10, 1792; m. Margaret Robinson of St. George, Oct. 29, 1818; r. Rock., a caulker. 7, Eliza, d. young. 8, Elizabeth, m. Ephraim Robinson; r. St. George. By 2d wife. 9, Sarah; 10, Chloe, d. young. 11, Thomas, m. 1st, Rachel Vinal, 2d, Lucy (Vinal) Burton; r. C. 12, Sarah. 13, James, m. Lucy Vinal; r. & d. C. 14, Chloe; 15, Alfred; 16, Elbridge; all d. young. 17, John R., m. Lydia Bradford; r. C. 18, Lucy, d. young. 19, William, (3d), m. Miss Hyler; r. C., d. New Orleans.

Matthew's ch. 1, Capt. Alfred, b. Dec. 13, 1818; m. 1st, Elionai L. Healey, Ap. 26, '46, 2d, Sarah A. Luce, April 1, '53; r. Rock., died, murdered in Kingston, Jamaica, Sept. 6, 1860, on board his barque *Alvarado*, by his crew. 2, Susanna R., born July 29, 1821; m. John Bartlett, Oct. 29, '46; r. Rock. 3, Nancy R., b. April 2, 1825; m. Lysander Fales; r. Rock. 4, Margaret, b. Aug. 7, '27; m. William G. Paul; r. Rock. 5, George, b. Sept. 16, '29; m. Lucy E. Clark, July 2, '48; r. Rock. 6, Capt. Benjamin, (4th), b. March 15, '35; m. Jane E. Oliver of W., April 4, '61; r. Rockland.

Capt. Alfred's ch. 1, Mayalan M., b. June 4, 1845, d. Sept. 2, '47. 2, Elionai L., b. Feb. 3, d. April 27, '49. By 2d wife. 3, Hiram C., b. June 14, '54. 4, Annie M., b. Sept. 30, '58, d Feb. 9, '63.

George's ch. 1, Henry F., b. Aug. 7, 1849. 2, George E., b. May 28, 1856.

BURTON, Elbridge, a branch of the same family, b. ab. 1826; c. from Cushing; m. Lucinda Stahl of W., p. Dec. 13, 1852; r. Th., corporal and com. sergeant in 1st Maine Cavalry.

BUTLER, Phinehas, m. Bathsheba Graves; c. from Framingham, Mass., to Old Th., at or before 1785. Their ch. 1, John, b. Feb. 10, 1756; was bound to Dr. Taylor till 21 years old, & c. to what is now Union in 1774; m. Lucy Robbins of Th.; p. Feb. 14, 1778; c. to Th. & d. Feb. 6, 1840, 2, Phinehas, (2d), b. April 8, 1758; c. to U., under Taylor, enlisted under Burton, three years, and joined the army Feb. 1777; m. Melia Robbins of Th.; p. Oct. 18, 1781; r. S. Th. & d. Sept. 25, 1852, a. 94 1-2 yrs. 3, ? Anna, m. John Tyngs, & c. here from Needham as early as 1785, with her son, Henry Clinton Tyngs. 4, Dr. Joseph, b. April, 1764; m. Margaret Martin of Bristol; was also bound to Taylor; c. to U. but rem. with his son Martin, to Pennsylvania, where he spent the last years of his life.

John's ch. 1, James, b. Nov. 8, 1778; m. Mary Gray; p. May 9, 1806; r. Rock, a farmer, & d. Jan. 6, 1861. 2, Lucy, b. March 15, 1780; m. David Gay; r. Rock., & d. April 3, 1860. 3, John, (2d), b. May 18, 1781; m., r., & d. Smithfield, R. I.; had 3 sons. 4, Betsey, b. Aug. 22, 1783; m. Richard Smith; r. & d. Rock. 5, Hannah, b. June 17, 1785; m. Capt. John Spear, (2d); r. Rock., & d. July 4, 1856. 6, Briggs, b. March 3, 1787; m. Ruth Rowell, Feb. 3, 1817; r. S. Th., & d. June 5, 1852. 7, Alden, b. Dec. 7, 1788, d. Oct. 15, 1792. 8, Otis, b. March 9, & d. April 29, 1790, or '91. 9, Brackett, b. in Th. Jan. 28, 1793; m. 1st, Nancy Mathews, Dec. 25, 1816, 2d, Eliza Kelloch of W., Jan. 1, 1834; r. S. Th., rem. Indiana. 10, Samuel Brinton, b. April 18, 1795; m. Harriet Perry, Jan. 24, 1822; r. S. Th., a farmer. 11, Charles, b. Feb. 12, 1798; m. Jane H. Russ of Cam. Feb. 1, 1825; r. Th., & d. June 3, 1858. 12, Susan, b. Aug. 29, and died Sept. 15, 1800.

Phinehas, (2d)'s ch. 1, William, b. April 11, 1782; m. 1st, Judith Loring, p. Nov. 22, 1804, 2d, Jane Singer, Aug. 3, '38; r. Rock., a farmer. 2, Sarah, b. April 20, 1784, d. Nov. 26, 1792. 3, Shepard, b. March 21, 1786, d. Dec. 17, 1795. 4, Phinehas, (3d), b. April 13, 1788; m. 1st, Catharine Ulmer of Th., Sept. 12, 1808, 2d, Hannah Demerritt of Liberty, 1833, 3d, Silence Jameson of W.; r. U. & d. Sept. 12, '55. 5, Melia; b. Feb. 23, 1790, d. Sept. 9, '92. 6, George, b. Aug. 27, 1792; m. Mima Robbins of U. Feb. 24, 1820; r. Th. 7, Levi, b. Jan. 22, 1795; m. 1st, Lucy Tolman of Th. April 17, '17, 2d, Mary Walker; r. Appleton. 8, Melia, b. Oct. 18, 1797, m. Dea. Samuel Dean, Dec. 24, 1829; r. S. Th. 9, Joanna C., b. Oct. 20, 1800; m. Israel Dean, & d. Oct. 15, 1859. 10, Walter, b. Nov. 22, '02; m. Joanna Packard of Nobleboro'; r. Rock., rem. & d. in Minnesota, '59.

Dr. Joseph's ch. 1, Nancy, b. Feb. 18, 1790; m. Pelatiah Pease; r. & d. Appleton. 2, John, (3d), b. Jan. 28, 1792; m. Sally Ulmer of Th., 1814; d. Sept. 16, '31. 3, Martin, b. Mar. 12, 1794; rem. Penn. 4, Susanna, b. June 25, 1796; m. ——— Hooper; r. & d. St. G. 5. Peggy, b. Dec. 9, 1798; m. Daniel Rokes of Appleton, April, '19. 6, Mary, b. Feb. 25, 1802; m. ——— Sprague. 7, William, b. Nov. 15, & d. Dec. 5, 1805; & probably others.

Fourth Generation.

James's ch. 1, Capt. Anson, b. ab. 1809; m. Hannah T. Hunstable of Boston; r. Rock., a master mariner. 2, Sophronia, m. Matthias Cushman; r. Rock. 3, Calvin, m. Virintha Ross, Nov. 29, 1835; r. Rock. and d. July 7, 1848. 4, Mary, m. J. Wheaton Sayward; r. California. 5, James, (2d), r. Rock., a quarryman. 6, Lucy Jane, m. ——— Meserve. 7, Emily A., m. George G. Woodward, Nov. 5, 1848; r. Boston.

John, (2d)'s ch., 1, John, (4th), m. Phebe W. Hart, 1836; r. Th. 2, Charles, b. Feb. 19, 1811; m. Jane W. Harrington; r. Rock., a quarryman; and d. Jan. 26, '61. 3, ——— ———, b. & r. in Smithfield.

Brigg's ch. 1, Alfred, b. Dec. 23, 1817; m. 1st, Catherine B. Haskell, 1849, 2d, Delia Lash, May 25, '55; r. Rock., and d. April 27, '56. 2, Charles S., b. Oct. 3, '19; r. California. 3, William R., b. June 3, '22; m. Julia Sartelle; r. S. Th., a farmer. 4, Oliver, b. May 22, 1826; m. 1st, Hannah Page, 2d, ——— Page, r. Boston. 5, Briggs M., b. Oct., '28; m. and r. Boston. 6, Horace J., b. April 6, '34; m. Frances Nowell, March, '59; r. S. Th., a farmer.

Brackett's ch. by 1st wife. 1, Miriam; m. Samuel Russ; r. Boston. 2, Lucy R., m. 1st, Capt. S. Andrews Bradbury, 2d, Gilbert Perry; r. Ohio. 3, Olive, m. a Mr. Keating; r. Ohio. 4, Nancy M., m. Capt. Charles Bradbury; r. S. Th. 5, Amanda, m. a Mr. Boston, and r. Boston. By 2d wife. 6, Alden B., m. and r. Indiana. 7, Harriet E., m. and r. Indiana. 8, Rosetta; 9, Aurelia; 10, Leander; 11, Josephine; 12, Elizabeth; all r, Indiana.

Sam'l Brinton's ch. 1, Harriet N., b. Nov. 3, 1822; married Otis McLean, Nov. 23, 1851; r. S. Th. 2, Samuel B., (2d), b. Nov. 30, 1823; m. Hannah J. Meservey, Dec. 2, 1847; r. S. Th., a carpenter. 3, Eliza P., b. Feb 12, '26; m. William Butler, (2d); r. Rock. 4, Alden G., b. March 18, '28; r. California. 5, Israel P., b. Aug. 6,

'30, r. S. Th. a blacksmith. 6, Henry B., b. May 20, '32; m. Mary Lawrence; r. Castine. 7, Robert E., b. March 16, '34; m. Eliza M. Healey, Jan. 13, '61; r. Th. 8, Ellen G., b. Aug. 19, '37. 9, Alvin N., b. July 5, '40. 10, William F., b. ab. 1844.

Charles's ch. 1, Lucy Jane, b. April 14, 1826; m. Washington Robbins; r. S. Th. 2, Charles E., Esq, b. April 20, 1828; entered H. U., but did not graduate on account of failing health; m. Harriet M. Kelley, 1861; r. Th., an attorney at law. 3, William H., born April 8, and d. June 9, 1831. 4, William T., b. May 19, 1832, died May 5, 1858. 5, Sarah E., b. March 12, 1835, d. May 8, 1857. 6, Roswell B., b. Jan. 6, 1837, d. Jan. 11, 1838. 7, Isabella C., b. Aug. 7, 1839; r. Th. 8 and 9, twins, b. Dec. 19, 1841; Xavier, r. Th., a student; Albert, r. S. Th.

William's ch. by 1st wife. 1, Shepard R., b. Oct., 1805, d. Jan. 1, 1806. 2, Julia, b. Feb. 28, 1807; m. James Dean, r. S. Th. 3, Maria, b. March 6, 1809; m. 1st, Capt. Job Perry, 2d, Jesse K. Dean; r. S. Th. 4, Melia R., b. April 25, 1811; m. 1st, Capt. Henry H. Fales, 2d, Elkanah S. Smith; r. N. Billerica. 5, Orris R., b. June 15, 1813; m. Mary Ann Ingraham, Nov. 15, 1835; r. Rock., a farmer. 6, Margaret B., b. June 28, 1815; m. Mark Perry; r. Rock. 7, William, (2d), b. July 30, 1817; m. Eliza P. Butler, Nov. 8, 1843; r. Rock., a farmer. 8, Sophia, b. Dec. 27, 1819; m. Hiram Worcester, Aug. 28, 1843, r. S. Th. 9, Bradford B., b. April 18, 1822; m. Helen M. Stevens; r. Rock., a farmer. 10, Fanny N, b. June 1, 1825; m. Orris B. Ulmer, r. Rock. Judith, the mother, d. Feb. 7, 1838.

Phinehas, (3d)'s ch. by 1st wife. 1, George W., b. June 10, 1809; m. Eleanor Collins; r. Union, & had 8 ch. for which see Mr. Sibley's interesting History of Union. 2, Elioenai C., b. Sept. 11, 1810; m. Israel Melay, p. July 2, '36. 3, Thomas J., b. July 18, '12; m. Harriet Kinney of Liberty in 1834; r. S. Th. 4, Sally Ulmer, b. Aug. 8, 1814; m. Hon. John Spear; r. Rock. 5, Eunice Gallop, b. April 16, 1816; m. Samuel Dodge; rem. & d. in Weld, July 21, '50. 6, Catharine S., b. May 1, '18; m. Isaac Simmons; r. Rock. 7, Joanna D., b. July 17, '20; m. William Ellems; r. Th. 8, Mima R., b. Sept. 11, '22, d. July 17, '50. 9, Lucy T., b. Jan. 20, '25; m. Richard Smith, (2d); r. Rock., & d. Sept. 27, '50. 10, Hannah R., b. Nov. 15, '26; m. ——— Pressy; r. Deer Isle. 11, Phinehas S., b. March 9, '28, d. Jan. 7, '32. 12, Maria J., b. April 23, '30; r. & d. Union. 13, Phinehas W., b. Jan. 6, '34; m. in Lynn, Mass. 14, Melea E., b. Jan. 4, '35, d. Sept. 26, '49.

George's ch. 1, Ruth P., b. Sept. 7, 1821; m. Albert Sleeper, Sept. 2, '44. 2, Catharine U., b. April 22, '22; m. William G. Colby, Sept. 8, '44. 3, George W., b. Feb. 22, '26; m. Mary E. Getchell, July 20, '56; r. Rock., rem. California. 4, Walter, (2d), b. June 12, '29; r. Th., a farmer. 5, Caroline A., b. March 22, '32; m. Capt. Henry Johnson of S. Th., Nov. 10, '55; r. Th. 6, Jason R., b. Jan. 16, '35; r. California. 7, Laura A., b. June 17, '37; m. Joseph G. Gookins of S. Th., Nov. 22, '56. 8, Lucinda A., b. Nov. 21, '39. 9, Shepard, (2d), b. ab. '45; r. Th., on homestead.

Walter's ch. Levitt or Levi, a mariner. The mother died June 21, 1851, aged 44.

John, (3d)'s ch. 1, Elizabeth, b. Sept. 28, 1814; m. Ezra Martin; r. Rock., & d. Oct. 6, '49. 2, Margaret, b. Sept. 22, '17; m. Augustine Drake . S. Th. 3, Harriet, b. Dec. 18, '20; m. William Blackington, p. Jaly 31, '38. 4, Jane, b. April 13, '22. 5, Matthias, b Aug.

7, '24. 6, Nancy, b. April 21, '27; m. James C. Linscott; r. Th., & rem. 7, Ephraim, b. Oct. 17, 1829.

Fifth Generation.

Capt. Anson's ch. 1, H. Augusta, b. May 21, 1837; r. Rock. 2, Maria Theresa, b. March 17, 1839. 3, Edward A., b. July 25, 1841; a mariner, appt. master's mate, U. S. N., Feb. 1862. 4, Abby M., b. ab. 1843; m. John R. Burpee; r. Rock. 5, Lucy H., b. ab. 1846. 6, Bardus R., b. ab. 1850. 7, Albert, b. ab. 1852.

Calvin's ch. 1, Andrew C., m. Mary E. Weymouth, Feb, 4, 1855; r. Rock. 2, Caroline F., b. Jan. 4, 1837. 3, Celinda A, b. Dec. 19, 1839, d. April 15, 1851. The mother d. April 16, 1851, aged 32.

John, (4th)'s ch. 1, Ferdinand, b. ab. 1839; r. Th. 2, Lydia A., b. ab. 1841; m. William Fish of Rock. 3, Arimona, b. ab. 1845. 4, Lumon, b. ab. '47. 5, Lucena D., b. ab. '52. 6, Malvina, b. ab. '54.

Charles's ch. 1, Mary F., b. April 12, 1838; m. Roscoe Martin; r. Rock. 2, Frederic, b. March 3, 1839; r. Rock., a quarryman. 3, Alfred H., b. April 29, 1840; a quarryman. 4, Josephine E., b. June 9, 1841. 5, Oceana E., b. ab 1844, d.. Nov. 21, 1857. 6, Emma A., b. ab. 1847. 7, Eddie H., b. ab. 1854.

William R.'s ch. 1, Charles W., b. ab. 1858. 2, Sarah O., b. ab. 1859.

Horace S.'s ch. 1, Kate, b. ab. 1860. Perhaps others.

Samuel B., (2d)'s ch. 1, Lewis M., b. ab. 1849. 2, Julia E., b. ab. 1850.

Orris R.'s ch. 1, Orris E., b. April 11, 1837. 2, Lillias A., b. Aug. 1, 1839; m. James T. Tolman; r. Rock. 3, Susan A., b. Dec. 19, 1841. 4, Leland M., b. ab. 1846. 5, Preston E. W., b. March, 1851, d. April 3, 1853. 6, Frederic A., b. Dec. 1854, d. Sept. 19, '55. 7, Mary E. S., b. ab. 1855.

William, (2d)'s ch. 1, Adelbert J., b. ab. 1847. 2, Helen A., b. ab. 1850. 3, Alden B., b. ab. 1858.

Thomas J.'s ch. 1, Andrew J., b. ab. 1836; r. S. Th. 2, Martha J., b. ab. 1841. 3, Ephraim K., b. ab. 1843; soldier of 4th Maine.

George W.'s ch. Lovesta A., b. ab. 1857.

BUTLER, John, (5th), b. Sept. 17, 1794, a grandson of David Creighton of Th., & brought up in his family; m. 1st, Mary, dau. of Allen Stone of Union, who was b. in Ashby, Mass., & d. Feb. 11, 1844, 2d, Rachel Spear of W. Aug. 24, '45; r. Th., a truckman, sexton, &c. His ch. by 1st wife. 1, Hannah, b. Oct. 4, 1818, a deaf mute, educated at the Institution of the Deaf and Dumb, Hartford, Con.; r. Th. 2, John, b. Sept. 19, '20; deaf mute, d. July 30, '43. 3, Samuel, b. Jan. 24, '23, d. Sept. 11, '26. 4, James, b. Oct. 19, '25, d. Oct. 15, '58. 5, Josiah H., b. May 30. '28; m. Susan Amelia Kaler, Jan., 1, 1860; r. Th.

BUTLER, John, of Union, (son of Christopher, from Edgartown, Mass., and Lydia, his wife, who settled in Union,) m. Hannah Hawthorn of Cushing. Their ch. 1, William, m. Lois Newbert; r. U.? 2, Lydia, m. Andrus Dwinel of Orono. 3, Selina, b. Feb. 11, '08; m. 1st, William Bartlett of Th. Sept. 20, '32, 2d, John O'Neil; r. Th. 4. Gorham, b. Nov. 20, '09; m. 1st, Mrs. Catharine (Gallop) Palmer of Th., Nov., '45, 2d, ? Lucinda R. Fuller, 3d, Amelia Fuller, May, '61; r. W., and '60 in Rock., a butcher. 5, Ward, b. Aug. 18, '11; m. Lucinda R. Hawes; r. Rock., a quarryman. 6, Elbridge, died young. 7, Christopher, b. May 18, 1820; m. Sarah Healey, of Th., r. Rockland.

Gorham's ch. by 1st wife. 1, John P., b. Sept., 1846. 2, Frederic U., b. ab. 1852.

Christopher's ch. 1, Lydia A., b. Aug. 14, 1846. 2, William Oscar, b. Aug. 29, 1848.

BUTLER, Rev. Nathaniel, b. 1824, son of Rev. John, (who d. in Franklin, Ohio, July 1, 1856, aged 67, but formerly from Maine), m. Jennette, daughter of Hon. Stephen Emery; a Baptist minister in Eastport many years; rem. Rock., private secretary to Vice President Hamlin; rem. Auburn. Their ch. 1, Jeanie, b. ab. 1851. 2, Nathaniel, (2d), b. ab. 1853.

BUTLER, John, b. ab. 1833, came from New Vineyard, Me.; m. Mary C. Moody; r. Rock., a joiner. Their ch. 1, Lendall M., b. Feb. 2, and d. July 17, 1858.

BYRAM, Willard W., b. ab. 1821, in Yarmouth, Me.; married 1st, Mary T. Field of Gardiner, 2d, Sarah A. Saunders of Swanville, March 10, 1859; r. Th., since 1855, a music teacher, &c. His ch. by 1st wife. 1, Ella, b. in Gardiner, May 4, 1844. 2, Mary C., b. Sept. 1846. 3, Anna L., b. Sept. 1848.

CABLES; of this family three brothers c. here from Cohasset, Mass. 1, Charles H., b. ab. 1818; m. Mary Ann Haskell of Rock., Nov. 1837; r. Rock., a carriage maker. 2, Capt. George H., b. ab. 1822; m. Nancy H. Grant of Rock., April 3, 1850; r. Rock., appt. acting master U. S. sloop *St. Louis*, Feb. 1862. 3, Capt. John F., m. Priscilla E. Grant of Rock., Feb. 14, 1850; r. Rock.

Charles H.'s ch. 1, John H., b. ab. 1845. 2, Ann P., b. ab. '47. 3, Charles H., (2d) b. ab. '51.

Capt. George H.'s ch. 1, David F., b. ab 1854. 2, Clara W., b. ab. '56. 3, Georgietta, b. ab. '58.

Capt. John F.'s ch. 1, Alvah H.. b. Feb. 1854, d. Nov. 10, '59. 2, Ada, b. April, 1857, d. July 4, '63.

CALL, Francis, b. ab. 1802, in New York, as was Henrietta, his wife; r. Rock., a lime burner. Of their ch. 1, Josephine, b. 1834, d. June 28, '62.

CALDERWOOD, Asa, b. ab. 1800; a son of Capt. Mark Calderwood of Vinalhaven; m. Barbara Brown of Vinalhaven; r. Rock., a blacksmith. Their ch. 1, Levi, b. Sept. 1, 1830 in Rock.; m. Ellen Mills, of Vinalhaven; went to Brazil to work in a sugar mill, and not heard from since 1862. 2, John A., b. March 7, '31; m. Emily E. Upham of Cam.; p. July 25, '53; r. Rock., a blacksmith. 3, Margaret M., b. Nov. 21, '35; m. Orlando B. Jones, r. Rock. 4, George A., b. Dec. 22, '37.

John A.'s ch. 1 & 2, twins, b. ab. 1856; Margaret O. & Ina F.; The mother d June 26, 1863.

CAMPBELL; of this family, (probably of Scottish origin,) four brothers c. from Ballyglass, Sligo Co., Ireland. 1, James, b. 1781; c. in 1818 to Portland, thence to Th., with his brother; & d. July 27, 1823. 2, Robert, a coach factor blacksmith, c. 1818 to Portland, did business about 7 yrs in Hallowell, c. to Th., which he left in 1831 for N. O. 3, William b. Dec. 15, 1794; c. to Quebec, 1817, in British ship *Royal Sam*; to Th., July 8, '20; m. Nancy Bradford of Th., Sept. 19, '21; commenced the tailor's business which he still continues, bought the Thatcher house in 1822, now r. at Prison Corner in the house he built in '40. 4, Matthew A., (name changed from Patrick) came to Portland 1818, thence to Th., a tin-plate worker; m. Experience (Orbeton) Keith, April 26, '26; went to N. O. about 1830.

William's ch. 1, William (2d) b. July 5, 1822, d. Nov. 27, '26; 2, James B., b. Jan. 12, '25; r. Th. and d. May 16, '61. 3, Capt. Robert N., b. Dec. 1, '26; m. Mary C. Perkins, July 8, '51; lost at sea with all on board, in the bark *Mandarin*, which was last spoken, Dec. 10, '53, in a gale off Mobile, with six feet of water in her hold. 4, Nancy J., b. Oct. 18, '28; m. Nathaniel Woodcock, (2d) r. Th. and d. May 16, '64. 5, William A., b. March 8, '31; m. Mary E. O'Brien, July 21, '56; r. Th., a sailmaker, and merchant, &c. 6, John H., b. Sept. 8, '37.

Capt. Robert N.'s ch. Mary C., rem., and d. in Damariscotta.

CAMPBELL; of this family, two brothers originated in Bowdoin, Me., viz: 1, Leonard, b. in Bowdoin ab. 1815; c. hither, m. Hannah Eliza Condon, p. Sept. 20, 1845; r. Rock., cooper, &c. 2, George, b. ab. 1822 in B., m. Mary V. Stevens, Oct. 1, 1843; r. Rock., teamster, &c.

Leonard's ch. 1, Albert, b. ab. 1846. 2, Fannie, b. ab. 1849. 3, Leonard, (2d), b. ab. '51. 4, James, b. ab. '53. 5, Julia, b. ab. '55. 6, Elvira A., b. Sept. 2, '57, d. Nov. 27, '58. The mother died April 19, 1858, a. 32 yrs., 11 dys.

George's ch. 1, Leslie, b. ab. 1846. 2, Arthur L., b. March 20, '50, d. July 29, '59. 3, Ella V., b. 1851, d. July 10, '53. 4, George, (2d), b. ab. '56. 5, Adilla, b. ab. '59. 6, Sidney, b. Feb. 8, '63, d. Jan. 27, '64.

CAMPBELL, Thomas B., b. ab. 1833, c. from New York; m. Mary F. Keith, Sept. 13, '54; r. Th., a soldier in 4th Me. reg., &c. Their ch. 1, Maria, b. July 26, '55, d. Nov. 13, '56. 2, Adelai.

CAMPBELL, George, (2d), b. ab. 1830; m. Lucy F. Davis, July 10, 1859; r. Rock., a teamster.

CANDAGE, Heman W., b. in Blue Hill, Me.; m. Susan B. Ladd; c. to Rock. to r. in 1847. Their ch. 1, Hiram S., was lost overboard from sch. *Samuel Rankin*, March 12, '56. 2, Horace E. b. ab. '38; m. Esther Kennedy, March 1, '62; r. Rock, a mariner. 3, Avery L., b. ab. '40; was corporal in the 4th Me. Reg.; killed at Fredericksburg, Dec. 13, '62. 4, Oliver W., b. ab. 1842; d. Oct. 28, '64, in the foundered schr. *Onatavia*. 5, Cynthia A., b. ab. 1844. 6, Almira M., b. ab '45; m. Reuben S. Ames; r. Rock. 7, Byron W. b. ab. '47; r. Rock., enlisted in U. S. navy. 8, Abby Emeline, b. ab. '49. 9, Charles A., b. ab. 1852.

CANN, Charles, b. 1821 in England; m. Abigail Smith of Eng.; c. from N. B.; r. S. Th., a farmer, Their ch. 1, Amelia, b. ab. 1847, in Eng; r. S. Th. 2, Eliza, b. 1849 in N. B.; r. S. Th.

CARLE, Peter, b. ab. 1836, in Ireland; m. Margaret Murphy? of I.; r. Rock., a lime burner. Their ch. 1, Mary E., b. ab. 1853. 2, James H., b. ab. 1856. 3, Kate E., b. ab. 1859.

CARLETON, Enoch, b. in Methuen, Mass., Dec. 1800; c. to Cam. and, after residing awhile there, at Eastport, Machias, &c.; m. Susan Brown of Wal., came to r. Th., Feb. 1835, superintended the shoemaking in State Prison from 1833 to 1861; and since carries on that business for himself and keeps a shoe store. Their ch. 1, David, b.

in Wal., ab. 1828; r. Th., a mariner, and d. Feb. 15, '64. 2, Charles H., b. in Wal., Dec. 1829, d. Nov. 23, 1845. 3, Gorham, b. in Wal., r. Th., a mariner. 4, Harriet, b. in Wal., m. William Andrews; r. Th. 5, Edward B., b. Sept. 2, 1835; m. Sarah E. Fales, Oct. 4, '56; r. Th. 6, Elizabeth S., b. Aug. 27, '37; m. Edward L. Dillingham; r. Th. 7, Maria, b. July 1, 1841, d. Aug. 27, 1842.

Edward B.'s ch. 1, George Ernest, d. an infant, March, 1858. 2, Flora Maria, b. 1859.

CARNEY, Thomas, m. Nellie O'Murphy; c. from Cork, Ireland; r. & d. at Broad Cove, Cushing. Of their ch. 1, James, c. to what is now Th., & r. some time at Beech Woods; m. Mary McLellan, p. Dec. 5, 1778; rem. Lower town, and d. in St. George. 2, Mary, m. 1st, John Shibles, 2d, John Dillaway; r. Th., and d. Aug. 1799. 3, Margaret, m. 1st, Waldo Henderson, 2d, —— Rawley; r. & d. St. G.

James's ch. 1, Sarah, born at Beech Woods, Nov, 1780; m. Capt. Joseph Gilchrist; r. Th. 2, Thomas, d. at sea, in a man of war. 3, James, (2d), m. Nancy Lash; rem. from Cushing to S. Thomaston, and was lost at sea. 4, McLellan, died at sea.

James, (2d)'s ch. 1, Capt. George L., b. ab. 1813; m. Sarah J. Nicholson, May 9, 1842; r. Th., a master mariner. 2, James, (3d). 3, Clementine C., m. Henry Nash of Boston, Sept. 29, '46. 4, Mary E., m. Joseph B. Williams; r. Thomaston.

Capt. George L.'s ch. 1, Walter, b. ab. 1844. 2, Elizabeth, b. ab. '46. 3, Ida, b. ab. '48. 4, George D., d. March 9, '59.

CARNEY, James, born in Ireland; m. Jane McLain of the same country, 1829; r. Th. about 20 years; and rem. with all his family to Michigan about 1850. Their ch. 1, James, (2d), b. May 9, 1830; killed in Th., April 26, '47, by the accidental discharge of a gun. 2, Daniel, b. April 12, 1832. 3, Mary Jane, b. Aug. 5, '35. 4, Nancy, b. April 6, '37. 5, Edward, b. Aug. 5, '39. 6, Thomas, b. Nov. 2, '41.

CARR, Moses S., b. July 16, 1809; m. Mary M. Montgomery of S. Th.; p. Nov. 16, '33; r, some time in Rock., but rem. Knox, Knox county, Ill. Their ch. b. here. 1, Sarah E., b. Feb. 16, '35. 2, Therese S., b. March 29, '37; 3, Helena P., b. Dec. 14, '42.

CARR, Benjamin, b. 1802; c. from Palermo to Th. as warden of State Prison, '42, had been representative and councillor; m. Roxanna Marden of Palermo, 2d, Mrs. Nancy McLellan, March, '49; & d. Jan. 11, 54. His ch. by 1st wife. 1, George F., m. Maria E. Stowe of Oldtown, Sept. 12, '54; r. Boston. 2, Helen M., m. Elliott Singer; r. Brooklyn, N. Y. 3. Flavel W., b. Dec. '35; r. Brooklyn, a soldier in 5th N. Y reg., was wounded in battle of Weldon Railroad, & d. on board transport, Oct. 30, '64, at Fortress Monroe. 4, Angela Estelle, r. Brooklyn. 5, Thomas A., b. in Th., Aug. 4, '40. 6, Benjamin F., b. Dec. 6, '42; r. Th., Lieut. in 2d Maine Battery. 7, Alphonso, b. June 6, '43, d. Sept. 16, '44. 8, Charles E. The mother d. April 22, '48.

CARR, John, a dry goods peddler, b. 1834; c. from Ireland to Th. with his mother & sisters; 1, Mary, r. Th. 2, Kate; m. John Bowman; r. Th. 3, Bridget, rem. & m. in California.

CARRIEL, Leander T., son of Stephen of Union, b. Feb. 12, 1831; m. Catharine ———; r. Rock. Their ch. Charles, b. ab. 1857.

CARROLL, Alice, b. in Ireland; r. Rock., a widow with 3 ch. 1, William, b. ab. 1855. 2, Mary, b. ab. '57. 3, Thomas, b. ab. '59.

CARTER, James, b. ab. 1795; place of origin not ascertained; m. Ruth ——— ; r. Rock. Their ch. 1, Francis M., b. ab. 1833. 2, Ann M., b. ab. '36.

CARVER, Lt. Col. Lorenzo D., b. ab. 1825, in Vinalhaven, a son of Melzar & Joanna (Snowman) Carver, who rem. Montville in their son's childhood; c. from Montville to Rock.; m. Catherine Willis, Nov., '47; r. Rock., a shipbuilder & officer in the 4th Me. reg. Of his brothers, formerly of Rock., Alden S. & Albert, rem. California, where, at Goldspring, the former was shot by some Irishmen, who disputed his brother's claim there.

Lt. Col. Lorenzo D.'s ch. 1, Melzar W., b. ab. 1850. 2, Gracia F., b. ab. '53.

CARY, Daniel, & Lucinda, his wife, were early in Old Th. and had recorded here their ch. Mary E., b. May 18, 1843.

CASE, Rev. Isaac, b. ab. 1761; came from Harpswell to S. Th., as a pioneer Baptist preacher; m. Joanna Snow, p. June 23, 1785; r. Castine, &c., was living in 1848 at Readfield in his 87th year. Their ch. 1, Joanna, m. Rev. Philip Weaver; r. Mercer, & d. in Belgrade. 2, Hannah, m. Ralph Haley; r. Newcastle. 3, Dr. Isaac, (2d), m. Abigail Page of Readfield; r. Kenduskeag. 4, Ambrose, b. ab. 1790; m. Susan Sawyer of Litchfield. 2d, Hannah (Spear) Robbins, Jan. 16, 1836; r. Rock., a truckman. 5, William, m. Eliza Hubbard of Readfield; d. at Little Rock, Ark. 6, Betsey, m. Joshua Lane; r. & died at Readfield. 7, Mary, m. Joseph Prescott of Readfield; rem. Arkansas. 8, Eunice, m. Dr. John Yeaton of Belgrade. 9, Louisa, m. Hiram Rockwood of Belgrade. 10, Elisha S., m. Joanna Jenkins; r. Readfield.

Ambrose's ch. 1, George W., b. ab. 1821; m. Emma Smith, Mar. 11, '47; r. Rock., a truckman, &c. 2, Lt. Col. John S., b. ab. '23; m. Lucy C. White, Aug. 4, 1852; r. Rock., a merchant, division inspector of Maine militia, &c. 3, Nancy, m. Samuel Winston; r. Manchester, Me. By 2d wife. 4, Charles A., b. Oct. 29, 1836, died Oct. 11, 1839. 5, Mary E., b. Feb. 8, 1839; m. Albert R. Reeve of New York city, Oct. 28, 1858. 6, Frank, b. ab. 1843; r. Rockland.

George W.'s ch. 1, Laura A. b. ab. 1848. 2, Lucia E., b. ab. '50.

Col. John S.'s ch. Emily W., b. ab. 1856.

CASWELL, Charles, b. ab. 1820, in N. H.; m. Mrs. Isabel S. Choate of S. Th., Nov. 30, 1848; r. Rock., a shoemaker. Their ch. 1, Mary I., b. ab. 1851. 2, Eliza F., b. ab. 1853.

CATES, Ambrose, b. Aug. 24, 1802; came from Machiasport; m. Grace ——— ; r. Rock., a truckman, & d. Jan. 25, 1859. Nathaniel, a nephew, came from Machiasport; m. 2d, Fanny Rich, Nov. 25, 1838; r. Rockland.

Ambrose's ch. recorded here. Susan E., born Sept. 9, 1840. The mother died Nov. 2, 1858, aged about 44.

Nathaniel's ch. Franklin E., born May, and died June, 1849.

CATES, Willard, b. ab. 1821, in Thorndike, Me.; m. 1st, Mary Blethen, 2d, Mary E., (Sullivan) Spear; r. Rock., keeps livery stable, &c. His ch. by 1st wife. 1, Mary, b. ab. 1845. 2, Flora, b. Feb. 28, 1847, d. March 5, 1860. 3, Julius S., b. ab. 1851. 4, Willard L., b. ab. 1855. 5, Mandana E., b. ab. 1857. 6, E. Bartlett, b. 1859.

CATLAND; of this family, 2 brothers came from Boothbay. 1, Joshua Sawyer, b. March 20, 1805; came to Th., 1835; m. Mary J.

Crane of W., Feb. 9, 1837; r. Th., a carpenter. 2, Dea. Joseph, b. ab. 1808; m. Sarah A. Robinson of C., Aug. 7, 1832; r. Th., a joiner.

Joshua Sawyer's ch. 1, Susan A., b. Dec. 19, 1837. 2, Mary Abbie, b. May 31, 1839. 3, Luther, b. Feb. 3, 1841, d. Nov. 17, 1842. 4, Lucy H., b. Nov. 3, 1844. 5, Lizzie M., b. Sept. 4, 1846. 6, Sawyer, b. Oct. 15, 1848, d. Dec. 4, 1853.

Dea. Joseph's ch. 1, John R., born Nov. 13, 1834; m. Lucy A. Young, Oct. 6, 1859; r. Th., a joiner. 2, Joseph E., b. Aug. 11, '36; m. Ann Medora Moody, Oct. 17, 1857; r. Th., a carpenter, & soldier. 3, Nehemiah Boynton, b. Jan. 19, 1840; r. Th., a joiner, & soldier in 1st Me. Cavalry; d. June 12, 1863. 4, William L., b. ab. '45; r. Th.

John R.'s ch. Eunice, b. ab. 1860.

Joseph E.'s ch. Osgood S., b. ab. 1859.

CHADBOURNE, Thomas W., b. ab. 1817; came from Edgecomb or Boothbay; m. Emma D. Arnold, March 10, 1858; r. Rockland, a police officer, high sheriff in 1858; m. again & rem. Boston. Lovell P., a brother; came to Th., where his 1st wife d.; m. 2d, Dosliska H. Willard at Harrison, Me., 1838; rem. W. and elsewhere.

Thomas W.'s ch. 1, Eveline C., b. ab. 1840. 2, Edward P. 3, Sarah A., b. ab. 1844; m. C. M. Tibbetts; r. Rock. 4, B. Walter. 5, Theodore I. 6, Ella Jane.

CHANDLER, Dr. Charles Chauncy, b. 1774, c. from Vermont; m. Lovicy Miller, of Linc., practised medicine Belfast and Warren, and d. in W. Sept. 12, 1833. Their ch. 1, Lucius Henry, Esq., graduate Waterville Coll. 1831; m. Susan A. Robbins of Northhampton Co., Va., practised law many years in Th., rem. Boston and Norfolk, Va., ret. to Rockland, August, 1861, appointed consul at Matanzas, Cuba, the same year, district attorney for E. Dist,. Va., 1863, and removed his family thither in the following June. 2, Mary Ann, m. Samuel I. Lovejoy; r. Rock. 3, Martha J., m. Francis Cobb; r. Rock. 4, Edwin, r. Rock., a mariner.

Lucius H.'s ch. b in Th. 1, Chauncy L., b. Sept. 13, d. Sept. 24, 1834. 2, Maria K., b. Dec. 4, 1835. 3, Sarah F., b. April 8, 1837. 4, Esther L., b. Oct. 7, 1838. 5, Thomas D., b. March 10, 1840, died March 30, 1841. 6, Susan. 7, Henry. 8, William T.

CHANDLER, Cyrus C., b. ab. 1822; came from Winthrop, Me.; m. Mary J. Keen, Aug. 16, 1846; r. Rock., a druggist, cashier, &c.

CHANDLER, Henry G., b. ab. 1824; came from Knox; m. Priscilla T. Snowdeal; r. S. Th., a carpenter. Their ch. 1, Oscar A., b. ab. 1848. 2, Emily L., b. ab. 1856.

CHANDLER, George W., b. ab. 1822; m. Rebecca ——; & r. Rock., a mariner. Their ch. 1, Eliza, b. ab. 1850. 2, Susan, b. ab. 1852. 3, George H., b. ab. 1858.

CHANEY, John, b. ab. 1825, in Ireland, as was Harriet his wife; r. Th. Their ch. Fanny, b. in 1860.

CHAPLES, James, b. ab. 1793, in St. George; m. Sarah Fuller, of Warren, where he r. but rem. Th., a shoemaker. Their ch. 1, Oliver, m. and r. Th., where he was killed July 10, 1848, by falling from staging of a vessel. 2, Hannah. 3, Addison. 4, Albion, d. Nov. 6, '49, in W. 5, Harriet, b. ab. 1834; m. Edward Hyler; r. Th. 6, Andrew F. The mother died March 19, 1861.

CHAPLES, George W., b. ab. 1810, in St. George; a distant branch of the same family; m. Eliza Crouse, p. Aug. 25, '32; r.

Rock. Their ch. 1, Charles, b. ab. 1843. 2, Almond, b. ab. '45. 3, Erastus, b. ab. '47. 4, James M., b. ab. '49.

CHAPLES, Benjamin A., b. ab. 1824, in St. George, of the same family; m. Nancy Witham, 1846; r. Rock., a quarryman. Their ch. 1, N. Winfield, b. ab. 1852. 2, Adelia S., b. Oct., '58, d. Nov. 1, 1864.

CHAPMAN, William, son of John, of Scituate, Mass.; c. first to Wal., thence in 1786 to what is now S. Th.; m. Deborah Caswell; and died before 1792. Their ch. 1, Deborah, m. Thomas Farr, 2d, Andrew Eveleth; r. and d. in Bangor. 2, Abigail, r. and d. in China, Me. 3, Lucy m. Thomas Russ in 1804, 2d, ——— Bradbury; r. and d. in Leeds, Me. 4, Capt. William, (2d), m. and r. in S. Th., was lost at sea. 5, Isaac, r. on homestead, rem. China. 6, Ralph, b. ab. 1788; m. Abigail Cooper, Dec. 17, 1817; r. S. Th., a stone layer, &c. 7, Prudence, m. George Fish; r. Dover, Me. 8, Mary, m., r., and d. in China. 9, Achsa, r. and d. in N. Y.

Ralph's ch. 1, Angeline, b. April 3, 1817, d. July 4, 33. 2, Lydia B., b. Feb. 8, '19: m. Capt. Harvey Perry. 3, Wm. Nelson, b. Dec. 30, '20; soldier in 4th Me., Reg. 4, Lucinda, b. April 20, 1823; m. Capt. Jonas K. Bartlett; r. S. Th. 5, Antoinette, b. April 7, '25; m. Samuel Bartlett; r. S. Th. 6, Ralph James, b. Feb. 13, '27; rem. California. 7, Edwin George, b. Feb. 13, '29; r. S. Th., a carpenter, corporal in 28th Me. Reg. &c.

CHAPMAN, Robert, b. ab. 1788; c. from Nobleboro'; m. Edie Flint; r. Th., a merchant, and d. July 26, 1855. Their ch. 1, Isaac, m. ——— Chapman at Damariscotta; r. Th., & Brooklyn, N. Y.; a merchant, &c., firm Flint, Chapman & Co. 2, Benjamin F., (adopted by his uncle, and took by Leg. Act the name of Flint. See Flint family. 3. Edmund B., b. July 27, 1827; m. Elsie Levensaler, June 17, 1855; r. Th., shipbuilder, of the firm of Levensaler, Walsh, & Co., d. July 20, 1858. 4. Mary Olivia, m. Capt. Dunbar Henderson; r. Th. 5, Capt. James F., m. Olive R. Levensaler, June 30, 1858; r. Th. The mother d. May 27, 1855.

Isaac's ch. 1, James Raymond, b. May, 1851, d. Jan. 21, 1855.

Edmund B.'s ch. 1, Edie, b. ab. 1856. 2, Josie, d. young.

Capt. James F.'s ch. 1, Edmund B., (2d), b. ab. 1859. 2, James, d. Sept. 13, 1861.

CHAPMAN, Stephen H., b. ab. 1825 in Nobleboro'; m, Emeline ———; r. Rock., a lecturer, &c.; first vol. in 4th Me. Reg. and d. at Bull Run, July 21, 1861. Their ch. 1, Cevosta V., b. ab. 1850. 2, Caravena, b. ab. 1852. 3, Mary L., b. ab. 1854. 4, Nellie, b. ab. 1856. 5, Aroline, b. 1858.

CHAPMAN, Edward T., son of Rev. Nathaniel, b. ab. 1830, grad. Bowd. Coll. 1857; a teacher here; paymaster on gunboat Com. Jones, destroyed with her May 6, 1864, on James River.

CHASE, Dr. Charles T., b. in Vassalboro'; grad. Bowd. Coll. 1839; M. D. Harvard University, 1846; c. to Th., m. Adelaide C. Ruggles, Sept. 15, 1852; r. Th. in successful practice of his profession.

CHASE, Dr. Ebenezer P., b. in Livermore, Sept. 17, 1831; m. Charlotte W. Owen of Brunswick; r. Rock., a surgeon dentist. Their ch. James E., b. Feb. 2, 1861.

CHRISTIAN, Peter, b. ab. 1818 in Denmark, Europe; m. Mary

E. ——— ; r. S. Th., a mariner. Their ch. 1, Austin M., b. ab. 1850. 2, George Bargreen, b. Oct. 6, 1852, d. June 30, 1858. 3, Hannah A., b. ab. 1854.

CILLEY, Hon. Jonathan, b. at Nottingham, N. H., July 2, 1802, (son of Greenleaf Cilley & grandson of Col. Joseph, who commanded a N. H. regiment during the Revolution,) grad. Bowd. Coll. '25 ; admitted attorney at law, '28 ; opened an office in Th., Sept. '28 ; m. Deborah Prince, April 2, '29 ; Speaker of the House in Me., '35 to '37 ; M. C. from Lincoln District, '38, & d. near Washington, Feb. 24, '38. Their ch. 1, Commander Greenleaf, b. Oct. 27, '29 ; r. Th., entered U. S. navy, &, rising in rank, took command, Oct., '63, of the iron clad monitor, *Catskill*. 2, Jane N., b. July 31, '31, d. May 19, '36 3, Bowdoin L., b. Sept. 1, '33, d. June 25, '34. 4, Lt. Col. Jona. Prince, b. Dec. 29, '35 ; declining a cadetship at W. Point, he grad. at Bowd. Coll., '58 ; was admitted to the bar at Rock., '60 ; entered on the practice of law at Th., but soon became Capt. of co. B., 1st Me. Cavalry, promoted to Maj & Lt. Col. ; wounded a second time in '64. 5, Julia D., b. Dec. 20, '37 ; r. Bath.

CILLEY, Charles H., b. June 7, 1836, in Jackson, Me., son of Rev. Joseph L. Cilley ; m. Mary E. Killsa, Nov. 14, '56 ; r. Rock., a joiner, painter, &c. Their ch. 1, Lottie E., b. Feb. 4, '57. 2, Helen A., b. in Rock. Nov. 19, '59.

CLARK, Dr. Daniel, c. with Larissa, his wife, from N. Yarmouth to Th., as a physician, in 1821, & after two years rem. Portland. Of their ch. Homer Johnson, d. in Th. of consumption, Aug. 12, '22.

CLARK, Benjamin, c. early to Th. as a potter ; m. Betsey Perkins Brown ; p. Jan. 12, 1797 ; r. & d. Th. Their ch. 1, Lydia D. 2, Eliza P. 3, Ebenezer ; all rem. Ohio with their mother & step-father Charles Bradford.

CLARK, Benjamin, b. ab. 1812 ; c. from Kingston, N. H. to St. G. ; m. Mary Stover ; r. Rock., a lime manufacturer. Their ch. 1, Sarah F., b. Aug. 30, '35, d. June 20, '52. 2, Orris, or Horace R., b. Oct. 24, '36 ; m. Catherine ——— ; r. Rock., a lime burner. 3, William, b. Aug. 26, '38 ; r. Rock., a lime burner. 4, Nathan, b. May 8, '40 ; r. Rock., a lime burner. 5, Nancy J., b. ab. '42 ; m. Samandel W. Cushman, Feb. 2, '62. 6, Charles, b. ab. '44, a soldier of the 4th Me. reg., killed at Bull Run, Aug. 29, '62. 7, Adelaide, b. ab. '46. 8, John, b. ab. '48. 9, Benjamin, (2d), b. ab. '50. 10, Edwin, b. ab. '55. Horace R.'s ch. Julia F., b. ab. 1857.

CLARK, Charles, b. in Newburyport, Mass., 1799 ; m. Jane Patterson of Belfast ; c. thence to Rock., where he was a baker from 1833 to Nov. 1851, then a flour & corn dealer, till his death, May 3, 1862. Their ch. 1, Jane, b. ab. '22 ; m. Capt. John W. Haskell ; r. Rock., & d. June 4, '59. 2, Charles W., b. ab. '28, d. June 23, '63. 3, Rosilla P. b. March 4, '33, d. Oct., '51. 4, George A., b. Sept. 4, '39 ; r. Rock., a clerk, &c.

CLARK, David, c. from Hanover, Mass. ; m. Delanah P. Maker ; p. Aug. 20, 1818, 2d, Hannah Bryant, Jan. 11, '51, 3d, Susan Perry of Vinalhaven, '52 ; r. S. Th., the Islands, &c, His ch. by 1st wife. 1, Hannah P., b. Sept. 29, '20. 2, Capt. Joshua G., b. Aug. 27, '21 ; m. Miranda M. Heard, May 22, '51 ; r. S. Th. 3, Jonathan M., b. March 11, '24 ; m. Hannah H. Hawes ; p. Sept. 1. '47 ; r. S. Th. a carpenter. 4, Tryphena B., b. April 5, '27 ; m. James R. Maker ; r.

S. Th. 5, Sarah E., b. April 25, '31; m. Eben W. Robbins, April 25, 1851.

Capt. Joshua G.'s ch. 1, Kate E., b. ab. 1852. 2, George P., b. ab. '54. 3, Julia B., b. ab. '56.

Jonathan M.'s ch. 1, Priscilla, b. ab. 1848. 2, Catharine, b. ab. 1852. 3. Alforetta, b. ab. 1853. 4, Miranda, b. ab. 1855.

CLARK; of this family two brothers c. from Union; 1, James W., b. ab. 1832; m. Rhoda A. Black, June 18, 1854; r. Rock., a fish-dealer. 2, Joseph L., b. ab. 1836; m. Mary J. H. Black; r. Rock., a teamster, &c.

James W.'s ch. 1, Cyrus W., b. ab. 1855. 2, Etta A., b. ab. 1858.

Joseph L.'s ch. 1, Arthur E. F., b. ab. 1858. 2, Clarence F., b. ab. 1860.

CLARK, Nathaniel C., b. ab. 1822, son of Joseph of Warren; purchased the Ulmer mill, and r. Th. some years, rem. with his family.

CLARK, O. A., came recently from St. George; m. Elizabeth A. Harding; r. Rock.

CLARK, George, b. ab. 1816; m. Louisa ——; r. Rock., a lime burner. Their ch. 1, Luther, b. ab. 1841. 2, Harriet L., b ab. 1843. 3, Julia E., b. ab. 1846. 4, Garrofilia, b. ab 1848. 5, George, (2d), b. Sept., 1855, and d. May 18, 1858. 6, George, (3d), b. ab. '59.

CLARK, Samuel S., b. ab. 1830, in Mt. Desert; m. Eliza T. Glover, Feb. 23, 1854; r. Rock., a painter; was in the South when the rebellion com.; was pressed into rebel army of Miss., taken at Vicksburg, and ret. home. Their ch. 1, Abbie C., b. ab. 1855. 2, Ernest W., b. ab. 1858.

CLARK, William, b. ab. 1835, in England; m. Wealthy Flanders, Sept. 2, 1853; r. Rock., a lime burner. Their ch. 1, Edwin, b. ab. 1855. 2, Caroline, b. ab. 1859.

CLARKSON, John, c. to S. Th., with Mary, his wife, from N. Y.; was a mariner, and, after residing here 10 or 12 years, was lost in the br. *Maine*, 1844. Their ch. 1, Lydia, b. Dec. 23, 1831; 2, Mary, b. June 26, 1833; 3, William F., b. April 14, 1836; 4, John, (2d), b. Feb. 24, 1838; 5, Elizabeth, b. March 19, 1840; all rem. and r. in different parts of Mass.

CLAY, Dr. R. Richard, c. from Portland, m. Mary N. (Young) Smalley of Th., Aug. 22, 1861; r. Th., well known as a lecturer on consumption and its cure.

CLEAVELAND, Samuel T., b. ab. 1825 in Camden, m. 1st, Caroline Pottle of Searsmont, 2d, Melinda M. Tolman of Cam.; r. Rock., a patent lime kiln builder; rem. and trades in Cam. Their ch. 1, Sidney L., b. ab. 1849. 2, Elethea C., b. ab. 1855. 3, Mary I, b. ab. 1859.

CLEMENTS, Tilley H., b. ab. 1796 in Berwick, Me.; m. Philena, dau. of Philip Hanson of Th.; r. Rock., a lime burner, &c. Their ch. 1, Mary Ann H., b. April 9, 1824, d. June 9, 1836. 2, Philip H., b. Oct. 12, 1826; r. Rock., a grocery merchant.

CLINTON, Henry, b. ab. 1834, in N. Y.; m. Emma F. Buckland, Dec. 13, 1858; r. Th., a mariner. Their ch. Georgiana, b. ab. 1859.

CLOUGH, David H., b. ab. 1793; came from Fall River, Mass., to what is now Rockland; mar. Miriam Palmer, Dec. 22, 1812; r. Th. Their ch. 1, Amos, b. Sept. 25, 1813; m. Mary K. Tilson, Oct. 13,

1839; r. Th., rem. California. 2, Josiah, b. March 24, 1818; mar. Lydia Hammond, Nov. 26, 1846, and d. by poison, Sept. 12, 1859. 3, Eliza J., b. ab. 1824; m. Ezekiel G. Dodge, Jr., r. Th. 4, David H., (2d), m. Eleanor Crandon, Sept. 15, 1850; r. Hope. 5, Susan E., m. John Palmer; r. Th. 6, Henry, rem. California. 7, Mary Ann; r. Th. 8, Daniel P., b. Dec. 7, '37; r. Th., a mariner, soldier of 4th Maine, and 38th New York, d. at Falmouth, Va., Feb. 9, '63.

Amos's ch. 1, Sarah, F., b. Aug. 31, 1840; r. Th. 2, John T., b. March 19, 1842; r. Th., in U. S. navy. 3, Henrietta, b. ab. 1844. 4, Frederic, b. ab. '46. 5, Franklin, b. ab. '48. 6, Charles, b. ab. '50.

Josiah's ch. 1, Horace C. 2, Eliza J. 3, Edward F., b. ab. 1852. 4, Ellen E., b. ab. 1858.

CLOUGH, Capt. Stephen, m. Sarah Decker; came from Wiscasset; r. Th. & d. in the South West, 1817. His sister, Elizabeth, m. 2d, John Paine, r. Th., and d. Aug. 7, 1834.

Capt. Stephen's ch. 1, Sarah D., b. July 5, 1790; m. 1st, Jonathan Bowman of Wiscasset, 2d, Rev. Job Washburn; r. Th., and d. April 24, 1846. 2, Eliza L. St. Barbs, m. Hon. William McLellan; r. Warren, and d. in Belfast. 3, H. Antoinette, m. Rev. Jonathan Adams, of Woolwich, July 16, 1821. The mother m. 2d, Capt. John Pendleton, of Cam. June 24, 1836.

CLOUGH, Benjamin, b. ab. 1812; c. from Camden; married 1st, Wealthy Tolman, April 26, 1835, 2d, Rebecca S. Jones, June 6, 1852; r. Rock. His ch. by 2d wife. John, b. ab. 1854.

CLOUGH, Stephen, b. ab. 1830, in Cam., nephew of Benjamin; m. Amanda M. ———; r. Rock., a lime burner. Leander, a brother, b. in Cam. ab. 1834; also r. Rock. with Mary, his wife, is a mariner.

Stephen's ch. 1, Joseph F., b. ab. 1852. 2, William D., b. ab. 1854. 3, Frances R., b. ab. '56. 4, Ann M., b. ab. '58. 5, Cora E., b. ab. '60.

CLOUSE, George W., b. ab. 1822, c. to Rock.; m. Mary T. Jackson, July 9, 1855; r. Rock., a carpenter. Their ch. 1, Ellen I., b. June 7, 1856, died Jan. 15, 1861. 2, Charles A., b, ab. 1859.

CLUSKY, John, b. about 1838, in Ireland; m. Hannah ———, r. Th. in 1860.

COBB, Capt. Barnabas, b. 1760, in Plympton, Mass., c. with his family from Carver to W. in 1802; & d. July 9, 1807. He m. Jerusha Cobb of Plymouth, whose grandfather, Ebenezer Cobb, d. at Kingston, Dec. 8, 1801, aged 107 years, 8 months, and 6 days. Capt. Barnabas's ch. 1, Clarissa, b. March 27, 1786; m. Capt. Matthew Beverage; r. Hope. 2, Hannah, b. Nov. 27, 1787; m. Alexander Lermond, (4th), of W., & d. April 28, 1840. 3, Sophia, b. Dec. 23, '89; m. George Andrews; r. W., & d. Jan. 20, 1864, in Th. 4, Ebenezer, b. Oct. 9, 1793; m. Patience M. Gilmore, Jan. 18, 1818; r. Union, a landlord, &c. 5, Eleazer Crocker, b. Oct. 4, 1798; m. Harriet Counce, Dec. 1827; r. Th., a farmer.

Eleazer C.'s ch. 1, Susan, b. ab. 1830; m. Henry Lermond; r. Th. 2, Edmund E., b. April 9, 1832; m. Matilda Boggs of W., Jan. 15, 1855, &. d. Feb. 10, 1856. 3, Albion, b. June 11, 1834; m. & r. Th. or Boston. 4, Emily, b. July 7, 1837; m. John A. Patterson of W., Nov. 18, 1860. 5, Lawson, b. Oct. 1, 1839; m. Harriet R., dau. of Capt. J. H. Kelleran, Nov. 10, 1864; r. Th.

COBB, Francis, of Portland, m. Jane Snow of Th.; r. & d. Portland. Their ch. 1, Mary, b. ab. 1808; m. Capt. George W. Wallace; r. Knox st., Th. 2, Ambrose S., b. ab. 1811; m. Vesta Jane Dunbar of W., Jan. 28, 1841; r. Rock., a joiner, superintendant of lime manufactory, &c. 3, Betsey, m. Albert Counce; r. W. 4, Capt. Edward, m. Lydia Berry of Bath, April 16, 1841; r. Rock., rem. to Kansas. 5, Capt. Francis, (2d), b. ab. 1818; m. Martha Jane Chandler, Oct. 8, 1839; r. Rock., a ship chandlery merchant, lime manufacturer, &c., in firm of Cobb, Wight & Case.

Ambrose S.'s ch. 1, William S., b. in W., d. young. 2, Nelson B., b. ab. 1845. 3, Mary Elizabeth, b. April 19, 1847.

Capt. Edward's ch. 1, Edward, (2d), b. 1840, d., lost at sea, June 30, 1858. 2, a daughter.

Capt. Francis, (2d)'s ch. 1, Mary A. C., born Nov. 11, 1840. 2, Frank K., b. ab. '43; r. Rock., a clerk, &c. 3, Louisa H., b. ab. '45. 4, Maria F., b. ab. '47. 5, Charles C. W., b. ab. '50. 6, Jennie W., b. ab. '54. 7, Maynard S., b. April 23, & d. Nov. 3, '56. 8, William T., b. ab. '57. 9, Martha F., b. ab. '59.

COBB, Alfred B., b. ab. 1826, in Hartland, Vt.; m. Nizaula M. Bartlett of N. H.; r. Rock., a marble manufacturer. Their ch. Lizzie W., b. ab. 1859.

COBB, John C. Esq., b. ab. 1838; came as a lawyer to S. Th., ab. 1860, enlisted and had a lieutenant's commission in the army, but resigned and returned to South Thomaston or Rockland.

COBURN, Charles, came from Dracut, Mass., m. Elizabeth Simonton, March 7, 1808; r. Th., and d. June 2, 1813. Their ch. 1, Justus, b. Nov. 8, 1808; m. in N. York, Mary ——— of Holland, Eu., r. Th., a rigger, &c., & d. from a fall, Oct. 5, 1859. 2, John S., b. Jan. 6, 1811; m. Sarah F. Levensaler, Dec. 17, 1837; r. Rock., a mason, alderman, &c.

Justus's ch. 1, Charles, (2d), b. ab. 1847. 2, Catharine, b. about 1849.

John S.'s ch. 1, Mary L., born Jan. 6, 1839; m. Capt. William J. Wilson; r. Th. 2, Sarah E., b. Nov. 22, 1840. 3, Abbie A., b. ab. 1844. 4, Emma, b. ab. 1857.

COBURN, William, b. ab. 1828; of a different family from preceding; m. Mary J. ———; r. S. Th., a farmer. Their ch. Rancel, b. ab. 1839.

COCHRAN, Dr. James, whose ancestor came over in the Scotch Irish colony of Londonderrry, N. H., was b. ab. 1777, in Windham, N. H.; m. Jane Moore, of Standish, Me., studied med. M. D. ——— Coll., r. and prac. med. many years in Rock., where he died Oct. 7, 1860. Their ch. 1, James (2d), born in Limington, Maine, m. Eliza McClure of Waldo. 2, Jane M., m. I. T. Hovey; r. Rock. 3, Elizabeth, b. in Standish; m. Rufus Day of Gardiner. 4, Mary M. H., b., as also all the succeeding, in Monmouth, Me., m. Henry S. Dearborn of Monmouth, p. Nov. 6, 1835; who d. 1839, and she r. Rock., with one child, Marietta M., b. ab. 1839. 5, L. H. M., mar. Sarah Hooper of Kennebunk, 2d, Augusta Patten; and d. at Melrose, Mass., Oct. 1860. 6, Hon. John C., b. ab. 1810; m. Susan Snowman of Sedgwick, May 8, '51; r. Rock., attorney, municipal judge, &c., d. Feb. 21, '55. 7, Ann U. D., m. Isaiah A. Jones; r. Rock. 8. Marietta C., b. ab. 1814; m. I. T. Hovey; r. Rock., and d. Jan. 1839. 9, Margaret A., m. Emery Sawyer, of Brooks. 10, Erasmus H., m. Hannah B. Ayer of Freedom; r. Rock., insurance agent, &c. 11, Delia E. W., born Nov. 15, 1820; m. C. V. R. Boynton; r. R. and died Feb. 29, 1857.

12, Sarah L., d. 1841. 13, George W., d. aged 2 years, in Monmouth. 14, George W., (2d), r. Rock., a trunkmaker, agent, &c.

Erasmus H.'s ch. Ellen J., b. ab. 1844.

COCHRAN, Gen. William S., b. in Belfast, Oct. 13, 1816; rem. Wiscasset; m. Maria L. Blaisdell of Bristol, 2d, Abby M. Rhoades, March 20, 1863; r. Wal., where he was representative, bank commissioner, sailmaker, &c., rem. Rock., 1860, & d. Nov. 23, '64. His ch. by 1st wife. 1, William T., b. ab. 1841; m. Lydia M. Jameson, July 16, '63; r. Rock. 2, Abby M., b. ab. '46. 3, Frank L., b. ab. '57. The mother d. Aug. 29, '62; a. 43.

COCHRAN, Jeremiah, b. 1827, in Ireland, as was Mary, his wife. r. Rock. Their ch. 1, James, b. ab. 1857. 2, John, b. ab. 1859.

COCHRAN, James, b. 1831, in Ireland; m. Anastasia Grennan, 1853; r. Rock., a marble worker. Their ch. 1, Margaret A., b. '56, d. Feb. 2, '64. 2, Mary E., b. ab. '57. The mother d. May 23, '57.

COCHRAN, James R. or H., of Rock., m. Ellen M. Berry, of Belfast, Nov. 5, 1849.

COFFIN, Augustus, b. ab. 1827; m. Ann ——; r. S. Th. Their ch. 1, Sarah I., b. ab. 1856. 2, Louisa I., b. ab. '58. 3, George A., b. ab. '59.

COFFRAN, Dr. Charles H., b. ab. 1819; M. D., Botanic Med. Coll. of Ohio, attended med. lectures H. U., practised med. 7 years in Weymouth, Mass.; came to Rock.; m. Jane Witham; r. & practised med. Rock. till, in 1861, rem. Suisun, Solano Co., since Fairfield, California. Their ch. 1, Ada A., b. ab. 1845; m. in Cal., William K. Solto, county recorder, Jan. 4, '64. 2, Adriana, b. ab. '46. 3, Albina H., b. ab. '48; m. in Fairfield, Cal., Hiram W. Blanchard, May 10, '64. 4, Charles A., b. ab. '50.

COGAN, Michael, b. ab. 1825, in Ireland, as was Julia his wife; r. Rock. Their ch. 1, Mary, b. ab. 1852. 2, John, b. ab. '54. 3, William, b. ab. '56. 4, Michael, (2d), b. ab. '58. 5, Robert, b. ab. '60.

COKELY, Cornelius, b. ab. 1830, in Ireland, as was Catharine his wife; r. Rock., a lime burner. John of Rock., probably a brother, had a thumb shot off and was otherwise wounded, May 5, 1864, in battle of Williamsburg.

Cornelius's ch. 1, Catharine, b. ab. 1857. 2, John, (2d), b. ab. '58. 3, Mary, b. ab. '59.

COLBURN, John, b. ab. 1825; m. 1st, Frances E. ——, who d. April 12, '53, a. 23; 2d, Julia A. Head, May 13, '55; r. Rock., a joiner. His ch. by 2d wife. 1, Willard, b. ab. 1858. 2, Nellie, b. ab. 1860.

COLBY, Dr. Zenas, b. Dec. 30, 1797, son of Benjamin J. & Rebecca Colby of Embden; m. 1st, Sophia Chamberlain; 2d, Lucy L. Kidder of Albion, p. Sept. 7, 1853; r. Rock., in practice of medicine since 1846; & d. Dec. 30, 1861. His 2d wife d. Sept. 8, '60. His ch. by 1st wife. 1, Mary, deceased. 2, Francis, m. & d. leaving 2 ch. 3, Adelaide, b. ab. 1832; m. Frederic W. Libbey; r. Rock. 4, Orrin S., b. Nov. 15, '34, d. March 7, '54. 5, Mary, b. ab. '35.

COLBY, William G., of a different family, b. in Liberty, Me., ab. 1829; m. Catharine U. Butler; r. Rock., a mariner. Their ch. 1, William F., b. ab. 1846. 2, Albion C., b. ab. 1848; enlisted in the army. 3, Charles C., b. ab. 1850. 4, Edward L., b. ab. 1854. 5, Emery J., b. ab. 1859.

COLLAMORE; this family originated in Bristol. Peter, b. ab. 1801; m. Rizpah ——; r. Rock. Benjamin, b. ab. 1825; m. Elizabeth Murphy, July 13, 1852; r. Rock., a lime burner. John, b. ab. 1832; m. Margaret Richardson, p. Sept. 29, 1853; r. Rock.

Peter's ch. 1, Thomas, b. ab. 1839. 2, Priscilla, b. ab. 1846. 3, Mary, b. ab. 1848.

Benjamin's ch. 1, Hannah J., b. ab 1853. 2, Benjamin F., b. ab. 1855. 3, Leonard F., b. ab. 1858. 4, Patience, b. ab. 1860.

John's ch. 1, Margaret E., b. ab. 1857. 2, Emma A., b. ab. 1858.

COLLAMORE, Andrew J., b. ab. 1831, in Friendship; m. Ann Church of Yarmouth, Nov. 5, 1859; r. Th., a peddler, soldier of 1st Me. Cavalry. Their ch. Jane A., b. ab. 1851.

COLE, Capt. William, b. Aug. 18, 1791; c. from Nashville, Tenn., and commenced trade at Mill River; m. Mary G. Dodge, Jan. 20, 1825; rem. his business to Rock., where he d. April 22, 1849. John P., his brother, born 1801, in Virginia; c. from Nashville to Th., a few years later, trading at the same place; m. Lavinia Southworth, July 1, 1828; rem. to Illinois, but ret. 1856; r. Th.; a merchant; rem. in 1862 to Mass.

Capt. William's ch. 1, Mary E., b. Dec. 1, 1826, d. May 5, 1851. 2, Winslow, b. Aug. 3. and d. Aug. 5, 1829. 3, Rebecca W., b. Nov. 1, and d. Nov. 2, 1830. 4, Susan W., b. Sept. 20, 1831; m. Capt. Artemas W. Watts, r. Th. 5, Sarah F., b. July 29, 1833, d. March 10, 1852. 6, William J., b. Aug. 16, 1835; r. Th.; rem. California. 7, Eveline W., b. April 30, 1837; r. Th. 8, Garnet G., b. May 30, 1838, d. June following. 9, Caroline, b. Dec. 20, 1839; r. Th. and d. Oct. 13, 1831. 10, Harriet A., b. July 18, 1841, d. Aug. 23, 1842. 11, Henrietta, b. Aug 23, & d. Aug. 30, 1842. 12, Randall, b. 1846, d. Aug. 12, '52.

John P.'s ch. 1, Lavinia S., b. Jan. 4, 1829; m. Benjamin Ayer of Boston; r. Th. 2, Adelia F., b. May 23, '32; m. J. Augustus Hersey of Wiscasset, Sept. 3, 1855. 3, John W., b. April 20, '34; r. Th., a clerk; rem. California, 1861. 4, James D., b. Aug. 1, '36; r. Th., a clerk, enlisted in cavalry; rem. Mass. 5, Adelaide, b. Sept. 4, 1840; m. Lysander Hill, Esq.; r. Alexandria, Va.

COLE, John F., b. in Wal., 1799; c. to Th., learned and carried on the marble manufacture; m. Clementina Bryant, Nov. 6, '25; r. Th., and d. Nov. 6, '31. Sarah, a sister, b. 1793; m. Charles Starrett, r. Th. John F.'s ch. 1, John J., b. Aug 6, & d. Sept. 4, 1826. 2, Sarah Clementina, b. July 20, '27. 3, John Andrew, b. Oct. 16, '29; rem. California with his mother & the family. 4, Mary Catharine, b. Oct. 8, '31.

COLLEY, Capt. Thomas, b. 1781; m. Mary Cook; came from St. George, and purchased Samuel Weed's farm; r. S. Th., and died at Maracaibo, March 3, 1834. His widow died Sept. 24, 1843, aged 61. Their ch. 1, Capt. Thomas, (2d), m. Eliza Singer, Jan. 11, 1825; was lost at sea, Oct. 1826, in sch. *Dolphin*, leaving but 1 child which d. 1827, an infant. 2, Margaret, m. William Williams; r. S. Th.. 3, Capt. John, m. Deborah Look of Addison, p. Aug. 6, '26; r. Cam. 4, Mary W., b. June, 1805; m. William Stackpole; r. Th., and d. April 3, '43. 5, Nathaniel, d. in 1827, on Rainsford Island, of small pox. 6, Capt. James S., b. ab. 1810; m. 1st, Rebecca C. Blackington, July 23, '32; 2d, Harriet G. (Webb) Sprague, March 1, '63; r. Cambridge, Mass. 7, Benjamin E., m. Elizabeth Norton; r. Somerville, Mass., a piano forte manufacturer. 8, Capt. Ebenezer, m. Eleanor Harding, Feb. 5, 1838; and died at New Orleans, Feb. 1848. 9, Caroline, m. Charles C. Rider of Wiscasset, 1834; r. & died in Boston. 10, Eliza Ann, m. David Jackins, jr., of Edgecomb, 1841; r. & died Wiscasset. 11, Capt. William, m. Mary Small, Oct. 26, 1845; r. Th.

Capt. John's ch. 1, William J., b. Nov. 8, 1829, a mariner. 2, Mary E., b. July 17, '32; m. ——— Thorndike; r. Cam. 3, Louisa L., b. Oct. 9, '34; r. Cam. 4, Stephen B., b. May 12, '39, a mariner. 5, Margaret, m. ——— Thorndike of Camden.

Capt. James S.'s ch. 1, Belmore D., b. March 14, 1837; r. Th., a mariner. 2, Franklin, b. June 29, '40, d. March 12, '42. 3, James, b. March 31, & d. Aug. 12, '42. 4, Clara Rebecca, b. April 11, '44; r. Th. 5, James Thomas, b. July 9, '46, d. April 19, '53. 6, Zora E., b. April, & died Oct. 18, '48.

Capt. William's ch. 1, William J., b. ab. 1850. 2, Edward, b. ab. '52. 3, Charles Frederic, b. April 18, & died Sept. 9, '54. 4, Lewis, born 1859.

COLLINS; of this family, ch. of Martin & Jeanette Collins, there r. in Rock. 1, Salome. 2, Ibrook A., b. ab. 1823, a truckman, &c. 3, Converse C. G., b. ab. 1825, a book agent.

COLLINS, George, came to Old Th. early; m. Adaline Blackington, Feb. 10, 1820; & had 1 child recorded here, viz.: Sarah T., born March 24, 1824. There was also here of the name, Zerah C. Collins, born Oct. 30, died Feb. 23, '54. Also

COLLINS, Levi, born in New Hampshire, June 15, 1792; married Thankful B. Spear, March 4, 1850; r. Rockland, & died Sept. 16, '57.

COLLINS, Richard, (colored), b. ab. 1840, d. at Rock., April 21, '61

COLSON, Joseph, c. from Bath to Th., in 1824; m. Eliza T. Fales, May 22, 1826; carried on sailmaking, &c., rem. Boston in 1837, thence to Glen Falls, N. Y., & thence to N. O. & California. Their ch. 1, Joseph W., b. March 24, 1827; m. Ann Herdman of Liverpool, Eng. 2, Sarah Clough, b. Feb. 6, '29; m. 1st, John V. Mitchell of Calais, Me., 2d, Wm. H. Bryan, of S. Carolina, and has ch. by 1st husband, viz.: Volney, b. at N. O.; & by 2d husband, Eulalie L., d. in Georgia; Wm. Herbert; John Arthur; Rosa C., b. in South Carolina, and Ernest V., d. in Miss. 3, Ann J, b. Feb. 18, '31; r. New Orleans & Th. 4, Rebecca C., b. Jan. 2, '33; m. Edward L. Robinson, r. Th. 5, William J., b. March 31, '35. 6, James E., b. Glen Falls, and died there Aug. 31, '39. 7, P. Eubertus, b. Glen Falls, and d. Feb. 14, '63.

COLSON, Thomas, b. ab. 1811 in Kennebec county; m. Sarah W. Tighe of Bath, p. Dec. 22. '38, 2d, Charlotte A. Blaisdell of Cam., Aug. 7, 1851; r, Rock., lime manufacturer. His ch. by 1st wife. 1, James W., b. April 7, 1839, d. Dec. 25, '40. 2, Charles T., b. June 6, '41; r. Rock., a cabinet maker. 3, Benjamin W., b. ab. '43; r. Rock., a cabinet maker. 4, John, b. ab. '47. 5, Sarah F., b. May, 1849, d. March 22, '57. By 2d wife. 6, Abby, b. March & d. Sept. 18, 56. 7, David, b. ab. '57. 8, Herbert W., b. ab. '59.

COMERY; of this Warren family, Alexander, b. ab. 1810; m. Catharine Mathews of Wal., r. Th., a ship carpenter. William, a brother, b. ab. 1817; m. Susan A. Singer, March 1, 49; r. Th., a painter. An uncle of these, John Comery, b. in Wal., c. to Th. in age, & d. Feb. 18, 1861.

Alexander's ch. 1, Harvey S., b. Dec. 27, 1837, a soldier, &c. 2, Helen M., b Sept. 2, '39; m. Charles W. Peabody; r. Th. 3, William H., b ab. '44; enlisted in U. S. Navy. 4, Maria H., b. ab. 52.

William's ch. 1, Mary A., b. ab. 1850. 2, Anna R., b. ab. '58.

COMSTOCK, James, c. from Eastport or Argyle; m. Nancy Vose, r. Th Their ch. Edwin, b. ab. 1852.

CONANT, Marlborough, a descendant of Roger, of Plymouth, and son of John and Deborah (Perkins) Conant, was b. at Bridgewater, Mass., Oct. 14, 1775; c. to r. in Th. May 30, '95; m. 1st, Mary Dunbar, (who d. 1796), 2d, Peronella Fales, of Th., 3d, Mrs. Catharine Keen, Aug. 9, '21; r. Th., a joiner, & d. Nov 21, '22. His ch. by 2d wife. 1 & 2, twins, b. March 30, 1800, Emily m. William S. Kimball; rem. Illinois; and Camilla, m. 1st, ——— Hall, 2d, Edward Newbert r. Belfast. 3, John P., b Oct. 6, 1801, d. Oct. 1, '02. 4, David Fales, b. Oct 3, '02; m. Sabra Rankin, Oct. 20, '25; r. Rock., a lime burner, &c. 5 & 6, twins, b. Dec. 31, '03; Mary probably d. young, Anna, m. Hon. Nathaniel Meservey; r. Rock. 7, Oliva, b. March 16, '06; m. Nelson Spear; r. Rock 8, Juliet, b. Dec. 6, '07; m. Samuel Hall; r. S. Th. 9, Oliver, b. Sept. 20, '09; d. Oct. 27, '17. 10, Lucy b. Jan. 11, '12, d. Aug. 20, '20. 11, Melinda T., b. April 1st, '14; m. James May, p. March 26, '33. 12, Sarah J., b. April 18, and d. Aug. 13, '16, at the same time with her mother.

David F.'s ch. 1, Capt. Oliver J., b. Dec. 14, 1825; m. Nancy P. Ames, Dec. 20, '47; r. Rock., a merchant, officer in the 4th Me. reg., &c. 2, Melissa, b. Feb. 9, '30; m. James Kelley, Nov. 20, '51. 3, Capt. Charles H. b. Sept. 7, '34; m. Carrie A. Thomas, May 26, '61; r. Rock., a caulker, officer of 4th Me. reg.; killed in battle, May 6, '64. 5, Hannah, b. April 12, '40, d. Feb. 24, '54. 6, William Eugene, b. August 31, '43, soldier of U. S. Sharpshooters, wounded & d. Nov. 23, 1862.

Capt. Oliver J.'s ch. 1, Etta O., b. ab. 1857. 2, Anna.

CONDON, Joseph, b. July 8, 1794, in Friendship; m. Frances R Hall; r. Rock., a merchant, & d. July 22, '53. Their ch. 1, Julia A., b. Feb. 25, '31, d. Aug. 23, '53. 2, Melissa T., b. May 17, '33; m. Enoch Davies; r. Rock. 3, John T., b. March 4, '35, d. Feb. 17, '36. 4, Amelia H., b. Dec. 21, 36. There are, or were, also, in Rockland, (perhaps sons of Joseph, but not recorded here,) 1, Capt. Thomas, d. at sea. in ship *Elizabeth Kimball*, ab. 1858. 2, Seth C. recently of the U. S. navy.

CONKLIN, John, b. ab. 1825, in Ireland, as was Catharine, his wife; r. Rock., a lime burner. Their ch. 1, John G., b. ab. '52. 2, Michael E., b. ab. '54. 3, William H., b. ab. '56. 4, Patrick S., b. ab. 1858.

CONLUN, John, b. ab. 1813, in Ireland, as was Ellen, his wife (who d. April 4, '64); r. Th., a shoemaker. Their ch. Martha, b. ab. '47.

CONNER; of this family, two brothers c. here early, from Newburyport, Mass. 1, David, m. Betsey Bryant, August 12, 1802; r. Th., a cooper, & rem.? 2, Eliphalet, b ab. 1770; m. ——— Bryant; r. Th., a cooper, rem. Cam., and d. in Rock. July 11, 1854. Of Eliphalet's ch; 1, Joseph, m. Miss Fowler, rem. west. 2, Elizabeth. 3. Mary, rem. Cam.

CONNER, Charles A., b. ab. 1834; m. Sarah J. Robbins, July 6 '58; r. Rock, a lime burner. Their ch. Willie A., b. March, 1859, d. Sept. 24, '60.

CONARY, David H., b. ab. 1799, c. from Deer Isle; m. Susan Small; r. Rock., and engaged in the fishery. Of their ch. 1, Capt. Harvey, b. ab. 1820 in Deer Isle; m. Emma Conary, his cousin; r. Rock. 2, Capt Samuel S, b. ab. 1829; m. Maria S. (Mosman) Hewes, Nov. 5, 60; r. Rock. 3, David E., b. ab. 1844; r. Rock. 4, Joshua S., b. ab. 1846; r. Rock.

Capt. Harvey's ch. 1, William, b. ab. 1849. 2, Alden, b. ab. '51. 3, Edgar H., b. Oct. 11, '56, d. Sept. 1, '57. 4, Emma, b. ab. '58.

Capt. Samuel S.'s ch. 1, F. Clifton, b. May 30, d. Dec. 1, 1861. 2, Eddie P., b. Nov. 17, '63, d. Oct. 24, '64.

CONNICK, William, b. ab. 1813; r. with Ellen, his wife, in Rock., 1860; a lime burner. Their ch. 1, Susan M, b. 1845. 2, Allen, b. '47. 3, Harriet E., b. '49. 4, Sarah N., b. Oct 1851, d. Jan. 12, '53. 5, Mary, b. '56. 6, Sophronia F., b. '60.

CONWAY, Joseph, b. ab. 1835, r. Rock., in 1860; a mariner.

COOK, Fuller G., b. 1814, in Newburyport, Mass., m. Charlotte A. Stevens, of Waterville; r. Rock., an apothecary. Their ch. Helen, b. ab. 1841.

COOK, Winchell M., b. ab. 1830, in Eppingham, N. H.; m. Maria T. Ruggles, Sept., 1850; r. Th., a merchant. Their ch. 1, Herbert Ruggles, b. Oct. 1851, d. May 4, 1855. 2, Clara, b. ab. 1857.

COOKE, John H., b. 1827; m. Lucy A. Hosmer, Jan. 10, '52; r. Rock., & d. June 28, '54. Their ch. 1, Frederic E, b. ab. 1853. 2, John C., b. ab. '55.

COOMBS, George, son of Stephen, whose parents were French, was b. r. & d. at New Meadows, now Brunswick, Me. He m. Abigail Berry, and had [sons.] 1, Peter, a deaf mute, m. ——— Berry, had 3 ch. settled in Brunswick. 2, George, (2d), m. ——— Parsley, had 5 sons & 6 daughters; settled in Bath. 3, Benjamin, m. ——— Sawyer, had 6 sons and 6 daughters; settled in New Gloucester. 4, Asa, m. ——— Thomas, had 7 sons & 3 daughters. r. New Meadows. 5, Lt. Joseph, b. in Brunswick, March 10, 1752, O. S.; came and settled at Wessaweskeag, 1773; m. Elizabeth Gamble, June 6, 1776, by Rev. J. Urquhart; built mills, burnt lime, and engaged in shipbuilding; r. S. Th. till his death, Nov 22, 1817. 6, Thomas, m. ——— Coombs, had 4 sons & 3 daughters; settled in Whitefield, Me. [And daughters.] 7, Joanna, m. ——— Coombs, had 4 sons and 4 daughters, r. Portland. 8, Abigail, m. Thomas Berry; r. & d. Portland. 9, Betsey, m. ——— Cowing; r. Lisbon, Me. 10, Isabella, m. ——— Donahue; r. Brunswick.

Of George, (2d)'s ch. 1, Abiezer, born in Brunswick; came to S. Thomaston; m. Sarah Randall.

Lieut. Joseph's ch. 1, Capt. Archibald G, born June 4, 1777; m. Nancy Mingerson, March 28, 1798; r. S. Th, lost at sea in sloop *Asa*, Oct. 28, 1818. 2, Capt. Joseph, (2d), b. June 3, 1779; m. Sylvia Randall, Feb. 2, 1809; r. S. Th, became blind and insane; & d. June 22, '41. 3, Isabella, b. April 9, 1781; m Hezekiah Prince, Esq.; r. Th, and died Dec. 2, 1840. 4, Col. George, b. Dec. 19, 1783 or '85; m. Rebecca A., daughter of Dr. Oliver Mann of Castine, p. Nov. 19, '08; r. S. Th., a millwright, shipbuilder, and farmer; and died May 13, '23. 5, Elizabeth, b. Nov. 18, 1787; m. James Dow; r. and died Th. 6, Nancy, b. Dec. 31, 1789; m. Capt. Samuel Fuller; r. Th., and has been its chief and sometimes only milliner more than 50 years. 7,

Abigail, b. Jan. 10, 1792; m. Joseph Berry; r. Th., and died July 9, '45. 8, Washington, b. May 18, 1794, died March 18, '97. 9, Asa, b. Aug. 28, '96; m. Lucretia Mann, Dec. 28, '23; r. S. Th., a farmer, trader, lightkeeper, &c.

Abiezer's ch. 1, Moses, b. May 3, 1809, died young 2, Abiezer, (2d), b. March 3, '13; m. Rebecca Bradbury, Oct. 8, '44; r. S. Th., d. at sea, 1847.

Capt. Archibald G.'s ch. 1, Henry, b. April 24, 1798; died on the coast of Africa, March 24, '25. 2, George W., b. June 7, 1800; m. Elsie Haskell; r. S. Th., a farmer. 3, Archibald G., (2d), b. April 15, '02; lost with his father, Oct. 28, '18. 4, Joseph, (3d), b. Nov. 8, '04; rem. Illinois 5, Nancy, b. Sept. 17, '07; m. Atwood Levensaler; r. Th, and died Dec. 8, '62. 6, Capt. John M., b. Sept. 3, '09; m. Almeda Litchfield, Aug. 17, '37, 2d, Matilda P. Litchfield, Sept. 29, '45; r. Th., and died out South. 7, Isabella P., b. July 18, '11. The mother died Aug. 18, '19, aged 44.

Col. George's ch. 1, George, (2d), b. Jan. 6, 1810; r. S. Th., a truckman. 2, Oliver M., b. Feb. 21, d. May 8, '11. 3, Perez M., b. March 22, '12; m. Eliza Administer of Lynn, Mass., Oct. 19, '41. 4, Hezekiah P., b. Sept. 1, '13; began to learn printer's trade of E. Moody, in Th., 1828; went on a whaling voyage, &c.; m. Lucinda Spofford, Aug. 14, '42; r. Th., publisher of the *Recorder*, register of deeds, &c., and died April 2?, '53. 5, Lucy, A., b. Aug. 17, '15; m. Capt. Richard Hayden; r. S. Th. 6, Elizabeth G., born May 21, '17; m. Capt. Sylvester Healey; r. Th. 7, Archibald G., (3d), b. Dec. 22, '18; m. Harriet Kelloch, July 24, '39; r. S. Th. 8, Lucretia M., b. April 22, '22; m. Capt. Edward Long. 9, Rebecca M., born Sept. 30, '23; m. Artemas W. Wall, Sept. 15, '44.

Asa's ch. 1, Mary J., b. March 17, '24; d. Sept. 14, '26. 2, Asa F., b. Aug. 17, '25; r. S. Th., a carpenter. 3 & 4, twins, b. May 17, '27; Oliver, r. Cal., Eliza P., m. Charles G. Snelling; r. S. Th. 5, Abby, b. May 21, '29; m. Frank Parker, r. S. Th. 6, Samuel F., b. April 16, '31; m. Rachel Boyd, Oct. 1, '54; r. S. Th., a trader; rem. Seattle, Washington Territory. 7, Thomas P., b. Nov. 8, '36; r. S. Th., a stone-cutter.

Fourth Generation.

George W.'s ch. 1, ——— d. April 15, '26. 2, Caroline M., b. March 13, '28; d. Nov. 22, '46. 3 & 4, twins, b. ab. 1832, Capt. Joseph A., r. S. Th.; lost with his vessel, schr. *Leo*, Dec., 1862; Francis T., m. Ellen D. Duncan, May 13, '62; r. S. Th., a mariner, entered U. S. Navy. 5, William H., b. ab. '35; r. S. Th., a joiner.

Capt. John M.'s ch. by 1st wife. 1, Helen A., b. April 2, '39; m. Julius A Litchfield; r. Rock., and d. April 19, '59. 2, John H., b. July 9, '41; r. Boston. 3, N. Almeda, r. Brewer.

Hezekiah P.'s ch. Charles S., b. March 16, 1844.

Archibald G. (3d's), ch. 1, William A., b. April 21, 1841. 2, Mingerson. 3, a daughter, r. Indiana. 4, Archibald, b. Jan., 1846, died Oct. 27, '47. 5, Esther L., b. July, 1848, d. Sept. 1850.

Samuel F.'s ch. 1, Louisa, b. '55. 2, Anna, b. April, '56, d. June 17, '62. 3, Abbie F., b. ab. '57. 4, Arthur, b. ab. '59.

Fifth Generation.

Francis T.'s ch. 1, Willie Linwood, b. Aug. 9, & d. Aug. 30, 1863.

COOMBS, Hosea, b. in Islesboro', Me., Dec 15, 1811; m. Harriet

Drinkwater of Northport, Dec. 15, '39; r. Rock., a blacksmith. Thatcher, a brother, also c. here, r. & d. Rock., & Almira, his widow, also d. here Sept. 16, '64.

Hosea's ch. 1, Hosea Ensign, b. Aug. 11, '41; soldier of 4th Me. reg. 2, Harriet T., b. Jan. 29, '43. 3, Otis D., b. Aug. 15, '46. 4, Charles S., b. ab. '49. 5, Eva M., b. ab. '51. 6. Ada A., b. ab. '58.

Thatcher's ch. 1, Faustina A., b. ab. 1842. 2, Sylvena A., b. ab. 44; m Llewellyn R. Smith of Portland, July 1, '64. 3, Daniel P., b. ab '46. 4, Fields F., b. ab. '53.

COOMBS, Levi G., b. Feb. 17, 1813, in Vinalhaven; m. 1st, Maria F., who d July 15, '44, 2d, Catharine ——; r. S. Th, a shoemaker, & d. July 5, '61. His ch. by 1st wife. 1, Mary E., b. July 25, 1835. 2, Ann Maria, b. July 20, '37; m. Joshua Marshall of Cam., 1852. 3, Arethusa T., b. Sept. 17, '39; m. Wm. R. Jacobs, r. Rock. 4, Charles T., b. Nov. 16, 1840. 5, Levi A., b. April 10, '42; a shoemaker, soldier of 2d Me. Reg. 6, Bertha C., b. ab. '45. 7, Cora, b. ab. '50. 8, Ada K., b. ab. '58.

COOMBS, Abraham B., b. ab 1824, probably also from Vinalhaven; r. with Mary A., his wife, in S. Th., a carpenter. Their ch. Julia F., b. ab. 1859.

COOPER, Benjamin, b. 1757, c, from Cambridge, Mass.; m. Lydia Bartlett; settled S. Th., and d. April 19, 1843; a. 86. His wife d. May 2, 1821, a. 67.

Their ch. 1, Mary, d. unm. 2, Lydia, m. John Heald, Oct. 30, '17; r. and d. Hope. 3, Priscilla, m. Johnson Pillsbury; rem. Wisconsin. 4, Benjamin, (2d), m Hannah Pillsbury, p April 2, 1808; r. Morrill, Me. 5, Abigail, b. 1785; m. Ralph Chapman; r. S. Th. & d. April 9, 1859. 6, William, d. young. 7, George B., b. Dec. 16, 1789; m. Sarah R. Killsa, p M. 19, 1818; r. S. Th., & d. July 8, 1858. 8, Hannah, m. Charles Dyer; r. S. Th. 9, Susan, m. Charles Sherman, Aug. 11, 1816; r. Hope. 10, Sarah, m. 1st, Capt. Nathaniel Sleeper, 2d, Hiram Brewster; r. Rock.

Benjamin, (2d's). ch. 1, Rhoda, r. Morrill. 2, Mary, m. 1st, Jos. Frost, 2d, —— Fletcher; r. Morrill. 3, Almira, m. & r. Morrill. 4, Fidelle, m. & r. Boothbay. 5, Lydia, m. —— Bailey, in the west. 6, Hannah, m. Phinehas Pillsbury. 7, Benjamin, (3d), m. r. & d. Morrill. 8, William, m. & r. Morrill.

George B.'s ch. 1, Nancy H., b. Dec. 7, 1818; r. S. Th. 2, Eliza B., b. April 15, '20; m. Oliver H Perry; r. Rock. 3, George B., (2d), b. March 28, '22; d. at sea. 4, John Edward, b. Jan. 14, '24, d. May 5, '31. 5, Richard B., b May 2, '26, d. July 29, '46. 6, Lois K., b. April 21, '28; m. Geo. Hall, (2d); r. S. Th. 7, Sarah, b. Feb 10, '30; m. Edward C. Spalding; r. S. Th. 8. Capt. Edward B., r. S. Th.

COOPER, Leonard, b in Pittston, Me.; m. Sarah Longfellow; & came from Windsor to Th. Their ch. 1, Mary. 2, Caroline, m. Abner Mitchell; r. Windsor. 3, Elvira, m. Caleb Buckland, and died Dec. 27, '52. 4, Hiram. 5, Sarah, m. Charles Woodcock; r. & died Th. 6, Leonard, (2d), m. Jane E. Wallace, Oct. 7, '56; r. Th. 7, Elizabeth, m. Edward Gould of Bangor. 8, Octavia, m. Charles Woodcock; r. Th. 9, Hannah, m. Henry Howes of Belfast. 10, Melissa Ann, b. June 28, 1841.

COOPER, Thomas W., b. ab. 1826, in Montville; m. Ursula J.

Stevens; ? r. Rock., a livery stable keeper. Their ch. Marcellus A., b. ab. 1835; r. Rockland.

COPELAND; of the sons of Nathaniel of W., (for family in full, see annals of Warren). 1. Rev. Nathaniel, m. Lydia A. Philbrook, was dismissed from the Albion and received by Th. Bapt church, Feb. 4, 1854, and has been an evangelist since in various places. 2, Chas., m. and r. in Warren. 3, Capt. Oliver, m. r. & d. in Warren. 4, Capt. John, b. Feb. 29, 1792; m. Lucy Malcolm of C.; r. Th., a hotel-keeper, deputy sheriff, '33 & '34, &c.; d. May 30, '62. 3, Moses, b. Jan. 6, 1801; m. Sarah Andrews of W., Sept. 23, '27; r. Th., a tanner, &c; rem. S. Th.

Rev. Nathaniel's ch. 1, Rev. William H., m. Lucinda Loyd; r. S. Berwick, a Baptist minister. 2, Mary, d. in Albion. 3, Nathaniel, m. Lydia Lowe; r. Th., a ship joiner; rem. Conn. 4, Almira, m. Cyrus Shaw, r. and d. China, Me. 5, Oliver E, b. ab. 1831, m. Rebecca J. Fulmer of C., p. Oct. 11, '54; r. Th., a joiner, soldier, &c. 6, John, a soldier, in the army. 7, Mary, m. Jos. Denton; r. East Boston.

Of Charles's ch. there c. here; 1, Lieut. Leroy, b. in W. ab. 1819; m. Rachel Copeland of W., r. Th.; a ship carpenter, officer in 21st regiment, &c.

Capt. Oliver's ch. 1, Edwin, b. 1821, d. Sept. 28, '25. 2, Maria, b. ab. 1823; m. S. Emerson Smith, Esq., r. Th. 3, George, m. Mary F. Munroe, Dec. 1, '53; r. Th. 4, Mary Jane, r. Th. By 2d wife. 5, Adelia Lois, b. ab. 1831, d. Jan. 5, '54.

Capt. John's ch. 1, Sarah A., b. Nov. 16, '25, d. Oct. 9, '30.

Moses's ch. 1, John Lewis, b. Sept. 6, 1829; r. S. Th., a farmer, brick manufacturer, &c. 2, Mary Ann, b. July 24, '30; m. Capt. Thomas Williams; r. S. Th. 3, Horatio G., b. Feb. 4, '34; m. Hannah F. Hathorn, Oct. 24, '55; r. S. Th., a brick manufacturer, carpenter, &c.

Oliver E.'s ch. 1, Frederic E., b. ab. 1856. 2, George A, b. ab. '57. 3, Mary, b. '59.

Leroy's ch. 1, Augusta C., b. ab. 1848. 2, Hilliard L., b. ab. '52. 3, Amelia J., b. ab. '56.

George's ch. 1, Lizzie, b. May, 1855, d. Nov. 10, '59. 2, Charles, b. ab. '59.

Horatio G.'s ch. 1, Flora A., b. ab. 1857. 2, Frederic.

CORBET, Charles B., b. ab. 1835; r. with Caroline, his wife, in Rock., 1860; a shoemaker. Their ch. Carrie E., b. ab. 1858.

CORELL, Ezekiel, b. ab. 1820; m. Susan ———; r. Rock. in '60; a mariner. Their ch. 1, Harriet A., b. ab. 1848. 2, Sarah F., b. ab. '50. 3, Mary E., b. ab. '52. 4, Susan A., b. ab. '54. 5, Elvira, b. ab. '57.

CORSON, Henry, b. ab. 1804; r. Rock., a gardener, in 1860; with Annie his wife. Their ch. Susan J., b. ab. 1845.

Of this name, also, Elisha H., jr., b. ab. 1829; perhaps a son of preceding; m. Cyrena Richards; r. Rock., a lime burner. Their ch. 1, Frances E., b. ab. 1852. 2, Charles H., b. ab. '55. 3, Anson F., b. ab. '57. 4, Amos O., b. ab. '58. 5, Flora A., b. ab. '60.

CORTHELL, Rev. William, son of Jonathan of Cam.; m. Sarah A. Allen of Th.; p. Nov. 30, '48; r. Th., a printer, &c.; rem. & became a Baptist minister, being ordained at S. Waldoboro', March 4, '57.

COTHRELL, Daniel L., b. ab. 1804; r. with Bethia his wife, in Rock.; a caulker.

COTTAR, William, b. ab. 1806, in Ireland, m. Ellen ——; r. Rock. Their ch. 1, William, (2d), b. Aug. 1832, d. March 27, '58. 2, Patrick, b. ab. 1835; r. Rock., a mariner. 3, James, b. April 3, '40; r. Rock., a mariner, enlisted in U. S. Navy. 4, Ellen, b. April 5, '42. 5, John, b. ab. '45. 6, Michael, b. ab. '51.

COTTON, Oliver M., b. ab. 1822; m. Mary Clough of Cam., r. Rock. Their ch. 1, Joseph C., b. ab. 1841; a mariner, enlisted in U. S. Navy. 2, Diana J., b. ab. '43. 3, William J., b. ab. '46. 4, Susan, b. ab. '51. 5, Rebecca, b. ab. '53. 6, Mary M., b. ab. '56. 7, Carrie E., b. ab. '60. Of this name, also, Horatio Q., perhaps a brother to Oliver M., was b. ab. 1827; m. Emma ——; r. Rock., a painter. Their ch. Eliza A., b. ab. 1849.

COUNCE, Samuel, b. 1741; m. Hannah Sumner; c. from Milton, Mass.; r. Warren, and d. March 12, 1800. His widow d. June 23, 1817, a. 80. Their ch. 1, Lemuel, b. in Milton, Nov. 25, 1760; m. Hannah Davis; r. Warren, and d. July 24, 1802. 2, Hannah, b. Sept. 17, '63, in Milton; m. Josiah Ingraham, r. Rock., and d. June 29, '42. 3, Jacob, m. Sarah Bachelder, p. July 9, '96; r. C., & d. Jan. 18, 1832. 4, Mary, b. Feb. 1766, r. Rock., & d. Nov. 5, 1849. 5, Eunice, b. Jan. 5, '71, r. W., & d. April 6, 1853. 6, John Holland, b. June 2, '76; m. Kezia Jordan, Jan. 8, 1806; r. W., & d. March 10, 1849. For the family in full, see "Annals of Warren."

Lemuel's ch. 1, Samuel, (2d), b. 1788; m. Sarah Payson, 1808; r. W., & d. Oct. 1852. 2, Jacob, b. 1790; drowned at sea, about '07. 3, Edward, d. young, of canker-rash. 4, Rufus C., b. June 8, 1795; m. Lucy Healy Spear, June 5, 1820; r. Th., a ship builder, &c. 5, Judah, b. June 16, 1797; m. Hannah Smith of C.; r. C. & d. Philadelphia, Oct. 1843. 6, Lemuel, (2d), died in infancy.

Of John H.'s ch., the 5th, Capt. Edwin S., b. ab. 1822; m. Sarah Alice Scrivener of Topsham, March, '50; rem. Th.; built the house on Knox st. now occupied by Amos Walker, & d. Dec. 10, '54. His widow m. 2d, Lewis T. Merrow of Bowdoinham, Feb. 12, '58.

Fourth Generation.

Of Samuel, (2d)'s 9 ch., the 7th, Lemuel, (3d), b. ab. 1820; m. Sarah F. Hilt, Jan. 30, '46; r. Rock., Superintendant of the city poor farm, &c.

Rufus C.'s ch. 1, Rufus Harvey, b. Aug. 19, 1821; m. Sarah P. Edgarton, June 3, '46; r. Th., a carver, &c. 2, Lucy Ann, b. Sept. 10, '22; m. Capt. Elkanah Stackpole; r. Th. 3, Barnabas Webb, b. Sept. 22, '24; m. Mary S. Ward of Spencer, Mass., Nov. 7, '55; r. Th., a merchant, &c. 4, Emily Spear, b. March 17, 1827; m. Elisha Linnell; r. Th. 5, Richard Spear, b. Dec. 24, '28, d. May 5, '33.

Of Judah's ch., 1, John, a mariner, r. Th.; 2, Edwin R., m. Mary Eliza Fales, Aug. 13, '64; r. Th., enlisted in U. S. navy.

Capt. Edwin S.'s ch. 1, Frederic E., b. April 10, 1851. 2, Charles E., b. June 8, 1852.

Fifth Generation.

Lemuel, (3d)'s ch. 1, Azira M., b. ab. 1848. 2, Lucy F., b. July 5, '58, d. June 18, '63. 3, Clifford.

COWING, Daniel, b. in Lisbon, Me., June 18, 1796; c. hither, m.

Dolly Ulmer, Jan. 17, 1822, 2d, Mrs. Sarah Holmes, Sept. 25, '52; r. Rock., & d. Feb. 13, '61. His ch. by 1st wife. 1, Jane E., b. July 22, '22, d. Oct. 29, '33. 2, Susan, b. July 24, '24, d. Sept. 14, '40. 3, Caroline Ann, b. May 23, '27; m. Capt. Orrin P. Mitchell; r. Rock. 4, Daniel, (2d), b. June 5, '29, probably d. young. 5, Andrew C., b. Feb. 8, 1832. 6, Harrison U., b. March 15, '34, sergeant in 4th Me. reg., killed July 1, '62, near Richmond, Va. 7, Christiana I., b. July 3, '36, d. March 18, '56. 8, Edmund S., b. July 20, '40; r. Rock., a teamster. 9, Lucy J., b. Oct. 31, 1842; m, Charles H. Waldron of Frankfort, Oct. 3, 1863.

COX, Capt. John, c. from Nobleboro'; m. Susan Robinson, July 9, 1844; r. Th., & d. It is believed, was lost overboard on passage to Norfolk, Nov. 7, 1851. Their ch. 1, Mary E., b. June 22, 1845. 2, Susan Ann, b. Aug. 31, 1847.

COX, William, b. ab. 1810, c. from Cork, Ireland, with his wife, about 1832; r. Rock., a gardener. His wife died June 21, 1858, in Rockland, aged 58.

CRABTREE, George F., b. ab. 1822, in North Haven, adopted son of Benjamin Crabtree of that place; m. Clementine McLoon, Nov. 13, '52; r. Rock., grocery merchant. Their ch. 1, Marietta, b. ab. 1854. 2, Helen, b. ab. 1855.

CRAIG, Samuel L., b. ab. 1796; c. from Nova Scotia, a joiner, & with Sarah J., his wife, r. Rock., where their son, John L., b. Feb. 14, 1842, d. March 29, 1857; family since removed to Rockport.

CRAWFORD, Capt. George W., b. April 3, 1806, son of Capt. James & Margaret (Rivers) Crawford of Warren; m. Mary B. Leeds, Nov. 3, 1833; followed the sea, rem. Th., where, after residing a time in Illinois, he carried on an iron foundry, &c., and died May 4, 1860. Their ch. 1, William C., b. March 27, 1835; m. Catharine L. Jameson; r. Th., an iron founder. 2, George M., b. Sept. 15, '37; r. Th., foundry man. 3, Mary L., b. Oct. 10, '39, d. Feb. 12, '42. 4, Mary L., b. March 28, '43, d. April 19, '57. 5, Emma Caroline, b. May 24, '45, d. July 12, '47. 6, John L., b. May 9, '47. 7, Emma L., b. April 7, '49. 8, Eliza L., b. Nov. 6, '50. 9, Spofford J. L., b. May 17, '53.

CRAWFORD, Oliver, son of Dea. Archibald & Eleanor (Parsons) Crawford of Warren; r. many years in Th., a joiner; m. Betsey, dau. of Lieut. Isaac Bartlett of Cam., Dec. 15, 1825, 2d, Eliza Sargent; rem. South with his family and died in Apalachicola, Fla.

CRAWFORD, Capt. Rufus C., b. ab. 1832, son of Charles, Esq., of Searsmont; came to Th.; m. Isabella P. Edgarton, Aug. 7, 1849; since removed, it is believed. Their ch. 1, Charles E., b. April 29, '50. 2, Alfred, b. ab. 1853.

CRAWFORD, Isaac, b. 1801, in Ireland; m. Rachel Rinds, Nov. 14, '22; r. Th., & d. April 4, '41. Their ch. 1, Margaret A., b. June 11, '23; m. Henry P. Wethaby of Grafton, Sept. 3, '43. 2, Deborah, b. '24, d. Nov. 25, '25. 3, Leanora L., b. Dec. 26, '25. 4, Isaac W., b. March 8, '27; 5, Catharine, b. Dec. 19, '29; 6, Joseph H., b. Feb. 27, & d. March 8, '31; 7, John, b. April 2, '32; 8, Charles, b. Dec. 3, '33; 9, Almeda, b. March 5, '36; 10, Emerson F., b. July 5, '38; 11, Nathaniel, b. April, '41; rem. with their mother to Buffalo, N. Y.

CREEGAN, Patrick, b. ab. 1810, in the North of Ireland; m. Margaret Hanly; r. Th. Their ch. 1, Mary, died young. 2, Peter, died in 1859.

CRESSY, John, b. in New York, Oct. 1815; m. Lovina H. Nutt, Dec. 25, '39; r. Rock., a lime burner, &c. Their ch. 1, William Thurlo, b. March 5, 1842; m. Betsey Ann Burns of Albion, March 8, '64; r. Rock., a soldier, &c. 2, Aurelius W., b. Oct. 28, '44. 3, Mary Ellen, b. Oct. 28, '51, d. Aug. 4, '54. 4, Harriet M., b. ab. '56.

CRIE, (originally McCrie), John, b. in Scotland, was a soldier in a Scottish regiment at what is now Castine, & deserted toward the close of the revolutionary war, became an American citizen, and settled at Matinicus. Of his ch. 1, Eben, m. and settled at Matinicus. 2, John, (2d), b. Feb. 12, 1788; r. a time in Rock., but perhaps returned to Matinicus, where Julia Ann his wife d. Aug. 30, 1858. 3, Reuben, m. and r. Matinicus.

Of the ch. of Eben. 1, Hiram H., b. ab. 1825, at Matinicus; m. Abby J. Trafton of Camden; r. Rock., a variety merchant, &c. 2, Esther, m. Rev. Josiah I. Brown; r. Rock., rem. East Pittston.

John, (2d)'s ch. 1, Isaac H., b. ab. 1831, at Matinicus; m. Mary Helen Hall of Matinicus; r. S. Th. Others perhaps were born at Matinicus; those recorded here were, 2, Hiram Albert, b. 1839, died April 14, '49. 3, Charles G., b. Feb. 27, '41. 4, Eben W., b. Oct. 19, '42, d. Aug. 12, '49. 5, Sarah A., b. Feb. 1849, d. Aug. 29, '50. 6, Julietta, b. 1850, d. Dec. 29, '56.

Reuben's ch. 1, Reuben F., b. ab. 1841; m. Floretta E. Tolman; is clerk in the 2d Maine Battery.

Hiram H.'s ch. 1, Alzira L.. b. ab. 1851. 2, Mary S., b. ab. '53. 3, Rufus A., b. ab. '55. 4, Henry A., b. May 28, '57, d. July 23, '58. 5 & 6, twins, b. March 25, '60, Alfred K., d. Aug. 22, '61; Hiram A., r. Rockland.

CREIGHTON, David, one of the first Scotch Irish settlers, m. and r. W., and was killed by the Indians in the war of 1744 at the old Fort here. Their ch. 1, Abraham, probably d. young. 2, Samuel, m. Lucretia Howell, of Bridgewater, r. W. where he d. by drowning, Nov. 10, 1783. 3, David, (2d), b. in Upper St. Georges, now W., Jan. 2, 1736; m. Mary Gamble, Dec. 19, 1770, according to town record, but 1769, county records; r. Th. and d. Aug. 29, 1811. Of Samuel's ch. 1, John, b. March 24, 1774; m. Joanna Jordan, Oct. 2, 1803; r. and d. W. For the Samuel branch in full, see Annals of Warren..

David's ch. 1, Samuel, (2d), b. Oct. 3, 1771; m. Susanna Davis, p. May 12, 1798; r. at the Meadows; and d. Sept. 19, 1832. 2, David, (3d), b. May 18, 1772; d. unm. in Jan., 1843. 3, Mary, b. Feb. 27, 1774; m. James Gordon of Cam., p. May 3, 1792. 4, James Glascow, b. Nov. 7, 1775; a mariner, d. unm. ab. 1833. 5, Robert, born Sept. 5, 1777; d. unm. 6, Nancy, b. Sept 11, 1785; r. Th. and died June 6, 1855. 7, Elizabeth, b. Jan. 11, 1788, m. Elijah Ripley of Hope; d. in autumn of 1859.

Fourth Generation.

Of John's ch., there came to Th. 1, Capt. Ebenezer, b. ab. 1812; m. Mary Adaline Robinson, A. 29, '35; rem. Th., built house on Main street, in '60; & d. Aug. 4, '63. 2, Capt. James A., b. about 1821; m. Emily Meservey, Jan. 1, 1849; r. T., a master mariner, wholesale merchant, &c.

Samuel, (2d)'s ch. 1, James, m. Mary (Robinson) Jenks, July 29, 1824; r. Th. & d. in the South, June, 1840. 2, Jane, m. Simeon Dunbar; r. Th. 3, Henry, b. in 1795; married Candace Brown, Oct. 22,

1826; r. Th. and d. June 27, '45. 4, Eunice, m. Edward Blackington; r. Th. & d. Dec. 1842. 5, William, a sufferer from epilepsy, d. in 1822 or '3.

Fifth Generation.

Capt. Ebenezer's ch. 1, Ebenezer J., b. ab. 1840. 2, Emily J., b. '42, d. Feb. 4, '54.

Capt. James A's ch. 1, Emma, b. ab. 1850. 2, Clara, b. ab. '51. 3, James Edwin, b. April 30, '53, d. Sept. 14, '54. 4, Harriet b. ab. '55. 5, John. 6, Elizabeth.

James's ch. 1, Sarah F., b. July 20, 1825; m. John L. Johnson; r. Th. 2, Orris L., b. March 29, '28, d. April 20, 1838. 3, Ann S., b. July 13, '30; m. George W. Standish of W., Nov. 6, '50; r. Th. 4, Medora B., b. April 13, '32.

Henry's ch. 1, Mary, b. Feb. 12, 1827. 2, Margaret, b. June 30, 1830; both rem., it is believed, to Mass. 3, William, b. March 9, '32, d. March 9, '35. 4, Almira, b. April 22, '33, died Jan. 16, 1835. 5. Sarah, b. Jan. 12, '37, removed Mass. or elsewhe e. 6, Julia Ann, adopted by A. Rice, Esq., and name changed to Rice, March 24, '53; see Rice family. 7, Cleora, b. Oct. 9, '42; rem. Mass.

CREIGHTON, James, b. ab. 1824; m. Martha J. ——; r. Rock., a teamster. Their ch. 1, Lucy J., b. ab. 1846. 2, John F., b. ab '48. 3, James S., b. ab. '51.

CROCKETT, Jonathan, born at Falmouth, now Portland, July 2, 1741, O. S.; m. Elionai Robbins, Jan. 18, 1763; was one of the first settlers of what is now Rockland, and died April 20, 1829, aged 88. His brother Nathaniel came 1st to Vinalhaven, thence to Ash Point, S. Th., where he was one of the first settlers; m. Eunice Cooper; & died in Ohio.

Jonathan's ch. 1, John, b. Oct. 28, 1765; m. Rebecca Blackington, p. Jan. 31, 1789; r. Rock., and died in 1807. 2, Jonathan, (2d), b. Aug. 24, 1768, d. Oct. 6, 1775. 3, Benjamin A., b. April 26, 1771; m. Eunice Crockett, p. Dec. 23, 1793; r. Rock., & d. March 3, 1813, 4, Enos, b. Nov. 6, 1773, d. Oct. 11, 1775. 5, Otis, b. June 21, 1776, d. May 7, 1777. 6, William, b. Feb. 23, 1778, d. April 24, 1798. 7, Dea. David, (2d), Esq., b. March 13, 1780; m. Abigail Crockett, Jan. 26, 1804; r. Rock., a master mariner, &c., and d. June 13, 1854. 8, Robert J., born Dec. 3, 1782; m. Dorcas Holmes, July 23, 1805; r. Rock., and d. Aug. 31, 1849. 9, George, b. July 6, 1785; d. at sea. 10, Elionai, b. Nov. 9, 1788, d. Sept. 25, 1800.

Nathaniel's ch. 1, Lucy, b. Aug. 3, 1772; m. Nathaniel Emery; rem. and died in Unity. 2, Eunice, b. Feb. 17, 1775; m. Benjamin Crockett; rem. and d. in Ohio. 3, Margaret, b. in Vinalhaven, Nov. 22, 1776; m. Thomas Rendell; and d. in Ohio. 4, Capt. David, m. Sarah Heard, Dec. 29, 1803; d. in New York. 5, Thomas, m. Sally Godding, Oct. 10, 1805; r. Rock., and d. May 18, 1816. 6, Lydia, m. David Wooster of N. H. 7, Capt. Jonathan, (3d), b. 1780; m. Catharine Ulmer, March 3, 1803; r. Rock. ? and died June 12, 1851. 8, Jane, b. Jan. 15, 1786; m. Benjamin Packard, (2d); r. & d. at Ash Point, S. Th. 9, Nathaniel, (2d), b. Dec. 26, 1787; died at sea. 10, Asa, b. Feb. 15, 1790; m. Miriam Keating, p. Jan. 1, 1817; rem. and d. in Ohio. 11, Enos, (2d), b. April 16, 1793; m. Lydia McLoon, p. April 30, 1818, 2d, Mrs. Leadbetter of Linc., rem. and r. on a farm in Lincolnville. 12, Mary, b. 1795, d. young. 13, Capt. James, b. April 9, 1798; m. Mary Haskell, Jan. 10, 1822; rem. Ohio.

Third Generation.

John's ch. 1, Nancy, born Dec. 10, 1789; m. Ephraim Perry of Vinalhaven, Nov. 15, 1818; r. Rock., and d. Dec. 22, 1861. 2, Hon. Knott, b. Jan. 15, 1792; r. Rock., was the first city mayor, president of Lime Rock Bank, one of the Fremont presidential electors, 1856, &c., and died unm., Sept. 6, 1857. 3, Rebecca, b. Jan. 13, 1794; m. Tileston Healey; r. Rock., and d. Feb. 12, 1851. 4, Elionai, b. Sept. 4, 1796; m. Capt. John Lindsey; r. Rock. 5, Edward, b. Feb. 3, 1799; m. Harriet Spear, Nov. 20, 1821; r. Rock., lost at sea, March 26, 1830. 6, Sophia, b. Dec. 5, 1801; r. Rock. 7, George, (2d), b. March 7, 1804, died young.

Benjamin's A.'s ch. 1, Oliver, b. Dec. 15, 1794; m. Bethana Nutt of Cam., 1818; rem. up country. 2, Sally, b. May 7, 1796, d. April 7, 1799. 3, John, (2d), b. Dec. 6, 1797; m. Eunice Rendell of Belmont, 1823; rem. Ohio. 4, Nancy, b. Nov. 21, '99; rem. Ohio. 5, Barbara, b. Jan. 2, 1801; m. Otis Barrows; r. Rock. 6, Avis, b. June 30, 1803; m. William Bartlett of Searsmont, Dec. 31, 1826; rem. & d. Ohio. 7, Eunice, b. Nov. 26, 1804; m. William Rendell of Belmont; rem. Ohio. 8, Jonathan, (4th), b. Aug. 24, 1806; m. Hannah Perry, Nov. 1, 1829; rem. & m. 2d wife in Ohio. 9, Nath'l, (3d), b. March 18, 1808; m. Sally Amsbury, May 12, 1833; rem. Ohio. 10, Benjamin A., b. Oct. 10, 1810; m. Margaret S. Amsbury, July 6, 1834; rem. Napoleon, Ohio. 11, Enos, (3d), b. Oct. 1812, d. Feb. 1, 1813.

David, Esq.'s ch. 1, Charles, b. March 19, 1804; m. 1st, Susan R. Ulmer, March 18, '27, 2d. Elethea Cobb of Warren, June 17, '55; r. Rock., a lime manufacturer, city mayor, &c. 2, Celia, b. Dec. 17, '05; m. Angus Gillis, Aug. 20, '51; rem. Ohio. 3, Cornelia, b. Feb 20, '08; m. Ebenezer Brown of Cam. '25; r. Rock. 4, Cephas, b. Nov. 6, '11; m. Emily M. Cox, Jan. 19, '37; rem. Lincolnville. 5, Cyrenius, b. May 18, '14; m. Eliza C. Holmes, p. Oct. 28, '36; r. Rock., a quarryman. The mother died Nov. 28, 1862, aged 80.

Robert J.'s ch. 1, George, (3d), b. Dec. 5, 1805; m. Amanda Simmons; d. at sea, Aug. 25, '47 2, Capt. Elijah, b. March 30, '07; m. Roxanna Cox, Dec. 20, '27, & d. from exposure, Jan. 27, '48. 3, Elionai, b. Aug. 16, '12; m. Capt. George D. Wooster; r. Rock. & died Mar. 9, '47. 4, Capt. Robert, b. Oct. 5, '15; m. Lucy Achorn, Nov. 7, '39; r. Rock., 5, Amos H., b. June 3, '20; m. Salmantha Sylvester, Oct., 1845; r. California. 6, Mary H., b. Feb. 5, '22; m. Henry Brown,; r. Rock., and d. Aug. 24, '49.

Capt. David's ch. 1, Jane, b. Nov. 3, 1804; m. Nathan Pillsbury. 2, Lucy H., b. May 11, '06; married Charles Spalding; r. S. Th. 3, Sarah, b. July 30, '07, d. Feb. 3, '40. 4, Thomas C., b. Nov. 15, '08; r. S. Th., in fish business. 5, Moses H., b. June 15, '10; m. Hannah Spalding, Dec. 23, '30; r. & d. S. Th.? 6, Abigail H., b. Dec. 15, '11; m. Stephen Foster; r. S. Th. 7, David A., b. Aug. 19, '13; m. Eliza D. Rowell, Jan. 18, '43; r. S. Th., a butcher, &c. 8, William H., b. Sept. 2, '14; m. Harriet Heard, Nov. 6, '42; r. S. Th., boarding house keeper, &c. 9, Eunice C., b. Aug. 7, '17, d. July 7, '39. 10, Margaret H., b Nov. 17, '19; m. Nathan Witham; r. S. Th.

Capt. Jonathan, (3d)'s ch. 1, James, (2d), b. March 19, 1803; m. Mary Spofford, Oct. 20, '25; r. Mt. Desert, 2, Hannah, b. Oct. 5, '04, d. Jan. 27, '05. 3, Capt Jonathan, (5th), b. April 10, '06; m. Nancy Spear, p. Jan. 21, '26; died Dec. 27, '45, at Havana when returning from Europe in command of ship *Medora*. 4, Capt. John, (3d), born

Nov. 3, '08; m. 1st, Margaret Watson, 2d, Mary A. Carle of Cam., 1839; r. Rock., a lime manufacturer, &c. 5, Capt. Asa, (2d), born Dec. 7, '10; m. 1st, Pamelia Lovejoy, Aug. 27, 1831, 2d, Elvira Robbins, July 16, '43; r. Rock, a lime manu'r, &c. 6, Capt. Nath'l, (4th), b. Jan. 17, '13; m. Lucy Ames, March 5, '35; r. Rock. 7, Enos, (4th), b. June 29, '15; married Mary J. Pitts, of U., '38; r. Rock., a photographist. 8, Jacob, b. Oct. 11, '17; d. July 22, '29. 9, Catharine C., b. Dec. 25, '19; m. John T. Berry; r. Rock. 10, Sylvanus C., b. April 6, '23, d. Oct. 7, '41. 11, Mary Nancy, b. Aug. 15, '25; m. John P. Wise; r. Rock. 12, Lucy M., b. Oct. 20, '28; m. Jabez B. Greenhalgh; r. Rock.

Of Asa's ch. who mostly rem. Ohio, 1, Delinsha, mar. Ivory W. Holbrook of R. July 15, 1860.

Enos, (2d)'s ch. 1, Mary, b. Feb. 26, 1819; m. Gen. Wm. H. Titcomb, Jan. 4, '44; r. Rock.

Capt. James's ch. 1, George, (4th), b. Feb. 8, 1823; 2, Almira, b. March 16, '24; 3, Josiah, b. March 9, '26; 4, Nathaniel, (5th), b. Dec. 21, '27; 5, Edwin, b. Feb. 2, '29; all rem. to Ohio.

Fourth Generation.

Capt. Edward's ch. 1, Rebecca, b. Jan. 28, 1824; m. Simon W. Litchfield; & d. March 15, '49.

Oliver's ch. 1, Asa, (3d), b. Aug. 18, 1819; rem. & m. in Ohio. 2, Martha, b. May 13, '21; 3, Mary, b. Feb. 10, '23; 4, Oliver, (2d), b. Feb. 1, '25; 5, Bethana, b. Sept. 20, '27; 6, Ruth, b. Aug. 1, '29; all rem. up country.

John, (2d)'s, ch 1, Maria B., b. March 30, 1824; 2, Albina, b. May 1, '27; 3, Adelia, b. Feb. 19, '29; all rem. Ohio.

Capt. Jonathan, (4th)'s, ch. 1, Nancy H., b. July 21, 1826; m. Hiram B. Williams of Belfast, Nov. 16, '45; r. Bangor. 2, Amanda S., b. Aug. 26, '28; m. Capt. Geo. W. Brown; r. Rock. 3, Eveline, b. May 26, '31; m. 1st, J. M. Murphy, May 28, '50; rem. and m., 2d, in the South. 4, Wm. Edward, b. April 21, '34; m. H. Jane Marshal, July 8, '54; r. Rock. a shopkeeper. 5, Medora, r. Rock. 6, Albert T., b. ab. '44; r. Rock., enlisted in U. S. Navy.

Nathaniel, (3d)'s, ch. 1, Edward, b. April 18, 1836; 2, Arthur, b. Oct. 1837; both rem. to Ohio. 3, Irving, b. March 18, '39; d. Feb. 29, 1840.

Benjamin A.'s ch. 1, Benjamin, rem. Ohio. 2, Oliver A, b. 1835, d. Nov. 2, '58, at Maumee City, Ohio.

Charles's ch. by 1st wife. 1. Alden, b. Sept. 27, 1830; m., in Ohio, Nellie V. Conner; enlisted in 4th Me. Reg; became division wagon master. 2, George, 5th, b. March 15, '32; d. Rock., Dec. 4, '47. 3, Frederic, b. March 13, '36; m. Caroline T. Knowlton; r. Rock., a mariner. 4, Charles R., b. March 12, and d March 17, '42. 5, Caroline D., b. ab. '44. 6, Ella S., b. ab. '47. 7, Charles F., b. ab. '50. By 2d wife. 8, William L., b. Oct. 25, '56. 9, Stanley, b. Feb. 19, '59; d. Nov. 10, '60.

Cephas's ch. 1, Adriel, b. March 11, 1838; 2, Abby, b. Oct. 15, '39; 3, Elizabeth R., b. Feb. 10, '40; all rem. Lincolnville.

Cyrenius's ch. 1, Warren L., b. May 26, 1837; m. Sylvania Sherer, Oct. 29, '59; r. Rock., a mariner. 2, Franklin, b. Aug. 6, '38; r. Rock., a mariner. 3, Alfred, b. Oct. 30, '39; r. Rock., a mariner, enlisted in U. S. Navy. 4, David Edwin, b. Feb. 1842; r. Rock., a mariner. 5, Adelaide, b. ab. '45. 6, Sarah, b. ab. '53.

George, (3d)'s, ch. David G., b. Nov. 11, 1841, d. Oct. 1, '42.

Elijah's ch. 1, James F., b. May 15, '28, d. July 28, '56, of yellow fever, when mate of bark *Hanson Gregory*. 2, Capt. Elijah D., b. April 20, '30; m. Caroline E. Achorn, Aug. 30, '57; r. Rock. 3, Alexander C., b. Aug. 25, '32; r. Rock., entered the U. S. Navy. 4, Harriet, b. Oct. 17, '34; m. Knott Rankin, r. Rock. 5, Amanda E., b. Sept. 2, '37. 6, Mary B., b. June 1, '40; m. Joseph H. Kalloch; r. Rock. 7, Jennie C., b. April 23, '43; m. Capt. W. W. Achorn; r. Rock. 8, Frances H., b. Aug. 23, '46.

Capt. Robert's ch. 1, Amos F., b. July 16, 1840; r. Rock., a W. I. goods dealer. 2, Charles Albert, b. Nov. 16, '42; r. Rock. 3, George E., b. July 2, '45, d. Feb. 13, '58. 4, Robert H., b. April 29, 1849. 5, Arthur, b. May 4, '54. 6, Louisa, b. Feb. 21, '59.

Moses H.'s ch. 1, Capt. William S., b. Oct. 4, 1831; m. Abigail Hayden, Nov. 4, '53; r. S. Th. 2, Moses H., (2d), b. Dec. 5, 1833; d. at N. Y., March 13, '50. 3, Norman L., enlisted in the army.

David A.'s ch. 1, Oliver H., b. ab. 1844. 2, Sarah Jane, b. ab. '50.

William H.'s ch. 1, William Henry, b. March, 1843, d. Aug. 26, '44. 2, Oscar, b. ab. '45. 3, Frederic, b. ab. '47. 4, Lizzie, b. ab. '49. 5, Laura A., b. ab. '51. 6, Francis, b. ab. '53.

James, (2d)'s ch. 1, Ann Maria S., b. Dec. 11, 1826; m. Abner B. Weeks; r. Rock. 2, Frances H., b. Aug. 28, 1828, d. Aug. 20, 1829. 3, Charles S., b. July 10, '30; m. Mary V. Flint, March 18, 1854; r. Rock., a mason. 4, James H., b. Aug. 21 '32, d. April 7, 1853. 5, John T., b. Jan. 27, '35; m. Julia S. Freeman, June 3, '56; r. Rock. 6, Julia Ada, b. Feb. 25, '37. 7, Ellen S., b. Aug. 3, '39.

Capt. John, (3d)'s ch. by 1st wife, 1, Capt. William S., (2d), b. Nov. or Feb. 17, 1828; m. Desire E. Rankin; r. Rock. 2, John, (4th), b. Oct. 28, '30. 3, Eliza W., b. Aug. 20, '32; m. George L. Smith, '51; r. Rock. By 2d wife. 4, Sylvanus, b. May 18, '42; r. Rock., a mariner. 5, Alice, b. ab. 1853.

Capt. Asa, (2d)'s ch. 1, Hannibal, b. Mar. 3, 1834, d. Rock. Jan. 3, '53. 2, Delileia, b. Oct. 5, 1835, d. July 31, 1837. 3, Imogene, b. May 11, 1837. 4, Jonathan, (6th), b. Nov. 23, 1839; m. Melissa A. Dean, May 12, '60; r. Rock., a tin plate worker; entered U. S. army. 5, Stephen D., b. March 26, d. Sept. 6, '42. By 2d wife. 5, Charles M., b. ab. '49. 6, Caroline O., b. ab. '51.

Capt. Nathaniel, (4th)'s ch. 1, Pembroke, b. July 9, 1835; rem. California. 2, Lieut. Edgar, b. Dec. 6, '37; r. Rock., a mariner; officer in co. D, U. S. Sharpshooters, 3, Cleaveland, b. ab. '43. 4, Catharine U., b. ab. '47.

Enos, (3d)'s ch. 1, Frank H., b. ab. 1845. 2, Alfred, b. ab. 1846. 3, Eliza J., b. ab. '47. 4, Mary W., b. ab. '52. 5, Fannie, b. ab. '56.

Fifth Generation.

Alden's ch. Brenda, b. Sept. 3, 1854, d. March 15, 1857.

Frederic's ch. 1, Eugene, b. ab. 1855. 2, Albert, b. ab. 1859.

Capt. Elijah's ch. 1, George, b. ab. 1859. 2, Willie, b. Sept. 2, '61. d. July 16, 1863.

Capt. William S.'s ch. 1, Alice Dell, b. April 17, 1854. 2, George B., b. Sept. 13, 1856. 3, Luther H., b. April 14, 1858.

Charles S.'s ch. Charles A., b. ab. 1859.

Capt. William S., (2d)'s ch. 1, Ida V., b. ab. 1854. 2, William, b. ab. 1857. 3, Margaret E., b. ab. 1859.

Jonathan, (6th)'s ch. 1 & 2, twins, b. July 22, 1861, Wilbert Clifford, d. Sept. 25, & Herbert Alton, d. Sept. 27, 1861. 3, Clifford R.

CROCKETT, George W., of a different family, came from Vinalhaven; m. Ann Lindsey of Fox Islands; r. Rock., and died at sea. Their ch. 1, Capt. Augustine W., b. ab. 1828; m. Harriet L. Hall, p. Aug. 10 '49; r. Rock. 2, George H., b. March 13, & d. Aug. 19, 1834. 3, Mary E., b. June 18, '36. 4, George H., b. Jan. 30, '38; corporal in 23d Mass. Reg., d. at Newbern, N. C., April 20, '62; much beloved by all his company. 5, James A., b. Nov. 18, '41.

Capt. Augustine W.'s ch. Marietta, b. ab. 1854.

CROCKER, Capt. John, b. ab. 1807; came from Machias; m. Mary J. Croner, April 13, '30; r. Rock., a ship master. Their ch. 1, Aldana C., b. Jan. 21, '31; m. Joseph H. D. Blake of Boston, March 6, '50, & d. 1854. 2, Niles T., b. Aug. 17, '32; r. Rock., enlisted in U. S. navy. 3, John L., b. May 28, '34; m. Mary A. Fuller, May 31, '56; r. Rock., a mariner. 4, Jonathan W., b. Sept. 17, '38; m. Annie Spear, May 20, '63; r. Rock., enlisted in U. S. navy. 5, Mary C., b. ab. 1847.

John L.'s ch. Jennie, b. 1856.

CROCKER, Thomas, b. ab. 1820; c. from Brooksville, Me.; r. Rock., a lime burner.

CRONER, Rev. Frederic, from Germany, preached awhile at Waldoboro'; m. there Mary Ulmer, and left the country. Their ch. 1, Catharine, b. May 14, (record blank). 2, Frederic, (2d), m. Eliza Havener, p. Sept. 26, 1808; r. Rock., and d. Aug. 18, '27. 3, Hannah, b. Feb. 23, (remainder of record blank).

Frederic, (2d)'s ch. Mary J., b. Jan. 5, 1809; m. Capt. J. Crocker; r. Rockland.

CROSBY, Robert, b. ab. 1823; m. Laura ———; r. Th., a mariner. Their ch. 1, Sarah E., b. ab. 1855. 2, Frank H., b. ab. '59.

CROSS, Elias, b. ab. 1808; r. with Nancy his wife in S. Th, 1860. Their ch. 1, Elias F., b. ab. 1838; m. N. Elizabeth ———; r. S. Th., a mariner. 2, George E., b. ab. '41; r. S. Th. 3, Sarah F. I., b. ab. '45; m. Stillman N. Robinson; r. S. Th. 4, Mary M., b. ab. '47. 5, Althea A., b. ab. '50. 6, William I. R., b. ab. '56.

Elias F.'s ch. Roderic L., b. ab. 1859.

CROSS, Josiah H., b. ab. 1815; r. with Lydia H., his wife, in Rock., 1860; a carver.

CROUCH, Capt. David, b. ab. 1752, in Boston; came early to Old Th.; m. Joanna Jordan, p. May 9, 1777; r. S. Th., and died March 3, 1829. Their ch. 1, William, died at sea. 2, Capt. Ephraim, b. Oct. 1782; m. Elsie Snow, p. March 13, 1819; r. S. Th., and d. Aug. 24, 1858. 3, Elisha, died at sea. 4, Capt. David, (2d), b. March, 1787; m. Mary Phinney of Boston; r. Rock. & d. Jan. 16, 1864. 5, Susan, m. William Wheeler of St. George, p. Dec. 24, 1818. 6, Joanna, m. Nathaniel Wheeler of St. Geo., p. Dec. 5, 1820. 7, Mary, m. George Fales; r. Th. 8, a son, died young.

Capt. Ephraim's ch. 1, Susan, born May 10, 1820; m. Simon D. Graves; r. S. Th. 2, William, b. Sept. 17, '21, d. Jan. 15, '28. 3, Ephraim, (2d), b. Feb 17, '22, d. Nov. 27, '34. 4, John S., b. Nov. 8, '24; m. Mary A. Hatch, April 24, '55; r. Th., a rigger. 5, Margaret S., b. Sept. 3, '27; m. Mortimer Sartelle in Boston. 6, Nancy M., b. May 26, '28; r. S. Th. 7, Elsie A., b. Nov. 5, '33, d. Nov. 15, '34. 8, Effie J., b. March 22, '36; r. S. Th. 9, George T., b. Sept. 18, '38, d. Feb. 15, '41. 10, Charles, b. July 19, '42; r. S. Th.

Capt. David, (2d)'s, ch. 1, Huldah L., b, ab. 1831; m. Demerrick Spear; r. Rock. 2, Charlotte, b. March 8, '35, d. April, 1846.

CROUCH, Alden, of a different family; m. Mary Cox of W., p. June 18, 1803; r. W. and Th., & d. S. Th. His widow, b. ab. 1778, r. Rock. Their ch. 1, Mary, m. John Winslow, r. W. & rem. 2, Charlotte, m. & rem. 3, Capt. Alden, (2d), b. ab. 1814; m. Marg. Ingraham, Sept. 25, '42; r. Rock., & d. at sea in sch. *Lucretia*, Dec. 7, '50. 4, George, d. at sea. 5, Rebecca H., b. ab. 1822; m. 1st, Capt. Abraham Simonton, 2d, David M. Webster; r. Rock.

Capt. Alden's ch. 1, Mary O., b ab. 1844. 2, Alden W., b. ab. '47. 3, George W., b. ab. '50.

CROWLEY, Cornelius, b. ab. 1820, in Cork, I., son of James and Mary (Ryan) Crowley; m. Catharine Callahan; r. Rock., an umbrella mender, &c. James, a brother, also c. & r. Rock., with his mother.

Cornelius's ch. 1, Ellen, b. 1851. 2, Mary Ann, b. '53. 3, James Henry, b. June, 1855, d. Dec., '59. 4, John, b. Feb., d. Dec. '58. 5, Catharine, b. ab. '59.

CROWLEY, Michael, b. ab. 1821, c. with Ellen, his wife, from Cork Co., I.; r. Th. Their ch. 1, Mary, b. ab. 1848. 2, John, b. ab. '53. 3, Kate, b. ab. '55. 4, Margaret, b ab. '57.

CROWLEY, Patrick, b. ab. 1820 in Ireland, as was Mary A., his wife; r. Rock.; a soldier of 4th Maine Reg.; d. from wounds, at Washington, May 29, '64; was brought home and buried with distinguished honors at Rock., June 23d. Their ch. James, b. ab. '59.

CROWLEY, William, b. ab. 1828 in Ireland, as was Ellen, his wife; r. Rock. Their ch. James, b. in Mass., ab. 1853.

CUMMINGS, F. L., m. Emma A. ——; r. Rock., in firm of Cables & Cummings, carriage-makers. Of their ch. Addie A., b. May, & d. Nov. 25, 1863.

CUMMINGS, Levi, b. ab. 1813; r. with Jane H., his wife, in Rock., in 1860; a quarryman. Their ch. 1, Wallace, b. ab. 1846. 2, William E., b. ab. '47.

CUNNINGHAM, George, b. ab. 1818; m. Sarah ——, r. Rock., a lime burner. Their ch. 1, Catharine, b. ab. 1835. 2, Sarah J., b. ab. '41. 3, George Alonzo, b. July 17, '49, d. May 7, '64.

CUNNINGHAM, Asa, b. ab. 1831; m. Priscilla Whitton, April 30, '53; r. Rock., a lime burner. Their ch. 1, Aldana, b. ab. 1855. 2, Edgar E., b. ab. '57.

CURLING, Capt. Sanders, b. ab. 1818; in Liverpool, Eng., c. to Th. ab. 1830; m. 1st, Almira C. Robinson, p. Aug. 19, '37; 2d, Almira R. McLellan, Oct. 28, '47; r. Th. His ch. by 1st wife. 1, Almira C., b. April 23, 1840; m. Capt. Edwin Watts, r. Th. 2, Ada R., b. March, 1843, d. Nov. 24, '44. 3, Helen A., b. ab. '45; m. Capt. John B. Henery, Nov. 18, '63; r. Th. 4, Charles S., b. Aug. 6, '48, d. Sept. 28, '53. By 2d wife. 5, Frank E., b. ab. '51. 6, Caroline, b. ab. '53. 7, Sanders E., b. '55.

CURLING, Daniel, m. Mary Sullivan, c. from Cork, Ireland, to Th. 1830; rem. and d. N. Y.

CURRAN, Patrick, b. in Cork county, Ireland, 1810; c. to Th., July 7, 1832; m. Sarah Kenneston, Jan. 10, '37; r. Th., a sexton, &c. Their ch. 1, Edmond, b. Feb. 4, and d. Oct. 8, 1838. 2, William J., b. Nov. 15, '39, d. April 9, '62. 3, Sarah E., b. Nov. 29, '41, d. Sept. 30, '60. 4, Henry, b. Dec. 25, '43; r. Th. 5, Mary A., b. Dec. 15, '45. 6, Amelia F., b. March 3, '48. 7, Almira F., b. Nov. 30, '49, d. Jan., 1850. 8, Richard E., b. Feb. 2, '52. 9, Edwin S., b. June 20, '55. 10, Coraetta, b. April 9, '58.

CURTIS, Cornelius, b. ab. 1817 in Ireland, as was Catharine, his wife, r. Rock. Their ch. 1, Daniel, b. ab. 1844. 2, Hannora, b. ab. '49. 3, Mary, b. ab. '56 4, Cornelius, (2d), b. ab. '57. 5, William.

CURTIS, Blynn, m. Sarah Robinson, Jan. 18, '46; r. & d. S. Th. Their ch. 1, Harriet A., b. ab. '47. 2, John B., b. ab. '51. 3, Harrison, b, ab. '56.

CUSHING, Dr. Isaiah, came, it is believed, from Scituate, or vicinity; graduated at Harvard University, 1798; practiced medicine in Th.; rem. to Nobleboro'; m. Hannah Vose of Th.; p. April 23, 1808; ret. Th., & d. 1819. Their ch. 1, Edwin, b. 1810; m. Hannah Irene Vose, July 7, '40; r. W. 2, Robert Thaxter, b. 1812; m. Sarah C. Paine, Nov. 5, '36; r. Th., a joiner, &c., and d. Jan. 16, '40, on the Mississippi. 5, James Otis, b. July 1, '14; m. Clementine B. Woodcock, Dec. 18, '45; r. Th., shipbuilder. 4, Hannah Elizabeth, b. Oct. 16, '16; m. Arunah Robbins, (2d); r. Rock..

Edwin's ch. 1, Leslie. 2, Martha E., d. 1864.

Robert Thaxter's ch. 1, Sarah E., b Oct. 14, 1837. 2, Henry T., b. April 11, 1839.

James O.'s ch. 1, Edwin O., b. Oct. 3, 1846, enlisted in U. S. navy. 2, Henrietta, b. Oct. '50. 3, Frederic, b. Feb. '53. 4, Charles H., b. May 3, 1858.

CUSHING, McCobb, b. in Camden, ? Jan. 18, 1819; m. Mary M. Whittier of Readfield; r. Rock., a lime burner, soldier of 4th Me. reg. Their ch. 1, James B., b Sept. 29, '47. 2, Ella C., b Jan. 16, '53. The mother died March 4, 1864.

CUSHMAN, Matthias, b. ab. 1812, in Waldoboro'; m. Sophronia Butler, March 12, 1835; r. Rock., Blackington's Corner, a farmer. Their ch. 1, Anson B., b. Aug. 11, 1836; m. Lizzie Pease of Rock., Oct. 20, '60; r. Rock. 2, Benjamin F., b. Aug. 14, '39; m. Ellen E. Barnes of Cam., Feb. 13, '64; r. Rock. 3, Emma, died young. 4, Reuben H., b. ab. '49.

CUTLER, Abner, came probably from Camden; m. 1st, Margaret Young; 2d, Mary (Frye) Lovies, June 22, 1838; r. Rock., rem. & d. Illinois. His ch. by 1st wife. 1, Vilenia, b. April 23, 1811; m. Jos. Wooster; r. Rock. 2, Capt. Irel, b. March 26, '13; m. Mary J. Sleeper, p. Dec. 15, '38; r. Th.. 3, Alvin, b. Sept. 19, '15; m. Mary A. Spalding, p. Oct. 21, '37. 4, Abner, (2d), b. Aug. 6, '17; m. Maria P. Farr, June 2, '41; rem. Bristol. 5, Sarah A., b. April 21, '25; m. John Morrison, p. Oct. 11, '45. 6, Rosina K., b. April 12, '28. 7, Mary, b. June 14, '31; m. Alexander B. Munroe, jr., of Bristol, Feb. 9, '52.

Capt. Irel's ch. 1, Abigail F., b. Oct. 28, 1842. 2, Josephine, b. ab. 1846. 3, George, b. ab. 1849.

CUTLER, Ethelbert N., b. Feb. 19, 1828, son of Nelson Cutler of U.; m. Frances Thayer; ? r. Rock., a horse dealer. Their ch. Ella A., b. ab. 1855.

DAGGETT, Thurston, b. Nov. 28, 1820, son of Ebenezer Daggett, of Union; m. Rachel Mitchell; r. S. Th., inventor and proprietor of

Dagget's Bone & Nerve Liniment, soldier, &c. Their ch. 1, Alonzo, b. ab. 1844, soldier in 28th Me. Reg. 2, George M., b. ab. '45. 3, Rachel, b. ab. '47. 4, Edwin W., b. ab. '52. 5, Sarah F., b. ab. '54.

DAGGETT, Aramander, b. ab. 1823; m. Arletta B., ——— ; who d. April 23, '64, aged about 40; r. Rock., a carpenter. Their ch. 1, George R., b. ab. 1850. 2, Willard, b. '52.

DAILEY, Capt. Andrew F., b. ab. 1822, in Camden; m. Hannah Benner; r. Rock.

DAVIES, Enoch, b. ab. 1829; m. Melissa T. Condon, Feb. 12, '57; r. Rock., a pump and block maker. Their ch. John F., b. ab. '59.

DAVIS, Oscar, oldest son of Wilbur Davis of Union; b. ab. 1830; m. Emily S. Tolman; r. Rock., a shipwright, dairy farmer, &c. Their ch. Frederic J., b. April 7, 1855.

DAVIS, Charles M., b. ab. 1835, in Lincolnville; m. Sarah Atkins; r. Rock., a blacksmith, artificer in Baker's D. C. cavalry, d. at Washington, D. C., March 24, '64. Their ch. Ernest C., b. ab. '58.

DAVIS, James, b. ab. 1812; m. Mrs. Susanna (Robinson) Hawes, of Cam., Sept. 25, 1836; r. Rock., a teamster. Their ch. 1, Mary E., b. Dec. 8, 1838; r. Rock. 2, Susan A., b. July 7, '40, d. April 30, '41. 3, Margaret A., b. April 28, '42. 4, Hannah S., b. ab. '47. 5, Georgiana, b. ab. '51.

DAVIS, James, b. ab. 1805; m. Appria ——— ; r. Rock., a lime burner. Their ch. 1, Kimball H., b. ab. 1833; married Clarinda N. Pease, March 31, '53; r. Rock., a mariner, 2, Henry, b. ab., '41; r. Rock., a mariner. 3, Charles Albert, b. Oct. 6, '42; r. Rock., a lime burner and soldier, returned home and d May 20, '64.
Kimball's ch. 1, Elizabeth A., b. ab. 1859.

DAVIS, Jonas S., b. ab. 1816, son of Daniel Davis of Washington, Me.; m. 1st, ——— ———, 2d, Mrs. Margaret (Ingraham) Crouch, r. R., a teamster. His ch. by 1st wife. 1, Sarah J., b. ab. '40. 2, Waite Ann, b. '44; m. Nathan F. Carruth of Chelsea, May 5, '63. By 2d wife. 3, Amanda M., b. June and d. Sept. 3, '53. 4, Effie, b. about '54. 5, Frederic S., b. ab. '57. 1, Elthea R., b. ab. '59.

DAVIS, William, b. ab. 1823; m. Clarissa ——— ; r. Rockland, a lime burner. Their ch. 1, Alden, b. ab. 1845. 2, Charles, b. about '48. 3, Lois, b. '51. 4, Adrian, b. '54. 5, George W., b. '57.

DAVIS, Michael, b. ab. 1824; m. Margaret, (who was b. ab. 1829, in London, Eng.,) r. Rock., a mariner. Their ch. 1, John H., b. '55. 2, Joanna, b. ab. '59.

DAY, Rufus F., b. April, 1834; m. Martha J. Boyd, July 5, 1857; r. Rock., a lime burner, and soldier of 4th Me. Reg., d. of typhoid, Aug. 18, '62, at Point Lookout, Md. Their ch. 1, Franklin A., b. ab. 1858. 2, Charles E., b. Nov. 2, '59, died May 16, '62.

DAY, Jacob Goodwin, b. ab. 1806; m. Rhoda ——— ; r Rock., a coroner, &c. Of their ch. 1, Samuel Q., b. ab. 1836; m. Nancy Kenneston, Feb. 22, '54; r. R., a blacksmith. 2, Frederic, b. ab. '46.
Samuel Q.'s ch. 1, Frank, b. ab. 1855. 2, Leforest, b. ab. '57. 3, Minnie E., b. July 7, and d. Sept. 1855. 4, Percy J., b. April 27, d. July 31, 1862.

DAY, Marius, b. ab. 1818; came from Damariscotta; m. 2d, Nancy M. (Page) Rivers, July, 1856; r. Th., a carpenter. His ch. by 1st wife. Emma, b. ab. 1855.

DAY, Thomas W., b. 1794, at Mount Desert; m. Susan W. Morey of Deer Isle; r. Rock., & d. Dec. 26, 1859. Their ch. 1, John, long absent at sea. 2, Patience, m. Twisden Bowden. 3, Hannah, m. Hozier Hesper; r. Boston. 4, Addison, b. ab. 1816; m. Matilda Douglass of Boston; r. Rockland, a carpenter. 5, Vespasian, b. ab. 1818; m. 1st, Mary Douglass, 2d, Martha B. Jordan; r. Rock., a carpenter. 6, Edmund, m. Abigail Gilley; r. Mt. Desert. 7, William, b. ab. 1821; m. Charlotte Grant; r. Rock., a carpenter. 8, Thomas, b. ab. 1823; m. Huldah Robinson of Ellsworth; r. Rock., a brick maker. 9, Gilbert. 10, Eliza, m. Miles Tinker; r. Ellsworth. 11, Otis B., b. ab. 1834; m. Victoria Clark of Northport, Nov. 2, 1863; r. Rock. 12, S. Newell, b. ab. 1838; m. Harriet Clark; r. Rock.

Addison's ch. 1, John, b. ab. 1838, a mariner. 2, Caroline, b. ab. '41. 3, Hannah, b ab. '45. 4, Mary A., b. ab. '47. 5, Charles R., b. ab. '50. 6, Elizabeth, b. ab. '56.

Vespasian's ch. 1, Sewall L., b. ab. 1841; r. Rock., a mariner, now in U. S. navy. 2, Edwin, b. Feb. 28, '42, d. Nov. 21, '58. 3, Ella M., b. ab. '53. 4, Chester F., b. ab. '55. 5, Caroline, b. ab. '58.

William's ch. 1, George William, b. ab. 1850. 2, Helen A., b. April, '52, d. Nov. 25, '58. 3, Julia H., b. ab. '54. 4, Alfred T., b. July 22, '58, d. Aug. 5, '63. 5, John C., b. Oct. 16, '60, d. Aug. 29, 1863.

Thomas's ch. 1, Fillmore, b. ab. 1855. 2, Ruth E., b. ab. 1856. 3, Tyler, b. ab. '58. 4, Thomas, b. ab. '60.

DAY, Alpheus, b. ab. 1818; m. Almira ———; r. Rock., a carpenter. Their ch. 1, Ardalissa, b. ab. 1847. 2, Amanda J., b. ab. '50. 3, Mary O., b. ab. '52. 4, Calvin A., b. ab. '56. 5, Alden H., b. ab. 1858.

DAY, Algernon, b. ab. 1834; m. Amanda E. Smith, July 8, 1856; r. Rock., a lime burner. Their ch. Cora Anna, b. ab. 1857.

DEAN, Capt. Jonas, b. in New Meadows, now Brunswick, Sept. 5, 1765; came early to Th.; m. Ruth Small of Harpswell, p. Jan. 30, '89; r. S. Th., a farmer, militia officer, &c., & d. March 7, 1846. Their ch. 1, Col. Benjamin S., b. Aug. 7, 1790; m. Elizabeth Fales, March 4, 1814; r. Th., a joiner, architect of Th. Cong. church, &c.; rem. Bangor. 2, Dea. Samuel, b. May 22, 1792; m. Melia Butler, p. Nov. 30, 1818; r. S. Th., a farmer, &c. 3, William, b. Feb. 7, 1794, d. in Chesapeake Bay, Oct. 5, 1817. 4, Israel, b. April 7, '96; m. 1st, Joanna C. Butler, p. Sept. 16, 1820, 2d, Mrs. Hester A. Johnson, p. Feb. 12, 1861; r. S. Th., a farmer, recently rem. 5, Ephraim, b. Feb. 21, 1798; m. Lucy McLoon, p. May 25, '22; r. S. Th., a farmer, &c. 6, Mary, b. Feb. 20, 1800; m. 1st, Anthony Hall, Nov. 11, '19, 2d, Francis Haskell; r. S. Th. 7, Jonas, (2d), b. June 25, '02; m. Julia Butler, Nov. 24, '25; r. Rock., a limeburner. 8, Sarah, b. Sept. 6, '04; m. Alden Gay, & d. Dec. 2, '59. 9, Nancy G., b. June 15, '07; m. John Graves, & d. Jan. 1, '48. 10, Louisa, b. Aug. 16, '09; m. Franklin B. Sartelle. 11, ? Elionai, b. ab. '11; r. S. Th.

Col. Benjamin S.'s ch. 1, Elizabeth A., b. Dec. 17, 1814; m. Andrew Wiggin of Bangor. 2, Erastus S., b. April 9, '16; m. & d. in Boston. 3, Hannah F., b. Jan. 27, '19; m. Artemas Edgery; rem. California. 4, Wm. Jonas, b. Dec. 16, '26; m. twice; rem. Bangor.

Dea. Samuel's ch. 1, Amelia R., b. Sept. 28, 1819, d. Oct. 4, '26. 2, Mary G., b. Nov. 11, '21, d. Sept. 19, '26.

Israel's ch. 1, Ruth S., b. Nov. 12, 1821; m. Capt. Ephraim Bartlett,; r. S. Th. 2, Elvira, b. Aug. 15, '23; m. James Merrill; r. Boston. 3, Maria B., b. Aug. 15, '25, d. in Mobile, April 6, '50. 4, Capt. Samuel, (2d), b. Aug. 1, '27; m. Hannah J. Sleeper, '54, & d. in Havana, Aug. 10, '58, master of the bk. *Charles Brewer*. 5, Sarah Louisa, b. Aug. 27, '30; m John S. Pierce; r. S. Th. 6, George B., b. Aug. 13, '32, d. April 22, '52. 7, Mary Emily, b. Aug. 7, 1838. 8, Edwin W., b. June, '43, d. Sept. 27, '50.

Ephraim's ch. 1, Mary Elizabeth, b. Sept. 17, 1823; m. Samuel Wiggin; r. S. Th. 2, Ephraim, (2d), b. Jan. 6, '25; m. Clementine J Spalding, Sept. 5, '51; r. S. Th., a merchant. 3, John H., b. April 14, '27; m. Lavona McKenny, 1854; r. S. Th., a merchant. 4, Lucy T., b. June 10, '32. 5, Lydia F., b. July 17, '39.

Jonas, (2d)'s ch. 1 William B., b. Dec. 7, 1826; m. Mary A. Scribner, July 31, '50; r. Rock., a caulker. 2, Mary J., b. Sept. 20, '28; m. Erastus Welt; r. Rock. 3, Otis R., b. Nov 10, '30; m. & r. Lynn, Mass. 4, Amariah K., b. March 23, '33; m. Clara Rollins; r. Rock., a caulker. 5, Julia L., b. May 28, '35; m. Benjamin Cushman, 1854; r. Bloomfield, Me. 6, Leander N., b. April 10, '38; r. Lynn. 7, Caroline, r. Lynn. 8, Emma P., b. ab. '45. 9, Clara A, b. April, 1848, d. Aug. 26, 1854. 10, Abby Johnson, b. ab. 1850.

Fourth Generation.

Samuel, (2d)'s ch. 1, Eliza Maria, b. ab. 1854. 2, Celia, b. ab. '58.

Ephraim, (2d)'s ch. 1, Cora Etta, b. ab. 1852. 2, Frederic E., b. ab. '54 3, George B., b. ab. '56. 4, Hattie B., b. ab. '58. 5, Emeline.

John H.'s ch. 1, Willard Harris. 2, Alvin F. 3, Benjamin W., b. 1859.

William B.'s ch. Clara E. b. ab. 1859.

Amariah K.'s ch. Nellie, b. ab. 1859.

DEAN, Luke, whose father was b. in Dedham, Mass., and grandfather in England, was himself b. in Francestown, N. H., Sept. 30, 1808; m. Thankful Burgess of China; r. Rock., a quarryman. Their ch. 1, Roxana, b. Dec. 17, 1830; m. Samuel R. Ulmer; r. Rock. 2, Delphas, b. March 25, '32; m. Ephraim J. Ulmer, r. Rock., & d. May 25, '58. 3, William F., b. Oct. 12, '33; m. Marilla Mosman, Nov. 26, '54; r. Rock., a teamster; rem. California, but ret. 1864. 4, Elizabeth E., b. Aug. 16, '35; m. Dexter S. Morse, r. Th. 5, Charles H., b. Feb. 1, '37; m. Ellen Tolman, Jan. 12, '62; r. Rock. 6, Mary J., b. May 14, '40; m. C. D. Smalley; r. Rock. 7 & 8, twins, b. June 9, '43, Alonzo W., r. Rock., & Melissa A., m. Jona. Crockett; r. Rock. 9, John H., b. Oct. 8, '46, r. Rock., enlisted in the army.

DEAN, Alanson, b. ab. 1797, m. Elizabeth Mosman; r. Rock. Their ch. 1, Harriet, b. Jan. 22, 1822; m. J. W. Ormsby, r. Rock. 2, Charles, b. March 28, '24; d. of consumption. 3, Alanson, (2d), b. July 1, '26; r. Rock., & d. in Augusta, Feb. 16, '61. 4, Mary, b. March 28, '29; d. of consumption. 5, Melinda, b. April 13, '31; r. Rock. 6, Hanson, b. March 3, '34; r. Rock., a farmer. 7, Caroline E., b. Feb. 12, '40, d. young.

DEAN, Benjamin F., b. Feb. 12, 1813, son of Isaiah Dean of Lincolnville; m. Susan U. Spear, p. Feb. 28, '34; r. Rock., lost sight in quarrying; since a peddler, sawyer, &c. Their ch. 1, Ellen A., b. April 13, '34; m. James R. Durden; r. Rock. 2, Elbridge S., b. May 26, '36; r. Rock., a mariner. 3, Mary A., b. Oct. 11, '38; r. Rock. 4, Ida F., b. ab. '51. 5, Ernest F., b. May, '31, & d. Aug. 27, 1855.

DEAN, Capt. Oscar P., b. ab. 1835; r. S. Th.

DELANO, Sandford, came from Friendship; m. Harriet Winchenbach, 2d, Columbia Black; traded a few years in W., rem. and kept victualling saloon in Th., where his 1st wife d. Sept. 14, 1863. His ch. by 1st wife. 1, Asa. 2, Olive. 3, Ada. 4 & 5, twins, Hattie & ———, both died young. By 2d wife. 6, Judith.

DEMUTH, Jacob, b. 1780, came from Wal. to Union, 1796, to Th., 1798; was a ship carpenter; mar. Mehitable, an adopted or natural daughter of Dr. E. G. Dodge, Sept. 14, 1805; r. Th., & died Dec. 26, 1863. Their ch. 1, Seth, m. Mary Watton, of Friend., & d. Dec. 19, '44. 2, Ezekiel D., b. ab. 1809; m. Caroline J. Copeland of Warren, May 6, '32; r. Th., a mason. 3, Jane Ann, m. George W. Fales; r. Washington, D. C. 4, Charles S, b. 1813; m. Eliza Robinson, pub. Aug. 29, '32; r. Th., and d. Nov. 26, '35. 5, Julia F., b. '15, d. April 24, '37. 6, James, m. & r. N. Orleans. 7, Hermon Fisher, d. 1845.

Ezekiel D.'s ch. 1, Frances O., b. Dec. 20, 1833; m. John B. Rogers of Hampden, Oct. 27, '53. 2, Sarah E., b. Dec. 9, '35; m. John C. Delano, Oct. 27, '53; r. St. Geo. 3, Charles L., b. Sept. 13, '37; m. Mary Hart, r. Th., a mason. 4, Caroline O., b. Jan. 5, '40; m. Samuel B. Flint; r. Th. 5, Aroline E., b. March 10, '42. 6, Ezekiel Frank, b. ab. '44, musician in 2d Me. Battery. 7, Julia, b. ab. '48. 8, James, b. ab. '50. 9, Susan E., b. ab. '53. The mother d. June 20, '61.

DENNIS, Selah G., b. 1820, in Fairhaven, Vt., m. Bethia Thorndike, July 19, 1847; r. Rockland, landlord of Commercial House, Thorndike Hotel, 1856; rem. to Boston, Commercial House, March, '62, r. Hallowell. Their ch. 1, George M., b. ab. 1849. 2, Charles S., b. ab. '51. 3, James B., b. ab. '53. 4, Frank C., b. ab. '55. 5, Augustus, b. ab. '58.

DENNIS, Samuel D., name changed from Twitchell by Leg. act., was b. ab., 1821, in Dixmont, Me.; m. Tamson D. Rowe, July 14, 1850; r. Rock., a shoe manufacturer.

DERBY, Rufus, b. ab. 1800; m. Harriet ———, r. Rock., a teamster. Their ch. 1, Charles H., b. Dec., 1840; a lime burner, soldier in 2d Me. Battery, & d. at Washington, D. C., Sept. '62. 2, Samuel, b. ab. '42; r. Rock., also enlisted in the army. 3, Mary A., b. about '45. 4, Sarah E., b. ab. '47.

DEVINE, Stephen A., b. ab. 1825; m. Olive H. Hall, March 16, 1851, r. Rock., a foundry moulder. Their ch. Flora E., born about 1852. 2, Edith N., b. ab. '56. 3, Lewis W., b. '58.

DILL, Asa, b. ab. 1809, in Franklin Co, Me.; m. Maria Pillsbury; r. Rock., a truckman. Their ch. 1, Thomas B., b. about 1838; r. Rock., a mariner. 2, Elzada M., b. ab. 1840. 3, Lauretta J., b. ab. '43. 4, Ambrose, b. Dec. 26, '45, r. Rock., a soldier of 2d Me. Cavarly, d. at N. Orleans, Oct. 10, '64. 5, George A., b. about '47. 6, Goodwin A., b. ab. '50. 7, John, b. ab. '52.

DILLAWAY, John, b. 1733; c. from Boston to Th., and m. about 1778, Mary, widow of John Shibles; was a cooper, some years an innholder, filled many town offices, and d. June 12, 1803. Their ch. 1, Betsey, b. May 1, 1779, d. young. 2, Samuel, b. April 22, 1782; m. 1st, Anna Farrington of War. June 6, 1805; 2d, Mrs. Hall, rem. and d. in Linc. 3, Polly, b. Dec. 20, 1785; m. John Robinson of C. rem. & d. Hope.

Samuel's ch. by 1st wife. 1, Eliza, mar. Sandford Libbey, r. Cam. And others probably by 2d wife.

DILLINGHAM, Edward L., born about 1837, son of Bernard and Sarah (Lincoln) Dillingham of Warren ; mar. Elizabeth S. Carleton, Jan. 24, '61 ; r. Th., a merchant in firm of Chapman, Flint & Co.

DILLON, James W., b. ab. 1834, in Ireland; r. with Ellen T., his wife, in Rock., a marble worker. Their ch. Harriet, b. ab. 1859.

DIMOND, James, b. ab. 1822, in Connaught, Ireland; m. Bridget Thornton; r. Th. Their ch. 1, John, b. ab. 1849. 2, Mary J., b. ab. '52. 3, Francis, b. ab. '58.

DINSMORE, Israel, b. ab. 1788; m. Abigail ———, and had a family of ch. in Cherryfield; m. 2d, Jane (Snow) Cobb of S. Th.; r. & kept public house in Cherryfield, Warren, & Th., & d. in the latter, July 29, 1849. Of his ch. by 1st wife, there came here. 1, Nancy, b. ab. 1821, d. at New Orleans, May 10, 1844. 2, Richard C., b. ab. 1827; m. Sarah A. Chase of Whiting, Washington county; r. Th., a carpenter, soldier of the 21st Me. Reg., &c. His ch. by 2d wife. 3, Maria F., b. March 6, 1836, in W.; m. Joseph L. Reed, Jan. 26, '51; r. Th., and died May 26, 1856.

Richard C.'s ch. 1, Stephen E., b. Dec. 1847, d. Aug. 23, '50. 2, Abbie, b. ab. '52. 3, Elizabeth, b. ab. 1860.

DINSMORE, Sam'l Frederic, b. ab. 1817; m. Mary K. Pillsbury; r. S. Th. Their ch. 1, Mary A., b. ab. 1851. 2, George F., b. ab. '52. 3, Sarah A., b. ab. '54. 4, Helen A., b. ab. '56. 5, William E., b. ab. '57. 6, Hermon S., b. ab. '58. 7, Minnie S., b. March, & died Oct. 1, 1860.

DINSMORE, William, b. ab. 1820; m. Nancy Sprague, Jan. 9, '53; r. Rock., a lime burner. Their ch. 1, Elnora, b. Feb. 1854; d. July 29, '61. 2, Edwin, b. ab. 1856.

DOANE, John B., b. ab. 1804; m. 1st, Dorcas ———; (who died Nov. 29, 1858); 2d, Susan A. ———; r. Rock., a truckman. His ch. by 1st wife. 1, Rebecca R., b. ab. 1847. 2, Fanny J., b. ab. '49. 3, Julia E., b. ab. '57.

DOCKHAM, Henry, b. ab. 1825; r. with Julia his wife, in Rock., a rigger. Their ch. 1, Emma, b. ab. 1850. 2, Daniel, b. ab. 1853. 3, Pamelia, b. ab. 1857.

DODGE, Dr. Ezekiel Goddard, b. 1765, son of Rev. Ezekiel Dodge of Abington, Mass.; m. Susanna Winslow of Vinalhaven, p. Aug. 8, 1798; prac. med. in Th. 30 years; besides engaging in trade, representing the town in the legislature and exerting a strong influence there as well as in this part of the commonwealth; he died Aug. 5, 1819. His widow died Oct. 31, 1848. Their ch. 1, Nathaniel C., b. March 9, & d. March, 1799. 2, Ezekiel G., (2d), b. Aug. 29, 1800; m. 1st, Mrs. Harriet Gilchrist, p. Sept. 15, '27; 2d, Eliza J. Clough, Dec. 18, '49; r. Th., a painter, farmer, &c. 3, Mary G., b. Dec. 23, '01; m. Capt. William Cole; r. Th. 4, Penelope W., b. & d. Jan. 3, '03. 5, Capt. Josiah W., b. Jan. 14, '04; m. Eunice Graves, March 27, '36; officer in militia, a merchant at Owl's Head, &c., and d. after only 5 days sickness, Feb. 20, '49. 6, Penelope K., b. May 6, '06, d. Feb. 6, '07. 7, Thomas B., b. Sept. 1, '08, d. Sept. 3, '09. 8, Robert G., b. April 5, '10; m. Mrs. Studley of Camden; r. Hope.

Capt. Josiah's ch. 1, Josiah W., (2d), b. March 27, 1836; rem. & m. in California. 2, Henry C., b. Jan. 10, '36; 3, Deborah N., b. Oct. 5, '39; 4, Ezekiel G., (3d), b. Jan. 4, '42; 5, Mary; all rem. & r. California.

Robert G.'s ch. 1, Susanna, m. James Moody; r. Linc. 2, Ezekiel G., (4th), m. & r. Lynn, Mass. 3, William C., m. Sarah Hutchinson of Danville, Me.

DODGE, Robert L., came from Edgecomb or Brunswick, Me.; m. Louisa Fales, May 21, 1829; r. Th., a cabinet maker; rem. Brunswick. Their ch. 1, Hezekiah, b. May 13, '30; 2, Harriet L., b. Nov. 12, '32; 3, Elizabeth P., b. Oct. 12, '35; 4, Frances V., b. Oct. 15, '37; 5, Arthur J., b. Nov. 24, '41; all rem. with their parents.

DODGE, Mark Z., c. from Islesboro', Me.; m. Sarah Knowlton, March 22, 1832; r. and d. Rock. Their ch. recorded here. Ephraim M., b. Sept. 9, 1832.

DODGE, Elbridge H., b. ab. 1824, in Islesboro', Me.; m. Lucy M. Spalding, July 4, 1848; r. Rock., a lime burner. Their ch. 1, Eldridge F., b. ab. 1843. 2, Margaret E., b. ab. '49. 3, Peter, b. ab. '56. 4 & 5, twins, b. Dec. 1859, George N., d. Aug. 13, '61, & Saul.

DODGE, Capt. Jonathan B., b. ab. 1795; m. Deborah ———; r. Rock., a master mariner. Their ch. 1, Mary E., b. ab. 1833. 2, Henrietta C., b. ab. 1838. 3, Adrian, b. ab. '41; r. Rock., a mariner. 4, Alvin H., b. ab. '45. 5, Edwin G., b. ab. '48.

DODGE, Samuel B., c. from Waldoboro' or Bristol; m. Eliza (Robinson) Demuth, May, 1838; r. Rock., a shoemaker, but bought a farm in and rem. Montville. Their ch. b. here. 1, Ann E., b. April 16, 1839. 2, Mary T., b. July 23, '49? both rem.

DODGE, Oakes A. G., m. 1st, Amanda M. Lermond of W.; c. to Th; m. 2d, Matilda R. Shibles, p. Sept. 17, 1853; & d. in Milton, Florida, Sept., 1858. His ch. by 1st wife. 1, Elizabeth, b. & d. '52. By 2d wife. 2, Wilbur, b. ab. 1855. 3, Florida, b. ab. '58.

DOE, Ezekiel, b. ab. 1826; m. Sarah L. Andrews; c. hither and bought the I. Brown lot; r. S. Th., a farmer, &c. Their ch. 1, Frances Ella, b. ab. 1853. 2, Frederic B., b. ab. '57. Of this name, also, Dr. Theophilus, b. ab. 1794, r. with his wife in Rock., 1860, & prac. med., but rem. Their ch. 1, Mary E., b. ab. 1835; m. S. K. Whiting; r. Winthrop. 2, Erastus A. b. ab. 1837. 3, Caroline A., b. ab. '39.

DOLAN, Felix C., b. ab. 1819, in Ireland, as was Margaret his wife; r. Rock. Their ch. 1, John J., b. ab. 1853. 2, Martin A., b. ab. '57.

DONAHUE, William, b. ab. 1820, in Ireland, as was Ellen his wife; r. Rock., a lime burner. Their ch. 1, James, b. ab. 1840. 2, Catharine, b. June 23, '45, d. July 8, '62. 3, Parfect, b. ab. '48, in Maine. 4, Ellen, b. ab. '50. 5, William, b. ab. '52. 6, Timothy, b. Nov. 30, '54, d. by drowning, Jan. 18, '60. 7, John, b. ab. '57.

DONOVAN, Daniel, c. from Ireland, with Julia, his wife; killed in a quarry, Aug. 8, 1845, leaving ch. 1, Daniel, (2d), b. ab. 1830 in Ireland; r. Rock., with Hannah his wife. 2, Joanna, b. Aug. 25, 1839. 3, Anoca, b. Jan. 18, d. Aug. 29, '42.

Daniel, (2d)'s, ch. Hannah, b. in Maine, ab. 1857.

DONOVAN, William, b. ab. 1823, in Ireland, as was Ellen his wife; r. Th. Their ch. 1, Michael, b. ab. 1849. 2, Ellen, b. ab. '51. 3, Jeremiah. 4, William, (2d). 5, Margaret.

DONOVAN, Michael, b. ab. 1825, in Ireland; m. Ellen ———;

r. Rock. Their ch. 1, Mary, b. ab. 1853. 2, Patrick, b. ab. '55. 3, Cornelius, b. ab. '56. 4, Catharine, b. ab. '58. 5, Michael J., b. ab. 1860.

DOVETON, Henry A., b. Feb. 28, 1836, in Jamestown, St. Helena; m. Mary A. Turner, of Rock., Oct. 29, '56; r. Rock., a mariner, and d. Sept. 25, '63. Their ch. 1, Lizzie May, b. Sept. 25, & d. Oct 16, '58. 2, Charlie E., b. May 12, '60, d. Aug. 23, '61. 3, Annie A., b. Oct. 25, '62.

DOW, Capt. James, came from the British Provinces; m. Elizabeth Coombs, p. March 17, 1806; r. & d. S. Th. a militia officer, &c. Their ch. 1, Abigail C., m. William L. Hayden; r. S. Th. 2, Capt. George C., b. ab. 1808; m. Catharine P. Wade, Dec. 12, '33, 2d, Sarah J. (Packard) Fales, July 26, '62; was thought, in 1830, to have perished in Peru, but survives many adventures, both by sea & land; & r. Th. 3, Capt. James, m. Julia Thorndike, p. Aug. 24, '35; r. S. Th.; rem. California.

Capt. George C.'s ch. by 1st wife. 1, Catharine L., b. June 26, 1835; m. Charles Redman; r. S. Th. 2, Capt. George, b. Aug. 27, '37; m. Mary D. Dyer, July 26, '62; r. Th. 3, Emily E., b. May 20, '40, d. Sept. 21, '43. 4, Octavia W., b. ab. '44. 5, Mary Emma, b. ab. 1846.

Capt. James's ch. 1, Helen, b. ab. 1839. 2, Frederic, b. ab. '43. 3, John B., b. 1845, d. Sept. 1846. 4, Caroline, b. ab. 1860.

DOW, Phinehas, b. ab. 1813, in Jefferson, Me.; m Delight Young, p. Feb. 26. '39; r. Th., a carpenter. Otis L., a cousin, b. ab. 1799; m. and r. Rock., a wheelwright.

Phinehas's ch. 1, Maria, b. Oct 7, 1839; r. Th. 2, Dana Y., b. May 4, '41; r. Th., a mariner, soldier of 4th Maine reg. 3, Israel, b. ab. '43. 4, Edwin, b. ab. '45. 5, Ebenezer S., b. Sept. 3, '46, died Sept. 17, '47. 5, Lucy, b. ab. '50. 6, Emily, b. ab. '54. 7, Ebenezer, b. ab. 1857.

Of Otis L.'s ch. 1, Herbert J., b. ab. 1839; r. Rockland, a wheelwright, soldier of Co. B, 4th Me. Reg., wounded Aug. 29, 1862. 4, Byron J., b. ab. 1843. 5, Ella F., b. ab. 1845. Perhaps also, of his older ch. might have been, 1, Joseph, m. Martha Thompson, p. Nov. 8, 1845. 2, Sarah J., m. Joseph H. Yeaton of Wal., p. Sept. 14, '52.

DOYLE, William, b. about 1832; mar. Sarah ———; r. Rock., a mariner. Their ch. 1, Laura, b. ab. 1854. 2, Frank, b. ab. '57.

DRAKE, Spencer, came from Sharon, Mass., to old Th., m. Jane Kelloch of St. George, p. Feb. 28, 1806; r. and d. S. Th. Their ch. 1, Augustine, b. ab. 1809; m. Margaret Butler of U., Sept. 14, '36; r. S. Th., a blacksmith, &c. 2, Relief, m. Capt. William Gray; r. & d. S. Th. 3, Hartford, lost at the age of 19 years at sea with Capt. James Sayward. 4, Margaret, m. Fullerton Kelloch; r. Th. 5, Elbridge, d. in Spain, aged 21 years. 6, Jackson, d. young.

Augustine's ch. 1, Elbridge Freeman, b. Dec. 11, 1838; r. S. Th., a blacksmith. 2, Washington R., born March 11, '41; r. S. Th., a blacksmith. 3, Lillias, b. ab. '43. 4, Spencer, (2d), b. ab. '46. 5, Augustine, b. March & d. Nov. 30, '48. 6, Harriet, b ab. '50. 7, Harrison, b. ab. '52. 8, Melvin, b. ab. '55. 9, Amariah, b. ab. '57. 10, a daughter, b. in '60.

DRAKE, Dr. Oramel L, came from Union, a dentist, to Th., & d. of fever, Dec. 8, 1858.

DREW, Joseph, b. Nov. 1771, c. from Dresden, Me., and with his son settled on a part of the Geo. Sayward farm, S. Th., where he d. May 8, 1849.

DREW, Capt. Albert, b. in Waterville, Me., 1798; m. in Newport, R. I., Mrs. Mary (Jeffers) Vaughan; c. from China, Me., & r. Rock. Their ch. 1, Laura C., m. Jonathan White, Nov. 14, 1845; r. Sullivan. 2, John A., b. Nov., 1829, d. when returning from Baltimore, June 9, '51. 3, Henry C., m. Sarah E. Everett, p. Jan. 21, '54; r. Ophir, Nevada Territory. 4, George A., m. Mary M. Mosman, Nov. 24, '58; r. Rock., a joiner, rem. California. 5, Mary A., b. in R. I., d. aged 11 yrs. 6, William H., b. in China, July, 1837, d. of yellow fever, on passage from Havana to Mobile, Dec. 25, 1857. 7, Otis, b. in Rock., May 25, '40; drowned, 1859, in James river.

Henry C.'s ch. 1, Ella, d. young. 2, Albert.

George A.'s ch. 1, Mary E., b. July 30, 1860. 2, Frank Alton, b. Nov. 25, '61.

DRINKWATER, Capt. James, b. ab. 1807, in Northport, Me.; m. Henrietta Philbrook of Islesboro'; r. Rock., in maritime pursuits. Their ch. 1, Sylvina, b. ab. 1827, d. April 10, 1862. 2, Alice J., m. Charles H. Paine; r. Hallowell. 3, Capt. James Jefferson, b. ab. '32; m. Susan K. Boyd, Oct. 1, '55; r. Rock. 4, Daniel D., b. April, 1834, died June 20, '58. 5, Sarah A., m. S. P. Merrill. 6, Rose B., deceased. 7, Louisa, A., b. ab. '44. 8, Lucy A., b. ab. '46. 9, Thomas T., b. ab. '48, d. at Bangor, April 10, 61, knocked overboard by vessel's boom. 10, Leonora, b. ab. '51.

Capt. James J.'s ch. 1, Mary Bell, b. ab. 1856. 2, Minnie, b. ab. '58. 3, Judson.

DRISCOLL, Timothy, b. ab. 1820 in Ireland, as was Catharine his wife; r. Rock., a soldier in 6th Battery. Their ch. 1, James, b. ab. 1846. 2, Cornelius, b. ab. '54. 3, Joseph, b. ab. '58.

DRUMMOND, Richard, b. ab. 1825, in Ireland, as was Elizabeth his wife; r. Rock., a shoemaker.

DRYNAL, John, b. ab. 1810 in Cork, Ireland, m. Catharine Murphy; r. & d. Th. Their ch. 1, Ellen, b. ab. 1848. 2, Joanna, b. ab. '50. 3, John, b. ab. '56. 4, George, b. ab. '58.

DUNBAR, Henry K., son of Daniel and Abigail (Kingman) Dunbar, of Warren, m. Sarah Bridges of S. Th., May 26, 1800, r. W., & d. July 9, 1805. Their ch. 1, Samuel, m. Mary Howard, June 1, 1823; r. W. but rem. 2, John B., m. Eliza Kenney, of St. George, p. Oct. 23, '24; r. Th., rem. St. Geo. and d. 1847. 3, Simeon, b. ab. 1804; m. Jane Creighton of Th., Oct. 5, '24; r. Th. 4, Henry K., (2d), m and r. in Eastport.

Samuel's ch. 1, Henry K., (3d), r. Mass., a tailor. 2, Thomas, r. W., a shipwright, rem. Cal.

John B.'s ch. 1, Sarah J., b. Nov. 12, 1825; 2, Mary E., b. Aug 4, '30; 3, John H., b. Feb. 11, '32; m. Ruth E. Harris, Aug. 17, '51; r. St. George. 4, William, b. March 5, '36; m. Nancy Gardner, Oct. 23, '53; all probably r. St. George.

Simeon's ch. 1, Mary Jane, b. ab. 1825; m. Henry T. Rivers; r. Th. and d. Aug. 12, '52. 2, Simeon, b. ab. 1834; m. Albina B. Weeks, Aug. 18, '54; r. Th., a mariner. 3, George, b. ab. '36; r. Th., a mariner. 4, Elizabeth, d. in Th. 5. Ellen, b. '40, d. Feb. 1, '54. 6, Eliza, b. ab. '48, r. Th.

DUNBAR, Richard, son of Asa & Jane (Butler) Dunbar, of W.; m. Catharine L. Copeland, Jan. 3, 1828, 2d, Fanny L. (Willis) Bentley; r. Th. a farmer. His ch. by 1st wife. 1, Joseph, d. young. 2, Charles, b. ab. 1833; r. Th. a mariner. 3, Alexander C., b. ab. '36; m. Aldana E. Jones of U., p. Dec. 19, '61; r. W., a painter and factory man. 4, Helen W., b. ab. '39; m. Eben C. Oxton of Cam., Jan. 1, '63. By 2d wife. 5, Nancy, b. ab. '43. 6, Oliver, b. ab. '46. 7, Frank, b. ab. '48.

DUNBAR, Joseph, of the 4th Me. Reg., m. in Belfast, Emma J. Burgess, April 16, 1864, r. Rock.

DUNCAN, John, m. r. & d. in Northport, Me. Of his ch. 1, Ingraham, b. ab. 1796, in Northport; m. Rebecca N. Perry, r. Rock., a caulker, &c. 2, Samuel, m., r. & d. Northport. 3, Capt. George W., b. Feb., 1802; m. Hannah Simonton, Jan. 26, '30; r. Rock. and died Dec. 7, 1851.

Ingraham's ch. 1, John W., m. Louisa Rooks of Linc. 2, Capt. Charles C., b. ab. 1830; m. Hattie P. Farrow of Belfast; r. Rock. & d. April, '61, drowned at the stranding of his vessel on Squam Beach. 3, George Merrill, b. ab. '33; m. Ellen Thomas, Nov. 1, '59, r. Rock., a caulker, &c. 4, Alphonso A., b. ab. '37; r. Rock., a caulker, &c. 5, Hudson, b. March 15, '43, d. July 11, '56. 6, Ferdinand P., b. ab. '46. 7 & 8, twins, b. ab. '49, Lorana L., r. Rock., Eldora, d. young.

Of Samuel's ch. Capt. Samuel, m. Lucinda Achorn, Sept. 24, '40; r. Rock., rem. New York.

Capt. George W.'s ch. 1, George I., b. ab. 1831; m. Sarah E. Knowles, Jan. 11, '53, 2d, Loraine Simonton, July 22, '62; r. Rock., a mariner. 2, Albion K. P., b. Feb. 28, '36, died, lost at sea, June 20, '58. 3, Hazen Franklin, b. April 26, '38. 4, Delora E. L., b. Nov. 16, '40; m. Frank T. Coombs; r. S. Th. 3, Freeman S., b ab. '43; r. Rock. 4, Mary A., b. ab. '46. 5, Isaac S., b. May, '51, d March 31, 1852.

Capt. Charles C.'s ch. Hattie P., b. ab. 1860.

Capt. Samuel's ch. b. in Rockland. Orrin C., b. July 2, 1842.

George I.'s ch. by 1st wife. Etta E., b. May, and d. Oct. 18, 1855.

DUNCAN, James, of a different family, b. ab. 1811, in Deer Isle, Me.; m. 1st, Lucretia Lane, 2d, Jane E. Low, Feb. 7, '56; r. Rock. His ch. by 1st wife. 1, Lavinia E., b. ab. 1832; m. Greenleaf Childs, March 28, '62; r. Rock. 2, Susan, b. ab. '40. 3, James E., b. ab. '43; r. Rock., a mariner. 4, Willis, b. ab. '53. The mother d. May 12, 1854. By 2d wife. 5, Lucretia, b. ab. '56. 6, Mary F., b. '58. 7, Vesta, b. Aug. 24, '60, d. Sept. 11, '61. 8, Simon L., b. June 20, '62, d. Aug. 20, '64.

DUNLAP, Robert, was at E. Th., in 1830, a merchant in Co. with E. Hall.

DUNN, Thomas W., b. ab. 1825, in Boston; son of Thomas & Abigail C. (Elliott) Dunn; came to Th., 1837; m. Eliza A. Giles of St. George, p. Feb. 18, '47; r. Th., a sailmaker. Their ch. 1, John G., b. ab. 1848. 2, Sarah A., b. ab. '50. 3, Thomas W., (2d), b. ab. '52. 4, Ann E., b. ab. '56. 5, Robert K., b. ab. '57.

DUNN, John G., b. ab. 1823, in Milton, Mass.; m. 1st, Ann M. Hall of Bath, (who d. Dec. 31, 1856, aged 26 yrs. 9 mos. & 29 days); 2d, Lizzie W. Collamore, June 11, '57; r. Rock., a stone cutter, &c. His ch. by 1st wife. 1, Adaline A., b. ab. 1849. 2, Ann M., b. ab.

'51. 3, Edmund J. B., b. ab. '53. 4, Georgiana, b. April 30, '55, d. May 16, '58. By 2d wife. 5, Cora E., b. ab.' 58. 6 & 7, twins, b. Dec. 27, '59, Jenny B., d. May 10, '60 ; Minnie C. ; r. Rock.

DUNNING, Capt. Robert, came from Harpswell; m. Elizabeth Bucklin of W., p. Feb. 14, 1794 ; r. S. Th., was lost at sea ab. 1800. Their ch. 1, Robert, (2d), b. ab. 1795 ; m. 1st, Mary Rowell, Jan. 9, 1817, 2d, Nancy (Horn) Boyd, April 13, '44 ; r. S. Th., a fish dealer, &c. 2, Margaret, m. Anthony Mathews ; r. S. Th.. 3, Sally, m. Rice Rowell ; r. and died S. Th.

Robert, (2d)'s, ch. 1, William, b. Oct. 25, 1817, d. Aug. 1, 1841. 2, Henrietta, b. Oct. 22, '19, d. unm. 3, Nathaniel, b. March 26, '22, d. Oct. 25, '41. 4, Robert, (3d), b. Sept. 6, '28 ; m. Aurelia Norton of St. George, Aug. 28, '53 ; r. S. Th., a sailmaker. 5, Betsey R., b. Dec. 26, '31 ; m. Oliver S. Quimby, Feb. 17, '53 ; r. Cam. 6, Sarah M.. b. March 25, '36 ; m. Daniel E. Wilson of Bradford, Me., Nov. 26, '56. 7 & 8, twins, and perhaps some others, died in infancy.

Robert, (3d)'s, ch. 1, Charles L., b. ab. 1856. 2, Emeline E., b. ab. 1858.

DUNNING, John T., b. ab. 1818, in New Brunswick ; m. Jane C. Arey ; ? r. S. Th., a carpenter. Their ch. 1, Stephen A., b. ab. '51. 2, Edwin B., b. ab. '59.

DUNNING, Henry T., b. ab. 1831, in New Brunswick ; m. Elizabeth S. Arey, May 28, '54 ; r. S. Th., a carpenter, soldier of 28th Me. Reg., since enlisted in U. S. Navy at Rock. Their ch. 1, Bradford, b ab. 1855. 2, Elva, b. ab. '59.

DUNTON, Abram, b. ab. 1822, in Hope ; m. Nancy Conant ; r. Rock., a cigar manufacturer. Their ch. 1, Silas P., b. ab. 1849. 2, Hiram A., b. ab. 1851. 3, Chloe S., b. ab. 1857.

DURDEN, James R., b. ab. 1834, in Bermuda ; m. Ellen A. Dean, 1854 ; r. Rock., a boat builder. Their ch. 1, Lizzie E., b. ab. 1857. 2, Charles H., b. ab. 1859.

DURGIN, James S., b. ab. 1816 ; m. Ruth ——— ; r. Rockland, a lime burner, soldier of 20th Me. Reg. Their ch. 1, Lucinda, b. ab. 1842 ; r. Rock. 2, Mary J., b. ab. 1844 ; m. John Blethen, of Frankfort, Feb. 27, '64. 3, Aurilla, b. ab. '47. 4, Rebecca, b. ab. '49. 5, Frances, b. ab. '53. 6, Sophia, b. ab. '59.

DURGIN, Munroe, b. ab. 1828 ; c. from Lubec, Me.; m. Rebecca Lincoln ; r. Th., soldier of 2d Me. battery, &c. Their ch. 1, Daniel, b. ab. 1851. 2, Mary A., b. ab. 1858.

DUTTON, Daniel, b. ab. 1808, in Readfield ; m. Helen Colby of Embden ; r. Rock., a gardener, &c. Their ch. 1, Johnson L., born Sept. 1830 ; m. Sarah H. Dutton ; r. Rock., a joiner, and d. March 11, 1861.

Johnson L.'s ch. 1, Daniel W., b. ab. '56. 2, Mary H., b. ab. '58.

DWIGHT, Col. Sullivan, b. March 29, 1783, c. from Shirley, Mass. to Th. about 1810 ; m. Betsey Marsh of Bath, p. Aug. 18, 1820 ; r. Th., a marble worker and manufacturer, militia officer, &c.; and died June 12, 1853. Their ch. 1, Caroline F. K., b. Dec. 5, '21 ; m. Edward C. Selden ; r. Th., and d. Aug. 24, 1854. 2, Henrietta L. M., b. March, 1823, d. March 31, '43. 3, Francis S., b. March 21, '25 ; d. June 2, '42. 4, Helen M., b. Aug. 6, '30, died Feb. 21, '45. The mother d. in Brooklyn, New York, May 22, 1858, aged 65.

DWINEL, Andrus, b. ab. 1797, in Orono, Me., mar. Lydia Butler, May 2, 1833; r. Rock. Their ch. Charles A., b. ab. 1848.

DYER; of the sons of Anthony, from Vinalhaven, it is believed, there c. hither, 1, Isaac; m. Susan Eastman, p. Aug. 19, 1815; r. S. Th., and probably rem. or died. 2, Capt. Charles, m. Hannah Cooper, Dec. 15, 1816; r. S. Th. and d. Aug. 10, '48.

Isaac's ch. 1, Asa C., b. Oct. 10, 1818; m. Martha Arey, July 17, '45; r. & d. S. Th. 2, Charles, (2d), b. Jan. 10, '20.

Capt. Charles's ch. 1, William Anthony, b. July 5, '17; m. Julia Arey, Jan. 1, '39; r. S. Th., a carpenter. 2, Benjamin C., b. March 14, '19. 3, Sarah Frances, b. Oct. 1, '22; m. Capt. Richard Harlow; r. S. Th. 4, Cathleen B., b. ab. '26; m. Ebenezer Arey; r. S. Th. 5, Marcia A. P., b. ab. '28; m. Eli P. Hall; r. Rock. 6, ? Charles, (3d), b. ab. '30; r. S. Th., a mariner.

Asa C.'s ch. 1, Ernestine, b. ab. 1848. 2, Manford, b. about 1850. 3, Edgar, b. ab. 1858.

William Anthony's ch. 1, Julia B., b. July 10, 1841; r. S. Th. 2, Alden W., b. Nov. 7, 1842; r. S. Th. a mariner, soldier of 19th Me. reg &c. 3, Liuellia A., b. ab. 1844; m. Mark Douglas of Vinalhaven, Sept. 20, 1863. 4, Louisa F., b. ab. 1846. 5, Alvarius A, born ab. 1848. 6, Medora L., b. ab. 1850. 7, Charles A., born 1852. 8, Josephine A., b. ab. 1854. 9 & 10, twins, b. ab. 1850; Leslie H. & Wesley H.

Charles, (2d)'s ch. 1, Lizzie A., b. 1858, d. Dec., 1859. 2, a son, b. 1860.

DYER, Asa, b. ab. 1811, son of Eben Dyer of North Haven; m. Jane M. Beverage of that place; r. Rock., a ship carpenter. Their ch. 1, Rosiltha, b. ab. '36. 2, Edwin B., b. ab. '41. 3, Lizzie J., b. ab. '46.

DYER, Christopher, b. ab. 1815; c. from Cape Elizabeth with wife & family; r. some time, & built vessels, in Rock., but rem. Portland. Benjamin F., also from same place, was here temporarily, and rem. Portland. Woodbury P., a boat builder, was here also; m. Malvina A. Brewster, Aug. 27, '53; rem. Portland.

EARLE, Halford S., b. ab. 1812, in Brunswick, Me.; m. Elizabeth Barker of New Bedford; r. Rock., postmaster, stevedore, &c.; but has removed recently to California. Their ch. 1, Henry H., b. ab. '44. 2, George F, b. ab. '46. 3, Annie B., b. ab.. '48. 4, John B., b. ab. '50. 5, Clara B., b. ab. '52; all rem. Cal.

EASTMAN, Philip, c. early, r. & d. in S. Th. Of his ch., we have noted, 1, John, b. Nov. 2, 1792; m. Abigail Munroe, Jan. 27, 1825; r. S. Th., and d. Feb. 10, 1856. 2, Susan, m. Isaac Dyer; r. S. Th. 3, Mehitable, m. Ezekiel Post; r. S. Th. 4, Mary, m. Nathan Pillsbury, (2d), r. S. Th. 5, Abigail, m. Joseph Kalloch; r. S. Th. 6, Hannah, m. Benjamin Stevens; r. Northport. Capt. Enoch, b. April, 1811; m. Harriet N. Washburn, June 27, '35; r. Rockport, and d. in Th., Nov. 14, '45.

John's ch. 1, Mary P., b. Dec. 30, 1826, d. May 16, '33. 2, Susan M., b. Feb. 14, '27; m. Israel Witham of S. Th. 3, Hannah S., b. May 11, 1828. 4, John M., b. Oct. 18, 1834; r. Rock., now in U. S. navy. 5, Abigail M., b. May 8, 1837.

EASTMAN, Joseph, b. ab. 1822; m. Mary M. Bradford, Oct. 7, 1857; r. Rock., a grain merchant. Their ch. 1, George B., b. Dec. 25, 1862, d. Aug. 19, 1863.

EASTMAN, Augustus, b. ab. 1834; m. Mary ——; r. Th., Their ch. 1, Nathaniel B., b. ab. 1859.

EASTIS, William, was here in 1795, & p. Oct. 7th, to Mary Philbrook of Vinalhaven.

EATON, Joseph, m. Mercy Nichols; c. from N. H.; r. & d. Monmouth, Me. Their ch. 1, James, b. Aug. 14, 1785; c. to Th. ab. 1815; m. Hannah Day of Monmouth; r. Th. and d. very suddenly, Sept. 3, 1828. 2, Joseph, d. at sea. 3, Mary, m. 1st, William Kelly, 2d, John Moody; r. and d. Monmouth. 4, Mehitable, d. unm. 5, Hubbard, c. to Th., m. Charlotte Frye of Bucksport; r. Th. & d. 1827, his wife having d. Oct. 30, '26, without ch. 6, Parker, d. unm. 7, Mercy, m. Henry Day, d. in Th. 8, Hannah P., m. Francis Weeks of Harlem, (now China,) Dec. 30, '21; r. Patten, Me. The mother d. in Th. Dec. 18, '25, a. 70.

James's ch. 1, Antoinette, b. May 9, 1819; m. Capt. Edwin S. Snow; r. St. Mary's, Texas. 2, Sarah F., b. June 9, '22; r. Th. 3, James N., b. Sept. 23, '24, d. at St. Thomas, W. I., March 5, '41. 4, Agarista A., b. July 16, '27, d. Sept. 13, '46.

EDGARTON, Otis, b. ab. 1797; came from Lancaster, Mass., ab. 1819; m. Mary H. Fales; r. Th., a marble manufacturer. Their ch. 1, Sarah P., b. July 12, 1823; m. R. Harvey Counce; r. Th. 2, Isabella P., b. Aug. 19, '25; m. Rufus C. Crawford; r. Th.. 3, Eliza M., b. Dec. 2, '27, d Jan. 13, '51. 4, Augustina, b. April 5, '30; m. Capt. Isaac M. Vose; r. Th. 5, James P., b. Nov. 21, '32; m. Augustina E Graffam, Dec. 21, '56; r. Th., a carpenter. 6, George W., b. April 11, '35; r. Th., a marble worker and carver, &c. 7, David R., b. Oct. 12, '37; m. Ophelia M. Taft of Uxbridge, Mass., April 28, '64; r. Th., a painter. 8, Lucy A., b. Sept. 22, '41; m. Alfred E. Robinson; r. Th.

EDGECOMB, Eleazer, b. in Scarboro', Me., March 1, 1802; m. Rebecca Carleton of Whitefield, Nov. 12, '29; c. to E. Th., now Rock., '37; & d. March 16, '58. Their ch. 1, Ellery C., b. in Appleton, July 19, & d. Aug. 28, '30. 2, Cordelia, b. Aug. 27, '31. 3, David C., b. June 8, '33, lost at sea, ab. Dec. 1, '49. 4, Imelda, b. April 5, '35, in Appleton; m. C. C. Crook of Vt., Dec. 5, '52; r. Chelsea, Mass. 5, Adelbert, b. in Rock. Feb. 12, '39, went south, a bridge and railroad builder. 6, Warren C., b. April 15, d. Sept. 18, '45. 7, Jos. Warren, b. March 13, '47, enlisted in U. S. Navy. 8, Helena F., b. Jan. 15, & d. May 19, '54.

EDWARDS, Alexander, b. Nov. 2, 1818, in parish of Kinneff, county of Kincardineshire, Scotland; came here, m. Mary A. Morton, May 20, '49; r. Th., a carpenter. Their ch. Rodney, b. ab. '50.

ELDRIDGE, Littleton R., b. ab. 1823, in Bucksport, Me.; m. H. Jane Dow; r. Rock., a lime burner, &c. Of their ch.. Richard A., b. ab. '44; r. Rock., a mariner.

ELDRIDGE, Amos, b. ab. 1830, in Millbridge, Me.; m. Elizabeth Strout; r. Rock., in U. S. Navy. Their ch. 1, Henry, b. ab. '47. 2, Jefferson, b. ab. '50. 3, Louis, b. ab. '51. 4, Tilton, b. ab. '55. 5, Jeannette, b. ab. '58.

ELLEMS, Rev. John, b. in Carlisle, Mass.; m. Hannah Ulmer, p. Aug. 16, 1807, 2d, Lucy Brewster; was a local Methodist preacher in Camden; rem. Rock. & d. April, '43. His ch. by 2d wife. 1, Capt. William B., b. Dec. 12, '18; m. Joanna Butler of U., July 5, '39; r.

Th. & d. in Havana, Jan. 14, '58. 2, Capt. Henry T., b. Oct. 5, '20; m. Sarah J. Eaton of Sedgwick, April 12, '46, 2d, Julia —— of Richmond, Va.; r. Rock. 3, Cyrus, b. Nov. 8, '21, lost at sea April 24, '37. 4, Capt. Ira B., b. in Cam., Aug. 30, '23; m. Caroline H. Getchell, Aug. 22, '47; r. Rock., an alderman, &c. 5, Joseph, b. in Cam., Feb. 14, '27; m. Jane Gardner, Nov. 30, '49; r. Rock., a stevedore, &c. 6, Mary, b. March 30, & d. Sept. 20, '29. 7, Mary C., b. April 1, '30, d. Feb. 11, '36. 8, John E., b. Dec. 18, '32, in Rock.; m. Sarah A. Smith of Vinalhaven, p. March 26, '52; r. Rock., a mariner, now in U. S. Navy. 9, Hannah, b. Dec. 21, '36.

Capt. William B.'s ch. 1, Marcia, b. Jan. 6, & d. Feb. 28, 1840. 2, Clara, b. Oct. 23, '42. 3, Kevern S., b. March 27, '48, d. April 12, '49.

Capt. Henry T.'s ch. by 1st wife. 1, Elizabeth E., b. Jan. 30, '47 d. Oct. 26, 1854. By 2d wife. 2, Herbert, b. ab. '56. 3, Virginia, b. ab. '59, in N. J.

Capt. Ira B.'s ch. 1, Clara, b. ab. 1848. 2, Helen L., b. ab. '50. 3, Caroline A., b. ab. '59.

Joseph's ch. 1, Lucy J., b. ab. 1851. 2, Oscar F., b. April 30, '56, d. Oct. 8, 57. 3, Oscar M., b. ab. '59.

John E.'s ch. 1, Georgiana, b. ab. 1853. 2, Emma S., b. ab. '55. 3, Clarabelle, b. ab. 57.

ELLEMS, Augustine E., b. ab. 1838, of a different family; m. Rose B. ——; r. Rock. Of their ch. Alice E., b. Mar. & d. Aug. 11, '60.

ELLIOTT, Ambrose, b. ab. 1778; m. Sarah Choate; c. from Portland to what is now S. Thomaston, where he d. in Jan., 1827. Their ch. 1, William Henry, b. March 25, 1810; m. 1st, Mary Jordan, May 10, '32, 2d, Hannah (Emery) Arey, Nov. 7, '44; r. S. Th., a mariner, & d. July, '59. 2, Hannah, m. 1st, Ebenezer Jordan, 2d, Matthew P. Barton; r. S. Th. 3, Sarah Ann, b. Aug. 31, '13, in Portland; m. Martin Keith; r. & d. Th., leaving one son, b. ab. 1846, whom she gave to her sister Susan, and who took the name of George E. Elliott, and r. Th. 4, Abigail, b. Nov. 14, '14; m. Leonard Johnson, Aug. 1, '30; r. Boston. 5, Ambrose, (2d), b. Sept. 21, '17; r. & d. S. Th. 6, Susan, b. Aug. 29, '19; r. Th. 7, Mary Elizabeth, b. June 10, '26; r. Boston. The mother m. 2d, Ebenezer Jordan of S. Th., 3d, William Jackson of W.; r. Th.

William H.'s ch. by 1st wife. 1, Mary A., b. May 16, 1834, died Oct. 24, '36. 2, Caroline, b. Nov. 1, '35, d. April 6, '36. 3, William, F., b. May 16, '37; m. Laura A. Sweetland, r. Rock., a mariner, now in the U. S. navy. 4, Hester E., b. July 29, '41, d. Sept. 11, '42. By 2d wife. 5, Laura, b. ab. '45. 6, John, b. ab. '48. 7, Henry, b. ab. 1851.

ELLIOTT, John, b. in Halifax, Mass., 1768; m. in Boston, Abigail Kneeland, 1796; rem. Wiscasset, 1797, to Th. in 1855, and died Dec. 19, 1862, aged 94. Their ch. 1, Abigail C., b. ab. 1797; m. Thomas Dunn, and d. in Boston, 1821. 2, Eliza, b. 1799; m. P. Call; r. Th. 3, Sarah K., b. 1801; m. Samuel Goodridge, 1826; r. & died Th. 4, John, (2d), b. '03; mar. Eliza N. Robinson, July 22, '27; r. Th., in Knox st., a blockmaker. 5, Richard, b. March 12, '05; m. Elionai D. Copeland of W., Oct. 4, '34; r. Th., a blockmaker, & d. Jan. 27, '59. 6, Mary Ann, b. '07; m. Robert Walsh; r. Th. 7, Adaline, born '09; m. William Nutter. 8, Samuel, b. '12; c. to Th., m. Irene Robinson, p. May 19, '35; rem. Mobile in 1839, and to Florida in 1854. 9, Henry, b. 1814, r. Wiscasset. The mother d. in 1842, aged 68.

John, (2d)'s ch. 1, John Henry, b. March 22, 1828; died Oct. 29, '49. 2, Sarah G., (adopted) b. '38; d. Jan. 5, '59. 3, John Henry, (adopted) b. '49, r. Th.

Richard's ch. 1, James W., b. Jan. 11, 1836, d. Sept 3, '47. 2, Oliver G., b. May 1, '37; r. Th., a sailmaker; lost at sea April 2, 1861. 3. George W. b. Nov. 12, '39; r. Th., a sailmaker. 4, Elizabeth.

Samuel's ch. 1, Susan Abigail. 2, Sarah G., b. May, 1838, died Jan. 5, '59. 3, Edwin R. 4, Alathea F. 5, Letitia. 6, Alfred B. 7, John Henry. 8, Amelia, N. 9, Martha K.

ELLIOTT, William D., son of Charles Elliott, of Knox, m. Mrs. Jane Kalloch, Dec. 29, 1857; traded awhile in Th., and returned to Knox.

ELLIS, Reuben N., b. ab. 1822, in Blue Hill, Me.; was in 1860 a variety merchant, r. Rock., with Orillia his wife, and ch. 1, Fannie, b. ab. 1845; 2, Minnie, b. ab. '59, but has since rem.

ELLIS, Edwin, b. ab. 1813; m. Elizabeth Henderson, of Belfast; inn keeper at the Georges Hotel, and returned Belfast, 1861.

ELLISON, Andrew, from England, came to Th. as a tailor, mar. Mary Cobb, Oct. 16, 1808; built a house on Main Street, but after r. here many years, rem. to and became a merchant tailor in Boston. Of their ch. 1, Andrew, (2d), was baptised he e April 28, 1811. 2, Mary Elizabeth; 3, William Sharswood, both bap. July 25, '13. 4, Frances, bap. April 28, '15; all rem. to Boston.

ELWELL, Capt. Andrew G., b. ab. 1819, came from St. George; probably descended, as well as others of the name mentioned below, from William, one of the 1st settlers of Meduncook, now Friendship; m. Hannah T. Maker of Th., Aug. 16, 1838; r. Rock., a pilot, lost at sea, with all on board, Oct. 1859, in the sch. *Mary Farnsworth*, coming from Pictou. Their ch. 1, Horace S., b. May 12, 1839; r. Rock., a mariner. 2, Charles H., b. June 5, '41; r, Rockland, a mariner. 3, Joshua C., b. ab. 1845; r. Rock., a mariner. 4, Clara I., b. ab. 1850. 5, William, b. ab. 1853.

ELWELL, James H., b. ab. 1826; m. Elizabeth B. Duncan, Nov. 1848; r. Rock., a joiner. Their ch. 1, Frederic, b. ab. 1850. 2, Eugene, b. ab. '54.

ELWELL, Samuel H., b. ab. 1821; c. from St. George; m. Jane C. ———, or Susan P. Elwell, Sept., 1844; r. Rockland, a mariner. Their ch. Reuben E., b. ab. 1846.

ELWELL, Iddo K., b. ab 1825; m. Lucy ———; r. Rock., a mariner, recently entered the U. S. navy. Their ch. Cora A., b. ab. 1855.

EMERY, George, b. ab. 1763, in Kittery, Me.; c. after the Revolution to what is now South Thomaston; m. Sarah Dean; and d. ab. 1846. Lucy, a sister, who m. Nathan Pillsbury, also c. here not far from the same time; and Nathaniel, a brother, b. April 20, 1772, settled here, Dec., 1789; but rem. and died in Thorndike, Me., 1862.

George's ch. 1, Sarah, m. John Whitcher; rem. Belfast. 2, Louisa, m. Nathaniel Graves, July 11, 1809; r. St. G., and d. March 29, '52. 3, Capt. John, b. ab. 1788; m. 1st, Hannah Post, p. Aug. 27, 1814; 2d, Mrs. Margaret (Crie) Bartlett, Nov. 20, '34; r. S. Th. 4, Dennis, m. in Nova Scotia; r. Belfast. 5, Jonas, b. Jan. 27, 1793; m. 1st, Abigail Sleeper, Oct. 17, 1816; 2d, Miss Kalloch; r. Belfast,

& d. May 27, '64. 6, George, (2d), b. 1795; m. 1st, Nancy Sleeper, Dec. 17, 1820; 2d, Rebecca Maddocks, 1826; r. S. Th., a farmer. 7, Nathaniel, (2d), d. unm. 8, Capt. Daniel, b. July 21, 1802; m. Sophia Sleeper, Sept. 6, '27; r. S. Th. 9, William D., b. June 15, '04; m. Hannah E. Pratt of Dunstable, Mass.; r. Boston. 10, Mary, m. Joseph Pillsbury, (3d); r. Rock. 11, Lucy, m. Archibald C. Lowell; 2d, Jonathan Post; r. and d. S. Th. 12, Rev. Ephraim U., a Baptist minister at Unity and other places; m. at Islesboro', Mrs. Temperance Pruda, p. July 2, '32.

Nathaniel's ch. 1, Anna, b. Nov. 21, 1792; 2, Elioenai, b. Nov. 30, '94; m. David Packard; 3, Tristram, b. April 26, '96; 4, Levi, b. Sept. 22, '98; all probably rem. Thorndike. 5, Thomas, b. Sept. 22, 1802, d. April 1, '03.

Capt. John's ch. by 1st wife. 1, Eliza H., b. Nov. 27, '15; m. Benjamin F. Webster; r. S. Th. 2, Capt. William S., b. Oct. 10, '17; m. Lucy I. Spalding, July 7, '39; rem. Cal. 3, Hannah, b. Oct. 4, '19; m. Alden B. Arey; r. S. Th. 4, Emily A., b. Jan. 2, 1823; m. Capt. Elias Sleeper; r. S. Th. & d. July 17, '50. 5, Sarah M., b. May 17, '24, d. Sept. 1826. 6, Capt. John A., b. March 7, '29; m. Kate S. Thorndike, June 21, '55; r. S. Th. 7, Mary S., b. June 27, '31; m. Nathan P. Webster, Jan. 1, '52; d. Dec. 14, '52. 8, Alvan S., b. March 13, '33. By 2d wife. 9, Susan E., b. Nov., 1835. 10, Richard A., b. Nov. 13, '37, d. young? 11, Richard B., b. '39; was a member of Baptist church from childhood, became a soldier of the 2d Me. Battery, for duty's sake, and d. Nov. 26,'62, at Brooks Station, Va. 12, Capt. B. Alden, b. ab. '41; m. Elizabeth O. Maddocks, March 8, '64; r. S. Th. 13, Samuel A., b. ab. '43, r. S. Th., a mariner.

Of Jonas's ch. 1, Capt. George, (3d), m. Susan D. Graves, Dec. 7, '42; r. Th.

George, (2d)'s, ch. 1, Eveline, b. Oct. 7, 1821; m. Charles Sherman; & d. Aug. 18, '43. 2, Edwin Thomas, b. April 27, '23; m. Susan M. Perry, Feb. 18, '47; r. S. Th., a truckman. By 2d wife. 3, John, (2d), b. Sept. 1, '27; m. Melissa L. Arey, June 1857; r. S. Th., a mariner. 4, Joseph M., b. March 27, '29; m. Mary Masters; r. S. Th., a carpenter. 5, George W., b. Sept. 29, '30; r. S. Th., a farmer. 6 & 7, twins, b. May 6, '32, Nancy Rosetta and Harrietta. 8, Lucy, b. April 14, '34, d. June 3, '52. Rebecca, the mother, d. April 13, '56, a. 62.

Capt. Daniel's ch. 1, Abigail, b. April 13, '33, d. Jan. 25, '42. 2, Sarah, b. May 21, '35; r. S. Th. 3, Bethiah, b. July 31, '37; r. S. Th. 4, Daniel W., b. Jan. 9, '39; a mariner, d. in Mexico, July 30, '60. 5, Harrison, b. April 30, '41; a mariner. 6, Clara, b. Oct. 24, '43. 7, Sophia, b. March 9, '46. 8, Knott, b. March 13, '48. 9, Abbie, b. Sept. 6, '53.

William D.'s ch. 1, Harriet E., b. in Boston, March 28, 1827; 2, Albert T., b. in S. Th., Oct. 7, '29; 3, Catharine R., b. in S. Th., May 17, '31; 4, Mary H., b. May 21, '33; 5, William N, b. in S. Th., May 25, '36; all probably rem. Boston.

Fourth Generation.

Capt. William S.'s ch. 1, Eleanor S., b. Feb. 20, and d. April 14, 1840. 2, William Edward, b. Feb. 21, '42.

Capt. George, (3d)'s, ch. 1, Evelina P. 2, Edwin R. 3, Lizzie C. 4, Silliam M. 5, Walter. 6, Arthur. 7, Nellie.

Edwin Thomas's ch. Edwin G., b. ab. 1851.

Joseph M.'s ch 1, Georgiana, b. ab. '53. 2, Charles O., b. ab. '55. 3, Joseph, b. ab. '57.

EMERY, Alonzo, c. with his wife from Hampden, Me ; kept the Owl's Head hotel in 1839 and '40 ; rem. Mass. Their ch. b. here· Josiah L., b. Sept. 1, 1839. Clarissa L., the mother, d. Dec. 22, '40.

EMERY, William, b. ab. 1828, came from Portland; m. Marilla Ames, Oct. 14, 1856 ; r. Rock., a mariner. Their ch. Charles, b. ab. 1859.

EMERSON, Thomas, b. in Dublin, Ireland; c. to Thomaston as a teacher; m. Lydia Morse, May 18, 1789; sailed for Ireland in June, 1790, and d. before his return. Their only son, John, b. July 30, 1789; grad. H. U., 1816; m. Mary Walls, July, 1829; rem. & prac. law in Montville. His ch. 1, Margaret Catharine, m. & rem. Burnham. 2, Almatia, m. ——— Follett, r. Montville. 3, Jennie, m. a Whitmarsh, r. Beverly. 4, Elizabeth. 5, Augusta.

EMERSON, Capt. Joseph, b. ab. 1800; c. from Edgecomb, Me., m. 1st, Rebecca Robinson, p. Oct. 21, 1826, 2d, Mrs. Mary E. Bright of Hampden, April 3, '44 ; r. Th., rem. and d. in San Francisco, Cal., Dec. 31, 1860. His ch. by 1st wife. 1, Mary Ann, b. Aug. 22, 1827; 2, Wm. James R., b. March 28, '29; m. Eliza James, of London, England, Sept. 30, '54; 3, Joseph Edwin R., b. May, 1832; 4, Julia Hortense, b. May 21, 1834 ; all probably rem. 5, Rebecca, b. May9, '36, d. Nov. 30, '55. 6, Elizabeth, b. June 18, '38, d. Oct. 11, '38. The mother b. June 16, 1806, d. Oct. 3, 1838.

EMPEROR, James, b. ab. 1828, in Ireland, as was Catharine, his wife; r. Rock. Their ch. 1, Ellen, b. ab. '56. 2, John, b. ab. '59.

ERSKINE, Abiel, b. ab. 1813, in Jefferson, Me.; m. Lucinda Borneman of Wal.; r. Rock., a joiner, &c. Their ch. 1, Royal G., b. ab. 1843; r. Rock., enlisted in U. S. navy. 2, Lincoln H., b. ab. '45. 3, Mary B., b. ab. '49. 4, Roswell, b. ab. '51. 5, Clarabelle, b. ab. '53. 6, Eugene, b. '55, d. May 13, '57. 7, Cora Emma, b. ab '59.

ESTABROOK, Dr. Theodore L., son of Dr. Joseph H. & Caroline (Jacobs) Estabrook of Camden, b. in Cam studied medicine & grad. at New York University; r. and prac. med. in Rock. since 1859.

ESTEN, Dr. John, b. Nov. 6, 1824, in Burrillville, Providence co., R. I.; m. Rebecca Day of Smithfield, R. I.; r. and prac. med. in Rock. Their ch. Nellie E., b. Aug. 1, 1850.

EUGLEY, Jacob A., b. ab 1830, in Waldoboro'; m. Martha A. ———; r. Rock., a carpenter. Their ch. 1, Webster L., b. ab. '57. 2, Susan E., b. ab. '59.

EVANS, Dr. Warren R., b in Norway, Me.; c. to Th. 1863, as a dentist.

EVANS, Elisha, c. to Th. from Sackville, N. S., with Betsey, his wife; and ret. thither after having r. here, as appears from the record of his 9 ch., from 1826 to 1841. All ret. to Sackville, as did also William A. Evans, who r. here some years.

EVERETT, David, b. ab. 1785, in Massachusetts; m. here Jane Bartlett, Nov. 3, 1808; r. S. Th., a farmer, &c. Their ch. 1, Mary, b March 1, 1810, d. March 13, '12. 2, Mary, b. March 10, '12, died April 15, '44. 3, Jeannette G., b. Aug. 30, '14; m. Adrian Child of Harpswell, Sept. 23, '42; rem. West. 4, Prudence C., b. Jan. 27, '17; m. Capt. Alfred Sherman of Hope; r. S. Th. 5, Meletiah, b.

Oct., 1821, d. Sept. 25, '26. 6, David B., b. July 16, '26; m. Clementine Fales; rem. Brooklyn, N. Y. 7, Samuel G., b. Nov. 3, '28; m. Susan E. Emery, Nov., 1856; r. S. Th. a mariner. 8, Sarah Ellen, b. Nov. 23, '34; m. Henry Drew; rem. West.

Of David B.'s ch. Fannie E., b. June, 1858, d. June 26, '61.

Samuel G.'s ch. Adrian C., b. ab. 1858.

EVERETT, Edward, b. ab. 1828, in Montville; m. Helen T. Keating, June 13, '56; r. Rock., in mercantile business. Their ch. John C., b. ab. '57.

EVERTON, Zephaniah, b. in 1764; was a soldier of the Revolution; c. from Gilmanton, N. H. to Th.; worked at the mills in U., 1791-3; m. Margaret Watson, Jan. 25, 1798; was long the toll gatherer at the lower bridge in Th., where he d July 26, 1841. Their ch. 1. Oliver, b. Aug. 9, 1798: enlisted at Portsmouth in U. S. service, 1816, received a furlough to visit his parents, & has never since been heard from. 2. Mary, b. March 1, 1801, d. of measles, April 9, '09. 3, William, b. May 3, 1803, d. of consumption, May 3, '46. 4, Margaret, b. Jan. 9, 1806, d. March 12, '42. 5, Maria, b. Dec 9, '08; r. Th. 6, John, b. 1812, d. five days old. 7, Eliza A., b. 1814, d. nine months old.

FAHEY, Thomas, b. Limerick, Ireland, 1811; m. Mary Savage; came hither '35-'6; r. Th., a laborer. Their ch. 1, Thomas, b. ab., '41. 2, John, b. ab. '43. 3, Michael, b. ab. '45. 4, Frances, b. ab. 49. 5, Mary, b. ab. '50. 6, James, b. ab. '53. 7, Catharine, b. ab. 1856.

FAIRFIELD, John, b. about 1839, r. with Mary A., his wife, in Rock., a mariner.

FALES, Nathaniel, of Bradford, Mass., (who was the son of James Fales, (3d), who was the son of James, (2d), who was the son of Jas. 1st, who came from the ancient town of Chester, in England, and settled in Walpole, Mass.) m. Elizabeth Atwood, and died Sept. 28, 1737. His wife, Elizabeth (or Jenney) d. in Bradford, 1782, aged 83 or 84. Their ch. 1, Atwood, b. March 10, 1723, (O. S. as are all the succeeding births of this generation) r. at Amherst, N. S. and Th., and d. at the former place, Feb. 8, 1805, aged about 82. 2, Elizabeth, b. Nov. 21, 1725; m. it is presumed, in Mass., and died March 12, 1808, a. 82. 3, Capt. Nathaniel, b. Jan. 2, 1727; m. Sarah Badger, at Norwich, May 18, 1749; settled in Th., where he r. and d. April 13, 1797, aged 70. 4, Ebenezer, b. Feb. 8, 1729; remained probably in Mass., and d. Nov. 30, 1798, aged ab. 70. 5, James, b. March 4, 1731, d. Feb. 13, 1756. 6, David, Esq., physician, and surveyor, b. June 9, 1733; mar. 1st, Hannah Thorp at Dedham, 1761, by Rev. Thomas Balch; settled in St. Georges, now Th., m. 2d, to Zibiah Partridge, June 6, 1782, by Mason Wheaton, Esq.; & d. April 4, '22. a. ab. 89. 7, Sarah, b. April 6, 1735; m. it is presumed, and remained in Mass.; d. Jan. 28, 1817, a. ab. 82. 8 & 9, twins, b. Sept. 21, 1737, Samuel, d. Oct. 21, 1737, and John Brock, d. Sept. 23, 1737.

Atwood's ch. 1, James, (2d), m. r. & d. in Nova Scotia. 2, John, m. Hannah Fales, p. Sept. 15, 1786; r. Beech Woods, Th., but ret. and d. in Nova Scotia. 3, Samuel, b. ab. 1756; m. Mary McLean from Mass., r. Th., at Beechwoods, and d. Sept. 29, 1841.

Capt. Nathaniel's ch. 1, Elizabeth, b. at Norwich, Jan. 25, 1750; m. Simeon Daniels at Franklin or Holliston, where she died. 2, Nathaniel, (2d), b. at Norwich, Oct. 25, 1752; m. to Zilpah Robbins by Mason Wheaton, Esq., Dec. 1781; r. Th., and d. June 19, 1834, aged 82. 3, Sarah, b. at Pepperel, March 18, '55, m. 1st, Elisha Partridge, 2d, James Stackpole; r. Th., and d. Nov. 19, 1834. 4, James, b. at Providence, R. I., Aug. 21 ,57; m. Deidamia Jenks, p. July 27, '86; r. Th., and d. April 13, 1842. 5, Rhoda, b. at Norwich, March 27, '60; m. Oliver Smith; r. Th., a tailoress, supporting her ch. by her industry; & d. June 2, 1839. 6, Hannah, b. at Norwich, Oct. 2, '62; m. John Fales, r. Th. and Nova Scotia. 7, Capt. David, Jr., b. at Norwich, Dec. 23, 1764; m. by Rev. Joseph Eckley, to Abigail Webb of Boston, Aug. 14, 1788; r. Th., and d. Sept. 6, 1845. The mother was b. at Norwich, Sept. 14, 1726; r. and d. Th.

David Esq.'s ch. by 1st wife. 1, Peronella, b. March 9, 1762, and d. June 24, 1764. 2, Willard, b. May 31, '63, d. July 7, '64. 3, Cynthia, b. July 27, '64, d. Dec. 24, '94. 4, Melinda, b. Dec. 26, '66; m. Dea. Perez Tilson, r. Th., & d. June 4, 1820. 5, Leonard, b. June 10, '68; m. Nancy James of Warren, Aug. 26, '90; r. Th., a constable, sheriff, &c., and d. Nov. 18, 1826. 6, Willard, b. Dec. 4, 1769; m. Harriet Webb of Warren, Aug. 21, 1800; r. Th., and d. Oct. 15, 1853. 7, Atwood, (2d), b. Feb. 10, 1772, d. Sept. 28, 1794. 8, Capt. William, b. July 30, 1773; m. Anna Woodcock, p. Dec. 13, 1798, r. Th., a seaman, and d. Oct. 12, 1826. 9, Peronella, b. Feb. 17, '75; m. Marlborough Conant; r. Th., and d. Aug. 13, 1816. 10, David S., Esq., b. May 12, '76; m. Mrs. Sally Bryant, March 8, 1807; r. Th. and d. March 5, 1846. 11, Hannah, b. June 15, '77, d. March 1, '81, of throat distemper. 12, Oliver, b. Nov. 17, '78; m. Mary Spear, Dec. 14, 1817; r. Rock., a merchant from 1807, and d. Dec. 10, 1858. Hannah, the mother, was b. Oct. 17, 1739, at Dedham, and d. July 11, '79, in the 40th year of her age. By 2d wife. 13, Asa, b. April 16, '83; m. 1st, Elizabeth Battle, Jan. 6, 1814, rem. to Strong; m. again, and d. Dec. 29, 1827. 14, Hannah, b. May 23, '85; d. suddenly of the disease then called *angina pectoris*, Sept. 18, '31. 15, Eusebius, b. June 24, '86; m. Sarah E. Haskell, June 15, 1826; and d. suddenly while at work in his garden, of the same disease as his sister, May 7, 1831. 16, Elisha, b. March 15, '88; m. Polly Lynn Gilchrist of St. George, Dec. 13, 1810; r. Th., and d. May 27, '63. 17, Elizabeth, b. Feb. 7, 1790; m. Col. Benjamin S. Dean; r. Bangor, and d. Dec. 12, 1857. 18, George, b. Dec. 1, '91; m. Mary Crouch, Sept. 3, 1815; r. Th., and d. Dec. 10, 1835. 19, Susanna, b. July 15, '93; r. Th., and d. June 4, 1844. 20, Cynthia, b. March 2, '95; m. 1st, Wm. Spalding, 2d, John M. Foster, of Bangor, Oct. 28, 1844; and d. July 5, 1855. 21, Julia, b. Nov. 22, '97; m. Whiting Hawes of Union, April 20, 1842; and d. Dec. 5, '63. 22, Thomas, b. May 14, '99, d. March 20, 1818. 23, Miriam, b. Dec. 28, 1800; m. ——— Titcomb, r. Cincinnati, Ohio, and had dau. Miriam bap. here, Nov. 9, 1834. 24, Philip Atwood, b. Feb. 22, 1803; m. Sarah Spalding, Feb. 7, '24; r. S. Th., a farmer. 25, (adopted grandchild), Nancy, m. Capt. James M. Blackington; r. Th.

Third Generation, in Thomaston.

John's ch. 1, Rev. Reuben, b. ab. 1788; entered H. U., but did not grad. on account of ill-health; possessed a strong desire for a knowledge of the oriental languages and for travelling in the East, was a proficient in Greek and Hebrew, took deep interest in theological subjects, was at times a Universalist preacher, was some years at the head of a collegiate institution in Nova Scotia, was the author of "Perigrinus in his Childhood," an epic poem, published at Boston by Geo. W. Briggs, which reached a 3d edition in 1849, and which exhibits his early mental struggles against the doctrines of Calvinism, and, as he expresses it, the

"Brief outlines of the fortunes of his life,
From youth's fair morning, till his cherished hopes
Completely vanished, like the morning dews;
And these sole expectations now remained,—
To glide along unnoticed and unknown,
To make life's final exit unobserved;
And mingle, in oblivion, with the dust,
Without a speaking marble o'er his bed,
To show that Perigrinus ever lived."

His nervous sensibility was great, his eccentricities, at times, amounted to insanity, and he died at the Thomaston poor-house in the month of Feb., 1864. 2, Irene, m. Ira Hussey of Cam., p. Dec. 7, '05. 3, Betsey, m. in Nova Scotia. 4, Arvilla. 5, James, (3d), rem. Nova Scotia.

Samuel's ch. 1, Mary, b. May 1, 1798; m. Abner Dunton of Lincolnville, March 7, 1816. 2, Ebenezer, b. Sept. 12, 1800; m. Mary Perkins of Windsor, July 3, '34; r. Beech Woods, Th., a stone cutter, &c. 3, Samuel H., b. March 5, '03; m. Asenath Trask, '32; r. Beech Woods, Th., & d. Jan. 29, '51. 4, Elibeus, b. July 30, '05; m. Elizabeth Simmons of Wal., '29; r. Beech Woods, Th., & d. July 25, '53, a fortnight after his return from California. 5, Catharine, b. June 2, '07; m. William Hall, r. Boston; joined the Mormons, & died among them at Beaver Isle. 6, Allen, b. March 6, '10; went to sea & never returned. 7, Sophia, b. March 2, '12; r. Portland. 8, John, (2d), b. Sept. 9, '15; d. at sea. 9, Sylvester, b. June 9, '20, d. July 10, '45, killed instantly by explosion in lime quarry. The mother d. Dec. '55.

Nathaniel, (2d)'s ch. 1, Sarah, born April 6, 1783; m. Darius Brewster; r. Rock., and d. May 3, 1844. 2, Nathaniel, (3d), b. June 28, 1785; m. 1st, Nancy Robinson, July 17, 1806; 2d, Sarah (Crawford) Page of Warren, April 1, 1852; r. Beech Woods, a farmer, &c. 3, Lucy, b. Nov. 15, 1787; m. Simon Blood, Dec. 22, 1808; rem. & d. Lincolnville. 4, Nancy, b. March 31, 1790; m. Lewis Robbins of Union, Feb. 5, 1811; r. Linc. 5, Priscilla, b. Sept. 2, 1792, d. Feb. 26, 1800. 6, Lucinda, b. Nov. 30, 1794; m. Simeon Blood; r. Th. 7, Joanna, b. Dec. 12, 1797, d. Sept. 1, 1801. 8, Deborah R., b. Nov. 14, 1801; m. Joshua Richardson, May 15, 1819.

James's ch. 1, Beriah, d. young. 2, David J., d. young. 3, Beriah, m. Jesse Rice, Dec. 4, 1817; rem. Union River. 4, Marcus, d., aged 23 or 24 years.

Capt. David, jr.'s ch. 1 & 2, twins, b. Oct. 21, 1789; d. same day. 3, Edward, b. Nov. 21, '90; d. same month. 4, Barnabas, b. March 5, '92; m. 1st, July 23, 1818, Diadama, sister of E. Phinney, Esq., was for many years in his office, rem. & did business at Washington, D. C., thence to Havana where he m. 2d, Mrs. Mary Ann McArdel, April 13, 1831, whose coffee plantation at Camarioca, Cuba, he changed into a sugar plantation and managed till his death, Oct. 1, or 20, 1840. 5, Noyes, b. Jan. 16, '94; m. Lydia Fountain of St. Geo.; r. Th., a mariner, &c. 6, Nathan W., b. Jan. 28, '96; m. 1st, Mrs. Elizabeth Mayo, dau. of Charles B. Davis of Washington, D. C., June 3, 1823; 2d, Mrs. ———; r. Washington, D. C. 7, Harriet, b. Nov.

14, '97; m. Joseph L. Gilchrist, Sept. 25, 1816. 8, Mary Holmes, b. Oct. 19, '99; m. Otis Edgarton; r. Th. and d. July 17, '61. 9, Capt. Edward, b. Sept. 16, 1801; m. 1st, Sarah Parker, May 4, 1835; 2d, Mary Kendall, June 8, '47; r. Shirley, Mass., rem. California. 10 & 11, twins, b. Jan. 2, '04; David, (4th), d. young, and George Washington, who m. Jane A. Demuth, May 12, '33; r. Washington, D. C. 12, Lewis T., b. June 17, '05; m. Antoinette Washburn, June 5, '32; r. Washington, D. C. 13, William Holmes, b. —— 27, '07; m. Sarah Jenkins of Boston, Nov., 1834; rem. and d. in Ohio. 14, Louisa, b. May 10, '10; m. Robert L. Dodge; r. Brunswick.

Leonard's ch. 1, Capt. William James, b. at Warren, Oct. 6, 1791; m. Eliza Ayers of New Orleans, and a native of Chichester, Del.; r. Th., a ship master & owner. 2, Atwood, (2d), b. Jan. 15, '94; traded in Th., rem. and d. in Baltimore, Aug. 31, 1825. 3, Eliza T., b. Feb. 22, '96; m. Joseph Colson; r. New Orleans, and d. Feb. 19, 1862. 4, Capt. Edmund, b. June 28, '98; d. at Charleston, S. C., Aug. 11, 1824, of yellow fever. 5, David Thorp, b. Sept. 28, 1800; m. Eliza A. Bishop, 1829; r. a time in Lowell, ret. & r. Th. on the old place of his grandfather, Dr. D. Fales. 6, Almond, b. Jan. 6, '03; died in Charleston, S. C., Aug. 11, '24. 7, Oliver, (2d), b. Aug. 10, '05; m. Sarah Pendleton of Northport, p. Jan. 14, '34; r. Augusta, Me. 8, Nancy James, b. Nov. 8, or Dec. 5, '09; m. Hon. Edward Robinson; r. Th., and d. Oct. 23, or April 23, 1845. 9, Penelope G., b. March 31, '12; m. Hon. Edward Robinson; r. Th. 10, Capt. Arthur Mac., b. July 28, '14; m. Sarah Frank Robinson, Jan. 18, '49; r. Th., a shipmaster. 11, Ormond Leonard, b. Aug. 30, '19, d. Aug. 19, '22, by drowning. The mother died March 6, '43.

Willard's ch. 1, Willard, (2d), b. July 26, 1801, d. Sept. 1, '02. 2, Capt. Henry H., b. May 5, '03; m. Melia Butler, Aug. 26, '32; r. Th. & d. Oct. 18, '34. 3, Benjamin W., b. April 25, '05; m. Hannah T. McKellar of St. George, Sept. 24, '40. 4, Harriet W., b. March 24 '07; m. Ephraim Hall, (3d); r. Readfield; rem. Wayne. 5, Willard, (3d), b. April 18, '09; m. Margaret P. Washburn, p. June 26, '37; r. New York. 6, Josiah, b. March 4, 12; m. Roxanna Poland, p. Oct. 21, '48; r. Th., a carpenter. 7, John H., b. March 26, '17, d. May 18, '48. 8, Lydia W., b. March 21, '19; r. Th.

Capt. William's ch. 1, Charles, (natural or adopted,) b. Nov. 19, 1794; was a mariner, entered the U. S. Navy, became a gunner, and is supposed to have died in the service. 2, Hon. Beder, b. Sept. 14, '03; m. Nancy F. King, p. Aug. 4, '32; r. Th., Judge of Probate for Lincoln county, 1856, the first chosen by the people; magistrate, administrator, &c. 3, Hannah Thorp, b. June 24, '05; m. Ebenezer McIntyre; r. Warren. 4, Seba, b. Sept. 1, '07; r. Th., and d. April 19, '55. 5, Zibiah P., b. Aug. 9, '10; m. Josiah Sanborn of Belfast, ab. 1828; r. Belfast. 6, Avis, b. Sept. 10, '15; m. James H. Winslow; r. Th., and died Jan. 7, '44.

David S. Esq.'s ch. 1, Oscar, b. Nov. 25, 1807; r. California, unm. 2, Albert Cushing, b. Nov. 23, '09; m. Lucinda Gates, p. Nov. 18, '36; r. Th., a mason, &c. 3, Sarah V., b. Feb. 17, '12, d. Nov. 26, '27. 4, George David, b. Dec. 12, '14; rem. and d. at Martinez, Cal., Dec. 20, '54. 5, Capt. Orris, b. March 20, '17; m. Clementine B. Webb, June 27, '47; r. Martinez, Cal. 6, Lavinia S., b. April 4, '20; m. Charles G. Smith; r. California. 7, Mary Spencer, b. July 11, '24, d. Sept. 1, '25. 8, David T., (natural or adopted), m. Sarah A.

Palmer, Aug. 27, '35; rem. Illinois, and thence to Portland, Oregon, over the Rocky Mountains, where he was obliged to winter, suffering much and losing his cattle.

Oliver's ch. 1, Mary Thomas, b. Sept. 30, 1818; m. 1st, James Fogg, Esq., 2d, Dr. Hebbard of Boston or vicinity. 2, Oliver Bailey, b. Sept 9, '21; m. 1st, Maria L. Robinson, Sept. 11, '50; 2d, Emma A. Sprague, May 29, '57; r. Rock., a merchant, &c. 3, Edward S., b. Dec. 26, '30, d. Feb. 27, '38. 4, Julia Melinda, b. Feb. 17, '34; m. Dr. Herbert C. Bradford of Auburn, Me., Nov. 23, '57.

Asa's ch. 1, Capt. Washburn, b. Oct. 3, 1814; m. Rachel Gates, Feb. 25, '44; r. Th., and was lost at sea in 1860 on passage from New Orleans to Liverpool with his wife and child, his ship *St. Patrick*, and all on board. 2, Ann Eliza, b. in Strong, July 4, '17; m. 1st, Joseph Ulmer, 1837; 2d, Dr. J E. Hunt; r. Nashua, N. H. 3, Susan, m. William M. Sartelle; r. Rock. 4, David, (3d), Esq., m. in Augusta; r. and practises law in Saco.

Eusebius, (3d)'s ch. 1, Wyman Eusebius, b. July 19, 1830.

Elisha's ch. 1, Juliana, b. April 20, 1813; m. Col. George A. Starr; r. Th. and d. Aug. 13, '36. 2, Joseph, b. Nov. 17, 1814, d. out South, Jan 21, '48. 3, Elisha Partridge, b. Jan. 5, '17; m. Agnes Handley, March 27, 1844, r. Th. a mason, livery stable-keeper, &c. 4, Thomas, b. Nov. 8, 1818; m. Margaret Williams, March 11, '44. r. Th., and d. Aug. 28, '44. 5, Mitchell, b. July 7, '21; m. Martha H. Kelleran, Feb. 6, '50, d. Oct. 18, '51. 6, Benjamin D., b. June 17, '23, died at N. O., May 21, '48. 7, Lucy S., b. Jan. 14, '26, m. James Payson of Cushing, Jan. 5, '45. 8, Henry, b. Oct. 8, '28; m. Eliza J. White, Feb. 13, '53; r. Rock. 9, Almira H., b. March 21, '31; m. William M. Vanstone. 10, Augustus S., b. July 4, '33; m. Lucretia Jameson; r. Cushing, a merchant, post-master, &c. 11, Mary, b. Feb. 5, '36. The mother d. Nov. 13, '45, a. 49.

George's ch. 1, Capt. Ephraim C., b. July 1, 1816; m. Hannah M. Wyman of Brooklyn, 1853, & d. May 22, '57, at the Chincha Is. 2, Mary Ann, b. Oct. 13, '17; m. Thomas Rose; r. Th. 3, Capt. Wm., (2d), b. March 24, '19; m. Catharine W. Bennett, Sept. 20, '43; r. Th., in Government naval service. 4, George H., b. Oct. 18, '20; m. in N. O., r. Brooklyn, N. Y. 5, Emily J., b. Sept. 7, 22. 6, Cynthia, b. Sept. 27, '24; d. Oct. 18, '61. 7, Margaret H., b. Nov. 7, '26; m. Capt. Silas O. Pierce, of Rock., Oct. 3, '49. 8, Clementine C., born Sept. 13, '28; m. David R. Everett, of S. Th.; r. Brooklyn, N. Y. 9, Eliza A., b. Sept. 14, '30, d. Dec. 11, '35. 10, Sarah V., b. Nov. 4, '32; m. Cyrus P. Shaw, of Rock., Nov. 4, '51; r. S. Th. 11, Edmund, b. Sept 23, '35; r. Th., a mariner.

Philip Atwood's ch. 1, Charles Atwood, b. Sept. 30, 1824; m. Nancy Robinson, Jan. 9, '49; r. Rock., a mariner. 2, John Henniker, b. May 20, '26; drowned at New York, Aug. 16, '50. 3, Elizabeth D., b. Dec. 26, '29; m. Capt. Robert P. Guptill; r. Rock. 4, Hannah A., b. Feb. 18, '33; m. Warren Rowell; r. S. Th.

Fourth Generation.

Ebenezer's ch. 1, Leonard K. or, as recorded, Lermond H., b. Oct. 23, 1834; r. Th., a mariner, soldier of 1st Me. Cavalry, &c. 2, Sarah M., b. June 23, '36; m. Edward Carleton; r. Th. 3, Nelson S., b. May 5, '38; r. Th., a mariner, sergeant in 7th Me. Reg. 4, Fenelon M., b. Aug. 3, '40; a mariner, soldier of the 1st Me. Cavalry, killed in battle, at Charles City Court House, April, 1864. 5, John L., b.

Jan. 28, '43; r. Th., a painter, soldier in 1st Reg. D. C. Cavalry, &c. 6, Sylvester L., b. Jan 21, '45; r. Th., a soldier of the 21st Me. Reg., killed near Port Hudson, June 7, '63. 7, Elwyn H., b. Dec. 5, '48. 8, Laura E., b. July 12, '51. 9, Susan L., b. May 26, '56.

Samuel H.'s ch. 1, Sylvanus C., b. July 1, 1833, d. June 23, '35. 2, Emerson F., b. Oct. 11, '34; r. Th., a mason, soldier of 4th Me. Reg., &c. 3, Albert S., b. June 3, '36; r. Th., and d. Nov. 29, '45. 4, Cyrus V., b. Sept. 9, '37, died Sept. 4, '56. 5, Asenath Mary, b. April 7, '39; m. John Frank Clark, and d. Oct. 4, '56. 6, Elizabeth J., b. March 28, '40; m. Andrew J. Grant, March 20, '58. 7, Margaret C., b. Nov. 16, '41; r. Th. 9, Samuel W., b. ab. '43; r. Th., soldier of 4th Me. Reg., since in U. S. Navy. 9, Frances, b. ab. '45. 10, Alfred C., b. ab. '48; r. Th., entered U. S. Navy. 11, Sophronia W., b. March 28, '50, died Oct. 22, '62.

Elibeus's ch. 1, William H., b. June 21, 1829; m. Pamelia A. Oliver, July 25, '52; r. Th., an overseer in State Prison, and d. Dec. 7, '60. 2, Mary A., b. Feb. 7, 31; m. George G. Carter of Portland, Feb. 20, '50. 3, Lauriton G., b. Sept. 12, '32; r. Th., a carpenter, &c. 4, Adney A., b. June 1, '34; r. Th., a mariner, soldier in 2d Me. Battery. 5, Sarah E., b. April 13, '36. 6, Gilman W., b. June 9, '38; r. Th., a peddler, soldier in 35th Mass. Reg., &c. 7, Malvina B., b. Jan., 1842. The mother died April 22, '53.

Nathaniel, (3d)'s ch. by 1st wife. 1, Jane R., b. Sept. 13, 1806; m. Samuel Albee; studied medicine in Female Medical College, Boston, and prac. med. in Rock. 2, Alice R., b. June 28, '08; m. Seth Vose; r. Th., on homestead. 3, Nathaniel, (4th), b. June 18, '10; m. Mary P. Morse, p. June 21, '35; rem. California. 4, Rufus S., Esq., b. Dec. 26, '12; m. Julia A. Thompson in Lowell, 1838; r. Th., and d. June 25, '58. 5, Rebecca C., b. Nov. 2, '14; m. Capt. Wellman Spear; r. Rock. 6, Burton, b. July 10, '17; m. 1st, Sarah Mosman, Dec., '38; 2d, Maribah Ann Thurston, Dec. 7, '41, who died June 19, '48; 3d, Rachel D. Bisbee of War, Jan. 9, '49; rem. California. 7, Nancy, b. Aug. 25, '19; m. Moses H. Watts; r. Th. 8, Sophia A., b. April 26, '22; m. William E. Whitney. 9, Newell, b. Feb. 27, '25, d. Dec. 11, '47, at Charlestown, Mass.

Barnabas's ch. 1, A. Ann, b. April 30, 1819; m. John Damon of Charlestown, Mass. 2, Joseph, b. Jan. 22, and d. Aug. 6, '21. By 2d wife. 3, Charlotte, b. Feb. 22, '32. 4, Mary A., b. Nov. 7, '33. 5, David Henry, b. Feb. 16, '40.

Noyes's ch. 1, Edward, (2d), b. Aug. 4, 1818, d. March 20, '35. 2, Barnabas, (2d), b. Jan. 18, '20, d. abroad. 3, Otis E., b. Jan. 29, '22; m. Sarah E. Rivers, Sept. 21, '41; r. St. Geo. 4, Abigail A., b. Jan. 15, '24; m. ——— Haskell. 5, Antoinette, b. Dec. 20, '25, died Sept. 20, '26. 6, Nelson, b. Aug. 19, '27; m. Sarah G. Piper, Nov. 26, '48, and d. Nov. 14, '53, lost at sea from ship *R L. Gilchrist* on passage to New Orleans. 7, William P., b. May 20, '29, d. in Mexico. ? 8, Sophronia, b. May 27, '31, d. May 5, '37. 9, Helen M., b. Dec. 26, '33. 10 & 11, twins, b. Jan 23, '36; Clementine N., d. May 26, '42, Catharine, d. Feb. 10, '37. 12, Almeda, b. Sept. 15, '37, died April 30, '61. 13, Ann E., b. Jan. 15, '40; r. Th. 14, Mary T., b. March 21, '42.

Nathan W.'s ch. by 1st wife. 1, Charlotte L., b. Sept. 5, 1824, d. May 16, '33. 2, William Ryland, b. Sept. 10, '26. 3, Nathan, born April 15, '29. 4, Henry R., b. March 29, '32. 5, Mary V., b. June 29, '35.

Capt. Edward's ch. by 1st wife. Sarah Jane, b. Dec. 22, 1832.

Of Lewis T.'s ch. 1, Judson W., b. 1837, d. Oct. 16, '43. 2, Lewis M., b. 1842, d. Dec. 19, '43.

Of William Holmes's ch. Sarah, m. William L. Packard; r. Th.

David Thorp's ch. 1, Ann E., b. Oct. 6, 1831, d. March 14, '47. 2, Penelope J., b. Dec 21, '33, d. March 19, '51. 3, Ellen M., b. Sept. 19, '36, d. Jan. 20, '51. 4, Frances A., b. Jan. 20, '39, d. Sept. 18, '56. 5, Eveline A., b. Sept. 26, '41, d. Feb. 18, '54. 6, Emma, born May 3, '46; r. Th. The mother died Nov. 18, '48, in Lowell, Mass.

Capt. Arthur Mac.'s ch. 1, Annie James, b. Dec. 25, 1853. 2, Alida, b. Dec., 1858.

Benjamin W.'s ch. 1, Harriet W., b. May 31, 1841, died April '44. 2, Benjamin T., b. Feb. 12, '43.

Willard (3d)'s ch. 1, Mary J., b. April 30, 1838. 2, Eugene H., b. March 10, '40. 3, Grenville, b. Sept. 4, '41.

Josiah's ch. 1, Eliza J., b. ab. 1850. 2, Harriet, b. ab. 1851. 3, Charlotte, b. ab. '53. 4, Emily, b. ab. '59.

Hon. Beder's ch. 1, Ada, b. June 30, 1833; r. Th. 2, Oswyn, b. Sept. 8, '35, d. July 21, '58. 3, Jonathan Cilley, born Dec. 30, '36; grad. Waterville Coll., 1858; is a teacher, &c., at the South; m. Maggie A. Cleland, of Lebanon, Kentucky, Nov. 8, 1862. 4, Jane Singer, b. Feb. 15, '42, d. Dec. 18, '44. The mother d. Sept. 23, '62, a. 60.

Albert Cushing's ch. 1, Mary S., b. Oct. 15, 1837, d. Dec. 1, '55. 2, Orris H., b. April 13, '40; r. Th., a mariner, entered U. S. navy. 3, Sarah G., b. ab. '45. 4, Anna, b. ab. '51. 5, John, b. ab. '53.

Capt. Orris's ch. Nisida Stewart, b. in California, May 25, 1848.

Oliver B.'s ch. by 1st wife. 1, Mary A., b. April 9, 1852, d. April 23, '53. 2, Maria Louisa, b. Feb. 5, '54, d. May 3, '57. By 2d wife, 3, Albert Barnes, b. May 17, '60.

Capt. Washburn's ch. 1, Frederic, lost at sea, with his parents, in 1860. 2, Ann Maria. 3, John Gates.

Elisha P.'s ch. 1, Alice Virginia, b. Sept. 21, 1845. 2, Agnes Louisa, b. Dec. 29, '46.

Thomas's ch. Thomas J., b. July 19, 1840.

Augustus S.'s ch. 1, Joseph. 2, Elisha. 3, Alice. 4, ———.

Henry's ch. 1, Adelaide C., b. Dec. 4, 1854. 2, Mary H., b, Oct. 7, 1858.

Capt. William, (2d)'s ch. 1, Caroline A., b. about 1846. 2, Mary E., b. ab. '49. 3, Edward R., d. at N. Orleans, at the age of 10 yrs.

Charles Atwood's ch. Thomas C., b. ab. 1850.

Fifth Generation.

William H.'s ch. 1, Rosilla, b. April, 1854. 2, Abby A. born Jan. '55, d. July 14, '57. 3, Susan A., b. March '57.

Rufus S.'s ch. 1, Imogene E., b. Sept. 3, 1838, d. Nov. 12, '41. 2, Rufus Orlando, b. Jan. 12, '40; r. Th., sergeant in the 4th Me. reg., d. Nov., 1863, of starvation in a rebel prison at Richmond, Va. 3, Eugene, b. June 2, and d. Aug. 20, '42. 4, Imogene, b. ab. '45. 5, Eugene, b. ab. '47. 6, Nancy, b. ab. '51. 7, Anna D., b. ab. '53. 8, Fanny F., b. ab. '55.

Burton's ch. by 1st wife. 1, Burton A., b. April 25, 1840, d. June 11, '44. By 2d wife. 2, Nathaniel, (5th), r. California. 3, Sarah, r. Rock. 4, Mary A., r. Th. By 3d wife. 5, Newell, (2d), r. Warren. 6, Sophia, r. California.

FALES, James, b. Oct. 11, 1785, son of Eliphalet Fales;* (who was the son of James, (3d), of Dedham, Mass., who was the son of James, (2d), of Dedham, who was the son of James, (1st), of Walpole, who c. from Chester, England, as was before mentioned,) was one of the early settlers in what is now Rock., m. Sybil Robbins, Oct. 30, 1771; & d. Jan. 27, 1827; a. 81. Their ch. 1, Oliver, b. Aug. 22, 1772, d. Aug. 24, '74. 2, Lucy, b. July 3, '74; m. 1st, John Crockett of Bristol, p. Sept. 4, 1802, 2d, Ebenezer Thompson, rem. Hope. 3, Sabra, b. Oct. 28, '76; d. Sept. 16, 1800. 4, Abigail, b. Jan. 14, '79; r. Rock. 5, James, (3d), b. April 14, '81; m. Sarah Howland; r. Rock. 6, Polly, b. Oct. 28, '83, d. Sept. 23, '92. 7, Sybil, b. Feb. 16, '86, d. Sept. 26, '92. 8, Dea. Waterman, b. April 7, '92; m. Sybil Robbins; r. Rock., a farmer,* &c.

Dea. Waterman's ch. 1, Lysander, b. Jan. 21, 1822; m. Nancy R. Burton, Nov. 5, 1845; r. Rock., a truckman, &c. 2, Philander, b. March 21, '24; r. Rock., a mariner. 3, Philetus, b. May 7, '25; grad. Dartmouth Coll., 1849; is president of a college in St. Louis, Mo., where he m. and resides. 4, Oliver James, b. Feb. 29, '28, d. Jan. 6, '52. 5, Hannah, E., b. Nov. 21, '29. 6, Ariadne, b. Aug. 17, '31; r. Rock. 7, Francisco A., b. Dec. 9, '37; rem. California. 8, Orpheus, b. June 16, '45.

Lysander's ch. 1, Fernando S., b. Feb. 2, 1846. 2, Leonardo D., b. May 2, '48. 3, Ida G., b. May 3, '56.

Philetus's ch. 1, Frank L., b. in St. Louis, Sept. 23, '62, d. Oct. 13, '63.

FALES, Adrian C., b. ab. 1811, (name changed by act of Leg. 1841, from Adriel Cox); m. Catharine B. Ulmer; r. Rock., a farmer. Their ch. 1, Albert N., b. ab. 1843; r. Rock., entered U. S. navy. 2, Sarah C., b. ab. '45. 3, James H., b. ab. '47. 4, William, b. Dec. 5, 1852, d. Oct. 19, '58. 5, Charles, b. ab. '55.

FARLEY, William Jewett, Esq., b. in Waldoboro', ab. 1802, son of Hon. Joseph Farley, collector of customs; grad. Bowd. coll. 1820; m. 1st, Alice McKeen of Brunswick, p. May 10, 1826, 2d, Sarah E. Foster, Dec. 10, '29; c. to Th. 1825; a lawyer, and d. June 15, '39. His ch. by 2d wife. 1, John, 2, Alice McKeen, 3, Benjamin Emerson; all d. in infancy.

FARNHAM, David, b. May 16, 1804, c. from Lincolnville, m. Mary Richards; r. Rock., and d. Jan. 3, '62. Their ch. 1, Jeremiah W., b. ab. 1830, r. Rock., a mariner. 2, Anselm D., b. ab. 1832; m. Sarah M. Moore, 1854; r. Rock., a mariner. 3, Joseph M., b. ab. 36; r. Rock., a mariner. 4, James G., b. June, 1839. 5, Georgiana, b. ab. 1846.

Anselm D.'s ch. 1, Sarah A., b. ab. 1853. 2, Lucy Ardell, b. Dec., 1858, d. Oct. 18, '60.

FARNHAM, Capt. Andrew, m. Ann M. Ackley, Nov. 15, 1861; r. Rock, a master mariner.

---

* Dea. Fales enlisted in 1813, with some 15 others, under Lieut. Robbins, who, however, being promoted in the regular service, did not accompany them in their one year's campaign. They went from here to Portland with Ensign Farnsworth, and thence up the Lakes and on our northern frontier, where they had some sharp encounters with Indians and others in the woods. Of those fifteen, the following only, from the same village, are recollected by him, (but their names were not received in season for insertion at page 295, Vol. 1st), viz.: John Ham, James Watson, John Ulmer, Jonathan Spear, David Maker, and ——— Prime; many of them enlisting again or dying in the service.

FARNSWORTH, William A., b. in Waldoboro', ab. 1815, son of Capt. William & grandson of Col. William & Elizabeth (Rutherford) Farnsworth; m. Mary, dau. of William Sprague of Wal.; r. Rock., a merchant and business man. Their ch. 1, Josephine, b. ab. 1837. 2, Lucy, b. ab. '39. 3, James, b. ab. '41. 4, William S., b. 1849, d. Oct. 23, '56. 5, Fanny, b. ab. '53. 6, Joseph F., b. Dec. '57, d. Jan. 25, '63.

FARNSWORTH, Theodore H., of a different family, b. ab. 1817; m. Almira B. Marston; r. Rock., a mariner, soldier, &c. Their ch. 1, Caroline A., b. ab. '44. 2, George R., b. ab. '48. 3, Edgar T., b. ab. '51. 4, Emma U., b. ab. '53. 5, Frank W., b. ab. '55.

FARR, William C., (probably a son of Thomas Farr, who was in South Thomaston, m. Deborah Chapman, & d. early,) was b. ab. 1798; m. 1st. Eunice ———, 2d, Susan M. Paul, p. Sept. 4, 1853; r. S. Th., a farmer. His ch. by 1st wife. 1,? William C., (2d), b. ab. '36; r. S. Th., a mariner, soldier of 4th Me. reg., &c. 2, Caroline, b. ab. '38. 3, ———, b. July 18, '40, d. July 18, '42. 4, Rachel, d. April 21, '41. 5, Celeste, b. ab. '44. 6, Eunice, b. ab. '48. By 2d wife. 7, Ida, b. ab. '56. 8, a daughter, b. 1860, unnamed when census was taken.

FARRINGTON; of this Warren family there came here three brothers, sons of Abner, (2d), viz., 1, Percy L., b. ab. 1815; m. Mary Lermond of W., 2d, Susan E. Achorn, Sept. 7, '43; r. Rock., a carpenter, &c. 2, Silas b. ab. '18; m. Mary E. Ulmer, April 22, '43; r. Rock., a blacksmith. 3, Allen P., b. ab. '24; m. Lucinda Spear, Oct. 26, '45, 2d, Maria S. Ulmer, 3d, Margaret ———; r. Rock., a restaurateur, sergeant in 4th Me. reg.

Percy L.'s ch. by 2d wife. 1, Alden L., b. ab. 1844; r. Rock., a teamster, soldier of 2d Me. Battery, &c. 2, Charles P., b. ab. '48; r. Rock. 3, Eva E., b. ab. '51. 4, Ellis F., b. ab. '53. 5, Crosby W., b. ab. '55.

Silas's ch. 1, Jacob U., b. ab. 1844; r. Rock., a soldier of 2d Me. Battery. 2, George A., b. ab. '46. 3, Mary F., b. ab. '48.

Allen P.'s ch. 1, Hiram A., b. ab. 1849. 2, Ada M. b. ab. '51. 3, Florence E., b. ab. '54. 4, Eli P., b. ab. '56. 5, Mary A., b. ab. '58.

FARRIS, Robert, b. ab. 1836, mar. Amelia Boggs, of Union, Oct. '57; r. Rock., a shipwright. Their ch. 1, Henry, born about '59. 2, Ada, b. Feb. 17, and d. March 20, '62.

FARROW, William, Jr., b. ab. 1827 in Islesboro, Me.; m. Marcia O. Spear; r. Rock., a sailmaker. Their ch. Cora E., b. ab. '52.

FARWELL, Henry, (son of Josiah and Lydia (Farnsworth) Farwell, of Charlestown, No. 4, N. H.) came to Winslow, Me., (where his elder brother and parents had before settled but had returned after six months), m. 1st, Ann Pattee, 2d, Margaret Pattee; rem. Unity in the then wilderness, where he took up a tract of land and built mills. His ch. by 1st wife. 1, Lydia, mar. Joseph Rich, of Thorndike. 2, Josiah, m. Susan Storer, of Lisbon. 3, Betsey, m. Sam'l Cates, of Thorndike, 2d, Levi Dyer, of Unity. 4, Ebenezer, m. Relief Gullifer, of Vassalboro'. 5, Antiope, m. Daniel McManners of Unity. 6, Oliver, m. Nancy Barker of Montville, r. and d. in Unity. 7, Henry, mar. Louisa Wright of Jackson; came to Rock. and d. in 1840. 8, Margaret, m. John Woodsam of Searsmont. 9, d. an infant. By 2d wife. 10, Jewett, m. Harriet White, of Albion. 11, d. an infant. 12, Ann, c. and d. in Rock. 13, Hon. Nathan A., b. 1812; m. Jerusha G. Thomas, Dec. 10, '37; r. Rock., senator 1861, president of the senate from 1863 to 1864; and was, in 1864, appointed U. S. senator to fill the vacancy caused by Hon. William Pitt Fessenden's resignation. 14, Hon. Moses Willard,* b. June 4, 1814; m. Eliza White, of Albion, 2d, Mary E. Daniels, of U., r. Rockland, Judge of Municipal Court, &c. 15, Hon. Joseph, b. 1816; m. Abby A. R. Spofford, Mar. 8, 1844, 2d, Mrs. Samantha O. (Sylvester) Crockett, May 9, '57; r. Rock., senator 1853, high Sheriff April, 1854, councillor, '64, &c. 16, William, d. unm. 17, Eliza T., b. 1820; m. Charles R. Mallard, r. R. and d. Feb. 7, '64. 18, Thomas R., d. unm. 19, Charles A., m. Matty Blair, of Spring Hill, Alabama; r. Lumpkin, Ga. 20, Louisa, V., mar. Amos Muzzy, of Unity. 21, Deborah A., mar. Richard A. Milliken, of N. Orleans, Oct. 6, 1864.

Of Oliver's ch., his only son, Freeman B., b. in Unity ab. 1828; m. Mary W. Pressey, Sept. 6, 1850; r. Rock., a grocer, &c.

Henry's ch. 1, Cornelia L., m. Charles Brown of Belfast; rem. California. 2, Wealthy W., d. young. 3, Capt. Henry M.

Hon. Nathan A.'s ch. 1, Mary E., b. June 28, 1837, died Feb. 23, '38. 2, Clara A., b. Jan. 18, '39. 3, Annie E., b. July 16, '41. 4, Fannie E. 5, Lucy M. 6, Marcia W. 7, Nathan T. 8, Jessie Benton, b. Feb. '56, d. Jan. '57. 9, Jennie B., d. young. 10, Charles, b. '59, d. July 12, '61.

Hon. Moses W.'s ch. 1, Thomas R., b. Jan. 7, 1835, died Nov. 9, '54. 2, Celinda, b. Nov., '36, d. May 31, '54. 3, Eliza, died young. 4, Gracia A., d. Oct. 24, '56. 5, Oaks A., d. young. 6, Helen A., b. 1842.

Hon. Joseph's ch. by 1st wife. 1, Lieut. William S. b. March 16, 1845; r. Rockland, officer in Capt. Chase's company of D. C. cavalry. 2, Joseph Henry, b. Dec. 17, '46, d. Jan. 12, '54.

FAYER, George, c. with Mary his wife from Ireland to Th., but rem. Illinois, his wife having d. in Th., Dec. 14, 1842. Their ch. James, b. Nov. 21, 1841.

FEELEY, Terance, b. in North of Ireland ab. 1810; m. Alice

---

* This gentleman, who with his brothers has attained to so many offices of trust, writes to the compiler that "we, the Farwell boys, had no advantages, only a common country school education, of from six to twelve weeks in a year; we had to haul the wood, cut it, and take care of a large stock of cattle, and, at the same time, travel more than a mile to school over the coldest of all hills to the old log school-house with its rock chimney where the schools were, for the most part. kept. We commenced the world without a cent I was married when but nineteen, without a cent in my pocket or a home to go to. This, (1864), is my sixteenth year that I have been steamboat agent; for 14 years I was agent of about all the boats that ran on these waters; a part of the time I had 18 boats a week,—they have been in here every hour in the night and day, and I never was sick, away from home, or caught napping, so but what I was on the wharf to meet them. I have collected more than $100,000 for the boats; — can tell every cent I ever collected, who I collected it of, who I paid it to, and what I paid for all the freight that ever came or went to and from here and to whom consigned. I have not wet my lips with anything stronger than coffee for 42 years. And now at 50 years of age. I have enough to eat, drink and to wear, and I thank Heaven for it. I will now make a prophecy: I expect to live to see this rebellion put down, the shackles struck from every slave on the American continent, the public debt and interest all paid, and these United States to contain 100,000,000 of people."

McLune; r. Th., a laborer. Matthew, a brother, also c. to, r. and d. Th., where Ellen, his widow, r. still.

Terance's ch. 1, Mary, b. ab. 1848. 2, Nancy, b. ab. '50.

Matthew's ch. 1, James, b. ab. 1853. 2, Mary, b. ab. 1854. 3, Matthew, b. ab. '56.

FERNALD, Chase, b. June 24, 1801, in Loudon, N. H.; c. to Th. Oct. 8, 1822; m. by H. Knox, Esq., to Nancy Benner, Nov. 19, '27; r. Th., a carpenter. Their ch. 1, Roxana B., b. Sept. 8, 1828; m. 1st, Gideon Young, and 2d, Charles P. Lenfest; r. Th. 2, Frances Sarah, b. April 13, '30; m. Nicholas H. Lenfest; r. Th. 3, George S., b. April 17, 1835; r. Th., a carpenter. 4, Ambrose S., b. April 15, '38, d. Sept. 4, '39. 5, Augusta C., b. May 24, '42. 6, Enoch C., b. May 25, '45.

FERNALD, Rev. Oliver Jordan, b. in Boston, Nov., 1822; studied at H. U., and grad. at Cambridge The. School, 1847; ord. pastor of Unitarian church in Th., 1848; m. Susan M. B. Ludwig, April 30, '49; built the house on Main St., where his family now reside; and d. May 8, '61. Their ch. 1, William L., b. Feb. 24, 1850. 2, Minnie, b. '52. 3, Margaret, b. '54. 4, Mary, b. '56. 5, Susan, b. ab. '58.

FERNALD, James, b. May 25, 1797; m. Sarah Calderwood; was a merchant at Vinalhaven; rem. late in life to Rock., and d. Oct. 20, 1861. Of their ch. 1, Emeline F., b. July 27, 1836; m. Wm. H. Glover; r. Rock., and d. Feb. 4, '61.

FERRAND; of this family two brothers c. from Sandy River, ab. 1826; viz: 1, Franklin, b. Sept. 16, 1802; m. Cordelia Austin, Nov. 27, 1828; r. Th., and d. very suddenly, July 26, '55. 2, Harrison, b. ab. 1806, c. here at the age of 20 yrs., m. Nancy Ingraham, p. March 5, '34, 2d, Orinda F. Ingraham, p. June 17, '37; r. Rock., a farmer.

Franklin's ch. 1, Aaron Austin, b. May 25, 1835; r. Th., a farmer, and soldier of 20th Me. Reg. 2, Olive Sophia, b. Jan. 1, '37; r. Th. 3, William F., b. Feb. 28, '39, d. Oct. 20, '43. 4, Harriet A., b. June 9, '41.

Harrison's ch. by 1st wife. 1, Susan, b. Feb. 28, and d. March 28, 1836. By 2d wife. 2, Susan I., b. Dec. 15, '38; m. Thomas W. Hix, (2d), r. Th. or Rock. 3, Gardner L., b. Jan. 16, '39; m. Helen Martin of U., Oct. 3, '63; r Rock, a mariner and soldier. 4, Harrison, (2d), b. Feb. 28, '42. 5, Nancy I., b. ab. '45. 6, William H., b. Sept. 24, '50, d. May 9, '61. 7, Eva E., b. Nov., 1854, d. Aug. 22, 1861.

FERRIN, Patrick, b. ab. 1814, in Ireland; m. Nancy Hanly; r. Th. Their ch. 1, Rose, b. ab. 1841. 2, Patrick, (2d), b. ab. 1848.

FESSENDEN, Rev. Samuel Clement, b. ab. 1815, son of Gen. Samuel Fessenden of Portland; grad. Bowdoin College, 1834, and Bangor The. Seminary, 1837; m. Mary A. G., daughter of Joshua & Marcia (Grosvenor) Abee of Bangor, p. Aug. 3, 1838; r. Rock., pastor of Congregational church of Rock. from 1838 to 1855, member of Congress from Sept., 1860 to 1862, &c. There also came hither three brothers, cousins to Hon. Samuel C., & sons of Ebenezer T. Fessenden of Fryeburg, Me., viz.: 1, Caleb P., b. in Fryeburg, ab. 1818; m. Abby A. Wiggin of Limerick, Me., April 1, '45; r. Rock., a druggist, &c. 2, Edward E., b. ab. 1820; r. Rock., a druggist. 3, William, b. ab. 1824, in Fryeburg; m. Mary Dunleve of Saco; r. Rock., an attorney at law, appointed paymaster of 4th Me. Reg., rem. Washington, D. C.

Hon. Samuel C.'s ch. 1, Margaret G. A., born Dec. 1, 1839. 2, Capt. Joshua A, born Feb. 15, '41, officer in Guenther's Battery, in Grant's army. 3, Eliza G., b. ab. '43. 4, Lucy W., b. ab. '45. 5, Samuel, b. ab. '47. 6, Mary E., b. ab. '49. 7, Deborah C., b. ab. '51. 8, Susan S., b. ab. '53. 9, Seth G., b. ab. '55. 10, Oliver G., b. ab. '56. 11, Abbie C., b. ab. '59.

William's ch. 1, Ina D., b. Nov., 1854, d. June 29, '58. 2, William C., b. 1860, d. young.

FEYLER, John, b. ab. 1800, in Waldoboro'; m. Elizabeth Palmer, April 11, '33; r. S. Th., a farmer. Their ch. 1, Augusta R., b. April 24, 1834. 2, James L., b. Feb. 8, '36; r. Th. 3, Palmer, b. Sept. 17, '39, d. Feb. 20, '42. 4, Caroline, b. '44. 5, Oscar L., b. July 16, '46, died of diphtheria, March 26, '63. 6, Helen I., b. Feb. 9, '51, died of diphtheria, April 4, '63.

FEYLER, Charles, born 1793, son of Charles of Waldoboro'; m. Catharine Neubert; came to W. from Washington, a farmer, rem. Th., and d. July 2, 1861. Their ch. 1, Michael, m. Sarah Chapman of Jefferson; r. Rock. 2, George L., b. ab. 1822; m. Lydia (Allen) Paul, Oct. 9, '53; r. Th., a soldier, &c., rem. Hope. 3, Mary C., b. ab. '30; m. Capt. David Oliver; r. Th. 4 & 5, twins, b. '33, William H., m. Lorinda Woodcock, Jan. 27, '56; r. Th., Godfrey J., m. Love Jane Kuhn, July 30, '59; r. Th. 6, Martha J., b. ab. '37.

Michael's ch. 1, Mary C. 2, Michael Aden. 3, Alice. 4, Carrie.

George's ch. 1, Charles H., b. ab. 1855. 2, James H., b. ab. '58. 3, George A., b. '60.

William H.'s ch. 1, Eben O., b. ab. 1857. 2, William O., b. '59. 3, Frazier Head, b. Aug. 20, '61.

FEYLER, Capt. John S., b. ab. 1832, son of John of Waldoboro'; m. Bertha E. Storer, June 29, '56; r. Th., a mariner. Their ch. Elizabeth, b. ab. 1857.

FIELDS, Isaac J., b. ab. 1818, in Waldoboro', m. Nancy Walsh; r. Rock., a quarryman. Charles, a brother, b. ab. 1826, m. Hannah Spalding, Aug. 5, '49; r. Rock., a lime burner; deceased.

Isaac J.'s ch. 1, Albert L., b. ab. 1845; r. Rock., a soldier in 2d Me. Cavalry. 2, Mary E., b. ab. '49. 3, Lewis b. ab. '52. 4, John, b. ab. '54. 5, Emma, b. ab. '56. 6, Theodore, b. '58.

Charles's ch. 1, Nancy I., b. ab. 1849. 2, Charles E, b. ab. '51. 3, John, b. ab. '53. 4, Catharine Georgiana, b. ab. '55. 5, Alfred W., b. ab. '57.

FILES; of this family, three brothers, (it is believed,) came to this place; viz., 1, Solomon S., b. ab. 1820; m. Adaline A. ——; r. Rock., a mason. 2, George W., b. ab. '22; m. Susan J. ——; r. Rock., a carpenter. 3, Thomas, b. ab. '27; m. Laura F. Johnson, Oct. 30, '54; r. Rock., a joiner.

Solomon S.'s ch. 1, Flora E., b. ab. 1848. 2, Ann M., b. ab. '52. 3, Gratia.

Thomas's ch. George T.

FISK, Galen, b. Oct. 16, 1810, (son of John Fisk of Camden, but who died in Readfield,) m. Sarah ——; r. S. Th. and d. Sept. 22, '59. Their ch. 1, Charles, b. ab. '36; m. Sarah McKellar, Feb. '59; r. S. Th., a butcher. 2, Amos, b. ab. '38; r. S. Th., a mariner, soldier of the 1st Me. Cavalry. 3, Lewis, b. ab. '40. 4, Irene, b. ab. '42; m. Capt. O. R. Perry; r. S. Th. 5, Olive, b. ab. '44. 6. George Franklin, b. ab. '46. 7, Merrill, b. ab. '49. 8, Laretta, b. ab. '52. 9, Emma, b. ab. '59.

FISK, Capt. Moses, b. ab. 1817. (son of Benjamin Fisk of Camden and cousin of Galen,) m. Harriet S. Ingraham, Jan. 23, '48; r. Rock., Their ch. 1, William H., b. ab '51. 2, Eva H., b. ab. '54. 3, Nancy I., b. ab. '56. 4, Caro S., b. ab. '58. 5, Hattie. b. ab. '59.

FISH, Capt. William, third son of Ebenezer and Deborah (Church) Fish of Duxbury, Mass.; m. Mary Sprague; followed coasting, purchased of John Crawford and removed with his family, in 1780, to the Fish farm, so called, in Waldoboro', Me. Their ch. I, Dea. Abel, b. 1772, was one of the first settlers of Hope, with wife and two children, (had 10 in all); m. 2d, Mrs. Sylvia Coombs, Dec. 26, 1841, 3d, Isabella (Hayden) Snow, March 26, '43; r, 12 years in S. Th. & d. July 12, '55. 2, Samuel, whose son, Joseph P., was b. 1800; c. from Wal.; m. Jane Young; r. Th., a wholesale and retail merchant in Rockland and Herring Gut, St. G. 3, Church, r. & d. unm. on the homestead, in Wal. 4, Sally, r. on the same homestead in Wal. 5, William, m. & r. Wal.

Of Dea. Abel's 10 ch. 1, Willis, m. & r. Hope, and his son, Joseph P., (2d), b. ab. 1826, m. Sarah M. Pendleton; r. Rock., a grocery merchant.

Joseph P.'s ch. 1, Joseph Wm., d. July 7, 1841. 2, Loretto, m. Charles W. Stimpson; r. Th. 3, H. Kendrick, b. ab. '35; r. Th.

Joseph P. (2d)'s ch. 1, Marion A., b. ab. 1851. 2, Willoughby G., b. ab. '54. 3, Albert M., b. ab. 57.

FISH, Joseph B., b. ab. 1832; m. Abby M. Ames of North Haven, p. April 19, '54; r. Rock., in 1860, a dry goods peddler. Their ch. 1, Lizzie. 2, Henry A.

FISH, Job, c. from Pembroke, Mass., with Lydia, his wife, in 1806, to r. in Th., where he had recorded, their ch. 1, Thomas, b. Oct. 31, 1806; Job, (2d), b. July 17, 1808; 3, Almira, b. March 26, 1810; but probably rem.

FITZGERALD; of the ch. of John, of Waldoboro' (see Annals of Warren) 1, John, m. Sarah Keating of Hope, in 1830; r. Warren, a tailor, rem. and d. Whitefield. 2, Andrew, m. Sarah Fuller, of W., r. Wal., a farmer. 3, Sophia, m. Philip Hanly, of Bristol; removed to & r. Thomaston.

John's ch. 1, George, d. by drowning at sea. 2, John, (2d), m. Ann Caroline ———, of Norfolk, Va., rem. California. 3, Francis, m. Sarah Hanly; r. Boston. 4, William, lately in U. S. employ at Fort Warren. 5, Edwin, b, ab. 1827; m. Francis Morton; r. Th., a carpenter. 6, Anastatia, r. Boston. 7, Lewis, in U. S. navy, or other Government employ.

Andrew's ch. 1, Elizabeth, m. Richard Flanagan; r. and d. Damariscotta. 2, Jane, m. William Morton; r. F. 3, Nancy, died young. 4, Andrew, (2d), d. young. 5, William, (2d), b. ab. 1822; m. Margaret Hanly, pub. Oct. 30, '48; r. Th. a wheel-wright. 6, Margaret, mar. Capt. William Parsons; r. Wal. 7, John, (3d), b. ab. 1825; m. Roxana Keating, of Searsmont, Oct. 1852; r. Th., a blacksmith, and d. Nov. 2, '62. 8, Andrew, (2d), d. young. 9, Sarah, m. David Williams; r. W. 10, Helen, m. Joseph Mathews, of W., r. Th., or Wal. 11, Lucretia, m. Charles Fogler; r. Wal.

Edwin's ch. 1, Mary, b. ab. 1854. 2, Sarah, b. ab. '56. 3, Grace. 4, George.

William, (2d's ch. 1, Sarah Elizabeth. 2, Mary Emma. 3, Wm. Dennis.

John, (3d)'s ch. 1, Francis Allen. 2, Edward K. 3, Elizabeth J.

FLAGG, Elizabeth, b. ab. 1798; r. Rock., a widow. Ch. 1, William H., b. ab. 1828; r. Rock., a lime burner. 2, Harriet A., b. ab. 1834, d. Aug. 18, '57.

FLANDERS, Albert A. b. ab. 1837; m. Mary A. Boyd, Aug. 3, '58; r. Rock., a mariner. Their ch. William, C., b. ab. '59.

FLANIGAN, James, b. about 1832, in Ireland, as was Mary his wife; r. Rock., a tailor. Their ch. Thomas, b. ab. 1859. Of this name also, Richard, r. Th., was sergeant in 21st Me. reg.

FLETCHER, Rev. Nathan C., b. in Newburyport, Mass., Nov. 1, 1810; was a Universalist minister at Rock, at Belfast, and other places; sup. school committee of Th. 9 years in succession; Bank commissioner in 1837; executive councillor, 1839 and '40; furnished rules and regulations for government of Insane Hospital, 1839; was auditor, &c. of Madawaska war accounts, 1840; appointed chaplain in U. S. navy, 1845; m. Lucy A. Prescott, of Monmouth, 1829; r. Camden. Their ch. 1, Eliza J., b. April 26, 1831; m. Capt. Wm. H. Thorndike; r. Rock. 2, Adelaide Ruggles, born Feb. 25, '33, in Lisbon, Me., r. Cam. 3, Edwin C., b. in Th., March 8, '35; m. A. Antoinette Pitcher, of Belfast, 1856; r. Cam. 4, Ann F., b. in Belfast, 1853.

FLETCHER, Bryan W., b. ab. 1829; m. Hannah R. Harden, Dec. 12, 1850; r. Rock., a joiner, and soldier of 4th Maine reg., killed in battle July 21, '61. Their ch. 1, Charles L., b. about '52. 2, Susan H., b. ab. '57. 3, Josiah, b. ab. '59.

FLEMING, Capt. Edward, b. ab. 1830, in England; m. Elizabeth A. Kenniston, Feb. 1851; r. Rock., lost at sea, as supposed, in 1862? his vessel having been last seen 12 miles from Thatcher's Is. Their ch. 1, Lauriette, b ab. 1851. 2, Mary Elonai, b. ab. '57, d. May, 1862. 3, Elizabeth A., b. ab. '59.

FLING, George F., b. Nov. 10, 1824, in Gardiner, Me.; m. Julia E. Russ, of Cam., 1849; r. Rock., a portrait painter, &c. Their ch. 1, Frances J., b. ab. '50. 2, Charles W., b. ab. '51. 3, Abby F., b. ab. '53. 4, George R., b. ab. '57.

FLINT; of this family, two brothers came early from Nobleboro', Me., to W. and thence to Th. 1, Dea. Benjamin, b. ab. 1785; m. Elizabeth Kinsman; r. Th., a caulker at first, afterwards one of the firm of Chapman, Flint & Co., rem. & r. Brooklyn, N. Y. His wife d. Sept. 9, '42, aged 57. 2, William, b. ab. 1788; m. Fanny Clapp; r. Th., a caulker, rem. Rockland about 1836.

Dea. Benjamin's ch. 1, (sister's son, adopted), Benjamin, jr., b. ab. 1825; m. 1st, Sarah Tobey of Portland, who d. Dec. 8, '53; 2d, Frances E. Scrivener of Topsham, Sept. 14, '56; r. Th. & New York, merchant, shipbuilder, &c., firm of Chapman, Flint & Co.

William's ch. 1, William, (2d), b. ab. 1816; m. Lucy Healey, Aug. 22, '34; r. Th., a merchant. 2, Priscilla, m. John Kirkpatrick; r. Rock. 3, Zaetta Z., m. Capt. Andrew Pressy, 1837; r. Rock. 4, Joseph G., b. May 26, '20, d. June 3, '21. 5, Harriet N. W., b. Sept. 4, '22; m. James F. Tarbox; r. Th. 6, John E., b. April 4, '26; m.

Emeline D. Holmes, Sept. 19, '47; r. Rock., a shop-keeper, and died May 30, '60, from injuries, by being stabbed, 3 days before. 7, Nathaniel C., b. ab. 1828; m. Olivia N. Spear, May 13, '50; r. Rock., rem. California, a caulker. 8, Joseph Henry, b. ab. '30; m. Ruxby M. Robinson of W., May 22, '53; r. Rock. 9, Samuel P., b. Dec. 27, '32; d. by drowning, March 23, '38. 10, Mary Augusta; r. Rock.

William, (2d)'s ch. 1, William H., born June 1, 1835; m. Martha McCallum, Feb. 8, '58; r. Th., a caulker. 2, Augusta C., b. April 4, '37, d. Oct. 9, '58. 3, Samuel Brainard, b. March 6, '39; m. Caroline O. Demuth, May, '62; r. Th., a clerk in 1860. 4, Adelia, born April 4, '43. 5, Lucy A., b. Sept. 10, '45. 6, John, (2d), b. ab. '54. 7, Carrie, b. ab. '57.

Joseph H.'s ch. 1, Clara, b. Jan. 12, d. March 20, '55. 2, Julia V., b. July 13, '58, d. Dec. 19, '59. 3, ———. 4, ———. 5, ———. The mother d. Aug. 10, '64, her neck being broken by a fall down her chamber stairs.

FLINT, James H., (a nephew of Dea. Benjamin & William), m. Charlotte Hodgman; also came to Th. & d. May 5, 1854. Their ch. recorded here, but all probably rem. were,—1, Mary, b. Aug. 13, '25. 2, Louisa, b. Nov. 5, '27. 3, James, (2d), b. Nov. 8, '30. 4, Josephine, b. Feb. 25, '33. 5, Nancy, b. June 17, '35. 6, Leander, b. Oct. 22, '38, d. July 5, '42. 7, Jane, b. May 17, '41, d. July 24, '42.

FLINT, Thomas, b. ab. 1825, in Damariscotta, Me.; m. Nancy J. Hall; r. Rock., a caulker. Their ch. 1, Frank, b. ab. '57. 2, Carrie, b. ab. '59.

FLINTON, Capt. Thomas, b. in Scarboro', England; m. Harriet Marshall of St. G., Aug. 10, '34; r. Th., the Islands, &c. Their ch. recorded here. 1, Mary A., b. May 6, '37, p. to Augustus L. Gilchrist, Aug. 2, '58; and d. by drowning, Aug. 7, '58. 2, Ellen P., b. Oct. 22, '39; m. Joshua Thompson of F., Nov., 1861. 3, Henrietta, b. Aug. 7, '41; m. William Rice Davis, Oct. 24, '60; r. St. George.

FLOYD, John, b. ab. 1805, in Ireland, as was Lydia, his wife; r. Rock., a shoemaker. Their ch. Patrick, b. ab. 1850.

FLYE, Capt. Jerome B., b. ab. 1815, in Brooklin, Me., m. Laura Waterhouse; r. Rock., a ship carpenter. Capt. Daniel P., a brother, b. ab. 1822; m. 1st, Lucina Croxford, 2d, Ruth McLaughlin, April 27, '62; r. Rock.. a truckman.

Capt. Jerome B.'s ch. 1, Myron W., b. ab. 1844. 2, Shepherd L., b. ab. '48. 3, Evans H., b. about '50. 4, Jerome R., b. ab. '54.

Capt. Daniel P.'s ch. by 1st wife. William P., born 1858. The mother d. April 29, '61, aged 34.

FOGERTY, Samuel, b. 1794, son of Moses of St. George; m. Jane Watts of that place, c. to Th. prior to 1834, when he was road surveyor; d. March 13, 1848. Their ch. 1, Harriet N., m. Edmund Copeland; r. W., & d. Aug. 24, '64. 2, Clarissa, b. 1821, d. Jan. 16, '41. 3, Sarah J., b. Aug. 7, 1823; m. Alexander W. Brown; r. Th. 4, Charles Atwood, b. Dec., 1825, d. Feb. 16, '32. 5, Woodman, b. ab. 1831; r. Th., a seaman.

FOGERTY, John, b. ab. 1831, of the same St. George family, probably; m. Cornelia M. Remick, Nov. 15, '57; r. Rock., a blacksmith. Their ch. Louisa, b. ab. 1860.

FOGG, Rev. Samuel, b. March 9, 1787, in Raymond, N. H., r. S. Th., a while, with Charlotte, his wife, but rem. with their ch., recorded here, viz: 1, Samuel Dow, b in Readfield, March 5, 1818. 2, Catharine C , b. Th., July 18, '22. 3, Abigail, b. Jan. 25, '25.

FOGG; of this family, 2 brothers c. from Cornville, Me., viz.: Isaiah, m. Charlotte Hall; r. Th., rem. St. George, in 1842, and r. at Seal Harbor. Timothy, traded many years at Mill River, Th.; m. 1st, Mary Miller of W., Nov. 14, 1830, 2d, Catharine P. Robinson, p. Aug. 26, 1836; but rem. California, sailing from Th. in Nov., 1849, in brig *Perfect*.

Isaiah's ch. 1, Philena R., m. Capt. Eben A. Thorndike; r. S. Th. 2, Arabelle O., m. Capt. Frederic Thorndike; r. S. Th. 3, Jelison K., b. 1834, d. Oct. 31, '39. 4, Alvan K., b. April 13, '40; m. Emily L. Lewis; r. S. Th., & d. Feb. 22, '63; 5, Adriana, b. Nov., '41, d. April 26, '42. 6, Charlotte. 7, Georgiana, b. Oct., 1845, d. Feb. 25, '53. Perhaps others, and these noted may not be in proper order.

Timothy's ch. 1, Mary F., b. Aug. 18, 1831; m. Henry R. Green of Spencer, Mass., May 18, '53. 2, Margaret M., b. April 13, '33; m. and r. in Spencer. 3, Angelica D., b. March 2, and d. June 16, '35. By 2d wife. 4, Esther S., b. Dec. 25, '37; rem. California. 5, Catharine, b. Aug. 26, '39, d. Sept. 25, '40. 6, Richard W., b. Aug. 31, '41, d. Feb. 7, '42. 7, Shepley. 8, Lucian. 9, Lillian; all rem. 10, one other, b. in California.

FOGG, James, Esq., b. ab. 1815, in Berwick, Me., grad. Bowd. Coll., 1841; m. Mary T. Fales, March 30, '44; teacher of first High School in Rock.; stud. law with H. C. Lowell; was a popular lawyer, merchant in firm of Fogg & Fales; rem. 1846 to N. Y., where he was senior of the firm of Fogg & Brothers, and d. at Hudson, N. Y., Aug., 1855.

FOLSOM, Moses, c. from Cornish, Me., with his 1st wife, who d. here; m. 2d, Mrs. Betsey Morse, April 20, 1840; r. Th., but ret. to & d. in Cornish. His ch. by 2d wife. 1, Emily, b. April 21, 1842. The mother d. Sept. 6, '54, a. 33.

FORSYTH, E. W., with Sarah M., his wife, r. Rock., and lost by death their ch. Nellie, b. Jan. & d. Aug. 28, 1861.

FOSS, William B., b. 1819; m. Sophronia Joy; r. Rock., a mariner, & soldier, killed July 21, '61. Their ch. 1, Caroline, b. ab. 1858. 2, Susan, b. ab. '59.

FOSSETT, George, b. ab. 1815; c. from Union, Me.; m. Sarah Townsend, June, 1844; r. Rock. Their ch. 1, Stephen H., b. ab. 1845. 2, Margaret, b. ab. '47. 3, Sarah F., b. ab. '54. 4, George I., b. Sept. 28, '60, d. March 21, '61.

FOSTER, James O. L., Esq., b. ab. 1818, educated in Machias; m. Eveline Ingalls of Bethel, Me.; c. from Lewiston to R., not far from 1850, an attorney and counsellor at law; was some time in partnership with Mr. Lowell; and d. in N. Y., Jan. 15, or 22, 1855.

FOSTER, Stephen, b. ab. 1811; m. Abigail H. Crockett; r. S. Th., engaged in the fishery. Their ch. 1, Ellen, b. ab. 1845. 2, Stephen, (2d), b. ab. '46. 3 & 4, twins, b. ab. '50; Clarence & Clara. 5, Edgar, b. ab. '52. 6, Thomas C., b. '53, d. Oct. 20, '56.

FOSTER, Major Robert, son of Edward, did business in Amesbury, N. H., and Newburyport, Mass.; m. Maria, dau. of Col. Benjamin Emerson of Hampstead, N. H.; came to S. Union about 1812; purchased farm, mills, and kept for a time the only store in U.; rem. Th., where he r. and was in business some years, but rem. and d. at West Chester, Penn. His wife d. in Th., July 1, 1831, aged 54. Their ch. 1, Robert N., m. Sarah J. Marsh of Bath, June 3, 1824; r. as a merchant in Th., then in New York, & d. in Bloomfield, N. J. 2, Martha J., b. 1803, d. in Th., May 2, 1832. 3, Maria, r. in Bloomfield, N. J. 4, Sarah, m. William J. Farley, Esq.; rem. and r. West Chester. 5, Benjamin Emerson, d. in New York. 6, Edward, (3d), b. 1810, died Dec. 26, 1831, in Th. 7, Henry True, m. in Philadelphia, and r. in Beardstown, Ill. 8, Abner, m. and r. Beardstown, Ill. 9, Caroline D., bap. with the two preceding, April 6, 1828; m. Dr. —— Davis; r. Bloomfield, N. J.

Of Robert N.'s ch. 1, Robert, (2d), m. Alida P. Robinson, Oct. 15, 1853; a teacher, &c., r. Bloomfield, N. J. 2, Maria, m. Charles M. Davis of Bloomfield, Oct. 6, 1851.

FOSTER, Amos, b. 1787 or '86, ? in Gloucester, Mass.; m. 1st, Mary ———, who d. Sept. 7, 1850, aged 58; 2d, Mrs. Nancy Parkman of Cam., Oct. 9, 1853; r. Gleason St., Th., a shoemaker, and d. Sept. 20, '61. His ch. by 1st wife. 1, Mary E., b. Aug. 24, '11; m. Capt. Joseph Norris; r. Th., rem. St. Paul, Min. 2, Emily T., born Aug. 11, '15; m. George Gay, April 5, '43; r. Union. 3, Lucy J., b. May 25, '18; m. David B. Foster of Groveland, Mass, Oct. 9, '53. 4, Benjamin T., b. April 29, '21; m. Susan M. Harrington, Sept. 12, '47; r. Th., a farmer. 5, William A., b. April 11, '25; m. Harriet A. Spear, Dec. 24, '48; r. Rock., and died Nov. 29, '58.

Benjamin T.'s ch. 1, Emily, b. ab. 1850. 2, Clara, b. ab. '52. 3, Lucy, b. ab. '54. 4, Mary, b. ab. '57. 5, Frank, b. ab. '59.

William A.'s ch. 1, Addie W., b. ab. 1850. 2, Charles E, b. ab. 1856.

FOSTER, John W., b. ab. 1810, in Machias, Me.; m. 1st, Caroline Rackliff, July 12, 1840; 2d, Mrs. Maria Simonton, Nov. 7, 1847; r. Rock., a shop-keeper. His ch. by 1st wife. 1, Emily, b. Dec. 2, '40. By 2d wife. 2, Isaac I, b. ab. '49. 3, Freeman F., b. ab. '51.

FOUNTAIN, Jacob, b. ab. 1798, in St. George, Me., it is believed; m. 1st, Mary R., (who d. in April, 1836); 2d, Hepzibah Morse, July 2, '36; r. S. Th. His ch. by 1st wife. 1, ? Lorenzo, b. ab. 1827; m. Keturah ———; r. Th., a carpenter. 2, Hannah P., b. Jan. 13, '30; m. Matthew K. Davis of St G., Oct. 1, '53. 3, Mary A., b. March 8, 31. 4, Serg't William, b. March 19, '33; r. S. Th., mariner, soldier in 4th Me. Reg. By 2d wife. 5, Barney, d. Sept. 26, '37. 6, John F., b. Dec., 1838, d. at Fortress Monroe, Aug. 25, '62, lost overboard from sch. *Bengal*. 7, Jacob M., b. ab. 1846.

Lorenzo's ch. Nancy J., b. ab. 1859.

FREEMAN, Capt. Reuben, b. in Mt. Desert, Me.; m. Sophia Atherton; r. Rock., and was lost at sea. Their ch. 1, Julia S., b. ab. 1838; r. Rock. 2, Isabel, m. Capt. G. A. Bailey; r. Rock. 3, George A., b. ab. '44; r. Rock., a mariner, entered U. S. Navy. 4, Hilton, b. ab. '48; r. Rock..

FREEMAN, John, b. ab. 1831, in England; m. Eliza C. ——— of Nova Scotia; r. Rock. Their ch. 1, William K., b. ab. '55. 2, John H., b. ab. '59. 3, Anna B., b. July 14, and died Oct. 17, '63.

FREEMAN, Gilman S., (colored,) b. ab. 1832; m. Charlotte Smith, Aug. 24, 1855; r. Th.

FRENCH, Dr. Jacob K., b. in Andover, Mass., July, 1776; studied medicine with Dr. Jacob Kittredge of Brookfield, Mass.; came to Thomaston in 1803; m. Mary Jenks in '04; r. & practiced medicine in Th. & d. July 28, '49. Their ch. 1, Maria, b. Feb. 15, '05; m. Geo. W. French of Tewksbury, Mass.; rem. to Wisconsin. 2, Mary A., b. Sept. 13, '07; m. Levi W. Hopkins; r. Boston, & d. May 23, '63. 3, James, J., b. Dec. 12, '09, d. Sept. 20, '33. 4, Theodore, b. Dec. 5, '11; m. Louisa R. Ulrick of Portland, p. Oct. 13, '45; r. Th., a furniture dealer, &c. 5, Sarah, b. June 27, '15; m. Henry French; r. Tewksbury. 6, Dr. William Kittredge, b. June 10, '20; prac. med. in Warren, 1849 — 50, and went to Europe; now r. N. Y. 7, George W., Esq., b. Aug. 11, '23; studied law in office of Hon. J, Ruggles; m. Harriet T. Palmer of Rock., June 6, 1850; r. Th., an attorney at law, &c.

Theodore's ch. 1, John W., b. Nov. 8, 1846. 2, T. Porter, b. April 6, '47, d. Aug. 19, '49. 3, George E., b. April 7, '48. 4, Frederic O., b. Dec. 9, '50. 5, Ulrick, b. March 14, '52. 6, Franklin I., b. Jan. 1, '54, d. Oct. 14, '57. 7, Nella Celeste, b. July 29, '56, d. Oct. 27, '57. 8, Herbert M., b. Dec. 14, '58, d. Dec. 25, '60. 9, Milton H., b. June 29, '60.

FRENCH; of this family, three brothers came from Massachusetts to this place. 1, Jonathan M., b. ab. 1823; m. Mary Saunders; r. Rock. 2, Capt. James H., b. ab. '30; m. Mahala Hart of St. George, Oct. 26, '52; r. Rock. 3, Capt. Ezra F., m. Emma F. May, June 10, '63; r. Rock., where his wife d April 26, '64, aged 18.

Jonathan M.'s ch. 1, Sarah J., b. ab. 1848. 2, Charles M., b. ab. '52. 3, Leroy F., b. ab. '58.

Capt. James H.'s ch. James A., b. ab. 1857.

FROHOCK, Joseph, b. ab. 1814, in Lincolnville, Me.; m. Olive L. Calderwood; r. Rock. Their ch. 1, Mary S., b. ab. 1843. 2, Jos. E., b. ab. '45. 3, Olive R., b. ab. '47. 4, John R., b. ab. '48. 5, Nettie S., b. ab. '50. 6, Henry M., b. ab. '55.

FROST, Samuel P., b. ab. 1822, in Standish, Me.; m. Harriet S. Hooper, March 2, '52; r. Rock., a shoe merchant. Their ch. 1, Emma J., b. Dec. 5, '53. 2, Hattie, b. June 16, '61.

FRYE, James Lowell, m. Alice Nutter of N. H.; c. from Kittery to Prospect, and thence to North Haven. Their ch. 1, Joseph, went to sea, m. and remained in Europe. 2, Mary, m. ——— Lovis, 2d, Abner Cutler; rem. Illinois, and m. again. 3, Alice Maria, m. 1st, Thomas Pierce, 2d, Ephraim Perry; r. Rock. 4, James, m. Abigail Casper; r. Rock. 5, William, m. Betsey Ames; r. & d. Searsmont. 6, Sally, m. Samuel Ayers; r. & d. Camden. 7, Hannah, m. Lemuel Ames; r. Cam. 8, Dr. Thomas, b. 1814; grad. Waterville College, stud. med. with Dr. Potter of Waterville, and grad at N. Y. Med. University; practiced 3 years in Cherokee nation, Arkansas, &c.; m. Susan M. Arey of Frankfort, April, 1851; r. and prac. med. in Rock. since 1847.

Of James's 11 ch. there c. here. 1, Delia b. ab. 1821; m. Joshua Thomas; r. S. Th. 2, Lucy, m. Capt. David Ames; r. Rock.

William's ch. 1, Susan, m. George W. Birding; r. S. Th. 2, Amanda, m. William H. Post; r. Rock. 3, Joseph, m. Lydia A. Leistner, 1856; r. Washington, Me. 4, Ruth, m. George Post; r. Rock. 5, Eben A., b. Feb. 2?, '38; m. Lavinia Snowdeal; r. S. Th., a peddler, and died July 3, '63.

Dr. Thomas's ch. 1, Charles R., b. Nov. 7, 1852. 2, Samuel F., b. Dec. 13, '58, d. Sept. 17, '59. 3, Annie Frances, b. Oct. 27, '61.

FRYE, Wakefield G., Esq., son of Robie Frye of Montville, Me.; grad. Waterville, attorney & counsellor at law, Rock., editor of Gazette, &c.; m. Annie E. Arey of Frankfort, Oct. 25, '55; rem. Belfast, where he is Deputy Collector, &c.

FULLER, Jesse, b. 1748; m. Ruth, dau. of Kimball Prince; r. & d. Lincolnville, Me. Their ch. 1, Joshua, b. 1778; c. to Th. from Castine; appren. to joiner's trade, with H. Prince, 1794; m. Nancy Adams, at Owl's Head, p. Nov. 26, 1808; r. S. Th., Castine, &c., and is now deceased. 2, Deborah. 3, Capt. Samuel, b. 1782; c. to Th., also learned joiner's trade; m. Nancy Coombs, p. July 9, 1806; in May, 1807, went to St. George, and traded in company with H. Prince, Esq.; ret. Th., traded at Mill River; followed coasting, r. a time in Boston, ret. Th., was dept. sheriff from 1815 to 1821, postmaster, 1st reg. of deeds in E. district, Lincoln Co., &c., and d. Nov. 4, 1846. 4, Jesse, d. young. 5, Noah; 6, Ruth; 7, John; 8, Rebecca; 9 & 10, Barnabas and Kimball; 11, Martha; 12, Sarah; 13, Jesse; whose marriages and places of residence have not been furnished the compiler.

Joshua's ch. 1, Nancy A., b. Dec. 16, 1809; m. Capt. Thomas McLellan; r. Th. and d. July 2, '42. 2, Joshua A., b. ab. 1811; m. 1st, Susan N. Robinson, Feb. 4, '41; 2d, Mrs. Joanna R. Foote of Boston, Dec. 5, '55. 3d, Harriet L. Rogers, 1860; r. Th., a merchant. 3, Adeline P., b. July 26, '13; d. in Th., Nov. 12, '40. 4, Abbott. 5, Silas M. 6, Thomas S. 7, Harriet N. 8, Rebecca. m. Chas. H. Averill, in Castine, Nov. 4, '45. 9, Ellen S.

Capt. Samuel's ch. 1, George W., b. May 23, and d. July 1, 1808. 2, Col. Sylvester H., b. Castine, Nov 19, '09; m. Amelia D. Holmes, April 8, '37; r. Th., kept tavern Rock. and Owl's Head; and d. Jan. 10, '55. 3, Asa C., b. March 8, '12; m., 1st, Mary J. Snow, July 5, '46, 2d, Ann B. Snow, Oct. 25, '57; r. Th., a trader. 4, Caroline S., b. Oct. 30, '14; m. Edwin Rose; r. a time in Wiscasset, ret. Th. 5, Nancy, b. Aug. 19, '16; m. Chas. N. Hopkins, March 31, '45; and d. by drowning, Sept., '60. 5, Sarah L., b. Dec. 3, '18; m. Capt. Jeremiah Murray, April 7, '42; r. Cal. 7, Mary S., b. March 18, '21, m. Capt. John T. Spofford; r. Rock. 8, Isabella B. P., b. June 20, '23, in Boston; m. Capt. William John Singer; d. in ship *Alice Counce* on passage from Melbourne to Callao, bur. in Th., July 20, '61. 9, Rev. Samuel A., b. July 10, '25; m. Susan E. Greenlaw of Knox, p. May 12, '55; artist, and Methodist minister. 10, Ruth J., b. Nov. 2, '27; music teacher, asst. register of deeds, and d. April 19, '50. 11, Abby B., b. March 4, '30; m. Levi B. Miller; r. Chelsea. 12, Jane G., b. Oct. 4, '42; m. Capt. William J. Singer; r. Th.

Joshua A.'s ch. 1, Ellen M., b. May & d. Sept. 26, '44. 2, George R., b. Sept. '46. 3, Frances R., b Oct., '47, d. Aug. 23, '48. 4, Susan A., b. Dec. '51, d. Jan. 1, '52. By 2d wife. 5, Jennie A., b. ab. '56.

Col. Sylvester H.'s ch. 1, Mary A., b. May 13, 1838; m. 1st, Capt. John L. Crocker, 2d, ——— Luce of Boston. 2, Charles H., b. Sept. 25, '39; rem. California. 3, Frances B., b. Jan. 31, '41; m. Judson Kelloch; r. Th. 4, Martha M.; r. Boston. 5, Caroline Rose; r. Boston.

Asa C.'s ch. 1, Jane C., b. ab. 1847. 2, Caroline, b. ab. '48. 3, Frederic G., b. ab. '50. 4, William F., b. ab. '52. 5, Nancy, b. April 17, '53. d. April 30, '56. 6, Julia A., b. ab. '55. 7, Lizzie J., b. ab. '57. By 2d wife. 8, Sylvester F., b. '60.

FULLER, William Oliver, b. ab. 1815, son of Peter Fuller, Esq., and Phebe (Dunbar) Fuller of Warren, Me., m. Bethia C. Snow.

Aug. 12, 1841; r. Rock., a merchant. His brother, Daniel D., b. ab. 1817, in W., m. Mary White, of Boston; r. Boston, a druggist, &c., rem. Rock. 1863.

William Oliver's ch. 1, Delia S., b. ab. 1842. 2, Martha C., b. ab. '44. 3, Ambrose C., b. ab. '46, was lost overboard from ship *Rochambeau*, Sept. 1861. 4, Mary, b. ab. '53. 5, William O., (2d), b. ab. '56.

Daniel D.'s ch. Mary W.

FULLER, Isaac, (2d), b. in Warren, Feb. 22, 1803, son of Isaac & Anna (Boggs) Fuller; m. 1st, Avis Cummings, 2d, Thankful Williams, March 18, 1849; r. Rock., a farmer. Their ch. 1, Amelia, b. ab 1841. 2, Ford, b. ab. '43. 3, Martha, b. ab. '50.

FULLER, James W., b. ab. 1818, m. Lavinia S. ———; r. Rock., a caulker, & rem. Their ch. 1, Sarah E., b. ab. 1845. 2, Lewis W., b. ab. '47. 3, Adelaide, b. ab. '49. 4, Abel M., b. ab. '51. 5, Alonzo A., b. ab. '53. 6, William C., b. ab. '56. 7, Arthur L., b. ab. '59.

FULLERTON, William, m. Jane McCobb, r. and died Cushing, at Fullerton's Point, near Broad Cove. Their ch. 1, Mary, b. Oct. 29, 1772; m. 1st, Faithful Singer, 2d, Samuel Hawthorn of Cushing, Oct 31, 1815; and d. at Thomaston, Nov. 16, 1858. 2, William, (2d), m. ——— Montgomery, of Cushing, d. at Boothbay. 3, Jane, mar. Alexander Kelloch, of St George. Jane, the mother, m. 2d., James Carven, of Warren, rem. Burnham, Feb. 28, 1814; and since deceased.

FURBISH, Joseph, b. ab. 1813; m. 1st, Angelia M. Perry, Oct. 31, 1834, 2d, Louise A. Wight, of E. Medway, Jan. 12, '54; r. Rock., a stove merchant. His ch. by 1st wife. 1, Joseph H., b. Aug. 9, & d. Sept. 9, 1835. 2, Capt. Mauran P., b. Dec 18, '37; m. Annie M. Parsons, of Bangor, Sept. 12, '62; r. Rock., and d. Dec. 10, '64, perishing with all his crew, five in number, in the sch. *Lion*, wrecked at Simmon's Point, near Nahant, in a snow storm. 3, Capt. Frederic, b. Feb. 22, '38; r. Rock., entered U. S. navy, 1862, as master's mate, promoted to acting ensign, and d. at N. Orleans, of yellow fever, Oct. 26, '63. 4, Emma S. C., b. Sept. 22, '42; r. Rock. 5, Richard P., b. ab. '49. 6, Joseph, b. Oct. 15, and d. Dec. 19, '51. By 2d wife. 7, Clara L., b. ab. '59.

GABRILL, John, b. ab. 1809, in Washington county, Me.; m. 2d, Catharine Huntley, Feb. 21, 1855; r. Th., Beech Woods. His chil. according to census of 1860. 1, Martha, b. ab. 1847. 2, John, b. ab. 1853.

GALLOP, Benjamin A., b. 1796, in the State of N. York; m. 1st, Eunice Ulmer, Sept. 2, 1816, 2d, Eliza J. Fuller; r. old Th., removed U. and Illinois, but ret. and d. in Rock., April 20, 1846. His ch. by 1st wife. 1, Matthias, b. May 2, 1817, d. March 16, '29. 2, Catharine, b. Nov. 10, '19; m. 1st, Benjamin B. Palmer, 2d, Gorham Butler, of Union, and d. in W. 3, Elizabeth, b. June 3, '22, d. Sept. 9, '26. 4, Cordelia A. b. Feb. 28, '25; m. Wm. H. Blood; r. Th. 5, Susan, b. April 26, '27; m. Lewis Stevenson; r. Carthage, Ill. 6, Benjamin, b. ab, '30, d. '33. The mother d. Jan. 28, '36. By 2d wife. 7, Adaline A., b. 1837; d. in Th., Sept. 24, '63, from a broken leg and injuries received by being thrown from a carriage at Rock., July 4, '63. 8, Margaret J., b. '38, m. a Mr. Metcalf; r. Lowell, Mass. 9, Edwin C., b. July 28, '40; r. Searsmont. 10, Mary Helen, b. Feb. '42.

GAMBLE, Thomas, m. Margaret Scott, r. and d. in the north of Ireland. Of their ch. 1, Archibald, c. early to St. George's, and was the first settler on the Buckland farm in Warren; m. Isabella (Asbell) Galloway, r. and d. Warren, and was buried in old Pres. graveyard ab. 1779. 2, Mary, b. 1697; m. Wm. Starrett in Ireland, c. with first settlers to St. Georges; r. Warren, and d. April, 1783.

Archibald's ch. 1, Ann, (alias Nancy), b. in the old fort in Th., in 1743 or '4; m. John Mingerson of Boston; (who fled from that place at the commencement of the revolution and took up land in Warren, but ret., or went into the army, and d. about 1780,) spent her latter years in S. Th., and d. Feb 15, 1830. 2, Thomas, impressed and d. in the British navy. 3, Mary, b. at Lexington, Mass., whither her mother had gone for safety during her confinement, Wed. May 28, 1746; m. David Creighton; r. & d. in Th. 4, Robert, lost at sea in 1770. 5, Margaret, b. Aug. 12, 1751; m. Nathan Buckland, of W., Sept. 4, 1770; and d. March 20, 1839, a. 88. 6, Elizabeth, b. June 3, 1754, or according to D. Fales, Esq., in Th. records, June 11, 1755, at W., but according to an obituary in the Th. Recorder, in the old block-house, or Fort, whither the family had fled from an Indian alarm and where she remained till seven years old; m. Lieut. Joseph Coombs; and d. at S. Th., Dec. 29, 1845, aged, according to the same obituary, 90 yrs., 6 mos., and 7 days.

GAMMON, Daniel W., b. ab. 1823; r. Rock., a jewelry peddler in 1860, but rem. with Maria C., his wife, and ch., Rebecca C., b. ab. 1854; Caroline M., b. ab. '56; and George E., b. ab. '59.

GARDNER, Nathaniel, was in Old Th., and m. by Rev. E. Snow, to Eleanor Foster of Muscle Ridge Isls., Aug. 22, 1803. Their ch. recorded here. 1, William, b. June 3, 1804. 2, Nathaniel, (2d), b. Aug. 12, 1806.

GARDNER, Benjamin B., b. ab. 1833; m. Nancy F. Spear; Sept. 19, 1854; r. Rock., a teamster, soldier in 2d Me. Battery. Their ch. William B., b. ab. '58.

GARLAND, Rev. Jonathan M., m. Rebecca C. Jewell of Westport, 1862; r. S. Th., whilst laboring as a minister of the Methodist E. church.

GARVIN, or Gavin, William, b. ab. 1822 in Ireland; as was Mary, his wife; r. Rock., a carver. Their ch. 1, Mary, b. ab. 1852. 2, William, (2d), b. ab. '54. 3, John H., b. March, 1856, d. Sept. 11, '59.

GATES, Dea. John M., b. 1784; c. from Barre, Mass., to W.; m. Sarah Cobb, Aug. 21, 1808; r. a while on a lot of unimproved land at Greene, Me.; carried on the saddler's business, the clothing and grist mills at W.; was innkeeper a few years at Portland; resumed his trade in Th., where he was postmaster, &c, and d. Aug 19, 1854. Their ch. 1, Charity, b. Feb. 9, 1809; r. Th. 2, Horatio, b. at Greene, July 9, '11, d. at sea, March, 1832. 3, Capt. Barnabas C. b. Feb. 1, 1814; m. Eliza A. Bunker, Dec. 23, 1841; and d. at sea, between Gaudaloupe and N. O., Nov. 24, '52. 4, Lucinda, b. March 13, 1816; m. Albert Cushing Fales,; r. Th. 5, Capt. Miles, b. Aug. 13, 1818; m. at N. O, Nancy A. Hedrick, of Marietta, Ohio, Nov. 10, '55; r. Th., on homestead. 6, Rachel, b. June 30, 1820, m. Capt. Washburn Fales, and was lost at sea with him in 1860. 7, Sarah M., b. Jan. 18, 1831; r. Th.

Capt. Barnabas's ch. 1, Edward Y., b. Jan. 22, '44; r. Th., entered U. S. navy. 2, Sarah Ann W., b. Dec. 24, '45.

Capt. Miles's ch. 1, Francis M., b. ab. 1857. 2, Edmund C., b. ab '58.

GAY, David, b. in Attleboro', Mass., October 3, 1769; came to this place, 1790; m. Lucy Butler, Jan. 28, 1802; r. Rock., a merchant, &c. and d. March 19, 1855. Of his brothers, there c. to this vicinity, 1, Ephraim, who m. Sally Keen, Dec. 18, 1803; r. Rock. and Cam., d. without ch. 2, Asa, m. and r. Cam., rem. Ohio.

David's ch. 1, Alden, b. Oct. 31, 1802; m. 1st, Sarah Dean, Nov. 30, 1826, 2d, Eliza J. (Wormell) Long, May 31, '64; r. Th. 2, Hanson, b. July 1, '04, d. July 24, '36. 3, Oliver, b. Dec. 1, '06, d. Aug. 22, '28. 4, David, (2d), b. Jan. 4, '09; m. Ann, daughter of Nicholas Davis, of Belmont, pub. Aug. 28, '35; r. Th. 5, Fisher, b. Dec. 25, '10; m. Leonora D. Hewett, Jan. 8, '46; r. Rock., a gardener. 6, Henrietta B., b. Jan. 29, '13; m. Capt. Jere. Jameson; r. Rock. 7, William, b. June 6, '15; m. Eliza Jane Boyd, February 7, '47; r. Rock., a lime manufacturer. 8, Lucy, b. Dec. 31, '18; m. Samuel Rankin; r. Rock. 9, and 10, twins, b. Sept. 7, 21, Sarah, r. Rock., and Ephraim, m. Anna S. Case, Sept. 26, '46; r. Rock., a grocery merchant. 11, John S., b. Nov. 22, '25; mar. Thankful Perry of Gouldsboro'; r. Gouldsboro'.

Alden's ch. 1, Alden M., b. March 20, 1828, d. May 25, 1854. 2, Oliver, (2d), b. March 17, '29; m. Frances E. Spear, Sept. '51; r. Rock., a grocery merchant. 3, Alfred, b. July 21, '30; m. Frances I. Sweat, p. Sept. 22, '55; r. Th. 4, Sarah B., b. Feb. 9, '33; m. Robert J. Barrett; r. Th. 5, Gilman, b. July 2, '35; r. St. Albans, Vt. 6, William Freeman, b. Dec. 18, '36; m. Henrietta Stevens, Sept. 19, '58; r. Th., a soldier in 21st Me. reg., &c. 7, Henry N., b. March 2, '39; r. Th. 8, Lucy A., b. Jan 21, '40; r. Th. 9, Horace H., b. July 14 '42; r. Th., a soldier in 21st Me. reg., &c.

David, (2d)'s ch. Edwin, b. ab. 1837; r. Th.

Fisher's ch. 1, Ella F., b. ab. 1847. 2, Mary L., b. ab. '58.

William's ch. 1, Ann E., b. ab. 1847. 2, William H., b. ab. '49. 3, George, b. ab. '52.

Ephraim's ch. 1, Grace L., b. ab. 1848. 2, Albert C., b. ab. '51. 3, Isaac, b. ab, '53. 4, Minnie B., b. ab. '57.

Fourth Generation.

Oliver's ch. 1 & 2, both d. in infancy.

Alfred's ch. 1, Lizzie E., b. ab. 1857. 2, Cora E., b. ab. '59.

GAY, John C., b. ab. 1827; c. from Union; m. Martha H. Stinson, July, '50; r. Th., Their ch. 1, Alphonso, b. ab. '51. 2, Mary I., b. ab. '53. 3, Laura E., b. ab. '55. 4, Anna, b. ab. '57. 5, Joseph, b. ab. '60.

GAY, Mark, b. ab. 1800, of the Friendship family; m. Sarah M. Watts; r. Th., a truckman. Their ch. Jane E., b. ab. 1834.

GEER, David R, b. ab. 1820, in Connecticut; m. 1st, Ann E. ———, 2d, Lucy L. Kelloch, Oct. 1, 1853; r. S. Th., a stone cutter, &c. His ch. by 1st wife. 1, Eliza F., b. ab. 1847. 2, Maria E., b. ab. '49. 3, Edwin A., b. ab. '51. The mother d. March 28, 1852, a. 27. By 2d wife. 4, Henry F., b. ab. '53. 5, Mary Rose, b. Dec., 1854, died Nov. 22, '55. 6, James H., b. ab. '55. 7, Charles H., b. March 10, and d. Sept. 18, '56. 8, George L., b. ab. '57. 9, William H., b. ab. '59. 10, Eva Jane, b. Oct. 6, and d. Nov. 13, '61.

GIOFRAY, Joseph L., b. ab. 1823, in Italy; c. hither, m. Susan

A. Drinkwater, p. Oct. 24, '50; r. Rock., a barber and hair dresser. Their ch. 1, Edward Leo, b. Oct. 7, 1853 and died June 17, '58. 2, Nathan C., b. Nov. 6, '57, d. May 2, '58. 3, Emma F., b. ab. '59.

GERMAINE, Dr. Charles N., b. in Boston, Mass., 1825; M. D. Harvard University, 1850; the same year admitted Fellow of Mass. Medical Society; came in 1853 to Rock. and immediately entered into practice as a physician; has filled many important offices, and ranks high, in the Masonic order; was, in 1862, appointed Examining Surgeon of drafted men for Knox county, and 1863, Examining Surgeon for the State, of applicants for pensions; m. in 1853, Mary J. Barker, a native of Hartford, Ct., favorably known for her zeal in the cause of the suffering soldier. Their ch. 1, Julia Blanche B., b. 1855, d. Jan. 9, '57. 2, Charles I., b. March, 1856, d. Jan. 20, '57. 3, Oliver W. H., b. Jan., 1858, died Aug. 13, '59.

GERRY, Seth S., b. ab. 1822, in Robbinston, Me.; c. to Th., m. Olivia M. Felt of Robbinston, June 30, 1851; r. Th., a ship builder. Their ch. 1, Charles, b. ab. 1853. 2, Catharine, b. ab. '57. 3, George, b. ab. '59.

GERRY, Richard C., b. ab. 1820; r. in 1860, in Rock., with Catharine C., his wife. Their ch. Olive M., b. ab. 1854.

GERRY, Michael, b. ab. 1820, in Ireland, as was Catharine, his wife; r. Rock. Their ch. 1, Thomas, b. ab. 1852. 2, William, b. ab. '55.

GETCHELL, Capt. Josiah, b. ab. 1796, in Brunswick, Me.; m. 1st, Achsah Randall, p. Oct. 27, 1820; 2d, Mrs. Caroline F. Emery of Portland, p. Jan. 5, 1827; r. Rock., a shop-keeper. His ch. by 1st wife. 1, Sarah E., b. March 11, '22; m. John Clark of Owl's Head. 2, a daughter, d. Aug. 1, 1826, aged 11 mos. By 2d wife. 3, Caroline H., b. Nov. 6, '27; m. Capt. Ira B. Ellems; r. Rock. 4, Sylvia, b. May 6, '29; m. Henry E. Ingraham; r. Rock. 5, Mary E., b. Oct. 6, '31; m. George W. Butler; r. California. 6, Josiah D., b. April 9, '34; left Rock. ab. 1852, went to Canton, China, has not been heard from since. 7, Ann, b. Dec. 7, '36, d. Nov. 11, '55. 8, Josephine, b. July 4, '40.

GETCHELL; of this family there were also in Rock., in 1850, J. W. & Sarah S. Getchell, who lost by death their ch. 1, Washington, b. March, 1830, d. at Havana, July 27, '50. 2, Marcus F., b. June, 1844, died Sept. 2, '49.

GHENTNER, George W., b. Feb. 8, 1814; r. Rock. with Sarah, his wife, & d. July 19, 1861. Their ch. Eugene M., b. ab. 1843.

GILCHRIST, Samuel, m. Hannah Robinson; went into the army and was wounded in a skirmish, at Harlem, during Washington's retreat from N. Y., the British ball remaining in his side to the day of his death; r. and d. St. George. An uncle, it is believed, of Samuel, r. in early times on the McLean or Andrews farm in W.

Samuel's ch. 1, Capt. John, m. Margaret Fogerty, Jan. 30, 1800; r. St. George. 2, William, b. Aug. 1780; m. Betsey Norwood; r. Montville, and d. 1860. 3, Capt. Joseph, b. in Cush., May 20, 1782; m. Sarah Carney, Jan. 6, 1803; c. to Th. Aug. 15, 1823, or '4; a wealthy retired mariner, and d. Sept. 7, 1864. 4, Hugh, m. 1st, Betsey Hall, 2d, Hannah Clemonds, in Knox, whither he rem. and m. a 3d time. 5, Samuel, (2d), m. Lydia Smalley; r. St. George. 6, Archibald, d. young. 7, James, m. Deborah Robinson; r. Cushing. 8, Alexander, m. 1st, Margaret Hyler, 2d, —— McKellar; r. & d. St. G.,

Aug. 8, '44. 9, Robert, m. Betsey Hall; r. St Geo. 10, Sarah, m. Jas. Linnekin; r. St. Geo., first house from Th. line. 11, George, m. Martha Linnekin; r. St. Geo.

Capt. Joseph's ch. 1, Mary, m. Lewis Spear of W, June 27, 1827. 2, Nancy, b. 1806, m. Capt, Samuel Creighton of W., and d. Oct., 1859, at Brooklyn, N. Y. 3, Harriet, b. ab. 1808; m. Caleb Levensaler; r. Th. 4, James, (2d), b. ab. 1811; m. Rebecca Kelleran; r. Th., a lumber dealer, &c. 2, Capt. Levi B., m. 1st, Catharine Webb, Nov. 23, 1843; 2d, Hortentia E. Harrington of Rock., Sept. 28, '51; r. Th., ship master and builder. 6, Eliza, m. Capt. Joseph S. Burgess of W.; r. N. Y. 7, Joseph, (2d), m. Martha Ann Vinal, Aug. 7,1842; lost at sea, April 28, '49, on passage from Havre to N. Y., 1st mate of ship *John Hancock*. 8, Capt. Raymond L., m. 1st, Harriet B. Jordan, May 30, 1853; 2d, Rebecca W. Jordan, Oct. 28, 1856; r. Th.

James's ch. 1, Samuel C., drowned in George's River, Aug. 7, 1858. 2, Augustus S., p. to Mary A. Flinton, Aug. 2, 1858, and perished with her and his brother by drowning, Aug. 7, 1858. 3, Faustina D., b. 1841; d. April 2, '62. 4, Winfield Scott, b. ab. 1843. 5, Charles H., b. ab. '49. 6, Ella R., b. ab. '52.

Capt. Levi B.'s ch. by 1st wife. 1, Webb Bliss, d. Sept. 29, '44. 2, Frederic Eugene, b. ab. 1847. By 2d wife. 3, Morisse Bliss, b. March 24, '53, d. Oct. 31, '54.

Joseph's ch. 1, Caleb Levensaler, b ab. 1843. 2, Mary Anna, b. ab. '46. 3, Adelia F., b. ab. '48.

Capt. Raymond B.'s ch. by 2d wife. Clarence.

GILCHRIST, Capt. Cornelius, of one of the St. George branches of the same family; m. 1st, Harriet N. Hall, Oct. 14, 1849, 2d, Mary Hart of St. George, Oct. 7, '54; r. S. Th.

GILLEY, Capt. Lewis W., b. ab. 1812, in Eden, Mt. Desert; m. an English lady; c, hither in 1849; r. Th. Their ch. 1, Mary A. b. ab. '39. 2, Adelaide, b. ab. '41. 3, Caroline, b. ab. '43; m. R. W. Burton, jr,. of Albany, N. Y., Nov. 15, '64. 4, Lewis, b. ab. '45. 5, William E. H., b. April, '47, d. May 9, '52. 6, Emma, b. ab. '51. 7, William, b. ab. '54. 8, Lowell, b. ab. '56, d. Jan. 1, '62.

GILMAN, Jeremiah, b. in Gilmanton, N. H., Oct. 14, 1804; c. to Th. in 1827; m. Jane (Robinson) Whitney, June 1, 1828; r. Beech Woods, Th., overseer of almshouse, &c. Their ch. 1, Jane A., b. Aug. 20, '29, d. Sept. 3, '30. 2, Col. Jeremiah H., b. Nov. 11, '31; grad. West Point Military Academy; m. in Gardiner, Kate Rogers of Bath, Nov. 3, '57; officer in the army. 3, Sophronia, b. Nov. 21, & d. Dec. 12, '33.

Col. Jeremiah H.'s ch. Howard K.

GINN, Jonathan C., b. ab. 1824; m Eliza ———; r. S. Th., engaged in fishery. Their ch. 1, Hiram Y., b. ab. '46. 2, Alonzo P. b. ab. '49. 3, Frances I., b. ab. '52. 4, Ann, b. ab. '54. 5, Rebecca, b. ab. '56. 6, Rebecca, b. ab. '59.

GITTIGAN, Patrick, b. ab. 1833, in Ireland, as was Nancy, his wife, in New Brunswick; r. Rock. Their ch. 1, Thomas, b. ab. '52. 2, John I., b. ab. '55. 3, Charles, b. ab. '57.

GLEASON, Col. John, b. July 22, 1746, in Framingham, Mass., where he was one of the selectmen; m. Anna Ames of Holliston; rem. to U. in May, 1805, & d. Sept. 20, '27. Their ch. b. in Framingham. 1, John, Esq., b, Mar. 31, 1771; c. to Th. in the employ of Gen. Knox; m. 1st, Mrs. Sarah Mitchell, a sister to Com. Samuel Tucker,

2d, Jane Paine, May 9, '27; was a surveyor, innkeeper, the first President of Thomaston Bank, &c., and died Nov. 25, '31. 2, Molly, b. July 27, 1773; m. 1st, Capt. Nathan Miles of Barrettstown, Sept. 21, 1801, 2d, Ebenezer Scott Young of Th. & d. June 16, '49. 3, Lydia, m. Joseph Morse, & d. in Union. 4, Micajah, m. Polly Cole of Sherburne; settled, as a clothier, in Union, & d. June 19, '23. 5, Calvin, m. Sally Rice of Natick, Mass.; c. to Union, '05, & d. '50. 6, Anna, m. Joshua Underwood of Holliston. 7, Rebecca, m. Jonathan Morse, & d. in Union, '41. 8, Olive, b. July 20, 1784; m. Micah Stone, & d. at Warren, March 1, '12. 9, Hitty, m. John Hemenway of Royalston, & rem. to Union. 10, Aaron, b. Feb. 17, 1791; came to Thomaston, a clothier, m. Rachel Metcalf of Hope, p. May 5, '18, & d. in Jay, Jan. 16, '19, his wife & only child having died Dec. 17, '18. [See Barry's Framingham and Sibley's Union.]

John, Esq.'s ch. 1, Henry K., b. Sept. 1, 1797; m. Ann Maria Hastings, Jan. 21, 1822; r. Th., & d. Jan. 11, '34. 2, John T., b. April 30, '01; m. Waity Ann Sleeper; r. Th. & N. Y., now collector of customs at Port Royal, S. C. 3, George W., b. Feb. 22, '04; m. Catharine Kuhn, Dec. 10, '27, 2d, Elizabeth Achorn, p. Nov. 2, '44; rem. to Waldoboro'. The mother died March 4, 1826, aged 63.

Henry K.'s ch. 1, Capt. John Henry, b. Dec. 6, 1823; m. Sarah L. Harrington of Rockland, Jan. 8, '57; r. Th., now in U. S. naval service. 2, Sarah Jane, b. Nov. 28, '27; m. Capt. William Hewes; r. Th. 3, Elizabeth C., b. Aug. 8, '33; r. Th.

George W.'s ch. 1, Sarah K., b. May 21, 1829; m. George Farnsworth, March, '49; r. Wal. & d. Nov. 19, '49. 2, George K., b. May 21, '31; m. Almira D. Morse of Appleton, p. May 20, '54; r. Th., soldier in 2d Me. Battery. 3, John K., b. July 21, '37, d. in Wal. Oct. 6, '53. 4, Victoria K., b. Sept. 16, '39, d. Aug. '40. 5, Mary K., b. Sept. 7, '42. The mother died June 16, '43, aged 38.

Capt. John Henry's ch. 1, Ann W., b. ab. 1859. 2, ———, d. Feb. 8, '62.

George K.'s ch. 1, Francisco, b. ab. 1855. 2, Florence, b. ab. '56.

GLOVER, Charles, b. ab. 1796, came probably from Vinalhaven; m. Almira W. Sayward, Sept. 27, 1821; r. Rock., a joiner, &c. Others of this name have probably r. here, as Lucy, widow of Thomas, died May 10, 1818, in 59th year of her age. Charles's ch. 1, George S., b. March 23, 1822, d. July 6, '45. 2, Susan S., born Oct. 9, '23, died March 15, '37. 3, Bethia, b. Oct. 2, '25; m. Capt. Alden T. Sherman; r. Rock. 4, Mary G., b. Dec. 20, '27; m. William B. Staples; r. Rock. 5, Capt. Thomas B., b. Dec. 18, '29; m. Elvira S. Wheeler, Nov. 8, '51; r. Rock., officer in 4th Me. reg,. &c. 6, Capt. Charles, (2d), b. Feb. 3, '33; m. Jerusha A. Stetson, Oct. 28, '54; r. Rock. 7, William H., b. Dec. 14, '34; m. 1st, Emeline Fernald, Aug 11, '59; 2d, Julia F. Fernald, Nov. 9, '62, r. Rock., a joiner. 8, Eliza T., b. Nov. 13, '36; m. Samuel L. Clark, Feb. 7, '54; r. Rock. 9, Edward K., b. Nov. 14, '39; mar. Sarah A. Fernald, April 14, '63; r. Rock., a joiner. 10, Lucy A., b. March 11, '42. 11, Abby A., b. Nov. '44, d. April, 1852.

Capt. Thomas B.'s ch. Francis, b. ab. 1852.

GLOYD, Col. David, b. 1766, m. 1st, Celia Smith, 2d, Susannah Reed; came from Abington, Mass., as a tanner; r. Th. & Rock., and d. Dec. 6, 1849. His ch. by 1st wife. 1, Celia, m. Elias Hunt, r. in the State of New York. 2, David, (2d), m. Mary Ripley, of Abington. By 2d wife. 3, Susanna, b. Dec. 25, 1796; m. James Walsh;

r. Rock., and d. April 12, 1858. 4, Spencer, m. Myra Nash; and d. at N. Orleans. 5, Sarah, m. Joseph Cleverly, r. Abington. 6, Mary, m. Joshua Allen; r. Th. 7, Capt. George W., b. ab. 1804; married Julia Marsh, Oct. 10, 1830, r. Th. 8, Charlotte, d. young. 9, Chas., rem. Cincinnati, O., last heard from in 1835, at Cuba, having been wrecked on his passage from Boston to N. Orleans. 10, Henry, died of yellow fever at New Haven, on his return from S. Carolina. Susanna, the mother, b. in Abington, 1771, d. June 1, 1824.

Capt. George W.'s ch. 1, George G., b. June 24, 1832, d. Oct. 4, '53. 2, Julia A., b. Nov. 26, '33; m. William H. Hatch, February 25, '55; r. Th. 3, Charles H., b. Aug. 26, '35; r. Th., a mariner, soldier in 2d Me. Battery, &c. 4, Franklin, b. Sept. 26, '37; r. Th., a seaman. 5, Sarah C., b. April 26, '40, d. April 17, '42. 6, William H. b. Aug. 26, '41; r. Th., a mariner, soldier of the 19th Me. reg., died at hospital in Washington, D. C., Nov. 16, '64. 7, Oscar, b. ab. 1846; r. Thomaston.

GODDING, John, born in Mansfield, Mass., came from Fox Is. to what is now Rockland during the revolution; m. Suviah Lucas from Mass., and d. Dec. 30, 1816. Their ch. 1, John, (2d), born Nov. 4, 1776; m. Nancy Killsa, Jan. 25, 1798; rem. to Waldo, Me., and died ab. 1862. 2, Betsey, b. Aug. 4, 1784; m. 1st, Samuel Lindsey, 2d, Hatevil Pease; r. Th., and d. Dec. 28, 1850? 3, Hatch, b. Aug. 10, 1786; m. Catharine Teal, of St. George, Oct. 6, 1810; r. Rock. and d. before 1815, lost at sea. 4, Sally, b. Sept. 14, 1788; m. 1st, Thos. Crockett, 2d, Elibeus Partridge; r. Rock., and d. ab. 1849. 5, Lucy Jane, b. June 14, 1793, d. April 18, buried the 19th, 1817.

John, (2d)'s ch. 1, John, (3d), b. April 19, 1798; mar. and rem. Waldo. 2, Hugh K., b. Oct. 16, 1801; m. and rem. Linc. 3, Sabra Killsa, b. July 24, 1805; m. and r. Northport.

GODFREY, John, b. ab. 1804, in Nova Scotia, and c. from thence with Ruth his wife, and family; r. Rock., a ship joiner. Their ch. b. in Nova Scotia. 1, William B., b. ab. 1839. 2, Edward C., b. ab. '42. 3, Lucretia, b. ab. '44. 4, Bethia I, b. ab. '46. 5, John J., b. ab. '48, d. Jan. 8, '64. 6, Charles D., b. ab. '52.

GOODELL, James E., b. ab. 1835, in Northport, Me.; m. Sabra A. Day, July, 1855; r. Rock. a mariner, &c. Their ch. 1, Emma J., b. ab. 1853. 2, Ida M., b. ab. '59.

GOODWIN, Dr. Jacob Scammon, grad. Dartmouth College, 1811, MD. 1814; came from Readfield to what is now Rock., rem. & d. Th. Their ch. 1, Julia Annette, m. ——— Yeaton; r. Vermont. 2, Eliza J.; 3, William, m. & r. in Boston; 4, Jacob B.; 5, Eliab Stone; 6, Daniel F.; 7, Sarah; 8, John; 9, Roby Hewett; 10, Wade Hampton; all rem. Boston with their widowed mother.

GORDEN, William W., b. ab. 1824, on Staten Island; m. Cyrena Achorn; r. Rock., an ice dealer. Their ch. 1, Orestes, b. ab. 1846. 2, Francis, b. ab. '47. 3, Lewis, b. ab. '49. 4, Eugene, b. ab. '51. 5, Ada, b. ab. '53. 6, Emma, b. ab. '55. 7, Annie, b. ab. '57. 8, Mary, b. ab. '59.

GOTT, Capt. John, b. ab. 1809, on Swan Island, Me.; m. Abigail Merchant; r. Rock. Capt. Joseph, a brother, m. & r. Swan Island.

Of Capt. John's ch. 1, Capt. David J., b. ab. 1834; m. Lydia J. Ingraham, Jan. 30, '55; r. Rock. 2, Caroline, b. ab. '38; r. Rock. 3, Mary J., b. ab. '40; m. Wilbert Boynton, March 30, '64; r. Rock.

Of Capt. Joseph's ch. Rodney J., b. ab. 1836, on Swan Island; m. Nancy E. Joice; r. Rock., a carpenter.

Capt. David J.'s ch. Mary Ella, b. Sept. 17, 1856, d. Nov. 23, '61.

GOULD, John, (son of William, and descendant of a Welsh ship-master who settled in Pembroke, Mass., about 1664, the first of the family in America), bought land in Winchester, N. H., 1763, built saw, grist, and clothing mills, was wealthy and noted for great obstinacy and physical strength, sometimes, it is said, taking with his fingers a barrel of cider by the chimes and lifting it so that he could drink out of the bung-hole. His oldest son, Thomas, b. in Pembroke, 1753; attended school 8 weeks only, but became learned, especially in natural philosophy and history; r. Winchester, and d. ab. 1830. His only son, Thomas, (2d), b. March 7, 1785; m. Abigail Briggs, a teacher, and of an ancient Brattleboro' family; was educated for a teacher and physician, but took the home farm, devoting much time to geological and other pursuits.

Thomas, (2d)'s ch. 1, Edwin P., d. aged 3 years. 2, Harriet Augusta, m. Willard C. Brigham; r. Rindge, N. H. 3, Abigail Nims, a successful teacher, d. in 1843. 4, Albert Palmer, Esq., b. Aug. 30, 1821, on the old homestead in Winchester; m. 1st, Perley Bryant of Franklin county, Mass.; 2d, Elizabeth D. Robinson of Th., Jan. 4, 1853; came to Maine, 1845, to Th., 1848, attorney at law. 5, Henry, m. & r. Winchester, a joiner. 6, Elizabeth H., died, aged 5 years.

Albert P., Esq.'s ch. by 1st wife. 1, Flora Elizabeth, b. ab. 1845, d. March 10, '62. 2, Abbie Augusta. 3, Mary Amelia. The mother d. March 7, '52, aged 33 years.

GOULD; of this Freedom, Me. family, perhaps descended from the same Pembroke ship-master, 3 brothers came to this place. 1, Edward, b. ab. 1815, in Freedom; m. Jane R. Bowker of Bangor; r. Rock., & d. Aug. 14, 1850. 2, Stephen, b. ab. 1819, in Freedom; r. Rock., a lime manufacturer. 3, Benjamin, b. ab. 1822; m. Elmira Smith, Dec. 25, '46; r. Rock., a lime manufacturer.

Edward's ch. 1, Charlotte, b. Feb. 18, 1839. 2, Rozetta Jane, b. Sept. 3, '41. 3, Almeda S., b. ab. '45.

Benjamin's ch. 1, Leforest, b. ab. 1848. 2, Frederic, b. ab. '57.

GOULD, John M., b. ab. 1825; came from Hillsboro', N. H.; m. Caroline Flye of Sedgwick; r. Rock., a dry goods merchant. Their ch. 1, Carrie W., b. ab. 1853. 2, Howard, b. ab. '55.

GOWEN, Nathaniel B., b. ab. 1823, in Union; m. Elizabeth H. Marshall; r. Rock., a lime burner, soldier in 4th Me. Reg., and died Dec., 1861, a prisoner in Richmond, Va.

GOWEN, Bradford, b. ab. 1825; m. Margaret ——; r. Rock., a truckman, &c. Their ch. 1, John W., b. ab. 1849. 2, Mary F., b. ab. '51. 3, Charles A., b. ab. '53. 4, George E., b Dec., '55, d. Oct. 22, '56. 5, Ellena, b. April, '59, d. Oct. 1, '60.

GRAFFAM; the father of this family r. on Matinic, & d. on one of the Muscle Ridge islands. His ch. 1, George, m. Margaret Spalding, May 6, 1806; r. S. Th. & d. in Th. 2, Pierce, removed. 3, Capt. Jacob, m. —— Andrews, and was one of the early settlers, and, it is said, founder, of Rockport.

George's ch. 1, John, b. 1807, d. 1825 by a fall from aloft, at sea. 2, Capt. James A., b. April 5, 1809; m. Mary Antoinette Bennett, July 13, '32; r. Th., a painter. 3, Nancy S., b. July 12, 1811; mar. Robert Bramhall; r. Rock. 4, Susan I., b. May 9, 1815; mar. John

Monk, '33; and d. May 16, '50. 5, William C., b. Nov. 1, '17; mar. Martha F. Burns, April 19, '46; r. Rockport. 6, Matilda S., b. Feb. 7, '20. 7, Lyman S., b. Jan. 20, '23; r. N. Orleans. 8, Lucy C., born Nov. 28, '23; m. Peleg Thomas, April 19, 1844; r. S. Th.

James A.'s ch. 1, Augustina, b. Jan. 2, 1837; mar. James P. Edgarton; r. Th. 2, Dexter, b. Aug. 23, '40. 3, Antoinette, b. about '44. 4, Ellen, b. ab. '46. 5, Almond B., b. ab. '47.

GRAFTON, Joseph, came from St. George, married Nancy Montgomery; r. Th., and was lost at sea. Their ch. 1, John M., d. in '56, lost at sea in the barque *Livorno*. 2, Henrietta, b. ab. '46. 3, Isaac M., b. ab. '47. 4, Lucy, b. ab. '49. 5, Helen, b. ab. '51.

GRAFTON, John H., b. ab. 1827, son of John and Almira (Webb) Grafton, of Warren and Union; m. Clara F. Spofford, Sept. 17, '56; r. Rock., a painter, enlisted in the U. S. navy. Their ch. 1, Clara, b. ab. '57. 2, Charles W., b. ab. '59.

GRAHAM, Levi N., b. ab. 1812; m. Eliza T. Skinner, pub. Sept. 16, '45; r. Rock., a quarryman. Their ch. 1, Sarah, b. ab. '48. 2, William, b. ab. '49. 3, Laura, b. ab. '55.

GRAHAM, ———, came with Fanny, his wife, from Ireland; r. Th. and British Provinces, and d. His widow r. Rock. Their chil. 1, Norman, b. ab. 1857. 2, John, b. ab. '59. Their father's brother, William, also r. Rock., a ship carpenter.

GRANT, John, came from Cape Cod to Fox Islands in 1785; m. Lydia Haskell of S. Th., and had 7 ch. of whom, there settled here, 1, Capt. David, b. 1801; m. Priscilla Ames; came to Rock., 1830, & d. at New York, Oct., 1851. 2, Capt. John, b. in 1805; m. Hannah Lindsey; came to Rock. to r. in 1838. 3, Capt. William, b. 1816; m. Elsie Brown; came to Rock., 1843, and was lost at sea, Dec., 1859.

Capt. David's ch. 1, a daughter, died young. 2, John S., b. in 1823; m. Mary C. Ulmer, Dec. 19, 1843; r. Rock., a mariner. 3, Abner E., m. Mary J. Childs, June 22, '45; r. Rock., & d. at sea, Oct. 26, '59. 4, Abby, m. Franklin Achorn; r. Rock. 5, Goodwin, b. 1829; m. Emma F. Dill, Oct. 27, '50; r. Rock., a mariner. 6, Nancy H., m. Capt. George H. Cables; r. Rock. 7, Priscilla E., m. Capt. John F. Cables; r. Rock.

Capt. John's ch. 1, Deborah L., m. Capt. Knott C. Perry; r. Rock. 2, Capt. David W., m. Elizabeth W. ——— of North Haven; r. Rock. 3, Mahala J., m. & r. in Hohokus, N. J. 4, Capt. Isaac H., b. 1835; m. Amanda M. Thompson, Oct. 16, '54; r. Rock. 5, John F., b. July 20, '38; r. Rock., a mariner, now in U. S. service. 6, Jarvis B., b. Oct. 22, '40; mariner, and volunteer soldier, died, killed at Bull Run, July 21, '61. 7, William, b. Jan. 10, '43; r. Rock., a mariner. 8, Mary B., b. ab. '46. 9, Susan E., b. ab. '48.

Capt. William's ch. 1, Charles, b. ab. 1848. 2, Clara, b. ab. '51. 3, Frederic, b. ab. '54.

John S.'s ch. 1, David E., b. 1845, mate of bark *A. H. Kimball*, drowned, Dec. 10, '60, on passage to New Orleans. 2, Isaac A., b. ab. '47. 3, Dora E., b. '53. 4, Mary F., b. '56. 5, George F., b. '59.

Goodwin's ch. 1, Frank A., b. ab. 1851. 2, Ella P., b. ab. '53. 3, Eva M., b. ab. '57.

Capt. David W.'s ch. 1, Hannah E., b. ab. 1854. 2, Deborah P., b. '56. 3, Matthew A., b. '58.

Capt. Isaac H.'s ch. Malvina, b. July, 1855, d. Aug. 8, '56.

GRANT, Hiram, b. Dec. 10, 1789; came from Berwick; m. Betsey Biskey of St. G.; r. Beech Woods, Th., & d. Nov. 20, 1862. Their ch. 1, William Joshua, b. 1823; m. Hannah A. Willis, Feb. 13, '44; r. California. 2, Mary Jane, m. Francis Burrill; r. Ct. 3, Eliza A., m. Walter Sutherland, now a soldier of the U. S., r. and d. Th. 4, Michael B., b. ab. 1829; m. Mary E. Achorn, Nov. 20, '52; r. Rock., a lime burner. 5, Hiram, (2d), b. 1833; m. Margaret A. Gilson, July 24, '53; r. Th. 6, A. Jackson, b. 1835; m. Elizabeth J. Fales, March 28, '58; r. Rock. 7, Frances Elvina, m. Charles Richardson; r. Rock. and died. 8, J. Catharine, m. John Hull, p. June 21, '56; r. Damariscotta. 9, John B., b. 1842, soldier in the 21st Me. Reg. 10, Martha W.; r. Th. 11, Angie R., m. William H. Keene; r. Rock. 12, Rachel, b. ab. '49.

William Joshua's ch. 1, Mary E., b. ab. 1845. 2, William A., b. '47. 3, Edwin S., b. '49.

Michael B.'s ch. 1, Willie H., b. May 25, 1855, d. Dec. 2, '56. 2, Charles L., b. Nov. 10, '59, d. Sept. 27, '60.

Hiram, (2d)'s ch. 1, Albert G., b. 1854. 2, Ernest, b. '59.

Andrew Jackson's ch. Cyrus N., b. 1859.

GRANT, James, b. ab. 1821; m. Celia ———; r. Rock. Their ch. 1, William H., b. ab. 1846. 2, Jane W., b. ab. '50. 3, Hannah S., b. ab. '53. 4, Eugene C., b. ab. '57.

GRANT, Daniel, b. ab. 1830, in Nova Scotia; r. S. Th., with Margaret S., his wife. Their ch. Calvin C., b. ab. 1859.

GRAVES; of this family two brothers came here from Deerfield, N. H., viz.: William, b. ab. 1778; m. Mary ———; r. S. Th. and d. April 16, 1849. Nathaniel, b. ab. 1788; m. Louisa Emery, July 11, 1809; r. S. Th., on road to St. George, and d. Jan. 8, '55.

William's ch. 1, Eunice, b. Oct. 18, 1800; mar. Capt. Josiah W. Dodge; rem. San Francisco, Cal. 2, John, b. May 27, '03; m. 1st, Nancy G. Dean, Nov. 8, '27, 2d, Mrs. Lydia W. Smith, p. June 14, '51; r S. Th., a joiner, &c. 3, Joseph, b. April 2, '05; m. Caroline S. Snow; r. S. Th., a farmer. 4, Parley, b. Sept. 26, '07; m. Mercy Williams, May 22, '45; r. S. Th., a farmer, rem. ? California. 5, Lydia, b. June 1, '10; r. Th. 6, Mary, b. Aug. 27, '12; m. Isaac Hall; r. Rock. 7, William D., b. July 31, '15; m. Mary S Graves of St. George, Dec. 16, '38; r. S. Th., and d. April, 1849. 8, Simon D., b. July 28, '18; m. Susan W. Crouch, Dec. 7, '41; r. S. Th., a carpenter, &c. 9 and 10, twins, b. Sept. 24, '21; Susan D, m. Capt. Geo. Emery; r. Th. Halsey H., lost at sea in the Gulf of Mexico. The mother d. March 19, 1842, aged 62.

Nathaniel's ch. 1, Lydia, mar. Oliver Wheeler of St. George. 2, George E., m. Lucy Harrington, Jan. 1838; r. Rock., or St. George. [A George Graves d. at Rock. April 25, '57, aged 47.] 3, Elizabeth, mar. Benjamin Thompson; r. S. Th. 4, Mary S., mar. William D. Graves, r. Aroostook. 5, Dennis, b. 1818, d. at sea Sept. 5, '43. 6, Margaret, m. Oliver Butler; r. Hope. 7, Edward, m. Martha Arey; r. S. Th. 8 and 9, twins, b. April 1826; Nathaniel, (2d), died at St. George, by suicide Sept. 12, '55; Josiah, d. at Mazatlan harbor, June 1, '51. 10, Sophia. 11, Louisa Maria.

John's ch. by 1st wife. 1, John, (2d), b. Sept. 7, 1828; r. Rock., ? soldier in the army. ? 2, Thomas J., b. Oct. 23, '30; r. S. Th. 3, Louisa D., b. Sept. 7, '32; m. 1st, Tileston P. Noyes, of Rock., 2d, Solomon Stahl; rem. Appleton. 4, Adeline, b. April 7, '34; m. John

H. Bennett, Sept. 19, '64. 5, Ephraim D., b. Dec. 25, '35; r. Rock. 6, Sarah A., b. Aug. 1, '38, d. March 12, '41. 7, Elizabeth W., b. April 15, '40. 8, Lorenzo A., b. May 4, '42; r. S. Th. 9, Algernon, b. ab. '45. 10, Stearns, b. ab. '47. By 2d wife. 11, Nancy, b. ab. '52.

Joseph's ch. 1, Orris, b. July 21, 1839; r. S. Th., a mariner. 2, Harriet, b. May 25, '42. 3, Emily, b. ab. '44. 4, Frederic, b. ab '46; r. S. Th., soldier of 2d Me. Battery, d. July 5, '62. 5, William, b. ab. '48. 6, Irving, b. ab. '51. 7, Edwin, b. ab. '53. 8, Ava, b. ab. '56.

Parley's ch. 1, Nathaniel, ? d. at New Orleans. 2, Archibald, b. ab. 1835; r. S. Th., a joiner.

Simon D.'s ch. 1, Sarah, b. Oct. 18, 1842. 2, Maria, b. ab. '43. 3, Oscar, b. ab. '45; r. S. Th., a mariner. 4, Lewis, b. ab. '46. 5, Halsey, b. ab. '48. 6, Francis, b. ab '50. 7, Laura, b. ab. '53. 8, Ella, b. ab. '55. 9, Charles, b. ab. '57. 10, a son, b. in 1860.

William D.'s ch. Lillias, b. Sept. 8, 1839.

GRAY, Leverett, b. in Yarmouth, Mass., in 1776; m. Rebecca Sears; came to reside in Thomaston, with his wife, in May, 1803; r. S. Th., a joiner, & d. Feb. 8, '42. He had brothers, Edward, who also came to Thomaston, and Capt. John, who resided on the Cape; also a sister who married Capt. Joshua Adams.

Leverett's ch. 1, Betsey. b. Jan. 17, 1803, m. Ezekiel Hall, April 18, '22; r. S. Th. 2, Joshua, b. Jan. 21, '06; r. S. Th., & d. Dec. 31, '57, unm. 3, Capt. William, b. Oct. 19, '07; m. 1st, Relief Drake, June 20, '40, 2d, Mary Ann Titus, Jan. 1, '52; r. S. Th., a farmer, & d. Nov. 18, '60. 4, Capt. Oliver, b. Oct. 27, '09; m. Lydia Merriman, p. March 7, '35, r. S. Th. & d. April 12, '45. 5, Nancy, b. Aug. 24, '11; m. Thomas Rendall and rem. to Ohio. 6, Shepard, b. April 9, '14; m. 1st, Hannah Thorndike; 2d, Emeline Butler, April 12, '41, 3d, Mary W. Sherman, Aug. 2, '46; r. S. Th., a farmer. 7, Rebecca, b. June 4, '16; m Capt. Nathan Sleeper; r. Rock. 8, George S., b. Aug. 27, '19; m. 1st, Eliza P. Sherman, 2d, M. Jeanette Paul, May 19, '51; r. S. Th., a joiner. 9, Caroline, b. Nov. 25, '26; m. 1st, John McMullen of N. S., Jan. 1, 1846; 2d, Benjamin Knowlton; r. Rock. The mother, b. Feb., 1783, d. in Rock., June 3, 1853.

Capt. William's ch. by 1st wife. 1, Nancy Jane, b. ab. 1844. 2, Helen, b. ab. '47. By 2d wife. 3, a son, d. young. 4, Leverett H., b. ab. 1856.

Capt. Oliver's ch. 1, John, b. ab. 1837; r. S. Th. 2, Oliver, (2d), b. ab. 1840.

Shepard's ch. 1, Charles. 2, Elizabeth. 3, a son, d. young. By 3d wife. 4, Adelaide L., b. ab. '47. 5, Clara Agnes, b. ab. '50. 6, Livingston, b. ab. '56.

George S.'s ch. by 1st wife. 1, Edward T., b. April 25, 1842; r. S. Th. 2, Mary A., b. March, and d. July, 1845. By 2d wife. 3, Eliza M., b. ab. 1847.

GRAY, Capt. Alfred, b. ab. 1838; m. Nancy Spalding, June 4, '58; r. Rock., and d., lost from the sch. *Orrin Cowl*, burnt at Sandy Hook, Jan. 1, '62. Their ch. Ella, b. ab. 1859.

GRAY, George H., b. ab. 1835; m. Emily ——; r. Rock., a shoemaker. Their ch. Thomas, b. ab. 1857.

GRAY, Andrew J., b. ab. 1830, in Brooksville, Me.; m. Caroline Grindle; r. Rock. Their ch. 1, Ada C., b. ab. 1855. 2, Arthur L., b. ab. 1859.

GRAY, Stillman, b. ab. 1835; m. Hannah E. ——; r. Rock., a lime burner, &c. Their ch. Charles W., b. ab. 1859.

GRAY, Francis, b. ab. 1772; came with his wife in 1847 or '8 from county of Sligo, Ireland, to r. with his ch. who had preceded him to America; r. Th., and d. Sept. 10, 1864, aged 92. Their ch. 1, Edward, m. and r. Ireland. 2, Dominic, b. ab. 1812; came to Th., m. Hannah Jones, Feb. 12, 1848; r. Th. 3, Luke, m. Sarah Brazier of C.; r. Th. 4, Patrick, m. Mary Henery, Sept. 27, 1847; r. Th. 5, Catharine, m. Daniel Preston, and died on passage to America. 6, Honoria, r. Th. 7, Frank, r. Th. 8, James, m. Mary Jane Doherty of Appleton; r. W., a blacksmith. Honoria, the mother, d. in Th., Nov. 28, 1862.

Dominic's ch. 1, Kate, b. ab 1848. 2, Daniel, b. ab. '50. 3, Ann, b. ab. '53. 4, Ellen, b. ab. '55. 5, Mary Jane, b. ab. '58, and d. Oct. 17, '61. 6, Nellie, and perhaps others.

Luke's ch. 1, Lizzie. 2, Silas John.

Patrick's ch. 1, Mary A., b. '49. 2, Eliza, b. '51. 3, Charles, b. '54.

James's ch. 1, Laura A., b. 1858. 2, Ellis S., b. '63.

GRAY, Edward, b. ab. 1805, in Ireland; r. Rock., with Mary, his wife. Their ch. 1, Patrick, b. ab. 1842. 2, Jane, b. ab. '44.

GREELEY, Elbridge E., b. ab. 1813, in Palermo, Me.; mar. 1st, Asenath Longfellow, 2d, Betsey ——; r. Rock. His ch. by 1st wife. 1, Anthony N., b. ab. 1840; r. Rock., a soldier in the army. 2, Lucina A., b. ab. '43. 3, Almond E., b. ab. '46; also entered the army. 4, Betsey M., b. ab. '49. 5, Forest, b. Feb. & d. Nov. 18, '55.

GREEN, William, m. Barbara Deago, and came from England to Plymouth, Mass., where he r. and had ch. born, but settled about the commencement of the Revolution in old Th., at Simonton's Point, on the farm lately owned by Capt. Jonathan Small; was sometimes drafted into the army, was a drummer and drummed for Gen. Wadsworth; at other times boiled salt for a living; about the close of the war lost his English wife and buried her at the Stackpole grave-yard, near; m. 2d, (p. Sept. 23, 1790), Lucy, daughter of Asa and Joanna Thomas of Friendship, brother to Jesse Thomas, a family from near Plymouth, Mass., and after Oct. 10, 1790, removed and settled near Fredericton, N. B., with his family and sister Eliza, who had also come here and kept a grocery in the Dunning house.

William's ch. by 1st wife. 1, Isaac; 2, Lydia; both rem. N. B. 3, John, or Jonny, m. at the residence of Gen. Knox, in New York, Dorcas Bidda, from England, who had been a domestic in the General's family; r. here, and later at Boston, where he d. ab. July, 1855; his wife having d. there about 1838. 4, Barbara; 5, Betsey; 6, Benjamin; all b. in Plymouth; 7, William, Jr., b. in Th.; all rem. with their father; who had a numerous family by his 2d wife.

John's ch. 1, Maria, m. Abram Wendell, of Boston, removed New York and d. leaving two daughters. 2, Eliza, m. Moses S. Robinson of C., rem. and d. in N. York, without ch.. 3, Cornelius Cooledge.

GREEN, Capt. Ballard, b. about 1787, a twin brother of Gardner Green, and brother of Peter H. Green of Bath, and Nathaniel Green of Topsham, both in turn high sheriffs of Lincoln county; came to Thomaston in 1819, from Topsham, and was a merchant at the present O'Brien wharf, in firm of Green & Merrill; mar. Jane A. Noyes or Norris, of Brunswick, p. May 15, 1819; and d. Feb. 10, '31. Their ch. 1, Elizabeth Titcomb, b. 1821, died in Brunswick, March, 1829. 2, Gardner, b. Sept. 22, '27, d. Aug. 19, '29. 3, Charles Ballard; 4, Harriet N.; both rem. Brunswick. 5, Albert, b. Aug., 1830, d. Jan. 18, '31. The mother d. Feb. 6, '32; aged 37.

GREENHALGH, Rev. Thomas, c. from England to this country in the print-making business, left it, and about $1200 per annum, and became a Methodist minister, receiving the first year a *salary of* $50; m. thrice; rem. Hampden, Me. Of his ch. 1, Lieut. Jabez B., b. ab. 1827; m. Lucy M. Crockett, May 13, '49; r. Rock., a saddler and harness maker, officer in 4th Me. reg., &c. 2, Capt. Charles B., b. ab. '33; r. Rock., saddler and harness maker, till he entered on military life, officer of the 4th Me., &c., since clerk in Thorndike House, &c. 3, Joseph, m. Margaret E. Miller, Feb. 27, '64; r. Rock.

Lieut. Jabez B.'s ch. 1, Charles J., b. ab. 1852. 2, Sylvanus, b. Oct. and d. Dec. 9, '55. 3, Fred. Thomas, b. April 23, and died Oct. 2, '57. 4, Lizzie K., b. ab. '59.

GREGORY, William, b. 1731; m. Experience Robbins; c. from Walpole, about 1762, to St. George's fort, & r. Th. seven years; rem. 1770 to Clam Cove, Camden, where he was the first settler, as also the first in Camden after Richards, & d. March, 1824, aged 93; buried at Rockland, in the Tolman graveyard. Their ch. 1, Elizabeth, b. 1755; m. Isaiah Tolman, (2d),; r. Rock. and d. Aug. 2, 1830. 2, William (2d), d. young. 3, Experience, d. young. 4, Experience, b. Sept. 19, 1760; m. Samuel Tolman; r. Rock. and d. Feb. 19, 1828. 5, Capt. William, (3d), b. in Walpole, Jan. 1, 1762; m. Melia Tolman, Oct. 23, 1784; r. Cam. 6, Francis, d. young. 7, Mary b. 1766; m. Capt. William Spear, r. Rock. & d. Nov. 2, 1839. 8, Capt. John, b. June 21, 1769; m. Elizabeth Simonton; r. Clam Cove. 9, Josiah, b. May 5, 1771; r. Appleton. 10, Olive, m. Daniel Andrews; r. & d. Cam. 11, Luther, d. young. 12, Luther, b. May 17, 1780; m. Jane McLoon, April 28, 1803.

Of Capt. William, (3d)'s ch. Calvin, b. 1801; m. Theresa Maker, Dec. 31, '21; r. Rock.

Capt. John's ch. 1, Mary S., m. Ebenezer Cleaveland; r. Cam. 2, Frances A., b. June 29, 1794; m. Jeremiah Berry; r. Rock. and died March 24, 1857. 3, William, (4th), m. Rebecca Damon of Westminster, Mass.; r. Cam. 4, Clarissa, m. John Bird; r. Rock. 5, Capt. John, (2d), b. 1799; m. Phebe M. Young; r. Rock. 6, Celinda, m. Michael Achorn; r. Rock. 7, P. Hanson, m. Mary Barrows; r. Cam. 8, Hiram, m. Mary Manning, p. Oct. 24, '33; r. Cam. 9, Capt. Isaac, b. '06; m. Merriel Ingraham, p. Sept. 20, '28; r. Rock.

Third Generation.

Calvin's ch. 1, Melinda A,, m. George Jackson; r. Rock. 2, Mary Ann, m. 1st, John Stover, 2d, John Hall; r. Rock. 3, Caroline C., m. James Morton; r. Rock. 4, Pamelia J., m. Capt. William N. Andrews; r. Rock. 5, Capt. Robert, b. '35; m. Margaret Dumont, Sept. 24, '52; r. Rock. 6, Capt. Calvin, m. Sarah Kuhn, Aug. 24, '54; lost, with his wife, in his sch. *Chance*, July, 1858. 7, Samuel H.,b. ab. '42; r. R. soldier of 20th Me. reg. 8, Amos, b. June, '44, d. Aug. 2, '62.

Of Wm., (4th)'s ch. 1, Mark, b. Aug., 1826; m. Maria ——; r. Rock., and d. Nov. 21, '59.

Capt. John, (2d)'s ch. 1, Joseph, b. March 5, 1834, died May 22, '35. 2, Araminta, b. Sept. 31, '35; m. George W. Sargent, Dec. 4, '53; r. E. Boston. 3, Capt. Weston, b. April 20, '37; mar. Irene A. Lincoln, r. Rock., appointed master's mate in the U. S. N., in Feb. '62. 4, John F., b. March 8, '41; m. Louisa Boynton, June 10, '62; r. Rock., a mariner. 5, Jane Y., m. Capt. Elkanah S. Hall; r. Rock. 6, Emma L. 7, Joseph D., d. young. 8, Almeda, d. young.

P. Hanson's ch. 1, Lucinda, m. Capt. Charles Sylvester; r. Cam. 2, Capt. George, mar. Olive Achorn, Aug. 3, '52; r. Rock. 3, Capt. Hanson, b. 1832; m. Mary A. Merrifield, Nov. 8, '53; r. Rock. 4, Capt. Jeremiah, m. Emily S. Kirk, Aug. 20, '54; r. Rock., a mariner. 5, Belinda, mar. Leonard Hall; r. Rock. 6, Rebecca, mar. Adoniram Packard, r. Rock. 7, Henry, rem. California.

Dea. Isaac's ch. 1, Melinda, d. Feb. 15, 1836. 2, Joseph I., born July 21, '37, d. April 20, '38. 3, Frances, b. April 2, '39; m. Alfred Burns, r. Rock. 4, Isaac, (2d), b. March 3, '41; a clerk. 5, Mary Melinda, b. Feb. 20, '43. 6, Lucy, b. '45.

Fourth Generation.

Capt. Robert's ch. 1, Clarence E., b. April, 1855, d. May 16, '56. 2, Addie A. 3, John C. 4 and 5, twins, born 1859, Albert E., and Winfred A., d. young.

Mark's ch. 1, George, (2d), b. ab. 1850. 2, Martha J., b. Feb.'55, d. Sept. 9, '57. 3, Harriet, b. ab. '57. The mother mar. 2d, George Kingman of Waltham, Me., Aug. 19, '60.

Capt. George's ch. Cora E., b. ab. 1853.

Capt. Hanson's ch. Lizzie, b. ab. 1854.

Jeremiah's ch. 1, Alice A., b. ab. 1855. 2, Alvestine, b. ab. '57. 3, Katie O., b. ab. '59.

GRIFFIN, George, b. ab. 1800; m. 1st, Lucinda T. ———, who d. Mar. 23, '58, 2d, Almira Bailey, Oct. 28, '60; r. Rock, a lime burner, &c.

GROSS, Henry, born about 1811, in Orland, Me., mar. 1st, Abigail Hutchings, 2d, Joanna French; r. Rock., a joiner, &c. His chil. by 1st wife. 1, Joseph, b. ab. 1833; m. Mrs. Hannah J. Hart; r. Rock., a lime burner, &c. 2, Andrew, ? born about '37; r. Rock., in fishery business. By 2d wife, 3, Vienna, b. ab. '50. 4, Henry, b. ab. '53. 5, Elnora, b. May 1, '55, d. May 8, '56. 6, Emma, b. ab. '57.

Joseph's ch. 1, Alzina, b. ab. '58. 2, Mary T., b. ab. '60.

GROVER, Capt. James, m Susan Rosilla Tyler, Feb. 27, 1834; r. Rock., and when master of the *Mary K. Kendall*, died Sept., 1853, at Jamaica, 18 persons out of the barque, including the captain's wife and child, dying in a few weeks. Their ch. 1, Edmund A., b. Sept. 25, 1836, d. in Kingston, Ja., Sept., 1853. 2, Samuel A., b. Nov. 18, 1838, d. July 18, '46. 3, Lucy F., b. Aug. 25, 1840, d. Aug. 28, '46.

GROVER, Edmund, b. ab. 1796; r. Rock., & d. by suicide, June 10, 1857; Lucy, his widow, b ab. 1797; r. Rock.

GROVER, Capt. Nathan, was in Rock. & m. Mrs. Lucy B. Brewster of Cam., Dec. 16, 1857.

GROVER, Capt. Joseph, m. Caroline Snow, June 1, 1837.

GRUNDY, Richard W., with Jane P., his wife, was in the place ab. 1842, & had recorded here their ch. William, b. Dec. 27, 1842.

GUPTILL, Capt. Nathaniel, b. ab. 1792; came from Lubec; m. Eleanor Spear, Dec. 22, 1817; r. Rock., & d. April 5, '57. Their ch. 1, Joseph, b. Dec. 16, 1821. 2, Eleanor A., b. April 13, '23; r. Rock. 3, Capt. Robert P., b. Dec. 1, '25; m. Elizabeth D. Fales, Sept. 30, '48; r. Rock., a master mariner. 4, Phylotia C., b. March 11, '28; m. Winchester T. Rice of Cam., p. Sept. 19, '46. 5, Wallis, b. May 19, '32. 6, John, b. Aug. 1, '34.

Capt. Robert R.'s ch. 1, Albert D., b. ab. 1850. 2, Charles C., b. ab. '54. 3, Robert C., b. ab. '58.

HAHN, Jacob, of German descent, b. Nov. 30, 1811; mar. and r. Rock., a blacksmith; and d. April 13, '64. His ch. 1, Eva A., b. ab. 1853. 2, Myron, b. ab. 1855. 3, Benjamin, b. ab. 1859. There was also in Rock., Edward P. Hahn, who lost Avis, his wife, March 3, '61, & m. 2d, Mary E. Frohock, of Linc., Aug. 10, '62.

HAHN, Sylvester, b. ab. 1834, in Waldoboro'; m. Mary A. Shibles, Oct. 31, '55; r. Th., a blacksmith. Their ch. Rowland, b. ab. '58.

HALL, ———, a baker by trade, came over from England about 1722 and settled in State (then King) street, Boston, but removed to New Meadows or Harpswell, ab. 1737. His ch. 1, Isaac born about 1725; married Miss Coombs of New Meadows; was a soldier at the taking of Louisburg, also in Revolution; r. a time in old Thomaston, settled and d. in St. George. 2, Joseph. 3, Nathaniel.

Isaac's ch. 1, Caleb, m. Hannah Snow; r. St. George and d. Feb. 8, 1814. 2, Rev. Isaac, (2d), m. Sarah Saywood; had charge of the Baptist church in Knox. 3, Rev. Ephraim, mar. Polly Snow; was many years the Baptist minister in St. George, and d. Oct. 5, 1809. 4, Dea. Peter, m. Polly Pierson; r. and d. St. George. 5, Lewis, b. Feb. 28, 1765; m. Anna or Hannah Dyer; r. S. Th., and d. Nov. 4, 1845. 6, Elijah, Esq., m. 1st, Betsey Robinson, 2d, Rebecca (Mann) Coombs, p. May 1, 1828; r. and d. St. George. 7, Mehitable, m. a Stover; r. and d. St. George. 8, Joanna, m. John Curtis; r. and d. St. George.

Caleb's ch. 1, Isaac, (3d), mar. Ann Anderson of W., r. St. Geo. 2, Elijah, (2d), b. Jan. 18, 1777; m. Betsey (Buckland) Dunning, 2d, Mary Wheeler; r. S. Th., a farmer, on the Dunning lot. 3, Ephraim, (2d). 4, Elisha. 5, Lewis, (2d). 6, Caleb, (2d). 7, Rebecca, m. Michael Fountain; r. St. Geo. 8, Samuel. 9, Jeremiah.

Dea. Peter's ch. 1, Joanna. 2, Joseph. 3, Bethia. 4, Dea. Peter, (2d), b. ab. 1797; mar. 1st, Sally Perry, 2d, Mary (Kelloch) Marsh, Nov. 15, 18 9; r. Rock., a fish dealer. 5, Mary. 6, Lucy. 7, Rachel. 8, Sally. 9, Daniel.

Lewis's ch. 1, Anthony D., b. Sept. 9, 1795; m. Mary Dean, Nov. 11, 1819; r. S. Th., and d. June 17, 1835. 2, Ezekiel D., b. Oct. 29, 1797; m. Betsey Gray, April 18, 1822; r. S. Th., a farmer. 3, Geo. D., b. June 24, 1800; m. Mary Ann Sleeper, Jan. 10, 1828; r. S. Th., and d. Feb. 25, '42. 4, Susan D., b. Jan. 24, 1802; mar. Thomas B. Perry; r. S. Th. 5, Lewis, (3d), b. Dec. 26, 1803; mar. Hannah McLellan, Sept. 1, '34; r. Rock, and d. Oct. 20, '58. 6, Ephraim, (3d), b. Dec. 10, '05; m. Harriet W. Fales, pub. Oct. 30, '34; was a merchant in Rock. 1846; rem. Readfield, and to Wayne. 7, Nancy D. b. Jan. 25, 1809, mar. 1st, George Bartlett, 2d, John Brown. 8, Eliza H., b. Aug. 5, '11; m. Alvan Heard, 2d, David Haskell; and d. May 23, '56. 9, Elijah, (3d), b. Jan. 26, '14; m. Mary O. Crawford of W., Nov. 10, '42; r. Rockland.

Fifth Generation.

Elijah, (2d)'s ch. 1, George, b. Jan. 29, 1802; m. Ardea Monk of Winthrop, p. Jan. 27, '31; 2, Ephraim, (4th), b. Aug. 6, 1806; m. Catharine A. Spear, Oct. 3, '30; r. Rock, a farmer. 3, Sylva, b. Feb. 6, '10. 4, Mary, b. Dec. 25, '15. 5, Harriet, b. Dec. 26, '21. 6, Caroline, b. March 12, '23. 7, Nathan B., b. Oct. 16, '25; r. S. Th., a mariner. 8, Isaac S., b. Oct. 17, '27; r. So. Th., a farmer. 9, Elijah H., b. Jan. 16, '29. 10, Sarah, b. June 9, '31, died Dec. 4, '46. 11, Albion K. P., b. Oct. 17, '35.

Of Elisha's ch. 1, George B., b. ab. 1827; mar. Mary A. Stover, May 12, '54; r. Rock., a mariner. 2, John, m. Asenath Pierson.

Dea. Peter, (2d)'s ch. by 1st wife. 1, Eli P., b. Nov. 18, 1822; m. Martha A. or Maria A. Dyer, Nov. 20, '46; r. Rock., a ship carpenter. 2, Capt. Albion K. P., b. Sept. 3, '24; m. Margaret J. Pinkham of Boothbay, p. Aug. 23, '51; r. Rock., & d. Oct. 4, '54. 3, Mary J., b. Sept. 12, '26, d. Aug. 11, '52. 4, Merrill, b. Nov. 21, '28, d. Feb. 4, '53. 5, Leander, b. Nov. 21, '32, d. Oct. 29, '34. 6, Harriet E., b. July 26, '34. 7, Alfred, b. 1839, d. March 10, '54. 8, Jane, b. ab. 1844.

Anthony D.'s ch. 1, William D., b. May 1, 1820; m. Catharine Cassady; r. St. Louis, Mo. 2, Capt. Edwin L., b. June 22, '21; m.? Julia Paul, p. Nov. 3, '53; r. S. Th., lost at sea. 3, Ann E., b. Oct. 20, '22; m. Silas S. Low of Bangor, March 15, '43. 4, Anthony D., (2d), b. Aug. 28, '24; m. Hannah Butman; rem. Lynn, Mass. 5, Mary S., b. April 20, '26, d. June 17, '28. 6, Ephraim H., b. May 27, '28. 7, Robert Livingstone, b. Jan. 13, '30. 8, Frederic C., b. Sept. 9, '32, d. Nov. 18, '48. 9, Mary S., b. Nov. 26, and d. Dec. 25, '35.

Ezekiel D.'s ch. 1, Leverett G., b. March 9, 1823; m. Catharine Mason of Salem, Nov. 18, '57; r. S. Th., a carpenter, &c. 2, Elizabeth, b. Jan. 23, '27; m. 1st, Elisha Prescott, Nov. 7, '47; 2d, Samuel Bryant. 3, Ezekiel D., (2d), b. March 14, '28; m. Caroline E. Kalloch, June, '56; r. S. Th., a merchant, &c; rem. West. 4, Oliver G. Esq., b. March 8, '34; m. S. Frances White, Dec. 25, '58; r. Rock., attorney at law, register of probate, &c. 5, Emily, b. June 8, '35; m. Capt. Henry F. Hix; r. Rock. 6, Caroline A., b. May 29, '38, d. Feb. 1, '46.

George D.'s ch. 1, Capt. Charles M., b. July 12, 1828; m. Louisa K. Boyd, 1853; r. S. Th. 2, George, b. Sept. 28, '30; rem. Cal. 3, Elias, b. May 24, '32, d. Oct. 17, '36. 4, Andrews B., b. May 26, '37; rem. Cal. 5, Albert S., b. Oct. 17, '40; r. S. Th., a caulker.

Lewis, (3d)'s ch. 1, Emeline M., b. July 28, 1835; m. Rev. George Slattery; r. Rock., rem. 2, Kendall K., b. Jan. 14, '37, d. Aug. 15, '38. 3, Anna, b. April, '38, d. Dec. 19, '39. 4, Sarah. 5, Celia A., b. ab. '48.

Ephraim, (3d)'s ch. 1, Hannah Elizabeth, b. ab. 1834; m. Dr. Seth E. Benson; r. Rock. 2, John. 3, George, (2d), m. Lois B. Cooper, Jan. 25, '45; d. at Panama, April 29, '49.

Elijah, (3d)'s ch. 1, Samuel L., b. ab. 1843; r. Rock., entered U. S. Navy. 2, Charles A., b. ab. '47. 3, Frank L., b. ab. '53. 4, Lizzie B., b. ab. '56. 5, Frederic M., b. ab. '58. The mother died April 21, '58, aged 38.

Sixth Generation.

Ephraim, (4th)'s ch. 1, John S., b. ab. 1843, a druggist, soldier in Sharpshooters, &c. 2, George M., b. ab. '52.

George B.'s ch. 1, John A., b. ab. 1855. 2 & 3, twins, b. ab. '59, Addie P., & Ada T.

Eli P.'s ch. 1, Eli L., b. ab. 1847. 2, Alvin M., b. ab. '49.

Capt. Albion K. P.'s ch. Harriet Ann, b. Nov., 1853, d. Aug. 11, 1854.

Ezekiel D., (2d)'s ch. Woodbury K., b. ab. 1858.

Oliver G. Esq.'s ch. Edith, b. Oct. 22, 1859.

Capt. Charles M.'s ch. 1, Lizzie, b. ab. 1854. 2, Mary b. ab. '58. 3, a son, b. 1860.

George, (2d)'s ch. 1, Francis S., b. ab. 1847. 2, Geo. L., b. ab. '49.

HALL; of this same St. George family, but of the sons of Archibald whose parents we have not ascertained,—Elijah H., b. in St. G., m. Louisa M. Hosmer, July 16, 1848; r. Rock., a ship carpenter. Their ch. 1, Clara E., b. ab. 1850. 2, Augustus E., b. July, '51, d. March 20, '53. 3, Fannie M., b. ab. '55. 4, Frank W., b. Dec. 2, '61, died Feb. 17, '62.

HALL; of this Matinicus family, 1, John, b. ab. 1779; m. Olive Tolman, r. Matinicus & Rock., or S. Th. 2, George, m. Elizabeth Burgess, May 19, '04.

John's ch. 1, Fanny, m. Joseph Condon; r. Rock. 2, Capt. Hiram, b. ab. 1805; m. Mary Hix, Oct. 2, '31; r. Rock. 3, Isaac T., b. ab. '07; m. Sarah Hahn of Wal., p. Nov. 4, '37; r. Rock., a peddler, &c. 4, Samuel, b. March 19, '09; m. Julia Conant, April 1, '32; r. S. Th., a mariner. 5, John, (2d), m. Margaret Watson, r. Rock., a mariner, lost at sea. 6, George, (2d), m. Lois Cooper; r. & d. S. Th.

Of George's ch. of Matinicus. Calvin, b. there, ab. 1811, m. Lydia W. Kendall, ; r. Rock., a merchant.

Capt. Hiram's ch. 1, Sarah Thomas, b. Aug. 20, 1832; m. Capt. William M. Munroe; r. Rock. 2, Capt. Hiram, (2d), b. Oct. 12, '34; m. Susan E. Snow, Jan. 1, '53; r. Rock. 3, John B., b. Aug. 20, '36; r. Rock., a mariner. 4, Joseph Weston, b. April 13, '38; r. Rock., a mariner. 5, Hezekiah H., b. June 15, '41; r. Rock., a mariner. 6, Richard C., b. ab. '44; r. Rock., a mariner. 7, Joshua B., b. ab '50.

Isaac T.'s ch. 1, Olive C., b. Jan. 26, 1839; m. George T. Perry; r. Rock. 2, Frederic John, b. Sept. 21, '40; r. Rock., a blacksmith. 3, Addie Mary, b. Sept. 4, '42; m. Thomas Dermot, March 1, '63; r. Rock. 4, Sarah E., b. ab. '48. 5, Simon H., b. ab. '50. 6, Isaac G., b. ab. '52. 7, Sidney, b. ab. '54.

Samuel's ch. 1, Samuel E., b. Dec. 12, 1833; m. Julia M. ——; r. S. Th., a mariner. 2, Louisa Ann, b. April 30, '35; m. Noyce Savage of Rock., p. in '63. 3, Isaac Albion, b. June 16, '40; r. S. Th., a mariner. 4, William L., b. ab. '44.

Calvin's ch. 1, Sophia R., b. ab. 1835; m. Capt. George G. Jameson; r. Rock. 2, Aurelius, b. Jan. '44, d. by drowning, May 12, '54. 3, Capt. Elkanah S., b. ab. '47; m. Jane Y. Gregory, June 26, '63; r. Rock. 4, Lenora J., m. James G. Simonton; r. Rock. 5, Castera. 6, Faustina B., b. July 10, '52, d. Nov. 6, '58.

Capt. Hiram, (2d)'s ch. May Belle, b. Dec., 1861, d. Oct. 6, '62.

Samuel E.'s ch. 1, Marietta, b. ab. 1855. 2, Maynard W., b. ab. '57. 3, a son, b. '60.

HALL, Isaac B., jr., of a different family, r. & d. in Rock. His widow, Mary B. Hall, r. Rock. Their ch. 1, Emily, b. ab. 1837; r. Rock. 2, Ellen L., b. ab. '38; m. Capt. Levi N. Verrill; r. Rock. 3, William S., b. ab. '40; r. Rock., a mariner. 4, Augusta, b. ab. '42; m. Capt. David Ames; r. Rock. 5, Samuel Larkin, b. ab. Aug. 21, '44; r. Rock., a printer, & d. April 23, '62. 6, Charles, b. ab. '46. 7, Hudson, b. ab. '50.

HALL, Jonathan, c. from Camden, m. Mahala St. Clair; r. Rock., about 1831, but probably returned to Camden, or died here. Their ch. recorded here. 1, Timothy, b. Dec. 31, '28, in Cam. 2, Olive, b. in Cam. July 18, '30. 3, Flora E., b. in Th., April 21, '32.

HALL, Nahum H., b. Dec. 4, 1828; c. from Gouldsboro', Me.; m. Lydia M. Witham, Nov. 21, '52; r. Rock., a botanic medicine dealer, & soldier of 28th Me. reg.; d. Sept. 6, '63, at home, of hydrophobia;

caused by a cat's bite, received when absent in the service. Their ch. Sarah E., b. ab. 1853.

HALL, John, b. ab. 1812, (son perhaps of John of Camden, who m. Mary Smith of Northport, April 29, 1803); m. Cyrena ——; r. Rock., a lime burner. Their ch. 1, Martha J., b. ab. 1837; r. Rock. 2, Albert M., b. April 12, '39; m. Mary L. Gray, Nov. 10, '58; r. Rock., & d. March 10, '59. 3, Edward, b. July 16, '42; r. Rock., a lime burner, soldier, &c. 4, Elsie F., b. ab. '45. 5, Mary E., b. April 23, '47, d, Feb. 25, '57. 6, Harriet A., b. ab. '49. 7 and 8, twins, b. Dec. 23, '54, George W., d. Feb. 8, '55, Clara R.; r. Rock. 9, Juliette F., b. '58, d. July 13, '64. 10, ——, d. Jan. 2, '62.

HALL, Jeremiah, b. ab. 1826; m. 1st, —— ——, 2d, Hannah E. Alley of Lynn, Mass., Oct. 29, '63; r. Rock., a lime burner. His ch. by 1st wife. 1, Almond B., b. ab. 1856. 2, Frederic H., b. ab. 1858.

HALL, Ambrose A., b. ab. 1827; m. Elvira A. ——; r. Rock., a shoemaker. Their ch. 1, Leander B., b. Jan., 1856, d. April 26, '60. 2, Angeline, b. ab. '58. 3, Frederic, b. '60.

HALL, Edmund S., b. ab. 1830; m. Hattie E. Childs, Nov. 3, '56; r. Rock., a shoemaker. Their ch. Eva L., b. ab. 1860.

HALL, Isaiah, b. ab. 1826; m. Sarah E. Sanders, Dec. 3, '54; r. Rock., a lime burner. Their ch. 1, Nathan, b. ab. 1856. 2, Elmore, b. ab. '58.

HALL, Lorenzo, b. ab. 1819; m. 2d, Mrs. Hannah Holbrook, Nov. 26, '48; r. Rock., a mariner. His ch. 1, Nelson, b. ab. 1841, a mariner, soldier, &c. 2 & 3, twins, b. ab. '43, Antoinette & Priscilla R. 4, Mary E., b. ab. '46. By 2d wife. 5, Charles E., b. ab. '52. 6, Merritt, b. ab. '54. 7, Melissa C., b. ab. '56.

HALL, William C., b. ab. 1828; m. Mary M. ——; r. Rock., a joiner. Their ch. Jenny M., b. July, and d. Aug. 28, 1861.

HALL, James, b. ab. 1814; m. Mahala ——; r. Rock. Their ch. 1, Mary V., b. ab. 1846. 2, Susie E., b. ab. '50.

HALL, James F., b. ab. 1833; m. Rebecca N. Ingalls, Sept. 9, '58; r. Rock., a mariner. Their ch. John M., b. 1860.

HALL, Edward, b. ab. 1827, in England, as was Catharine, his wife, in Ireland; r. Th., a carpenter, soldier in the 4th Me. Reg., &c. Their ch. 1, Vesper, b. ab. 1858. 2, Robert, b. ab. '60.

HALLOWELL, Capt. Reuel, b. ab. 1815, in Windsor, Me.; m. Emily Linn; r. Th., a master mariner. Their ch. 1, Leroy, b. ab. 1840; r. Th., a mariner. 2, George O., b. ab. '42. 3, Emily F., b. ab. '44. 4, Abbie L., b. ab. '46. 5, Reuel, b. ab. '48. 6, Ellen T., b. ab. '50. 7, Nathaniel, b. ab. '52. 8, Susan W., b. ab. '54. 9, William B., b. ab. '59.

HAM, Thomas, was a house holder at the incorporation of Old Th., but rem., and of him we have learned nothing more.

HAM, John, b. April, 1794, in Shepley, N. H.; came here, was a soldier under Gen. Scott at Lundy's Lane in the war of 1812; m. Mary McAllister, p. May 1, 1822; r. Rock., & d. Feb. 27, '64. Their ch. 1, Capt. Joseph N., b. March 28, 1823; m. Olive J. Berry, Nov. 17, '45; r. Rock. 2, Lydia J., b. May 30, '25, d. Jan., 1840. 3, William, b. May 6, '27, left home, quite young, and has never been heard from. 4, Lucy, b. Aug. 19, '29; m. John Karl; r. S. Th. 5, Lillias, b. Aug. 4, '31; rem. California, where she m. a Mr. Drush. 6, Sarah T., b. Aug. 2, '35; m. Charles Mathews, Jan. 1, '52; rem. California. 7, Elizabeth H., b. Aug. 7, '37; m. Anselm Davis; r. Rock. 8, John H., b. July 10, '43; m. Caroline E. Gott, May 28, '62; r. Rock., was a soldier in the 4th Me. Reg., and wounded at Williamsburg, May 5, '62, and a mariner since his honorable discharge. 9, Frank W., b. ab. 1845; a soldier of 2d Me. Battery.

Capt. Joseph N.'s ch. 1, Edith E., b. ab. 1854. 2, Leonard S., b. ab. '55. 3, Abbie H., b. ab. '57.

HAM, Edward P., b. ab. 1835; m. Avis ——— ; r. Rock., a joiner. Their ch. Addie E., b. ab. 1857.

HAMILTON, Alvah, c. hither; m. Caroline B. Lindsey, June 3, 1846; r. Rock., a stove dealer; rem. California. Their ch. Alvah, (2d), b. ab. 1849; r. Rock.

HAMMOND, Samuel, b. in 1770; m. Polly Blye, Feb. 19, 1800; r. at the Meadows; and d. Sept. 26, 1826. Their ch. 1, Edward, b. June 12, 1802; m. Susan Ulmer, Oct. 2, '28; r. Rock., and d. March 12, '34. 2, Mary, b. Jan. 20, '07; m. Benjamin Bartlett; r. Rock., & died May 2, '58. 3, John, born May 28, '10; m. Susan (Ulmer) Hammond, May 31, '31; r. Rock., and d. Oct. 19, '46. 4, James, b. Aug. 30, '14; m. Mrs. Eliza J. Gallop, p. Oct. 1, '46; r. Rock. 5, Henry, b. July 3, '17, d. unm. 6, Lydia, b. Aug. 12, '20; m. Josiah Clough of Th. 7, Susan, b. April 17, '25, d. Sept. 24, '26.

Edward's ch. 1, Harriet E., b. May 20, 1829; m. Thomas Brimigion; r. Rock. 2, Mary, b. Dec. 18, '31, d. Sept. 30, '32.

John's ch. 1, Henry, (2d), b. July 7, 1836; m. Adeline M. Seidlinger, Aug. 4, '61; r. Rock., a quarryman. 2, Eunice A., b. June 30, '38. 3, Julia Ann, b. Feb. 24, '40, d. Oct. 12, '41. 4, Mira, b. April 7, '42, d. Jan. 5, '63.

HANAKY, Augustus, came to what is now Rockland; m. Catharine (Ulmer) Seyers; and d. Aug. 31, 1841. Of their ch. Edgar A., b. ab. 1836; r. Rock., sergeant in 2d Me. Cavalry.

HANCOCK, Sewall, c. from St. George, Me., to which John, his father, had come as a trader; m. Lydia Jenks, p. Nov. 1, 1817, r. Th. and d. April 14, 1840. Their ch. 1, Leander W., b. Sept. 13, 1818; m. and went to the Red River; d. in Texas. 2, James William, b. May 6, 1620, ? rem. Texas. 3, Harriet Lydia, m. and r. in Medford, Mass. 4, ———, b. in 1824, d. Sept. 5, '25, of dysentery.

HANDLEY, John, from Holland, Europe, m. Lucy Lewis, from Wales, England; r. Georges Fort, Th., and Canton, Mass. Their ch. 1, Henry, killed by the Indians, 1756. 2, Joseph, killed at the same time with his brother. 3, Hannah. 4, William, r. and died in Roxbury. 5, Samuel, lost at sea. 6, Nancy, m. Simeon Hyler of C. 7, Lucy, m. ——— Hawthorn of Bangor; was drowned by the upsetting of a sail-boat in mouth of the river, when coming to St. Geo. on a visit. 8, Jane, mar. John Whipple of Boston. 9, John, mar. Mary Etheredge; took up lots No. 29 and 30 of wild land in Middle Neck, in upper part of St. Geo., where he r. and d., a mason, having done the mason work on the Knox mansion, &c.

John's ch. 1, Nancy, m. Ephraim Linnekin of C. 2, Mary, born Oct. 19, 1777; mar. 1st, Geo. Lash, 2d, John Harrington of S. Th., rem. St. Geo. and d. Nov. 16, 1861. 3, John, (2d), died aged 9 mos.

4, William, m. Nancy McKellar of St. George. 5, Jane, mar. James Weed, r. Appleton. 6, Capt. Simon, m. Jane Glidden; r. New Castle. 7, Henry, (2d), m. Mary Carney; r. Boothbay. 8, Lucinda, m. John Leeds; r. W. 9, John, (3d), b. Feb. 3, 1791; m. Eliza Hall of St. Geoorge, r. Rock., a stone mason; and died very suddenly, July 11, 1859.

John, (3d)'s ch. 1, Capt. Freeman C., mar. Catharine V. Ulmer, Aug. 29, 1858; r. Rock. 2, Elijah H., b. ab. 1833; mar. Orrana L. Ingraham of Cam. Feb. 15, '59; r. Rock., a mariner. The mother d. May 12, '61, aged 58.

HANLEY, John H., b. ab. 1820; c. from Hope; mar. Lydia W. Beverage of Fox Is., Nov. 18, '49; r. Rock., a clerk. Their ch. Addie W., b. Jan. 1, '52.

HANLEY; of this Bristol family, 1, Roger, m. Mary Fitzgerald; r. and d. Bristol. 2, John, m. Sarah Hanly; r. Bristol. 3, Philip, m. Sophia Fitzgerald; r. and d. Bristol.

Roger's ch. 1, William, m. Nancy Hatch; r. Bristol, homestead. 2, John, (2d), m. Mary Lawley; r. & d. Damariscotta. 3, James R., b. ab. 1809; m. 1st, Eliza Schenk, 2d, Bathsheba Ludwig; r. Rock., a mason. 4, Roger, d. young. 5, Jerome, d. young. 6, Roger, died young. 7, Roger, (4th), mar. Catharine C. Clark; r. Chelsea, Mass. 8, Felicitas, m. John Rafter; r. Damariscotta. 9, Francis A., b. ab. 1820; m. Martha P. Lermond, Dec. 25, 1848, 2d, Maria J. (Lermond) Welsby, July, 1853; r. Th., a joiner, light-keeper on Monhegan, &c. 10, Mary, m. Michael Furlong; r. Dam. 11, Sophia Ann, d. unm. 12, Theresa, m. Peter Connell; r. and d. Damariscotta.

John's ch. 1, Mary, m. George Starrett; r. Th. 2, Sarah Ann, d. young. 3, Margaret, m. William Fitzgerald; r. Th. 4, Sarah. 5, John, d. young. 6, Dennis R., m. Anastatia Hazelton.

Philip's ch. 1, Philip George, b. ab. 1825; m. Sarah Keating, p. Jan. 10, '57; r. Th., a blacksmith. 2, Sophia Kate, r. Boston. 3, Jos. W., b. ab. 1830; m. Catharine Fall, April 12, '56; r. Th., a carpenter. 4, Anastatia, m. William Levensaler; r. Boston. 5, Sarah Elizabeth. 6, Silas, m. Adeliza Bradford, 1864; r. Th.

James R.'s ch. by 1st wife. 1, Addie S., b. ab. 1839; m. Joseph W. Jackson; r. Rock. 2, James S., b. ab. '41, a mariner. 3, Augustus V., a soldier in 4th Me. reg. & U. S. regular Battery. 4, Danville, d. young.

Francis A.'s ch. 1, Florence May, b. Sept. 24, 1849. By 2d wife. 2, Frank, b. July 27, '54. 3, Martha, b. May 18, '57.

Philip George's ch. 1, Lizzie, d. young. 2, William Augustine. 3, George Vincent. 4, Philip Eugene.

Joseph W.'s ch. 1, Joseph Edwin. 2, Ann Estelle. 3, Oswald, b. March, 1860.

HANLY, Patrick, b. ab. 1820; c. from the north of Ireland, with his wife, Mary, & r. Th. Michael, a brother, also came here, but died in 1856. Patrick's ch. 1, Kate, b. in Ireland, ab. '45. 2, George, b. ab. 1847, in Maine. 3, Peter, b. ab. '49. 4, Margaret, born about 1852.

HANSON, James F., b. ab. 1795; m. Abigail Robinson of Boston, Dec. 30, 1823; r. Th. & d. Feb. 4, '31. Their ch. 1, Capt. William S., b. ab. '24; m. Josephine ———, of Paris, France; r. Rock., in U. S. naval service. 2, Catharine, b. ab. '26; m. Capt. Oliver Sleeper; r. Rock. 3, Mary F. S., b. July '28, d. Oct. 20, '30.

Capt. William S.'s ch. 1, Mary, b. ab. 1852, in N. York. 2, Abby, b. ab. '58.

HANSON, Philip, b. May 27, 1774, in Dover, N. H., c. to Th., m. Mary Hastings, Jan. 6, 1799; r. Th., a merchant, &c., and d. July 27, 1804. Their ch. 1, Mary Ann, b. May 18, '03; m. Samuel Howard of Dover, March 3, '25. 2, Philena, b. Sept. 3, '04; m. Tilley Clements, r. Rock.

HARDEN, Freeman, b. in Pembroke, Mass., Aug. 4, 1783; c. to old Th. in 1799; m. Hannah Rankin, April 22, '06; r. Rock., a leading man, and early friend of temperance; and d. Nov. 22, '48. Their ch. 1, Freeman, (2d), b. June 30, '06; m. Ruth R. Spear, Nov. 9, '26; r. Rock , a farmer, &c. 2, Hannah I., b. Aug. 6, '15; m. Dudley P. Spofford; r. Rock.

Freeman, (2d)'s ch. 1, Heman P., b. Aug. 9, 1827; m. Martha A. J. Trueworthy, Nov. 2, 1851; r. Rock., in the mercantile line. 2, Capt. John, b. April 30, '29; m. Sarah J. Pillsbury, Dec. 16, '51; r. Rock., employed in U. S. naval service. 3 & 4, twins, b. May 1, '34; Edwin A., d. May 2, '34, Helen A., d. Oct. 2, '34. 5, Clarence F., b. Sept. 4, & d. Sept. 6, '38. 6, R. Frances E., b. May 8, '46. 7, George N., b. Jan. 31, '51.

Capt. John F.'s ch. 1, Charles F., b. ab. 1854. 2, Albert R., b. Oct. '57, d. Sept. 8, '59.

HARDING, John, b. 1825, son of Phillips C. Harding of Union; m. Elizabeth Oliver, Nov. 26, '51; r. Th., a butcher. Their ch. 1, Oliver C., b. Jan. 26, '54. 2, John Alden, b. March 27, '56, d. Oct. 3, '57. 3, Ida May, b. Aug. 5, '58. 4, Eliza F., b. April 6, '61.

HARDING, Otis, came from Abington, Mass.; m. Margaret Blackington, Jan. 1, 1817; r. Th., and died Aug. 23, 1834. Their ch. 1, Eleanor, born Oct. 16, 1818; m. Ebenezer Colley, Feb. 4, 1838; 2d, Samuel F. Johnston, p. Dec. 15 '49, rem. Mass. 2, Harriet, b. March 9, '21; 3, Matilda, b. Jan. 24, '23; m. ——— Prouty; 4, Maria, born Dec. 11, 26; all m. and r. Abington, and other places in Mass.

HARDING, Dr. Elisha, b. 1796; M. D. at Brown University, 1819; came to Union in the spring of that year, from Franklin, Mass.; m. Amelia Hawes of U.; prac. med. there till 1842, when he rem. Rock., continued his practice; and d. May 6, 1850. His widow d. at Rock., April 3, 1852. Their ch. 1, Harriet A. b. June 7, 1820, d. Aug. 2, '26. 2, Nathaniel Miller, b. Feb. 9, 22; m. Sarah W. Cobb of Union, June 13, '39; r. Rock., and d. Oct. 24, '58.

Nathaniel M's ch. 1, Amelia Alwilder, b. Nov. 3, 1841, d. May 13, '42. 2, Lewis Cobb, b. July 31, '49, d. Feb. 28, '51.

HARDING, William, b. ab. 1830; m. Vesta ———; r. Rock., a teamster. Their ch. 1, Emily, b. ab. 1858. 2, George, b. ab. 1859.

HARDING, Josiah, b. ab. 1796; m. Lucinda ———; r. Rockland, in the fish business. Of their ch. 1, Lieut Eben, b. ab. 1833; mar. Almira Grover, May 21, '51; r. Rock., keeper of fish market, 1860; since in the 4th Me. Reg., now rem. 2, William H., born ab. 1842; m. Sarah C. Fales, April 22, '63; r. Rock., a fisherman, rem. recently. 3, Mary M , b. ab. '45.

Eben's ch. 1, Lucinda, b. ab. 1852. 2, Henry N., b. ab. '54. 3, Charles E., b. ab. '56.

HARDY, Capt. Weston, born 1807; came from Bremen, Me., mar. Maria H. Arnold of B., Jan. 25, 1846; r. Rock. Benjamin, Esq., a brother, b. ab. 1812, m. Elizabeth M. Arnold, March 7, '44; r. Rock., attorney at law.

Capt. Weston's ch. 1, William W., b. ab. 1847; r. Rock., in U. S. Navy. 2, Charles S., b. ab. '52.

Benjamin, Esq.'s ch. 1, Henry F., b. ab. 1854. 2 and 3, twins, b. ab. 1859, Emma I. and Albert.

HARLOW, Capt. Richard F., b. ab. 1818, came from New York; m. Sarah F. Dyer, Oct. 18, '41; r. S. Th. Their ch. 1, Richard B., b. July 2, '42; r. S. Th., a mariner. 2, Hannah F., b. ab. 1845. 3, Charles, b. ab. 1847. 4, Silas M., b. ab. 1849. 5, Edwin W., b. ab. 1851. 6, Frederic W., b. ab. 1854. 7, Oscar G., born ab. 1856. 8, William H., b. ab. 1859.

HARPER, Reuben A., b. ab. 1827; m. Mary S. Henderson, Oct. 19, '51., r. Rock., a lime burner, &c. Their ch. 1, Emma J., b. ab. 1854. 2, an infant, d. Dec. 21, '57. 3, Edward, b. ab. '59.

HARRINGTON, Asa, b. in Worcester, Mass.; m. Asenath Brown; r. Uxbridge, Mass., Barre, Vt., and Acworth, N. H., where he died. Of their 8 ch, 4 came to Maine. 1, Asa, (2d), m. Betsey Watts of St. Geo.; r. and d. Appleton. 2, Benjamin, d. unm. in Machias. 3, Steward, m. Rosanna Robinson of St. Geo.; r. W. and Th., where he d. Sept. 30, 1845. 4, Panthea, b. in Acworth, Jan. 18, 1795; mar. Jacob Allen, p. Nov. 5, 1829; r. Th. & d. Nov. 2, '62. Her husband, we have learned, on the excellent authority of T. J. Rider of Th., during the printing of this Table, but too late for insertion in the proper place, was the only ch. of Jacob & Lucy Allen (cousins) of Gloucester, Mass., b. Aug. 28, 1763; m. 1st. in Millbridge, or Marsh Bay, or Frankfort, whence he came to Th., 1826, & was the first man that ever built pound-weirs in George's River for catching alewives; had been a local Free Will Baptist or Methodist preacher; m. again here and d. Aug. 23, 1858; having had by 1st wife a son Jacob, who r. in Millbridge; a dau. Sally, who r. in Bangor; and 6 other ch.

Asa, (2d),'s ch. 1, Asenath, m. Isaac A. Willis, and d. Dec. 27, 1832. 2, Benjamin, m. and rem. Illinois. 3, Mary J., m. Maddin L. Willis; r. Th. 4, Asa, (3d), m. ——— ———, and r. Searsmont. 5, Susan M., m. Benjamin T. Foster; r. Th. 6, Giles, m. Lucy Davis; r. Belfast. 7, Elizabeth, m. Alden M. Harrington; r. Th. and died March 18, '64.

Steward's ch. 1, Charles S., b. Nov. 26, 1818; m. Sarah McCarter, Aug. 29, '48; r. Th., a mariner. 2, Jane R., b. Aug. 12, 20; m. Simon Watts; r. Th. 3, Joseph R., b. May 9, '23. 4, Harriet T., b. May 23, '25; m. Dexter W. Hildreth; rem. California. 5, Alden M., b. July 4, '27; m. Elizabeth Harrington; r. Th., a mariner. 6, Lovicy C., b. Feb. 10, '30; m. and r. California. 7, Albert Chandler, b. Nov. 10, '32; r. Th., a mariner. 8, Mary F. D., b. Feb. 10, '35; m. and r. Portland.

Charles S.'s ch. 1, George, b. ab. 1849. 2, Harriet, b. '51. 3, Joshua R., b. '53. 4, Abbie, b. '55. 5, Frank Chandler, b. June 6, '57, d. June 18, '58.

Alden M.'s ch. Marcia, b. ab. 1857.

HARRINGTON, Jacob, b. ab. 1778; c. with Betsey his wife from Damariscotta, Me.; r. Rock., and d. Nov. 16, 1854. Their ch. 1, Joel W., b. ab. 1804; m. Rebecca Melcher of Newcastle, 2d, Mrs. Elizabeth Barstow, Feb., 1831; r. Th., a hat and fur dealer. 2, Theron W., m. Henrietta N. Cox; ret. Damariscotta, 1843. 3, Adaline,

m. James Partridge; r. Th. 4, Francis, b. ab. 1816; m. Sarah A. Holmes, Sept. 18, '37; r. Rock., a pump & block maker. 5, Isabella D., m. Martin Labe; r. Rock., as does also their mother, with her.

Joel W.'s ch. by 2d wife. 1, Mary R., b. Dec. 4, 1831; m. T. A. Wentworth; r. Rock. 2, Caroline A., b. July 4, '34. 3, Oliver B., b. Nov. 2, and d. Dec. 14, '36. 4, Leanora C., b. Feb. 25, '39.

Theron W.'s ch. 1, Theron, b. ab. 1830, and d. of cholera in Bankoke, Siam, March 10, '63. 2, Harriet N., b. Aug. 19, '33; 3, Elizabeth C., b. June 20, '36; both rem. Damariscotta. 4, Helen, b. April 2, '41, d. July 15, '42.

Francis's ch. 1, Emily G., b. June 4, 1838; m. George F. Kaler; r. Rock. 2, Sarah F., b. Jan. 23, '42; r. Rock. 3, William H., b. ab. '47. 4, Ada M. 5, Anna L. 6, Charles M.

HARRINGTON, John, c. from Boothbay; m. Mary Handly, and d. in S. Th. Of his ch. 1, Asa, b. Sept. 21, 1818; m. Eliza Kelloch, Dec. 23, '30; r. S. Th.

Asa's ch. 1, Charles, b. Jan. 1, 1834, d. Feb. 16, '35. 2, Nancy B., b. Dec. 29, '34; mar. John B. Haley, Dec. 7, '54; r. S. Th. 3, Charles B., b Nov. 14, '36; r. S. Th., a mariner. 4, James, b. March 2, '39 5, Isaac B., b May 8, '41. 6, Waldo. 7, Susan.

HARRINGTON, Charles, b. 1792; c. from Mass.; m. Margaret Keen, p. Jan. 1, 1824; r. Rock., a merchant, and died Dec. 12, 1847. Their ch. 1, John K., b. Jan. 3, '25, d. Feb. 15, '48. 2, Charles A., b. Oct. 13, '26; m. Priscilla Sears, Jan. 14, '51, 2d, Caroline E. Jones, May 26, '57; r. Rock., a merchant, but rem. 1864. 3, Elliott T., b. Feb. 3, '28; m. Sophronia Achorn, 1848; r. Rock., and d. May 12, '51. 4, Harriet A., b. April 26, '29; m. Albion P. Mosman; r. Rock. and d. Oct. 15, '58. 5, Susan M., b. Aug. 31, '30, d. Nov. 23, '36. 6, Orissa Ann, died young. 7, Hortense, b. Feb. 25, '34; m. Capt. Levi B. Gilchrist; r. Th. 8, M. Maria, b. Oct. 23, '35; m. Charles Ingraham; r. Rock. 9, Sarah L., b. May 9, '37; m. Capt. John H. Gleason; r. Th. 10, M. Victoria, b. June 13, '39; m. Capt. Arthur Prince; r. Th. 11, Julia A., b. Oct. 28, '41; m. Charles Waterman; r. Th.

Charles A.'s ch. 1, Eva H., b. ab. 1852. 2, Edith, b. ab. '54. By 2d wife. 3, Emma H., b. ab. '59.

HARRINGTON, Timothy, b. ab. 1810; came with Mary his wife, from Ireland; r. Rock. Their ch. 1, Mary M., b. ab. 1844. 2, Timothy, b. ab. '51. 3, Margaret, b. ab. '54. 4, Jeremiah, b. ab. '56. 5, James, b. ab. '59.

HARRINGTON, John, b. ab. 1829; came with Hannah, his wife, from Ireland; r. Rock. Their ch. 1, Margaret, b. ab. 1857. 2, John, (2d), b. ab. '58.

HARRIS; of this family, two brothers came here from Germany. 1, Edward, b. ab. 1821; m. Ottilie Matthias of Brooklyn, N. Y., June 17, '55; r. Rock., a merchant. 2, Julius, b. ab '27, in Prussia, but now a naturalized citizen of the U. S.; m. Theresa Peavey; r. Rock. a merchant.

Edward's ch. 1, Zerlina, b. May 14, 1855. 2, Jacob C., b. Nov. 17, '57. 3, Edward, b. ab. '59.

Julius's ch. 1, Anselm M., b. ab. 1858. 2, Solomon K., b. Oct. 23, 1860.

HART, Rev. Henry A., from Portland, graduate Waterville Coll. 1857, Newton, The. Sem., 1860; m. Nellie M. Hanson of Portland,

July 10, '60; r. Rockland, pastor of first Baptist Ch. Their ch. 1, Howard Sumner, b. June 26, and d. July 17, '64.

HASKELL, Francis, b. 1749, an early inhabitant of Old Th., c., it is believed, from Deer Isle; m. 1st, Lydia Crockett, 2d, Jane Stimson; r. Ash Point, S. Th., a farmer, &c., and d. July 14, 1842, a. 93. His ch. by 1st wife. 1, Lydia, m. John Grant; r. Vinalhaven. 2, David, lost at sea with Capt. Dunning. 3, Lucy, b. Oct. 14, 1781, in Th., m. Abraham Simonton; and d. May 23, 1832. By 2d wife, 4, Capt. John, b. 1785; m. Mary Jordan of Harrington, p. Sept. 15, 1810; r. S. Th. 5, Betsey, b. Aug. 15, 1787; m. Coit Ingraham; & d. April 16, 1814. 6, Hannah, b. 1789; m. William Kelloch; r. S. Th., and d. Nov. 28, 1845. 7, Capt. Francis, (2d); m. 1st Mary Kelloch, Jan. 23, 1817, 2d, Mrs. Mary Hall; was in command of schr. *Mars*, and d. Nov. 21, '46, being found drowned in Boston harbor. 8, Ruth, m. Samuel Thayer, 2d, ? James Dusten, pub. Dec. 21, '32. 9, Capt. Thomas, b. ab. 1796; mar. Betsey Kelloch, Feb. 2, 1822; r. S. Th., a farmer. 10, Elsa, m. George W. Coombs; r. S. Th. 11, Jane, m. Ambrose Kelloch; r. S. Th. 12, Abigail, m. ——— Perkins, r. Boston. 13, Capt. David, (2d), b. July 17, 1809; m. 1st, Keziah Packard, Jan. 10, 1828; 2d, Eliza K. (Hall) Heard; r. S. Th., a mariner, like most of his brothers, and d. Nov. 3, '54. Jane, the mother, d. May 13, '44, a. 77.

Capt. John's ch. 1, Alfred, b. July 27, 1814; m. 1st, Nancy P. Heard, 2d, Hannah M. Philbrook, Nov. 27, 1843; r. S. Th., a wheelwright. 2, Eliza J., b. April 18, '16; m. Nathaniel Merriman; r. S. Th. 3, Catharine, b. Sept. 3, '18, d. Dec. 30, '24. 4, Mary A., born Oct. 16, '20; m. Charles H. Cables, r. Rock. 5, Noyes P., born June 21, 23; m. Eveline Bartlett; r. S. Th., a carpenter.

Capt. Francis, (2d)'s ch. by 2d wife. 1, Caroline S., b. Dec. 16, 1836. 2, Elbridge F., b. Aug. 9, 1840.

Capt. Thomas's ch. 1, Mary Jane, b. July 4, 1823; r. S. Th. 2, Hannah, b. May 30, '35; m. Capt. Samuel A. Thompson; r. S. Th. 3, George C., b. Oct. 24, '30; m. Eliza E. Miller of L. C., r. S.Th., a mariner. 4, Lydia M., b. Sept. 12, '34; r. S. Th. 5, William T., b. Jan. 12, '38; r. S. Th., a mariner.

Capt. David, (2d)'s ch. 1, Capt. Benjamin F., b. Oct. 8, 1828; m. Cornelia L. Shepherd, June 8, '49; r. S. Th. 2, Amanda Jane, born April 7, '31; m. Magnus Ventress of Boston, Oct. 19, '51. 3, Catharine C., b. July 3, '33; m. Thomas McLain. 4, James P., born July 10, '36; m. Helen M. Ventress, Nov. 24, '56; died Jan. 19, '57, lost overboard from barque *Tidal Wave*.

Fourth Generation.

Alfred's ch. by 2d wife. 1, Alfred D., b. ab. 1845. 2, Nancy M., b. ab. '47. 3, John D., b. ab. '49. 4, Francena H., b. ab. '51. 5, Mira A., b. ab. '55.

Noyes P.'s ch. Mary E. b. ab. 1853.

George C.'s ch. Edward T., b. ab. 1860.

HASKELL, Josiah, b. ab. 1758, c. early to what is now Rockland, before the incorporation of old Thomaston, with his wife Abigail, who d. Jan. 7, 1830, a. 65; m. 2d, Abigail Berry, Sept. 5, '30; r. Rock., & d. May 5, '44, a. 86. His ch. by 1st wife. 1, John W., b. ab. '10; m. 1st, Mary J. Branton, p. Nov. 21, '33, 2d, Eliza J. Clark, Jan. 5, '41; r. Rock., a mariner, soldier in the 4th Me. reg., &c.

John W.'s ch. by 1st wife. 1, Mary J., b. Aug. 15, 1837, d. Dec.

14, '38. The mother d. March 16, '39. By 2d wife. 2, George, b. Oct. 2, '42, r. Rock., a mariner. 3, Charles, b. ab. '48 ; r. Rock., a soldier in 28th Me. reg. 4, Edwin, b. ab. '51. 5, John, b. ab. 1854.

HASKELL, Col. John, c. from Greenwich, Mass. ; m. Sarah D. Sampson of Wal. ; r. Th., as a merchant, militia officer, &c., & d. 1834 or '35. Had brothers, viz., Tilson, Ira, & William, the last of whom came to Waldoboro', and removed to Windsor.

Col. John's ch. 1, Sarah Elizabeth, b. Feb. 11. 1810; m. 1st, Eusebius Fales, 2d, Charles Loring; r. Portland. 2, John E., b. Feb. 1, '11 ; m. & r. Cass co., Virginia. 3, Mary S., b. Nov. 13, '13 ; m. Edmund Wilson, Esq. ; r. Th. 4, Martha B., b. Nov. 3, '18 ; m. Shubael Waldo; r. Th. 5, Susan Lovett, b. July 16, '21 ; m. Col. Wm. Bennett; r. Th., & d. May 20, '53. 6, Capt. Charles W. T., b. Oct. 1, '23; m. Mary U. Black; r. Ellsworth. The mother d. at Bucksport, Jan. 21, '50, a. 66 yrs., & 6 months.

HASKELL, Daniel C., b. ab. 1808, in China, Me. ; m. 1st, Hannah Sleeper, p. Aug. 24, '31. 2d, Jane R. Perry, March 16, '36 ; r. Rock., a lime manufacturer. His ch. by 1st wife. 1, Samuel S., b. April 5, '33 ; m. Olive G. Vaughan, Feb. 16, '58 ; r. Rock., in lime business. 2, Daniel O., b. Sept. 8, '34; m. Caroline Bennett or Babb, Dec. 11, '58 ; r. Rock. By 2d wife 3, William O., b. Feb. 8, '37; m. Hannah A. Haskell, Jan. 12, '62; r. Rock., a mariner. 4, Charles H., b. July 15, '38; m. Faustina D. Morse, April 6, '62 ; r. Rock., a farmer. 5, Albert E., b. Jan. 14, '40 ; m. Susan Hilt; r. Rock. 6, Amariah K., b. ab. '43 ; m. Adelaide Whitcher, Feb. 14, '63 ; r. Rock.

Samuel S.'s ch. Charles A., b. ab. 1859.

HASKELL, William, born 1822 ; m. Emeline ——— ; r. Rock., a joiner.

HASSAN, Samuel, b. ab. 1798 ; m. Martha (Richards) Pendleton; r. Rock. Of his ch. 1, Samuel, (2d). b. ab. 1821 ; m. Harriet Spear, p. Nov. 21, '40 ; r. Rock., a lime burner, &c.

Samuel, (2d)'s ch. 1, Charles, born Jan. 25, 1843 ; a mariner. 2, Martha A., b. ab., '45. 3, Susan F., b. ab. '47. 4, Joseph, b. ab. '52. 5, Rebecca A., b. Dec. 17, '54, d. Sept. 1, '56. 5, Stephen R., b. ab. 1857.

HASTINGS, ———, of Boston, m. Mary Lushe; r. & d. in Boston. Their ch. who c to Th. (with their mother, who m. 2d, Spencer Vose), 1, Mary, b. March, 1770, mar. 1st, Philip Hanson, 2d, Dr. Isaac Bernard ; r. Rock., & d. Nov. 11, 1849. 2, Nancy, m. Stephen Thompson, r. Th.

HASTINGS, Benjamin, c. from Lexington, Mass. to Th., m. Jerusha, widow of Capt. Alexander Pease, p. June 6, 1801 ; r. Th. where his wife kept tavern in Wadsworth street many years ; enlisted and d. in the army of 1812. Their ch. 1, Ann Maria, b. ab. 1802 ; m. Henry K. Gleason ; r. Th. Jerusha, the mother, d. Sept. 27, 1839, aged 80.

HASTINGS, T. Matthew, b. 1823 ; (son of Thaddeus, who mar. Hannah Vaughan, and r. and d. Hope), m. Abby O. Trull, Jan. 10, 1853 ; r. Th., a carpenter, and d. Feb. 23, '61. Their ch. 1, Caroline, b. Oct. 12, '53. 2, Alton B., b. '57. 3, Samuel, b. '60.

HASTY, Joseph, c. here from Shapleigh, Me., before 1812 ; r. unm. and d. in Rock., on what was afterwards the McIntosh place, burnt in 1862.

HATCH, Rowland, b. ab. 1803; came from Nobleboro', Me.; m. 1st, Mary, daughter of Capt. Thomas Brackett of Bristol, 2d, her sister, Charlotte Brackett, Feb. 26, '29; r. Th., a blacksmith. His ch. by 1st wife. 1, Elizabeth S., b. Sept. 14, 1824; mar. John Ellis of Halifax, N. S., Nov. 19, '46; r. Charlestown, Mass. 2, Charlotte B., b. Aug. 17, '26, d. Oct. 6, '31. The mother d. Sept 13, '27. By 2d wife. 3, Mary J., b. March 1, '31, d. June 25, '42. 4, William H., b Aug. 6, '32; m. Julia A. Gloyd, Feb. 25, '55; r. Th., a tin plate worker, rem. 5, Arthur J., b. Dec. 4, '34; m. Olive Liscomb, Nov. 12, '56; r. Th., in tin and stove business.

William H.'s ch. 1, Roland H., b. Dec. 16, 1855. 2, Lizzie E., b. July 12, '57. 3, Charles, b. '60.

Arthur J.'s ch. Elizabeth B., b. ab. 1859.

HATCH, Nathan, m. Jane Stetson, March 3, 1819; r. and d. Robbinston, Me. Their ch. 1, Nathan, (2d), b. June, 1824; m. Nancy J. Stearns, Sept. 13, '48; r. Th., and d. Nov. 8, '54. 2, William L., m. Harriet M. Trussell, Jan. 21, '52; r. Th., a carpenter, &c. 3, Mary A., m. John S. Crouch; r. Th.

Nathan, (2d)'s ch. 1, Mary A., b. ab. 1849. 2, Charles H., b. Feb. '51, d. March 25, '52. 3, Wilbur F., b. ab. '53. The mother d. Feb. 24, '59, aged 31.

William L.'s ch. 1, Frederic, b. ab. 1853. 2, Clara, b. ab. '56. 3, Nathan, (3d), b. ab. '58.

HATCH, Stephen, born in Gorham, Me., May 10, 1786; mar. 1st, Mercy Dyer, March 5, 1807; 2d, Diadema Smith of Steuben; rem. Eastport, and in 1829, Dec. 13th, to what is now Rockland, where he r. and d. July 4, 1858. His ch. by 1st wife, who was born in Stroudwater, June 25, 1787, were: 1, Eliza Jane, b Jan. 19, 1808; m. Capt. Luther Kendall; r. Rock., and d. April 13, 1858. 2, Asa D., born in Gorham, Oct. 16, 1810; m. Abigail S Irish, 1832, 2d, Mercy Irish; rem. San Francisco, Cal. 3, Stephen N., b. in Eastport, Jan. 15, '12; m. Lydia S. Thomas, Sept. 25, '33; r. Rock., cashier of North Bank, &c. 4, George L., b. Oct. 10, '14; m. Elvira Daggett, Oct. 31, '41; r. New York. By 2d wife, who d. Oct. 12, 1849, aged 59 years. 5, Capt. William S., b. ab. 1820; m. Abbie C. Berry, Sept. 11, '43; r. Rock. 6, Josiah H., rem. California. 7, Mary C, m. and r. New Jersey. 8, Margaret E., b. April 26, '32, in Rock.; r. New Jersey. 9, Loring W., b. Dec. 26, '34; m. Annie Coombs, July 22, '56; r. Rock., a mariner.

Stephen N.'s ch. 1, Lucy H., b. Feb. 28, 1834. 2, Hannah Adelia, b. Oct. 25, '35, d. Sept. 12, '60. 3, Julia A., b. Jan. 13, '41, d. March 11, '42.

George L.'s ch. Charles L., b. Aug. 29, 1842, and perhaps others.

Capt. William S.'s ch. Henry U., b. ab. 1848.

Loring W.'s ch. George N., b. ab. 1857.

HATCH, Hiram, b. ab. 1814, in China, Me., son of Sylvanus Hatch, jr., c. to Rock., 1849; m. Eliza Ann Haskell of Livermore, March 23, '51; r. Rock., a millinery merchant. Their ch. 1, Nathan Grover, b. June 22, 1853, d. Nov. 14, '57. 2, Ann E., b. Sept 2, '58, d. Sept. 12, '61. 3, Jessie Waters, b. Sept. 8, '61.

HATCH, Hiram F., b. ab. 1817, of a different family; m Nancy C. Davis; r. Rock., a joiner, &c., rem. California. Their ch. 1, Georgiana, b. ab. 1847. 2 & 3, twins, b. ab. '49, Orrin D., and Warren [illegible].

HATCH, Samuel, b. ab. 1816; m. Mary B. ——— ; r. Rock., a

oiner. Their ch. 1, Wilton B., b. ab. 1839. 2, Mary E., b. ab. 41. 3, Ella B., b. ab. '51. 4, Arabelle, b. ab. '53. 5, George E., b. ab. '55. 6, Freeman L., b. April 21, '58, d. Dec. 4, '63.

HATCH, Henry, b ab. 1829 ; m. Hannah ——— ; r. Rock., a carpenter. Their ch. 1, Ronelle, b. ab. 1856. 2, Estelle, b. ab. '58.

HATCH, Leonard C., b. ab. 1833 ; m. Eliza E. ——— ; r. Rock., a joiner. Their ch. William, b. ab. 1855.

HATCH, Andrew, b. ab. 1835 ; m. Ruth B. ——— ; r. S. Th., a carpenter. Their ch. 1, Sarah F., b. ab. 1851. 2, Mary E., b. ab. '56. 3, Albert C. F., b. ab. '59.

HAVENER, (original German spelling, Heibener,) William H., b. ab. 1815 ; m. 1st, Clara L. Roberts of Brooks, p. Feb. 16, '41, 2d, Lucretia W., ———, (who died Dec. 29, 1860, a. 28,) 3d, Alice S. Trundy, March 17, '61 ; r. Rock., a meat dealer, &c. His ch. by 1st wife. 1, Clara F., b. ab. 1842, r. Rock. 2, Charles H., b. ab. 1844. 3, Abby F., b. ab. '48. 4, William, b. ab. '50. 5, Mary E., b. about '52. The mother d. June 4, '57, aged 36.

HAVENER, Capt Joseph Albert, b. ab. 1829 ; cousin of William H., and son of Joseph Albert Havener, of Waldoboro' ; mar. 1st, Eveline M. Paine, Aug. 29, 1853, 2d, Charlotte B. Wallace ; r. Th. His ch. by 2d wife. Clara E , b. ab. 1859.

HAVENER, James A , b. ab. 1816, came, it is believed, from Belfast, with Olive B., his wife ; r. Rock., a shoemaker. Their ch. 1, Emma A., b. ab. '44 ; m. J. Y. Wing, Nov. 10, '63. 2, Herbert C., b. ab. '47. 3, Ada, b. ab '50. 4, Anna D., b. ab. '54.

HAVENER, Richmond H., b. ab. 1826 ; mar. Harriet ——— ; r. Rock., a teamster. Their ch. 1, John W., b. ab. 1852. 2, Arabella K., b. ab. '54. 3, Hattie F., b. ab. '56.

HAWES, Capt. Robert, b. ab. 1807, (probably a son of Robert, of Cushing, who m. Lydia Kelloch of Th., June 10, 1802,) m. and r. Rock., a mariner. Of his ch. recorded here, Lucinda was b. May 27, 1834. Annis, the mother, d. in Rock., Sept. 10, 1861, a. 47 y. 8 m. 11 d.

HAWES, George W., b. ab. 1828, m. Mary Warren of Freedom, p. Dec. 15, '52 ; r. Rock., a mariner. Their ch. 1, Reuel, b. ab. '54. 2, Samuel, b. ab. '56.

HAWK, John B., a native of Germany, came to the W. Indies, and, in 1773, to this country ; was a soldier of the Revolution ; m. Sarah ———, of N. B., r. W., and d. Feb. 3, 1824. Their ch. 1, Mary, m. Joseph Hodgkins ; r. and d. Damariscotta. 2, Martha, mar. ——— Burns ; and r. Damariscotta. 3, Capt. John, b. Feb. 11, 1791 ; spent his youth in W. ; m. Harriet Blackington of Th., May 15, 1815 ; commanded a coaster, was captured, and sometime a prisoner at Halifax, in the war of 1812 ; r. Th., and d. at St. Augustine, Oct. 18, 1839 ; (Recorder) Oct. 18, 1840. 4, Sarah, kept boarding house, &c. ; m. in Boston. 4, Deborah,? probably d. young.

Capt. John's ch. 1, Harriet G., b. Nov. 5, 1817 ; mar. Dr. Daniel Rose, r. Th. and d. May 5, 1861. 2, Lucy W., b. July 18, '20 ; mar. Wilmot Rose ; r. Th. 3, James D., b. July 22, '23 ; lost at sea from sch. *Frances Ellen*, Jan. 1846. 4, John, (2d), b. Aug. 23, '26 ; r. California ; 5, Sarah F., b. Aug. 27, '28 ; probably d. young. 6, Mandana, b. Dec. 16, '33 ; mar. S. Parker Swett of Georgetown, Nov. 1,

'57; r. Bath and Th. 7, Laura J., b. Aug. 15, '35, r. Th. 8, Susan L., b. Jan. 9, '37; m. Lieut. James H. Hewett; r. Th.

HATHORN, or Hawthorne; of this Cushing family, Rebecca, m. J. Harvey Healey, r. Rock. 2, Mercy, m. Hon. Halsey Healey; r. Th., and d. June 12, 1829. Of their brothers, Capt. James, who m. and r. St. Geo., and Capt, Alexander, who m. Keturah Watts, r. Th., and d. in N. York, were both masters of Col. Healey's vessels, sailing many years from this place.

Of Capt. James's ch.. 1, Halsey H., m. Sarah Montgomery of C., r. and d. Th. 2, Mercy, b. July, 1811; m. Rev. Amariah Kalloch, and d. March 27, 1833.

Of Capt. Alexander's ch. 1, ———, is a ship master in St. Geo. 2, Catharine, b. Aug 1824, d. Oct. 17, 1825.

Halsey H.'s ch. 1, Sarah M., b. 1836; r. Th. 2, Hannah F. N., b. March 6, '38; m. Horatio G. Copeland; r. S. Th. 3, William M., b. Feb. 25, 39; r. Th. a teacher, soldier of 4th Me. Reg. 3, Halsey H., (2d), b. ab. 1846; r. Th., in U. S. navy.

HATHORN, Andrew J., b. ab. 1830, son of Capt. Aaron of Cushing; mar. Olive L. Kelloch; r. Rock , a sailmaker. Their ch. Alice, b. ab. 1857.

HAYDEN, William, m. Sarah Wade; r. & d. Scituate, Mass.; his widow c., with her children, to Th., now S. Th., & d. Jan. 16, '31, a. 82. Their ch. 1, Mabel, m. Stephen Sweatland; r. Hope. 2, Luther, b. April 19, 1769, in Scituate; m. Martha Jones, p. Nov. 22, '93; r. S. Th., a ship carpenter, & d. Sept. 19, 1852. 2, Ruth, b. Oct. 6, 1770; m. Capt. Isaac Snow; r. S. Th., and d. Oct. 3, 1832. 4, Sally, m. William Bryant; r. & d. S. Th. ? 5, Rebecca, m. Rev. Tristram Jordan; rem. Denmark, Me.

Luther's ch. 1, Sarah W., b. July 12, 1794, d. April 30, 1849. 2, Eliza F., b. Feb. 22, '96; m. Robert Heard; r. S. Th.. 3, Mary, b. May 23, '98; m. Percy Lermond; r. Warren. 4, Isabel, b. May 26, 1800; m. 1st, William Snow, 2d, Abel Fish; r. S. Th. 5, William L., b. Sept. 24, 1802; m. Abigail C. Dow, July 31, '31; r. S. Th., a ship carpenter and builder. 6, Capt. Luther, (2d), b. Nov. 15, '04; m. 1st, Hannah Randall, Aug. 24, '30, 2d, Adaline (Heald) French of Linc.; r. New York. 7, Alden, b April 18, '07, d. Sept. 1, '13. 8, Capt. Richard, b. June 26, '10; m. Lucy Coombs, Oct. 13, '33; r. S. Th., a carpenter. 9, Ann Maria, b. Dec. 13, '12; m. William Kelloch; r. S. Th. 10, John, b. July 31, '16, d. Feb. 3, '44. 11, Ezekiel G., b. April 4, '19, d. Nov. 14, '37. The mother, b. Sept. 19, 1774. d. Nov. 14, 1828.

William L.'s ch. 1, Abigail A., b. Feb. 14, 1832; m. Capt. William S. Crockett; r. S. Th. 2, William John, b. Sept. 8, '33; r. S. Th., a carpenter. 3, Luther James, b. Sept. 12, '35, left Boston, Dec. 19, '62, in sch. *Leo*, of Rock., which has never since been heard from. 4, George Dow, b. April 14, '37; r. S. Th., a caulker. 5, Julia D., b. Feb. 25, '39. 6, Mary Eliza, born Feb. 12, '41. 7, Frederic, born March 29, '43. 8, Charles M., b. Sept. 19, '45. 9, Sarah Martha, b. Aug, 28, '47, d. Jan. 4, '50. 10, Arthur Prince, b. Jan. 5, and died March 21, '52.

Capt. Luther, (2d)'s ch. by 1st wife. 1, Hannah, b. Oct. 23, 1841. By 2d wife. 2, Adaline. 3, Beulah J. 4, Henry Adelbert. 5, Elden B. 6, Laura F.

Capt. Richard's ch. 1, Martha R., b. Aug. 7, 1834; mar. Lieut.

George W. Kelloch of W., Dec. 20, '57; d. April 6, '60. 2, Richard A. b. July 17, '36; r. Oregon. 3, Archibald C., b. April 10, '38, d. Aug. 27, '39. 4, Nancy F., b. July 26, '40, died March 27, '42. 5, Mary, b. ab. '45. 6, Alden, (2d), b. ab. 49. 7, Adelia, b. ab. '53.

HAYDEN, John, c. to Th. as an apprentice to E. Moores, watchmaker, about 1824; and after a time returned to Bath, Me., where he m. and r. in the possession of wealth and influence.

HEAD, Capt. Wm. Augustus, b. ab. 1828; m. Mary F. Ingraham, p. Nov. 5, '53; r. Rock., and died Oct. 1859. His widow mar. 2d, Leonard Kidder, Oct. 6, '63.

HEALD, Enoch H., b. Sept. 16, 1823, in Hope, Me., m. Malvina Mosman, Sept. 16, '49; r. Rock., a saloon or shop keeper. Their ch. 1, Laura C., b. July 12, 1850. 2, Freddy L., b. Aug. 24, '52, d. Dec. 23, '58. 3, Adelaide M., b. Feb. 16, '54.

HEALEY, Sergt. Eliphaz, b. Feb. 18, 1755, in Attleboro', Mass.; m. Lucy Robinson; was an officer of the Revolution; c. to this place in 1780 and bought, in connection with his brother-in-law, N. Woodcock, the J. Alexander lot, at Oyster River, but settled west of the Meadows, Th., a farmer; and d. Oct. 10, 1833. Welcome, a brother, m. Jemimah Blackington; c. also to Th., settling near; was a farmer, and d. Feb. 18, 1842. Rebecca, a sister, born 1757; mar. Nathaniel Woodcock; r. Th. and d. May 30, 1813. Recompense, another brother, m., r., and d. Attleboro', but his daughter Mary came here, m. Asa Bennett; r. Th. and d. April 24, 1852.

Sergeant Eliphaz's ch. 1, Penninah, b. ab. 1779; m. Elkanah Spear, r. Rock. 2, Melinda, b. Dec. 1, 1780; m. Leonard Smith; r. Th. and d. June 1, 1853. 3, James Harvey, b. Jan. 1783; m. Rebecca Hawthorn of St. George, p. Sept. 24, 1808; r. Rock., a farmer, & d. Dec. 7, '57. 4, Hon. or Col. Thomas Halsey, b. ab. 1786; seems to have dropped the Thomas from his name; m. 1st, Mercy Hawthorn of St. George, p. Nov. 22, 1806, 2d, Mary M. (Marsh) Sprague, March 11, '30; r. Th., merchant, ship-builder &c., and d. Jan. 11, '62. 5, Tileston, b. May 9, 1793; m Rebecca Crockett, Feb. 9, '15; r. Rock. and d. Sept. 1852. The mother d. March 29, '39, a. 80.

Welcome's ch. 1, Eunice, b. ab. 1791; m. Henry McIntosh; r. Rock 2, Margaret, m. Arunah Robbins; r. Th. 3, Nathaniel W. b. Aug. 11 1797; m. Adeline Fogler, Jan. '28; r. Rock. & d. without ch. Feb. 16, '57. 4, Hannah S, b. Dec. 9, 1799; m. Capt. John Vose; r. Rock. and d. Dec. 8, '60. 5, Calista, b. ab '01; m. 1st, Dennis Long, 2d, Joseph Copeland of War. Aug. 29, '46; r. Rock. 6, Ziba Pope, d. unm. 7, George, b ab. '14; mar. Mary J. Thomas, Feb 2, '43; r. Th. and d. Oct. 13. '45. The mother d March 29, '39, a 79.

James Harvey's ch. 1, Amanda F. born May 17, '09; m. 1st, Asa Ulmer, 2d, Aaron Wood; r. Rock. 2, Oscar F. b. Jan. 1, '11, mar. Elizabeth A. Munroe; Aug. 7, '36; r Rock. a quarryman. 3, Betsey H. b. July 14, '13; m Jerome Watson; r Linc. 4, Penninah S., b. Sept. 25, '16; mar. Joseph T. Thomas; r. Rock. 5, Alexander H., b. Dec. 29, '18; probably d. young or rem. 6, Henry H, born Apr. 23, '21; m. and r. Prospect, Me. 7, Halsey H., b March 9, '23. 8, Sally R, born March 3. '26; m. Christopher Butler, Sept. 14, '45. 9, Mary Jane, b. Sept. 15, '28.

Col. Halsey's ch. by 1st wife. 1, Catharine P., b March 29, 1807; m. Col. George A. Starr; r. Th 2, Capt. G. Dodge, b. Nov. 18, '08; m. Charlotte A Mitchell, June 23, '44; r. Th. and d. July 3, '58 near

Cairo, on his way home from N. O.; was buried at Paducah. 3, T. Halsey, Jr., b. Oct. 7, '10; m. Eliza C. McLellan, June 28, '34; & d. of yellow fever at N. Orleans Oct. 13, '37. 4, Capt. Sylvester, b. Oct. 9, '12; m. Elizabeth G. Coombs, Feb. '38; r. Th., ship master, &c. 5, Lucy, b. May 27, '15; m. William Flint, Jr.; r. Th. 6, Susan D., b. July 20, '17; m. Joel Levansaler; r. Th. 7, Mary Ann, b. Oct. 29, '19; m. David A. Sawyer, Apr. 3, '38; r. Cape Elizabeth. 8, Penelope W., b. Dec. 26, '21; m. Joseph B. Woodbury of Cape Elizabeth, Aug. 14, '45. 9, Sarah S., b. June 5, '24; m. Charles T. Starrett; r. Th. 10, Mercy A., b. March 29, '29; d. March 24, '33. By 2d wife. 11, Wm. S. Dwight, b. Dec. 30, '30; m. Betsey Y. Drinkwater of Cumberland, Feb. 13, '56; r. Th. a cabinet maker. 12, Richard S., b. July 16, '32; d. March 13, '33. 13, Augusta, born Jan 15, '34, d. Feb. 3, '37. 14, Augusta M., b. Sept. 4, '35; m. Jacob C. Barker of Portland, Aug. 19, '63, and rem. to Portland. 15, Henrietta, b. July 4, '37, d. Apr. 14, '41.

Tileston's ch. 1, Eliphaz C., b. Aug. 27, 1816, d. Sept. 17, '19. 2, Capt. Edward C., b. Jan. 5, '19; m. Sarah R. Spear, Sept. 5, '44; r. Rock., in U. S. naval service. 3, Harriet B., b. March 20, 1821; m. Joshua C. Worcester, & d. May 24, '61. 4, Elioenai L., b. May 27, '23; m. Alfred Burton; r. Rock., & d. Feb. 16, '49. 5, Capt. Russell S., b. Nov. 2, '27; went to California, 1851, where he was mate of steamer *Cortez*, and commanded the b'k *Charles Devins*, but died in Rock., Aug. 23, '58. 6, Capt. Egbert P., b. May 2, '30; r. Rock. 7, Tileston, (2d), b. March 25, '34, d. in West Indies. 8, Julia A., b. July 15, '36; r. Rock.,

George's ch. 1, Sarah, d. June 2, 1853. 2, Julia, b. ab. '44; r. Th.

Third Generation.

Oscar F.'s ch. 1, Oscar D, b. Jan. 3, 1838; m. Elvira S. Hosmer, Nov. 16, '59; r. Rock., a mariner. 2, Mary E., b. Oct. 28, '39; m. Capt. Israel Pease; r. Rock. 3, Jairus M., b. Feb. 17, '42; m. Huldah C. Demuth, May 10, '64; r. Rock., now in U. S. navy. 4, Sarah F., b. ab. '44. 5, Lucy J., b. ab. '46. 6, Rebecca A., b. ab. '48. 7, Clara M., b. ab. '50. 8, ———, d. young.

G. Dodge's ch. 1, Rodolphus T., b. Oct. 1, 1848, d. Oct. 20, '52. 2, E. Augustina, b. Jan. 3, & d. Sept. 18, '51. 3, Lucy Kate, b. Nov. 15, '53, d. Jan. 23, '54. 4, Martha Eugenia, b. in N. O., March 25, '55. 5, George Adelbert, b. Feb. 14, '57.

Halsey, jr.'s ch. 1, Ann E, b. April 12, 1835; m. Frank Walcott; r. Boston. 2, Deborah H., b. March 5, '37; m. William Kendall; r. Boston.

Sylvester's ch. 1, Eliza McLellan, b Jan. 6, 1839; m. Robert E. Butler; r. Th. 2, Mary Emor, b. Oct. 16, '49, d. Jan. 24, '54.

William S. Dwight's ch. 1, William Addison, b. Feb. 5, 1857. 2, Edwin Sprague, b. Oct. 1, '59.

Edward C's ch. 1, Emily M., b. ab. 1846. 2, Charles E. b. ab. '52. 3, Lucy C., b. Sept. 25, '57, d. Nov. 29, '58. 4, William H., b ab. '59.

HEALY, Patrick, d. Feb. 8, 1844, in the 28th year of his age, and was buried in Thomaston cemetery.

HEARD, William, c. at an early date before the Revolution, from New Hampshire (with his brother James, who, after awhile returned to N. H) was a mason by trade; m. Abigail (Crockett) Killsa, r. & d. Ash Pt., S Th. Their ch. 1, Sally, b. June 9, 1776; m. Capt. David Crockett; r. S. Th. and d. March 12, 1861. 2, John, b. Apr. 6, '79;

m. Lucy W. Heard, Dec. 13 1807; r. & d. S. Th. 3, William, (2d,) b. Dec. 23, '81, r. S. Th. a farmer. 4, David, b. Feb. 5, '85; r. S. Th. 5, Lucy, b. Nov. 5, '87; r. S. Th. 6, Moses, b. June 1, '90; m. Elioenai Perry, p. Sept. 10, 1817; r. S. Th. a farmer. 7, Robert, b. July 6, '92; m. Betsey Hayden, p. Nov. 20, 1815; r. S. Th., a farmer. 8, Oliver, b. Aug. 24, '94; m. Lucy W. Smith of Vinalhaven, p. Dec. 23, 1822; d. Sept. 25, 1836. 9, Abigail, b. Apr. 28, '96; m. Ambrose Snow, (3d), and r. Th. 10, Margaret C., born Dec. 16, '99; d. Jan. 24, 1848.

John's ch. 1, Eliza, m. Thomas Jenkins; r. Lincoln, Aroostook county, Me. 2, Abigail, m. Ezekiel Crockett; r. & d. Rock. 3, Lucy, m. Hiram Allen; r. Lincoln. 4, William, (2d), r. Swanville, Me. 5 Oliver, (2d), r. Swanville.

Moses' ch. 1, Nancy Perry, b. Sept. 4, 1818; m. Alfred Haskell, r. S. Th. and d. July 22, '42. 2, Mary, b. March 25, '20; r. S. Th. 3, Oliver, (2d), b. Dec. 25, '21; r. S. Th. a mariner. 4, Margaret Miranda, b. May 25, '29; m. Joshua G. Clark. 5, Caroline Matilda, born July 24, '31; m. V. F. Hinkley, r. S. Th. 6, Julia B., born Sept. 25, '33; m. Charles W. Rackliff; r. S. Th. The mother d. Jan. 27, '57; a. 61.

Robert's ch. 1, Alvan, b. Sept. 12, 1816; m. Eliza H. Hall, p. Aug. 23, '38; r. S. Th. d. June 15, '46. 2, Harriet, b. Sept. 23, '18; m. Wm. H. Crockett; r. S. Th. 3, Robert Henry, b. Jan. 10, '21; m. Ruth Rowell, Dec. 25, '45; r. S. Th., a boatman, &c. 4, Sarah Elizabeth, b. May 13, '23, d. Jan. 25, '30. 5, Luther H., b. July 16, '33; m. Jane Harvey of England, Sept, 27, '59; r. S. Th., a mariner.

Oliver's ch. 1, Abigail Amanda, b. Aug. 19. '25; m. Moses Shaw; r, S. Th. 2, James A., b. Feb. 5, '27, d. Apr. 11, '55.

Fourth Generation.

Alvan's ch. 1, Ann Eliza, b. May 25, 1841; m. Sidney Bird; r. Rock.

Robert Henry's ch. 1, Charles Spalding, b. Nov. 23, 1848; died Apr. 20, '49. 2, Henry Edward, b. Nov. 10, '50. 3, Charles W., b. Feb. 11, '52. 4, Emma E., b. July 3, '56. 5, Alice W., b. ab. '58.

Luther H.'s ch. Jeanie Elizabeth, b. May 23, 1860.

HEARSEY, Luther, b. ab. 1773; was here early in some part of old Th. and d. Nov. 24, 1828. His wife d. Sept. 13, '25,

HEATH, Samuel, b. ab. 1825, in Jefferson, Me., m. Ruth Ann W. Murphy; r. Rock., soldier of 4th Me. Regt., d. Oct. 1, 1862. Their ch. 1, Henrietta J., b. ab. 1851. 2, Atwell S., b. ab. '54. 3, Willie E, b. ab. '59.

HEMENWAY, Bickford N., b. ab. 1823, in Searsmont, Me.; m. Emeline P. Woodcock; r. Rock., a joiner. Their ch. 1, Avis A., b. ab. 1846. 2, Melville D., b. ab. '47. 3, Edith, b. ab. '59.

HEMENWAY, William S., b. ab. 1827, in Camden, cousin of preceding; m. Julia G. Crabtree of Hope; r. Rock., a fruit dealer. Their ch. Martha L., b. Feb. 12, '54, d. April 22, '57.

HENDERSON, Capt. Thomas, from Round Pond, Bristol, was one of the first settlers of the upper St. Georges, now Warren, but, in a few years, removed to Pleasant Point, where he commanded a garrison and blockhouse in the war of 1744; m. the widow of the celebrated Col. David Dunbar, surveyor of the King's woods, Governor of Sagadahoc, &c ; r. & d. C. His son, Dunbar, succeeded to the estate, and was commander of the garrison there in 1756; r. & d. C. His ch. were — 1, Capt. Robert, m. Jane Young; r. Pleasant Point, followed the sea, was at St. Domingo at the time of the conflagration, and, after years of adventure, was drowned near home, on a fishing excursion, in 1812. 2, Thomas, (2d), m. Betsey Rivers; r. St. George. 3, Jabez, m. ——— Malcolm; r. St. G. 4, William, m. ——— Nichols.

Capt. Robert's ch. 1, James, killed at sea, by accident. 2 & 3, twins, b. 1790; Capt. Dunbar, (2d), m. Sarah Burton, July 18, 1815; r. Th., in the house where his widow still resides, & d. at sea, July 20, '29, off the Tortugas, in his ship, *William & John*, bound to Europe. Capt. William, (2d), m. Lucy Vose, Jan. 30, 1815; r. Th., & d, Aug. 31, '27. 4, Elizabeth, b. ab. 1794; m. 1st. Capt. Bartholomew Kelleran of C., Nov. 15, '14, 2d, Samuel Allen of Th. & d. Dec. 5, '51.

Of Jabez's ch. 1, Robert, (2d), b. ab. 1793; m. Elizabeth O'Brien, of W., r. C., Th., and Belfast, where he died by drowning, Dec. 3, 1855.

Fifth Generation.

Capt. Dunbar, (2d)'s ch. 1, Capt. James, b. about 1817; mar. 1st, Sarah J. Singer, Oct., 1841, 2d, Mrs. Sarah J. Robinson, May 13, '54; r. Th., a ship master. 2, Ann E., m. Col. William Bennett; r. Th. 3, Susan; r. Th. 4, Capt. Dunbar, (2d), b. ab. 1826; m. Olivia Chapman, July 25, '56; r. Th., a ship master, like most of the family.

Capt. William's ch. 1, Capt. William, (3d), born Oct., 1816; m. Olivia Chapman, July 25, '46; r, Th. and d. Feb. 19, '55. 2, Lucy, m. Rev. John Humphrey of Charlestown, Mass, July 2, '45. 3, Robert, b. Sept. 1819, d. March 10, '25. 4, Mary, m. a Mr. Bullard; r. Mass. 5, James, b. Aug., 1824, d. Jan. 28, '25

Robert, (2d)'s ch. 1, Jane O., b. March 24, 1811, d. July 27, 1831, 2, Capt. Edward, b. March 9, 1813; m. Hannah Holland in Belfast, and d. in Cohasset, Mass. 3, John, b. Feb. 28, d. May 4, 1815. 4, Elizabeth, b. Feb. 3, 1817; m. Edwin Ellis; r. Th., rem. Belfast. 5, Thomas O., b. Sept. 14, '19; went to sea and not heard from. 6, Seth O'B., b. Dec. 11, '22; m. Octavia Lovejoy, r. Th., was landlord of Knox hotel. 7, Sarah R., b. June 16, '24; m. Alexander Crawford; r. War., and has ch. Oliver Crawford, b. Oct. 12, '45; Edwin E., b. Jan. 8, '48, d. April 9, '50; Ellen F., b. April 9, '50; Inez, b. Aug. 10, '52; Eliza M., b. March 4, '55; Charles E., b. Sept. 17, '57; and Willie J., b. May 17, '54, d. spring of '62. 8, Susan B., b. Dec. 20, 1826, d. Aug. 15, '27. 9, Ellen M., b. Sept. 24, 1827; mar. James Teague; r. W., and has ch. George; Frederic; and Adelia.

Sixth Generation.

Capt. James's ch. by 2d wife. Ann G., b. ab. 1856.

Capt. William, (3d)'s ch. 1, William Oliver, b. Dec. 10, 1848. 2, Edward, b. Jan. 31, d. April 7, '53. 3, Lucy A., b. ab. '55.

Seth O'B.'s ch. 1, Emma J., b. Jan. 21, 1845; m. Lieut. William K. Bickford, Nov. 1, '63. 2, Robert F., b. Sept., 1849. 3, Abbie, b. June 10, '51.

HENDERSON, Elbridge D., of the same family & said to be half brother of Capt. William Henderson of Th., was born in St George; m. Elizabeth D. Hall; r. &. d. Rock., where his widow now resides. Their ch. 1, Alonzo, b. ab. 1842; r. Rock., a mariner. 2, Charles, b. ab. '53; r. Rock.

HENDERSON, John, b., it is thought, in Oldtown or vicinity; m.

1st, Alice McKenney of Madison, Me ; came to this place ab. 1844; m. 2d, Jacintha Davis, Dec. 6, '51 ; r. Rock., a lime burner, &c., died May, 1855. His ch. by 1st wife, who d. Sept. 1, 1850, aged 48. 1, John W., b. Sept. 29, 1829, d. Nov. 17, '49. 2, Capt. Thomas J., b. May 14, '31; m. Elizabeth Squires, Jan. 2, '48 ; r. Rock., and served 18 months in 2d Reg. U. S. Sharpshooters. 3, Lincoln L., b. July 6, '33; m. Catharine T. Dodge, April 12, '53; r. Rock. 4, Mary S., b. May 14, '36; m. R. A. Harper; r. Rock. 5, Samuel J., b. April 11, '38; m. Anne S. Campbell, Sept. 15, '61; r. Rock.

Capt. Thomas J.'s ch. 1, Ellen E., b. ab. 1849. 2, Emma F., b. ab. '51. 3, Orrin M., b. April, '53, d. Aug. 30, '57. 4, William T., b. ab. '55.

Lincoln L.'s ch. 1, Charles E., b. ab. 1854. 2, Mary A., b. ab. '56. 3, Lincoln b. ab. '59.

Samuel J.'s ch. Edward Herbert, b. Aug. & d. Dec. 2, 1862.

HENERY; of this family, (sometimes written Henrys,) James, b. 1805, in Sligo county, Ireland, about 16 miles from the sea-coast, was educated as an engineer; m. Mary McHugh; came here in 1840; r. Th., & built at Beech Woods, ab. '56. John, a cousin, b. ab. '20; m. Catharine O'Brien; c. here ab. '50; r. Th., having purchased the Linscott house.

James's ch. 1, Eleanor, d. young. 2, Ann, d. young. 3, Capt. John C., b. Aug. 23, '39; r. Th., a master mariner. 4, James, d. at sea of yellow fever, aged 17. 5, Charles P., b. Feb. 5, '44, entered the U. S. navy. 6, Frederic T., b. Dec. 30, '45. 7, Joseph, b. March 11, '47. 8, Mary, b. March 23, '50. 9, Andrew, b. June 8, '52. 10, Sarah, b. Aug. 3, '54. 11, Bernard, b. March 20, '57.

John's ch. 1, Capt. John B., b. Nov., 1839; m. Helen A. Curling, Nov. 18, '63; r. Th., sails a British barque. 2, Bartholomew, b. ab. '41; r. Th., a mariner. 3, Ann, b. ab. '43. 4, Adelia, b. ab. '45. 5, Maria, b. ab. '50. 6, Sarah, b. ab. '54. 7, Susan, b. ab. '57. 8, Matilda, b. '59.

HENRAHAN; of this family two brothers came from Limerick, Ireland; 1, John, b. ab. 1812; came here early, & m. Eleanor O'Neil, p. July 12, '38; r. Th., a quarry owner, &c. 2, Cornelius, b. ab. '23; m. Catharine, dau. of Archibald Brown, r. Rock., a lime manufacturer, &c. Mary, their mother, d. at Rockland, Oct. 8, '58, a. ab. 77, having m. 2d, John Henrahan, who also d. here. Michael, a cousin of these, also came here, with Catharine, his wife; r. Rock., a quarry man.

John's ch. 1, Mary A., b. July 25, 1839. 2, John, (2d), b. June 12, '41. 3, James, b. ab. 1843. 4, Ellena, b. ab. '46.

Michael's ch. 1, Joanna, b. ab. 1844. 2, Bridget, b. ab. 1846. 3, Mary, b. ab. '49. 4, Ellen, b. ab. '52. 5, Michael, 2d, b. ab. '54. 6, Catharine, b. ab. '57. 7, John, (3d), b. ab. '59.

HERRICK, Joel, b. ab. 1805, in Sedgwick, Me.; m. Jane, dau. of Isaac Hall of St. G.; r. Rock., agent for marble works, Their ch. 1, Lillias, b. ab. '42; m. George A. Bramhall; r. Rock. 2, Elijah, b. ab. '44. 3, Frances J., b, ab. '46. 4 Emma J, b. Feb. 12, '53.

HERRICK, Joseph F., b. ab. 1823, in Northport, son of Joseph Herrick; m. Amanda M. Herrick; r. Rock., a lime burner. Their ch. 1, Henry W. b, ab, '54. 2, Abby E., b. ab. '56. 3, Alice J., b. ab, 1858,

HEWETT, Dea. Waterman, born in Vinalhaven, ab. 1767; m. Patience Keen, Jan. 30, '92; r. Cam., and d. Sept. 1851. Their ch. 1, Sarah S., m. Charles Lowell, Esq.; r. and d. Rock.? 2, Harvey, m. Miriam Hunt; rem. Ill., where, near Peoria he was murdered, Oct. 12, 1850, and robbed of $1500. 3, Waterman T., m. Sarah W. Parsons; r. Old Th. and d. at Miami, Mo., March 22, '49. 4, Rachel, m. Seth Hunt; r. and d. Cam. 5, Ephraim G., b. ab. 1800; m. Diana Spring, r. Rock., a truckman, &c. 6, Capt. Peter A., b. ab. 1802; m. Jane M. Thorndike of Hope, p. Sept. 9, '34; r. Rock. 7, Joseph, b. ab, '04; m. Nancy Marsh, Sept. 16, '27; r. Rock., a merchant, ship-owner, &c. 8, Patience. 9, Ann, m. William Perry; r. and d. Cam.? 10, Alvan, m. Eliza A. Rankin. 11, Eliza, mar. Henry Craig of Augusta. 12, Leander, m. Felicity Paul of Natchez, Miss. and is now deceased. 13, Leverett, m. Sarah Hewett, and is deceased.

Of Waterman T.'s ch. Flora, b. ab. 1850.

Ephraim G.'s ch. 1, Albion E., born ab. 1825; mar. Rebecca W. Wilie, April 2, '49; r. Rock., a teamster, &c. 2, William W., b. ab. 1828; mar. Martha L. Babbage, Sept. 2, '49; r. Rock., a truckman. 3, Waterman, (2d), born ab. 1836; r. Rock. 5, Leonora, mar. Fisher Gay; r. Rock.

Capt. Peter A.'s ch. 1 & 2, twins, b. Aug. 11, 1836; Leander, d. Aug. 13, '36; Leverett, d. Aug. 12, '36. 3, Eliza, b. Nov. 19, '39. 4, Leonidas, b. Oct. 31, '43; d. at Oswego, N. Y., Sept. 24, '64.

Joseph's ch. Hudson J., b. June 21, 1829; m. Sarah C. Simpson of N. Y., r. Rock., a ship owner.

Fourth Generation

Albion E.'s ch. 1, Helen, b. ab. 1852. 2, Frank, b. ab. '55.

William W.'s ch. 1, Alfred W., b. ab. 1850. 2, Charles E., b. ab. '52. 3, Clara L., b. ab. '54. 4, Frederic E., b. ab. '56. 5, Melinda, b. ab. '58.

Hudson J.'s ch. 1, Joseph H., b. March and d. Aug. 21, 1851. 2, Hudson, b. ab. '52. 3, Jenny F., b. ab. '56. 4, Ralph, b. ab. '58. 5, Sarah, b. ab. '59.

HEWETT; of this family, there c. from Hope, three brothers, sons of John. 1, Capt. Marcus L., b. ab. 1825; m. Sarah Metcalf of Appleton; r. Th., a carpenter, officer in 21st Me. Regt. &c. 2, Thomas R., b. ab 1829; m. Elizabeth Thomas, p. May 14, '54; r. Th., a carpenter. 3, Lieut. James H., b. ab. 1835; m. Susan L. Hawk, Aug. '62; r. Th., an officer in army.

Capt. Marcus L.'s ch. 1, Albert W., b. ab. 1855. 2, George T., b. ab. '56. 3, Clara. 4, Charles M.

Thomas R.'s ch. 1. Lizzie T., b. April 27, 1855, d. in Boston, June 21, '64. 2, Catharine, b ab. '57. 3, Etta A., born April '59, d. July 31, '61.

HEWETT, William O., b. ab. 1822, son of William of Hope; mar. Adelia M. Perry of Hope, Sept. 27, 1846; r. Rock., a merchant. Anson, b. ab. 1830, a brother; mar. Frances H. Alford; r. Rock., a carpenter, soldier of 2d Me. Battery.

William O.'s ch. 1, Theodore E., b. ab. 1847. 2, Emily P., b. ab. '49. 3, Cora F., b. ab. '58.

HEWETT, Herbert or Hubbard, a cousin of preceding, b. in. Hope ab. 1816; m. Jane ——, r. Rock., a lime burner. Their ch. 1, George E., b. ab. 1837; m. Delphina Adams, Nov. 26, '63; r. Rock. 2, Jason B., b. ab. '41. 3, Sewall W., b. ab. '43, a soldier of 4th Me.

captured July 21, '61, and supposed to be dead. 4. Samuel, born ; b '44; r. Rock., discharged soldier of 2d Me. Battery, since enlisted in 2d Me. Cavalry. 5, Ephraim M., b. ab. '45; r. Rock., soldier in the U. S. regulars. 6, Nathan A., b. ab. '47; enlisted in 2d Me. Cavalry. 7, Frederic, b. ab. '49. 8, Rebecca, b. ab. '51. 9, Margaret E., b. ab. 1854.

HEWES, Capt. William, born ab. 1820, in Wales, G. Britain; m. Sarah J. Gleason, Nov. 17, 1847; r. Th., a master mariner. Their ch. 1, William (2d), b. ab. 1849. 2, Frederic G., b. March and d. Aug. 11, '51. 3, Maria G., b. ab. '53.

HEWLETT, George, b. in England ab. 1823; m. Eliza A. ———, of England, r. Rock., a mariner. Their ch. 1, William V., born ab. 1842. 2, George (2d), b. ab. '44. 3, Louisa, b. ab. '45. 4, Florence, b. ab. '47. 5, Charles, b. ab. '50, in England. 6, Amy, b. ab. '51, in N. York. 7, Fanny b. ab. '53; 8, Richard, b. ab. '55; both in New Brunswick. 9, Henry, b. ab. '60, here.

HIGGENS, Benjamin L., b. in Eden, Sept., 1812; m. in Philadelphia, Louisa Morley, in 1835; r. Rock., since 1848, a lime burner. Their ch. 1, Ellen R., b. April 8, 1836. 2, Zenas H., b. May 20, '38; m. Clarion F. Jameson, Jan., 1856; r. Rock., entered the U. S. Navy. 3, Nancy L., b. Sept. 14, '40; m. Henry M. Foss of Clarington, N. H., had 1 ch., Henry M., b. Feb. 6, & d. June 10, '64; r. Rock. 4, J. Milton, b. Jan. 8, '43, d. Jan. 5, '48. 5, Eben L., b. Oct. 15, '45; r. Rock., in 4th Me. Reg., since in U. S. Navy. 6, Sherman W., b. Oct. 2, '48. 7, Sarah E., b. Jan. 2, '50. 8, Benjamin F., b. March 12, '52. 9, Rosilla, b. Jan. 28, '54.

Zenas H.'s ch. 1, Ursilla, b. May, 1856, d. young. 2, Zenas L., b. Aug., '59. 3, Clara E., b. June 5, '63.

HIGGENS, Charles, b. ab. 1830, in Eagerlougher, Armagh county, Ireland; came hither in 1849; m. Emma Tall of Nova Scotia; r. Th., a peddler. Their ch. 1, Mary E., b. ab. 1855. 2, Emma C., b. ab. '57. 3, Rosanna, b. ab. '59.

HIGGENS, William T., b. ab. 1827; m. Orinda S. Allen, Oct. 28, '56; r. Rock., a mariner, in U. S. Navy.

HILDRETH, Abel, b. 1795; was left by his father (who was in Th. early but rem. to Bradford, Me., 1803; subsequently to New York and Ohio), in care of James D. Wheaton, by whom he was brought up; m. Betsey Coombs of Bowdoin, p. July 25, 1818; r. Th., a carpenter, or millwright, and d. Oct. 20, '62. Their ch. 1, Sarah J., b. Feb. 19, and d. Nov. 11, 1820. 2, Elizabeth T., b. Sept. 8, '21; m. James L. Howe of Boston, Oct. 5, '45; r. Portland. 3, Dexter W., b. March 1, '25; m. Harriet S. Harrington, Feb. 24, '50; rem. California. 4, Susan L., b. June 30, '27; m. Charles Freeman; r. Cal. 5, Sarah F., b. July 12, '29; m. Frank Sweat; r. Portland. 6, Abel C., b. June 26, '31; m. Mary A. Anderson; r. Boston. 7, Joseph E., b. Oct. 4, '33; m. twice, and r. Lynn. 8, Lewis G., b. Dec. 28, '35; r. Th., a carpenter, rem. Cal. 9, Emily M., b. May 19, '38; mar. Charles E. Lombard; r. Springfield, Mass.

HILL, Lysander, Esq., b. in Union, brought up by William Malcolm, Esq., of Cushing, grad. Bowd. Coll. 1858; studied law with Mr. Gould and commenced practice in Th., became an officer in the army; m. Adelaide C. Cole, Feb. 2, '64; r. Alexandria, Va., in practice of his profession.

HILL, Rev. Luther D., b. ab. 1825, in N. Y. State; r. Th. as pastor of Baptist church, but soon rem. with Eliza S., his wife, & ch., John E., Ella M., Charles I., & Hannah L.

HILLMAN, Whitten, b. ab. 1807, in New York; c. to this place; m. Harriet (Bernard) Ulmer; r. Rock., a mariner. Their ch. 1, Emeline M., b. Jan. '32, d. July 26, '53. 2, Mary F., b. April 6, '33; r. Rock. 2, Richard B., b. June 19, '36; m. Augusta J. Spear, Jan. 15, '56; r. Rock., a joiner.

Richard B.'s ch. Franklin K., b. ab. 1859.

HILLS, Edward, b. ab. 1822, in Union, son of Samuel, (2d), and grandson of Reuben Hills; m. Almena Drake; r. Th., high sheriff, &c. Austin, b. ab. 1824, son of Reuben, jr., & grandson of Reuben of Union; m. Harriet Heald; r. S. Th., a carpenter; rem. California.

Edward's ch. 1, Hiram A., b. ab. 1847. 2, Helen, b. ab. '50. 3, Caroline, b. ab. '52. 4, Charles Edward, b. Oct. 24, '54. 5, Fontanelle, b. July 3, '57. 6, Sidney W., b. ab. '59.

Austin's ch. 1, Austin H., b. ab. 1851. 2, Reuben W., b. ab. '56. 3, Ernest S., b. ab. '58.

HILLS, William H., b. Aug., 1805, in Rochester, Eng.; c. to this country when a boy; m. Ann ———; r. Rock., a sailmaker, went to St. John, N. B., for materials for his business, and was killed, Sept. 3, 1862, by a secession mob at that place on account of his devotion to the Union and Government of his adopted country. Their ch. 1, Ann E., b. March 17, 1833; grad. Mt. Holyoke seminary; died at Rock., July 27, '55. 2, Sarah L., b. Feb. 3, '35; d. May 9, '63. 3, Lucy G., b. Sept. 30, '36. 4, Julia L., b. Sept. 28, '38. 5, William H., (2d), b. July 1, '41, d. Aug. 12. '47. 6, Samuel C. F., b. Feb. 29, '43; soldier in 4th Me. Reg., d. at Rock., June 23, '64. 7, John G. E., b. Oct., '46, d. April, '47.

HILT, John, b. ab. 1819; (son of Philip and Mary (Fish) Hilt of Warren); m. Lydia Jones, p. May 15, 1847; r. Th., a shipbuilder, &c. Their ch. 1, Estelle, b. ab. 1850. 2, Agnes, b. ab. 1854.

HILT, John C., b. ab. 1820; (son of Henry and Mary (Crawford) Hilt of Warren); m. Nancy Toner, Jan. 2, '43; r. Rock., a shipbuilder, rem. Portland. Their ch. 1, Susan M., b. ab. 1846. 2, Henry, b. '49, d. Aug. 19, '50. 3, Ellen M., b. ab. '51. 4, Sarah C., b. ab. '57.

HINCH, James, b. ab. 1829, in Birkenhead, England; m. Catharine Fox of England; r. Th., a painter and photographist. Their ch. 1, William, b. ab. 1856. 2, James, b. ab. '57, d. of diphtheria, Feb. 3, '62. 3, John S., b. ab. '59, d. of diphtheria, Feb. 5, '62. 4, ———, d. diphtheria, Feb. 7, '62.

HINKLEY, Capt. Edmund B., b. ab. 1827; son of Capt. Samuel and Sarah (Wilson) Hinkley of W.; m. 1st Henrietta A. Lermond, Dec. 3, '50, (who d. Dec. 23, '55) 2d, Eliza A. O'Brien, Dec. 25, '61; r. Th., stove dealer, &c.

HINKLEY, Vespasian F., b. ab. 1821, in Blue Hill, Me., m. Caroline M. Heard, July, 1854, r. S. Th., a stone cutter, &c. His brother Shubael A., b. ab. 1828; also came to this place; m. Lizzie H. Spalding, April 27, '55; r. S. Th., a stone cutter, &c.

Vespasian F.'s ch. 1, Frederic, b. ab. 1856.

Shubael A.'s ch. 1, Fannie B., b. ab. 1857. 2, William, b. about 1859.

HIX, or Hicks, William, c. from England, while young; m. Lydia Woodbury; settled, r. & d. in Cape Elizabeth. Their son, Thomas, b. Oct. 27, 1756; m. Mary Jameson of Warren; settled in S. Th., & d. May 16, 1808.

Thomas's ch. 1, William, b. May 30, 1780, d. Feb. 20, 1791. 2, Dea. Thomas, (2d), born Aug. 14, 1782; m. Sally Holland, April 8, 1810; a master mariner, r. Rock., & d. Nov. 20, '61. 3, Capt. Samuel, b. Dec. 21, 1784, r. S. Th., a mariner, unm. and died April 12, 1849. 4, Sarah, b. Feb. 29, 1788; m. Barzillai Pierce; r. S. Th. and d. July 12, 1860. 5, Lydia, b. March 16, '90; m. Jeremiah Witham, June 5, 1814; r. S. Th. 6, Hannah, b. Jan. 8, '93, m. Abner Perry; r. & d. Cam. 7, Ann, b. Sept. 8, 1795, m. Jesse McLean, April 20, 1820; r. New Sharon, Me. 8, Rachel, b. Jan. 31, 1798; mar. John W. Hunt; r. Rock. 9, Capt. Isaac Jameson, born April 1, 1801; m. Mary Crane of Hope, July 22, 1824; r. S. Th., a mariner, &c. The mother, b. 1759, d. Aug. 26, 1839, aged 80.

Dea. Thomas, (2d)'s ch. 1, Mary, born Oct. 17, 1810; mar. Capt. Hiram Hall; r. Rock. 2, Thomas Woodbury, b. Nov. 27, '12; m. Susanna Ingraham of Cam., p. Nov. 8, '34; r. Rock., has been Warden State Prison, &c. 3, Capt. Samuel, (2d), b. Jan. 27, '15; lost at sea, Dec. 1, '37. 4, Martha M., born May 27, '17; mar. Capt. Joshua Bartlett; r. S. Th. 5, Capt. Hezekiah, b. May 16, '21; m. Abby or Hattie Ingraham; r. Rockland.

Capt. Isaac J.'s ch. 1, Capt. Isaac A., born July 30, 1826; mar. Amanda C. Emery, Sept. 27, '47; r. S. Th. 2, Capt. Henry Franklin, b. Jan. 17, '29; m. Emily Hall, Sept. 21, '54; r. Rock. 3, Oliver P., b. April 7, '31; m. Elethea M. Fisk, Dec. 13, '55; r. Rock., keeps meat market, &c. 4, Hannah C., b. Sept. 25, '33; r. S. Th. 5, Wm. B., b. Nov. 1, '36; m. Sarah M. Rhoades, Jan. 23, '64; r. S. Th., a joiner.

Thomas W.'s ch. 1, Thomas W., (3d), born April 18, 1836; mar. Susan I. Ferrand, Jan. 8, '59; r. Rock. 2, Orianna A., b. June 26, '38, d. Sept. 16, '40.

Capt. Hezekiah's ch. 1, Hezekiah L., b. Feb., 1845, d. Dec. 12, '46. 2, Samuel, b. ab. 1846. 3, Ada L., b. ab. '48. 4, Hezekiah, b. Sept., '49, d. Jan. 30, '54. 5, Eugene, b. ab. '55. 6, Hezekiah, (2d), born July 23, '58, d. Feb. 12, '63.

Capt. Isaac A.'s ch. 1, Eugene A., b. 1847, died March 4, '48. 2, George B., b. ab. '49. 3, Alvah W., b. ab. '53. 4, Althea F., b. ab. '5[illegible]. 5, Frederic L., b. ab. 1859.

Capt. Henry F.'s ch. 1, Frank Herbert, b. June, 1858, d. Aug. 4, '59. 2, Harry Irving.

Oliver P.'s ch. Galen F. b. ab. 1859.

HIX, George W., b. ab. 1831, in Mass., m. Mary E. Howard, Dec. 3, '58; r. Rock., a boat builder, &c. Their ch. Alice, b. ab. 1859.

HODGES, George W., b. ab. 1820, in Hallowell, Me.; m. Sarah M. Smiley; kept Thorndike Hotel, Rock., 1862–3, but rem. Their ch. George R., b. ab. 1843.

HODGKINS, Joseph, mar. 1st, Mary Hawk, 2d, Mrs. Jane Hammond; r. Damariscotta Mills. His ch. By 1st wife. 1, James, m. Elizabeth Brown; r. Nobleboro'. 2, Miles, m. Lucy Hatch; r. Nobleboro'. 3, Patience, m. Isaac Avery; r. Jefferson. 4, William, b. ab. 1822; c to Th., m. Joanna P. Robinson, July 2, '46; r. Booker St., a caulker. 5, Ezekiel, m. Betsey Morgan; r. Boothbay. 6, Almira, m.

Rev. Paris Rowell, min. of Meth. E. church. 7 & 8, twins, Amasa and Sarah E., who m. Edward Hutchins, April 20, '54 ; r. Dam.

William's ch. 1, Ann A., b. Jan. 22, '47, d. June 7, '49. 2, Ida E., b. '49. 3, Catharine, b. '51, d. Dec. 31, '53. 4, Frank F., b. Jan. 10, d. June 17, '53. 5, William, (2d), b. ab. '55. 6, Ambrose L., b. ab. 1858.

HODGMAN, David, c. from Ashby, Mass. to Cam., where he r. & d. He m. Lois Melvin from the neighborhood of Concord, Mass., who d. in Th. May 4, 1858, a. 80 y. and 6m.

Of their ch. 1, Isaac, born ab. 1814; c. from Newcastle, mar. 1st Sarah W. Starrett, Dec. 13, '38; 2d, Zilpha Bryant of Knox, April 11, '52 ; r. Th., a blacksmith.

Isaac's ch. by 1st wife. 1, Sarah C., b. Oct. 21, 1839; r. Th. 2, David J., b. April 23, '42 ; r. Th. 3, Isaac H., b. July 30, '49. The mother d. Aug. 2, '49. By 2d wife. 4, John C., b. ab. '53. 5, Mary L., b. ab. '56, a deaf mute.

HODSDON, Capt. Charles F., b. ab. 1824, in North Haven; mar. Sarah T. Lyman; r. Rock. Their ch. 1, W. Lyman, b. ab. '50. 2, Sarah C., b. ab. '54.

HOLBROOK, Capt. Jesse, whose ancestor emigrated to Plymouth, Mass., with the pilgrims in the *Mayflower*, was born in Islesboro', in Aug. 1787; m. Jane Hall of Georgetown; r. Northport, Bangor and Rock., where his wife d. Dec. 16, 1855, aged 68. Their ch. 1, Capt. John, b. ab. 1812, m. Eliza Kirkpatrick of W., r. Rock. 2, William, born '14; m. Hannah Leggett, p. July 10 '38; r. Rock., and is now deceased. 3, Jesse, (2d), rem. and r. Ohio. 4, Capt. Samuel H., b. April 8, '19, in Northport, as were the preceding; mar. in England, Catharine Rogers of Liverpool, April 11, '42 ; r. Rock., since '47. 5, Capt. Thomas K., b. ab. '22, in Bangor; m. Melissa Robinson, July 17, '51 ; r. Rock., 1860, since deceased.

Capt. John's ch. 1, Ibra W., b. ab. 1836; r. Rock., a mariner. 2, Orissa J., b. April 18, '37; r. Rock., a milliner. 3, Harriet E. b. Nov. 8, '38; m. Joseph Files, Nov. 24, '55. 4, Irene F., b. Dec. 30, '40; r. Rock. 5, William D., b. ab. '46.

William's ch. 1, Sarah B., b. Nov. 30, 1839. 2, William H., b. May 13, '41, d. April 12, '42. 3, Priscilla, b. Feb. 13, '43.

Capt. Samuel H.'s ch. 1, John, (2d), b. ab. 1847. 2, Sarah, b. ab. '51. 3, Samuel, b. ab. '53. 4, Emma, b. ab. '55. 5, Aurelia, b. ab. 1857.

Capt. Thomas K.'s ch. 1, Jane, b. ab. 1853. 2, Melissa E., b. Dec. '54, d. Jan. 25, '63. 3, Lizzie, b. ab. '56. 4, Ezra T. b. ab. '58.

HOLBROOK, Nathan, b. ab. 1813 in Penobscot, Me., m. 1st, Martha Vincent in Staffordshire, Eng., 2d, Sarah G. Huntress of Otisfield; r. Rock., and keeps the Rockland Exchange. Their ch. James B., b. ab. 1845.

Besides these families, there were also in Rock. in 1860, according to the census,

HOLBROOK, John F., b. ab. 1807, m. Lucy A. ——— ; r. Rock., a joiner.

HOLBROOK, Samuel, b. ab. 1826 ; m. Maria J. ———, r. Rock., an ostler. Their ch. 1, Frances, b. ab. 1852. 2, Ella V., b. ab. '53. 3, Melbourne A., b. ab. '54.

HOLDEN, Capt. Sylvanus, b. Sept. 1, 1813, in Bremen; m. in

Bristol, Catharine Fogler, 1840; r. Rock., since '52. Their ch., all b. in Bristol, 1, Samuel W., b. Oct. 6, '41. 2, Harriet, b. Sept. 22, '43, d. June 22, 1858. 3, Mary A., b. July 17, 1845, d. March 3, '59. 4, Margaret C., b. April 9, '47; m. Edwin Wade, Dec. 31, '64. 5, William, b. Sept. 16, '49. 6, Ella J., b. Dec. 2, '51. 7, Juliette, b. Feb. '59.

HOLLAND, Capt. John, came early, with his family, from Ipswich, Mass., settled at Ash Point, was a lace maker by trade, as well as mariner; r. & d. S. Th. Their ch. 1, Mary, b. in 1775, in Ipswich; m. Roland Wade; r. S. Th. & d. Oct., 1834. 2, Sarah, b. in Ipswich, Oct. 29, 1781; m. Dea. Thomas Hix; r. S. Th., was a member of the 1st Baptist church 40 or more years, & d. May 11, 1859. 3, Lucy, m. Lt. Joseph Perry; r. S. Th.

HOLMES, Elijah, b. in Stoughton, now Sharon, Mass., Sept. 29, 1764; c. to Union & m. 1st, Dorcas Partridge, Aug. 25, 1785; settled & built log house on the farm since owned by the late Obadiah Morse, and recently by Maj. James A. Ulmer; after several removals, came to what is now Rockland, March 15, 1792; before 1812, went to the British Provinces, m. a second time, and settled at Moose river, near Lubec, Me., but returned to Rockland in 1829, & d. Feb. 10, 1839. His ch. by 1st wife. 1, Dorcas, b. May 26, 1786, m. Robert J. Crockett; r. Rock. 2, Bernard, b. Jan. 1, 1788; m. Polly Havener, July 25, 1809; r. Rock., & d. Dec. 25, 1825. 3, Elijah E., b. Dec. 11, 1789; m. Sally Havener, June 1, 1817; r. Rock., & d. March 11, 1849. 4, Willoughby, b May 17, & d. July 18, 1792. 5, Hon. Charles, b. Aug. 20, '93, was apprenticed to the shoemaker's trade, but went privateering in the *Wasp*, (together with six other companions, among whom were Josiah Spalding, Elijah E. Holmes, and Paul Thorndike, whose names were not ascertained till page 293, vol. 1st, was printed;) returned home; m. Mary B. Prior, Jan. 30, '17, 2d, Abigail (Edwards) Ranks, Jan. 16, 1842; r. Rock., an active business man, senator in 1839-40, & d. May 17, '63. 6, Susanna, b. Dec. 29, '96, d. Feb. 8, '97. 7 & 8, twins, b. March 20, '98, Mary, m. Moses Gross of Orland, p. Dec. 2, '33, & d. May 26, '35; Hannah, d. Oct. 24, 1800. 9, Anna, b. March 31, & d. Oct. 22, 1800. 10, Amos, b. Feb. 14, '02, now deceased. 11, Oliver, b. May 12, '03; m. Catharine Achorn, Oct. 11, '27; r. Rock., a farmer. 12, George, b. Aug. 24, '05; removed & m. twice at Fall River, Mass., and was accidentally killed in a flume, in California, Aug. 6, 52, leaving a wife and six children in Fall River. 13, Robert, b. May 4, '08; removed to Massachusetts.

Bernard's ch. 1, William, b. Oct. 2, 1809; d. young by drowning. 2, Washington, b. Feb. 3, '11; drowned, Aug., '39, from sch. *Patriot*. 3, Caroline, b. Oct. 7, 1812; m. 1st, George C. Tate, 2d, Andrew J. Pierce; r. Rock. 4, Sarah, b. Oct. 3, '14; m Francis Harrington; r. Rock., 5, Catharine, b. Sept. 13, '16; m. Ephraim Knowlton; r. Rock.

Elijah E.'s ch. 1, Hannah, b. April 5, 1818; m. William C. Ramsey, p. Sept. 27, '35. 2, Eliza, b. March 17, '20; m. Cyrenius Crockett; r. Rock.

Hon. Charles's ch. by 1st wife. 1, Capt. Charles S., b. Jan. 17, 1818; m. Olive H. Condon, Dec. 18, '38; r. Rock., & perished in sch. *Lion*, Dec. 11, '64. 2, Amelia D., b. May 25, '19; m. 1st, Sylvester H. Fuller, 2d, Henry Luce; r. Rock. 3, Emeline, b. May 3, '28; m. John Flint; r. Rock. The mother d. Nov. 20, '40. By 2d wife. 4, George Edward, b. Jan. 3, '43; r. Rock., was a sergeant in 19th Me.

reg., d. from his wounds and an amputated leg, at Amory Square hospital, Washington, June 15, '64. 5, John Henry, b. Feb. 2, '45; r. Rock., 6, Albert P., b. Jan. 21, '48. 7, William, b. Oct. 12, '50, d. May 14, 1853. 8, Mary A., b. March 11, 1854, d. Aug. 6, '62. 9, William O., b. Aug. 13, '56.

Oliver's ch. 1, William, b. April, 1833, & d. in Placerville, Cal., Nov. 3, '52. 2, Orris, b. ab. '38. 3, Michael A., b. ab. '41. 4, Melinda A., b. ab. '47.

Capt. Charles S.'s ch. 1, Hiram C., b. —— 14, 1842; r. Rock., a mariner, soldier in 4th Me. reg., &c. 2, Bradford K., b. ab. '46; r. Rock., entered U. S. navy. 3, Charles, b. March, 1855, d. Sept. 18, '56. 4, Abbie F., b. ab. '59.

HOLMES, Mrs. Nancy, of a different family, b. ab. 1817; r. Rock., a widow. Her ch. 1, Angeline, b. ab. 1837; m. George H. Tighe; r. Rock. 2, Mary E., b. ab. '42; m. Charles L. Williams, Aug. 20, '60. 3. Jacob B., b. ab. '45; r. Rock., in the army.

HOOPER; of this North Haven family, there came to this place. 1, Capt. Watson, b. ab. 1820; m. Adelaide Maddocks, p. March 27, '54; r. S. Th. 2, Capt. Joel R., r. S. Th., & d. at sea, July 1858, on passage from New Orleans to New York. 3, Solomon, deceased. 4, Capt. Jeremiah, b. ab. 1833; m. Annie E. Webster, Dec. 21, '54; r. S. Th. 5, Capt. George Melvin, b. ab. 1839; m. Elvira H. Brewster, Nov. 17, '61; r. S. Th. 6, Albert, b. ab. 1841; r. S. Th., and d. at sea, June 28, '60.

Capt. Watson's ch. 1, Sidney, b. ab. 1855. 2, Edwina, b. ab. '57. 3, Minnie, b. ab. '59.

Capt. Jeremiah's ch. Capt. Horatio B., b. ab. 1841; m. Emma F. Webster, Oct. 27, '61; r. S. Th.

HOPKINS, James C., b. ab. 1792; r. here in 1860 with wife and family, but has since rem. to Portland. Of his ch. 1, Capt. Henry E., mar. Sylvenia N. ———; r. Rock. 2, Capt. Charles N., b. ab. 1822; m. Nancy B. ———; r. Rock., rem. Millbridge, Me. 3, Capt. George A., m. in Boston, Effie E. Wallace, Sept. 15, '57; r. Rock. 5, Caroline A., m. Robert L. Jackson; r. Rock.

Capt. Henry E.'s ch. 1, Herbert A., b. Oct., 1847, d. May 5, '50. 2, Herbert N., b. ab. '50. 3, Edwin F., b. ab. '56.

Capt. Charles N.'s ch. 1, Frank M., b. ab. 1846. 2, Charles W., b. ab. '48. 3, Edgar L., b. ab. '54.

Capt. George A.'s ch. Nellie W., b. June, and d. Aug. 20, 1860.

HOPKINS, Albert, of a different family, b. ab. 1832; m. Sophronia ———; r. Rock., a carpenter. Their ch. Ida, b. ab. 1856.

HOPKINS, Martin, b. ab. 1835; m. Rosalinda ———; r. Rock., a lime burner, and soldier in U. S. Sharpshooters, for a time. Their ch. 1, Mary E., b. ab. 1856. 2, Albert R., b. ab. 1859.

HOSMER, Anthony, b. Dec., 1793; came from Camden; r. Rock., with Mary, his wife, & d. in Aug., 1855. Their ch. 1, Frederic A., b. in Cam., Feb. 21, 1826. 2, Lucy A., b. June 15, '28; m. John H. Cooke; r. Rock. 3, Louisa E., b. Jan. 5, '30. 4, Achsah S., b. Feb. 21, '32; m. John D. Simmons; r. Rock. 5, Josiah Haskell, b. Jan. 22, '34, d. Nov. 18, '47.

HOVEY, Ivory, son of Dr. Ivory Hovey of Berwick, Me.; m. Mary, daughter of Manasseh Smith, Esq., of Wiscasset; r. in that place and Rock., rem. and m. 2d, in Dover, N. H., Mrs. Sarah Robinson, June

15, '52; but ret. & d. in Rock. His ch. by 1st wife. 1, Ivory T., b. May, 1803; m. 1st, Marietta Cochran, p. July 27, '37, 2d, Jane M. Cochran; r. Rock., a shoemaker, &c., died Sept. 5, '64. 2, Frances Eliza, m. Elbridge Pratt of Mobile, where she r. a widow with one daughter. 3, Manasseh S., b. ab. 1805; m. Maximilia Stinson of Deer Isle, May 7, '42; r. Rock., a merchant. 4, Mary Hannah, r. Rock., a teacher, &c. 5, Lucy Smith, r. Rock. 6, Olivia H., r. Rock. 7, Edwin S., Esq., m. 1st, Clarissa Reed of Orono, Nov. 3, '29; prac. law in Rock., from ab. 1826; rem. Wiscasset, as register of probate, ab. 1852; m. 2d, Susan Thresher; rem. & r. Portland. 8, Lydia Ann, m. Daniel Howard, Oct. 12, '56; r. Hope. 9, Susan Lord, m. Capt. William Spofford; r. Rock. 10, Joseph E., d. in New Orleans. 11, Sarah M., m. Robert D. Post of Mobile, July 31, '44; r. Mobile. The mother died April 21, '48, aged 72.

Ivory T.'s ch. by 1st wife. William, b. ab. 1839; r. Rock., an insurance clerk.

Manasseh S.'s ch. 1, Mary S., b. May 7, 1841; m. Romanzo W. Moore of Searsport, Dec. 28, '60. 2, Olive S., b. ab. '44. 3, Susan S., b. ab. '46. 4, Caroline S., b. ab. '48. 5, Edwenia, b. ab. '50. 6, Frances E., b. ab. '53. 7, Ella Maude, b. ab. '56.

Edwin S.'s ch. by 1st wife. 1, Edwin E., b. Oct. 22, 1830, d. Dec. 1845. 2, Mary E., b. May 23, & d. June 14, '32. 3, Ivory T., b. July 12, & d. 25, '33. 4, Maria Louisa, b. Dec. 14, '34, d. Aug. 22, '36. 5, Albert R., b. Aug. 2, '36; r. Portland, a soldier in the army. 6, Margaret L., b. Aug. 20, & d. Nov. 3, '38. 7, Joseph F., b. Feb. 13, & d. May 22, '40. 8, Milton H., b. March 13, & d. May 22, '41. 9, Clara M., b. May 1, '42; r. Portland. 10, Theodore F., r. Portland. 11, Emerson Waldo, r. Portland. 12, Caroline E., b. March, and d. June, 1846. The mother d. at Orono, Sept., 1850. By 2d wife. 13, Edwin S., (2d). 14, Louise S. 15, Belle Brandon.

HOWARD, Caleb, came from Bridgewater, Mass.; m. Catharine Romergar; r. and d. Wal., below the Dr. Brown place. Of his brothers, Capt. Joshua also c. to Wal., r. & d. down the Bay. 2, Daniel, m. and settled in St. George.

Caleb's ch. 1, Philip, lost at sea. 2, Elizabeth, b. 1755; m. 1st, a Howard of Wal., 2d, Josiah Mero; r. W. and d. Feb. 28, 1848. 3, James, b. 1767; c. to Th. ab. '92; m. Lydia (Morse) Emerson, p. Jan. 1793; r. Linc. and Th., d. Jan. 17, 1853. 4, Hannah, b. July 20, '73; m. Matthew Watson; r. Rock. 5, Julia Ann, b. March 20, '75; m. John Montgomery; r. W., and d. June 16, 1862. 6, George, mar. r. and d. in Castine. 7, Caleb, (2d), b. 1779; m. 1st, Mary Gerrish, 2d, Betsey (Howard) Blood; r. U. 8, Ruth, mar. John Bartlett of Wal., 2d, George Jameson,; r. and d. W. 9, Jane, m. John Peavey; r. & d. Belmont. 10, Margaret, b. 1785; m. John D. Morse; r. Th. & d. Sept. 15, 1840. 11, Daniel, (2d), m. Catharine Montgomery; r. U., rem. and d. St. George. 12, Susan, m. Thaddeus Sheperd; r. Union. 13, Joshua, (2d), m. Martha Howard of Gardiner, d. ab. 1830.

Capt. Joshua's ch. 1, Caleb, (3d), m. Agnes Robinson of St. Geo., and d. leaving one son, Caleb, (4th), who removed to Ohio with his mother and step-father, Robert Porterfield.

Daniel's ch. 1, Betsey, m. Abel Blood of Th., 2d. Caleb Howard, of U. 2, Mary, b. ab. 1786; m. David Watson, r. Rock. 3, Daniel, (3d), r. and d. St. George. 4, Joshua, (3d), r. St. George.

James's ch. 1, Freelove, b. Aug. 1, 1793; m. John Sterling; r. Th. and d. Dec. 15, '32. 2, Elizabeth, b. Jan. 24, '95; m. Capt. Thomas

Morison, p. June 15, '19; r. W. 3, Lucy, b. Sept. 1, '97; m. Richard Moore; r. Freedom. 4, Theodore P., b. Sept. 14, '99; m. 1st, Elizabeth (Robinson) Sayward, May 15, 182, 2d, Elethea Lindsey; r. Rock., a wheelwright, &c. 5, James Horace, b. June 22, 1801, d. Aug. 1828 in N. O. 6, Mary D., b. April 15, and d. Nov. 1803. 7, Maria Durand, b. Oct. 3, '05; m. John Blackington; r. Th., and d. Jan. 2, '52. 8, Margaret Catharine, b. Dec. 1, '07; m. Dodapher Richards; r. Searsmont, and d. May 25, '37.

Of Joshua (3d)'s ch. Capt. Daniel b. ab. 1830; m. Mary A. Meservey; r. Th.; had his ship burned by rebel privateers 1863.

Fourth Generation.

Theodore P.'s ch. 1, Theodore H., born Feb. 7, 1826, d. June 16, '45. 2, Henry Swasey, b. Nov. 12, '28, d. of consumption. By 2d wife. 3, John Barry, born ab. '44 (with a twin brother who d. an infant,) r. Rock. 4, Francis Elizabeth, b. ab. '45.

Capt. Daniel's ch. 1, Julia B., b. ab. 1855. 2, Lizzie A., b. ab. '58.

HOWARD, Ichabod A., b. ab. 1814, in Phillips, Me., son of Frederick and grandson of Joseph Howard, one of the first settlers of that town from Conn.; m. Olive Burns, and r. Rock., a lime burner, &c. Their ch. 1, Francis A., b. June 2, 1840. 2, Gardner L., b. July 8, '42. 3, Nancy, b. ab. '46. 4, Lucia, b. ab '59.

HOWARD, Henry, born ab. 1819, in Washington, Me., (son of Micah Howard, who was in Th. and m. Betsey Young of W., Jan. 20, 1809, but rem. Washington,) m. Hepzibah Turner; r. Rock., a lime manufacturer. Their ch. 1, Augusta R. b. ab. 1843. 2, Emma S. b. ab. '45. 3, Henry D., b. ab. '47. 4, Kendall, b. ab. '49. 5, Ada A., b. Sept. 9, '51, d. Aug. 18, '54. 6, Gracia A., b. Aug. 12, '56, d. Nov. 25, '57.

HOWARD, Elias, b. ab 1833, in Hallowell, Me., m. Nancy Snow; r. Rock., a mariner. Their ch. Clara E., b. ab. 1854.

HOWARD, Michael, b. ab. 1805, in Limerick county, Ireland; m. Ann Conklin, p. Sept. 4, 1855; r. Th. Their ch. 1, Michael (2d) b. ab. 1856. 2, Mary, b. ab. '58.

HOWE, Simeon, born ab. 1816, in Lincolnville; mar. Jane, dau. of John Comery; came here in 1849; r. Th., a stevedore, &c. Their ch. 1, Ellen, b. in 1840, d. May 21, '52. 2, Erastus, b. ab '41; r. Th., a mariner. 3, Stephen, b. ab. '56. 4, Edward, b. in June & d. in July, 1859.

HOWES, Lewis W., Esq., b. ab. 1821, prac. law in Belfast; mar. Clementine O. Allen, in Fayette, June, 1851; rem. and r. Rock., attorney and counsellor at law, appointed County Attorney of Knox, Jan., 1862, re-elected by the people and still continues. Their ch. 1, John A., b. ab. 1853. 2, Annie L., b. ab. '58.

HOWES; of this family two brothers came from Solon, Me., viz.: 1, Aaron, b. ab. 1821, in Solon; m. Hannah Heald of S. Solon, Oct. 24, '52; r. Rock., a lumber merchant. 2, Chandler, b. ab. 1832; m. Adelaide C. Pendleton of Rock.; r. Rock., a lumber merchant.

Aaron's ch. Lilian B., b. ab. 1856.

Chandler's ch. Frederic W., b. ab. 1857.

HOWLEY, Michael, b. ab. 1827, in Waterford county, Ireland; m. Aurelia Woodcock; r. Th. Their ch. 1, Ellen, b. ab. 1857. 2, Jas. H. b. ab. 1859.

HUDSON, John, came to old Th., m. Mrs. Abigail Kelloch, April 13, 1823, (who d. Sept., 1825, aged 30.)

HULL, Robert A., b. ab. 1830, son of Robert Hull of Bristol; m. 1st, Miss Erskine of Bristol, 2d, Julia F. Spear of W., Dec. 1, '60; r. Th., a carpenter. His ch. by 1st wife, Addie.

HUME, Eli, b. ab. 1808, in New Brunswick; m. Ellen ——— of Glasgow, Scot., r. Rock. Their ch. 1, John, b. about 1834; r. Rock., a mariner. 2, Ann, b. ab. '36. 3, Ellen, b. ab. '38. 4, Mary, b. ab. '41. 5, Jane, b. ab. '43. 6, Sarah, b. ab. '45. 7, David, b. ab. '48. 8, Peter, b. ab. '50. 9, Emeline, b. ab. '52. 10, Clara, b. ab. '55.

HUMPHREY, Benjamin, r. and d in Boston, a wealthy merchant, originally from Weymouth, m. Oriens, daughter of Maj. William Turner of Scituate, (who grad. H. U., 1767, raised a company and went into the Rev. service, was aid-de-camp to Maj. Gens. Heath and Knox, surveyed the town of Turner, Me., where he settled and died 1808,) and grand daughter of Rev. Charles Turner of Duxbury. Of their ch. 1, Henry B., born about 1812; was educated in the Boston schools, served 7 years in his father's counting-room against his own inclination which would have led him to college, was in trade eight years, amassing a sufficient fortune, spent four years from 1839 to '43, in travelling through Europe, Asia Minor, Egypt, across the desert to the Red Sea, thence to Petra, Syria, and Palestine; was appointed by Pres. Polk, consul at Alexandria, but declined; m. Pastora E., Mason; c. to Th., purchased the three story house in Wadsworth street, which he has renovated and filled with books, paintings, and all the spoils of travel.

HUNT; of this family, two brothers came to this place, viz.: — 1, John W., b. Feb. 11, 1800, in Lincolnville, Me., m. Rachel Hix, July 1, '30; r. Rock., a lime manufacturer, &c. 2, Elisha, b. ab. '12, in Belmont; m. Eunice Collamore; r. Rock., in lime business.

John W.'s ch. 1, Albina W., b. June 28, 1833; m. Capt. Joseph Thorndike; r. Rock. 2, John F., b. Jan. 29, '35; m. Ellen C., Shepherd; r. Rock. 3, Anna A., b. Jan. 9, '37. 4, Sidney P., b. Oct. 28, '39, a mariner. 5, Alfred I., b. Oct. 29, '41, a clerk.

Elisha's ch. 1, Abbie Jane, b. ab. 1844. 2, Thirza H., b. ab. '46.

John F.'s ch. Charles, b. ab. 1859.

HUNT, William, b. ab. 1819; m. Angeline ——; r. Rock. Their ch. 1, Charles W., b. ab. '49. 2, Mary E., b. ab. '51. 3, William, (2d), b. ab. '53. 4, Adelia F., b. ab. '57. 5, Kate S., b. ab. '59.

HUTCHINGS, William, b. ab. 1790; r. Rock., with Clara, his wife, was a shoemaker, & d. Feb. 14, 1859.

HUTCHINSON, Rev. E. W., son of Rev. David Hutchinson, was b. in Winslow, Me., Feb. 4, 1826; m. Nancy Woodsum of Albion, Oct. 19, '51; entered the ministry, Aug., '58, joined M. E. conference 1859; came to Rock., as pastor, in May, 1863. Their ch. 1, George A., b. in Winslow, Nov. 24, 1854. 2, Abby J., b. Dec. 3, 1856, in Winslow.

HYLER, Capt. Haunce R., b. in Cushing, March 27, 1790; m. Mary Shibles of Th., March 15, 1818; rem. Th., followed coasting, & d. Aug. 18, '32. Their ch. 1, Capt. Dodge, b. Sept. 14, '18, lost at sea, '46. 2, Eliza M., b. Nov. 17, '19; m. Capt. John M. Brown, & d. June 14, '56. 3, Helen A., b. April 9, '21; m. 1st, Capt. Simon B. Leeds of Warren, July 3, '42, (who was drowned at N. O., Sept. 17,

'42,) 2d, Capt. Rasmus Anderson, (who was also lost overboard in the Atlantic ocean); r. Th. 4, Capt. Alden B., b. Oct. 9, '22; m. Susan H. Reed of Newcastle, and d. in Liverpool, Eng., March 14, '55. 5, Priscilla, b. Aug. 27, '24; m. Capt. John M. Brown, Oct. 3, '59; r. Th. 6, Capt. William M., b. April 18, '26; r. Th., a master mariner. 7, Capt. J. Burnham, b. April 25, '28; m. Susan A. Fuller of S. Th., March 16, '51; r. Th., and d. of yellow fever, in Havana, Cuba, June 24, '58. 8. Margaret G., b. Oct. 7, '29; m. Capt. John Norebeck of Denmark, Eu., Sept. 13, '55, who d. July 18, '56, in Mobile, Ala. 9, Capt. Ballard G., b. July 30, '31; r. Th., a master mariner.

Capt. Alden B.'s ch. Abbie, b. ab. 1848.

Capt. J. Burnham's ch. 1, Emma B., b. ab. 1851. 2, Alvah, b. ab. '53. 3, Alida, b. ab. '55. 4, Burnham, b. ab. '57.

HYLER, Edward, b. ab. 1811, son of Jacob Hyler of Cushing; m. Harriet Chaples; r. Th. Their ch. 1, Sarah, b. ab. '55. 2, Lewis, b. ab. '56. 3, Andrew, b. ab. '58.

INGERSON, Willard, b. ab. 1817; m. Delilah ——, r. S. Th., engaged in the fish business. Their ch. 1, Augusta M., b. ab. 1844. 2, John M., b. ab. '46, 3, Josiah W, b. ab. '48. 4, Charles B., b. ab. '53. 5, Marietta J., b. ab '56. 6, Sidney D., b. ab. '58. 7, a daughter, b. in 1860.

INGRAHAM; of this, Gloucester, Mass., family, there c. hither 3 brothers and one sister, viz.: 1, Dea. Job, b. in G. Sept. 15, 1755; c. to Old Th., m. by Rev. J. Urquhart to Lucy Tolman, May 13, '78; settled on what is now the northernmost lot in S. Th., at the head of the bay, and d. Nov. 27, 1834. 2, Joseph, Esq., b. July 1, 1759; m. Bradbury Keen, July 1, '83; r. Rock. and d. Oct. 23, 1848, a. 90. 3, Capt. Josiah, b. Sept. 3, 1761, c. to Th. '81, with one brother and sister; m. Hannah Counce of W., by Col. Wheaton, Dec. 15, '85; settled on the lot between his two brothers, now the first in Rock., & d. Jan. 22, 1849. 4, Nancy, b. 1769, m. Jedediah Spalding; r. S. Th., and d. Jan. 11, 1832.

Dea. Job's ch. 1, Elizabeth, b. March 13, 1779; m. Joab Brown, rem. Unity. 2, Joseph, (2d), b. Dec. 29, '82, m. Nancy Spear, Oct. 9, 1804; 2d, Mrs. Lucy Hodgman of Cam., Jan. 15, '57; r. Rock., a farmer. 3, Job, (2d), b. Jan. 3, '85; m. 1st, Mary Crandon, Sept. 29, 1803; 2d, Nancy Young of Matinicus, Nov. 28, '11; r. Rockport. 4, Dea. Josiah, (2d), b. May 29, '86, m. Mrs. Abigail Young of Matinicus, May 11, 1809; r. Cam., and d. Sept. 6, '64. 5, Isaac, born June 29, '88, m. 1st. Susanna Crie of Matinicus, Dec. 9, 1813; 2d, Sarah (Libby) Norwood, 1836, 3d, Mrs. Octavia Masters; r. S. Th., a carpenter, and d. Feb 6, '62. 6, John, b. June 18, '90, m. Lydia Packard, Nov. 5, 1812; r. Cam., & d. Feb. 22, '63. 7, Bernard, b. Jan. 29, '93, mar. Hannah Crane of Hope, Dec. 7, 1815; r. Linc. 8, Lucy, b. April 22, '99, mar. Philip Thomas, Dec. 7, 1810; r. Linc. 9, Archibald C., b. Jan. 3, 1803, m. Eliza Oxton; r. and d. Cam.

Joseph Esq.'s ch. 1, Lydia, b. April 4, 1784, m. Thomas Tolman; r. Rock. 2, Coit, born Aug. 4, '87, m. Betsey Haskell, Oct. 6, 1810. 2d, Sally Witham, Sept. 9, '45; r. Rock., and d. Aug 27, '57. 3, Charles, b. June 16, '93; d. by drowning, May 9, '14. 4, Dea. Henry, b. April 23, '97, m. Mary Lindsey, Jan. 1, 1817; r. Rock., a farmer.

Capt. Josiah's ch. 1, Susan Hunt, b. June 29, 1794, m. 1st, Otis Robbins, Jr.; 2d, Major John Spear, r. Rock., and died Nov. 4, 1834. 2, Josiah, (3d), b. July 13, 1796, m. Harriet, dau. of Maj. J. Spear, June

17, 1818; r. Rock., and d. May 17, 1824. 3, Samuel, b. Nov. 9, '98, mar. Hannah I. Spear, Dec. 17, 1818; r. Rock., and d. at Martha's Vineyard of yellow fever, Nov. 4, 1819.

Third Generation.

Joseph, (2d)'s ch. 1, Meriel, b. Aug. 7, 1805, m. Isaac Gregory; r. Rock. 2, Joseph, (3d), b. May 27, '07, m. Julia A. Robbins, p. Oct. 9, '34; r. Rock., a farmer, & d. Jan. 27, '61. 3, William S., b. June 20, '10, m. Almira Vose, July 27, '33; r. Rock., a farmer. 4, Isaac, (2d), born June 24, '12, m. 1st, Susan Blackington, 2d, Abby Merrill; r. Rock., and d. Feb. 12, '59. 5, Nancy, born May 7, '15, m. Harrison Ferrand; d. March 1, '36. 6, Lucy Margaret, b. July 5, '17, m. Maj. Jona. Spear, (2d), r. Rock. 7, James S., b. July 25, '19, m. Mary C. Fassett of Union, Dec. 4, '42; r. Rock., a farmer. 8, Rufus C., born July 14, '21, m. Mary E. Rankin, Dec. 14, '43; r. Rock., lime burner. 9, Henry B., b. Nov. 8, '23, d. young. 10, Edwin, b. Feb. 7, '25, d. young. 11, Henry B., born Nov. 11, '27, m. Jane P. Hawes, p. Jan. 23, '47; r. Rock., a lime manufacturer. 12, Harriet S., born May 30, '29, m. Capt. Moses Fisk; r. Rock. 13, Harrison F., b. Dec. 1, '30, d. Sept. 1, '31.

Job (2d)'s ch. 1, Royal, b. ab. 1817, m. Harriet M. (who d. Dec. 26, '63, a. 46); r, Rock., a blacksmith. Probably others r. Rockport.

Isaac's ch. By 1st wife. 1, Betsey B., b. Dec. 1813, m. John Kellock; r. Rock., and d. Aug. 22, '61. 2, Orinda, b. Dec. 23, 1815, m. Harrison Ferrand; r. Rock. 3, Mary Ann, b. April 12, '17, m. Orris Butler; r. Rock. 4, A. Melvina, b. Aug. 15, '20, m. Josiah Ames; rem. California. 5, Margaret, b, April 12, '22, m. Capt. Alden Crouch, 2d, Jonas S. Davis; r. Rock. 6, Elathea, b. Jan. 26, '26, m. Josiah Rankin; d. in N. Orleans. 7, Capt. Isaac Thomas, b. July 12, '28, mar. Sophia R. Pillsbury, Oct. 26, '50; r. S. Th. The mother d. Nov. 26, 1835, a. 42.

Bernard's ch. 1, Melvina, b. May 10, 1818, d. Aug. 18, '20. 2 & 3, twins, b. Feb. 12, '20; Elizabeth C., m. Abner B. Weeks, r. and d. Rock.; Mary Jane, m. Samuel B. Perry; r. S. Th. 4, Ezekiel P., b. Nov. 30, '21. 5, Dea. Bernard Boyce, b. Nov. 23, '23; m. Elizabeth O. McIntosh, Dec. 2, '49; r. S. Th., a farmer. 6, Calvin C., b. July 6, '26; m. Lydia A. Pierce, Feb. 27, '49; r. S. Th., a merchant. 7, Margery McK., b. Dec. 21, '29; mar. Andrew J. Young; r. S. Th. 8, Hannah F., b. Feb. 3, '32; m. Robert C. Brann, r. S. Th. 9, Job P., b. March 25, '35; m. M. Nettie Holbrook, Sept. 1, '59; r. S. Th., a marble dealer.

Coit's ch. 1, Eliza, b. Nov. 20, 1811; r. Rock. 2, Charles, (2d), b. April 26, '14; m. Eleanor Brown, Oct. 17 '41; r. S. Th. 3, Capt. Joseph C., b. Sept. 3, '18; m. Mary E. Palmer, Oct. 17, '43; r. Rock., 4 and 5, twins, b. April 29, '24; Capt. David H., m. Catharine P. Vanstone, June 13, '44; r. Rock. Capt. Mark L., m. Julia A. Snow, Dec. 26, '45; r. Rock. 6, Harriet B., born Feb. 26, '27; mar. Henry Haywood, July 7, '46; r. Rock. 7 and 8, twins, born April 21, 1831; Capt. Otis, m. Lucy M. Stearns, Dec. 20, '51; r. Rock.; Capt. Orris R., m. Arlette H. Rollins, Dec. 22, '50; r. Rockland.

Dea. Henry's ch. 1, Ann L., b. April 25, 1819, d. April 26, 1836. 2, Achsah, born Dec. 2, '20; mar. Rev. Joseph Kalloch; r. Rock. 3, Henry Edwin, b. Aug. 25, '27; m. Sylvia R. Getchell, Nov. 10, '52; r. Rock., a farmer. 4, Oliver F., b. March 20, '37; r. Rock., attorney at law, vol. in Col. Mitchell's Kansas reg. 5, John N., b. Oct. 16, '39; m. Sarah L. Miller, Oct. 16, '63; r. Rock.

Josiah, (3d)'s ch. 1, Capt. John S., b. Aug. 28, 1820; m. Elvena M. Hewett; r. Rock., now commission merchant, South st., N. Y. 2, J. Albion, b. Feb. 2, 1824; m. Elizabeth Hall of Camden, Jan. 2, '53; r. Rock., a merchant, firm of Kimball & Ingraham.

Samuel's ch. 1, Capt. Samuel L., b. Oct. 9, 1819; m. Sophia Adams, July 1, '39; r. Rock. & d. Jan. 29, '56, on passage from Valparaiso to Boston. in b'k *Iddo Kimball*.

Fourth Generation.

Joseph, (3d)'s ch. 1, Mary S., b. ab. 1843. 2, Charles R., b. ab. '46. 3, Aldana, b. ab. '49.

William S.'s ch. 1, George W., b. July 4, 1838; m. Agnes A. Gregory, Sept. 16, '55; r. Rock., a milk dealer. 2, Lizzie J., b. ab. '41; m. Robert A. Palmer; r. Rock.

Isaac, (2d)'s ch. 1, Adoniram J., b. May 6, 1840. 2, ? Charles Milliken.

James S.'s ch. 1, Nancy E., b. ab. 1847. 2, James A., b. ab. '53. The mother d. Dec. 2, '62, aged 43.

Henry B.'s ch, Ella, b. ab. 1852.

Royal's ch. Flavilla B., b. ab. 1841.

Capt. Isaac Thomas's ch. 1, Cora, b. ab. 1854. 2, Clinton S., b. ab. 1856.

Dea. Bernard B.'s ch. 1, Albert H., b. ab. 1852. 2, Caroline I., b. ab. '56. 3, Alfred C., b. ab. '59.

Calvin C.'s ch. Abigail F., b. ab. 1857.

Charles C.'s ch. 1, Charles Coit, b. July 28, 1842. 2, Clarence J., b. ab. '45; m. Martha Arey, Jan. 2, '64; r. S. Th., soldier of 2d Me. Battery. 3, Clara A., b. ab. '49.

Capt. Joseph C.'s ch. 1, Ellen F., b. ab. 1847. 2, Adelaide C., b. June 16, '52, d. Feb. 5, '56. 3, Ida L., b. ab. '56. 4, Lizzie M. B., b. March 31, '59, d. April 27, '63. 5, Orris, b. March 16, and d. Dec. 3, '63.

Capt. David H.'s ch. 1, Harriet M,, b. ab. 1844. 2, Angenette H., b. ab. '47.

Capt. Mark L.'s ch. 1, Albert F., b. ab. 1847. 2, Annie C., b. ab. 1855.

Capt. Otis's ch. William, b. ab. 1856.

Capt. Orris R.'s ch. 1, Lester A., b. ab. 1852. 2, Frederic H. b. ab. '57.

H. Edwin's ch. Edwin, b. ab. 1855.

Capt. John S.'s ch. 1, Emma C., b. June 8, 1846. 2, Frederic H., b. Dec., 1848, d. July 7, '51. 3, Addie W., b. Jan. 13, '53. 4, Celeste H., b. April 17, '56.

J. Albion's ch. 1, Mary K., b. Nov. 30, 1853. 2, George S., b. Jan. 7, '56. 3, Edward, b. May 4, '60, d. Oct. 4, '60. 4, Eugene, b. March 17, '61, d. July 14, '61.

INGRAHAM, Rev. John Henniker, of a distant branch of the same family, (as was also Rev. J. H. Ingraham, the novelist), was b. in Portland, son of Hon. J. H. Ingraham, June 11, 1793; stud. theology with Dr. Payson; m. Abigail Guild, daughter of Hon. Daniel Cony of Augusta, Jan. 28, 1818; Congregational minister in Th. from 1817 to 1830; rem. Augusta, became a Baptist minister and teacher, was ten years chaplain of Insane hospital, &c., died April 13, 1864. Their ch. b. here. 1, Marcia Paulina C., b. Aug 27, 1819; m. ——— Ladd; r. Bangor. 2, Edward Tyng, b. June 15, '23; m. & r. a merchant in Bangor. 3, Joseph Sprague, b Oct. 29, '25. 4, Rev. John H., (2d), b. June 7, '28. Also, born after the parents removed from Thomaston. 5, Rev. Daniel C., b. ab. '30; grad. Bowd. Coll., '50, Bangor Theo. Sem., '56; an Episcopal minister; d. at Augusta, '60. 6, Cornelia, and perhaps others.

INGRAHAM, George H, b. ab. 1823, of a different family; m. Lavinia Reagan, Sept. 5, '50; r. Rock., a carpenter. Their ch. 1, George W., b. ab. '52. 2, Floretta C., b. Sept. 5, '53, d. Sept. 12, '54. 3, Anson L., b. ab. '60.

INGRAHAM, Richard B., b. ab. 1833; m. Lydia Dyer, July 29, '54; r. S. Th., a joiner. Their ch. 1, Gilbert, b. ab. '55. 2, Lizzie May, b. ab. 1857. 3, Clara E., b. Nov. 23, 1860, d. Oct. 13, 1861. 4, Watie A., b. Sept. 30, 1862, d. Dec. 27, 1863.

IRESON, George W. b. ab. 1812, in Mass., and, with Eliza J., his wife, r. Rock. a few years, ab. 1859, a trader, since rem. Their ch. Sarah M., b. ab. 1859.

IRONS, Freeman W., b. ab. 1821; m. Martha L. ——; r. Rock., a mariner, & rem. or d. His widow r. Rock. and keeps public house. Their ch. 1, John F., b. ab. 1846; in the U. S. Navy. 2, Melissa A., b. ab. 1849. 3, Katie O., b. ab. 1858.

JACKSON, William, a whip sawyer; m. & r. W., rem. & m. Sarah (Choate) Jordan, in Th., March 3, 1839; r. Th., & d. Nov. 7, 1844.

JACKSON, Robert L., b. ab. 1812, in Winthrop, Me., lost his 1st wife here, & m. 2d, Caroline A. Hopkins, Jan. 20, '52; r. Rock., a photographist. His ch. 1, Miller C., b. ab. '43. The mother died Oct. 18, '50, aged 36. By 2d wife. 2, Carrie, b. ab. '54. 3, Affie L., b. ab. 1857.

JACKSON; of this family two brothers c. from Derry, N. H. 1, Ebenezer T, b. ab. 1808, m. 1st, Mary B. Cotton, 2d Sarah E. Merriam, Oct. 12, '54; r. Rock., a joiner, &c. 2, Ivory, b. ab. 1820; c. to Rock., m. Mrs. Lavinia Burgess, Feb. 6, '51; r. Rock., a joiner.

Ebenezer T.'s ch. By 1st wife. 1, Edward C., born ab. 1831; r. Rock., a joiner. 2, Mary J., b. April 6, '35. 3, Caroline, b. Nov. 14, '38; r. Rock. 4, Edmund G., born Jan. 23, '42, died Jan. 21, '63. 5, Nancy H., b. April 2, '45, d, July 5, '54. The mother died Aug. 26, '52, a. 45. By 2d wife. 6, Clarence, b. ab. '55. 7, Cora, b. ab. '57. 8, Nellie b. ab. '59.

Ivory's ch. 1, Franklin P., b. ab. 1852. 2, William R. b. April 24, '53, d. March 3, '56. 3, Charles A., b. ab. Aug. '55. 4, Willard C., b. ab. '57. 5, Clarissa W., b. Dec. 6, '61, d. Aug. 10, '62.

JACKSON, Joseph, b. ab. 1813 in Belmont, Me., m. Mary J. Moody, r. Rock., a cooper, &c. Their ch. 1, Joseph W., b. ab. 1840, m. Addie S. Hanly, Oct. 10, '63; r. Rock., a clerk, &c. 2, Nahum R., born Dec. 1, '42; was a soldier of 19th Me. Reg., d. in hospital at Washington, Jan. 7, '63.

JACKSON, Amasa, born ab. 1828, mar. Eliza Hall, Sept. 1852; r. Rock., a lime burner and soldier of 4th Me. Reg., died at Baltimore, Nov. 29, '62. Their ch. 1, Charles M., b. ab. 1854. 2, Frederic E., b. ab. '57.

JACKSON, Alexander. S., b. ab. 1820, mar. Flora McDonald, May 30, '55; r. S. Th., a farmer. Their ch. 1, Lucinda, b. ab. 1851. 2, Sidney, b. ab. '56. 3, Franklin, b. ab. '59.

JACKSON, Bartlett, with his family r. in Th. some dozen years or more prior to 1862, when he was Treasurer of Knox county, &c., but has since removed.

JACKSON, John P., born 1781; mar. Margaret ——, r. Rock. Their ch. Margaret, b. ab. 1843; r. Rock.

JACKSON, Capt. George H., b. ab. 1822, in Brooksville, Me., m. Melinda A. Gregory; r. Rock., 1860 & before; since rem. St. George. Their ch. 1, Mary A., b. ab. 1843, m. Israel Curtis. 2, Sarah E.' b, ab. '45, m. William Holland. 3, Emma, b. ab. '47. 4, Caroline C., b. ab. '49. 5, John P., b. ab. '51. 6, Augusta M., b. ab. '53.

JACKSON, Nathaniel, born ab. 1797, m. Sarah ——; r. Rock. Their ch. 1, Samuel, b. ab. 1828, r. Rock., a fisherman, soldier of 4th Me. Regt., &c.

JACOBS; of this English family, probably of Jewish descent, and at first written Jacob; Nicholas, according to Daniel Cushing's record, "with his wife and 2 children and their cosen, Thomas Lincoln, weaver, came from *old* Hingham and settled in *this* Hingham in 1633." [See Barry's History of Hanover, Mass.] Of his 8 ch., the oldest, Capt. John, b. in Eng., m. 1st, Margery Eames, 2d, Mary Russell, Oct. 3, 1661, and had 14 ch. Of these, the 4th, Capt. David, b. June 20, 1664, m. 1st, Sarah Cushing, 2d, Mary Cushing; r. and d. Scituate; was a weaver, a deacon, a schoolmaster, and always employed in public affairs; of his 11 ch. 7th, Joshua, b. March 31, 1702, m. Mary James, April 7, 1726; r. and d. Scituate. The 4th of Joshua's 8 ch. Col. John, b. May 23, 1735, m. Hannah Tolman; r. Scituate, a mason and active officer in the Revolution.

Col. John's ch. 1, John, b. Sept. 22, 1759, m. Mabel Litchfield; r. Hanover, a blacksmith, rem. and died Carlisle, Mass. 2, Samuel, or Lemuel, b. June 10, '61, m. Sarah Randall; r. and d. Scituate, a shipwright. 3, Hannah, b. April 4, '63, m. Col. and Hon. Charles Turner, M. C.; r. 1853 in S. Scituate. 4, Sarah, b, Dec. 15, '64, m. Calvin Bailey of Hanover. 5. Francis, b. Oct. 2, '66. 6, Mary, b. July 20, '68, m. James Bourne. 7, Charles, b. May 26, '70, mar. Elizabeth Snelling; r. Boston, a carpenter. 8, Rowland, b. March 17, '72; c. to Th. about 1800, m. Anna Eames of Holliston, Mass.; r. Th., a blacksmith, and d. Dec. 11, 1857, a. 85 ys. 8 mos. 9, Walter, b. Dec. 27, '74, m. Elizabeth Turner; r. some years in Th., ab. 1808; a mason; rem. and d. Scituate. 10, Fanny b. Nov. 18, '76, r. 1853 in S. Scituate. 11, Warren, b. March 29, '78, m. Rachel Clapp, and was killed by falling from a building in Boston.

Rowland's ch. 1, Rowland, (2d), b. March 6, 1802; mar. Lois Young, June 30, 1825; r. Th., a blacksmith, shipbuilder, &c. 2, Mary Eames, b. June 20, '04, m, Paul Bradford; r. Th. 3, Joseph Warren, b. Sept. 23, '06, mar, Almira Boynton of Palermo, Oct. 14 '41; r. Th., a ship-builder, &c. 4, Ann, b. Sept. 18, '08, d. March 3, '38. 5, Hannah Tolman, b. March 12, 1811; r. Th. 6, John, b, Dec. 15, '13, m. Betsey Woodcock, Nov. 2, '41; r. Th., on homestead, a farmer, blacksmith, &c. 7, Walter, b. Feb. 18, '18, died Feb. 8, '19. The mother, b. June 30, 1776; d. May 21, 1864.

Rowland, (2d)'s ch. 1, Joseph Henry, b. Feb. 11, 1828; m. Ellen A. Hight of Wayne, May 29, '55; r. Th., a merchant. 2, Mary A., b. Feb. 21, '30; r. Th. 3, Caroline A., b. Nov. 29, '32; mar. Capt. Samuel C. Jordan; r. Th. & d. March 4, '61. 4, Theoxena, b. Aug. 9, '35, d. May 30, '39. 5, Lucy C., b. Sept. 10. '37, d. Sept. 24, 38. 6, Lucy Ann E., b. Aug. 29, '40, d. April 4, '48.

Joseph Warren's ch. 1, Ann, b. Oct. 16, 1842. 2, Walter E., b. Feb. 8, '44; r. Th., entered U. S. navy. 3, Mary Lois, b. Oct. 25, '45. 4, Almira, b. April 18, '48. 5, Lucy Emily, b. March 23, 1850. 6, George W., b. Aug. 25, '52. 7, Helena B., b. Dec. 4, '54. 8, Naomi B., b. Dec. 27, '56. 9, Sarah Leland, b. March 18, and d. July 16, 1860.

John's ch. Hannah M., b. Dec. 15, 1842.

Fourth Generation.

Joseph Henry's ch. 1, Edwin H. b. Jan. 15, and d. Nov. 17, 1857, 2, Charles Rowland, b. March, 1858, d. March 16, '62.

JACOBS, Samuel, Esq., son of Elisha, who was a son of Dr. Joseph, (who was the 9th child of Capt. David, before mentioned,) m. 1st, Margaret Stinson, settled in Camden, but was m. in Th. to his 2d wife Peggy McGlathery, March 19, 1789, by D. Fales, Esq., was a shipwright, representative, and d. Sept. 5, 1809. Ch. by 2d wife. 1, Samuel, (2d), lawyer, merchant, d. unm. 1835, a. 44. 2, Frederic, mar. Julia Cushing, and d. 1834, a. 39. 3, Robert, d. unm. 1829. 4, Bela, d. unm. 1849, a. 52. 5, Caroline, m. Dr. Joseph H. Estabrook, 1823, r. Camden.

JACOBS, William, b. ab. 1834; probably of this Camden branch, m. Arethusa T. Coombs; Nov. 13, '59; r. Rock., a quarryman.

JAMES, David M., Esq., b. ab. 1813; r. Rock., where he was city marshal, &c., but rem. and died in Conewango, Penn., Feb. 1, 1864.

JAMESON; of this family two or more brothers came from Cape Elizabeth, and in 1753 planted themselves on a point which took their name in Meduncook now Friendship, viz.: 1, Alexander, b. ab. 1728; m. Mary McLellan of Falmouth; r. on the farm in F. now owned by Emery Davis, and d. Jan., 1800. 2, Paul, m. Betsey, dau. of Patrick Pebbles of Warren; r. & d. on the farm in F. which his son Jeremiah and descendants have since occupied, formerly distinguished for one of the best orchards in these parts, now in decay. 3, Martha, a sister, m. Patrick Porterfield; r. Th., & d. in 1771. 4, Samuel, probably the oldest, had come earlier, was the first settler of Meduncook in 1743, and the father of Samuel, who mar. Sarah McLellan, and whose ch. settled in W., for which branch of the family see "Annals of Warren."

Alexander's ch. 1, Robert, b. April 1, 1746; m. 1st, Deborah Morton, Feb, 9, '69; 2d, Sarah Rivers, May 14, '86; r. F., and died Sept. 22, '32, leaving 137 descendants. 2, Martha, m. Wm. Motte, a school master, from France; r. and d. F. 3, Alexander, (2d), mar. Sarah Blackington of Th., p. Oct 10, '77, r. Clam Cove or Jameson's Point, and rem. Charleston, Me. 4, Mary, mar. Abraham Jones of Cam., p. Oct. 6, '81. 5, Ebenezer, mar. Catharine Morse, formerly *Demorse*, r. and d. F. 6, Margaret, m. Daniel Howard of Wal. r. & d. St. George. 7 and 8, d. young.

Paul's ch. 1, Robert, (2d), settled on and gave name to Jameson's Point, Rockland; m. 1st, Martha Porterfield of Cam., p. Dec. 30, 1780, 2d, Deborah Simmons, p. April 20, '91; & d. ab. 1828. 2, Chas. settled beside his brother, m. 1st, Ruth Horton, p. Nov. 13, '94, 2d, Agnes Hyler, Feb. 22, 1808; r. and d. Rock. 3, Capt. Paul, (2d), m. Sarah Parsons, was a seaman, r. on Burton's or Gay's Is., and d. aged about 30. 4, Jeremiah, r. F. and d. 1829, leaving 38 grand ch., 79 great grand ch., and 5 gr. gr. grand ch. 5, William, r. and d. F. 6, Isaac, r. and d. F.

Third Generation.

Robert's ch. 1, James, b. June 5, 1770; m. Elizabeth Storer, of Wal., 2d, Margaret Thompson of W., 3d, Mrs. Cedonia Winslow of Wal., and d. at Rock., Jan. 4, 1861, aged 90 y. 7 m. 2, John, mar. Abigail Cook; 2d, Celia Cook; 3d, Mrs. Esther Gardner; r. S. Th., rem. Matinic Is. & St. Geo., & d. in 1848. 3, Maria, m. 1st, Joseph Rivers, 2d, David Sweetland; r. & d. at Skowhegan. 4, Betsey, b. 1776; m. Samuel Rankin; r. Rock., & d. Feb. 4, '50. 5, Sarah, m. Stephen Lawry, 2d, Simeon Wotton of F., 3d, Soloman Fernald of N. H.; r. Charleston, Me. 6, Robert, (3d), m. 1st, Betsey Rivers of St. G., 2d, Lucy (Wheeler) Saywood, Dec. 1, 1833; was a farmer, r. and d. S. Th. 7, Sabra, born 1783, m. P. Pebbles Robinson; r. Warren. By 2d wife, 8, Moses, d. young. 9, Joseph, d. young. 10, Deborah, d. young. 11, Margaret, d. young. 12, Thurston W., m. Caroline Robinson of F., and d. in U. 1842. 12, Mary, m Capt. Henry Robinson; r. W. 13, Jane, mar. Capt. Simon Robinson; r. and d. in Friendship.

Robert, (2d)'s ch. by 2d wife. 1, Paul, (3d) a mariner, d. unm. 2, Martha, m. Capt. William Brewster; r. and d. Cam. 3, Elizabeth, m. Samuel McLaughlin; r. Rock., & d March 28, '49. 4, Isaac, (2d), m. Sarah Clough, July 1, 1832; r. and d. Cam. 5, Robert, (4th), m. Susan Clough of Cam., p. June 3, 1825; r. Rock. 6, Ruth, m. Wm. Clough; r. and died Cam. 7, Patrick, r. Rock. and Cam. 8, James, (2d), r. and d. Cam. 9, Diana, born Sept. 1811, mar. John Jones; r. Jameson's Point, just over the line in Cam., and d. Jan. 21, '62. 10, William, m. Harriet Grant, Nov. 15, 1856; r. Cam.

Charles's ch. by 2d wife. 1, Capt. Jeremiah, b. ab. 1809, m. 1st, Martha Gregory, March 6, 1836, 2d, Henrietta K. Gay, Jan 26, '61; r. Rock., a ship master, &c. 2, Charles, (2d), b. ab. 1811, m. 1st, Mary Tolman of Cam., p. May 28, '31, 2d, Cordelia Tolman, Oct. 7, '51; r, Rock., a farmer, &c. 3, Mark Dexter, m. Lydia Clough, p. July 30, '35; r. Cam. 4, Capt. Oliver, b. ab. 1815; m. Charlotte Smith, of Cam., p. Sept. 27, 1834; r. Rock 5, Mary, m. Geo. Johnson; r. R.

Fourth Generation.

James' ch. 1, Elizabeth, m James Burns; r. & d. Wal. 2, Abby, m. a Mr. Tibbets of Bath. 3, Catharine, m John Farnsworth; r. & d. Wal. 4, George, r. Wal., and d., supposed to have been killed by a vicious horse. 5, John, (2d), m. Rebecca Miller; r. Wal. or Windsor. 6, Deborah, m. Thomas Mitchell; r. and d. Union. 7, Henry, mar. Chloe Mero; r. and d. U. 8, Matthias, m. Sarah Law, 2d, Rebecca Storer; r. U. 9, Jane, r. Rock.

Of John's ch. 1, Elsie, m. Henry Stahl; r. Wal. 2, Lucy Ann, m. Benjamin Dillingham; r. Cam., rem. Framingham, Mass. 3, Ruby, r. Rock. By 2d wife. 4, Capt. Andrew, b. ab. 1803; m. Abby Morse of F.; r. Rock., ship master, owner, &c. 5, John, (3d), d. unm. 6, Margaret, m. Joseph Sweetland; r. Rock. 7, Mary Ann, m. James Murch; r. Rock. 8, Elijah C., m. Bertha Morse; r. Th., and died July 18, '46.

Robert, (3d)'s ch. 1, Capt. Thomas, b. Aug. 23, 1802, drowned at Marsailles, France. 2, Mary, b. July 14, '04, d. June 2, '30. 3, Abigail, b. March 2, '06; r. S. Th. 4, Sally, b. Nov. 11, '08; m. William Munroe; r. S. Th., Ash Point. 5, Hannah, b. Sept. 19, '10; m. Eben Sweetland, Oct. 13, '39; r. Rock, or S. Th. 6, Robert, (5th), b. June 17, '12; m. Louisa C. Sleeper; r. Rock., a ship carpenter. 7, Sylvester, b. June 14, '14, d. Feb. 10, '31. 8, Alexander, b. Feb. 7, '16, d. Aug. 7, '31. 9 & 10, twins, b. Sept. 7, '18; Ezekiel G., m. Nancy C. Wheeler of St. G., Nov. 25, '41; r. S. Th., a carpenter. (Susan W., m. Robert Gregory of Cam., 1837. 11, Eliza Jane, b. Oct. 20, '20.)* By 2d wife. 12, Mary Elizabeth, b. ab. 1835; m. Jacob Post; r. S. Th. 13, Sabra, b. 1837; r. S. Th. 14, Thomas Marcellus, b. ab. '39; r. S. Th., a farmer.

Isaac, (2d)'s ch. 1, Nelson, b. June 10, 1832; r. Cam., and d. at Insane Hospital, Augusta, Nov. 22, '62. 2, Rachel, m. Wm. Blackington; r. Cam. 3, Isaac, (3d), m. ——— Upham; r. Cam. 4, Robert, (6th), r. California. 5, Elizabeth, mar. Elbridge Pendleton; r. Rock. 6, Lydia M., m. William T. Cochran; r. Rock. 7, Charles, (3d); r. Rock.

Robert, (4th)'s ch. 1, Esther E., m. Capt. Isaac Smith; r. Cam., and d. June 19, '51. 2, Robert, (7th), r. California. 3, Almira, r. Cam. 4, Susan, m. Frank Shepherd; r. Rockport. 5, Isaac, (4th), r. Cam. 6, William J., b. March, 1840, d. by drowning at Delaware Breakwater, Sept. 22, '63. 7, Diana; r. Cam.

William's ch. 1, Ettie. 2, Dudley.

Capt. Jeremiah's ch. By 1st wife. 1, Clarian F., b. Aug. 3, 1836, m. Zenas H. Higgins; r. Rock. 2, Mary S., b. Nov. 8, '39. 3, Abigail T., b. Dec. 12, '42, d. Jan. 18, '43. 4, Lucy. 5, Albert H., b. ab. 1853.

Charles, (2d)'s ch. 1, George G., born Jan. 1, 1831, d. July, 1833. 2, Catherine E., b. April 1834, d. Dec. 1835. 3, Angeline A., b. Oct. 7, '36, m. Albert Burrell; r. Bucksport. 4, Charles A., b. Oct. 12, '38; r. Rock., soldier in 2d Me. Battery. 5, Orris J., b. Aug. 26, '40, m. L. Emma Blake of Montville, July 15, '60; r. Rock., now in U. S. navy. 6, John J. or M., b. July 24, '42, soldier in U. S. Sharpshooters. 7, William J., b. ab. '44. 8, Susan A., b. ab. '47.

M. Dexter's ch. 1. John, (4th). 2, Lucretia, mar. Augustus S. Fales; r. Cushing; 3, Dexter, (2d); 4, Isaac, (5th); 5, William; all r. Cam.

Capt. Oliver's ch. 1, Capt. George G., b. Feb. 9, 1835, m Sophia R. Hall, Oct. 9, '56; r. Rock. 2, Capt. Freeman H., b. Oct. 8, '37, m. Amelia Forman; r. Rock. 3, Oliver, (2d), b. March 29, '39, m. Mary Kelloch; r, Rock., a mariner. 4, Leonard, b. March 7, '41; r. Rock., entered the navy. 5, Margaret A., b. Nov. 1847, d. Feb. 18, '54. 6, ? Sidney M., b. ab. '57.

Sixth Generation.

Capt. Andrew's ch. 1, Capt. James L., b. ab. 1836; r. Rock., a master mariner. 2, Caroline L., b. ab. '42, m. Albert S. Gay of F. Aug. 28, '64.

Elijah's ch. 1, Allen, b. ab. 1844. 2, Elijah, (2d), b. ab. '47.

Robert, (5th)'s ch. 1, Ira Lee, b. ab. 1855.

Ezekiel G.'s ch. 1, Luella, b. ab. 1849. 2, William, b. ab. '56.

Capt. George G.'s ch. 1, Adelbert A., b. June 30, d. Feb. 6, 1859. 2, Lenora S., b. ab. '60.

JAMESON, Capt. David P., of the Warren branch of same family, b. Jan. 29, 1800, m. Penelope Jones; r. W., and d. Nov. 11, 1841. Of his sisters, Louisa and Anne F., teachers, r. Rock.

---

* Mrs. Sabra Robinson of W., a near relative, thinks the latter part of this record is erroneous; that the twins died unnamed, and that Susan W. and Eliza Jane are not of this family.

David P.'s ch. 1, Freeman, born 1826, d. July 11, '29. 2, John, (2d), b '28; r. Rock., a mariner, d. in N. O. 3, D. Erastus, b. ab. '30, r. Rock., a mariner. 4, Ormond F., b. ab. '33; r. Th., a joiner; rem. California. 5, Catherine L., b. ab. '37, m. William C. Crawford; r. Th. 6, Martha Isabel, b. ab. '42, m. Clarance D. Ulmer; r. Rock.

JAMESON, John, m. Lydia J. Collamore, Oct. 22, 1843; r. Rock. Their ch. 1, Sarah E., b. ab. 1855. 2, Mary A., b. '57, d. Nov. '59. 3, Lydia A., b. '60, d. Sept. 17, '61.

JENKS, Capt. David, b. in 1758, came, a refugee, from Nova Scotia, in time of the Revolution; m. Deborah Rhoades of Dedham; r. Fox Isl. & St. Georges lower town; c. to Th., 1786, a lime manufacturer, innholder, &c., d. Feb. 26, 1825. Simeon, a brother, also came from N. S.; m. 1st, Miss Nubbins of C., 2d, in Dover, N. H., whither he removed. Deidamia, a sister, m. James Fales, & r. Th.

Capt. David's ch. 1, David, (2d), b Dec. 31, 1783; m. Sarah R. Harrup, April 17, 1806; r. Th., & d. Nov. 15, '53. 2, James, b. Nov. 29, 1785; lost at sea. 3, Mary, b. Feb. 24, 1788; m. Dr. Jacob K. French; r. Th., 4, Lydia, b. June 12, 1790; m. Sewall Hancock; rem. Texas. 5, John, b. Jan. 10, 1793, d. March 12, 1834. 6, Henry, b. May 30, 1795; m. Mary Robinson, p. Sept. 12, 1818; r. Th., & d. in Mobile of yellow fever. The mother d. Dec. 28, 1821, a. 65.

Of Simeon's ch. 1, Robert was clerk for Col. Head, in W.; m. Lydia Rackliff, & d. in Aroostook. 2, a daughter; m. Jeremiah Proctor of Th., rem. Sennebeck. 3, James, r. awhile at Warren.

David, (2d)'s ch. 1, Thomas H., b. Nov. 6, 1806; m. & r. Mobile. 2, Angelina, b. Aug. 18, 1809; m. Lincoln Levensaler; r. Th., & d. Sept. 29, '58. 3, John W., b. Oct. 3, '11, d. Feb. 8, '20. 4, Sally D., b., Nov. 20, 1813; m. Capt. Ira Smith of Boston, Oct. 10, '31; rem. west. 5, Henry K., b. Sept. 29, '15, went to sea and was never heard from. 6, Lydia, b. Aug. 27, '18; m., in Cahawba, Alabama, Isaac B. Stone, a lawyer, & d. in Haynesville, May 10, 1852. 7, David K., b. Sept. 18, 1821; r. in Mobile. 8, Catharine P., b. June 27, 1824; m. John W. Smith of Boston, Aug. 7, 1848.

Henry's ch. 1, Deborah R., b. March 29, 1818, & d. Sept. 17, '43.

JENNISON, Dr. William, b. in Salem, Mass.; m., at Milford, Mary Staples, & d. at Brookfield, May 8, 1798 Their ch. 1, William. 2, Samuel, Esq., b. 1759; grad. H. U., 1774; m. Sally, dau. of Rev. Dr. Nathan Fiske, of Brookfield, Dec. 25, 1781; r. Th., & d. Sept. 1, 1826, buried at Rock. 3, John, a lawyer, settled in Boston, & d. of lung fever. 4, Timothy Lindall, M. D. of Cambridge. 5, Ebenezer, r. sometime in Union, a teacher and surveyor; m. Sarah Webb of Boston; rem. to Dixmont, where he was postmaster, & d. before 1851. 6, Mary, m. Jonathan Whipple of Cambridge. 7, Abigail.

JOHNSON, George, b. April 8, 1785, in Boston, rem. on to a farm in Mass., but came to what is now Rock., ab. 1804, where he worked at first for Mr. Spear; m. Abigail Tolman, May 3, 1808; r. Cam. & Rock. & d. July 25, '59. Their ch. 1, George, (2d), b. Feb. 10, '09; m. Mary Jameson; r. Rock., a rigger, and d. April 25, '62. 2, Isaiah T., b. May 4, '11; mar. Mary M. Morton, April 8, '35; r. Rock. since 1846, a lime burner, &c. 3, Veranus, died in 1846.

George, (2d)'s ch. 1, Laura F., b. Dec. 18, 1838; m. Thomas Files; r. Rock. 2, Ellen M., b. ab. 1845. And perhaps others unrecorded.

Isaiah T.'s ch. 1, Frederic O., b. Oct. 8, 1837. 2, Freeman, born Dec. 7, '40. 3, Abby A, b Jan. 1, '43. 4, George A., b. Dec. 27,

'46; r. Rock., in Coast Guards. 5, Almeda F., b. Dec. 8, '48. 6, Mary M., b. Nov. 13, '52. 7, Ella A., b. Nov. 16, '59.

JOHNSON, Capt. Leonard, b. ab. 1810, in South Thomaston; m. Abigail Elliott, p. May 22, '30; r. Rock., a mariner, &c. Their ch. 1, Almira, b. Nov. 10, 1833; mar. 1st, ——— Arey, 2d, Richard R. Rankin; r. Rock. 2, Abigail, b. July 24, '36, d. Sept. 4, '39. 3, Sarah, b. March 9, '39; r. Rock. 4, Hester, b. ab. '43. 5, Mary E., b. ab. '45. 6, Margaret A., b. July, 1850, d. March 4, '54. 7, Leonard F., b. ab. '55.

JOHNSON, John L. b. ab. 1825, in Perry, Me.; mar. Sarah F. Creighton of Th.; r. Th., a joiner, &c. Their ch. Edward S., born Aug. 3, 1858, died Sept. 18, '59.

JOHNSON, Pillsbury, b. ab. 1827, in Jefferson; m. Emma Ross; r. Rock., a joiner. Their ch. Mary E., b. ab. 1855.

JOHNSON, Capt. Henry, b. ab. 1825; m. Caroline A. Butler, Nov. 10, '55; r. Th. Their ch. 1, Frank, b. ab. 1857. 2, Merritt A., b ab. '59 3, Frederic J., b. Feb., '62, died Jan. 27, '63.

JOHNSON, Capt. William H., b. ab. 1826; m. Sarah A. ———; r. Rock. Their ch. 1, Ella L., b. ab. 1850. 2, Edgar L., b. ab. '53. 3, Albert E., b. ab. '55. 4, Charles H., b. ab. '57. 5, Lizzie F., b. ab. '59.

JOHNSON, Hudson, b. ab. 1827; m. Martha ———; r. Th., a carpenter. Their ch. 1, Martha L., b. ab. 1851. 2, A. Hudson, b. '60.

JOHNSON, Franklin, b. ab. 1835; m. Amelia ———; r. Rock., a lime burner, &c. Their ch. 1, John E., b. ab. 1848. 2, Harriet A., b. ab. '50.

JOHNSON, Andrew, b. ab. 1829, in Guttenburg, Sweden; mar. Jane A. Munroe, Dec., 1855; r. Rock. Their ch. 1, Nelson H., b. ab. 1857. 2, Elizabeth, b. ab. '58. 3, Alfred C., b. Oct., '59, d. April 17, '63. 4, Martha J., b. Nov. 17, '63, d. Sept. 4, '64.

JOHNSON, James, b. ab. 1815, in New York; m. Mary A. Over, Sept. 16, '46; r. Rock., a barber.

JOHNSTON, T. W., b. March 21, 1829, son of Thomas and Eliza Johnston of Washington, Me.; m. Margaret Robinson of Richmond, Me., took charge of the Thorndike Hotel, Rockland, in June, 1864. Their ch. 1, Mary Eva, b. April 20, 1852. 2, David W., b. Feb., 1858.

JONES, James, m. Eunice Brewster of old Th., p. Nov. 11, 1791; r. and d. in Camden. Their ch. 1, Crowell C., b. ab. 1793; mar. Rebecca Simonton, Jan. 20, 1820; r. Rock., a joiner, &c. 2, James, (2d), b. ab. 1805, m. Anne Simonton, of Rock., p. April 2, 1831; r. Rock. 3, John, m. Diana Jameson; r. Jameson's Pt., Cam. These had two sisters, viz.: 4, Lois, mar. John W. Burns; r. and d. Rock. 5, Sally, d. young.

Crowell C.'s ch. 1, Eunice B., b. May 31, and d. July 1, 1820. 2, Mary M. b. Aug. 20, '21, m. William G. Berry; r. Rock. 3, Harriet C., b. April 21, '26, d. Feb. 19, '34.

James, (2d)'s ch. 1, Dudley S., born March 16, 1832; r. Rock., a mariner. 2, Eunice B., b. Jan. 12, '34. 3, Lucy J., b. April, 1836, d. July 9, '56. 4, Margaret A., b. March 21, '38; r. Rock. 5, James, (3d), b. Nov. 17, '40; r. Rock., a mariner. 6, Maria M., b. Jan. 19, '42. 7, Abram, b. ab. '44. 8, Crowell, b. ab. '46. 9, William, b. ab.' 48. 10, Mary, b. ab. '51.

John's ch. 1, William, b. ab. 1830, d. Nov. 14, '47. 2, Rebecca, b. ab. '29, m. Benjamin Clough; r. Rock. 3, Mary, m. Cyrus V. R. Boynton; r. Rock. 4, Caroline E., mar. C. Aurelius Harrington; r. Rock. 5, Augusta, r. Cam. 6, Elsie, d. young.

JONES, Benjamin, b. Jan. 3, 1820, in West Camden; m. Ann C. Grant of North Haven, Oct. 24, '44; r. Rock., a painter, member of coast guards, &c. Their ch. Judson Bird, b. Sept. 4, 1853.

JONES, Nathaniel, b. ab. 1830, in Mercer, Me., son of Nathaniel and Phebe (Fletcher) Jones of that place; m. Sarah H. Woodcock of Searsmont; r. Rock., a joiner. Their ch. George E., b. ab. 1856.

JONES; of this family, two brothers, sons of Tobias Jones, a native of Brunswick, c. to this place, viz: 1, Isaiah A., b. ab. 1820, m. Anna U. D. Cochran; r. Rock., a grocery merchant. 2, Frank L., b. in China, May 30, 1826, m. Lucy A. Sylvester, Feb. 13, '54; r. Rock., a carpenter.

Isaiah A.'s ch. Everett A., b. ab. 1854.

Frank L.'s ch. 1, Nellie L., b. ab. 1855. 2, William L, b. ab. '58. 3, Lucy F., b. ab. '60.

JONES, James, b. in Alna, ab. 1810, m. Eliza Jones of Alna, Dec. 25, '42; r. Th., a merchant. Their ch. 1, Mary E., b. ab. 1843. 2, John Franklin, b. March 5, and d. Dec. 3, 1847. 3, Mary J., b. ab. 1849.

JONES, Orlando B., b. ab. 1825, c. from Auburn, m. Margaret M. Calderwood, Feb. 2, '57; r. Rock., a stone cutter, &c. Their ch. 1, Myrta L., b. April 22, 1858, d. Nov. 29, 63. 2, Roswell, b. ab. 1859.

JONES, Amos P., b. ab. 1818, in China, m. Marion Jones of China; r. Rock., a provision dealer. Their ch. 1, Mary C., b. ab. 1842. 2, Henry J., b. ab. '43. 3, Sarah A., b. ab. '54. 4, Florence C., b. ab. '60.

JONES, Franklin, b. ab. 1827, in Searsmont, Me., mar. Mary E. Neubert; r. Rock., a farmer, &c. Their ch. Rosalinda, b. 1852.

JORDAN; all the different families of the name in this place are probably descendants of Rev. Robert, an Episcopalian minister, who came from the west of England, in 1640, settled at Falmouth, m. Sarah, daughter of John Winter, and, at her death, became owner of a large estate there. He gave much trouble, by factious opposition to the government of Massachusetts, was finally driven off by the Indians, in 1675, and ended his days in Portsmouth, N. H., 1678, a. 68, leaving six sons. 1, John, who m. Elizabeth Stilesman, and who had by his father's will, Richmond's Isl. and land in Cape Elizabeth. 2, Robert, (2d), who had land confirmed to him in Cape Elizabeth, before conveyed. 3, Dominicus, who m. Hannah, dau. of Ralph Tristram, inherited 1000 acres of land in Spurwink, and was killed by Indians in 1703. 4, Jedediah, 1000 acres in Spurwink. 5, Samuel, 1100 acres in Spurwink. 6, Jeremiah. Their mother, Sarah, was at the same time willed "the ould plantation" in Spurwink, 1000 acres, & also the Nonsuch place in Scarboro'. The connecting links remain unknown; but Robert Jordan, son of Israel, and undoubtedly a descendant, came from Cape Elizabeth to Wessaweskeag before 1777; mar. Betsey Nutting of what is now C.; r. on the west side of the river, on the farm now occupied by Hanse Kelloch, and d. Dec. 20, 1802. Of his sisters, 1, Betsey, b. 1740; mar. Rev. Elisha Snow; r. S. Th. & d. July 27, 1834, a. 94. 2, Susan, b. 1742; m. Capt. Israel Jordan; r. S. Th. & d. Nov. 22, 1800. 3, Polly, m. Capt. Israel Lovett; r. S. Th. & d. in Linc. 4, Sally, m. ——— Brown; r. eastern part of the State. 5, Joanna, b. 1756; m. Capt. David Crouch; r. S. Th. & d. March 23, 1831. Their mother m. 2d, ——— Webb, & d. nearly 100 years old, in South Thomaston.

Robert's ch. 1, Joanna, m. John Creighton; r. & d. W 2, Capt. Ebenezer, (2d), b. 1782; m. Belinda Dunbar, July 26, 1808; r. W. & d. Oct. 17, '28. 3, Kezia, b. ab. 1785; m. John H. Counce of W.; rem. Th. '58. 4, Robert, (2d), m. 1st, Margaret Winchenbach, 2d, Betsey Palmer; r. Appleton, Brighton, Me., and Augusta,, a farmer, where he d. Oct., '60. 5, Capt. Oliver, b. ab. 1790; m. Susan Oakes; r. Th., a ship master, builder, owner, &c. 6, Capt. Ephraim, b. ab. 1792; m. Sarah Copeland; r. Th., retired master mariner. 7, Joshua, b. 1797; m. Mary Nutting, Oct. 28, '27; r. Th., a merchant, &c., & d. July 16, '34. 8, William, lost at sea at the age of 17.

Capt. Ebenezer's ch. 1, Eliza, m. John Freeman; r. Oldtown. 2, Phebe, m. Newell Blake; r. Oldtown. 3, Capt. George, b. Feb. 22, 1813; m. Betsey B. Masters, Oct. 12, '47; sold his ship at Cuxhaven, and, returning, was lost in steamer *Pacific*, which sailed from Liverpool, Jan. 23, '56. 4, Belinda, m. Silas Stowe of Stowe, Mass.; r. Oldtown. 5, Ebenezer, (4th), r. San Francisco, Cal, engaged in a steam ferry. 6, Sarah A., m ——— Dummer; r. & d. Oldtown.

Robert, (2d)'s ch. 1, Ebenezer, (3d) m. Phebe Knox; r. Brighton, Me. 2, Henry, r. & d. in Brighton. 3, Capt. William, (2d), b. ab. 1815; m. Mary Delano; r. Th., a ship master. 4, Eliza, m. John Tomlinson; r. Brighton. 5, Ephraim, (2d), lost at sea. 6, Margaret, b. ab. '20; m. Alexander Libbey, (2d), of W.; r. Rock. By 2d wife. 7, Martha. 8, Robert, (3d), m. & r. Augusta. 9, Kezia C., b. 1825, d. May 31, '51. 10, Harriet, m. George Wentworth, d. in N. O., '59. 11, Abigail, r. Augusta. 12, Oliver, (2d), r. Augusta. 13, Eben, ? r. Augusta.

Capt. Oliver's ch. 1, Ann M. b. Nov. 25, 1817; m. Capt. Charles Ranlett; r. Th. 2, Oliver W., b. Nov. 3, '21; m. Margaret J. Robinson, Nov. 6, '45; r. Th., a merchant. 3, Charles F., b. June 11, '23, d. at Havre, July 7, '44. 4, Capt. Joshna L, b April 7, '25; m. Joanna Jenkins of Boston, Oct. 12, '53, 2d, Harriet McCallum of War., June, 1861; r. Th. 5, Susan Amelia, b. May 12, '27; m. Capt. William Henderson; r. Th. 6, James S., b. July 12, '29, d. at New Orleans, Feb. 21, '50 7, Harriet B., b. April 27, '31; m. Capt. Raymond L. Gilchrist, & d. at New Orleans, Feb. 11, '54. 8, Capt. Samuel C., b. Sept. 14, '33; m. Caroline A. Jacobs, 2d, Lizzie F. Ranlett, July 14, '62; r. Th. 9, Rebecca W., b. Dec 22, '34; m. Capt. Raymond L. Gilchrist; r. Th. The mother died Feb. 13, '55, aged 60.

Capt. Ephraim's ch. 1, Elizabeth H., b Oct. 21, 1822; m. William Whitney; r. Th. 2, Susan P., b. Feb. 21, '25; m. Gardner Winslow, Oct. 30, '44; r. Th. 3, Sarah F., b. June 16, '30; r. Th.

Joshua's ch. 1, Mary T., b. Sept. 24, 1829; mar. 1st, Charles F. O'Brien, 2d, ——— Kelley, July, 1862. 2, Joshua T., b. 1832, died June 17, '35.

Fourth Generation.

Capt. George's ch. George E., b. Jan. 14, 1848, d. Sept. 26, '49.

Capt. William's ch. 1, Emily, b. ab. 1840. 2, Nettie, b. ab. '42; m. Edgar Stackpole; r. Th. 3, Lewis, b. ab. '45. 4, William, (3d), b. ab. '48. 5, Ann, b. ab. '51.

Oliver W.'s ch. 1, Clara M., b. Feb. 2, 1848. 2, Frederic O., b. Feb. 18, '50, & d. 3, Frank H., b. ab. '53.

Capt. Joshua L.'s ch. by 1st wife. 1, Clement. By 2d wife. 2, Herbert Duncan, b. June 10, 1863, died in W., July 12, 1864. The mother died July 22, '63.

Capt. Samuel C.'s ch. Clement O., b. 1855.

JORDAN, Rev. Tristram, b. ab. 1761; c. to S. Th, a shoemaker; m. Rebecca Hayden, p. Nov. 13, 1797; ordained as an evangelist by 1st Baptist church, 1802; & d. suddenly in Denmark, Me., Sept. 4, '26.

JORDAN, Capt. Israel, a cousin, it is believed, of Robert; m. Susanna Jordan; c. to what is now S. Th before 1777, from New Meadows or Cape Elizabeth; r. Ash Point, & d., being knocked overboard and lost when coming down from Boston in company with another vessel. Their ch. 1, Betsey, m. ——— Oaks; r. Blue Hill, and d. Bangor. 2, Israel, (2d), m. ——— Decker; r. Portland, & d. Bangor. 3, Polly, b. 1781 or 1778; m. Job Perry; r. S. Th., and d. April 17, 1857 or 1854. 4, Robert, m. Hannah Keating, rem. & d. in Ohio; of whose daus. Bethia, m. Daniel Barrett of Cam. 5, Ezekiel, d. at sea. 6, Capt. Joshua, m. Mrs. Apphia (Snow) Mathews; r. & d. Bangor; had a son, Joshua, jr., who mar. in Bangor, Catharine Ames, in March, 1846. 7, Simon, r. & d. Boston. 8, Susan, m. ——— Cummings of Portland. 9, Capt. John, mar. Nancy Killsa, p. Dec. 25, 1797; r. Boston. 10, Hannah, m. Josiah Haskell, (2d); r. and died Boston.

JORDAN, Ignatius, came early from Massachusetts to this place, and was much employed by Knox; m. Sally Sampson, pub. Oct. 24, 1794; r. and d. Th., and S. Th. Benjamin, a brother, was also here and worked for Knox. Ignatius's ch. 1, Zebulon, m. Mary Knowlton, (p. as Barrett) July 9, 1826; r. S. Th. and d. Sept. 30, 1840. 2, William, b. ab. 1804; m. 1st, Sarah D. Buckland, 1829, 2d, Rachel Rivers, 1841, 3d, Mary Ann Kenniston, 1860; r. W., rem. Th., a carpenter. 3, Abigail 4, Capt. Isley; 5, Rozella; 6, Sarah E.; 7, Benjamin, (2d), m, Sarah A. Rivers, March 27, 1845; mostly rem. Hope.

William's ch. 1, William M., mar. Rebecca W. Counce, June 25, 1853; r. W. or Th. 2, Mary C., b. ab. 1836; m. Rufus C. Sumner, Dec. 30, '60. 3, Leander. By 2d wife, 4, Amaziah, b. ab. 1845. 5, Nancy. 6, Sarah.

JORDAN, Capt. Ebenezer, a distant relative of Robert and Capt. Israel, and probably from the same region; m. 1st, Mary Packard, Oct. 16, 1804, 2d, Sarah (Choate) Elliott, Oct. 19, '28; r. and d. S. Th., Ash Pt. His widow mar. 2d, Wm. Jackson, and r. Th. Capt. Ebenezer's ch. 1, Ebenezer, (3d), b. July 27, 1805; m. Hannah Elliott, Feb. 7, '28; r. Ash Point, and d. 1858 or '59, from mortification caught from a diseased horse. 2, Benjamin, b. June 21, '07; m. Julia Johnson, Aug. 13, '52; r. S. Th. 3, Mary, b. Nov. 15, '09; m. Capt. Eben Walker; and d. Aug. 11, '42. 4, Isaac, b. Oct. 16, '11; r. S. Th., a shoemaker. 5, Lydia, b. Sept. 5, '13. 6, Nancy, b. April 8, '16, d. April 9, '23. 7, Maria, b. April 23, '18, d. June 1, '21. 8, John, b. Dec. 9, '23; m. Eunice Allen, April 25, '45, 2d, Mrs. Mary P. Keith, Feb. 6, '50, 3d, Elizabeth Havener, March 5, '56; r. S. Th., a mariner.

Ebenezer, (3d)'s ch. 1, Melissa, b. June 10, 1828, d. Nov. 22, '30. 2, Emeline, b. Sept. 4, '34; m. Montgomery Anderson of Rock., 2d, Ward Davis; r. S. Th. 3, Isaac, (2d), born Sept. 24, '37; r. S. Th., a peddler, &c, 4, Susan, b. March 27, '40.

JUMPER, Joseph, mar. Phebe Milliken, Oct. 19, 1817.; r. S. Th., but rem. Ohio, with their ch. 1, Alden H., b. Feb. 16, '19; 2, Mary E., b. July 31, '20; 3, Nancy, b. Oct. 18, '22; 4, Benjamin S., born July 11, '26; 5, George, b. Sept. 17, '31. 6, Lucy R., born Feb. 11, 1835.

KALER, John S., born in 1807, and probably descended from the German family of that name in Waldoboro'; m. Mary Twist, Nov. 10, 1833; r. Rock., and d. Nov. 6, '52. Their ch. 1, Susan P., b. March 30, 1836; r. Rock. 2, Elsa M., b. Dec. 31, '38; r. Rock. 3, Lewis S., b. Aug. 1, 1841, d. June 7, '42.

KALER, Robert, m. Nancy Rokes of W., p. Dec. 15, 1838, who d. in Rockland, Aug. 21, '64, aged 46. Of their ch. 1, Elmada, b. ab. 1848; 2, Samantha, b. ab. '54; r. Rockland.

KALER, George F., b. ab. 1835, in Camden; m. Emily G. Harrington, May 11, '59; r. Rock., a dry goods merchant.

KALER, Charles L., b. ab. 1831; m. Angeline F. ——; r. Rock., a joiner, &c. Their ch. Abbie E., b. ab. 1852.

KARL, John, b. ab. 1825, in Lapland, Europe; mar. Lucy Ham. April 26, 1849; r. S. Th., a painter. Their ch. 1, Mary, b. ab. 1850, 2, John A., b. ab. '52. 3, Joseph H., b. ab. '55. 4, Grace, b. ab. '58.

KAUFMAN; of this family from Mayen, Prussia, there came to this place; 1, Nathan, kept store several years in Th., rem., m. and r. Illinois. 2, Louis, b. ab 1828, m. Rebecca Mathews of N. York, June 4, '55; r. Rock., a dry goods merchant. 3, Joseph, in same business; r. Rock. 4, Fannie, m. Henry Strauss; r. Rock.

KEATING, Dea. Richard, b. 1751, in Kittery, Me., mar. Miriam Bridges; c with his family ab. 1773, from New Meadows to Wessaweskeag; r. S. Th., was a soldier of the Revolution, &c., d. April 22, 1839. His wife d. April, 1830, a. 77 years. Their ch. 1, Richard, (2d), b. Oct. 12, 1774, m. Mrs. Olive Mathews, p. Dec. 8, '98; r. S. Th., Hope and Adams, Ohio, where he deceased. 2, Capt. William, m. Bethia Thorndike, Feb. 19, 1800; r. S. Th., and d. at Havana of yellow fever. 3, Betsey, m. Samuel Bartlett, (2d), rem. and d. in Adams, Ohio. 5, Miriam, b. Sept. 14, 1786, m Capt. Joshua Bartlett; r. S. Th., and d. Sept. 26, 1860. 6, Rev. John, m. Eliza Mathews, p. July 4, 1807; became a Bapt. minister, rem. and d. in Adams Ohio, leaving a large family. 7, Jonas, d. unm. 8, Oliver, drowned in the Wessaweskeag. 9, Susan, b. Feb. 22, '94, mar. Capt. Joshua Thorndike; r. S. Th., and d. March 21, 1863.

Richard, (2d)'s ch. Miriam, b. April 12, 1800, m. Asa Crockett; r. Adams, O. 2, Sophia, b. May 21, '02, m. Jacob Mansfield of Hope; 2d, —— Hilt; r. Hope. 3, Hannah, b. April 1, '04; rem. Ohio, and m., 1st, a nephew of Gen. Lewis Cass, 2d, —— Stone of Ohio. 4, Harriet, b. Aug. 17, '06; rem. Ohio.

Capt. William's ch. 1, Joshua, d. Oct., 1826, at City Point, Va. 2, Capt. William, (2d), m. Mary T. Spalding, Feb. 29, 1832; r. Afton, Iowa. 3, Eliza, m. Charles W. Thorndike; r. Rock. 4, Capt. Richard, (3d) b. April 22, 1807, m. Lillias T. Snow, p. July 11, '32; r. S. Th., and Rock., and d. at Calcutta, June 3, '55, when in command of the India ship, *Kate Sweetland*. 5, Hannah, mar. William McLoon, (2d), r. Rock.

Rev. John's ch. 1, John M, b. Nov. 16, 1809, d. young. 2, Joseph M., b. Aug. 24, '12; 3, Asa Crockett, b. Sept. 12, '14. 4, Campbell Snow, b. April 8, '16; all rem. Ohio; while of those b. later, 5, Henry A., was here and m. in Rock., Susan M. Thorndike, Sept. 5, 1851.

Fourth Generation.

Capt. William, (2d)'s ch. 1, Joshua, (3d); r. Iowa. 2, Henry S., r. Iowa. 3, Bethia, b. ab. 1838; m. George Beyman; r. Ohio.

Capt. Richard, (3d)'s ch. 1, Richard Edwin, b. July 30, 1834, died July 25, '57. 2, Helen Taylor, b. June 13, '36; m. Edward Everett; r. Rock. or Boston. 3, Luella Austin, b. Nov. 10, '38; mar. Capt. Israel L. Snow; r. Rock. 4, Caroline A., b. Dec. 14, '41. 5, Willis S., b. June 9, '44. 6, George S., b. Jan. 3, '47, d. Aug. 29, '50. 7, Fanny Maria, b. Dec. 13, '48. 8, Henry, b. ab. 1852. 9, Adelia H., b. Feb., '54, d March 18, '55.

KEATING, William, of a different family, settled, r. and died in Hope. His ch. 1, James, m. and r. Whitefield, Me. 2, Sarah, mar. John Fitzgerald; r. W. and Whitefield. 3, William, (2d), m. and r. Hope. 4, Archibald. 5, John, m. and r. Hope. 6, Lewis. 7, George, m. and r. Hope.

Of James's ch. 1, George, b. ab. 1824; m. Helen M. Rivers of C , June 9, '59; r. Th. 2, Thomas, b. ab. 1827; m. Emeline A. Sidelinger, Nov. 29, '56; r. Th., a joiner, &c.

Of William's ch. Roxana, m. John Fitzgerald, (2d); r. Th.

Of John's ch. Agnes, r. Th , some years and kept milliner's shop in company with Miss H. Bradford, but m. and r. Hope.

Thomas's ch. 1, Maria, b. ab. 1858. 2, Isabel, b. ab. 1859.

KEEN, (or as sometimes spelled in early times Kein, or Kean), Josiah, a native of London, England, c. over to Boston, Mass., about 1640; afterwards r. in Hingham and Marshfield. Of his descendants, 1, Jacob, b. Nov. 21, 1731, in Pembroke, Mass.; m. his second cousin, Deborah, dau. of Isaac Keen of Pembroke, and soon after purchased Hog Island near the borders of what is now Bremen, Me., where he r. some years, but to the title of which difficulties soon were raised, & he employed a lawyer by the name of Bradbury, who managed so well that he named his eldest daughter *Bradbury;* but this lawyer dying, matters went against him, he lost his possession and his island home, left in a flat-boat or gondola with his family, his cow, and all his estate on board, stopped on the main in Bremen for a few months, and thence sailed along the indented coast of the State to what is now Rockland, settling on the west side of Tolman's or Chikawauka Lake. His brother John about the same time settled in the town of Turner. Jacob, besides being a hunter as before mentioned, was, we have since learned, an able seaman, capable of navigating a ship to any part of the world; was of a sandy complexion, with blue eyes and a stature of six feet; was noted for intelligence, muscular strength, and endurance, together with some eccentricities — receiving the New Testament, but rejecting the Old, and professing the Quaker faith without being a member of the Society; was injured by the fall upon him of the companion-doors at sea, from the effects of which, 8 years after, he died Oct. 10, 1788. His wife died July 20, 1825, aged 84, & leaving 14 ch., 87 grand ch., & 61 great grand ch., as stated in newspaper.

Jacob's ch. 1, Bradbury, b. 1757; m. Joseph Ingraham; r. Rock., and d. July 8, 1848, aged 91. 2, Mary, b. in Bristol, April 24, 1761; m. Major Otis Robbins; and moving into her new house, never spent a night away from it, from her marriage till her death, June 26, 1836, though on one occasion at least riding as far as Belfast on horseback. 3, Lydia, m. James Killsa; r. and d. Th. 4, Jacob, (2d), m. Hannah Adams, p. Dec. 12, 1786; r. Rock., and elsewhere. 5, Deborah, b. 1764; m. Rosamus Lowell; r. S. Th., & d. Feb. 4, 1838. 6, Elisha, was drowned at sea. 7, John, b. in Bristol, June 7, 1767; m. Hannah Packard, Oct. 4, '94; r. Rock., and d. by suicidal hanging, Aug. 26, 1829. 8, Rev. Josiah, m. 1st, Jane Wade, 2d, Phebe Gould; r. in Montville, Camden, and various places, as his calling led; and d. at the age of 86. 9, Patience, m. Dea. Waterman Hewett; r. and died Cam. 10, Capt. Peter, died of a wound received in the war of 1812, while in the act of firing a cannon at the enemy on board of a privateer. 11, Rev. Reuben, b. Oct., 1777; m. Lois Brewster; r. in Freedom; and d. at Cam., of cramp in the stomach when on a visit to his native region, March 17, 1852. 12, James, m. 1st, Polly Simmons of Wal. p. Jan. 5, '97, 2d, Peggy Dunbar; r. Cam., and d. April 1, 1848, by a fall from an upper story when on a visit to children in Mass. 13, Sally, m. Ephraim Gay; r. and d. Cam. 14, Isaac, b. 1787, d. of throat distemper, Oct., 1794. The whole family, most of whom arrived to upwards of three score and ten years, were noted for their temperance and abstaining from the use of tobacco.

Jacob, (2d)'s ch. 1, Rufus, m. 1st, Peggy Allen, p. May 29, 1809; 2d, Miss Conway; r. Rockport. 2, Jacob, (3d), d. young. 3, Hannah, m. James W. Blackington; r. Rock., and d. Nov. 18, 1839. 4, Hezekiah, r. N. Orleans. 5, Reuben, (2d). 6, Patience. 7, Ephraim, r. Cam. 8, Betsey. 9, Jane. 10, Washburn, r. in N. Y. 11, Caroline, m. Moses L. Simmons of Rock., and d. Nov. 30, '54. 12, Sophia.

John's ch. 1, Lucy, b. Nov. 4, 1794, m. 1st, Samuel Tyler of Cam., 2d, Abraham Simonton; r. Rock. 2, Elisha, b. May 13, '97, m. Priscilla Witham, June 9, 1822; r. Appleton. 3, Margaret, b. March 3, '99, m. Charles Harrington; r. Rock. 4, Susanna, b. Aug. 28, 1800. 5, Isaac, b. May 2, 1802, m. 1st, Martha M. Watson of Cam., p. Sept. 15, '34; 2d, Susan I. Tolman, p. Nov. 12, '39; r. Cam., and d. instantly, Nov. 8, '63 6, Bethiah, b. Feb., 1804, m. James Tolman; r. Cam. 7, John, (2d), b. Feb. 21, '06, mar. 1st, Sarah Brown of Cam., p. Nov. 8, '32, 2d, Harriet A. Reed, Oct. 14, '55; r. Rock., a farmer on the homestead. 8, Alden, d. young. 9, Waitstill, m. Randall Tolman; r. Cam. 10, Lydia.

Rev. Josiah's ch. By 1st wife. 1, Elsie, mar. Isaac Thompson of Montville. 2, Jane, m. a Rackliff of Montville. 3, Deborah, m. Edmund Daggett of Hope. By 2d wife. 4, Rev. Josiah, (2d), a Free Will Baptist minister. 5, Peter, (2d), a teacher of penmanship. 6, Esther, m. a Mr. Linscott, and is now deceased.

Rev. Reuben's ch. 1, Eunice B., m. Benjamin Spring; r. and d. West Cam., leaving 3 ch, viz.: Hattie K. Spring, Julia K. Spring, and Ephraim Albion Spring. 2, Comfort S., b. ab. 1811, in Cam., mar. Olive A. Lindsey, Oct. 30, '47; r. Rock., in shoe business. 3, Reuben L., Esq., m. Aurelia, dau. of Jonathan Parkhurst; is a lawyer of East Montville. 4, Dr. Alden T., m. Elizabeth Perry, a descendant of the Jarvis family of Cambridge, Mass., is in the practice of med. at Gorham. 5, Orris H., Esq., attorney at law in Freedom. 6, Harriet P., m. the late Levi Woods; r. Unity. 7, Julia Ann., d. young.

James' ch. By 1st wife. 1, Sally, m. a McCarrison. By 2d wife. 2, Joshua, r. in the Western States. 3, Joseph, supposed to be dead. 4, James, (2d), m. Caroline Schwartz, p. Nov. 7, 1835; r. Rock., a merchant, and d. falling suddenly in the street, April 5, 1848.

Fourth Generation.

John, (2d)'s ch. by 2d wife, 1, Nelson H., b. ab. 1837; r. Rock., a teacher. 2, Mary Ann, b. ab. '40; r. Rock., a teacher. The mother d. Oct. 20, '50. By 2d wife, 3, John Preston, b. ab. 1857.

Of James, (2d)'s ch. 1, Victorine M., b. ab. 1835; m Capt. Wilson Buckland; r. Rockland.

Comfort S.'s ch. Lois B., b. ab. 1859.

Dr. Alden T.'s ch. 1, Julia M.; 2, Lillie; 3, Jarvis Brewster; all r. Gorham.

Of the other descendants of this family we are not informed, but probably most of these that follow belong to it, though some have added *e* to the name.

KEENE, Wait W., b. ab. 1827, son of Capt. Wait W., and Huldah Keene of Bremen, who is either a descendant of John Keen of Turner, or Isaac of Pembroke, Mass.; m. Mary J. Varney of Bristol, Feb. 22, '53; r. Th, tin and stove dealer. Maj. Samuel T., a brother, b. ab. 1833, in Bremen; grad. Union Coll., New York, was preceptor Cherryfield academy 2 years, came to Th., and studied law, admitted to bar at Rock., 1860; m. Sarah F. Prince, March 1, '62; was an officer in the army, and, struck at Petersburg, by a musket ball in the breast, d. June 22, '64.

Wait W.'s ch. George, b. ab. 1859.

KEEN, Charles A., Jr., b. ab. 1825, son of Charles A. Keen of Appleton; m. Ann W. Hewett, Sept. 29, '53; r. Rock., keeps livery stable. Horatio N., a brother, mar. Elizabeth Johnson of Appleton; r. Rock, a shoe merchant.

Charles A., Jr.'s ch. Mary Rose, b. Nov. 13, 1858.

KEEN, William H., b. in Bremen, April 30, 1825; mar. Angie R. Grant, April 30, '63; r. Rock., a saloon keeper.

KEEN, Charles, b. ab. 1782, m, and r. Rock., and d. Oct. 5, 1860. Of his ch. 1. Newell, b. ab. 1819, mar. Maria ———; r. Rock, a blacksmith. 2, Harriet, b. ab '23, m Mr. Miller; r. Rock. 3, Alfred, b. ab. 1829, m. Jane ———; r. Rock., a rigger.

Alfred's ch. 1, Clara J., b. ab. 1852. 2, Alfred, (2d), b. ab. '54. 3, Anna, b. ab. '59.

KEEN, Dudley, b. ab. 1824, m. Rhoda Simmons; r. Rock..

KEEGAN, Patrick, b. ab. 1798, in Dublin, Ireland, came here, m. Hannah Parsons of Canaan, Vt., p. Oct. 13, 1827; r. and traded Th., Mill river, became wealthy, rem. and did business with less success in Boston awhile, but returned Th., and d. Aug. 3, '59, buried at Mt. Auburn. Their ch. 1, William, b. ab. 1830 2, Carrie M., b. ab. '32, m. John S. Ide of N. Y., Jan. 1, '63. 3, Mary E., mar. Dr. J. A. Harlow of Waynesboro', Ga., May 6, '55. 4, Sarah A., mar. A. M. Shurtleff of Boston, April 14, '56. 5, an infant, died Oct. 1838. 6, Alice, b. ab. 1840. 7, Anna, b. in Boston, ab. '42. 8, Dermot. 9, Vincent; all rem. to Mass., it is believed.

KEITH, David, b. in 1747; (the 4th in descent from Rev. James Keith, a Scotchman, who came over in 1662, at the age of 18, and was the first minister of Bridgewater, Mass.,) m. Sarah, dau of Jona. Copeland, 1769; r. & d. Bridgewater. Their ch. 1, Francis. 2, Bezer, both r. Easton, Mass. 3, Josiah, b. 1771; served his time as a tanner and shoemaker, with the father of the late Hon. Reuel Williams of Augusta; c. to Th., m. 1st, Sarah Robinson, 2d, Experience Orbeton, Dec. 6, 1804, & d. Oct. 23, '14. 4, Friend, also, c. to Th., m. Mary Bryant of Newcastle, p. April 13, '05; a painter by trade; r., in old age, with his son in Lynn, & d. 1863. Mitchell's History of Bridgewater says, there were probably other children of David; and it is certain there came to Thomaston, — 5, Susanna Kingman, m. Isaac W. Lincoln of Th. 6, Mary, m. Gilbert Tilson, and d. Feb. 7, 1846. Also, 7, Jerusha, m. ——— Quiggle, and had one son, Friend Quiggle, overseer of thread factory, in East Mansfield, where she d. Nov., '63, a. 84.

Josiah's ch. by 1st wife. 1, William R., b. ab. 1799; m. Anne M. Smith of Bangor, Oct. 3, 1842; r. Th., a successful merchant, builder, &c., now secretary of M. F. Insurance Co. 2, Susanna K., b. Dec. 6, 1800, d. May 26, '07. 3, Sarah, b. Dec., '02, d. April 1, '03. By 2d wife. 4, Sarah R., b. March 27, '06; m. Amos Barnes of Cam., Aug. '48. 5, Clementine B., b. Jan. 24, '08; m. Leander Starr; r. Rock.

Friend's ch. 1, Joseph B., b. Nov. 25, 1805; m. Asenath Swift; r. Th. and d. Oct. 7, '51. 2, Mary Adams, b. ab. '08; m. Capt. Hugh Peabody; r. Th. 3, Andrew J., b. Nov. 11, '10; m. Lydia Redlon, April 21, '33; r. Th. 4, David Kingman, b. March 27, '13; m. Mary P. Barnes, Nov. 2, '45; r. Th., is in the U. S. Navy. 5, Sarah B., b. May 20, '15, d. Aug. 1, '33. 6, Nathaniel C., b. Sept. 25, '17; m. Ruth Robinson Linneken of Rockland, Sept. 17, '43; r. Lynn, Mass. 7, William R., (2d), b. Jan. 4, '20; m. Fanny Black of Dublin, Feb. 14, '43; r. California. 8, Martha B., born Nov. 14, '22. 9, Josiah, (2d), b. March 22, '25, d. at sea, July 30, '43. 10, Friend H., b. Nov. 16, '27; r. Th., a painter.

Third Generation, or 7th from Rev. James.

Joseph B.'s ch. 1, Joseph Judson, m. M. Catharine Hoffsis of Wal. Oct. 15, '54; r. Rock., a teamster, &c. 2, Sarah B., m. A. Jackson Young; r. Montville. 3, Vesper J., b. ab. 1837; r. Th., a mariner. 4, Zipha S., b. ab. '40; r. Th., a mariner, soldier of the 4th Me. Reg., drowned, Nov. 15, '62. 5, Lydia Maria, b ab. '45; mar. Lorenzo J. Hall of W., Jan., '64. 6, Orianna or Aurelia, b. ab. '47.

Andrew J.'s ch. 1, Mary F., b. ab. 1824; mar. Thomas B. Campbell; r. Th. 2, Eliza H., b. ab. '27; m. Joseph T. Arnold of Wal., Oct. 15, 1855; r. Th.

Nathaniel C.'s ch. 1, Frank Harding. 2, Celia N. R.

William R., (2d)'s ch. 1, William Henry. 2, Hugh Peabody.

Joseph Judson's ch. 1, Hattie Jordan, d. young. 2, William, b. ab. 1859.

KEITH, John, b. ab. 1832, in Ireland, as was Mary his wife; r. Rock. Their ch. 1, Thomas, b. ab. 1852. 2, Matthew, b. ab. '56. 3, Edward, b. ab. '58. 4, Anna S., b. ab. '59.

KEIZER, or Kaizer, Edwin, b. ab. 1834, in Waldoboro'; m. Sarah C. Jackson of W., April 5, '54; r. Rock., a lime burner, corporal in 4th Me. Reg., &c. Of their ch. Leroy C., b. Jan. 8, '53, d. May 16, 1861.

KELLERAN, or Killeran, Hon. Edward, b. 1751, mar. Elizabeth Burton; r. Cush., and d. May 23, 1828, a. 77. Their ch. 1, Capt. Benjamin, b. 1775, mar. Mary Pendleton; r. and d. Cush. 2, Capt. Edward, m. Lucy Reed; r. Portland. 3, Nancy, m. Capt. John Hall, and d. May 22, 1847. 4. Rebecca, d. a. about 21. 5, Elizabeth, mar. William Malcolm of C. 6, Sarah, mar. Capt. James Parsons. 7,

Thomas, m. ——— Young of Cushing. 8, Capt. Bartholomew, m. Elizabeth Henderson, Nov. 15, '14; r. Th., lost at sea. 9, William, m. ——— Gay; d. in Boston. 10, Arthur, m. Mary Norton of C. 11, Elsie, r. Boston.

Capt. Benjamin's ch. 1, Capt Edward, m. Jane Ann Shibles, 1833; r. C. 2, Sarah P., m. Capt. James Vose; r. Th. 3, Rebecca, mar. James Gilchrist; r. Th. 4, Capt. James H., b. 1814; m. Margaret M. Huse of Cush., Sept. 1, 1839; r. Th. 5, Nancy M., b. 1811; m. Nathaniel Liscomb; r. Th., and d. March 22, '62. The mother died in Th, June 4, 1852, aged 73.

Capt. Bartholomew's ch. 1, Jane P., m. Joshua Brackett; r. Th. 2, Susan, b. March 29, 1838; m. Capt. Artemas W. Watts; and died Sept. 3, '56, at N. York. 3, Larissa J, m. S. Fessenden Allen; r. Th.

Capt. James H.'s ch. 1, Harriet R., b. ab. 1844, m. Lawson Cobb; r. Th. 2, James H., b. ab. '46. 3, Margaret A., b. ab. '49. 4, Franklin, b. ab. '51. 5, Isaac S, b. ab. '54. 6, Mary L., born ab. '55. 7, Edgar R., b. ab. '56. 8, Sarah, b. ab. '60.

KALLOCH, ———, with his two sons, David and Finley, c. from North of Ireland to Portsmouth, N. H, & rem. Philadelphia. Finley, m. Mary Young, and came with her father among the first settlers of what is now Warren, in 1735. Finley's ch. 1, David, (2d), b. 1725; m. 1st, Jane Boyd, 2d, Catharine (Cooper) Cox; r. W., and d. without ch. Feb. 18, 1802. 2, John, m. Isabella Cunningham of Arrowsic Is.; r. and d. St. George. 3, Mary, m. ——— Brown of Boston. 4, Matthew, m. Mary Robinson; rem. St. George, served under Com. Tucker in navy of Revolution, and d. March 22, 1824, aged about 90 years. 5, Alexander, b. 1740, m. Eleanora Gaut; r. W., & d. Feb. 14, 1826. 6, Margaret, m. ——— Boyd of Boothbay.

John's ch. 1, David, (3d), mar. 1st, Betsey Love of Boston, 2d, Polly (Ross) Kelloch, July 25, 1833; served as a soldier under Gen. Gates in 1777, and through both the wars with England; r. W. & St. G., & d. Jan., 1846, aged 91. 2, John, (2d); 3, James; both died in the army of the Revolution. 4, William, d. in Halifax prison, a captive soldier of the Revolution. 5, Margaret, mar. 1st, Dr. Nichols of St. Geo., 2d, Shepard Robbins; r. S. Th., & d. Sept. 7, 1848. 6, Alexander, (2d), m. Jane Fullerton of Boothbay; r. St. G. 7, George, m. Jane Boyd; r Boothbay; d in the army of 1812. 8, Matthew, (2d), m. Polly Forrest of Boston; r. & d. St. G. 9, Finley, (2d), m. Polly Hasey of New Meadows; r. & d. S. Th., 1st lot from St. Geo. 10, Moses, d. in West Indies. 11, Archibald, d. at St. George. 12, Joseph, d. in St. G. 13, Thomas, m. 1st, Sally Farnham of Boothbay, 2d, Effie Sterling of St. Geo. 14, Jane, b 1783; mar 1st, Spencer Drake, 2d, William McLoon, 3d, William Perry; r Th.

Matthew's ch. 1, Margaret, d. unmarried in St George. 2, Finley, (3d), m. r. and d. Camden. 3, Moses, m. 1st, Mehitable Hasey of New Meadows; 2, Lydia Sayward; r. S. Th., and d. ab. 1826. 4, Hanse, m. Sally Phinney; r. St. George. 5, Polly, mar. Adam Boyd of Broad Bay; r. and died St. George. 6, Katie, mar. David Boyd; r. and d. St. George. 7, Jane, m. Capt. Thos. Kenney; r. & d. St. George. 8, Sarah, m. Jacob Robinson; r. S. Th. & d. St. Geo.

Alexander's ch. 1, David Y., b. 1763; m. Mary Ross; r. W. and d. June 25, 1823 2, Margaret, b. 1766; m. Francis Young; r. W. & d. June 17, '26. 3, Alexander, (3d), b. Sept. 26, '70; m. Elizabeth Mero; r. W., where all his ch. were b., but rem. Rock., & d. May, '53, a. 82. 4, Mary, m. Moses Hawes of Union. 5, Jane, m. Joseph Jameson; rem. Senebec Pond. 6, Adam, m. Mary Butler; rem. China. 7, George, d. a. 19. 8, Samuel, b. ab. 1778; m. Lucy Lewis; r. W. 9, Sarah, d. a 13. 10, Rosanna, m. David Cummings of Union. 11, Benjamin, b. 1785; m. 1st, Esther Libbey, Nov. 5, 1805, 2d, Hannah (Nichols) Mallard, '33; r. W. & d. very suddenly, Jan. 2, '38.

Fourth Generation.

David, (3d)'s ch. by 1st wife. 1, John, (3d), m. Mary Stover of St. G.; r. S. Th. 2, James, (2d), m. Hannah Madding of St. G., Jan. 7, '08; r. & d. in Belfast or Waldo. 3, Jane, d. young. 4, William, (2d), b. ab. 1793; m. 1st, Susan Snow, 2d, Hannah Haskell, May 27, '32, 3d, Ann Maria Hayden, April 8, '46; r. S. Th., a mason, &c. 5. Rachel, m. Adam Boyd, jr., r. & d. Rock. 6, David, (4th), m. Eleanor Kelloch of St. George. The mother d. May 21, 1826.

Alexander, (2d)'s ch. 1, John, (4th), d. unm. at sea, Oct. 7, '41. 2, Singer, d. of yellow fever, returning from the W. Indies. 3, Nancy, m. George Harrington of S. Th.; r. St. G., 4, Mary, m. Daniel Meserve, Dec. 31, '35. 5, Capt. James, (3d), m. Louisa Kelloch; r. St. G. 6, Fullerton, b. ab. '10; m. Margaret Drake, Dec. 31, '35; r. Th., a carpenter. 7, Isabel, m. Daniel Kinney of St. G. 8, Alexander, (4th), m. Mary Ann Kelloch.

George's ch. 1, Washington, and three others; all r. Wal.

Matthew, (2d)'s ch. 1, Polly, m. Francis Haskell; r. & d. S. Th. 2, Ambrose, b. ab. 1797; m. Jane Haskell; r. S. Th., a merchant. 3, Hannah, d. young. 4, Betsey, m. Thomas Haskell; r. S. Th.

Finley, (2d)'s ch. 1, Isabella, m. William Sleeper; r. & d. S. Th. 2, Joseph, m. Abigail Eastman, July 17, 1817; r. & d. S. Th. 3, Archibald, d. in Virginia. 4, Mehitable, d. young. 5, Eleonai, d. unm. 6, Capt. Jesse, b. ab. '10; m. 1st, Elathea Lindsey, 2d, Sarah Lindsey, Dec. 20, '32; 3d, Julia A. Davis, Dec. 24, '58; r. Rock. 7, Mary, b. ab. '12; m. 1st. Albert Marsh, 2d, Dea. Peter Hall; r. Rock. 8, Lydia, m. Harrison Ulmer; r. Rock. 9, Nancy, m. Alden Blackington; r. Rock.

Thomas's ch. 1, Eleanor, m. David Kelloch, (4th); r. St. G. By 2d wife. 2, Farnham, m. ——— Rivers; r. Bangor 3, Jefferson, m. Emeline H. Blackington; r. S. Th., 4, Capt. Madison, m. Lovicy C. Fountain, May 1, 1840; r. St. G. 5, Elbridge G., b. ab. '16; m. Frances E. Blackington, Nov. 20, '47; r. Rock., a lime burner. 6, Joshua, m. & r. Eastport. 7, Jackson, b. '18; d. unm. at Providence, D. 22, '41.

Moses's ch. by 1st wife. 1, William, (3d), b. March 18, 1781; m. Catharine (Montgomery) Kelloch; r. S. Th. & d. Feb. 21, 1864. 2, Mehitable, m. John Hall of Knox. 3, Hannah, m. Benjamin Bump of Knox. By 2d wife. 4, John S., b. 1796; m. Catharine Montgomery of W.; r. S. Th. & d. Aug. 16, 1824, lost overboard at sea. 5, Dea. Hanse, (2d), b. 1800; m. Anora Montgomery, Feb. 8, '32; r. S. Th., a farmer. 6, Sarah, m. 1st. Barnabas Shea of St. G., Sept. 3, '26, 2d, Israel Elwell of St. G. 7, Charlotte, r. S. Th. 8, Moses, (2d), died young. 9, Eliza, m Asa Harrington of S. Th. 10, Abigail, b. '09; m. Barney Thomas; r. Th. 11, Jacob, d. unm. 12, Capt. James S., m. Mary Emeline McKellar, Oct. 11, '46; r. S. Th.; drowned in endeavoring to get ashore from his wrecked vessel. 13, Joshua, lost at sea.

Hanse's ch. 1, Matthew, (3d), d. unm. 2, Shepherd, d. unm. 3, Adam, m. Effie Linneken, d. at sea. 4, Josiah, m Jane Willie; r. St. G., d. at sea. 5, Hanse, (3d), d. in California. 6, William, d. at sea. 7, Warren D., b. ab. 1827; m. Susan A. Thompson, Aug. 9, 1856;

r. S. Th., a mariner, and was killed by accident on board ship at Buffalo, 1864. 8, Ludwig. 9, Jane Ann, m. Levi Kinney; r. Framingham, Mass. 10, Eliza Helen M., m. Henry Snow; r. St. G.

For David Y.'s ch., & most of the branches, see Annals of Warren.

Alexander, (3d)'s ch. 1, Dea. Mero, b. ab. 1801; m. Ruth Matthews, Oct 3, '22; r. W. 2, Rev. George, fitted himself for the ministry, but died not long after 1828. 3, Silas, b. ab. 1806; mar. Olive (Robbins) Maxey, June 20, '30; r. Rock., a truckman, city undertaker, &c. 4, Rev. Amariah, licensed by Warren Baptist church in Jan., 1830; m. 1st, Mercy Hathorn, 2d, Harriet Sleeper, Oct. 3, '33, 3d, Sarah Jane Hathorn, May 28, '42; was pastor of the 1st Baptist church, S. Th., from 1831 to '34, then of the 1st Baptist church, Rock.; rem. Augusta, where he was pastor of the church and Chaplain of House of Representatives, ret. Rock., sailed in Oct., 1849, for San Francisco, and d. at Hangtown or Placerville, June 16, '50. 5, Rev. Joseph, b. ab. 1814, ord. junior pastor of 1st Baptist church in St. Geo., Sept., 1841; m. Achsah Ingraham, Dec. 10, '37; pastor of 1st Baptist church in S. Th., from '45 to '55; in Wal., from '55 to '59; since at Rock. as pastor of 2d Baptist church. 6, Rosanna, mar. 1st, Henry Libbey of W., 2d James Hawthorn of St. G., 1831. 7, Jane, m. Samuel Southworth of Roxbury, April 6, 1828. 8, Eliza, mar. Brackett Butler; r. S. Th. 9, Nancy, m. Joseph S. Wall of St. Geo.; r. Rock. The mother died Sept. 3, '47, aged 76.

Fifth Generation.

John, (3d)'s ch. 1, Louisa, m. Capt. James Kelloch, (3d), of St. G. 2, John, (5th), b. ab. 1813; m. 1st, Angelina Vose, April 1, '38, 2d, Betsey B. Ingraham, July 4, '41; r. Rock., a quarryman, &c. 3, Oliver B., m. Clarissa L. Goldsmith, p. April 25, 1846; r. and d. in Lynn. 4, Rachel, mar. 1st ——— Orr of Lynn, (and had 2 ch., viz.: Sarah E., b. 1845, and George W., born '47, and both r. Rock.) 2d, Jefferson Kelloch; r. Rock. 5, Elizabeth, mar. and d. in Lynn. 6, James, b. ab. 1817, mar. Susan Ulmer, p. Oct. 4, '45; r. Rock., a truckman, &c. 7, George, (2d), b. ab. 1826, mar. Mary F. Wotton, Aug. 31, '51; r. Rock 8, Myrick, a deaf mute, r. Rock.

William, (2d)'s ch. By 1st wife. 1, Harriet, b. Jan. 15, 1823, m. Archibald G. Coombs; r. Indiana. 2, William, (3d), b. Aug. 27, '25, d. at sea in 1856. By 2d wife. 3, Susan S., b. Jan. 26, '29, m. Jesse Sleeper, (2d); r. S. Th. By 3d wife. 4, Eliza Paulina, b. Sept. 4, '47. 5, John Martin, b. Dec. 16, '49. 6, Maria Isabella, b. May 20, '51. 7, Mary Perry, b. May 30, '54.

Fullerton's ch. 1, Judson M., b. Oct. 2, 1836, m. Francis B. Fuller, Sept. 17, '60; r. Th., a teacher, &c. 2, Kendall, b. Dec. 29, '37, d. March 16, '40. 3, Bradford H., b. Aug. 28, '39, at St. George, as were the preceding; r. Th., a teacher. '4, Jane F., b. Dec. 29, '40,, d. March 3, '41. 5, Leander F., b. Jan. 22, '42; r. Th., now in U. S. navy. 6, Lillias, b. Dec. 14, '44. 7, Frederic A., b. Oct. 22, '46.

Ambrose's ch. 1, Lucy L., b. Oct. 4, 1824, m David R. Geyer; r. S. Th. 2, Capt. William H., b. June 11, '26, d. on the Mississippi, in brig *Sarah Lewis*, Dec. 22, '50. 3, Mary F., b. March 8, '28, m. Gilbert Rose of Lowell, Sept. 18, '53. 4, Ruth, b. Dec. 1, '31, m. Wm. Johnson, and d. in Marlboro', Mass., April 5, '63. 5, Amariah, (2d), b. Sept. 13, '33, m. Julia E. Perry, Feb. 14, '60; r. S. Th., a mariner. 6, Charles D., b. April 9, '36; m. Margaret R. Shaw, Jan. 1, '62; r. S. Th., a mariner. 7, Lydia Jane, b. Feb. 27, '38; r. S. Th.

Joseph's ch. 1, Joshua, b. Nov. 28, 1818, m. Frances ———, and rem. 2, Joseph, (2d), b. Oct. 23, '20; probably rem.

Capt. Jesse's ch. By 2d wife. 1, Sarah Elizabeth, born Sept. 23, 1833, d. Nov. 5, '38. 2, John L., b. Jan. 7, '36; r. Rock., a soldier in 4th Me. Regt., &c. 3, Alfred N., born Oct. 25, '40, mar. Angelia ———; r. Rock., a mariner, and soldier; killed at Ft. Butler, June 28, '63. 4, Joshua H., b. ab. 1844, soldier of 28th Me. Regt., wound- at Donaldsonville, June 28th, d. July 5, '63.

Elbridge G.'s ch. Everett, b. ab. 1855.

William (3d)'s ch. George H., b. Feb. 2, 1838, m. Mary E. Chaples; r. S. Th., a mariner.

John S.'s ch. 1, Julia Ann, b. March 26, 1825, mar. Thomas H. Wiggin; r. Rock., and rem. 2, Eliza J., b. June 1, 1827, m. James Renney from Scotland, April 13, '45; (who d. in Warren, leaving 2 ch. Julia F., b. July 1, 1847, and John M., b. Jan. 1849.)

Dea. Hanse, (2d)'s ch. 1, Edwin D., b. Nov. 15, 1833; r. S. Th., a mariner, & volunteer in U. S. N., d. at Chelsea, Mass, April 10, '63. 2, Alden M b. Feb. 9, '34; r. S. Th., a carpenter. 3, Irene, b. Jan. 25, '36, m. George Bradbury; r. S. Th. 4, Albert S., b. Oct. 10, '41; r. S. Th., a mariner. 5, Nancy M., b. ab. '43.

Capt. James S.'s ch. 1, James W., b. Aug. 1848, d. Nov. 15, '53. 2, Charles Winfield.

Warren D.'s ch. 1, Joseph W. 2, Annie E.

Silas's ch. 1, Oscar A., b. May 7, 1831, mar. Abbie C. Snow of Jackson, p. Oct. 10, '55; r. Rock, a blacksmith. 2, Silas E., b. Dec. 14, '33, m. Anna M. Stewart, Nov. 8, '57; r. Rock., a hackman, &c. 3, Olive L., b. May 11, '37, mar. Andrew J. Hathorn; r. Rock. 4, Mortimer, b. March 18, '40, d. Sept 4, '49.

Rev. Amariah's ch. by 1st wife. 1, Rev. Isaac S., entered Waterville college but did not graduate; m. Caroline E. Philbrook, Nov. 19, 1850; c. to Rock., and was ordained 1851, pastor of the 1st Baptist church till 1855, rem. Boston and took charge of Tremont st. Baptist church, Sept. 1855, had difficulty, left, and was admitted to bar at Leavenworth, Kansas, April, 1858, returned by invitation of his Boston church, in Sept. of the same year, has been since pastor of the Laight street Baptist church, N. Y., which he found feeble but left one of the largest of the city, in March, 1864, and went to take charge of important denominational and educational interests in Kansas. By 2d wife, 2, Caroline E., b Feb 5, '36; m. E. D. Hall; r. S. Th. 3, Amariah, (3d), b Dec. 22, '37. 4, George T., b. Aug. 4, '41, d. Jan. 19, '43. By 3d wife, 5, Mercy Jane, b. March 8, '43.

Rev. Joseph's ch. 1, Joseph Henry, born about 1839; m. Mary B. Crockett, Apr. 28, '63; r. Rock., a teacher, &c. 2, Frank S., b. ab. '51.

Sixth Generation.

John, (5th)'s ch. By 1st wife, 1, Orris, b. Feb. 3, 1839, d July 26, '57. By 2d wife, 2, Isaac I. b. April 9, '42; r. Rock., a quarryman. 3, Harrison, b. ab '43. 4, John A., b. ab. '44; corporal in Me. 4th reg., of a joyous and sportive disposition, and distinguished as a wag on the route to Washington; killed at Fredericksburg, Dec. 13, 1862.

James's ch. 1, Ada M., b. ab. 1849. 2, Hattie F., b. ab. 1854. 3, Lizzie C., b. ab. '58. 4, Herbert W., b. 1860.

George, (2d)'s ch. George F., b. ab. 1857.

Alfred N.'s ch. Frederic E., b. 1860.

Oscar A.'s ch. Charles M., b. ab. 1857.

KELLOGG, Dr. David, son of Rev. David Kellogg, of Framingham, Mass., studied medicine with his brother-in-law, Dr. Kittredge of that town; came to Th., m. Sarah Prince, Jan., 1823, and, after years of successful practice here, rem. in 1847 to Waukegan, Illinois, where he now resides. Their ch. 1, Frederic H., b. Aug. 20, 1823, m. Catharine Woodcock of Th., Aug. 14, 1850; and d. July 25, '53, at Philadelphia; mate of barque *Mandarin*. 2, Sarah B., b. Jan. 18, '27; rem. Waukegan, and m. —— Ferry. 3, Eliza P., b. Feb. 27, '29; rem. Ill., and mar. J. Y. Cony, or Cory, of Waukegan, Oct. 12, '52. 4, Charles, b. July 14, '31; 5, David, (2d), b. Feb. 23, '34; 6, George P., b. June 22, '36; 7, Gardner, b. Feb. 26, '39; 8, Edward N., b. ab. '42; 9, Ellen Hooper; all rem. Ill.

Frederic H.'s ch. Eliza Prince, b. July 20, 1850.

KELLY, Rufus, b. ab. 1810, in Freedom, Me.; m. Fidelia Russell; r. Rock., a lime burner. Their ch. 1, Oliver, b. ab. 1834, in Freedom; m. Mrs. Lydia Herbert; r. Rock. 2, Joseph, b. ab. '40; mar. Matilda E. Mills; r. Rock., a teamster. 3, Ellen, b. ab. '42. 4, Hannah, b. April, 1853, d. Jan. 2, '54. 5, Rufus, (2d), b. ab. '56. 6, Mary, b. ab. '58.

KELLY, David J., b. ab. 1821; m. Lydia ——; r. Th., a hackman, rem. Rock. Their ch. 1, Frances E., b. ab. 1843. 2, Sarah A., b. ab. '47. 3, Ianthe P., b. ab. '52. 4 and 5, twins, b. ab. '56, Frederic J. and Ida Jane. 6, Ada, b. ab. '58.

KELLY, John, b. ab. 1821, in England; came with Mary his wife, and r. S. Th., a stone cutter. Their ch. 1, Mary E., b. ab. 1854. 2, Catharine E., b. ab. '56. 3, Horace, b. ab. '59.

KEMP, John, b. ab. 1824; m. Margaret ——; r. Rock., a mariner. Their ch. 1, John F., b. ab. 1857. 2, William, b. ab. '59.

KENDALL, Capt. Luther, a native of Hope; m. Eliza Jane Hatch, Dec. 22, 1833; r. Rock., & d. Aug. 3, 1858. Their ch. 1, Elizabeth, b. July, 1834; m. George C. Harriman. 2, Edwin, b. April, and d. Oct., 1836. 3, Capt. George E., b. May, 1837; m. Sophia D. Baker of Steuben, Oct. 10, '60; r. Rock., a master mariner. 4, Rosiltha J., b. March, 1840, d. Oct. 31, '59. 5, Francisco T., b. May, 1842.

KENNEDY, Daniel, b. ab. 1808, in Ireland; m. Abigail ——; r. Rock., soldier in 4th Me Reg., &c. Their ch. 1, Capt. Thomas A., b. ab. 1836; m. 1st, Deborah W. Davis, Feb. 14, '61, 2d, Henrietta Saunders, Jan. 1, '65; r. Rock., a master mariner. 2, Esther, b. ab. '43. 3, David, b. ab. '45. 4, James, b. ab. '48. 5, Frederic, b. ab. '50. 6, Sarah, b. ab '53. 7, Paulena, b. ab. '55. 8, Nathan, b. ab. '59.

KENNEDY, Fardy, b. ab. 1815, in Ireland, as was Hannah his wife; r. Rock., a lime burner. Their ch. 1, Peter, b. ab. 1846. 2, James F., b. ab. 1850. 3, William H., b. ab. '54. 4, Bridget E., b. ab. 1859.

KENNEDY, James, b. ab. 1825; came from county of Waterford, Ireland; as did Mary his wife; r. Th., entered U. S. 1st Infantry. Their ch. 1, Catharine, b. ab. 1853. 2, John, b. ab. '55. 3 & 4, twins, b. ab. '57, George, & William.

KENNEY, John, b. ab. 1828, in St. George; ? m. Ann ——; r. Rock., a mariner. Their ch. 1, Josephine, b. ab. '53. 2, Thomas, b. ab. '55. 3, Ann E., b. ab. '57. 4, John, b. ab. '58. 5, Sarah A., b. ab. '60.

KENNISTON; of this family, 5 brothers came to Th. 1, Moses, c. from S. Berwick, m. Hannah Kenniston, rem. to and d. Appleton. 2, Samuel, m. Mrs. Nancy Young of Martha's Vineyard, Nov. 27, 1803, and was killed by caving in of a clay bank; had one son, Samuel, (2d), who r. Boston, which he has represented in Legislature. 3, Henry, b. Sept. 1789, m. Mary Stevens, p. Dec. 26, 1818; r. Th., and d. March 2, '59. 4, James, mar. Sally Robbins, April 20, 1809. 5, Theodore, both r. Th., awhile, but ret. to S. Berwick.

Moses's ch. Gustavus Myrick, b. Oct. 6, 1812, m. Louisa Sibley, Oct. 8, '37; r. Appleton.

Henry's ch. 1, Sarah, m. Patrick Curran; r. Th. 2, Elizabeth, b. Nov. 15, '23, m. Edward Fleming of Rock., Feb. 23, '51; r. Rock. 3, Almira, b. July 17, '26, m. Ambrose P. Melvin; r. Rock. 4, William, b. May 10, '30; has been, since 1857, in U S. cavalry. 5, Samuel J., b. Jan. 12, '33; r. Th., a mariner. 6, Elonai F., b. Aug. 5, '35, m. John McKenny; r. Th. 7, Edwin D., b. April 8, '38; r. Th., a caulker.

KENNISTON; of this, Mt. Desert, family, there c. here, 1, John S., b. ab. 1825, m. 1st, Elizabeth Robinson, Dec. 1, '50, 2d, S. Elizabeth Melvin, May 4, '56; r. Rock., a carpenter, &c., entered the army. 2, Charles H., b. ab. 1830, m. Nancy J. Babb, Nov. 25, '51; r. Rock., a carpenter. 3, William H., b. ab. 1832, m. Martha Jane Melvin; r. Rock., a teamster, now in the army.

Charles H.'s ch. 1, Charles E., b. ab. 1853. 2, Ella M., b. ab. '55.

KENNISTON, Mrs. Mehitable, born ab. 1807; r. Rock., a widow. Her ch. 1, William H., b. Sept. 21, 1840; r. Rock., and d. Nov. 29, '63. 2, Edward, b. ab. 1843.

KEOUGH, John, b. ab. 1820, in county of Sligo, Ireland, m. 1st, Mary Henery, 2d, Margaret Kavanagh; r. Th. His ch. By 1st wife. 1, Catharine, b. ab. 1836. 2, John, (2d), b. ab. '38; r. California. 3, Dennis, b. ab. '40. 4, Mary, b. ab. '42. By 2d wife. 5 & 6, twins, b. ab. '46, Owen and Ann C. 6, Edwin, b. ab. '52.

KIDD, David, b. ab. 1818; of Scottish origin it is believed, m. Eliza ———; r. Rock., a fisherman, now deceased. Their ch. 1, David, (2d), b. ab. 1840. 2, Hudson H., b ab. '46. 3, George T., b. ab. '52. 4, Eliza J., b. ab. '55.

KIEFF, or Kiff; of this name there were in old Th., about 1810, John, who m. Mary or Betsey Peabody; r. U., rem. Belmont, was a carpenter. Daniel, who r. at the mouth of the Wessaweskeag; William; and Ephraim. John's ch. 1, Alexander, b. in U., Feb. 21, 1798; mar. Bradbury I. Witham of Searsmont; r. Rock., a peddler, &c. 2, Jane, b. in Union, Aug. 29, '99; m. and r. Waldo, Me. 3, Mary, b. in Hope, May 4, 1801; m. probably, and r. Michigan. 4, Greenleaf, b. May 13, '03; d. in Belmont.

Alexander's ch. 1, John W., b. ab. 1825; mar. Nancy Sawyer of Montville; r. Rock., a soldier of the 4th Me. Reg., &c. 2, Abbie P, m. Horace Weeks; r. Mass. 3, Mary Jane, m. Cornelius Irish; r. Mass. 4, Agnes R. 5, Marcus R., mar. Victoria Starkey; r. Unity. 6, Alexander B., b. ab. 1837; m. Matilda Wentworth of S. Th., Feb. 27, '59; r. Rock., a shoemaker, soldier of 4th Me. Reg., &c. 7, Orlando S. 8, Cornelius I., b. ab. '50.

John W.'s ch. Charles G., b. ab. 1850.

Alexander B's ch. Minnie J., d. May 24, '61, an infant.

Daniel's ch. 1, Hannah G., m. Benjamin Brewster; r. Rock. 2, Sarah, m. Samuel Graves of S. Th. 3, Mary A., m. D. Hibberd; r. Belmont. 4. Abigail, m. John Bickford; r. Mt. Desert. 5, Daniel, killed in C. Crockett's lime quarry, ab. 1844.

KIEFF, James, born ab. 1820 in Ireland, mar. Bridget O'Brien, p. March 27, '53; r. Th., rem. Augusta. Their ch. 1, Ellen, born ab. 1856. 2, Michael, b. ab. '58. 3, Bridget, b. ab. '59.

KILLSA, Lieut. Hugh, born in Nottinghamshire, N. H., Jan. 26, 1749, O. S.; m. Lois Robbins; r. at Meadows, Rock., and d. Feb. 8, 1824. 2, James, a brother, c. later; m. Lydia Keen, Sept. 29, 1785; r. Meadows, Th., & d. June 25, 1792. 3, George, a brother, settled & d. by drowning at Owl's Head. 4. Sarah, a sister, b. March 24, 1761; m. Oliver Robbins, (2d), & d. Feb. 10, 1820. Another brother probably settled in Bristol. Mrs. Joseph Wilson of Damariscotta and others of the Bristol branch, write the name *Kelsey*.

Lieut. Hugh's ch. 1, John, d. young. 2, Nancy, m. John Godding, jr.; rem. & d. Waldo. 3, William, d. young. 4, Lois, d. young. 5, Mary, m. in '05, her cousin, James Killsa of Bristol, who was b. there in 1779; m. 1st, a Miss Wentworth, & d. Dec. 25, '06. 6, Sabra, m, Josiah Gregory of Corinth, p. Oct. 9, '33; r. & d. Appleton. 7, Hannah, d. young. 8, Hugh, (2d), d. young. 9, Sarah R., b. 1793; m. Geo. B. Cooper; r. S. Th. 10, Lois, m. Samuel Davis of Appleton.

James's ch. 1, William, b. Aug. 28, 1786; m. Catharine McLean of Boston; r. Th. & traded at Oyster river; rem. & d. in Ill. 2, Esther, b. Aug. 9, 1788; m. a Simmons; rem. Troy, N. Y. 3, Charles, b. March 24, 1790; d. unm. 4, John, b. Oct. 4, '91; m. r. & d. Augusta. 5, Charlotte, b. May 20, '93; m. Alex. Barrows, r. Rock,.

James of Bristol's ch. 1, Hugh, (3d), b. in Bristol, Jan. 30, 1807, m. Mahala (St. Clair) Hall, Aug. 6, 1835; r. Rock., a lime burner, &c.

William's ch. 1, William A., r. Th. as a merchant, rem. Canton, Fulton Co., Ill. 2, Mary Ann, m. Edmund B. Lermond; rem. with her ch. to Ill. 3, Erastus. 4, James, (3d). 5, Sarah. 6, Lawton. 7, Harriet, all rem. Ill.

Hugh (3d)'s ch. 1, Mary E., b. Nov. 12, 1836, m. Charles Cilley; r. Rock. 2, Louisa H., b. Sept. 17, '38, m. Benjamin F. Pottle, 2d. David Rich, July 6, '63; r. Rock. 3, William J., b. July 27, '41. 4, Orinda M., b. Sept. 26, '44, d. Nov. 18, '46. 5, Huldah A., b Aug. 5, '46, m. Emery Thorndike; r. Rock. 6, Lois D., b. Oct. 23, '49.

KIMBALL, William Story, son of Richard and Sally (Story) Kimball of Bath, Me., and descendant of Richard and Ursula Kimball, (who with 12 children, 4, of them twins, came from Yarmouth, England, in the *Elizabeth*, and settled, 1734, at old Ipswich, Mass.), was b. in Bath, July 19, 1792; learned cabinet maker's trade of George Beck, was a privateersman in the war of 1812, on board the *America*, of Salem; m. Emily Conant of Th., Sept. 17, '17; r. near Prison Corner, Th., north side Main St., worked at his trade, but in '53, rem to Riley, St. Clair county, Michigan. Their ch. 1, Joseph S., b. June 5, 1818, m. Mary D. Davis, Dec. 22, '39; rem. '53, and r. Riley, Mich. 2, Sarah S., b. Oct. 31, '19, m. Charles Dudley Starr of Riley, Mich. 3, William, b. Feb. 13, '21, d. in Charleston, S. C., Aug. 14, '40. 4, Charles, b. July 7, '23, d. at sea, July 24, '43. 5, Mary J., b. Sept. 20, '25, d. March 13, '26. 6, Emily, b., Jan. 20, '27, rem. Riley. 7, Moses C., b. April 21, '29, m. Marie De Cota, a Spanish lady of Lapaz, Mexican California; r. San Francisco. 8, Thomas Danforth, b.

July 18, '31, m. Almira C., dau. of William Preble of Whitefield. 9, Edward Brown, b. April 6, '33, d. May 8, '34. 10, Adah Lucy, b. March 9, '35; m. Henry Barker of Upper Alton, Ill. 11, Malvina Susan, b. Sept. 24, '37; m. Edwin Sprague; r. Rock. 12, William Edway, b. Oct. 24, '41. 13, Julia F., b. June 22, '44.

Joseph S.'s ch. 1, Mary E., b. Sept. 19, 1840, d. Aug. 5, '42. 2 & 3, twins, b. April 9, '43; Sarah Emily, & Mary Ellen, who m. Joshua Perry of Sterling, Mich., Dec., 1860. 4, Frances Ann, b. April 29, '45; 5, Joseph Thomas, b. March 31, '47; 6, Simon Shibles, b. April 5, '49; 7, William Benjamin, b. March 21, '53; 8 & 9, twins, Horace & Horatio, b. June 18, '55. 10, Martha Ada, b. Sept. 29, '58; all in Michigan.

KIMBALL, George W., b. ab. 1806, in Haverhill, N. H.; m. Olive B. Carlton; spent about four years in Philadelphia, New York, and New Orleans; came in 1833 to what is now Rock., where he engaged in trade till 1860; r. Rock., a retired merchant. Their ch. 1, Alice C., b. 1832; mar. John A. Meserve, Esq.; r. Rock. 2, George W., (2d), b. 1834; m. Elmira A. Achorn, April 28, '56; r. Rock., a boot & shoe merchant, deputy collector, &c.

KIMBALL, Capt. ———, m. Eleanor Martin; r. Head of the Bay; & perished by shipwreck off Seguin before 1788. Their ch. 1, Timothy, m. Diana Keen; r. and d. Bremen. 2, Sarah, m. Brotherton Daggett; r. & d. Union. 3, Samuel, d. at sea, drowned. Timothy's ch. 1, Robert K. 2, Samuel, m. Mercy Cushman; has ch., Timothy, William C., Daniel C., and one other; r. Long Island, Bremen. 3, Sophronia, b ab. 1815; mar. Martin Marsh; r. Rock. 4, Timothy, (2d), died young.

KIMBALL, Dea. Iddo, b. July 14, 1782; c. from Bradford, Mass., to what is now Rock., in the fall of 1808; m. Mary Robbins, Jan. 17, 1813; r. Rock., a merchant, &c., d. Jan. 1, '54. Their ch. 1, Hon. Iddo K., b. Nov. 29, 1813; mar. 1st, Mary H. Spear, Feb. 8, '35, 2d, Mary L. Trundy, Sept. 19, '52; r. Rock., a merchant, firm Kimball & Ingraham, State Senator, 1848, & '49, &c. 2, Alfred H., b. June 3, '16; m. Mary J. Bray of Deer Isle, Dec. 12, '48; r. Rock., president Rockland Bank, &c. 3, Bradford, b. Feb. 5, '19; m. Melinda Shaw of Rock., Sept. 25, '52; r. Vassalboro', a farmer, &c.

Hon. Iddo K.'s ch. 1, Mary T., b. April 22, 1836; m. Samuel W. Tate, and d. Feb. 13, '54. 2, Angeline E., b. Dec. 29, '39. 3, ? John K., b. '43, died July 10, '51, 4, Fannie, b. ab. '45. By 2d wife. 5, Clara, b. ab. '54. 6, Ida M., b. ab. '56. 7, Marietta, b. '60.

Alfred H.'s ch. 1, Bradford, (2d), b. ab. 1849. 2, Mary H., b. ab. '51. 3, Ada F., b. ab. '53. 4, Alfred Banks, b. Jan. 31, and d. Aug. 19, '61. 5 & 6, twins, b. Aug. 21, '62, Iddo K. jr., d. Aug. 27, '63; Emma B., d. Aug. 30, '63.

KIRKPATRICK, James, b. ab. 1776; youngest son of John, one of the first Scottish settlers of Warren, in 1753; m. Elizabeth Williams of Long Island; r. Rock. Their ch. 1, Charles W., m. Mary Babbage; r. Bangor. 2, Eliza, b. ab. 1811; m. Capt. John Holbrook; r. Rock. 3, Alfred, m. Harriet Leslie; r. Bangor. 4, Jane W., m. Robert Maker; r. Northport. 5, Mary, m. John T. Smith of Guilford, N. H. 6, Benjamin, b. ab. 1819; m. Clara or Chloe Cotton of Hope; r. Rock., a soldier in 2d Me. Battery. 7, Ann S., m. Parker Means; r. Belmont. 8, James, (2d), m. Josephine Thurston; r. Rock. 9, Hollis, m. Sarah Clough; r. Rock. 10, John, (4th), b. ab. 1827;

m. Mary E. Butler; r. Rock., a teamster. 11, Eleanor A. 12, Emily S. 13, Philena, m. Capt. Edward Rogers; r. Rock. 14, William F., r. Bangor.

Benjamin's ch. 1, George T., b. ab. 1849. 2, Daniel L., b. ab. '51. 3, Hattie O., b. ab. '55. 4, Chloe, b. ab. '60.

John, (4th)'s ch. 1, Sarah E., b. ab. '52. 2, William E., b. ab. '54.

KIRKPATRICK, John, (3d), son of John, (2d), and Nancy (Starrett) Kirkpatrick of Warren, b. in W. ab. 1814; m. Priscilla Flint of Rock., July 14, '38; r. Rock., a blacksmith. Frances J., a cousin, dau. of Thomas & Margaret (Starrett) Kirkpatrick of W.; r. Rock., and keeps millinery establishment. John, (3d)'s ch. 1, Ann, F., b. March 23, and d. Sept. 20, 1838. 2, Lucy, b. July 10, '40. 3, Edgar C., b. Feb. 22, '42; m. Ada B. Spear, April 3, '62; r. Rock., a blacksmith, soldier, &c. 4, Frances, b. ab. '43; m. James Feyler, Oct. 12, '62. 5, Lizzie T., b. ab. '46; mar. Thomas Devins, Jan. 12, '64; r. Rock. 6, Emma, b. ab. '48.

KITTRIDGE, Edwin, b. ab. 1813; m. Louisa ——; r. Rock., a joiner. Their ch. 1, Cora H., b. ab. 1843. 2, William H., b. ab. '47. 3, John W., b. ab. '51.

KNIGHT, John, b. ab. 1805; mar. Adaline P. ——; r. Rock. Their ch. 1 & 2, b. ab. 1837, John W., r. Rock., William J., mar. Georgiana Tibbets, June 29, '56; r. Rock., a clerk, &c. 3, Ada F., b. ab. '43. 4, Francis A., b. ab. '45; soldier in 2d Battery, and 2d Me. Cavalry.

KNOWLTON, Ephraim, came from Salem, Mass., to what is now Rock., ab. 1805; m. Mrs. Hannah Barrett, p. May 17, '06; a cooper, &c.; r. & d. Rock. Their ch. 1, Ephraim, (2d), b. ab. 1814; mar. Catharine Holmes, April 24, '34; r. Rock., engaged in fishery, &c. 2, Benjamin, b. ab. '17; m. 1st, Margaret Spalding of Linc., Nov. 1, '35, 2d, Mrs. Caroline S. McMullen, Oct. 5, '51; r. Rock., a grocery merchant. 3, Hannah, m. Benjamin Stone of Vinalhaven, July 22, '24. 4, Lucy, m. William Spalding; r. Rock. 5, Sarah, m. Mark Dodge of Islesboro', 2d, Sumner Allen of Montville, 3d, Moses Nickerson; r. Rock.

Ephraim, (2d)'s ch. 1, Caroline T. 2, Mary A., b. Oct. 18, 1838; m. Finley Boyd, July 12, '55; r. Rock. 3, Ellen M., b. May 9, '42. 4, Ann E., b. ab. '46. 5, Ephraim J., b. ab. '51. 6, Clara B., b. ab. '57.

Benjamin's ch. 1, William N., b. Feb. 26, 1836; m. Frances A. Worthley, Nov. '58; r. Rock., a truckman, soldier in 17th Me. reg., &c. 2, Susan I., b. Oct. 23, '38; m. Josiah Peabody. 3, Harriet H., b. Nov. 29, '41, d. Feb., '42. The mother d. Dec. 28, '50, a. 33. By 2d wife. 4, Franklin, b. ab. '52. 5, Emma H., b. ab. '54. 6, an infant, d. Aug. 4, '61.

Of William N.'s ch. Annie C., b. June 31, 1861, d. Aug. 4, '62.

KNOWLTON, John W., b. ab. 1822, in Belfast, Me.; m. Almira F. Ames; r. Rock., a carpenter. Their ch. 1, Edward A., b. ab. '47. 2, Frank M., b. ab. '51. 3, Ralph E., b. ab. '57. 4, John A., b. ab. '59.

KNOWLTON, Charles H., b. ab. 1825, in Liberty, Me.; m. 1st, Delinda Davis, Dec. 26, '47, (who d. Jan. 31, '54, a. 28,) r. Rock., a pump peddler. His ch. 1, Freeland C., b. ab. '49; r. Rock., entered U. S. navy. 2, Freeman P., b. ab. '54.

KNOWLES, Joseph, b. ab. 1800; c. from Northport; m. & r. Th. His ch. 1, Lewis, b. ab. '33, a teacher, &c. 2, Catharine, b. ab. '36.

3, Levi, b. ab. '38, a mariner. 4, Marcus, b. ab. '40, a mariner. 5, George C., b. ab. '42, soldier in 21st Me. reg., &c. 6, ? Clarena, b. ab. '55.

KNOX, Maj. Gen. Henry, b. in Boston of Scottish* parents July 25, 1750; lost his father while yet a boy; was educated in the common schools of Boston; labored as a bookbinder & stationer to maintain his mother, himself, and only brother, who d. young; m. Lucy Flucker June, '74; r. Boston & Philadelphia; was artillery officer in Revolution; secretary of war; secretary of the society of the Cincinnati; honorary A. M. Dartmouth Coll., '93; c., '95, to Th. & d. Oct. 25, '06. Their ch. 1, Lucy Fluker, b. in 1776; m. Hon. Ebenezer Thatcher; r. Th., W. & Bingham, d. at Montpelier, Th., Oct. 12, '54. 2, Henry Jackson, b. 1780, was an infant at Mt. Vernon during the seige of Yorktown; m. Eliza T. Read of Th., p. May 1, '03; had name changed to Henry, Feb. 11, '23; r. W. & Th. & d. very suddenly, without ch., Oct. 9, '32. His wife d. Dec. '25, or Jan. '26, a. 41, at Worcester, Mass. 3, Marcus Camillus, d. very suddenly, at the age of 8 years, in fits caused by sun stroke, at Philadelphia. 4, George Washington; 5, Marcus; 6, Washington; 7, H. W. Bingham; 8, Julia; 9, Caroline; 10, H. Augusta; 11, Julia Wadsworth; all died young, before their father, & many in infancy. 12, Caroline Fluker, b. in 1791; m. ab. 1808, James Swan of Boston, who d. here March 22, '36, 2d, Hon. John Holmes of Alfred, July 31, '37; r. Montpelier, Th. and d. without ch., Oct. 17, '51. The mother d. at 3 o'clock on the morning of June 20, 1824, aged 68.

LABE, Martin D., b. ab. 1822 in Waldoboro', m. Isabella D. Harrington, May '44; r. Rock., a joiner. Silas E., probably a brother, b. Oct. 12. '32, m. Lucinda S. Burns, Dec. 6, '55; r. Rock., a joiner, soldier of the 4th Me., and d. Feb. 4, '63.

Martin D.'s ch. 1, William F., b. Oct. 1846, d. March 21, '51. 2, Erastus P., b. ab. '52.

LACKEY, William, c. from Hingham, Mass,, early to Th., m. Olive Stackpole, p. April 2, 1788; r. Th., & d. July 5. '97. Their ch. 1, Jane, b. April 13, '88; 2, William, b. Feb. 12, '90; 3, Simeon, b. March 9, '92; all probably rem. Prospect. 4, Lucy, b. March 20, '94, d. July 20, '96. 5, Susan Stackpole, b. May 18, '96, and rem.

LADD, Daniel, b. ab. 1823; m. Sarah J. Benner of Wal., in 1853; r. Rock., a teamster.

LAMB, Benjamin, b. ab. 1811; in Lincolnville, m. Mary J. Dunnell; r. Rock., a lime burner, &c. His brother, Jacob W., also came here, m. Adelaide Dean; r. Rock.

Benjamin's ch. 1, Andrew D., b. ab. 1844, a mariner. 2, Amanda E., b. ab. '47. 3, George E., b. ab. '49. 4, Adelbert E., b. ab. '51. 5, Flora E., b. ab. '55.

LAMPSON, Jonathan, m. Mary Gross; c. from Derry, N. H., before 1780, and r. many years in Th., rem. to what is now Rock., had charge of Blackington's mill, and d. March 7, 1835. His wife d. Aug. 17, 1824. Their ch. 1, William, m. Mrs. Caroline Sidensberger; r. W., and died without ch., April 13, 1836. 2, Sally, m. Ignatius Jordan; r. and d. Th. 3, Martha, m. Capt. Matthias Isley, 2d, Thomas McIntyre; r. Th., and d. Nov. 16, 1856. 4, Mary, m. Adam Martin,

---

* Knox used to visit, as a relative, Mrs. Rawley of St. George, wife of one of the Scottish settlers of Warren.

p. Jan. 1, 1803; r. S. Th., rem. and d. Union. 5, Abigail, b. in May, 1775; r. Rock , and died Oct. 27, 1843. 6, Lucy W., mar. Franklin Stearns, July 10, 1814; rem. and died Burnham. 7, Ambrose, (an adopted grandson,) b. Sept. 13, 1796, m. Elsie Burns, Oct. 19, 1817; 2d, Eliza L. Bradley, June 9, 1850; r. Rock., a wheelwright, served in war of 1812 in place of Joseph Ingraham; and d. Dec. 1, 1861.

Ambrose's ch. By 1st wife. 1, Jonathan, (2d), b. June 1, 1818, d. Oct. 5, '26. 2, Edward I., b. Aug. 7, '19, m. Antoinette Brown, Feb. 27, '53; r. Rock., a quarryman. 3, Martin, b. April 7, '21, d. Oct. 7, '24. 4, Antoinette, b. March 22, '25, d. Oct. 7, '26. 5, Ambrose, (2d), b. April 22, 1827, m. Mary O. Tolman of Cam., May 14, '51, 2d, Ardell Ingraham, Aug., 1862; r. Rock., rem. Cam., a joiner. 6, Julia M., b. Oct. 22, '28, m. John Barrett; r. Rock. 7, Otis Manley, b. March 6, 1835; r. Rock., a wheelright, &c. The mother d. July 10, '48, a. 51 years.

Edward I.'s ch. 1, Elsie E., b. April 16, 1854. 2, Anna F., b. Dec. 7, '60.

Ambrose, (2d)'s ch. 1, Frederic U., b. July 23, '57. 2, Leslie, b. March 31, '61. The mother d. April 11, 1861.

LANDER, William, b. ab. 1824, in England, as was Sarah E., his wife, in N. S.; r. S. Th., a whip sawyer. Their ch. 1, Rosanna L., b. ab. '52. 2, Caroline M., b. ab. '55. 3, Nancy E., b. ab. '58.

LANDERS, Robert, b. ab. 1815, in Ireland, as was Mary, his wife; r. Rock. Their ch. 1, ? Thomas. 2, ? Michael. 3, Mary, b. ab. 1845. 4, Joanna, b. ab. '47. 5, Ellen, b. ab. '52. 6, Robert, b. ab. '56. 7, John, b. ab. '58. 8, William, b. ab. '59.

LANE, Joseph, b. in Marblehead, Mass., m. Betsey Flagg; r. in Bristol, Me., lately rem. Rock., where two of his sons had settled, viz.: 1, Joseph H., b, in Bristol ab. 1821, m. Melissa Erskine; r. Rock. 2, Philip H., b. in Bristol ab. 1835. m. Nancy Martin; r. Rock., a mariner.

Joseph H.'s ch. 1. Mary A., b. ab. 1854. 2, Exie, b. ab. '57.

Philip H.'s ch. Ida M., b. ab. 1858.

LANGELL, Ephraim, born in Nova Scotia, ab. 1823, m. Asenath Roberts, Oct. 25, '53; r. Rock., a shoemaker, soldier of 4th Me., &c.

LARRABEE, James, b. ab. 1797; m. Maria ———; r. Rock., lost his sight by explosion in lime quarry. Their ch. 1, John H., b. ab. 1827; m. Margaret R. Young, p. Sept. 26, '45; r. Rock., a truckman. 2, Mary Ann, b. ab. 1835; m. ——— Erskine; r. Rock. 3, Achsa R.; r. Rock. Of James's nephews there also came here from Knox, 3 brothers, viz.: 1, Otis, b. ab. 1823; m. Sarah J. Achorn, March 8, '49; r. Rock. 2, Solomon, b. ab. '25; m. Nancy Stevens, Aug. 13, '48; r. Rock., & d. April, 1863, from a stab received from one Foster with whom he got into a dispute when cutting timber. 3, Elias, b. in Knox, Nov. 6, 1829; m. H. Elizabeth Brewer, June 11, '53; r. Rock., a lime burner.

John H.'s ch. 1, Mary M., b. Aug. 15, 1846; m. Robert Jackson of Milford, Mass., Nov. 3, '64. 2, Marcia V., born Sept. 8, '48. 3, Valdora E., b. May '27, & d. Aug. 26, '51. 4, Charles Y., b. Feb. 28, '53. 5, James Augustus, b. March 25, '58. 6, Herbert Lincoln, born March 28, '61. 7, Orris B.. b. Feb. 25, '64.

Otis's ch. 1, Ruth A., b. ab. 1851. 2, William H., 3, Emery. 4, Eugene, b. ab. '59.

Solomon's ch. 1, Fidelia A., b. June, 1853, died Jan. 6, 60. 2, Mary E., b. ab. '55. 3, Frederic F., b. ab. '58. 4, Alden H., b. Dec., '62, died Oct. 27, '63.

Elias's ch. 1, Cora E., b. Aug 3, 1857. 2, Albert J., b. Jan. 25, '60. 3, Alfred, b. June 1, '62. The mother d. June 4, 1862, aged 32.

LASH, Casimir, of German descent, c. from Waldoboro', mar. 1st, Ann Malcolm of C., Dec. 26, 1824, 2d, Ann (Stetson) Eaton of Cam., p. Nov. 3, '37; r. Th., a painter, florist, &c., d. Sept. 22, '49. His ch. By 1st wife. 1, Delia D., b. Oct. 24, 1825, m. Alfred B. Butler of S. Th., 2d, ——— Dizer, of St. George; r. Th. 2, Octavia D., b. March 10, '28, m. Edward E. O'Brien; r. Th. 3, Alcander S., b. July 17, '30, m. Adelaide Reed of Belfast, March 3, '58; r. Th., a painter. 4, Laura D., b. June 1, '33, d. in Boston, Feb., '51. 5, Aroline H., born Aug. 16, '35, d. Feb. 29, '36. The mother d. April 13, 1836.

Alcander S.'s ch. John, b. ab. 1859.

LASH, John B., b. ab. 1822, c. from Wal., m. Anstruss E. Getchell, Dec. 1846; r. Th., a baker. Their ch. Anna B., b. ab. 1859.

LASSELL, or Laisdell, ———, was, with his family, the early and only occupant of, gave name to, and d. on Laisdell's Is., which lies between Cam. harbor and Long Is. Of his ch. 1, Ruth, m. Samuel Williams of Harpswell, p. May 22, 1777. 2, Lois, m. William Lermond of W., r. and d. W. 3, Deidamia, m. William Philbrook, pub. May 6, 1780; r. and d. Long Is. Also, probably, Joshua, who came from Vinalhaven to Cam., mar. ——— Philbrook, and had ch. 1, Robert, mar. 1st, Mrs. Elizabeth Robinson, 2d, a Hilt of Hope. 2, John. 3, Joshua, (2d), mar. Miss Sweetland of Hope. 4, Jeremiah, m. Miss Payson of Hope. 5, Hannah. 6, Betsey.

Robert's ch. 1, David, m. Lucy Crockett. 2, William, m. in Kirkland. 3, Mary, m. James M. Tibbits. 4, Jonathan, b. ab. 1819, mar. Delilah Spalding, Nov. 1, 1838; r. S. Th., a mariner. 5, Nancy.

Jonathan's ch. 1, George S., b. Feb. 15, 1842. 2, Charles A., b. ab. '44. 3, Sarah E., b. ab. '46. 4 & 5, twins, b. Dec. 13, '49; Hannah C., d. March 17, '62, and Bernard I. 6 & 7, twins, William and Ada, both died young. 8, Lucy T., b. ab. '55. 9, Jonathan, (2d), b. ab. '56. 10, Francis D., b. ab. '59.

LATTA, William, b. ab. 1818, in New Brunswick, as was Ann his wife in England; r. S. Th. Their ch. 1, ? James, b. ab. 1837, died July 21, '59. 2, Kate, b. ab. '43. 3, Lucretia, b. ab. '45. 4, Andrew, b. ab. '47. 5, Sophia, b. ab. '49. 6, Isabel, b. ab. '51. 7, William I., b. ab. '53. 8, Anson, b. ab. '56.

LAWRENCE, Archibald, b. ab. 1825, in Hope; m. Phebe Calief; r. Rock., a joiner. Their ch. 1, Ellen, b. April, 1847, died July 23, '61. 2, Emma, b. ab. '49. 3, Austin, b. ab. '53. 4, George, b. ab. '57. 5, Phebe, b. ab. '60.

LAWRENCE, Henry F., b. ab. 1835; mar. Emma J. Coombs, p. April 21, '53; r. Rock., a mariner. Their ch. 1, Emerette, b. ab. 1857. 2, Edwin, b. ab. '59.

LAWRENCE, Samuel, b. ab. 1835; m. Caroline H. Day, May 23, '53; r. Rock., a mariner. Their ch. Charles C., b. ab. 1860.

LAWRY, Samuel, b. July, 1805, probably in Friendship; m. Betsey Ann ———; r Rock., a joiner, and d. Dec. 11, 1860. Their ch. 1, Helen I., b. ab. 1834. 2, Llewellyn W., b. ab. '36. 3, Albert D., b. ab. '39. 4, Alonzo F., b. ab. '41. 5, Edwin H., b. ab. '43. 6, Lettie E., b. ab. '49. 7, Samuel W., b. ab. '57.

LAWRY, Robert, son of Robert Lawry of W.; mar. Emma L.

Walker of Hampden, Oct. 25, 1857; r. Th., a carpenter. Their ch. Elwin, b. ab. '59.

LEACH, Ambrose, son of Jerathmael of W.; m. Julia Littlehale, 1831; r. and d. U.; but his family rem. Rock. Their ch. 1, James L. 2, Frances E., r. Rock. 3, Ambrose A.

LEAVETT, Charles, b. ab. 1812; mar. Rebecca Fish of Hope; r. Rock., a joiner. Their ch. 1, Adolphus A., b. ab. 1844; r. Rock., soldier in 28th Me. Reg., lately re-enlisted. 2, Alvina, b. ab. '45. 3, Charles B., b. ab. '49. 4, Henry, b. ab. '51. 5, Medora A., b. ab. '53. 6, Frank, b. ab. '55.

LEAVETT, Silas, b. ab. 1824, in Augusta, Me., mar. Eliza Ann Wood; r. Rock., a lime burner, &c. Their ch. 1, Harriet M.; born Feb., 1850. d. March 2, '51. 2, Silas P., b. ab. '54.

LEIGHTON, Daniel, b. ab. 1805 in Mass., m. Sarah ——; r. S. Th., a mariner. Their ch. 1, Abiathar R., b. ab. 1839; r. S. Th., a farmer.

LEISTNER, Charles, b. ab. 1793, probably in Wal., m. Lucy ——; r. Rock. Their ch. 1, Priscilla H., b. ab. 1841. 2, Susan, b. ab. '44.

LENFEST; of this family there came from Washington, Me., two brothers; 1, Nicholas H., b. ab. 1817, m. Sarah F. Fernald, May 2, 1857; r. Th, a carpenter. 2, Charles P., b. ab. 1832, m. Roxana B. (Fernald) Young, Nov. 5, 1856; r. Th.

Nicholas H.'s ch. 1, Henry A., b. Jan. 25, 1858. 2, William C., b. May 13, 1860. 3, Ellen F., b. Aug. 12, 1862.

Charles P.'s ch. Merritt F., b. Dec. 26, 1858.

LEONARD, Mary, b. in Ireland, ab. 1820; r. S. Th., a widow. Her ch. 1, James, b. ab. '35; r. S. Th., a mariner. 2, Mary A., b. ab. '41.

LERMOND; for this family in full, see Annals of Warren. Of the sons of William, there c. here, 1, James, (3d), who m. Elizabeth Andrews, Dec. 15, 1800; r. Th., on the Porterfield place, & d. in W., '06. 2, Mary, m. E. S. Young; r. Th. & d. Oct. 19, '09. 3, George, b. ab. 1787; m. 1st, Lucy Vose, Nov. 18, 1819, 2d, Sarah Vose, Nov. 26, '32, (who d. Dec. 21, '55); r. Th., d Jan 5, '65. Of Alexander, (2d)'s ch. Ambrose, b. Nov. 28, 1800; m. Sarah Lermond, Dec. 25, 1828; was many years commissioner of Lincoln co.; rem. Th.: postmaster 8 years, merchant, &c. Of James, (3d)'s ch. 1, Sarah, b. '01; m. Ambrose Lermond; r. Th. & d. Dec. 4, '53. 2, Capt. Edward, b. '03; m. Eveline Parsons of C., p. Sept. 30, '30; r. Th., & d. March 2, '62. Of Alexander, (4th)'s ch. Edmund B., b. Oct. 12, 1807; m. Mary A. Killsa, Sept. '34; r. Th., a merchant, & d. at Philadelphia, May, '50, on his passage home from N. O. Of Joshua's ch. Albert G., b. June 26, '09; m. Elizabeth Nutting, p. June 9, '38; r. Th., a teacher, &c., d. May 14, '55. Of Alexander, (3d)'s ch. Charles, b. ab. '16; m. Rebecca C. Morton, Dec. 12, '41; r. Th.. a shipbuilder. Of Percy's ch. Henry, b. ab. '27; m. Susan Cobb; r. Th., a shipbuilder.

George's ch. 1, Oliver, (2d), lost at sea, March 9, 1839 2, Erastus, b. ab. '22; m. Emeline Woodcock, Jan. 30, '44; r. Th., a farmer. 3, Geo. Washington, m. Lucy A. Young, April 23, '45, d. California, '50.

Ambrose's ch. 1, William Edward, b. Oct. 5, 1829, d. of fever at N. Y., on passage from N. O., Oct. 5, '54. 2, Frances E. b. Sept. 16, '31. 3, Eveline, b. Oct. 23, '36.

Capt. Edward's ch. 1, Edward W., b. ab 1844, entered the navy. 2, Franklin, b. ab. '46.

Edmund B.'s ch. 1, Franklin; 2, Mary Helen ; 3, Maria J. L., all rem. to Canton, Ill.

Albert G.'s ch. 1, Mary Elizabeth, b. Oct. 11, 1839, d. April 15, '55. 2, Emma F., b. Oct. 20, '40: m. Joshua Wyllie; r. Th. 3, William James, b. June 4, '45 ; r. Th., a mariner. 4, Margaret H., b. Oct. 7, 1851.

Charles's ch. 1, Aroline C., b. Oct. 11, 1843. 2, Lauretta R., b. May 9, '46. 3, Levi M., b. June 22, '48. 4, Lizzie C., b. May 7, '50. 5, Charles Herbert, b. Aug. 26, '52. 6, Albert M., b. April 28, '55, d. O. 5, '58. 7, Alice M., b. May 15, '59. 8, Cora Ella, b. J. 16, '61.

Henry's ch. 1, Frederic, b. ab. 1852. 2, Merritt Alden, b. Oct. '60.

Erastus's ch. 1, Irene C., b. June 28, 1844. 2, Oliver G., b. Sept. 5, '47. 3, Adelaide W. b. Jan. 15, '57. 4, Ettie K., b. May 18, '59.

G. Washington's ch. 1, Elizabeth A., b. ab. 1846. 2, William G., b. ab. '49.

LERVEY, Capt. William, J., b. ab. 1824; m. Emily P. Snow, Jan. '47; r. Rock. Their ch. 1, Melvin F., b. ab. '48. 2, Abby C., b. ab. '51. 3, George, b. ab. '53. 4, John, b. ab. '56.

LEVENSALER, or Lebensaler, Adam, of German descent, b. Nov. 1773, c. from Waldoboro' to Th., before 1798; mar. Mary Turner of Wal., p. May 2, 1798, and d. June 16, 1849. Mary, his wife, a supposed descendant of one of the Mayflower pilgrims, d. Sept. 21, 1853, a. 79 years and 10 months. Their ch. 1, Barden T., b. 1798, mar. Ann J. Robinson, Aug. 21, 1828 ; r. Th., and died June 4, '52. 2, Hon. Atwood, b. Nov. 8, '99, mar. Nancy Coombs, Jan. 28, 1831; r. Th., a merchant, councillor, 1842, and '43, &c. 3, Lincoln, b. April 30, 1801, m. Angelina Jenks, 1834; r. Th., and d. on homestead, Jan. 12, '63. 4, Julia S., b. Oct. 25, '02, m. Thomas Howard; r. W. 5, Capt. Caleb, b. Aug. 14, '04, mar. Harriet Gilchrist of C., p. June 9, 1832; r. Th. 6, Leanora, b. Sept. 15, '06, m. William H. P. McLellan, Nov. 10, '33; r. N. O. 7, Elsie K., b. Jan. 14, '09 ; r. Th., and d. at W., Aug. 12, '62. 8, Michal, b. Nov. 19, '10, d. March 2, '17. 9, Sarah F., b. Dec. 17, '13, m. John S. Coburn; r. Rock. 10, Capt. Orris, b. Jan. 17, '17; perished by shipwreck, Feb. 11, '43.

Barden T.'s ch. 1. William B., b. June 10, 1829, mar. Anastasia Hanley of Bristol, Dec. 18, '59; r. Boston, a mariner. 2, Hester A., b. March 11, '31, d. Sept. 23, '42. 3, Edward R., b. April 21, '33; r. Th., a painter, &c. 4, Thomas H., b. Nov. 12, '34 ; r. Th., a mariner, entered the navy.

Hon. Atwood's ch. 1, Dr. Henry C., born April 15, 1831 ; M. D. Bowd. Coll., 1856 ; r. and practised med., St. George; appointed asst. surgeon of the 19th Me. Regt., promoted surgeon of the 8th Me. Regt., &c. 2, Mary T., b. Oct. 15, '32, m. Thomas S. Andrews of W., Nov. 30, '63 ; r. Th. 3, John C., b. May 7, '35; r. Th., Cashier of Georges Bank. 4, Augusta, b. Jan. 7, '37. 5, Adam P., b. April 13, '39; r. Th., a mariner. 6, Atwood J., b. March 3, '41. 7, Orris, b. ab. '43, d. Oct. 1, '64. 8, Nancy I., b. ab. '45. 9, Lucius C., b. Jan. 8, '50, d. Jan. 20, '54.

Lincoln's ch. 1, Frederic, r. Th., a mariner. 2, George D., b. Dec. 13, 1836; r. Th., a clerk, &c. 3, Julia F., b. Oct. 28, '38; r. Boston. 4, Francis, b. ab. '40. 5, Sarah A., b. April 6, '42, and died July 26, '43. 6, Charles L., b. ab. '43. 7, Caleb, (2d). 8, Lydia. 9, Thomas J., b. Jan. 18, '46, d. Sept. 29, '58. 10, Catharine, b. Oct. 5, '47, d. Sept. 21, '48. 11, John West, b. ab. '50.

Caleb's ch. 1, Elsie, b. Sept. 28, 1832, mar. Edmund B. Chapman; r. Th. 2, Olive R., b. Nov. 11, '34, m. Capt. James F. Chapman; r. Th. 3, Joseph G., b. April 19, '37; r. Th., a mariner. 4, Harriet, b. ab. '44. 5, Raymond, b. ab. '50.

William R.'s ch. Florence N., b. April, 1860.

LEVENSALER, Joel, b. ab. 1810 in Waldoboro'; mar. Susan D., Healey, Oct. 4, '33; r. Th., a marble worker, and died Feb. 5, '53. Their ch. 1, Dodge H., b. May 15, 1836, mar. Bertha A. Hall, Nov. 11,'58; r. Th., a mason. 2, Winfield, b. April 8, '39, d. Oct. 3, '43. 3, Mary Elizabeth, b. —— 23, '41; r. Th.

Dodge H.'s ch. Caroline F., b. ab. 1859.

LEWIS, Thomas, b. ab. 1804; m. Caroline S. ——; r. S. Th., a stone cutter. Their ch. Caroline M., b 1839; r. S. Th., a teacher.

LEWIS, Capt. James H., b. ab. 1824, in Bucksport, Me.; m. Clara Howes; r. Rock. Their ch. 1, Charles H., b. Oct. 24, 1854, d. June 28, '63, by drowning. 2, John W., b. April 4, '58.

LIBBEY, Joseph C., b. ab. 1806, in Limington, Me.; m. Lois M. Waterhouse; r. Rock., a merchant. Their ch. 1, Frederic W., b. ab. 1828; m. Abby W. Colby, Aug. 27, '49; r. Rock., musician in 6th Me. Reg., since in navy. 2, Helen, b. 1830, d. Nov. 13, '54. 3, Capt. Edwin, b. Feb. 28, '32; m. Mary F. Cook, Sept. 9, '56; r. Rock., officer in 4th Me., killed in battle of Wilderness, May 5, '64. 4, Capt. Arthur L., b. Dec. 29, '34; m. Ellen F. ——; r. Rock., officer in 4th Me. Reg., &c. 5, Lucius H., b. May 28, '39; r. Rock., a tin plate dealer. 6, Charles A., b. Aug. 24, '42; r. Rock., soldier in 4th Me., &c. 7, Frank Cobb, b. ab. 1844, a mariner.

Capt. Arthur L.'s ch. 1, Ella M., b. Aug. 19, 1855, d. Sept. 26, '56. 2, William A., b. ab. '57.

LIBBEY, Samuel, b. ab. 1786, son of Eliakim of Warren; m. Nancy Crawford, Dec. 13, 1812; rem. Rock., a merchant, &c. His wife, b. March 20, 1789, in W., d. Sept. 27, 1864. Their ch. 1, (adopted), Frances, r. Rock. Of the sons of James of Warren; 1, Alexander, (2d), b. ab. 1817; m. Margaret Jordan; r. Rock., a shipbuilder, rem. South. Their ch. 1, Eliza E. H. V., b. ab. 1843. 2, James A., b. ab. '57. 3, Virginia F., b. April 15, '59, d. Sept. 23, '60.

LIBBEY, Charles A., b. ab. 1822; m. Sarah A. ——; r. Rock., professor of music, asst. superintendent of State Reform School. Their ch. 1, Charles A., (2d), b. ab. 1848. 2, Sarah F, b. ab. '50.

LIBBEY, Michael, r. Th., some years, a merchant; m. Rebecca Frances Copeland of W., Nov. 6, 1843; rem. Boston.

LIDDY, Michael, c. from Limerick, Ireland, with Mary, his wife, to Th. in 1835 or '6, & d. Sept. 22, '49. Their ch. 1, John, came over with his parents, and d. June 21, '51, killed, blasting lime rock. 2, James, b. March 13, '31; r. Th., an ostler, &c. 3, Michael, (2d), b. ab. '37; r. Th., a mariner.

LINCOLN, Luther, c. from Hillsboro', N. H.; r. Th. unm., was a mason, merchant, lime inspector, &c., & d. Oct. 3, 1852. Isaac Watt, a brother, b. 1784; m. Susanna K. Keith, Jan. 2, 1806; r. Th., a mason, and d. Aug. 18, 1837. Isaac W.'s ch. 1, Joanna T., b. Oct. 12, 1810; m. David Cotton, Aug. 7, '30; r. Hope. 2, Ruth, b. May 20, '12; m. Jesse Tibbets; r. New Sharon. 3, Isaac, (2d), b. Sept. 6, '14, d. Oct. 19, '34. 4, Angerana, b. May 10, '16; m. 1st, Moses H. Cobbett of Belfast, Feb. 27, '31, 2d, James Tarbox of Th., &. rem. Lynn. 5, Jeanette, b. May 10, '18; m. W. Ramsdell; r. Roxbury, Mass. 6, John, b. Jan. 12, '20, d. July 31, '46. 7, Susan, b. Dec. 24, '23; m. Levi Cooper; r. Woburn, Mass. 8, Sarah, b. March 22, '25; mar. Cyrus S. Waterman of Hope, May 31, '45.

LINDSEY, John, b. in Old York about 1735; removed at the close of the French and Indian war to Fox Islands; m. Susanna Robinson; settled, r. and d. at what is now Rockland. Their ch. 1, Nathaniel, b. Sept. 8, 1768; m. Experience Ames of Fox Is., p. March 24, '92; r. S. Th., & d. Rock., Aug. 22, 1850. 2, John, (2d), b. May 20, '70; m. Miss Snow in Hampden; r. Frankfort and Bangor. 3, Martha, b. May 6, '72; m. William Perry; r. and d. Hope. 4, Samuel, born July 5, '74; m. Betsey Godding, Jan. 23, 1804; r. Rock., lost at sea. 5, Patience, b. July 19, '76; m. John Hastey, March 16, 1809. 6, Susanna, b. May 25, '80; m. Constant Rankin; rem. Frankfort. 7, Betsey, b. Aug. 24, '86; m. Robert Murdough, d. Dec. 29, 1808. 8, George, b. April 29, '92; mar. Rachel Simonton, Nov. 19, 1815, 2d, Sarah A. (Pillsbury) Cook, p. Jan. 31, 1835; r. Rock., landlord of the Lindsey House, &c.

Nathaniel's ch. 1, Capt. John, (3d), b. March 20, 1793; m. Elionai Crockett, Feb. 21, 1821; lost at sea, Aug. 1830. 2, Anna, born Nov. 15, '94; r. California. 3, Mary, b. Jan. 15, '98; m. Dea. Henry Ingraham; r. Rock. 4, Rebecca, b. Oct. 20, '99; r. Rock. & d. March, 1861. 5, Elethea, b. April 15, 1803; m. Theodore Howard; r. Rock. 6, Mark, b. ab. 1805; m. Mary Rankin, Oct. 30, '28; r. Rock., rem. Northport. 7, Sarah, b. July 20, '07; mar. Capt. Jesse Kalloch; r. Rock., and d. April 28, '58. 8, Priscilla, m. William T. Saywood; r. Rock., and d. Nov. 30, '52.

Of John, (2d)'s ch. 1, John, (4th), b. ab. 1814; m. Elsie J. Ellis, Oct. 4, 1840; r. Rock., a joiner. 2, Eliza Snow, b. June 18, '21, died at Rock., Jan. 16, '63.

Samuel's ch. 1, Thomas, b. Oct. 25, 1804, d. unm. 2, Capt. Israel, m. Harriet Prescott; rem. Bath. 3, Elsie, b. May, 1808; mar. Capt. John Bently, (2d), r. Th. and died May 30, '47; 4, Lucy, mar. John Pease, now deceased.

George's ch. 1, Olive A., b. Sept. 17, 1816; m. Comfort S. Keen; r. Rock. 2, Harriet S., b. Jan. 20, '20; mar. Samuel I. Thomas; r. Rock. 3, Clarissa E., b. Oct. 25, '28; r. Rock. 4, George N., born Nov. 26, '30; r. Rock. By 2d wife. 5, Joseph O., b. Dec. 8, '37, d. July 11, 1857.

Capt. John, (2d)'s ch. 1, Almira, born Nov. 28, 1821; mar. Capt. Azariah Stanley; r. Rock. 2, Caroline B., b. Dec. 13, '24; m. Alvah Hamilton; r. Rock. 3, Frances H., b. June 22, '29; d. March 17, '46. 4, Nancy, b. April 15, '34; r. Rockland.

Mark's ch. 1, Sarah F., b. March 19, 1830; m. Robert P. Havener of Frankfort, May 2, '47. 2, Marcia A., b. Feb. 8, '32; mar. John E. Moore, July 30, '54; and d. June 4, '56. 3, Elizabeth F., b. Nov. 13, '34; r. Rock. 4, John B., b. May 17, '39; 5, Edward, b. ab. 1843; 6, Talbot, b. ab. 1846; 7, Henry, b. ab. 1850; all rem. Northport.

John, (4th)'s ch. 1, Susan M., b. Aug. 26, 1841. 2, Edith J., b. ab. '52. 3, Frank Ellis, b. Feb. 26, '57, d. March 28, '59.

LINDSEY; there were also of this name, & probably connected with the foregoing, Sarah, b. ab. 1805; r. S. Th.; also Edwin, b. ab. '39; r. S. Th., a soldier of 4th Me. reg., d. Aug. 16, '62, at St. Luke's hospital, N. Y., of fever; also, Henry, b. ab '45; r. S. Th.

LINNEKIN, David. c. from St. George; m. Rachel Wheeler of St. G.; r. Th., on the Finley Kelloch lot. Their ch. 1, Angeline. 2, George. 3, Clara. 4, Barbara. 5, Charles.

LINNEKIN, Joshua S., b. in Appleton; m. Marietta Richardson, May 7, 1859 ; r. Th., a cooper.

LINN, Peter, b. ab. 1832; c. from Ireland with Ellen, his wife, r, Rock., a gas worker. Their ch. 1, James, b. ab. '58. 2, Annie, b. ab. '59.

LINNELL, Elisha, c. from Palermo, Me.: m. Emily S. Counce, Sept. 17, 1847; r. Th., a merchant, & d. July 18, '64. Their ch. 1, ———, b. Feb. 17, & d. Oct. 12, '51. 2, Charles C., b. ab.. '57. 3, Herbert, b. '59.

LINSCOTT, James C., b. ab. 1832, m. Nancy P. Butler, p. Jan. 27, '49; r. Th., a farmer, & rem. Their ch. 1, Sarah J., b. ab. '51. 2, William, b. ab. '53. 3, James W., b. ab. '55. 4, Cora E., b. ab. '57.

LISCOMB, Nathaniel, b. ab. 1806, c. from Cape Elizabeth in '25; m. Barbara Blackington, p. Feb. 16, '30, 2d, Nancy H. Kelleran, Oct. 15, '38; r. Th., a stove and tin plate dealer, &c. His ch. by 1st wife. 1, Orlando, b. Feb. 1, '28, d. Feb. 8, '38. 2, Abby M., m. Joel Emery, Jr. of Eden, Dec., '49. 3, John T., b. Sept. '31, d. Feb. 15, '32. 4, Olive, b. July, '36; m. Arthur J. Hatch; r. Th. By 2d wife, 5, Hezekiah C., b. March, 1840; r. Th., a soldier of 4th Me. reg. &c. 6, Eveline A., b. ab. '45. 7, Ettie F., b. ab. 1847.

LITCHFIELD, Benjamin, b. 1782; c. from Lewiston; m. Nancy McLellan; r. C. and U., and rem. Rock. 1854. Their ch. 1, Eliza Jane, b. in C., Sept. 30, 1810; m. Asa Morse; r. Rock. 2, Benjamin, (2d), born Aug. 26, 1812; mar. Ruth P. Williams of Orono, learned clothier's trade in W., r. Rock., a corn and flour dealer. 3, Simon M. C., b. ab. 1816; m. 1st, Rebecca Crockett, Feb. 10, '45; 2d, Hannah Clark, Jan. 3, '53; r. Rock., a joiner, &c. 4, Nancy M., m. Winslow Litchfield; r. Boston. 5, Orrin, d. young. 6, Almeda, b. Aug. 1818; m. Capt. John M. Coombs; r. Th., and d. Sept. 23, '43. 7, Matilda, mar. 1st, Capt. John M. Coombs, 2d, William Hopkins, r. Brewer. 8, Electa A., m. Hermon Mero; r. W. 9, Albee K., mar. Cerena Young of Cam., r. Boston. 10, Alden, m. Mary B. Allen of Hope, May 6, '55; r. Rock., a clerk, quartermaster of 20th Me. reg. 11, Silas C., b. 1834; r. Boston.

Benjamin, (2d)'s ch. 1, Capt. Julius B., b. Feb. 19, 1839; m. Helen A. Coombs, r. Rock., an officer in army, long an inmate of a rebel prison, though making many bold attempts to escape. 2, Henry A., b. Aug. 17, '41, a clerk. 3, Frederic P., b. Jan. 23, '44. 4, Emma C., b. April 16, '46. 5, Georgiana F., b. ab. 1849.

Simon M. C.'s ch. 1, Rebecca C. H. A., b. ab. 1846. 2, Ella, born ab. '56. 3, Edward M., b. April, and d. July 20, 1861.

LITTLE, Micajah, b. in Hampstead, Oct., 1762; m. Sarah Noyes of Atkinson, N. H., 2d, Miss Pottle of Kingston, N. H., r. Newburyport, came here, kept tavern, awhile, at Rockland, and died May 26, 1850. John, a cousin, m. Sarah Little of Atkinson, settled in Union, & d. Oct. 21, 1855. Micajah's ch. by 1st wife. 1, Mary, mar. a Mr. Kimball; r. Haverhill. 2, Eliza, b. ab. 1787; m. John Lovejoy; r. Rock. 3, Relief, m. Mr. Pingree, r. Newburyport. Others by 2d wife.

LONG, Michael, b. ab. 1736, m. and r. on the Finley Kelloch place, & d. in St. George, Oct., 1826, a. 90. Of his ch. 1, Catharine,

m. William Biskey. 2, Mary, m. a Simmons. 3, ? Betsey, born Aug. 15, 1783; m. Preserved Willis; r. Th. 4, Capt. Madding, m. and r. St. George. 5, Fanny, m. a Wyllie. ? 6, Capt. Dennis, b. May, 1797; m. Calista Healey, Feb. 11, 1819; r. Th., & d. June 27, '32.

Of Capt. Maddings's ch. 1, Capt. Edward, b. ab. 1822; m. Lucretia M. Coombs, Feb., 1860; r. Thomaston.

Dennis's ch. 1, Sylvanus H., b. Dec. 19, 1819, m. Eliza J. Wormell, April 22, '48; r. Th., and d. March 9, '61; killed by a premature explosion in lime quarry of Munroe, when touching off a seam blast. 2, Capt. Henry N., b. Nov. 3, '23, mar. Hannah C. Crane of W., July 7, '64; r. Th. 3, Meritt A., born April 8, '30, died Oct. 18, '32. 4, Americus N., b. May 6, '35, mar. Mary C. Whitney, Oct. 19, '50; r. Th. 5, Martha A. A., b. Feb. 24, and d. Oct. 3, '32.

Capt. Edward's ch. George, b. ab. 1851.

Sylvanus H.'s ch. 1, Almira, b. ab. 1849. 2, Henry N., b. March 4, died June 20, '50. 3, Alden, b. ab. '52. 4, Edgar, b. ab. '55. 5, Mary, b. ab. '59.

LONG, John, came from Martha's Vineyard, m. and r. in Cushing, had one son, Abraham, who, on his mother's 2d marriage with Capt. John Stizaker, was brought up by him, m. and r. C., but was drowned at Watson's Pt., May 27, 1803. Abraham's ch. 1, Hannah, mar. John McKenny; r. Rock. 2, John, (2d), d. at Mobile or on his passage thence.

LONG, Cynthia, born ab. 1815; r. Rock., a widow. Her ch. 1, Roscoe, b. ab. 1840, a mariner. 2, Theresa H., b. ab. '44. 3, Owen, b. ab. '47. 4, Henry, b. ab. '49.

LONG, Lieut., Hezekiah, an officer in 20th Me. Regt., now in Grant's army; r. Th., with Sarah H., his wife, and of their ch. 1, Frederic W., b. Nov. 16, 1852, died June 26, '64, by drowning in a lime quarry, at Rock.

LONGLEY, Rufus, b ab. 1830, m. Abby A. Saunders, April 26, '55; r. Rock., a mariner. Their ch. 1, Helen E., born ab. 1856. 2, Narcissa R., b. ab. '59. 3, Abby, b. Sept. 28, '62, d. June 8, '63.

LORD, Sabine, b. ab. 1826, in Surry, Me., m. Abby S. Swett; r. Rock., a joiner, &c. Andrew J., b. ab. 1831, mar. Susan F. (Penneman) Cook; r. Rock., a shipwright, rem. California. Sabine's ch. 1, Lilla D,. b. Feb. 1848, d. Nov. 4, '59. 2, Sabine F., b. ab. '51. 3, William S., b. ab. '54. 4, Otis A., b. ab. '54. 5, Herbert M., b. ab. '59.

LORING, Charles, c. from North Yarmouth, m. Sarah E. (Haskell) Fales, p. July 3, 1833, was a merchant many years in Th., but rem. to Portland, and d. Nov., 1856. J. G. Loring, a brother, bought Charles's stock of goods and went to trading in Th., Dec. 1829. Charles's ch. 1, George B., b. Sept. 19, 1834. 2, Sarah E., b. Oct. 9, '35. 3, Emma.

LORING, Jacob B., b. ab. 1834, in Perry, m. Caroline Young, of Th., Aug. 8, '54; r. Th., a joiner, and orderly sergeant in 1st Me. Cavalry. Their ch. 1, Susan, b. ab. 1855. 2, Cora, b. ab. '57. 3, Etta, b. ab. '59.

LOTHROP, Benjamin W., born in Searsmont, Jan 10, 1822, mar, Francis A. Washburn; c. here from Belfast; r. Rock., a merchant, &c. Capt. Sumner P., a brother, b. ab. 1826, also r. Rock., acting master, U. S. N,, died in Boston, June 15, '63. Benjamin W.'s ch. Carrie B., b. Oct. 1852.

LOTHROP; of this name, but of a different family, are also, 1, Thomas, b. ab. 1815, m. Lucy ——; r. Rock., a lime manufacturer. 2, Charles, b. ab. 1825, m. Frances ——; r. Rock., a lime burner. 3, George, b. ab. 1831, m. Helen ——; r. Rock., a lime burner. 4, John H., b. ab. '31, m. Ursilla Davis, April 12, '53; r. Rock., a lime burner. 5, Lorenzo D., b. ab. 1835, m. Anna Bryant, p. Feb. 1, '50; r. Rock., a lime burner, member of coast guards, &c.

George's ch. Edward, b. ab. 1856

John H.'s ch. 1, John T., b. ab. 1855. 2, Franklin C., b. Nov., 1856, d. April 16, 1858.

Lorenzo D's ch. 1, Lewis S., b. ab. 1852. 2, Luella V., b. about '56. 3, Mary A., b. Jan., 1859, d. Oct. 6, '61.

LOURRAINE, Peter, b. in Smyrna, ab. 1831; r. Rock., a stevedore, with Francesca M, his wife. Their ch. 1, Ella F., b. ab. 1855, 2, Jennie N., b. ab. '57. 3, Edith.

LOVE, Andrew, b. ab. 1814, in Ireland; m. Elizabeth ——; r. Rock., a lime burner. Their ch. 1, Edward, b. ab. 1841; r. Rock., a clerk, &c. 2, Ellen, b. ab. '48. 3, Albert C., b. ab. 1856.

LOVEJOY, John, b. 1778, in Andover, Mass.; c. to reside in what is now Rock., May 6, 1803; m. Eliza Little of Newburyport, p. Sept. 22, 1807; was long one of the active business men and merchants of Rock., & d. Oct. 17, '43. Dr. Enoch, a brother, b. 1783; stud. med. in Andover, Me., c. somewhat later; m. 1st, Martha Tilson, March 26, '12, 2d, Mrs. Margaret Porterfield, p. Nov. 6, '37; prac. med. many yrs. in Rock., and d. Nov. 17, '48. Their brother, Stephen, m. and r. in Andover, & his dau. Sarah, d. here, Sept. 10, '35, aged 22. John's ch. 1, John G., b. April 15, 1808; m. Margaret B. Bradley of Haverhill, p. Sept. 17, '36; r. Rock., a merchant. 2, Arthur, b. March 17, '12; m. Mary H. Reed of Orono; r. Rock., an expressman. 3, Benjamin H., b. 1814, d. April 24, '37. 4, Samuel I., b. April 21, '17; m. Mary A. Chandler, Jan. 6, '41; r. Rock., a commission broker. 5, Edward L., b. Dec. 17, '19; m. Margaret E. Porter of Cam.; r. Rock., a restaurateur, &c. 6, Francis P., b. April 17, '22; r. Rock., and d. suddenly in the stage coach, Dec. 20, '58. 7, Eliza A., b. April 21, '27, d. Oct. 20, '47.

Dr. Enoch's ch. 1, Abiel Wheaton, b. May 1, 1813; m. Eliza L. Russ; r. Cam. 2, Edwin P., b. 1815; m. Elioenai W. Robbins, p. Jan. 16, '38; r. Rock., a milk dealer in 1860. 3, Charles C., b. Feb. 23, '18; m. Caroline Keizer, May 20, '49; r. Rock., a quarry man, &c. 4, William F., b. Oct. 16, '25; m. Martha A. Hilt, Feb. 4, '55; r. Bethel, Me., a hotel keeper. 5, Helen A., b. June 6, '29; m. Leonard Benner; r. Rock. 6, Amasa P., b. Feb. 9, 34. ?

John G.'s ch. 1, George G., b. Oct. 3, 1839; a clerk. 2, Abby A., b. May 8, '42. 3, Joseph B., b. July, 1844, was employed in a Coast survey sch. in going aboard of which, Sept. 15, '62, the boat capsized and he was drowned. 4, Charles H., b. ab. '54.

Arthur L.'s ch. 1, Mary E., b. Sept. 1, 1841. 2, Sarah L., b. Jan. 6, '44. 3, Arthur Hazen, b. Aug. 31, '45, d. Feb. 11, '47. 4, Arthur G., b. June 20, '47. The mother d. March 21, '62, aged 41.

Samuel I's ch. 1, John, (2d), b. Dec. 22, 1842; r. Rock. 2, Samuel, b. ab. '44. 3, Henry L., b. ab. '45. 4, Herbert, b. ab. '47. 5, Frank C., b. ab. '57.

Edward L.'s ch. Seth F., b. ab. 1859.

Abiel W.'s ch. 1, Mary E. 2, Adelia.

Edwin P.'s ch. 1, Oliver E., b. June 12, 1841, d. March 5, '42. 2, Martha N., b. Oct. 9, '42; m. Thomas B. Spear; r. Rock. 3, Willie Tilson, b. Aug. 15, '53, d. April 28, '58. 4, Albion or Alvan W., b. ab. '46. 5, Sarah, b. ab. '51.

Charles C.'s ch. 1, Laura A., b. Nov. 13, '53, d. March 9, '56. 2, Ira T., b. ab. '57.

William T.'s ch. 1, Ferrand.? 2, William.

LOVETT, Capt. Israel, c. early to what is now S. Th.; m. Joanna Jordan; was a ship master; rem. after a long residence here, & d. in Lincolnville, April 6, 1825, aged 83. Their ch. 1, Bartholomew, m. Hannah Fling, p. Feb. 3, 1792; rem. Hallowell, and d. in Jefferson, aged 99 yrs. 2, Israel, (2d), m. Rebecca Dolliver, p. Aug. 21, 1794; and d. by drowning at Hallowell. 3, John J , m. Reliance Brown, p. March 8, 1798, & rem. 4, Sally, m. Leonard Wade, rem. Union. 5, Simon, m. Miss Decker; r. and built in Warren, rem. thence to Portland and thence to eastern part of State. 6, Mary, b. 1761; m. Col. John Glidden of Damariscotta, Jan. 27, 1812, and d. Oct. 1, 1829; buried at S. Th. 7, Jordan, app'd to joiner's trade, 1792, lost at sea with Capt. Dunning. 8, Ephraim, settled in St. Geo.; mar. Sophia Sherman, Nov. 5, 1813; rem. and d. Hope. 9, Robert, b. 1770; m. Nancy Martin, Nov. 21, 1799; rem. and d. Lincolnville. 10, Joseph, m. and r. Newburyport, Mass.

Of Israel, (2d)'s ch. 1, Jordan, (2d), m. Mrs. Katy Godding, Dec. 15, 1815; lost at sea with Capt. Archibald Coombs; his widow mar. Peter Houerman of Boston, p. Oct. 14, '23. 2, Stephen, a rigger, m. and with his wife r. for a time in Th., where was recorded the birth of their ch., Sally Ann, b. Dec. 18, 1824.

Of Ephraim's ch. 1, Albert G., b. ab. 1827; m. Adelaide Sleeper, Oct. 25, 1852, 2d, Anna A. Brown, Oct, 1857; r. Rock., a joiner. 2, Capt. Edwin; and probably others.

Robert's ch. 1, Mary, b March 2, 1801; m ——— Sweetland; r. Linc. 2, Margaret, b. Jan. 15, '03; m. Nathaniel B. Maddocks; r. S. Th. 3, Richard M., b. Feb. 8, '04; m Sally Martin of St. G.; r. Linc.

Albert G.'s ch. by 2d wife. Eva L., b. ab. 1859.

LOWE, Thomas, b. ab. 1801, in Vassalboro', Me.; m. 1st, Sarah B. Clifford, 2d, L. Adeliza Sterling, Feb. 25, 1850; r. Th., a shoemaker, soldier of 4th Me. Reg., &c. His ch. by 1st wife. 1, Augustus T., b. ab. 1825; m. Eunice P. Achorn of Camden; r. Rock., teacher of Grammar school 12 or more years, alderman, &c. 2, John Edward, r. & trades in Omaha, Nebraska. 3, Nancy C., m. Edward H. Orbeton; r. Rock. 4, Cordelia F., b. in Freedom, d. young in Cam. By 2d wife. 5, Clarence R., b. ab. '52. 6, Albion A., b. ab. '55.

Augustus T.'s ch. 1, Harriet A., b. ab. 1850. 2, Clara E., b. ab. '52. 3, William C., b. ab. '55. 4, Castera, b. ab. '59.

LOWELL, Rosamus, b. 1762; c. from Amesbury, Mass.; m Deborah Keen of Th., p. Jan. 24, 1786; r. S. Th., a farmer, "of regular and unimpeachable life," & d. July 27, 1829. Their ch. 1, Reuben B., b. Aug. 25, 1786, d. Sept. 14, 1812. 2, Rosamus K., b. Aug. 3, 1788; m. Lois Bartlett; rem. Farmington. 3, Hannah, b. Dec. 23, '90; m. Lieut. Ebenezer Childs, July 16, 1810; r. & d. Farmington. 4, Charles, Esq., b. Oct. 1, '93; stud. law, rem. Lubec ab. 1814; m. Sarah L. Hewett of Cam., May 11, '17, 2d, Mary Crawford of Castine; rem. Ellsworth and in 1826 established the *Independent Courier*, prac. law, r. and d. there. 5, Archibald C., b. Oct. 1, '95; mar. 1st,

Lucy Emery, p. May 17, 1817; rem. & m. 2d, in the British provinces. 6, Simeon, b. May 17, '97, d. June 14, '98. 7, Rev. Josiah J., b. May 10, '99; m. & r. a preacher in State of N. York. 8, Hon. Joshua A., b. March 20, 1801; stud. law and rem. to East Machias before Dec., 1823; m. there, Miranda Turner, Jan., 1827; has been representative to Congress, &c. 9, Mary, b. Jan. 14, and d. Nov. 28, '03. 10, Hon. Henry C., b. Sept. 1, '04; stud. law, m. Mercy Maker, July 27, '24; r. & prac. law in Rock. many years; rem. Faribault, Min., where he was Judge of the lower court, and d. suddenly, March 19, 1863. 11, Hon. Simeon B., b. July 29, '06; stud. law; m. Marion S. Goss, June 1, '28; r. & prac. law in Orono, is Judge of Probate, &c. 12, Lucy, m. Capt. Jonathan Post, d. May 29, '34.

Charles's ch. by 1st wife. 1, Julia A. H., b. July, 1818, d. at Rock. Jan. 3, '39. 2. Adelia Maria, b. '20; m. Robert Butcher; r. Galena, Ill., & d. May 3, '57.

Hon. Henry C.'s ch. 1, Agnes R., b. Feb. 5, 1825; m. William L. Pitts; rem. to his native S. C., where he is commissary in rebel army. 2, Rosamus C., b. Aug. 3, '26; m. Justina A. Beattie, May 22, '44; r. Rock., & d. April 9, '56. 3, Reuben K., b. Dec. 13, '27; m. Nancy A. Morgan, April 2, '48; r. Faribault. 4, Charles L., Esq., b. Oct. 3, '29; m. Georgiana Berry, May 29, '51; r. & prac. law Faribault. 5, Maria S., b. May 10, '31, d. Feb. 24, '38. 6, Caroline A., b. May 27, '36; r. Faribault.

Hon. Simeon B.'s ch. 1, Martha Ann, b. May 4, 1829. 2, John Q. A., b. Sept. 3, '30; 3, Daniel G., b. April 15, '33; 4, Miranda S., b. Dec. 7, '34, all rem.

Rosamus C.'s ch. 1, Julia, b. ab. 1846. 2, Joseph Hewett, b. March '47, d. Sept. 20, '49. 3, Oliver, b. ab. '55.

LOWELL, Benjamin A., Esq., c. from Hope, & r. some 5 or 6 y'rs in Th., a teacher, lawyer, &c., but rem. Illinois. Martha A., his wife, d. here, June 28, 1858, a. 35.

LUCE, Capt. Andrew G., b. in 1811, in North Haven, Me.; m. Rebecca Spear, Sept. 9, 1837; r. Rock. & d. Feb. 1860, of yellow fever. Their ch. 1, Capt. William Henry, b. Oct. 1, '39; m. Eliza U., dau. of S. D. Carlton of Cam., Jan. 3, '65; r. Rock., a ship master, lately in U. S. navy. 2, Mary F., b. April 16, '42. 3, Eliza E., b. ab. '46. 4, Charles E., b. ab. '54.

LUDWIG, Jacob, Esq., b. in Ninderrotte, Province of Dentz, Germany, in 1730; left there June, 1753, with his parents, Jose & Catharine (Klein) Ludwig, brother, Capt. Jos. Henry, (then 15 years old, who m. Catharine Eliz. Kaler, r. & d. Wal.,) & only sister, Margaretta, in Waldo's colony of sixty other families; touched at Cowes, Isle of Wight, where his father and several other passengers died and were buried on the coast of France, — arrived at Broad Bay, now Wal., in Sept. following; was the first town clerk, and selectman of the place, having a good German education, and after a time acquired English; was a joiner, served as sergeant in French and Indian war, as captain in 1776 at Machias; m. Margaret Hilt, and d. Jan. 1, 1826, a. 91 yrs., 5m. Their ch. 1, Catharine Elizabeth, m. Christian Hoffsis; r. Wal., and d. ab. 1846, a. 87. 2, Eliza, b. April 19, 1764, mar. Moses Robinson; r. and d. W. 3, Eve Catharine, m. Mathias Havener; r. and died Wal., a. 81. 4, Joseph Henry, (2d), b Feb. 2, '67, m. Sarah Winchenbach; r. and d. Wal. 5, Catharine, m. Charles Kaler, r. & d. Wal., a. 80. 6, Jane, m. Christopher Walch, and d. with her first child, a. 20. 7, Katy, b. March 5, '74, m. Michael Reed of St. Stephens, N. B. 8, Col. Jacob, b. Oct. 10, '76, m. Susan Hutchins, of C. r. and died Wal.,—the shortest period allotted to either of this large family, aside from Mrs. Walch, being 80 yrs., and the longest 95 yrs.

Of Joseph Henry, (2d)'s ch. Godfrey, b. ab. 1822; mar. Rebecca ——; r. Rock., a lime burner, &c.

Col. Jacob's ch. 1, Dr. William, b. 1798, M. D. Bowd. Coll. 1825; m. Lucy Whitney of Linc., Nov. 27, '29; r. and prac. med. Linc. ret. and died in Wal., Oct. 14, '49. 2, Hon. Moses R., b. Wal., ab. 1800; M D. Middlebury Coll., Vt., 1824; m. Sophia Balch of Haverhill, Mass., May 6, '30, 2d, Hannah C. (Robbins) Thomas, Nov. 12, '58; r. and prac. med. in Th. since April 25, '25;* state Senator 1865, &c. 3, Mary, m. Joseph Groton of Wal. 4, Orchard C., b. ab. 1802, mar. S, Jane Rokes of W., pub. July 5, '38; r. Rock., a meat dealer. 5, Bathsheba, b. ab. 1806, mar. James R. Hanley; r. Rock. 6, Newall W., m. Sarah Arnold; r. Wal. 7, Clarissa J., d. in July, 1851. 8, Dr. Gardner, M. D. Bowd. Coll., 1833; m. Elizabeth Lothrop; prac. med. many years in Rock., till 1852, rem., and has a good practice in Portland. 9, Warren, m. Mary C. Smith; r. Boston, a druggist, &c.

Dr. William's ch. 1, Clara W., born Dec., 1830, mar. Stephen R. Dennen of Andover, Mass., Nov. 22. '54. 2, Samuel W., d. in 1849.

Hon. Moses R.'s ch. By 1st wife. 1, Susan M. B., b. March 4, 1831, m. Rev. O. J. Fernald; r. Th. 2, William A. T., b. Aug. 26, and d. Sept. 10, '33. 3, Mary F., born June 16, '35, mar. Edward P. Merrill; r. Boston. 4, Moses M., b. July 15, '37, died at sea, Dec. 6, '58, on board bk. *Aurelia*. 5, Margaret G., b. Feb. 4, '40, d. Aug. 22, '46. The mother d. March 20, 1855, a. 48.

Orchard C.'s ch. 1, Susan E., b. Feb. 15, 1843. 2, Jacob, (3d), b. ab. '45; r. Rock. 3, John, b. ab. '48. 4, Gardner, (2d), b. ab. '50. 5, William, b. ab. '52. 6, Rebecca, b. ab. '55.

Godfrey's ch. Oliver, b. ab. 1853.

LUNT, John S., and Rebecca, his wife, r. Rock., and lost, by death, their ch., Martin, Sept. 25, 1864, aged 1 year.

McALLISTER, John, c. to what is now S. Th., and was here with his wife as early as 1792. Their ch. 1, Joseph, b. Sept. 18, '94; m. Ann ——, in Nova Scotia, where, & in N. B., he r. some time; ret. Rock., a truckman, & d. Feb. 7, 1863. 2, John, (2d), b. in 1796; m. Lydia Mathews; r. Linc. & Rock., & d. Aug. 10, '62. 3, Benjamin, b. 1799; m. & r. Hope, d. in Linc. Feb. 11, '39, from injury in a mill. 4, Mary, b. ab. 1802; m. John Ham; r. Rock 5, Israel, m. in Hope, rem. & d. Cam. 6, Jane, b. ab. 1810; m. John Pillsbury; r. Rock. 7, Lucy, m. —— Hall, now deceased. 8, Charity, m. Jos. Sweet-

* In the autumn of 1851, the Doctor visited Liverpool, London, Paris, Rotterdam, Frankfort, Cologne, and other parts of his *Vader-land*, from whence his letters were published in the Lincoln Miscellany, and re-published by several principal papers in the State; — one paragraph of which gives these impressions of the home of his ancestors. "Germany is a strange country With all its abundance of literature, and the prevalence of education, with, also, freedom of religous opinion, it is far from being a *free* country. The people are despotically ruled by great or petty Princes, and have only here and there a mock form of representative government. The lower classes are entirely destitute of the means of improving their condition. — Though a country from which more of the elements of freedom sprung, than any other, it is now, unquestionably, among the least free of all the nations of Christendom."

land; r. & d. S. Th., 9, Eliza, m. John Milliken of Rockport; r. Boston.

Joseph's ch. 1, John, (3d), b. in Mirimichi, N. B., ab. 1818; m. Abby P. Coombs; r. S. Th., a carpenter. 2, Joseph, (2d), b. ab. '31; r. S. Th., a carpenter, soldier in 1st Me Cavalry, &c.

John, (2d)'s ch. 1, William, b. Dec. 7, 1822, d. in Port au Prince, 1849. 2, Archibald, b. June, 1824. 3, Charles, b. April, 1826, d. in Italy, 1834. 4, Edwin S., b. Sept. 21, '28; m. Sarah E. Thompson of W., p. March 23, '48; r. Rock., a mariner. 5, Sarah S., b. 1830; m. John T. Bow of New Windsor, N. Y., Sept. 28, '61; r Lowell, Mass. 6, Mary Jane, b. 1832; m. William M. Munroe; r. Rock., and died Dec. 11, '55.

John, (3d)'s ch. 1, George A., b. ab. 1851. 2, Caroline, b. ab. '54. 3, Charles, b. ab. '56.

Edwin S.'s ch. 1, Clementine S., b. ab. 1854. 2, Joseph F., b. '56. 3, Cemantha, b. ab. '58.

McCAHORN, Archibald, b. in England ab. 1825; m. Abby W. Rivers, Sept. 8, '54; r. Th., a tailor, soldier in 4th Me., &c. Their ch. 1, Henry, b. ab. 1857. 2, Adelaide, b. ab. 1859.

McCALLUM, Alexander, b. in W. ab. 1800, son of John and Mary (Miller) McCallum from Scotland; m. Mehitable Jones, Nov. 27, '36; a successful ship-builder in W., rem. & continues the business in Th. Their ch. 1, Martha B, b. ab. 1838; m. James H. Flint; r. Th. 2, George B., b. ab. '40; r. Th. 3, Nelson, b. ab. '43. 4, Abbie F., b. ab. '45. 5, Edwin C., b. May 9, '47, died Jan. 16, '58.

McCANN, Simon, b. ab. 1825, in Ireland, as was Mary his wife; r. Rock., a lime burner, soldier of 21st Me. Reg., &c. Their ch. 1, Mary, b. ab. 1851. 2, Kate, b. ab. '54. 3, Hannah, b. ab. '55. 4, Edward, b. '57. 5, Mary, b. ab. '59.

McCARTY, Patrick, b. ab. 1810, in Ireland, as was Hannah his wife; r. Rock., a sawyer, and d. March 11, '61. Their ch. 1, Ellen, b. ab. '49. 2, Daniel, b. ab. '51. 3, Charles, b. '59, d. July 28, '61.

McCARTY, Florence, b. ab. 1812, in Ireland; m. Joanna ———; r. Rock., a lime burner. Their ch. 1, Jeremiah, b. ab. 1844. 2, Mary, b. '46. 3, Ellen, b. ab. '52. 4, Johannah, b. ab. '56.

McCAULIFF, Patrick, b. ab. 1820, in Ireland; m. Mary Bettermere, 1854; r. Rock. Their ch. 1, Sarah, b. ab. 1859. 2, Mary Ellen, b. ab. '60.

McCLURE, Col. Jacob, b. in Ohio, ab. 1832; m. H. Jennie Eldridge; r. Rock., a marble worker, officer in Me. Sharpshooters, &c. Their ch. 1, John B., b. ab. 1857. 2, Fuller I., b. ab. '59. 3, Jennie L., b. June, 1861, d. Nov. 25, '62.

McCOY, Alexander, b. ab. 1816, in Nova Scotia, as was Ann, his wife; r. Rock., a mariner, and perished in the wrecked sch., *Lion*, Dec. 11, '64. Their ch. 1, Catharine J., b. ab. 1843, m. William N. Rackliff; r. Rock. 2, Priscilla, b. ab. '45. 3, James H., b. ab '47.

McDADE, John, b. ab. 1822 in Ireland, as was Mary, his wife; r. Rock., a lime burner. Their ch. 1, Margaret, b. ab. 1853. 2, Catharine, b. ab. '55. 3, Ann M., b. ab. '57. 4, Mary E., b. ab. '59.

McDAVIT, James, b. ab. 1820, in Ireland, as was Mary, his wife; r. Rock., a lime burner, soldier in 4th Me., &c. Their ch. 1, Elizabeth, born ab. 1856. 2, Catharine, b. ab. '57. 3, James, b. ab. '59.

McDONALD. John, b. ab. 1828 in Shubenacatia, N. S., m. Isabella Ellis; r. Th. a ship builder. Their ch. Henry L., b. ab. 1853. 2. Edward, b. ab. '54. 3, John, b. ab. '56, d. in autumn of 1863. 4, an infant, deceased.

McDONALD, Charles, b. Oct., 1824, in England; mar. Mary Dimond, 1854; r. Rock., a blacksmith, and d. May 28, '64. Their ch. 1, Alexander, b. ab. '55. 2, Charles, b. ab. '57. 3, Mary, I., b. ab. '59.

McDONALD, Angus, b. ab. 1821, in N. Brunswick, as was Barbara, his wife; r. Rock., a mariner. Their ch. Geo. W., b. ab. 1859.

McDONALD, Daniel, b. ab. 1830, in Scotland, m. Mary McNaughton, Mar. 6, '57; r. Rock., a quarryman. Their ch. Annie, b. ab. 1858. Of this name, there also came here from Nova Scotia, Hugh McDonald, who was b. ab. 1830; mar. Hannah Sullivan, 1854; r. Th., a carpenter, and has ch. 1, Daniel, b. ab. 1856. 2, Hannah, b. ab. '59;—Also Daniel McDonald, (2d), who was b. ab. 1828, m. Mary Cullinem, 1855; r. Th., a carpenter, and has ch. 1, Mary E, b. ab. 1856. 2, Catharine, b. ab. '58. 3, Flora, b. ab. '60;—Also Angus McDonald, (2d), who was b. ab. 1830, in N. S, m. Bridget Quillering, 1853; r. Th., a mariner, and has ch. 1, Leonora, b. ab. 1857. 2, Hugh, b. ab. '59.

McGLOON, Daniel, b. ab. 1830, in Ireland, as was Ann, his wife; r. Th. Their ch. 1, Mary, b. ab. 1857. 2, William, b. ab. '59. Of this name also came here, Patrick McGloon, b. ab. 1828, in Ireland, m. Mary ——; r. Th. Their ch. 1, Patrick, b. ab. 1856. 2, Mary, b. ab. '59.

McINTOSH, William, c. from Philadelphia, with his wife in the employment of Gen. Knox; r. Th., but after Knox's death rem. and took charge of his grist mill in W., where, after some years, he left home in a desponding mood, and was supposed to have been drowned in Damariscotta Pond. Their ch. 1, Henry, b. ab. 1791; m. Cynthia Collins of C., p. Nov. 26, 1831, 2d, Sarah Robbins, p. Sept. 11, '24, 3d, Eunice Healey, p. Nov. 26, '31; r. Rock., a farmer. 2, Theodore B, b. 1793, d. in Th., Nov. 29, 1820. 3, Augustus, b. ab. 1807; r. Rock., a peddler, &c.

Henry's ch. by 1st wife. 1, William H., b. June 24, 1817; mar. Hannah H. Palmer, Jan 1, '39; r. Rock., a truckman. 2, George A., b. Aug. 13, '19; r. California. 3, Theodore B., b. Dec. 22, '20; m. Melinda H. Turner, Nov. 18, '46; r. Rock., a truckman, &c. 4, Joseph G., b. Feb. 10, '22; r. California. 5, Winthrop C., b. Oct. 7, '22; m. Lucretia Walsh, Oct. 7, '46; r. Rock., a truckman, &c. The mother d. Oct. 25, '22. By 2d wife. 6, Sarah E., b. July, '25, died Sept., '35. 7, Sampson, b. July 2, '27; was captured, as supposed, in California by the Indians, and either killed or held a prisoner. 8, Isaac R., b. May 6, '28; rem. to California, and came over, one of the company of California Cavalry. 9, Hannah E., born Nov., '29, died young. By 3d wife. 10, Elizabeth O., b. Dec. 27, '30; m. Bernard B. Ingraham; r. S. Th. 11, Cynthia I., b. May 8, '35; m. Robert A. B. Arey; r. Rock., and d. March 8, '60.

William H.'s ch. 1, Henry A., b. Feb. 9, 1842; r. Rock., a teamster. 2, Edward, b. ab. '44. 3, Eveline R., b. ab. '46. 4, Sarah E., b. Oct., '52, d. Nov. 30, '54.

Theodore B.'s ch. 1, Frank Hudson, b. Oct. 31, 1848. 2, Sidney T., b. June 11, '53.

Winthrop C.'s ch. 1, Hester M., b. ab. 1847. 2, Ida I., b. ab. '49. 3, Clara F., b. ab. '51. 4, Sarah A., b. ab. '56.

McINTOSH, John H., of a different family; m. Elsie M. Tolman, March 14, 1861; r. Rock.

McINTYRE, Thomas, came from North of Ireland with his wife; m. 2d, Martha (Lampson) Isley, Jan. 8, 1826; r. Th., and d. July 22, '37. His ch. 1, Matthew. 2, James, b. Jan. 20, '20, d. Jan. 2, '54. 3, Mary Ann, m. in Boston. 4, Catharine. 5, ———, b. '24, d. Sept. 20, '25. Of this name also, Peter McIntyre, b. ab. 1836, in Nova Scotia; r. Rock., a lime burner. Catharine, his wife, was born in Ireland. Their ch. Edward W., b. ab. 1859.

McKELLAR, Archibald, b. 1777, son of John & Martha (McCarter) McKellar, Esq., of St. Geo.; m. Jane Robinson, & d. in Rock., Jan. 22, 1863. Their ch. 1, Mary, m. Thomas Richardson, 2d, Capt. Alexander Gilchrist; r. and d. St. Geo. 2, John, (2d), b. ab. 1802; m. Harriet Trussell; r. Th., a brewer, &c. 3, Joseph, d. unm. 4, Betsey, m. Peter Williams, jr., 2d, Capt. Richard Davis; r. F. 5, Catharine, m. Perly Gray; r. & d. St. G. 6, Col. Archibald, b. ab. 1813; m. Catharine Sweetland, Dec. 9, '33, 2d, Caroline M. Bailey, Oct. 19, '51; was P. M. at S. Th., and in business with G. Thorndike; rem. Rock., where he has been city recorder, assistant Postmaster, &c.

John's ch. 1, Mary Emeline, m. Capt. James S. Kelloch; r. S. Th. 2, Jane, b. Nov. 8, '33; m. Andrew J. Hathorn; r. Th., & d. Jan. 23, '53. 3, William J., b. ab. 1843; r. Th., a student.

Col. Archibald's ch. 1, Eliza S., m. Lewis E. Beals; r. Bucksport. 2, James Frederic, b. ab. 1843; vol. soldier. By 2d wife. 3, George A., b. ab. '53. 4, Arthur B. 5, Charles M., b. Sept. 30, '60, died Sept. 14, '63.

McKENNY, John, b. ab. 1803; m. 1st, Sarah ———, 2d, Hannah Long, Feb. 22, '46; r. Rock., & d. March 17, 1853. Recorded, his ch. by 1st wife. 1, Clarissa, b. Aug. 17, '37. Also probably, though not recorded, John McKenny, (2d), who was b. ab. 1827, in Rock.; m. Elionai F. Keneston, Sept. 9, '52; r. Th., a mariner, and has ch. 1, Maria, b. ab. 1853. 2, Clara, b. ab. '55. 3, George, b. ab. '60. A child d. March 3, '62.

McKENNY, Charles, b. ab. 1811; m. Maria ———; r. S. Th., a stone cutter. Their ch. 1, William A., b. ab. 1839; 2, Henry H., b. ab. '41; stone cutters. 3, Frances E., b. ab '43. 4, George E., b. ab. '46. 5, Drusilla M., b. ab. '48. 6, Herbert N., b. ab. '51. 7, Charles, b. ab. '55. Of this name also Melinda McKenny, b. ab. 1816; r. Rock., a widow; and has ch. 1, Henry, b. ab. 1836; r. Rock., a mariner. 2, Mary L., b. ab. '43. 3, George W., b ab. '45. 4, Delia F., b. ab. '47. Also, George H. McKenny, b. ab. 1835; m. Henrietta Swift; r. Rock., a teamster. Of their ch. George F., b. in March, d. Sept. 14, 1860.

McKENNON, Capt. John F., b. ab. 1826; came from Deer Isle; mar. Frances Shaw of Th., Jan. 25, 1843, 2d, Ellen Morey; r. Rock. Their ch. 1, Helena F., b. ab. 1850. The mother d. Sept. 19, '59, aged 33.

McKNIGHT, Capt. Richard, came from Scotland; mar. Caroline Malcolm, April, 1852; r. Th. and Boston. Their ch. Elsie, b. 1854, died Nov. 12, '56.

McLAIN, Alvin, b. ab. 1830, in Appleton; m. Clementine Ulmer,

April 21, '50; r. Rock., a teamster. Their ch. 1, Alden, b. 1852. 2, William, b. '54. 3, Eliza, b. '57. 4, Frederic, b. '59.

McLAUGHLIN, Samuel, b. ab. 1797, in Camden; m. Elizabeth Jameson, p. Feb. 12, 1822, 2d, Sarah (Clough) Jameson, p. Dec. 6, '51; r. Rock. His ch. by 1st wife. 1, Elizabeth, b. Oct. 22, '22; m. John H. Young; r. Rock. 2, Patrick, b. Aug. 2, '24, d. young. 3, Baruch, b. & d. '25. 4, Ruth, b. Jan. 30, '26; m. Capt. D. P. Flye; r. Rock. 5, Isaac, b. May 10, '30; r. Rock. 6, Robert, b. Aug. 17, '32; r. Rock. 7 & 8, twins, b. Nov. 7, '34, Diana & Maria. 9, Samuel, (2d), b. '36. 10, William, b. May 7, '39. 11, John, b. ab. '42.

McLAUGHLIN, Michael, b. ab. 1810, in Ireland, as was Mary, his wife; r. Rock Their ch. 1, John, b. ab. '53. 2, Michael, (2d), b. ab. '56. Of this name, there are also, James McLaughlin, b. ab. '15; c. from Ireland, with Catharine, his wife; r. Rock., & has a ch., William, b. ab. '36, in Ireland, who m. Ellen ———, r. Rock., a dry goods peddler, & who has one ch., John F., b. ab. '59. Also Michael McLaughlin, (2d), b. ab. '30, in Ireland, as was Catharine, his wife; r. Rock. & has ch. 1, Mary, b. ab. '57. 2. Hannora, b. ab. '59. Also, James McLaughlin, (2d), b. ab. 1841, in Ireland; m. Catharine ———; r. Rock., a baker, soldier in 4th Me., &c. Their ch. 1, Ada M., b. ab. '58. 2, James E., b. ab. '60.

McLELLAN, Capt. George, m. Mary Webster of Portland, where he r., was a ship master, & d., lost at sea. Their ch. 1, Rachel, m. John Simonton; r. S. Th., & d. Dec. 3, 1838. 2, Capt. Thomas, b. ab. 1749; m. Hannah Dyer of Portland; c. to what is now S. Th., early; was a ship master, farmer, &c. 3, George, (2d), lost at sea with his father. 4, William, d. on board a prison ship in the revolutionary war. 5, Mary, m. James Carney; r. & d. C. 6, Sarah, m. John Nichols of Newcastle. 7, Capt Simon, m. Betsey Robinson; r. & d. C., a ship master. 8, Betsey, b. Oct. 29, 1767; m. Robert K. Shibles; r. Th. and died Nov. 11, 1846.

Capt. Thomas's ch. 1, George, (3d), b ab. 1783; m. Deborah Weed, Feb. 14, 1813; r. Th., a merchant, & d. Nov. 12, '28. 2, Hon. William, b. 1785; m. Eliza L. St. B. Clough, Oct. 28, 1810; r. W., a merchant & ship owner, & d. at Insane Hospital, Augusta, Oct. 8, '42. 3, Hannah, b. ab. 1788; m. Capt. William Robinson; r. Th. & d. Aug. 19, '63. 4, Ephraim, b. Feb. 4, 1792; m Caroline Wheeler; r. S. Th., a farmer, d. at Augusta, Dec. 4, '50. 5, Capt. Thomas, (2d), m. 1st, Lydia Adams, Feb. '23, 2d, Nancy A. Fuller of Castine, p. Feb. 22, '32, 3d, Mrs. Huldah M. Hobbs of Cam.; was a merchant, &c., in Th., rem. & r. Hamilton city, Hancock county, Ill., a man of wealth & standing, supervisor of the county, &c.

Capt. Simon's ch. 1, Capt. Isaac, m. Deborah (Weed) McLellan, Feb. 21, 1830; rem. Illinois, but ret. & r. Th., 2, Capt. Simon, (2d), m. Deborah Metcalf of F.; d., killed in Richmond. Va., Dec. 18, '28. 3, Nancy, b. ab. 1792; m. Benjamin Litchfield; r. Rock. 4, Capt. James, m. Mary Rivers; r. C.

Fourth Generation.

George's ch. 1, Eliza C., b. Jan. 2, 1814, m. T. Halsey Healy, (2d); r. Th. 2, Hannah D., b. Feb. 22, '16, m. Lewis Hall, (2d), of Rock.; r. Th. 3, Nancy B., born March 13, '18, mar. Isaac R. McLellan, 2d, Hon. Benjamin Carr, 3d, Hon. Thomas O'Brien; r. Th. 4, Emeline T., b. July 14, '20, m. Capt. Joseph Wilson; r. Th. 5, George W., b. May 10, '32, lost at sea, Feb. 11, '43.

Of Hon. William's ch. Capt. James B., b. ab. 1826, mar. Horatia Robinson, Aug., 1861; r. Th.

Ephraim's ch. 1, Charles A., b. May 22, 1822, m. Anna Mette of Detroit, Mich.; r. Placerville, Cal. 2, Almira R., b. Feb. 20, '23, m. Capt. Sanders Curling; r. Th.

Capt. Thomas's ch. by 1st wife. 1, a son, b. April, 1824, d. an infant. 2, Mary Adams, bap. May 4, '28; m. Benjamin Davis; r. Illinois. 3, Lydia Caroline, bap. May 4, '28; m. Crockett Wilson; r. Ill. 4, Adaline, rem. Ill. By 2d wife. 5, William. 6, Henry. 7, Adelia; all r. Illinois.

Capt. Isaac's ch. 1, Bertha D., b. May 24, 1831, m. Moses Stearns; rem. Libertyville. Ill. 2, Edwin B., b. June 11, '33, mar. Mary F. Quimby of Wal., p. Aug. 23, '53; r. S. Th., a painter.

Capt. Simon, (2d)'s ch. Ira, m. and r. Friendship.

Capt. James's ch. 2, Isaac R., m. Nancy B McLellan, March 31, 183[illegible]; r. and d. C. 2, Eliza, m. Thomas Vose Robinson; r. and d. C. 3, William, drowned when sailing out of the mouth of George's river.

Edwin B.'s ch. 1, Abby W., b. ab. 1858. 2, Geo. E, b. ab. '60.

Isaac R.'s ch. Celia, b. Oct. 1841, d. July 13, '44.

McLOON, William, b. in Bristol ab. 1774, m. Polly Mathews, 1796, 2d, Jane (Kelloch) Drake, Nov. 29, 1821; r. S. Th., a ship builder; and d. May 7, '31. His ch. By 1st wife. 1, Betsey, born at Clam Cove, March 29, 1797, m. John Sartelle; r. Rock. 2, Lucy, b. May 2, '99, m. Ephraim Dean; r. S. Th. 3, Lydia, b. Jan. 2, 1801, m. Enos Crockett; r. Rock., and d. Dec. 18, 1857. 4, Hon. William, b. Sept. 2, 1803, mar. Hannah T. Keating, p. July 27, '26; r. Rock., a ship-builder and owner, senator, &c. 5, Charles, b. March 2, 1809; m. Nancy Martin, p. Dec. 12, '33; r. S. Th., a ship-builder, &c.

Hon. William's ch. 1, Mary A, b. March 26, 1828, mar. Horace Williams; r. S. Th. 2, Louisa, b. Nov. 21, '29, m. John Fred Hatch, of Rock., Feb. 5, '51, and d. June 25, '53. 3, Clementine, b. Dec. 5, '31, m. George F. Crabtree; r. Rock. 4, Charles William, b. Sept. 6, '33; r. Rock. 5, Bethia, b. May 28, '37, m. S. F. Thayer of Boston, Nov. 18, '55. 6, Lucy, b. Feb. 1, '39, m. Capt. W. G. Allen, July 8, '63, in Cardiff, Wales. 7, Juliett, b. Jan. 31, '41, mar. Richard W. Trundy of N. Y., Jan. 6, '58; r. Rock. 8, Eliza E., b. April 17, '42; r. Rock. 9, Lauretta, b. Nov. 1843, d. May 27, '46. 10, Silas W., b. ab. '47. 11, Laura F., b. ab. '52.

Charles's ch. 1, Thomas, b. ab. 1835; r. S. Th., an artist. 2, Enos C., b. ab. '37; r. S. Th. 3, N. Adelaide, b. ab. '43. 4, Mary Adelia, b. ab. '48. 5, Charles Leroy, b. ab. '55.

McLOON, James, b. in Havre, France, 1828, m. here, Clara Foster, Aug. 9, '57; r. Rock., a truckman. Their ch. 1, Alice M., b. ab. 1858. 2, Clara E., b. ab. '60.

McMANUS, John, b. ab. 1815 in the North of Ireland, mar. Mary Hanly; r. Th. Their ch. 1, Michael, b. ab. 1838; r. Rock., a baker. 2, Larry, b. ab. '42. 3, John, b. ab. '46.

McMEYER, John, b. ab. 1822, in Ireland, as was Helen, his wife; r. Rock. Their ch. Michael, b. ab. 1852.

McMINN, George, b. ab. 1818 in Dumfrieshire, Scotland; mar. a lady of Nova Scotia; r. Th., a sawyer, lumberer in Maryland, &c. Their ch. 1, William, b. ab. 1845. 2, Eva E., b. ab. '49. 3, Roseltha J., b. Jan. 1851, d. Oct. 6, '56. 4, George, b. ab. '53. 5, Wellington, b. ab. '58. 6, Elizabeth, b. 1859.

McNAMARA, Timothy, b. ab. 1800, in Ireland, as was Mary, his wife; r. Rock. Their ch. 1, William, b. ab. 1833; mar. Catharine ———, r. Rock. 2, Patrick, b. ab. '40. 3, Kate, b. ab. '42. 4, John, b. ab. 1844.

William's ch. 1, Frances E., b. ab. 1857. 2, William A., b. ab. '60. Of this name, also, there are O'Brien McNamara, b. ab. 1806 in Ireland, as was Mary, his wife; r. Rock., and has ch. 1, Bridget, b. ab. 1851. 2, Mary J. 3, Ann. 4, Kate. 5, Margaret. 6, Ellen, b. ab. '60. Also, Anthony McNamara, b. ab. 1820, in Ireland; m. Ann Lines, p. June 6, '54; r. Rock. His ch. 1, Mary Ann, b. ab. 1857. 2, James, b. 1859.

McNIEL, Roderic J., b. ab. 1831 in Nova Scotia; mar. Martha J. Collamore, July 2, 1857; r. S. Th., a carpenter. Their ch. John F., b. ab. 1858.

MACOMBER; of this family, two brothers came from Dover, Me. 1, Samuel K., b. ab. 1830; m. Ellen A. Robinson of Montville, pub. May 3, 1854; r. Rock., a jeweller, &c. 2, George B., b. ab. '32; m. Adaline Rankin, Oct. 28, '59; r. Rock., a jeweller., &c. Of this name, also, Charles A., came, it is believed, from Boston, a merchant many years in Rockland, but removed about 1840.

Samuel K.'s ch. 1, Eva A., b. 1855. 2, Ellen A., b. ab. '59.

MADDOCKS; of this family, two brothers c. here from Lincolnville. 1, Nathaniel B., b. ab. 1804; m. Margaret Lovett; c. to S. Th. in May, '53, a ship builder and farmer. 2, Winthrop C., b. '07; m. Mary Rackliff; c. to South Thomaston in '52, where he r., a mariner.

Nathaniel B.'s ch. 1, Roxana L., m. Sewall H. Knights, Dec. 9, 1858; r. Minnesota. 2, Capt. Thomas B., born '35, mar. Caroline E. Perry, Dec. 25, '57; r. Owl's Head, S. Th. 3, Joseph G., b. '38; r. S. Th., a mariner, soldier of 19th Me. Regt. 4, Lizzie O., b. '40, m. Capt. B. A. Emery, March 8, '64; r. S. Th. 5, Ruth Ann, b. ab. '42.

Winthrop C.'s ch. 1, Helena, m. Edwin Maddocks; r. Hermon. 2, John, b. ab. 1832; r. Owls Head, a mariner. 3, Adelaide, m. Watson Hooper; r. Owl's Head. 4, Sarah, b. '36. 5, Capt. Samuel, b. '38; m. Mary K. St. Clair, Oct. 26, '62; r. S. Th. 6, Julia A., b. '40, m. John H. Skinner, June 16, '64; r. S. Th. 7, Henry, b. '42. 8, Frank R., b. '44, m. Mary E. Dyer, Oct. 16, '64. 9, Lewis, b. '50. 10, Eugene, b. '55.

Capt. Thomas B.'s ch. 1, Frank D. 2, Cora Edna.

MADDOCKS, William, b. 1810, in England; r. Rock., in 1860.

MAHONEY, John, b. ab. 1827, mar. Sarah ———; r. Rock., a lime burner.

MAKER; of this Cape Cod family, there came with their widowed mother, to this vicinity. 1, Jonathan, who settled 1791 in what is now S. Th., and m. Hannah Tenant. 2, David, m. Thankful Dowlf, settled in St. George. 3, Benjamin, m. and r. St. G. 4, Jerusha, m. a Davenport. 5, Rachel. 6, Betsey, m. a Burrows of Cam.

Jonathan's ch. 1, Ruth, m. Israel Gregory; r. and d. Muscle R. Is. 2, Delany F., mar. David Clark; r. and d. S. Th. 3, Eliza, mar. Daniel Elwell; r. St. G. 4, Mercy, mar. Hon. Henry C. Lowell; r. Faribault, Min. 5, Hannah, d. young. 6, Joshua T., m. and r. St. G. 7, Mary, m. Robert Elwell; r. St. G. 8, Theresa, b. ab. 1806; m. Calvin Gregory; r. Rock. 9, Jonathan, died unm. 10, Hannah, m. Capt. Andrew Elwell; r. Rock. 11, William R., b. ab. 1809; m. Sarah A. Kieff of St. G., Aug. 7, '39; r. S. Th., a fish dealer.

William R.'s ch. 1, Sarah E. b. June 2, 1840. 2, Delia A., born Feb. 3, '42. 3, Rebecca R., born April 3, '44, d. at Faribault, Min., Jan. 14, '64. 4, William A., b. ab. '47. 5, Mary A., b. ab. '49. 6, Reuben H., b. ab. '51. 7, Margaret F., b. ab. '56. 8, Harriet, b. ab. 1859.

MAKER, James R., b. ab. 1823, m. Tryphenia B. Clark; r. S. Th., in fish business. Their ch. 1, Israel M., b. ab. 1846. 2, Rosella S., b. ab. '48. 3, Ellis H., b. ab. '52. 4 & 5, twins, b. ab. '54, Alonzo and George C. 6, Sidney F., b. ab. '55.

MALCOLM, William H., b. ab. 1820, son of Capt. Andrew and Mary (Lowell) Malcolm of Warren, m. Maria A. Smith, p. June 26, '52; r. Th., a painter. Their ch. 1, Frank, b. ab. 1854. 2, Frederic, b. ab. 1856.

MALLARD, Edmund, b. in Warwick, Mass., c. to Union, traded there under the firm of Mallard & Chase, built and carried on paper mills, &c.; mar. Hannah Nichols of Th., and d. in Prescott, Canada West, June, 1830. Their ch. 1, Charles R., b. ab. 1815, mar. 1st, Louisa I. Perry, Aug. 27, '43, 2d, Eliza T. Farwell, Sept. 24, '50; r. sometime a merchant at Watervliet, N. Y., since r. Rock., secretary Insurance Co., &c. 2, Olive, m. Charles I. Loud; r. E. Boston.

Charles R.'s ch. by 1st wife. Clara, b. ab. 1845.

MANCHESTER, Jonathan, b. July 11, 1806, in Mt. Desert, mar. Betsey Rodick, Dec. 25, '30; r. Rock., since 1852, a fisherman, &c. Their ch. 1, David, b. June, 1832, mar. Sarah Rodick of Eden; r. Rock. 2, John, b. Feb. 1835, m. Clarissa Whitehouse; r. Rock., a painter. 3, Clara, m. Ephraim Wall; r. Eden. 4, Florinda, b. 1843; r. Rock., a milliner.

David's ch. 1, Ansel, b. ab. 1853. 2, Florinda, b. ab. '57. 3, Charles, b. ab. '59.

MANNING, Sylvester, was b. in Lancaster, Mass., May 12, 1782; c. to reside in Th., now Rock., in 1860, m Phebe Damon (who died March 7, 1835, a. '44); 2d, Ann Munroe, May 17, '35; r. Rock., and d. Dec. 8, 1838. John, a brother, ? b. in 1787, came to what is now Rock., m. Elizabeth Tolman, April 27, 1813, d. Nov. 9, 1822. Sylvester's ch. by 1st wife. 1, Ann, b. Feb. 1806, m. Elliott Tolman; r. Rock., and d. Aug. 24, '62. 2, Mary, b. Jan. 20, 1811, m. Hiram Gregory; r. Cam. 3, Martha, b. Aug. 7, '12, d. June 19, 1833. 4, Charles, b. Feb. 7, '14, m. Rebecca Wasgatt, March 18, '54; r. Rock., a lime burner, &c. 5, Timothy D., b. Aug. 12, '15, mar. Orinda F. Walker, Sept. 29, '44, 2d, Isabella T. Pitcher of Belfast, Oct. 14, '55; r. Rock., a lime burner, and died Nov. 21, '61. 6, Phebe, b. June 6, '17, m. Samuel Prescott of Hope, p. May 13, 1836. 7, Sylvester, (2d), b. Feb. 25, '19, mar. Louisa Fish, June, 1844; r. Rock., a truckman. 8, Elmira, b. Jan. 9, '21; r. Rock. 9, Susan, b. Oct. 18, '23, d. Oct. 1, '31. 10, Nancy, b. May 26, '25. 11, John, b. June 7, '27, m. Lavina H. Wasgatt, p. Oct. 8, '53; r. Rock., a mariner, and was drowned by the upsetting of a boat, in letting go an anchor, in Rock. harbor, April 5, '62. 12, Harriet, b. Feb. 17, '29, d. June 7, '50. 13, Rebecca, b. Sept. 27, '31, m. Capt. Lincoln Rhodes; r. Rock. 14, Augustus, b. April 29, '34.

Charles's ch. 1, Mary E., b. ab. 1855. 2, Albert F., b. ab. '57.

Timothy D.'s ch. 1, Edwin F. R., b. ab. 1847. 2, Emma I., born ab. '49. The mother d. Feb. 6, 1854, a. 33 yrs., 10 ms., 6d.

Sylvester (2d)'s ch. 1, William, b. ab. 1846. 2, Edward, b. ab. '48.

John's ch. 1, Almeretta P., b. 1854. 2, Allen M., b. '56. The mother m. 2d, Capt. Allen Merrill of Cam., Nov. 27, '63.

MANNING, Capt. James, b. ab. 1825, in N. Y., m. Elizabeth D. Rhodes, April 18, '52; r. Rock. Their ch. 1, Myra, b. ab. 1853. 2, James W., b. ab. '54. 3, Minnie, b. Sept. and d. Nov. 2, '59.

MANSFIELD, Dr. William P., b. ab. 1833, in Hope; m. Susan J. Huston; r. and prac. med. in Rock.. Their ch. 1, Nellie F., b. ab. 1856. 2, Charles E., b. ab. '58.

MARDEN, William H., b. ab. 1822; m. Angeline York, 1848; c. from Palermo; and r. Th., a tin plate worker. Jane, a sister, b. ab. 1817; also r. Th. Of this name, also, William T. Marden, b. ab. 1826; mar. Ann M. Larrabee, Aug. 1, 1849; r. Rock., a truckman. Their ch. 1, Emma F., b. ab. 1852. 2, Ellen M., b. ab. '53. 3, Carrie, b. ab. '56. 4, William G., b. ab. '58. 5, Rose, b. ab. '60.

MARKS, Warren, b. ab. 1811; m. Betsey E. Hubbard; r. S. Th. Their ch. 1, William A., b. ab. 1840; r. S. Th. 2, Maria L., b. ab. '44. 3, Hezekiah H., b. ab. '47. 4, Mary I., b. ab. '48. 5, Sarah A., b. ab. '50. 6, Gardner L., b. ab. '51. 7, George H., b. ab. '53. 8, Margaret E., b. ab. '55.

MARSH, Martin, b. in Holliston, Mass., April 27, 1771; came to what is now Rock., and settled on or near Madambettox Mt., since often called by his name; m. Ruth Hall, dau. of Mrs. D. Watson by a former husband, p. Nov. 12, 1798, & d. Sept. 30, 1835. His wife d. Feb. 20, '20, aged 47. Their ch. 1, Sylvia, b. June 10, 1799; mar. Capt. Abner Perry of Cam., p. June 8, 1829. 2, Gilbert H., b. March 10, '01; grad. Bowd. Coll., 1828; stud. theology at Andover, and d. there, Jan. 6, '32. 3, Albert, b. Dec. 8, '03; m. Mary Kelloch, May 9, '30; r. Rock., & d. April 6, '50. 4, Juliet M., b. Sept. 17, '06; m. George W. Gloyd; r. Rock. 5, Nancy, b. Nov. 20, '08; m. Joseph Hewett; r. Rock. 6, Martin, (2d), b. Dec. 10, '10; m. Sophronia Kimball, p. Aug. 25, '36; r. & d. Rock. 7, Lois F., b. Dec. 10, '13, died young.

Albert's ch. 1, George G., b. March 4, 1831; mar. Augusta A. Palmer, p. Jan. 11, '51. 2, Gilbert H., (2d), b. June 22, '33; mar. Eleanor B. Ulmer; r. Rock., a shopkeeper. 3, John B., b. March 4, '37; m. Hannah Ulmer, Dec. 10, '57; r. Rock., a teamster. 4, Leonard S., b. Nov. 22, '39, d. Feb. 19, '58.

Martin's ch. 1, Orinda D., b. Dec. 29, 1837. 2, Lois Emily, b. Aug. 23, '39. 3, Robert Norman, b. Oct. 20, '41, soldier in 2d Battery, &c. 4, Sylvia P., b. Feb. 5, '44. 5, Arvilla N., b. ab. '49. 6, Elizabeth O., b. ab. '53. 7, John A., b. June 24, '57, d. Aug. 27, '64.

Gilbert H.'s ch. Lewis E., b. ab. 1857.

John B.'s ch. Clarence S. b. ab. 1858.

MARSHALL, Robert, with Ruth, his wife, c. early to old Th., but, in 1803, made, in company with James (John ?) White of this place, the first clearing in the town of Bradford, Me., whither White moved his family in 1804, & Marshall in 1805, & where the latter was still living in '58. His ch. recorded here; 1, Olive, b. Aug. 27, 1797; 2, Maria, b. July 13, '99; & 3, Alden, b. Feb. 21, '04; all rem.

MARSHALL, Capt. Thomas, b. ab. 1800; came probably from St. George; m. Temperance ——; r. Rock. Their ch. 1, James A., b. ab. 1834; r. Rock., a mariner, entered the army. 2, ? Elizabeth A., mar. Freeman A. Kingsley, April 28, '61; r. Rock. 3, Sarah, b. ab.

1843. 4, Addie, b. ab. '45. Of this name also, & perhaps a brother, Capt. Richard Marshall, b. ab. 1802 ; m. Abigail Haskell, p. Oct. 28, '23 ; r. Rock. Their ch. 1, Charles, b. Sept. 19, 1824, d. April 19, '29. 2, Abigail W., b. Jan. 30, '26 ; m. Samuel H. Burpee ; r. Rock.

MARSTON, Samuel H., b. ab 1795, in Addison, Me.; mar. 1st, Elizabeth Shorey of N. H., 2d, Fanny N. (Rich) Cates,* March 28 1850 ; r. Rock., a carpenter, &c. His ch. by 1st wife. 1, Almira B , b. ab. 1824, in Sedgwick ; m. Theodore H. Farnsworth ; r. Rock. 2. Andrew J., mar. Catharine Hatch. 3 & 4, twins, Sarah & Mary. 5, Capt. Charles H., b. ab. 1830, in Sedgwick ; m. Margaret B. Ames, Dec. 3, '55 ; r. Rock. 6, Lois D., b. in Sedgwick ; m. Capt. H. W. Bullock ; r. Rock. 7, Lura E., b. in S.; m Judson Simonton ; r. Rock. By 2d wife. 8, Caroline E., b. ab '51. 9, Freeman S., b. ab. '53. 10, Melvin J., b. ab. '55. 11, Jennie B., b. ab. '59, d. Dec. 19, '64.

Capt. Charles H.'s ch. Charles I., b. ab. 1859.

MARTIN, Thomas, b. 1780, son of Richard, c. with his father from Marblehead to St. George, mar. Margaret McKellar, 2d, Bethiah (Thorndike) Keating, May 25, 1815 ; rem. S. Th., 1848. His ch. By 1st wife. 1, Richard, m. Mary A. Ogier of Cam. ; r. St. G. 2, Eliza, m. George O'Brien ; r. St. G. 3, Catharine W., b. 1809, m. James Sweetland ; r. S. Th. 4, John, b. 1810, m. Jane Young, Nov. 8, '40 ; r. S. Th., a mariner. 5, Sarah V., mar. Richard Martin Lovett ; r. Linc., in the same house where the 4th generation of both parents are living. 6, Nancy, m. Charles McLoon ; r. S. Th. By 2d wife. 7, Margaret, b. ab. 1819, m. Capt. Henry Spalding ; r. S. Th., and died June 11, '64. 8, Thomas, d. an infant. 9, Bethiah, m. Joseph Ames ; r. S. Th.

John's ch. 1, James Y., b. 1847. 2, Belmore C., b. '49. 3, Kate M., b. '56.

MARTIN, Ezra, b. ab. 1804, m. Elizabeth O Butler, Aug. 13, '37 ; r. Rock., many years sexton of 1st Baptist church, and d. Dec. 7, '59. Their ch. 1, Augustus, born Feb. 1, 1838 ; r. Rock., a teamster. 2, Elbridge, b. Jan. 22, '40. 3, John F., b. Dec. 1, '41 ; r. Rock., and d. April 5, '61. 4, Sarah E., b. May 15, '44 ; r. Rock. 5, James, born July, and d. Oct. 5, '49.

MARTIN, Eliphalet, m. 1st, Jane Pierce, Aug. 19, 1833, 2d, Emeline A. Conant of Orono, p. Aug. 3, '51 ; r. S. Th., and Rock. His ch. By 1st wife. 1, Almond G., b. June 9, '34. 2, Roscoe G., born Dec. 5, '35, m. Frances H. Butler, June 14, '60 ; r. Rock., a mariner. 3, Sarah I., b. Feb. 14, '38. 4, Alonzo C., b. Feb. 7, '40. 5. Archibald P., b. Oct. 31, '42.

MARTIN, Horace, b. 1804, in Appleton ; m. Abigail Nash ; r. Rock. Their ch. 1, Orlando, b. ab. 1839. 2, James, b. ab. 1846. Of this name, also, Allen F. Martin, b. ab. '20, mar. Mary ——— ; r. S. Th., was postmaster, &c., and had ch. 1, Ella K , b. ab. 1851. 2, Ada, b. ab. '58.—Also William F. Martin, b. ab. '27, m. Salome E. Sprague, Nov. 22, '52 ; r. S. Th , a joiner, and had ch. 1, William C., b. ab. '54. 2, D. Perry, b. ab. '57. Also Mrs. Clarissa Martin, b. ab. '23 ;

---

* Mrs. Marston originated in Cooper, Me., and m. 1st, Nathaniel Cates, who, it has been ascertained, too late for insertion in its proper place, had 3 ch. besides the one mentioned on page 173, viz.: 1, Harriet F , m. Zebulon Babb ; r. Rock. 2, Henrietta E., b. ab. 1842, m. John A Webster ; r. Rock. 3, Nathan H., r. Rock.

r. Rock., a widow, and has ch. 1, Clariette, b. ab. '50. 2, Mary F., b. ab. '59. 3, Adeline, b. Feb. and d. May 20, '64. Also, George D. Martin, b. ab. '09, m. Lydia Wooster; r. Rock. Also, Edward Martin, b. ab. '35 in Ireland, m. Sarah Mullen, Oct. 25, '53; r. Rock., a marble worker, and has ch. 1, Mary A., b. ab. '54. 2, Sarah I., b. '56. 3, Kate, b. ab. '58. 4, William, b. ab. '60.

MASON, Capt. Jonas, came from Unity, m. 1st, Abiah Prince, 2d, Rebecca Mathews, 1824, 3d, Jane Hathorn of St. G., p. July 30, '25; r. Th., a shoemaker, dept. sheriff, &c., lost his 3d wife, 1827, removed to Hermon, Me., rem. thence, and again m. 4th in N. Y.

MASON; of this family from Gouldsboro' or Blue Hill, there came here 3 brothers. 1, Thomas, m. Mary I. Green; r. and d. Rock. 2, James, b. ab. 1835, m. Irene Elwell, Nov. 17, '55; r. Rock. 3, Chas. b. ab. '37; m. Henrietta A. Miller, Aug. 6, 1857; r. Rock., a mariner.

James's ch. 1, Ada L., b. Dec., 1856, d. March 21, 1859. 2, Ada F., b. ab. 1859.

Charles's ch. 1, Charles I., b. ab. 1858. 2, Lizzie E., born Nov. 1860, d. Feb. 23, '62.

MASTERS, William, m. Octavia W. ——; r. Rock., a clock and watch maker, ab. 1830, constable 1834, &c., d. and his widow m. again in 1856. Their ch. 1, Betsey B., b. ab. 1829; m. 1st, Capt. George Jordan, 2d, Capt. James Watts; r. Th. 2, Ann C., b. Aug. 4, '32. 3, Octavia W., b. March 27, '34. 4, John H., b. Sept. 23, '36; died Dec. 22, '37. 4, Elvira O., b. Dec. 25, '38. 5, William O., b. Dec. 19, '40; r. S. Th., a mariner.

MATHEWS, Call, the ancestor of this family, with his wife, Catharine Campbell, and one brother, name unknown, emigrated to this country from Ireland. Of his descendants, (probably ch.), four came early to what is now S. Th., viz.; 1, Lieut. John, mar. Elizabeth, a cousin of Lieut. Joseph Coombs; c. from Plainfield, Ct., one of the first settlers at Wessaweskeag, and d. near the close of the Revolution. In 1788 his widow m. Samuel Sweetland of Wal. 2, James, m. and r. S. Th., died in 1802 or '3, being scalded to death in Heard's salt works. 3, Ruth, m. 1st. Mr. Tenant, 2d, William Rowell; r. S. Th., and d. in 1832. 4, Charles, who subsequently rem. to Linc.

Lieut. John's ch, 1, Joseph, m. Olive Lucas, p. Sept. 18, 1788, d, before '98, & was buried on Cape Cod. 2, Anthony, m. Sarah Spalding, p. Dec. 25, '88; r. S. Th., a farmer, & d. '90 or '91. 3, Lydia, b. 1768, m. John McAllister; r. Hope, and d. Rock., Sept. 2, 1852, a. 84. 4, John, (2d), m. Apphia Snow, p. April 30, 1803. 5, Polly, b. '86; m. William McLoon; r. S. Th., and d. April 14, 1820. 6, Lucy, m. William Spear of Brunswick. 7, Betsey, d. a. ab. '16. 8, Archibald, d. young.

James's ch. 1, William, m. Miriam Bachelder, p. March 28, 1792; with probably others: Edward Mathews, who was murdered in Waterville in 1848, by Dr. Coolidge, was a great grandson of James, and grandson of Capt. —— Mathews, who for many years commanded a ship sailing out of Bath.

Of Charles's ch. 1, Isaac, of Lincolnville, m. Sarah Snow, p. Oct. 31, 1818.

Joseph's ch. 1, Elizabeth, b. Dec. 2, 1789, m. John Keating, and rem. Ohio. 2, Nancy, b. Feb. 1, '92, m. Brackett Butler, & d. Aug. 21, or 16, 1827. 3, Anthony, (2d), b. Feb. 5, '94, m. 1st, Margaret Dunning, Jan. 3, 1816, 2d, Sarah Barrett of Hope, p. April 15, '17;

r. and d. Linc. 4, Olive, b. Sept. 1, 1796, m. Stephen Boardman; r. Hope.

Anthony's ch. 1. Ruth, b. June 2, 1790, m. Wymond Bradbury; r. S. Th., and d. Sept. 26, '61. 2, Archibald, b. 1792, d. in Havana, Sept. 2, 1806.

John, (2d)'s ch. 1, Apphia, b. ab. 1802, d. July 16, '25. 2, John,? (3d). b. ab. '16, m. Mary J. ——— ; r. Rock., a mariner.

John, (3d)'s ch. 1, Allen F., b. ab. 1839. 2, Hannah A., b. ab. '41. m. Charles Barrett; r. Rock. 3, Almond A., b. May 12, '44, d. Jan. 28, '46. 4, Atwood, b. ab. '47. 5, Faustina, born ab. '50. 6, Samuel, b. ab. '53. 7, Margaret, b. ab. '56.

MATHEWS, Isaac, b. ab. 1829, son of Major John, and Sarah (Doane) Mathews of Warren; m. Eliza A. Shibles, March 7, '44; r. Th., a blacksmith, &c. Their ch. 1, Laura A., b. ab. 1845. 2, Oliver D., b. ab. '48. 3, Alden H., b. ab. '54. 4, Alice B., b. ab. '59. Of this same Warren family, William O., b. ab. 1811, son of Robert Mathews, (2d), mar. Mary G. Hemanway of U., 1837, 2d, Lucy Ann French of W., April 7, '64; r. Rock., a brickmaker, &c. His ch. 1, Lieut. James M., born ab. '40; r. Rock., an officer in the Me. U. S. Sharpshooters. 2, Nathaniel C., b. ab. '43; r. Rock., a clerk, soldier of 4th Me. Regt., &c. 3, Sarah A., b. ab. '45, m. James M. Gordon of Chester, N. Y., Nov. 23, '63.

MATHEWS, George, b. ab. 1827, in Prussia; r. Rock., a furnishing merchant. 2, Dorothea, b. 1830, a sister; r. Rock. 3, Adolphus, b. ab. 1832 in Prussia, as was Henrietta his wife; r. Rock., a dry goods merchant, and has ch. Julius, b. ab. 1859, in Rock.

MATHEWSON, Daniel J., b. ab. 1826, m. Susan ——— ; r. Rock. Their ch. 1, Ada C., b. Feb. 1858, d. June 2, '59. 2, Francis L., b. ab. 1860.

MAXEY, Harvey, son of Lieut. Benjamin & Sarah (Fuller) Maxey of Attleboro' & Union, was b. April 30, 1782; m. Sally Eastman of Kingston, 1805; r. Union, on north part of Mill-farm; rem. & r. Th. Their ch. 1, John E., b. Aug. 7, 1806; m. Ann Adams; r. C. 2, Hannah, b. Jan. 4, '08; m. Reuben Hills; r. Linc. 3, Joseph, b. Oct. 29, '09, d. Jan., 1811. 4, Joseph, b. Jan. 29, '11; r. Th., a farmer. 5, Nancy E., b. 1812; m. Charles Hook; r. Danville, N. H. 6, Harvey, (2d), b. July 28, '14; m. Maria Staples; r. Th. 7, Josiah, born Jan. 22, '16, d. in Th., Feb. 9, '49. 8, Henry, b. March 10, '21; r. Th., a merchant in company with Henry O'Brien, now officer in the prison. 9 & 10, twins, b. July 1, '23; Sarah; & Cyrus, who m. Martha Boynton, Sept. 9, '50; r. Th., deputy warden of State prison, &c. The mother d. June 16, 1861, aged 76.

Harvey's ch. 1, George W., b. ab 1844; r. Th., entered the navy. 2, Harvey M., b. ab. '46. 3, James B., b. ab. '55.

Cyrus's ch. 1, Josiah, b. ab. 1851. 2, Charles, b. ab. '54. 3, Henry W., b. ab. '58.

MAYBERRY, Elijah N., came to Thomaston and m. Rebecca W. Palmer, Nov. 2. 1834, and d. in a foreign port, Oct. 10, '41. Their ch. 1, Mary A., b. June 25, 1837. 2, James O., b. June 27, '39. 3, Elijah N., b. Sept. 1, '41.

MAYO, or Mayhew, Daniel, b. ab. 1831, in Hampden; m. Alice L. Vose, June 1, '54; r. Th., a carpenter, &c. Their ch. 1, Cyrus, b. ab. 1855. 2, Eveline, b. ab. '58. 3, Seth V., b. June 24, '60, d. July 8, '61. 4, Angeline.

MEHAN; of this Warren family, sons of Patrick & Maria (Crawford) Mehan, there came to this place, 1, Capt. Francis, b. ab. 1827; m. Ethelda Coggans; r. Th., a ship master. 2, Niven C., b. ab. '29; m. Lucy Jane Annis, Jan. 13, '56; (who d. Oct. 18, '59, aged 25); r. Th., a ship builder. 3, John, b. ab. '31; m. Harriet C. Trueworthy, July 1, '60; r. Rock., a ship builder.

Capt. Francis's ch. 1, Alfred C., b. ab. '55. 2, Clifton A., b. ab. '57.

John's ch. ——, b. 1862.

MELVIN, Ambrose P., b. ab. 1822; came from South Reading, Mass.; m. Almira Kenniston, Oct. 15, 1848; r. Rock., a stone mason, soldier of 4th Me. Reg., &c. Their ch. 1, Joseph H., b. ab. 1851. 2, Lorilla E., b. March, 1853, d. April 18, '58. 3, Isaac F., b. July 2, '55, d. July 12, '64. 4, Lucy E, b. Feb. 17, '59, d. July 9, '60. 5, Ambrose P., (2d), b. July, and d. Dec. 23, '61.

MERO, James, b. ab. 1807; son of Zenas Mero of Hope; m. Mahala Bennett; r. Th., a blacksmith. Eben, a brother, also r. a time in Th., a shoemaker, and some time overseer in the State Prison. James's ch. 1, William, b. ab. 1837; r. Th., a mariner. 2, Ann, b. ab. '39. 3, James O., b. ab. '41; r. Th., a mariner. 4, Nancy J., b. ab. '43. 5, Elizabeth, b. ab. '45, d. July 18, '64. 6, Amelia, b. ab. '48. 7, Celia, b. ab. '50. 8, Catharine, b. ab. '53. 9, Walter Clarke, ? b. 1860.

MERRIAM, Matthew T., m. & r. Morrill, formerly Belmont. Of his ch. 1, Horace, b. ab. 1815; m. Mary P. Bailey; r. Rock., a ship builder, now absent doing business in Shanghai. 2, Jane S., b. 1825; m. Charles S. Rice; r. S. Th. 3, Sarah E., b. 1827; m. Eben T. Jackson; r. Rock. Horace's ch. 1, Melissa A., b. ab. 1843. 2, George A., b. Sept. 29, '45, d. Oct. 8, '58. 3, James H, b. Aug. 3, '47, d. June 15, '48. 4, Mary A., b. ab. '49; 5, Emma I., b. ab. '51; 6, Horace A., b. ab. '53; 7, Frederic, b. ab. '58; all r. Rock.

MERRICK, William, m. and r. Burnham, d. S. Th. Of his ch., there c. here, 1, George G., b. ab. 1814; m. Belinda (Watts) Thomas of W., 2d, Sarah A. Starrett of W., Oct. 22, '40; r. Th., a shipwright; 2, Gardner, b. ab. 1821; m. M. Susan Bailey, Oct. 17, '56; r. Th., a farmer; 3, Kendrick, b. ab. '24; m. Christiana Adams; r. S. Th., a farmer. 4, Cordelia, b. ab. '26; m. Edwin Starrett; r. S. Th.; 5, William C., m. Sarah A. Young, June 4, '56; r. Th., a joiner; all, except the 4th, rem. in 1862, to Libertyville, Ill.

George's ch. 1, G. Lermond, b. 1839; m Sarah A. Townsend, July 24, '62; r. Libertyville. By 2d wife 2, Belinda, b. ab. '41; m. E. O. Staples; r. Ill. 3, Augusta, b. May, 1843. 4, Almira E., b. Sept., '44, d. April 4, '47.

Gardner's ch. Gardner, (2d), b. ab. 1856.

Kendrick's ch. 1, Charles A., b. ab. 1852. 2, Cora, b. ab. '57. 3, Elvira A., b. ab. '59.

William C.'s ch. Walter H., b. ab. 1858.

MERRILL, Eli, m. Sarah M. George of Watertown, Mass., p. Oct. 28, 1819; traded in firm of Green & Merrill, at Knox's wharf, afterwards, by himself, at the upper corner; rem. to Portland & d. in N. Y., where his widow still resides.

MERRILL, Dr. John, b. ab. 1802, grad. Bowd. Coll., '27; c. from Topsham in 1825 to what is now Rock., where he has since been in successful practice of medicine; m. Paulina Sawtelle of Norridgewock, p. Sept. 18, '38; r. Rock. Their ch. 1, John Frederic, b. Oct. 21, '39, clerk in Rock. Bank, since in Washington, D. C. 2, Sarah L., b. Oct. 29, '42, d. Dec. 25, '43. 3, Edwin P., b. ab. 1845; r. Rock., entered the army.

MERRILL, Capt. John, b. in Bristol, in 1807; m. Nancy Holden of Bristol, in '24; r. Rock. Capt. Wilson, a brother, m. ——— Holden; r. Cam. or Rock. Capt. John's ch. 1, Hannah, m. John Fields of Boston, 2d, William Brown; r. Islesboro'. 2, Abby H., m. Isaac Ingraham, (2d),; r. Boston. 3, Edwin W., b. ab. 1838; m. Lydia Merrifield, Aug. 27, 1859; r. Rock., has a son, Anson, born '60. 4, Alonzo L., b. ab. 1847.

MERRILL, Moses W., b. ab. 1813; c. from South Reading; m. ——— Copeland of W., 2d, Catharine R. Patterson of W., p. May 6, '48; r. Rock., a painter, &c.

MERRILL, Edward P., b. in Portland ab. 1828; m. Mary F. Ludwig, Nov. 28, '55; r. & traded Th., rem. Biddeford & Boston. Their ch. 1, Mary, b. ab. '57. 2, Nellie, b. ab. '58.

MERRIMAN, Capt. Nathaniel, c. with Mary, his wife, from Harpswell; r. & d. S. Th. Their ch. 1, Hannah, b. ab. 1808; m. John S. Wade; r. S. Th., & d. 1862. 2, John, b. Aug. 8, 1811; m. Deborah Spring, April 17, '38; r. & d. S. Th. 3, Nathaniel, (2d), m. Eliza J. Haskell, Feb. 27, 1840; r. S. Th., a mariner. 4, Jacob, r. S. Th., a farmer. 5, Joel, r. S. Th. 6, Lydia, b. ab. '20; m. Capt. Oliver Gray; r. S. Th. 7, Fannie. 8, Elmira.

John's ch. 1, Frances L., b. July 1, 1838; r. S. Th. 2, William W., b. Dec. 31, '39; r. S. Th., a mariner. 3, Lydia M., b. Dec. 1841; r. S. Th. 4, Isaac W., b. ab. '44; r. S. Th., soldier of 19th Me., &c. 5, Lewis, b. ab. '46. 6, Helena, b. ab. '49.

Nathaniel, (2d)'s ch. 1, Mary Ann, b. Dec 14, 1840; r. S. Th. 2, Almira, b. Feb. 23, '43. 3, Nancy J., b. ab. '46.

MERROW, James R., b. ab. 1829, in Chesterville, Me.; m. 1st, Maria Reynolds, 2d, Mrs. Eliza A. Allen, p. Oct. 23, '63; r. Rock., a baker, shop keeper, &c. Their ch. 1, Emma F. S., b. ab. 1853. 2, Frederica B., b. ab. 1857.

MESSER, John B., b. Oct. 8, '26, son of Minot Messer of Union; m. Harriet L. Bachelder of Union; r. Rock., a merchant. Their ch. Matilda C., b. ab. '58. Of this name, also, R. W. Messer, r. Rock., a grocery merchant.

MESERVE, John A., Esq., b. 1828; c. from Richmond, Me.; m. Alice C. Kimball, Jan. 26, '52; r. Rock., an attorney at law. and Co. Attorney, 1861; ret. to Richmond, and d. Aug. 7, '62. Their ch. 1, Alice H., b. ab. '53. 2, John W., b. ab. '59.

MESERVEY, Col. Nathaniel, b. Oct. 28, 1795, in that part of Hope now Appleton, m. 1st, Susan Ulmer, p. Sept. 19, 1829, 2d, Anna Conant, published February 1, 1841; r. Rockland, was street engineer, Judge of the Municipal Court, 1860, &c., died August 24, 1864. His ch. by 1st wife. 1, Emily Jackson, born April 6, 1830, mar. Capt. James A. Creighton; r. Th. 2, John H., b. July 5, and d. Oct. 30, '36. By 2d wife 3, Nathaniel W., b. March 7, and d. Oct. 24, '42. 4, George Frederic, b. Aug 23, '43; m. Ellen O'Neal, July 13, '64; r. Rock., a marble worker, firm, McClure & Meservey. 5, William F., b. Oct. 9, '45. 6, Nathaniel H., b. July 10, '48.

MESERVEY, Dexter, b. ab. 1805; m. 1st, Betsey Kaler, 2d, Emily

Fisk of Liberty, 3d, Susan Flanagan; r. Rock., a lime burner. Of his ch. by 1st wife. 1, Mark Dexter, b. ab. 1829; m. Mary M. ———, r. Rock., a lime burner. 2, Arletta. 3, Benson.

Mark Dexter's ch. 1, Frederic E., b. ab. 1855. 2, Reuben L., b. ab. '57. 3, John A., b. ab. '59.

MESERVEY, Samuel L., b. ab. 1832 in Jefferson, Me., m. Elizabeth Richards; r. Rock., a blacksmith, sergeant in 4th Me. &c. Their ch. 1, Edward R., b. 1854, d. Nov. 2, '59. 2, Susan J., b. ab. 1857.

METCALF, or Medcalf, William, from Newburyport, Mass., mar. Sarah Day, r. & d. in Nobleboro', now Damariscotta. Their ch. 1, William, (2d), b. May 15, 1799; m. Mary Wormell, Dec. 2, 1824; r. Th., a pump and blockmaker. 2, Hon. Benjamin D., mar. Jane Lovett, r. Damariscotta. 3, Martha Ann, b. Nov. 16, 1804; m. Dea. Alexander Singer, r. W. 4, Samuel, m. Sarah Foster of Bristol; r. Damariscotta. 5, Robert D, b. 1815; m. Lucy A. Libby of Dam., r. Rock., a pump and blockmaker. Sarah, the mother, d. in W. April 6, 1849.

William, (2d)'s ch. 1, Sally Ann, b. Sept. 14, 1825; m. Bradford Oliver; r. Th. 2, Benjamin D., b. March 28, '27, d. in Chasta, Cal., Aug. 24, '51, for which he sailed in March, 1849. 3, Mary E., born Sept 7, '28, d. June 22, '42. 4, Martha C., born Feb. 23, '32; r. Th. 5, William A., b. Sept. 23, '33; m. Melina A. Morse of Rock., Oct. 27, '56; r. Th., a blockmaker. 6, Edward G., b. Aug. 25, and died Sept. 8, '35. 7, Daniel D., b. June 21, '37; r. Th., a mariner.

Robert D.'s ch. 1, Ann A., b. Aug. 1841. 2, Joseph L., born ab. '44; r. Rock., a mariner. 3, Leander N., b. ab. '46. 4, William A., (2d), b. ab. 1848.

William A.'s ch 1, Sidney H., b. ab. 1858. 2, Maurice, b. ab. '60.

MICHAELS, Henry P., b. Oct. 28, 1826; m. Sarah G ———; r. Rock., and d. Dec. 2, 1861.

MILLAY, William K., b. ab. 1821, in Somerset county; m. Mary J. ———; r. Rock., a quarryman; rem. S. Hope. Their ch. 1, William A., b. ab. 1850; 2, Charles A., b. ab. 1852. 3, Frederic C., b. ab. '54; all rem. 4, Herbert L., b. Feb. 21, '59, d. March 23, '60.

MILLIKEN, Charles W., b. ab. 1832; m. Eleanor U., ———; r. Rock., a ship machinist.

MILLER, Major Noah, (2d), son of Noah & Mary (Mills) Miller, of Lincolnville and of Scottish descent; m. Lucy Mahoney, &c., r. & d. Linc. Hon. Joel, a brother, b. in Linc. ab. 1784; c. to St. George, m. Elizabeth Robinson; rem. Th. ab. 1828; was warden of State Prison, senator 1828, judge of probate 1836, &c, and d. Sept. 10, '49. Lovicy, a sister, m. Dr. C. C. Chandler; and died at her sons' in Th. Feb. 3, 1843.

Of Major Noah's ch. 1, Noah, (3d), came to Th., m. Abigail E. Sellea, Sept. 1, 1836; r. and d. Thomaston.

Hon. Joel's ch. 1, Mary J., m. Hon. Nehemiah Boynton; r. Chelsea, Mass. 2, Sophronia, r. Th. 3, George, b ab. 1810; m. Julia (Robinson) Spear, p. Aug. 16, '34; r. Th., and died Aug. 20, '41. 4, William K., b. ab. 1812; r. Th., and d. Aug. 19, '32. 5, Leander, b. 1814; was a merchant in the firm of Boynton & Miller, at Th. and Boston; r. Chelsea, Mass., and d. there July 16, '50. 6, Levi B., m. Abby B. Fuller, Oct. 3, 1852; r. Chelsea, Mass. 7, Harriet N., b. 1823; m. Capt. George C. Snow; r. Th., and d. Sept. 24, '45. 8,

Amasa, b. ab. 1828; m. Margaret Eugenia, daughter of Eben. Young, Sept. 29, '59; r. Th., a painter, &c. 9, Edwin, b. in Th., June 10, '30, d. Nov. 26, '32.

Noah, (3d)'s ch. 1, Nathan L., mar. Hester C. Morton, Nov. 5, 1858; r. Th., a caulker. 2, Noah, (4th), b. Oct. 15, '38. 3, Edward R., born ab. '41; mar. Margaret J. Willard, July, 1862; r. Th., a mariner, &c.

George's ch. 1, Albion K., b. April 30, 1835. 2, George E., born July 28, '38, d. Aug. 28, '49. 3, Julia A., b. March 23, '40.

Nathan L.'s ch. Augustus, b. ab. 1859.

MILLER, Major Charles A., came from Skowhegan to Rock., was clerk of House of Rep., 1860, '1, & '2; clerk of courts, Knox county, '63; aid-de-camp and private secretary of Gov. Coburn; since in the army.

MILLER, Capt. Peter, b. ab. 1798, in the island of Bonholm, Denmark, (family name Peterson); leaving Europe, bought an American protection and sailed under the name of John Harris, but was naturalized as Peter Miller; m. 1st, Hepzibah (Nutting) Biskey, Sept. 6, 1830, 2d, Elizabeth (Nutting) Lermond, Sept. 15, '62; r. Th., a master mariner. His ch. by 1st wife. 1, Amanda, b. June 6, 1831; m. Capt. John Eureka Harding from Germany; r. Th. 2, William B., b. May 4, '33, d. Aug. 13, '38. 3, Joshua J., b. May 28, '38, d. Oct. 26, '40. 4, Hepzibah, d. young.

MILLER, James, b. Nov. 1, 1798, c. from Waldoboro' with Margaret, his wife, and r. Rock., a lime burner, &c. Of their ch. 1, Parker, b. ab. 1829, mar. Abbie M. Cram; r. Rock., a lime burner. 2, James B., b. ab. '32; r. Rock., a lime burner. 3, Denny, b. ab. '35; m. Olinda S. Burns, Oct. 10, '55; r. Rock. 4, Simon, born ab. '38; r. Rock., a lime burner. 5, Sarah J., b. May, '44, d. July 28, '54. Of the same Waldoboro' family and nephews to James, there came hither three brothers; 1, William E., b. in Wal. ab. 1812; mar. Exie or Achsah Coombs; r. Rock. 2, John E., b. in Wal., ab. 1817; m. Margaret Ginn; r. Rock., a shop keeper. 3, Warren F., m. Clara A. Edgarton of Dam., Nov. 6, '60; r. Rock., a shop keeper.

Parker's ch. 1, William C., b. ab. 1857. 2 and 3, twins, b. Aug '58, James A., d. Sept. 4, '60, Denny H., r. Rock.

Denny's ch. Deborah E., b. ab. 1857.

Wm. E.'s ch. 1, Emerson W., b. ab. 1843. 2 Mary E., b. ab. '47.

John E.'s ch. 1, Margaret E., b. ab. 1838. 2, John D., b. ab. '42, m. Julia H. Hovey, Oct. 28, '63; r. Rock. 3, Sarah I., b. ab. '44. 4, Amelia, b. ab. '46. 5, Martha W., b. ab. '48.

MILLER, Capt. Jacob, of a different family, b. ab. 1832, m. Susan ——; r. Rock, a master mariner. Their ch. 1, Frank L., b. ab. '56. 2, John, b. ab. '59.

MILLS, James, b. ab. 1783 in Massachusetts; m. Mary Hathorn, settled in St. G.; rem. Th. Of his ch. Capt. Harvey, b. ab. 1817, in St. G., m. 1st, Olive Fountain, 2d, Sarah Dizer, Dec. 2, '55, 3d, Mary Rhoda Adams; r. Th.

Capt. Harvey's ch. by 1st wife. Warren, b. ab. 1849.

MILLS, Capt. William H., c. from Vinalhaven; m. 1st, Emeline Dyer, 2d, Lydia C., (Lyman) Bunker; r. Rock. Hanson A., also, a brother, m. Mary Blackington, & r Th. but rem. Cam.; both having come, probably, since 1860, as neither were included in the census of that year. Of Capt. William H.'s 5 ch. 1, Eugene, is in U. S. navy.

MILLS, Amos, b. ab. 1803, in Nova Scotia, as was Rosanna, his wife, (who died here March 5, 1854, a. 48,) m. 2d, Judith ——— ; r. Rock., a shoemaker. Of his sons, probably, 1, William H., b. ab. '34, in N. Scotia; m. Sarah A. Godfrey of N. S., p. Feb. 3, '55; r. Rock, a mariner. 2, Oliver B., entered U. S. navy. William H.'s ch. 1, Lucy, b ab. '59. 2, Oliver B., b. Oct. 11, '62, d. April 19, '64.

MINNEHAM, John, b. ab. 1836, in Ireland; c. to Rock., with Mary, his mother, who d. Apr. 23, '64, a. 63. His ch. Mary, b. ab. '59.

MINK, Thos. W., b. ab. 1829, probably in Wal.; m. Jane U. Spear, Nov. 24, '53; r. Rock., a joiner. Their ch. Andrew b. ab. '57.

MITCHELL, Dea. Cyprian, (name changed from Twitchell by Legislative Act, March 14, 1843), was b. ab. 1800; m. Lucretia Davis, came from Freedom with his family to S. Th. and bought the Singer place, afterwards rem. Mill River. John, a brother; r. Montville.

Dea. Cyprian's ch. 1, Martha Jane, b. ab. 1821; m. Capt. Harris Stackpole; r. Th. 2, Capt. George Albion, b. ab. '23; m. Susan S. Bunker, July 22, '49, 2d, Mary K. Bunker, Oct. 29, '58; r. Th., & d. at Stockton, Cal., Sept. 1, '61. 3, Oakes Perry, b. '25; lost in brig *Maine*, 1844. 4, C. Amanda, b. ab. '27; m. Capt. Dodge Healey, 2d, Dr. Daniel Rose; r. Th. 5, Horace Chandler, b. June 2, '32, d. Aug. 8, '53, at New Orleans of yellow fever, mate of barque *Franklin*. 6, Adelbert Davis, b. ab. '41; r. Th., lost at sea, Oct., 1863, on passage to Halifax, N. S.

Of John's ch. David M., b ab. 1817; m. Elsie J. ———; r. Rock. a joiner, deputy sheriff, 1854, &c.

Capt. George A.'s ch. 1, Cora E., b. Nov. 21, 1851. By 2d wife. 2, George O., b. Aug. 8, '60.

David M.'s ch. 1, Elvira A., b. ab. 1846. 2. Frances H., b. ab. '49. 3, Hiram B., b. ab. '51. 4, James A., b. ab. '55. 5, Elsie C., b. ab. '59.

MITCHELL, Capt. Orrin P., b. ab. 1827, in Montville, (name changed from Twitchell, Aug. 2, '48); m. Caroline A. Cowing, Dec. 21, '51; r. Rock., a joiner, and officer in 4th Me. Reg. Their ch. 1, Carrie E., b. ab. 1853. 2, Nellie C., b. ab. '58.

MITCHELL, Capt. Steuben, son of Mrs. J. Gleason by a former marriage, c. with her, when a child, from Philadelphia; m. Margaret Gilchrist, May 17, 1817, 2d, Catharine Moody, Nov. 27, '43; r. Th., d. W. of small pox, Sept. 22, '60. His ch. by 1st wife. 1, Sarah T., m. E. Scott Young; r. St. G. 2, George G., b. ab. 1817; m. Abigail E. (Sellea) Miller, Nov. 1, '45; r. Th., & d. July 11, '62. 3, Lucy A., d. Aug. 9, '45. 4, Mary M. 5, Samuel Tucker, b. 1830, d. Feb. 8, '32. 6, Samuel T., b. Dec., 1832, d. May 6, '53. The mother d. July 9, '40, aged 44.

George G.'s ch. 1, Margaret, b. ab. 1844; m. J. K. Morton; r. Th. 2, Lucy A., b. ab. '48. 3, William F., b. ab. '52. 4, George B., b May 28, d. Feb. 8, '56.? 5, George, b. '59.

MITCHELL, Benjamin P., b. ab. 1825; came from Belfast; ? m. Mary W. Roberts, Sept. 16, '49; r. Rock., a shoemaker, soldier of 28th Me. Reg., &c. Their ch. 1, Benjamin E., b. ab. 1852. 2, Mary J., b. Nov. 22, '54, d. Feb. 15, '57. 3, Mary W., b. Aug. 31, '57, d. Sept. 21, '58. 4, Ida M., b. May, 1859, d. Oct. 29, '61.

MITCHELL, C. C., b. in Crete, Is. of Cyprus; r. a time in Th., & leaving a family in California, d. in Damariscotta, Sept. 2, 1856.

MOFFITT, Caleb G., b. ab. 1824, in Smithfield R. I., m. 1st, Louisa M. Norcross, 2d, Julia E. Whittier, Feb. 17, '63 ; r. Rock., a merchant tailor. His ch. By 1st wife. 1, Eugene, b. ab. 1848. 2, Ralph P., b. Dec., 1849, d. Sept. 5, '51 ; r. Rock., enlisted in army. 3, Angeline, b. ab. '53. 4, Caleb, b. ab. '59. The mother d. July 5, 1860, a. 37.

MOLECAMP, Cornelius, b. in Holland, 1806, m. Catharine ——; r. Th., and d. of consumption, July 2, 1859. His wife, b. in Ireland, d. Sept. 23, '62. Their ch. 1, Maria, born Oct. 10, '39 ; r. Th. 2, Catharine, b. June 14, '41, d. Nov. 21, '59. 3, Cornelius, (2d), b. ab. '43 ; r. Th. 4, Luke, b. ab. '45. 5, Franklin, b. ab. '47. 6, Mary A., b. ab. '50. 7, John, b. June, and d. Oct. '59.

MONK, Charles Robinson, came from Vassalboro', Me., mar. Mrs. Elizabeth Dowlf, pub. Sept. 28, 1822 ; r. Th., a trader. John, a brother, also came to Th., m. Susan Graffam, p. Oct. 2, '33, was a mariner, and d. at N. O., Nov. 1843.

Charles R.'s ch. 1, Mary A., b. Aug. 27, 1823, m. Mr. Swinburne of Boston. 2, George H., b. Feb. 4, '25, d. Jan. 20, '43.

John's ch. 1, Eugene, b. ab. 1842, a soldier of 8th Me., Reg., d. at Hilton Head, March 29, '63.

MONTGOMERY, William, son of Robert and Elizabeth (Cooper) Montgomery, of Warren, was b. March, 1772 ; m, Mary Rackliff of Boothbay ; removed to S. Th., on the place of John Jameson, and d. there, May 21, 1854. Of his nephews ; Percy, b. Nov. 22, 1817, son of John and Julia A. (Howard) Montgomery of W., m. Dolly Spear, Aug. 29, '41 ; r. Rock., a wheelwright, artificer in 2d Me. Battery, &c. Capt. Eber S., born ab. 1820, son of Robert, (2d), and Rachel (Whittier) Montgomery, m. Maria M. Helmerhausen, p. Oct. 18, '45 ; r. S. Th., a master mariner, in Govt. employ.

William's ch. 1, Anora, b. ab. 1803, m. Hans Kelloch ; r. S. Th. 2, Lydia A., b. 1808 ; r. S. Th.. 3, Capt. Benjamin R., b. May 19, 1810, followed the sea, but d. at home, of consumption, June 29, '42. 4, Mary, b. July 8, '13, m. Moses S. Carr of Rock., rem. Illinois. 5, Sarah G., b. March 18, '15, d. Feb. 22, '44. 6, Margaret, rem. California with her brother. 7, Chandler R., b. April 25, '21, m. Olive L. Whitmore of Linc., Dec. 9, '55, and rem. to California.

Percy's ch. 1, Eliza S., born ab. 1843. 2, Martha, b. ab. '46. 3, Charles R., b. ab. '56.

Capt. Eber S.'s ch. Stanley, b. ab. 1849.

MOODY, Daniel, b. ab. 1812, in Nobleboro', m. Mary —— ; r. Th., a carpenter, &c. George, a cousin, b. ab. 1810, mar. 1st, Lucy Trask, April 8, '32, who d. June 30, '34, 2d, Deborah Gilchrist of St. G., p. Jan. 2, '35 ; r. Th., a mason, &c.

Daniel's ch. 1, Ann M., b. Sept. 12, 1835, m. Joseph E. Catland ; r. Th. 2, Kendall W., b. July 1, '37, d. June 6, '55. 3, Mary A., b. ab. '46. 4, Abbie A., b. ab. '50.

George's ch. By 2d wife. 1, George A., b. Feb. 11, 1836, mar. Laura Partridge, Jan. 1861 ; r. Th., a caulker, soldier in 20th Me., &c. 2, Sylvanus, b. July 23, '37, d. April 20, '42. 3, Edward T., b. Feb. 8, '39, d. April 3, '42. 4, Lucy S., b. Feb. 28, '42. 5, Edward, b. ab. '44. 6, Franklin Halsey, b. ab. '46. 7, Mary, b. ab. '49. 8, Ellie, b. ab. '52.

MOODY, Nathaniel, b. ab. 1812, c. from Waldoboro', m. Sarah E.

True of Freedom; r. Th., dept. sheriff 1857, and again appt. Jan. 1863. Their ch. Sarah E., b. ab. 1857.

MOONEY, James, b. ab. 1830, in Ireland, as was Ann, his wife; r. Rock., a mariner. Their ch. John, b. ab. 1858.

MOORE, Abel, c. from China, Me.; m. Sarah G. Hanson of China, p. April 4, 1832; r. Th., and d. or rem. Alfred, a brother, also came to Th., a quarryman, and was killed, May, 1846, in quarry. Abel's ch. recorded here: 1, John, b. May 9, 1833. 2, Sarah A., born Feb. 10, '35. 3, Alice H., b. Nov., 1836. 4, Eliza J., b. Nov. 16, '38. 5, Mary B., b. May 11, '41, d. Jan. 20, '51. 6, Clara B., b. '43, d. Jan. 26, 1858.

MOORE, John Elbridge, b. ab. 1822, son of Richard and Lucy (Howard) Moore of Freedom; m. Martia A. Lindsey of Rock., July 30, '54; r. Th., and died Aug. 10, '60. Their ch. Henry A., born 1856; r. Freedom.

MOORE, Joel, b. in Southboro, Mass., July 15, 1768; m. Abigail Bubier, of Marblehead; came to Rock., and d. April 23, 1859, aged 90 y. 9 m. 8 d. Of this name, also, Isaac Moore, b. ab. 1824, mar. Elizabeth Amsden, ? r. Rockland, a marble worker, &c. Wilder C. Moore, b. ab. 1828; m. Caroline ———, r. Rock., a quarryman, &c. Alvah G. Moore, b. ab. 1830; m. Mary E. Runnels, March, 1855; r. Rock. John B. Moore, b. ab. 1835; m. Eliza J. ———; r. Rock., a mariner. Nathaniel Moore, mar. Rebecca Spofford; r. Georgetown, Mass., and Rock., a currier. Hafford S. Moore, b. ab. 1831; mar. Eliza A. ———; r. Rock., a shop keeper.

Isaac's ch. 1, Charles, b. ab. 1850. 2, Anna, b. ab. '54. 3, Ella, b. ab. '57.

Wilder C.'s ch. 1, Alfred R., b. ab. '54. 2, Mary Ann, b. ab. '60.

Alvah G.'s ch. Harriet P., b. ab. 1858.

John B.'s ch. 1, Winnie. 2, Mabel, b. April, 1858, d. Oct. 19, '60.

Hafford S.'s ch. 1, Charles H., b. ab. 1855. 2, Emma L., b. 1859, d. Jan. 1, '62.

MOORE, Charles, partly of African descent, but of most polished and gentlemanly manners, came to Th., lived as coachman, &c. in the family of Mr. Swan, 1826 and '7; went away and d. of dropsy in Havre, France, where he had arrived as steward of a packet ship. Edgar, a son of his, whose mother was Mary Smith of C., was born ab. 1827; m. a Crouse, and r. Friendship.

MORGAN, Littleton T., mar. Lydia B. Pierce of Northampton, Mass., 1847; r. Rock., in shoe business, but removed.

MORIN, or Morang, Simon, b. ab. 1828; mar. Betsey ———; r. Rock., a lime burner, soldier, &c.

MORRISON, John, b. ab. 1836, in Ireland; mar. Ann Cutler; r. Rock., a quarryman. Their ch. 1, John, b. Dec., 1845. 2, Lucy. 3, Isabel. 4, Ally. 5, William.

MORSE, Daniel, b. in Attleboro', June 9, 1743, O. S., m. Freelove Dexter, of Cumberland, R. I, Feb. 16, '69; came here early, r Th., a wheelwright, and d. Dec. 16, 1808. His wife b. March 25 1747, died June 16, 1824. Their ch. 1, Lydia, b. Aug. 1, 1769; mar. Thomas Emerson, 2d, James Howard; r. Th. & d. Jan. 29, 1850. 2, John D., b. Sept. 1, '71; m. Margaret Howard; r. Th., a farmer at Meadows, and d. March 9, 1841. 3, Lavinia D., b. Nov. 19, '72; m. John M.

Wight, 2d, Benjamin Tucker; and d. Aug. 11, 1850. 4, Daniel, (2d), b. Oct. 9, '74, d. July 10, '87. 5, Capt. Henry, b. May 3, '77; perished at sea. 6, Freelove, b. Oct. 4, '79; m. Boaz Brown; r. Th. & d. March 17, 1864. 7, Jabez, b. March 20, '82; m. Betsey Kaler, of Wal., 1826; and. d. Dec. 3, '38. 8, Lucy, born May 3, '84, d. March 23, '25. 9, James, b. April 25, '87; m. Hannah Mayo of Cam, Jan. 2, '11; r. Th., at Meadows, a farmer.

John D.'s ch. 1, Capt. John D., b. Feb. 13, 1800; m. Margaret U. Bartlett, Nov. 9, '33, 2d, Elizabeth Copeland of W., r. Th. 2, Sarah, b. Aug., 1805, d. Jan. 26, '08. 3, Daniel, (3d), b. Dec. 26, '09; m. Jane Austin, June 17, '41; r. Th., a farmer. 4, Almira, b. Nov. '11; m. Christian Kaler, '36; r. W., rem. Aroostook, '59. 5, Julia G., b. Nov. '14; m. James Harper; r. Worcester, Mass. 6, Mason W., b. Nov. 1815; m. Priscilla C. Rankin, p. Aug. 2, '40; a blacksmith, r. Minnesota. 7, Ann Maria, m. Henry Gleason; r. Watertown, Mass. 8, Henry, (2d), b. Nov., 1819; m. Caroline Moore; r. Th., a farmer. 9, Dexter S., b. 1821; m. Elizabeth Dean, Dec. 24, '53; r. Th. 10, Adaline, b. 1823, d. Sept. '25. 11, Margaret, b. July, 1826; m. Horatio Bartlett; r. Th., & d. March 6, '54. 12, Jabez, (2d), d. young. 13, Benjamin, b. March 6, '31; rem. California.

Jabez's ch. 1, Sarah J., b. April 22, 1830; m. and r. Bangor. 2, Noah, b. Jan. 27, '32; r. a merchant in Bangor. 3, Jabez, (3d), b. Feb. 3, '39; rem. California.

James's ch. 1, Mary P., b. Nov. 6, 1811; m. Nathaniel Fales; r. California. 2, Hannah, b. March 11, '14; m. Henry Brown; r. Th. 3, Eliza, b. Oct. 7, '16; m. Thomas Wentworth; r. Hope. 4, James, (2d), b. Nov. 21, '18; mar. Abby Nichols, Nov. 30, '51; r. Th., a farmer. 5, Maria, b. April 10, '21; m. William T. Gleason; r. Watertown, Mass. 6, Isaac, b. Aug. 16, '23, d. Sept. 6, '25. 7, William B., b. Feb. 3, '26; m. Martha Shorer of Palermo; r. Th., & d. March 13, '59. 8, Charles, b. Feb. 22, '29; m. Marcia Allen, Sept. 13, '54; r. Th., a farmer. 9, Amelia, b. Dec. 5, '31, d. March, '46. 10, Susan F., b. Nov. 11, '35; m. Lathley R. Nichols; r. Th.

Capt. John D.'s ch. by 2d wife. 1, Harris S., b. ab. 1849. 2, ———, b. 1860.

Daniel, (3d)'s ch. 1, John Dexter, b. April 6, 1842; r. Th., soldier in 20th Me. Reg., &c. 2, Richard W., b. June 25, d. Nov. 25, '43. 3, Louisa J., b. Oct. 16, & d. Dec. 4, '45. 4, Franklin, b. May, 1848. 5, Daniel H., b. Sept. 21, & d. Oct. 7, '55.

Mason W.'s ch. 1, Emma E., b. Dec. 16, 1841. 2, Charles H., b. March, '44, d. Dec. 20, '51. 3, Clara A., b. Feb., '46, d. Aug. 8, '60. 4, Richard, b. ab. '49. 5, Laura, b. ab. '51. 6, Josephine, b. ab. '54. 7, Jennie, b. ab. '56. 8, Edith E., b. ab. '58.

Henry, (2d)'s ch. 1, Merritt A., b. ab. 1845. 2, Margaret Amelia, b. ab. '47. 3, Frederic, b. ab. '50. 4, Henry P., b. June 25, '53, d. May 15, '54. 5, George S., b. ab. '57.

Dexter S.'s ch. 1, Charles W., b. ab. '55. 2, Flora E., b. ab. '58.

James, (2d)'s ch. Frank, b. ab. 1855.

William B.'s ch. 1, Ida, b. ab. '57. 2, William B., (2d), b. ab. '59.

Charles's ch. Jane, b. April, 1860.

MORSE, Obadiah, b. at Sherburne, Mass., Dec. 11, 1776; came to U., 1798; m. Sally Palmer, 2d, Phebe Carriel, and d. Aug. 8, 1837. His widow mar. Major James A. Ulmer; r. Th. Of his ch. by 1st wife. 1, Asa, b. Jan 27, 1809; m. Eliza J. Litchfield; c. to Rock., 1848; r. Pleasant street, a teamster, &c. 2, Obadiah, b. May 18, '13;

m. Chloe Copeland of W.; c. to Th. where he d. July 14, '47; being fatally injured, July 11th, by caving in of a clay bank at his brick-yard. Of the sons of Levi Morse of Union, 1, William Bradford, b. Aug. 24, 1813; m. Emma G. (Parsons) Ross, Oct. 12, '37; r. Rock., a lime manufacturer, & d. Nov. 8, '52. Of the sons of Moses Morse of U. Dexter P., b. ab. 1825; m. Emeline P. Eaton in 1858, and r. Rock., a melodian manufacturer.

Asa's ch. 1, Edwin P., b. July 20, 1836; r. Rock., corporal in U. S. Sharpshooters, &c. 2, Fostena, b. March 7, '38; m. Charles H. Haskell; r. Rock. 3, Argyl Dudley, b. March 28, '41; soldier of the Sharpshooters, &c. 4, William Spofford, b. Nov. 29, '43. 5, Sidney Adelbert, b. in Rock., Jan., 1851.

William Bradford's ch. 1, Penelope C., born Aug. 29, 1838. 2, Serg't William Henry, b. Jan. 1, '41; a clerk, and soldier of 28th Me. Reg., killed in battle, June 30, '63. 3, Charles Bradford, b. Dec. 24, '47; r. Rock.

MORSE, formerly DeMorse; of this Friendship family, 1, John, b. ab. 1804; m. Mrs. Eliza Hall, p. Oct. 31, '33; r. Th., a carpenter 2, Capt. Oliver, a cousin, b. ab. 1834; m. Catharine V. Haupt of Wal., May 25, '56; r. Th., a master mariner. 3, William, another cousin, b. ab. 1835; m. Ann Stevens, Dec. 8, '53; r. Th., a mariner.

John's ch. Elizabeth, b. ab. 1837.

Capt. Oliver's ch. Jane, b. ab. 1860.

William's ch. 1, Frederic, b. ab. 1856. 2, Frank, b. ab. '58.

MORSE, James M., b. ab. 1828; m. Rebecca J. Briggs, p. Aug. 22, '53; r. Rock, a teamster. Their ch. 1, Wilmot, b. July, '56, d. May 30, '57. 2, Florabelle, b. ab. '59. 3, Ida E., b. Oct. 10, '61, d. Aug. 29, '62. Of this name, also, Archibald C. Morse, b. ab. '34; m. Frances A. ——; r. Rock., a lime burner. Their ch. 1, William V., b. June 28, '56, d. March 9, '57. 2, Delora, b. ab. '58.

MORTON, Cornelius, c. from Kingston, Mass., early, to what is now Friendship; m. Jane Johnson; r. & d. F. Their ch. 1, Cornelius, (2d), m. Abiah Wadsworth; r. & d. F. 2, Joshua, m. Mercy Howard of Wal.; r. & d. Friendship. 3, Sarah. 4, Deborah, m. Robert Jameson of Friendship.

Of Joshua's ch. 1, Joshua, (2d), b. June 16, 1789 in F.; m. 1st, Jerusha Cobb of W., Oct. 29, 1812, 2d, Mary A. Davis of F., March 25, '32; came to Th. 1827, and began shipbuilding, continuing it, building by himself and in company with his son, building no less than 22 vessels; built the 2d house ever put up on Green St. 1826; rem. in 1840 to the Seavy house near his ship yard, and d. Jan. 25, '57. 2, Cornelius, (3d), m. 1st, Sally (Morton) Lawry, 2d, Nancy (Pitcher) Morse; r. F.

Joshua, (2d)'s ch. 1, Lucinda C., b. Aug. 7, 1813, m. Harvey G. Snow; r. N. Y., d. and was buried in Th., Nov. 20, '64. 2, Mary Ann, b. Feb. 17, 1815, m. Alexander Edwards; r. Th. 3, Charles C. b. Feb. 16, '17, m. Sarah Waterman of Wal., Aug. 8, '44; r. Th., a shipbuilder, in firm of J. & C. C. Morton, &c. 4, Albert, b. March 16, '20, m. Harriet M. Wiggen of Brooks, Nov., 1845; ship builder, in company with C. Lermond and L. B. Gilchrist; removed June, 1857, to W. Springfield, Mass., and d. March 26, '58. 5, Rebecca C., b. May 18, '22, m. Charles Lermond; r. Th. 6, Alzina W., b. Nov. 11, '24; r. Th., and N. Y. 7, Jerusha A., b. Nov. 15, '29, d. Nov. 22, '43. The mother, b. Nov. 5, 1786, d. Nov. 15, 1829. By 2d wife. 8, an infant, d. 9, Francis A , m. Edwin Fitzgerald; r. Th. 10, Margaret A., m. Washington Morton of F. 11, Joshua K., b. 1838, m. Margaret G. Mitchell, April 9, '64; r. Th., a ship carpenter. 12, William J., b. '41; r. Th., a carpenter, and mariner. 13, Hester, m. Nathan L. Miller; r. Th. 14, C. Aubigne. 15, Oliver A., b. Oct. 10, '48, d. Sept. 12, '49. 16, Florilla Olive.

Cornelius, (3d)'s ch. By 1st wife. 1, Nancy, m. 1st, Francis W. Rhoades of Rock., 2d, Dea. Isaac Robinson of War.; r. Rock. 2, Susan, m. John Sanborn; r. Prospect, rem. Dover. 3, Howard, b. ab. '16, m. Melinda Robinson, Oct. 9, '42; r. Th., a joiner. 4, Josephus B., b. ab. '21; r. Th.

Charles C.'s ch. 1, Sarah Ellen, b. Oct. 3, 1846. 2, Mary Thomas, b. Jan. 17, '51.

Albert's ch. 1, Harriet E., b. Nov. 16, 1846. 2, Ada M., b. Sept. 15, '48. 3, Albert O., born Dec. 26, '50, died Aug. 22, '52. 4, Eda Crockett, b. May, 1854, d. April '55. 5, a son, b. Sept. and d. Dec. 1857.

Howard's ch. 1, Orilla A., b. ab. 1847. 2, Clara E., b. July, and d. Sept., '53. 3, Clara Emma, b. ab. '58.

MORTON, James C., b. 1808, son of Zenas Morton of Eastport, m. Mehitable R. Morton of F.; r. Rock., a blacksmith. Their ch. 1, Leonese, b. ab. 1837. 2, Franklin, b. ab. '41. 3, Ella B., b. ab. '53.

MORTON, Robert, b. ab. 1822, in Bristol; m. Martha M. Bryant; r. Rock., a mariner. Their ch. 1, Frederic C., b. 1854. Capt. Jas., brother of Robert, b. in B. ab. 1828; m. Caroline C. Gregory, Feb. 14, 1848; r. Rock. Their ch. 1, James U., b. ab. 1849. 2, ——— b. '52, d. Jan. '53. 3, Helen F., b. ab. '56. Of this name, also, Enos B. Morton, b. in Bristol ab. 1822; m. Mary P. Lane; r. Rock., a mariner.

Enos B.'s ch. 1, Mary S., b. ab. 1847. 2, Enos B., (2d), b. about '51. 3, John M., b. ab. '53.

MOSHER, James W., b. ab. 1830 in N. Scotia, mar. Margaret J. Stone, July, 1852; r. S. Th., a carpenter. Their ch. 1, Lucy E., b. ab. 1853. 2, Frank H., b. ab. 1858.

MOSMAN, Aaron, b. Oct. 22, 1757, in Sudbury, Mass., came and settled south of Chickawauka Pond, where he had grist and other mills; was a rev. soldier; m. Hepzibah Hosmer, May 28, 1782, 2d, Sarah Gardner, June 16, 1814; and d. Nov. 27, 1840, aged 83. His ch. by 1st wife. 1, Hepzibah, mar. Nathaniel Packard; r. and d. Rock. 2, Capt. Reuben, m. Margaret Studley of Wal, pub. Jan. 31, 1808; r. Cam. and Rock., rem. and is supposed to be dead. 3, Mary, m. Daniel Packard, rem. Cam. 4, William, mar. Lucy Safford of Hope, Dec. 6, 1817; r. and d. Rock. 5, Aaron, (2d), m. Experience Andrews; r. Cam. 6, Betsey, b. Nov. 1, 1800; m. Alanson Dean, April 19, '21; r. and d. Rock. 7, Merrick, born Dec. 8, 1803; mar. Elizabeth Ott of Cam., Oct. 10, '24; r. Rock., on homestead; and d. Oct. 17, '47. The mother, b. in Concord, Mass., July 24, 1759, died June 11, 1812. The step-mother, b. April 11, 1778, in Edgecomb, Me., d. Oct. 28, 1844.

Capt. Reuben's ch. 1, Hannah S., m. James Murch, and d. June 15, 1840. 2, Mary S., m. Robert S. Stockbridge of Castine, Aug. 12, '32. 3, Reuben H., was mate of sch. *Ann*, and died on Nantucket, March 2, '29. 4, Elbridge, steward in same sch., and perished same time with his brother. 5, Capt. Gardner, mar. Sarah H. Shepherd,

May 16, '40, 2d, Emeline Ghentner, May 21, '43. 6, Sarah, m. Burton Fales, r. Th. and d. Dec. 30, '40. 7, Angeline. 8, Daniel.

William's ch. 1, Dillora, born March 14, 1820; mar. Charles Van Duyzer; r. Charlestown, Mass 2, Orris, b. Jan. 30, '22; r. Rock., a peddler, &c. 3, Albion K. Parris, b. April 1, '25; m. Harriet A. Harrington, 2d, Maria ——— of Charlestown, Mass.; r. Rock, a shipbuilder. 4, Catharine, m. Hezekiah Fuller; r. Hope. 5, Mary J., d. young. 6, James, m. & r. Natick, Mass. 7, Henry, m. & r. in California. 8, Judson, r. California. 9, William Reuben, m. & r. Hope.

Aaron, (2d)'s ch. Mial, m. Wealthy A. Clough, Dec. 22, 1855; r. Camden.

Merrick's ch. 1, Malvina, b. June 29, 1828; m. E. Hinkley Heald, Sept. 16, '49; r. Rock. 2, Miles, b. June 6, '30, d. Sept., 1848. 3, Mareuel, b. Jan. 5, '33; m. Bathsheba Ewell of Cam., Sept. 22, '53; r. Cam., a mariner. 4, Maria S., b. Aug. 10, '34; m. Cyrus Hughes, or Hewes, Aug. 24, '52, (who d. at sea, 1855, leaving 1 son, Herbert Leslie, b. ab. '55), m. 2d, Capt. Samuel Conary; r. Rock. 5, Marilla, b. Feb. 29, '36; mar. William F. Dean; r. Rock. 6, Ezekiel D., b. Aug. 26, '37; r. Rock., a teamster, &c. 7, Mary Marinda, b. July 27, '40; m. George A. Drew; r. Rock., rem. California. 8, Almeda S., b. Feb. 4, '45; r. Rock.

Of Capt. Gardner's ch. Gardner M., b. Sept., 1853, d. Jan. 16, '55.

Albion K. P.'s ch. by 1st wife. 1, Harriet, b. ab. 1849. 2, Charles.

MUNROE, or Monroe, Martin, c. from Spencer, Mass., to Th.; m. Eliza Martin, May 4, 1818; r. Th., worked in lime quarries, &c., but removed.? His nephew, Jairus, b. ab. 1795, came also from Spencer in 1815, m. Mary Bentley, Feb. 1, '18; worked at quarrying, and lost his sight, 1825; r. Th.

Martin's ch. 1, Solomon, d. at N. O., March 14, 1839. 2, Lafayette, b. 1823, d Oct. 10, '25. 3, James, r. N. O. 4, Capt. William M., b. 1827, m. Mary J. McAllister, Sept. 3, '51, 2d, Sarah T. Hall, Feb. 10, '59; r Rock., a master mariner. 5, Elizabeth, r. Rock. 6, Diana, b. ab. 1833; m. ——— Alley, (and has son, William L., b. ab. '55), 2d, James Sholler, Feb. 21, '61; r. Rock. 7, Jane Ann, b. ab. '34, m. J. Andrew Johnson; r. Rock.

Jairus's ch. 1, Elizabeth, b. Feb. 2, 1819, m. Oscar F. Healey; r. Rock. 2, Sally A., b. Feb. 4, '23, m. Capt. Harris Robinson, 2d, Capt. Austin Williams; r. Th. 3, Halsey H., b. Oct. 14, '27, m. Lucy H. Tozier, Sept. 11, '55; r. Thomaston, a farmer, inventor of improved rotary harrow, &c. 4, Mary F., b. Nov. 5, '32, m. George Copeland; r. Th. 5, John B., b. Oct. 13, '25, d. Sept. 20, '26. 6, Adelaide, b. May 20, '37. 7, Horace, b. Feb. 28, '39; r. Th., a teacher, soldier in 20th Me. Reg., &c.

MUNROE, Capt. William, of a different family, mar. Susan Dyer, Aug. 4, 1822, 2d, Sarah R. Jameson, Sept. 22, '44; r. S. Th. His ch. 1, Ann Maria, b. Feb. 12, '24. 2, William, b. Nov. 24, '25, d. Oct. 8, '38. 3, Sarah A., b. Aug., 1834. The mother d. Dec. 26, '38. By 2d wife. 4, Robert V., b. ab. 1846.

MURCH, James, came from Castine, m. Hannah Mosman, Oct. 24, 1837, 2d, Mary A. Jameson, Jan. 9, '41; r. and d. Rock.

MURPHY, Daniel, b. ab. 1806, in Cork, Ireland, m. Joanna Murphy; c. to Th. in 1832; r. Th. Their ch. 1, Timothy, b. May 2, 1837; r. Th., a mariner. 2, Daniel, (2d), b. April 4, '39; r. Th., a mariner. 3, Mary A., b. Nov. 2, '41. 4, Michael, b. ab. '44. 5, John, b. ab. '46.

Of this name also, John Murphy, b. ab. 1827, in Ireland, as was Margaret, his wife; r. Rock. Their ch. 1, John, (2d), b. ab. 1846. 2, Patrick, b. ab. '48. 3, Jeremiah, b. ab. '50. 4, Julius A., b. ab. '52. 5, Margaret, b. ab. '54. 6, Dennis, b. ab. '57. 7, Mary, b. '59.

MURPHY, Levi, b. ab. 1832, in St. Geo., m. Abby Bird; r. Rock., a mariner 1860, soldier in 4th Me. Regt., &c. Their ch. 1, Charles A., b. ab. 1855. 2, Corabelle, b. ab. '57. 3, Abby, b ab. '59.

MURRAY, Edward C., born ab. 1807, in Rhode Island, as was Amanda, his wife; r. Rock., a shoemaker. Their ch. 1, Ellen C., b. ab. 1837. 2, Abby S., b. ab. '39. 3, Edgar L., b. ab. '44. Of this name, also, Alexander Murray, b. ab. 1820, m. Matilda ——; r. Rock., a lime burner. Their ch. Alexander, (2d), b. ab. 1853.

MURRIN, Terence, b. ab. 1817, in Ireland, as was Bridget, his wife; r. Rock.

MYERS, Capt. Ephraim, b. ab. 1825, m. Annie E. Blaisdell, Sept. 13, '57; r. Rock., a mariner, rem. California.

NASH, Thomas, and Rebecca, his wife, came early to old Th., from Lincolnville, & had recorded here, their ch.; 1, Capt. Ezekiel R., b. May 1, 1834; m. Mrs. Catharine Stover, Nov. '56; r. Rock., a master mariner. 2, Winslow, b. April 6, d. Aug. 12, '42. Amos W., a nephew of Thomas, b. ab. '33, in Linc., m. Abby Nash; r. Rock., a mariner, entered the navy.

Capt. Ezekiel R.'s ch. 1, Frank, b. ab. 1857. 2, Catharine, b. ab. '59. Amos W.'s ch. 1, Elvira, b. ab. 1857. 2, Cora A., b. ab. '59.

NASH, Andrew J., b. ab. 1828; m. Martha L. Buckminster; ? r. Rock., a lime burner. Their ch. 1, Georgiana, b. ab. '53. 2, Elizabeth, b. ab. '58. 3, Ada A., b. Feb. '60, d. April 26, '61. 4, Lyman H., b. Sept. '61, d March 1, '62.

NEALLEY, Edward S. J., Esq., c. to Th., m. Lucy C. Prince, July 5, 1836, but soon rem. to Bath. Their ch. 1, Edward Bowdoin, b. in Th., July 22, '37; grad. Bowd. Coll., 1858; rem. Iowa. 2, Hezekiah P., b. in Bath, June 11, '40, d. Nov. 5, '41. 3, Henrietta P., d. young. 4. Greenleaf C. 5, Susan.

NELSON, Capt. Charles H., b. ab. 1829, in Edinburgh, Scotland, c. here, m. Maria Harrington, July 7, 1853; r. Rock., a master mariner. Their ch. 1, Isabella F., b. ab. '54. 2, Nellie A., b. ab. '56. 3, Arthur P., b. Jan. 4, '59, d. Aug. 15, '62.

NEWELL, Samuel J., b. ab. 1820; m. Nancy D. ——; r. Rock., in '60, a carriage manufacturer; since rem. China, Me. Their ch. 1, Arthur W., b. ab. '43, an ornamental painter. 2, Ellen E., b. ab. '48. 3, Milton A., b. ab. '52. 4, Eben P., b. ab. '56. 5, Effie F., b. ab. '59

NEUBERT, or Newbirt, Adam; m. 1st, Dorothy Storer, 2d, Lucy (Wentworth) Smith of Knox; r. Wal. An older brother, Michael, m. Mary Feyler; rem. Appleton, and, of his ch., John W., b. ab. 1819; m. Laura E. —— of Fox Isl.; r. Rock., a stone cutter, &c. Adam's ch. by 1st wife. 1, William F., b. '27; m. Mary L. Dunbar, Oct. 23, '64; r. W., a teacher, &c. 2, George G., b. 1828, d. in Wal., '56? 3, Andrew A., b. 1830; m. Arletta A. Penniman, Nov. 17, 1852; r. Rock., a ship carpenter, &c. 4, James W., b. '32; rem. Cal. '52, & m. there in '61. 5, Joel M. b. '36, d. at sea '57. The mother d. Feb. '46. Of other branches of this family, there also c. here, Alvan, b. ab. '28; m. Lydia M. Hall of Wal., r. Th., a mariner. Thomas A., son of Philip of Jefferson; m. Abby Robinson, '55; r. Th

John W.'s ch. 1, George G., b. ab. 1854. 2, Mary L. 3, Lizzie. 4, Frank E., b. Feb. 19, '60, d. Aug. 30, '61.

Andrew A.'s ch. 1, Alphonso, b. ab. 1854. 2, Fannie B. 3, Frederic W. 4, Etta E., b. Feb. 4, and died Oct. 4, '61.

Alvan's ch. Susan, b. ab. 1854.

NEWHALL, Jonathan, came from Lynn, Mass., to Union, before 1791, made the first horse-wagon ever built there; m. Hannah Peabody of W., rem. and died Washington, Me. Of their ch. 1, Jonathan, (2d), b. Aug. 12, 1799, m. 1st, Elizabeth D. Boyd of Wash., 2d, Margaret Yeates of Wal., came to S. Th., July, 1849, a jeweller, millwright, &c. 2, James, b. March 2, 1804, m. Mrs. Rebecca Bowles of Northport; r. S. Th., a teacher, &c. 3, Joseph, b. Dec. 9, 1807, m. 1st, Mary Neubert of Windsor, 2d, Priscilla Jameson of Wash.; r. S. Th., a millwright, &c.

Jonathan, (2d)'s ch. by 1st wife. 1, John B., b. 1828, d. in Calais, Milltown, Jan. 1849. 2, Oscar, d. in 1835. 3, Wilbert, b. Dec. 19, '30. 4, Mary E., b. 1832, d. 1835.

James's ch. 1, Harriet, b. ab. 1830; m. Harrison P. Babb; r. S. Th. 2, Hannah, m. ——— Hopkins of Wash. 3, James T., b. ab. 1833; mar. Alzena Trask, Sept. 23, '61; r. S. Th., a clerk, &c. 4, Catharine L., m. William M. Jordan of Cam., Sept. 16, '56; r. S. Th. 5, Ebenezer W., b. ab. '39, a mariner. 6, Margaret, b. ab. '45. 7, Ellen, b. ab. '47.

Joseph's ch. 1, Mary Elizabeth m. George Bond of Jefferson, June 25, '54; r. S. Th., rem. Presque Isle. 2, ———, d. young. 3, Ann Maria, b. ab. '32. 4, Harriet M., b. ab. '40; m. Emery L. Stetson, April 14, '61; r. S. Th.

NEWALL, Charles, b. ab. 1808; m. Louisa ———; r. Th., a peddler. Their ch. 1, Emma C., b. ab. 1844. 2, Mary, b. ab. '50. 3, Anna, b. ab. '56.

NICHOLS, Dr. ———, a native of Ireland, came to St. George; m. Margaret Kelloch, and d. St. G. His widow m. Shepard Robbins. His ch. 1, Hannah, m. 1st, Edmund Mallard of Union, 2d, Benjamin Kelloch of W., Aug. 27, 1833. 2, George, m. & r. Frankfort.

NICHOLS, Dr. Alonzo D., b. Sept., 1826, in Albany, N. Y.; came to r. in Rock., 1848, in connection with telegraph office; m. Catharine H. Achorn, Aug. 4, '52; was cashier of Lime Rock Bank, editor of Gazette, &c., d. Feb. 25, '63. Their ch. 1, Frances E., b. ab. '54. 2, Florence M., b. ab. '56. 3, Charlie H., d. Sept. 24, 1863.

NICHOLS, Lathley R., b. ab. 1832, in Prospect; mar. Susan T. Morse, Dec. 17, '53; r. Th., a carpenter. Their ch. 1, Charles, b. ab. 1856. 2, George, b. ab. '58.

NICHOLS, Nathaniel, b. ab. 1810, in Bucksport, Me.; m. Sarah Atwood; r. Rock., a mariner, &c. Noah, a brother, b. ab. 1813, in Bucksport; m. Sophronia Hilburn; r. Rock., a painter, &c.

Nathaniel's ch. Grace D., b. ab. 1848.

NICHOLS, P. P., b. in Georgetown; m. Burletta Rivers, June, 1861; r. Th.

NICHOLSON, William, b. March 2, 1791; came from Prescott, Lancashire, England; m. Susan Wyllie of C.; r. Th., a carpenter, & d. Oct. 17, 1860. Their ch. 1, John A., b. Jan. 4, 1818; r. Th., a carpenter. 2, Elizabeth, b. June 10, '19, d. in Boston, June 22, '40. 3, William H., b. March 27, '22, d. May 30, '24. 4, Sarah J., born

March 16, '23; m. Capt. George L. Carney; r. Th. 5, William H., b. April 27, d. June 2, '25. 6, William J., b. Sept. 29, '26, d. Nov. 14, '28. 7, Susan D., b. July 15, & d. Oct. 19, '28. 8, Lucy Frances, b. Aug. 18, 29; m. Thomas Russell; r. Th. 9, Thomas W., b. June 6, '32; r. Th., a mariner; & d. Jan., 1865. 10, Capt. George M., b. Jan. 27, '35; r. Th., a mariner. 11, Marcia F., b. July 27, '37. The mother d. Oct., 1849, aged 55.

NICHOLSON, Thomas, b. ab. 1821, in Sligo, Ireland; m. Mary Brennan; r. Th. Their ch. 1, John, b. ab. 1854. 2, James, b. ab. '56. 3, Mary Hattie, b. ab. '59.

NICKERSON, Moses, b. ab. 1826; c. from Perry; m. Sarah W. (Knowlton) Allen, April 20, '59; r. Rock., a mariner, &c.

NORRIS, Capt. Joseph, b. 1803; c. from Windsor; m. Mary E. Foster, p. Aug. 17, '33; r. Th., rem. St. Paul, Minnesota, 1861, where he d. Sept., 1861. Their ch. 1, Joseph, (2d), b. March 15, and died April 7, 1836. 2, Edward B., b. April 17, '38. 3, Joseph W., born April 20, '40. 4, William, b. ab. '46. 5, Robert, b. ab. '50. 6, Mary Ann, b. ab. '53; all rem.

NORTON, Amos A., b. ab. 1818; m. Hannah J. Bartlett, r. S. Th., in fishery business. Their ch. 1, Aldrick, b. ab. 1845. 2, Amos, b. ab. '47. 3, Joshua B., b. ab. '49. 4, Asahel, b. ab. '51. 5, William S., b. ab. '53. 6, Adelaide A., b. ab. '55. 7, Miriam B., born ab. '57. 8, Ruth, b. ab. '59. Of this name, also, Enoch Norton, b. ab. 1832; m. Mary A. Robinson, June 26, '56; r. S. Th., a mariner. Their ch. Joseph, b. ab. 1857.

NORTON, Edward B., b. in New Vineyard, Me., (whither his father c. from Martha's Vineyard, Mass.), c. to Th., m Rachel Moody, of Nobleboro', June 19, 1839; and d. Feb. 2, '57. Their ch. 1, Isaac E., b. March 1842, d. Sept. 21, '52. 2, Hezekiah Prince, b. Nov., '43; r. Thomaston.

NORWOOD, Isaac, b. ab. 1826; m. Mary A. Lothrop, p. June 14, '52; r. Rock., a mariner.

NUTT; of this family two cousins of Irish or Scotch Irish descent, came to this vicinity, viz.: Col. David, b. ab. 1738, m. and r. in Cam., was an actor in the Rev. War, and d. April 20, 1797, and was buried at the Tolman burying ground, Rock. John, m. twice, r. Cam., a farmer, rem. to Knox.

Of David's ch. 1, Nancy, m. George W. Bowers; r. & d. S. Th.

John's ch. 1, David, (2d), d. in Ohio, ab. 1813. 2, William, b. in Cam., May 27, 1790, m. Nancy Ladd of Belmont, March 25, 1813; came to Rock., 1848, farmer, lime burner, &c. 3, Joanna, mar. Wm. Harkness; r. and d. Cam. 4, Ashley, rem. Ohio, m. Nancy Gardner, and d. ab. 1856. 5, John, (2d), m. Jane Paul of Cam.; r. Cam. 6, Elijah, m. Mary McIntyre; r. Cam. 7, Nancy, mar. Capt. William Brewster; r. Cam. 8, Susan, m. Daniel Melvin; r. Hope.

William's ch. 1, David, (3d), b. July 5, 1813, d. Nov. 17, '24. 2, Lovina H., b. Aug. 29, '15, m. John Cressy; r. Rock. 3, William, (2d), b. June 27, '19; r. Rock., a mariner. 4, Louisa, born April 24, '22, m. Elihu Tilden of Linc., and d. Sept. 26, '53. 5, Nancy, b. May 6, '24, mar. Ephraim Perkins of Freedom. 7, Susan, b. Aug. 27, '26, m. Isaac M. Tilden, May 15, '45. 8, Hannah, b. Oct. 29, '28, m. Eben L. Higgens, and d. 1853. 9, Cornelia, b. April 7, '31, mar. John E. Pendleton, 1850. 10, Isaac F., b. Nov. 8, '35; r. Rock., a mariner.

John, (2d)'s ch. 1, Nancy, m. Elihu Tilden; r. Linc. 2, John, (3d), m. Eliza Miller; r. Cam. 3, James, m. Caroline Clark; r. Cam. 4, Mary J., m. Lawry Gardner; r. Cam. 5, Caroline, mar. Lorenzo Soule of Freedom. 6, Susan, m. Jeremiah Nutt; r. Cam.

Elijah's ch. 1, Jeremiah, m. Susan Nutt; r. Cam. 2, Alzade.

NUTTER, Lorenzo, b. ab. 1831, in Pembroke, Me., mar. Emeline Staples; r. Th., a joiner. Their ch. 1, Clifford, b. ab. '57. 2, Eliza, b. 1859, d. Feb., 1860.

NUTTING, Jonathan, m. 1st, ———, 2d, Mary Butler; r. and d. C. His ch. By 1st wife. 1, Silas, m. Elizabeth Gardner, May 25, 1818; r. C., and died in W. I. 2, Jonathan, (2d). 3, George. 4, Barbara, m. Jacob Hyler; r. and d. C. By 2d wife. 5, Capt. Ebenezer, lost at sea in the *Hercules*. 6, Hepzibah, b. May 15, 1799, mar. 1st, Capt. William Biskey, 2d, Capt. Peter Miller; r. Th., and d. Nov. 9, '61. 7, Thomas, lost at sea, as mate of the *Hercules*. 8, Mary, m. Joshua Jordan; r. and d. Th. 9, Eliza, mar. Alden Robinson; r. Cush. 10, Edward. 11, Clement, d. unm. 12, Freeman, m. r. Cush., and d. March 13, '46.

Silas's ch. 1, Elizabeth, b. ab. 1818, m. Albert G. Lermond, 2d, Capt. Peter Miller; r. Th.

O'BRIEN, John, b. 1755; c. from Craig, Ireland, as ship's steward, to Castine; was employed as a teacher by Mr. Beverage on the Fox Islands, by whose aid he escaped there from the British yoke; found his way to Warren, where he m. Mary, daughter of Col. Starrett, Nov. 14, 1785; r. W., a farmer & schoolmaster, on the place now occupied by his grandson, William L. O'Brien, & d. June 19, 1828. Their ch. 1, Elizabeth, m. Robert Henderson; r. Belfast & W. 2, Lewis, born June 5, 1788, d., shot, accidentally, in his father's barn, April 2, '05. 3, Mary, m. Archibald Crawford; r. W. 4, Hon. John, (2d), b 1791; m. Mary Ann George of Watertown, Mass., Sept. 30, '22; r. Th., a marble manufacturer, warden of prison, councillor, &c., d. Sept. 23, '50. 5, Hon. Edward, b. ab. 1793; m. Mary Starrett, May 16, '20; was long an active shipwright & liberal citizen in W.; rem. Th., 1847, continued ship-building, was State Senator, 1856, visited Europe and the home of his ancestors in 1862; r. Th., in the house he built on Main street, is president of the Georges Bank, &c. 6, James, b. 1795, d. Aug. 27, 1800. 7, Sarah, m. Otis Crocker of Machias, June 27, '24. 8, Seth, m. Nancy Lermond, Jan. 19, '26; r. W. 9, Rebecca, b. ab. 1801; m. Capt. Ichabod Boyles of St. G., Jan. 4, '21; r. Belfast, & d. May, 1846. 10, William A., b. 1803; m. Esther Gardner, p. Oct. 22, '31; r. W., and d. July 6, '37, without ch.; his widow r. Th. 11, George, m. Eliza Martin, p. Dec. 3, '32; r. St. G. 12, Hon. Thomas, m. 1st, Rebecca Malcolm of C., p. Nov. 1, '37, 2d, Nancy B. (McLellan) Carr, Jan. 5, '57; r. Th., has been in both branches Legislature, a trader, &c. 13, David, Esq., studied law in the office of E. Smith, Esq., Warren; m. Eliza A. Whitney of Boston; r. Th.

Hon. John's ch. 1, Susan Jones, b. July 31, 1823; r. Th. 2, Capt. John G., b. Jan. 12, '25; m. Margaret A. O'Brien of W., Aug. 5, '49. 3, Charles F., b. June 19, '27; m. Mary T. Jordan, Dec. 25, '51; r. Th., & d. July 26, '55. 4, Capt. Joseph Lee, b. Jan. 30, '29; m. 1st, Mary E. Bentley, Dec. 6, '50, 2d, Lizzie ———; r. Th. 5, Eli Merrill, b. March 25, '30; r. New York. 6, Edward K., b. Feb. 3, '33; mar. Lydia O. Masters, April 2, '56; r. Th., a merchant, in firm of O'Brien,

Burgess & Co. 7, Henry H., b. Dec. 5, '34 ; r. Th., a merchant, soldier in 20th Me. Reg., &c.

Hon. Edward's ch. 1, Jane S., b. Nov., 1821, d. Sept. 3, '55. 2, Edward Ellis, b. ab. 1829 ; m. Octavia D. Lash, Nov. 11, '50 ; r. Th. a merchant, in firm of O'Brien, Burgess & Co. 3, Mary E., b. ab. 1837 ; m. William A. Campbell ; r. Th.

Seth's ch. 1, Margaret A., m. Capt. John G. O'Brien ; r. W. 2, Thomas Lewis, r. W. 3, Otis C., b. in 1832 ; m. Jane E. Russell of Wal., Sept. 15, '57 ; r. War., and d. June 29, '60. 4, William L., r. War. 5, Rebecca, b. 1839, d. April 29, '42. 6, Oliver L., b. July, 1841, d. Nov. 22, '58.

George's ch. 1, Richard Morris. 2, William Thomas.

Hon. Thomas's ch. by 1st wife. 1, Thomas, (2d), b. April 4, & d. April 10, 1840. 2, Sarah Antoinette, b. Dec. 4, '41. 3, Frederic, b. ab. 1844. The mother d. Dec. 13, 1853, aged 50.

David, Esq.'s ch. 1, Eliza A., b. ab. 1833 ; m. Capt. E. B. Hinkley ; r. Th. 2, Frances, b. ab. 1838. 3, Mary, b. ab. '42. 4, Abby L., b. ab. '47. 5, Horace, b. ab. '49. 6, John, b. ab. '54, d. May 15, '59. 7, Alice, b. ab. '57.

Edward E.'s ch. 1, Frank Pierce, b. Nov. 15, 1852. 2, Freddie, b. 1854, d. Oct. 5, '58. 3, Mary Amelia, b. Sept. 12, '56, d. Oct. 5, '58. 4, Alida Maria, b. Oct. 1, '58. 5, an infant, d. Sept., 1862.

O'BRIEN, Stephen, b. ab. 1825, in Cork, Ireland ; m. Bridget —— ; r. Rock. Of this name, also, Edward, (2d), b. ab. 1810, c. with Mary E., his wife, from Ireland ; r. Rock. 2, Patrick, b. ab. '25, in Ireland, as was Mary, his wife ; r. Rock., a soldier of the 4th Me. reg., missing after the battle of Malvern Hill, July 1, '62. 3, Thomas, (2d), b. ab. '22, in Ireland, as was Helen, his wife ; r. Rock., a quarryman, soldier of the 4th Me., &c.

Stephen's ch. 1, Timothy, b. ab. 1844. 2, Cornelius, born ab. '46. 3, ? John, b. '53, d. '54. 4, Stephen, (2d), b. ab. '56. 5, William, b. ab. 1860.

Edward, (2d)'s ch. 1, Edward, (3d), b. Dec 22, 1852, d. Feb. 5, '61. 3, Julia A., b. ab. '57. 4, Joanna, b. ab. '59.

Patrick's ch. James, b. ab. 1853. The mother d. Oct. 24, '60, a. '40.

Thomas's ch. 1, John, b. ab. 1856. 2, Mary E., b. ab. '57.

O'CONNER, Timothy, b. ab. 1810, in Ireland ; m. Hannah Bartlett, Sept. 7, 1839 ; r. Rock., lost his sight by an explosion in a lime quarry. Their ch. 1, William H., b. ab. 1837 ; r. Rock. 2, Daniel, b. April 24, '40. 3, Mary F., b. ab. '43.

OLIVER, William, of Phipsburg ; m. Elizabeth Young of Cushing. David, a brother, m. & r. in Phipsburg or vicinity.

William's ch. 1 & 2, twins, David, (2d), m. Susan Rogers, r. Georgetown ; George, m. 2d, Susan Parker, r. Bangor. 3, William, (2d), m. Mary Sprague ; r. & d. Georgetown. 4, Margaret, m. Patrick Duley ; r. & d. Phipsburg. 5, Alexander, b. ab. 1794 ; m. Sarah Davis of W. ; r. Th. 5, Betsey, m. William Wallace ; r. Phipsburg. 6, Agnes, m. James Duley ; r. Phipsburg. 7, Robert, m. Eunice Oliver ; r. Freedom. 8, Palmer, b. ab. '02 ; came to W., m. 1st, Sophronia Spear, '30, 2d, Elizabeth Montgomery, '42 ; rem. Phipsburg.

Of David's ch. 1, Campbell, b. ab. 1794 ; m. Lydia Bearce ; r. Th. 2, Bartlett, c. to W. ; m. Eliza P. Patterson, p. Aug. 29, '29, 2d, Mrs. Elsie J. Gilchrist, Nov. 11, '51 ; r. C.

Of William, (2d)'s ch. Loring, b. 1828 ; m. Susan Oliver ; r. Th., carpenter.

Alexander's ch. 1, Elizabeth, m. John Harding, Nov. 26, 1851 ;

r. Th. & d. Aug. 1863. 2, Palmer, (2d), m. Philena Ann Oliver of Georgetown, p. Feb. 24, '56; r. Bath. 3, Pamelia Ann, b. '32; m. William Henry Fales; r. Th. 4, Philinda, m. David Oliver; r. Bath, has 1 child, Frederic Eugene. 5, Joseph B., b. Feb. 5, '41; m. Sarah J. Delano, March 23, '61; r. Th, a soldier in 2d Me. Battery.

Robert's ch. 1, Hannah E., d. young. 2, Robert M., b. 1830; m. Sarah J. Barlow, Dec. 30, '55; r. Rock., a ship carpenter. 3, Addison, c. to Rockland in '56; m. Mary B. Mehan of W., Dec. 3, '62. 4, William Henry, r. Rock., a ship carpenter. 5, Warren Y; 6, Margery S.; 7, Benjamin F.; 8, Wesley; all r. Freedom. 9, M. Ella, d. young.

Campbell's ch. 1, Bradford, b. ab. 1822; m. S. Ann Metcalf, May 4, 49; r. Th, a blacksmith. 2, Silas; r. Th., N. Y., &c. 3, Langley, r. Th., &c. 4, Susan, m. Loring Oliver; r. Th. 5, Harriet, r. Th.

Bartlett's ch. by 1st wife. 1, Capt. David, b. Nov. 6, 1830; mar. Mary C. Feyler, Aug. 30, '52; r. Th. 2, Ebenezer, b. Jan., 1835. 3, Cyrus, b. Feb., 1837, d. at sea. 4, Eliza A., b. March 1, '40; mar. Elmas Hoffsis of W., p. Nov. 19, '63. 5, Scott, b. April 15, '42.

Loring's ch. 1, William, b. ab. 1854. 2, Cora, b. ab. '57. 3, Esther, b. ab. '59.

Palmer's ch. Willie P., b. ab. 1858.

Joseph B.'s ch. ——, b. Aug., 1861.

Capt. David's ch. 1, Cecilia, b. March 13, 1854. 2, Alton Vesper, b. March 17, '56. 3, Edwin P., b. Oct. 31, '58. 4, Mary C., b. Aug. 14, '62.

Robert M.'s ch. 1, Nathan H., b. Feb. & d. May 13, '58. 2, Ada E., b. '60.

Bradford's ch. 1, Carrie E., b. ab. 1851. 2, Hattie A., b. ab. '54. 3, Lawrence, b. 1857, d. Oct. 26, '58. 4, Mary, b. ab. '59. 5, Alice, b. 1861, d. 1862.

O'NEILL, James, b. 1766 in Creuykills, parish of Amlish, county Sligo, Ireland; c. to Philadelphia, thence to Th., early in the century, became wealthy, left valuable quarries and other estate to his ch. and d. June 24, 1859. Eleanor, his wife, was b. 1770 in Ballyshannon, Donegal county, Ireland, and d. in Th., Dec. 13, 1859. Their ch. 1, Mary, b. '09, d. Aug 10, '31. 2, John, b. in Philadelphia, 1811, m. Selina Bartlett, Sept. 7, '41; r. Th., and d. Feb. 3, '61. 3, Ann, mar. Joseph Newman, p. June 22, '32. 4, Eleanor, m. John Henrahan; r. Th. 5, Catharine, d. young.

John's ch. 1, Ellen, b. April 4, 1842, m. George F. Meservey; r. Rock. 2, Hannah, b. ab. 1844. 3, John, (2d), b. ab. '48. 4, Jane, b. ab. '52. 5, Mary, b. ab. '54.

O'NEILL, Wm. Henry, m. Martha Albee, July 29, 1828; r. Rock., soldier of 4th Me. Reg., d. Oct. 15, '63. Their ch. Jane E., b. Nov. 23, 1835.

ORBETON; of this family, two brothers c. early to what is now S. Th. 1, James, m. Mary Fellows of Georgetown, p. Oct. 2, 1785; r. on the William Montgomery place, and d. before 1803. 2, Jonathan, mar. —— Thompson; r. on the farm next adjoining Deacon Keating's; rem. Cam.

Jonathan's ch. 1, Betsey, m. William Paul; r. and d. S. Th. 2, Mary, m. Samuel Paul; r. and d. S. Th. 3, Isaac, mar. —— Andrews; rem. Cam. 4, Experience, m. Josiah Keith, 2d, Matthew A. Campbell; r. Th., and d. Dec. 30, 1859. 5, Mercy, m. Stephen Post;

r. S. Th. 6, Lydia, m. Benjamin Jones, 2d, ——— Barmer, from Ireland; rem. Cam. 7, James, died at sea. 8, Olive, mar. and rem. 9, Sarah, m. Samuel Packard; r. and d. Rock.

Of Isaac's ch. 1, Isaac, (2d), b. ab. 1820, m. Francis B. Achorn, Sept. 7, 1843; r. Rock., a farmer. 2, Edward H., b. ab. '28, in W. Cam., m. Nancy C. Lowe, Aug., '49; r. Rock., a joiner, &c.

Isaac, (2d)'s ch. 1, Mary M., b. ab. 1844, m. James Fosset of U., Oct. 7, '62. 2, William T., b. ab. '49.

ORDWAY, Charles D., b. ab. 1818, m. Mary E. ———; r. Rock., a mariner. Their ch. 1, Frederic, b. ab. 1840; r. Rock., a mariner, entered the navy. 2, Elizabeth. b. ab. '41. 3, Georgiana, b. ab. '43. 4, Franklin, b. ab. '48. 5, Mary E., b. ab. '53. 6, Flora E., b. ab. 1856.

ORFF, Edward, b. ab. 1833, m. Jane E. Wagner, May 23, '53; r. Rock., a mariner.

ORMSBEE, James W., b. ab. 1821, in Seekonk, Mass., m. Harriet W. Deane, Dec. 12, 1847; r. Rock., was a member of city council, &c. Their ch. Helen E., b. ab. 1853.

ORNE; of this family, two brothers c. to this place. 1, James, b. ab. 1825, mar. Ellice ———; r. Rock., a lime burner, &c. 2, Capt. William A., m. Mrs. Alice Morse, Dec. 17, 1848; r. Rock.

James's ch. 1, Augusta M., b. ab. 1846. 2, Henry D., b. '49, d. April 27, '51. 3, George, b. ab. '55. 4, John F., b. May, & d. Aug. 10, 1857.

William A.'s ch. Frank C., b. July, 1858, d. June 6, '59.

OSGOOD, Thomas K., b. ab. 1828, in N. Hampshire, m. Francis M. Snow, Sept. 6, '52; r. Rock., a teacher, &c, dept. collector of customs, now paymaster in U. S. Army. Their ch. 1, Mary L., b. ab. 1854. 2, Alice M. b. ab. '57.

OTT, Peter, came with his family from Germany, r. a time in Boston, was one of the first settlers of Rockport, where he died at a great age, having been blind some years. His ch. 1, Elizabeth, b. 1764; m. William Harkness, r. Cam. and d. Nov. 6, 1856. 2, Peter, (2d), m. r. and d. Cam. Peter, (2d)'s ch. 1, Samuel, a soldier in the war of 1812, d. of putrid fever when stationed at Castine. 2, William, a soldier at Plattsburg, &c., a year and a half; c. home and enlisted for the war, d. at Castine five weeks after his brother. 3, John, drowned at Cam., a. ab. 21. 4, Daniel, also enlisted during the war, returned after the peace, mar. Phebe, dau. of Adjt. Jonathan Allen; r. Cam., Rock., &c. 5, Mary, b. 1797, m. John Smith, and d. June 7, 1863; r. War. 6, Elizabeth, b. 1799, mar. Merrick Mosman; r. Rock. 7, Frances, m. Capt. Luther H. Snow; r. Rock. 8, Naomi, b. 1805, m. John Walsh, r. Rock., and d. Oct. 23, 1856.

Daniel's ch. 1, Daniel, (2d), b. ab. 1819; mar. 1st, Elizabeth E. ———, 2d, Achsah Post, Dec. 16, 1860; r. S. Th. 2, Samuel, b. ab. '21; m. Margaret L. ———; r. S. Th., a fisherman. 3, Mary, b. ab. '23; m. Henry Richardson; r. Rock. 5, Jonathan, and 9 others not ascertained.

Daniel, (2d)'s ch. 1, George W., b. ab. 1843. 2, Lizzie S., mar. George S. Ames of Cam., Dec. 18, '64. The mother d. April, 1860, aged 57.

Samuel, (2d)'s ch. Phebe E., b. ab. 1846.

OVERLOCK, James, b. ab. 1813, in Waldoboro'; m. Phebe Jones

of W.; r. Th., a joiner, &c. Their ch. 1, I. Albion, b. Dec., 1843, d. April 6, '59. 2, Hollis M., b. ab. '49. 3, Frederic, b. ab. 1855, d. Dec., 1862, of diphtheria. 4, George A., b. ab '59, d. of diphtheria, Dec., 1862.

OWEN, David, b. ab. 1820, in Wales, Eng., mar. Rebecca (Bradbury) Coombs, p. April 30, '50; r. S. Th., a mariner. Their ch. 1, Wymond, b. ab. '53. 2, Caroline, b. ab. '57.

PACKARD, Benjamin, a son of Solomon of Bridgewater, (who was the 5th ch. of Zacheus, who was the 3d ch. of Samuel, who came with his wife and child from Windham, England, in ship *Diligent*, of Ipswich, and in 1638 settled at Hingham, Mass., afterwards at Bridgewater, and d. 1684,) was b. Aug. 22, 1743, in Bridgewater, mar. 1st, Ruth Leach, came to St. George's river, where, his wife being lost at sea, m. 2d, Anna (James) Patterson; rem. to Ash Pt., m. 3d, Polly Crockett, p. March 25, 1780; a joiner, &c., r. and d. S. Th.

Benjamin's ch. by 2d wife. 1, Catharine, b. Oct. 3, 1773, mar. Capt. William Robinson; r. C., and Th., d. April 17, 1851. 2, Benjamin, d. young. By 3d wife. 3, Mary, m. Capt. Eben Jordan; r. S. Th., and d. May 24, 1825. 4, Benjamin, (2d), m. Jane Crockett, p. Nov. 7, 1807; r. and d. S. Th. 5, Isaac, b. 1784, m. Lucy Cooper of Vinalhaven, p. Sept. 3, 1814; r. S. Th., d. May 17, '26. 6, David, m. Elionai Emery, Dec. 12, '16; r. and d. S. Th?. 7, Lydia, mar. John Ingraham; r. Cam.

Benjamin, (2d)'s ch. 1, Bethia, d. young. 2, Kezia, b. July 17, 1809, m. David Haskell; r. S. Th., and d. March 12, '46, 3, Lucy, H. b. Feb. 1811; m. Harvey G. Snow; r. S. Th. d., July 13, '37. 4, Samuel, d. young. 5, James, b. 1816, d. at sea, in brig *Danube*, Feb. 11, '39. 6, Asa, absent 20 yrs. or more, on whaling and sea voyages.

Isaac's ch. 1, Nancy, b. Sept. 6, 1815. 2, Hiram, b. Jan. 15, '17. 3, Philena, b. Nov. 3, '18. 4, Irena, b. May 15, '22. 5, Francis F., all rem. with their widowed mother to North Haven.

David's ch. Alonzo, rem. to Ohio.

PACKARD, Samuel, (probably a son of Samuel of Easton, Mass., who was the eldest son of Samuel, (4th), of Bridgewater, eldest son of Samuel, (3d), who was the eldest son of Samuel, (2d), the 2d ch. of Samuel, (1st), from Hingham, before mentioned,) came from Easton to F. and Wal., thence to Th., m. Bethia Waters; r. and d. in what is now Rock. Their ch. 1, Hannah, b. June 7, 1775, mar. John Keen; r. Rock., and d. May 22, 1842. 2, James, b. ab. 1777, mar. Sarah (Watson) Horton, Dec. 25, 1803; r. Rock., a farmer, &c. 3, Nathaniel, m. Hepzibah Mosman, March 17, '03; r. and d. Rock. 4, Daniel, m. Polly Mosman, April 3, '06, 2d, ——— Waterman; r. & d. Cam. 5, Mary, m. Henry Perry, March 14, '02; r. and d. Cam. 6, Bethia, m. Daniel Brewster; r. and d. Hope. 7, Samuel, (2d), b. ab. 1787, m. 1st, Sarah Orbeton, 2d, Harriet (Young) Fletcher, pub. Nov. 15, '22; r. Rock., a farmer. 8, John, mar. Abigail Waterman, May 22, '14; r. and d. Cam.

James's ch. 1, Samuel, (3d), mar. Anna Tolman of Cam., July 4, 1822, 2d, Eliza J. Falkingham, or Patterson, 1856; r. Th., W., and now Rock., a farmer. 2, Mary, m. Simmons Barrows, p. June 12, 1824; r. F.

Nathaniel's ch. 1, Henry, b. Nov. 3, 1805, mar. Jane Kieff, Aug. 13, '29; r. Rock. 2, Lozier, b. April 21, '10, m. Henrietta Sleeper, Aug. 11, '33; r. in South. 3, Erastus F., b. Aug. 9, '12, d. Sept.

28, '38. 4, Lorenzo, b. Jan. 20, '19, m. Ann Colmar, p. Sept. 23, '55; r. Rock., soldier in 4th Me., &c. 5, Capt. Merrick M., b. March 16, '22, m. Harriet A. Bird, Nov. 24, '50; r. Rock.

Daniel's ch. 1, Reuben, b. Feb., 1806, d. Oct. 21, '12. 2, Daniel, (2d), m. Zillah Tolman, Jan. 8, '32; r. Cam. 3, Capt. Joseph, b. ab. 1817, m. Sarah Brewster; r. Rock. 4, Capt. Alden, mar. Mary Achorn; r. Rock. 5, Capt. Isaac, m. Floretta Frost of Rock.; r. Rock., all master mariners.

Samuel, (2d)'s ch. by 2d wife. 1, Lycidia, m. Stephen Frost; r. Cam. 2, Harriet, m. George Studley; r. Cam. 3, Eliza, m. Ezekiel Vinal; r. Cam. 4, Samuel E., b. ab. 1827, m. Esther E. Vinal, July 16, '57; r. Rock., a farmer.

John's ch. 1, Capt. John, (2d), b. Aug., 1815, m. Lucy J. Ulmer, May 24, '42; r. Rock., a master mariner. 2, Oren, m. Eliza Hewett; r. Cam. 3, Hannah H., m. Jeremiah Tolman, (3d); r. Rock. 4, Sarah O., m. ——— Fales, and r. Lowell, Mass. 5, Drusilla E., b. ab. '22, m. Alden Tyler; r. Rock.

Samuel, (3d)'s ch. 1, Sylvia, m. George? Studley; r. Rock. 2, Albert, m. Nancy J. Vinal, p. Jan. 25, 1850; r. Rock. 3, Irena, mar. Huse Tolman; r. and d. Cam. 4, Angelia, m. John Studley, p. May 26, '47. 5, Leander, m. Lucy Ellen McIntyre, Nov. 3, '56; r. War. 6, Lucy A., r. W. 7, James W., b. ab. '43; r. Rock., a musician in 19th Me. Reg., and d. of fever, Dec. 18, 1862.

Henry's ch. 1, Hepzibah, b. Dec. 7, 1829. 2, Jerome, b. Jan. 22, '31; r. Rock. 3, Henry, (2d), born Aug. 9, '32, d. May 9, '37. 4, Alonzo, b. March 15, and d. April 30, '34. 5, Angeline, b. Nov. 23, '35, m. James Barnes, p. May 5, '54.

Lozier's ch. 1, Oscar H., b. May 6, 1834, m. Augusta M. Hewett, Nov. 17, '55; r. Rock. 2, Ardelle C., b. Nov. 17, '35, m. John Griffith, Dec. 5, '54. 3, Orissa A., b. Dec. 2, '37. 4, Lucy O., b. Nov. 8, '39. 5, Erastus F., b. Oct. 5, '41.

Capt. Merrick M.'s ch. 1, Ella, b. ab. '51. 2, Clarence, b. ab. '53.

Of Daniel, (2d)'s ch. Capt. Alden, b. ab. 1832; m. Mary Achorn of Cam.; r. Rock.

Capt. Joseph's ch. 1, Benjamin F., b. ab. 1843. 2, Eunice C., b. ab. '48. 3, Joseph L., b. ab. '55.

Samuel E.'s ch. 1, Harriet M., b. ab. '52. 2, William F., b. ab. '59.

Capt. John, (2d)'s ch. 1, Frederic A., b. ab. 1843; a painter. 2, Charles A., b. Feb. 18, '45, d. Dec. 12, '64. 3, Lucy A., b. ab. '47. 4, Helen Leona, b. 1849, d. May 14, '51.

Oscar H.'s ch. Eugene, b. March, 1858, d. Aug. 15, '59.

Capt. Alden's ch. Margaret Viola.

PACKARD, Daniel L., b. March 23, 1812, in Ipswich, Mass.; m. Eliza Flitner of Pittston, Aug. 10, '34; came here in 1848; r. Th., a joiner. Their ch. 1, William L., b. in Nobleboro', Sept. 4, 1835; m. Sarah Fales, Nov. 6, '62; r. Th. 2, Angeline, b. Sept. 4, '39, d. Sept. 1, '40. 3, Edna Ann, b. in Wiscasset, July 1, '41, d. Aug. 25, '44. 4, Joseph H., b. June 30, '43, d. Sept. 18, '48.

PACKARD, Horace B., m. Mrs. Susan Clark, Oct. 19, 1864; r. Rock.

PAINE, John, b. in Boston, May 29, 1763; traded in Bristol; m. 1st, Catharine Leistner, Jan 7, 1795, 2d, at Wiscasset, Elizabeth (Clough) Huse, Sept. 25, 1800, 3d, Ann (Greenough) Bright of Boston, July 17, 1836; c. to Th., 1805, where he was long a merchant;

& d. suddenly, dropping in the street whilst engaged in conversation, April 5, 1841. There also came with or after him to Th., his mother, Bethia; his brother, Snow Paine, b. Feb. 4, 1774, who traded a long time at the Prison Corner, & d. unm., Feb. 23, 1855; and two sisters, Hannah; & Jane, who m. John Gleason, Esq., & d. May 12, '40, a. 62.

John's ch. by 1st wife. 1, Capt. John Gray, b. March 21, 1797; m. Susan Bowers, Jan. 27, '28; r. Th., & d. Jan. 27, '41. 2, Catharine, b. May 30, '99, d. by drowning, Aug. 21, '24. By 2d wife. 3, Jane, b. Aug. 20, d. Oct. 17, 1801. 4, William Henry, b. Jan. 16, '04, d. at Th., Jan. 24, '11. 5, Elizabeth, b. July 4, '05, d. at Bristol, Jan. 20, '06. 6, Susan A., b. Nov. 19, '06, d. March 10, '07. 7, Jane, b. Nov. 8, '07; m. G. Webster Shibles; r. Th., & d. April 15, '38. 8, Elizabeth, b. Feb. 5, '09; built and r. in Wadsworth street, Th. 9, Sarah Clough, b. May 27, '13; m. R. Thaxter Cushing; r. Th.

Capt. John G.'s ch. 1, Susan Gray; r. Th.. 2, John Thomas; r. Th.; m. Sarah N. Teel of C., April 11, 1863. 3, Catharine Brown; r. Th. 4, Peter M., b. March 24, 1835, and d. April 6, 1859.

PAINE, Henry, Esq., born 1793, in Vernon, Ct.; rem. Amherst, Mass., grad. Waterville college, 1823; commenced teaching, 1812; taught in Vassalboro'; S. Th., 1821; Eastport, 1823; Windsor, Vt.; was preceptor of Monmouth academy from 1827, 4 yrs.; of Waterville do., 4 or 5 yrs.; of China do., 10 yrs.; of Rock. select schools, 5 yrs.; of Th. academy, 7 yrs.; and now teaches in a department of Rock. high school; m. Evelina Bacon; r. Rock. Their ch. 1, Charles H., b. Jan. 13, 1829; m. Alice Drinkwater of Rock., Aug. 12, 1852, printer, publisher of Th. Advertiser, &c.; r. Th., Damariscotta, Bath, and now Hallowell. 2, Evelina M., b. July 30, '30; m. Capt. Joseph A. Havener of Rock., & d. Oct. 27, '55. 3, Lydia J., b. ab. '34. 4, Louisa J., b. ab. '36. 5, William E., b. ab. '38. 6, Isabel M., b. ab. '40

PAINE, Josiah, b. ab. 1833, in Mt. Desert; m. Ellen Kennedy; r. Rock., soldier in 28th Me. Reg., &c. Their ch. 1, Thomas Irving, b. 1857, d. Oct., 1862. 2, Charles, b. 1859.

PAINE, Daniel, b. ab. 1813, in Strong; m. Elizabeth Redlon, Oct. 29, 1845; r. Th.

PALMER, Daniel, mar. ——— Goudy; c. from Bristol, Me., and settled early, west of the Meadows. Their ch. 1, Daniel, (2d), b. 1774, in Bristol, m. Rebecca Blackington, Oct. 4, '04; r. Th., and d. Jan. 18, '56. 2, Mercy, m. John, or Daniel Ray. 3, John, d. unm. 4, Mary, mar. ——— Crockett; r. and d. in Jackson or vicinity. 5, Amos, d. unm. 6, James, d. unm. 7, Hannah, m. George White; r. and d. Th. 8, Sarah, mar. Abraham Bradford; r. and d. Cam. 9, Miriam, m. David H. Clough; r. Th. 10, Elizabeth, d. young. 11, Jane, m. Eben Boynton of Cam.; r. and d. Th.

Daniel, (2d)'s ch. 1, Benjamin B., b. April 15, 1805, m. 1st, Catharine Gallop, 1837, 2d, Sophia Blackington, July 4, '46; r. Th., at Meadows. 2, Elizabeth, b. July 15, '07, mar. John Feyler, April 11, '33; r. S. Th. 3, James W., b. March 10, '09, d. in '37. 4 & 5, twins, b. March 15, '12; John, m. Susan E. Clough, p. April 16, '60; r. Meadows, a farmer; Sarah A., m. David T. Fales, rem. Ill., and now r. Portland, Oregon. 6, Sullivan D., b. March 15, '14, d. Jan. 15, '15. 7, Rebecca W., b. Jan. 25, '16, m. 1st, Elijah Mayberry, 2d, G. Webster Shibles; r. Th. 8, Hannah H., b. July 1, '18, m. William McIntosh; r. Rock. 9, Eunice H., b. Aug. 16, '20, m. Simeon Blood, (2d); r. Rock., and d. Aug. 28, '64. 10, Henry O., b. April 23, and

d. May 23, '24. 11, Eleanor M, b. March 7, '26, m. Capt. Joseph C. Ingraham; r. Rock.

Benjamin B.'s ch. By 1st wife. 1, Benjamin F., b. ab. 1837, m. Harriet Sterling, Feb. 16, '60; r. Th., a soldier of 4th Me. Regt. 2, Helen M., b. Nov. 16, '38, d. March 5, '40. 3, Albion Dudley, born Oct. 31, '41; r. Th., soldier in 1st Me. Cavalry, &c. By 2d wife. 4, Emma, b. ab. '47.

John's ch. Carrie Elthura.

Benjamin F.'s ch. Samuel, b. ab. 1860.

PALMER, Robert A., b. ab. 1836, m. Lizzie J. Ingraham, Sept. 20, '57; r. Rock., a corn and flour merchant, serg't in 28th Me., &c.

PALMER, Joseph, c. from Litchfield, Me., mar. Ann Blackington, Oct. 13, 1823, and r. sometime at Beech Woods, Th; had ch. recorded here, viz.: 1, Joseph E., b. Feb. 1, '24. 2, Frederic, b. April 11, '25, d. Dec. 5, '39. 3, George A., d. April 17, '39; but the family rem. to Pelham, Mass.

PALMER, Daniel, born ab. 1816, in Hopkinton, N. H., mar. 1st, ———, 2d, Asenath Plummer in Augusta, May 21, 1852; c. to Th., was overseer in Prison shoe-shop, 1859, since orderly sergeant in 21st Me. Reg. His ch. by 1st wife. 1, Charles S., b. ab. 1844, soldier in Mass. 35th or 40th Reg. 2, Edwin L., b. ab. '51.

PALMER, William, b. ab. 1834 in England, as was Alice, his wife in Ireland; r. Rock.

PALMER, Greenleaf W., b. ab. 1820, mar. Elizabeth ———; r. Rock., a medicine agent. Their ch. 1, Eugene W., b. ab. 1846. 2, Mary E., b. ab. '51. 3, Ella F., b. ab. '59.

PARKER, Josiah, c. to S. Th.; m. 1st, ——— ———, 2d, Mercy Stetson, Oct. 8, 1820; r. S. Th., rem. Lowell, Mass., there being recorded here; his ch. by 1st wife. 1, Eliza Ann, b. March 2, 1820. By 2d wife. 2, Mary Jane, b. April 1, 1821; m. Charles Newcomb of Rock., p. April 1, '52.

PARKER, Andrew H., b. ab. 1826, in Blue Hill, Me.; m. Lucy A. Eaton; r. Rock., a lime burner, &c. Of this name also, Frank Parker, b. ab. 1829; m. Abby Coombs, Dec. 6, '57; r. S. Th., a mariner. Frank's ch. Frank O., b. ab. 1859.

PARKS, William I., b. ab. 1830, in New Brunswick; m. Christina McLain of Araisaig, N. S.; r. Rock.

PARTRIDGE, Elisha, son of Edward & Sarah, born at Medfield, July or Aug. 8, 1734; m. Dorcas Pond, 1756, 2d, Sarah Fales, Jan. 28, '79; r. on Col. Wheaton's place in U., 1786, left P. Robbins's for home, Jan. 1, '87, on horseback, & was found dead upon the ground, probably from apoplexy; his horse returning riderless. His ch. 1, Simeon, b. May 19, 1758. 2, Zibiah, b. June 18, '60; m. David Fales, Esq.; r. Th., and d. Dec. 21, 1830. 3, Judith, b. March 17, '62. 4, Miriam, b. Aug. 25, '64. 5, Dorcas, b. March 30, '67; mar. Elijah Holmes; r. & d. Rock. 6, Elisha, (2d), b. Jan. 1, '70. By 2d wife. 7, Elibeus, b. Nov. 14, '79, in Franklin, as were the preceding; mar. 1st, Prudence Brown, Nov. 13, 1808, 2d, Mrs. Sarah Crockett, March 2, 1817; r. a time in Ohio, but ret. & d. Dec. 12, '40. 8, Dea. James, b. Sept. 10, '82, in U.; m. 1st, Betsey Brown, Oct. 11, 1804, 2d, Sarah G. Vose, Aug. 8, 1838; r. Rock., & d. Nov. 3, '60. 9, Sarah, b July 4, '86; r. Rock.

Elibeus's ch. by 1st wife. 1, Elisha, (3d), b. May 9, 1811; now deceased. 2, Samuel, b. April 8, '16, in Ohio; m. Lucy Simonton, p. Jan. 12, '40; r. Rock., and d. Aug. 18, '41. By 2d wife. 3, Asa, b. April 16, '22, in Ohio; mar. Mrs. Abigail Colamore; r. Rock., rem. British Provinces. 4, Biancy, b. Feb. 22, '24, in O.; m. Albion G. Achorn; and rem. Mass., or California. 5, Lucy G., b. June 1, '27, in Th.; m. Albion G. Achorn; r. and d. Rock.

Dea. James's ch. 1, Simeon, (2d), b. Nov. 25, 1805; m. Mary A. Spofford, p. March 8, '28, 2d, Mrs. Harriet Crockett, p. Oct. 18, '34; r. Rock., and d. March 1, '56. 2, Alma, b. July 10, '08, d. March 3, '33. 3, Rev. Seavey William, b. May 21, '12; stud. 1831, '2, & '3, at Me. Wesleyan Seminary, Kent's Hill; was licensed at Rock., 1838; and commenced his labors at Th.; m. Hester A. C. Hinkley of Hallowell; and, after faithful and efficient labors in various stations of the M. E. Church, d. at Rock., Aug. 6, '60. 4, Eliza, b. Oct. 20, '15; m. William S. Wyllie; taught in the South, & died at New London, Ct., leaving one dau. Eliza R. Wyllie, b. ab. 1846, who r. Rock.. 5, James, (2d), b. Jan. 9, '18; m. Adeline G. Harrington, Dec. 11, '38; r. Th., a painter. 6, Mary J., b. July 16, '20; m. Hon. N. A. Burpee; r. Rock. 7, Abigail Ann, b. Feb. 29, '28, d. May 5, '51.

Samuel's ch. Mary E., b. April 29, '41, d. April 7, '53.

Asa's ch. 1, Sylvanus C., b. ab. 1841, a mariner. 2, Mary E., b. ab. '45. 3, George S., b. ab. '52.

Simeon's ch. by 1st wife. Rebecca, b. Sept. 20, 1832; m. Andrew G. Reed of Hampden, p. Dec. 2, '52.

Rev. Seavey William's ch. Eugene, b. ab. 1843.

James, (2d)'s ch. 1, Laura Isabel, b. Feb. 27, 1840. 2, James L., b. ab. '44. 3, Frank A., b. ab. '53.

PARTRIDGE, Abram W., b. ab. 1816; m. Elizabeth Weeks, 2d, Betsey Lansil; r. Th., a harness maker. Their ch. Charles, b. ab. '50.

PATTEN, Abel W., Esq., b. ab. 1788; m. Mrs. Sarah N. Bailey; ? r. Rock. & d. March 23, 1858. Of his ch. 1, Sarah E., m. in S. Th. April 18, '47, Daniel C. Prescott, corporal of 9th U. S. infantry. 2, John F., b. ab. '39; r. Rock., a mariner, & perhaps others.

PATTERSON, John, b. ab. 1816, in Vermont; m, Lydia Williston, Oct. 27, '54; r. Rock., a stone cutter, &c. His ch. by a former wife. 1 & 2, twins, b. ab. '47, Betsey & Charlotte. 3, Martha, b. ab. '51.

PATTERSON, Mrs. Nancy, b. ab. 1800; r. Rock., a widow. Her ch. 1, Sarah E, b. ab. 1836. 2, John F., b. ab. 1840; r. Rock., a mariner. 3, Belle A., b. ab. '42; m. Erastus R. Perry of Boston, Sept. 16, '63. 4, Amos P., b. ab. '44; r. Rock., a mariner.

PATTERSON, George S., b. ab. 1827, in Louisiana; m. Catharine C. Stover, Aug. 7, '59; r. Rock., a mariner.

PAUL, Robert, c. at the age of 18, an apprentice boy, of Scottish origin, from the north of Ireland, in the ship "*Grand Design*," which was wrecked on Mt. Desert about 1740, was taken off, after much suffering, carried, with the survivors, (except 16, who stopped at this river,) to Bristol, where he m. a Miss Patterson, r. & d. His ch. 1, John, b. 1763; m. Polly Philbrook, p. May 9, 1795; r. S. Th., & d. May 25, 1838. 2, Matthew, m., r. & d. Franklin county, Me. 3, Jane, m., r. & d. Sandy river. 4, Samuel, m. Mary Orbeton, p. Dec. 9, 1799; r. & d. S. Th. 5, Betsey, m., r. & d. Kennebec. 6, Hugh, m. Lydia Wade; r. & d. Bristol. 7, William, m. 1st, Betsey Orbeton, p. May

9, 1795; r. S. Th., & was a ship builder & active man some time, but went away to British Provinces, m. again, ret. & d. in poorhouse. 8, James, m. Patty Hutchings; r. & d. Cam. 9, Nancy, m. Thomas Foster; r. & d. Montville. 10, Alexander, m. & r. Montville, &c., and d. in Bangor.

John's ch. 1, James, (2d), b. 1795; m. Mary J. Wilson, p. Jan. 4, 1822; r. Ash point, S. Th. 2 & 3, twins, Daniel N., m. Susan M. Wilson, p. Oct. 26, '33; r. & d. Ash point; Martin K., mar. Dorcas Philbrook of Bangor, p. Sept. 12, '31; rem. & d. Frankfort. 4, Alexander, (2d), was washed overboard from br. *Samuel & John*, Capt. Emery, Jan. 2, '27, on voyage to Mobile.

Samuel's ch. 1, Hannah, b. May 11, 1801. 2, Isaac, b. July 4, '03, d. June 15, 1834. 3, Olive, b. June 6, 1805; m. David Robbins; r. Rock. 4, Eliza, b. Dec. 1, '07, deceased. 5, Joseph, b. July, '09; m. Mary A. Winslow of Wal., p. Sept. 16, 1837, 2d, Lydia J. Allen, Oct. 14, '49, lost his sight, April 4, '48, in lime rock quarry; r. Rock., and died July 30, 1852.

William's ch. 1, Achsah, b. Aug., 1800; m. Robert Perry; r. S. Th. & d. May 21, '56. 2, Eliza B., b. '06, d. June 17, '47. 3, Asenath, b. April, '14; m. Samuel B. Perry, & d. June 6, '40.

Fourth Generation.

James, (2d)'s ch. 1, Robert, b. Oct. 29, 1822; m. Lucy T. Fogler, Sept. 30, '46; r. S. Th., a mariner. 2, Mary Janette, b. Jan. 18, '26; m. George S. Gray; r. S. Th. 3, Capt. Josiah W., b. ab. '28; rem. N. Y., has sailed several steam ships to China, &c. 4, Clara M.

Daniel N.'s ch. 1, Capt. Charles S., b. Oct. 14, 1834; m. Lillias M. Snow, May 3, '59; r. Rock. 2, Harriet N. b. Dec. 16, 1836. 3, Laurette, b. Feb. 18, '39. 4, Henry J., b. Jan. 11, '41; r. S. Th., a mariner. 5, Selim, b. ab. '43; r. S. Th., a mariner.

Robert's ch. 1, Albert M., b. 1850. 2, Josiah O., b. 1852.

Capt. Charles S.'s ch. Amanda, b. 1860.

PEABODY; for this family in full, see "Annals of Warren," or, fuller still, the "Peabody Genealogy." Of the sons of Parent, there came to Th., from Hope, 1, John, who m. Lydia Curtis of U.; r. Th., and d. at N. O., Dec. 29, 1848. 2, Jesse, m. Elizabeth Rose, June 12, '40; r. Th., and d. in N. O., April 8, '53. Of the sons of Nathan Peabody, there came hither, 1, Capt. Hugh W., who m. Mary A. Keith of Th., p. July 9, '33; r. Th., and d. at sea, Jan. '47, on his passage from Liverpool to Charleston, S. C., master of ship *Rochester*, of Bath.

John's ch. 1, Elvira D., b. May 3, 1831, m. George C. Sanborn, of Wal., June 11, '50. 2, Jesse, (2d), b. Dec. 19, '32, m. Emily Rutledge; r. Th., a blacksmith. 3, Charles W., b. Feb. 28, '35, m. Mary H. Comery, Nov. 28, '63; r. Th. 4, Elizabeth, b. Dec. 10, '36, mar. Simon Shibles, (2d); r. Th. 5, Lucy, b. Aug. 6, and d. Aug. 28, '38. 6, John, (2d), b. June 30, & d. July 27, '42. Mother d. June 1, '45.

Jesse's ch. 1, Lucinda, b. July, 1840. 2, Frances E.. b. April, & d. Sept., '42. 3, Jane E., b. ab. '45, d. May 26, '60. 4, George E., b. ab. '50. 5, Jesse W., b. ab. '52. One of the sons d. in Dec. '63.

Capt. Hugh W.'s ch. 1, Hugh Edes, b. April 20, 1834, a mariner and soldier. 2, Mary A., b. April 15, '36. 3, Lucy V., b. April 30, '39. 4, William K. 5, Josiah K.

Jesse, (2d)'s ch. 1, Charles R., b. ab. 1855. 2, Jesse E., b. ab. '57. 3, Lucy E., b. ab. '60.

PEABODY, Cyrus or Josiah, of the same family, b. ab. 1824, mar. Susan J., Knowlton, June 6, '54; r. Rock., a lime burner, entered the army. Their ch. 1, Fanny M., b. ab. '55. 2, Wm., b. ab. '58.

PEASE, Havilla, c. from Vinalhaven, mar. 2d, Betsey (Godding) Lindsey, p. Oct. 17, 1818; r. and d.? Rock. Of his ch. by 1st wife. 1, Seba, b. Jan. 1805, m. Mary C. ——; r. Rock., and d. March 17, '64. And probably others. By 2d wife. 1, Hatch, b. Jan. 25, '20, m. Catharine Meloney, Aug. 30, '44; r. Th. 2, Harriet, b. March 21, '24, m. Joel R. Thompson; r. Th.

Seba's ch. 1, Lieut. Havilla, (2d), b. ab. 1827; r. Rock., a mariner, officer in 4th Me., &c. 2, Jesse H., b. ab. '35; r. Rock., a mariner.

PEASE, Capt. Israel L., b. ab. 1836, m. Mary E. Healey, June 18, '60; r. Rock., a mariner, Of this name also, Lorenzo C. Pease, b. ab. 1827, in Appleton, came ab. 1853 to Rock., with Adeliza, his wife; r. Rock., a corn and flour merchant, and died Appleton, Dec. 14, '63. Their ch. Frank, b. ab. 1859.

PECK, William, b. ab. 1806, in New Brunswick, as was Ruth, his wife; r. Rock., a truckman. Their ch. 1, George, b. ab. 1834; a truckman. 2, Chandler, b. ab. '47. 3, Mary S., b. ab. '52.

PENDLETON, Capt. William, b. Aug. 14, 1779; m. & r. Hope; & d. in Rock., April 30, 1856. Of his sons. 1, William, (2d), b. ab. 1809, in Hope; m. Mary Bartlett; r. Rock., manufacturer and dealer in botanic and other medicines. 2, E. Wood, b. ab. 1811, in Hope; m. 1st, or 2d, Emily P. Hunt, p. Nov. 17, 1838, 3d, Susan H. Sherman, March, 1848; r. Rock., a merchant. 3, Capt. Littleton M., m. Elizabeth Crane, p. Dec. 27, 1840; r. Rock. 4, Capt. Ambrose, b. in Hope; m. Priscilla Pendleton, Aug. 26, '42; r. Rock., rem. City Is., N. Y. There also came here from Northport, 3 brothers, cousins to the above, viz.: 1, Job, b. May 16, 1815, in N.; m. Louisa A. Howard; r. Rock., a carpenter, & d. Jan. 7, '62. 2, Capt. Benjamin G., b. ab. 1827, in N.; m. Nancy J. Patterson; r. Rock. 3, James N., b. ab. 1830; m. Helen M. Farrow, June 26, '54; r. Rock., a joiner, and soldier, killed in battle, May 5, '64.

William, (2d)'s ch. 1, William R., b. ab. 1840; mar. Helen H. Spalding, Dec. 3, '61; r. Rock., a mariner. 2, Frances A., b. ab. '42. 3, Ellen A., b. ab. '44. 4, ? Charles, b. ab. '50.

E. Wood's ch. 1, Adelaide C., m. Chandler Howes of Frankfort, Nov., 1854. 2, Cornelia, b. ab. '45. By 3d wife. 3, George W., b. ab. '51. 4, Annabelle.

Capt. Littleton M.'s ch. 1, Capt. Albert C., b. May 8, 1842; mar. Caroline D. Crockett, Jan. 31, '64; r. Rock. 2, Mary E., b. March, 1854, d. Feb. 4, '58. 3, Willie B., b. April 18, '57, d. Feb. 8, '58.

Job's ch. 1, Louisa E., b. March, 1842, d. Nov. 27, '54. 2, Sandford H., b. ab. '45; r. Rock., entered the army. 3, Helena C., b. ab. '48. 4, F. Eugene, b. March 15, and d. Sept. 8, '53.

Capt. Benjamin G.'s ch. Lucy A., b. ab. 1858.

James N.'s ch. 1, Joseph Hosmer, b. Oct. 7, 1856, d. June 9, '58. 2, Lucy H., b. ab. '59.

PENNIMAN, Capt. Silas, came from Hingham, Mass.; m. Fanny M. Ulmer, May 1, 1826; r. Rock., & d. at Charleston, S. C., Sept. 24, 1838. Their ch. 1, Silas M., b. Oct 19, 1826, d. Nov. 24, '38. 2, Susan F., b. Aug. 4, '28; m. S. P. Cook, Oct. 13, '41, 2d, Andrew J. Lord; rem. California, & d. April 9, '64. 3, Capt. Hiram G., b. Dec. 23, '31; m. Lydia A. Coombs, July 19, '49; rem. Mauston, Juneau county, Wis. 4, Rufus L., b. Jan. 3, '32; m. Sarah H. ———, who d. Nov. 6, '56, aged 28. 5, Albion P., b. Oct. 13, '33, d. Oct. 21, '34. 6, Asahel W., born Aug. 13, '35; r. Rock., a mariner. 7, Arletta Amitia, b. March 18, '37; m. Andrew A. Newbert; r. Rock. 8, Silas H., b. June 3, '39, d. June 2, '40, perished at sea; & with him Henry T. Penniman, connection not ascertained.

Of Capt. Hiram G.'s ch. Ella F., b. Jan. 9, 1858, d. Sept. 13, '62.

PERKINS, Dea. Asa, b. 1798; mar. Mary Day of Damariscotta; c. from Windsor, Me., about 1830; r. Th., clerk of the State Prison. Their ch. 1, Alonzo, b. 1822; m. Martha D. Goodenow of Ashland, Mass., Nov. 10, 1846; r. Th., a sash and blind dealer, volunteer in Me. Cavalry, c. home sick with typhoid and died Aug. 24, 1862. 2, Anthony, m. Eliza J. Adams, Jan. 20, '48; r. San Francisco. 3, G. Barton, b. 1825; m. Nancy R. Delano, Dec. 8, '53; r. Th., a carpenter; soldier of the 1st Me. Cavalry; d. at home Oct. 21, '64. His wife d. May 6, '61. 4, Mary C., b. June 5, 1831; m. 1st, Capt. Robert Campbell, 2d, ——— Hall; r. Damariscotta. 5, Rev. Asa, born Dec. 1, '34; grad. Waterville Coll., 1856, and Newton The. Sem., 1860; ordained at Rockport, Sept. 12, '60, a Bapt. minister. 6, Francis O., b. May 15, 1836, r. Th., a soldier of the 21st Reg., d. at New Orleans in 1863. The mother d. July 4, 1864.

Alonzo's ch. 1, Edward E., b. 1851. 2, Alice N., b. '53. 3, Robert C., b. ab. '55. 4, George A., b. ab. '57.

PERKINS, Heman N., b. ab. 1832, in Penobscot; m. Lorinda Mason; r. Rock., a lime burner, &c. Their ch. 1, Oriana, b. 1849. 2, Mary E., b. ab. '52. 3, Clara E., b. ab. '54.

PERRY, Job, born at Marshfield, Mass., mar. 3d, Abigail Ford; r. Georgetown, Boothbay, and S. Th., where he d. ab. 1789. His ch. by 1st wife. 1, Simeon, d. young. 2, Polly, m. ——— Pinkham; r. Boothbay, and d. at an advanced age leaving many descendants. By 3d wife. 3, David, died in the army of the Revolution. 4, Hannah, m. a Harrington; r. and d. Boothbay, or vicinity. 5, Lieut. Joseph, b. 1761, in Marshfield; m. Jemima, dau. of Dr. Brown of Fox Is., p. Nov. 10, 1785, 2d, Lucy Holland; r. S. Th., and d. Jan. 18, 1853. 6, Eli, r. and d. Phipsburg. 7, Job, (2d), b. in Georgetown, April 21, 1762; m. Polly Jordan, p. Aug. 3, '92; r. S. Th. and d. Dec. 19, '41. 8, Abigail, m. Robert Thorndike; r. and d S. Th. 9, William, born in Boothbay, 1771; m. Polly Randall, p. Sept. 5, 1794, 2d, Mrs. Jane McLoon, Nov. 25, 1834; r. S. Th., and d. Jan. 29, 1853. 10, Mercy, m a Ford, r. and d. Ohio.

Lieut. Joseph's ch. 1, David, born March 17, 1788; r. S. Th., a mariner, &c. 2, Capt. Abner, b. Aug. 6, '89; m. Hannah Hix, Jan. 13, 1820, 2d, Sylvia Marsh; r. Cam., lost with his vessel, being run over off Portland by a steamer. 3, Charlotte, b. May 31, '91, d April 22, 1805. 4, Sally, b. May 25, '93; m. Elliott Tolman; r. and died Rock. 5, Joseph, (2d), b. Aug 1, '97; m. Lydia Jordan, Oct. 14, 1832, 2d, Susan Young, May 17, 1846; r. and d. Vinalhaven. 6, Capt. Thomas B., b. Aug. 1, 1800; m. Susan D. Hall, Dec. 2, '32; r. Rock., and d. Dec. 24, '41. 7, Samuel, b. May 6, 1802; m. Susan Twist, Feb 12, '29, and d. Feb. 4, '40. The mother d April 15, 1807, aged 45. By 2d wife. 8, Capt. Mark, b. Jan. 15, 1811; mar. Margaret Butler, Jan. 22, '37; r. Rock., was sergeant, &c. in 4th Me. reg. 9, Oliver H., b. May 25, 1812; mar. Eliza B. Cooper, Jan. 26, 1837; r. Rock., a merchant. 10, Capt. Harvey, b. May 5, 1814; m. Lydia B.

Chapman, Jan. 17, '39 ; r. Rock., rem. 11, Eliza K., b. Feb. 5, '19, m. Capt. Isaac K. Thomas; r. Rock. 12, Capt. John, b. July 3, '21; m. Harriet Wooster, Jan. 25, '45; r. Rock., a ship master, &c. 13, Susan Maria, b. Oct. 22, '25 ; m. Edwin Thomas Emery, r. S. Th.

Job's ch. 1, Capt. Israel J., b. Dec. 6, 1792, mar. Eliza K. Spear, Jan. 24, 1821 ; r. Rock., & d. May 31, '52. 2, Betsey, born Oct. 14, '94, d. young. 3, Capt. Robert, b. Nov. 10, '96, mar. Achsah Paul, Dec. 2, 1819, 2d, Mrs. Frost; r. S. Th., rem. and d. in West. 4, Ezekiel, b. July 15, 1800, m. Eliza Beecher of Martha's Vineyard, Oct. 17, 1827; r. Rock., and d. Dec. 19, '54. 5, Harriet, b. Sept. 10, 1802, m. Samuel B. Butler; r. S. Th. 6, Capt. Job, (2d), b. July 13, '05, m. Maria Butler, Nov. 14, 1830, and d. lost at sea on his return from Mobile. 7, Susan, b. Oct. 3, '07, m. Elkanah S. Smith, and d. Nov; 21, '34. 8, Mary, b. June 11, '09, m. Ebenezer Sweat, Aug. 25, '30. rem. and d. in Muscatine, Iowa, Feb. 9, '62. 9, Capt. Samuel B., b. June 30, '11, m. Aseneth Paul, Dec. 4, '33, 2d, Mary J. Ingraham, Dec. 24, '40; r. S. Th., rem. Vinalhaven. 10, Joshua, b. Jan. 10, '15. d. March, 1835, lost overboard from ship *Franklin*.

William's ch. By 1st. wife. 1, Sally, b. Oct. 5, 1796, m. Dea. Peter Hall; r. Rock., and d. Nov. 15, 1858. 2, Polly, b. Aug. 13, '98, m. Jacob Fountain; r. Rock., and d. April 24, '35. 3, William, (2d), b. June 13, 1800, m. Oliva D. Fountain of St. George, 1829, 2d, Sarah J. Seavy, p. March 15, '60 ; r. Rock., keeper of alms-house, &c. 4, Eli, b. April 9, 1802, m. Alice M. (Frye) Prior; r. Rock., a trader, &c. 5, Jane, b. March 13, 1804, m. Daniel C. Haskell; r. Rock. 6, Hannah, b. April 20, '06, m. Jonathan Crockett, (3d); r. Rock., & d. Aug. 20, '41. 7, Lucy, b. Nov. 18, '08, d. July 31, '10. 8, Benjamin, b. Feb. 10, '11, d. Aug. 25, '15.

Capt. Thomas B.'s ch. 1, George T., b. Sept.. 17, 1833; m. Clara O. Hall, Jan. 28, '60; r. Rock., a caulker. 2, Horace S., b. Aug. 21, '36; r. Rock., a mariner. 3, Elijah H., b. March 14, '40; r. Rock., a clerk.

Capt. Mark's ch. 1, Albert J., b. Jan. 29, 1838, d. Dec. 29, '42. 2, Emma R., b. Nov. 10, '39, d. Jan. 5, '42. 3, Frances A., b. April, '42. 4, Lewis B., b. Jan. 30, '45, d. Feb. 1, '48.

Oliver H.'s ch. 1, Oliver L., b. Aug. 13, 1838, d. Sept. 27, '41. 2, Helen B., b. Feb. 27. '42, d. Feb. 25, '44. 3, Frederic L., b. Aug., 1844, d. April 20, '47. 4, Oliver H, (2d), b. ab. '48. 5, Heman H., b. Jan. 28, '52, d. Oct. 22, '61. 6, Cora, b. ab. '58.

Capt. Harvey's ch. 1, Abby, b. March, 1840. And others.

Capt. John's ch. 1, Georgiana, b 1846. 2, Clara E, b. 1849. 3, Hattie H., b. 1857.

Capt. Israel J.'s ch. 1, Israel J., (2d), b. April 17, 1822; m. Hannah D. Fowler; r. Rock., landlord of Atlantic House, &c. 2, Leonard S., b. June 11, '24, d. Dec. 23, '42. 3, Harriet Ann, b. Sept. 1, '26; m. Rufus R. Woodbridge, March 8, '46, & d. May 29, '52, hers and her father's funeral being held in one day and house. 4, Margaret S., b. July 29, '28 ; m. Jesse R. Richardson; r. Rock. 5 & 6, twins, b. Aug. 13, '31; Helen L., d. Aug. 5, '33; Hester A., m. Capt. Joseph T. Berry; r. and d. Rock. 7, Van Buren, b. Feb. 21, '35, d. Aug. 21, '39. 8, Edgar A., b. Oct. 21, '38; r. Rock., a clerk, vol'd Sept., 1861, became Sergeant Major of 8th Me. Reg., and d. at Tybee Is., of typhoid, May, 1862. 9, Albert W., b. Nov. 26, '40; r. Rock., a marble worker.

Capt. Robert's ch. 1, Louisa J., b. Oct. 5, 1820; mar. Charles R.

Mallard; r. Rock., & d. June 16, '47. 2, Nancy J., b. Sept. 17, '27, r. Rock., & d. Oct. 31, '62.

Ezekiel's ch. 1, James C., b. July 22, 1828; r. Rock., a paper hanger, &c. 2, Erastus B.. b. March 11, '30; m. Amelia A. Patterson, Sept. 16, 1863; r. Boston. 3, Sarah B., b. Oct. 12, '31, d. Aug. 21, '33. 4, Ezekiel I., b. Oct. 27, '33; r. Rock., a soldier of 28th Me., since in navy. 5, Orlando G., b. Nov. 12, '35; r. Rock., a mariner. 6, Hester, b. Nov. 13, '37, d. March 10, '40. 7, Gardner, b. June 29, & d. July 10, '40. 8, Ambrose C., b. Dec. 4, '42; r. Rock., a saloon keeper. 9, Eliza J., b. Dec. '47, d. March 19, '51.

Capt. Job, (3d)'s ch. 1, Capt. Gilbert H., b. Dec. 26, 1831; r. S. Th., officer in the army. 2, Dr. Henry F., b. Jan. 10, '34; went west, taught, studied medicine, engaged in lumbering, was appointed, May, '61, agent on Dayton & Mich. R. R., & is now a lieut. in co. G, 38th Indiana reg. 3, Oscar R., b. Oct. 4, 1835; m. Irene R. Fisk, April, '62; r. S. Th., member of Coast Guards, &c. 4, Adelaide, m. Andrew J. Erskine; r. Rock.

Capt. Samuel B.'s ch. 1, Leander L., b. May 17, 1833; r. California. 2, Julia E., b. 1835; m. Amariah Kalloch, (2d); r. S. Th. 3, Frank B., b. '40; killed by a fall from aloft; Sept. 17, 1863, off Nantucket shoals. By 2d wife, 4 & 5, twins, b. Nov. 30, 1843; Charles Mallard, d. Feb. 12, '49; Emeline, r. Rock. 6, Eber M., b. ab. '49.

William, (2d)'s ch. 1, Lovisa J., b. Dec. 1, 1830, d. Dec. 9, '36. 2, Sarah Olive, b. Feb. 23, '33, d. June 30, '37. 3, Benjamin, born Nov. 15, '34, d. Dec. 30, '35. 4, Wm. Henry, b. July 8, '35, d. April 13, '37. 5, George H., b. March 18, '37, d. July 14, '38. 6, Lieut. John Fairfield, b. Feb. 4, '39; r. S. Th., a teacher, and officer in army, m. Olive A. Fisk, Nov. 7, '63. 7, Caroline, b. in St. George, April 26, '41, d. March 3, '50. 8, Sergt. Eli R., b. '43; r. S. Th., entered the army. 9, William R., b. '45. 10, Oscar, b. ab. '47. 11, Mary Florence, b. '56. By 2d wife. 12, Fanny, b. June 7, '63, d. April 3, '64.

Eli's ch. Delia Maria, b. Sept. and d. Nov. 1836.

PERRY, John, of a different family, c. from Cape Cod, to Fox Is, about 1773, and, in the war of 1812, to what is now Rock. Of his 13 ch there settled here, 1, Capt. Ephraim, b. 1788, m. Nancy Crockett, Nov. 15, 1814; r. Rock., and d. May 10, '62. 2, Capt. Robert, (2d), mar. Dolly Spear, Aug. 1, 1821, 2d, Millicent Eaton, Sept. 2, '27; r. Rock., and d. of fever, at N. Y., Jan. 31, '51. 3, Lucy, b. 1785, mar. Capt Benjamin Thomas; r. Rock., and d. Feb. 23, 1851.

Capt. Ephraim's ch. 1, Angelia M., b. March 20, 1815, m. Joseph Furbish; r. Rock., and d. Nov. 4, '51. 2, Sophia C., b. May 10, '17; r. Rock. 3, Capt. Knott C., b. April 27, '20, m. Deborah L. Grant, July 18, '43; r. Rock. 4, Ephraim M., born Feb. 2, '23; r. Rock., a photographist, and d. Jan. 17, '62. 5, John J., b. Jan. 26, '25, mar. Mary F. Cowl of Brooklyn, N. Y., Aug. 4, '52; r. Rock., a merchant. 6, Oliver A., b. March 15, '28, d. April 9, '29.

Capt. Robert, (2d)'s ch. 1, Harriet, b. May 5, 1822, d. July 14, '29. 2, Dolly, b. April 30, '24; mar. Patrick W. Walsh; r. Rock. By 2d wife. 3, Edward C., b. Jan. 15, '29, d. May 3, '32. 4, Jasper, b. Dec. 10, '30, d. Sept. 11, '31. 5, George W. or F., b. Jan. 11, '32, mar. Adecia Spear, Nov. 28, '59; r. Rock., a teacher, &c 6, Chas. C, b. Apr. 24, '33; r. Rock., a mariner, soldier of 4th Me, &c. 7, Mary E, b. June 23, '36. 8, Robert Frank, b. Oct. 28, '37, m. Eliza J. Aldrich, Feb. 2, '62; r. Rock., a sailmaker. 9, Oren C., b. April 29, '39. 10, Edward, b. Oct. 28, '42, d.? young. 11, Lucy Ann, b. ab. '45.

Capt. Knott C.'s ch. 1, Ephraim, b. ab. 1844. 2, Frederic W., b. ab. '49. 3, Rebecca C., b. ab. '51. 4, Ellen E., b. ab. '54. 5, Angelia R., b. March 4, '59, d. March 24, '60.

John J.'s ch. 1, Jarvis C., b. ab. '57. 2, Orrin F., b. ab. '59. 3, John J., b. ab. '60.

George's ch. George, b. 1860.

PERRY, Capt. Nathaniel, of Roxbury, Mass., settled early in S. Th. His ch. 1, Nathaniel, (2d), b. in Roxbury, 1816, m. Louisa G., Pillsbury; r. S. Th., a mariner. 2, George F., m. a dau. of Henry Achorn; r. Mass. 3, Mary, m. Peter Christian; r. Boston.

Nathaniel, (2d)'s ch. George F., b. 1849.

PERRY, Chandler F., b. ab. 1813; c. from New Meadows, 1854 to Owl's Head, S. Th., m. Sarah ——; was a farmer, and one of the first volunteers in the 4th Me. reg., a prisoner and hospital nurse at Richmond, Va., and d. Nov. 27, '61. Their ch. 1, Chandler F., (2d), b. 1836; m. Miss Young of Matinicus; r. S. Th., a mariner and vol. soldier, killed in battle, July, 1863. 2, Mary Ann, born ab. '39; m. Daniel Pierce of Munroe, Oct., 1864. 3, Capt. William Henry H., b. ab. '41; m. Sarah C. Arey, Nov. 27, '62; r. S. Th. 4, Levi J., b. ab. '42, a mariner, corporal in 4th Me. reg., &c. 5, Elizabeth, m. Thomas Maddocks; r. S. Th. 6, Harriet C., b. ab. 1857.

PERRY, William, (3d), c. from Cam. or Hope; m. Lucinda Havener; r. Rock., a truckman. Their ch. 1, Lieut. William A., b. ab. 1831; m. Marion W. Brown, April 24, 1853; r. Rock., a caulker, officer in the army, &c. 2, ? Abner A., entered U. S. navy. 3, ? Estelle H., b. '46, d. April 14, '60. 4, Ella H., b. ab. '49. 5, Mary E., b. ab. '52. 6, Charles W., b. ab. 1855.

Lieut. William A.'s ch. Cornelia A., b. 1856.

PERRY, Rev. David, of a North Haven family, b. 1822; m. Miss Rogers of Lincolnville; was Bapt. minister in Cam., Union, and S. Th., and d. in Boston, May 27, 1859. Their ch. Celia, b. ab. 1849.

PERRY, Upton, b. ab. 1811; c. from Camden; m. Sarah A. Spencer; r. Rock. Their ch. 1, James N., b. ab. 1844. 2, Justina J., b. ab. '50. 3, Laurietta, b. ab. '52. 4, George W., born ab. '55. 5, Manly H., b. ab. '58.

PERRY, Benjamin, m. Peggy Tolman, r. and d. Camden. Their ch. 1, Martha, m. Oliver Graffam of Camden. 2, Joseph E., b. ab. 1827; m. Araminta Philbrook of Matinicus; r. S. Th., a carpenter. 3, Chesley B., m. Margaret Philbrook; r. Matinicus.

Joseph E.'s ch. 1, Franklin, b. ab. 1855. 2 & 3, twins, b. ab. '57, Wesley L., and Leforest C. 4, Martha, b. ab. 1858.

PETERSON, John, b. 1822, in Sweden, Europe; m. Almira Burnham, July 11, 1853; r. Th., a mariner. Their ch. 1, Albertina, b. ab. 1855. 2, Mary S., b. ab. 1859.

PHILBRICK, Walter, b. ab. 1805; m. Rachel Sheldon, ? r. Rock. Their ch. 1, James G., b. ab. 1831; m. Amelia Seavey, Feb. 8, '61; r. Rock. 2, William A., b. Dec. 26, '33, volunteer in 4th Me. reg. & d. at Alexandria, Va., Dec. 16, '61, of fever. 3, Benjamin Franklin, b. ab. '36, r. Rock., soldier in 4th Me., reg. 4, Martha J., b. ab. '43. Of this name, also, Enoch S. Philbrick, born ab. 1820; mar. Eunice ——; r. Rock., a lime burner, soldier in 4th Me., &c. Their ch. 1, Mary M., b. Aug. 14, 1839; m. Samuel Haskell; r. Rock., and d. Nov. 26, '57. 2, Celesta, b. ab. 1844.

PHILBROOK, Jeremiah, mar. Sarah Leadbetter; r. and d. N. H. Their ch. 1, Mary, m. William Estes; r. and d. Portland. 2, Jeremiah, (2d), b. May 27, 1777; m. Hannah Hasey; r. S. Th., and d. June 30, 1861. 3, Phinehas, m. Lydia Young; r. and d. N. H. 4, Sarah, m. Ezra Burgess; r. & d. Searsmont. 5, Susan, m. Alexander Young; r. N. H. 6, David, m. Joanna Andrews; r. Th. 7, Hannah, m. Eben. Young; r. N. H. 8, Daniel, m. Rachel Young; r. & d. N. H. 9, William, m. Rachel Norton; r. O. 10, Ezekiel, m. Martha Young; r. Freeport. 11, Elisha, a land surveyor and agent in Michigan. 12, Jesse, died young.

Jeremiah, (2d)'s ch. 1, Jesse, b. Aug. 27, 1804; mar. Rose Ann Lindsey, Dec. 20, '27, 2d, Nancy Davis, Nov. 28, '41; r. S. Th., rem. back of Bangor. 2, Samuel, b. April 28, '06; m. Rebecca Hunt, p. Nov. 21, '35; r. S. Th., a farmer. 3, William Hafse, b. Sept. 28, '08; m. Joanna Dolph of Beverly, Dec. 5, '33; r. S. Th , a farmer. 4, Jeremiah H., b. July 13, '10; m. Mary H Pratt, Dec. 25, '39; r. S. Th., a cooper. 5, Nancy, b. Sept. 22, '12; mar. David Robinson, Jan. 9, '45; rem. East 6, Julia, b. March 24, '15; m. Nathaniel Ash; r. S. Th. 7, Oliver F., b. April 10, '17; m. Sarah Pratt, Oct. 13, '37, 2d, Mrs. Mary J. Jackson of Rock., Dec. 15, '60; r. S. Th. 8, Joseph W., b. May 12, '19; m. Emily K. Petty; r. S. Th. 9, Hannah, born March 21, '21; m. Alfred Haskell. 10, Levi, b. July 27, '23; died young. 11, Charles J., b. March 21, '27; mar. Olive Buckman, Jan. 19, '59; r. S. Th., a mariner.

David's ch. 1, Susan, m. Daniel Hall; r. S. Th. 2, Sabra, mar. George Lawrence; r. Searsmont. 3, Rufus, m. Sarah Andrews; r. St. G. 4, Ruth, d. unm. 5, Sarah, d. unm. 6, Deborah, d. young. 7, David, (2d), d. unm. 8, Elizabeth, mar. ——— Turner; r. West Newton, Mass. 9, Isadore F., m. Reuben White, jr.; r. Boston. 10, Lilias, m. J. Harvey Boggs; r. Th. 11, Isaac, mar. Harriet Maxey; r. St. George.

Third Generation.

Jesse's ch. William, b. 1830; drowned in well, Sept. 6, 1832.

Samuel's ch. 1, Horace S , b. Oct. 31, 1836, d. Dec. 18, '61, lost overboard from sch. *Peru*, in Portsmouth harbor. 2, Julia M , b. Aug. 28, '39; m. Capt. Israel A. Thorndike; r. S. Th. 3, Levi A., b. Sept. 3, '41; r. S. Th., soldier in 4th Me., &c. 4, Sarah E., d. Aug. 18, '48. 5, Franklin, b. ab. '48. 6, Oscar, b. ab. '52. 7, Emma I., b. ab. '55.

William H's ch. 1, Lucy A , b. Sept. 6, 1834. 2, Catharine A., b. Sept. 16, '36. 3, Margary, b. Oct. 5, '38; r. S. Th. 4, Paulina M., b. Aug. 2, '40; m. Wm. A Vose, Oct. 31, '64; r. S. Th. 5, Cordelia F, b. Feb. 10, '42. 6, William J., b. 1844; r. S. Th., soldier in 1st Cavalry, d. March 1, '63. 7, Ada, b. Oct., and d. Nov. 16, '48. 8, James A., b. ab. '50.

Jeremiah H.'s ch. 1, Dudley S., b. Oct. 24, 1840; m. Jennie Kalloch, May 7, '64; r. S. Th., a mariner. 2, Joseph M., b. May 23, '42, d. Aug. 22, '55. 3, Mary A., b. ab. '49. 4, Lucy E., b. ab. '57.

Oliver F.'s ch. Matilda, b. ab. 1839; mar. George Mayo, Oct. 26, '64; r. S Th. The mother d. in May, 1860.

Joseph W.'s ch. 1, Georgiana, b. ab. 1846. 2, Charles M., b. '48. 3, Malvina H., b. July, 1850, d. Nov. 27, '54. 4, Julia E., b. '55. 5, Manford, b. '57. 6, Harriet E , b. '59. The mother d. March 29, '61, aged 37.

PHILBROOK, Benjamin, b. ab. 1822, in Northport; m. Elizabeth

Maddocks; r. Rock., a joiner. Their ch. 1, Inez, b. ab. 1851. 2, Egbert, b. 1853, d. Oct. 10, '54. 3, Mabel, b. ab. '57. 4, Frances H., b. ab. '59. 5, Willie O., b. Nov., 1860, and d. June 4, '61. Of this name, also, John Philbrook, m. Clementine Thorndike; r. Old Th., & d. in New York. Their ch. 1, Harriet P., b. Nov. 29, 1841, died March 7, '42. 2, Lucy C., b. Nov. 15, '42.

PHILLIPS, George H., b. ab. 1821, in Mass.; m. Mary J. Bennett, Feb. 20, '48; r. Rock., a painter & glazier. Their ch. 1, John L., b. ab. 1851. 2, Edgar, b. ab. '53. 3, Ella F., b. ab. '55. 4, Minnie, b. '57. 5, Samuel M., b. Oct. 5, '59, d. Oct. 17, '61. Of this name, also, there were here, Calvin S. Phillips, who m. Abigail M. Greeley of Palermo, p. Oct. 10, 1836, 2d, Mary H. Scammon, May 4, '51; r. Rock.? and Aaron Phillips, who m. Mary Wood, p. Jan. 8, 1839; & of whose ch,, there was recorded here, 1, Adelbert, b. May 25, 1841.

PIERCE, Barzillai, b. 1779; c from Bangor, Me.; m. Jane Turner, June 10, 1802, 2d, Sarah Hix, Dec. 29, '33; r. S. Th., a farmer, & d. Oct. 24, '61. Joseph, his father, also d. at S. Th., Sept. 2, '03, a. 65. Barzillai's ch. by 1st wife. 1, William, b. Jan. 13, '03; m. Mercy J. Pratt of Corinth, p. Oct. 27, '27; r. S. Th. 2, Israel S., b. Jan. 1, '05; m. Mary Snow of Nobleboro', Oct. 23, '28; r. Rock., d. March 18, '51. 3, John, b. Feb. 1, '07, r. S. Th. & d. Sept. 30, '46. 4, Jane, b. Dec. 28, '09; m. Eliphalet Martin, & d. in S. Th., Jan. 19, '51. 5, Joseph S., b. Feb. 5, '11; m. Margaret Snow, Jan. 16, '36; r. Rock., in lime business. 6, Archibald, b. Jan. 24, '13, d. May 7, '35, at N. Orleans. 7, George W., b. May 13, 1816; m. Nancy F., Martin of Linc., p. Oct. 27, '47, 2d, Mrs. Harriet N. McLane, Dec. 8, '61; r. S. Th., a farmer, &c. 8, Nancy C., b. Nov. 14, '19, d. at S. Th., March 28, '43, 9, Charles G., b. June 12, '23; r. California. The mother d. Feb. 5. '33, a. 54.

William's ch. 1, John S., b. Aug. 26, 1828; m. Sarah L. Dean, July 20, '51; r. S. Th., a farmer, &c. 2, Samuel D., b. April 27, '32, d. at sea, 1852. 3, Almira S., b. April 14, '39, m. Elbridge F. Haskell, p. Oct. 27, '59; r. Bangor.

Israel S.'s ch. 1, Nathaniel I., b. Aug. 5, 1830, d. at sea ab. 1845. 2, Israel T., b. Jan. 8, '34, m. and d. at N. York. 3, Mary H., b. Sept. 30, '35; r. N. York. 4, Caroline E., born Sept. 24, '37, mar. ——— Thompson; r. N. Y. 5, George W., (2d), b. April 12, '39, d. at N. Y. 6, Susan A., b. June 22, '41; r. N. Y. The mother m. 2d, David Pettingill, Oct. 2, '52, and rem. N. Y.

Joseph S.'s ch. 1, Joseph H., b. March 7, 1839; r. Rock., a lime burner, &c, entered U. S. Navy. 2, Rosanna C., b. Aug. 15, '40; r. Rock. 3, Margaret A., b. Oct. 21, '42; r. Rock. 4, Delia, b. May 7, 1844.

George W.'s ch. 1, Sidney H., b. ab. 1849. 2, Sarah T., b. ab. '52. 3, Anna F., b. ab. '54. 4, Emma E., b. ab. '56; all r. S. Th.

John S.'s ch. 1, Samuel, b. ab. 1853. 2, Edwin, b. ab. '55.

PIERCE, Capt. Jacob L., b. ab. 1797; came from Southport, Me., m. Mary L. Day; r. Rock. Of his ch. 1, Capt. William D., b. ab. 1822, m. Emma A. Varney of U., June 7, '49; r. S. Th., a master mariner. Their ch. 1, Wm. M., b. ab. 1850. 2, Charles W., b. ab. '52.

PIERCE, Capt. Joseph, b. ab. 1800, c. from Bucksport, m. Sophia Moore of Bucksport; r. Rock., and d. Aug. 9, 1853, late of br. *Swan*. Their ch. 1, Frances, b. Oct. 31, 1831, m. Hezekiah W. Wight; r. Rock. 2, Helen S., b. March 1, '33; r. Rock., a dress maker. 3,

Imogene, b. Feb. 15, '37 ; r. Rock., a milliner. 4, Edwin, b. May 1, '39, a mariner. 5, Reuel, b. Oct. 20, '40, d. July 31, '42. 6, Joseph O., b. ab. '46 ; r. Rock., entered U. S. Navy.

PIERCE, Andrew J., b. ab. 1821, mar. Caroline (Holmes) Tate, Sept. 19, '59 ; r. Th., a photographist.

PIERCE, Albanius L., (colored), m. Hannah Peters of War., Sept. 6, 1857 ; r. Th., a barber.

PILLSBURY, Joseph, m. Sarah Emery; c. from Kittery, and settled early at Ash Point, was a blacksmith, r. and died S. Th. Dea. Nathan, a brother, and also a blacksmith, was b. in Elliot, formerly Kittery, 1760 ; served in the Rev. War upwards of six years, came to Th. soon after the war; m. Lucy Emery, p. Jan. 16, '88 ; r. Ash Pt., and d. May 23, 1826.

Joseph's ch. 1, Samuel, lost at sea with Capt. Dunning. 2, Betsey, m. Stephen Frost; r. and d. S. Th. 3, Johnson, mar. Priscilla Cooper, p. Dec. 7, 1798 ; r. S. Th. & Cam., a blacksmith ; d. at Linc. 4, Joseph, (2d), m. Phebe Dunham of Martha's Vineyard ; r. S. Th. and St. George, where he d. suddenly, July 13, 1822. His widow d. at Rock., March 5, '48, aged 69. 5, Sarah, mar. William Randall of Prospect, 1812 ; r. and d. Prospect. 6, John, m. Mary Kelloch, Sept. 27, 1808 ; r. and d. S. Th., a blacksmith. 7, Hannah, mar. Benjamin Cooper, (2d), r. Belmont. 8, Nathan, (2d), m. Mary Eastman, May 16, 1811 ; r. Dixmont and Belfast. 9, Margaret, m. Robert Alexander ; r. and d. Indiana.

Dea. Nathan's ch. 1, Nathaniel, m. Cynthia Brown, p. Oct. 2, 1817 ; r. S. Th., rem. and d. Rock. 2, Sarah, b. 1794 ; r. Rock., and d. Oct. 21, '62. 3, Joseph, (3d), m. Mary Emery, p. Aug. 17, 1816 ; r. and d. Rock. 4, Samuel, (2d), d. suddenly at Ash Point, Feb. 7, 1823. 5, Nathan (3d), b. ab. 1805, m. Jane Crockett, Jan. 14, 1828 ; r. Rock., a merchant, &c.

Johnson's ch. 1, Johnson, (2d), b. May 8, 1804 ; m. Mary Simmons ; r. S. Th., a retired mariner. 2, Mary, m. 1st, a Mr. Simmons, 2d, Nathan Frost, 3d, Robert Perry ; r. S. Thomaston.

Joseph, (2d)'s ch. 1, Sarah Ann, mar. 1st, a Mr. Cook of Boston, 2d, George Lindsey ; r. Rock. 2, John, (2d), b. ab. 1807 ; m. Jane McAlister, Sept. 20, 1830 ; r. Rock., a farmer. 3, Joseph, (3d), born ab. 1809 ; r. Rock. 4, Samuel, (3d), born ab. 1811 ; mar. Sarah M. Spalding of Phipsburg, March 1, '32 ; r. Rock. 5, George W., mar. 1st, Emeline D. Pillsbury of Northport, p. March 17, '38 ; 2d, Arzelia McLain, July 6, '56 ; r. Rock., a merchant, &c. To the families of this name the city is indebted for several important improvements.

John's ch. 1, Mary, m. Hezekiah Stover of St. George, pub. Dec. 16, '26 ; r. and d. St. George. 2, Jane, d. young, in Boston. 3, Hannah, m. Ephraim Snow, (2d) ; r. Rock. 4, Capt. Dennis, b. Nov. 14, 1814 ; m. Matilda Sweetland, May 8, '42 ; r. S. Th., and d. Oct. 24, '52. 5, Mehitable, b. ab. 1817 ; m. Andrew Whitcher ; r. S. Th. 6, George, d. young.

Nathaniel's ch. 1, Amos, b. Aug. 25, 1818, lost at sea Feb. 14, '41. 2, Lydia, b. April 17, '20, and d. Rock., Dec. 25, '39. 3, Lucretia, b. March 28, '22 ; r. Rock. 4, Capt. Oliver B., b. April 6, '24 ; mar. Phebe W. Adams, Oct. 7, '58 ; r. Rock., has crossed the Atlantic 42 times, besides making the passage between this country and Fayal 37 times during the 10 years spent in that trade. 5, Nathaniel E., born Feb. 15, '26 ; d. unm. 6, Cynthia A., b. Feb. 13, '28. 7, Reuben, b. Feb. 14, '30 ; m. Martha L. Ulmer, Nov. 26, '54 ; r. Rockland.

Joseph, (3d)'s ch. 1, Louisa K., b. Sept. 16, 1817; m. Nathaniel Perry of Salem, p. Sept. 7, '46; r. S. Th. 2, Henry, b. Sept. 25, '18½; m. Lydia M. Adams, Aug. 26, '49; r. S. Th., a mariner. 3, Lucinda M., b. May 1, '24; m. & r. at the West. 4, Sarah J., b. Aug. 16, '26; m. ——— Perry; r. Boston. 5, S. Nathan, b. Oct. 8, '28, d. Aug. 24, '31. 6, Hannah Lowell, b. Jan. 4, '31; r. S. Th. 7, Josephine, born March 2, '34; m. & r. Mass. 8, Lucy A., b. Jan. 2, '41; mar. Seth Ayer; r. S. Th.

Fourth Generation.

Johnson, (2d)'s ch. 1, Sophia R., b. in Belmont, May 3, 1832; m. Isaac Thomas Ingraham; r. S. Th. 2, Hannah, b. Sept. 29, '35; m. Abraham Brann; r. S. Th. 3, Hiram G., b. Jan. 26, '37; m. Sarah A. Wentworth, Jan. 12, '63; r. S. Th., a mariner. 4, Charles E., b. Jan. 19, '39; r. S. Th. 5, Mary E., b. Sept. 26, '41. 6, Helen, b. '42, d. April 16, '59. 7, Almeida, b. ab. '44.

John, (2d)'s ch. 1, Sarah J., b. Dec. 18, 1831; m. Capt. J. F. Harden; r. Rock. 2, John L., b. July 12, d. Sept. 18, '33. 3, E. Adelia, b. Aug. 1, '34; m. C. A. Barrett of Placer county, Cal., Sept. 5, '63. 4, Capt. John Russell, b. Sept. 10, '36; mar. 2d, ? Jane A. Benner, April 7, '60; r. Rock. 5, Lucy E., b. Oct. 10, '38; mar. Rufus T. Hall, Feb. 13, '64; r. Rock. 6, Delora B., b. May 3, '40; r. Rock. 7, Charles H., b. March 7, '42; r. Rock., a sailmaker. 8, Montoro M., b. ab. 1846; r. Rock., entered U. S. Navy.

Samuel's ch. 1, Mary K., b. Sept. 18, 1832; m. Samuel Frederic Dinsmore; r. S. Th. 2, Ann A. C., b. Feb. 11, '34, d. July 4, '53. 3, George W., b. March 9, '36; r. Rock. 4, Statira, b. Nov. 19, '38; m. John H. D. Anderson, Aug. 19, '54; r. Rock. 5, Phebe F., b. June 18, '40, d. Dec. 28, '41. 6, Frances E., b. Oct. 30, '42. 7, Helen L., b. ab. '49.

George W.'s ch. 1, Helen M., b. 1839; m. Somers McNeil, Nov. 16, '56; r. California. 2, Thaddeus S., b. Oct. 17, '40; r. Rock., a mariner, soldier of 4th Me., &c. 3, Faustina, b. ab. '43. 4, Georgie E., b. Oct., 1845, d. Aug. 24, '60. 5, Aliscena F., b. ab. '47. The mother d. Oct. 6, '50, aged 37. By 2d wife. 6, Lewis M., b. ab. '57. 7, Knott C., b. ab. '59.

Capt. Dennis's ch. 1, Oliver, b. ab. 1843. 2, Augustus, b. ab. '46. 3, Sidney, b. ab. '49. 4, Matilda, b. ab. '52.

Capt. Oliver B.'s ch. John O., b. ab. 1860.

Henry's ch. Moses, b. ab. 1851.

Capt. John R.'s ch. 1, Edwin. 2, Caroline. 3, Oliver. 4, Katie. 5, Lilian. 6, Anna R., b. 1863, d. Nov. 17, '64.

PILLSBURY, Capt. Thomas R., b. ab 1820, in Northport; mar. Mary Brown, p. Dec. 10, '44; r. Rock. Their ch. 1, Leanora F., b. ab. 1847. 2, Edgar T., b. ab. '50. 3, Addie E., b. ab. '58.

PILLSBURY, Capt. Benjamin A., b. ab. 1832, in Belfast; m. Jane M. T. ——— of Liverpool, Eng.; r. Rock. Their ch. 1, Ellen C., b. ab. 1854. 2, Mary A, b. Feb. & d. July 19, '57. 3, Byron S., b. ab. '58. 4, Bennie W., b. Dec. '31, '61, d. Jan. 6, '63.

PIPER, Capt. David Norris, b. Aug. 23 1796 in Loudon, N. H., c. here in 1819, m. Eliza Gleason of Union, in 1821; r. Th., a clothier, deputy sheriff, now in the meat business. Their ch. 1, Aaron G., b. Feb. 27, 1822, m. Eliza Lois Young, Aug. 20, '57; r. Th., a joiner. 2, Sarah Jane, b. Dec. 3, '23, m. Nelson Fales; r. Th. 3, Mary E., b.

Jan., 1825, m. Barnabas Webb; rem. California. 4, Martha F., b. March 20, '28, m. George W. Beverage; r. Th., and d. April 24, '64. 5, David N., (2d), b. Jan., 1831; r. Th.

Aaron G.'s ch. 1, Marion G., b. ab. 1858. 2, Herbert Nelson, b. ab. '60. 3, Ora, b. ab. '62.

PINKHAM, Asa G., b. ab. 1826, in Steuben, Me., m. Deborah W. Buckminster; r. Rock., a lime burner, &c. Their ch. 1, Abbie, b. ab. 1843. 2, Eugene A., b. ab. '49. 3, Edna F., b. ab. '57. 4, Clara E., b. Aug., '60, d. Jan. 23, '62.

PISTON, Capt. Anthony E., b. ab. 1820, in Italy, mar. Experience Hamor of Eden, Me.; r. Rock., a master mariner. Their ch. 1, Marietta P., b. Feb. and d. March 11, '55. 2, Delia M., b. ab. '57. 3, Agnes L., b. ab. '59. 4, Susan G., b. Aug. 18, 1861, d. April 26, '62. 5, Anthony E., b. Feb., and d. Aug., '63.

PITTS, Abner, b. ab. 1780, m., and, after some years residence in W. & U., c. to Rock., a saddler, &c., d. Dec. 8, 1853. Of his ch. 1, William M., b. ab. 1826, m. Eliza H. Liniken of Boothbay, 1846; r. Rock., a farmer, but rem. to New York, with his ch. 1, Acelia, b. ab. 1848. 2, Lauretta, b. ab. '50. 3, Malcolm L., b. ab. '53. 4, Elton, b. ab. '57. Of this name also, William L., came here, mar. Agnes R. Lowell, Oct. 14, '47; r. Rock., cashier of Ship-builder's Bank, and ret. to his native Carolina.

PLACE, Darius, b. ab 1807; m. Jane ——; r. Rock., a shoemaker. Of their ch. 1, Darius, (2d), b. ab. 1831; m. Mrs. Lucy E. Richards, Dec. 1, '61; r. Rock., a shoemaker. 2, ? James H., soldier in 19th Me. reg., &c. 3? George H., in U. S. regulars. 4, Charles E., b. ab. '43; r. Rock., a shoemaker.

POLAND, Henry L., b. ab. 1829; m. Phebe A. ——; r. Rock., a mariner. Their ch. 1, James A., b. ab. 1856. 2, Marietta, b. July 30, '60, d. July 10, '62.

POMEROY, Francis G., b. ab. 1821; m. Jerusha ——; r. Rock., a ship carpenter. Their ch. 1, John W., b. 1845. 2, Amanda L., b. ab. '47. 3, Rebecca, b. ab. '49. 4, Cyrus L., b. ab. '51. 5, Francis, b. ab. '53. 6, Mary E., b. ab '56. 7, Rufus, b. ab. '59.

POPE, Rev. Joseph, grad. H. U., 1770; was long the settled Cong. minister in Spencer, Mass.; m. —— ——, & d. 1826. Of his ch. 1, Joseph, Esq., was Counsellor at Law in Portland. 2, Charles, b. 1780; c. to Union as a merchant; rem. Th., continued trade, taught school, was deputy sheriff, &c., & d Oct. 21, 1842. 3, William, came at the same time, was partner in business with his brother Charles; m. Eliza Prince, p. Oct. 19, 1817; ret. to Spencer, having had ch. b. in Th. 1, Ann E., b. Nov. 12, 1818; m. R. Vaile, April 16, '40; rem. & d. Indiana. 2, Isabella, b. Dec. 17, '20, d. June 30, '24. Also, b. in Spencer, 3, Joseph, b. Aug. 14, '22. 4, Lucretia H., b. Sept. 17, '24. 5, Sarah A., b. Jan. 17, '27.

PORTER, John, b. ab. 1807, in Salem, Mass.; m. Almira Barnard of Th., Nov. 16, 1834; r. Th. and carried on the tailor's business; rem. Belfast and Rock., where he commenced the Rockland Gazette, of which he, in company with his son for a time, and recently with E. E. Wortman, is still the publisher. Their ch. 1, Helen S., b. ab. 1836; m. Capt. William A. Barker, r. Rock. 2, Greenleaf, b. about 1838; m. Augusta C. Brown of Chesterville, Me., June 12, '61; r. Rock., assistant publisher, &c., is recently of the U. S. Navy. 3, Harriet W., b. ab. 1840; m. John W. Brown, Nov. 12, '61. 4, John B., b. ab. 1845.

Greenleaf's ch. George Greenleaf, b. March, & d. July 18, 1862. The mother d. June 8, 1862.

PORTER, Benjamin, m. Lucretia Achorn, March 24, 1825, r. Camden, and d. May 5, 1851, having jumped from the sch. *Fountain* in a fit of insanity. Of his ch. 1, Capt. Isaac A., m. 1st, Juliet M. ———, who d. Nov. 5, 1850, at Rock., a. 19 yrs., 2d, Mary C Coburn of W., July 6, '52; r. Rock., and was lost at sea, July 2, '55 2, ? Capt. Michael O., b. ab. 1829; m. Helen M. Ulmer; r. Rock., and d. Sept. 25, '59.

PORTER, John, (2d), b. ab. 1825, in Nova Scotia, as was Lydia, his wife, at the Bay of Chaleur; r. Rock., a ship carpenter. Their ch. 1, Margaret A., b. July 17, 1849, d. July 27, '56. 2, J. Newton, b. June, 1851, d. Sept. 18, '52. 3, John N., b. ab. '53. 4, Joseph M., b. ab. '57. 5, Margaret E., b. ab. '59.

PORTERFIELD, Capt. Patrick, came from North of Ireland about 1749, & settled on Mr. North's Lot, No. 48; m. 1st, Martha Jameson, 2d, Mary (Webster) McLellan; & d. Oct. 3, 1799, aged 77. His 2d wife d. Aug. 28, 1797, aged 70. His ch. by 1st wife. 1, William, m. & d. in Cam., one of whose sons, Patrick, d. Jan. 27, 1811, aged 12, and was buried in Rock. 2, John, perished at sea with Patterson, 1770. ? 3, Elizabeth, b. Sept., 1754; m. Capt. James Watson; r. and d. Th. 4, Catharine, mar. ——— Upham. 5, Ruth, mar. Benjamin Buckland; r. and d. Cam. 6, Martha, b. May 7, 1748; mar. Robert Jameson; r. in what is now Rock., and d. on afternoon of June 16, 1789. 7, Nancy, m. John Shibles, (2d), rem. Ohio. 8, Adj. Robert, m. Agnes (Robinson) Howard of C., Nov. 30, 1797; r. Th. and W., rem. Ohio, with their son, William, (2d), and four other ch. The mother d. in 1771.

POST, Stephen, b. in Seabrook, Ct., m. 1st, Mrs. Eunice Hambley, p. at Th., Feb. 29, 1780; c. from N. Scotia to Th., Jan. 25, 1781, m. 2d, Abigail (Crane) Montgomery of W., p. Aug. 13, 1792, 3d, Mrs. Hannah Dyer, June 28, '95; r. S. Th., and died Dec. 9, 1834. His widow d. at Owl's Head, Jan. 1846, a. 90 y., 8 m., having had 9 ch., 67 grand ch., 87 gr. grand ch., and 2 gr., gr., gd. ch. His ch. By 1st wife. 1, Zachariah, b. in Cornwallis, N. S., Jan. 27, 1780, m. Abigail Witham, Aug. 6, 1808; r. S. Th., & d. July 24, '33. 2, Stephen, (2d), b. Feb. 25, '81, m. Mercy ———, (who d. Feb. 20, 1864, a. 75,); r. and d. S. Th. 3, Eunice, b. June 17, '83, m. James Sweetland; r. S. Th., and d. June 3, 1827. 4, Jane, b. June 4, '85, m. 1st, Nathaniel Sleeper, p. Dec. 1, 1818, 2d, Timothy Wellman; r. Rock., and d. April 2, '37. 5, Anna, b. Aug. 4, '86. 6, Capt. Ezekiel, b. March 13, '88, m. 1st, Mehitable Eastman, Oct. 23, 1814, 2d, Mary Snow, Nov. 4, '20; r. Th., and d. Jan. 10, '37. 7, Enoch, b. April 10, '91, m. Mary Curtis, p. April 19, 1817; r. S. Th, and d. Aug. 3, '42. By 2d wife. 8, Phebe, born Dec. 21, '94; r. in War. By 3d wife. 9, Hannah, b. May 11, '96, m. John Emery, Sept. 29, 1814; r. S. Th., and d. May 8, '34. 10, William, (natural or adopted), m. Susan Kalloch; r. S. Th.

Zachariah's ch. 1, Ezekiel G., b. June 16, 1810, d. Sept 24, '26. 2, Lowla, b. Aug. 19, '14. 3, Catharine, b. April 15, '17. 3, Zachariah, (2d), b. Jan. 17, '20. 4, Abigail W., b. April 20, '22, m. Hanson or Hirah? Hawes, March 15, '46. 5, Ira C., b. Sept. 22, '27. 6,

Josiah W. D., b. July 30, '30, m. Abby H. ——— ; r. S Th., a mariner. 7, Charles W., b. March 7, '33, d. Nov. 19, '38.

Stephen, (2d)'s ch. 1, Capt. Jonathan, b. April 18, 1807, m. 1st, Lucy Lowell, April 2, '29, 2d, Mary Simonton, Dec. 31, '34 ; r. Rock., and d. Jan. 20, '59. 2, Jane, b. Dec. 10, '08, m. John W. Burns ; r. Rock., and d. Jan. 20, '47. 3, Sally, b. Jan. 13, '10, m. Moses Benner of Wal., March 23, '34. 4, Nancy, b. Oct. 6, '12, m. Henry York ; r. Rock. 5, Enoch, (2d), b. June 5, '14, m. Hannah F. Sumner of U., Jan . 21, '51 ; r. S. Th., a mariner. 6, Stephen, (3d), b. Nov. 11, '16; r. S, Th., and d. Jan. 26, '62, found d. in B. Ingraham's field, near the cove at S. End, Rock. 7, Isaac, b. Feb. 12, '19. m. Elizabeth, a lady of Germany ; r. S. Th., a mariner. 8. Freeman, b. June 6, '21, d. by drowning, Nov. 23, '40. 9, Julia Ann, b. Aug. 13, '23, mar. George Bradshaw, March 15, '54. 10, Achsah, b. Sept. 16, 25, mar. Daniel Ott ; r. S. Th. 11, Eunice, b. June 14, '29, mar. John W. Burns ; r. Rock., and d. Aug. 30, '59. 12, William Henry, b. Aug. 4, 31, m. Amanda E. Frye, p. Sept. 17, '52 , r. Rock., a mariner. 13, George W., b. April 30, '33, m. Ruth Frye, July 19, '60 ; r. Rock., a mariner.

Capt. Ezekiel's ch. By 1st wife. 1, Matilda, b. ab. 1815, d. April 10, '39 ?. By 2d wife. 2, Capt. Alex. Campbell, b. 1824, m. Jane A. Blood, Nov. 21, '48 ; r. Th., and d. Feb. 8, '63. 3, William Francis, b. 1827, d. at sea in brig *Roger Lynn*, Jan. 6, '55. 4, Edward E., b. ab. '32 ; r. Th., a mariner, &c.

Enoch's ch. 1, Elizabeth, b. March 18, 1818, m. Daniel Kieff, Sept. 16, '41. 2, Atwood K., b. Jan. 1, '20, d , lost at sea, Nov. 26, '38. 3, Nancy, b. July 26, '26. 4, Elijah G., b. July 25, '28. 5, Albert, b. July 1, '31, d. May 23, '40.

William's ch. 1, Charlotte K., b. Dec. 25, 1825, m. Ebenezer Williams ; r. Rock. 2, Capt. George R., b. ab. '27, mar. Lydia Beals, March 31, '48 ; r. S. Th. 3, John K., m. Harriet P. Snowdeal, Sept. 7, '51 ; r. S. Th. 4, Capt. Hanson or Hanse, K., b. Aug. 8, '30, m. Mary E. Braley, Feb. 12, '57 ; r. Rock., and d. Oct. 7, '58. 5, Thos. W. ; r. S. Th. 6, Jacob, b. ab. '38, m. M. Elizabeth Jameson, Nov. 23, '59 ; r. Th., a quarryman.

Josiah W. D.'s ch. 1, Frederic L., b. ab. 1855. 2, Franklin W., b. ab. 1859.

Capt. Jonathan's ch. by 1st wife. 1, Capt. Daniel, b. April 27, 1830 ; m. Margaret B. Simonton, Feb. 10, '52 ; r. Rock. & d. Jan. 11, '63. 2, Capt. Ephraim E., b. Jan. 31, '32 ; m. Melissa Simonton, Jan. 24, '55 ; r. Rock.

Isaac's ch. 1, Lucy I., b. ab. 1852. 2, Freeman I., b. ab. '54. 3, Clara A., b. ab. '58. 4, Isaac L , b. 1860.

William H.'s ch. 1, Lizzie M., b. May 23, 1853, d. Oct. 9, '54. 2, Josephine, b. ab. '56. 3, William A., b. ab. '58.

Capt. Alexander C.'s ch. 1, Mary F., b. March 24, 1850. 2, Walter E., b. Nov. 15, '52, d. Nov. 10, '53. 3, Frederic C., b. Jan. 7, & d. July 3, '55, in Havana. 4, Lucinda J., b. March 24, 1857. 5, Herbert N., b. April 17, '59.

Capt. Daniel's ch. 1, Lucy M., b. ab. 1853. 2, Mary, b. ab. 1856. 3, Eveline A., b. June '62, d. April 11, '63.

Capt. Ephraim E.'s ch. Margaret, b. ab 1846.

Capt. George R.'s ch. 1, George T., b. Dec., 1849, d. Feb. 28, '52. 2, David, b. ab. '52. 3, Alice, b. ab. '55.

Capt. Hanson K.'s ch. Frederic K., b. June 27, '57, d. Feb. 10, '59.

Jacob's ch. Llewellyn, b. in 1860.

POTTLE, Andrew D , b. ab. 1810, in Searsmont, Me. ; m. 1st, Harriet Smith, 2d, Susan Pease ; r. Rock., a shoemaker. Their ch. 1, Harriet, b. ab. '36 ; m. Charles Spear; r. Rock. 2, Benjamin F., b. ab. '38 ; m. Louisa H. Killsa; r. Rock., a volunteer in 4th Me. reg., d. at Harrison's Landing, of fever, July 12, 1862. 3, Frederic A., m. Hannah J. Tibbetts; r. Bangor. 4, Mary E., b. ab. '42. 5, Andrew D., (2d), b. ab. '44, a mariner, soldier in 4th & 28th Me. reg., &c. 5, Frances E., b. ab. '46, all r. Rock.

Benjamin F.'s ch. William F., b. in 1860.

PRATT, Capt. James W., b. Oct. 21, 1816, son of Oliver & Joanna G. (Titus) Pratt of Union; m. Martha Linniken; r. Rock., a ship master. Their ch. 1, Miller. b. ab. '40, a mariner. 2, Bainbridge, b. ab. '41. 3, Melvin, b. ab. '46. Of this name, also, Daniel or David Pratt, b. ab. '30 ; m. Sarah C. ——— ; r. Rock., a joiner.

PRESCOTT; of this family there is reason to believe that all or nearly all of the name in this country have sprung from James, of English birth, who came over and settled in Hampton, N. H., about 1665. His son Jonathan had a son, Capt. Jonathan, (2d), who was in the royal army under Sir William Pepperell at the siege of Louisburg, where he d. of fever about 1744, & left at least one son, Micah, whose son Stephen was b. in Epping, N. H., July 24, 1763 ; m. Rachel Rundlet in 1784; settled in Gilmanton, N. H., where he had 12 ch., but rem. about 1806 to Liberty, Me., and died Oct. 19, 1861.

Of Stephen's ch., 9 of whom were still living in 1864, the 5th, viz., Stephen, (2d), Esq., was b. Jan. 14, 1791 ; m. Betsey, dau. of Ezekiel & Mary True, Sept. 20, 1818 ; rem. from Liberty to Rock., and m. 2d, Priscilla (Ames) Grant, Nov. 13, 1852 ; r. Rock. His ch. by 1st wife. 1, John T., b. June 20, 1819 ; m. Lydia, dau. of Benjamin & Hannah Brooks of Searsmont, Oct. 30, '45 ; came to Rock. in May, 1853 ; and d. Nov. 13, '54. 2, Dr. Paul T., b. Oct. 11, '21 ; studied medicine with Drs. Hollis & N. P. Munroe of Belfast; grad. Jefferson, Med. Coll., Philadelphia, 1850 ; commenced practice in Rock., 1852 ; m. 1st, Sept. 20, '55, Harriet M., dau. of Benjamin F. & Mary Fairbanks, (b. in Hope, Sept. 2, 1829, d. Aug. 16, '62, at Rockland,) 2d, Mary J. Arnold, June, 1864 ; r. & prac. Rock. 3, Mary J., b. Dec. 24, '26 ; m. George W. Prescott, Aug. 24, '52 ; r. Liberty, having 2 ch., viz., Lizzie M., b. April 26, '58, & John, b. April 16, '59. 4, Charles S., b. May 4, '29, d. at Liberty, Oct. 4, '42. The mother b. in Salisbury, Mass., d. in Liberty, March 29, '51.

PRESCOTT, Royal, b. ab. 1818 ; m. Mary E. ——— ; r. Rock., a joiner, soldier of 4th Me., &c. Their ch. 1, Georgiana, b. ab. 1844. 2, Oscar, b. ab. '46. 3, Harrison, b. ab. '49. 4, Washington, b. ab. '52. 5, Wealthy, b. ab. '55. 6, Medora, b. ab. '57. Of this name, also, Elisha Prescott, b. ab 1811 ; m. Elizabeth Wall, Nov. 7, '47 ; r. S. Th., d. in California, Nov. 16, '50.

PRESCOTT, Moses, came from Sandwich, N. H. ; mar. 1st, Olive Orbeton, 2d, Susan Perry of Cam., Sept. 21, 1821 ; r. Cam. & Rock., a joiner. His ch. by 1st wife. 1, Harriet, mar. Israel Lindsey ; r. Rock. and Bath. 2, Francie, m. Joseph Lombard; r. Bath. By 2d wife. 3, Lucinda. 4, Ann, m. William Brown; r. and d. Th. 5, Moses, (2d), b. Oct., 1826 ; m. Mary Richards; r. Rock., and d. Dec. 25, '54. 6, ? Stephen, b. ab. 1829 ; m. Mary J. ——— ; r. Rock., a lime burner. 7, Lydia J., mar. George H. Allen; r. Th. 8, Elvira,

m. Eli Colson; r. Belfast. 9, Mary Elizabeth, b. March 17, '43. 10, Susan, d. young.

Stephen's ch. 1, Harriet C., b. ab. 1851. 2, Stephen G., b. ab. '54. 3, Albert T., b. ab. '58. 4, Washington, b. 1860.

PRESSEY, Capt. Andrew, b. ab. 1817, in Deer Isle; came to this place; m. Zaetta Z. Flint, p. Oct. 17, 1837; r. Rock. Of his sisters there came here, 1, Sophronia S., m. Alexander M. Snow; r. Rock. 2, Olinda A, mar. Charles W. Snow; r. Rock. 3, Harriet W., born 1824; m. Isaac C. Abbott; r. Rock, & d. Oct. 2, '63. 4, Mary W., m. Freeman B Farwell, d. in Unity, 1863.

Capt. Andrew's ch. 1, Andrew B., b. March 15, 1838; m. Sarah Andrews, May 1, '61; r. Rock., a mariner, soldier of 4th Me., &c., entered U. S. Navy. 2, William A., b. Jan. 23, '40; r. Rock., a mariner, entered the Navy. 3, Charles H., b. ab. '45; a mariner. 4, Flora, b. ab. '52. 5, Thaniel, b. ab. '59.

PRESTON, Daniel, c. from Ireland; m. 1st, Catharine Gray, 2d, Jane Derrick; r. Th. & d. Sept. 6, 1859. His ch. 1, Dominic, b. ab. '39, a mariner. 2, Luke, b. ab. '41. 3, Daniel, b. ab. '55. 4, Amelia, b. ab. 58.

PRICE, Charles, b. ab. 1836, in Jersey, Eng., as was Sarah A., his wife, in New Brunswick; r. Rock., a stevedore. Their ch. 1, Jeneva, b. ab. '57. 2, Minnie, b. ab. '59. 3, Charles, (2d), b. in '60. 4, Sarah A., b. March, & d. April 12, '63.

PRIEST, Wesley H., with Maria, his wife, r. in Rock. & lost, by death, Aug. 18, 1864, a son, Charles A., aged 5 months, 9 days.

PRINCE, John, (son of Rev. John of East Strafford. Eng.,) c. over & d. at Hull, Mass., Aug 6, 1676. Of his 12 ch., the 12th, Thomas, bap. Aug. 3, 1658, m. Ruth Thomas, (qr. Turner?) r. Scituate, & had Thomas; Benjamin, who probably settled at North Yarmouth; & Job, who, b. 1695, m. Abigail ———, & had a son, Kimball Prince, b. May 9, 1726; m. Deborah, dau. of Dea. John Fuller, Nov. 13, 1749; r. Kingston, Mass, & d. 1814. Deborah, his wife, was b. Dec. 25, 1729, & d. March 4, 1826.

Kimball's ch. 1, Christopher, b. July 22, 1751; m. & r. N. Y. 2, Kimball, (2d), b. July 20, 1753; m. & r. New London, Ct., & d. 1824. 3, Sarah, b. Jan. 15, 1756. 4, Ruth, b. Aug. 7, 1758; m. Jesse Fuller; r. Hebron, Me. 5, Deborah, b. July 13, 1760. 6, Noah, b. Jan. 18, 1763; m. & r. Va. & near Athens in Georgia. 7, Job, b March 22, 1765; m. & r. in Buckfield, Me. 8, John, b. Feb. 23, 1768, m. & r. Kingston, & d. in 1824. 9, Hon. Hezekiah, b. Feb. 7, 1771, in Kingston; c. to Th., m Isabella Coombs, Jan. 4, 1798; r. Th., senator & member of the council, &c., &c., & d. Dec. 27, 1840.

Hezekiah, Esq.'s ch. 1, Eliza, b. Oct. 14, 1798; m. William Pope; rem. Spencer, Mass., and d. July 25, 1828. 2, Hezekiah, (2d), Esq., b. Oct. 8, 1800, m. Henrietta Marsh of Bath, Oct. 23, '28; r. Th., custom house inspector, secretary of Ins. Co., &c., & d. July 28, '43. 3, Sarah, b. July 20, '02, mar. Dr. David Kellogg; rem. Waukegan, Ill., and d. May 3, '57. 4, Isabella, b. Feb. 10, '05, m. J. Bentley H. Starr; rem. and r. Spencer, Mass. 5, Deborah, b. July 6, '08, mar. Hon. Jonathan Cilley; r. Th., and d. Aug. 14, '44. 6, Lucy C., b. in St. George, as were the preceding, Aug. 25, '10, m. E. S. J. Neally; rem. Bath, and d. Sept. 17, '53. 7, Joseph, b. in Th., Sept. 16, '14, grad. Bowd. College, 1835; was a teacher in the South, m. Lucinda A. Walker of Monroe, Ga., Sept. 12, '37, & d. there when just ready to enter on the practice of medicine, Sept. 10, '43. 8, Capt. George, b. in Th., Aug. 9, '17, m. Lucy M. Rice of Eastport, April 29, '45; r. Th., where he was a merchant, went whaling voyage, was a ship-master, editor of Th. Recorder, author of "Rambles in Chili," &c.; rem. and r. Bath, cashier of Bank, and Capt. of Co. K., in 1st Reg. Cavalry. 9, Nancy Pope, b. in Th., May 25, '20, m. Rev. Lorenzo B. Allen, son of Rev. William, of Jefferson, Oct. 19, '42, rem. Burlington, Iowa, and d. in 1858. 10, Christopher, Esq., b. in Th., July 31, '22, m. Marion W. Webb, May 3, '46; r. Th., on homestead, engaged in insurance, &c.

Hezekiah, (2d), Esq.'s ch. 1, Capt. Arthur, b. March 10, 1830, m. Victoria Harrington of Rock. April 29, '56; r. Th. 2, Eliza, b. Jan. 30, '32. 3, Thomas, b. Feb. 16, '34; rem. Vandalia, Ind. 4, Henrietta, b. Oct. 6, '35. 5, Sarah F., b. Jan. 16, '40, m. Maj. S. T. Keene; r. Th. 6, Isabella, b. June, 1842, d. Aug. 15, '43.

Capt. George's ch. Maria, b. in Th.

Christopher Esq.'s ch. Edmund W., b. March 19, 1847.

Capt. Arthur's ch. Arthur Frank, b. 1858

PROCTOR, Daniel, b. ab. 1830, m. Eliza Carver, p. March 5, '51; r. Rock., a lime burner, &c. Their ch. 1, Lillias, b. ab. 1854. 2, Elizabeth, b. Dec. '56, d. June 9, '58. 3, Daniel L., b. June, and d. Nov. 9, '62.

QUIN, Oliver A., and Martha were here and had recorded their child, viz., Oliver, born Jan. 31, 1841. Perhaps there were others. John Quin d. in Th., July 1, 1864, aged 21.

RACKLIFF, William, ? m. r. and d. on Rackliff's Is., near S. Th. Of his ch. 1, William, (2d), m. Eleanor Eustis, Feb. 7, 1803; r. and d. S. Th. 2, Lydia, b. 1788; m. Robert Jenks; r. W. & d. Dec. 19, 1838. 3, John, r. St. George. 4, Samuel, b. 1796; m. Mary ———; r. Rock., near Sherer's Mills; and d. Dec. 28, 1859. 5, Martha, mar. ——— Linnekin; r. St. Geo. 6, James, b. ab. 1800; m. 1st, Rachel Chaples, 2d, Roxana Fogler of Windsor, March 23, '43; r. Ash Pt., and now Rock. 7, Betsey; 8, Mary, both of whom, it is believed, m. Elwells of St. George.

Of William, (2d)'s ch., we are not informed; but it is believed 3 of his sons, Samuel, Ezekiel, & James, were drowned at Wessaweskeag. Freeman Rackliff, perhaps his son or grandson, m. Hannah C. Maker, May 1, 1853; r. S. Th.

Samuel's ch. 1, William, (3d), b. May 20, 1817, d. Nov. 3, 1833. 2, Ezekiel, b. April 1, '19; m. Mary Pearson of St. Geo., Oct. 4, '44; r. Rock., a lime burner, soldier in 19th Me. Reg., &c. 3, James H., b. March 4, '21; mar. Almira Elwell, Aug. 2, '45; r. Rock., a lime burner, soldier in 4th Me., since re-enlisted. 4, Samuel, (2d), born April 21, '24. 5, Betsey, b. Oct. 26, '25; m. Gilford Young, Dec. 4, '50. 6, Capt. Jeremiah P., b. Dec. 18, '27; mar. Mrs. Hannah F. Andrews, March 14, '51; r. Rock., or S. Th., a mariner, entered the army. 7, Elisha, b. Dec. 30, '29. 8, Nancy, b Jan. 7, '33, d. Dec. 6, '35. 9, William N., b. Sept. 9, '39; mar. Catharine McCoy, Oct. 13, '63; r. Rock., a lime burner, soldier in 4th Me. Reg., &c.

James's ch. by 1st wife. 1, John, m. Catharine Payson; r. Hope. 2, Oliver, b. ab. 1832; m. Olive or Alice Benner, p. April 5, '51; r. Rock., a lime burner. 3, Elizabeth, m. Alfred Carleton, Dec. 23, '49; rem. Des Moines, Iowa. 4, Hannah, b. Dec. 13, '39; m. T. Jefferson Brown; r. Rock. 5, Isaac, d. in Th. The mother d. Oct. 21, '42.

By 2d wife. 6, Rebecca, b. ab. 1846. 7, William Alvan, b. ab. '48; r. Rock., in Coast Guards.

Freeman's ch. 1, Esther E., b. ab. 1857. 2, Willis P., b. ab. '59.

Ezekiel's ch. 1, Artemas H., b. ab. 1848. 2, Albert, b. ab. '50. 3, Effie L., b. ab. '53. 4, George W., b. Dec, 1855, d. Sept. 4, '56. 5, Mary E., b. April, 1858, d. May 29, '59.

James H.'s ch. 1, Mary E., b. ab. 1848. 2, Nancy H., b. ab. '50. 3, Annie L., b. ab. '53. 4, Margaret A., b. ab. '55. 5, William F., b. April 6, 1857, d. May 5, '60.

Capt. Jeremiah P.'s ch. Ella, b. ab. 1852.

Oliver's ch. 1, Mary F., b. Sept., 1852, d. Nov. 23, '60. 2, George S., b. ab. '54. 3, Ellen B., b. ab. '59.

RACKLIFF, Charles W., b. ab. 1830, probably of the same family; came from Muscle Ridge Point; m. Julia B. Heard, p. Dec. 3, '52; r. S. Th., a stone cutter, soldier of 28th Me., &c. Their ch. 1, Ida, b. Sept. 13, 1853, d. June 28, '55. 2, Eleonai E., b. ab. '59.

RAFTER, Daniel, b ab. 1812, in Jefferson; m. Antoinette Andrews of W., Jan. 18, '41; r. Th., a shipwright; rem. Libertyville, Illinois. Their ch 1, Benedict Fenwick, b. ab. 1842. 2, Mary, b. ab. '47. 3, James, d. young. 4, Antoinette, d. Jan., 1861.

RAMSEY, William, was here early, and with Hannah, his wife, had recorded their ch. 1, Sarah, b. April 25, 1838. 2, Crowell J., b. Oct. 29, '39; perhaps rem. Of this name, also, John Ramsey, printer, r. here; m. Burnice B. Bourke of Bath, p. June 15, '33; but soon rem.

RANDALL, Job, b. 1772, c. from Easton, Mass., a carpenter; m. Peggy Glover, July 14, 1806; built a house in Wadsworth st, Th., r. there & S. Th., & d. Dec. 15, '37. There came with him, his sisters, Silvia, who, b. 1788, m. 1st, Joseph Coombs, 2d, Abel Fish, & d. Oct. 2, 1842; Achsah, b. 1800, m. Capt. Josiah Getchell; r. S. Th., & d. Sept. 23, '26; & Sally, m. 1st Abiezer Coombs, 2d, Roland Wade.

RANKIN, Capt. Constant, b. at old York, April 17, 1747, O. S., April 28, N. S; m. 1st, Patience Dinstow, 2d, Mary Tolman, Aug. 22, 1775, the same year he settled here; r. Rock., & d. Dec. 19, 1831. His ch. by 1st wife. 1, Hannah, m. ——— Stone; r. & d. Augusta. 2, Priscilla, m. Samuel Cummings; r. & d. Augusta. 3, James, afflicted with epilepsy, r. & d. Rock. By 2d wife. 4, Samuel, b. May 4, 1776, m. Elizabeth Jameson, Nov. 15, 1802; r. Rock, & d. April 7, '42. 5, Constant, 2d, b. Oct. 4, 1778; m. Susannah Lindsey, Aug. 6, 1802; r. Rock. & d. in Frankfort. 6, Mary, b. Oct. 12, 1781; m. Ellithan Taylor; r. & d. Albion. 7, Joseph, b Oct. 14, 1784; a mariner many years, & d. abroad. 8, Hannah, b. Sept. 21, 1786; m. Freeman Harden; r. Rock. & d. Aug. 1, 1862. 9, Andrew, b. Dec. 26, 1788; was one of those mentioned on p. 293, vol. 1st, who shipped on board the privateer *Dart* of Portland, and, during her cruise, was put on board a vessel which they captured, but which was retaken by the enemy, before they could bring her in, and, with the rest of the prize crew, was made prisoner, but returned, & m. 1st, Betsey Burns, July 2, 1812, 2d, Mary (Havener) Holmes, March 13, 1828; r. Rock. 10, Esther, b. April 24, 1791; m. 1st, Israel Gardner, Nov. 7, 1811, 2d, Joseph Walker of Albion; r. Aroostook county.

Samuel's ch. 1, Sabra, b. June 18, 1803; m. David F. Conant; r. Rock. & d. Oct., '59. 2, Constant, (3d), b. April 26, '05; m. Harriet Stevens, Aug. 9, '27; r. Rock., a lime burner, &c. 3, Elizabeth, b. Oct. 2, '07; m. Ephraim Ulmer; r. Rock. & d. Oct. 4, '49. 4, Samuel, (2d), b. Feb. 11, '10; m. Olive Ames of Vin., p. March 8, 1831, 2d, Lucy Gay, July 1, '49; r. Rock., a lime manufacturer. 5, Mary, b. Aug. 14, '12; m. Mark Lindsey; r. Rock. 6, Joseph or Josiah W., b. Oct. 18, '13; m. Elethea L. Ingraham, Oct. 12, '48, d. in N. O.

Constant, (2d)'s ch. 1, Clementina, b. Aug. 15, 1803; m. James Havener, Sept. 5, '18; r. Frankfort. 2 & 3, twins, b. May 20, '05; Richard, m. & r. Frankfort; & Robert, m. 1st, Desire K. ———, who d. at Richmond, Va., Jan. 18, '45, 2d, Abby B. Wardwell or Wadsworth, Jan. 24, '46; was com. merchant, firm of Rankin & Whitlock, Richmond, Va., '45, since deceased. 4, Presina, b. April 10, '08; m. Benjamin Kelly, Feb. 18, '58; r. Belfast. 5, Fidelia, m. William A. Kimball, p. Nov. 4, '44; r. Isle Haut. 6, Susan, m. & rem. west. 7, Priscilla, m. Mason Morse; r. Th., and perhaps others.

Andrew's ch. by 1st wife. 1, Relief, b. Jan. 10, 1813, d. May 28, '25. 2, Richmond, b. Nov. 11, '14. 3, Robert R., b. April 8, '17, d. Jan. 30, '18. 4, Hannah, b. Dec. 8, '18; m. Daniel Blake of Th., Sept. 11, '42. 5, Eliza A., b. Sept. 10, '21; m. Alvan Hewett; r. Rock. 6, Harriet, b. Sept. 15, '24. By 2d wife. 7, Mary A., b. Nov. 14, 1828, d. May 30, '30. 8, Almerin, b. Feb. 2, & d. June 1, '30. 9, Knott C., b. Dec. 4, '31; m. Harriet Crockett, Jan. 12, '53; r. Rock., a caulker.

Constant, (3d)'s ch. 1, Mary E., b. July 1, 1828, m. Rufus C. Ingraham; r. Rock. 2, John Edwin, born March 24, '30, mar. Theresa Young; r. Cam.? 3, Richard R., b. June 24, '32, m. Almira (Johnson) Arey; r. Rock. 4, William H., b. July 13, '34, mar. Eliza J. Heald, Jan. 3, '56, 2d, Effie J. Clouse, Oct. 15, '63; r. Rock., a truckman. 5, Harriet Adeline, b. Sept. 5, '36, m. George B. Macomber; r. Rock. 6, Lieut. Kendall K., b. Jan. 7, '39, m. Margia D. Achorn, Oct. 30, '64; r. Rock., a caulker, officer in 4th Me. Reg., &c. 7, Leonard C, b. Dec. 5, '41; r. Rock.. a soldier of 4th Me. Reg., killed in battle of Wilderness, May 5, '64. 8, Samuel D., b. ab. '47.

Samuel, (2d)'s ch. By 1st wife. 1, Albert. By 2d wife. 2, Florence A., b. ab '51.

Knott C's ch. 1, Edward C., b. ab. 1854. 2, Augustus, b. ab. '59.

RANKS, John, b ab. 1811, m. Abby Edwards of Manchester, Mass., Aug. 1, '37; r. Rock., a time, and d. July 11, '39. Their ch. Bethia F. E., b. June 10, '38, d. Oct. 6, '42. His widow, b. June 16, '14, m. Hon. Charles Holmes; r. Rock.

RANLETT, Capt. Charles E., b. ab. 1817, in Montville, & when his mother, (a cousin of the late Hon. Edward Everett, and a well educated woman,) married Capt. Joseph Watts of St. George, rem. thither, became a seaman and ship-master; m. Elizabeth Stearns of St. George, 2d, Ann Maria Jordan, March, '46; c. to Th., engaged in ship building and other business, till 1863, when he took command of his new bk., *Sunbeam.* His ch. By 1st wife. 1, Elizabeth F., b. ab. '42, m. Capt. Samuel C. Jordan; r. Th. The mother, b. Oct. 6, '20, d. at sea, June 4, '44. By 2d wife. 2, Charles O., b. Jan, 17, '47, d. at Calcutta. Oct. 14, '51. 3, Allie, d. young. 4, Alice, b. ab. '53. 5, Charles O., b. Aug., '54, d. May, '59. 6, F. Jas., b. ab. '58.

RANLETT, David, b. ab. 1822, m. Cyrena C. Brown, April 11, '52; r. Rock., a lime burner, &c. Their ch. 1, William D., b. April 11, '49, d. Aug. 9, '53. 2, Martha, b. ab. '55. 3, David E., b. ab. '58.

READ, Nathan A., b. ab. 1810, c. from Attleboro, Mass., to Th., mar. Reliance W. Williams, pub. Nov. 22, '32, a ship carpenter, &c., visited California, but ret., and r. Th. Their ch. 1, Alvan A., born

Sept. 30, '33; r. Th. 2, Sarah F., b. March 27, '36, mar Charles E. Hovey, Sept. 24, '55; r. Wal. 3, Marietta, b. ab. '44. 4, William Henry, b ab. 1847; r. Th., entered U. S. Navy. Of this name, also, Isaác L. Read, was here with Ann his wife in 1842, and had recorded of their ch. 1, Isaac, (2d), b. Dec. 18, 1838.

REARDEN, John, b. ab. 1830, in Ireland, as was Mary, his wife; r. Rock. Their ch. 1, Mary, b. ab. 1857. 2, Timothy, b. ab. '59.

REDLON, Nathan, came to Th., and traded many years at Paine's Corner; mar. 1st, Elizabeth Brown of W., Nov. 26, 1837, 2d, Mary Martin of U., Sept. 7, '51; built the house now that of A. P. Gould, Esq., but rem. China, Me. His ch. By 1st wife. 1, James, b. May 12, and d. June 1, '38. 2, George M., b. March 28, '39; r. Th., corporal in 4th Me. Reg., wounded near Centerville, Sept. 1, d. Oct. 19, '62, at Washington. 3, Frances A., b. Sept. 28, '40; r. China. 4, Julia, b. Aug. 20, '42, d. Sept. 12, '43. 5, Frederic, r. China. The mother d. Feb. 3, '47.

REDMAN, Lorenzo, b. ab. 1815; c. from Cherryfield with Mary, his wife; r. Th., a blacksmith. Their ch. 1, John, b. ab. 1838, a teacher. 2, Charles, b. ab. 1840, d. Oct. 5, '61. 3, Lorenzo, b. ab. 1842; r. Th., soldier in 20th Me., &c. 4, Mary E., b. ab. '44. The mother d. Oct. 4, 1861.

REDMAN, Charles P., b. ab. 1834; c. from Belfast, mar. Kate S. Dow, May 22, '56; r. S. Th., a sailmaker, &c. Their ch. Emma K., b. ab. 1857.

REED, Joseph, b. ab. 1826, in Ellsworth; m. 1st, Maria S. Dinsmore, 2d, Elizabeth Mulligan, p. Nov. 25, '59; r. Th., and kept Knox Hotel, rem. Boston. His ch. by 1st wife. 1, ———. 2, Jennie, b. ab. 1855. By 2d wife. 2, Atwood J., b. 1860.

REED, Andrew J., b. ab. 1821, in Hampden; m. Rebecca S. Partridge, Dec. 2, '52; r. Th., a joiner. Their ch. 1, Clarence E., b. ab. 1853. 2, Albert C., b. ab. 1858. Of this name, also, John Reed, b. ab. 1830; r. Rock., with Susan, his wife, in 1860; since rem. Their ch. 1, Mary E., b. ab. 1855. 2, George H., b. ab. '59. Charles A. & Elvira I. Reed were also here in 1860, with their ch., Helen T., b. ab. 1851; and Hattie D., b. ab. 1854.

REED, James, b. ab. 1834, in Waldoboro', of German ancestry. m. Abigail Welt of Wal.; r. Th. Their ch. 1, Frank, b. ab. 1860; Of this name, also, John Reed, b. ab. 1817, in Scotland, as was Elizabeth, his wife; r. Rock. Their ch. 1, Benjamin A., b. ab. 1847. 2, Mary A., b. ab. '59. ?

RENDELL, John, b. in Old England; m. Jane Clark; came first to Round Pond, Bristol, afterwards to St. George's, or Th., r. what is now S. Th., & d. in Feb., 1781. His wife was b. in Ireland, April 1, 1733, & d. Nov. 5, 1801. Their ch. (sons), 1, James, b. at Round Pond, May 8, 1759; m. by Rev. J. Urquhart, to Polly, dau. of Thomas & Susanna Toburn, April 4. '83; r. and probably d. S. Th. 2, John, (2d), m. Sarah Toburn of Fox Islands, Aug. 2, 1785; & d. in 1785. 3, Thomas, b. at Bristol, March 10, 1769; m. Peggy Crockett, Jan. 25, '98; & d. S. Th., or rem. Belmont. 4, William, m. Jenny Farr, p. at Th., Nov. 18, 1796. (daus.), 5, Margaret. 6, Hannah. 7, Jane, m. John White, p. Nov. 10, 1789; r. S. Th., 1790, rem. Bradford. 8, Mary, b. 1771; mar. William Perry; r. S. Th., & d. March 20, 1832. 9, Sally, m. Benjamin Sleeper; r. & d. S. Th.

James's ch. 1, James, (2d), b. & d. 1783; 2, Susanna, b. Jan. 29, '85; 3, John, (3d), b. Oct. 29, '86; 4, Jane, b. Nov. 29, '88; all probably rem. 5, James, (3d), b. Sept. 6, '91; m. Hannah Sleeper, Oct. 31, 1820; when he r. Prospect. 6, Israel, b. July 4, '93. 7, William, (2d), b. Aug. 18, '95; m. Sally Pillsbury, July 29, 1812; when he r. Prospect. 8, Polly, b. Aug. 15, '97; 9, Nancy, b. Aug. 15, '99; both probably rem. 10, Hannah, b. Jan. 8, 1802; m. Capt. Luther Hayden; & d. Jan. 1, 1842. 11, Ambrose, b. June 1, '04; probably rem.

Thomas's ch. 1, Abigail, b. Nov. 1, 1798. 2, William, (3d), born March 28, 1800; m. Eunice Crockett, Dec. 19, '22; when he r. Belmont. 3, Eunice, b. Jan. 21, '02; m. John Crockett. 4, Jane, born April 14, '03; 5, David Crockett, b. Dec. 17, '04; both probably rem. 6, Thomas, (2d), b. Dec. 10, '06; m. Nancy Gray, Sept. 24, '29; and rem. Ohio. 7, Louisa, b. Oct. 29, '11; 8, Mary B., b. Oct. 23, '13; 9, Nancy, b. Feb. 21, '16; 10, Sally, b. July 13, '18; all probably rem.

James, (3d)'s ch. 1, Benjamin S., b. Oct. 21, 1821. 2, Mary Elizabeth, b. Feb. 1, 1824. 3, Caroline, b. Sept. 2, '23.

William, (2d ?)'s ch. 1, Eliza Dummer, b. Dec. 17, 1823. 2, William Edwin, b. Nov. 19, '27.

Thomas, (2d)'s ch. 1, Leverett G., b. Aug. 10, 1830; 2, William Thomas, b. Nov. 12, '31; 4, George, b. Jan. 4, '36; 5, Rebecca C., b. Nov. 27, '38; all probably rem.

RHOADES, George, mar. Abigail Lincoln; r. and d. Bristol, a ship builder. Their ch. 1, Capt. Lincoln, m. in N. C., and d. abroad. 2, Capt. George, m. his brother's widow, and d. abroad. 3, Cornelius, mar. Nancy Wellman; r. and died Bremen; five of whose sons have joined their country's army in the war for the Union, and four of them given their lives in the service. 4, Jacob L., m. Miss Tirrell; r. and d. Northport. 5, Nancy, m. ——— Collins; r. and d. in neighborhood of Bangor. 6, Orris, m. Ann Worth; r. Northport. 7, Francis W., b. 1800, m. Nancy Morton; r. Rock., a ship builder, and d. Dec. 5, '54, leaving a vessel which he had begun, for his son Wm. G., then 18 yrs. old, to finish, as he had likewise done for *his* father, at the time of *his* death in Bristol.

Of Jacob L.'s ch. 1, Capt. Wm. Henry, b. ab. 1820, in Northport, m. 1st, Mary J. Brackett of Belfast, Feb., 1847, 2d, Mary H. Hills, Jan. 31, '61; r. Rock. 2, George J., mar. Mary A. H. Hall, Aug., 1854; r. Rock. or Cal.

Of Orris's ch., probably. 1, Capt. Hector, b. ab. 1818, in Northport, m. Sarah A. Brackett of Belfast; r. Rock. 2, Capt. Lincoln, (2d), b. ab. '21, m. Rebecca G. Manning, Dec. 15, '55; r. Rock. A cousin of these, Capt. Orris, perhaps a son of Jacob L., was born in Northport ab. '15, m. Lucy E. Woodbury; r. Rock.

Francis W.'s ch. 1, Mary Francis, b. March, 1832, mar. Sanford Burkett, of Wal.; r. Rock., a widow, with one dau., Ella F., b. Feb. '54. 2, Albert K., b. Jan., 1834, m. Addie M. Bradford, July 8, '58; r. Nebraska City, a soldier at Pittsburg Landing, and other battles. 3, William G., b. May, 1836, m. Addie T. Durgen, of Bath, Nov. 25, '61; r. Rock., a shipwright. 4, Ira O., b. Oct. 21, '37, a soldier, d. at Cincinnati, O., May 11, '62. 5, Sarah M., b. Jan., 1840, m. William B. Hix; r. Rock. 6, Galen M., b. Sept., 1843; r. Rock., entered the navy. 7, Daniel W., b. Sept., 1845. 8, Ellis A., b. Dec., 1848.

Capt. William Henry's ch. By 1st wife. 1, Laura J., b. ab. 1848, 2, Hiram, b. ab. 1849. By 2d wife. 3, Lizzie May. 4, a dau. b. '64,

Capt. Orris's ch. 1, Gideon, b. ab. 1842; r. Rock., a mariner. 2, Nancy Ellen, b. ab. '44. 3, James E. b. ab. '47. 4, Ella, b. ab. '52,

Capt. Hector's ch. 1, Sarah E., b. in May, and d. Aug., 1855. 2, Eugene A., b. ab. '57.
Capt. Lincoln's ch. Francis, b. ab. 1857.
Albert K.'s ch. Effie A., b. April, 1861.

RHOADES; of this name and probably connected with the preceding, there are also, 1, Henry P., b. ab. 1819, m. Susan E. ——; r. Rock., a carpenter, &c. 2, Charles, b. ab. 1830, m. Abbie ——; r. Rock., a foundry engineer, soldier of 20th Me., &c. Henry P.'s ch. 1, James E, b. ab. 1846; r. Rock., entered the army. 2, Louisa, b. ab. '48. 3, Hiram, b. ab. '50. 4, Joseph, b. ab. '53. 5, Hannah, b. ab '56. Of this name also, Sanford Rhodes, b. ab. 1813, in Washington, Me., m. Mary Russell of Warren; r. Rock., a lime burner, &c. Their ch. Warren N., b. ab. 1843.

RHONEY, Mrs. Mary, b. ab. 1832; r. S. Th. Her ch. 1, Ada J., b. ab. 1853. 2, Mary E., b. ab. '55. 3, William E., b. ab. '57.

RICE, Abner, (a descendant of the Edmond Rice, who emigrated from Burkhamstead, England, in 1638,) was born in Holden, Mass., 1792, son of Elijah Rice, mar. Lucy Washburn of Kingston, Mass., 1719; came to Th. the same year, followed the blacksmith business at Mill river, till 1831, when he commenced trade at Paine's Corner, where he resides, much interested in mechanical inventions. Their ch. (Adopted.) Julia Ann, b. June 12, 1840, m. Lewis Spear, April 9, '59; r. Warren.

RICE, Warren W., a descendant, probably of the same Edmond, & son of Noah and Sarah (Shattuck) Rice of Union, m. Caroline Gould of Norridgewock; c. to Th., June, 1863, as warden of State Prison. Charles A., his brother, b. 1825, m. Jane S. Merriman; r. S. Th., a carpenter.
Charles A.'s ch. 1, Wilbert H., b. Aug. 1856. 2, Abby W., b. May 1, '58.

RICH, Albert, b. ab. 1835, in Orrington, mar. Onera Hewett; r. Rock. Their ch. Alphonso, b. ab. 1858.

RICHARDS, Joseph, son of Dodapher, one of the early settlers in Cam., mar Elizabeth Young, r. and d. Lincolnville. Their ch. 1, Olive, m. Phinehas Manning, and r. Linc. 2, Deborah, mar. Ephraim Boggs of War.; r. Cam. 3, Martha, born 1787, mar. 1st, —— Pendleton, 2d, Samuel Hassan; r. Rock., and d, Sept. 15, '55. 4, Ruth, m. Josiah Richards; r. Searsmont, and d. 1836. 5, Nehemiah, m. 1st, Nancy Farnham, 2d, Betsey Levansaler; r. Linc. 6, Rev. David, m. Susan Ginn; r. Frankfort a Methodist minister. 7, Isaac, b. 1796; m. Lydia Milliken; r. Linc.; rem. Monmouth, & d. Oct. 18, '56. 8, Amos, m. Phebe Wadsworth; r. Linc. 9, Mary, b. ab. '02; m. David Farnham; r Rock. 10, Gideon Y., m. Louisa Parker of W.; r. Belmont, a teacher, &c. 11, Stephen, b. ab. 1804; m. 1st, Nancy Harding, 2d, —— Maddocks, 3d, Cordelia Dean of Linc.; r. Rock., has been city marshal, &c. 12, James G., b. Dec. 21, 1806; m. Eveline Heald; r. Rock.
Of the sons of Dodapher, (2d), of Searsmont, brother of Joseph, Dodapher, (3d), b. ab. 1806; m. Margaret Maddocks, May 5, '39; r. Rock., entered the navy. Of this name, also, Jonas W., a son of Benjamin Richards, was b. in Bristol, ab. '18, m. Sarah Erskine; r. Rock.
Nehemiah's ch. 1, Almond, r. Aroostook Co. 2, Mary, m. Richard Maddocks; r. Linc. 3, Farnham, b. ab. 1820; m. Mary Wads-

worth; r. Rock., a lime burner. 4, Nancy, mar. Jacob Anderson; r. Cam. 5, Ruth, m. and r. Cam. 6, Frances, and perhaps others, r. Lincolnville.

Of Amos's ch. 1, Zealor W., b. ab. 1827; m. Lauretta A. Craig, Jan. 29, 1853; r. Rock., a mariner. 2, Cyrena, m. Elisha H. Corson, r. Rockland.

Stephen's ch. 1, James, b. 1829; m. Sarah J. ———, r. Rock. 2, Mary, m. Warren Milliken of Linc.; r. Rockland.

James G.'s ch. 1, Francis W., m. Annie Heald; r. Linc. 2, Adolphus, b. 1835; m. Martha Richards, May 8, '58; r. Rock., a mariner, soldier of 2d Battery, &c. 3, James Emerson, m. Ann E. Knowlton, March 19, '61; r. Rock. 4, Lauretta, m. Oscar Snow; r. Linc. 5, Albert. 6, Henrietta A. 7, Adelia. 8, George. 9, Frederic; all rem. Lincolnville.

Dodapher, (3d)'s ch. 1, Horatio N., b. ab. 1841; r. Rock., a quarryman, soldier of 4th Me., &c. 2, Martha M.; born May 28, '42. 3, Frank, b. ab. '45. 4, John, b. ab. '48. 5, Victoria, b. about '51. 6, Liberty, b. ab. '55. 7, Edwin S., b. '59.

Jonas W.'s ch. 1, Robert E., b. ab. 1849. 2, Ida J., b. ab. 1855. 3, Willie M., b. June and d. Sept. '59.

Farnham's ch. 1, Charles, born ab. 1847. 2, Louisa, born '49. 3, Emma J., b. ab. '51. 4, Alfred, b. ab. '53. 5 & 6, twins, b. ab. '55, Viola and Victoria.

Zealor W.'s ch. 1, Wilbert L., b. Dec. 16, 1853, d. May 22, 1855. 2, Clinton L., b. ab. 1856. 3, Ann M. W., b. 1859.

James's ch. Ada R., b. ab. 1859.

Adolphus's ch. Carrie E., b. ab. 1859.

RICHARDSON, Joshua, b. March, 1796; came from Litchfield, Me.; m. Deborah Fales, p. May 15, 1819; & d. Oct. 1, 1851. Their ch. 1, Sarah, b. March 4, 1822, d. Aug. 14, '23. 2, William J., b. Sept. 6, '27; m. Sarah Lewis, Jan, 22, '53; r. Rock., & d. in California, May 17, '50. 3, Jane M., b. Dec. 25, '32; m. Samuel Thomas, Nov. 25, '52; r. War. 4 & 5, twins, b. June 2, '36; Edward, d. Jan. 3, '37, Edwin, died young.? 6, Henrietta, b. Sept. 18, '40; mar. Joshua Linnekin; r. Th.

RICHARDSON, Joseph B., came from Cushing; m. Ann ———; r. Old Th., and had recorded here their ch. 1, Warren, b. March 1, 1826. 2, Halsey, b. Oct. 8, '29. 3, John A., b. Jan. 1, '31; m. Nancy E. Lane of Bristol, Sept. 11, '52; r. Rock. 4, Mercy A., b. May 30, '33. 5, James G., b. April 28, '36.

John A.'s ch. 1, Cyrena E., b. ab. 1854. 2, Nancy J., b. ab. '55. 3, John A., (2d), b. ab. '57. 4, William T., b. ab. '59.

RICHARDSON, Dr. Joel, b. ab. 1819, son of Daniel Richardson of Eden, Me; studied medicine, completing his studies at Edinburgh and Paris, Europe, in 1861; m. Isabelle M. Heath of Tremont, Me.; came here in 1853, was appointed surgeon of 9th Me. Reg., but resigned, and practices medicine Rock. Their ch. 1, Lewis, (2d), b. ab. 1849. 2, Lilla Bell, b. Oct. 4, 1850, died Aug. 23, '63.

RICHARDSON, Lewis, b. ab. 1815, in Moultonboro', N. H.; c. here about 1840, commenced the Lime Rock Gazette, firm of Richardson & Porter, but soon withdrew; m. Frances E. Condon, Jan. 3, '47; r. Rock. Their ch. 1, Sarah F., b. Jan. 1, 1850, d. Aug. 1, '52. 2, Emma J., b. ab. '55. 3, Abbott L., b. ab. '57. 4, Lewis F., b. ab. '59. 5, Ella, b. April 17, and died March 9, 1861.

RICHARDSON, Justus R , b. ab. 1826, in Jefferson, Me.; m. Emily R. Erskine; r. Rock., a teamster. Their ch. 1, Ida M., b. ab. 1857. 2, Frank G., b. ab. 1859.

RICHARDSON, Jesse R., b. ab. 1828, in Bath, Me.; m. Margaret S. Perry, Nov. 23, '47; r. Rock., a mason, &c. Their ch. 1, Fred. Herbert, b. June, 1850, d. March 24, '53. 2, Albert A., b. ab. 1856. 3, Charles, b. ab. '59. Of this name, also, Peter Richardson, b. ab. 1800; r. Rock. and d. March 15, 1855. Of his ch. 1, Peter, b. ab. 1842; r. Rock., a mariner. Also of the same name, Henry Richardson, b. ab. 1822, in Mt. Desert; mar. Mary Ott; r. Rock., a mariner, soldier of 2d Battery, &c. Their ch. 1, Mary E., b. ab. 1846. 2, Phebe A., b. ab '48. 3, Catharine A., b. ab. '50. 4, Harriet J., b. ab. '52. 5, Octavia, b. ab. '54. 6, William H., b. ab. '56.

RICHIE, Enoch S., b. ab. 1830; m. Annie ——; r. Rock., a carpenter. Their ch. 1, John A., b. ab. 1852. 2, Eugene C., b. ab. '56.

RICKERING, William, b. ab. 1827; m. Margaret ——; r. Rock. a mariner. Their ch. 1, Augusta S., b. ab. 1850. 2, Ada F., b. ab. 1856.

RIDER, Nathaniel, a lineal descendant of Samuel of Yarmouth, Mass., (who in 1643 was one of 18 able to bear arms, and was mar. Dec. 23, 1656, to Sarah, dau. of Robert Bartlett of Plymouth, Mass , who came over in the *Ann*, in July, 1623); m. Priscilla Bradford of Plympton, who was 5th in descent from Gov. William Bradford, through his son William, the deputy governor and major; r. & probably d. Halifax, Mass., where their son, Capt. John Bradford Rider, was b. Nov. 9, 1778; came first to Th. in 1793, as apprentice to Capt. Richard Bosworth of Halifax, assisted that season and in '94 to build a house at Herring Gut for John Hupper, that at Mill River for H. J. Knox, jr., by Hatch & Tilson, commonly called the Stimpson House, and the E. Scott Young house at Oyster River; settled here in May, 1800; mar. Feb. 14, 1805, Nancy, dau. of Joel & Margaret (Shaw) White, and descendant of the Peregrine White, b. in the *Mayflower* in Cape Cod Harbor; m. 2d, Mary (Simonton) Wiggin, July 29, 1819; r. Th., a joiner, artillery officer, worked on most of the buildings put up in Knox's time and later; died Jan. 9, '45, aged 66.

Capt. John B.'s ch. 1, Thomas J., b. July 17, 1806; mar. Jane (Wilson) Smith, Jan. 17, '36; r. Th., a joiner, prison guard, &c. 2, Nancy, b. Dec. 18, '07; m Charles White, May 27, '29; r. Halifax, Mass. 3, Lurania, b. Jan. 14, '10; d. in Th., of erysipelas, June 10, '29. 4, Margaret, b. Oct. 25, '11; m. John Bonney, June 20, '46; r. Plympton, Mass. 5, John B., (2d), b. Aug. 25, '14; mar. Elizabeth Asmet Colcord, Nov. 28, '37; r. S. New Market, N. H. 6, Soveiah, b. Oct. 25, '16; m. Harrison Fuller, Nov. 3, '47; r. N. Bridgewater, d. Jan. 6, '60. The mother, b. Feb. 5, 1779, d. July 4, 1818, aged 39.

Thomas J.'s ch. 1, Jane, b. July 31, 1837. 2, John T., b. June 20, '46. 3, Nancy Elizabeth, b. April 4, '48. 4, Alice Carpenter, b. March 10, '53.

John B., (2d)'s ch. 1, Sarah E., b. Sept. 30, 1838. 2, John F. C., b. July 6, '42. 3, Cada Augusta, b. Aug. 16, '49.

RILEY, Thomas, b. ab. 1825, in Ireland, as was Margaret, his wife; r. Rock. Their ch. 1 & 2, twins, b. ab 1856; Mary & Margaret. 3, Joanna, b. ab. '58. 4, Ellen, b. ab. '60.

RIPLEY, Lieut. Henry O , b. in Appleton, ab. 1841; c. with his widowed mother to Rock., was a printer, and officer of 4th Me. Reg., d. at Washington, D. C., May 24, or June 7, 1864, from a wound in the lungs. Of this name, also, Archelaus Ripley, b. ab. 1789, and Margaret, his wife; r. Rock., in 1860.

RIVERS, Joseph, came from the North of Ireland; mar. Margaret Robinson; settled and d. in Cushing. Their ch. 1, Thomas, mar. Katie Furness; r. & d. C. 2, Mary, m. Dennis Fogerty of St. Geo. 3, Moses, m. Hannah Carney; r. & d. C. 4, Archibald, mar. Nancy Gardner of Boston. 5, Betsey, m. Thomas Henderson of St. G. 6, Sarah, m. Robert Jameson of F. 7, Joseph, (2d), m. Maria Jameson; r. & d. C. 8, Margaret, mar. Capt. James Crawford; r. & d. W. Of the sons of Thomas. 1, Dennis, m. and r. C., and had sons, viz.: 1, Richard. 2, James H., m. Elizabeth A. Leman of Boston, 2d, Nancy Vose, Nov., 1838; r. Th., was deputy collector of customs, commission merchant some years at Mobile & Boston. Of the ch. of Moses. 1, Joshua, m. and r. in C., and had ch. 1, Robert, b. ab. 1816; mar. Nancy M. Page of C.; r. W., rem. Th., & d. Sept. 10, '54. 2, Rachel, m. William Jordan; r. & d. Th. 3, Sarah A., m. Benjamin Jordan; rem. Hope. Thomas, also, of the same family, (descent not ascertained), b. ab. 1809; m. Amelia ———; r. S. Th., in fish business.

Of Richard's sons. 1, Capt. William W., m. Louisa B. Russell of Wal., Nov. 18, 1858; r. Th., and d. in 1862, his wife having d. previously, and an only child died April 28, '63.

James H.'s ch. by 1st wife. 1, Henry T., b. ab. 1825; m. Mary J. Dunbar, Aug. 20, '51; a commission merchant at Mobile, since clerk in U. S. Navy. 2, Edward R., b. ab. 1827; m. Eliza Aldrich of New Bedford; r. Th. & Mobile. 3, Sarah G., m. William H. Church, Sept. 2, '46; r. N. York. 4, William E., a soldier in 13th Mass. Reg. 5, Elizabeth A., b. May 5, '36; m. Capt. Albert J. Aldrich of N. Bedford, Nov. 18, '54; r. Th. The mother d. April 15, '38. By 2d wife. 6, Julia S., b. Sept. 29, '39; mar. Augustus O. Robinson; r. Th. 7, Col. Charles C., b. March 26, '41; officer in 11th Mass. Reg.; mar. Hannah M. Jacobs, Jan. 24, '65; r. Th. 8, George M., entered the U. S. Navy. 9, Frank. 10, Mary.

Robert's ch. 1, Burletta, b. ab. 1841; m. P. P. Nichols; r. Th. 2, Evander, b. June, 1844, d. in W., Jan., 1845. 3, Evander, (2d), b. in W., 1846.

Thomas's ch. 1, Israel, b. ab. 1842; r. S. Th., a mariner, member of Coast Guards, &c. 2, Sarah, b. ab. '44. 3, Richard T., b. ab. '46. 4, Dennis, b. ab '48. 5, Ruth H., b. ab. '51. 6, Amos, b. ab. '54. 7, Hiram, b. ab. '56. 8, Caskaline, b. ab. '59.

ROBERTS, Leonard, b. ab. 1813; m. Avis ———; r. Rock., a mariner. Their ch. 1, Benjamin P., b. ab. '40. 2, Mary S., b. ab. '49. 3, Leonard C., b. ab. '52. 4, Charles W., b. ab. '55. 5, Avis H., b. ab. '58.

ROBBINS, Ebenezer, of Walpole, Mass., son of William & Priscilla, from which pair, according to Mr. Sibley's History of Union, all of the Robbins name in this vicinity descended, was b. May 19, 1691; m. 1st, Mary ———, 2d, Experience Holmes, & d. in Walpole, July 3 or 6, 1762. His ch. by 1st wife. 1, Mary, b. Nov. 12, '20, d. July 18, '46. 2, Sarah, b Oct. 23, '22. 3, Ebenezer, (2d), b. Sept. 11, '24; c. to Fox Isl. before the Revolution, & came off, as many others did at the time, to get away from the British; settled in Union in '79, & d. March 1, '98. 4, Oliver, b. Oct. 1 or 30, 1727: m. 1st, Elioenai Shepard of Wrentham, c. to St. George's, now Th., m. 2d, Mrs. Chloe Blackington of Attleboro', in '75, was p. Feb. 22, '92, to Mrs. Ama Maxcy of Union, & d. March 27, '92. By 2d wife. 5, Philip, b. Aug. 20, '30; r. and d. U. 6, Margaret. 7, Benoni. 8, Experience, b. June 2, 1735; m. William Gregory; r. Cam. & d. June 30, 1827; bur. Rock. 9, Josiah, r. and d. U. And 5 others.

Ebenezer, (2d)'s ch. 1, Zilpah, b. at Cumberland, R. I., Nov. 29, 1758; m. Nathaniel Fales of Th. & d. Oct., 22, 1827. 2, Bela, b. May 2, 1761; m. Margaret Meservey; r. U. & d. April 19, 1831. 2, Philip, (2d). 3, Molly. 4, Azubah, b. 1752; m. William Hays; r. W. & d. March 7, 1832.

Oliver's ch. by 1st wife. 1, Elioenai, b. April 20, 1747; m. Jonathan Crockett; r. & d. Rock. 2, Sybell, b. Aug. 30, 1749; m. James Fales of Rock. & d. May 27, 1825. 3, Oliver, (2d), b. Aug. 22, '51; m. Sarah Killsa of Bristol, Feb. 28, 1780, by Alexander Nichols, Esq.; r. W. of the meadows, & d. July 8, 1829. 4, Lois, b. March 10, 1754; m. Lt. Hugh Killsa; r. Th. & d. Dec. 21, 1837. 5, Lucy, b. July 18, 1756; m. John Butler, & d. Jan. 29, 1840. 6, Major Otis, b. Oct. 20, 1758; m. Mary Keen, Oct. 28, '84, by Mason Wheaton, & d. May 1, 1840. 7, Sabra, b. Jan. 26, 1761, at Attleboro', as were all the preceding; m. Comfort Barrows, & d. June 4, 1840. 8, Mella, b. May 11, 1764, at S. Th., the first white child born east of Mill river; m. Phinehas Butler; r. Th. & d. April 2, 1852. 9, Joseph, b. July 26, '68, d. instantly. 10, Shepard, b. May 31, '72; m. Peggy (Kelloch) Nichols of Th., p. Nov. 24, 1804, r. 1st lot in S. Th. & d. Nov. 1, or 26, '37. The mother d. May 31, '72, & was b. in Wrentham, Aug. 1, 1727. By 2d wife. 11, Ruth, b. '77, d. in Brownsville. 12, Betsey, b. Feb. 25, '79; m. Simon Brown; rem. to Brownsville. 13, Rufus, b. Oct. 23, '85; m. Hannah Thompson of Eden, p. Feb. 20, 1808; traded for a time in Th. & rem. Eastward. Chloe, the mother, d. 1790.

Third Generation.

Oliver, (2d)'s ch. 1, Elioenai, b. June 18, 1781; m. John Wright of Barrettstown, July 28, 1800. 2, Oliver, (3d), b July 31, 1783, d. in the W. I. 3, Robert, b. May 22, '86; m. —— Ray, had wood wharf & store in Boston; r. near Boston. 4, Araunah, or, as often spelled, Arunah, b. March 24, '90; m. Margaret Healey, p. Oct. 10, 1818; r. Th., a farmer. 5, Isaac C., b. Aug. 17, '92; m. Sally Spear; r. Th. 6, Sarah, b July 23, '95; m. Henry McIntosh; r. Rock. & d. Dec. 3, 1829. 7, Eleanor, b. Feb. 10, 1797; m. ——— Barstow; r. Vt. 8, Sybell, b. Aug. 31, 1799; m. Waterman Fales; r. Rock. 9, Shepard, (2d), b. Feb. 3, 1802; m. & r. in Boston.

Maj. Otis's ch. 1, Capt. Otis, Jr., Esq., b. Sept. 1, 1785, m. Susan H. Ingraham, March 30, 1815; r. Th., and died July 9, '22. 2, Mary, b. April 2, '87, m. Iddo Kimball; r. Rock. 3, Susan, b. Aug. 17, '91, d. April 30, '49. 4, Orris, b. Oct. 12, '95, d. Jan. 22, '96. 5, Viram B., b. April 11, '97, m. Patience (Otis) Simonton, Sept. 25, 1842; r. S. Th., a farmer. 6, Orris, (2d), b. Feb. 7, '99, m. Hannah (Spear) Ingraham, Nov. 30, 1828; r. Th., and d. June 4, 1833.

Shepard's ch. 1, Dea. Oliver, (natural or adopted) born Dec. 17, 1796, m. 1st, Nancy Brown, Nov. 18, 1827, 2d, Esther Starr, Sept. 8, '49; r. Th., a merchant, and d. Aug. 2, '51. 2, Shepard K., b. ab. 1805; r. on homestead and d. unm. June 19, '36. 3, Washington, b. ab. 1808, m. Lucy J. Butler, Sept. 25, '51; r. Th., a farmer.

Rufus's ch. 1, a dau., m. and r. Brownsville.

Fourth Generation.

Arunah's ch. 1, Julia A., b. Nov. 2, 1813, m. Joseph Ingraham; r. Rock. 2, Arunah, (2d), b. March 24, '19, m. Hannah E. Cushing, Dec. 18, '42; r. Th., a farmer. 3, Charles K., b. Sept. 22, '21; r. Th., a farmer. 4, Margaret, b. June 17, '24.

Isaac C.'s ch. 1, Harriet S., b. Dec. 22, 1817, m. Rufus K. Blackington; r. Rock. 2, Elionai W., b. April 25, '19, m. Edwin T. Lovejoy; r. Rock. 3, Adela H., b. March 17, '22, m. Charles Sherer; r. Rock. 4, Oliver S., b. Feb. 24, '24, mar. Eliza Bishop of Braintree, Mass.; r. Th., a farmer.

Otis, Jr., Esq.'s ch. 1, Hannah Coit, b. May 15, 1816, m. 1st, Hon. Wm. Thomas, 2d, Dr. M. R. Ludwig; r. Th. 2, Horace Hudson, b. Jan. 8, '18, mar. Sophia B. Wooster, Dec. 21, '43; r. Rock., a farmer, and d. Aug. 2, '59. 3, John H. C., b. Feb. 4, '19, m. Mary A. Keen; r. Th., a farmer. 4, Otis I., b. May 17, '21, and d. next day.

Orris, (2d)'s ch. Orris K., b. May 15, 1829, d. Jan. 6, '34.

Dea. Oliver, (4th)'s ch. 1, Oliver J., b. Oct. 11, 1828; rem. Mass. 2, Charles E., b. Oct. 2, '30, d. Oct. 5, '47. 3, William H., b. Oct. 17, '32; r. Th., a cabinet maker. 4, Bertha Maria, b. Dec. 22, '34. 5, Marcia E., b. Feb. 24, '38. 6, Shepard K., b. Nov. 10, '40.

Washington's ch. Lucy Shepard, b. ab. 1857.

Arunah, (2d)'s ch. 1, Sarah A., b. ab. 1844. 2, Edwin O. b. ab. '47. 3, ? Lucy, b. ab. '49.

Oliver S.'s ch. Henry S., b. ab. 1858.

Horace H.'s ch. 1, Clara M., b. Oct., 1844, d. April 9, '46. 2, Geo. Hiram, b. ab. '46. 3, Julia H., b. ab. '48. 4, John T. R., b. Feb. 5, '49. 5 and 6, twins, b. Jan. 1852, Anna L., and Lauretta.

John H. C.'s ch. 1, Gilbert J., b. ab. 1852. 2, Frank, b. ab. '55. 3, Frederic H., b. ab. '57. 4, Charles, b. ab. '59.

ROBBINS, Lieut. Nathaniel A., b. Aug. 24, '34, son of Willard Robbins of Union, grad. Bowdoin Coll., 1857, admitted to the bar at Rockland, Oct., 1860; enlisted and became an officer in 4th Me. reg., taken prisoner, July, 1863, and, despite attempts at escape, was still, at the opening of 1865, enduring the slow starvation of a rebel prison. A cousin of his, Edward K. Robbins, b. April 9, 1839, son of Nathaniel, of Union, r. Rock., a druggist. Of this name, also, William J., b. ab. 1830, son of Lewis Robbins of Hope; mar. Mary E. Nash of Wal, r. Th., a joiner; and has one ch. Ellison, b. ab. 1856. Milton Robbins, b. ab. 1833, in Appleton; m. Julia Conant; r. S. Th., a carpenter. Their ch. 1, Lauraette, b. ab. 1852. 2, Alvinza, b. ab. '54. 3, Osmond, b. ab. '56. 4, Cora E., b. ab. '58.

ROBBINS, Rufus G. b. ab. 1806, r. Rock., a shop keeper in 1860. His ch. 1, Margaret, b. ab 1836. 2, Rufus G., (2d), b. ab. 1838; m. Mary E. Lamb of Cam., June, 1861; r. Rock., a soldier of 4th Me. reg., &c. 3, Mary A., b. ab. '40. 4, William, born ab. '42. 5, John, b. ab. 1844. Of this name, also, David Robbins, born ab. 1807; mar. Olive ———, who died May 9, 1859, a. 53; r. Rock., a lime burner, and had with him one son, William J., b. ab. '58. There was also here, Daniel Robbins, b. ab. 1808; m. Eliza Sheldon; r. Rock., a wheelwright, soldier of 2d Battery, and re-enlisted. Their ch. 1, Daniel O., b. ab. 1849. 2, Joseph W., b. Jan. 1851, d. Feb. 14, '54. Also, James G. Robbins, b. ab. 1831; m. Sarah E. ———; r. Rock., a mariner. Their ch. 1, Henrietta, b. ab. 1853. 2, Chloe E., b. ab. '55. 3, Agnes M., b. ab. '57. Capt. George Robbins, b. ab. 1804;

m. 1st, Mary Witham, 2d, Sarah (Hartford) Andrews, r. Cam., War., and, of late, Rockland. His ch. by 1st wife. 1, Orinda, m. Francis Allen of Lewiston. 2, Benjamin Otis. 3, Lydia J., m. John Copeland; r. Rock. 4, James P., b. ab. 1836; mar. Cynthia Henderson, Oct. 21, '59; r. Rock., a lime burner., soldier of 4th Me., &c. 5, Sarah H., r. Rock. 6, Charles W.

ROBINSON, Dr. Moses, of the Scotch Irish emigration, came first to what is now Cushing, afterwards, to W., with the first settlers; d. and was buried there in the 1st graveyard, by the old Pres. meeting-house. Capt. Andrew, probably a brother, died and was buried at the old Fort, 1742. Dr. Moses's ch. (sons.) 1, Joseph, m. Mary McFetheridge; not *McKoun*, as in Annals of Warren; r. C., and d. aged about 78. 2, Moses, (2d), m. ——— McFarlane; r. & d. C. 3, John, m. Sarah Carver, descendant of Gov. Carver of Plymouth; r. & d. Pleasant Pt. Cove, C. 4, Major Hanse, m. Bridget or Priscilla Hyler, r. & d. C.* 5, Archibald, born Jan. 31, 1737; the first white male ch. at what is now W., m. Margaret Watson; r. C. and d. Feb. 25, 1820 6, William, b. ab. 1738, or the latter part of 1737, m. Mrs. Rebecca (Rea) Minot, Nov. 3, 1767; r. W. and died April 23, 1813. (daus.) 7, Margaret, m. Joseph Rivers of C. 8, Mary, m. Matthew Kelloch; r. & d. St. George. 9, Jane, m. ——— Bennett; r. Rock., and perished in a snow storm, in 1770.

Joseph's ch. 1, Hannah, m. Samuel Gilchrist; r. and d. St George. 2, Sarah, d. unm. 3, Mary, d. young. 4, Moses, (3d), b. 1756, died 1777, said to be the first buried in the old grave yard, in Cushing. 5, John, (2d), lost at sea. 6, Joseph, (2d), d. in W. Indies. 7, Elizabeth, m. Elijah Hall; r. and died St. Geo. 8, Archibald, (2d), mar. Sarah Hutchins; r. and d. C. 9, Jane, d. unm. in St. Geo., aged 75 or 80.

Moses's (2d)'s ch. 1, Moses, (4th), m. Jane Burton, r. C., and d. Appleton. 2, John, (3d), m. Nancy or Harriet Payson; r. St. Geo. 3, Mary m. Capt. Samuel Watts; r. and died St. George. 4, Joseph, (3d), b. Feb., 1755; m. Jane Lewis; r. St. Geo., and d. March 4, '43. 5, Matthew, m. Hannah Sterling of Bristol; r. 1st, at McCobb's Narrows, but rem. over nearer F.; r. and d. C. 6, Betsey, mar. William Burton; r. and d. C. 7, Nancy, m. 1st. Capt. Simon McLellan, 2d, James McCarter; r. C. 8, Isaac, m. Sarah Rivers; r. & d. C., widow m. Samuel Payson. 9, Andrew, m. Margaret Lewis,; r. C., rem. & d. Union.

John's ch. 1, Reuben, d. unm. 2, Robert, d. unm. 3, John Carver, m. Betsey Hyler; r. and d. C. 4, Capt. Alexander, m. Polly

---

* It was on his lot, near McCobb's Narrows, we believe, that, when first taken possession of, there was found what has always been called the "Old Cellar," but which, from recent examination, made by Mr. I. S. Burton, appears to have claims to much greater interest than is usually attached to that class of ruins. The first huts of the settlers here, were usually without cellars, or, at most, with only a slight, unwalled, excavation, entered by a trap door in the middle of the room. But this was a deep and capacious structure, 40 feet in length, and at this day not less than 9 feet in depth; well walled, when first discovered, with hewn timber, since crumbled to dust; and situated on a point projecting into the river, with a cove on one side, to which a subterranean passage, with similar walls and depth, led from the main structure. What was its design, and by whom it was built, whether by early French traders, or as a retreat for pirates frequenting the coast, remains uncertain.

Page; r. and d. Pleasant Pt. C. 5, Charles, m. Alice Robinson; r. and d. C. 6, Betsey, m. Moses Rivers. 7, Sarah.

Major Hanse's ch. 1, Priscilla, m. ——— Gardner; r. and d. C. 2, Margaret, b. 1763; m. John Roakes; r. W., and d. April 19, 1806. 3, Simeon, m. Hannah Hyler; r. C. 4, Agnes, m. 1st, Caleb Howard, 2d, Rob. Porterfield; rem. Ohio. 5, Betsey, m. Cornelius Hyler; r. & d. C. 7, Hanse, (2d), mar. Lucy Hyler; r. C. 8, Capt. Moses, (5th), b. 1773; m. Priscilla Hyler; r. C. and d., lost overboard June, 1833, from sloop *Orient*, on passage from E. Th. to Bangor. 9, John, (4th), m. Polly Dillaway; r. and d. Hope. 10, Thomas, m. a Collamore; r. and d. Liberty. 11, Jacob, m. 1st, Nancy, (or, as the town records have it, Anomeriah) Robinson, who died Oct. 28, 1795, 2d, Sarah Kelloch, p. Dec. 1, 1796; r. S. Th. and d. April 6, 1813.

Archibald's ch. 1, Capt. William, (2d), born Nov. 27, 1762; mar. Catharine Packard, Oct. 3, '93; r. C. and d. June 26, 1822. 2, Mary, b. Sept. 27, '64; d. unm. 3, Elizabeth, b. Aug. 17, '66; mar. Dea. James Fisher; r. W., and d. Oct. 1849. 4, Margaret b. Aug. 17, '68, m. 1st, William Watson, 2d, John A. Ruscoe, July 27, 1805; r. Th., and d. F., 1822. 5, Capt. James, b. Sept. 25, '70; m. Rachel, dau. of Lieut James Thompson of Cranberry Is., (a Rev. soldier who d. in Friendship, Dec. 1, 1837, aged 93,) r. C. and Rock. and d. March 11, 1831. 6, Capt. John H., b. Jan. 11, '73, m. Jane Sumner of War.; r. C., & d. Nov. 1, 1837. 7, Sarah, b. March 21, '75, m. Josiah Keith; r. Th., and d. May 3, 1803. 8, Lucy, b. Oct. 8, '77, m. William W. French; r. and d. W. 9, Nancy, b. July 2, '80; r. Th., and d. Feb. 18, 1861. 10, Capt. Archibald, (3d), born Jan. 8, '83, mar. 1st, Elizabeth Vose, 2d, Mary Vose, p. May 16, 1811; r. Cush., and d. in W. I.

William's ch. 1, Moses, (5th), b. Oct., 1769; m. Elizabeth Ludwig of Wal.; r. War., a farmer, & d. Dec. 19, 1858. 2, P. Pebbles, b. 1775; m. Sabra Jameson; r. W., & d. Dec. 20, 1824. 3, Capt. William, (3d), b. Oct. 3, '79; m. Hannah McLellan, p. March 22, 1806; r. Th., & d. Oct. 11, '45. 4, Hannah, m. William Watton of F. 5, Mary, m. Christian Kaler of Wal. 6, Daniel, b. 1785, d. Nov. 5, 1809.

Fourth Generation.

Archibald, (2d)'s ch. 1, Samuel, a soldier on the Lakes, and d. of fever after peace but before his return. 2, Robert, d. in 1813. 3, Mary, b. ab. 1797; m. 1st, Henry Jenks, 2d, James Creighton; r. Th. 3, Archibald, (4th), mar. Elizabeth Curtis, Dec. 10, 1824; r. Th., on the place now occupied by his widow, and d. June, 1845. 4, Sarah, m. —— Felch of Natick, Mass. 5, Susan, m. Chas. S. Brown; r. R.

Moses, (4th)'s ch. 1, Alice, m. 1st, Charles Robinson, 2d, James Hackelton; r. and d. Bristol. 2, Elizabeth, b. 1785; m. 1st, William Sayward, 2d, Theodore Howard; r. Rock., & d. April 29, 1842. 3, Rebecca, m. Solomon Comstock; r. & d. Argyle, Me. 4, Nancy, m. Nathaniel Fales, (3d); r. Th., & d. Sept. 19, 1850. 5, Jane, m. 1st, Haynes Whitney, 2d, Jeremiah Gilman; r. Th. 6, Maria, d. young. 7, Susanna, d. in Argyle. 8, Charlotte, mar. Thomas Ellis, Jan. 25, 1821; r. & d Argyle. 9, Benjamin B., b. 1819; m. Abigail Pottle; r. Appleton, rem.? Rock. 10, Sarah, m. Joseph Pottle, Jan. 25, 1821; r. and died Montville.

John, (3d)'s ch. 1, John, (4th), m. Nancy Robinson of C.; r. St. G. 2, Ephraim, m. Betsey Burton; r. St. G. 3, Mary, mar. Adam Wyllie; r. & d. St. G. 4, Margaret, b. June 12, 1797; m. Matthew

32*

Burton; r. Rock. 5, Moses, (6th), b. ab. 1800; m. Hannah Hall; r. Rock., rem. St. G., a carpenter, &c. 6, Isaac, m. Mary Wyllie; r. St. G. 7, George, died unm.

Joseph, (3d)'s ch. 1, Mary, d. young. 2, Andrew, (2d), m. 1st, Nancy Burton, 2d, Polly Fuller; r. St. G, and d. March, 1860. 3, Jane, m. Archibald McKellar; r. & d. St. G. 4, Capt. George, born April 14, 1784; m. Susan Norwood, (who it is somewhat remarkable was born the same year, month, day, and time of day with himself); r. Th., a ship master, tanner, &c. 5, Margaret, m. Dea. John Miller; r. & d. W. 6, Elizabeth, m. Hon. Joel Miller; r. Th. 7, Rosanna, m. Steward Harrington; r. Th. 8, Joseph, (4th), m. Abigail Ames; r. & d. St. G. 9, Edward, m. Hannah Fuller; r. St. G.

Matthew's ch. 1, Capt. Moses, (6th), m. 1st, Jane, dau. of Jesse Thomas of Cam., 2d, Eliza Green, 3d, Maria Diamond; r. Rock., & d. in South America. 2, Capt. Henry, b. Jan. 4, 1796; mar. Mary Jameson of F.; r. F. and War. where he d. July 21, 1860. 3, Capt. Simon, b. Oct. 8, '97; m. 1st, Jane Jameson, 2d, Hannah Storer of C.; r. Th., and d. Aug. 20, 1861. 4, Caroline, m. 1st, Thurston W. Jameson, 2d, Josiah Sterling; r. F. 5, Eliza, m. Josephus Bradford of Bradford's Is. 6, Dea. Isaac, b. ab. 1803; m. Clarinda A. Copeland, June 11, 1829, 2d, Mrs. Nancy (Morton) Rhoades, p. Dec. 5, 1861; r. War., and d. Jan. 22, '63. 7, Capt. James, (2d), m. Susan Ann Robinson; r. Th., and d. in Pensacola, Oct. 26, 1834. 8, Jesse, m. Eliza Robinson; r. C.

Isaac's ch. Rachel, m. William Parsons; r. Cush.

Andrew's ch. 1, Lewis, m. ——— Fairbanks, of Hope; r. and d. Bradford. 2, John L., m. Hannah Burton, Jan. 16, 1814; removed Union, r. and d. Searsmont. 3. Yarley, rem., m. and d. in the South. 4, Margaret, d. in Cush. 5, Jane, m. James Hall of W.; r. Boston. 6, Ephraim, d. in Cush. unm. 7, Mary, m. William H. Webb, Jr., of War.; r. Boston. 8, Agnes, m. and r. Boston.

John Carver's ch. 1, Nancy, d. unm. 2, William, d. unm. 3, Elizabeth, m. 1st, ——— Hoffsis, 2d, James Grant. 4, Carver, died unm. 5, ———, m. James Grant.

Capt. Alexander's ch. 1, Elsie, r. Cush. 2, Alexander, (2d), d. a. about 21. 3, Hannah, m. Moses Rivers; r. Cush. 4, Hope, mar. Hermon Casualis or Castilleux; r. Cush. 5, Eliza, mar. Capt. Jesse Robinson. 6, Arthur, m. Eliza McLellan; r. Cush., at Pleasant Pt. 7, Dolly, d. in C. 8, George, (2d), m. and r. C. 9, Mary, mar. Mr. Pitcher of Wal. 10, Harriet, r. Boston.

Simeon's ch. 1, Barbara, m. Capt. William Hyler; r. Cush. 2, Capt. John, (5th), m. Abigail Parsons, became a Mormon, rem Salt Lake. 3, Agnes, m. Cornelius Robinson; r. and d C. 4, Hannah, m. William Wyllie; r. and d. C. 5, Capt. Oliver, mar. Matilda Shibles, Nov. 6, 1825; came to Th. and d. 1846, lost at sea, in a gale, with all on board. 6, Peggy, m. Capt. Henry Ulmer; r. and d. Rock. 7, Simeon, (2d), d. unm 8, Lawrence, lost overboard at sea.

Hanse, (2d)'s ch. 1, Nancy, m. John Robinson, (4th); r. St. G. 2, Simon, (2d), m. Polly Wyllie; r. & d. C. 3, Deborah, mar. James Gilchrist; r. St. G. 4, Jacob, (2d), m. Hannah Carney; r. C.

Capt. Moses, (5th)'s ch. 1, Ann, m. ——— Grafton; r. Rock. or C. 2, Cornelius, m. Agnes Robinson; r. and d. C. 3, Mason, m. 1st, Rachel Hyler, 2d, her sister; r. and d. C. 4, Louisa, mar. Anthony Libbey; r. and d. W. 5, Moses, (6th), m. Rachel Elwell, r. C. and Salt Lake. 6, Emeline. 7, Paulinda. 8, Edward. 9, Hannah, died unmarried.

Jacob's ch. By 2d wife. 1, Nancy, b. Jan. 4, 1799, m. —— Beals, it is believed, and rem. Mass. 2, Priscilla, b. July 2, 1800. 3, Mary, b. April 26, 1802 4, Hanse, (3d), b. Aug. 18, 1804. 5, Sarah, born July 14, '06. 6, Susan, b. Dec. 15, '08, m. —— Hawes, 2d, James Davis; r. Rock 7, Jacob, (2d), b. June 26, '11, d. July 2, '38, his skull being broken when blasting kilnwood in Th. 8, Mathew, (2d), b. Aug. 8, '13, probably rem. St. George with most of the family.

Capt. William, (2d)'s ch. 1, Marlborough, b. April 26, 1794, lost off Newport, on Briton's reef, Nov. 27, 1815; in a Boston vessel, the crew all perishing, save one. 2, Hon. Edward, b. Nov. 25, '96; mar. 1st, Joanna A. Parsons of C., April 25, 1821, 2d, Nancy J. Fales, May 29, '28, 3d, Penelope G. Fales, Jan. 15, '46; r. Th., a ship master, merchant, &c., State Senator, 1836; M. C., 1838; Presidential elector, 1840; candidate for Governor, 1843 & '4; d. Feb 19, 1857. 3, Eben, b. June 13, '98, d. in Salem, Mass., Oct. 20, 1820. 4, Ann James, b. May 25, 1800; m. Barden T. Levensaler; r. Th.. 5, William, (4th), b. July 17, '02; mar. Eliza Parsons of C.; r. Th., & d. Nov. 27, '47. 6, Capt. Oliver, (2d), b. Feb. 17, '05; m. Margaret Patterson, Aug. 6, '35; r. Th., ship master, cashier of Th. Bank, &c. 7, Hester, b. Aug. 8, '07; m. Abner Knowles, Esq.; r. Bangor and Th. 8, Harlow, b. July 1, '10; r. Th. 9, Catharine, b. Nov. 27, '11; m. Timothy Fogg; rem. California. 10, Benjamin, b. Nov. 13, '14; m. Sarah E. Washburn, Dec. 25, '44; r. Th., keeps livery stable, &c.

Capt. James's ch. 1, Anne, b. in C., Sept., 1798; m. Capt. Barnabas Webb; r. Th. 2, Edmund, b. June 25, 1800, died by drowning, May 9, 1814. 3, Julia, b. May 1, '04; mar. Dexter Bennett; r. Th. 4, Rebecca, b. June 16, '06; m. Joseph Emerson, Nov. 30, '26, d. Oct. 2, '38. 5, Capt. James, (3d), b. Nov. 20, '08; m. Margaret M. Spear, Sept. 18, '32; r. Rock. 6, Capt. Joshua A., b. May 8, '11; m. & r. a time, near the Mississippi River; ret. and r. Rock. 7, Capt. David W., b. 1813; m. Mary A. Fuller of or near Boothbay, Nov. 26, '36; r. Rock., all master mariners. 8, Barnabas W., b. Dec. 8, '15; r. Rock. & d. at New Orleans, Sept. 18, '64. 9, Eliza, b. Dec. 18, '18; m. 1st, Charles S. Demuth, 2d, Samuel B. Dodge; rem. Montville. 10, Capt. William W., b. July 28, '20; r. Rock., a ship master. The mother d. at Rock., Aug. 9, '53, aged 77.

Capt. John W.'s ch. 1, Capt. Alden, b. Feb. 1, 1801; mar. Eliza Nutting, March 11, '34; r. C., and d. July 30, '53. 2, Sarah Ann, b. June 13, '07; m. Dea. Joseph Catland; r. Th. 3, Mary Adaline, b. May 27, '10; m. Capt. Ebenezer Creighton of War.; r. Th. 4, Seth, b. Dec. 8, '12, d. Sept. 23, '30. 5, Edmund Buxton, b. Aug. 30, '16, d. at New Orleans, Jan. 2, '38. 6, Ebenezer Archibald, b. June 25, '21, d. Jan. 9, '53. The mother died suddenly, July 4, '48.

Capt. Archibald, (3d)'s ch. 1, Susan Ann, b. 1809; m. 1st, Capt. James Robinson, 2d, Capt. John Cox; r. Th. 2, Rufus Vose, went to sea and has not been heard from. By 2d wife. 3, Thomas Vose, m. 1st, Eliza Ann McLellan of C., 2d, Jane McIntyre; r. C. 4, Mary E., m. Henry Bradford; rem. Nebraska. 5, Lucy J. 6, James, mar. Lydia M. Hyler of C.

For Moses, (5th)'s and P. Pebbles's descendants, see Annals of Warren.

Capt. William, (3d)'s ch. 1, Capt. George W., b. Oct. 27, 1807; m Lucretia B., daughter of Peter Stone of Castine, Oct. 1, '33; r. Th., a master mariner. 2, Julia, b. Oct. 23, '09; m. Capt. Richard Spear, 2d, George Miller, 3d, John Griffin. 3, Electa P., b. April 26, '13;

m. Phinehas Tyler; r. Th. & d. since '55. 4, Jackson, b. Feb, 26, '15, & d. Feb. 18, '16. 5, Almira, b. '17; m. Capt. Sanders Curling; r. Th. & d. Aug. 29, '46. 6, Capt. William Jackson, b. Jan. 21, '20; m. Sarah Simonton of Portland, Sept. 23, '47; d ? Aug. 18, '50, at sea in brig *Irvin*. 7, Eliza A., b. Feb. 7, '23; m. 1st, Capt. Thomas Allen, Sept., '47, 2d, Capt. William Slater; r. Th. 8, Thomas M., b. March 17, '25, d. in New York, June 29, 1852.

Fifth Generation.

Archibald, (4th)'s ch. 1, Mary A., b. Nov. 22, 1826, d. Sept. 1, '27. 2, Charles B., b. Feb. 15, '29, d. ab. '49, of cholera, returning from Europe. 3, Susan L., b. Oct. 15, '32; m. Andrew J. Benner, p. Sept. 26, '53, & d. Nov. 17, '61. 4, Ann E., b. July 22, '35; r. Th.

Benjamin B.'s ch. 1, Calvin, r. Appleton. 2, Eliza J., b. ab. 1849; r. Rock.

Moses, (6th)'s ch. 1, Ambrose H., b. June 12, 1824; m. Mary J. (Green) Mason, Dec. 14, '51; r. Rock., provision dealer, &c. 2, Julia A., m. Alexander Hathorn; r. St. G. 3, Elizabeth; m. John Kenniston; r. Rock. & d. Jan. 12, '55. 4, Lovisa, m. ——— Wellington; r. Lexington, Mass. 5, Hannah, b. Nov. 8, '35, d. Dec. '54. 6, Elijah, b. Nov. 21, '36, d. Jan. 18, '37. 7, Caroline, b. Aug. 15, '39; r. Lexington. 8, Margaret, b. Feb. 16, & d. April 2, 1842. 9, Eliza, b. ab. 1844. 10, Mary, b. ab. 1846.

Andrew, (2d)'s ch. 1, Jane, m. Phinley Kelloch; rem. Oregon. 2, William B., b. ab. 1807; m. Eleanor Clark; r. Rock., a carpenter, &c. 3, Nancy, m. Samuel Tobey; r. Machias. 4, Eliza, d. young. By 2d wife. 5, Sarah; 6, Hannah, both dead. 7, James F., m. Catharine Clark; r. St. G. 8, Mary, m. James Wylie; r. St. G. 9, Almira, m. Lincoln Gilchrist; r. St. G.

Capt. George's ch. 1, Eliza N., b. July 7, 1806; m. John Elliott, (2d); r. Th. 2, Oliver, b. July 13, '08, d. July 5, '10. 3, Joel M., b. May 12, '10; m. Ann Burgoyne; r. E. Cambridge, Mass. 4, Irene, b. Aug. 27, '12; m. Samuel Elliott; r. Mobile, d. in Florida. 5, Albert, b. May 12, '14; m. Mary E. Gault, p. Nov. 7, 1835; rem. Ellsworth. 6, Israel, b. Nov. 16, '16, d. young. 7, Alden, (2d), b. June 9, '18; m. Mary A. Bates of Boston; r. E. Cambridge. 8, Susan N., b. April 23, '20; m. Joshua A. Fuller; r. Th. & d. May 28, 1855. 9, George I., b. June 10, '22; m. Helen M. Stackpole, June 9, '50; r. Th., a druggist, &c. 10, Capt. Edwin A., b. Dec. 31, '24; m. Amelia Waldo, Nov. 28, '55; r. Th., a master mariner. 11, Arthur E., b. May 7, '28; m. Georgianne Woodward, r. S. Boston.

Edward's ch. 1, Nathan, lost at sea in brig *Amanda*, 1843. 2, Edward, (2d), d. young. 3, John, d. young. 4, Elsie, m. John, son of Ephraim Robinson; r. St. G. 5, Abigail, d. young. 6, Mary E., b. ab. '32; m. Thomas Walsh; r. Th. 7, Sarah, d. young. 8, Edward, (3d), m. Nancy Wylie; r. St. G. 9, Clara.

Capt. Henry's ch. Thurston J., b. ab. 1843; m. Abbie J. Williams, Aug. 7, '62; a soldier of 20th Me, reg., d. in Virginia.

Capt. Simon's ch. by 1st wife. 1, Melinda, m. Howard Morton; r. Th. By 2d wife. 2, Simon, (2d), b. Feb. 14, & d. Feb. 27, '33. 3, Hannah Jane, b. Aug. 31, '35. 4, Willard W., b. ab. 1837.

Capt. James, (2d)'s ch. 1, Levi L., b. March 6, 1831. 2, James W., b. April 21, 1833.

Capt. Oliver's ch. 1, Harriet, b. Sept. 28, 1826; m. Capt. John B. Roney; r. Th. 2, R. Killpatrick, b. Sept. 14, 1827; m. Ellen Allen,

Dec. 19, '50 ; r Th. 3, Charlotte, b. March 21, 1829 ; m. Henderson C. Miller, Sept. 30, '49 ; r. Wal. 4, Mary A., b. Dec. 21, 1832 ; m. William Woodcock; r. Th. 5, Oliver, (3d), b. May 10, 1835; m. Mary Bohndel, Sept., '62 ; r. Th., a mariner. 6, George Henry, b. April 1, '38 ; r. Th., a mariner.

Hon. Edward's ch. by 1st wife. 1, Sarah Frances, b. in C., April 26, 1822 ; m. Capt. Arthur M. Fales ; r. Th. 2, Catharine P., born May, 1824, d. Sept. 22, '25. By 2d wife. 3, Joanna E., b. Dec. 23, '29 ; d. Oct. 16, '39. 4, Maria Louisa, b. Oct 5, '31 ; mar. Oliver B. Fales ; r. Rock., and d. April 11, '54. 5, Alida P., b. June 18, '33 ; m. Robert Foster of Bloomfield, N. J., Oct. 15, '53 ; and died Oct. 3, 1856. 6, Lieut. Edward L., b. Feb. 2, '35 ; m. Rebecca Colson, Feb., 1864 ; r. Th., a mariner ; officer in the 20th Mass. Reg., &c. 7, Nancy Isadore J., b. Oct. 1, '36 ; r. Th. 8, Frederic A., b. Jan. 16, '40 ; m. Mary A. Barnard, March 23, '64 ; r. Vineland, N. J., an orchardist. 9, Julia Wilder, b. Jan. 4, '42. 10, Ella, b. April 9, and d. April 29, '44. By 3d wife, 11, Caroline Dwight, b. ab. 1848.

William (4th)'s ch. 1, Joanna P., b. June 3, 1829 ; mar. William Hodgkins ; r. Th. 2, Sarah C., b. Dec. 18, '33 ; mar. Waterman M. Robbins, Aug. 3, '51, and d. April 10, '54. 3, William P., b. Dec. 3, 1836 ; m. & r. in the West, sails on the Lakes. 4, Lermond, b. Nov. 12, '40, d. Jan. 28, '41. 5, Ada E., b. July 28, '42, d. March 19, '61. 6, Mary H., b. Dec. 16, '45. 7, Oliver, (2d), b. July 30, and died Sept. 14, 1848.

Capt. Oliver, (2d)'s ch. Augustus Oliver, b. Feb. 19, 1840 ; mar. Julia S. Rivers, Oct., '63 ; r. Th., asst. cashier.

Capt. James, (3d)'s ch. James F., m. Nancy J. Sweetser, Sept. 28, '59 ; r. Rock., a painter, &c.

Capt. Joshua A.'ch. 1, Julia A., b. March 7, 1841, d. Oct. 17, '61. 2, Catharine, b. ab. '43. 3, Mary E., b. ab. '50. 4, Willie H., b. ab. '52. 5, Clara E., b. ab '55. 6, Frederic C., b. ab. 1858.

Capt. David W.'s ch. 1, Franklin F., b. June 16, 1838, d. March 2, 1856, lost overboard in a gale, from sch. *St. Lawrence*. 2, David E., b. May 22, 1839.

Capt. George W.'s ch. 1, Ada L., b. Oct. 11, 1835, d. July 28, '40. 2, Horatia W., b. Aug. 8, '41 ; m. Capt. James B. McLellan ; r. Th. 3, George Lucretius, b. March 6, '43. 4, Adelle, b. 1845 ; m. Capt. William H. Robinson of Auburndale ; & d. Sept. 24, 1864, drowned a few months after her marriage, at Gabarus Bay, when leaving the wreck of her husband's vessel. 5, Mary S., born ab. '47. 6, Anah, b. ab. '49. 7, Sarah J., b. ab. '53.

Ambrose H.'s ch. 1, Lizzie D., b. May 10, 1856. 2, Albert, (2d), b. Oct. 7, 1858.

Albert's ch. 1, Albert C., b. Sept. 4, 1836. 2, Edward F.

George I.'s ch. 1, Helen, b. ab. 1852. 2, Fannie, b. ab. 1859.

Capt. Edwin A.'s ch. Eddie Stetson, b. Dec. 17, 1854, d. March 20, 1858.

R. Killpatrick's ch. Lucy Ellen, b. Dec. 8, 1855, d. March 29, '64.

ROBINSON, Capt. Richard, born in North Wales, G. B., Nov. 5, 1788, came when a boy with Capt. Tobey, and was apprenticed to Miles Cobb of War., where he r. sometime ; m. Jane, dau. of Capt. J. Wyllie, became commander of one of Cobb's vessels ; but rem. Th. was long a ship master here, president of Th. Bank 21 years, &c., and d. June 6, or 8, 1857. Ellen, a sister, b. ab. 1795, came later, and r. Th.

Capt. Richard's ch. 1, Mary, b. Aug. 31, 1815, m. Capt. Ambrose

Snow, (4th), r. N. Y. 2, Capt. Richard, (2d), b. Aug. 13, '17, mar. Mary Wentworth of Lincolnville, Aug. 26, '40; r. Auburndale, Mass., a retired ship master. 3, Capt. Harris, b. Feb. 2, '20, in War. as were the two preceding, m. Sally A. Munroe, July 13, '45, and d. at sea. in command of ship *Arvum*, July 12, '47. 4, Margaret, b. Feb. 18, '22, m. Oliver W. Jordan, (who d. Feb. 5, '65); r. Th. 4, Esther Jane, b. June 29, '24, d. Nov. 1, '26. 5, Elizabeth D., born Sept. 26, '26, m. Albert P. Gould, Esq.; r. Th. 6 and 7, twins, b. March 16, '29; Susan, r. Th., and Sarah, who d. Nov. 9, '32. 8, John Owen, b. July 7, '31, grad. Bowd. Coll., 1854, m. Clementine Yates, Nov. 28, '54; r. and prac. law Th., but rem. Mahanoy City, Penn., and engaged in coal mines. 9, William S., b. July 24, '35, d. Nov. 4, '40.

Capt. Richard, (2d)'s ch. 1, Capt. William Harris, m. Adele Robinson, April 28, 1864; r. Auburndale, master mariner. 2, Richard, (3d); r. Auburndale. 3, Charles.

Capt. Harris's ch. Ellen M., b. ab. 1847; r. Th.

John O.'s ch. 1, Lizzie, b. ab. 1856. 2, Alfred, b. '58, d. Apr. '62. 3, Catharine, b. April, and d. Sept. 1, '60. 4, John Clement.

ROBINSON, ——, came with his wife, from England, to Boston, Mass., afterwards to this place, & r. awhile, in early times, at the old Fort. Their ch. 1, Susanna, b. 1748, m. John Lindsey; r. Rock., and d. Jan. 9, 1826. 2, George, m. Mary Quinham of Boston, rem. to Cam., thence to what is now S. Th., about 1807, afterwards to Mt. Desert, and died with his wife in Harrington, about 1834. George's ch. 1, Betsey, m. 1st, —— Goodspeed, 2d —— Speed. 2, Nathaniel, mar. Elizabeth Derry of Cam.; r. S. Th., and d. Sept. 5, 1854. 3, George, (2d), m. Julia or Susanna Chaples of St. George. 4, Lucy, m. James Harvey. 5, Robert, rem. Northport, mar. his 2d wife in Lynn. 6, William, m. Betsey Brewer of Boothbay; rem. East. 7, Thomas, m. in Mass. 8, Patience, m. —— Johnson of Appleton. 9, John, m. Ann Jordan, rem. East. 10, Samuel, m. Minda Jackson of N. B.

Nathaniel's ch. 1, John, (2d), b. ab 1800, m. Nancy Bryant, Nov. 9, '20; r. S. Th., a farmer, &c. 2, ? Nancy, b. ab. 1802, m. David Beals; rem. Boston. 3, Nathaniel, (2d), b. 1804; r. S. Th., was found dead by the meadow road, supposed murdered for his money, Sept. 4, '54. 4, Benjamin, m. Nancy M. Littlefield of Castine, p. July 28, 1828; r. Newburyport.

John, (2d)'s ch. 1, Sarah, b. March 12, '21, m. Blinn Curtis; r. S. Th. 2, Nancy, b. July 4, '23, m. Charles A Fales; r. Rock. 3, Elizabeth D., b. Feb. 6, '26, m. Zolmany Sewall, March 10, '46. 4, David, b. March 4, and d. Sept. 30, '28. 5, Mary, b. Aug. 3, '29, m. Enoch Norton; r. S. Th. 6, Capt. John R., b. Feb. 1, '32, mar. N. Maria Snow, March 8, '53; r. S. Th, a master mariner, &c. 7, Hannah, b. May 22, '34, and d. Aug. 27, '38. 8, Harrison B., b. Jan. 25, '37, m. Emily S. Bryant, Nov. 16, '58; r. S. Th., and d. June 25, '61. 9, Joseph, born Nov. 7, '39; r. S. Th., a mariner. 10, Delilah, born March 17, '42. 11, Adeline E., b. June 2, '45; r. S. Th.

Capt. John R.'s ch. Alma E., b. ab. 1854.

Harrison B.'s ch. Annie, b. ab. 1859.

ROBINSON, Edward W., came from Munson, Me., mar. Harriet Watts, May 21, 1848; r. Th., a tailor, P. Master, &c. Of his brothers; George W., also c. to Th., m. at Newport, Esther E. Benner, Jan. 18, '47. 2, Lyman, lost at sea in ship *R. L. Gilchrist*, April, 1854. 3, Alfred W., born ab. 1832, mar. Lucy Edgarton, Oct. 7, '59; r. Th., a tailor.

Edward W.'s ch. 1, Samuel, b. ab. 1850. 2, Clara, b. ab. 1852. George W.'s ch. George Winfield, b. Jan. 1848, d. Sept. 9, '49.

ROBINSON, Warren, b. ab. 1826, in Union, son of John, and grandson of James, mar. Mercy Bridges, Jan. 31,' 52; r. Rock., a meat dealer. Their ch. 1, Fanny, b. Feb. 9, 1854, d. Oct. 14, '56. 2, Frank, b. Oct., '57, d. Jan. 17, '63. 3, Frank, b. ab. '58. Of this name, also, Stillman Robinson, b. ab. 1836, m. Sarah F. Cross, Aug. 22, '60; r. S. Th., soldier in 28th Me. Reg. Also Charles A., soldier in 8th Me. Reg.

ROGERS, Capt. Howland, b. in 1764; came from Marshfield early to Th. as a ship carpenter; mar. Hannah Bradford; rem. to Medford, Mass., where he d. March 1, 1814. Their ch. 1, Capt. Thomas, who commanded the steamer *Patent*, &c.; rem. Boston. 2, Mehitable, m. Ephraim Wood; r. Cam. 3, Nancy, mar. Oakes Perry; r. Cam. 4, Hannah, m. Simon Hunt; r. Cam.

ROGERS, Capt. Edward, b. ab. 1829; m. Philena N. Kirkpatrick, Aug. 27, 1853; r. Rock., a master mariner, now in navy. Their ch. 1, Carrie E., b. ab. 1856. 2, John Walter, b. ab. '58. 3, Mary E., b. Sept. 28, '61, d. May 5, '63.

ROGERS, Lieut. Elisha S., b. ab. 1818, in New Brunswick; mar. Sarah J. ——; r. Rock., a teamster, officer in 4th Me., &c. Their ch. 1, Avis G., b. ab. 1849. 2, Emeline A., b. ab. 1851.

ROLLINS, Alfred, b. ab. 1800, in Poland, Me.; soon rem. to Jay, from whence he came to Th.; m. Mira Tillson, p. Aug. 24, 1832; r. Th., a mariner, &c. Their ch. 1, Capt. Charles A., b June 7, 1833; r. Th., a merchant, officer in 4th Me. Reg., &c. 2, Frederic A., born March 31, '36; r. Th., a clerk, 1860. 3, Aroline Amelia, b. April, 1845, d. Dec. 5, or 12, '46.

ROLLINS, Stacy, b. ab. 1797, & with Damaris, his wife, r. Rock. in 1860. Of their ch. 1, Marcellus M., b. ab. 1837; r. Rock.

ROKES, Robert, (son of Isaac, & grandson of Daniel of W.); m. Elizabeth Neubert; r. Appleton, and d., killed by lightning, Aug. 25, 1840. Their ch. 1, Gilbert U., b. 1827; m. Caroline Morse of U.; r. Rock., was taken with typhoid when on the James River, & d. at Boston, Aug. 7, '62. 2, Adelia A., m. Benjamin Eastman; r. U. 3, Emerson, m. Aldana Neubert of Wal., Sept. 1, '55; r. Rock., and has 1 ch., Frank. 4, R. Marcus, b. Oct. 22, '33, d. Sept. 5, '55, in Rock. 5, Leander, m. Zilpha E. Daniels of U., Sept. 28, '61; r. S. Th., having purchased the D. Vaughan farm.

RONEY, Capt. John B., came from Holstein, Denmark; m. Harriet Robinson of Th., Aug., 1846; r. Th, a master mariner. Their ch. 1, Nelson, b. ab. 1848. 2, John, b. ab. '52. 3, Ellen, b. ab. '54. 4, Maria, b. ab. '56. 5, Lizzie C., b. Oct. 17, '59, d. Nov. 28, '60.

ROSE, Hon. Daniel, b. in 1771; m. 1st, Miss Hammond, 2d, Olive Peaseley; was in service of U. S. as engineer in war of 1812; a physician, magistrate, surveyor, &c., in Boothbay; rem. Th., July, 1823, as the first warden of the State Prison, was president of the Senate from 1822 to '24, and acting governor of Maine from Jan. 2, to Jan. 5, 1822; land agent, &c., d. Oct. 25, '33. His ch. by 2d wife. 1, Edwin, m. Caroline S. Fuller, Oct. 9, 1834; rem. Wiscasset, clerk of courts Lincoln county, 1859 & '60; ret. Th. 2, Olive, b. ab. 1810; r. Th. 3, Dr. Daniel, (2d), b. ab. 1813; M. D. Bowd. Coll. 1837; m.

1st, Harriet G. Hawk, Oct. 28, '37, 2d, C. Amanda (Mitchell) Healey, Jan. 28, '63; r. & prac. med. Th. 4, Elizabeth, m. Jesse Peabody; r. Th. 5, Thomas, b. ab. 1819; mar. Mary Ann Fales, Oct. 12, '41; r. Th., a surveyor, &c. 6, Wilmot, b. ab. 1822; mar. Lucy S. Hawk, Nov. 29, '49; r. Th., a painter. 7, Martha J., b. in Th., Feb. 6, '24; m. John Shibles; r. Th. The mother d. Sept. 11, 1844, aged 56.

Edwin's ch. 1, Caroline E., b. March 10, 1836. 2, Edwin T., b. Jan. 10, d. Oct. 10, '38. 3, Samuel F., b. Oct. 11, '39. 4, Olive, b. March 16, '42. 5, Henrietta D., b. 1844, d. Dec. 8, '51.

Dr. Daniel, (2d)'s ch. 1, Harriet O., b. Sept. 13, 1838. 2, Hester A., b. Jan. 28, '43, d. March 2, '50. 3, Daniel S., b. ab. '46. 4, John E. b. ab. '47. 5, Catharine, b. ab. 1849.

Thomas's ch. 1, Mary Eliza, born July 11, 1842, d. May 4, '44. 2, Francis W., b. ab. '44. 3, Henry T., b. ab. '45. 4, Annie J., born Sept. 1, '59, d. Dec. 25, '63.

ROSELAND, Andrew, b. ab. 1820, in Guttenburg, Sweden, as was Martha, his wife, in England, ab. 1825; r. Rock., a rigger.

ROSS, Ezekiel, Esq., b. ab. 1830 in Jefferson; grad. Bowd. Coll. 1855; c. to Rock., taught high school 1857, studied law in Gould's office, admitted to the bar in 1858; r. Rock., an attorney at law, &c.

ROSS, John, c. from New Meadows to S. Th., m. ——— Mathews, and d. early. Their ch. 1, Mary, m. 1st, David Y. Kelloch of W., 2d, David Kelloch, (3d), and d. in W., Sept. 1860. 2, Catharine, m. William Patten, p. Sept. 3, 1795; rem. Lincolnville.

ROSS, Freeman, b. in New Sharon, m. Angela (Wheeler) Gilchrist, r. W., c. to Th. 1863. Their ch. 1, Ardelle, born ab. '51. 2, Ann Maria. 3. Harriet. 4, Charles F. 5, Fred. Oscar, d. July 2, '61. 6, Frank.

ROUSE, Dr. James, b. ab. 1822, in Virginia, m. 1st, ———, (who d. Aug., 1857, in Rock.), 2d, Mary E. ———; r. Rock., & S. Th., prac. med., went to British Provinces. His ch. by 1st wife. 1, Helen M., b. 1853. 2, Avis A., b. '54. By 2d wife. 3, James W.

ROWE; of this family, Capt. Joshua N., of Rock., m. Caroline A. S. Keating, Feb. 5, 1865; was appointed acting master in U. S. ship *St. Louis*; and Adelbert Rowe, of Rock., entered the navy also.

ROWELL, William, b. in 1755; m. Mrs. Ruth (Matthews) Tennant; came from Nottingham, N. H, to Th. directly after the revolution; was a soldier at Bunker Hill; and died Sept. 30, 1811. Ruth, his widow, d. in 1832. Their ch. 1, Betsey, mar. William Russ of Cam. and d. 1854. 2, William, (2d), d. by drowning, aged 3 yrs. 3, Rice, b. April 27, 1789; m. 1st, Sally Dunning, Feb. 8, 1816, 2d, Mrs. Eunice (Davis) Allen, Dec. 30, 1839, 3d, Sally (Holmes) Ally, 1856; r. S. Th., a caulker, &c., d. in April, 1863. 4, John, d. young. 5, Ruth, b. ab. 1792; m. Briggs Butler; r. S. Th., and d. Jan. 4, 1853. 6, Mary, b. 1794, m. Robert Dunning, (2d); and d. July 4, 1842.

Rice's ch. 1, Eliza D., b. Nov. 23, 1816; m. David A. Crockett. 2, William, b. March 22, '18; mar. Mary Ellen Bartlett; r. S. Th., a caulker, rem. Ohio. 3, Robert D., b. March 21, '21, d. April 6, '31. 4, Ruth, b. Dec. 25, '24, m. Robert H. Heard. 5, Margaret, born Oct. 26, '27, d. April 2, '41. 6, Warren R., b. Oct. 24, '29; m. Hannah Ann Fales, April 8, '52; r. S. Th., a caulker, &c. 7, Luther H., b. May 10, '33; m. Sarah Mathews of Linc., April 28, '56, r. S. Th. a caulker, &c. 8, Hannah H., b. Nov. 19, '36; r. S. Th. 9, Mary, b. July 14, '39; r. S. Th.

William's ch. 1, Adelphus, b. Feb. 12, 1843. 2, Almenzer, born April 5, '45. 3, Frank B., b. April 12, '47. 4, Rice, (2d), b. Jan. 12, '52, & d. Oct. 29, '52. 5, Henry S., b. Nov. 16, '53, & d. Dec. 2, '55. 6, Mary E., b. Sept. 21, '56. 7, Margaret, b. Nov. 1, '58.

Warren R.'s ch. 1, Warren R., (2d), b. ab. 1856. 2, Nathan C., b. ab. '57.

Luther H.'s ch. 1, Frederic, b. ab. 1857. 2, Ida, b. ab. '59.

RUGGLES, Hon. John, b. in Westboro', Mass., ab. 1790; grad. Brown University, 1813; stud. law with Gov. Levi Lincoln at Worcester, as also, before graduating, with Estes Howe, Esq., of Westboro'; commenced practice in Skowhegan, 1815; came to Th., 1818; was speaker of the house of representatives from 1825 to '29, and again in 1831 and '32; judge of the District Court; senator in Congress from 1834 to 1840; m. Margaret George of Watertown; r. Th., a counsellor at law. Their ch. 1, Adelaide C., b. June 11, 1825; mar. Dr. Charles T. Chase; r. Th. 2, Maria, b. Feb. 8, '27; m. Winchell M. Cook; r. Th. 3, John, (2d), b. Jan. 30, '28; r. Chicago, Ill., a merchant. 4, Margaret G., b. March 10, '31, d. Sept. 7, '59.

RUSS, William, came early to what is now S. Th.; mar. Betsey Rowell, p. Jan. 21, 1799; but rem. Cam. Thomas, also, was here, & m. Lucy Chapman, p. May 14, 1804. Of William's ch. 1, Jane H., b. ab. 1802; m. Charles Butler; r. Th.

RUSSELL; of the sons of Thomas & Theresa (Fitzgerald) Russell of Waldoboro'. 1, William, b. ab. 1824; m. 1st, Mary F. Bickmore of F., 2d, L. Maria (Hahn) Havener, Oct. 21, '52; r. Rock., a blacksmith, rem. Cam. since 1860. 2, Thomas, (2d), b. ab. 1828; mar. Frances Nicholson, Feb., 1859; r. Th., a carpenter.

William's ch. by 1st wife. 1, Mary A., b. ab. 1847. 2, Frank W., b. ab. '51. By 2d wife. 3, Ellen K., b. ab. '54. 4, Frederic T., b. ab. '56.

Thomas's ch. Helen, b. April, 1860.

RUSSELL, John, b. ab. 1823, in Ireland; r. Rock., a mariner. Frank, b. ab. 1828, in Ireland, as was Margaret, his wife; r. Rock. Frank's ch. 1, William, b. ab. 1858.

RYDELL, Henry, came from Ireland; r. Th., a tailor, and d. Nov. 5, 1861.

SADDLER, Moses B., b. ab. 1815; m. Eunice ———; r. Rock., a fisherman. Their ch. 1, Sylvanus N., b. ab. 1840, a mariner, soldier of 4th Me., &c. 2, Lorenzo D., b. Aug., 1841; died, lost overboard from sch. *Caroline*, March 21, '61. 3, Flora L., b. ab. '55.

SAFFORD, Gustavus A., b. ab. 1836, in Hope; mar. Almatia A. Rhoades; r. Rock., a merchant, firm of Hewett & Safford.

ST. CLAIR, James, b. 1777, in Meredith, N. H.; m. Sarah Wiggen, landed at Owl's Head, Dec. 25, 1803, was a joiner, and worked on various houses in Th., W., &c.; r. U., was more than 50 yrs. a member of the Baptist church; & d. June 25, 1858, in S. Th., where his widow still resides. Their ch. 1, Lavinia, m. Benjamin Burgess; r. Matinicus. 2, Mary, m. Sion Payson; r. Freedom. 3, George W., b. April 22, 1806; m. Sabra Hall, 2d Eliza (Smith) Brewster of Cam., 1853; r. S. Th., a farmer, &c. 4, James M., mar. Miss Payson; r. Hope. 5, Erastus, m. ——— Bowley; r. Hope. 6 & 7, twins, b. ab. 1811; Thirza, m. Capt. Isaac Tolman; r. S. Th.; Mahala, m. Jonathan Hall of Cam., 2d, Hugh Killsa; r. Rock. 8, Sarah, m. Samuel Crie from Matinicus; r. & d. Rock. 9, Lucy, m. Abijah T. Metcalf; r. Hope, & d. 1863. 10, Abigail, m. Samuel Hastings; r. Hope. 11, Guilford D., b. ab. 1825; m. Leonora Payson; r. Rock., a carpenter.

George W.'s ch. 1, Emery J., b. ab. 1835; m. Caroline S. Long, 1862; r. S. Th., a carpenter. 2, Mary H., b. ab. '37; mar. Capt. Samuel Maddocks; r. S. Th. 3, Gilbert M., b. ab. '39; r. S. Th. By 2d wife. 4, George H.

Guilford D.'s ch. 1, Ashley, b. ab. 1847; r. Rock., entered the army. 2, Laureston, b. ab. '51. 3, Eva, b. ab. '53. 4, Leonora E., b. ab. '55. Of this name, also, Andrew H. of Rock., entered the army.

SAMPSON, or Sansom, Abram, born ab. 1816, in Ireland, as was Mary, his wife; r. Rock., an ostler. Their ch. 1, John, b. ab. 1845. 2, William, b. ab. '47; r. Rock., entered the navy.

SANBORN, Capt. Daniel, b. March 7, 1796, in Steuben, Me., was in revenue service before 1812, entered the U. S. Navy 1814, and served in the Algerine war, under Com. Morris, then, in 1817, the merchant service; c. here with Mary, his wife, m. 2d, Lucy H. Ulmer, Oct. 17, 1847; r. Rock., and d. July 30, '64. Of his ch. By 1st wife. George C., b. Aug. 23, 1839, m. Fannie P., dau. of the late Alden W. Jones of Boston, Oct. 20, '61.

SARGENT, Hon. William G., c. here from Portland; m. Angie E. Haines, a dau. in law of John May, Esq., of Winthrop; r. Rock., an attorney at law, judge in municipal court, &c., rem. Kansas.

SARGENT, Simeon, b. ab. 1829; c. from Bow, N. H; mar. Mary E. Thorndike, Oct. 14, '58; r. S. Th., a stone cutter. Their ch. Mabel E., b. Oct., 1859, d. in Bow, Sept. 23, '61.

SARTELLE, or Sawtelle, John, b. May, 1783, m. 1st, ———, 2d, Betsey McLoon; c. from Concord, Mass., to Cam., rem. Rock., and d. S. Th., Oct. 20, 1852. Of his ch. By 1st wife. 1, Franklin B., b. ab. 1805; m. Louisa Dean, Jan. 1, '32; r. S. Th. By 2d wife. 2, Capt. William M., b. Oct. 28, 1818, m. Susan Fales, Oct. 8, '41; r. Rock., and d. at Savannah, Ga., April 19, '53, when master of brig *Coral* of Bath.

Franklin B.'s ch. 1, William F., b. Aug. 29, 1833; r. S. Th., a mariner. 2, Sarah, b. March 29, '36, m. Henry E. Ames of Jeff., p. June 15, '59. 3, Eugene F., b. April 16, '41; r. S. Th.

Capt. William M.'s ch. 1, Frank Cleaveland, b. Dec. 30, 1841; r. Rock., a mariner. 2, Wm. Constantine, b. May 2, '44; r. Rock., a mariner. 3, Florence A., b. Aug., '46, d, Jan. 6, '52. 4, Mary E., b. ab. '50. 5, Susan F., b. Dec. 21, '52, d. Sept. 22, '64.

SAUNDERS, Jacob P., m. Charlotte Harriman; b. and r. in Orland, Me. Their ch. 1, Joseph, b. or r. in Bucksport, m. Sarah L. Gavett. 2, Levi, born in Orland ab. 1829, mar. 1st, Miss Arnold, 2d, Hannah Trueworthy; r. Rock. 3, Jacob C., b. ab. '41, m. Sarah R., Holbrook; r. Rock., a mariner. 4, Isaac S., b. in Orland ab. '43; r. Rock., a mariner, soldier of 4th Me., d. in, or after the service. 5, John E., born in Orland; r. Rock., entered the army. Of this name, also, Mrs. Elizabeth Saunders; r. Rock., a widow, and of her ch. 1, Thomas C., b. ab. '38; r. Rock., a mariner, soldier of 4th Me., since in the navy or army. 2, Lucy A., b. ab. '46; 3, Henrietta, b. ab. '49; both r. Rock.

Levi's ch. 1, Almira E., b. ab. 1853. 2, Willis P., b. ab. '55. 3,

Enoch S., b. ab. '57. 4, Eugene L., b. Sept. 20, '59, d. Sept. 25, '60. 5, Ada Estelle, b. '61, d. Sept. 13, '63.

Jacob C.'s ch. Alice, b. ab. 1859.

SAUNDERS, Robert, b. ab. 1810, in Ireland, as was Bridget, his wife; r. Rock. Their ch. 1, Robert, (2d), b. ab. 1852. 2, Mary, b. ab. 1856.

SAVAGE, Capt. John, b. ab. 1822, in Mt. Desert, m. 1st, Martha A. Hodgdon, 2d, Almira (Robinson) Whitmore of Mt. Desert; r. Rock., and d. April 12, '62. His ch. John W., b. ab. 1850. Ch. of 2d wife. 1, James F. Whitmore, b. ab. '44. 2, Caroline Whitmore, b. ab. '47; r. Rock.

SAVAGE, Warren, b. ab. 1823, in Hampden, Me., m. Lois A. Simmons of Appleton; r. Rock., a peddler, &c. Their ch. 1, Asbury C., b. ab. 1846. 2, Tileston I., b. ab. '49. 3, Orinda B., b. ab. '52. 4, James E., b. ab. '55. 5, William L., b. ab. '58.

SAVAGE, James, b. ab. 1836, in Ireland, m. Sarah Carney, April 6, '59; r. Rock., a gardener. James Savage, (2d), b. ab. '37, in Ireland, as was Kate his wife; r. Rock., and has ch. Kate, b. ab. '48.

SAWYER, Benjamin W., b. ab. 1805; r. Rock. some years, but rem., was unm., a cabinet manufacturer. Benjamin W. Sawyer, (2d), b. ab. 1811, in Belfast; m. Nancy J. H. Robinson, p. Aug. 13, '36; r. Rock., furniture dealer, firm of Sawyer & Colson. Of this name, also, Sylvester H., b. ab. 1830, mar. Abby S. Bean, Jan. 23, '55; r. Rock., a joiner, &c. Also John A., m. Mary Helen Austin, of Th., Jan. 1, '63.

Benjamin W., (2d)'s ch. 1, Frederic M., b, Feb. 20, 1839; r. Rock., officer in 5th N. Y. Cavalry. 2, Adjt. Charles F., b. Jan. 26, '42; r. Rock., officer in 4th Me., &c. 3, Helen L., b. ab. '44, mar. Capt. Wm. Wright; r. Rock.

Sylvester H.'s ch. Frederic, b. ab. 1857.

SAYWARD, Richard, c with his wife from Gloucester, Mass., after the peace of 1783; r. & d. S. Th. Their ch. 1, George, m. Lydia Snow, Nov. 23, 1802. r. S. Th., at Wessaweskeag. 2, John, went to sea, & d. in the W. I. 3, Lydia, b. ab. 1774; m. Moses Kelloch; r. S. Th. 4, Sarah, m. Rev. Isaac Hall of St. G.; rem. Knox. 5, Richard, m. Eliza Bradford, p. Sept. 9, '08; rem. Union. 6, Capt. William, m. Elizabeth Robinson, Dec. 24, '12; r. Th., now deceased. 7, Joseph, m. Martha Wheeler of St. G., p. Dec. 3, '13; rem. Burnham. 8, Capt. James, m. Lucy Wheeler of St. G., p. July 4, '18; was lost at sea, May '30. 9, Susanna, m. James Littlehale, p. Aug. 22, '07; r. & d. U. 10, Judith, m. Abiel Gay of U., Jan. 15, '16; r. Waldo.

Of George's ch. 1, Joseph, (2d), m. & r. Thorndike. 2, Almira W., m. Charles Glover; r. Rock.

William's ch. 1, Capt. William T., b. ab. 1813; m. Priscilla H. Lindsey, p. Sept. 13, '34; r. Rock., an active business man, dep. sheriff under Burgess and Cunningham, was among the first to visit California, 2 years; ret. '55, & settled, since, there or in Oregon. 2, James Wheaton, m. Mary E. Butler, Feb. 14, '41; r. Rock., a joiner, rem. & r. San Francisco, California.

Of Capt. James's ch. 1, Lucy A., m. Francis Harding of U., June 16, '50. 2, Wm. H., m. Mary A. P. Merriam, April 1, '55; r. S. Th.

Capt. William T.'s ch. 1, Ophelia P., b. Aug. 27, 1836, d. Aug. 1, '46. 2, Alfred R., b. Nov. '44, d. Jan. 27, '46.

Of Joseph, (2d)'s ch. 1, Albert T., b. in Th. ab. 1822; m. Elizabeth Burns; r. Rock., a saloon keeper.

SCANLIN, Bartholomew, b. in Sligo, Ireland, ab. 1834; m. Mary Armstrong; r. Th. Their ch. 1, Mary, b. ab. '49. 2, Martin, b. ab. '50. 3, Nancy, b. ab. '52.

SEARS, Capt. James, c. from Camden; m. Sophia Bernard; r. in what is now Rockland, & d. Jan. 19, 1810, lost at sea. Their ch. 1, Dr. John B , b. March 26, 1807; m. Priscilla Wotton of W., p. Feb. 22, '30; r. Rock., manufacturing Sears' Blood Root Pills, &c., doing an extensive business ab. '33, but rem. to Illinois and California.

Dr. John B.'s ch. 1, Mary Kimball, b. Nov. 30, 1830; m. Samuel M. Veazie; r. Rock. 2, Priscilla, b. March 26, '32; m. Charles A. Harrington; r. Rock. & d. Oct. 6, 1854. 3, John B., (2d), b. March 25, '34; 4, Richard W., b. Nov. 5, '36; probably rem. 5, James F., b. Jan. 30, '39, d. Dec. 20, '59, killed on the burning of the Commercial House. 6, Benjamin F. b. April 3, '42.

SEAVEY, Gideon, b. May, 1784; c. from Beverly or Rye, as a blacksmith; m. Mary Brown of Th., March 25, 1803, built a shop & house in W.; ret. Th.; r. Wadsworth house; built that now occupied by Mrs. Morton, & d. Nov. 3, '38. Their ch. 1, Eliza Ann, m. Martin Barnes, who is a clothing merchant in Boston. 2, William B., b. May, '08 or '6; lost at sea, Sept. '46. 3, Mary Jane, m. Ludolph George Fogg, p. July 9, '36; rem. & d. in Boston.

SEAVEY, William, b. ab. 1799; m. Sarah ——— ; r. Rock., a carpenter. Their ch. 1, William, (2d), b. Sept. 5, 1827; m. Amelia Tucker, p. May 25, '54; r. Rock. & d. Sept. 18, '58. 2, ? Josiah, b. ab. 1835; r. Rock., a carpenter. 3, Joel A., b. ab. '38; m. Barbara D. Sawyer, Feb. 23, '61; r. Rock., a steam-mill engineer. 4, Alora, b. ab. '40. 5, Lucy Ann, b. ab. '42. 6, James, b. ab. '46.

SELDEN, Edward C., came from Norridgewock; m. Caroline F. H. Dwight, Aug. 13, 1848; r. Th., a merchant, but rem. California. Their ch. 1, Edward D., b. Sept. 22, 1851.

SELLEA, Nathan, came from Saco to Th. in 1819; mar. Abigail Wormell; r. Th., a potter, but after 5 or 6 years, d. of consumption. Their ch. 1, Mary Ann, r. in Portland. 2, Lucy P., mar. Henry H. Watts; r. Th. 3, Abigail E., mar. 1st, Noah Miller, 2d, George G. Mitchell; r. Th.

SEWALL, George Washington, b. ab. 1832, in China, Me.; mar. there, Lucy E. ——— ; r. Rock., a lime burner. Their ch. 1, Alden H., b. ab. 1858. 2, George W., b. Aug. 19, '59, d. Sept. 19, '60. 3, Oren A., b. Oct., 1861, d. Jan. 24, '62.

SHADY, John, b. ab. 1810, in Ireland, as was Jane, his wife; r. Rock., a lime burner. Their ch. 1, Margaret, b. ab. 1841. 2, Mary, b. '43. 3, Joanna, b. '45. 4, Ann Jane, b. '49. 5, Patrick, b. '53. 6, Catharine, b. '55. 7, Michael, b. '57. 8, Elizabeth, b. '59.

SHALER, Capt. David, a native of Holland; m. Alice McKnights; r. Th., a master mariner.

SHAW, Capt. Zenas, b. ab. 1827; came from St. George; m. 1st, Nancy F. Elwell, Jan. 12, '49, 2d, Mrs. Lois Fletcher, May 2, '58; r. Rock. His ch. by 1st wife. 1, George F., b. ab. 1849. 2, Sarah C., b. ab. '50. 3, Joseph, b. ab. '52. 4, Edwin, b. ab. '54. By 2d wife.

5, Lois M., b. Feb. 21, & d. March 21, '59. 6, Charles, b. Sept. 14, '60, d. Jan. 17, '61.

SHAW, Moses, b. ab. 1824, in Holderness, N. H.; came to this place and mar. Abigail A. Heard, Nov. 15, '50; r. S. Th., a farmer, soldier of 28th Me., &c. Their ch. 1, Charles, b. ab. 1851. 2, Albert, b. '53. 3, James H., b. Nov. 30, '55, d. Feb. 22, '62. 4, Eugene, b. '57. 5, Laura, b. '59. 6, Moses, b. March 2, '63, d. March 20, '64.

SHAW, Albert J., came from Albion; r. Rock., a merchant.

SHAW, Seth P., b. ab. 1829; m. Sarah B. Fales, Nov. 4, '51; r. S. Th., a painter. Their ch. 1, Ella R., b. ab. 1853. 2, Alice W., b. ab '56. 3, Allan K., b. ab. '58. Of this name there were also here John and Jane Shaw, of whose ch. 1, William J., b. Sept. 25, 1829, d. Aug., '32. 2, Ann, b. March, 1830, d. Aug., '31.

SHEA, Thomas, b. ab. 1822, in Ireland; m. Mary ——; r. Rock. Their ch. William F., b. ab. 1860.

SHIELDS, Charles, b. ab. 1808, in Ireland, as was Ann, his wife; r Rock., a lime burner. Their ch. 1, William J., b. June 1, 1840; r. Rock., an ostler. 2, Mary A., b. Dec. 31, '42. 3, Emma J. 4, Eliza F. 5, Charles A., b. ab. '48. 6, John H., b. ab. '50.

SHELDON, Abiel, b. ab. 1808; m. Mary ——; r. Rock., a fisherman, &c. Their ch. 1, William H., b. 1829; m. Susan M. Alley, p. June 1, '52; r. Rock., a mariner. 2, Rachel, b. 1831; m. James W. Walsh; r. Rock. 3, Lydia K., b. ab. 1833, died Sept., 1850. 4, Josiah H., b. '35, a mariner. 5, Moses, b. ab. '37; r. S. Th., a fisherman. 6, Vinson R., b. ab. '39, a mariner.

William H.'s ch. 1, Lucy E., b. ab. 1854. 2, Mary F., b. '56. 3, Mercy J., b. '58. 4, Susan, b. '60.

SHEPHERD, William W., b. ab. 1821, in Jefferson; m. Flora E. Hall, Feb., 1850; r. Rock., a carpenter, &c. Their ch. 1, Albert J., b. ab. 1852. 2, Ida E., b. ab. '54.

SHEPHERD, Elbridge G., b. ab. 1810; m. Harriet S. Ulmer, Sept. 15, 1831; r. Rock., and d. Sept. 2, '53. Their ch. 1, Susan C., b. Feb. 11, '33, d. May 7, '56.

SHERER, Reuben, b. July 9, 1783; came from Enfield, Mass., and early settled on the farm where he ever after resided; m Sabra Barrows, Jan. 14, 1808; r. Rock., a farmer, and d. Jan. 27, '63; having been for many years one of the largest tax payers in the city. Their ch. 1, Otis R., b. July 19, 1808; m. Elvira Tolman, p. July 24, '37; r. Rock., a farmer, lime manufacturer, &c. 2, Ann F., b. Oct. 4, '10; m. Isaac Ames; r. Rock., and d. April 15, '62. 3, Sabra, b. May 26, '13; m. John Brown; r. Rock., & d. June, '52. 4, Reuben, (2d), b. Nov. 20, '16; mar. Orinda F. Daggett, Nov. 15, '43; r. Rock., a farmer, lime manufacturer, &c. 5, Bradish D., b. Oct. 24, '19; mar. Susan T. Keen, p. Oct. 21, '44; r. Rock., a farmer, &c. 6, Charles, b. Feb. 20, '23; m. Adelia H. Robbins, Oct. 1, '46; r. Rock., a farmer, &c. 7, John M., b. Sept. 3, '25; m. Mary Lucas of U., Dec. 22, '50; r. Rock., a farmer. 8, Louisa R., b. May 8, '28; m. Josiah Tolman; r. Rock.

Otis R.'s ch. 1, Sylvania, b. April 8, 1838; m. Warren Crockett; r. Rock. 2, Josiah T., b. Oct. 23, '39; r. Rock., entered the navy. 3, Margaret A., b. July 18, '41; m. Wilson Boggs; r. Rock. 4, Mary S., b. Sept. 10, '43, d. Feb. 18, '44. 5, Mary, b. ab. '46. 6, Elvira,

b. ab. '49. 7, Orrin T., b. ab. '53. 8, Imogene, b. May 25, and died July 23, '55.

Bradish D.'s ch. 1, Charles M., b. ab. 1846. 2, Sabra A., b. ab. '48. 3, Harriet A., b. ab. '50. 4, Alden N., b. Nov. 8, '55, d. Jan. 23, '61.

Charles's ch. 1, Oliver R., b. Jan., 1853, d. April 8, '54. 2, Alvin N., b. Feb. 8, & d. Oct. 24, '55. 3, Corinda, b. ab. '57. 4, Eleanor, b. ab. '59.

John M.'s ch. 1, Frederic A., b. ab. 1852. 2, Willard L., b. ab. '54. 3, Edgar A., b. '59.

SHERMAN, Nathan, b. ab. 1765; c. from Marshfield, Mass., mar. Bethia Thomas of Marshfield, settled about 1787, at the head of the Bay, now in S. Th., and d. May 21, 1851. His wife d. in Mass., Oct. 19, 1826, a. 61. Their ch. 1, Nathan, (2d), b. ab. 1785, m. Hannah B. Cobb of Cam.; r. Rock., having had the misfortune to lose his sight. 2, Abigail, b. ab. 1788, mar. Jeremiah Sleeper; r. Rock. 3, Bethia, b. ab. 1790, d. a. 16. 4, Sophia, m. Capt. Ephraim Lovett; r. St. G., and Hope, now deceased. 5, Deborah, d. at the age of 12 yrs. 6, Charles, m. Susan Cooper, Aug. 11, 1816; r. and d. Hope. 7, Abijah, b. ab. 1799, m. 1st, Hannah Wilson of St. G., pub. Feb. 10, 1819, 2d, Mrs. Palmer of Cam.; r. S. Th., a farmer, rem. Washington, Me. 8, Asa, mar. Olive Pottle of Linc, pub. Nov. 16, 1827. 9, Nancy, b. ab. 1807, m. J. Sumner Wentworth; r. S. Th. 10, Thomas, m. 1st, Margaret Henderson of St. G., 2d, Phebe Holbrook, p. Nov. 26, 1840; r. in Ohio.

Nathan, (2d)'s ch. 1, Ardra C., m. Isaiah Neal; r. Searsmont. 2, Mary Cordelia, b. Feb. 3, 1818, m. ——— Rankin; r. Rock. 3, Abigail M., b. Dec. 18, '22, m. Jonathan Thompson, April 2, '48; r. Belmont or vicinity. 4, Caroline A., b. Nov. 27, '24, m. Capt. Edwin Lovett of N. York, Sept. 12, '44. 5, Lucy C., b. ab. '26, m. John W. Norwood, June 16, '47; r. Rock., and has one dau., Mesella, born in 1849. 6, Frank, rem. and m. in the West. 7, Elizabeth, mar. 1st, Almond Judkins, Aug. 25, '51, and 2d, in Cal. 8, William.

Of Charles's ch. 1, Capt. Alfred, c. from Hope, mar. Prudence C. Everett; r. S. Th., and d. at his father's in Hope, June 20, 1858. 2, Cyrus, b. ab. '24, m. 1st, Harriet B. Lewis of S. Th., p. Nov. 6, '53, 2d, Emily A. Perkins, Nov. 11, '62; r. Rock., a carpenter.

Abijah's ch. 1, Mary W., b. Oct. 14, 1819, m. Shepard Gray; r. S. Th. 2, Eliza B., b. Jan. 20, '21, m. George S. Gray; r. S Th., & d. Dec. 30, '46. 3, Justus E., b Oct. 1, '28, m Rebecca Keen, June 23, '50; r. Rock., a painter, &c. 4, Capt. Alden T., b. Feb. 24, '31, m. Bethia B. Glover, Oct. 17, '43; r. Rock., a master mariner.

Thomas's ch. by 2d wife. Jane H., b. Jan. 17, 1842.

Cpat. Alfred's ch. 1, Ida I., b. ab. 1846. 2, Edward E., b. ab. '48. 3, Mary H., b. ab. '50. 4, Alfred, b. ab. '55.

Cyrus's ch. By 1st wife. 1, Henrietta, b. ab. 1854. 2, Sarah E., b. ab. 1856. 3, Hattie A., b. May, '58, d. June 11, '61. The mother d. Feb. 27, '62, a. 35.

Justus E.'s ch. 1, Euretta E., b. ab. 1852. 2, Minnie, b. ab. '59.

Capt. Alden T.'s ch. 1, George A., b. ab. 1845. 2, Sophia L., b. Feb. 1847, d. March 19, '49. 3, Ellen F., b. '48, d. Oct. 9, '61. 4, Myra W., b. ab. '53. 5, Emma E., b. ab. '55.

SHERMAN, Alpheus, b. ab. 1823, came from Washington, Me., in 1837, mar. Mary C., Whitcomb of Yarmouth, Aug. 31, '51; r. Th., a shipbuilder. Their ch. 1, Franklin P., b. ab. '52. 2, Angeletta, b. ab. '54. 3, William S., b. ab. '57. 4, Emma, b. ab. '59.

SHERWELL, Samuel P., m. 1st, Julia A. Sweetland, 2d, Huldah H. Tabor, Sept. 30, 1832; r. S. Th., but probably rem.

SHIBLES, John, son of John and Elizabeth (Killpatrick) Shibles, was b. at Pemaquid in 1732, c. to Th. with his mother in 1736; m. Mary Carney & d. Feb. 7, '77, a. 45. Their ch. 1, Thomas, b. April 15, 1766; m. Sally (Holbrook) Coffin, Aug. 20, 1800; r. & d. Th. 2, Robert, b. Dec. 29, '68; m. Betsey McLellan, p. June 17, '90; r. Th. & d. June 21, 1837. 3, John, (3d), b. April 3, 1770; m. Nancy Porterfield, p. July 25, '92; rem. & d. in the west. 4, James, b. May 22, '73; m. Betsey Rawley, May 16, 1800; rem. & d. U., June 17, 1843. 5, David, b. Feb. 4, '76; m. Katy Buckland of Cam., p. Oct. 6, '96; r. Searsmont. The mother m. 2d, John Dilloway; r. Th. & d. Aug. 1799.

Thomas's ch. 1, Ezekiel, b. Sept. 5, & d. Sept. 11, 1801. 2, Priscilla, b. Dec. 31, 1802. 3, Naaman H., b. Jan. 6, 1805, in Camden, whither the family removed.

Robert's ch. 1, Mary, b. Oct. 2, 1790; m. Capt. Haunce R. Hyler, May 15, 1818; r. Th. 2, Capt. Simon M., b. Feb. 13, 1792; m. Sally Achorn, p. May 15, 1819; r. Th., a master mariner, farmer, &c. 3, John, b. Dec. 30, '93; drowned in George's river, April 20, 1813. 4, Harriet M., b. Jan. 19, '96; m. 1st, Capt. James Burnham, 2d, Capt. Charles Walker; r. Th. 5, Charlotte, b. Feb. 28, '98; r. Th. 6, Eliza M., b. April 24, 1800; m. Edward Kaler, Dec. 28, '23; r. Wal. 7, Maria Matilda, b. Aug. 22, 1802; m. Capt. Oliver Robinson; r. Th. 8 & 9, twins, b. April 18, '05, George Webster, m. Jane Paine, 2d, Rebecca (Palmer) Mayberry, June 29, '44; r. Th., a rigger, inventor of improvement in reefing and furling topsails; Robert Killpatrick, m. Abigail Butler, '32; drowned at sea, Feb. 26, '51. 10, Jane P. A. C., b. May 13, '07; m. Capt. Edward Kelleran; r. C. 11, Arthur J. C., b. Oct. 3, 1811, d. Dec. 4, 1828.

Capt. Simon M.'s ch. 1, John, (4th), b. Nov. 23, 1821; m. Martha J. Rose, Nov. 25, '49; r. Th., a farmer. 2, Eliza A., b. Nov. 8, '23; m. Isaac Mathews; r. Th. 3, Simon, b. Sept. 27, '26; m. Elizabeth Peabody, Oct. 15, '51; r. Th., a carpenter. 4, Arthur Joseph, b. May 13, '29; r. Th., a carpenter. 5, Warren J., b. Feb. 5, d. July 27, '32. 6, Hanse H., b. Aug. 18, '33; m. Helen J. Young of C., June 8, '54; r. Th., a carpenter. 7, Mary A., b. June 21, '36; m. Sylvester Hahn of Wal., Oct. 31, 1855.

George Webster's ch. 1, Lucina Paine, (adopted,) b. April 4, 1829; m. 1st, Capt. David Brown, 2d, Horace Muzzey of Searsmont, Feb. 11, '63; r. Th., and d. Sept. 18, '64. 2, H. Hyler, b. Jan. 12, '31; r. Th. 3, George Webster, (2d), b. Jan. 26, '32, d. Aug. 15, '53. 4, Matilda, b. Aug. 20, '33; m. Oakes A. Dodge; r. Mass. 5, Elizabeth, b. April 10, '35; m. Leander Woodcock; r. Th. 6, Jane, b. Jan. 24, '37; m. Matthew Webb; r. Th. By 2d wife. 7, Eldora, b. ab. '45. 8, Julietta, b. ab. '47. 9, Richard Irving, b. ab. '50. 10, Geo. W., (3d), b. ab. '52.

R. Killpatrick's ch. 1, Sarah A., b. Aug. 31, 1833. 2, Warren J., b. Dec. 29, '34, mar. Ann Hyler of C., Oct. 31, '55; r. Th., a blacksmith. 3, Helen H., b. April 12, '37, d. Aug. 30, '40. 4, Robert K., (2d), b. June 16, '38; r. Th., a blacksmith. 5, Edward E., b. May 12, '40, d. March 29, '41. 6, Edward E., (2d), b. Feb. 7, '42. 7, Helen, b. '48, d. Dec. 13, '61. 8, Charles Henry, b. ab. '49.

John's ch. 1, Daniel R., b. ab. 1853. 2, Olive R., b. ab. '55. 3, William, b. ab. '57.

Simon's ch. 1, Virginia, b. ab. 1852. 2, Mary E., b. ab. '54. 3, Peter P., b. ab. '59.

Haunce H.'s ch. Frederic W., b. ab. 1855.

SHIBLES, John, of a different, or distant branch of the same family, b. ab. 1821, mar. Angeline ——; r. Rock., a lime burner. Their ch. 1, Jane, b. ab. 1846. 2, Moses W., b. ab. '48. 3, Ann P. b. ab. '50. 4, James, b. ab. '53. 5, Peter, b. ab. '57.

SHUMAN; of this Wal. family of German descent, 1, Zenas G., b. Aug. 15, 1815; r. Rock., with Julia, his wife, and d. Feb. 10, '64. 2, Simon, b. ab. 1816, m. Sophronia ——; r. Th. 3, Nelson, b. ab. '26, m. Mary A. Levansaler, July 31, '52; r. Rock., a joiner. Of this name, also, James M. Shuman; r. S. Th., and entered the army.

Zenas G.'s ch. 1, Frank, b. ab. 1845. 2, Mary J., b. ab. '47. 3, Flora, b. ab '53. 4, George, b. ab. '57. 5, Zenas, b. ab. '60.

Simon's ch. 1, George, b. ab. 1838, mar. Julia ——; r. Th. 2, Clara, b. ab. '47. 3, John.

Nelson's ch. Newell A. b. ab. 1853.

SIDELINGER, Elijah, b. ab. 1816, probably in Wal., and of German descent, m. Mary ——; r. Rock., a lime burner. Their ch. 1, Abby N., b. ab. 1841. 2, Alvina, b. ab. '45. 3, Jane, b. ab. '48. 4, Amasa, b. ab. '50. 5, Ethal, b. ab. '55. 6, Remely.

SIMMONS, Henry B., b. ab. 1808, in Waldoboro', m. Sarah Ludwig; r. Th., a blacksmith. Their ch. 1, Boyd, b. ab. '46. 2, George, b. ab. '48. Of the same family, or name, John A. Simmons, b. ab. '11, in Waldoboro', m. Jane Ann Bennett; r. Rock., a joiner, &c. John A.'s ch. 1, Charles T., b. ab. '37. 2, Gilman T., b. ab. '43; r. Rock. entered the navy. 3, Ada A., b. July 13, '47. 4, George, b. April '51, d. July 31, '54. Of this name, also, Cyrus R. Simmons, b. in Hope, '18, m. Elizabeth Chapman of Appleton; r. Rock., a joiner. Cyrus R.'s ch. 1, Francena, b. ab. 1846. 2, Adriana, b. ab. '48. 3, Elden, b. ab. '54. Also, Gershom Simmons, b. ab. '19, in Mass., m. Lydia ——; r. Th., a cooper. Gershom's ch. 1, Julia F., b. ab. '48. 2, Abbie P., b. ab. '50. 3, Mary E., b. ab. '52. 4, Hattie B., b. ab. '55. 5, Edward H., b. ab. '58.

SIMMONS, Luther, b. ab. 27, in Union, m. Mary J. Andrews of W., June 18, '54; r. Th., a ship carpenter and builder. Their ch. 1, Effie J., b. 1860. Of this Union family, also, Moses L. Simmons, b. ab. 1825, in U., m. 1st, Caroline Keen, 2d, Mrs. Olive D., widow of Algernon Simmons, Nov. 19, '56; r. Rock., a teamster. His ch. by 1st wife. 1, Marietta, b. ab. 1853. By 2d wife, 2, Algenora, b. Aug. 12, '58, d. July 7, '61. Of this name, also, James B. Simmons, b. ab. 1828; mar. Nancy Bisbee of W., p. Sept. 29, '53; r. Rock., a lime burner, soldier in 28th Me., &c. James B.'s ch. 1, Elvona, b. Aug., 1854, d. June 25, '56. 2, Clara Ella, b. ab. '57. Of the same name, John D. Simmons, b. ab. 1834; mar. Achsah S. Hosmer; r. Rock., a mason. John D.'s ch. 1, Ralph K., b. July 17, 1855, died Sept. 26, '61. 2, Lizzie, b. ab. '57. There was also, Isaac Simmons, b. ab. 1820; m. Catharine S. Butler; r. Rock., a lime burner, lately rem. with his family to California. Isaac's ch. 1, Wilbert, b. ab. 1839, a mariner. 2, Margaret N., b. Jan., 1842, d. Oct. 11, '53. 3, Hanson B., b. ab. '44; soldier of 4th Me. Reg. 4, ——, b. 1846; drowned, July 29, '54. 5, Charles E. 6, Cassie U. 7, Frank W.

SIMONTON; of this family there came hither from Falmouth or Portland two brothers; 1, John, m. Rachel McLellan; r. & d. S. Th. 2, James, m. in Falmouth, Susan Gross; settled and d. in Camden. There also came later, their sister, Elizabeth, b. Jan. 13, 1772; mar. Capt. John Gregory; r. Cam., and d. Nov. 4, 1857, leaving 8 ch., 50 grand ch., 71 great grand ch., and 4 gr. gr. grand ch. And their brother, Abraham, b. April 18, 1778; m. 1st, Lucy Haskell, Sept. 1, 1803, 2d, Mrs. Lucy Tyler; r. Rock., and d. Oct. 25, '51.

John's ch. 1, Mary, b. June 13, 1774; m. William Howe Wiggin, 2d, Capt. J. B. Rider; r. Th. & Rock. & d. March 1, 1863. 2, Capt. George, b. 1779; r. Th., unm., & d. March 5, 1831. 3, Capt. Patrick, m. & r. in Virginia or North Carolina. 4, Hannah, b. 1785; m. John Spofford; r. Rock. 5, Elizabeth, b. 1787; mar. Charles Coburn, 2d, Patrick Woodcock; r. Th., and d. March 10, 1853. 6, Rachel, mar. George Lindsey; r. and d. Rock. 7, Capt. John, (2d), mar. Patience Otis; r. Th., & d. in Boston or New York of small-pox in 1830. 8, Rebecca, m. Crowell Jones; r. Rock.

James's ch. 1, William, Esq., m. Elizabeth (Roberts) Leland; r. & d. Cam. 2, Margaret, m. 1st, Mr. Fiske; rem. Ohio, but ret., and m. 2d, Daniel Howard of St. G. 3, James, (2d), m. Mrs. Morse; r. & d. Cam. 4, Susan, mar. Josiah Hemenway. 5, Abraham, born in Cam.; m. Sarah Townsend; r. & d. Cam. 6, Joanna, m. Dea. William Brown; r. Cam. 7, John, m. Elizabeth Richards; r. & d. Cam. 8, Sarah, m. Daniel Ames; r. Cam. 9, Dr. Putnam, mar. Elizabeth Eaton; r. and prac. med. in Searsport. 10, Charlotte, mar. William Burkett; r. East Boston.

Abraham's ch. 1, Jane, b. Dec. 3, 1803; m. Capt. Isaac Bullock. 2, Capt. Francis H., b. Oct. 26, '05; m. Melissa Bullock of Northport, p. July 10, '31; r. Rock., a master mariner. 3, Anne, b. Jan. 14, '07; m. James Jones, jr.; r. Rock. 4, Hannah, b. Oct. 14, '08; m. Capt. George W Duncan; r. Rock., & d. Dec. 12, '61. 5, Mary, b. Oct. 2, '11; m. Jonathan Post; r. Rock. 6, Maria, b. June 11, '14. 7, Capt. Abraham, (2d), b. April 17, '16; mar. Rebecca H. Crouch, Dec. 27, '44; r. Rock., & d. at New London, Sept. 30, '54. 8, Lucy, b. June 12, '18; m. Samuel Partridge, 2d, Elijah M. Averill; and d. Nov. 25, '53. 9, Capt. Freeman H., b. March 17, '21; m. Sarah E. Rich, Sept. 19, '43; r. Rock., & d. July 8, '59, very suddenly. 10, Margaret, b. Jan. 24, '24; mar. Capt. Daniel E. Post; r. Rock. 11, Isaac B., b. March 5, '28, d. Jan. 29, '52. By 2d wife. 12, James G., b. ab. 1836; m. Lenora J. Hall, July 18, '55; r. Rock., wagoner in 28th Me., &c.

Capt. John, (2d)'s ch. George, (2d), d. at sea, July, 1847. The mother m. 2d, Viram B. Robbins; r. S. Th. & d. Nov. 22, '64.

William, Esq.'s ch. 1, Eliza Ann, m. Robert White of Belfast. 2, Sarah G., m. Capt. James W. Clark; r. & d. Cam. 3, Margaret J., m. Capt. James W. Clark; r Cam. 4, William P., mar. Harriet A. Sawtelle; r. Cam. 5, Thaddeus R., Esq., mar. Josephine Hall of Brunswick; r. Cam., attorney at law, collector of customs, &c. 6, Lavinia G., m. Andrew E. Clark; r. Cam. 7, Theodore E., b. Aug. 24, 1833; mar. Ellen S. Wadlin of Belfast, July 27, '57; r. Rock., a dry goods merchant. 8, Frederic J., b. July 24, '36; mar. Flora J., dau. of S. G. Adams of Cam., Nov. 24, '63; r. Rock., a merchant. 9, Harriet A., r. Cam.

Capt. Francis H.'s ch. 1, Capt. Judson, b. May 2, 1832; m. Lura E. Marston, Jan. 24, '55; r. Rock. 2, Melissa, b. Nov. 27, '33; m. Capt. Ephraim E. Post; r. Rock. 3, Francis W., b. Nov. 4, '35, d.

May 30, '48. 4, Lucy E., b. Feb. 5, '38 ; r. Rock. 5, Loraim, b. July 3, '39 ; r. Rock. 6, Abraham K., b Feb. 7, '43 ; r. Rock., entered the navy. 7, Samuel, b. ab. '48. 8, Robert, b. ab. '50. The mother d. Aug. 5, 1858, aged 50.

Capt. Abraham, (2d)'s ch. 1, William A., b. ab. 1847. 2, Cora E., b. ab. '52.

Capt. Freeman H.'s ch. 1, Lugilla F., b. March, 1847, d. Dec. 15, '49. 2, James F., b. May, '49, d. Dec. 15, '51. 3, Eugene, b. May, '53, d. Oct. 3, '54. The mother d. Sept. 15, '58.

SINGER, Faithful, (whose father came from North of Ireland, but went back, and never returned), was b. at Edgecomb, m. Mary Fullerton; r. Edgecomb, and d. in W. Indies in 1810. His mother m. 2d, ——— Williams, and left ch. in Edgecomb. His widow m. 2d. —— Hawthorn, and d. in Th.

Faithful's ch. 1, Jane, b. ab. 1794, m William Butler; r. Rock. 2 and 3, twins, b. Jan. 8, 1797, Hon. William, mar. Mary Bridges, p. Aug. 22, 1818 ; r. Th., where he has long been a master mariner, merchant, and business man, president of Georges Ins. Co., was Councillor 1841, Pres. Elector in 1856, &c. ; John, d. at Mobile, July 17, 1826. 4, Susan, b. ab. 1799, d. at Th., April 12, 1830. 5, Dea. Alexander, b. July 13, 1801, m. 1st, Hannah Comery, who, with her infant, d. Sept. 14, 1829, a. 30, 2d, Martha Ann Metcalf, July 5, '30 ; r. Th., rem. W. 6, Eliza, b. ab. 1805, m. Capt. Thomas Colley, (2d) ; r. Th.

Hon. William's ch. 1, Mary J., b. Nov. 16, 1819, m. Capt. James Henderson, Oct. 7, '41, d. March 25, '50. 2, Capt. William J., born March 9, '22, m. Isabella Fuller, Sept. '47, 2d, Jane G. Fuller, March '62 ; r. Th., master mariner, &c. 3, Samuel S., born Sept. 3, '25, d. Aug. 7, 1851. 4, Sarah C., b. Aug. 28, '31, d. April 7, '58. 5, Edward R., b. Dec. 2, '33, m. Helen M. Carr, Feb. 28, '57 ; r. N. Y., a ship chandler, ret. Th., a jeweler, &c. 6, Henrietta, b. Nov. 4, '37, d. Dec. 23, '52

Dea. Alexander's ch. by 1st wife. 1, Eliza Colley, b. 1827, died Sept. 22, '31. 2, Susan? b. 1829, d. young. By 2d wife. 3, Susan Ann, b. July 11, '31, m. William Comery, of W., r. Thomaston. 4, Sarah E., b. April 23, '35, m. Robert Creamer, (2d), of Wal., Sept. 31, '62. 5, Alexander, (2d), b. Feb. 1, '37 ; r. Washington, D. C., a sutler, &c. 6, Mary Eliza, b. June 30, '43. 7, William Frederic, b. Dec. 6, '44.

Capt. William J.'s ch. 1, Ida E., b. ab. 1847. 2, Thomas Sprague, b. ab. 1850.

SINGHI, Francis A. D., b. in Lucca, Italy, ab. 1804 ; c. here and mar. Susan Ulmer, Feb. 10, '33 ; r. Rock., a barber, musician, &c. Their ch. 1, Lieut. John F., b. Nov. 10, '33, m. Francis A. Blackington, Feb. 13, '56 ; r. Rock., a leader of brigade band in U. S. Army, &c. 2, Ferdinand G., b. Jan. 4, '35, mar. Lizzie Swan, Nov. 29, '57 ; r. Rock., a barber, &c. 3, Wellington G., b. Aug. 4, '37. 4, Angelo B., b. Oct. 11, and d. Nov. 23, '38. 5, Angelo L., b. Oct. 31, '39, d. July 28, '40. 6, Vittrice H., b. Oct. 8, '41. 7, Lucinda C., b. Oct. 13, '45, d. Dec. 10, '48. 8, Martin U., b. May 4, '47 ; entered the navy and was stated to have perished in the *Congress*, March 8, '62. 9, Florence E., b. ab. '50. 10, George B. B., b. and d. 1856.

Ferdinand G.'s ch. 1, Lizzie E., b. ab. 1858. 2, Francis A. D., (2d), b. ab. '59.

SLATER, Capt. William, b. ab. 1818, in Washington, Me., mar. Eliza A. Robinson; r. Th, a master mariner. Their ch. William T., b. ab. 1852.

SLEEPER, Benjamin, m. Hannah Hasey; was a shoemaker, came from N. H. to New Meadows, and d. there, being one, or a descendant of one of three brothers, who c. from England, one of whom settled in Massachusetts, and another in Pennsylvania. Benjamin's ch. 1, Nathaniel, b. 1762; c. here with his widowed mother and brothers about 1788; m. 1st, Nancy Thomas, Nov. 28, 1796, 2d, Jane Post; r. S. Th., at Ash Pt., d Oct. 24, 1825. 2, William, went to sea young, and not heard from. 3, Benjamin, (2d), m. 1st, Sally Rendall, April 10, 1800, 2d, Pamelia C. Greeley, Oct. 13, '31; r. and d. S. Th., Owl's Head. 4, Jeremiah, b. ab. 1781, m. Abigail Sherman, March 18, '04; r. Rock. 5, John, d. young. 6, Jesse, b. 1787, mar. 1st, Rebecca Bridges, p. Dec. 18, 1808, 2d, Mrs. Mary S. Haskell, Nov, 1852; r. S. Th., a caulker, &c.

Nathaniel's ch. by 1st wife. 1, Abigail, b. Nov. 19, 1797, m. Jonas Emery, and d. July 25, 1819. 2, William, b. May 11, '99, m. Isabella Kelloch, Feb. 20, 1820, and d. Oct. 9, '22. 3, Nancy, b. Nov. 2, '01, m. George Emery, Esq.; r. S. Th., and d. May, 1825. 4, Capt. Nathaniel, (2d), b. Sept. 15, '03, m. Sarah A. Cooper, Nov. 1, '27; r. S. Th., and d. April 11, '30, lost at sea. 5, Stephen P., b. Oct. 15, '05, d. of dysentery, Oct. 25, '25. 6, Charles, b. May 11, '07, d. April 11, '30, of consumption, as have most of the family. 7, Hannah, b. March 27, '10, m. Daniel C. Haskell; r. and d. Rock 8, Capt. Samuel B., b. Feb. 14, '12, m. Lucy Ann Pilsbury, Nov. 26, '35; r. Rock, and d. April 1, '51. 9, Henrietta Maria, b. Aug. 28, '14. 10, Benjamin, (2d), b. May 18, '16; r. and d S. Th. By 2d wife 11, Elvira T., b April 18, '19; d. in Th., Dec. 22, '55. 12, Mary Jane, b. Dec. 22, '20, m. Capt. Irel Cutler; r. Th., and d. Aug. 17, '61. 13, Abigail E., b. Aug. 29, or 31, '22 14, a dau., b. March, and d. Oct. 17, '25, of dysentery.

Benjamin, (2d)'s ch. by 1st wife. 1 and 2, twins, b. Sept. 21, 1800; Hannah, m. 1st, James Rendell, 2d, Jacob Clifford of Prospect, July 12, '31; Jenny, m. and r. Prospect. 3, Sally, b. Aug. 2, '02, m. Samuel Nichols, jr., of Prospect, Dec. 1, '25. By 2d wife. 4, Benjamin F, b. April 11, '33, m. Adelia Grimes, Oct. 18, '52; r. Mass. 5, Melissa Maria, b. June 20, '35; m. & r. Cal. 6, Marinda N., b. Sept. 20, '37, m. Capt. David B. Clifford of Prospect, Dec. 4, '52, sailed from Bath with her husband, and was never heard from. 7, Burnam C, b. Aug. 6, '39; r. Owl's Head, S. Th., a farmer, soldier of 4th Me., &c. 8, Caroline Ellen, b. Feb 3, '40; r. S. Th.? 9, Helen A., b. ab. '45; r. S. Th.

Jeremiah's ch. 1, Capt. John, b. June 18, 1805, m. Mercy Beverage of Vinalhaven, Aug. 3, '31; r. and d. Rock. 2, Sophia, b. Aug. 2, '07, m. Capt. Daniel Emery; r. S. Th. 3, Capt. Jeremiah, (2d), b. Sept. 2, '09, m. Mary Ann Amsbury, p. Jan. 9, '37; r. S. Th., Owl's Head. 4, Capt. Nathan, b. Dec. 7, '12, m. Rebecca Gray, p. Oct. 16, '38; r. Rock. 5, Capt. Oliver, b. Dec. 18, '14, m. Catharine Hanson, May 28, '48; r. Rock. 6, Capt. Alfred, b. Jan. 9, '17, m. Lydia J. Pendleton; r. Rock. 7, Joseph, b Feb. 3, and d. June, 1818. 8, Lavinia, b. Sept. 22, '22, m. William K. Sherman of Cam., May 30, '41; r. Cam., and Linc. 9, Bethiah, b. Oct 18, '25, d. Oct. 13, '26. 10, Capt. William, b. Aug. 14, '27, mar. Rebecca F. Cobb of W.; r. Rock., all master mariners. 11, Marietta, b. June 12, '33; r. Rock.

Jesse's ch. 1, Mary Ann, m. George D. Hall; r. S. Th. 2, Harriet, b. ab. 1810; m. Rev. Amariah Kalloch; r. Rock., & d. July 14, 1843. 3, Capt. Elias P., b. ab. 1815; mar. 1st, Helen M. Thorndike, 1839; 2d, Emily Emery; 3d, Eliza A. Thorndike of Dixmont, p. Nov. 10, '51; r. S. Th. 4, Capt. Albert, m. Ruth P. Butler, Sept. 2, '42; r. S. Th., both master mariners. 5, Arethusa, b. ab. 1819; m. Hon. George Thorndike; r. Rock. 6, Jesse, (2d), b. ab. 1824; m. Susan E. Kelloch, Oct. 17, '52; r. S. Th., a caulker. 7, Sarah E., m. Oliver Sweetland; r. S. Th. 8, Hannah Jane, m. Samuel Dean; r. S. Th.

Capt. Nathaniel, (2d)'s ch. Capt. Samuel A. b. April 4, 1829; m. Aldana C. Havener, June 17, '51; r. Rock., a master mariner.

Capt. Samuel B.'s ch. Nancy, b. ab. 1845.

Capt. John's ch. 1, Capt. Henry J., b. June 27, 1832; m. Lucretia Waterman of North Haven, Jan. 10, '57; r. Rock., in naval service. 2, Adelaide, b. Nov. 18, '33; m. Albert G. Lovett; r. Rock.

Capt. Jeremiah, (2d)'s ch. 1, Eugene B., b. July 6, 1838, d. July 6, '43. 2, Otis H., b. May 3, '39; r. S. Th., a mariner. 3, Abby, b. Oct. 2, '41, d. Sept. 18, '42. 4, Jeremiah W., b. ab. '43.

Capt. Nathan's ch. 1, Irving R., b. Oct. 15, 1840; r. Rock., a mariner. 2, Aramantha, b. Sept., '43, d. Oct. 9, '46. 3, Rebecca E., b. ab. '47. 4, Ida J., b. ab. '49, d. April 18, '51. 5, Winfield S., b. ab. '54.

Capt. Oliver's ch. 1, James F. 2, William H.

Capt. Alfred's ch. Isabel A.

Capt. William's ch. George W.

Capt. Elias P.'s ch. 1, William E. By 2d wife. 2, Emily H., b. 1850, d. March 3, '53. By 3d wife. 3, George T. 4, Henrietta S.

Capt. Albert's ch. 1, Mary A. 2, Ella J. 3, Elida A. 4, Laura A.

Jesse, (2d)'s ch. 1, Willard F. 2, Kate M.

Samuel A.'s ch. Edith M., b. June, 1855, d. Dec. 7, '58.

Capt. Henry J.'s ch. Clarie Helen, b. July 23, d. Nov. 12, 1863.

Of this name, also, Nathaniel Sleeper, b. ab. 1790; probably of a different family; r. Rock. in 1860.

SMALL; the ancestor of this family m. Mary Lassell; r. Cape Elizabeth, and d. at sea. Their ch. 1, Dea. Benjamin, b. May, 1769, m. Mary Fling, p. Nov. 22, '93, c. here with his mother, brother and sister; r. S. Th., and d. March 21, 1821. 2, Jonathan, ret. to Cape Elizabeth, m. and had one dau., who m. Dea. Colby; r. and d. Richmond, Me. 3, Ruth, b. Nov. 24, 1767, m. Capt. Jonas Dean; r. S. Th., was one of the early converts of Rev. I. Case, and a devoted member of the Baptist ch. for more than 75 years, and d. at her son Samuel's, June 11, 1861, leaving 49 grand ch., and 46 gr. grand ch.

Dea. Benjamin's ch. 1, Capt. Jonathan, (2d), b. Aug. 17, 1791, mar. 1st, Rebecca Otis, 2d, Betsey (Wheeler) Small, April 7, '44, 3d, Thankful (Otis) Williams, p. July 20, '47; r. S. Th., a farmer, and d. May 30, '62. 2, Mary, b. 1801, d. Oct. 11, '19. 3, Benjamin, (2d), mar. Mary C. Otis, p. Feb. 3, '18; r. Belfast. 4, John, d. at sea. 5, Edward, m. Betsey Wheeler, p. Sept. 25, '22, d. abroad. 6, Hannah F., m. Oliver Wheeler; r. S. Th. 7, Rev. Ephraim H., m. Eliza B. Sayward, p. April 22, '34; r. Union, a Meth. minister. 8, Shepard R., b. ab. '13, m. 1st, Margaret Ames, pub. April 14, '37, 2d, Olive Ames, Nov. 1856; r. S. Th., a carpenter. The mother d. Jan. 11, '38, a. 65.

Capt. Jonathan, (2d)'s ch. By 1st wife. John W., born May 12, 1818, mar. Caroline O. Simonton, Oct. 31, '43; r. Th., a shipbuilder. The mother d. Oct. 1, '42, a. 47.

Edward's ch. 1, Mary S., b. March 21, 1824. 2, Emeline, b. Oct. 1, '25; m. Cyrus P. Johnson of Lowell, April 14, '50. 3, Capt. Edward, (2d), b. Nov. 27, '29; m. Sarah E. Small, Jan., '60; r. S. Th., a master mariner. 4, Elizabeth, b. July 12, '31.

Shepherd R.'s ch. 1, Gilbert, b. Oct. 24, 1838; rem. Cal. 2, Sarah E., b. Nov. 28, '39; m. Capt. Edward Small, r. S. Th.

John W.'s ch. 1, Francis, b. ab. 1846; r. Th. 2, Frederic, b. ab. '48. 3, Seth, b. March, & d. June 18, '50. 4, John Bradford, b. ab. '54. 4, Charles Emerson, b. ab. '57.

Capt. Edward, (2d)'s ch. Arthur A., b. Dec. 11, 1860, d. Jan. 28, 1861.

SMALL, Capt. Jackson, b. ab. 1835, in Deer Isle; m. Adaline M. Hall of St. G., June 17, '55; r. Rock., a master mariner. Their ch. Lilla, b. ab. 1859.

SMALLEY, Capt. William W., b. 1822, in St. Geo.; m. Mary N. Young; r. Th. & d. Oct. '59. Of this name, also, C. David Smalley, b. ab. '25, in Reading, Vt.; m. 1st, Mary E., Carpenter, 2d, Mary J. Dean; r. Rock., a tailor. His ch. by 1st wife. 1 & 2, twins, b. ab. '52, Willis and Frederic.

SMART, Henry A., b. ab. 1805; m. Eliza Thorndike; r. Rock., a joiner, &c. Their ch. 1, Eliza J., b. Feb. 18, 1832; m Capt. Nelson P. Spear; r. Rock. 2, Fannie, b. ab. 1846; r. Rock.

SMITH, Oliver, b. in Norton, Mass., served his time as blacksmith in Easton; c. here and had a shop near Mill River; m. Rhoda Fales, p. Sept. 19, 1778; r. and d. Thomaston. His younger brother, Abiathar, also c. to Th., mar. 1st, Hannah Coffee, and again in Fox Is., where he rem. after many years, and died at Isle Haut. Oliver's ch. 1, Betsey, died young. 2, Ebenezer, learned blacksmith's trade of J. Mero in W, d. unm. in Rock. or S. Th., Feb. 1, 1829. 3, Oliver, (2d), b. July 18, 1784; m. Catharine Stevens of Penobscot, p. March 18, '11; r. Belmont, Linc, Hope, and now Th. 4, Abigail, m. Isaac Dunton of Linc. 5, John, d. young. 6, Rufus, d. at N. O. 7, Betsey, m. Almond Bennett; r. Th., and d. May 6, 1852. 8, Joanna, mar. Marcus Bennett.

Abiathar's ch. by 1st wife. 1, Barbara, mar. John Horton of Camden, p. Nov. 15, 1798. 2, George, m. & r. Isle Haut. 3, Simeon, m. & r. Isle Haut. 4, Abiathar, (2d), m Nancy Thompson; r. Cam. 5, Hannah, m. Elisha Holbrook; r. & d. Islands. 6, James. 7, Charles. 8, Coffee. By 2d wife. 9, Susan. 10, Mary, and others rem.

Oliver, (2d)'s ch. 1, Harriet, m. Andrew Pottle; r. & d. Linc. 2, Rufus, m. & r. Alabama. 3, Joel B., m. Bethia Morton, p. June 3, 1847; r. F. 4, Moses, m. ——— Ross; was in the Naval service, Charlestown, Mass., before 1861. 5, Mercy I., mar. Daniel G. Andrews, July 27, '45; r. Rockport. 6, Almira, m. 1st, Joseph Lombard, May 26, '46, 2d, William Higgins, r. Richmond, d. Rockport. 7, Andrew, d. young.

SMITH, Jonathan, b. in Smithfield, R. I., Aug. 9, 1742, O. S., m. Elizabeth McDougle, March 28, 1776, by Rev. J. Urquhart; c. to r. in Th., April, 1778; and d. ab. 1814. Elizabeth, his wife, was born at St. George's Fort, now Th., June 22, 1743, and d. June 11, 1804. Their ch. 1, Leonard, b. March 29, 1780; m. 1st, Submit Fuller, of Attleboro', Aug. 1, 1802, 2d, Melinda Healey, May 28, 1805; r. Th. & d. Nov. 1, '64, a. 84. 2, Richard, b. July 20, '83; m. Betsey Butler, April 16, 1807; r. Rock., and d. June 23, 1827,

Leonard's ch. by 1st wife. 1, John, b. March 21, 1803; m. Mary Ott of Cam., Nov. 14, '25; r. W., & d. Dec. 26, '57. 2, Richard, (2d), b. Feb. 5, 1805; m. Jane L. Wilson, Oct. 19, '28; and d. Oct. 23, '33. By 2d wife. 3, Submit, b. July 12, '06; m. 1st, Jackson Turner, 2d, Capt. Samuel Getchell, Nov. 28, '51; r. Rock. and d. July 31, '59. 4, Melinda, b. Jan. 3, 1808, d. Aug. 12, '11. 5, Leonard, (2d), b. April 12, '13; m. Ann Y. McIntyre, Nov. 10, '50; r. C., and d. Oct. 6, '53. 6, Tileston H., b. Jan. 19, '15, m. 1st, Mary C. Starrett, July 8, '38, 2d, Emma D. Brown, July 31, '57; r. Th., lumber dealer, teacher, carpenter, &c. 6, Charles G., b. June 29, '18; m. Lavinia S. Fales, Dec. 3, '42; r. Th., a joiner, &c.; rem. California, and purchased a farm. 7, Albert M., b. Sept. 5, '21; m. Roxana B. Waugh, April 30, '46; d. in California, Oct. 24, 1852.

Richard's ch. 1, Elkanah S., born Jan. 2, 1810, mar. 1st, Susan J. Perry, Feb. 27, 1834, 2d, Melia R. (Butler) Fales, Sept. 21, 1837; r. Rock., has been postmaster, alderman, &c, rem. N. Billerica, Mass. 2, Betsey B., b. July 22, '13; m. ——— Watson from Boston. 3, Melinda H. b. Jan. 19, 1816, m. Gilman Woodward. 4, Capt. Richard M., b. Aug. 18, 1818; m. 1st, Lucy T. Butler, April 4, 1843, 2d, Fannie Sterling, Dec. 25, '51; r. Rockland.

Of John's ch. 1, Albert b. in W., r. Rock., a teacher of music and penmanship, and dealer in piano fortes, & other musical instruments.

Richard, (2d)'s ch. Charles R., b. July 21, 1830, lost at sea.

Leonard, (2d)'s ch. 1, Melinda H., b. June 12, and died Sept. 4, 1852. 2, Ann M., b. ab. 1853.

Tileston H.'s ch. by 1st wife. 1, Mary T., b. May 1, 1839, d. April 2, '57. 2, Lucy C., b. Jan. 30, '47, d. June 7, '54. 3, Francis T., b. Jan.. 21, '49. 4, Frederic R., b. Aug. 20, '51, d. Aug. 18, '59. By 2d wife. 5, Albert H., b. Jan. 19, 1859.

Charles G.'s ch. 1, Lucy Vose, b. Nov. 2, 1846; 2, Lavinia Gertrude, b. July 22, '55; 3, Charles G., (2d), b. Aug. 10, '57; all r. Cal.

Albert M.'s ch. 1, Emma. 2, Hannah R.

Elkanah S.'s ch. 1, Clinton P., b. Nov. 19, 1834; m. Helen Sterling, Sept. 19, '58; r. Rock., a mariner. By 2d wife. 2, William H., b. May 25, '39; r. Rock., a clerk. 3, Susan E., b. July 27, '41. 4, Coburn S., b. ab. '44. 5, Judson H., b. Feb., 1846, d. Feb. 20, '48. 6, Julia Ella, b. '48, d. Aug. 14, '54. 7, Larissa M. 8, Edgar E.

Capt. Richard M.'s ch. 1, Frederic M., b. ab. 1845. 2, Richard F., b. ab. '47. By 2d wife. 3, Elora, b. 1860.

Clinton P.'s ch. George E., b. ab. 1859.

SMITH, Charles, b. ab. 1810; came from Sandy River; mar. Jane H. Watson, p. Dec. 7, '33; r. Rock., a joiner. Their ch. 1, Cyrus S., b. Sept 19, 1835; r. Rock. 2, Charles A., b. April 5, '38, d. Nov. 16, '41. 3, George M., b. Jan. 20, '41; m. Miss Maxey; r. Rock., a farmer, soldier of 4th Me., &c. 4, Jerome W., b. ab. '43. 5, Charles L., b. ab. '52. 6, Mary C., b. ab. '54.

SMITH, Capt. Wooster, b. ab. 1806; came from Fox Islands; m. Mercy S. Thomas; r. S. Th., a master mariner. Their ch. 1, Oliver H., b. May 18, 1834, d. May 3, '38. 2, David V., b. Aug. 15, '35; m. Julia A. Shea, June 16, '55; r. S. Th. 3, William T., b. Aug. 10, '36, d. May 14, '37. 4, Mercy W., b. July 7, '38; m. Samuel Gross; r. S. Th. 5, Wooster, (2d), b. ab. '43; r. S. Th. 6, Willard, b. ab. '45; m. Adelaide Robinson in 1862; r. S. Th. 7 & 8, twins, b. Sept. 1846, Otis O., d. Dec. 21, '46, and Eliza T., m. Albert Gross of Rock., Jan. 11, '65. 9, Sarah, b. ab. '48.

David V.'s ch. 1, Ella F., b. ab. 1856. 2, Adelaide, b. ab. '57. 3, Frank H., b. ab. '59.

SMITH, Samuel Emerson, Esq , b. 1821; son of Edwin & Caroline (Head) Smith of Warren; grad. Bowd. Coll., 1839; stud. law in his father's office; mar. Maria Copeland of W.; prac. sometime in W., rem. Th., as cashier of Georges Bank, 1852-3; and d. Dec. 5, '55, of fever. Their ch. 1, Osgood Frazier, b. Dec. 25, 1846, d. Nov. 28, '57. 2, Ella M., b. ab. '50. 3, Clarence Sidney, b. ab. '52. 4, Alice, b. March, '54, d. Dec 8, '57. 5, S. Emerson, (2d), b. '56.

SMITH; of this Rhode Island family 3 brothers, sons of Sylvester Smith, came to this place. 1, Leprelet, m. Mercy ——; r. Rock., and carried on considerable business, but rem. to the West. 2, Lewis was here early with Maria, his wife, but rem. to Worcester, Mass. 3, Charles W., m. 1st, Almira Achorn, Dec. 26, 1833, 2d, Betsey Currier, Jan. 1, '43; rem. to West Camden.

Leprelet's ch. 1, Ann Emma, b. Nov. 20, 1828; mar. George W. Case, March 11, '47; r. Rock. 2, James L. or R., b. April 20, '30; mar. Margaret A. Kaler, p. March 15, '52; r. Rock., a truckman, &c. 3, Lucia A., b. Sept. 18, '32. 4, Lewis L., b. June 21, '37; m. Susan Seidlinger, April 5, '59; r. Rock., corporal in 2d Me. Battery, since in navy. 5, Anna E., d. June, 1830.

Lewis's ch. 1, George L., born Oct. 9, 1826, d. June 10, '30. 2, Manly S., b. June 11, '28. 3, Abigail P., b. Aug. 4, '31. 4, Elliott, b. July 31, '33 5, Jesse, b. March 22, '36. 6, John W., b. May 16, '39. 7, Harriet E., b. June 15, '41; all probably rem.

Charles W.'s ch. By 1st wife. Chas. W., (2d), b. Nov. 13, 1835.

James R.'s ch. 1, Mercy A., b. ab. 1852. 2, Cassian A., b. ab. '55. 3, Minnie M., b. ab. '59.

Lewis L.'s ch. Emma, b. ab. 1859.

SMITH, Jacob, b. ab. 1792, c. from Matinicus, m. Jane Toppy of Matinicus, by Elder Snow, 1812; r. Rock. Of their ch. 1, Jacob, (2d), ? b. ab. 1821, mar. Almira T. Burgess; r. Rock., a mariner. 2, Isaac, m. Martha Manning, 2d, Esther Jameson; r. Rock.? 3, Timothy, b. ab. 1828, in Cam., m. Nancy Clough; r. Rock., now in U. S. Navy. 4, Nancy, b. ab. '37.

Jacob, (2d)'s ch. 1, Henry A., b. Aug. 29, 1842, m. Arletta Adams; r. Rock., now in U. S. Navy. 2, Sarah, b. ab. '45. 3, George, b. ab. '48. 4, Frederic, b. ab. '56.

SMITH, Reuben G., b. ab. 1805, in Freedom, Me., m. Eliza Gregory; r. Rock. Their ch. 1, Albert E., b. ab. 1828, m. Lydia M., Beals, Aug. 7, '55; r Rock., a blacksmith. 2, Alfred G., b. ab. 1830, m. 1st, Mary A. Munroe, Nov. 21, '52, 2d, Angeline Russell; r. Rock. a cooper, &c. 3, ? Wesley F., b. ab. '43; r. Rock., entered the U. S. Navy. 4, Esther A., b. ab. '47; r. Rock.

Albert E.'s ch. 1, Ada I., b. ab. 1856. 2, Luella, b. Aug. and d. Nov. 13, '59.

Alfred G.'s ch. 1, Sanford M., b. ab. 1854. 2, Alfred F., b. ab. '58.

SMITH, Capt. Sylvanus N., b. ab. 1824, mar. Clara S. ——; r. Rock., a master mariner. Their ch. 1, Helen A., b. Oct. 17, 1858, d. Feb. 5, '60. 2, Laura E, b. Dec. 1859, d. July 15, '63. Of this name, also, Charles I. Smith, b. ab. 1835, mar. Helen M. ——; r. Rock., a lime burner, &c. Their ch. John S., b. ab. 1859. And of this name, George L. Smith, b. June 8, 1826, son of Isaac S. Smith of Dexter, Me., m. Eliza W. Crockett; r. Rock.

SNELLING, Charles G., b. ab. 1834, m. Eliza P. Coombs, Dec. 16, '52; r. S. Th., a teacher, supervisor of schools, &c. Their ch. Charles A., b. ab. 1855.

SNOW; of this family, 1, Rev. or Elder Elisha, was b. in Brunswick, March 26, 1739, O. S.; m. Betsey Jordan at Cape Elizabeth, Dec. 6, 1759; settled in S. Th. & d. Jan. 30, 1832, a. 93. 2, Polly, m. Rev. Ephraim Hall; r. & d. St. G. 3, Joseph, c. with his family from New Meadows; settled, r. & d. in S. Th. 4, Samuel, was here early, but probably ret. 5, Hannah, m. Caleb Hall; r. & d. St. Geo. Their father, Dea. Isaac Snow, also, c. to S. Th. in his old age, & d. in 1799, at his dau. Hannah's in St. George.

Rev. Elisha's ch. 1, Capt. Ephraim, b. Oct. 14, 1760, mar. Jenny McKown of Bristol, p. July 17, 1785; rem. Boston. 2, Capt. Robert, b. March 14, '62; m. Susan Mingerson; rem. St. George, and d. Feb. 17, 1803. 3, Capt. Ambrose, b. March 2, 1765; m. Fanny (Campbell) Archibald; and d. April 11, 1802. 4, Joanna, b. Jan. 2, '67; m. Rev. Isaac Case; and d. probably in Readfield. 5, Elisha, (2d), Esq., born May 29, '69; mar. 1st, Achsah Stetson, Oct. 10, '93; 2d, Nancy McKown, Sept. 25, '96; 3d, Lillias Taylor Mingerson, Aug. 14, 1806; 4th, Hannah, (Day) Eaton, Aug. 7, '31; r. S. Th. and Th., a merchant, d. Jan. 20, 1843. 6, Capt. Israel, b. Oct. 2, '71, at Harpswell, as were the five preceding; m. Hannah Snow, p. Nov. 15, '93; rem. Bangor and d. Sept., 1863, the oldest citizen and Mason in the place. 7, Capt. Isaac, b. at S. Th., Nov. 19, '73; m. Ruth Hayden, p. June 25, '95; & d. at Philadelphia, March 28, 1820. 8, Polly, b. Nov. 27, '75; m. Capt. James Spalding; r. S. Th., and d. suddenly, Aug. 24, 1851. 9, Larkin, b. Jan. 24, '78; m. Nancy Willis of Boston, p. Oct. 6, 1802; r. Boston, a merchant, and d. April, 1846. He, as well as Elisha, had commanded vessels; so that all of the seven brothers might be termed master mariners, or captains.

Joseph's ch. 1, Nathaniel. 2, Benjamin, b. 1764; mar. 1st, Lucy Davis of War., p. Nov. 14, '92, 2d, Elizabeth (Copeland) Wiggen of War., p. April 5, 1811; r. S. Th., d. Oct. 24, '25. 3, Joseph, (2d), m. Margaret Snow, Jan. 1, 1826, (who d. July 13, '27, aged 24); r. S. Th. 4, Daniel, m. Mrs. Sarah Mathews, p. Sept. 25, '93; rem. Linc. 5, Hannah, m. Capt. Israel Snow; r. Bangor. 6, Lydia B., b. '75; m. George Sayward; and d. in Rock, Oct. 27, 1855. 7, Apphia, m. 1st, John Mathews, 2d, Joshua Jordan; rem. Bangor.

Third Generation.

Capt. Ephraim's ch. 1, Betsey, b. July, 1787, d. Dec, '91. 2, Larkin, (2d), b. '89, d. Feb. 6, '97. 3, Alexander. 4, John McK., b. Feb. 15, '93; d. in Boston, Dec., 1842. 5, Margaret, b. Feb. 11, '94; mar. Edward Williams. 6, Nancy, b. March 10, '96; d. unm. 7, Julia, b. July 30, '99; m. ——— Topliffe. 8, Jane, b. Jan. 27, '01; d. unm. 9 & 10, twins, Eliza & Maria, the latter of whom m. Dr. Bellows of Charlestown, Mass.

Capt. Robert's ch. 1, Robert, probably d. young. 2, John, mar. Sarah Wilson, p. Jan. 26, 1817; & d. Sept. 25, '36, or Aug. 27, '37, drowned in mouth of Kennebec River. 3, Elizabeth, mar. 1st, Eben Thorndike, 2d, Mr. Clark; r. St. Geo. 4, Capt. Israel, (2d), b. May 31, '01; mar. Lucy W. Thorndike, p. Aug. 7, '24; r. Rock., master mariner. 5, Nancy, m. William Stackpole; rem. Illinois. 6, Susan, m. William Kelloch, Dec. 20, '21; r. & d. St. Geo.

Capt. Ambrose's ch. 1, Capt. Robert, (2d), b. 1788; m. 1st, Hannah Thorndike, 2d, Sarah P. Washburn, Aug. 12, 1828; r. Th., & d. Aug. 28, '48. 2, Jenny, b. ab. 1791; m. 1st, Francis Cobb of Portland, 2d, Israel Dinsmore of Cherryfield; rem. thence to War., & in 1843 to Th., kept Knox Hotel. 3, Campbell, d. young. 4, William, rem. & m. 1st, in Columbia, Me., & 2d, in N. S. 5, Mary, b. ab. '96; m. Capt. Ezekiel Post; r. Th. 6, Ambrose, (2d), m. 1st, Catharine Handly of Wal., p. Feb. 2, '30, 2d, Mrs. Sarah Scholfield of Cambridgeport, Aug. 12, '47; a joiner, r. Cambridge, Mass. 7, Capt. Thomas A., m. Catharine Campbell; r. Th., ship master, hotel keeper, &c., rem. New Orleans, in the business and commerce of which, especially the tow-boat enterprise, he took a conspicuous part; & d. there, Sept. 6, 1856. The mother d. Dec. 24, '42, aged 83.

Elisha, (2d), Esq.'s ch. 1 and 2, twins, b. Sept. 23, 1794, Ambrose, (3d), m. 1st, Abigail Heard, 2d, Frances ———, and d. in Michigan, where he has r. as also at Deer Isle, and other places; Mary S., m., r. and d. Seal Harbor. 3, Achsah, b. April 2, 1796; r. Rock. By 2d wife. 4, Jane M., b. Sept. 19, '97, m. Benjamin Safford, Sept. 5, 1822; r. Hope. 5, Larkin, (2d), Esq., b. Sept. 27, '99, mar. Alice Small of Deer Isle; r. Rock., a lime manufacturer, and leading business man, d. Oct. 19, 1861. 6, Alexander McKown, b. April 10, '03, mar. Sophronia S. Pressey of Deer Isle, p. July 12, '34; r. Rock., a merchant, &c. 7, Charles Willis, b. April 4, '04, m. Olinda A. Pressey, p. March 28, '34; r. Rock., a merchant, &c. 8, Nancy, b. March 10, '06, m. Rev. Eben Myrick of Sedgwick, Jan. 28, '29, and d. Feb. 14, '30. The mother d. March 20, '06, a. 36. By 3d wife. 9, Elisha, (3d), b. June 19, '07, d. May 18, '26, when just ready to graduate at Watervillle Coll. 10, Archibald Gamble, b Sept. 8, '09, mar. Eliza Thorndike, '33, and d suddenly in Boston, July 24, '34. 11, Lillias T., b. Sept. 13, '11, m. Capt. Richard Keating, (3d); r. Rock., and d. Jan. 15, '64. 12, Caroline, b. Aug. 11, '14, d. April 6, '15. 13, Capt. Edwin L., b. April 21, '16, mar. Antoinette Eaton, May 27, '38; r. Milton, Fa, rem. Texas. 14, Caroline M., b. Aug. 13, '18, m. Eben Alden, (2d); r. Rock. 15, Capt. George C., b. Oct. 25, '20, m. Harriet N. Miller, June 23, '44, and d. Aug. 21, '46. 16, Adaline, born Aug. 9, '22, d. Nov. 2, '44. 17, Maria Louisa, born Sept. 5, '24; r. Rock. The mother d. Jan. 25, '31, a. 48. By 4th wife. 18, Sergt. Elisha M., b. Dec. 3, '33, merchant at the South, ret. to Th., officer in 21st Me., killed by accident, Nov. 15, '62, at N. Y. 19, Eliza T., b. Oct. 14, '35, m. Nathan A. Packard, Oct. 17, '57; r. Searsmont.

Capt. Israel's ch. 1, Betsey. 2, Hannah. 3, Sophia. 4, John. 5, Isaac. 6, Susan. 7, George. 8, Joseph. 9, Charles. 10, Elisha; mostly residents of Bangor or vicinity.

Capt. Isaac's ch. 1, Capt. Elisha, (4th), m. Mary Sartelle of Cam., p. April 28, 1821; r. Rock. 2, Capt. Luther H., b. ab. 1800, mar. Frances Ott of Cam., p. Nov. 28, '23; r. Rock., both master mariners. 3, Sarah W., m. John Sweetzer; r. Wisconsin. 4, Rebecca J., mar. Joseph North, Dec. 11, '28. 5, Harvey Gilmore, m. 1st, Lucy H. Packard, 1835, 2d, Lucinda Morton, July 29, '38; r. N. Y. 6, Ephraim, (2d), b. ab. '08, m. Hannah Pillsbury, Sept. 12, '23; r. Rock., a mariner. 7, Nancy W., m. Beza Sweetzer; r. Rock. 8, Eliza, b. 1812, m. Paul Wentworth, p. Sept 25, '29, and d. in Rock., April 10, '44. 9, William. 10, James.

Larkin's ch. 1, Ephraim Larkin, a well known citizen of Boston, taking great interest in the old volunteer fire department, was, according to the newspapers, the original person that answered to the question, "Who struck Billy Patterson?" rem. N. Y., where he was clerk of one of the N. Y. courts, auctioneer, assembly man, &c., d. in Nov. 1860. 2, Margaret. 3, George. 4, Henry. 5, Mary.

Benjamin's ch. 1, Polly, m. Mr. Hawes of Joy. 2, William, born Oct. 9, 1794, m. Isabel Hayden, July 12, '29 ; r. S. Th., and d. Aug. 17, '38. 3, Rufus, b. Jan. 13, '97, m. Cordelia Wiggen, Sept 23, '27; r. S. Th. 4, Nancy, rem. east. 5, Elsie, b. ab. 1799 ; mar. Capt. Ephraim Crouch ; r. S. Th. 6, John, d. young. 7, Margaret, mar. Joseph Snow, (2d), Jan. 1, '1826 ; r. and d. S. Th. By 2d wife. 8, Lucy, m. Martin Mink of Wal. 9, Moses, b. ab. '15, m. Sarah Foster, Oct. 8, '37 ; r. S. Th., a mariner.

Daniel's ch. 1, Israel, (3d), b. July 28, 1794, m. Mary Mathews of Linc. 1820 ; r. Linc, and d. May 11, '34.* 2, Sarah, b. April 17, '96, m. Isaac Mathews of Linc., and d. Sept. 15, '60. 3, Lydia, b. May 13. '98, m. John McAllister, (2d) ; r. Linc. and Rock. 4, James S., d. in infancy. 5, Henry, b. June 10, '04, m. Mary Thomas of Linc., and d. Nov. 29, '41, wrecked in Long Is. Sound. 6, Margaret S., b. Jan 18, '06, m. Joseph S Pierce ; r. Rock. 7, Samuel B., b. Oct. 1, '08, m. Sarah Hilt of Hope, Jan. 16, '36 ; r. Augusta.

Fourth Generation.

John's ch. 1, Caroline, b. Jan. 1818 ; m. Joseph Graves ; r. S. Th. & d. March 13, '56. 2, Robert, (3d), b. ab. '21 ; m. Margaret Harrington, Dec. 1, '44 ; r. S. Th., a farmer. 3, Susan P., b. ab. '26 ; m. Joseph R. Walker ; r. Rock. 4, Lucy, m. Nathaniel Bassett ; r. Waldo & St. Geo. 5, Hannah L., m. Woodbury Davis, Nov. 13, '49 ; r. Waldo. 6, Henry, m. Eliza H. M. Kelloch ; r. St. George.

Capt. Israel, (2d)'s ch. 1, Elvira P., b. Jan. 25, 1825 ; m. Joshua K. Thorndike ; r. Cal. 2, Lavinia M., b. Oct. 24, 1826 ; r. Rock. 3, Capt Israel L., b. May 28, '29 ; m. Luella A. Keating, Nov. 20, '56 ; r. Rock., a ship master. 4, Lucy A., b. Jan. 11, '32 ; m. Capt. George L. Snow ; r. Rock. 5, Susan E , b. April 8, '34 ; mar. Capt. Hiram Hall, (2d) ; r. Rock. 6, Eliza T., b. May 19, '37 ; r. Cal. 7, Lydia T., b. Sept. 3, '39. 8, Charles W., (2d), b. May 9, '42 ; acting ensign in U. S. Navy, d. in New Orleans, of typhoid, Sept. 14, '64.

Capt. Robert, (2d)'s ch. by 1st wife. 1, Capt. Ambrose, (4th), b. Jan. 28, 1813 ; m. Mary Robinson, March 16, '36 ; r. Th., a ship master, &c., rem. to N. Y., com. merchant in firm of Snow & Burgess ; r. Williamsburg. 2, Mary Jane, b. Nov. 29, '16 ; m. John Bailey, & d. March 27, 1853. 3, Bethia C., b. April 22, 1823 ; m. William Oliver Fuller ; r. Rock. By 2d wife. 4, Capt. Robert R., b. Nov. 12, '31 ; m. Sarah E. Spear of W., Sept. 16, '57 ; r. Th., a master mariner. 5, Henry A., b. Aug. 5, '34, d. June 15, '60. 6, William R., b. Oct. 3, & d. Oct. 17, 1836.

Ambrose, (2d)'s ch. by 1st wife. 1, Robert William, d. young. 2, John, (2d). 3, Frances A., m. Ambrose Weeks ; rem. west. The mother d. Dec. 12, '42, a. 33.

Capt. Thomas A.'s ch. 1, Horatio, d. July 29, 1827. 2, Mary E., b. Aug. 2, '27, d July '31. 3, James C., b. June 17, '30, d. June 1, '31. 4, Susan F., b. Aug. 2, '32 ; 5, Louisa M., b. Sept., 23, '34 ; m. Capt. Richard Francis, Oct., '52 ; 6, William T., b. Aug. 10, '36 ; all rem. to N. O. 7, Joseph F., b. May 30, '39, d. Sept. 16, '40. 8, Colin C., b. Sept. 25, '41 ; rem. to N. O.

Ambrose, (3d)'s ch. 1, Abigail H., b. Jan. 20, 1829 ; m. Capt. Alden T. Spear ; r. Rock. & d. Nov. 30, '59. 2, Alexander, b. ab. '33 ;

r. Rock., a mariner. 3, Lillias M., b. ab. '35; m. Charles S. Paul; r. Rock. 4, Alonzo, b. ab. '37; r. Rock., a mariner. Probably others.

Larkin, (2d), Esq.'s ch. 1, Mary L., b. 1825, d. March 14, '45. 2, Capt. George L., b. ab. '28; m. Lucy A. Snow, Nov. 20, '54; r. Rock., a master mariner. 3, Frances Myrick, b. Oct. 16, '30; m. T. K. Osgood, Esq.; r. Rock. 4, Edward A., b. May 4, '33; mar. Sarah M. Read, Sept. 11, '55; r. Rock. 5, William M, b. May 8, '37; r. Rock., a merchant, entered 3d Wisconsin Reg., &c.

Alexander M.'s ch. 1, Charles M., b. Sept. 8, 1835; r. Rock., a merchant. 2, Andrew, b. March 8, & d. April 9, '38. 3, Celeste P., b. Feb. 14, '39. 4, Sidney, b. Jan. 6, '41. 5, Alice S., b. ab. '44. 6, Ebenezer A., b. ab. '49.

Charles W.'s ch. 1, Nancy J., b. Dec. 12, 1836, d. April 20, '38. 2, Greenleaf, b. May 28, '40, d. July 24, '41. 3, Laura Jane, b. Oct. 14, 1843; r. Rockland.

Capt. Edwin L.'s ch. Lucius Edwin, b. March 21, 1839, d. in Florida, Sept. 21, '53. Perhaps others.

Capt. Elisha, (4th)'s ch. 1, Capt. Isaac, (2d), b. Nov. 7, 1821; m. Pamelia Farr, Oct. 29, '43; r. S. Th., a master mariner. 2, Mary J., b. Sept. 9, '22; mar. Asa C. Fuller; r. Th., and died Aug. 1, '57. 3, Frederic G., b. March 20, '24, d. July 20, '44. 4, Julia A., born June 21, '26; m. Capt. Mark L. Ingraham; r. Rock. 5, Elizabeth, born March 20, '28; m. Amos L. Thompson; r. Rock. 6, John, (2d), b. June 24, '30; r. S. Th. 7, Capt. B. Franklin, b. Nov. 9, '32; mar. Rebecca G. Meservey, Dec. 7, '56; r. Rock. 8, Hannah, b. Nov. 10, '34, d. Nov. '37. 9, Ann B., b. April 21, '39; m. Asa C. Fuller; r. Th. 10, Frederic G., b. July 21, '42; r. Rock., entered the navy. The mother d. May 31, '58, a. 58.

Capt. Luther H.'s ch. 1, Lydia J., b. Oct. 22, 1824; m. 1st, Crawford A. Stover, 2d, John Bowden; r. Rock., rem. 2, Emily, b. Sept. 15, '26; m. Capt. William Lervey; r. Rock. 3, Maria, b. Sept. 13, '30; m. Caleb Stover; r. Rock. 4, Nancy, b. Dec. 4, '32; m. Elias Charles Howard; r. Rock. 5, Edwin, b. Nov. 14, '34; m. Sarah J. Fuller; r. Rock., a mariner, soldier of 4th Me., &c. 6, Harvey G., b. Oct. 14, '36, d. Oct. 31, '37. 7, Frances, b. March 20, '40, d. Oct. 19, '41. 8, William, (2d), b. ab. '44. 9, Mary Frank, b. ab. 1846.

Ephraim, (2d)'s ch. 1, Arthur L., b. Oct. 5, 1835; mar. in Liverpool; r. Rock., a mariner. 2, Adelaide F., b. July 27, '37; mar. Z. Pope Vose, Esq., r. Rock. 3, Mary F., b. May 21, '39; mar. Francis Tighe, Dec. 11, '61; r. Rock. 4, Laura Ann, b. May 4, '41, d. May 31, '42. 5, Albert Sidney, b. ab. 1846; entered U. S. N. Academy, Newport, R. I., Dec. 2, 1861.

William's ch. 1, N. Maria H., b. May 26, 1830; m. Capt John R. Robinson; r. S. Th. 2, William H., b. April 11, '33; m. Harriet T. Norton of St. George, Oct. 16, '53; r. S. Th., a carpenter, &c. 3, John M., b. Sept. 26, and d. Nov. 4, '36. 4, Robert H., b. Sept. 26, '37, d. Sept. 10, 1838.

Rufus's ch. 1, Martha H., b. Dec. 10, 1827; m. Samuel Cole of Lewiston. 2, Hannah P., b. June 4, '30; r. S. Th. 2, Sarah E., b. July 15, '34; mar. Randal Benner of Wal. 3, Edmund, b. Oct. 27, '36, d. March 17, '39. 4, Lucy Anne, b. Jan. 21, '39. 6, Julia D., b. March 16, 1842.

Moses's ch. 1, Stephen F., b. Sept. 3, 1839, d. March 14, '42. 2, Stephen, b. Aug., '42, d. Jan. 15, '44. 3, Mary Lucy, b. Jan. 27, '45, d. April 20, '49. 4, Ira M., b. Oct. 10, '48, r. S. Th. 5, Ann Augusta, b. April 14, 1852, d. April 15, '53. 6, Albert F., b. May 27, 1857.

Fifth Generation.

Robert, (3d)'s ch. 1, Flora, b. ab. 1848. 2, Eben, b. ab. '50. 3, Nancy, b. ab. '52. 4, William H., (2d), b. ab. '54. 5, Rose K., b. ab. '56. 6, Sarah, b. ab. '58. 7, a daughter, b. 1860.

Capt. Israel L.'s ch. 1, Frank E., b. ab. 1858. 2, Richard K., b. ab. 1859.

Capt. Ambrose, (4th)'s ch. 1, Adelia, b. Sept. 5, 1837, d. Oct. 13, '40; 2, Alfred D., b. Sept. 26, '40; 3, Louis; 4, Richard; 5, William; all r. New York.

John, (2d)'s ch. Henry S., b. Feb. 5, 1836.

Capt. Robert R.'s ch. Henry Lewis, b. ab. 1859.

Capt. George L.'s ch. 1, Mary L., b. ab. 1856. 2, Florence, b. ab. '58. 3, Lillian, b. Dec., '59, d. Sept. 28, '60.

Edward A.'s ch. Emily R., b. 1856, d. Aug. 26, '61.

Capt. Isaac, (2d)'s ch. 1, Roscoe G., b. ab. 1845. 2, Julian, b. ab. '50. 3, Lester, b. ab '52. 4, Emma G., b. ab. '54. 5, Ada, b. ab. '57.

Capt. B. Franklin's ch. Rebecca E., b. ab. 1859.

Edwin's ch. Ira R., b. ab. 1859.

William H.'s ch. Helen M., b. ab. 1859.

SNOWDEAL, John, m. Elizabeth Bridges; came from Waldoboro' to what is now S. Th. before 1804; was a soldier of the Revolution; & d. March 11, 1838. Their ch. 1, Mary, m. Godfrey Overlock; r. Liberty. 2, William, m. r. & d. Wal. 3, Elizabeth, m. Ashbee Goddard, Oct. 15, 1809; r. Illinois. 4, Catharine, m. ——— Goddard; & rem. to Illinois. 5, Hannah, m. Matthew Kelloch, p. Dec. 9, '18; r. Machias. 6, George, mar. Hannah Thorndike, Nov. 24, '25. 7, John, (2d), m. Mary Harrington of St. G., Jan., 13, '29; r. S. Th., & Saco, d. March 12, '38. 8, Edward, b. ab. 1806; m. Mary A. Wall, p. July 3, '33; r. S. Th., a joiner.

George's ch. 1, Almira, m. Frank Bartlett; r. Ohio. 2, Priscilla m. Henry G. Chandler; r. S. Th. 3, Eliza M., m. Robert Speed, p. Sept. 6, '47; r. Rock. 4, Anna Frances, m. Henry McAllister. 5, George, (2d), r. S. Th., soldier in 4th Me.; &c. 6, Charles, m. Harriet Knowles; r. Belfast. 7, William H.; r. California. 8, Thomas H., b. March, 1837; r. S. Th., vol. soldier of 4th Me., killed April 16, '62, at Yorktown. 9, Eben, d. young.

John, (2d)'s ch 1, Lucy Jane, b. June 18, 1829; m. ——— Porter; r. Houlton. 2, Harriet, b. Jan. 22, '31; mar. John K. Post; r. Rock. 3, Mary A.; 4, Helen; 5, Ada; all r. Rock. 6, Irene, mar. ——— Baker; r. Saco. 7, Alvan. 8, George. 9, Estelle.

Edward's ch. 1, Elizabeth, b. Jan. 15, 1834; m. ——— Neubert; r. Cutler. 2, Catharine, b. Feb. 28, '35; m. ——— Clark; r. Rock. 3, Nancy J., b. Feb. 21, '36; m. William Norton, Dec. 1, '60; r. S. Th., & Matinicus. 4 & 5, twins, b. Dec. 24, '37; Sarah, m. Zebulon Kinney of St. George, Dec. 15, '61. Olivia, mar. ——— Neubert; r. Cutler. 6, Lavinia, b. July 25, '39; m. Eben A. Frye; r. S. Th. 7, Joseph, b. Oct. 23, '41; r. S. Th., a mariner. 8, Lydia M., b. ab. '43. 9, Thomas E., b. ab. '45; r. S. Th., soldier in 4th Me., &c. 10, William, b. ab. '47. 11, Charles, b. ab. '51. 12, Jackson, b. ab. '53. 13, Eveline, b. ab. '55.

SOUTHWORTH, William, b. in 1766; came from Duxbury, Mass. to Wal., where he worked for W. Thomas, Esq.; m. Lucy Wheaton; c. to r. in Th., 1806; was a blacksmith, and d. Dec. 13, 1851. Their ch. 1, Lavinia, b. ab. 1805; mar. John P. Cole; r. Th., rem. Mass. 2, Lucy, b. in Th., Oct. 12, 1807; r. Th., or Mass.

SPALDING, Timothy, m. Margaret Mathews, c. here from New Meadows, ab. 1787 ; r. and d. S. Th. Their ch. 1, Jedediah, b. ab. 1765, m. Anne Ingraham, Nov. 21, '87 ; r. S. Th., and d. Dec., 1843. 2, Sarah, b. Oct., '67, m. Anthony Mathews, 2d, Daniel Snow; r. S. Th. and Hope. 3, Capt. James, b. at Phipsburg, Aug. 23, '68, mar. Mary Snow, July 28, '96 ; r. S. Th., a master mariner, rem. Ohio, but d. at Rock., July 15, 1853, in 85th year. 4, Ruth, mar. Capt. John Bryant ; r. S. Th.

Jedediah's ch. 1, Margaret, b. Jan. 15, 1789, m. George Graffam ; r. S. Th. 2, James, (2d), b. Aug. 22, '90, m. Hannah Chute of Portland, p. March 9, 1814, d. without ch. Aug. 5, '44. His wife d. May 3, '48, a. 53. 3, Capt. Josiah, b. Jan. 20, '93, m. Eleanor Bartlett, Sept. 4, 1817 ; r. S. Th., and d. March 15, '29, lost overboard, when master of sch. *Leo*. 4, Timothy, (2d), b. Nov. 21, '95, d. July 10, '08. 5, Job, b. Jan. 26, '97, m. Mary L. Sylvester, Nov. 23, '28 ; r. S. Th., & d. Oct. 4, '29. 6, William, b. Jan. 17, '99, m. Cynthia Fales, p. Jan., 1829 ; r. S. Th., a mill manager, and d. Sept. 21, '30. 7, Sarah, born Jan. 17, 1801, m. P. Atwood Fales; r. S. Th. 8, Joseph I., b. Oct. 21, '02, m. Rachel P. Quimby, March 14, '33, rem.? 9, Capt. Chas., b. Jan. 1, '05, m. Lucy H. Crockett, Aug. 1, '27 ; r. S. Th., & d. Dec. 19, '46. 10, Hannah, b. March 4, '08, m. Moses Crockett; r. S. Th.

Capt. James's ch. 1, Larkin, b. Sept. 1, 1797, m. Mary A. Patrick of N. O., 1834 ; r. Ohio and N. O., where he d. Sept. 27, '62, of consumption. 2, Jedediah, (2d), born April 11, '99, d. on Staten Is., N. Y., Sept., 1821. 3, Matilda, b. July 21, '01, m. Ephraim S. Bartlett, rem. Ohio, 1838. 4, Dr. Joshua A., b. Aug. 17, '04 ; killed, 1847, in the attack on Maj. Lally by the Rancheros, at the National Bridge, Mexico, where, and in S. America, he had travelled much. 5, Capt. Archibald C., b. Aug. 19, '06, m. Lucy Kaler of Wal., Nov. 22, '43 ; r. Rock., a master mariner, was in business in N. Y. sometime, and since 1861, has been of the Pension bureau at Washington, D. C. 6 and 7, twins, b. May 31, '08, Eliza, d. S. Th., July 19, '56, Margaret, m. Isaac W. Small of Cherryfield, Oct. 1, '33, rem Ohio, '37, now r. Rock., had one ch. Eliza A. Small, b. May 29, '36, m. Capt. O. Merrill White; r. Rock. 8, Mary T., b. Sept. 18, '11, m. William Keating, rem. 1837 ; r. Iowa. 9, Capt. Henry C., b. Feb. 9, '15, m. Margaret Martin of St. George, Aug. 19, '38 ; r. S. Th., a master mariner.

Capt. Josiah's ch. 1, Harriet S., b. March 20, 1818, mar. ——— Bartlett; r. Cal. 2, Lucy S., b. March 23, '20, mar. William S. Emery; r. Cal. 3, Capt. Edward C., born Sept. 26, '21, mar. Sarah H. Cooper, May 11, '47 ; r. S. Th., a master mariner. 4, Josiah, (2d), b. Dec. 29, '25, m. Eliza S. Palmer, Oct. 18, '49 ; r. S. Th. 5, Ira Gilman, b. April 13, '28, d. Nov. 26, '50, at New Orleans, when mate of bark *Mary Adelia*, Capt. A. C. Spalding. 6, Clementine, b. Oct. 30, '29 ; m. Ephraim Dean ; r. S. Th.

Joseph I.'s ch. 1, Oliver H., b. Jan. 12, 1834. 2, Emeline, b. June 11, '35. 3, Ann E., b. July 14, '36. 4, Jona. Cilley, b. March 18, '38, all rem.? 5, Edwin Warren, b. May 1, '39, d. Sept. 10, '40. 6, Lilias, b. Nov. 26, '40. 7, Nancy M., b. Sept 15, '42. 8, Sarah F., b. March, 1844. 9, Hannah C. 10, Ardell.

Capt. Charles's ch. 1, Maria N., b. May 31, 1828, m. Capt. Nathan L. Witham; r. S. Th., and d. Jan. 18, '54. 2, Sarah E., b. Jan. 27, '30, m. Shubael A., Hinkley; r. S. Th.

Larkin's ch. 1, William, b. Jan. 7, 1836, in Texas. 2, George, b. March 12, '38, d. in Ohio. 3, Matilda, b. in Ohio, deceased. 4, John,

b. March 17, '42. 5, Lucy, b. June 16, '44. 6, Amanda, born Aug. 22, 1847.

Capt. Archibald C.'s ch. 1, Grace D., b. May 18, 1847; r. Rock. 2, Alice, b. April 15, '51, d. Oct. 4, '52.

Capt. Henry C.'s ch. 1, Elizabeth, b. Nov., 1839, d. March 9, '41. 2, Elizabeth R., b. Ang., 1844. 3, James Henry, b. Oct. 12, '48, d. Oct. 25, '50. 4, Kate, b. Oct., 1849. 5, Joshua S., b. ab. 1856. 6, Henrietta, b. Nov., 1858.

Capt. Edward C.'s ch. 1, E. Cooper, b. ab. 1848. 2, Clara O., b. ab. '50.

SPALDING; of this Phipsburg family, four brothers came to this place. 1, Robert, b. ab. 1794; m. Asenath Barrett of Ipswich; r. Rock., a cooper, &c. 2, John, b. ab. 1797; m. Eleanor Lovett of Orono, Dec. 25, 1828; r. Rock., & was lost at sea, March 26, '30. 3, Joseph, b. ab. 1800; m. 1st, Mary Elizabeth Webber of Vinalhaven, Aug. 30, '29, 2d, Salome Stone, p. Feb. 27, '35; r. Rock. 4, Stephen, m. Mary Lovett of Orono. Besides these, there c. here, 1, William, a cousin of preceding, & son of Samuel, b. ab. 1803, in Lincolnville; m. Lucy Knowlton, Jan. 16, '28; r. Rock., a lime burner. 2, Capt. Charles, b. ab. '18, in Linc.; m. Harriet N. Bucklin, Oct. 1, '41; r. Rock., a mariner. 3, Ebenezer D., b. ab..'18; m. Cemantha ——; r. Rock., a brickmaker. 4, Nathan, son of Asa, b. ab. '32; m. Catharine Ulmer, p. Sept. 18, '52; r. Rock.

Robert's ch. 1, Margaret, b. Feb. 27, 1820; m. John Johnson, & d. at Orono, Oct. 30, '54. 2, James L., b. Nov. 25, '22; m. Mary M. Kenniston, Sept. 8, '57. 3, Stephen, (2d), b. July 30, '26, d. Feb. 4, '29. 4, Victorine, b. Aug. 28, '29; m. Simon Gorden, May 29, '53; r. Rock. 5, John R., b. May 30, '32; m. Susan A. Pottle, or Pettie, Dec. 31, '63; r. Rock., a mariner. 6, Robert B., b. May 19, '35; r. Rock., a mariner, soldier of 2d Me. Battery, re-enlisted. 7, Delmoca, b. April 10, '39. 8, Asenath, b. April 25, '41.

John's ch. Stephen, (3d), b. Nov. 12, 1829.

Joseph's ch. by 1st wife. 1, Mary L., b. June 3, 1830; m. Frederic S. Sweetland; r. Rock. 2, Frances M, b. Nov. 17, '32. The mother d. Dec. 23, '32. By 2d wife. 3, Deloma, b. April 24, '36.

William's ch. 1, Hannah, b. May 28, 1828; m. Charles Fields; r. Rock. 2, Lucy M., b. Jan. 18, '31; m. Elbridge H. Dodge; r. Rock. 3, William, (3d), b. Oct. 15, '34; m. Sarah Ames, p. Oct. 29, '53; r. Rock. 4, Mary E., b. April 5, 1838, d. Aug. 19, 1853. 5, Nancy, b. March 4, '40; m. Capt. Alfred Gray; r. Rock., 6, Charles Henry, b. ab. '44; r. Rock., soldier of 2d Me. Battery, re-enlisted. 7, Harriet, b. ab. 1846.

Capt. Charles's ch. 1, Sylvanus C., b. Feb. 8, 1843; r. Rock. 2, Harriet M., b. ab. '45. 3, Ada Alona, b. Jan., '49, d. Sept. 16, '51. 4, Ada A., b. ab. '53. 5, Mary T., b. ab. '57.

Ebenezer D.'s ch. Alice J., b. ab. 1852.

Nathan's ch. 1, Susan, b. ab. 1853. 2, Lydia, b. ab. '56. 3, Melissa, b. ab. '59.

William, (3d)'s ch. 1, Eva D., b. ab 1855. 2, Lizzie E., b. ab. '57. 3, George W., b. ab. '59.

Of this name, also, Mrs. Abigail Spalding, b. ab. 1795; r. Rock., a widow. Of her ch. 1, William, b. ab. 1824; r. Rock., a mariner. 2, John L., b. ab. '38; m. Jane ——; r. Rock., a mariner.

SPEAR, Capt. Jonathan, b. at Braintree, Mass., June 19, 1726, or

1723, ? m. 1st, Miss Dexter, 2d, Miss Brown of Smithfield, came to the old Fort and m. 3d, Margaret M. Dougle, Nov., 1762, by J. North, Esq., r. what is now Rock., & d. Oct. 10, 1811, a. according to gravestone, 88 yrs. 4 mos. Margaret, his third wife, was born at the Fort, now Th., March 12, 1746, O. S., and d. Sept. 22, 1811, bur. at Tolman cemetery. His ch. by 1st wife. 1, Hannah, b. 1758; mar. Thomas Stevens; and d. Sept. 12, 1830. By 3d wife. 2, Capt. William, born March 25, 1764; mar. Polly Gregory; r. Meadows, rem. Shore, now Rock. city, and d. April 28, '20. 3, Jonathan, (2d), b. Oct. 22, '66; m. Anne Howes, p. May 15, '88; r. Rock., & d. Sept. 8, 1847, a. 81. 4, Isaac, b. March 19, '69; m. Ann Simonton; r. Rock., and d. Aug. 20, 1836. 5, Joseph, b. Sept. 16, '71; m. Dolly Reed, pub. Nov. 29, '92; r. Rock., and d. May, 1819. 6 and 7, twins, born Sept. 22, '75; Maj. John, Esq., m. Ruth Stoddard, p. June 19, '97, 2d, Susan H. (Ingraham) Robbins, Sept. 24, 1827, 3d, Sarah U. Butler; r. Rock., and d. Eagle Is., where he was light keeper, Jan. 6, 1848; was inspector general of lime, State senator, &c. Eleanor, m. John Blackington; and d. March 14, 1843. 8, Capt. Elkanah, b. March 18, '78; m. Penninah Healey, June 1, 1800; r. Rock., on the farm where he was born; and d. July 19, '55. 9, Richard, b. Nov. 28, '80, d. Aug. 31, '91. 9, Nancy, b. March 29, '83; m. Joseph Ingraham; r. Rock. and d. June 29, 1856. 10, Polly, b. July 11, '86; mar. James Stackpole, Jr., and d. Sept. 1, 1855.

Capt. William's ch. 1, William, d. June 2, 1788, a. 11 days. 2, Hannah, d. young. 3, Capt. John, (2d), b. May 25, '89; m. Hannah Butler, Nov. 1, 1809; r. Rock., a master mariner, and died April 23, '63. 4, Rebecca, b. March 18, '92, d. Jan. 11, '94. 5, Capt. William, (2d), b. Oct. 20, '95; m. Jane Ulmer, Nov. 19, 1815; r. Rock., and d. July 5, 1838. 6, Capt. Mark D., b. Jan. 15, '97; mar. Betsey Hyler, Sept. 5, 1816; r. Rock., and d. Aug. 26, 1825; both master mariners. 7, Mary, b. Jan. 16, '99; m. Oliver Fales; r. Rock. 8, Hannah, b. March 26, 1801; m. Samuel C. Ingraham, 2d, Orris Robbins, 3d, Ambrose Case; r. Rock. 9, Harriet, born April 6, 1803; mar. Edward Crockett, 2d, Simeon Partridge; r. Rock., and d. April 23, '64. 10, Archibald G. C., b. April 25, 1805; m. Angelica Bronton; r. Rock., a pilot, &c. 11, Nancy, b. July 22, 1807; m. Capt. Jonathan Crockett; r. Rock.

Jonathan, (2d)'s ch. 1, Jonathan, (3d), b. Aug. 17, '91; lost at sea with Capt. Sears. 2, Betsey, b. July 19, '94; mar. Rufus Spear; r. Rock., and d. March 4, 1828. 3, Isaac, (2d), b. May 8, '96; died by drowning, May 9th, 1814. 4, Anna, b. Jan. 23, 1801, d. Oct. 1819. 5, Lucretia, b. Aug. 11, 1802; m. William Blaisdell; r. Rock. 6, Capt. Wellman, b. Aug. 13, 1809; m. Rebecca C. Fales; r. Rock., a ship master. The mother d. Jan. 29, 1853, aged ab. 86.

Isaac's ch. 1, Margaret, b. Sept. 3, 1791, d. July 12, '94. 2, Richard, b. Sept. 4, '93, d. July 19, '94. 3, Eleanor, b. June 16, '95; m. Nat. Guptill; r. Rock., and d. May 27, '54. 4, Richard, b. April 5, '97, d. March 18, 1809. 5, Joseph, (2d), b. July 11, 1800; m. Sarah Haskell, June 20, '22; r. Rock., a lime manufacturer. 6, Dolly, b. March 12, 1803; m. Capt. Robert Perry, and d. Aug. 2, '24. 7, Geo. W., b. May 6, '10; m. Abby Fuller; r. Rock., & d. Nov. 15, '62. 8, Elizabeth, b. April 17, 1813; r. Rockland.

Joseph's ch. 1, James, b. Oct. 15, 1793; m. Eliza Ulmer, Nov. 14, 1816, 2d, Betsey Boynton; r. Th., a farmer. 2, Rufus, born Dec. 15, '94; m. Betsey Spear, Nov. 5, 1815, d. in '34. 3, Henry, b. March 6,

'97; m. Sarah Anderson of Deerfield, Mass., r. N. York, in shoe business. 4, Alexander, b. July, 1800; m. Margaret Bennett, Oct. 10, '26; d. in California, Sept. '51. 5, Capt. Charles S., b. ab. 1802; m. Frances A. Fuller; and d. at N. York, of small pox, Oct. 6, '45. 6, Pearl S., b. ab. 1804; m. 1st, in Georgetown, S. C., 2d, Frances D. Wilcox of Portland, April 17, '57; r. Portland. The mother d. Aug. 19, '28, aged 51.

Maj. John's ch. by 1st wife. 1, Sally, b. Dec. 6, 1797; m. Isaac C. Robbins, Dec. 25, '16; & d. April 5, '48. 2, Harriet, b. Jan. 28, '99; m. 1st, Josiah Ingraham, 2d, Oliver White; r. Rock. 3, Demerrick, b. Dec. 6, 1800, a student at law, but d. Dec. 22, '25. 4, Leonard, b. May 7, '02, d. Sept. 19, '18. 5, Eliza K., b. March 5, '04; m. Israel I. Perry; r. Rock. 6, Capt. Nelson, b. Feb. 22, '06; m. Olivia Conant; r. Rock. 7, John, (3d), b. June 7, '07; m. Thankful Wright; & d. at New York, Aug. 21, '43. 8, Ruth R., b. May 15, '09; mar. Freeman Harden; r. Rock. 9, Margaret M., b. April 9, '12; m. Capt. James Robinson; & d. Jan. 30, '42. The mother d. June 5, '26, aged 47. By 3d wife. 10, Leonard J., b. July 22, & d. Dec. 28, '36. 11, Isora D., b. Feb. 17, '38; m. William F. Rollins of Cam., Dec. 3, '54. 12, Freeman H., b. Jan. 29, '40; r. Rock., a mariner.

Capt. Elkanah's ch. 1, Lucy H., b. May 27, 1801; mar. Rufus C. Counce; r. Th. 2, Capt. Richard, (3d), b. Jan. 2, '03; m. Julia Robinson, May 5, '29; & d. July 21, '31. 3, Harvey H., b. April 10, '05; m. Jane R. Spofford, Sept. 1, '29; rem. Pelham, N. H. 4, Elkanah, (2d), b. Jan. 3, '07; mar. Maria Spofford in 1831; r. Rock., a bookseller, &c. 5, Emily, b. March 22, '09; m. Jonathan White; r. Rock. 6, Otis R., b. Feb. 17, '11, d. Nov. 30, '29. 7, Maj. Jonathan, (4th), b. Jan. 1, '13; m. Lucy M. Ingraham, Dec., 1836; r. Rock., a farmer, &c. 8, Russell, b. March 3, '15, d. March 30, '29. 9, Sally Reed, b. July 22, '17; m. Capt. Edward C. Healey; r. Rock.

Fourth Generation.

Capt. John, (2d)'s ch. 1, Catharine A., b. Dec. 31, 1812; mar. Ephraim Hall; r. Rock. 2, Mary Hannah, b. May 15, '15; m. Hon. I. K. Kimball; & d. June 24, '51. 3, Capt. John Alden, b. May 5, '17; m. Nancy A. Clark, July 13, '48; r. Rock. 4, Capt. Alfred K., b. July 1, '20; m. Nancy M. Thorndike, Nov. 29, '49, 2d, Angeline A. Thorndike, Dec. 31, '61; r. Rock. 5, Edward C., b. Jan. 3, '23, d. Aug. 21, '26.

Capt. William, (3d)'s ch. 1, Susan U., b. Feb. 19, 1816; m. Benj. F. Dean; r. Rock., & d. May 29, '58. 2, Capt. Philip U., b. March 27, '18; m. Mary C. Hatch, Oct. 4, '42; r. Rock. 3, Lucy A., b. May 23, '21, d. April 5, '36. 4, Oliver F., d. Aug. 6, '26. 5, Capt. Alden T., b. March 18, '26; m. Abby H. Snow; r. Rock., sailing master in U. S. N., appt. Nov., 1861; promoted for gallantry, to Act. Lieut. Commanding, & d. Sept., 1863. 6, Harriet E., b. Oct. 27, '28; mar. Alexander Young, ? Nov. 14, '55. 7, Emily Jane, b. Nov. 12, '33, d. Sept. 22, '52.

Capt. Mark D.'s ch. 1, William Henry, b. Dec. 15, 1816. 2, Rebecca, b. April 8, '20; m. Capt. Andrew G. Luce; r. Rock. 3, Mark A., b. Oct. 31, '22, d. Aug. 26, '26. 4, Harris R., b. April 22, '25; r. Rock., a clerk, &c.

Archibald G. C.'s ch. 1, Olivia N., b. April 9, 1830; mar. Dr. Alonzo Garcelon of Lewiston, Jan. 13, '59. 2, Caroline F., b. July 7, '32; mar. William S. Frye, Feb. 27, '53. 3, Emeline A., b. Aug.

22, '37; r. Rock. 4, Julia C., b. Oct. 3, '39; r. Rock. 5, William E., b. ab '48.

Capt. Wellman's ch. 1, Jepson O., b. April 25, 1837, d. June 30, '48. 2, Madelah F., b. Oct. 27, '39. 3, Wellman C., b. June 27, '42. 4, Jonathan I., b. April, '45, d. July 31, '46. 5, Lucretia A., b. ab. '48. 6, Luke A., b. ab. '51.

Capt. Joseph, (2d)'s ch. 1, Isaac, b. June 25, 1822, d. April 19, '29. 2, Ann M., b. Oct. 27, '23, d. July 7, '27. 3, Elvira H., b. July 7, '25, mar. Ithamer Bowles, March 18, '47. 4, Mary C., b. Oct. 18, '27, m. Heman H. Burpee; r. Rock. 5, Harriet A., b. Oct. 7, '29, m. William T. Foster; r. Rock. 6, Emeline, b. Aug., 1831, d. Oct., '32. 7, Joseph, (3d), b. Aug., and d. Sept. 30, '33. 8, Emma, b. March 4, '36, m. Horace A. Chase of Bucksport, Oct. 12, '60. 9, Leonidas, b Feb. 15, '38; r. Rock, a mariner, lost overboard, Dec. 26, '61, from bk. *Jenny Pitts.* 10, Josiah C., b. Jan. 18, '40; r. Rock., a soldier of 4th Me., &c. 11, George A., b. June 18, '42.

George W.'s ch. 1, Isaac, (2d), b. Feb. 18, 1835, d. June 30, '51. 2, George C., born Jan. 4, '38; r. Rock., and d. March 15, '61. 3, Sarah Ann E., b. May 20, '42; 4, Almira E., b. ab. '46; both r. Rock.

James's ch. 1, Margaret, b. April 9, 1817; m. Capt. Samuel B. Stackpole, '39, d. May 31, '51. 2, Joseph, (4th), b. June 15, '19, d. Sept. 1, '20. 3, Asa, b. Aug. 26, '21; m. Sarah J. Fields, p. June 12, '45, 2d, Susan J. Saunders of Belmont; r. Fox Isl., a quarry man. 4, Dolly, b. Sept. 22, '23; m. Percy Montgomery; r. Rock. & d. Aug. 23, '61. 5, Lucinda, b. Jan. 2, 1825; m. Allen P. Farrington, & d. with her twin babes, July 24, '46. 6, Eliza, b. July 13, '28, d. June, '36. 7, James, (2d), b. May 4, '30; m. Mary E. Sullivan, Feb., '56; r. Rock. & d. July 7, '60. 8, Frances, b. Oct. 17, '33; m. Oliver Gay; r. Rock. 9, Hannah, b. Sept. 14, '35; m. David Brown of Damariscotta, Feb. 18, '60; r. Rock. 10, Jane, b. March 7, '38; m. Thomas Mink of Wal.; r. Rock. By 2d wife. 11, Oliver B., b. March 3, '42; m. Elizabeth, dau. of Chris. Butler; r. Rock., soldier of 2d Me. Battery, &c. 12, Pearl H., b. Nov. 3, '45; entered the army. 13, Lucretia A., b. Oct. 26, '47; m. William H. Clifford from Waterville; r. Rock 14, Sarah E., b. April 21, '47.

Rufus's ch. 1, Charles, b. Aug. 14, 1816; m. Harriet J. Pottle, & d., lost at sea, from ship *St. Patrick*, Dec., '60. 2, Julia, b. Feb. 14, '18; m. John Crie; r. Rock. 3, Harriet b. July 29, '23; m. Samuel Hassan; r. Rock.

Alexander's ch. 1, Alexander, (2d), b. Jan. 19, 1827; m. Sarah C. Adams, Sept. 9, '52; r. Th., a mariner. 2, Andrew J., b. May 23, '29, d. July 15, '54. 3, Laura A., b. Oct. 11, '31; m. Robert Crosby, June 10, '53; r. Rock. 4, Moses C., b. May 8, 1834, d. Nov. 25, 1843. 5, Thomas S., b. May 28, '36. 6, Sarah E., b. June 11, '38. 7, Penelope, b. Sept. 21, '40.

Charles S.'s ch. 1, Eliza Vose, b. April 8, 1833, d. Dec. 14, '39. 2, Lucy S., b. Jan. 9, '35. 3, Vivian K., b. June 29, '36. 4, Emily W., b. April 9, '39.

Capt. Nelson's ch. 1, Demerrick, (2d), or M.? b. June 30, 1827; m. Ledonia Crouch, Sept. 2, '49; r. Rock., soldier in N. Y. Cavalry. 2, Marcia, b. Jan. 6, '29; m. William Farrow, jr., May 19, '48. 3, ? Capt. Nelson P., b. ab. '32; m. Eliza J. Smart; r. Rock. 4, Cleaveland B., b. April 6, '35, d. Feb. 11, '39. 5, Roscoe, b. Feb. 27, '37; r. Rock., a mariner. 6, Adecia, b. Jan. 6, '41; m. George W. Perry; r. Rock. 7, Margaret, b. June 15, '43.

John, (3d)'s ch. 1, John D., b. in Hope, Nov. 2, 1832. 2, Clara F., b. Oct. 23, '34, d. Dec. 7, '39. 3, Victorine H., b. Feb. 13, '37; m. Charles H. Knowlton; r. Rock. 4, Morgiana, b. March 31, & d. Sept. 26, '39. 5, Lenora, b. May 19, '41, d. April 9, '54. 6, Ada B., b. ab. '44; r. Rock.

Capt. Richard, (3d)'s ch. William R., b. Jan. 25, 1830.

Harvey H.'s ch. 1, Julia A., b. Oct. 8, 1830. 2, Thomas S., born March 28, '34. 3, Otis G., b. May 15, '35; mar. Clarinda Spofford; r. Rock., corporal in 4th Me., since in the navy.

Elkanah, (2d)'s ch. 1, Lt. Col. Edward R., b. Jan. 1, 1833; mar. Ellen C. Haynes of Winthrop, Dec. 16, '54; r. Rock., a bookseller & stationer; on the Governor's staff, 1864, &c. 2, Julia S., b. July 8, '40; r. Rock.

Major Jonathan, (4th)'s ch. 1, Nancy F., b. May 23, 1837; mar. Benjamin D. Gardner, Sept. 10, '53. 2, Richard C., b. March 22, '39, d. Rock., Sept. 14, '58. 3, Thomas Benton, b. Jan. 4, '41; mar. Martha A. Lovejoy, June 13, '63; r. Rock., soldier in 4th Me., &c. 4, Elkanah, (3d), b. Dec. 15, '45. 5, Harriet, b. April 16, '47.

Capt. John A.'s ch. 1, Alfred K., b. ab. 1849. 2, Maynard S., b. ab. '51.

Capt. Philip U.'s ch. 1, Sereno T., b. ab. 1850. 2, Edwin E., b. ab. '53.

Asa's ch. 1, William, b. ab. 1850. 2, Frank, b. ab. '56. The mother d. March 23, '58, aged 36. By 2d wife. 3, James. 4, Jane.

James, (2d)'s ch. Arthur L., b. ab. 1857.

Charles's ch. 1, Ella G., b ab. 1854. 2, Emma M., b. ab. '56. 3, Susan L., b. ab. '59.

Alexander, (2d)'s ch. 1, Fanny E., b. ab. 1857. 2, Cora M., b. ab. '59.

Otis G.'s ch. Ellen J., b. ab. 1859.

Lt. Col. Edward R.'s ch. 1, Ellen M., b. Feb., 1858. 2, Edward D., b. Oct., '59. 3, Fanny, b. April 5, and died Aug. 18, '62. The mother d. Feb 28, '63, aged about 28.

SPEAR; of this Warren family, no relation to the preceding; 1, Capt. Arthur, b. ab. 1817, son of Capt. David; m. Lucy A. Spear of War.; r. Th., a master mariner. 2, Alexander, son of Alexander of W.; mar. Rosanna Studley; r. Th., a mariner. Also of the sons of John Spear, (3d), of W. 1, Thomas W., b. ab. 1818; mar. Sarah T. Collins, Nov. 4, '47; r. Rock., a teamster. 2, Silas, b. March, 1825; m. Julia A. Simmons; r. Rock., and d. Jan. 14, '62.

Capt. Arthur's ch. Frederic, b. ab. 1846; r. Th.

Alexander's ch. 1, Moses, b. ab. 1849. 2, Cora, b. ab. '53. 3, Sarah, b. ab. '54. 4, Vesta, b. ab. '55. 5, Alice, b. ab. '57.

Thomas W.'s ch. 1, Erastus A., b. ab. 1848. 2, Wilmot R., b. ab. '52. 3, Lucy A., b. ab. '56. 4, Herbert, b. ab. '58.

Silas's ch. 1, Dudley K., b. ab. 1850. 2, Rhoda K., b. ab. '51. 3, Benjamin P., b. ab. '52. Of this name, also, Edward P. Spear, & Abigail R., his wife, had recorded here their ch. 1, Helen P., born March 14, 1836. 2, Mary Z., b. May 2, '41.

SPEED, John F., b. ab. 1828; m. Angeline C. Dyer, p. March 19, '53; r. S. Th., a mariner. Their ch. 1, Henry I., b. ab. 1855. 2, Jeremiah B., b. ab. '58.

SPOFFORD,* Thomas, (oldest son of Thomas of Andover, who

---

* The name is of Anglo Saxon origin, from *spaw*, a mineral spring or water, and *ford*, a passage across it.

was 2d son of Samuel of Bradford, who was 4th son of Samuel of Rowley, who was the 3d son of John and Elizabeth Spofford, the first of the name in America, who came from England in 1638, and settled at Rowley, Mass.); mar. Esther Pearl and settled in Pelham, N. H. Their ch. 1, Thomas, (3d), b. May, 1772; m. Nancy Sears; came to Rock., 1851 or '2, a shoemaker, and d. Aug. 11, 1854. 2, Charles, b. Dec. 25, '76; came to Old Th., 1800; m. Lucy Reed, Oct., 1805; r. Rock., and d. Oct. 1, '19. 3, Pearl, came to Bucksport, 1801; mar. Sarah Averill in Boston, settled in Deer Isle, merchant, representative 9 years, postmaster 22 years. 4, Dudley, b. Dec. 20, '79; mar. Mary Atwood; r. Pelham, and had 17 ch. in little more than 25 years. 5, John, b. Feb. 21, '83; came here 1803; m. Hannah Simonton, Sept. 27, '08; r. Rock., since 1807, shoemaker, merchant, postmaster 15 yrs. &c. 6, Frederic, m. Mary Perkins, 1806; r. & traded Deer Isle, and was lost, coming from Boston in sch. *Shakspear*, with 22 others. 7, Abigail; and, by 2d wife, m. about 1794, 8, Sophia, died 1823.

Thomas, (3d)'s ch. 1, Philena, b. Dec. 14, 1800; m. Samuel Kimball. 2, Mary Ann, b. April 25, '03; m. Simeon Partridge; r. Rock. & d. April 3, '54. 3, Abigail R., b. April 2, '05; m. Charles Coburn. 4, Thomas, (4th), m. Eliza Hildreth. 5, Eliza J., m. Jonathan White. 6, Jane R., b. June 29, '11; m. Harvey H. Spear; r. Pelham. 7, Rebecca A., b. March 25, '13; mar. Nathaniel C. Moore; r. Rock. 8, James R., b. and d. 1815.

Charles's ch. 1, Mary, b. Aug. 6, 1806; m. James Crockett, (2d); r. Rock. 2, Julia A., b., Dec. 7, '09; m. Fred. Conway, Oct. 22, '29; d. Cam. 3, Maria, b. Oct. 7, or April 1, '13; m. Elkanah Spear, (2d); r. Rock. 4, Lucinda, b. Feb. 16, '16; m. H. P. Coombs; r. Th. 5, Sophia, b. Jan. 24, '19; grad. Mt Holyoke, 1847; r. Rock., teacher, &c. The mother, b. in Kingston, N. B., Oct. 28, '87, d. Feb. 14, 1857.

Pearl's ch. 1, Capt. Frederic P., m. Caroline E. Haskell, May 4, 1845; r. Deer Isle. 2, Charles A., grad. Bowd. Coll., 1849; mar. ——— Haskell; r. Deer Isle, attorney, speaker of Me. House, 1857. 3, Capt. Edward B., m. & r. D. I. 4, Capt. George W., m. Lucy A. Howard, March 7, '57; r. D. I. 5, William, m. r. and trades, D. I. 6, Henry, died young. 7, Sarah H., mar. Dr. Amos A. Herrick; r. Sedgwick. 8, Eliza, m. Dr. William F. Collins, Nov. 18, '52.

John's ch. 1, Capt. William, b. Jan. 8, 1808; m. Susan H. Hovey, p. June 12, '35; r. Rock. 2, Harriet, b. Sept. 25, '09; m. W. E. Tolman; r. Rock. 3, Capt. Dudley P., b. Jan. 20, '12; m Hannah I. Harden, p. June 10, '34; r. Rock. 4, Hannah, b. July 2, '15, d. June 26, '42. 5, Capt. John T., b. May 19, '19; m. Mary S. Fuller, Sept. 26, '47; r. Rock., all ship masters. 6, Abby A. R., b. Sept. 25, '24; m. Hon. Joseph Farwell; r. Rock., and d. Dec. 6, '52.

Capt. William's ch. Clarinda, b. ab. 1841; m. Otis G. Spear; r. R.

Capt. Dudley P.'s ch. 1, Edner Pearl, b. Jan. 10, 1836; r. Rock. 2, Clara F., b. Oct. 29, '38; m. John H. Grafton; r. Rock. 3, John F., b. ab. '41; r. Rock., a mariner. 4, Dudley P., b. ab. '43. 5, Harriet E., b. ab. '47. 6, Harden, b. ab. '50. 7, William, (2d), b. ab. '54. 8, George K., b. ab. '57. 9, Nathaniel A., b. ab. '60.

Capt. John T.'s ch. 1, Samuel F., b. ab. 1851. 2, Franklin M., b. '55. 3, Hannah J., b. '59.

SPRAGUE, Joseph, Esq., b. 1788, grad. Bowd. coll. 1808; c. from Bath and commenced the practice of law at Th. about 1812; m. Mary Marsh of Bath, p. Sept. 8, '15; r. Th. & d. Sept. 21, '26. Their ch. 1, Joseph Manning, b. July 25, '16; r. Th. & d. Nov. 23, '37, knocked overboard near N. O., when mate of the brig *Paragon*. 2, Capt. John Oakman, b. Feb. 24, '18; m. 1st, Lucretia D. Mitchell, June 28, '46, 2d, Isabella Rannie of Glasgow, Scotland; r. Th., a ship master. 3, Capt. James Thomas, b. Jan. 26, 1820: m. Harriet G. Webb, Sept. 16, 1847; r Th. & d. Feb. 5, 1852. 4, Sarah M., b. Dec. 17, '21; m. Leonard C. Stetson; r. Th. 5, William H. D., b. Sept. 25, '23, & d. Jan. 12, 1824.

Capt. John O.'s ch. 1, Mary, b. ab. 1847. 2, Sarah, b. ab. 1849. 3, Charles, b. ab. 1855.

SPRAGUE, Eli, b. ab. 1819, c. from Hope; m. Sarah T. Carkin; r. Rock., a blacksmith. Their ch. 1, Edward A., b. March 21, '43; was in Texas on the breaking out of the rebellion, on business, bought a horse and tried to escape, but was taken back and impressed in the rebel army till the battle of Shiloh, when he escaped into the Federal lines; c. home, joined the 28th Me. Reg., in which he was made prisoner and exchanged; re-enlisted in 31st Me. Reg., color sergeant, promoted for gallantry to Lieut. and was killed in battle, Sept. 30, '64. 2, Ellen A., b. ab. 1846. 3, Edwin A., b. ab. 1848.

SPRAGUE; of the sons of Nathaniel of Appleton, who m. a dau. of Fergus McLain; r. a time in Miramichi, N. B., & d in A., Feb. 17, '65, a. 75; there came here, 1, Alden, b. ab. 1826 in Searsmont; m. Lavinia B. Mansfield; learned printer's business; r. Rock., editor of the Democrat and Free Press, treasurer of Knox county 1862, '3, &c. 2, Edwin, b. ab. '34; m. Malvina S. Kimball; r. Rock., printer and publisher of the Democrat and Free Press.

Alden's ch. 1, Charles, b. ab. 1854. 2, Caroline M., b. ab. '56. 3, Annie K., b. ab. '58. 4, Alden, (2d), b. ab. '59.

Edwin's ch. Ida K., b. ab. 1859, d. July 14, 1860. Of this name, also, William Sprague, born ab. 1803, and Almira, his wife, r. Rock. Also, Hiram J., b. ab. 1836, m. Dorcas E. ——— ; r. Rock., a mariner.

William's ch. 1, Rhoda A., b. ab. 1847. 2, James F., b. ab. '53.

Hiram J.'s ch. Cora A., b. Aug. 3, and d. Sept. 6, 1860.

STACKPOLE, James, b. at Somersworth, N. H., May 1, 1744, O. S., m. 1st, at Harpswell, Judith Thompson, May 18, '67; c. early to Th., a carpenter, &c., mar. 2d, Sarah (Fales) Partridge, Nov. 23, '97; and d., we believe, at a good old age. Judith, his 1st wife, was b. at Brunswick, Feb. 8, 1743, d. April 13, '97. His ch. by 1st wife. 1, Olive, b. April 27, 1768; m. 1st, Capt. William Lackey, 2d, William Staples of Prospect, pub. Jan. 21, '99; r. and d. Prospect. 2, Aaron, b. April 13, and d. May 1, '70. 3, Aaron, (2d), b. Aug. 7, '71; m. Hannah Young, p. March 20, '94; rem. & d. Belmont. 4, an infant, born and d. Nov. 13, '73. 5, Joseph, b. Oct. 26, '74, d. unm. March 17, 1836. 6, Elizabeth, b. Jan. 24, '77, died Nov. 24, '78. 7, James, (2d), b. May 17, '80; m. 1st, Sally Hawes of Union, April 10, 1804, 2d, Mary Spear; r. Th. and d. June 21, '37. 8, Cornelius, b. June 7, '82; mar. Mary Richardson of Portland, pub. Nov. 25, 1810; 2d, in Whitefield, rem. Lewiston, where he r. in 1830, and died in Washington, in 1849. 9, Betsey, b. June 4, '85; m. George Vose, rem. Castine, and d. April 3, 1841. 10, William, b. Dec. 20, '87; mar. 1st, Hannah Sidensberger of Wal, July 30, 1814, 2d, Nancy Snow, pub. May 28, 1819; rem. Illinois. 11, Judith, b. April 8, '90; m. James D. Wheaton; r. Th. and d. March 17, 1858.

James, (2d)'s ch. by 2d wife. 1, William (2d), b. Jan. 21, 1805; mar. Mary W. Colley, Dec. 18, '33, 2d, Louisa Austin, Jan. 26, '45;

r. Th., a farmer, &c. 2, Capt. James, (3d), b. May 25, '08; m. Mary Curtis of Cam., April 14, '39. 3, Capt Elkanah, b. April 24, 1809; mar. 1st, Sarah Ann Webb, Oct. 10, '39, 2d, Lucy A. Counce, June 24, '48; r. Th., and d. struck by a wave, Jan. 19, '52. 4, Capt. Samuel B., b. April 24, 1811; m. 1st, Margaret U. Spear, June 5, '36, 2d, Sarah Knight of Edgecomb, Oct., '51; was keeper of White Head light, 1853, &c.; rem. North Yarmouth. 5, Margaret, b. Sept. 8, '13, d. Dec 11, '37. 6, Capt. Harris, b. June 8, '16; m. Martha J. Mitchell, July 25, '41; r. Th., a merchant. 7, Washburn, born April 28, '18, d. at sea on passage from N. O., May 8, '42. 8, Mary, b. April 13, '20, d. Oct. 29, '41. 9, Henry S., b. Oct. 3, '22, died Oct. 22, '25. 10, Harriet B., b. Aug. 13, '24, d. Jan. 22, '26. 11, Sarah W., born July 20, '26; m. Edwin Thomas of Weymouth, Mass., Oct. 31, '50. 12, Harriet E., b. Nov. 28, '29, d. Nov. 14, '48. 13, Oliver B., born March 4, '33; removed.

Of Cornelius's ch. by 1st wife there were, 1, Absalom. By 2d wife, 2, Laura, m. Alexander D. Lees of Portland, Sept. 26, 1861; and probably others.

William (2d)'s ch. 1, Thomas W., b. Sept. 19, 1834; r. California. 2, Elkanah, (2d), b. Sept. 29, '35; r. Th., a mariner. 3, Edgar, b. March 14, '37; m. Antoinette Jordan, Oct. 15, '62; r. Th., a merchant. 4, Henrietta, b. Feb 9, '39, d. Aug. 25, '40.

Capt. Samuel B.'s ch. by 1st wife. 1, Eliza A. B., m. Richard B. Kelly of Rock., June 13, 1854. 2, Harris, (2d), d. in Portland. 3, Edwin. 4, Charles S., b. '46, d. April 2, '47. 5, Eugene. 6, Sarah. 7, Margaret. By 2d wife, one or more.

Capt. Elkanah's ch. Frances P. B., b. Aug. 2, & d. Aug. 20, 1840.

Capt. Harris's ch. Frederic W., b. April 28, 1844.

STACKPOLE, John, b. 1782, of a different family, c. from Berwick; settled in what is now S. Th.; m. Ruth Brown, Feb. 19, 1807, was a tailor, & d. March 9, '54. Their ch. 1, John M., b. Jan. 4, '08; m. & r. Nantucket; ret. Th. & d. Aug. 11, '44, on passage from N. O. as 1st mate of the *Montpelier*. 2, Nancy B., b. Sept. 24, '09; m. Rev. Kilborn Holt, Nov. 11, '44; r. Ashland, Mass. & d. Aug 29, '57. 3, Hanson, b. Sept. 3, '11; r. S. Th., fell from aloft at sea, & d. Dec. 12, '35. 4, Louise, b. March 20, '13; r. Boston. 5, Alden, b. April 17, '15; a mariner; rem. Australia. 6, Catharine, b. April 20, '16; m. Joshua Haynes of Boston, May, '56; r. Chicago, Ill. 7, Bethiah, or Bertha, b. March 4, '19; rem. '51. 8, Sarah S., b. Feb. 6, '21; r. Th. 9, Isabella P., b. April 26, '23, d. May 1, '40. 10, Lucy P., b. April 19, '25; m. Richard D. Starr; r. Th. 11, Helen M., b. March 18, '30; m. George I. Robinson; r. Th., and d. April 15, 1859. 12, Elizabeth Ann, b. April 14, '32; r. Th. 13, Amelia H., b. April 5, '36; mar. Samuel Whitcomb; r. Th. 14, Theodocia I., b. July 29, 1839; r. Th.

John M.'s ch. 1, Edward P., r. Nantucket. 2, Charles M. or A., r. Th., entered U. S. navy; 3, Henry C.; 4, Albert D.; all mostly r. Nantucket, mariners, the last a soldier in the army.

STAIRFORD, Patrick, c. from Dublin, Ireland, m. Martha Keating; r. S. Th.

STAHL; of this Waldoboro' family, whose ancestor c. from Germany, there c. here, 1, Solomon, b. ab. 1818, m. 1st, ———, 2d, Louisa (Graves) Noyes, June 20, '58; r. Rock., rem. Appleton. 2, Isaac, son of Charles of Warren, was b. in W. ab. '28; m. Mary E. Jackson, May 29, '53; r. Rock., a lime burner, soldier of 4th Me., &c.

Solomon's ch. 1, Mary J., b. April 14, 1838, d. April 17, '63. 2, Huldah M., b. ab. '40. 3, Warren, b. ab. '42. 4, Lorenzo, b. ab. '44. 5, Solomon, (2d), b. ab. '46. 6, Sarah, b. ab. '48. 7, George, b. ab. '50. 8, Angus, b. ab. '52. 9, Annie, b. ab. '55.

Isaac's ch. 1, Delphina, b. 1856, d. Jan. 22, '59. 2, Rosilla, b. ab. 1859.

STANLEY, Azariah, b. ab. 1814, in Vinalhaven; m. 1st, Almira Cooper, 2d, Almira A. Lindsey, Oct. 31, '47 ; r. Rock., a lumber dealer. Their ch. 1, Lucy A., b. June 20, 1841. 2, Hannah E., b. ab. '45. The mother d. Feb. 24, '46, aged 25. By 2d wife. 3, William, b. ab. 1854. 4, Caroline H., b. ab. '57. 5, Frances L., b. ab. '59. Of this name, also, Benjamin & Abigail Stanley were here, and had recorded their ch. Benjamin, b. Nov. 31, 1842.

STANTON, Nathan, b. ab. 1820, in R. I.; m. Adeline ——— ; r. S. Th., a stone cutter. Their ch. 1, Jonathan W., b. ab. 1848. 2, Nathan E., b. ab. '50. 3, Thomas U., b May, '52, d. Jan. 12, '62. 4, George W., b. ab. '54. 5, Elvira A., b. ab. '56. 6, Arementa F., b. ab. '59.

STAPLES, William B., b. ab. 1824, in Sedgwick, Me.; mar. Mary G. Glover, July 26, '46 ; r. Rock., a mariner. Their ch. 1, Isadore M., b. Nov. 4, '47, d. Dec. 23, '49. 2, Izora B., b. ab. '50. 3, Addie F., b. ab. '52. 4, Hattie M., b. ab. '59.

STAPLES, Edmund M., b. in Gorham, of English ancestors who settled at Piscataqua River, came to Th., April 23, 1820, carried on blacksmith business; mar. Ann M. Ulmer, Dec. 16, 1822, 2d, Mrs. Harriet (Staples) Dow of Biddeford; rem. Sept. 14, '54 with his family to Libertyville, Ill. Their ch. 1, Capt. Willard W., b. Oct. 24, 1823; m. Caroline A. Leeds of War, June 20, '49 ; r. Th. 2, Andrew U., b. June 1, '26, d. May 27, '27. 3, Andrew F., b. June 25, '28 ; r. California, since 1849. 4, Joseph U., b. Jan. 4, '32, d. June 15, '56, ? of yellow fever, mate of ship *Harriet* of Bath. 5, Stephen M., b. July 31, & d. Oct. 12, '34. 6, Edmund O., b. Oct. 26, '36 ; r. Illinois; m. Belinda Merrick, 1863. 7, Albert P., b. May 23, '39 ; r. Ca.. By 2d wife. 8, an infant who d. at same time with its mother.

Capt. Willard W.'s ch. 1, Willard, b. ab. 1850. 2, Frederic, b. ab. 1857.

STAPLES, Thomas A., b. ab. 1827, in Portland; mar. Lucy Ann Richards; r. Rock., a ship carpenter. Their ch. 1, Julia A., b. ab. 1842. Of this name, also, George A. Staples; r. Rock., corporal in 4th Me., &c.

STARR, Rev. Robert C., b. Feb., 1779, in Bridgewater, Mass.; m. 1st, Mary Eustace, 2d, Jane D. (McLellan) Barker of Bath; r. Jay & Warren; a joiner by trade, but became a minister of the Baptist faith at Friendship, Woolwich, New Gloucester, and other places; rem. in 1859 from Wayne to r. with his ch. in Th., where he d. Dec. 11, '62. His 2d wife d. in Th., May, 1860, a. 85. His ch. by 1st wife. 1, J. Bentley H., b. ab. 1803; m. Isabella Prince, June 24, '27; r. Th., a jeweller, &c., d. Nov 24, '36. 2, Almira, m. Capt. John Barker of Woolwich. 3, Col. George Augustus, b. in Warren, June 24, '08 ; m. 1st, Juliana Fales, p. June 2, '32, 2d, Catharine Healey, Feb. 13, '37 ; r. Th., a mason, militia officer, &c, senator, 1861, elected again, 1863, but d. at Portland, Oct. 7, '63. 4, James, b. Jan. 18, '12, d. in 1821. 5, Leander, b. in W., Jan. 16, '14; m. Clementine B. Keith,

p. Sept. 3, '34; r. Rock., a jeweller, & d. June 5, '54. 6, Esther E., b. in W., Aug. 8, '16; m. Oliver Robbins, (4th); r. Th. 7, Richard D., b. ab. '21; m. Lucy P. Stackpole, May 7, '46; r. Th., a cabinet maker and furniture dealer.

J. Bentley H.'s ch. 1, John B., b. Sept. 5, 1828; r. Spencer, Mass. 2, Mary I., b. Jan. 9, '30; mar. Erastus F. Jones of Spencer, June 9, '50. 3, Hezekiah P., b. Jan. 14, '32; r. Spencer.

Col. George Augustus's ch. 1, George R., b. June 15, 1835, died Jan. 19, '55. By 2d wife. 2, Joseph S., b. May 25, '38, d. May 22, '42. 3, Lucius C., b. June 29, '41; r. Th., a mariner.

Leander's ch. William R. K., b. Aug. 26, 1836; r. Rock.

Richard D.'s ch. 1, Helen Florence, b. Oct. 31, 1849. 2, Charles D., b. May 5, '53.

STARRETT; for this family in full, see Annals of Warren. Of the sons of Thomas, Charles, b. 1793, m. Sarah Cole of Wal., p. Sept. 30, 1815; learned tailor's trade of A. Ellison; r. Th. & d. Jan. 25, '57. Of the sons of John of W., who d. Jan. 18, '56, leaving a valuable legacy towards the erection of a Catholic church in Th.; 1, George F., b. ab. '14; m. Mary Hanley of Bristol; r. Th., a carpenter & joiner. 2, Edwin F., b. ab. '21; m. Cornelia Merrick; r. S. Th., a farmer, &c. Of the ch. of Lewis of W., who was b. May 2, 1783, & d. April 13, '63; 1, Dea. Cephas, b. ab. 1809; m. Mary Tolman, p. March 21, '37; r. Rock., long a successful ship builder. 2, Sanford, b. ab. 1813; m. Sarah Ghentner; r. Rock., also a ship builder. 4, Stephen B., b. ab. 1815; r. W. and Th., ship joiner and owner. 5, William E., b. ab. 1820; m. Mary A. Haveuer, Oct. 18, '43; r. Rock., a carpenter. 7, Catharine R., m. Rufus C. Thomas; r. Rock. Of the sons of Edward of W. 1, Oliver, b. ab. 1830; m. Emma ———; r. Rock., a carpenter.

Charles's ch. 1, Sarah W., b. Oct. 24, 1816; m. Isaac Hodgman; r. Th., and d. Aug. 2, '49. 2, Mary C., b. March 13, '18; m. Tileston H. Smith; r. Th., and d. July 3, '56. 3, Charles T., b. May 30, 1820; mar. Sarah S. Healey; r. Th., furniture dealer, &c., rem. Dedham, Mass. 4, John C., b. April 11, '23, d. July 17, '32. 5, David J., b. June 5, '25; m. Martha Ann Harrington, Nov. 14, '49; r. Th., bookseller, teacher, inventer of patent coal sifter, &c.

George F.'s ch. 1, Silas J., b. ab. 1846. 2, Agnes, b. 1849, died March 9, 1850. 3, William G., b. ab. '50. 4, Mary E, b. ab. 1852.

Edwin F.'s ch. 1, Alton L., b. Jan., 1850, died Dec. 31, '51. 2, Florence E., b. ab. '52. 3, George E., b. ab. '54. 4, Alice I., b. ab. '58. 5, Danville, b. ab. 1859.

Sanford's ch. 1, Edgar, b. April, 1847, d. Dec. 9, '52. 2, Mary A., b. ab. '52. 3, Cephas S., b. July '54, d. Oct. 4, '55. 4, Alice P., b. ab. 1858.

Oliver's ch. Addie, b. ab. 1858.

Charles T.'s ch. 1, Mary Augusta, b. July 9, 1845. 2, Maria W., b. Sept. 23, '47. 3, Charles H., b. March 27, '52, d. Oct. 11, '57. 4 & 5, twins, b. Nov. 26, '56, Adelia Flint, and Lizzie Stetson. 6, Adelaide C., b. ab. 1859.

David J.'s ch. 1, Anna T., b. ab. 1851. 2, Clara A., b. ab. '54. 3, Charles C., b. ab. '56. 4, William J., b. ab. 1859.

STEARNS, Ezekiel, came to Th., m. 1st, Jane Ulmer, July 24, '27, 2d, Elizabeth M. Osborn of Belfast, April 28, '33; r. Th., overseer in State Prison under Rose, and to end of Miller's term, as wardens;

rem. and d. in Levant. Stearns, Isaac, r. some time in old Th. or S. Th., lightkeeper, merchant, &c. Of this name, also, Albert I. Stearns of Rock., m. Emma L. Carpenter of Nashua, N. H., July 1, '63. Besides these, Mrs. Sarah Stearns, b. ab 1820, in Canada East; r. Rock., a widow. Her ch. 1, John, b. ab. 1841; r. Rock., a mariner. 2, Rachel, b. ab. 1845. 3, Nicholas, b. ab. 1848.

STERLING, John, b. ab. 1800, in Thomaston; mar. 1st, Freelove M. Howard, p. Feb. 22, '23, 2d, Mrs. Sarah (Calef) Blackington, Nov. 27, '34; r. Th., & d. June 18, '62. His ch. by 1st wife. 1, Margaret Josepha, b. ab. 1827; m. William Wasgatt; r. Rock. 2, Lavena, b. 1830, d. March 4, '64. 3, L. Adeliza, b. ab. 1833; m. Thomas Low; r. Rock. By 2d wife. 4, George, b. ab. 1835; mar. Lucy Moody, (who d. Oct. 25, '61); r. Th., soldier in 20th Me., &c. 5, Harriet, b. ab. 1837; mar. Benjamin F. Palmer; r. Th. 6, Ellis Gardner. 7, Hannah. 8, Delora. 9, Richard, r. Th., soldier of 30th Me., &c.

STETSON, William, (2d son of William of Scituate, who was the 3d son of Robert, who was the 2d son of Joseph of Scituate, who was the oldest son of Cornet Robert Stetson, one of the noted and valued members of Plymouth colony); was b. in Scituate ab. 1728; m. Mary Lincoln, July 19, '64; came to Th., mentioned Feb. 14, '87, as from Bristol, surveyor of lumber, 1794, &c. William's ch. 1, Caleb, b. 1765; m. Rebecca Cummings of St. Andrews, Sept. 9, '90; r. S. Th. & Robbinston, and d. Jan. 5, 1820. 2, Achsah, b. 1770; mar. Elisha Snow, (2d), Esq.,; r. S. Th., & d. May 16, '96. 3, Isaac. 4, Capt. Joseph, mar. Ann Battles; r. S. Th, d., lost at sea. 5, Samuel. 6, Stephen. 7, William, (2d). 8, Mercy, mar. Rev. Mr. Parker; rem. Lowell, Mass. 9, Lemuel.

Caleb's ch. 1, Hannah, b. Oct. 14, 1793; mar. Robert Huston of Bristol, Sept. 8, 1811, d. in Eastport, July 2, '33. 2, Mary, b. May 11, '95; m. Seth Gerry of Robbinston. 3, Achsah, b. July 4, '97; mar. William P. Lowe of Rob. 4, Elizabeth, b. June 16, '99; mar. Thomas Rogers of Eastport, and had Harriet L.; Thomas B.; and Jos. S. 5, Jane, b. May 2, '02; m. Nathan Hatch of Rob., 2d, Robert McFarland of Bloomfield. 6, Joseph Cummings, b. Oct. 14, '04; m. Harriet Brown; r. Cam. 7, Rebecca, b. June 22, '06; mar. Ichabod Stoddard of Perry. 8, Ann, b. April 18, '08; mar. Horatio Eaton of Cam, 2d, Casimir Lash; r. Th. 9, Moses P., b. March 23, '10; mar. Julia Kaler; r. Robbinston. 10, William, (3d), b. April 21, '13; m. Rachel G. Whitcomb of Eastport, May 15, '38, 2d, Sarah (Bugbee) Patten in Roxbury, Dec. 28, '59; c. to Th., where, since 1839, he has been a successful ship-builder, merchant, &c. 11, Samuel, (2d), born March 11, '14, d. young. 12, Leonard Cummings, b. March 17, '16; m. Sarah M. Sprague, Sept. 16, '40; r. Th., a merchant. 13, Sarah C., b. Oct. 17, '19; m. Augustus D. Merrick of Cam., Oct. 10, '47. The mother died Jan. 22, 1848.

William, (3d)'s ch. by 1st wife. 1, Joseph H., b. Sept. 27, 1839; r. Th., a mariner. 2, Louisa, b. Feb. 7, '41. 3, Elizabeth, b. Jan. 21, '44. 4, Charles Ward, b. Oct., '45, d. Dec. 4, '46. 5, Edward, b. '50, d. May 1, '62. The mother d. Dec. 9, '58. By 2d wife. 6, ———.

Leonard C.'s ch. 1, Henrietta, b. Nov. 26, 1840, d. Aug. 5, '59. 2, John Thomas, b. ab. '43; r. Th., entered the navy. 3, Mary Rebecca, b. ab. '45. 4, Harriet, b. ab. '47. Of this family, also, George Stetson, born Aug., 1797, (son of Gershom of Newcastle, the son of Matthew, (2d), the son of Matthew, (1st), the son of Benjamin, who was the son of Capt. Benjamin of Scituate, the 2d son of the Cornet);

m. Rosalinda Hatch; r. Washington, Me., rem. Rock., a carpenter. Of his 5 ch., there r. Rock., 1860, 1, George Franklin, b. ab. 1832; soldier in 4th Me., &c. 2, Hiram H., b. ab. 1840; m. Sarah I. ——— ; a mariner; had one ch. Florence.

STEVENS, Thomas, from vicinity of Providence; c. to Falmouth, & thence with his wife to Th., 1763. Their ch. 1, Nehemiah, mar. Nancy Blye, p. Aug. 20, 1789; r. & d. Th. 2, Thomas, (2d), b. ab. 1767; mar. Hannah Spear, p. June 23, 1788; r. Th., & d. March 22, 1830. 3, William d. ab. 1810. 4, Hannah, b. ab. 1777; m. Nathan Blackington; r. Rock. 5, Ephraim, b. ab. 1781; r. Rock. 6, Sarah, mar. Eben. Thompson of F., pub March 11, 1809. 7, Lucy Lewis, (adopted grand daughter), m. Samuel Kelloch of W. 8, Elizabeth. m. David Braley, 2d, Charles Wight; r. & d. Th.

Nehemiah's ch. 1, John, b. ab. 1794; mar. Eliza Tobey, Nov. 13, 1818, 2d, Mary Pease, 3d, Elsy Cummings; r. U. 2, James, b. 1796; soldier in 1812, &c.; m. Hannah Libbey, Jan. 13, 1825, 2d, Catharine H. Ladd, p. May 17, '44; r. W. 3, Dexter, lost at sea. 4, Harriet, b. Oct. 1, 1805; m. Constant Rankin; r. Rock.

Thomas, (2d)'s ch. 1, George W., b. July 26, 1793; mar. Rachel Vose of C., July 20, 1820; r. Th., and d. Feb. 12, '32. 2, Samuel, b. July 5, '95; m. Clarissa Hersey, p. Feb. 10, 1816, 2d, Catharine Hyler of C., Dec. 16, '17.

George W.'s ch. 1, Leonard S., b. Jan. 5, 1821; m. Mary E. Shaw, Dec. 15, '44, 2d, Laura E. Cookson, Oct. 3, '58; r. Rock., rem.? 2, John V., b July 11, '23, d. Aug. 1, '42. 3, Mary V., b. May 3, '25; m. George Campbell; r. Rock. 4, George S., b. Nov. 22, '29.

STEVENS, William, whose father was killed in the battle of Lexington; c. from Concord, N. H.; m. Sally Stevens; was a cooper by trade, r. Th., & d. March 29, 1826, aged 60. Their ch. 1, Charles, m. Hannah Tracy, Dec. 30, 1810; r. Gouldsboro'. 2, Nathaniel, m. Bathsheba Martin, p. Nov. 20, '18; r. Th., & d May, '28. 3, William K., b. ab. 1797; m Ann F. Bennet, Dec. 28, '20; r. Th. 4, Mary, mar. Henry Kenneston; r. Th. 5, Hiram K., b. ab. 1799; mar. 1st, Margaret Martin of Bristol, Dec. 11, '23, 2d, Eliza B. (Martin) Munroe, p. July 11, '46; r. Rock., a teamster, &c. 6, James, m. 1st, Betsey Beters, Nov., 1838, 2d, Mary (Cooper) Knights, Feb. 11, '46; r. Th. 7, Madison, b. 1800; m. Hannah Marr of Wash.; r. Th., and d. Nov. 2, '51.

Nathaniel's ch. 1, Eliza, m Felix Moran; r. Rock. 2, John.

William K.'s ch. 1, (adopted), John M., b. 1824, d. Aug. 1, '42. 2, Henrietta, b. ab. '39; m. William F. Gay; r. Th.

Hiram's ch. 1, Mary F., b. Dec. 4, 1824; m. John Reading; rem. Mass. 2, Ludwig, b. Feb. 3, '27; m Mary A. Brown, April 23, '53; r. Rock., a soldier in U. S. Army. 3, Madison, (2d), mar. Elizabeth Wagner of N. B., Dec., 1850; r. Rock., a corporal in 4th Me., killed Sept. 1, '62, near Centreville, Va. 4, Wallace, m. Sarah J. Gibson; r. Rock. 5, Hiram, (2d), m. Ann C. Long, July 11, '57; r. Rock., soldier of 4th Me., d. Oct. 24, '62.

James's ch by 2d wife. Helen. The mother d. May 17, '52, a. 37.

Madison's ch. 1, William C ; r. California. 2, Ann, b. Sept. 21, 1834; mar. William Morse; r. Th. 3, Charles M., b. April 2, '37; m. Sarah (Ghentner) KcKenny, July 14, '59; r. Th. 4, Solomon, b. March 4, '39; r. Th., a mariner. The mother d. Aug. 10, 1861.

Ludwig's ch. 1, William P., b. ab. 1853. 2, Frank L., b. ab. '56.

Madison, (2d)'s ch. Elsie M., b. ab. 1852.
Wallace's ch. George.
Hiram, (2d)'s ch. Margaret, b. Dec., 1859.

STEVENS, Isaac, of Scottish descent, b. in Wells in 1776; m. Lois, dau. of Nathaniel Low of English descent, r. & d. Waterville. Of their ch. 1, Hermon, Esq., b. April, 1807, in Waterville; graduate Waterville Coll., 1828; studied law with Hon. Timothy Boutelle of Waterville; c. hither in Sept., 1831, & r. Rock., a counsellor at law.

STEVENS; of this Lincolnville family, 2 brothers c. to this place. 1, George A., b. ab. 1818, in Linc.; mar. Mary U. Tyler; r. Rock., a joiner, &c. 2, Horatio G., b. ab. 1822; m. Amelia E. Jenson; r. R., a joiner; rem. Belfast, with his ch., Annie M., & George W.

George A.'s ch. 1, Helen A., b. Sept., 1843, d. March 3, '51. 2, Emma C., b. '45, d. Aug. 22, '54. 3, Lucy W., b. ab. '48. 4, Kate H., b. ab. '53. 5, F. Roscoe, b. Feb., '55, d. Sept. 4, '57. 6, Edgar, b. ab. '58.

STEVENS, Albert T., b. in Thorndike, Jan. 10, 1822; m. Bethia S. Hubbard, Dec. 24, '44, 2d, Mary E. (Cilley) Mitchell, April 22, '52; r. Rock., since Oct., '52, a carpenter. Their ch. 1, Charles A., b. Sept. 5, '47, d. Oct. 5, '49. 2, Henry M., b. July 25, '49. By 2d wife. 3, Mary G., b. Jan. 22, '48. 4, Frank A., b. May 17, '60, died Sept. 29, '61. 5, Robert F., b. Oct. 8, '62. Of this name, also, George W. Stevens, b. June, 1804; came from Machias; ? mar. Deborah T. ——; r. Rock., & d. Jan. 10, '61. Their ch. 1, Ellery G., b. ab. 1840; r. R., a teamster, soldier in 4th Me., &c. 2, Horace, b. ab '47.

STEWART, Capt. Thomas, b. ab. 1808, in Bristol; came here from Belfast; m. Olive H. Tolman; r. Rock. Their ch. 1, Thomas F., b. ab. 1841. 2, Jacob H. R., b. ab. 1850.

STIMPSON, Brown, b. in Reading, Mass., ab. 1788; m. Eliza K. Sawyer; came to Th. & r. Mill River, an apothecary, manufacturer of cordials, the celebrated Stimpson's Pills, &c., d. Aug. 23, 1838. Their ch. 1, Eliza Kidston, b. Aug. 12, 1812; r. Th. 2, Adam Orr, born Aug. 28, '14; drowned on his way home from school, Feb. 17, '21. 3, Capt. Charles Ward, b. May 20, '17; m. Rachel J. Field, Nov. 14, '44, 2d, Loretta Fish, Sept. 5, '53; r. Th. 4, Caroline Knox, b. Nov. 27, '19; m. Mr. Chipman of Halifax, N. S.; r. Montreal. 5, Rachel, b. Nov. 26, '21; d. young. 6, James E., b. ab. 1825; m. Sarah Robinson of Halifax; r. Th., an overseer in State Prison, &c. 7, William, r. Halifax, a merchant.

Capt. Charles W.'s ch. by 1st wife. 1, Mary Caroline, d. young. The mother d. Nov. 27, '51. By 2d wife. 2, Charles W., (2d), b. ab. '55. 3, Etta, b. ab. '59.

James E.'s ch. 1, William, b. ab. 1850. 2, Mary, b. ab. '53. 3, Minnie, b. ab. '60.

STINSON; of this Deer Isle family, as it is believed, Mrs. Olive S., r. Rock., a widow. Her ch. George W., b. ab. 1849.

STODDARD, George L., b. ab. 1827 in Perry, Me., mar. Emeline M. Gerry, Sept. 28, '52; r. Th., a carpenter; and d. June 22, 1863. Their ch. Caroline E., b. ab. 1858.

STONE, Micah, son of Abel and grandson of Micah of Framingham, Mass., b. in 1782; c. to Th. and W., a cabinet maker; m. Olive Gleason, of U., Oct. 7, 1804; ret. Framingham, where he d. ab. 1860.

Their ch. b. at W. 1, George, b Nov. 15, 1806; m. Mrs. Sarah

Hills, May 13, '35; r. Th., rem. Mass. 2, Henry, b. Sept. 22, 1808; rem. Framingham, or some part of Mass. 3, John Y., born Feb. 26, '10; m. Deborah Simonton, Nov. 2, '37; r. Th., and d. May 27, '53. 4, an infant, d. 3 days old, March 1, 1812.

John Y's ch. 1, Edwin A., b. Aug. 5, 1838, d. June 13, '39. 2, Mary P., b. July 4, '40. 3, Olive R., b. Nov. 20, '42. 4, Alice D., b. ab. '46. 5, John O., b. ab. '49. 6, Matilda, b. ab. '51. 7, Geo. H., b. ab. 1853.

STONE, James D., b. 1807, son of Allen and Hannah (Bennet) Stone, m. Eliza, daughter of John Comery; c. from Union, Nov., '51; r. Th. Their ch. 1, Amanda, b. May 1, 1833; m. Stephen Pettegrew; r. Lowell, d. Th. 2, Caroline F., b. March 11, '35; m. Geo. Bissell; r. Lowell and Vermont. 3, Orrin E., b. March 2, '37; r. Th., a carpenter. 4, Melzar John, b. Nov. 17, '39, died Sept. 29, '62. 5, Andrew K., b. Aug. 1, '41, a mariner. 6, Sarah M., born Feb. 7, '43. 7, Clara E., b. March 19, '46. 8, Gilman, b. March 10, '48. Of this name, also, Seth Stone, c. from Union; m. Clarissa or Rachel Simonton of Cam., r. in Th. a time, and rem. Cam. Their ch. 1, Franklin, b. June 21, 1838, r. Th., or Cam., a mariner. 2, Frederic, born Sept. 19, 1840.

STORY, George W., c. from Camden; m. Harriet W. Brewster; r. Rock., a teamster, &c. Their ch. Frank Bentley, b. June 15, '60.

STOVER, Caleb, of Long Cove, St. George; m. a Clark of Clark's Is., and was living in Rock. in 1861 or '2. Christopher, a brother, m. Pamelia ———; r. Rock., rem. and d. S. Th., or St. G.

Of Caleb's ch. 1, Capt. James, b. ab. 1810; m. Catharine Hall; r. Rock. & d. Jan. 2, '54. And, perhaps also, 2, Caleb, (2d), who was b. in St. George; m. Maria Snow; r. & d. Rock.

Christopher's ch. 1, John G., b. Oct. 6, 1821; m. Mary A. Gregory, April 21, '44; r. Rock. & d. Nov. 27, '52; 2, Isabel G., b. May 2, 1824; 3, Pamelia J., b. Dec. 4, '26; 4, Clarissa H., b. Oct. 1, '29; 5, Archibald H., b. Feb. 9, '31; mar. Lucy A. Taylor of Lewiston, Sept. 2, '55; 6, Mary E., b. Oct. 6, '34; 7, Jesse, b. Jan. 25, '37; 8, Charles W., b. July 25, '39; 9, William M., born April 16, '42; all probably removed.

Capt. James's ch. 1, James A., born June 19, 1837; mar. Elethea Skinner; r. Rock., a lime burner, &c. 2, Charles, b. Oct. 7, 1840, d. Sept. 19, '51. 3, Charles, b. Oct. 15, 1842.

Caleb, (2d)'s ch. 1, Ella, b. ab. 1851. 2, Elizabeth, b. ab. 1856.

John G.'s ch. 1, Lilias. 2, Agnes A.

James A.'s ch. 1, Henry, b. ab. 1858. 2, Alden, b. ab. '60. Of this name, also, Charles Stover, m. Catharine Seavey, Oct. 31, 1847; r. Rock. & d. April 3, '54. Andrew W. Stover, m. Abby M. Wiggin, p. Oct. 5, '61; r. S. Th., sergeant in 20th Me. reg., d. at N. York, July 1, '64, of wounds received at Petersburg, Va. And George Stover, b. ab. '33, m. Hattie ———; r. Rock., a teamster.

STOWE, Ephraim, m. Mary Ann Burns, Nov. 24, 1835; r. here, and had 3 ch. recorded, viz.: 1, Charles W., b. Dec. 3, 1836; 2, Ephraim H., b. Sept. 28, '38; 3, John B., b. Nov. 21, '40; but has probably rem.

STRAUSS, Henry, came from Lyons, France, grad. at the Paris University; mar. Fannie Kaufman; has been a tutor of modern languages, now merchant and peddler; r. Rock. Their ch. Isaac M., b. Sept. 17, 1861.

STROUT, Lemuel, b. ab. 1802, in Cape Elizabeth; mar. Louisa P. Cotton of Falmouth; r. Th., a boat builder, &c. Their ch. 1, Capt. James Charles, grad. Bowd. Coll., 1857, officer in 16th Me., &c. 2, Abby Ellen, b. June 21, '37, d. April 1, '54. 3, Alfred C., b. ab. '40; sergeant in 1st Me. Cavalry. 4, Sarah L., b. ab. '43.

STUDLEY, Pelatiah, b. ab. 1833, in Windsor; m. Harriet Walker, Jan. 13, '57; r. Th., a trader, farmer, &c. George, his brother, came since 1860, & r. Rock. Pelatiah's ch. 1, Isadore, b. ab. 1857. Of this name, also, Augustus & Benjamin C. Studley; r. Rock., soldiers of 4th Me., &c. And probably others.

SUTHERLAND, Alexander, b. ab. 1832, in Scotland; as was Jane, his wife, in N. S.; r. S. Th., a stone cutter. Their ch. 1, William, b. ab. 1860. Of this name, also, Walter Sutherland; r. Rock., soldier of 4th Me., &c.

SULLIVAN, Timothy, b. ab. 1810, in Ireland; as was Ellen, his wife; r. Rock. Their ch. 1, Jeremiah, b. ab. 1841; r. Rock., soldier of 4th Me., &c. 2, Timothy, (3d), b. ab. '44. 3, Margaret, b. ab. '48. 4, James, b. ab. '50, in Ireland. 5, Thomas, b. ab. '57, in America. Of this name, also, Patrick Sullivan, came from county of Waterford, Ireland; m. Jane Brady of Th., p. Aug. 18, 1851. Timothy Sullivan, (2d), b. ab. 1820; c. with wife Ellen from Ireland; r. Rock. and d. very suddenly, Feb. 23, '63. Daniel Sullivan, b. ab. 1825, in Ireland; m. Hannah ———; r. Rock. Jeremiah Sullivan, b. in Ireland ab. 1829; mar. Ann Cronan, p. June 7, '50; r. Rock. Michael Sullivan, b. ab. 1825, in Ireland, & Bridget, his wife; r. Rock. Their ch. 1, Thomas, b. ab. 1854. 2, Mary, b. ab. '58.

Timothy, (2d)'s ch. 1, Mary, b. ab. 1856. 2, Hannah, b. ab. '57. 3, Ellen, b. ab. '59.

Daniel's ch. 1, Mary, b. ab. 1851. 2, John, b. ab. '55. 3, Anna, b. ab. '57. 4, James, b. ab. '59.

Jeremiah's ch. 1, John, b. ab. 1851. 2, Edward, b. ab. '53. 3, William, b. ab. '56. 4, Jeremiah, (2d), b. ab. '59.

SUMNER, Capt. Seth, m. Hannah Hall, July 1, 1819; b. r. & d. in Warren. Their ch. 1, Rufus C., m. Mary C. Jordan, Dec., 1860; r. Th., a clerk, &c. 2, Capt. David H., m. Sarah F. Gerrish, Nov. 30, 1854; r. Th., ret. War., sailing master in navy, &c. 3, Francis M., b. ab. 1824; mar. Lucy J. Benner of Wal., Sept. 15, '56; r. Th., a merchant.

Capt. David H.'s ch. 1, David C., b. ab. 1856. 2, Benjamin G., b. ab. '59.

Francis M.'s ch. 1, Elizabeth F., b. ab. 1857. 2, Rufus M., b. ab. 1859.

SUMNER, Maynard, b. ab. 1822, in Dedham, Mass., son of Seth Sumner of Stoughton, Mass.; r. Rock., Secretary Ins. Company, &c.

SWEENEY; of this name, 1, Owen, b. ab. 1820, in Ireland; as was Margaret, his wife, in 1827, but who d. May 25, '62; r. Rock. 2, Francis, b. ab. 1825, in Ireland; m. Ellen Sharrow; r. Rock. 3, James, b. ab. 1825, in Ireland, as was Catharine, his wife, in New Brunswick; r. Rock.

Owen's ch. 1, Patrick, b. ab 1847. 2, John, b. ab. '51. 3, Mary A., b. ab. '55.

Francis's ch. 1, William, b. ab. 1852. 2, Francis, (2d), b. ab. '54. 3, Mary, b. ab. '56. 4, James, (2d), b. ab. '58. 5, Elizabeth, b. '60.

James's ch. Francis J., b. ab. 1859.

SWEETLAND, Samuel, came from New Meadows, m. 1st, ? ——— Gay of F., 2d, Mrs. Elizabeth, widow of Lieut. J. Mathews, Jan. 7, 1788; r. & d. Wal. His ch. 1, David, m. 2d, Maria (Jameson) Rivers; r. S. Th., rem. Farmington. 2, James, b. May, 1774; mar. 1st, Eunice Post, p. Sept. 24, 1801, 2d, Hannah (Palmer) White, Dec. 18, '28; r. S. Th., and d. Sept. 26, '51. 3, Samuel, (2d), rem. west. 4, John, went to sea & was never heard from. By 2d wife. 5, Charles, m. & r. on homestead in Waldoboro'.

Of David's ch. 1, Eben, b. ab. 1808; m. Hannah Jameson, Oct. 13, '39; r. S. Th., a farmer. 2, Joseph, b. ab. 1814; m. 1st, Charity McAllister, 2d, Margaret Jameson, Sept. 28, '34; r. Rock., a mariner.

James's ch. 1, Julia Ann, b. ab. 1802; m. Samuel P. Sherwell; r. S. Th. & d. Aug., '26. 2, James, (2d), b. ab. 1806; m. Kate Martin, March 7, '38; r. S. Th., a shipbuilder. 3, Archibald C., b. ab. '08; m. Elizabeth Sawen of W., July 22, '38; r. Rock. & d. May 23, '42. 4, Kate, m. Col. Arch. McKellar; r. S. Th. & d. in '50. 5, Matilda, m. Capt. Dennis Pillsbury; r. S. Th. & d. Oct. 21, '52. 6, Oliver, b. ab. '23; m. Sarah E Sleeper, Dec. 29, '46; r. S. Th., a shipwright. By 2d wife. 7, Alden W., mar. Mary E. Worth, April 24, '51; r. China. 8, Abner P., b. ab. '34; m. 1st, Abby E. Gerry, 2d, Achsa B. Larrabee, April 29, '61; r. Rock., a cigar manufacturer.

Joseph's ch. 1, Frederic S., b. ab. 1830; m. Mary L. Spalding, June 29, '52; r. Rock., a mariner, &c. 2, Celia A., b. Aug. 22, '39; r. Rock. 3, Olive F., b. Sept. 17, '42. 4, Judson J., b. ab. '46.

James, (2d)'s ch. 1, Henry S., b. Dec. 8, 1838; m. Amanda H. Thomas of Linc., July 3, '59; r. S. Th., a farmer. 2, Iraette, b. Oct. 2, '41; r. S. Th. 3, Archibald, (2d), b. ab. '44. 4, Cleora, b. ab. '56.

Abner P.'s ch. by 1st wife. Willard, b. May & d. Aug. 20, 1859.

Frederic S.'s ch. 1, Frederic H., b. ab. 1853. 2, Charles A.

Henry S's ch. Helen Eva.

SWEETLAND, Robert L., b. ab. 1821, c. from Searsmont, a grandson of Stephen of Hope; m. Elizabeth E. Whitten; r. Rock., a mariner. Their ch. 1, Charles E., b. ab. 1839. 2, Albro L., b. May 7, '44, d. Nov. 15, '50. 3, Mary E., b. ab. '49. 4, Frederic A., b. ab. '55.

SWEETZER, Beza, b. ab. 1807, in Gray, Me.; c. to this place, m. Nancy W. Snow, March 12, '35; r. Rock., a stone mason, &c. John, an older brother, m. Sarah W. Snow, Sept. 9, '21; rem. Wisconsin. Joel, b. '14, m. Roxalana Buxton, also came here and d. of consumption, Jan., 1840.

Beza's ch. 1, Charles M., b. ab. 1840. 2, Harvey A., b. ab. '55.

SWETT, or Sweat, Ebenezer, m. Mary Perry, Aug. 25, 1830, was here some years, but rem. Muscatine, Iowa. Their ch. 1, Mary E., b. June 25, 1831; m. Nehemiah J. Kelly, March 10, '50. 2, Avis, b. Oct. 4, '37; 3, Asbury C., b. July 2, '42; all probably rem.

SWETT, John D., mar. Clarissa L. Torrey, Sept. 22, 1839; r. Th., built on Lowell St., was a joiner and d. Nov. 26, '58. Their ch. 1, George W., b. ab. 1844. 2, Charles Otis, b. Dec. 7, '49, d. Sept. 22, '50. 3, Maria W., b. ab. 1853.

SWETT, Lorenzo, of a different family, b. ab. 1809, in Buckfield; m. Celestia H. Case; was engaged in powder mills, in Camden, rem. and r. Th., at Meadows. Their ch. 1, Frances Isadore, b. ab. 1837; m. Alfred Gay; r. Th. 2, Isabelle, b. ab. '42. 3 Adelaide, b. about '44. 4, Ella, b. ab. 1853.

SWIFT, Joseph and Abigail were here early, and had recorded their ch. 1, Catharine E., b. Oct. 3, 1824. 2, William J. S., b. May 28, '26 ; 3, Mary F., b. July 13, '28, d. Oct. 20, '30. 4, Charles F., b. July 21, '41 ; probably removed.

SWIFT, Zipha, b. at Foxboro', 1770 ; r. Canton, c. to Cush. 1800, thence to War. ; m. Deborah Morton ; and d. Jan. 10, 1829. Their ch. 1, Lyman, b. March 30, 1804 ; m. Eliz. Moore, July 5, '29, 2d, Maria Thomas, '51 ; r. Th. 2, Joshua, b. Feb. 1, '06 ; mar. Abigail (Robinson) Hanson, p. June 26, '32 ; r. Rock., a truckman. 3, Asenath, m. Joseph Keith ; r. Th. 4, Jirah, or Jairah, b. Jan. 18, '09 ; m. Mary Lewis, Oct. 29, '47 ; (who d. June 7, '63,) r. Th. 5, William, b. Aug. 10, '12 ; m. and r. Belfast. 6, Jane M., b. Sept. 1, '14 ; mar. Charles Hilt of St. George, Nov. 29, '40. 7, Chauncy, mar. and r Frankfort. 8, Adam Kinsley, b. June 12, '19 ; m. Mary A. W. Copeland, Nov. 14, '44 ; 2d, ——— Morse, r. Th. 9, Elizabeth, m. Milton Stevens, of Dixmont. 10, Lavinia W., mar. Francis R. Barlow ; r. Rockland.

Lyman's ch. 1, Charles, killed in Boston. By 2d wife. 2, William, b. ab. 1850. 3, Jason, b. ab. '52. 4, Frederic, b. ab. '57. 5, Benjamin, b. ab. 1860.

Joshua's ch. 1, Joshua E , mar. Mary J. Lysler ; r. Brooklyn, N. Y. 2, Asenath A., m. Seth Crane, Nov. 10, '55, r. War. 3, Henrietta, b. ab. '35 ; m. George H. McKenney ; r. Rock. 4, Harriet F., b ab. '39, r. Rockland.

Jirah's ch. (adopted,) Josephine, b. ab. 1852.

Ad. Kinsley's ch. 1, Faustina, b. ab. 1847. 2, Rose, b. ab. 1852. 3, Vesper, b. ab. 1859.

SYLVESTER, Chas. A., Esq., b. ab. 1797, in Winchendon, Mass. ; m. 1st, Judith Horr, 2d, Martha B. Stevens, p. May 31, 1852 ; r. Rock., attorney at law, dept. sheriff, 1846, &c.• His ch. by 1st wife. 1, Capt. Charles A., (2d), b. ab. 1822 ; m. Lucinda D. Gregory, Feb. 20, '49 ; r. Rock. 2, Evelina. 3, Samantha O., m. 1st, Amos H. Crockett, 2d, Hon. Joseph Farwell ; r. Rock. 3, E. Angenette, m. Samuel H. Tyler ; r. Rock. 4, Lucy Ann, m. F. L. Jones ; r. Rock. The mother d. April 29, 1850, a. 55.

Capt. Charles A.'s ch. 1, George A., b. about 1850. 2, Nathaniel G., b. ab. '51. 3, Jessie, d. Jan. 4, '54. 4, Charles E., b. ab. '54. 5, Mary, b. ab. '56. 6, Joseph F.

SYLVESTER, Asa, b. ab. 1824, son of Asa of Freedom ; m. Martha Drake of Albion ; r. Rock., a confectioner. Their ch. 1, Arthur, b. ab. '53. 2, William D., b. Nov. 23, 1859, d. Sept. 7, '60. Of this family, also, Roscoe G. Sylvester, b. ab. 1836, son of Enoch of Freedom ; m. Helen M. Johnson ; r. Rock., a harness maker. Of their ch. Sarah F., b. Aug. and d. Oct. 9, 1860.

TALBOT, Charles, b. ab. 1820, in Ireland ; mar. Celia Henery, p. Aug. 30, '55 ; r. Th. Their ch. 1, a daughter, b. 1857, drowned July, 1859. 2, Mary R., b. ab. 1859.

TAPPAN, Moses, b. ab. 1821 ; m. Elsie ——— ; r. Rock., a mariner, 1860, since rem. Their ch. 1, Laura E., b. ab. 1847. 2, Etta F., b. ab. '53.

TARBOX, James, b. in Biddeford, Me., 1797 ; learned the potter's trade of John Aulds of that place ; c. to Th. in 1819 ; m. 1st, Elizabeth Wormell, Jan. 2, 1823, 2d, Mrs. Angeretta (Lincoln) Corbitt,

Aug., 1854; r. Th. His ch. by 1st wife. 1, James F., b. Dec. 4, 1823; mar. Harriet Flint of Rock., Sept. 4, '47; r. Th. 2, George William, b. Sept. 2, '25; m. Sarah Clapp of Newcastle, July 2, '55; r. Portland. 3 & 4, twins, b. Jan. 20, '28; Caroline, mar. William T. Fowler of Th.; r. Salem, Mass., & Cornelia, m. Henry E. Buckmar of Belfast, June 27, '64.

James F.'s ch. Elizabeth, b. ab. 1850.

TARR, Abraham, b. in Whitefield, Me.; r. here a time with Rebecca, his wife; rem. Waldoboro'. Calvin, his brother, m. Emeline W. ——— ; r. Rock., and d. Oct. 14, 1856.

Abraham's ch. 1, Edward, b. April 16, 1839; 2, Elizabeth, b. Feb. 25, '41; probably rem.

Calvin's ch. 1, Albert H., b. Dec. 4, 1839; mar. Lydia Ooster, p. Aug. 2, '59; r. Rock., sergeant in 2d Me., since in navy. 2, Nancy R., b. Aug. 1, '42. 3, Oren R., b. Oct. 30, '43, d. May 13, '55. 4, Caroline A., b. 1852, d. May 28, '57.

TATE, Capt. Thomas T., m. and r. Salem, Mass. Of his sons. 1, Capt. William, b. April, 1792; m. Mary ———; r. Rock., but rem. Newburyport, where he d. May 25, 1857. 2, George C., m. Caroline Holmes, pub. April 23, '31; r. Rock., but probably rem. 3, Capt. Thomas T., (2d), b. ab. 1814; mar. 1st, Catharine (Ulmer) Hanaky, Oct. 3, '47, 2d, Martha A. Knights, March 19, '54; r. Rock.

Capt. William's ch. 1, William Pierce, b. Sept., 1826, d. April 22, '48. 2, Sarah W., b. Dec. 10, '30. 3, Albert W., b. Jan. 24, '34, d. Sept. 11, '42. 4, Hannah E., b. Nov. 23, '35; probably rem.

George C.'s ch. 1, George B., b. May 19, & d. Aug. 6, 1837. 2, Delia S., b. Jan. 21, '40; m. B. W. Caryl of San Francisco, Sept. 19, '57. 3, George N., b. May 28, '42.

Capt. Thomas T.'s ch. George T., b. ab. 1855.

TAYLOR, Dudley H., b. ab. 1797, in Gardiner, Me.; mar. Bertha W. Taylor; r. Rock. Their ch. 1, Gates, b. ab. 1829, in Shelburn, N. H.; m. Abigail Bowdoin; r. Rock. 2, Solomon, b. ab. 1831, in Gardiner; m. Sophia Boynton; r. Rock., soldier in 19th Me., &c. 3, George F., b. ab. 1835, in G.; m. Elizabeth Boynton; r. Rock., soldier in 4th Me. 4, Simeon, b. in G. ab. 1839; m. Elizabeth Lint; r. Rock., a mariner, soldier of 4th Me., &c.

Solomon's ch. 1, Allena F., b. ab. 1851. 2, Elizabeth A., b. ab. '55. 3, Wilbert J., b. June, 1857, d. Oct. 28, '62.

Of George F.'s ch. 1, Matilda, b. June, 1859, d. Aug. 21, '60. Of this name, also, Ellithan Taylor, c. to r. here in 1807; m. Mary Rankin, Feb. 1, '10; after a time rem. Albion; had recorded here their ch. Joseph, b. Aug. 13, 1810. Robert H. Taylor, also, b. ab. 1821, in Ireland; mar. Abby R. Higgens, March 5, '59; r. S. Th., a stone cutter. Their ch. 1, John, b. ab. 1844. 2, Francis, b. '46. 3, Robert H., b. ab. '54. Of this name, also, Simon P. Taylor; r. Rock., soldier of 4th Me., &c.

THAYER, Samuel, came from Vinalhaven to S. Th.; mar. Ruth Haskell, Dec. 16, 1818; r. Ash Point, a mariner, & d. Sept. 10, '29. Their ch. 1, Clementine, b. Oct. 22, 1819, d. Sept. 2, '30. 2, Capt. John, b. Jan. 16, '21; m. Eliza Paulina Eckell, Oct. 11, '46; r. Rock. 3, Capt. Samuel, (2d), b. Aug. 22, '23; m. 1st, Deborah ———, 2d, Lucinda S. Bridges, Sept. 26, '47; r. S. Th. 4, David, b. Aug. 9, '25; m. Marietta Farr, July 22, '52; r. S. Th.? 5 and 6, twins, b.

Nov. 1, '28, Susan and Sylvia, both d. Sept. 10, '29. 7, Mary Jane, b. Nov. 22, '29; m. John Maddocks of U., Jan. 17, '47.

Capt. John's ch. 1, Josephine A., b. ab. '50. 2, Marion, b. ab. '54.

Capt. Samuel's ch. 1, Malinda, b. May 14, 1842. By 2d wife. 2, Alphonso, b. ab. '50. 3, Alforetta, b. Nov. 28, '51, d. May 11, '53. 4, E. Eugene, b. ab. '56. 5, Annette, b. ab. '58.

THACHER, Rev. Thomas, (whose father, Peter, was minister of Salisbury in England,) c. to New England, at the age of 15, with his uncle Anthony, became minister of the church in Weymouth, 1644, and, in 1669, of the Old South church in Boston; had sons, 1, Thomas, d. young. 2, Rev. Peter, settled in Milton; rem. & probably d. in England. 3, Rev. Ralph, minister of Chilmark, Mass.; purchased land in 1706, & rem. in 1714, to Lebanon in Ct., where he had given farms to his three sons, Thomas, Ralph & Peter. Peter's ch. 1, Rodolphus, m. & r. Lebanon; d. a. 46, leaving two orphan ch. 2, Abigail, b. in 1723, adopted her elder brother's orphans, devoted her little property to their support & the education of the son in college; r. with him after his marriage, beloved & revered, & d. at Kennebunk, Me., in 1813, a. 90. 3, Hon. Josiah of Gorham, Me. Perhaps others.

Rodolphus's ch. 1, Mary, b. ab. 1776, d. before 1795. 2, Hon. Stephen, b. in 1774, an orphan when 14 yrs. old, and adopted by his aunt, as before stated; grad. Yale coll. 1795; stud. theology with Rev. Dr. Howard of Springfield; was a teacher there, at Suffield, Ct., & at Beverly, Mass., where he preached in 1798 & 9, afterwards in Barnstable; rem. Kennebunk, engaged in trade, was a warm supporter of Pres. Jefferson, was Judge of Probate, 1807, to '18, & postmaster, '10 to '18, when he was appointed Collector of Passamaquoddy district, rem. to Lubec, was twice reappointed, holding the office 12 years; was an indefatigable classical student even to the last year of his life; deeply religious in youth, as a Calvinist, & equally so as a Unitarian, to life's close; public spirited, throwing the whole weight of his energetic nature into the cause of education, improved highway & mail & postal systems, & of progress in morals, manners, temperance, & freedom; m. in 1804, Harriet, dau. of Col. Esaias Preble of York; rem. in 1856, to Rock., where he r. & d. Feb. 19, 1859.

Hon. Stephen's ch. 1, George Washington, Esq., b. in 1805; r. Rock., counsellor at law, d. of consumption, Nov. 19, '64. 2, 3, & 4, a son & daus., d. in infancy. 5, Peter, Esq., b. ab. '11, grad. Bowd. Coll., 1831; m. Margaret Louisa, dau. of Judge Barrett Potter, of Portland; r. Rock., attorney at law, member of Me. Hist. Society, &c. 6, Mary, mar. William B. Smith, of Machias, and d. at that place in 1838. 7, Emily Bliss, m. Edmund A. Souder; r. Philadelphia. 8, Joseph Storer, d. at Lubec, a. 2 yrs. 9, Ralph Partridge Preble, d. at Lubec, a. 7 yrs. 10, Harriet, m. Capt. Edward Mellus of Salem, Mass, (who d. in Foo Choo, China, 1856, when in command of steamship *Antelope*) and d. at Lubec, 1855, leaving one son, Edward Lindon Mellus, who r. Rock. 11, Priscilla Josephine, d. at Lubec, a. 20 yrs. 12, Joseph Anderson, m. Nancy Wilder; r. Zambrota, Min., a State senator, commissioner of enrolment in 1st Cong. District. 13, Ralph Partridge Emilius, r. Rock., counsellor at law. 14, Abigail Lindon.

Peter, Esq.'s ch. 1, Francis S., b. ab. 1842, ent. Bowd. Coll. 1862, but left on account of ill health and r. Minnesota. 2, Mary P., b. ab. '44. 3, Stephen, (2d), b. ab. '46. 4, Annie B., b. ab. '48. 5, Geo. W., (2d), b. ab. '50. 6, Harriet P., b. ab. '52. 7, Margaret J., b. ab. '54. 8, Henry W. L., b. ab. 1858.

THATCHER, Samuel, (a branch, probably, of the preceding family, though spelling the name differently) admitted freeman, 1642, in Watertown, Mass., where he was selectman, deacon, and four years a representative; m. Hannah ———, and died Nov. 30, 1669. Of their ch. 1, Lieut. Samuel, born Oct. 20, 1648, admitted freeman, April 18, 1690, m. and r. Watertown; and d. Oct. 21, 1726. Lieut. Samuel's ch. 1, Mary. 2, Samuel, (2d). 3, John; 4, Hannah, died young. 5, Mary, d. young. 6, Abigail. 7, Mary. 8, Sarah. 9, Ebenezer, b. 1703; mar. Susanna Spring, 1731; r. Watertown, and died 1757. Ebenezer's ch. 1, Samuel, (3d), b. ab. 1732; mar. Mary Brown of Lexington; r. and represented Cambridge, Mass., and d. 1792. 2, Sarah. 3, Ebenezer, (2d). 4, Mary, m. ——— Goddard.

Samuel, (3d)'s ch. 1, Susanna, b. 1755; mar. Jesse Putnam. 2, Ebenezer, (3d), b. & d. 1759. 3, Mary, b. 1767, m. Thomas Mayhew, d. 1805. 4, Elizabeth, b. 1771. 5, Hon. Samuel, (4th), b. 1776; grad. H. U. '93; mar. Sally Brown of Concord, 1800; settled in W., a lawyer, rep. in Congress, &c.; rem. Brewer & Bangor. 6, Hon. Ebenezer, b. 1778; grad. H. U. 1798; m. Lucy F. Knox; came to Th., attorney at law, judge of court of common pleas, militia officer, &c.; rem. and d. Bingham, June 12, 1841.

Hon. Ebenezer's ch. 1, Julia K., b. 1805; m. Rev. Oren Sikes; r. Mercer, Bedford, Mass., &c., d. Aug. 30, '53. 2, Commodore Henry Knox, bap. April 11, '09; grad. West Point Mil. Academy, 1827; has risen in the U. S. Navy to his present high standing; commanded the frigate *Colorado* at the storming of Fort Fisher, Wilmington, &c.; m. & r. Mass. 3, Charles, b. Feb., 1809, d. Oct. 8, '10. 4, Lucy Anna, bap. Aug. 3, '10; took by Legislative act the name of Leeson, and r. Mercer. 5, Mary Henrietta, b. 1811; m. Rev. George C. Hyde; was principal many years of the Female High School at Syracuse, N. Y., & d. Aug. 30, '53, leaving 2 daughters, Henrietta C., & Mary P. Hyde. 6, Caroline F., m. ——— Smith, & rem. 7, James Swan, bap. Aug. 9, 1815; admitted to the bar, 1840; entered U. S. N., and, as purser, perished in the *Grampus*, March 18, '43. 8, Harriet Elizabeth, mar. George B. Page of Belgrade, Oct. 28, '41, and d. Feb. 18, '47.

THOMAS, the ancestor of this family, came from Scotland and settled at Plymouth, Mass. Of his sons, or, more probably, his *grandsons*, Joshua, b. in Duxbury, Mass. m. Mercy Ozier, Ogier, or Osyer, r. & d. Duxbury. Of Joshua's ch. 1, Peleg, b. in Duxbury, rem. m. & settled in Vinalhaven. 2, Joshua, (2d), b. in Duxbury, m. and settled in Vinalhaven. Of Peleg's ch. 1, Capt. Benjamin, m. Lucy Perry; r. Vinalhaven; was lost at sea, Sept. 15, 1819, in sch. *Thomas*, bound for Fredericksburg with plaster; & his widow rem. Rock. with her family in 1824. 2, Dea. George, m. Peggy Vinal; r. Rock., and built ships many years, but rem. to Quincy Point, Mass., ab. 1854.?

Joshua (2d)'s ch. 1, Mercy S., b. in Bristol ab. 1812; m. Capt. Wooster Smith; r. S. Th., and d. Aug. 17, 1855. 2, Capt. Peleg, b. in Duxbury; m. Lucy Grafton of Liverpool, Eng.; r. Rock., awhile, rem. S. Th., & has ch., names not ascertained. 3, Capt. Isaac K., b. in Duxbury ab. 1816; c. to Rock. ab. 1828; m. Eliza K. Perry, p. May 19, '39; r. Rock. 4, Capt. Joshua, m. Delia Frye; r. S. Th., all mariners.

Benjamin's ch. 1, Roxana, m. Howland Dyer, 1830; r. Vinalhaven. 2, Julia G., b. ab. 1809; mar. Willard S. Blackington; r. Rock. 3, Lydia S., m. Stephen N. Hatch; r. Rock. 4, Hon. William, b. 1812; m. Hannah C. Robbins, April 16, '36; r. Rock., merchant, State senator, 1841; & d. May 20, '49. 5, Jerusha G., m. Hon. Nathan A. Farwell; r. Rock. 6, Robert P., b. ab. 1817; m. 1st, Charlotte Tolman, p. June 6, '40, 2d, Lydia M. Tolman. p. May 24, '45, 3d, Martha H. Johnson, June 12, '59; r. Rock., a lime manufacturer, &c.

Dea. George's ch. 1, Charlotte V., b. Oct. 5, 1820, probably died young. 2, Mary, b. Dec. 15, '22; m. D. Howard Bills, rem. Quincy, & d. Nov. 15, '64. 3, Penelope, b. Sept. 4, '26. 4, Joshua, b. Nov. 13, '27, d. young. 5, Eliza J., b. Dec. 2, '28; m. 1st, ——— Thomas, 2d, B. Bryant of Quincy, Jan. 1, '56. 6, George E., b. Sept. 4, & d. Sept. 8, '31. 7, George H., b. May 19, '33; mar. Elizabeth J. Sias, Sept. 9, '54; r. Quincy. 8, Loretta, b. April 30, '36. 9, Theodore, b. Oct. 15, 39. The mother d. at Quincy Pt., July 6, '57, aged 59.

Capt. Isaac K.'s ch. 1, Edmund W., b. July 28, 1840, m. Almeda B. Flemming, Oct. 4, '63; r. Rock., a mariner, soldier of 4th Me., &c. 2, Kendall K., b. May 30, '44, m. Mary E. Holbrook, Aug. 16, '64; r. Boston.

Capt. Joshua's ch. 1, Lydia F., b. ab. 1847. 2, Joshua, (4th), b. ab. 1852.

Hon. William's ch. 1, Frederic, b. July 25, and d. Nov. 3, 1837. 2, Capt. Albert F., b. April 20, '39; r. Th., officer in 2d Me. Battery. 3, William O., b. June 20, '42, d. young.

Robert P.'s ch. 1, Ellen M., b. Nov. 1, 1840; m. Charles Duncan; r. Rock. 2, Susan Marilla, b. April 1, 1842. 3, Sarah Francis. 4, Clara. 5, Lucy. 6, Isabella W., b. May 14, '55, d. Nov. 22, '58. 7, Charles.

Joshua's ch. 1, Lydia F., b. ab. 1847. 2, Joshua, (6th), b. ab. '52.

THOMAS, John, m. Lucy Davis; r. and d. Lincolnville. Of their ch. there c. to Rock. four sons. 1 Franklin, b. ab. 1817; mar. Sarah H. Wooster, Dec. 9, '38; r. Rock. 2, Joseph T., b. ab. 1820; mar. Penninah S. Healey, p. Sept. 7, '38; r. Th., a quarryman. 3, Jacob, m. Mary J. Witham; r. Th. 4, Rufus C., b. ab. 1825; m. Catharine B. Starrett of War. March 28, 1850; r. Rock., a carpenter.

Franklin's ch. George F., b. March 18, 1840; r. Rockland, corporal in 2d Me. Battery, &c.

Joseph T.'s ch. 1, John H., b. Sept. 31, 1840; soldier of 4th Me. reg., &c. 2, Margaret, b. ab. '43. 3, Lucy, b. ab. '46. 4, William H., b. ab. 1851.

Jacob's ch. Roscoe, b. ab. 1844.

Rufus C.'s ch. 1, Josephine, b. June, 1853. 2, Mary Ann, born Sept., 1855. 3, Martha Frances, b. Aug. 1857.

THOMAS, Edward, b. in Friendship about 1800; m. Melinda Tilson, Sept. 3, 1830; came from Camden here, a clothier, &c., r. Th. Their ch. 1, Mary b. ab. 1823; m. George Healey; r. Th. 2, Edward, b. ab. 1837. 3, Reuel, b. ab. 1839; officer in 20th Me., wounded May, 1864.

THOMAS, Samuel, b. ab. 1813, in Vinalhaven; son of Cushing Thomas of Marshfield, Mass.; m. Mary Beverage, p. April 20, 1836; r. Rock., a mariner. Their ch. 1, Arabella B., b. April 21, 1838. 2, Mary E., b. ab. '45. 3, William K., b. ab. 1849.

THOMAS, Leander, b. ab. 1834; m. Fanny L. Thomas of Linc., Feb. 7, '58; r. Rock., a merchant. Their ch. Herbert L., b. ab. '59.

THOMAS, David, b. ab. 1805, m. 1st, Mary, (who d. Feb. 16, '40), 2d, Isabel Davis, May 23, '41, 3d, Mrs. Emeline W. Tarr, Feb. 9, '58; r. Rock. His ch. 1, William I., b. Aug. 5, 1829, [a William perished in sch. *Lion*, Dec. 10, '64,] 2, Elbridge S., b. March, 1831; r.

Rock., a mariner. 3, Edward, b. Nov. 10, & d. Nov. 26, '36. 4, Ellen L., b. '37, d. Sept. 18, '38. By 2d wife. 5, Orlando Orrin, b. Nov. 4, '41; r. Rock., a soldier of 4th Me., &c. 6, Marcellus S., b. ab. 1846. 7, Adelbert, b. ab. 1851.

THOMAS, David, (2d), b. ab. 1810; m. Elizabeth A. ——— ; r. Rock., a stevedore, &c. Their ch. 1, Eliza J., b. ab. '39. 2, Cinderella, b. ab. '41; m. Martin V. Warren; r. Rock. 3, Ruth C., b. ab. '43. 4, Benjamin D., b. ab. '45.

THOMAS, Ellerson, b. ab. 1817; m. Elizabeth Foster of S. Th., Oct. 30, '47; r. Rock., a lime burner, &c. Their ch. 1, Ellerson, b. April 12, '48, d. Dec. 14, '64. 2, Elizabeth, d. Oct. 12, '49. 3, Sarah Lizzie, b. March 1, '50. 4, Julia Ann, b. May 7, '53. 5, Calvin, b. Jan. 30, & d. July 28, '57. 6, Emily F., b. April 29, & d. May 22, '60.

THOMAS, Barney, c. from Ireland; m. Abigail Kelloch, p. March 18, 1830; r. Th., a rigger, & d. from a fall, Dec. 26, 1851. Their ch. 1, Elizabeth, b. Oct. 23, '30; m. Thomas R. Hewett; r. Th. 2, James H., b. Feb. 12, '36; m. Adelaide Jackson, Oct. 18, '60; r. Th., a carpenter & soldier in the 4th Me., d. in 1862. 3, Abby, b. Jan. 15, & d. Jan. 28, '38. 4, Marietta, b. Jan. 30, '39; r. Th. 5, Susan Amelia, b. July 7, 1842. 6, Abner B., member of 1st Me. Cavalry, &c. 7, Joshua L., b. ab. '48. 8, Ambrose L., b. ab. '51.

James H.'s ch. Frank.

THOMAS, Samuel I., b. ab. 1820, in Eden, Me.; m. Harriet S. Lindsey, Aug. 31, '45; r. Rock., a blacksmith. Their ch. 1, Edward H., b. ab. '47. 2, Clara L., b. ab. '49. 3, Charles H., b. ab. '52. 4, Alice L., b. ab. '56. 5, Frank C., d. Jan. 30, '59.

THOMAS, Jacob U., b. ab. 1802; c. from Searsmont; m. Deborah S. ——— ; r. Rock., a carpenter, &c. Of their ch. Albert G., b. ab. '37; r. Rock. And, of this name, Franklin B. Thomas, b. ab. '36; r. Rock., with Clara S., his wife, & their ch. Hattie E., b. ab. '57; was a soldier of 7th Me., &c.

THOMPSON, John, c. from Londonderry, N. H., to St. George's Lower Town, and m. Mary Gordon. Their ch. 1, Jane, mar. John Hart; r. and d. St. George. 2, William, mar. 1st, Nellie Gordon, (who d. March 9, 1796, a. 35,) 2d, Betsey Harrup of Cam., p. May 2, 1796, settled early, r. and d. in what is now Rock. 3, Dea. John, b. ab. 1768, mar. Susan Hart, p. Dec. 15, '91, 2d, Mrs. Mary Small, 3d, Mrs. Martha Marshall, Dec 13, 1838; r. S. Th., and d. June 27, '43. 4, Mary, m. Thomas Briggs; r. and d. Cam. 5, Ebenezer, m. Mary Gordon, 2d, Lucy (Fales) Crockett, 1817; c. from Lower St. Georges to Th., in 1785; rem. and d. Hope.

William's ch. 1, Ruth, m. in 1806, Abner Lee, a stage driver here in early times; rem. Ellsworth. 2, Nellie, m. and d. Cam. 3, William, (2d), m. and r. Oldtown. 4, John, (3d), m. Martha Nutt, July 27, 1800, rem. eastward.

Dea. John's ch. 1, Ebenezer, (2d), m, Mehitable Lawrence of W., p. Feb 27, 1817; r. Th., and d. at N. O., May, 1849. 2, Susan, mar. James Wall; r. and d. St. G. 3, John, (3d), mar. Sarah Bright; r. Gouldsboro'. 4, Eleanor, m. Nathan Pease of Appleton, p. Sept. 5, 1818, 2d, John Hart; r. St. G. 5, Rosanna, m. Jesse Hart; r. St. G. 6, Capt. Simon M. G., b. Sept., 1804, m. Abigail Kaler, p. Nov. 3, 1826; r. S. Th., and d. April 7, '59. 7, Sarah, m. Leonard Hooper; r. St. G. 8, Capt. Benjamin, m. Elizabeth J. Graves, June 30, 1844; r. S. Th., and d. at sea ab. '51. The mother d. June 3, 1833, a. 64.

Ebenezer's ch. 1, Nancy, m. Isaac Flagg; r. and d. Belmont. 2, Jane, m. Sluman Lawrence; r. W., and d. Jan. 13, 1861. 3, Margaret, m. James Jameson, p. Feb. 2, '40; r. & d. Rock. 4, Eleanor, born May 2, 1793, m. Joshua Lawrence; r. W. 5, Mary E., b. Nov. 25, '98, m. Capt. John B. Booker; r. Rock., and W. 6, Freelove, mar. Richard Howard; r. Castine, d. Belfast. 7, Trustim, m. Susan Sumner, Nov. 13, 1823; r. W., and d. Rock.

Ebenezer (2d)'s ch. 1, Joel R., m. Harriet Pease, July 14, 1844; r. Th., and d. Dec. 5, '56. 2, Amos L., b. ab. 1818, mar. Elizabeth Snow, Jan. 31, '46; r. Rock., soldier of the 4th Me., &c. 3, Capt. Samuel Albee, b. ab. '21, m. Hannah Haskell, July 21, '50; r. S. Th., a master mariner. 4, Jasper. 5, Susan. 6, Julia A., m. Rufus S. Fales of Th. 7, Mehitable, m. a Mr. Cotton of Boston. 8, Anastasia, m. and r. eastward.

Capt. Simon M. G.'s ch. 1, Charles W. d. unm. a. 26 years. 2, Sarah, m. Thomas Gordon of Linc., rem. Ohio. 3, Susan A., mar. Warren D. Kelloch; r. and d. S. Th. 4, Wm., m. Mary A. Hawes, p. Aug. 11, 1855; r. St. G. 5, Harriet E., b. April, 1834, d. Feb. 14, '51. 6, George Augustus, b. ab. '41; rem., m. and d. eastward. 7, Miles, b. ab. 1845, rem. eastward.

Trustim's ch. 1, Tileston, killed at sea, by falling into the ship's hold. 2, Sarah E., b. ab. 1829, m. Edwin S. McAllister; r. Rock.

Joel R.'s ch. 1, Rowena, b. ab. 1846. 2, Roselle, b. ab. '48. 3, Alvin Otis, b. Feb. 27, '49. 4, Mary E., b. ab. '51. 5, Ann, b. ab. '53. 6, Augustina. 7, Augusta.

Amos L.'s ch. 1, Mary E., b. ab. 1846. 2, Harriet A., b. ab. '48. 3, Cecilia M., b. ab. '54. 4, Franklin N., b. ab. '58.

Capt. S. Albee's ch. 1, Lathley N., b. ab. 1851. 2, Lizzie E., b. ab. '55.

THOMPSON, John, (5th in descent from John who came when six yrs. old with his father from England to Plymouth, Mass., May, 1623), was b. in Halifax, Mass., Feb. 14, 1725; m. Betty Fuller; was found frozen to death, Jan. 8, '77, in Plympton, on road home from Plymouth. John's ch. 1, Susanna. 2, Thaddeus. 3, Nathan, deaf mute, r. & d. Kennebec Co. 4, Zacheus, deaf mute, owned, r. & d. homestead. 5, Elizabeth. 6, Stephen, b. in Halifax, April 10, '74, and not in *Bridgewater*, as intimated on page 214, vol. 1, from the best information then obtained; came first to Th., 1793, as an apprentice to Capt. R. Bosworth of Halifax; m. Nancy Hastings, Jan. 5, 1800; r. Mill River, Th , a joiner & framer; & d. Nov. 15, '34. His widow d. ab. 1836. Their ch. 1, George L., rem. & d. East Abington, Mass. 2, Henry H. 3, William, b. ab. 1805; m. Mary Rice Washburn; r. Th., & d. Sept., 1847; had one ch., Henry W., who d. Dec. 13, '52, a. ab. 18. 4, Susan T., b. March, 1807; m. John Peters of Boston, p. May 3, '34. 5, Elizabeth B., b. 1810; m. in E. Abington. 6, Andrew L., rem. m. r. and has ch. in E. Abington. 7, Nancy H., b. Jan. 7, '15; m. in E. Abington, & d. April, 1844. 8, Mary, d. ? young. [Thompson Genealogy and com. of T. J. Rider, Esq., of Th., a genealogist of correct and extensive information.]

THOMPSON, Capt. Augustine, b. Nov. 25, 1835, son of James of Union; m. ——— Linnekin, 2d, ——— Stewart, July 4, '62; r. Rock. a blacksmith, organist, officer of 28th Me. Reg., &c. George W. Thompson, a 2d cousin of the preceding, b. ab. 1825; mar. Julia A. Benner of Wal., Oct. 16, '53; r. Th., a ship carpenter. George W.'s ch. Bertrina, b. ab. 1856.

THOMPSON, Elias, b. & brought up in Strong; m. Cynthia Paine of Strong; r. Th., a truckman, &c. Their ch. 1, Cynthia Ann, b. Jan. 24, 1839. 2, Helen E., b. June 1, '44. 3, Theresa Emma, born Oct. 1, '48.

THOMPSON, William, b. ab. 1805; came from Canton, Me.; m. Lucy (Winslow) Tillson, Jan. 27, '59; r. Rock., on site of the old Tillson tavern, a lumber dealer.

THOMPSON; of the sons of Benjamin of Frankfort, 1, James, b. ab. 1823; mar. Adelia Ulmer, Feb. 7, '50; r. Rock., a clerk, &c. 2, William, (2d), b. ab. 1828; mar. Zilpha H. Pease, June 25, '54; r. Rock., a quarryman, &c. James's ch. 1, Susan J., b. ab. 1850. 2, Hattie F., b. ab. '51. 3, Lucy H., b. ab. '53. 4, James Nelson, b. ab. '60. William, (2d)'s ch. 1, Coraetta, b. ab. 1855. 2, Frank E., b. Sept. 1, '58, d. June 7, '63.

THOMPSON, William T., b. ab. 1832, in Bucksport, Me.; mar. Mary E. Ames of Searsport; r. Rock., in mercantile business. Their ch. 1, Hattie M., b. ab. 1855. Of this name, also, Benjamin Thompson, b. ab. 1856; r. S. Th., a mariner, &c., with Antoinette, his wife, and ch., Cora, b. ab. 1856, and James W., b. ab '60. Also, Joseph Thompson, b. in Th.; m. Eliza (Everton) Whitney, p. July 8, 1833; r. & d. Rock. Joseph's ch. 1, Emeline, b. April 22, 1834. 2, Joseph, (2d), b. Sept. 2, '35; r. Rock., soldier of 4th Me., &c. 3, Parthena A., b. May 20, '38; all r. Rock. with their mother. Of the same name, also, Henry Thompson, b. ab. 1832, in Sweden, as was Mary, his wife, in England; r. Rock., entered the navy; their ch. William H., b. April 1, 1856, d. April 21, '61.

THORNDIKE; according to a family tradition, the founder of this family in England, was from Germany or the Low Countries, a ditcher, who introduced there the system of *dikes* and *thorn* hedges, and thus obtained the name. It was first brought to this country by John, the son of Francis, and brother of Herbert, prebendary of Westminster, being 5th in descent from William of *Great* or *Little* Carlton, Lincolnshire, Eng. He, John, born in Great Carlton, c. from Ipswich, England, about 1629, was one of the first settlers of Ipswich, Mass., 1633, where he r., a leading man, 35 yrs., but, displeased with the marriage of his only son, returned with his daughters to England. Paul, his son, m. Mary Patch, April 28, 1668; r. Beverly, Mass., in which, a promontory took from him the name of *Paul's Head;* he had ch. 1, Mary, m. Robert Morgan. 2, Elizabeth, m. Isaac Woodberry. 3, Hannah, m. William Pride. 4, John, (2d), b. Jan. 22, 1675; m. 1st, Joanna (Larkin) Dodge, 2d, Christiana West; r. Beverly, & d. March 23, 1760. 5, Paul, m. Mary Batchelder; r. and d. Beverly. 6, Herbert, m. Sarah Herrick, 2d, Abby Sallows. 7, Martha, mar. Richard Thissell.

John, (2d)'s ch. 1, Robert, b. Feb. 4, 1697; m. Elizabeth Woodberry, 1718; r. Beverly, rem. Cape Elizabeth. 2, Paul, m. Mehitable Woodberry. 3, John, (3d), m. Eliz. Ober. 4, Joanna, m. a Lovett. 5, James, m. Anne Ober. 6, Herbert, m. Abby Ober. 7, Edward. 8, Sarah, m. Joshua Thorndike. By 2d wife. 9, Anne. 10, Mary.

Robert's ch. 1, Ebenezer, born July 9, 1719; mar. Lydia Herrick, Sept. 5, '50; r. Cape Elizabeth, came to S. Th. and St. Geo., and died Feb. 4, 1819. 2, Joanna, b. July 11, 1721; mar. Israel Jordan, 2d, —— Webb, c. in age to, & d. in S. Th., aged ab. 100. 3, Hannah,

d. young. 4, Ruth. 5, Hannah; all born and recorded in Beverly. 6, Robert, (2d), b. 1730, in Beverly; m. Deborah Wallace of Cape Elizabeth; c. from Falmouth to Cam. with his 7 ch. and d. Dec. 10, 1834, a. 104. 7, Paul, probably b. at C. Elizabeth; m. there Bathsheba Emery; c. also to and d. in Cam. 8, John, (4th), m. and settled in Cam. and left descendants. 9, Lucy, m. Capt. Joseph Wallace and settled at Harrington. Some of these, after the first six, may be wrongly numbered.

Ebenezer's ch. 1, Cushing; 2, Ebenezer, both d. young. 3, Capt. Joshua, b. March 12, 1755; m. Hannah Nutting, Aug. 23, '80; was a rev. soldier, r. St. G., and d. Dec. 25, 1823. 4, Lydia, b. May 22, 1757; m. Azor Roundy; r. and d. St. Geo. 5, Benjamin, b. May 4, '59; m. Priscilla Woodbury; r. Matinic; and d. in S. Th., 1834. 6, Robert, (3d), b. April 22, '61; m. Anna Dyer, of C. Elizabeth, 2d, Abigail Hadley of Gloucester, 1789, 3d, Abby Perry; r. Th., was a rev. soldier, & d. Jan. 20, 1843. 7, Hannah, m. Ephraim Dyer; r. & d. Sullivan, Me. 8, Elizabeth. 9, Mary. 10, Ruth, b. Aug. 10, 1767; m. Francis Yates; r. & d. Cambridge. 11, Ebenezer, b. July 11, '69; m. Sarah White. 12, John, b. June 3, 1771.

Robert's (of Camden) ch. 1, Mary, m. John McKellar. 2, John, m. Mary Annis. 3, Lucy, m. Lewis Ogier, of French descent, from Quebec; r. Cam. 4, Deborah, m. Capt. Andrew Malcolm; r. & d. War. 5, Joanna, m. 1st, Thomas Garish, p. in Th., Oct. 10, 1785, 2d, ——— Annis; r. & d. Cam. 6, Mehitable, m. James Richards; r. & d. Cam. 7, Patience, m. William Moody, p. in Th., Oct. 3, '87; r. & d. Linc. 8, Robert, (2d), b. in Cam. Sept. 17, '73; m. 1st, ———, 2d, Mrs. Porterfield of Cam., 3d, Mary Thomas, 4th, ——— Farnham; r. Cam. & d. 1860. 9, Eliza, m. ——— Hardy. 10, Joseph Wallace, m. Sarah ———; r. Cam. 11, Herbert, m. a Harrington. 12, James, b. July, 1779; m. a Richards.

Paul's ch. 1, Abigail, b. 1766; m. Samuel Crane, p. in Th., Aug. 4, '85; r. War. & d. July 25, 1823. 2, Elizabeth, m. John Stanford of Cape Elizabeth. 3, Moses, m. Rebecca Proctor, & r. in Salem. 4, Paul, (2d), m. Isabel Boggs; r. & d. Cam. 5, Sarah, m. Reuben Barrett; r. Hope. 6, Hannah, m. Robert Boggs; r. W. & d. Nov. 12, '43. 7, Ebenezer, (2d), m. Mary Thorndike; r. Cam. 8, Larkin, m. Mary Stanford of Cape Eliz. 9, Israel, m. in Cohasset; r. Scituate, Mass. 10, John, (2d), m. Elizabeth Hart; r. U. 11, Joanna, m. 1st, a Preble, 2d, a Daily; r. & d. Linc. 12, Bathsheba, m. Capt. Thompson of Cam., who d. suddenly, soon after marriage, and was soon followed by his wife, as suddenly, while sitting in her chair at breakfast, and after relating a remarkable dream. 13, Lucy, m. ——— Eells of Cam.

Sixth New England Generation.

Capt. Joshua's ch. 1, Bethia, b. May 23, 1781; m. William Keating, 2d, Thomas Martin of St. G.; r. S. Th. 2, Capt. Joshua, (2d), b. April 3, '87; m. Susan Keating, March 19, 1812; r. S. Th., a retired master mariner. 3, Hannah, b. July 16, '89; m. Capt. Robert Snow; r. and d. Th. 4, Eben, b. Aug. 26, '91; m. Betsey Snow; r. St. G., and d. Sept., 1819. 5, George, b. March 31, '93; d. at Turks Island, 1815. 6, Eliza, b. Jan. 4, '99, d. Sept., 1803. The mother, b. June 21, 1764, d. Jan. 12, 1852.

Benjamin's ch. 1, Joseph, b. March 5, 1792. 2, Charles W., b. March 10, '94; m. Eliza Keating, April 26, 1822; r. Rock., & d. Dec. 15, '50. 3, Ruth, b. June 10, '96; m. Thomas G. McKellar; r. St.

G. ? 4, Hannah, b. Feb. 5, '99; m. George Snowdeal; r. S. Th. 5, Benjamin, b. June 9, 1801. 6, Lucy W., b. Sept. 11, '03; m. Israel Snow; r. Rock. 7, Eliza, b. Dec. 22, '05; mar. Henry A. Smart; r. Rock. 8, Thomas W., b. March 31, '08. 9, William K., b. July 14, '10. 10, Eben, b. Nov. 6, '13. 11, Lydia, b. April 16, '16; m. Archibald Fisher of War., & d.

Robert, (3d)'s ch. 1, Lydia, b. Oct. 23, 1782, d. 1837. 2, Robert, (4th), b. Jan. 4, '84, d. Feb. 5, 1816. 3, Anna, b. Dec. 26, '86. died Jan. 8, '87. By 2d wife. 4, Asa, b. Aug. 13, '90, d. March 6, 1803. 5, Anna, b. Jan. 12, '92, d. Oct., '93. 6, Charlotte, b. Aug. 3, '93, m. Asahel Gilbert in W. Cambridge, Dec., 1827. 7, Mary, b. July 5, '95. 8, John, b. Feb. 17, '99, d. April 1, 1816. 9, William, b. Dec. 13, '98, mar. Margery Dyer, Aug. 31, 1823; r. Portland, since 1815. 10, Capt. Henry, b. Dec. 6, 1800, d. Aug. 12, 1827, lost at sea. 11, Capt. Israel, b. Dec. 1, '02, m. Mary A. Van Buskirk; r. S. Th., and d. April 18, '59. By 3d wife. 12, Cushing, b. Jan. 16. '04; r. Rock. 13, Harriet, b. Sept. 19, '06, mar. Cornelius Kreamer of Wal., April 12, '40. 14, Lucy, b. March 29, '09. 15, Joseph P., b. June 9, '15.

The Camden branches are from necessity here omitted, but of Herbert's ch., there came to Rock , 1, William N., b. in Cam., 1810, mar. Chloe Barns of Cam , and r. Rock. 2, Jane Malcolm, mar. Peter A. Hewitt; r. Rock. Also of Larkin's ch. 1, Paul, (3d), born Cam. 1827, mar. Lucinda Norwood, 2d, Ellen Havener, Sept. 25, '59; r. Rock., a carpenter, &c. 2, Emery, mar. Huldah A. Killsa; r. Rock., keeps livery stable. And, of the sons of James, the son of Robert, (2d), of Cam., James F., c. from Cam., m. Lucy S. Ulmer, Oct. 13, '25; r. Rock., entered the navy.

Seventh Generation.

Capt. Joshua, (2d)'s ch. 1, Hon. George, b. Nov. 5, 1814, m. Arethusa Sleeper, Nov. 6, '36, shipbuilder in S. Th. for many yrs. till '48, having built 19 vessels on his own account, was State senator '50 to '55, councillor '59 and '60, was in '61 the first volunteer from Maine, being in Cassius M. Clay's battalion for the defence of Washington, D. C., rem to Rock., sailed the India ship, *Kate Sweetland*, was clerk of courts, 1864, but resigned and took command of ship *Otago*, in '65. 2, Eliza, b. March 22, '16, m. Archibald G. Snow, and d. at St. Geo., May 6, '36. 3, Julia, b Jan. 23, '18, m. Capt. James Dow; r. S. Th. 4, Helen M., b. Nov. 11, '19, m. Capt. Elias P. Sleeper; r. S. Th., and d. June 11, '47. 5, Capt. Charles Wm., b June 9, '22, lost at sea in br. *Maine*, Dec. 11, '44. 6, Joshua K., b. April 26, '24, mar. Elvira P. Snow, Dec. 20, '45, rem. Cal. and Puget's Sound, Washington T'y. 7, Capt. Eben A., b. March 22, '26, m. Philura R. Fogg; r. S. Th., a ship master. 8, Susan Maria, b. Aug. 26, '29, mar. Henry Augustus Keating; r. Ohio. 9, Capt. Frederic, b. May 19, '31, m. Arabella O. Fogg, March 16, '54; r. S. Th., a ship master.

Charles W.'s ch. 1, Capt. William H., b. July 3, 1823; m. 1st, Melinda Achorn, July 19, '47, 2d, Eliza J. Fletcher of Belfast, '52; r. Rock., keeps livery stables, &c. 2, Charles W,, (2d), b. Feb. 15, '25; r. Rock. & d. Nov. 11, '64. 3, Capt. Joseph, b. May 18, '27; m. Albina W. Hunt, June 21, '57; r. Rock. 4, Bethiah, b. July 25, '29; m. Selah G. Dennis, rem. Hallowell. 5, Nancy M. b. Feb. 13, '31; m. Capt. Alfred K. Spear; r. Rock. & d. Jan. 3, '61. 6, Eliza F., b. March 4, 1833. 7, Angelina A., b. July 6, 1836; m. Capt. Alfred K. Spear; r. Rock. 8, Hannah M. b. July 25, '38. 9, Emma L., b. April 16, '42. 10, Melinda A. b. ab. 1848.

William's ch. 1, John B., b. Dec. 12, 1824. in Portland; m. Arvilla J. Jordan, March 19, '50; r. Portland. 2, Benjamin F., b. Feb. 15, '27. 3, Martha A., b. May 3, '29. 4, William H., (2d), b. Oct. 29, '30, d. young. 5, Robert, (5th), b. April 1, '33. 6, William H, (3d), b. Dec. 16, '34, d. young. 7, William H, (4th), b. April 20, '37.

Capt. Israel's ch. 1, Capt. Israel A., b. July 7, 1832; m. Julia M. Philbrook, Feb. 8, '62; r. S. Th., a master mariner. 2, Mary E., b. Jan. 20, '35; m. Simeon Sargent; r. S Th. 3, Abigail A., b. March 18, '37; m. John D. Currier, Sept. 15, '58; r. S. Th. 4, Frances Ellen, b. April 25, '39; r. S. Th. 5, Robert Henry, b. April 9, '41; r. S. Th., a farmer, &c. 6, Annie M. b. 1843, died in Concord, N. H., Nov. 5, '61. 7, Melville L., b. ab. '46. 8, Loretta C., b. ab. '48. 9, Susan L., b. April '51, d. Feb. 18, '52. 10, George A., b. ab. '53.

William N.'s ch. 1, Daraxa, b. ab. 1839. 2, Harriet, b. ab. '42. 3, Lucy, b. ab. '47. 4, Isaac, b. ab. '49.

Paul, (3d)'s ch. 1, Jacob, b. 1843. 2, Frederic, b. 1847, drowned Feb. 19, '63, at the N. marine railway, Rock., where he had gone to find his father at his work.

James F.'s ch. Mary E., m. S. Watson Veazie; r. Rock.

Eighth. Generation.

Hon. George's ch. 1, Lane, b. Feb. 20, 1844; r. Rock. 2, Chas. Wm. b. June 11, '46. 3, George Leslie, b. Nov. 5, '48. 4, Joshua, b. April 1, '51. 5, Alice Augusta, b. Dec. 15, '53. 6, Eliza Snow, b. July 20, '56. 7, Arthur H., b. March 30, '58. 8, Frederic Keating, b April 6, 1861.

Capt. Eben A.'s ch. 1, Ava, b. ab. 1849. 2, Estella, b. ab. 1852. 3, Delia, b. ab. '54. 4, Helen, b. ab. 1858.

Capt. Frederic's ch. Adella F., b. ab. 1855.

Capt. William H.'s ch. 1, William H., b. April 8, 1848, d. young. 2, Walter H., b. May 29, '54. 3, Ralph W. E., b. June 12, '57.

Capt. Joseph's ch. Josephine A., b. Sept. 9, 1858.

John B.'s ch. 1, Martha E., b. Dec. 17, 1853. 2, John W., born Jan. 21, '56. 3, Charles S. b. Jan. 21, '58. Of this family, also, Alden U. Thorndike, r. Rock., entered the army, and James E. Thorndike, r. Rock., corporal in 2d Battery, re-enlisted, &c.

THORNTON; of this family two brothers came from Ireland; 1, Thomas, b. ab. 1830; m. Bridget ———, of the same country; r. Th. 2, John, b. ab. 1836, in Ireland, as was Mary, his wife; r. Rockland. Thomas's ch. 1, Mary, b. ab. 1855 in Th. 2, Bridget, b. ab. '57. 3, Bennett, b. ab. 1860.

John's ch. 1, Bridget, b. ab. 1858. 2, John, (2d), b. ab. '59.

THURLOW, Moody E., b. ab. 1811, in Hallowell; c. to this place ab. 1841; mar. Martha C. Hutchinson; r. Rock., a merchant tailor. Their ch. 1, Annie M., b. ab. 1837. 2, Sarah L., b. ab. 1838. 3, George M., b. Sept. 22, '39; r. Rock., a mariner. 4, Martha Augusta, b. April 8, '41, d. Sept. 28, '59. 5, Edward W., b. ab. 1843, a mariner.

THURSTON, Capt. Thomas F., b. in Bristol ab. 1822; mar. Alice V. Albee, March 12, '48; r. Rock., rem. Wiscasset. Their ch. 1, Flora, b. May 17, & d. June 14, 1849. 2, Samuel Albee, b. in Rock., June 9, and d. Sept. 10, '50. 3, Eliza P., b. in Rock., March 7, '54. 4, Edwin A., b. in Rock., Dec. 11, '56. 5, Russell, b. in Bristol, Oct. 5, '61. 6, Paulina Jane, b. April 2, '63.

THURSTON, Philo, b. ab. 1820, son of Philo Thurston of Union; m. Olive Robbins, Jan 11, '34; r. Rock., engaged in iron foundry. Their ch. 1, Willis E., b Oct. 19, 1849, d. March 21, '62. Of this name, also, William J Thurston, b. ab. 1823; r. Rock., a sergeant in 28th Me., &c. Martha, his wife, d. Aug. 13, 1860, aged 38.

TIBBETTS; of this family two brothers c. to this place, viz.: 1, Samuel, b. ab. 1811, in Bristol, Me.; m. Maria W. Morrill; r. Rock., keeps a meat market, &c. 2, Alpheus Chandler, b. ab. 1820, in Windsor; mar. Elizabeth F. Farrow of Belfast, p. July 27, 1840; r. Rock., a sailmaker, &c.

Samuel's ch. 1, Charles M., b. ab. 1833; mar. S. Augusta Chadbourne, July 2, '62; r. Rock, a meat dealer, &c. 2, Chloe M., b. ab. '39. 3, Henry G., b. Nov. 4, '42; m. Mary A. Burns, June 1, '61; r. Rock., a sailmaker, musician in 4th Me., &c. 4, Horace J., b. ab. '44. 5, George W., b. ab. '46. 6, Samuel, jr., b. ab. '48. 7, Abbie F., b. ab. '49. 8, Joseph U., b. May, 1851, died March 23, '52. 9, Thomas E., b. ab. '53.

Alpheus C.'s ch. 1, Hannah E., b. Aug. 17, 1841; m. Capt. Samuel P. Wilson; r. Rock. 2, Helen A., b. ab. '45. 3, Albert C., b. ab. '50. 4, Minnie C., b. ab. '54. 5, William F., b. ab. '58. 6, Walter, died young.

TILDEN, Samuel B., b. ab. 1821, in Belmont, Me.; m. Ann McDonald; r. Rock., a cooper, &c.

TILLSON, or as spelled by the earlier settlers, Tilson; of this family, there c. to this place, 1, William, b. in Halifax, Mass., April 25, 1754, m. Anna Haskell, c. to what is now Rock., before 1795, was an inn holder at Brown's Corner, a soldier of the Revolution, &c., d. June 28, 1841. 2, Dea. Perez, b. at Halifax in 1765, c. to r. in Th., in May, 1795, mar. 1st, Melinda Fales, Feb. 23, '97, 2d, Mrs. Lucy Holmes, p. Oct. 28, 1831, and d. Oct. 5, '52, aged 87. 3, Gilbert, a nephew, came later to Th., m. Mary Keith, June 7, 1812, was a shoemaker by trade; r. and d. Th.

William's ch. 1, Martha, b. 1792, m. Dr. Enoch Lovejoy; r. Rock., and d. June 19, 1834. 2, William Fearing, b. Jan. 31, 1803, m. Jane Davis of U., 1829, 2d, Lucy Winslow of Wal, p. Sept. 19, '33; r. Rock, and d. Sept. 10, '51. 3, Henry Knox, b. Feb. 28, '05, d. young.

Dea. Perez's ch. 1, Myra, b. Feb. 22, 1798, m. Alfred Rollins; r. Th. 2, Melinda F., b. Oct. 19, '99, m. Edward Thomas; r. Th. 3, Perez, (2d), b. Oct. 21, 1803, m. 1st, Ruth W. Sweetland of Hope, Nov. 16, '25, 2d, Martha Sawyer of C. Elizabeth, '33, 3d, Harriet Collins of Portland, June 9, '47; r. Th., a farmer, &c. 4, Hannah Thorp, b. Nov. 21, '05; r. Th. 5, Col. Edward C., b. March 15, '07, mar. Mary P. Sawyer of Scarboro', p. Nov. 22, '32, an active man in Th., but rem., and r. Centralia, Boon Co., Mo. 6, Capt. Charles S., born March 11, '10, m. Mary J. Dyer of Portland, p. Sept. 15, '38; r. Th., a master mariner, and d. March 27, '56.

William F.'s ch. 1, Brig. Gen. Davis, born April 17, 1830, grad. West Point, m. Margaret E. Achorn, Aug. 4, '52; r. Rock, a civil engineer, Adjt. Gen. of Me. 1859—60, collector of customs, &c, raised the 2d Me. or Tillson's battery, of which he was Captain, and has risen rapidly to his present high rank as an artillery officer. By 2d wife. 2, Mary A., b. ab. '35, m. Dr. William A. Banks; r. Rock. 3, Lincoln, b. ab. '38, m. Ada, dau. of David Ames; r. Rock. The mother m. 2d, Wm. Thompson and r. Rock.

Perez, (2d)'s ch. 1, Ruth S., b. Oct. 16, 1832, d. April 23, '54. By 2d wife. 2, Juliana F , b. Dec. 18, '36 ; r. Th. 3, Perez Henry, b. April 19, '39 ; volunteered in the 4th Me. Reg., and was killed at Manassas, July 21, '61. 4, Ethan S., b. Aug. 27, '41 ; r. Th., a student. The mother d. Dec. 5, '45. By 3d wife. 5, Ge rge C., b. Aug. 17, 1848, d March 12, '49. 6, John S., b. Dec. 27, '50. 7, George W., b. Dec. 18, '52. 8, Harriet, b. ab. '54.

Col. Edward C.'s ch. 1, Mary M., b Oct. 29, 1833, d. Oct. 16, '34, 2, Elizabeth M., b. June 4, '35 ; removed with her parents. 3, Mary Ann H., b. July 16, '37 ; rem. and m. William R. Davis of Piedmont, Va., Jan. 20, '63. 4, Edward Francis, b. Sept. 17, '39 ; rem., entered the army, was wounded and taken to Richmond, had a leg amputated, and d. from its effects. 5, Emeline M., b. ab. 1842, rem. Missouri.

Capt. Charles S.'s ch. 1, Sarah M., b July 26, 1839. 2, Fannie J., b. June 24, '42. 3, Charles H., b. July 17, '46. 4, Mary A., b. April 13, '55.

Gilbert's ch. 1, Mary, m. Amos Clough ; r. Rock. 2, Martha G., d. Dec. 31, 1855. 3, Susan K., m. David Lewis, Jan. 21, 1849, died ? Dec. 8, '50.

Gen. Davis's ch. Jennie C., b. ab. 1856.

TINKER, Richard, Esq., b. June 18, 1795 ; m. Mehitable Jellison, Feb., 1824 ; was senator and sheriff of Hancock county, c. from Ellsworth to Th as warden of the State Prison, '61 ; & as such was murdered by a convict, May 14, '63. Their ch. 1, Charlotte J., b. Sept. 20, '26 ; m. E. C. Milliken, Jan., '52 ; r. Boston. 2, George W., b. Jan. 30, '28. 3, Mary Agnes, b. July 18, 1831, a teacher, writer, &c. 4, Caroline A., b. June 5, '33 ; m. James M. Bartlett, Nov. 22, '57 ; r. Ellsworth. 5, Hettie C., b. Feb. 8, '35, d. in Th. Aug. 12, '62. 6, Louise, b. June 1, '37 ; a teacher in Boston. 7, Richard H., b. April 20, '39 ; 8, Charles, b. Jan. 22, '41 ; 9, Sarah E., b. April 15, '43 ; 10, Helen, b. Aug. 19, '45 ; all ret. to Ellsworth, after their father's death, taking their dead with them. The mother d. in Th. Nov. 26, '62.

TITCOMB, Maj. Gen. William H., b. ab. 1820, c. here from Boston' where he had been a merchant ; m. Mary Crockett, Jan. 4, 1844 ; r. Rock., cashier of Rock. Bank, officer of 2d Division of Me. Militia, &c. Their ch. 1, Mary A., b. March 6, 1845, d. March 7, 1857. 2, Fannie M., b. ab. 1847.

TITUS, Elijah, b. ab. 1812, in Digby, N. S. ; m. Eunice ——— of Westport, N. S. ; r. Rock., a gardener, &c. Abraham Titus, b. ab. '16, in N. S., c. with Phebe A., his wife & 7 ch.; r. S. Th., in fishery. Elijah's ch. 1, Capt. Wellington J , b. ab. '39 ; m. Lydia A. Bowden, March 16, '64 ; r. Rock. 2, Ezekiel M., b. ab. '41 ; r. Rock ; 3, John W., b. ab. '43 ; r. Rock. ; both soldiers of 4th Me., &c. 4, Lalia, b. ab. '45 ; mar. Serg't Charles H. Miller, March 5, '64 ; r. Rock. 5, George, b. ab. '48. 6, Phebe, b. ab. '50. 7, Caroline, b. ab. '52. 8, Clara, b. ab. '54.

Abraham's ch. 1, Frances A., b. Dec. 1835, d Oct. 17, 1850. 2, Charles, b. ab. '41 ; r. S. Th., soldier in 28th Me., re-enlisted. 3, Henrietta, b. ab. '44. 4 & 5, twins, b. ab. 1846 ; William, r. S. Th., Edward, entered the army. 6, Jane, b. ab. '50. 7, George, b. in N. S., ab. '52. 8, Frances, b. in Maine, ab. '54. 9, Susan T., b. Sept. 15, '56, d. Feb. 1, '57.

TOBEY, William, b. ab. 1817, c. from Portland ; m. Lucinda Flint ; r. Th., a sailmaker. Their ch. 1, William, b. ab. 1846. 2, Sarah E.

b. ab. '48. 3, George W., b. March 8, & d. March 31, '50. 4, Martha E., b. ab. '52. 5, Abbie F., b. ab. '54. 6, Lucinda J., b. ab. '56. 7, Charles E., b. ab. '58. 8, Frank, b. ab. '59.

TOBEY, Nathaniel, jr., son of Nathaniel Tobey of Jefferson, Me., m Sarah E. Hinkley of W., May, 1853 ; c. to Th., a joiner, rem. ab. '60, to Magnolia, Miss., ret. in '64, & r. Th. Of his brothers, 1, Alberti, b. ab. '35, r. Th., a joiner. 2, West, m. Eveline H. Wyllie of W., p. Aug. 3, '63 ; r. Th.

TOBURN, Thomas, c. from Fox Islands; r Rock. & d. Nov. 30, 1845. Mary, his wife, d. June 9, '38, a. 62. Of their ch. 1, ———, m. ——— Arey; r. S. Th. 2, Thomas, jr., m. Barbara A. Reaver, Feb. 3, '61 ; r. Rock., soldier of 15th Me , &c. 3, John, r. Rock. & d. Sept., 1848.

TOLMAN, Isaiah, b. in Stoughton, Mass., May 28, 1721 ; m. 1st, Hannah ———, (who was b. Nov. 10, 1725) ; c. with his family in 1769, and took up 500 acres around the pond long named Tolman's, now Chikawauka Lake, m. 2d, Margaret Robbins, 3d, Jane Philbrook of Vinalhaven; rem. in his latter days and d. at Matinic. His ch. by 1st wife. 1, Hannah, b. July 7, 1746 ; mar. ——— Stone of U. 2, Mary, b. Feb. 15, '48 ; m. Constant Rankin; r. & d. Rock. 3, Isaiah, (2d), b. June 26, '51 ; m. Elizabeth Gregory ; r. Rock., & d. Nov. 15, 1823. 4, Jeremiah, b. Feb. 8, '53 ; m. Martha, dau. of John Calderwood, Jan. 26, '84 ; r. Rock., & d. Nov. 25, 1827. 5, Samuel, b. Jan. 24, '55 ; m. Experience Gregory of Cam., p. April 15, '85 ; r. Rock., rem. & d Cam., Feb. 18, 1826. 6, Experience, b. Aug. 15, '56 ; mar. ——— Bowen of U. 7, Elijah, b. July 18, '58, d. young. 8, Esther, b. July 19, '58, d. young. By 2d wife. 9, Lucy, b. June 11, '60 ; m. Dea. Job Ingraham ; r. Rock., & d. Aug., 1846. 10, Curtis, b. May 26, '62 ; m. Ann Harrington, Sept. 22, '85 ; r. Rock , a Rev. soldier, & d. Feb. 24, 1852. 11, Melea, b. Aug. 11, '64 ; mar. Capt. William Gregory of Cam., & d. Feb. 9, 1856. 12, Elijah, b. Sept. 7, '66 ; m. Mrs. Sally Woodward of Cam., Nov. 12, '97 ; r. & d. Cam. 13, Katie, b. Sept. 11, '68 ; m. Dr. Isaac Bernard ; r. & d Rock. 14, Nathaniel, b. Oct. 9, '70, d. young. 15, Peggy, b. April 28, '73 ; m. Capt. Jos. Young, settled in Cam., & d. June 25, 1829 ; bur. in Rock. 16, Abigail, b Nov. 24, '75 ; m. George Johnson ; r. Rock. 17, Capt. Isaac, b. Feb 28, '78 ; m. Eunice Young of Matinicus, where he d. Aug. 20, 1855. 18, Luther, b. March 27, '80 ; m. Jane Young ; r. & d. at Matinicus. 19, Olive, b. Sept. 1, '83 ; m. John Hall ; r. Rock. By 3d wife. 20, Lydia, m. Samuel Haskell of Gorham ; and r. in Knox. One other, died young, making 21 in all.

Isaiah, (2d)'s ch. 1, Frances, b. April 11, 1775, d. Sept. 9, 1826. 2, Capt. Samuel, (2d), b. Jan 16, '77 ; mar. Nancy ———; r. Cam. 3, Calvin, b. March 1, '79 ; m. Eunice Gay, Nov. 20, 1804 ; r. Rock.? & d. Dec. 18, '54. 4, Josiah, b. May 19, '81 ; m. Mary Achorn, Jan., 1804 ; r. Rock., a farmer, &c., & d. Nov. 12, '52. 5, Betsey, b. April 20, '83 ; m. Benjamin Brewster of Cam. 6, Polly, b April 9, '85, d. Aug 30, '94. 7, Amos, b. Nov. 3, '89, d. Nov. 7, '92. 8, Esther, b. Feb. 7, '94 ; m. Walter Edmunds, p. Aug. 1, 1814 ; rem. Burnham and died. 9, Lucy, b. Oct. 6, '96 ; m. Levi Butler.

Jeremiah's ch. 1, Thomas, b. Nov. 20, 1784 ; m. Lydia Ingraham, Dec. 3, 1810 ; r. Rock., & d. May 23, '53. 2, Elizabeth, b. Oct. 3, '88 ; m. John Manning, April 27, 1813 ; r. Cam., & d. Feb. 2, '39. 3, Jeremiah, (2d), b. Sept. 19, 93, d. April 24, '94. 4, Mark, b. Sept.

23, & d. Oct. 7, '95. 6, James, b. March 29, '97; mar. Bethia Keen, Sept. 12, 1822; r. California. The mother d. Feb. 5, 1839, aged 81 years, 8 months, 8 days.

Samuel's ch. 1, William, b. May 28, 1786, m. 1st, Catharine Burns of Wal., p. June 15, 1807, 2d, Mrs. Martha Greenlaw, May 16, '19; settled and d. in Cam. 2, Isaiah, (3d), b. March 22, '88, probably d. young. 3, Joseph, b. Aug. 10, '89, mar. Bethia Brown, March 26, 1818; r. Cam. 4, Shepherd. b. Sept. 10, '92, mar. Jane Phinney of Eastport, April 25, 1816; r. and d. Cam. 5, Asenath, b. Aug. 17, '95, m. Moses Kelloch of St. G.; r. Cam. 6, Hannah, b. Feb. 21, '99, m. Joshua Bradshaw; r. and d. Cam. 7, Isaac, (2d), b. Jan. 2, 1802, d. young.

Curtis's ch. 1, David H., b. March 15, 1786, m. Katie Johnson, May 26, 1805; r. Cam., & d. Feb. 9, '63. 2, William Elliott, b. Feb. 26, '90; m. 1st, Sally Perry, May 28, 1815, 2d, Ann (Munroe) Manning, Dec. 25, '42; r. Rock., a blacksmith. 3, John Minot, b. ab. 1792, mar. 1st, Elizabeth Norwood of Cam., Sept. 12, 1822, 2d, Mrs. Catharine Hunt; r. Cam. The mother d. April 29, 1832, aged 70.

Elijah's ch. Peggy or Margaret, m. Benjamin Perry of Cam.

Capt. Isaac's ch. 1, Matilda, m. Alexander Philbrook of Islesboro'; r. Matinicus. 2, Hanson, b. ab. 1806, m. Margaret A. Tolman, Nov. 2, '31; r. Rock. 3, Almira, m. Josiah Achorn; r. and d. Rock. 4, Margaret R., m. Lewis Leadbetter; r. North Haven. 5, Olive H., m. Capt. Thomas Stewart; r. Rock. 5, Lisetta, m. Lewis Ames; r. & d. Matinicus. 7, Isaac, (2d), m. Susan Crie; r. Matinicus. 8, Iddo K., m. Sally Susan Ames of North Haven; r. Matinicus. 9, Harriet C., m. Jonathan Norton of St. G.; r. Matinicus.

Luther's ch. 1, Job, m. Lucy Studly of Bremen; r. and d. Bremen. 2, Luther, (2d), m. Sally Roberts of Matinicus; r. Matinicus. 3, Jefferson, d. unm. 4, Elliott, m. Sarah Ozier of Bremen; r. Bremen.

Fourth Generation.

Calvin's ch. 1, Archibald, b. May 25, 1806; m. Mercy Perry, May 9, '30. 2, Calvin, (2d), b. Feb. 12, '09; m. Margaret Kaler of Wal., p. Sept. 28, '31; r. & d. Rock. 3, Zillah W., b. Feb. 5, '11; m. Daniel Packard, (2d), of Cam. 4, Orissa W., b. April 19, '13; m. Josiah Achorn, & d. Dec. 27, '42. 5, Wealthy G., b. June 26, '16; m. Benjamin Clough; r. & d. Rock. The mother d. Jan. 1, '54, a. 76.

Josiah's ch. 1, Margaret A., b. Nov. 2, '05; m. Hanson Tolman; r. Rock. 2, Isaac, (3d), b. Aug. 6, '07; m. Mary J. Packard, p. Sept. 17, '32; r. Blackington's corner, Rock., a farmer. 3, Walter E., b. Nov. 18, '10; m. Harriet Spofford, p. April 2, '36; r. Rock., a merchant. 4, Elvira, b. March 26, 1813; m. Otis Sherer; r. Rock. 5, Mary, b. March 10, '16; m. Dea. Cephas Starrett; r. Rock. 6, Josiah, (2d), b. March 14, 1822; m. Louisa R. Sherer, Sept. 21, 1848; r. Rock., a farmer. 7, Orrin P., b. Dec. 18, 1829; m. Mary Scholes of N. B., Aug. 7, '53; r. homestead, Rock., a farmer.

Thomas's ch. 1, Jeremiah, (3d), Esq., b. Nov. 3, 1811; m. Hannah K. Packard of Cam., April 5, '38; r. Rock., a farmer, &c., assistant assessor of U. S. Internal revenue for 5th District. 2, Martha B., b. May 8, '13; m. Capt. Jesse Ames; r. Rock. & Minnesota. 3, Lydia Maria, b. Oct. 20, '17; m. Alexander Martin of Cam., Dec. 20, 1840. 4, Clarinda, b. Sept. 10, '19; mar. John Wyman, p. Feb. 21, '37; r. Millbridge. 5, Marietta, b. April 8, '22; m. Jos. F. Allen; r. Rock.

6, Harriet A., b. April 3, '24; m. Capt. Allen Linnell; r. Cam. 7, Julia, b. Nov. 21, '25; m. Amos Barrett of Cam., Feb. 18, '51.

James's ch. 1, Lanson D., b. Feb. 24, 1823. 2, Susan, b. Sept. 27, '24. 3, Hannah E., b. April 10, '26. 4, James T., b. Dec. 9, '28; mar. Lillias A. Butler, Aug. 25, '60; r. Th., a farmer, &c. 5, John Jeremiah, b. March, 1831, d. in Cam., Sept. 15, '51.

William's ch. 1, Capt. Isaac, (4th), b. ab. 1809; mar. Thirza or Louisa St. Clair; r. S. Th., Owl's Head, fish dealer, &c. 2, Mary, m. Charles Jameson; r. and d. Rock. 3, Cordelia, m. Charles Jameson; r. Rock. 4, Sarah, m. Frederic Andrews. 5, Caroline, m. William Achorn; r. Rock. 6, Martha, m. Aaron Kelloch; r. East Machias.

Joseph's ch. 1, Maria, m. William Barnes; r. & d. Cam. 2, Harriet, m. Luther Hemenway; r. Cam. 3, Antoinette; r. Cam., with her father. 4, Warren, r. and d. unm., Cam.

Shepherd's ch. 1, Capt. Alvin, b. March 31, 1818; m. Lucy Ann Tyler of Cam., 2d, Lizzie M. Sumner April 8, '54; r. Rock., d. at sea, Oct. 20, '64. 2, Exia, m. Elithan Young; r. Cam. 3, Susan, m. Isaac Keen; r. & d. Cam. 4, Huse, m. 1st, Irene Packard, 2d, Lorina Brewster; r. Cam. 5, Orinda, m. Ambrose Lampson, jr.; r. & d. R.

David H.'s ch. 1, Ann, m. Samuel Packard; r. and d. Th. or W. 2, Louisa, mar. Benjamin Crandon; r. Cam. 3, Otis, mar. Abigail Barnes; r. Cam. 4, Irene, m. Amos Fisk; r. Cam. By 2d wife. 5, David H., jr.; r. Cam., now in the army. 6, Lucy, r. Cam.

William Elliott's ch. by 1st wife. 1, Abner P., m. Emily Grover, June 24, 1845; r. and d. Rock. 2, Charlotte, m. Robert P. Thomas; r. and d. Rock. 3, Marilla, d. unm. 4, Joshua, d. young. 5, Lucy A., d. young. 6, Emeline, d. young. 7, Charles H., b. Nov. 12, '25; r. Rock., & d. April 23, '58. 8, Lydia M., b. Aug. 25, '27; m. Robert P. Thomas, p. May 24, '45; r. Rock., & d. July 22, '58. 9, Emily, b. ab. '29; m. Oscar Davis; r. Rock. 10, Sarah E., mar. Rev. George Watts of St. George. 11, Margaret E., d. young.

John Minot's ch. 1, Minot, m. Augusta McKellar; r. W., lost an arm in defence of his country. 2, Danson, m. and r. California. 3, Orinda, m. r. & d. in Massachusetts. 4, Henry H., d. in California. 5, Sarah F.; 6, David; 7, Hiram; all 3 d. young. The mother died Aug. 15, '35, a. 33. By 2d wife. 8, Albert, d. in the army. 9, John r. California. 10, Lisana, m. Albert Tolman; r. Cam.

Calvin, (2d)'s ch. 1, Calvin N., b. Aug. 12, 1832; r. Rock., a mariner. 2, Otis G., b. Dec. 29, '33; r. Rock., a mariner. 3, Franklin, b. Sept. 29, '35; r. Rock., a farmer, corporal of 2d Me. Battery, &c. 4, Oscar, b. April 19, '38; r. Rock., a mariner. 5, Elsie M., b. Sept. 15, '39; m. John H. McIntosh; r. Rock. 6, Helen A., b. Sept. 7, '41. 7, Orissa A., b. Jan. 10, '43.

Isaac, (3d)'s ch. 1, Alonzo, b. May 4, & d. May 6, 1841. 2, Benton I., b. ab. '44. 3, Almond S., b. ab. '48. 4, Ella A., b. ab. '52.

Walter E.'s ch. 1, Norman S., b. April 5, 1837; r. Rock., a farmer, &c. 2, George, b. Jan. 22, 1839; m. Eliza A. Collins of Deer Isle, Nov., '62; r. Rock., a merchant in firm of Tolman & Sons. 3, Walter, b. Jan. 31, '41; r. Rock., a merchant in same firm. 4, Mary Hannah, b. Jan. 25, '46; r. Rock.

Josiah's ch. 1, Charles E., b. Nov. 30, 1850, d. March 10, '57. 2, Alfred, b. ab. '53. 3, Hiram, b. ab. '56. 4, Harriet A., b. ab. '59.

Orrin P.'s ch. Eudora, b. June 22, 1854.

Jeremiah, (3d)'s ch. 1, Ellen E., b. Dec. 24, 1838; m. Charles H. Dean; r. Rock. 2, Thomas M., b. March 19, '42; appointed a cadet at West Point, March, '61. 3, John D., b. Oct. 3, '43. 4, Jeremiah A., b. May 13, '55. 5, Jesse, b. June 3, '58.

Capt. Isaac, (4th)'s ch. 1, ? Sarah C., m. H. P. Philbrook, Dec. 23, 1851. 2, ? Henry E., b. ab. '36; m. Frances S. Adams, Nov. 10, '57; r. S. Th. & d. Aug., '59, of southern fever. 3, ? Guilford, b. ab. '39, d. at Brooklyn, N. Y., Sept. 11, '63. 4, Almira, b. ab. '41. 5, Ezekiel, b. ab. '43. 6, Wilfred, b. ab. 1845. 7, Charles, b. ab. 1848. 8, Herbert, b. ab. 1850. 9, Laura H., b. ab. 1852.

Capt. Alvin's ch. 1, John C., b. ab. 1848. 2, Lucille W. b. ab '59.

TONER, James, b. ab. 1816, son of Charles of Warren, but remained with grandparents, in Ireland, till 1837; m. in N. Y., rem. to Rock., a foundry man, and d. July 21, '59. His ch. 1, James, b. ab. 1846. 2, Charles, b. ab. '48. 3, William H., b. ab. 51. 4, Sarah, b. ab. '54. 5, Isaac B., b. '55, d. July 23, '61, by drowning, as did his father, grandmother, and only uncle. The mother d. Sept. 4, '63, aged 42.

TORREY, Capt. Charles, b. ab. 1819 in Deer Isle, m. Ann P. Barker, April 5, '42; r. Rock., a master mariner. Their ch. 1, Charles A. M., b. Jan. 13, '43; r. Rock. 2, George A., b. ab '45. 3, Helen F., b. ab. '48.

TORREY, Joseph G., b. ab. 1820 in Hanson, Mass., mar. Nancy Caryl of Vermont; r. Rock, a brass founder. Their ch. 1, Helen M., b. ab. 1844, 2, George E., b. ab. '52. 3, Willard C., b. ab. '55. 4, Olive B., b. Jan. '59, d. July 10, '61. Of this name, also, there was here early Elijah Torrey, b. 1776, mar. Hannah Baker; r. here some years, a blacksmith, rem. Belfast before 1816, and d. July 27, '25, bur. under Masonic form. Ch. recorded here. 1, Leander Lozier, b. Oct. 7, 1806, d. March 12, '10. 2, Emeline C., b. Dec. 20, '08. 3, James Madison, b. Jan. 29, '11; r. here a time with Elizabeth T., his wife, and had ch., viz.: Sarah E., b. Jan. 13, '40, and George F., d. Aug. 11, '42; probably rem. 4, Erastus N., b. July 2, '13.

TOTMAN, Samuel S., b. ab. 1826 in Bath, mar. Francis E. Labe, April 16, '53; r. Rock., a mason, soldier of 4th Me., &c. Their ch. Fannie, b. ab. 1858.

TOWLE, Gorham R., b. ab. 1832 in Hartland, Me., m. Elizabeth B. Hunt; r. Rock., a stage driver, &c.

TOWNE, Asahel, b. ab. 1821, m. Nancy J. French; r. Rock., soldier of 4th Me., killed in battle, July 21, '61. Their ch. 1, Michael E., b. ab. 1846, entered the army. 2, Moses A., b. April '48, d. Aug. 15, '58. 3, Flora, b. ab. '54. 4, Ada M., b. ab. '58.

TRACY, Rev. A. P., b. in Vassalboro', March 18, 1838, m. S. M. Eastman of Canton, July 22, '53; entered Waterville Coll., but did not grad. on account of ill health; r. Rock., pastor of F. W. Bapt. ch. Their ch. 1, Frank Edwin, b. in Webster, July 9, '54. 2, Mary Eva, b. in W. Gardiner, Aug. 19, '55. 3, Edward P., b. in S. Montville, May 3, '57. 4, Hattie Ella, b. in Linc., Oct. 11, '58. 5, Annie F., b. in Hallowell, Jan. 10, and d. Dec. 11, '60. 6, Flora C., b. in H. April 22, '61. 7, James L. Phillips, b. in China, June 17, '63, d. Aug. 31, '64. Of this name, also, Michael Tracy; r. Rock., entered the army.

TRAFTON, Josiah, b. ab. 1813, in Camden; mar. Lovisa Shorey, Nov. 21, '39; r. Rock., a lime burner, &c. Their ch. 1, Roseltha. 2, William H., b. Nov. 14, 1842. 3, Abby, b. ab. '44. 4, Leonidas, b. ab. '47.

TRASK, Alfred, b. in Jefferson, ab. 1817; m. Lydia, dau. of Thomas Kennedy; r. S. Th., on George's river side; a farmer, &c. Their ch. 1, Alzena, b. ab. 1842; m. James T. Newhall; r. S. Th. 2, Almira D., b. June, 1843, d. Feb., 1860. 3, Lucinda K., b. ab. '45. Of this name, also, Daniel Trask of Th., m. Nancy M. Hatch, March 19, '53.

TRIPP, Stewart, b. ab. 1831, in Jefferson, Me.; m. Margaret, dau. of John or Thomas Linneken of St. G., p. Jan. 21, '53; r. S. Th., a blacksmith.

TROWBRIDGE, Robert, b. ab. 1826, son of John Trowbridge of Wal.; m. Miss Lambright; r. Rock., a ship-builder, inspector of customs, &c. Their ch. Frederic K., b. ab. 1852.

TRUE, Lewis M., b. ab. 1805, in North Yarmouth, Me.; m. Eliza Titcomb; r. Rock., a carpenter, &c. Their ch. 1, Cora F., b. ab. 1836; a teacher, & d. in N. Yarmouth, May 4, '63. 2, Edward E., b. ab. '39; r. Rock., entered the navy. 3, Marcia S., b. ab. '42.

TRUE, Daniel M., b. ab. 1826, in Montville; m. Julia A. ———; r. Th., overseer in State Prison, &c. Their ch. 1, Martha E., b. ab. 1850. 2, Etta, b. ab. '52. 3, Israel C., b. ab. '55. 4, Julia, b. ab. '57.

TRUEWORTHY, William S., b. July 11, 1801, in North Haven; m. Sophronia Trueworthy; r. Rock., and d. Dec. 3, 1860. Their ch. 1, Harriet C., b. 1836; mar. John Mehan; r. Rock. 2, Acel E, b. 1839; m. Acelia H. Worthing, Feb. 4, '61; r. Rock., a mariner. 3, Erastus A., b. 1841, d. Dec. 18, 1860, from an accidental fall into the hold of the ship *Chimborazo.*

TRUNDY, John W., b. Nov. 30, 1796; mar. Hannah ———; r. Rock., & d. April 4, 1860. Of their ch. 1, Alice, b. ab. 1826; mar. ——— Bradley; r. Rock., a widow and has one ch., Alice, b. ab '50. There also r. Rock., Lucy A. Trundy, b. ab. 1836; 2, Susan H., b. ab. '40; 3, Benj. F., b. ab. '42; r. Rock., a sailmaker, entered navy.

TRUSSELL, Joshua, came from Camden with his wife to S. Th., & bought the Abel Fish place; afterwards rem. & d. in St. Geo. Their ch. 1, Capt. Moses, m. ——— Meloney; r. Th., a master mariner, rem. New Orleans. 2, Elizabeth, mar. William Watts; r. Th. 3, Harriet, b. ab. 1808; m. John McKellar; r. Th. 4, Dr. Joshua W., b. ab. 1811; m. ——— Lawrence; r. War., rem. Rock., a dentist. 5, Capt. Samuel, m. & r. St. G., kept the Ocean House, &c. 6, Roselle, m. ——— Vose; r. Th. 7, Mary, m. and r. St. George.

Dr. Joshua W.'s ch. 1, Theresa M., b. ab. 1839. 2, Orlando S., r. Rock., entered the navy. 3, Helen, b. in W., as were the preceding. 4, Frederic, b. ab. 1847, d. Jan. 20, '54. 5, Edward F., b. ab. 1851.

TUCKER, Benjamin, b. ab. 1779, on Copp's Hill, Boston; came to this place, m. Lavinia (Morse) Wight; r. Th., at Beech Woods and at Watson's Pt., a cooper, and d. Sept. 4, 1846. Their ch. 1, Mary A., b. Sept. 7, 1808; r. Th., and d. Oct. 14, '60. 2, John, born April 30, '12, m. Julia M. Dow, May 3, '62; r. Th. 3, Isaac H., b. June 4, '14, and d. July 4, '15. Others of this name, perhaps, r. Rock., as Bolin F. Tucker of Rock., entered navy.

TUPPER, Charles F., b. ab. 1834, in New Brunswick, as was Elizabeth, his wife; r. Rock., a merchant, formerly Methodist minister. Their ch. 1, William, b. ab. 1848. 2, George, b. ab. '49. 3, Melvina, b. ab. '51. 4, Even, b. ab. '54. 5, Melissa, b. ab. '56.

TURNER, Jackson, b. Sept. 1, 1803, in Old Th., m Submit Smith, Aug. 1, '24; r. Rock., and d. April 11, '41. Their ch. 1, Orville R., b. March 4, '25, d. Oct. 28, '44. 2, Melinda H., b. Sept. 14, '26, m Theodore B. McIntosh; r. Rock. 3, Andrew Jackson, b. Dec. 19, '28, m. Mary E. Ackley, Dec. 25, '50; r. Rock., and San Francisco, where he m. 2d, Anna M. Starbird, Oct. 4, '59. 4, Leonard S., born May 22, '31, d. in California, Sept., 1850. 5, Henry M., b. May 11, '33, d. in Rock., July 28, '56. 6, Theodore B., b. Aug. 13, 35, died April 27, '47. 7, Theron Tileston, b. Sept. 27, '37, m. Julia A. Whitten, Aug. 8, '59; r. Rock., a mariner. 8, M. Augusta, b. Aug. 15, '39, m. Henry A. Doveton; r. Rock., rem. California. 9, Lavinia F., b. Aug. 27, '41, d. April 19, '62.

T. Tileston's ch. 1, Ada, b. Aug. 12, & d. Sept. 1, 1862. Of this name, also, James Turner, b. ab. 1812, m. Margaret Achorn, Nov. 2, '43; r. Rock., was a soldier of the 4th Me. Reg., and d. in Virginia by sickness, Aug. 30, '61. Their ch. 1, Almira, b. ab. 1845. 2, Lavinia, b. ab. '47. 3, Clara, b. ab. '50. 4, Lydia, b. ab. '52. Of the same name, John W. Turner, of the 2d Me. Battery, m. Flavilla V. Ingraham, Feb. 7, '63; r. Rock., re-enlisted in army.

TUTTLE, George W., b. ab. 1821, in Perry, Me., m. Emily Loring; r. Th., photographist. Their ch. 1, Florence, b. ab. 1848. 2, Laura, b. ab. '51. 3, George, b. ab. '58. Of this name, also, James F. Tuttle; r. Rock., soldier of 4th Me.

TYLER, Samuel, of Camden, m. Lucy Keen of Rock., March 30, 1814; r. and d. Belfast. Of their sons. 1, Alden L., b. ab. '20, in Belfast, m. Drusilla E. Packard, June 18, '44; r. Rock., a teacher, &c., elected Clerk of Courts for Knox county, 1864. 2, Samuel H., b. ab. '25, in Belfast, m. Elizabeth A. Sylvester, Jan. 24, '50; r. Rock., a merchant.

Alden L.'s ch. 1, Helen, b. ab. 1845. 2, Sarah, b. ab. '48. 3, Mary, b. ab. '50. 4, John, b. ab. '53. 5 & 6, twins, b. ab. '58, Lemuel and Samuel.

Samuel H.'s ch. 1, Francis O., b. ab. 1851. 2, Henry H., b. ab. '56. 3, Samuel A., b. ab. '58. 4, Charles A., b. Nov. 27, '60, died June 11, '61.

TYLER, Phinehas, b. in 1798, c. from Boston to Union, m. there Louisa Alden in 1823, rem. Th., and traded many years, m. 2d, Electa P. Robinson, May 9, '32; and d. at Rock., Sept. 28, '56. His ch. 1, William P., b. March 30, '24. 2, Edwin, b. Oct. 25, '25. By 2d wife. 3, Louisa A., b. May 6, '33, m. Charles E. Bliss of Wal., April 2, '55. 4, Julia C., b. May 29, '35. 5, Lucretia G., b. Dec. 27, '37. 6, Clara H., b. Aug. 25, '39. 7, Lucy C., b. July 2, '42.

TYLER, Capt. Peter P., b. ab. 1802, m. Phebe ———; r. Rock, a steamer pilot. Their ch. 1, Joseph, b. ab. '40, a painter. 2, Peter, b. ab. '42. 3, Ellen, b. ab. '44. 4, Elizabeth, b. ab. '46. 5, Benjamin, b. ab. '48.

ULMER, Capt. John, b. in Germany in 1736; c. to Waldoboro' in 1740; m. Catharine Remilly; rem. to what is now Rock & d. Aug., 1809, a. 73. His brothers, Capt. Philip M., & Gen. George, settled at Ducktrap; the latter was b. in 1755, was a soldier of the revolution, Maj. Gen. of 6th division of the militia, sheriff of Hancock county, senator of Mass. & Maine, & d Jan., 1826. Capt. John's ch. 1, George, m. Mrs. Mary Beckett, 2d, Miriam Townsend, Sept. 2, 1824; r. Rock., a lime burner, &c., rem. Cam. & Hope, where he died. 2, Mary, m.

Peter Schwartz; r. & d. Wal. 3, John, (2d), b. 1763; m. Eunice Barrows, p. Dec. 27, '88, 2d, Chloe Barrows, April 16, 1820, 3d, Anne Andrews of St. G., Sept. 19, '30; rem. Burnham, ret. & d. Jan. 15, '31, in Ulmer's mill, as was supposed, from arsenic, which was kept in the mill for the purpose of destroying rats, & was taken by mistake, for other medicine, on an attack of sickness in the night. 4, Margaret· b. Sept. 16, 1765; m. Jacob Achorn; r. Rock. & d. April 25, 1849. 5 & 6, twins; Hannah, m. Henry Hyler, r. & d. Castine; Jacob, m, Margaret Schwartz; r. Rock., built mills, &c. and d. Dec. 7, '48. 7, Matthias, m. Betsey Demuth; r. Rock. & d. April 8, 1841. 8, Mary, m. 1st, Rev. Frederic Croner, 2d, Isaac Brown; r. Rock. 9, Maj. Philip, m. Susan Schwartz; r. Rock., a deputy sheriff, militia officer, &c., & d. Sept. 6, '45. 10, Andrew, b. 1778; m. 1st, Jane Overlock, July 25, 1799, 2d, Lucy Brown, in 1839; a farmer, &c.; r. in the heart of Rock. city, & d. April 10, 1845. 11, Sarah, m. William Brown; r. & d. Cam. 12, Capt. Martin, b. Jan., 1783; m. Susan Stoddard, p. Oct. 1, 1803; r. Rock. & d. Oct 4, '30. 13, Catharine, b. May 10, 1785; m. Capt. Jona. Crockett; r. Rock., and d. Jan. 31, 1863, The mother died Sept. 14, 1824, aged 83.

Third Generation.

George's ch. by 1st wife. 1, Isaac B., d July 20, 1839. By 2d wife. 2, George, (2d), m. & r. in Hope, d. Aug. '27. 3, Martin; 4, Isaac, both settled, m. & d. in or near Belmont. 5, Eliza, m. ——— Annis; r. & d. Cam. 6, Sarah, m. ——— Bryant; r. & d. Cam. 7, Catharine, m. Abel Tyler; r. & d. Cam. Perhaps others.

John, (2d)'s ch. 1, Capt. John, (3d), m. Lydia Torrey; rem. to Burnham.

Jacob's ch. 1, Hannah, b. 1797; m. Knott Bartlett; & d. Feb. 23, 1842. 2, Eliza, m. 1st, James Spear, 2d, ——— Boynton; r. and d. Th. 3, Jacob S., b. ab. 1803; mar. Mary Hosmer of Cam., p. Sept. 22, '23; r. Rock., a farmer. 4, Polly, b. 1805, d Rock., March 21, '55. 5, Gilbert, b. July 20, '07; mar. in 1829, Mary Ann Kuhn of Bremen, (who was b. Nov. 27, 1805); r. Rock., a farmer. 6, Margaret, m. R. Robinson Richards, March 6, '31; r. & d. Rock. 7, Asa, b. ab. 1809; m. Amanda F. Healey, Sept. 15, '33; r. Rock., and d. May 21, '38. 8, Enos C., mar. Catharine Fields, p. Nov. 21, '35; r. Rock., and d. Oct. 28, '47. The mother died Jan. 9, 1848, aged 74.

Matthias's ch. 1, Catharine, b. Oct. 19, 1793; m. Phinehas Butler, (3d); r. & d. U. 2, Sarah, b. April 18, '95; mar. John Butler of U. 3, Eunice, b. Feb. 3, '97; m Benjamin A. Gallop; r. Rock., and d. Jan. 28, 1835. 4, Jenny, b. Feb. 9, & d. Sept. 19, 1800. 5, Ephraim, b. March 14, '01; m. Elizabeth Rankin, Dec. 5, '22; r. Rock., & d. March 20, '58. 6, Susanna, b June 30, '03; m. Edmund Hammond, 2d, John Hammond; r. Rock. 7, Major James A., b. April 14, '05; mar. Catharine Black, p. Nov. 16, '26, 2d, Phebe (Carriel) Morse, p. April 14, '47; r. Rock., in quarry business. 8, Eliza, b. March 18, '07; m. John Richards, p. March 22, '24; r. Cam. 9, Mary Ann, b. March 20. '09; m. Elias Dodge; r. & d. Strong. 10, Matthias, (2d), b Aug. 11, & d. Aug. 18, '11. The mother d. April 14, '60, aged 91 years, 10 months.

Major Philip's ch. 1, Capt. Jacob, (2d), b. Feb. 9, 1794; m. Harriet Bernard, July 31, 1814; r. Rock., & d. Sept. 20, '29. 2, Jane, b. March 15, '96; m. William Spear, (3d); r. Rock. 3, Philip, (2d), b. May 30, '98, d. Aug., 1802. 4, Charles, b. May 13, 1801; mar. Mrs.

Mary Thayer, p. July 24, '21; r. Rock., & d. Oct. 2, '39. 5, Lucy S., b. Sept. 1, '03; mar. James F. Thorndike, Oct. 13, '25; r. & d. Rock. 6, Alden, b. July 28, '05; m. Eliza Wooster, Jan. 14, '27; r. Rock., general inspector of lime, &c. 7, Philip, (3d), b. May 18, '07; mar. Mary W. Thorndike, p. May 19, '29; r. Rock., & d. Feb. 3, '31. 8, Susan R, b. Dec. 7, '09; m. Hon. Charles Crockett; r. Rock, and d. in Boston, Feb. 24, '55 9, Harriet, b. Feb. 28, '12; m. Elbridge G. Shepherd; r. Rock., & d. Dec. 15, '63. 10, Gen. William S., b Jan. 15, '14; m. Louisa B. Poor, p. March 25, '35; r. Rock., & d. May 4, '45. 11, Julian, b. Feb. 18, & d. July 27, '17. 12, John R., b. Sept. 28, '18; mar. Sarah Young of Cam., p. May 18, '39; r. Rock. The mother died Dec. 27, '55, aged 79 years, 11 months, 21 days.

Andrew's ch. 1, Dolly, b. Dec. 11, 1798; m. Daniel Cowing; r. Rock., & d. May 19, '52. 2, Ann M., b. Dec. 28, 1800; m. Edmund P. Staples; r. Th., & d. May 2, '47. 3, Susanna, b. Feb. 14, '03; m. Col. Nathaniel Meservey; r. Rock., and d July 19, '36. 4, Jane, b. Oct. 14, '04; m. Ezekiel Stearns, July 4, '27; r. Th., & d. March 16, '32. 5, Andrew, (2d), b. July 29, '08; m. Lucinda B. Thomas, Oct. 5, '35; r. Rock., a lime manufacturer. 6, Joseph, b. Sept. 15, '10; m. Ann E. Fales, Sept. 17, '37; rem. San Francisco, and d. Nov. 1, '50. 7, Harrison, b. Feb. 14, '14, m. Lydia Kelloch, Oct. 22, '35; r. Rock., and d. Oct. 28, '50. 8, Catharine, b March 11, '16, mar. Eliphalet Seyers, p. Sept. 13, '34, 2d, Augustus Hanaky, 3d, Capt Thos. Tate, and d. Rock. The mother d. Jan. 29, '39.

Capt. Martin's ch. 1, Capt. Henry H., b. Feb. 7, 1804, m. Margaret Robinson of C., p. Jan. 18, '24, 2d, Mrs. Eliza Spear, Sept. 13, '29, 3d, Lucy Black; r. Rock., a master mariner, like his father and all his 5 brothers. 2, Fanny, b. April 21, '05, m. Capt. Silas Penniman, 2d, George J. Burns; r. Rock. 3, Capt. Levi S., b. Sept. 9, '06, mar. Clarissa Simonton, April 6, '29, and d. of yellow fever at Mobile, Nov. 3, '43. 4, Caroline, b. Nov. 12, '07, m. Capt. Henry Verrill; r. Rock. 5, Capt. Bernard, b. Sept. 12, '09, m. Hannah Adams, Aug. 4, '34; r. Rock. 6, Susan, b. Oct. 8, '11, m. Francis A. D. Singhi; r. Rock. 7, Mary, b. Dec. 20, '13, d. June 6, '29. 8, Capt. Matthias, (3d), b. April 14, '15, mar. Mary Ann Ripley; r. Rock., and d. Nov. 28, '40. 9, Capt. Martin, (2d), b. Oct. 14, '16, m. Zoa Pease, p. Oct. 3, '37; r. Rock., and d. Aug. 25, '49. 10, Capt. Asahel, b. Sept. 12, '18, lost at sea, Nov. 24, '38.? The mother d. May 27, '58, aged 80.

Fourth Generation.

Jacob S.'s ch. 1, Mary E., b. Dec. 1, 1824, mar. Silas Farrington; r. Rock. 2, Anson, b. July 21, '26, d. Nov. 17, '47. 3, Gilman L., b. Dec. 19, '27, m. M. Elizabeth Palmer; r. Rock., in quarry business. 4, Emily H., b. April 12, '30, mar. Edward F. Blackington; r. Rock. 5, Harriet S., b. May 19, '34, m. Lorenzo D. Martin, July 2, '54; r. Rock. 6 and 7, twins, b. May 20, '38, Sarah M., m. Oliver B. Ulmer; r. Rock., and Frances S., m. William N. Ulmer; r. Rock.

Gilbert's ch. 1, Maria S., b. Oct. 19, 1830, m. Allen P. Farrington; r. and d. Rock. 2, Mary Ann, b. Sept. 2, '32, m. John S. Robbins, Dec. 2, '49; r. Th. 3, Margaret, b. Nov. 2, '34; r. Rock. 4, Oliver B., b. July 18, '36, m. Sarah M. Ulmer, Sept. 3, '56; r. Rock., in quarry business. 5, Frederic H., b. Oct. 31, '39, m. Mary E. Feyler, Sept. 16, '61; r. Th., a farmer, soldier in 2d Me. Battery, re-enlisted. 6, Jacob U., b. Oct. 8, '41, mar. Helen M. Wagner, Nov. 21, '63; r. Rock., a farmer. 7, Asa, (2d), b. ab. '44. 8, Sarah J., b. ab. '50. 9, Gilbert, (2d), b. ab. '53.

Asa's ch. 1 and 2, twins, b. March 17, 1834; Adelia, mar. James Thompson; r. Rock., Angelia, d. Jan. 22, '35. 3, William, b. Feb. 22, and d. Nov. 19, '36. 4, Almira J., b. Nov. 30, '37, mar. Ezekiel Winslow; r. Rock.

Enos C.'s ch. 1, Eleanor B., born July 24, 1836, mar. Gilbert H. Marsh; r. Rock. 2, Lewis S., b. June 25, '38, m. Melissa, dau. of Capt. Holt; r. Rock. 3, Leander, b. July 24, and d. Aug. 14, '41. 4, Hannah, b. June 28, '42, m. John B. Marsh; r. Rock.?

Ephraim's ch. 1, Sabra R., b. Nov. 18, 1823, m. John M. Alden; r. Rock. 2, Ephraim J., b. April 30, '26, m. 1st, Martha J. Proctor, p. April 24, '47, 2d, Delphus Dean, March 17, '51, 3d, Sophia Robinson; r. Rock., in quarry business. 3, Samuel R., b. Oct. 6, '28, m. Rosanna Dean; r. Rock., in quarry business. 4, Elizabeth, b. Jan. 23, '31, d. Oct. 4, '49. 5, Almira P., b. June 18, '33, mar. Lawrence C. Burkett; r. Rock. 6, James W., b. April 24, '38, m. Mary A. Millikin, Aug., 1861; r. Rock. 7, Abby M., b. ab. '46. 8, Mary Ellen, b. ab. '48.

Maj. James A.'s ch. By 1st wife. 1, Frederic Thomas, b. Sept. 28, 1827, m. Mary F. Morse, Jan. 19, '51; r. Rock., a teamster, &c. 2, Caroline B., b. Sept. 2, '30, m. Knott M. Bartlett, d. April 1, '53. 3, Matthias, (4th), b. Feb. 25, '32; r. Rock., in quarry business. 4, Martha L., b. April 15, '35, m. Reuben Pillsbury; r. Rock. 5, Violetta, b. March 6, and d. Aug. 21, '40. By 2d wife. 6, Matilda M., b. Oct. 8, '48.

Capt. Jacob, (2d)'s ch. 1, Catharine, b Jan. 2, 1814, m. Adriel C. Fales; r. Rock. 2, Orris B., b. Dec. 12, '16, mar. Fanny N. Butler, Nov. 25, '41; r. Rock., a farmer, &c. 3, Charles, (2d), b. March 23, '18, d. Sept. 23, '32. 4, Alden, (2d), b. Feb. 18, '20, d. Nov. 25, '39. 5, Edward E., b. Jan. 4, '27, m. Lucinda Overlock, July 26, '51; r. Rock., a joiner. 6, Susan C., born June 8, '29, mar. James Kelloch; r. Rock.

Charles's ch. 1, Lucy J., b. March 10, 1820, m. Capt. John Packard; r. Rock. 2, Julia A., b. March 10, '22. 3, Malvina M., b. Dec. 25, '23, m. Capt. Hanson Bird; r. Rock. 4, Capt. Charles C., b. Nov. 8, '25; r. Rock., a master mariner. 5, Capt. William H., b. April 20, '27; r. Rock., and d. at Williamsburg, N. Y., Aug. 16, '56. 6, Harriet A., b. Aug. 19, '30, m. Alden Brown; r. Rock. 7, Philip T., b. March 22, '33, m. Catharine Tolman of Cam., Sept. 18, '53; r. Rock. 8, Edwin L., b. March 2, '35, deceased. 9. Hiram F., b. Aug. 19, '37, m. Melissa H. Hookson, Aug. 22, '58; r. Rock., a painter, &c. The mother d. Oct. 2, '38.

Alden's ch. 1, Clementine, b. Feb. 27, 1829, m. Alvan McLain; r. Rock. 2, Eliza F., b. ab. '43; r. Rock. 3, Franklin, b. ab. '45.

Gen. William S.'s ch. 1, Capt. William N., b. Jan. 4, 1836, m. F. Sophia Ulmer; r. Rock., a W. I. Goods dealer, officer in 2d Me. Battery. 2, Horatio A., b. June 4, '37, mar. and r. Rock., soldier in 4th Me., since in navy. 3, Arthur, b. Sept. 26, '42; r. Rock., entered the navy. 4, Francis H, b. ab. '44; r. Rock., soldier in 2d Me. Battery, &c.

John R.'s ch. 1, Edgar O., b. Jan. 21, 1839; r. Rock., corporal in 28th Me. Reg, re-enlisted. 2, Albert F., b. Dec. 4, 1840; r. Rock., entered the navy.

Andrew, (2d)'s ch. 1, Mary Lucinda, b. Sept. 5, 1835; m. Michae. A. Achorn; r. Rock. 2, Judith E., b. Nov. 17, '38; m. Harvey N. Greely of Bangor, Jan. 8, '61. 3, Augustus Hanaky, b. Sept. 4, '41;

r. Rock., soldier in 28th Me., &c. 4, Ann Charlotte, b. 1844, died March 8, '46.

Joseph's ch. 1, Calphurnia P., b. April 15, 1838. 2, Clarence D., b. Feb. 17, '40; m. Martha J. Jameson, April 1, '61; r. Rock., quartermaster in 1st Cavalry, &c. 3, Caslon F., b. Dec. 17, '47, d. May 15, '55. The mother m. 2d, Dr. J. E. Hunt, and rem.

Harrison's ch. 1, Wyman W., b. Dec. 30, 1838; m. Emily Hall, June 16, '61; r. Rock., a mariner, corporal in 4th Me. Reg., &c. 2, Mary E., b. Jan. 21, '41; m. Capt. John D. Cornwall of New York, Aug. 24, '58; has one son, (Horace B., b. ab. '57); r. Rock. 3, Frances K., b. Aug. 16, '43. 4, Joseph H., b. Sept. 20, '49.

Capt. Levi S.'s ch. 1, Mary B., b. Feb. 21, 1830; r. Bangor. 2, Sears S., b. Feb. 14, '33; m. Lucinda Blood, May 31, '57; r. Rock., telegraph operator, &c.; rem. Presque Isle. 3, Augusta, b. April 14, '36; mar. Ransom Pierce, Sept. 11, '53. 4, Barnard U., b. Dec. 12, '37; died of yellow fever, at sea, in sch. *Hardscrabble*, March, 1856. 5, Matthias U., b. April 26, '41; r. Rock. The mother died April 6, '60, aged 52.

Capt. Bernard's ch. 1, Helen M., b. March 20, 1835; mar. Capt. Michael O. Porter; r. Rock. 2, James B., b. Feb. 12, '37; r. Rock., killed at sea, May, 1860, by a fall from aloft. 3, Caroline V., b. Mar. 24, '39; m. Freeman C. Hanley; r. Rock. 4, Frances P., b. April 7, '42; r. Rock. 5, Marion, b. ab. '46. 6, Addie, b. ab. '49. 7, George, b. ab. '52.

Capt. Martin, (2d)'s ch. 1, Alonzo N., b. Feb. 20, 1841; soldier of 4th Me., &c.

Fifth Generation.

Gilman L.'s ch. 1, Clarence E., b. ab. '54. 2, Lizzie E., b. ab. '56.

Oliver B.'s ch. 1, Sarah F., b. Sept. 23, and d. Nov. 25, 1857. 2, Heber A., b. ab. '59.

Ephraim J.'s ch. by 1st wife. 1, William, b. April, 1848, d. Oct. 9, '49. 2, Elizabeth, b. ab. '50. By 2d wife. 3, Martha D., b. ab. '52. By 3d wife. 4, George H., b. ab. '59.

Frederic T.'s ch. George Herbert, b. Nov. 9, '55, d. Aug. 17, '58.

Orris B.'s ch. 1, Addie, b. ab. 1844. 2, Clara, b. ab. '46. 3, Helen, b. ab. '50. 4, Adriel, b. ab. '55.

Edward E.'s ch. 1, Elvira L., b. May 25, 1853, d. March 15, '62. 2, Orris E., b. ab. '58.

Hiram F.'s ch Clara E., b. ab. 1859.

William N.'s ch. William E., b. ab. 1859.

Sears S.'s ch. 1, Frank Blair, b. Nov. 30, 1858, d. Feb. '60. 2, Harry N., b. Sept. 25, '60, d. Oct. 7, '63.

VANSTONE, James, b. ab. 1784, in England, a wheelwright by trade, m. Harriet Robinson, p. Feb. 14, 1818; kept tavern at Prison corner, Th., rem. and r. Rock. Their ch. 1, James, (2d), b. May 9, 1818, d. Oct. 29, '37. 2, Samuel, b. Sept. 21, '19, d. at Mobile, Nov. 1, or 30, '39. 3, Catharine P., b. Sept. 26, '21, m. Capt. David H. Ingraham; r. Rock. 4, William M., b. Sept. 21, '23, m. Almira H. Fales, July 18, '47. 5, Alinda F., or Melinda, b. Sept. 6, '27, d. Nov. 22, or Dec. 21, '45. 6, Mary A., b. Oct. 18, '41; r. Rock.

VARNEY, Richard, b. Nov. 1, 1807; r. Rock., and d. Feb. 10, '59. Harriet D., his wife, d. Oct. 14, '58, a. 51. Alfred S. Varney, r. S. Th., soldier of 8th Me., &c.

VAUGHAN, Daniel, b. Dec. 10, 1787, son of James of Carver, Mass., c. to Warren, where he taught school, was an assessor, m. 1st, Polly Dunham of Plymouth, 2d, Nancy Spear of W., June 24, 1829, rem. Th., and d. at Rock., Oct. 24, '60, found dead in his bed. His ch. 1, Stetson, mar. Olive Gleason of U.; r. Abington, Mass. 2, Nancy, m. and r. Abington. 3, George, d. unm. 4, Mary Ann, b. Oct. 10, 1818, m. Horace Williams; r. S. Th., and d. March 1, '47. By 2d wife. 5, Olive G., b. ab. '34, m. Samuel S. Haskell; r. Rock. 6, Agnes C., b. July 21, '37. Nancy, the mother, d. Jan. 30, '55, a. 59.

VEAZIE, Abiezer, m. and r. Camden. Of his sons, 1, Capt. Sewell Watson, b. ab. 1825 in Cam., m. Mary E. Thorndike of Cam.; r. Rock., a mariner. 2, Samuel M., b. ab. 1830 in Cam., m. Mary K. Sears, Dec. 21, '51; r. Rock., a stove dealer. 3, Abiezer, (2d), (or Abijah, as in Adjt. Gen's Report,) b. ab. '32, m. Freelove Richards; r. Rock., soldier in 4th Me., re-enlisted.

Sewell W.'s ch. Sarah, b. ab. 1851.

Samuel M.'s ch. Morris C., b. ab. 1859.

Abiezer's ch. Freelove A., b. ab. 1852.

VERRILL; of this Vinalhaven family, there came to this place, 1, Capt. Henry, b. ab. 1806 in V., m. Caroline Ulmer, Aug. 14, '31; r. Rock., a master mariner. 2, Jacob A., a brother, m. Mary R. Fogerty, p. Aug. 14, '35; r. Rock.? Of their cousins. 1, Thomas, b. Sept. 29, 1805 in Vinalhaven, mar. Harriet ——, who was born Aug. 1, 1809; r. Rock., a lime burner, &c. 2, David, m. Emeline Morrill, p. July 29, '40; r. Rock.?

Capt. Henry's ch. 1, Capt. Henry S., b. Jan. 14, 1833, m. Margaret E. Porter, May 10, '54; r. Rock., and d. at sea, April 2, '55. 2, Margaret, b. May 1, '35, m. Capt. Albert F. Ames; r. Rock. 3, Capt. Levi U., b. Oct. 24, '37, m. Ellen L. Hall, Sept. 19, '63; r. Rock. 4, Emma K., b. ab. '49.

Thomas's ch. 1, John N., b. Oct. 14, 1833; r. Rock., d. Mar. 12, '60. 2, Maria, b. March 3, '37, m. Wesley H. Priest, Aug. 10, '62; r. Rock. 3, Joseph Edwin, b. Aug. 3, '39, mar. —— Metcalf; r. Rock., a carver, soldier in a Mass. Reg., &c. 4, Clara H., b. April 30, '42, d. March 17, '49.

VESPER, or Wesberg, Capt. Peter, b. ab. 1807, in Slape, Sweden, c. here in 1817; m. 1st, Catharine Pitcher, (who d. May 18, '43,) 2d, Almira Morse of Friendship, Nov. 10, '44; r. Th., a ship master. His ch. by 1st wife. 1, Ambrose, b. ab. 1836; r. Th., a mariner. By 2d wife. 2, Oliver M., b. ab. '45. 3, Randall N., b. ab. '47, d. in May, '63. 4, Allen or Alton H., b. ab. '50. 5, Charles P., b. ab. '57.

VINAL, Oliver M., b. ab. 1823, in Waldoboro'; m. Arcan, dau. of Dr. Hill of C., Nov. 20, '47; r. Th., a carpenter, school teacher & superintendent. Newell E., a brother, b. ab. '34; r. Th., a carpenter.

Oliver M.'s ch., William E., b. ab. 1850.

VOSE, Jonathan, of Milton; m. 1st, Mary ——, and had ch. 1, Seth, b. Jan. 4, 1733-4; m. Rachel Copeland; c. east in 1763; r. & d. in Cushing. 2, Samuel; 3, Jonathan, (2d); 4, Hannah; 5, Jane; 6, Thomas, probably d. in infancy; 7, Mary; 8, Jesse; 9, Ebenezer; 10, Jemima; 11, Kezia; all remained in Milton. (By his 2d wife, Mary ——;) 12, Capt. Thomas, b. May 8, 1753; m. Sarah George; was an officer in the Revolution; c. to Th., a merchant, &c., d. Dec. 28, 1810. 13, Mary, b. Sept. 29, 1755. [Milton Records.]

Seth's ch. 1, Elijah, b. Aug. 1, 1766 ; m. Sarah Andrews ; r. W., a farmer, & d. April 10, 1840. 2, Mary, b. 1770 ; m. 1st, John McIntyre, 2d, Dea. Calvin Crane ; r. W. & d. May 13, 1843. 3, Seth, (2d), b. 1772 ; r. W., a farmer ; m. Lydia Delano, & d. Oct. 18, 1846. 4, Ebenezer, b. 1774 ; r. Th.; m. 1st, Nancy Lermond of W., Jan. 14, 1802, 2d, Sarah (Bridges) Dunbar, May 9, 1812 ; r. Th., a joiner, rem. Montville & d. May 21, '29. 5, David, b. Feb. 8, 1776 ; m. Alice L. Eastman ; rem. Montville, a farmer, & d. Feb. 25, 1844. 6, Elizabeth, m. Capt. Arch. Robinson of C. 7, Hannah, m. Dr. Isaiah Cushing ; r. Th. & d. Oct. 24, 1816. 8, Rufus, d young. 9, William, m. Jane McCarter, April 7, '14 ; r. C. 10, Capt. John, b. 1784 ; m. 1st, Mary Hyler, Aug. 11, '14, 2d, Hannah S. Healey, Dec. '34 ; r. C. & Rock., & d. in Cushing, May 7, '39. 11, Rachel, b. Aug. 20, '93 ; m. George W. Stevens ; r. Rock.

Capt. Thomas's ch. 1, Mary, b. Sept. 26, 1785 ; m. Capt. Archibald Robinson of C., p. May 16, 1811, & d. Jan. 2, '54. 2, Sarah, b. Sept. 28, 1787, d. Nov. '93. 3, Margaret, b. Sept. 28, '89, d. Nov. '93. 4, Lucy, b. April 23, 1791 ; m. Capt. William Henderson of C., Jan. 30, 1815 ; r. Th. & d. July 19, '25. 5, Thomas, (2d), b. Jan. 1, & d. Nov., '93. 6, Sarah P., b. Oct. 4, 1794 ; m. Dea. James Partridge ; r. Rock. 7, Thomas P., b. Sept. 13, 1796 ; r. Th., a merchant, &c. ; d. unm. May 10, 1832. 8, William, (2d), b. Dec. 24, '98 ; r. Th. in the homestead, Wadsworth st. 9, James, b. March 23, 1800 ; m. Sophia Andrews of W., Jan. 10, '33 ; r. Wadsworth st. The mother d. Feb. 20, '35, a. 79.

For Elijah's, Seth, (2d)'s and Ebenezer's ch., see Annals of Warren.

David's ch. 1, Capt. Burton, b. Sept. 21, 1797 ; mar. Elizabeth Bentley, Nov. 17, 1822 ; r. Th., and d. May 23, '40, at New Orleans. 2, Mehitable, b. Sept. 26, '99 ; m. John Evans of Montville. 3, Capt. Edward K., b. June 6, 1801 ; m. Eliza L. Spear, Oct. 7, '27, 2d, Mary Clements, 3d, Belinda M. Clements ; r. Th., rem. Montville. 4, Seth, (4th), b. May 29, '03 ; m. Alice R. Fales, Sept. 18, '28 ; r. Th., a farmer, &c. 5, Benjamin, b. April 23, '05 ; m. Lucinda Clements, 2d, Jane P. Avery of Whitefield ; r. Th , a carpenter, sheriff, &c. 6, Elijah, (2d), Esq., b. March 19, '07 ; m. Mary True, June 4, '43, prac. law, & r. U. 7, Sarah E., b. Feb. 18, '09 ; mar. Nathan Haskell of Knox. 8, Rufus, b. March 8, '11 ; m. Eliza T. Ayer, and d. Nov. 11, '42. 9, Bartholomew K., b. March 19, '13 ; mar. Sarah T. Haskell. 10, David, (2d), b. May 11, '15, d. April 13, '39. 11, Alice L., d. a. 2 years. 12, Cyrus N., b. Dec. 21, '19, d. July, '42.

William's ch. 1, Capt. James, b. June, 1814 ; mar. Sarah P. Kelleran, June 21, '42, d. March 31, '50, drowned near Mobile. 2, Alfred, b. May 5, '16 ; m. Catharine M. McIntyre, Sept., 1843 ; r. Th., & d. Feb. 22, '53. 3, Edwin, m. Irene Counce, March 31, '57 ; r. C. 4, Robert, m. Mary (Young) Robinson ; r. C. 5, Belinda ; r. C.

Capt. John's ch. 1, Almira, b. Feb. 2, 1815 ; m. William S. Ingraham ; r. Rock. 2, Angelina, b. March 10, '18 ; mar. John Kelloch, (4th) ; r. Rock., & d. June 11, '40. 3, Pamela J., b. Nov. 1, '22, d. Oct. 14, '25. The mother d. Oct. 23, 1823, aged 27 years, 9 months. By 2d wife. 4, Z. Pope, b. Sept. 26, 1835 ; mar. Adelaide F. Snow, July 25, '64 ; r. Rock., editor of Rockland Gazette, Youth's Temperance Visitor, &c.

James's ch. 1, Lucy, b. June 6, 1833 ; m. John W. Mathews, p. Nov. 25, '51 ; r. W. 2, Thomas O., b. March 26, '36. 3, Oliver A., b. Sept. 25, '37 ; m. Cordelia M. Watts, Jan. 12, '61 ; r. Th. 4, Maria

A., b. March 26, '42. 5, Benjamin, born Aug. 22, 1846, died April 27, 1847.

Capt. Burton's ch. 1, Edward K., b. June 24, 1824, d. Jan. 15, '44, at Staten Island. 2, Sarah A., b. Oct. 28, '26, d. Aug. 5, '33. 3, Capt. Isaac M., b. Jan. 6, '29; m. Augustina Edgarton, Sept. 26, '55; r. Th., & d. at New York, suddenly, Aug. 6, or 7, '61. 4, Susan C., b. March 27, '35; r. Th. 5, John B., b. Dec. 2, '36, d. Nov. 3, '38. 6 & 7, twins, b. in Knox, July 29, '32; Thomas B., d. Aug. 24, '33, Elizabeth, d Aug. 5, '33. 8, Mary E., b. May 21, '39, d. Ap'l 2, '42.

Benjamin's ch. 1, James C., b. ab. 1830; m. Abby M. Hix, Dec. 27, '63; r. Th. 2, Sarah E., b. ab. '34. 3, Marcia P., d. young. 4, Dolly C., b. ab. '39. By 2d wife. 5, Celia M., b. ab. '44. 6, Wallace, b. ab. '47. 7, Frank, b. ab. '49. 8, Emma W., b. Dec. 24, '51, d. July 29, '57. 9, Marcia A., b. Dec. 22, '55, d. Aug. 1, '57.

Seth, (4th)'s ch. 1, Eliza L., d. Sept. 5, 1841. 2, Nancy F., b. ab. '32; m. James Comstock; r. Th. 3, Alice L., b. April 25, '36; m. Daniel Mayo; r. Th. 4, David, (2d), b. ab. '43; r. Th., entered the navy.

Capt. James's ch. 1, Emma L., b. ab. 1843. 2, Ambrose, b. May 24, '45, d. Aug. 16, '53. 3, James B., b. ab. '50.

Capt. Alfred's ch. Laura C., b. 1844, d. Jan. 6, '50.

Capt. Isaac M.'s ch. Ida, b. ab. 1854.

VOSE, Spencer, b. 1754, a cousin, it is believed, of Seth and Capt. Thomas; m. Mary (Lushe) Hastings; came from Attleboro' to Th., about 1790; a tanner, &c., d. Dec. 13, 1806. Their ch. 1, Sally, b. Aug. 3, 1782; m. Joseph Bryant of Newcastle, Jan. 5, 1800, 2d, David S. Fales of Th., & d. Aug. 10, 1853. 2, George, b. May 4, 1785; m. Betsey Stackpole, March 5, 1807; rem. Castine. The mother died Jan. 28, 1818, aged 73.

WADE, Philip, came from Scituate, Mass, m. 1st, ——— ———, 2d, Mary Simmons of W., June 5, 1808; r. Wal. and Union. His ch. by 1st wife. 1, Lydia, b. 1769; m. Hugh Paul; r. Bristol, and died July 20, 1851, aged 82. 2, Roland, b. May, 1771; c. to S. Th., mar. Mary Holland, pub. May 4, 1798, 2d, Sarah (Randall) Coombs, June 29, 1835; r. S. Th., a ship carpenter, and d. in S. Danvers, Nov. 10, 1855. 3, Capt. Leonard, ; m. Sally Lovett, p. Nov. 5, 1799; r. S. Th., a master mariner, rem. Union. 4, Philip, m. and r. Friendship, but rem. 5, Levi, m. Deborah Nash; r. Wal., and d. when his only son, Moses Ellis Wade of War. was 8 years old; his widow m. 2d, Philip Stahl of W., and 3d, Brotherton Daggett of U.

Roland's ch. 1, Jane, b. June 19, 1799; m. Zebedee, or Edmund W. Wood; r. Boston and South Danvers. 2, John H., b. March 17, 1801; mar. Eunice Getchell of Brunswick, Jan. 19, '26, 2d, Hannah Merriman of Owls Head, Aug. 3, '45; r. S. Th. 3, Daniel, b. Dec. 19, 1802, d. Sept. 13, '04. 4, Margaret, b. Feb. 8, and d. Oct. 13, '05. 5, Nancy M., born Feb. 24, '08; mar. Samuel Waters of Boston. 6, Catharine P., b. Jan. 1, '10; m. George C. Dow; and d June 23, '59. 7, Capt. Joseph S., b. Sept. 21, '12; m. Rosina Ranlett of St. George, p. Dec. 10, '37; rem. Montville. 8, William B., b. Dec. 4, '16; mar. Mary Ann Witham, Aug. 22, '43; and d. in Florida.

John H.'s ch. by 1st wife. 1, Achsa Jane, b. ab. 1827; m. William Henry Witham; r. Rock. 2, Lorenzo, lost at sea. 3, John E., b. ab. '31; r. Rock., sergeant in U. S. sharp shooters, &c.

Capt. Joseph S.'s ch. 1, Cynthia J., b. Sept. 13, 1839. 2, Mary J., b. Aug. 18, '42. 3, Alfred, b. April, '45, d. Jan. 30, '50. 4, Josephus; 5, Emma; 6, Charlotte R.; all rem. Montville.

William B.'s ch. 1, Edmund J., b. ab. 1845; r. S. Th., a mariner. 2, William R., b. ab. '47. 3, Franklin S., b. ab. '49. Of this name, also, Edwin Wade, mar. Margaret C. Holden, Dec. 31, '64; r. Rock., soldier of 4th Me., &c.

WAGNER, Andrew, b. ab. 1806, in Waldoboro'; m. Elsie Stimpson; r. Rock., a lime burner. Their ch. 1, William L., b. ab. 1833; m. Lorinda M. Wyman, June 6, '63; r. Rock., a lime burner, &c.

WAIT, John W., came from Calais, Me., m. Mary Pettigrove; r. S. Th. Of their ch. Alice E. D , was b. Feb 8, 1861.

WAKEFIELD, Rev. John, born ab. 1797, in Bath, Me., mar. Ann Prior of Bath, 1821; was Bap. minister at Th. and of Warren from 1820 to '27; forced by ill health to leave the ministry, he went into trade; rem. Rock. 1844, a bookseller, afterwards corn and flour merchant, rem. Portland 1860, returned Rock. '63. Their ch. 1, Elizabeth, b. ab. 1822; m. Miles C. Andrews; r. Rock. 2, Olivia B., b. ab. '25; r. Rock., an artist. 3, Ann, b. ab. '27; m. William C. Burgess; r. Th. 4, Maria J., b. Nov., '29, d. June 27, '52. 5, Virginia W., b. ab. 1842.

WALCH, John, b. ab. 1820, in Ireland, mar. in Appleton, Mary or Sarah Richardson; r. Th. Their ch. 1, John, b. ab. 1857. 2, Mary, b. ab. 1858.

WALDO, Shubael, came from Wellington, Ct., m. Martha B. Haskell, Nov. 15, 1835; r. Th., a merchant, &c. Their ch. 1, Amelia, b. Feb. 7, 1838; mar. Capt. Edwin A. Robinson; r. Th. 2, Frederic D., b. March 27, '43; r. Th., entered the navy. 3, Martha, b. June 29, '45. 4, Maria, b. Jan., 1849. 5, Annie or Fannie S., born May 20, 1850.

WALKER; of the sons of Amos Walker of Union, there c. here, 1, Amos, (2d), b. ab. 1816; mar. Eliza Starrett of W., 2d, Susan A. Clements of Ellsworth, pub. Sept. 8, '50, 3d, Mary Caroline Bailey of Pawtucket, Oct. 16, '54; r. Th., a ship builder. 2, Col. Elijah, b. ab. 1818; m. Susan E. Brown of Rock. Nov. 3, '44; r. Rock., a lumber merchant, officer in the army, &c.

Amos's ch. by 1st wife. 1, John, b. ab. 1845. 2, Susan Caroline, b. ab. 1847. The mother d. Oct. 30, '49. By 2d wife. 3, Eliza S., b. ab. '51. The mother d. Aug. 29, '53. By 3d wife. 4, Amos B., b. Nov. 5, 1855, d. of diphtheria, Nov. 7, '62.

Col. Elijah's ch. 1, William H., b. ab. 1846. 2, Narcissa R., b. ab. '48. 3, Ireson B., b. ab. '50. 4, Winfield S., b. ab. 52. 5, Frank, b. ab. '56. 6, Annie B., b. ab. '59.

WALKER, Capt. Ebenezer, b. ab. 1808 in Canaan, ? Me., m. Margaret Douglass, March 7, '31; r. Rock., a lime burner, &c. His ch. 1, Mary Eliza, b. Nov. 23, '34. 2, Rhoda Ann, born Nov. 6, '36. 3, John Fairfield, b. Dec. 15, '38, m. Mary A. Lamb, Nov. 30, '58; r. Rock., musician in 4th Me., &c.

WALKER, Capt. Charles, b. in London, England, 1798, son of a mathematical instrument maker; c. to Th. in the war of 1812, mar. Harriet M. (Shibles) Burnham, p. Nov. 9, '33; r. Th., & d. Nov. 18, '44. Their ch. 1, Betsey, b. May 19, '35. 2, Harriet, b. July 30, '38, m. Peletiah M. Studley, Jan. 13, '57; r. Th. 3, Charles, b. Feb. 19, '40; r. Th.

WALKER, Abel, b. in Wilton, Me., Sept. 26, 1811, m. 1st, Louisa Lake of New Sharon, Sept. 2, '38, 2d, Mary Clark of Wilton, Sept.

29, '43; r. Rock., since Dec. 31, '59, a mill manager, &c. His ch. By 2d wife. 1, Louisa L., b. in Wilton, Dec. 28, '44. 2, Malvina F., b. Feb. 26, '46. 3, E. Clark, b. in Wilton, April 16, '48. 4, Catharine E., b. in Dixfield, July 24, '57. Of this name, also, Joseph R. Walker, b. ab. 1826, mar. Susan P. Snow, July 25, '52; r. Rock., a carpenter. Their ch. 1, Lizzie, b. ab. 1853. 2, Winthrop T., born Aug. 29, '56.

WALL; of this St. George family, two brothers c. to this place, 1, Capt. Aaron S., b. in St. G., m. Elsie F. Watts; r. awhile in Th., and rem. to Ashland, Mass. 2, Joseph S., b. ab. 1810 in St. G., mar. Nancy L. Kelloch, p. Nov. 4, '36; r. Rock., a merchant.

Capt. Aaron S.'s ch. recorded here. 1, Ellen, b. Nov. 17, 1836, d. May 5, '46. 2, Edwin, b. Dec. 17, '38, d. April 1, '39. 3, Aaron F., b. May 10, '42.

Joseph S.'s ch. 1, ? Leonard, b. 1840, d. Nov. 30, '63. 2, Olive, b. ab. '43. 3, George E., b. ab. '45; r. Rock., sergeant in 4th Me. Reg., &c. 4, Vinal E., b. ab. '47; r. Rock., corporal in 20th Me. 5, Frank, d. July 31, '62.

WALLACE, Capt. James, b. ab. 1820 in Cape Small Point, Phipsburg, Me., m. Bethana Bucklin of Cam., p. March 27, '41; r. Rock. Their ch. 1, Adelaide, b. ab. '44. 2, Helen, b. ab. '50. 3, Arthur, b. ab. '52. 4, Nellie, b. ab. '54.

WALLACE, Capt. Joseph, of Cape Ann, m. Lucy Thorndike of Cape Elizabeth, where he r. awhile, took down in his vessel the first 16 settlers of Machias, settled in what is now Harrington, where he traded, was major in the militia, and d. a. 92. His only child, Col. Joseph, m. Deborah Smith of Machias, and d. at Harrington, about 1845. Of his 5 sons, and 2 dau., 1, Capt. George W., b. ab. '01, m. Mary Cobb, came from Cherryfield to W., ab. 1837, rem. Th., 18 ,0. His ch. 1, Capt. Francis C., b. ab. '33, m. Jennie Watts of Great Britain; r. Th. 2, Jane C., b. ab. '35, m. Leonard Cooper; r. Th. 3, Charlotte B., b. ab. '38, m. Capt. Albert Havener; r. Th. 4, Joseph W., b. in W., ab. '40, d. June 26, '59, of yellow fever at Havana. 5, Given B., b. ab. '42, a soldier in 1st D. C. Cavalry. 6, Mary Helen, b. Jan. 1, '44; m. Serg't Leander Robinson, p. Aug. 28, '63; r. W. 7, George E., b. ab. '46. 8, Fanny S., b. ab. '49. 9, Albert H., b. ab. '50. 10, Eva A., b. Sept. 30, and d. Nov. 4, '53.

WALLACE, Reuben, b. ab. 1829, in Waldoboro'; m. Arvilla A. Lothrop; r. Rock., a lime burner. Their ch. 1, Sarah H., b. ab. 1855. 2, Lucy A. E., b. ab. '58. 3, Hattie E., b. Feb., & d. March 26, '60. 4, Winfield S., b. Oct. 11, '61, d. Nov. 1, '63.

WALSH, William, b. 1765; c. from Dublin, Ireland, in 1774, and, after some time, to Th.; m. Sarah Pressy, p July 8, '89; r. Rock., a schoolmaster; d. June 30, 1837. His widow d. Feb. 19, 1844, a. 73. Their ch. 1, James, m. Susanna Gloyd, Jan. 23, '25; r. Rock., a farmer. 2, Lawrence, m. Eliza Harrington; d. in the army or navy, ab. 1813 or 14. 3, William, (2d), m. Nancy Watson, May 9, '16; r. Rock. & d. Jan. 22, '36. 4, John, b. ab. 1800; m. Naomi Ott of Cam. April 14, '25; r. Rock. 5, Robert, b. '03; m. Mary Ann Elliott, p. Oct. 25, '34; r. Th., a successful shipbuilder & business man; d. instantly, July 20, 1864. 6, Sarah, m. David Boyd, and rem. Ohio. 7, Alice, b. Nov. 28, 1819; m. Simon Benner, 2d, Oliver Rackliff; r. Rock.

James's ch. 1, Susanna, b. Aug. 27, 1825; m. Franklin P. Witham; r. Rock. 2, Spencer G., b. Sept. 3, '27; m. Hannah M. Keen, Dec. 17, '48; r. Rock., a farmer, soldier in 2d Me. Battery, &c.

William, (2d)'s ch. 1, Patrick W., b. Aug. 12, 1816; m. Dolly Perry, June 26, '42; r. Rock., a merchant. 2, James W., b. Dec. 31, '18; m. Mary J. or Rachel Sheldon, Feb. 18, '47; r. Rock. & d. Jan. 31, '63. 3, Capt. William, (3d), b. Sept. 16, '22; m. Mary F. Blaisdell, Jan. 1, '48, d. Nov., '57, supposed murdered for his money, at Portsmouth, N. H., where his body was found. 4, Bradish W., b. June 10, '24, d. Aug. 15, '57. 5, George S., b. July 4, '27; r. Rock., a lime burner. 6, Enos C., b. Aug. 22, '30; r. Rock., a lime burner. 7, Susan, b. Feb. 20, '35, d. July 10, '41

John's ch. 1, Nancy, b. June 10, 1825; m. I. J. Fields; r. Rock. 2, Thomas, b. Dec. 28, '26; m. Mary E. Robinson; r. Rock., a lime burner. 3, Robert, (2d), b. May 22, '28; m. Lydia Fields, p. March 16, '50, 2d, Maria Flanders, Dec. 30, '58; r. Rock., a joiner, soldier, &c. 4, Mary, b. Dec. 16, '29. 5, Merrick, b. Dec. 16, '33, d. March 14, '36. 6, Alvina, b. June 4, & d. June 28, '34. 7, John, (2d), b. Sept. 4, '36; was mate of a ship and died at sea.

Robert's ch. 1, Robert K., b. Sept. 3, 1835, d. Nov. 21, 1855. 2, Edwin, b. Sept. 24, '37; r. Th., a merchant. 3, Ann E., b. March 2, '41. 4, Richard E., b. ab. '45. 5, Alfred, b. ab. '51.

Spencer G.'s ch. 1, Augusta I., b. ab. 1850. 2, Susan G., b. ab. '52. 3, Priscilla K., b. ab. '54. 4, Raymond R., b. ab. '56. 5, William J., b. ab. '58.

Patrick W.'s ch. 1, Harvey S., b. ab. 1845; r. Rock., entered U. S. Navy. 2, ? Patrick, b. ab. '47; r. Rock., entered the navy. 3, ? Frank, b. ab. '49.

James W.'s ch. 1, Franklin, b. ab. 1848. 2, Frederic, b. ab. '50. 3, Emma.

Thomas's ch. Abby L., b. ab. 1859.

WARD, Nathaniel C., b. ab. 1814; mar. twice; r. Rock., a shop keeper. Ch. 1, Nathaniel, b. ab 1848. 2, Ellen S., b. ab. '51. 3, Edward S., b. ab. '54. 4, Francis C., b. ab. '58.

WARREN, Augustus, b. ab. 1836; r. Rock., a blacksmith, some time; but rem. to Augusta. Martin V. Warren mar. Cinderella Thomas of Rock., Nov. 27, '64.

WASGATT, George W., b. ab. 1824, in Tremont, Mt. Desert; m. 1st, Lucy Shorey, Jan. 11, '54, 2d, Susan G Conary; r. Rock., a mariner, soldier in 8th Me., &c. 2, William, b. ab. 1829; m. Margaret J. Sterling, April 16, '55; r. Rock., a mariner, soldier in 2d Cavalry, &c. William's ch. 1, Alvah H., b. ab. 1852. 2, Llewellyn, b. ab. '56. 3, Charles F., d. Feb., 1859.

WASHBURN, Rev. Job, came from Kingston, Mass., m. Sally D. (Clough) Bowman, p. March 12, 1812; was a shoemaker in St. Geo., a merchant in Th., where he became the minister of the 2d Baptist church, from 1822 to '41; rem. Cam., and m. 2d, Betsey, widow of William Carleton, May 8, 1848; r. Cam. Kimball, a brother, mar. Mary Stevenson; r. Taunton, Kingston, and Providence. Lucy, a sister, m. Abner Rice, and r. Th.; also, Sarah P., a sister, mar. Capt. Robert Snow; r. Th.

Rev. Job's ch. by 1st wife. 1, Antoinette, b. Jan. 13, 1818; mar. Lewis T. Fales; r. Washington, D. C. 2, Harriet N, b. Oct. 18, '15; m. 1st, Capt. Enoch Eastman of Rockport, 2d, S. Dexter Carleton of Cam., July 15, '47 3, Capt. Judson R. or E., b. Oct. 18, '17; mar.

Sarah L. Biskey, March 11, '45 ; r. Th., a master mariner. 4, John W., b. Jan. 12, and d. Oct. 2, '20. 5, Isabella P., b. Aug. 18, '21 ; m. Eben E. Carleton, Nov. 26, '39 ; r. Cam. 6, Sarah E., b. Sept. 27, '23 ; mar. Benj. Robinson, r. Th. 7, Lucy R., b. July 9, '25, d. Sept. 12, '26. 8, Mary S., b. April 2, and d. April 23, '27. 9, Job Kimball, born Feb. 10, '28 ; r. Cam. 10, Wm. Henry, b. Nov. 27, '29 ; m. Josephine S. Verrill, Dec. 12, '56 ; r. Cam., a sail maker ; 11, Abby P., born April 28, '32 ; m. Augustus C. Carleton of Cam., Dec. 7, 1851.

Of Kimball's ch. 1, Margaret, m. Willard Fales, (2d), r. Th. and d. N. Y. 2, Mary, R., b. 1814 ; m. William Thompson ; r. Th., and d. March 25, '44. 3, George K., c. to Th., m. Abigail K. Dunn, June 22, '42 ; r. Knox St., a sailmaker. 4, Capt. Charles P. or B., r. sometime in Th., mar. Sarah L., dau. of Horace Breed of Boston, Feb. 23, '52, 2d, Lydia Hatch of Rock., where he resides, a sailing master in U. S. N.

Capt. Judson R.'s ch. 1, Katie B., b. ab. 1846. 2, Mary, b. ab. '50. 3, Judson, b. ab. '52.

George K.'s ch. 1, George S., b. ab. 1843. 2, Frank, b. ab. '45. 3, Charles, b. ab. '48. 4, Edward P., b. ab. '52. 5, Wm., b. ab. '56.

WASS, Alexander H., b. ab. 1825 in Addison, Me., mar. Elizabeth S. ——— ; r. Rock., a millinery merchant, rem. Cal. with their son, Alexander H., (2d), b. ab. '59.

WATERHOUSE, Ezra, b. ab. 1822, in Liberty, Me., m. Nancy J. Orbeton ; r. Rock., a joiner. Their ch. 1, Louisa, b. ab. '50. 2, William, b. ab. '56. 3, Isaac O., b. '59.

WATERMAN, Samuel H., b. Jan., 1824, in Waldoboro', m. Olive Frances Adams, Jan., 1847 ; r. Th., a house and ship joiner, and d. at Wal., Sept. 11, '49. His wife d. Feb. 26, '57 Charles, a brother, also c. and r. Th., a ship builder, & m. Julia A. Harrington, June 16, '63. Samuel H.'s ch. 1, Charles Wm., b. Sept. 14, '48, d. Sept. 19, '49. 2, Samuel M.

WATERMAN, Winslow, b. ab. 1817 in North Haven, m. Emily A. Sampson ; r. Rock., a carpenter, &c. Albion P., b. ab. 1825, mar. Lucy A. Thomas, March 25, '52 ; r. Rock., a merchant. Of their sisters it is believed, three r. Rock., Lucy, Mary A., and Julia. Adeline, also d. in Rock., Dec. 31, '61.

Winslow's ch. 1, Warren S., b. ab. 1850. 2, Maria K. 3, Lucy A., b. ab. '58.

Albion P.'s ch. 1, Hattie E., b. Jan. 6, 1855, d. Feb. 14, '57. 2, Frederic, b. ab. '56.

WATERS, Eugene, b. in Waterville, ab. 1834 ; r. Rock.. a member of 4th Me. Reg. and State guards, was a merchant, and d. Aug. 27, '64, found dead in his bed.

WATTS, William, c. in the Scotch Irish emigration of 1719 ; m. Margaret McLellan of Casco ; r. & d. Boston, or neighboring islands. Their ch. 1, John, b. on Long Island, Boston Harbor, 1740 or '42 ; m. Elizabeth McNeal of Boston ; c. to W., 1764, r. there & d. Aug. 10, 1817. For his descendants, see Annals of Warren. 2, Capt. Samuel, b. on Long Island ; m. Mary Robinson, Dec. 22, 1772 ; r. & d. St. G. 3, a dau. d. unm. in Mass. The mother m. 2d, Samuel Gilchrist, & r. awhile on the McLean or S. Andrews lot, in what is now Warren. Capt. Samuel's ch. 1, Capt. Joseph, b. Sept. 27, 1773 ; m. Sarah Stone of Linc., 2d, Cynthia (Everett) Ranlett ; r. St. Geo. & d. Sept. 7, 1841. 2, Margaret, b. July 27, '75 ; m. Moses Fogerty ; r. &

d. St. G. 3, Jane, b. June 23, '77 ; m. Joshua Smalley; r. & d. St. G. 4, Capt. John, b March 20, '79 ; m. Hannah Smalley; r. & d. St. G., a master mariner. 5, Samuel, (2d), b. April 12, 1781; d. at Guadaloupe, from a cut & ensuing mortification. 6, Moses, b. June 5, '83 ; m. Catharine McKellar, 2d, Polly Fogerty; rem. & d. Montville. 7, Mary, b. July 11, '85 ; d. with throat distemper. 8, Capt. William, b. Dec. 11, '87 ; m. Jane, dau. of Thomas Henderson of St. G.; r. Th., a carpenter, militia officer, &c. 9, George, b. March 16, '90 ; m. Mary Giles; r. St. G. 10, Elizabeth, b. July 20, '92 ; m. Asa Harrington ; r. & d. Appleton. 11, Sarah, b. April 2, '95 ; m. Paul Giles, 2d, Mark Gay of C.; r. Th., & d. Nov., 1859.

Capt. Joseph's ch. 1, Mary, m. Isaac Thompson of Montville, & d. leaving but one child ; viz., J. W. Thompson, Esq., an active business man in Stockton, Me. 2. Jane, b. ab. 1798 ; m. Samuel Fogerty; r. Th. 3, Rachel, m. George Watts of W. ; rem. & d. Harrington, Me., (having had 5 ch. of whom the 4th, George, rem. with his father to Oregon, & 5th, Rachel, m. William Beckett of Th.; rem. Cal.) 4, Sarah, b. June 16, 1801 ; m. Charles Watts of Warren, (who d. Feb. 24, '63, a. 64,) r. W. 5, Elizabeth, m. 1st, John Giles, 2d, John Teal; r. St. G. 6, Capt. Wm., (2d), b. ab. '05 ; m. Elizabeth Trussell of St. G.; r. Th., a master mariner. 7, Joseph, (2d), m. Cyrena Luke of St. Geo. 8, Nancy, m. Dea. Joseph Simmons of St. G, 2d, William Gilchrist of St. Geo. 9, Capt. Samuel, (3d), b. ab. '11 ; m. Clarissa Mills of St. G.; r. Th., a ship builder & merchant, for a time under the firm of Watts, O'Brien & Co., & since by himself. 10, Capt. George, (2d), lost at sea in sch. *E. O'Brien* 11, Capt. Alfred, b. April 25, '16 ; m. Elizabeth W. Brown, July 20, 1843 ; r. Th. since '38, a master mariner. By 2d wife. 12, Capt. John, (3d), m. Eliza Davis; r. East Boston, Mass.

Capt John's ch. 1, Samuel, (4th), Esq., m. Sarah Linnekin; r. St. G. 2, Capt. Joshua, m. Lucy Hall, 2d, Cyrena Clark ; r. St. G. 3, Ketura, m. Capt. Alex. Hathorn, 2d, Albion Wall of St Geo. 4, Mary ; 5, David, both d. young. 6, Lydia; m. Capt Eben Farnham of Boothbay. 7, Hannah, m Capt. ——— Robinson of Belfast; r. St. G. 8, John, (4th), b. ab. '14 ; m. Sarah Linnekin of Belfast; r. Tenant's Harbor, St. G., & now Rock., a merchant. 9, Edward, died young. 10, David P., m. Mary J. Harrington ; r. St. George.

Moses's ch. 1, Isaac, m. a Foster; r. Knox. 2, Wiers, m a Foster; r. Montville. 3, Levi, m. a McLaughlin; r. Montville. 4, Catharine, m. a Smith; r. Freedom. 5, Eli, mar. and r. St. George. 6, Sarah, mar. and r. St. George 7, Archibald, mar. Mary J. French of St. Geo. 8, Moses, (2d), m. Mary E. Long, r. St. George.

Capt. William's ch. 1, Capt. Artemas W., b. ab 1814; mar. Susan Kelleran, p. Sept. 12, '35, 2d, Susan W. Cole, d. Dec. 6, '58 ; r. Th., a master mariner. 2, Henry H. Y., b. ab. '16; m. Lucy P. Sellea, Oct. 1, '37 ; r. Th., a caulker. 3, Clementine; r. Th. 4, Elizabeth, d. in April, '45. 5, Lucy A., b. 1824, d. Feb. 25, '56. 6, Nancy J., b. & d. Dec., 1829. 7, Mary Frances, b. Oct. 5, '30, d. March 19, '52.

George's ch. 1, Elsie F., m. Capt. Aaron Wall; r. Th. 2, Capt. James, mar. Catharine Woodcock, July 10, '42, 2d, Betsey (Masters) Jordan, Nov. 5, '56 ; r. Th., a master mariner. 3, Capt. George, (3d), m. Lucy Fountain, of St. George. 4, Capt. William Henry, b. St G., May 15, 1821 ; mar. Bessie Fountain; r. Th, and died Dec. 23, '62, drowned on passage from Callao to Cowes. 5, Capt. Edward, (2d), m. Emeline Gilchrist; r. St. Geo. 6, Robert, drowned young, having slidden on his handsled into a curbless well. 7, Capt. Charles D.; m. Mary A. Dizer of St. George; r. Th., and d. in Boston, Feb. 1, '63. 8, Capt. Robert G., m. Rachel M. Simonton, Nov. 18, '49; r. Th., a master mariner. 9, Jackson, m. Penelope Hathorn; r. St. G. 10, Simon, mar. Jane R. Harrington, Sept. 21, '49; r. Th. 11, Julia A., m. Capt. Gideon Young; r. Th. 12, Cyrena, mar. Capt. Leonard Henderson of St. G. 13 and 14, Jane and Whitney, twins, d. young. 15, Paul G., r. St. G. 16, ———, d. young.

Fifth Generation.

Capt. William, (2d)'s ch. 1, Harriet, m. Edward W. Robinson; r. Th. 2, Joshua T., b. ab. 1832; r. Th., a mariner. 3, Capt. Edwin, b. ab. '35; m. Almira C. Curling; r. Th. 4, William, (3d), b. March 4, '37; d. Oct. 24, '60, lost overboard on voyage to Europe. 5, Joseph Melvin, b. March 24, '39, d. April 19, '60, killed by a fall from aloft, five days out, on passage from Liverpool to N. Y. 6, M. Elizabeth, b. April 9, '42. 7, Rose A.

Joseph's ch. 1, Ann L., m. Capt. Adam Parsons of St. Geo. 2, George W., d. young. 3, Cyrena. 4, Lilias, d. young. 5, Susanna. 6, Joseph, (2d). 7th, Samuel, (5th). 8, Luke.

Capt. Samuel, (3d)'s ch. 1, Mary Jane. 2, Sarah. 3, Clarissa, b. June, 1844, d. Feb. 12, '47. 4, Adelaide, b. April, and d. Sept. 1, '46. 5, Clara, b. July, '47, d. Sept. 2, '48. 6, Emma, b. ab '49. 7, James Harvey, b. March, and d. Nov. 27, '52. 8, Alice, b. '54, d. Oct. 21, 1856.

Capt. Alfred's ch. 1, Edward Brown, b. June 1, 1844. 2, Iada Maria, b. Aug. 3, '52. 3, Sarah Stone, b. April 2, 1857.

Capt. John's ch. One son, only, name not ascertained.

Capt. Artemas W.'s ch. by 1st wife. 1, Susan A., born Nov. 17, 1837, d. April 30, '53. 2, Bartholomew K., b. ab. '44. The mother d. Sept. 3, 1856.

Henry H. Y.'s ch. 1, Calvin N., b. March 23, 1839, r. Th. 2, Oscar, b. April 16, '41; a mariner. 3, Lucy J., b. ab. '47. 4, Abby, b. ab. '48. 5, Orris, b. ab. '49. 6, Leander, b. ab. 1850.

Capt. James's ch. by 1st wife. 1, Charles W., b. April, 1846, d. in Weston, Ct., March 4, '55. 2, Mary G., b. ab. '44; r. St. Geo. 3, William J., b. May, and d. Oct. 26, '47. 4, Adelia C., b. ab. 1848.

Capt. William Henry's ch. 1, Elsie Jane, born June 5, 1845. 2, Ellen Augusta, b. April 27, '47, d. at N. O., Jan. 6, 1850. 3, Mary Ada, b. Oct. 11, '50. 4, Flora E., b. March 13, '53. 5, William J., b. Nov. 14, '59. 6, Alice, b. Sept. 6, 1862.

Capt. Charles D.'s ch. Everett, b. ab 1851. The mother d. March 1, 1861.

Capt. Robert G.'s ch. 1, Seth, b. June 18, 1850. 2, Robert Alton, b. ab. '52. 3, Viram R., b. ab. '55. 4, John Bentley, b. ab. '58.

Simon's ch. Rosanna S., b. July 20, 1850, d. Oct. 15, '59. Of the Warren branch of this family, Samuel Watts, (5th), son of Samuel of W.; m. Eveline Farrington, Aug. 27, 1829, 2d, Mary ———; r. Beech Woods & Cobb's Mills. Their ch. 1, Angeline, m. David A. Linnekin of Appleton, Aug. 11, '56. 2, Emeline, m. Dexter Burkett; r. Th. 3, Mary, b. ab. '34. 4, William E., b. ab. '39; m. Nancy Ellen Copeland of W.; r. Th. 5, Cordelia M., b. ab. '42; m. Oliver A. Vose; r. Th. 6, Frances A., b. ab. '45.

WATTS, George, a rigger, c. to Th. with his wife and family from Portsmouth, N. H., and after a time rem. Newburyport, or elsewhere.

Their ch. 1, Moses H., b. Jan. 2, 1818, in S. Berwick; mar. Nancy Fales, April 18, '43; r. Th., a carpenter, &c. 2, George, (2d), b. in Portsmouth, July 14, '22; m. Sarah E. Bisbee, p. July 14, '49; r. Rock., & Th., and d. July 12, '61. 3, Samuel C., b. in Portsmouth, Oct. 13, '24. 4, Julia C., b. in Th., July 16, '27. 5, Henrietta, b. Sept. 10, '29. 6, Joseph S., b. June 29, '32.

Moses H.'s ch. 1 & 2, twins, b. ab. 1844, Ann Eunice & George Newell. 3, Julietta, b. ab. '48. 4, Clara E , b. ab. '50. 5, Emma, b. ab. '53. 6, Moses F., b. ab. '57.

George's ch. 1, Henrietta, b. ab. 1853. 2, Esther, b. ab. '55. 3, Oscar, b. ab. '57.

WATSON, William, c. from the North of Ireland, & r. first at Falmouth, Scarboro' or vicinity; rem. here from Scarboro', Aug. 26, 1753; m. twice; r. Watson's Point, now Th., and d. Sept. 21, 1768. His ch. by 1st wife. 1, Capt. John, b. May 18, 1731; m. & r. Scarboro', killed by the Indians. 2, William, (2d), b. March 6, '33, at Falmouth; m. Margaret Lermond, Dec., 1762, by John North, Esq.; r. Th., at Watson's Point; & d. ab. 1805. 3, Jane or Jean, b. July 5, '35; m. Major Hatevil Libbey; r. Warren, and d. Sept. 26, 1819. 4, Mary, b. June 28, 17—; probably m. in Scarboro'. 5, Margaret, b. Aug. 22, '43; m. Archibald Robinson of C., & d. Sept. 1, 1817. By 2d wife. 6, Capt. James, b. July 25, '45; m. Elizabeth Porterfield; r. & d. Th., at Watson's Point; a mariner, &c. 7, Elizabeth, b. Feb. 11, '50; probably m. in Scarboro'. 8, David, b. Jan. 25, '52; m. Martha (Hathorn) Hall of St. G.; r. & d. Rock. 9, Matthew, b. June 13, 1754; lost at sea with Capt. Tucker, March 30, 1785. ?

William, (2d)'s ch. 1, Mary, b. Oct. 29, 1763; r. unm. on the homestead, and d. March 24, 1849. 2, John, (2d), b. Oct. 26, '65, d. at sea, Sept. 25, 1800. 3, Margaret, b. Nov. 18, '67, m. Zephaniah Everton; r. at Th. toll-bridge, and d. April 24, 1845. 4, William, (3d), b. Oct. 23, '69, m. Margaret Robinson, and d. Oct. 16, 1802. 5, Nancy, b. Feb. 25, '72, d. July 18, '96. 6, James, (2d), b. Jan. 29, '75; r. War., and d. March 26, 1837. 7, Alexander, b. Jan. 7, '78, d. July 14, 1804. 8, Elizabeth, b. March 3, '82, m. Edward Brown; r. Th., and d. Sept. 8, 1809. The mother, b. at War., 1738, d. Aug. 21, 1804.

Capt. James's ch. 1, Isaac, b. Nov. 15, 1777, d. unm. Jan. 28, 1808. 2, Ruth, b. Sept. 1, '80, deceased. 3, Martha, b. March 13, '83, d. unm. 4, Catren, or Catharine, b. Aug. 28, '85, mar. Patrick Woodcock, and d. Nov. 10, 1819. 5, Simon, b. April 16, '88, mar. ——— of Northport. 6, Nancy, b. Aug , 1791, m. William Walsh, (2d); r. Rock. 7, Mary, b. April 7, '94; r. Th., a painter, & d. Feb. 27, 1864. 8, ———, b. Oct. 5, '97, d. July 18, '98. 9, Bradbury, b. July 20, '99, lost in brig *Hercules*.

David's ch. 1, Sally, b. ab. 1778, m. James Packard; r. Rock., & d. Jan. 22, '64. 2, Matthew, (2d), m. Hannah Howard, pub. June 5, 1795; r. and d. Rock. 3, Elizabeth, m. Capt James Blackington, & d. Oct. 9, 1848. 4, Martha, m. William Tolman; r. and d. Cam. 5, Mary, m. William Grover, June 23, 1803; r. and d. Cape Ann. 6, David, (2d), b. Oct. 5, '86, m. Mary Howard of St. G., Jan. 14, 1810; r. Rock., a farmer. 7, James, (3d), m. Eunice Porter, 2d, Amelia Parker, p. Aug. 17, 1836; r. and d. Cam. His widow, r. S. Th.

Fourth Generation.

William, (3d)'s ch. 1, Clarissa, b. Aug. 19, 1793, m. James Young

Esq.; r. Cush., and d. Oct. 5, 1858. 2, Asenath, or Essie, b. Sept., 1801, d. Nov. 12, 1848.

Mathew's ch. 1, Martha, mar. Luther Tolman, and d. one week after, a. about 23. 2, James, (4th), b. 1803, m. in the South; r. Rock., and d. Jan. 23, '30. 3, Eliza, m. Capt. Life Wilson; r. Illinois. 4, Mary, m. Haywood Read, Oct. 12, '31; r. & d. Bangor. 5, Margaret, m. Capt. John Crockett, (3d); r. and d. Rock. 6, Jeremiah, a mariner, died unm., on a voyage home, after getting into the harbor inside of Owl's Head. 7, Thomas, d. young. 8, Sarah, b. 1816, d. March 13, '29.

David, (2d)'s ch. 1, Jerome, b. Nov. 30, 1810, m. Betsey Healey, June 23, '33; r. Rock., rem. Linc. 2, Jane, b. Sept. 20, '13, mar. Charles Smith; r. Rock. 3, Margaret, m. John Hall; r. Rock.

James, (3d)'s ch. by 2d wife. 1, Edwin, m. on Fox Is., and died Cam. 2, Jerome, (2d); r. Rock., soldier in 4th Me., having early in Sept., 1862, already fought in 7 battles, and many since. 3, Martha. 4, Wellman, b. ab. '49; r. S. Th.

Fifth Generation.

Jerome's ch. 1, Jerome, (3d), b. April 16, 1834, d. July 29, '41. 2, Harvey H., b. Dec 13, '35, m. Melissa Buzzell; r. Rock., a mariner. 3, David, (3d), b. Jan. 20, and d. Jan. 30, '38. 4, David A., b. Jan. 17, and d. March 2, '41. 5, Gardner L., b. Oct. 9, '42; r. Cal. 6, John. 7, David, (3d), b. May, 1846, killed by accidental discharge of a gun, Nov. 23, '62. 8, Charles. 9, Loring Wilson. 10, Wm. F.

WEBB, Barnabas, of Boston, b. in 1729; m. Mary Holmes, Sept. 6, '59; and d. in '95, a. 66. Mary, his wife, b. March 16, 1741, d. at her son's in Warren, April 24, 1833, a. 92. Their ch. 1, Mary, b. Oct. 23, 1761, d. Sept. 12, '62. 2, Dr. Benjamin, b. Feb. 13, '63; c. to War. in 1784 or '5; m. 1st, Catharine Gregg, 2d, Sarah Boggs in 1795; rem. to Th., & in 1813 to Ohio, near Zanesville, where he m. 3d, a widow lady, & d. Feb. 26, 1834, a. 71. 3, Rebecca, b. April 23, '64, d. Sept. 7, '65. 4, Elizabeth, b. July 14, '66, d. Oct. 12, '79. 5, Abigail, b. Dec. 8, '67; m. Capt. David Fales, jr.; r. Th., & d. Nov. 27, 1858. 6, Sally, b. April 16, '69; m. Ebenezer Jennison, Esq.; r. Th. 7, Nathan, b. April 18, '71, d. Oct. 23, '95. 8, Dea. William Holmes, b. Oct. 16, '73; c. to Warren ab. '95, where he m. Ann Seids ab. 1802, 2d, Mrs. Lucy Burton, Dec. 20, 1826; r. W. 9, Thomas, b. Oct. 13, '75, d. Nov. 6, '77. 10, Harriet, b. Feb. 25, '77; m. Willard Fales & r. Th. 11, Lydia, b. April 16, '79; r. Th., long a store keeper at Mill River, & d. Oct. 7, 1864. 12, Barnabas, (2d), b. Oct. 20, '80, d. next day. 13, Barnabas, (3d), b. Nov. 9, '81, d. Nov. 8, '82. 14, Mary, b. Dec. 4, '86; r. & traded War., rem. & r. Th., a shop keeper. Of the above numerous family there were, April 16, 1864, five still living, aged, respectively, 95, 91, 87, 85, and 77 years.

Dr. Benjamin's ch. by 1st wife. 1, Polly, b. April 13, 1788; m. John Hussey in 1805; r. Jefferson. 2, Capt. Barnabas, (4th), b. June 19, '89; mar. Ann Robinson of Rock., Oct. 11, 1815; r. Th., a ship master, ship owner, &c., & d. Aug. 9, 1863. By 2d wife. 3, Benjamin, (2d), b. Aug., 1797; r. & m. in Ohio. 4, Nathan, (2d), b. July 17, '99, d. Jan. 6, 1802. 5, Nathan, (3d), b. Aug. 26, 1802; m. & r. in Ohio.

Capt. Barnabas's ch. 1, Capt. Edmund R., b. Jan. 22, 1816, mar. Sarah Woodhull, Dec. 22, '50, & d. Dec. 10, '53, in N. York, of fever contracted while in command of ship *Chimborazo*. 2, Sarah Ann, b,

Jan. 15, '18; m. Capt. Elkanah Stackpole; r. Th., & d. Jan. 27, '46. 3 & 4, twins, b. Feb. 9, '21, Clementine, m. Capt. Orris Fales, June, 1847; d. at Martinez, Cal., Feb. 18, '55; Catharine, m. Capt. Levi B. Gilchrist, Nov. 23, '43; d. April 6, '47. 5, Harriet Gilchrist, b. Feb. 14, '23; m. 1st, Capt. James Thomas Sprague, 2d, Capt. James W. Colley; r. Cambridge, Mass. 6, Barnabas, (5th), b. May 15, '25; m. Mary E. Piper, Sept. 18, '48; went to California in 1854. 7, Marion W., b. July 8, '27; m. Christopher Prince; r. Th. 8, Franklin, b. April 21, '33. 9, Francis P. B., b. Aug. 29, & d. Sept. 8, '39.

Capt. Edmund R.'s ch. Edmund Standish, b. June, 1852; r. Bangor.

WEBSTER; of this family, two brothers c. from Waldo county. 1, David M., b. ab. 1807; m. 1st, Bathsheba H. Rider of Vinalhaven, p. Aug. 21, '33, 2d, Rebecca H. Crouch, June 5, '57; r. Rock., a joiner, &c. 2, Benjamin F., b. ab '10; m. Eliza H. Emery, p. Oct. 11, '34; r. S. Th., a carpenter.

David M.'s ch. by 1st wife. 1, George, b. Nov. 1, 1835. 2, John A., b. Dec. 10, '37; m. Henrietta E. Cates, April 28, '60; r. Rock., a mariner. 3, Emily, b. Dec. 13, '39; r. Rock. 4, Osbirt H., b. May 6, & d. Sept. 6, '42. 5, Mary, b. ab. '47. By 2d wife. 6, Julia. 7, Charles A., b. Aug. 6, '58, d. Oct. 10, '61.

Benjamin F.'s ch. 1, Margaret, b. 1835; r. S. Th. 2, Hannah M., b. May 29, '36; r. S. Th. 3, Ann Eliza, b. April 16, '38; m. Capt. Jere. Hooper; r. S. Th. 4, Emma F., b. ab. '44; mar. Horatio B. Hooper, r. S. Th.. 5, Lydia E., b. ab. '46. 6, Eveline, b. ab. 1848.

WEED, Dea. James, b. at Brunswick, July 17, 1753; c. early to Th., m. Annah Williams of Harpswell, July 17, '77; settled at S. Th., on the road to St. George; was a tanner and farmer; rem. and d. in Knox. His widow d. there about 1857, aged 98. Of his sisters. 1, Reliance, b. at B., Oct. 7, 1754; m. Dea. Samuel Brown; c. to Th., and d. Dec. 5, '76. 2, Ruth, b. at Harpswell, May 4, 1760; died Th. Sept. 25, '88. Dea. James's ch. 1, Daniel, b. May 13, 1778; mar. Polly Mingerson, p. Jan. 26, '99; r. Knox. 2, James, (2d), b. May 12, '80; m. Jane Handly; rem. & r. Appleton. 3, Betsey, b. May 29, '82; m. John Geyer, p. March 16, 1802; r. Friendship. 4, Samuel, b. May 18, '84; m. Nancy Carven of W., p. Nov. 3, 1809, rem. and d. Burnham or Knox. 5, Sarah, b. Feb. 11, '86, d. Jan. 19, '87. 6, Ruth, b. Nov. 9, '87; m. Mr. Young; r. Bristol. 7, Reliance, b. Oct. 23, '89; m. Noah P. Fuller of Hebron, Feb. 21, 1808; r. Hope. 8, Judith, b. Dec. 5, '91; m. Judah Delano of Friendship, Jan. 24, 1810. 9, Adam, b. Oct. 14, '93, d. Oct. 17, '96. 10, Deborah, b. Oct. 5, '96; m. Capt. Geo. McLellan, 2d, Capt. Isaac McLellan; r. Th. 11, Adam, b. Sept. 30, '97; m. 1st, Sarah? Pendleton, 2d, ———, 3d, Jane Otis of St. George. 12, Abner, b. May 4, 1800; removed, it is believed, to Knox. 13, Hannah, born May 3, '02; m. Ezekiel D. Williams; r. Burnham.

Daniel's ch. 1, Nancy, b. Dec. 18, 1799, d. Feb. 1, 1804. 2, Polly, b. Dec. 20, 1802, d. April 5, 1804. 3, Jenny, b. Dec. 20, 1804; and others probably in Knox

James, (2d)'s ch. Nancy, b. Dec. 31, 1805, rem. to Appleton.

WEED, Levi, born Oct. 25, 1808, in Deer Isle, son of William and Mary (Eaton) Weed of that place; m. Sarah C. Duncan; c. to Rock. in June, 1853, to S. Th. in April 1857; a farmer. Joseph, his cousin, b. at Deer Isle ab. '08; m. Eunice D., sister of Levi Weed; r. Rock. a lime burner, and soldier of the 4th Me. reg. David D., also, son of

Daniel and grandson of William above named, b. at Deer Isle about 1832; m. Pamelia C. Bray; r. Rock., a mariner.

Levi's ch. 1, James D., b. at Deer Isle, Dec. 4, 1837, m. Sarah E. Stover of St. G., July 6, '62; r. S. Th. 2, John E., b. Feb. 3, '40, a soldier of the 20th Me. Reg. 3, Mary E., b. July 9, '42. 4, Sarah A., b. Feb. 23, '45. 5, Levi A., b. Feb. 25, '47. 6, Susan F., b. Feb. 18, '51. 7, Eliza H., b. at Rock., Aug. 21, '53. 8, Leslie V., b. at S. Th., April 3, '59. The mother was b. at Deer Isle, Feb. 26, '18.

Joseph's ch. 1, Joseph, (2d), ? b. ab. 1833; r. Rock. 2, Thurlow, b. ab. 1839, soldier of 4th Me., &c. 3, ? Luther, b. ab. 1850. 4, Hester A., b. ab. '52.

David D.'s ch. 1, Mercy S., b. ab. 1855. 2, David E., b. ab. '57. 3, Emeretta, b. ab. '59.

James D.'s ch. Carrie Florence, b. Dec. 20, 1863.

WEEKS, Leander, b. in Jefferson, ab. 1823; m. Mary Jane Ross; c. to Rock. in 1852, where he r., a merchant, at first in company with William J. Bond, and now by himself. Jackson Weeks, a cousin, b. in Jefferson, ab. '22, also r. Rock. and m. Clarissa Bird, Aug. 27, '54. Leander's ch. 1, George, b. ab. '48. 2, Alphonso R., b. ab. '50. 3, Jennie M. b. ab. '59. 4, Frank L. Of this name, also, & probably of another branch of the same family, Edwin Weeks, b. in Jefferson, ab. '21; m. Mary A. Overlock of Wal.; r. Th., a mason. Edwin's ch. 1, Alfred, b. ab. '51. 2, James E., b. ab. '54. 3, Emma F., b. ab. '58. 4, an infant, d. Sept. 1, 1861.

WEEKS, Abner B., b. ab. 1813; c. from Bath, m. Elizabeth C. Ingraham, Oct. 10, '41, 2d, Ann M. Crockett, Jan. 27, '47; r. Rock., a mason, inventor of Weeks's patent lime kiln, &c. His ch. by 2d wife. 1, William b. ab. '48. 2, Sophia S., b. ab. '50. 3, Charles E., b. ab. '58. 4, Mary C., b. Oct. 21, '61, d. April 8, '64.

WELCH, William, & Sarah, his wife, were here early & had 2 ch. entered on the Th. records. 1, Amanda S., b. April 27, 1838. 2, Lucy E., b. Oct. 29, '41. Of this name, also, Peter Welch, b. ab. '16; m. Susanna ———; r. Rock., a lime burner. Their ch. 1, James, b. ab. '40; r. Rock., a lime burner. 2, Ephraim, b. ab. '42; r. Rock., a lime burner. 3, Lucinda C., b. ab. '45. 4, Jane S., b. ab. '48. 5, Isaac, b. ab. '52. Also, of the same name, Thomas Welch, b. ab. '30, in Ireland, as was Margaret, his wife, ab. '35; r. Rock., an ostler. Their ch. 1, Patrick, b. ab. '51. 2 & 3, twins, b. ab. '53, Georgiana & Elizabeth. 4, Thomas, (2d), b. ab. '55. 5, James, (2d), b. ab. '58.

WELLMAN, Timothy, Esq., b. in 1781; c. from Salem, Mass.; m. 1st, Jane (Post) Sleeper, Oct. 15, 1833, 2d, Phebe R. Burns, p. Feb. 2, '39; r. Rock. & d. May 14, '42, leaving one daughter only.

WELSBY, Capt. William N., b. Sept. 21, 1803, in Prescott, England, son of William & Margaret (Nicholson) Welsby; c. in 1816 to Th., when a boy of 7 years; m. Maria J. Lermond of W., Jan. 26, '45; was drowned at Trinidad de Cuba, May 12, 1847, when in command of sch. *Linnell*. Their ch. Margaret Alice, b. March 8, 1846.

WELLINGTON, James, b. ab. 1822; m. Eliza ———; r. Rock. Their ch. Louisa, b. ab. '42. 2, Charles V., b. ab. '44. 3, Lucy F., b. ab. '50.

WELT, Erastus, of German descent, c. from Waldoboro'; m. Mary J. Dean, Nov. 16, 1848; r. Rock., a carpenter. Their ch. 1, Willie

E., b. March, '52, d. Aug. 20, '54. 2, Merrill G., b. ab. '54. 3, Julietta, b. ab. 1858.

WENTWORTH, John Sumner, b. ab. 1806, in Mass., m. Nancy Sherman, Oct. 27, 1829; r. S. Th., a farmer, &c. Their ch. 1, Nelson F., b. April 15, 1831; r. S. Th., a farmer, &c. 2, Thomas A., b. ab. '33, in Brooks, Me., m. Mary R. Harrington, Dec. 4, '57; r. Rock., hat, cap and fur dealer. 3, Arabella, b. May 11, '38, m. Lewis Childs of Rock., Oct. 2, '59. 4, John S., (2d), b. June 15, '41, d. at Rock., Aug. 21, '57. 5, Sarah A., b. ab. '43, m. H. G. Pillsbury; r. S. Th. 6, William B., b. ab. '48.

Of Thomas A.'s ch. Alice, b. March, and d. Aug., 1859.

WENTWORTH, Cyrus, b. ab. 1826, in Hope, m. Maria Mehan of W.; r. Rock., a ship carpenter. Of this name also, Charles O., and Robert E. Wentworth; r. Rock., soldiers, one of the 7th Me., re-enlisted, and the other of the 8th Me. Reg.; also, J. A. Wentworth, entered the navy.

WEST, Hosea, b. ab. 1821, in Frankfort, Me., m. Ann Mehitable Boynton; r. Rock., soldier of 19th Me., &c. Their ch. 1, Mary H., b. ab. 1848. 2, Hosea A., b. ab. '50. 3, Georgiana, b. ab. '52. 4, John F., b. ab. '57. 5, Ocena, b. ab. '59.

WEYMOUTH, Nehemiah, b. ab. 1811, m. Joanna ———; r. Rock. in 1860, a lime manufacturer, as did also Martin Weymouth, probably a brother, b. ab. 1815,, and also a lime manufacturer. Of this name, also, Alfred D. Weymouth, b. ab. '35, m. Melissa E. Young, Aug. 14, '59; r. Rock.

Alfred D.'s ch. Alfred, b. ab. 1860.

WHALEN, John, b. ab. 1829, in Ireland, as was Nancy, his wife; r. Rock., a quarry man. Their ch. Ellen, b. ab. 1827. Daniel Whalen, also of Rock., entered the army.

WHEATON, Col. Mason, Esq., b. ab. 1736, m. Lavinia Dexter of Providence; c. to St. George's, now Th., 1762 or 3, was long a leading man of business and political influence; and d. Sept. 15, 1812. Their ch. 1, James D., Esq. b. Feb., 1767, m. Judith Stackpole, July 30, 1832; r. Th., and d. Sept. 17, 1847. 2, Lucy, b, 1769, m. Wm. Southworth; r. Th., and d. April 23, 1844.

James D. Esq.'s ch. Lavinia J. M., b. Dec. 24, 1834; r. Th.

WHEELER, David of St. George; m. Hannah Hart; r. St. G., & d. Dec. 10, 1843. Their ch. 1, Oliver, b. Sept. 25, 1802; m. Hannah F. Small, May 29, '36; r. S. Th., a farmer, &c. 2, Betsey, born Dec. 7, '03; m. Capt. Edward Small, 2d, Capt. Jonathan Small; r. S. Th., & d. Jan. 29, '47. 3, John H., b. Dec. 28, '11; m. Eliza Bryant of St. G., Jan. 26, '36; r. Rock., a lime manufacturer. 4, Joseph S., b. ab. 1813; m. Martha Stover of St. G.; r. Rock., a lime manufacturer. 5, Deborah, m. Isaac A. Willis; r. Th.

Oliver's ch. 1, Ira G., b. Aug. 28, 1837. 2, Leander S., b. Dec. 18, '38; r. S. Th. 3, Silas C., b. March 30, '40, d. Dec. 11, '46. 4, Darius, b. ab. '43.

John H.'s ch. 1, Julia Ann, b. Jan. 12, 1837; mar. Thomas Ashcroft, Nov. 17, '55; r. Rock., and has one son, John W. Ashcroft, b. ab. 1857.

Joseph S.'s ch. 1, Elvira, b. Feb. 21, 1835; m. Thomas B. Glover; r. Rock. 2, Henry P., b. March 2, '37; m. Phebe Orbine, July 19, '56, 2d, ? in Boston, Maria Ford, June 14, '58; r. Rock., a lime burner.

3, Alvan, b. June 21, '40, d. Sept. 4, '41. 4, Amariah, b. ab. 1843. 5, Gardner, b. ab. 1851.

Henry P.'s ch. Caroline, b. ab. 1859. Of this name, also, Robert Wheeler, b. ab. 1823; m. Eunice ——; r. Rock., a joiner. Their ch. 1, Marcella, b. ab. 1853. 2, Eugene, b. ab. '55.

WHITCHER, or Whittier, John, came to what is now S. Th.; m. Sarah Emery, Dec. 27, 1804; rem. to Northport. Of their ch. 1, Joshua, b. ab. 1813; mar. Sabra ——; r. S. Th., a mariner. 2, ? Andrew, came from Northport; m. Mehitable Pillsbury, July 27, '41; r. S. Th., and d. or rem. 3, ? John H., b. ab. 1820; mar. Eliza A. ——; r. Rock., a mariner.

Joshua's ch. 1, Ellen, b. ab. 1840; mar. Winthrop F. Ames of Vinalhaven, Nov. 6, '60. 2, Adelaide, b. ab. '42. 3, Mary, b. ab. '44. 4, Sabra, b. ab. '46. 5, Joshua, b. ab. '50. 6, Emma, b. ab. '52. 7, Charles, b. ab. '54. 8, Fremont, b. ab. '56.

Of Andrew's ch. 1, Andrew T., b. Nov. 18, 1842; r. S. Th., a mariner, and d. by a fall from aloft, April 2, '64, on passage from San Francisco to Oregon.

John H.'s ch. 1, George W., b. ab. 1852. 2, Ida M., b. ab. '55.

WHITCOMB, Henry, b. ab. 1797; came from Hope to S. Th.; m. Sarah A. R. Elliott, p. April 26, 1838; r. S. Th., a farmer, &c. Their ch. 1, Hannah A., b. May 27, 1841; m. Sidney W. Oakes of Gloucester, Mass., Feb. 12, '60; r. S. Th. 2, Angeline, b. ab. '44. 3, Mahala, b. ab. '51.

WHITCOMB, Samuel, b. ab. 1833; c. from Worcester, Mass.; m. Amelia H. Stackpole, Sept. 5, '56; r. Th., a ship carpenter. John G., a brother, b. ab. '35; m. Mary J. Fountain, June 30, '56; r. Th., a ship carpenter. Of this name, also, Ambrose Whitcomb, b. ab. 1836; m. Martha Oliver of W.; r. Th., wagoner in 20th Me. Reg., &c.

WHITE, Oliver, son of Major George of North Haven, m. Harriet (Spear) Ingraham, June 17, 1828; r. Rock., and d. at N. Y., Aug., 1839. George W., a nephew, b. in North Haven, 1821, m. Damaris, dau. of Abram Ripley of Appleton; r. S. Th., and Rock., a teacher in various places, editor, register of deeds for Knox county, 1860 and '62.

Oliver's ch. 1, Harriet A., b. March 16, 1829. 2, Eliza J., b. Nov. 17, '30, m. Henry M. Fales; r. Rock. 3, Capt. Oliver M., b. June 19, '34, mar. Eliza A. Small, May 29, '56; r. Rock., and d. at sea of yellow fever, July 22, '59. 4, Sarah F., b. March 29, '36, m. Oliver G. Hall; r. Rock. 5, Charles, b. Sept. 22, '38, d. Sept., 1841.

George W.'s ch. 1, John W., b. ab. 1850. 2, Harriet K., b. ab. '54. 3, Eda E., b. ab. '57.

WHITE, Jonathan, b. in 1805, c. from Belfast, m. Emily Spear, p. Oct. 21, '31; r. Rock., a lime manufacturer. Their ch. Lucy C., b. May 19, '34, m. John S. Case; r. Rock.

WHITE, Capt. John T., b. 1818, c. from North Carolina, m. Hannah Pressey, March 25, '38, did business in Rock., was a com. merchant in N. Y., ret. Rock., and d. Dec. 29, '56. Their ch. 1, Adelaide, b. July 25, '39, d. Dec. 30, '55. 2, Mauncell, b. Nov. 15, '41, d. April 29, '61. 3, Mary, b. ab. '48.

WHITEHOUSE, Jacob, b. ab. 1830, m. Mary McLaughlin of W., p. Aug. 21, '54; r. Rock., a carpenter. Their ch. 1, Alice, b. ab. 1856. 2, Arvilla W., b. ab. '58.

WHITING, Manasseh S., Esq., son of John of Union; r. Rock., a while, rem. San Francisco, Cal., where he was said to be an active business man, and nominated for State senator 1862. Of this name, also, Sullivan K. Whiting, b. ab. '32, m. Mary E. Doe; r. Rock., a merchant, enlisted as musician in 4th Me. Reg., since rem. Winthrop, Me. Sullivan K.'s ch. Frances D., b. ab. 1857.

WHITNEY, Haynes, b. Dec. 1788, c. from Woodstock, Vt., to Th., m. Jane Robinson, Jan. 24, 1816; settled at Beech Woods, and died suddenly from bilious colic, Sept. 18, '25. Calvin, a brother, c. later, m. Eliza Everton, and d. Oct. 1832.

Haynes's ch. 1, William, b. Oct. 29, 1816, m. Eliza Brown, Sept. 16, '39, 2d, Elizabeth Jordan, April 24, '62; r. Th., a farmer, &c. 2, Maria R., b. June 24, '18, m. Joseph C. Stafford, Oct. 20, '44; r. Boston, and d. at St. Louis, Mo., 1845. 3, Charles R.. b. Jan. 16, '20, m. Mary Thurston; r. Rock., a lime manufacturer. 4, Reuben K., b. Nov. 10, '23, d. lost overboard from bk. *Valhalla*, Dec., 1838. 5, Elizabeth H., b. Nov. 22, '25, mar. 1st, Charles A. Green of Boston, Sept. 1, '44, 2d, Stephen Styles of Cambridge, Mass.

Calvin's ch. 1, Calvin F., b. April 7, 1816; r. Cam. 2, Henry, b. April 25, '18, d. in the South. 3, William E., b. Jan. 23, '22, m. Sophia A. Fales, Dec. 29, '42; r. Th., a merchant, &c. 4, Joshua G., b. Nov. 10, '23; r. Rock., soldier in 4th Me, &c. 5, John K., born June 19, '26, m. and r. Th., went to California. 6, Mary E., b. July 31, '30, m. Americus Long; r. Th. 7, Joshua, b. ab. '33; r. Rock. The mother, m. 2d; Joseph Thompson; r. R., & d. Feb. 20, '61, a. 61.

William's ch. 1, Frances I., b. Sept. 12, 1842, d. June 18, '48. 2, Eliza J., b. ab. '45. 3, Olena, b. ab. '47. 4, Charles G., b. ab. '52. 5, Andrew F., b. ab. '56.

Charles R.'s ch. 1, Mary, b. ab. 1856. 2, Lizzie, b. ab. '57.

William E.'s ch. 1, Lydstone, b. Feb. 1843, d. July 21, '57. 2, Calvin H., b. ab. '45. 3, William J., b. ab. '47. 4, Rebecca Ann, b. Jan. 16, d. Dec. 8, '49. 5, Francis M., born and d. Oct. 13, '53. 6, Aroline, b. ab. '55. 7, Alice R., b. ab. '58.

WHITNEY, Ezra, b. ab. 1823; m. & r. Rock., a tin plate peddler, &c. His ch. 1, Cornelia A., b. ab. 1844. 2, Celestia A., b. ab. '49.

WHITTON, Nathan, b. in Unity ab. 1828; m. Mary N. McAllister; r. Rock., an ambrotypist, 3 or 4 years about 1860; rem. Belfast. Ephraim, his brother, m. Priscilla Harding; r. Rock., ab. six years, but rem. & m. 2d, in California. Nathan's ch. 1, Leonora S., b. ab. 1850. 2, Roscoe N., b. ab. '56.

WHITTON, Nathan, b. ab. 1828, in Gouldsborough; m. Rebecca Small; r. Rock, in fishery business. Their ch. 1, Larkin S., b. ab. 1844. 2, Monselle W., b. ab. '48.

WHITTON, Hiram, b. ab. 1832, in China, Me.; m. Abigail Burns, p. Nov. 2, 1850; r. Rock., a teamster, wagoner in 19th Me. Reg., &c. Their ch. Frederic A., b. June, 1859, d. Jan. 23, '63.

WIGGIN, Capt. Jonathan, b. in Stratham, N. H., Jan. 19, 1740; m. 1st, Mary Little in Newbury, Oct. 10, 1761, 2d, Mehitable Thurston, 3d, Mrs. Mary Mason; r. and d. about 1810, in Stratham; which township had been granted to an ancestor, Andrew Wiggin, who m. a dau. of Gov. Bradstreet. Capt. Jonathan's ch. by 1st wife. 1, Elizabeth, b. Oct. 10, 1762; m. Stephen Thurston, who was a soldier under Gen. Wayne at the time of Arnold's treason; lived in the marriage state 75 years, and d. in Madison, Me., a. ab. 97, leaving many descendants, to the 5th generation. 2, Mary, b. July 30, 1767; mar. Levi Barker; r. Stratham, & d. leaving 8 ch. By 2d wife. 3, Edmund, b. May 30, 1772; c. here 1794; m. Elizabeth Copeland of W., June 12, 1800; r. and d. Th., being a clerk and assistant in Knox & Vose's store. 4, Mehitable, b. Aug. 18, 1773; m. Samuel Marble; r. and d. Stratham. 5, Abigail, b. March 22, 1775; m. Thomas Chase; r. and d. Stratham. 6, William Howe, b. Dec. 16, 1776; c. here ab. 1795; mar. Mary Simonton, Dec 13, 1804; r. Th., overseer of lime business; & d. Jan. 20, 1811. 7, Sarah, b. Sept. 18, 1778; m. James St. Clair; r. S. Th. 8, Clarissa, b. Oct. 15, 1780; m. Stephen Bowman; r. and d. Stratham. 9, Augusta, b. Aug. 15, 1782; m. Jacob Wiggin; r. and d. Stratham.

Edmund's ch. 1, Augusta, m. Edward Mink; r. Waldoboro'. 2, Cordelia, m. Rufus Snow; r. S. Th.

William Howe's ch. 1, Hon. George S., b. Sept. 28, 1805; learned the mason's trade of Jere. Berry, and industriously worked his way to places of trust and eminence; m. Lydia W. Amsbury, March 16, '33; r. Rock., city mayor seven years & re-elected 1865. 2, Clarissa, b. April 26, '07; m. George B. Wormell; r. Th. 3, William Howe, (2d), b. Aug. 14, '09; died June 16, '39, by drowning.

Hon. George S.'s ch. 1, Oliver A., b. March 8, 1835; m. Charlotte Carman; r. Rock., stage agent, livery stable keeper, &c. 2, George Howe, b. May 20, '47; r. Rock.

WIGGIN, Thomas M., b. ab. 1818, probably of a distant branch of the same family; came from China, Me.; m. Mary J. ——; r. Rock., a lime burner. Their ch. 1, Lizzie B., b. ab. 1843. 2, Chas. T., d. Jan. 29, '49. 3, Lucius H., b. ab. '53.

WIGGIN, Thomas S., b. ab. 1825; c. from Brooks, Me.; m. Julia A. Kelloch of W.; r. Rock., a shoemaker, rem. Portsmouth, N. H. Samuel, also from Brooks; m. Elizabeth Dean, May 23, 1842; r. S. Th., a shoemaker, and died May 15, 1860.

Thomas S.'s ch. 1, Thomas D., b. Sept. 30, 1851. 2, Fannie I., b. Jan. 28, '54. 3, Alice Catharine, b. Feb. 20, and d. Aug. 16, '56.

Samuel's ch. 1, Charles M., b. May 14, 1842; mar. Josephine B. Allen, Oct. 11, '63; r. S. Th. 2, Abby M., b. ab. '44; m. Andrew W. Stover, Oct. 12, '61; r. S. Th. 3, Ruth A., b. ab. '46. 4, Henry, b. ab. '50.

WIGGIN, Nathan, b. ab. 1835; c. from Fryeburg; m. Sarah E ——; r. Rock., a druggist, &c. Of this name, also, Abiathar K. Wiggin of Rock., entered the army.

WIGHT, John M., b. in Wrentham, now Foxboro', Mass., had been in the army; was in Union 1787; c. to Th., m. Lavinia Morse, Jan. 20, 1793, engaged in trade, was sur. of lime 1796, taught school near the head of Tolman's Pond, left the place and his family, Dec. 6, '99. Their ch. 1, Daniel M., b. April 18, '93, followed the sea. 2, James W., b. Oct. 29, '95, brought up in Wal., mar. in Boston, went to sea. 3, Henry M., b. March 15, '98, d. in the army, at Burlington, Vt., in war of 1812. 4 and 5, twins, b. March 9, 1800, Charles, m. Elizabeth (Stevens) Braley, Sept. 7, '28, and lost his sight whilst blasting rock on the islands, before 1838; r. Th., and d. suddenly in a store, Feb. 7, '54; — Osmond, drowned at sea; had been low-spirited during the voyage, in consequence of a dream, (which he refused to tell till he should get ashore;) heaving the line, as if to sound, while the crew were at supper, he fell overboard, and, taking no notice of a line thrown to him, sunk without a struggle.

Charles's ch. 1, Charles O., b. July 24, 1829. 2, Elizabeth A., b. Nov. 25, '31. 3, Lavinia T., born Jan. 28, '34, d. July 16, '53. 4, Henrietta S., b. Nov. 2, '36, d. Jan. 22, '37. The mother d. April 4, '54.

WIGHT, Hezekiah W., b. ab. 1832, in Penobscot, Me., ; r. Rock., a merchant, lime manufacturer, &c., now in firm of Cobb, Wight & Case; m. Frances S. Pierce, Oct. 8, '54. Their ch. 1, Frederic W., b. ab. '58. 2, Jennie C., b. May, 1862, d. Jan. 26, '63.

WIGHT, James, b. in Lowell, Mass., m. Emma E. Burpee, Nov. 24, '64; r. Rock., a machinist.

WIGHT; of this family, 3 brothers c. from Windsor, Me. 1, Hiram, b. ab. 1815, m. Mary Elizabeth Kelleran, Nov, 1842; r. Th., a trader, &c. 2, Charles, r. in S. Th. a while and carried on bakery. 3, John B., b. ab. '25, m. Sarah Jane Lash of Wal., Jan. 21, '54; r. Th. some time, a baker in Wadsworth St.

Hiram's ch. 1, William F., b. ab. 1843, m. Lucy Fuller, Oct. 30, '64; r. Th., a soldier of the 20th Me. Reg, &c. 2, Henderson K., b. Sept. 30, '45, d. Oct. 7, '46. 3, Mary, b. ab. '48. 4, Ernest, b. ab. '50. 5, Emma, b. ab. '52. 6, George M., b. Sept. '54, d. May 9, '57. 7, Martha W., b. May 16, and d. June 23, '58. 8, Ellen, b. '60.

Of John B.'s ch. Willie, b. 1855, d. June 27, '58.

WILLARD, James Frederic, b. ab. 1822 in Portland, mar. Olive Post; r. Th., a boat builder, &c. Their ch. 1, Margaret J., b. ab. 1844, m. Edward F. Miller, June 29, '62; r. Th. 2, Charles, b. ab. '49. 3, Alfred V., b. July '52, d. Jan. 24, '54. 4, Penelope. b. in '60.

WILLIAMS; of this Harpswell family there came to Th., 3 brothers. 1, Benjamin, m. Jane Otis, ab. 1790; r. and d. S. Th., on the 8th lot from St. G. line; a tanner. 2, Dea. Daniel, b. May 14, '75, m. Hannah Page, c. here ab. 1805; r. on the lot below his brother's, S. Th., and d. June 13, 1858. 3, Peter, c. to Th. 1806, mar. Margaret Bucklin of W.; r. Th., Wadsworth Street, a joiner, &c. Another brother, George, m. and r. Durham, Me. Mercy, their mother, d. in Th., Sept., 1825, a. 94.

Benjamin's ch. 1, Ebenezer, m. Thankful Otis of St. G., Nov. 26, 1810; rem. & d. Burnham, Me. 2, Nancy, m. Jas. Harvey Haynes, of Milo, Nov. 28, '23, rem. Burnham, and d. Ill. 3, Benjamin, (2d), mar. Fanny Williams, Dec., 1818; r. and d. Freedom or Knox. 4, Deborah, d. unm. 5, and 6, twins, b. March 30 and 31, '05, George S., m. Sarah Hall of St. G., p. Oct. 7, '28; r. S. Th., on homestead; Peter, (2d), m. Betsey McKeller, p. Dec. 17, '31; r. homestead, and died Aug. 20, '60, by a fall, whilst running in pursuit of his sheep in the pasture. 7, Ezekiel D., mar. Hannah Weed in Burnham; rem. Minnesota. 8, Hezekiah, m. ——— Ulmer; r. Ill.

Dea. Daniel's ch. 1, William, b. Dec. 2, 1798, m. Margaret Colly, Jan. 13, 1825; r. S. Th., a joiner, &c. 2, Fanny, b. Sept. 5, 1800, m. Benjamin Williams, (2d); r. and d. Freedom. 3, Eliza, b. July 2, '02, d. Jan. 10, '20. 4, Mercy, b. Feb. 13, '04, m. Perley Graves; r. S. Th., rem. Cal. 5, Reliance, b. April 7, '06, mar. Nathan Read; r. Th. 6, Solomon, b. Oct. 15, '07, d. June 30, '29. 7, Daniel, (2d), b. Aug. 4, '09, m. Rachel Lawry; r. Frankfort. 8, Oliver, b. Aug. 16, '11; rem. Australia. 9, Horace, b. Sept. 20, '15, mar. 1st, Mary Ann Vaughan, Dec. 16, '44, 2d, Mary H. McLoon, Jan. 1, '50; r. S. Th., a ship builder, and d. July 30, '58. The mother was b. April 17, 1772 in Harpswell; d. Sept. 19, 1858.

Peter's ch. 1, Calista, b. Aug. 1, 1809; r. Th. 2, Joseph B., born April 5, '11, m. Mary E. Carney, Oct. 25, '57; r. Th., in the Hastings house, a trader. 3, Andrew, b. May 27, '13, m. Frances Dean of N. Y.; r. Medford, Mass. 4, Sarah E., b. Dec. 25, '15, d. July 19, '17. 5, Margaret, b. Nov. 29, '18, m. ——— Loring; r. Boston, 6, Geo. M. L., b. Oct. 9, '21, d. Oct. 7, '25. 7, Mary A., b. May 15, '24, d. Nov. 22, '25. The mother d. March 7, '64, a. 80.

Of Ebenezer's ch. 1, Ebenezer O., b. 1823, m. Charlotte K. Post, July 14, '52; r. Rock., a shipwright, and d. Sept. 17, '63, from a fall in Starrett's ship yard.

George S.'s ch. 1, Elizabeth, b. Nov. 28, 1830. 2, Sarah, b. May 18, '32; r. S. Th. 3, George E., b. Sept. 14, '33, m. Susan H. Libby of Cam., 1858; r. S. Th., a farmer, entered the navy. 4, James, b. April 19, '35. 5, Isaac H., b. Dec. 16, '36, m. Lovisa H. Edwards of Cam., Sept. 11, '59; r. S. Th. 6, Maria, b. May 1, '39, mar. S. A. Sweetland of Boston, Sept. 29, '63. 7, Edwin, (2d), b. March 4, '42; r. S. Th.

Peter, (2d)'s ch. 1, Edwin, b. Nov. 3, and died Dec. 15, 1834. 2, Benjamin, (3d), b. Feb. 22, '36; r. S. Th., a student. 3, John, born Jan. 24, '38; r. S. Th., a mariner. 4, Ferroline M., b. May 23, '40, m. Dr. John T., Main of Unity, March 3, '59. 5, Frederic O., b. Aug. 7, '42. 6, Nathan H., b. ab. '48. The mother mar. 2d, Capt. Richard Davis of Harbor Is., Dec. 17, '62.

William's ch. 1, Mary Ann, b. Oct. 21, 1825; r. S. Th. 2, Capt. Thomas C., b. June 14, '29, m. Mary A. Copeland, Dec. 28, '51; r. S. Th., a ship master. 3, Margaret C., b. Aug. 31, '31; r. S. Th. 4, Adelaide or Adeline, b. Feb. 13, '34, d. Aug. 25, '64. 5, Wm. John, b. July 4, '40; r. S. Th., a mariner. 6, Charles E., b. ab. '46.

Horace's ch. by 2d wife. 1, Charles M. 2, William. 3, Fanny D., b. March 17, and died Oct. 6, '53.

Joseph B.'s ch. 1, Simon Lewis. 2, ———. 3 and 4, twins, b. ab. 1862.

Andrew's ch. 1, Joseph. 2, William.

Fourth Generation.

Ebenezer O.'s ch. Ardella E., b. ab. 1860.

George E.'s ch. Loring, b. ab. 1859.

Capt. Thomas C.'s ch. 1, Thomas, (2d), b. ab. 1853. 2, Horatio Herbert, b. ab. '55.

WILLIAMS, Col. Timothy, b. ab. 1805; c. first from Woolwich to Starks when 14 years of age, thence to what is now Rock.; m. Jane H. Blackington, July 3, 1842; r. Rock., in 2d house from Th., is interested in lime-quarries and lime business. His brother, Capt. Austin, b. in Woolwich, in 1813; also came to Th.; m. Sarah (Munroe) Robinson, Nov., 1853; r. Th., a ship master.

Col. Timothy's ch. 1, Warren G., b. ab. 1843. 2, Mary J., b. ab. '45. 3, Maynard S., b. ab. '56. 4, Annie L., b. Aug. 1, d. Aug. 25, '61.

Capt. Austin's ch. 1, Harris R., b. in 1854. 2, Charles A., born March, 1856, d. Oct. 25, '57.

WILLIAMS, Capt. Charles, b. in England ab. 1830; came from Brandon, Vt.; m. Julia F. Foster of Cape Cod; r. Th., a master mariner. Their ch. 1, Charles E., b. ab. 1857. 2, Lena, b. ab. 1859.

WILLIAMS, Sandford, b. ab. 1820, in Warren, son of Jesse and Rachel (Copeland) Williams of W.; m. Angeline B. Crane of W.; r. Th., a shipbuilder.

WILLIAMS, Seth N., b. ab. 1820, in Augusta; m. Annie Luce; r. Rock., a photographist. Their ch. Frank, b. Sept., 1859. Williams, Charles, also b. in Augusta, ab. 1820; mar. Sarah Booden; r. Rock., a shoemaker, &c. Their ch. 1, Mary Ann, b. ab. 1844. 2, Lydia, b. ab. '46. 3, Sarah, b. ab. '48. 4, Marcia E., b. ab. '52. 5, Georgietta, b. ab. '54. 6, Abbie J., b. ab. '57. 7, Hannah F., b. ab. 1859.

WILLIAMS, Henry, b. ab. 1810, in England, as was Louisa C., his wife; r. Rock., a mariner. Their ch. 1, Louisa M., b. in Mass., ab. 1854. 2, Adelaide J., b. in New York, ab. '57. 3, Marietta, b. April 21, '59, d. Sept. 10, '60. Of this name, also, James Williams, b. ab. 1829; mar. Charlotte ———; r. Rock., a mariner. James's ch. 1, Reuben, b. ab. '52. 2, Maria J., b. ab. '54. 3, James R., b. ab. '56. 4, Eliza A., b. ab. '58.

WILLIAMSON, Warren, b. ab. 1822, in Mercer, Me.; mar. 1st, Margaret C. ———; (who d. April 19, '58, aged 35 years, 8 months) 2d, Mary ———; r. Rock., a quarryman; rem. California. Their ch. Charles E., b. Aug. 20, 1850, d. Sept. 30, '57.

WILLIS, Preserved, b. April 12, 1780; c. from Taunton, Mass., burnt and inspected lime for Knox; m. Betsey Long of St. Geo., p. Sept. 2, 1805; r. west of Meadows; & d. Feb. 28, 1849. His widow still r. in his house built by D. Palmer, as she has done for nearly 60 years. Their ch. 1, Isaac A., b. May 10, 1806; mar. Asenath Harrington, 1830, 2d, Deborah Wheeler, Dec. 20, '32; r. Th. 2, Fanny L., b. Sept. 13, '08; m. 1st, Thomas J. Bentley, 2d, Richard Dunbar; r. Th. 3, Madding L., b. June 19, '12; mar. Mary J. Harrington, p. Nov. 13, '37; r. Rock., a lime burner. 4, Anna, b. Nov. 25, '14; m. Joshua Grant; r. Th. 5, Arunah, d. at New Orleans. 6, Dennis L., b. Aug. 26, '18; a mariner. 7, Hannah A., b. Oct. 22, '22; m. William H. Grant; r. California. 8, Mary C., b. Sept. 22, '26; m. Lt. Col. Lorenzo D. Carver; r. Rock. 9, Asenath E., b. July 8, '32, d. March 2, '52.

Isaac A.'s ch. 1, Thomas J., b. Aug. 27, 1832. By 2d wife. 2, Asenath M., b. May 1, '33; m. Edward Boyles; r. Rock. 3, Abner N., b. May 23, & d. July 2, '34. 4, Edward A., b. May 17, '35; an overseer in State Prison, &c. 5, Albion K., b. April 17, '39; m. Rebecca Poland of F., Sept. 30, '60; r. Th. 6, Charles E., b. April 4, '39; r. Th., a mariner. 7, Henry A., b. Jan. 16, '40; r. Th., a painter, corporal, &c., in 1st Me. Cavalry. 8, Frances H., b. Oct. 11, '41, d. Feb. 7, '42. 9, Isaac Dexter, b. Aug. 21, '47 10, Mary Frances, b. Nov. 16, '49. 11, (adopted), William L., b. Sept. 22, '50.

Madding L.'s ch. 1, Asa S., b. Nov. 8, 1839; a lime burner. 2, Arunah, b. Oct. 1, '41; r. Rock., soldier in 4th Me., &c. 3, Ellerson C., b. ab. '44; a mariner. 4, Sarah G., b. April 22, '46, d. Oct. 3, '49. 5, Mary H., b. April, 1848, d. Oct. 1, '49. 6, Sarah G., b. July 12, & d. Oct. 1, '50. 7, Mary I., b. ab. '51. 8, Franklin, b. ab. '53.

WILLOUGHBY, Jonathan S., b. ab. 1823, in Nashua, N. H., m. Jennie E., dau. of G. Bailey, Feb. 11, '60; r. Rock., a millinery and dry goods merchant.

WILSON, William, son of John Wilson of Acworth, N. H., (who was a lineal descendent from Rev. John Wilson, who came over from England in the *Arbella* in 1630, at the instance of Gov. Winthrop, & was a preacher of note in Wilson's Lane, Boston, Mass.;) m. Elizabeth ———, and settled in St. George. Of William's ch. 1, Jane L., b. in St. G., Aug. 26, 1809, m. 1st, Richard Smith, 2d, Thomas J. Rider;

r. Th. 2, Capt. Joseph, b in St. G., March 14, '12, m. Emeline Titcomb McLellan, Oct. 18, '38; r. Th., and d. at sea, of apoplexy, in ship *Mountaineer*, Dec. 30, '60. Their ch. 1, Capt. William J., born Aug. 14, '39, m. Mary L. Coburn, July 18, '62; r. Th., a master mariner. 2, Eliza Emma, b. April 10, '41, d. Aug. 26, '50. 3, George McLellan, b. June 22, '46. 4, Frederic, b. July 30, '48, d. Sept. 1, '50. 5, Frank Lewis, b. May 24, '50.

Capt. William J.'s ch. Sarah Emma, b. Oct. 1864.

WILSON, Capt. Life, b. Sept. 22, 1799, in Warren, m. Eliza Watson, p. Oct. 12, 1823; long a ship master in Th., rem. Ill. Their ch. 1, Life, r. Ill. 2, James W., b. ab. 1830, m. Abby F. Young, June 24, '58; r. Th., a mariner. 3, Mary. 4, Edward. 5, William. 6, Clara. 7, Ann Maria; all r. Ill. James W.'s ch. Mary J., d. Feb. 5, '63.

WILSON, Edmund, Esq., b. ab. 1813, in Cornish, Me., studied law with Hon. Joseph Howard and Hon. E. Shepley, Portland; was county attorney 1842, collector of customs, Wal. district, appt. March 1846, m. Mary S. Haskell, Dec. 1, '42; r. and prac. law Th. Their ch. Bion Bradbury, b. ab. 1855.

WILSON, William, b. ab. 1820, in Industry, Franklin Co., m. Luzerne Chase of Livermore; c. from Hallowell to Rock. in 1852, where he r. and does business, as a merchant, &c., at first in firm of Wm. Wilson & Co., now Wilson & Norton. His ch. 1, Capt. Samuel P., b. 1842, m. Hannah E. Tibbets, Dec. 24, '63; r. Rock. 2, Lottie A.,? m. Hiram F. Huntington of Atkinson, Dec. 30, '63. 3, Annie C., d. June 25, '55. 4, William C., b. ab. '56.

WILSON, Capt. Richard H., b. ab. 1820, m. Clara D. Norton, p. Jan. 15, '50, 2d, Louisa B. Ulmer, pub. Aug. 4, '52, 3d, Delana Cummings, Dec. 21, '60; r. Rock. Of his ch. by 2d wife. Addie L., b. Aug. 1855, d. Feb. 13, '62. Of this name also, Wilson, John M.; r. Rock., asst. quartermaster in U. S. Sharpshooters, re-enlisted. Samuel Wilson, soldier in 10th Me.; John Wilson, in the navy, both of R.

WINCHENBACH, Henry W., b. ab. 1793, son of Henry & Mary (Woltz) Winchenbach of Warren; m. Agnes Spear, Oct. 15, 1818; r. Rock., a truckman. Their ch. 1, Robert W., m. Almira E. Stahl. 2, Sarah J. 3, John S.

WINSLOW, James H., b. ab. 1820; c. from Nobleboro'; m. 1st, Avis B. Fales, Dec. 18, 1842, 2d, Patience Braley, Nov. 2, '44, 3d, Marilla Hussey, April 24, '53; r. Th., a carpenter. Cyrus N., a brother, c. to Th.; m. Sarah Ghentner, Aug. 21, '42; ret. Nobleboro'. James H.'s ch. by 2d wife. William J., b. ab. 1846. The mother d. Nov. 17, 1847.

WINSLOW; of this Waldoboro' family, 5 brothers settled here. 1, David, b. ab. 1822; m. Sarah F. Benner, Dec. 5, '49; r. Rock., in quarry business. 2, Edbert, b. ab. 1824; m. Mary Walter; r. Rock. 3, Ezekiel, b. ab. 1831; m. Almira J. Ulmer, Aug. 20, '54; r. Rock., a soldier in 1st Cavalry. 4, Charles. 5, Jacob, r. Rock., a soldier of 4th Me. Reg., &c.

David's ch. 1, Reuben L., b. ab. 1851. 2, Frances A., b. ab. '53. 3, William H., b. ab. '55. 4, Marcena, b. ab. '57. 5, Hannah L., b. ab. '59.

Ezekiel's ch. 1, William S., b. ab. 1855. 2, Herbert L., b. ab. '58. 3, Mary A., b. '60.

WISE, John P., b. in Kennebunk, Me, July 5, 1817, son of Dr. John and Sophia (Paul) Wise; m. Mary N. Crockett, May 19, '44; r. Rock., a stove dealer, seedsman, &c. Their ch. 1, Henry M., born March 6, 1847. 2, Flora M., b. April 1, '49.

WITHAM, or Whitham, Benjamin, c. from Blue Hill, Me., to S. Th., m. Sarah Philbrook, May 16, 1789, & d. May 7, 1848. His wife d. May 15, 1838. Their ch. 1, Jeremiah, b. Nov. 16, 1789, m. Lydia Hix, p. May 6, 1814; r. S. Th., drowned Aug. 11, '40. 2, Abigail, b. Aug. 25, '91, m. Zachariah Post; r. S. Th. 3, Benjamin, (2d), b. July 16, '93, m. 1st, Nancy Paul, July 6, 1815, when he r. Northport, 2d, Catharine Fogler, Oct. 10, '19, when he r. Cam.; died in Rock., Aug. 29, '56. 4, Sally, b. Nov. 25, '95, mar.? John Thomas, Jr., of Searsmont, p. March 18, '22, 2d, Coit Ingraham; r. and d. Rock. 5, Philbrook, b. May 9, '97, d. at Mirimichi, N. B. 6, Pamelia, b. March 29, '99. 7, Priscilla, b. May 16, '01, m. Elisha Keen; r. Appleton. 8, Polly, b. Sept. 7, '03, m. George Robbins; r. and d. W. 9, Bradbury, b. Sept. 26, '05, m. Alexander Kiff; r. Rock. 10, Jane, b. Feb. 6, '08; d. young. 11, Henry P., b. April 11, '10, m. 1st, Nancy Fogler, 2d, Rebecca Elwell of St. G., Aug 26, '38, 3d, Eliza A. Mann, May 6, '49; r. Rock.

Jeremiah's ch. 1, Capt. Nathan L., b. March 9, 1815, mar. 1st, Eliza A. Stearns, p. July 23, '38, 2d, Maria N. Spaulding, p. May 25, 1849; r. S. Th., and d. May 7, '56. 2, Capt. William H., b. May 21, '17, m. Achsa J. Wade, June 18, '44; r. Rock., a master mariner. 3, Jane, b. Sept. 11, '19, m. Dr. Charles Coffran; r. Rock. and Cal. 4, Mary Ann, b. Sept. 5, '21, m. William Wade; r. S. Th. 5, Lydia M., m. Nahum H. Hall; r. Rock.

Benjamin's ch. by 1st wife. 1, Eliza, d. young. 2, Nancy, d. unm. By 2d wife. 3, Mary J., b. May 23, 1822, m. Jacob Thomas; r. Th. 4, Henry P., b. Oct. 31, '24, d. unm. 5, Nathaniel H., b. May 15, '27, d. Feb. 10, '46. 6, Philip U., b. April 18, '31, mar. Ellen Cram, Oct. 6, '55; r. Rock., a teamster. 7, Elkanah S., b. Jan. 17, '37, died unm. 8, Odbury Miles, b. April 4, '41, m. Ellen Pease, Jan. 29, '64; r. Rock., soldier of 2d Me. Battery, re-enlisted.

Henry P.'s ch. 1, Nancy, b. Jan. 4, 1830, m. Benjamin A. Chaples; r. Rock. 2, Franklin P., b. Sept. 4, '33, m. Susanna R. Walsh, Aug. 16, '56; r. Rock., soldier in 2d Me. Battery. By 2d wife. 3, Charles P., b. March 10, '39, d young. 4, Eliza A., b. '41, d. Oct. 2, '49. 5, Susan W., b. Oct. 2, '44, d. Sept. 25, '49. The mother died Aug. 2, '47, a. 28. By 3d wife. 6, Albert M., b. Sept. 5, '49. 7, Leforest, d. Oct. 26, '53. 8, Edgar D., b. Dec. 9, '54, d. Sept. 2, '55. 9, Edo C., b. Aug. 19, '59.

Capt. Nathan L.'s ch. 1, Mary E., b. May 13, 1840, d. Dec. 19, '41. 2, George F., b. Oct. 16, '41. By 2d wife. 3, Maria T., b. ab. 1855.

William H.'s ch. 1, William, b. ab. 1846. 2, Woodbury A., b. ab. '50. 3, Edmund H.

Philip's ch. 1, Esmerilda, b. ab. 1856. 2, Mary E., b. ab. '58. Of this name, also, Isaac Witham, b. ab. 1812; mar. Susan Eastis, April 7, '46; r. Rock., a mariner.

WITHINGTON, Ephraim A., b. ab. 1825, in Camden; m. Dolly G. Miller; r. Rock., a joiner, &c. Their ch. 1, Benjamin B., b. ab. '49. 2, Caroline H., b. ab. '54. 3, Augusta B., b. ab. '56. 4, Dolly G., b. '60.

WOLFF, Charles, b. ab. 1830, in Baden, Germany; m. Christiana Martin of Germany; r. Th., engineer in U. S. Navy. Their ch. 1, Charles, b. here ab. 1853. 2, John, b. ab. '55. 3, George, b. ab. '57. 4, Augusta, b. ab. '59.

WOOD, Capt. James B., b. ab. 1822, in China, Me.; m. Abigail K. Pierce; r. S. Th. Their ch. 1, Jacob F., b. Aug. 15, 1842; r. S. Th., a mariner. 2, Clara M., b. ab. '44. 3, Razada F., b. May, '48, d. Aug. 29, '49.

WOOD, Zebedee, b. ab. 1800; mar. Mary Shea, Sept. 8, '33; r. Rock., & d. April 8, '50. His widow d. Aug. 2, '60, a. 49. Their ch. 1, Halsey, b. March 22, 1834; m. Mary J. ——— ; r. Rock., a mariner. 2, Charles F., b. ab. '36; m. Mary ——— ; r. Rock., a corporal in 4th Me., &c. 3, Henry, b. Oct. 11, '38; r. Rock., entered the navy.

WOOD, Aaron, b. ab. 1817; mar. Amanda F. (Healey) Ulmer, Sept. 1, '30; r. Rock., in quarry business. Their ch. 1, George W., b. Jan. 22, 1840; r. Rock., soldier of 4th Me., & re-enlisted, died at Alexandria, Va., July 20, '64. 2, Rebecca K., b. April 6, '41. 3, Jerome B., b. ab. '43; r. Rock., soldier of 2d Me. Battery, re-enlisted. 4, Mary E., b. ab. '46. 5, Orville T., b. ab. '48. 6, James H., b. ab. '51. Of this name, also, Amos P. Wood of Rock.; mar. Abbie D. Davenport, Oct. 20, '63; entered the navy. And Samuel A. Wood of Rock., soldier of 4th Me., d. Dec. 13, '62. Also Jonas Wood, b. ab. 1825; c. from Kennebec; ? m. Rachel Ames, 2d Anginette Harwood, Nov. 29, '64; r. Rock., in quarry business. James's ch. 1, Charles P., b. ab. '45; entered the army. 2, Emma G., b. ab. '48. 3, Ada U., b. May 6, '51, d. Oct. 26, '56. 4, Edgar L., b. Jan., '56, d. June 18, '57. 5, Jennie A., b. ab. '58.

WOODARD, Nathan C, b. ab. 1815; was landlord of the White Mountain House in Gorham, of the Commercial House, Rock., and took the census of Rock., 1860; m. Ann M. Washburn. Their ch. 1, Moses E., b. ab. 1846. 2, Annette, b. ab. '48. 3, Frederic, b. ab. '50. 4, Frank L., b. ab. '56.

WOODCOCK, Nathaniel, b. 1750; m. Rebecca Healey; came from Attleboro', Mass., and purchased, in 1780, one-half the John Alexander lot, Th., on which he r. & d. Jan, 1826, a. 76. Israel, a brother, was in Th. in 1774, when he worked for James Fales, 6 months, for £90; but ret. and m. in the State of New York. A sister of theirs, Eunice, b. March 28, 1743; m. Benjamin Blackington; r. Rock., and d. June 19, 1815.

Nathaniel's ch. 1, Anna, b. in Attleboro', Dec. 22, 1777; m. Capt. William Fales; r. Th., & d. Oct. 10, 1816. 2, Patrick, b. 1782; m. 1st, Catharine Watson, May 5, 1803, 2d, Elizabeth (Simonton) Coburn, Oct. 29, '20; r. Th., a farmer, & d. April 23, '52. 3, Huldah, d. young. 4, Nathaniel, (2d), d. young. 5, Nathan, b. ab. 1793; m. Margaret Waning, Feb. 4, 1813; r. Th., a farmer.

Patrick's ch. by 1st wife. 1, George, b. Jan. 13, 1804; m. Chloe Pitcher of F. or Wal.; r. Th. 2, James, b. Feb. 4, '06; m. Sarah S. Robbins of U., 1828; r. Th., & d. Aug. 31, or July 28, 1837. 3, Casper F., b. July 1, '07, d. May 8, '15. By 2d wife. 4, Elizabeth, (adopted), b. Jan. 29, '17; m. John W. Jacobs; r. Th. 5, Catharine, b. May 31, '21; m. Capt. James Watts; r. Th., & d. Jan. 20, '56. 6, William, b. April 15, '24; m. Mary A. Robinson, July 18, '50; r. & d. Th.; his widow is a milliner on Main st., Th. 7, Charles, b. June

11, '28; m. 1st, Sarah Cooper, Sept. 3, '51, 2d, Octavia Cooper, Nov. 15, '59; r. Th., a mariner.

Nathan's ch. 1, Israel, b. July 1, 1813; m. Cordelia C. Kaler, p. Aug. 25, '53; r. Th., on homestead. 2, Rebecca, b. July 21, '15, d. Aug. 24, '16. 3, Nathaniel, (3d), b. July 23, '17; mar. Nancy A. Campbell, Sept. 12, '44; r. Th., a blacksmith. 4, Sarah, b. Jan. 23, '19; m. Edward G. Libbey of W., Aug. 11, '44. 5, Emeline, b. Jan. 27, '23; m. Erastus Lermond; r. Th. 6, Clementine, b. Feb. 5, '25; m. James O. Cushing; r. Th. 7 & 8, twins, b. May 4, '28, W. Leander, m. Elizabeth P. Shibles, Sept. 26, '54; r. Th., soldier in 21st Me. Reg., & 2d Cavalry; Alexander, d. Oct. 31, '35. 9, Catharine, b. Jan. 7, '31; mar. Frederic H. Kellogg; r. Th. 10, Antoinette, b. June 2, '33; m. John W. Tozier, May 17, '54; r. Hudson.

Of George's ch. 1, Patrick, (2d), m. Mary (Williams) Copperholt, Jan. 20, 1856; r. Th. 2, Lorinda, m. Wm. H. Feyler; r. Th. 3, Irene, m. Michael Howley; r. Th. 4, Catharine, b. ab. 1842. 5 and 6, twins, b. ab. '44, Casper and George. 7, Llewellyn, b. ab. '46. 8, Julia, b. ab. '48.

James's ch. 1, Leanora L., b. Feb. 17, 1830; m. Isaac Kaler. 2, Esther M., b. Jan. 16, '32; m. Edmund B. Wyllie; r. W., & d. Sept. 10, '58. 3, Moses Ludwig, m. Mary J. Robinson, p. Sept. 7, '56; r. Cush. 4, Harriet, d. young.

William's ch. 1, Estelle, or Adelle, b. ab. 1854. 2, Ann, b. ab. '56. 3, Clara, b. ab. '58. 4, Hezekiah P., b. May, 1860.

Charles's ch. by 1st wife. Charles Leonard, r. Thomaston.

Israel's ch. 1, Mary Eva, b. April 8, 1855. 2, Ada Frances, born Oct. 25, '57. 3, Emma L., b. March 3, 1858.

Nathaniel, (3d)'s ch. 1, Lucy E., b. ab. 1846. 2, Adelaide, b. ab. '48. 3, Orris D., b. ab. '50. 4, Adelia, b. ab. '53. 5, Ida May, b. ab. '58.

W. Leander's ch. 1, Alexander, b. Aug. 31, 1855. 2, Samuel H., b. June 4, '57. 3, Webster, b. Oct., 1859.

WOODHULL, Rev. Richard, b. in Conn.; grad. Bowd. Coll. 1827; and stud. theology at Bangor The. Seminary; m. Sarah Forbes; was long the minister of the Th. Cong. Church; rem. Bangor, and has since been agent of the Am. Bible Society. Their ch. 1, Sarah F., b. June 14, 1830; m. Capt. Edmund R. Webb, 2d, Philip Coombs, of Bangor, Jan. 3, 1856; r. Bangor. 2, Caroline Augusta, born Jan. 29, '32; m. Rev. Wm. C. Pond of Bangor, Sept. 28, '52, and rem. Cal. 3, Richard S., b. Sept. 27, '33, d. July 5, '52. 4, Helen, b. June 12, '36; mar. Rev. W. Pickard of Groveland, Mass., June 14, '54. 5, Frances, b. Nov. 30, '38, d. Nov. 8, '43. 6, Lucy, b. Sept. 3, '40. 7, Mary Elizabeth, b. May 16, '44. 8, Edward F., b. April 16, '47. 9, Harriet N., b. Feb. 27, & d. Sept. 23, '49. 10, Arthur Wm., b. April 19, '51, d. at Bangor Oct. 9, 1856.

WOLTZ, Simon, m. Elizabeth Thompson, Oct. 15, 1854; r. S. Th.

WOOSTER, (sometimes written Worcester); of this family; 1, Nathaniel, m., r. and perhaps d. in North Haven, Me. 2, Joseph, b. Nov. 31, 1759, m. Mary ———; r. North Haven, but rem. Rock., where he d. June 22, 1843, aged 84, and, as well as his wife, (who d. March 31, 1845, aged 74,) was buried in Rock.

Of Nathaniel's ch. 1, Capt. John C., b. in North Haven, m. Hannah Amsbury; r. Rock., and d. Feb. 8, 1841. 2, Capt. George D., b. ab. 1804, m. 1st, Elionai Crockett, p. Oct. 10, 1835, 2d, Amanda W. (Simmons) Crockett, Oct. 16, '48; r. Rock., master mariner, &c.,

rem. S. Th., as light keeper at Owl's Head. 3, Benjamin F., m. Drusilla Perry; r. Rock., but probably rem. 4, Oliver, m. & r. N. Haven.

Of Joseph's ch. 1, Joseph, (2d), b. ab. 1805, in North Haven, m. Vilenia Cutler; r. Rock., in lime business. 2, Joshua C., b. ab. '14, in North Haven; m. 1st, Harriet B. Healey, Sept. 21, '42, 2d, Orinda M. Smith, Dec. 4, '64; r. Rock., a lime burner, &c.

Capt. John C.'s ch. 1, Marian H., b. April 29, 1828, m. George Mallett of W.; r. Rockport. 2, Margaret A., b. July 5, '34, m. Alexander Huke; r. Rockport.

Capt. George D.'s ch. by 1st wife. 1, George F., b. July 22, 1836, d. March 18, '54. 2, John H., b. Nov. 21, '40, d. Jan. 2, '42. 3, Robert C., b. ab. '45. By 2d wife. 4, Joseph T., b. ab. '51. 5, Caroline A., b. Aug. 20, '53, d. May 27, '54. 6, Oliver A., b. Sept. 16, and d. Oct. 13, '56.

Benjamin F.'s ch. recorded here. Drusilla A., b. April 3, 1842.

Joseph's ch. 1, Sarah F., b. March 15, 1838, mar. Seth E. Condon of Matinicus, Feb. 26, '56; r. Rock. 2, Judson, b. April 23, '40; r. Rock. in lime business. 3, Alden F., b. ab. '42; r. Rock., soldier in 4th Me.. &c. 4, Margaret A., b. ab. '47.

Joshua C.'s ch. 1, Edward R., b. ab. 1843; r. Rock., entered the U. S. Navy. 2, ? William E., b. ab. '51. 3, ? Julia A., b. Dec. 1858, d. Sept. 13, '64.

WOOSTER, George, b. May 12, 1785, m. Julia Bernard, 1818; r. Rock., and d. Oct. 27, 1854. Their ch. 1, Hiram, b. July 30, 1818; m. Sophia Butler, Aug. 28, '43; r. S. Th., a mariner. 2, Sophia B., b. Sept. 5, '20, m. Horace H. Robbins; r. Rock. 3, Harriet, b. Dec. 15, '26, m. Capt. John Perry; r. S. Th. 4, Susan M., b. Nov. 21, '38.

WORMELL, Joseph, c. with his wife from England, and settled, first, at Grand Menan, but rem. & d. in Falmouth. Their ch. 1, Ebenezer. 2, Nathaniel. 3, John. 4, William, rem. with his parents to Falmouth; m. Elizabeth Bresto, or Barstow, of Concord, Mass.; r. and d. Falmouth, a caulker. 5, Benjamin. 6, Susan, m. ——— Richardson of Mt. Desert. 7, Mary, m. Gamaliel Pote, 2d, ——— Patrick. 8, one other. William's ch. 1, Edward. 2, Sophia, m. Samuel Kinney, a brush maker from Westbrook, came with her family to Th., but d. ab. 1836, in Westbrook, where her husband afterwards dropped dead in his shop. Of her ch., one dau., Lucy A. Kinney, r. S. Th., the other 3 d. young. 3, William. 4, Hannah. 5, Mary, m. William Metcalf; r. Th. 6, Abigail, m. Nathan Sellea; r. Th. & d. April 18, 1836. 7, George Bresto, b. ab. 1800; learned the comb making trade; c. from Falmouth, 1819; m. Clarissa Wiggin of Rock., p. Sept. 20, 1828; r. Th., a carpenter. 8, Elizabeth, m. James Tarbox; r. Th. & d. Sept. 14, '45. 9, Charles, b. ab. '04; m. Charlotte Kuhn of Wal., Nov. 20, '24; r. Th., a carpenter. 10, Joseph, m. Martha Doughty of Sangerville; r. Dexter.

George B.'s ch. 1, Harriet M., mar. Dana R. Young; r. Th. 2, George, b. ab. 1832; r. Th., a mariner. 3, William, (3d), b. ab. '35; r. Th., a mariner. 4, Antoinette, b. ab. '38. 5, Oliver, b. ab. '42. 6, Lydia, b. ab. '45. 7, Moses Ludwig, b. ab. '47, d. Dec. 3, 1864.

Charles's ch. 1, Eliza J., b. Aug. 25, 1830, m. Sylvanus H. Long, 2d, Alden Gay; r. Th. The mother d. Feb. 26, '58.

WORTH, Aseph, b. ab. 1810, in Nova Scotia, as were Mary, his wife & their 4 eldest ch.; r. S. Th., a carpenter. Their ch. 1, Sarah E., b. ab. 1844. 2, Mary I., b. ab. '46. 3, Rachel A., b. ab. '48. 4,

Benjamin Howard, b. ab '50. 5, Amos, b. here, ab. '53. 6, Peter H., b. ab. '56. 7, James H,, b. ab. '58.

WORTMAN, Lieut. Elijah E., b. ab. 1829, in Houlton, Me., mar. Mary J. Perley; r. Rock., publisher, in Co. with J. Porter, of Rock. Gazette. His ch. 1 Clarence P., b. ab. 1852. 2, Ada, b. March 26, and d. Aug. 29, '55. 3, Marietta, b. ab. '59.

WOTTON, Moses, b. ab. 1828, in Friendship, ? m. Anna E. ———; r. Rock., a painter. Their ch. Mary Helen, b. May, 1860, d. March 11, 1864.

WRIGHT, William S., b. ab. 1836, mar. Martha J. Hahn, Nov. 7, '58; r. Rock., a blacksmith. Their ch. 1, Mary E., b. June 4, '59, d. Sept. 25, '64. 2, William H., b. March 26, and d. Oct. 16, 1864. Of this name also, Capt. William Wright, m. Helen L. Sawyer, Sept. 20, 1863; r. Rock., acting master in navy. Also James Wright of Rock., was a musician in 2d Me. Reg.

WYATT, Thomas, b. ab. 1815 in Nova Scotia, as was Mary, his wife; r. Rock., a fisherman, soldier, killed on a gunboat in bombardment of Fort St. Charles, June 16, 1862. Their ch. 1, Mary A., b. ab. 1846. 2, Phebe, b. ab. 1848. 3, William B., b. ab. 1850. 4, Lucy, b. ab. 1855. 5, George? Thomas, b. ab. 1858, d. Jan. 14, 1863. 6, Jenny Lind, b. Aug., 1860, d. Feb. 27, 1864.

WYLLIE, John A., b. July 24, 1817; son of Capt. Alexander Wyllie of Warren, m. Eliza Andrews, Nov. 10, 1843, rem. Th., and took charge of Georges Hotel. Their ch. 1, Alanson. 2, Orilla I., b. June, 1849, d. March 23, 1864. 3, Iola. 4, Alice.

WYLLIE, Isaac, b. ab. 1821, c. from St. George, with Mary Jane, his wife; r. Rock., a mariner. Their ch. Sarah Maria, b. Oct., 1854, d. Sept. 1855. Of this name also, Ephraim Wyllie or Wilie; r. Rock., entered the navy.

WYNNE, Dominic, b. ab. 1830 in Ireland, m. Mary ——— ; r. Th. John, a brother, b. ab. 1828; also r. Th. Dominic's ch. 1, Ann, b. ab. 1857. 2, James, b. ab. 1859.

YEATON, Capt. Wm., b. ab. 1825, in Isle of Haut; mar. Eliza J. Sawyer; r. Rock. Their ch. 1, Martha H., b. 1848, died April 27, '54. 2, Ellen, b. ab, '53. 3, Charles C., b. July 24, & d. Aug. 6, '56.

YORK, Henry, b. ab. 1814; m. Nancy Post, Aug. 5, '49; r. Rock., kept a shop in 1860. Their ch. 1, Ann K., b. ab. 1852. 2, Helen M. W., b. ab. 1856.

YOUNG, Ebenezer Scott, born Aug. 25, 1772; came from Scituate, Mass., a mason by trade, m. 1st, Mary, daughter of Wm. Lermond of W., Jan. 24, 1799, 2d, Molly (Gleason) Miles of Hope, pub. Sept. 6, 1810; r. and built on the place now owned by Capt. D. Oliver; & d. Oct. 15, 1829. Joseph, a brother, also c. to Th. & d. Oct. 20, 1835. Eben Scott's ch. by 1st wife. 1, William, b. Oct. 23, 1799; m. Eliza Philbrick of Hope; r. Th. 2, Lois, b. Nov. 25, 1801; mar. Rowland Jacobs, (2d); r. Th. 3, Alexander, b. Sept. 19, '04; m. 1st, Angelina Blackington, July 15, '31; 2d, Nancy Collamore of F., March 24, 1854; r. Th., deputy sheriff, &c., kept hotel at Herring Gut. 4, Lucy Ann, b. Jan. 19, '07; d. May 20, '10. The mother d. Oct. 18, 1809, aged 30. The step-mother d. June 15, '49, aged 76.

William's ch. 1, Enoch P., b. ab. 1825; m. Ellen Kelleran, Jan. 29, '54; r. Th., a mariner. 2, Mary A., b. Jan. 19, '28; m. Cyrus H.

Shaw of China, Jan. 8, '52. 3, Lucia M., b. Feb. 8, '32; m. Hiram H. Boynton; r. and d. Th. 4, Albina F., b. ab. '34, mar. Hiram H. Boynton; r. Th. 5, Eliza Lois, b. Aug. 2, '36; m. Aaron Piper; r. Th. 6, Lucy A., b. June 11, '39; m. John A. Catland; r. Th. 7, Rowland J., b. May 28, '41, d. Sept. 15, '42.

Alexander's ch. by 1st wife. Abby Frances, b. ab. 1834; m. Jas. Wilson; r. Thomaston.

Enoch P.'s ch. 1, Thomas K., b. ab. 1857. 2, Enoch D., b. ab. 59.

YOUNG, Gideon, b. Feb., 1787, in Scituate, Mass., a nephew of Eben Scott Young; came as a joiner and framer from Minot to Th., with Roxey, his wife, and three ch. b. in Minot; r. Th., and d. June 30, 1854. Two of his brothers c. to this vicinity, viz.: Allen Young to Warren, and Christopher Young to Union. Gideon's ch. 1, Olive B., b. Sept. 2, 1810, d. Sept. 11, '30. 2, Delight, born Sept. 21, 1813; m. Phinehas Dow; r. Th. 3, Ebenezer Scott, (2d), b. Nov. 30, 1816, in Minot, as were the preceding; mar. Sally T. Mitchell, April 7, '39; r. St. George. 4, John S., b. May 21, 1819; m. Sarah Hall, Oct. 29, 1849; r. Th. 5, Lucy A., b. July 23, 1822; mar. Geo. Washington Lermond; r. Th. 6, Gideon, (2d), b. Jan. 23, 1825; m. Roxana B. Fernald, July 3, 1847; r. Th. and died Sept. 7, 1854. 7, Dana R., b. July 16, 1827; m. Harriet M. Wormell, Oct. 29, 1853; r. Th. 8, Andrew J., b. Sept. 12, 1831; m. Sarah B. Keith, Jan. 23, 1854; r. Montville. 9, Oliver, b. Jan. 9, 1834, probably d. young.

E. Scott, (2d)'s ch. 1, Margaret Eugene, b. Jan. 5, 1840. 2, Martha B., b. Nov. 23, '41, d. Feb. 25, '64. 3, Sarah, b. '44, d. Sept., '59. 4, Julia S., b. Oct. 15, '51, d. Aug. 13, '52.

John S.'s ch. 1 & 2, twins, b. Aug. 29, 1851, Danbury L., d. Oct. 7, '57; George, r. Th. 3, Lysander, b. May 22, '55, d. Jan. 18, '56. 4, Frederic, b. ab. '57. 5, Roxana, b. ab. '59.

Of A. Jackson's ch. Carrie Ella, b. Jan. 28, 1855, d. July 11, '57.

YOUNG, Caleb, came from Lancaster, Mass., worked in Old Th. and vicinity awhile; mar. Susanna Manning, Feb. 12, 1812; enlisted for the war of 1812; ret. and settled in Camden.

YOUNG, Capt. Robert, b. ab. 1800, in Cushing, son of Francis Young; mar. Eliza Kelleran, Oct 10, '27; r. Th., long a trader on Wadsworth st. Their ch. 1, Clementine W., b. Sept. 4, 1830. 2, George P., b. April 25, '32, died at sea, Dec. 7, '49, on board brig *J. H. Whipple*. 3, Sarah A., b. Feb. 8, '34; m. William C. Merrick; rem. Libertyville, Ill. 4, Robert K., b. Jan. 14, '36; mar. Penelope H. Spear, Dec. 19, '57; r. Th., a blacksmith. 5, Mary E., b. March 24, '38; m. Capt. Daniel H. Adams; r. Th. 6, Adelaide L., b. Oct. 7, 1840.

Robert K.'s ch. 1, Ida Delia, b. April 4, 1858. 2, Robert, (2d), b. Jan., 1860.

YOUNG, Capt. Abraham, also probably from Cushing; r. Th., awhile, where Nancy, his wife, d. Feb. 28, 1833, aged 32; and he m. 2d, Louisa Marshall, p. Dec. 21, '34.

YOUNG, Daniel, b. ab. 1830; r. Th. in 1860, with Harriet, his wife. Their ch. 1, Clara, b. ab. 1855. 2, Ada, b. ab. '57. 3, Harriet, b. ab. '59.

YOUNG, Reuben H., b. ab. 1822, in Massachusetts; mar. Martha Wetherbee; ? came from Monroe, Me., to Rock., a gas manufacturer; ret. Monroe. Their ch. Clementine A., b. ab. 1855.

YOUNG; of this Lincolnville family, there came here 5 brothers, viz.: 1, Joseph T., b. ab. 1820; in Linc., m. Martha J. Peabody of W.; r. Rock. a teacher. 2, Capt. Ralph W., b. ab. 1824; m. Martha E. Howard; r. Rock., a carpenter, became an officer of the 6th Me. Reg., and was killed by a shot, May 3, '63. 3, Frederic B. W., b. ab. 1827; m. Mary Jane Howard; r. Rock., a carpenter. 4, Capt. James, m. Fannie Richards; r. Rock. 5, John W. or E., r. Rock., a soldier in 2d Mass. Reg.

Joseph T.'s ch 1, Levander A., b. ab. 1846. 2, Joseph F., b. ab. '53. 3, Wilbur C., b. ab. '59.

Capt. Ralph W.'s ch. 1, Charlotte B., b. ab. 1852. 2, George W., b. ab. '58.

Frederic B. W.'s ch. Marietta, b. ab. 1859.

YOUNG; there also came here from Lincolnville, related probably to the preceding family, 2 brothers, 1, John H. b. ab. 1825, in Linc.; m. Elizabeth McLaughlin; r. Rock., a carpenter, soldier in 4th Me., &c. 2, Andrew J., b. ab. 1829, in Linc.; mar. Margie K. Ingraham, Aug. 16, '55; r. S. Th., a carpenter.

John H.'s ch. 1, Charlotte E., b. ab. 1848. 2, Ella J., b. ab. '52.

Andrew J's ch. Effie E., b. ab. 1859.

YOUNG; of the sons of William of Warren, there came hither, 1, Wellington Gay, b. ab. 1813; mar. Mahala Sylvester of Montville, 1847; r. Rock. since 1853, a shoemaker and carpenter. 2, Daniel, b. ab. 1815; m. Judith ———; r. Th., a harness maker.

Daniel's ch. 1, Oscar A., b. ab. 1847; r. Th., entered the navy. 2, Frank, b. ab. '55. 3, Emma, b. Oct. and d. April 19, '59.

YOUNG, Aurelius, b. ab. 1824, in Union; m. Sarah G. Bachelder; r. Rock., deputy sheriff, &c. Their ch. 1, Charles E. b. ab. 1852. 2, Lizzie I., b. ab. '59.

THE END.

www.ingramcontent.com/pod-product-compliance
Lightning Source LLC
LaVergne TN
LVHW020930110826
845150LV00004B/818

* 9 7 8 1 4 2 5 5 5 3 2 0 3 *